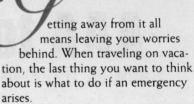

Connecticut Massachusetts Rhode Island

Valid through April 2000

Published by:
AAA Publishing
1000 AAA Drive
Heathrow, FL 32746-5063
Copyright AAA 1999.

The publisher is not responsible for changes that occur after publication. Published for the exclusive use of members. Not for sale.

Send Written Comments to:
AAA Member Comments
Box 61, 1000 AAA Drive
Heathrow, FL 32746-5063

Advertising Rate and Circulation Information
Call: (407) 444-8280

Printed in the USA by Quebecor Printing, Buffalo, NY

 Printed on recyclable paper. Please recycle whenever possible.

Stock #4607

Connecticut
Massachusetts
Rhode Island

Featured Information

Rhode Island

4

© 1998, Promus Hotels, Inc.

Congratulations. You made it.

It's a place where you can kick off your shoes and take it easy.

Where you can take a load off your mind as well as your feet.

Where you can relax, because you know we don't.

Call 1-800-HAMPTON® or visit us at hampton-inn.com.

We make it easy to take it easy.℠

When it comes to personal trip planning, nobody beats trained AAA travel counselors.

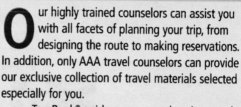

O ur highly trained counselors can assist you with all facets of planning your trip, from designing the route to making reservations. In addition, only AAA travel counselors can provide our exclusive collection of travel materials selected especially for you.

TourBook® guides are comprehensive travel guides listing AAA-approved attractions, lodgings and restaurants. In addition to the coveted diamond ratings, you'll find descriptions of towns and cities and information on discounts available only to AAA members. TourBooks are updated annually and cover every state and province in the United States and Canada.

TripTik® routings trace your route mile-by-mile and are clearly marked with the vital information you need while on the road, such as highway exits and rest stops. These handy spiral-bound maps are custom-configured by your AAA travel counselor and can highlight the quickest, shortest or most scenic routes, as well as highway construction projects along the way.

O nly AAA offers an integrated travel information system that is tailored to your individual needs.

Sheet maps are updated annually and cover every state and province, plus regional areas throughout North America. An extensive network of road reporters and club staff work with AAA cartographers to ensure that AAA maps are the most detailed and accurate maps available.

CampBook® guides list AAA-approved camping and RV facilities, both public and private, throughout the United States and Canada.

So the next time you're planning a trip, remember to visit your local AAA travel counselor, and *Travel With Someone You Trust.®*

TRUST the AAA TourBook for objective travel information. Follow the pages of TourBook Navigator to thoroughly understand this unique member benefit.

Each attraction, lodging and restaurant is listed on the basis of merit alone after careful evaluation, approval and rating by one of our full-time inspectors or, in rare cases, a designated representative.

Annual lodging inspections are unannounced and conducted on site by random room sample. Learn how to use the diamonds on pages 14-15.

An establishment's decision to advertise in TourBooks has no bearing on its inspection, evaluation or rating. Advertising for services or products does not imply AAA endorsement.

Casino gambling establishments not contained within hotels, as well as recreational activities of a participatory nature (requiring physical exertion or special skills), are not inspected but are presented in a bulleted format for informational purposes.

All information in this TourBook was reviewed for accuracy before publication. However, since changes inevitably occur between annual editions, we suggest you contact establishments directly to confirm prices and schedules.

How the TourBook is Organized

Geographic listing is used for accuracy and consistency. This means attractions, lodgings and restaurants are listed under the city or town in which they physically are located—or in some cases under the nearest recognized city or town. See the comprehensive City Index on page 486 for an A-to-Z list of towns in this TourBook.

Most listings are alphabetically organized by state or province, city, and establishment name. Reflecting contemporary travel patterns, TourBooks cluster information in two additional ways that illustrate geographic relationships among major travel targets:

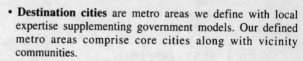

- **Destination cities** are metro areas we define with local expertise supplementing government models. Our defined metro areas comprise core cities along with vicinity communities.

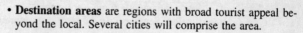

- **Destination areas** are regions with broad tourist appeal beyond the local. Several cities will comprise the area.

Note: If a city is grouped in a destination vicinity section, the city name will still appear at its alphabetical location in the book—and a handy cross reference will give the exact page on which listings for that city begin.

Map illustrations at the beginning of their sections orient you to these major destinations. A color bar across the top of the page indicates you are in a destination section.

Additional color tabs on the sides of pages are coded to a state or province. Match the color tabs to easily switch from attractions to lodgings and restaurants.

Sample Lodging Listing

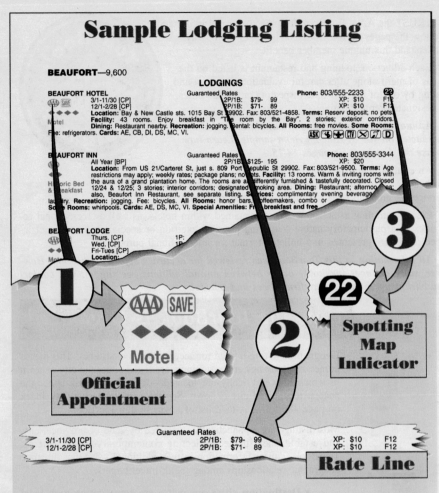

BEAUFORT—9,600

LODGINGS

BEAUFORT HOTEL ⏺ Guaranteed Rates ⏺ **Phone:** 803/555-2233 [22]
AAA SAVE ⏺ 3/1-11/30 [CP] ⏺ 2P/1B: $79- 99 ⏺ XP: $10 ⏺ F12
⏺ 12/1-2/28 [CP] ⏺ 2P/1B: $71- 89 ⏺ XP: $10 ⏺ F12
◆◆◆ **Location:** Bay & New Castle sts. 1015 Bay St 29902. Fax: 803/521-4858. **Terms:** Reserv deposit; no pets.
Motel **Facility:** 43 rooms. Enjoy breakfast in "The room by the Bay". 2 stories; exterior corridors.
Dining: Restaurant nearby. **Recreation:** jogging. **Rental:** bicycles. **All Rooms:** free movies. **Some Rooms:**
Fee: refrigerators. **Cards:** AE, CB, DI, DS, MC, VI.

BEAUFORT INN ⏺ Guaranteed Rates ⏺ **Phone:** 803/555-3344
AAA ⏺ All Year [BP] ⏺ 2P/1B: $125- 195 ⏺ XP: $20
◆◆ **Location:** From US 21/Carteret St, just s. 809 Port Republic St 29902. Fax: 803/521-9500. **Terms:** Age
restrictions may apply; weekly rates; package plans; no pets. **Facility:** 13 rooms. Warm & inviting rooms with
Historic Bed the aura of a grand plantation home. The rooms are differently furnished & tastefully decorated. Closed
& Breakfast 12/24 & 12/25; 3 stories; interior corridors; designated smoking area. **Dining:** Restaurant; afternoon tea;
also, Beaufort Inn Restaurant, see separate listing. **Services:** complimentary evening beverage
laundry. **Recreation:** jogging. Fee: bicycles. **All Rooms:** honor bars, coffeemakers, combo or
Some **Rooms:** whirlpools. **Cards:** AE, DS, MC, VI. **Special Amenities:** Free breakfast and free

BEAUFORT LODGE
AAA ⏺ Thurs. [CP] ⏺ 1P:
◆◆ ⏺ Wed. [CP] ⏺ 1P:
Motel ⏺ Fri-Tues [CP]
Location:

① → AAA SAVE ◆◆◆ Motel
Official Appointment

③ → [22]
Spotting Map Indicator

② →
	Guaranteed Rates			
3/1-11/30 [CP]	2P/1B:	$79- 99	XP: $10	F12
12/1-2/28 [CP]	2P/1B:	$71- 89	XP: $10	F12

Rate Line

---

① ◆◆◆ or ◆◆◆ The number of diamonds—not the color—informs you of the overall level of quality in a lodging's amenities and service. More diamond details on pages 14-15.

Motel or Motel Diamond ratings are applied in the context of lodging type, or classification. See pages 16-17 for our Lodging Classifications.

AAA or AAA indicates our Official Appointment (OA) lodgings. The OA Program permits properties to display and advertise the AAA or AAA emblem. **We highlight these properties with red diamonds and classification**. OAs have a special interest in serving members like you. Some OA listings include special amenities such as free breakfast; early check-in/late check-out; free room upgrade or preferred room, such as ocean view or poolside (subject to availability); free local phone calls; and free daily newspaper. This does not imply that only these properties offer these amenities. The AAA or AAA sign helps traveling members find accommodations that want member business.

Discounts

[SAVE] is used to highlight Official Appointment properties that guarantee members a minimum 10% discount off the published TourBook rates.

[SAVE] appears in "icon row" below the listing and indicates that the following Show Your Card & Save® chain partners provide special values to our members: Choice Hotels, Days Inn, Hilton, Hyatt and La Quinta. Individual properties in these chains appearing in the TourBook have been inspected and approved by AAA. Be sure to read "How to Get the Best Room Rates," page 12.

[S/D] identifies establishments offering a senior discount with either the Guaranteed Rates or Rates Subject to Change options (see below). Where [S/D] appears in "icon row," a minimum discount of 10% off the prevailing or guaranteed rates is available to members who are 60 or older.

[ASK] in "icon row" below the listing points out the many TourBook properties that offer discounts to members even though the lodgings do not participate in a formal discount program. The [ASK] is another reminder to *ask* about available discounts when making your reservations or at check-in.

NOTE: Discounts normally offered at some lodgings may not apply during special events or holiday periods. Special rates and discounts may not apply to all room types.

Rate Lines and Rate Options

Rate Lines

Shown from left to right: dates the rates are effective, any meal plan included, the number of Persons/Beds allowed/provided, the rates charged, the extra person (XP) charge and any applicable family plan indicator. (See next page for meal and family plan codes.) Rates are for typical or standard rooms, not special units.

Rate Options

If a lodging chooses not to offer a discount to our members, then it must select one of the following rate options:

> **Guaranteed Rates**—The establishment guarantees our members will not be charged more than the maximum rates printed in the TourBook.
>
> **Rates Subject to Change**—Rates may vary for the life of the TourBook but are guaranteed not to exceed a 15% increase on the printed rates.

Printed rates are based on rack rates and last room availability and are rounded to the nearest dollar. Rates do not include taxes and discounts. U.S. rates are in U.S. dollars; rates for Canadian lodgings are in Canadian dollars. Lodgings may temporarily increase room rates or modify policies during a special event or holiday.

Always Verify Rates and Discounts

To obtain published rates or discounts, you must identify yourself as a AAA or CAA member and request them when making reservations. The SAVE or senior discounts may not be used in conjunction with other discounts. Show your card at registration and verify the room rate.

[22] are numerals used to locate, or "spot," lodgings on maps we provide for larger cities. We spot restaurants with black numerals on white background ovals [22] .

What the Icons Mean

Member Services

- ⛾ Cocktail Lounge
- 🍽 Restaurant on Premises
- 🍽 Restaurant off Premises (walking distance)
- 🛎 24 Hour Room Service
- 🎷 Nightclub
- 🎭 Entertainment
- ✈ Transportation to Airport
- 🐕 Pets Allowed

Special Features

- 🧸 Child Care
- 💼 Business Services
- 🧺 Laundry Service
- ♿ Fully Accessible
- ♿ Semi-Accessible
- 🚿 Roll-in Showers
- 👂 Hearing Impaired
- 🅿 Valet Parking

Room Amenities

- ☕ Coffee Maker in Room
- 🍾 Honor Bar
- 💻 Data Port/Modem Line
- 📺 No Cable TV
- 🎬 Movies
- VCR VCR
- 📻 Radio
- ✖ Non-Smoking Rooms
- ▢ Microwaves
- 🔌 Refrigerator
- ❄ No Air Conditioning
- ☎ No Telephones

Sports/Recreation

- 🏊 Pool
- 🏋 Fitness Center
- 🎾 Recreation Facilities

Safety Features

- Ⓢ Sprinklers
- Ⓓ Smoke Detectors
- 🅾 Safe

Fees may be charged for some of the services represented by the icons listed above; please inquire when making reservations. Check-in times are shown in the listing only if they are after 3 p.m.; check-out times are shown only if they are before 10 a.m. Parking is on the premises and free unless otherwise noted. If a pet icon is not present, assume that the property does not accept pets; although deposits and fees are stated in the listing, check policies and restrictions when making reservations.

Meal Plan Indicators

CP = Continental Plan of pastry, juice and another beverage or may offer expanded breakfast items
BP = Breakfast Plan of full hot breakfast
AP = American Plan of three meals daily
MAP = Modified American Plan of two meals daily
EP = European Plan, where rate includes only room

Family Plan Indicators

The establishment may limit the number of children to whom the family plan applies.
F17 = children 17 and under stay free (age displayed will reflect property's policy)
D17 = discount for children 17 and under
F = children stay free
D = discounts for children

Access for Disabled Travelers

Qualified properties listed in this book have symbols indicating they are either *Fully Accessible or Semi-Accessible*. This two-tiered standard was developed to meet members' varying degrees of accessibility needs.

Fully Accessible properties meet the needs of those who are significantly disabled and primarily confined to a wheelchair. A fully accessible lodging will provide at least one guest room meeting the designated criteria. A traveler with these disabilities will be able to park and access public areas, including restrooms, check-in facilities and at least one food and beverage outlet. A *Fully Accessible* restaurant indicates that parking, dining rooms and restrooms are accessible.

Semi-Accessible properties meet the needs of those who are disabled but have some mobility and are not confined to a wheelchair. Such travelers would include people using a cane or walker, or a disabled individual with good mobility but a limited arm or hand range of motion. A *Semi-Accessible* lodging will provide at least one guest room meeting the designated criteria. A traveler with these disabilities will be able to park and access public areas, including restrooms, check-in facilities and at least one food and beverage outlet. A *Semi-Accessible* restaurant indicates that parking, dining rooms and restrooms are accessible.

This symbol indicates a property with the following equipment available for *Hearing Impaired* travelers: TDD at front desk or switchboard; visual notification of fire alarm, incoming telephone calls, door knock or bell; closed caption decoder available; text telephone or TDD available for guest room use; telephone amplification device available, with shelf and electric outlet next to guest room telephone.

AAA/CAA urges members with disabilities to always phone ahead to fully understand the accommodation's offerings. Some properties do not fully comply with AAA/CAA's exacting accessibility standards but may offer some property design standards that meet the needs of some guests with disabilities.

AAA/CAA does not evaluate recreational facilities, banquet rooms or convention and meeting facilities for accessibility. Call a property directly to inquire about your needs for these areas.

The criteria used by AAA/CAA do not represent the full scope of the Americans With Disabilities Act of 1990 Accessibility Guidelines (ADAAG); they are, however, consistent with the ADAAG. Members can obtain from their local AAA/CAA club the AAA brochure "Accessibility Criteria for Travelers With Disabilities," which describes the specific criteria pertaining to the *Fully Accessible* and *Semi-Accessible* standards.

The Americans With Disabilities Act (ADA) prohibits businesses that serve the public from discriminating against persons with disabilities who are aided by service animals. Some businesses have mistakenly denied access to their properties to persons with disabilities who use service animals. ADA has priority over all state and local laws, as well as a business owner's standard of business, that might bar animals from the premises. Businesses must permit guests and their service animal entry, as well as allow service animals to accompany guests to all public areas of a property. A property is permitted to ask whether the animal is a service animal or a pet, or whether a guest has a disability. The property may not, however, ask questions about the nature of a disability or require proof of one.

How to Get the Best Room Rates

You'll find the best room rate if you book your reservation in advance with the help of a travel counselor or agent at your local AAA/CAA office.

If you're not yet ready to make firm vacation plans or if you prefer a more spontaneous trip, take advantage of the partnerships that preferred hotel chains have arranged with AAA. Call the toll-free numbers on the opposite page that have been set up exclusively for the purpose of reserving with these *Show Your Card & Save*® chain partners.

Even if you were unable to make a reservation, be sure to show your membership card at the desk and ask if you're being offered the lowest rate available for that time. Many lodgings offer reduced rates to members.

Making Reservations

Give Proper Identification

When making reservations, you must identify yourself as a AAA/CAA member. Give all pertinent information about your planned stay. Request written confirmation to guarantee: type of room, rate, dates of stay, and cancellation and refund policies. **Note:** Age restrictions may apply.

Confirm Deposit, Refund and Cancellation Policies

Most establishments give full deposit refunds if they have been notified at least 48 hours before the normal check-in time. However, when making reservations, confirm the property's deposit, cancellation and refund policies. Some properties may charge a cancellation or handling fee. When this applies, "handling fee imposed" will appear in the listing. If you cancel too late, you have little recourse if a refund is denied. When an establishment requires a full or partial payment in advance, and your trip is cut short, a refund may not be given.

When canceling reservations, call the lodging immediately. Make a note of the date and time you called, the cancellation number if there is one, and the name of the person who handled the cancellation. If your AAA/CAA club made your reservation, allow them to make the cancellation for you as well so you will have proof of cancellation.

Review Charges for Appropriate Rates

When you are charged more than the rate listed in the TourBook, under the option **Guaranteed Rates,** or you qualify for the **Senior Discount** and did not receive it, question the additional charge. If management refuses to adhere to the published rate, pay for the room and submit your receipt and membership number to AAA/CAA *within 30 days.* Include all pertinent information: dates of stay, rate paid, itemized paid receipts, number of persons in your party, the room number you occupied, and list any extra room equipment used. A refund of the amount paid in excess of the stated maximum will be made if our investigation indicates that unjustified charging has occurred.

Get the Room You Reserved

When you find your room is not as specified, and you have written confirmation of reservations for a certain type of accommodation, you should be given the option of choosing a different room or finding one elsewhere. Should you choose to go elsewhere and a refund is refused or resisted, submit the matter to AAA/CAA *within 30 days* along with complete documentation, including your reasons for refusing the room and copies of your written confirmation and any receipts or canceled checks associated with this problem.

Preferred Lodging Partners

Call the member-only toll-free numbers or your club to get these member benefits.

Choice Hotel brands
(800) 228-1222 ◄

SAVE Save 10% at Sleep, Comfort, Quality and Econo Lodge
SAVE Save 20% at Clarion Hotels and Clarion Carriage House Inns
SAVE Guaranteed stay - If you're not satisfied with your stay, it's free

Days Inn
(800) 432-9755 ◄

SAVE Guaranteed lowest rates available for dates of stay when booked in advance

Hilton Worldwide
(800) 916-2221 ◄

SAVE Guaranteed lowest rates available for dates of stay when booked in advance

Hyatt Hotels
(800) 532-1496 ◄

SAVE Guaranteed lowest rates available for dates of stay when booked in advance
SAVE Receive second dinner entree at half-price in Hyatt dining room when staying at the hotel

La Quinta Inns
(800) 221-4731 ◄

SAVE Guaranteed lowest public rate for dates of stay for standard room
SAVE Children under 18 and spouse sharing room stay free
SAVE Guaranteed stay - If you're not satisfied with your stay, it's free

Red Roof Inns
(877) 222-7663 ◄

SAVE Save 10% at all Red Roof Inns
SAVE Guaranteed stay - If you're not happy with your night's stay and the problem can't be corrected, it's free

Special rates and discounts may not apply to all room types. Not available to groups and cannot be combined with other discounts. Restrictions apply to stay guarantees. Valid AAA/ CAA membership card must be presented at check-in. Offers good at time of publication; chains and offers may change without notice.

Show Your Card & Save

The Lodging Diamonds

AAA-RATED® lodgings are evaluated annually during unannounced visits by full-time inspectors. Properties must satisfy a set of minimum requirements that reflect the basic lodging needs members have identified. An increased number of diamonds reflects higher levels of quality in service and amenities.

The few lodgings with [FYI] in place of diamonds are included as an "informational only" service for members. It indicates that a property has not been rated for one or more of the following reasons: too new to rate; under construction; under major renovation; not inspected; or may not meet all AAA requirements.

Properties meet all Listing Requirements. They are clean and well-maintained.

Properties maintain the attributes offered at the one diamond level while showing noticeable enhancements in room decor and quality of furnishings.

Properties show a marked upgrade in physical attributes, services and comfort. Additional amenities, services and facilities may be offered.

Properties reflect an exceptional degree of hospitality, service and attention to detail, while offering upscale facilities and a variety of amenities.

Property facilities and operations exemplify an impeccable standard of excellence while exceeding guest expectations in hospitality and service. These renowned properties are both striking and luxurious, offering many extra amenities.

The Restaurant Diamonds

Diamond ratings are assigned based on conditions noted at the time of the evaluation. Food quality is the most critical to the overall rating, but other factors also are considered, such as service and atmosphere. Restaurants are classified by cuisine type. Some listings include additional information, such as the availability of a senior citizen menu, children's menu or "early bird specials," if offered at least 5 days a week. The dinner price range is approximate and includes a salad or appetizer, an entree, a vegetable and a non-alcoholic beverage for one person. Taxes and tip are not included. *Note: Major restaurant chains are not listed due to their widespread recognition.*

Provides a simple, family or specialty meal in clean, pleasant surroundings. Food is basic and wholesome. Service is casual, limited or self-serve. Decor is informal.

More extensive menus for family or adult dining. Food is prepared with standard ingredients. Service is attentive but may be informal, casual, limited or self-serve. The decor presents a unified theme that is comfortable but also may be trendy, casual or upbeat.

An upscale or special family dining experience. Food is cooked to order and creatively prepared with quality ingredients. A wine list is available. A skilled, often uniformed staff provides service. The usually professional and inviting decor projects a trendy, upbeat, casual or formal atmosphere.

A high degree of sophistication, thus creating an adult dining experience. Complex food is creatively presented. An extensive wine list is offered. The service staff, often formally attired, is professionally trained. The decor is distinctive, stylish and elegant; some establishments are casual while still offering refinement or formality.

A memorable occasion—the ultimate in adult dining. Food shows the highest culinary skills, evident in all areas of preparation and presentation. An extensive wine list is available. A professional staff—often in formal attire—provides flawless and pampering service. The decor has classic details, often formal, and reflects comfort and luxury.

Lodging Classifications

AAA inspectors evaluate lodgings based on classification, since all lodging types by definition do not provide the same level of service and facilities. Thus, hotels are rated in comparison to other hotels–and so on. A lodging's classification appears beneath its diamond rating in the listing.

Motel
(limited service)

Low-rise or multistory establishment offering limited public and recreational facilities.

Hotel
(full service)

Usually high-rise establishments, offering a full range of on-premises food and beverage service, cocktail lounge, entertainment, conference facilities, business services, shops and recreational activities. Wide range of services provided by uniformed staff on duty 24 hours. Parking arrangements vary.

Motor Inn
(moderate service)

Single or multistory establishment offering on-premises food and beverage service. Meeting and banquet facilities and some recreational activities. Usually complimentary on-site parking.

Bed and Breakfast
(limited service)

Usually smaller establishments emphasizing a more personal relationship between operators and guests, leading to an "at home" feeling. Guest units tend to be individually decorated. Rooms may not include some modern amenities such as televisions and telephones, and may have a shared bathroom. Usually owner-operated, with a common room or parlor, separate from the innkeeper's living quarters, where guests and operators can interact during evening and breakfast hours. Evening office closures are normal. A continental or full, hot breakfast is served and is included in the room rate.

Country Inn
(moderate service)

Although similar in definition to a bed and breakfast, country inns are usually larger in size, provide more spacious public areas and offer a dining facility that serves at least breakfast and dinner. May be located in a rural setting or downtown area.

Apartment
(limited service)

Establishments that primarily offer transient guest accommodations with one or more bedrooms, a living room, a full kitchen and an eating area. Studio-type apartments may combine the sleeping and living areas into one room.

Condominium
(limited service)

Establishments that primarily offer guest accommodations that are privately owned by individuals and available for rent. These can include apartment-style units or homes. A variety of room styles and decor treatments as well as limited housekeeping service is typical. May have off-site registration.

Lodging Classifications

Complex
(service varies depending on type of lodgings)

A combination of two or more types of lodging classifications.

Lodge
(moderate service)

Typically two or more stories with all facilities in one building, rustic decor. Located in vacation, ski, fishing areas, etc. Usually has food and beverage service.

Resort
(full service)

Geared to vacation travelers. It is a destination offering varied food and beverage outlets, specialty shops, meeting or conference facilities, entertainment, and extensive recreational facilities for special interests such as golf, tennis, skiing, fishing and water sports. Assorted social and recreational programs are typically offered in season, and a variety of package plans are usually available, including meal plans incorporated into the rates. Larger resorts may offer a variety of guest accommodations.

Cottage
(limited service)

Establishments that primarily provide individual housing units that may offer one or more separate sleeping rooms, a living room and cooking facilities. Usually incorporate rustic decor treatments and are geared to vacationers.

Ranch
(moderate service)

Often offers rustic decor treatments and food and beverage facilities. Entertainment and recreational activities are geared to a Western-style adventure vacation. May provide some meeting facilities.

Subclassifications

The following are subclassifications that may appear along with the classifications listed above to provide a more specific description of the lodging:

Suite

One or more bedrooms and a living room/sitting area, which is closed off by a full wall. *Note:* May not have a partition bedroom door.

Extended Stay

Properties catering to longer-term guest stays. Will have kitchens or efficiencies. May have a separate living room area, evening office closure and limited housekeeping services.

Historic

Accommodations in restored structures built prior to 1920, reflecting the ambiance of yesteryear and the surrounding area. Antique furnishings complement the overall decor of the property. Rooms may lack some modern amenities and may have shared bathrooms.

Guest Safety

Precautions Can Save A Vacation!

Travelers are faced with the task of protecting themselves while in a strange environment. Although there is no way to guarantee absolute protection from crime, the experts—law enforcement officials—advise travelers to take a pro-active approach to securing their property and ensuring their safety.

1 Make sure the hotel desk clerk does not announce your room number; if so, quietly request a new room assignment.

2 Ask front desk personnel which areas of town to avoid and what, if any, special precautions should be taken when driving a rental car (some criminals target tourists driving rental cars).

3 Never open the door to a stranger; use the peephole and request identification. If you are still unsure, call the front desk to verify the identity of the person and the purpose of his/her visit.

4 Carry money separately from credit cards or use a "fanny pack." Carry your purse close to your body and your wallet in an inside coat or front trouser pocket. Never leave luggage unattended, and use your business address, if possible, on luggage tags.

5 Beware of distractions staged by would-be scam artists, especially groups of children that surround you or a stranger who accidentally spills something on you. They may be lifting your wallet.

6 If using an automatic teller machine (ATM), choose one in a well-lit area with plenty of foot traffic, such as one at a grocery store. Law enforcement officials suggest that machines inside establishments are generally safer to use.

7 Use room safes or safety deposit boxes provided by the hotel. Store all valuables out of sight, even when you are in the room.

8 Law enforcement agencies consider card-key (electronic) door locks the most secure.

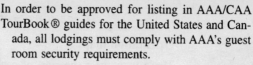

Guest Safety

In order to be approved for listing in AAA/CAA TourBook® guides for the United States and Canada, all lodgings must comply with AAA's guest room security requirements.

In response to AAA/CAA members' concern about their safety at properties, AAA RATED® accommodations must have deadbolt locks on all guest room entry doors and connecting room doors.

If the area outside the guest room door is not visible from inside the room through a window or door panel, viewports must be installed on all guest room entry doors. Bed and breakfast properties and country inns are not required to have viewports. Ground floor and easily accessible sliding doors must be equipped with some other type of secondary security locks.

Field inspectors view a percentage of rooms at each property. It is not feasible for the inspectors to evaluate every room in every lodging establishment. So, AAA cannot guarantee that there are working locks on all doors and windows in all guest rooms.

Because of the highly specialized skills needed to conduct professional fire safety inspections, AAA/CAA inspectors cannot assess fire safety. However, guest rooms in U.S. lodging properties must be equipped with an operational, single-station smoke detector, and all public areas must have operational smoke detectors or an automatic sprinkler system. **Note:** Some Canadian lodgings are an exception to this requirement. There may be some Canadian properties that were approved prior to 1988 that use heat sensors in place of smoke detectors and/or automatic sprinkler systems.

Since all U.S. lodgings must be equipped as described above, no special notation is made in the U.S. listings. Canadian listings reflect with icons (shown on page 8) the type of fire safety equipment provided. A AAA/CAA inspector has evaluated a sampling of the rooms to verify this equipment is in place. For additional fire safety information read the page posted on the back of your guest room door, or write:

National Fire Protection Association,
1 Batterymarch Park, P.O. Box 9101,
Quincy, MA 02269-9101.

TourBook Maps

Attractions Section

Orientation maps

These maps near the start of each Attractions section show only those places we call points of interest. Stars accent towns with "must see" attractions. And the black ovals with white numerals locate items listed in the nearby Recreation Areas chart.

Defined metro and destination area maps

These maps illustrate key travel areas defined by local travel experts. Communities shown have listings for AAA approved attractions.

National park maps

These maps represent the area in and around the park. Some campground sites and lodges spotted on the maps do not meet AAA/CAA criteria, but are shown for members who nevertheless wish to stay there.

City maps

These maps show areas where numerous points of interest are concentrated and indicate their location in relation to major roads, parks, airports and other landmarks.

Walking or self-guiding tour maps

These maps correspond to specific routes described in TourBook text.

Driving Distance Maps

Driving distance maps

These maps located in the Featured Information section of the book are intended to be used only for trip-distance and driving-time planning.

TourBook Maps

Lodgings & Restaurants Section

State or province orientation maps

These maps appear before the property listings in the Lodgings & Restaurants section of selected TourBooks. These maps show the relative positions of major metropolitan areas and the vicinity towns in those areas.

Area maps

These maps denote large geographical areas in which there are many towns containing lodgings and/or restaurants. Due to these maps' small scale, lodgings and restaurants are not shown; towns with lodgings and/or restaurants are printed in magenta type.

Defined metro and destination area maps

These maps illustrate key travel areas defined by local travel experts. Communities shown have listings for AAA RATED® lodgings and/or restaurants.

Spotting maps

These maps show the location of lodgings and restaurants. Lodgings are spotted with a black-background numeral (**20**, for example); restaurants are spotted with a white-background numeral (**20**, for example). Spotting map indexes have been placed after the main city heading to provide the user with a convenient method to identify what an area has to offer at a glance. The index references the map page number where the property is spotted, indicates if a property is an Official Appointment and contains an advertising reference if applicable. It also lists the property's diamond rating, high season rate range and listing page number.

Downtown/city spotting maps

These maps are provided when spotted facilities are very concentrated. Starred points of interest also appear on these maps.

Vicinity spotting maps

These maps spot those properties that are outside the downtown or city area. Major roads, landmarks, airports and starred points of interest are shown on vicinity spotting maps as well. The names of suburban communities that have AAA RATED® accommodations are shown in magenta type.

Sample Attraction Listing

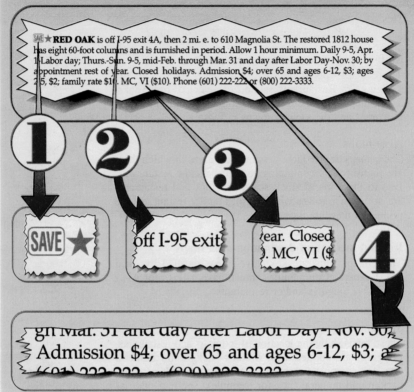

RED OAK is off I-95 exit 4A, then 2 mi. e. to 610 Magnolia St. The restored 1812 house has eight 60-foot columns and is furnished in period. Allow 1 hour minimum. Daily 9-5, Apr. 1-Labor day; Thurs.-Sun. 9-5, mid-Feb. through Mar. 31 and day after Labor Day-Nov. 30; by appointment rest of year. Closed holidays. Admission $4; over 65 and ages 6-12, $3; ages 2-5, $2; family rate $10. MC, VI ($10). Phone (601) 222-222 or (800) 222-3333.

SAVE ★

off I-95 exit

ear. Closed .). MC, VI ($

gh Mar. 31 and day after Labor Day-Nov. 30; Admission $4; over 65 and ages 6-12, $3; a (601) 222-222 or (800) 222-3333

(1) SAVE participants offer AAA/CAA cardholders and up to six family members at least 10% off admission for the validity period of the TourBook. Present your card at the admissions desk. A list of participating attractions appears in the Indexes section of the book. The SAVE discount may not be used in conjunction with other discounts. Discounts may not apply during special events or particular days or seasons.

★ —Attraction is of exceptional interest and quality.

(2) Unless otherwise specified, directions are given from the center of town, using the following highway designations: I (interstate highway), US (federal highway), Hwy. (Canadian highway), SR (state route), CR (county road), FM (farm to market road), FR (forest road), MM (mile marker).

(3) AE=American Express   DS=Discover   MC=MasterCard
CB=Carte Blanche   JC=Japanese Credit Bureau   VI=VISA
DI=Diners Club
Minimum amounts that may be charged appear in parentheses when applicable.

(4) Admission prices are quoted *without* sales tax. Children under the lowest age specified are admitted free when accompanied by an adult. Days, months and age groups written with a hyphen are *inclusive*. Prices pertaining to attractions in the United States are quoted in U.S. dollars; Canadian province and territory attraction prices are quoted in Canadian dollars.

Confirm Prices and Schedules

All information was reviewed for accuracy before publication. However, since changes often occur between annual editions, please use the phone numbers in the listings to confirm prices and schedules.

Attraction Partners

These Show Your Card & Save® attraction partners provide the listed member benefits. Admission tickets that offer greater discounts may be available for purchase at the local AAA club.

Universal Studios (Florida and Hollywood)

Save $3 on admission at the gate

Save 10% on selected souvenirs and dining

SeaWorld/Busch Gardens

Save at SeaWorld, Busch Gardens, Sesame Place, Water Country U.S.A. and Adventure Island

Save 10% on general admission

Save 10% at a selected restaurant and retail shops inside the park

Offers at the attractions listed above are good at the time of publication and are subject to change without notice.

Golden Passports

Citizens or permanent residents of the United States who are 62 and older can obtain Golden Age Passports for a one-time $10 fee. The Golden Eagle Passport is available to everyone, despite country of origin; it costs $50 annually. Golden Access Passports are free to citizens or permanent residents of the United States (regardless of age) who are medically blind or permanently disabled. All cover entrance fees for the holder and accompanying passengers in a private vehicle to all national parks and historic sites, monuments and battlefields within the U.S. national park system, plus half off camping and other fees. Apply in person at most federally operated areas.

Connecticut

Center of Culture

Feed your creative appetite in museums, theaters, concert halls and craft shops

Take It Easy

Stroll a secluded beach, drive a country road or browse for antiques

Sailing Back in Time

See the sights and learn about history on a narrated cruise

Author, Author

Tour the Hartford homes of Mark Twain and Harriet Beecher Stowe

Go Yale!

It's ivy-covered buildings and Gothic dormitories are among New Haven's many charms

a small package

G ood things come in small packages.

And packages don't come much smaller than gracious Connecticut, which surpasses only Rhode Island and Delaware in size.

There's the southwestern corner, home to celebrities and commuters who enjoy having easy access to the Big Apple without having to sacrifice privacy and space.

The fertile Connecticut River Valley nurtured the talents of authors Harriet Beecher Stowe and Mark Twain, both of whom kept homes in Hartford. It also fueled the eccentricities of actor William Gillette, whose peculiar 24-room castle on a hilltop overlooking the river is open for tours.

The wooded Litchfield Hills boast lush, green valleys; the magnificent 250-foot cascade of Kent Falls; and a pair of romantic covered bridges over the peaceful Housatonic River.

New Haven is Connecticut's intellectual hub. Home to prestigious Yale University, the city is the birthplace of the lollipop, the corkscrew and the steamboat.

A rich maritime history punctuates the personality of Mystic, most noted for its re-created mid-1800s seaport.

The state's emerging locale is the Quiet Corner, a collection of tranquil northeastern towns that share an authentic Colonial feel.

Take the time to unwrap Connecticut. It's a worthwhile delight.

Starting in 1810, when the Hartford Fire Insurance Co. was incorporated as the country's first such business, insurance has been key to Connecticut's economy.

Scads of other providers—among them Mutual Insurance Co., Connecticut Mutual Life Insurance Co., Aetna Life Insurance Co., Travelers Insurance and Connecticut General Life Insurance Co.—have been founded in the state to insure everything from cars and houses to health and life.

Can these companies ensure a delightful escape from the day-to-day grind?

Probably not. But it's highly likely that Connecticut can.

The scenery is spectacular. SR 169, one of Connecticut's two national scenic byways, wends through dense forests, quaint towns and acres of farmland between the Massachusetts border and the Quiet Corner region, in the northeastern quadrant. The other so-designated road is Merritt Parkway, a 38-mile route in southwestern Connecticut lined with interesting bridges.

Get in touch with the outdoors at a nature center. They're in Bristol, Canton, Derby, Litchfield, Manchester, Mystic, New Canaan, New Haven, Stamford and West-port. Factor in audubon centers, and you can add Fairfield, Greenwich and Sharon to that lengthy list.

Breathtaking cascades splash splendor into the landscape. Visit Kent to see the impressive Kent Falls, which tumbles 250 feet over rock ledges. For more watery views, take a cruise along the Connecticut River, among the tiny Thimble Islands or in Long Island Sound.

That "Mystical" Appeal

Aquatic sightseeing also is popular in Mystic, where water defines the city's past. Penguins, beluga whales and dolphins are among the residents at Mystic Marinelife Aquarium. The houses, shops and buildings that make up Mystic Seaport paint a picture of 19th-century life, while the local maritime museum displays such items as ship models and figureheads.

Nearby Groton sustains this focus in a museum that houses the world's first nuclear-powered submarine.

Other aspects of history are recounted, too. Trace Revolutionary War events at the Christopher Leffingwell House in Norwich, Fort Griswold State Park in Groton, Shaw

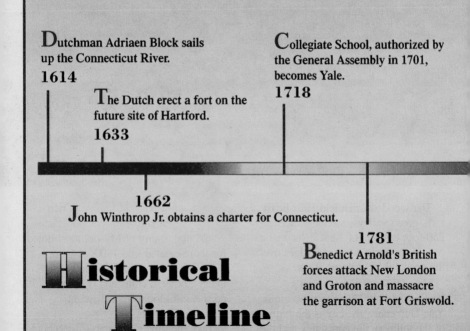

Dutchman Adriaen Block sails up the Connecticut River.
1614

The Dutch erect a fort on the future site of Hartford.
1633

Collegiate School, authorized by the General Assembly in 1701, becomes Yale.
1718

1662
John Winthrop Jr. obtains a charter for Connecticut.

1781
Benedict Arnold's British forces attack New London and Groton and massacre the garrison at Fort Griswold.

Historical Timeline

Mansion in New London and Webb-Deane-Stevens Museum in Wethersfield.

Learn about the military at the U.S. Coast Guard Academy's visitor pavilion in New London or at The Company of Military Historians in Westbrook. Explore American Indian heritage at such places as Fort Shantok State Park in Uncasville, Mohegan Indian Burial Ground in Norwich, Somers Mountain Indian Museum in Somers and The Institute for American Indian Studies in Washington.

The Constitution State is the birthplace of plenty of creative folks, such as showman P.T. Barnum and the diminutive spotlight of his circus, Gen. Tom Thumb (a.k.a. Charles Thurwood Stratton), both of Bridgeport; author Harriet Beecher Stowe, of Litchfield; and lexicographer Noah Webster, of West Hartford.

Also originating here were numerous inventions, including the Colt revolver, portable typewriter, sewing machine, can opener, lollipop, Frisbee, vacuum cleaner, Polaroid camera, helicopter and color TV.

A Who's Who of Nutmeggers

Noted nutmeggers, as Connecticut residents colloquially are dubbed, include Mark Twain, who lived 27 years in Hartford, and Nobel Prize-winning playwright Eugene O'Neill, who was raised in New London. The castle that is the centerpiece of Gillette Castle State Park was the home of William Gillette. The eccentric actor, who designed unique locks for each of the doors to castle rooms, implored his family not to sell the estate to some "blithering saphead" upon his death.

There are places to view exquisite art. Impressionist pieces by such masters as Mary Cassatt, Edgar Degas and Edouard Manet decorate the walls of Farmington's Hill-Stead Museum. New Britain Museum of American Art includes works by Winslow Homer and James McNeill Whistler. At New Haven's Yale University Art Gallery you'll find paintings by Claude Monet, Pablo Picasso and Vincent van Gogh.

If crafts are more your style, stop by Bittersweet Farm in Branford, Brookfield Craft Center in Brookfield or Silvermine Guild Arts Center in New Canaan.

In Connecticut, you'll run out of acreage before you deplete your options for fun.

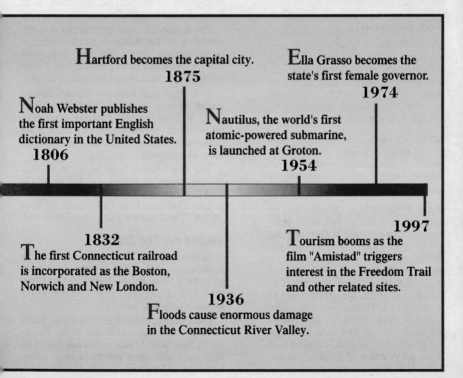

Hartford becomes the capital city.
1875

Ella Grasso becomes the state's first female governor.
1974

Noah Webster publishes the first important English dictionary in the United States.
1806

Nautilus, the world's first atomic-powered submarine, is launched at Groton.
1954

1832
The first Connecticut railroad is incorporated as the Boston, Norwich and New London.

1997
Tourism booms as the film "Amistad" triggers interest in the Freedom Trail and other related sites.

1936
Floods cause enormous damage in the Connecticut River Valley.

FAST FACTS

POPULATION: 3,269,900.

AREA: 5,009 square miles; ranks 48th.

CAPITAL: Hartford.

HIGHEST POINT: 2,380 ft., Mount Frissell, in Salisbury.

LOWEST POINT: Sea level, Long Island Sound.

TIME ZONE: Eastern. DST.

MINIMUM AGE FOR DRIVERS: 16.

SEAT BELT/CHILD RESTRAINT LAWS: Seat belts are required for driver and front-seat passengers; child restraints are required for under age 4.

HELMETS FOR MOTORCYCLISTS: Required for rider and passenger under 18.

RADAR DETECTORS: Permitted.

FIREARMS LAWS: Vary by state and/or county. Contact the Board of Firearms, 251 Maxim Rd., Hartford, CT 06114; phone (860) 566-7078.

HOLIDAYS: Jan. 1; Martin Luther King Jr.'s Birthday, Jan. (3rd Mon.); Lincoln's Birthday, Feb. 11; Presidents' Day, Feb. (3rd Mon.); Memorial Day, May (last Mon.); July 4; Labor Day; Columbus Day, Oct. (2nd Mon.); Veterans Day, Nov. 11; Thanksgiving; Dec. 25.

TAXES: Connecticut's statewide sales tax is 6 percent. There is an Admissions Tax of 10 percent on most places of amusement; the rate is 5 percent on goods and services at any cabaret.

STATE INFORMATION CENTERS on I-95 northbound at Darien and North Stonington; I-84 eastbound at Danbury; and I-84 westbound at Willington are open year-round 8-6. Centers northbound on I-95 at Westbrook and I-84 eastbound at Southington are open Memorial Day through Labor Day 8-6. Centers on I-91 northbound at Middletown and southbound at Wallingford are not staffed but have tourism literature available. Visitor information also is available in Terminals A and B of Bradley International Airport, Windsor Locks.

Recreation

Although small in size, Connecticut is plenty big on recreation.

State parks along the rocky coast boast beautiful sandy beaches. Whether you prefer **swimming** or just sprawling on a towel, Hammonasset Beach, west of Clinton, Rocky Neck, near Niantic, and Sherwood Island, in Westport, all fit the bill.

Long Island Sound is the top destination for water lovers. Forget about your troubles while **boating** in the sparkling blue waters, or cast your **fishing** line to see if the bluefish, striped bass and flounder are biting. You can charter a boat from many towns along the shore.

Also a lure for boaters are the Thimble Islands, a cluster of many tiny islands just offshore from Branford.

Inland, you'll find lots more water—more than 80 lakes and ponds and more than 300 miles of rivers and streams. Avid anglers head to the western upland region and to the Farmington and Housatonic rivers, where bass as well as brown and rainbow trout nearly always are running. Only fly fishing is permitted on the section of the Housatonic in Housatonic Meadows State Park, in Cornwall Bridge.

For a leisurely way to pass the day, try **canoeing** or **kayaking** on the Connecticut or Housatonic rivers. Or just float your woes away while **tubing** on the lazy Farmington River, near New Hartford.

Don an oxygen tank and flippers and go **scuba diving** at Lake Waramaug State Park, in New Preston; Pachaug State Forest, north of Voluntown; Rocky Neck State Park, near Niantic; or Stratton Brook State Park, in Simsbury.

The Constitution State boasts more than its fair share of waterfalls. **Hiking** trails lead to Chapman Falls, at Devil's Hopyard in East Haddam; Kent Falls, north of Kent on US 7; and Shelter Falls, near Mansfield.

Taking on The Trail

Serious trekkers can take on a stretch of the Appalachian Trail, which follows the Housatonic for a while before veering east to Cornwall, then turning north near Lakeville to the Massachusetts state line.

Other hiking routes lead to vantage points offering spectacular countryside vistas. Neighboring New York, Massachusetts and Rhode Island are visible from the tower atop Talcott Mountain, in Simsbury.

It's also perfectly acceptable to **climb** all over the sleeping giant rock formation at Sleeping Giant State Park, in Hamden. A 1.6-mile trail on the "left hip" of the resting body leads to an four-story observation tower.

Outstanding paths at Canaan Mountain, near Canaan, and Topsmead State Forest, east of Litchfield, attract **horseback riding** enthusiasts. A 3-mile **bicycling** trail awaits cyclists at Lock 12 Historical Park, in Cheshire. Mountain biking is among the biggest draws at Nepaug State Forest, east of Torrington.

To maximize any outdoor experience, plan your trip around the Columbus Day holiday, when fall foliage usually is at its most vibrant.

Ready to Chill Out

When the temperature drops, fun-seekers head for the slopes. **Downhill skiing** resorts—Mohawk Mountain, off SR 4 near Cornwall; Mount Southington, near Hartford; Powder Ridge, in Middlefield; Ski Sundown, in New Hartford; and Woodbury Ski Area, in Woodbury—cater to skiers of all abilities.

Cross-country skiing and **snowshoeing** are other winter diversions. Visit Macedonia Brook State Park in Kent, Putnam Memorial State Park in West Redding or Squantz Pond State Park in New Fairfield. Kick your cold-weather thrills up a notch by **snowmobiling** through state forests such as Cockaponset, west of Chester; Natchaug, south of Phoenixville; or Peoples, north of Pleasant Valley.

There are plenty of places to bed down for the night if you go **camping** in Connecticut. Particularly interesting are campsites at Hurd, Gillette Castle and Selden Island state parks; they are accessible only by canoe and require you to obtain a permit in advance. For more information about camping in Connecticut, *see the AAA Northeastern CampBook.*

Recreational Activities

Throughout the TourBook, you may notice a Recreational Activities heading with bulleted listings of recreation-oriented establishments listed underneath. Since normal AAA inspection criteria cannot be applied, these establishments are presented for information only. Age, height and weight restrictions may apply. Reservations are often recommended and sometimes required. Visitors should phone or write the attraction for additional information, and the address and phone number are provided for this purpose.

FOR YOUR INFORMATION

FURTHER INFORMATION FOR VISITORS:
State of Connecticut Department of Economic and Community Development
505 Hudson St.
Hartford, CT 06106
(800) 282-6863

RECREATION INFORMATION:
State of Connecticut Department of Environmental Protection
79 Elm St.
Hartford, CT 06102
(860) 424-3200

DID YOU KNOW?

First printed in 1764, The Hartford Courant is the oldest newspaper in the United States.

From 1703 to 1875 Connecticut had two capitals: Hartford and New Haven.

The original name of Connecticut, "Quinnehtukqut," was derived from the Algonquin Indian word for "beside the long tidal river."

What is considered to be the world's first written constitution, the Fundamental Orders, was created in 1639 by the English settlements that made up the Connecticut Colony. That is why Connecticut is often referred to as "The Constitution State."

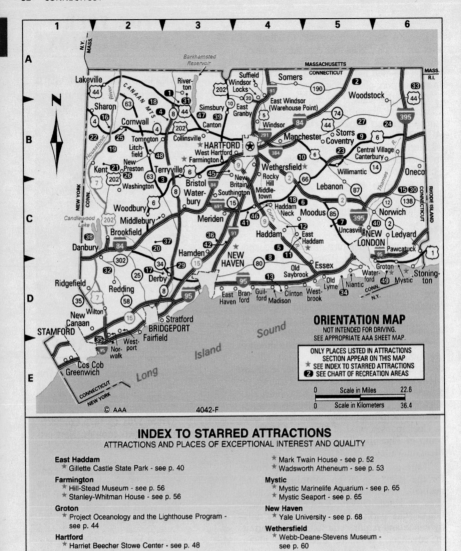

INDEX TO STARRED ATTRACTIONS
ATTRACTIONS AND PLACES OF EXCEPTIONAL INTEREST AND QUALITY

Can't resist the call of the wild?

Make your trip doubly enjoyable with the help of a AAA CampBook.

RECREATION AREAS

	MAP LOCATION	CAMPING	PICNICKING	HIKING TRAILS	BOATING	BOAT RAMP	BOAT RENTAL	FISHING	SWIMMING	PETS ON LEASH	BICYCLE TRAILS	WINTER SPORTS	VISITOR CENTER	LODGE/CABINS	FOOD SERVICE
STATE															
American Legion (A-3) 782 acres 1 mi. n. of Pleasant Valley on West River Rd.	1	•	•	•				•		•		•			
Bigelow Hollow (A-5) 513 acres 2 mi. n. of Union on SR 197.	2		•	•	•	•		•							
Black Rock (C-2) 444 acres 3 mi. s.w. of Thomaston on US 6.	3	•	•	•				•	•			•			•
Bluff Point Coastal Reserve (D-6) 806 acres 5 mi. s.e. of Groton off US 1.	49		•	•				•							
Burr Pond (B-2) 438 acres 5 mi. n. of Torrington off SR 8.	4	•	•	•	•	•	•	•	•						
Chatfield Hollow (D-4) 356 acres 1.5 mi. w. of Killingworth on SR 80. Ice skating; horse trails.	8	•	•	•				•	•			•			•
Cockaponset (C-4) 15,652 acres 3 mi. w. of Chester on SR 148. Snowmobiling.	5		•	•				•	•	•		•			
Day Pond (C-4) 180 acres .5 mi. n. of Westchester on SR 149. Horse trails.	6		•	•				•	•	•					
Devil's Hopyard (C-5) 860 acres 3 mi. n. of North Plain off SR 82.	7	•	•	•				•							
Gay City (B-5) 1,569 acres 8 mi. s.e. of Manchester on SR 85. Ice skating; horse trails.	10		•	•				•	•	•		•			
Gillette Castle (C-4) 184 acres 2.5 mi. s. off SR 82, then 1.7 mi. w., overlooking the Connecticut River. Historic. Scenic. *(See East Haddam p. 40)*	11		•	•				•							•
Haddam Meadows (C-4) 175 acres 3 mi. s. of Higganum on SR 154.	12		•		•	•		•							
Hammonasset Beach (D-4) 923 acres 2 mi. e. of Madison off US 1; 1 mi. s. off I-95 exit 62. *(See Madison p. 63)*	13	•	•					•	•	•		•	•		•
Hopeville Pond (C-6) 554 acres s.e. of Hopeville on SR 201.	15	•	•	•	•	•	•	•	•						
Housatonic Meadows (B-2) 452 acres 1 mi. n. of Cornwall Bridge on US 7.	16	•	•	•				•							
Hurd (C-4) 884 acres w. of Haddam Neck off SR 151.	46		•	•				•		•		•			
Indian Well (D-2) 153 acres 2 mi. n.w. of Shelton on SR 110.	17		•	•	•	•		•	•						•
James L. Goodwin (B-5) 2,171 acres 3 miles east of South Chaplin on US 6. Horse trails.	9		•	•				•				•			
John A. Minetto (B-2) 678 acres 5 mi. n. of Torrington on SR 272. Ice skating.	18		•	•				•				•			
Kent Falls (B-2) 275 acres 4 mi. n.e. of Kent on US 7.	19		•	•				•							
Kettletown (C-2) 492 acres 6 mi. s. of Southbury off I-84 exit 15.	20	•	•	•				•	•						
Lake Waramaug (B-2) 95 acres 5 mi. n. of New Preston on Lake Waramaug Rd. (SR 478). Ice skating; scuba diving. *(See New Preston p. 70)*	21	•	•	•		•	•	•	•			•			
Macedonia Brook (B-1) 2,300 acres 4 mi. n.w. of Kent off SR 341.	22	•	•	•				•							
Mansfield Hollow (B-5) 2,328 acres 1 mi. e. of Mansfield Center off SR 89.	23		•	•	•	•		•		•		•			
Mashamoquet Brook (B-6) 860 acres 5 mi. s.w. of Putnam on US 44.	24	•	•	•				•	•						
Mohawk Mountain (B-2) 259 acres 6 mi. w. of Goshen off SR 4.	25		•	•								•			
Mount Tom (B-2) 232 acres 3.5 mi. w. of Bantam off US 202. Ice skating; scuba diving.	26		•	•				•	•						
Natchaug (B-5) 12,935 acres 4 mi. s. of Phoenixville on SR 198. Historic. Snowmobiling.	27		•	•				•		•		•			
Osbornedale (D-3) 350 acres 1 mi. n.w. of Derby off US 34. Ice skating.	29		•	•				•		•		•			
Pachaug (C-6) 23,938 acres 1 mi. n. of Voluntown.	30	•	•	•	•	•		•		•		•	•		
Penwood (B-4) 787 acres 4 mi. w. of Bloomfield on SR 185.	14		•	•							•	•			

RECREATION AREAS

	MAP LOCATION	CAMPING	PICNICKING	HIKING TRAILS	BOATING	BOAT RAMP	BOAT RENTAL	FISHING	SWIMMING	PETS ON LEASH	BICYCLE TRAILS	WINTER SPORTS	VISITOR CENTER	LODGE/CABINS	FOOD SERVICE
Peoples (B-3) 2,942 acres 1 mi. n. of Pleasant Valley on East River Rd. Snowmobiling.	31		●	●				●		●		●			
Putnam Memorial (D-2) 183 acres n. of Redding at SRs 107 and 58. Horse trails. *(See Redding p. 74)*	32		●	●				●		●		●			
Quaddick (A-6) 116 acres 7 mi. n.e. of Putnam off SR 44. Ice skating.	33		●	●	●	●		●	●	●		●			●
Rocky Neck (D-5) 710 acres 1 mi. e. of South Lyme off I-95 exit 72. Scuba diving.	34	●	●	●				●	●			●			●
Salmon River (C-4) 6,115 acres 1 mi. n. of Westchester; 2 mi. w. of SR 149 on River Rd. Historic.	18		●	●				●			●	●			
Sherwood Island (E-2) 234 acres 2 mi. s. of Westport off I-95 exit 18.	35		●					●	●				●		●
Sleeping Giant (C-3) 1,439 acres 3 mi. n. of Hamden off SR 10.	36		●	●				●		●					
Southford Falls (C-3) 120 acres 4 mi. s.w. of Southbury on SR 188.	37		●	●				●		●		●			
Squantz Pond (C-1) 172 acres 4 mi. n. of New Fairfield on SR 39.	38		●	●	●	●		●	●			●			●
Stratton Brook (B-3) 148 acres 2 mi. w. of Simsbury on SR 309.	39		●	●				●	●			●			
Topsmead (B-2) 511 acres 2 mi. e. on SR 118, e. on E. Litchfield Rd., then s. on Buell Rd. *(See Litchfield p. 63)*	48		●	●								●			
Wadsworth Falls (C-4) 285 acres 3 mi. s.w. of Middlefield on SR 157.	41		●	●				●	●	●		●			
Wharton Brook (C-3) 96 acres 2 mi. s. of Wallingford on US 5.	42		●					●	●	●					●
OTHER															
Lake McDonough (B-3) on SR 219 in New Hartford.	47		●	●	●		●	●	●	●					
Mohegan Park and Memorial Rose Garden (C-5) 380 acres e. of Norwich off SR 32 on Judd Rd. *(See Norwich p. 72)*	40		●	●				●	●						
Stanley Quarter Park (B-3) 225 acres in New Britain, n. of Central Park on Stanley St. *(See New Britain p. 58)*	45		●	●				●	●	●	●	●	●		

Is there a camping vacation in your future?

AAA CampBooks make

valuable additions

for AAA members

who enjoy

outdoor vacations.

Now You Can Count on AAA for Financial Services Too!

*N*ow, your AAA membership offers even more. Choose from a full range of financial products and services with special AAA member-only rates and features.

AAA Member Select℠ Prime Access℠ Credit Card

AAA Member Select℠ Rewards Credit Card

AAA Member Select℠ Platinum VISA® Credit Card

Auto Loans & Leasing	Market Rate Checking
Home Equity Loans[1]	Money Market Accounts
Personal Loans	Certificates of Deposit[2]

Financial Services

MAKE THE MOST OF YOUR MEMBERSHIP.℠

1-800-680-AAA4

24 HOURS A DAY. 7 DAYS A WEEK.

Available only through participating AAA clubs.

Equal Housing Lender

STARRED ATTRACTIONS

Gillette Castle State Park—The former estate of William Gillette—the American actor known for his portrayal of Sherlock Holmes—is patterned after the designs of medieval German castles. See East Haddam p. 40.

Harriet Beecher Stowe Center—Items belonging to the author of "Uncle Tom's Cabin" are displayed in the restored house. See Hartford p. 48.

Hill-Stead Museum—The paintings and etchings of Mary Cassatt, Edgar Degas, Eduoard Manet, Claude Monet and James McNeill Whistler are among the works in the Colonial-revival house. See Farmington p. 56.

Mark Twain House—The author lived for 17 years in the peculiar 19-room Victorian Gothic house, characterized by orange and black brick, towering turrets and large porches. See Hartford p. 52.

Mystic Marinelife Aquarium—Seals, sea lions and penguins are among the 3,500 sea creatures at the aquarium, which also features whale and dolphin demonstrations. See Mystic p. 65.

Mystic Seaport—Visitors gain an understanding of life in a seaport during the mid-19th century as they visit historic houses, shops and trade buildings. See Mystic p. 65.

DID YOU KNOW?

The first portable house in America was brought from Windsor to Plymouth in 1724.

Continued on page 38

Points of Interest

BRANFORD (D-4) pop. 27,600, elev. 17′

Established in 1644, the coastal village of Branford became a popular vacation spot at the turn of the 20th century. Short Beach, Branford Point, Indian Neck, Pine Orchard and Stony Creek—granite coves known as the "five fingers" of Branford—lured many summer vacationers.

Harrison House, 124 Main St., is a 1724 house with original period furnishings and local historical items and archives. Also featured are an herb garden and a barn with vintage farm implements. The house is open Thursday through Saturday afternoons in the summer. Phone (203) 488-4828.

Branford Chamber of Commerce: 230 E. Main St., P.O. Box 375, Branford, CT 06405; phone (203) 488-5500.

BITTERSWEET FARM, 779 E. Main St. (US 1), supports artists and artisans who work in restored farm buildings to create hand-blown glass, stained glass, metal sculptures, paintings, paper cuttings, handmade pottery, fiber arts, jewelry, shells and seasonal ornaments and decorations. Allow 1 hour, 30 minutes minimum. Tues.-Sat. 11-5, Sun. noon-5; closed Easter, Thanksgiving and Dec. 25. Free. Phone (203) 488-4689.

THIMBLE ISLANDS CRUISES, which depart the Stony Creek dock 3 mi. s. of I-95 exit 56, offers 45-minute narrated trips among the 25 tiny Thimble Islands.

Connecticut Sea Ventures boards at 25 minutes past the hour and departs at 40 minutes past the hour daily 10-5, Memorial Day-Labor Day. Fare $7; senior citizens $6; under 12, $3. Phone (203) 397-3921.

Sea Mist boards on the hour and departs on the quarter-hour Wed.-Mon. 10-4, June 1-Labor Day; Fri.-Sun. at noon, 2 and 4 in May and day after Labor Day-Columbus Day. Fare $8; over 61, $7; under 13, $3. Phone (203) 488-8905.

Volsunga IV leaves daily on the hour 11-4, Memorial Day-Columbus Day (weather permitting); phone to verify schedule. Fare $7; over 59, $6; under 12, $3. Phone (203) 488-9978 or 481-3345.

BRIDGEPORT (D-2) pop. 141,700, elev. 12′

Bridgeport, on a harbor formed by the Pequonnock River, first was settled in 1639 by residents of the older settlements of Fairfield and Stratford. Known as Newtown, then as Stratfield, the community was incorporated as the town of Bridgeport in 1821; by 1836 it had become a city. As in many New England seaport towns, its first economic activity was whaling, which gave way to industry with the coming of the railroad.

Bridgeport was the home of P.T. Barnum and the 1838 birthplace of Charles Thurwood Stratton, who was only 25 inches tall until he was in his teens and 40 inches tall at maturity. Billed as "General" Tom Thumb, Stratton was the main attraction of Barnum's "Greatest Show on Earth."

Coastal Fairfield County Convention & Visitors Bureau: 297 West Ave., Norwalk, CT 06850; phone (800) 866-7925.

THE BARNUM MUSEUM, 820 Main St., chronicles the life and times of P.T. Barnum. The three-story museum presents three themes—Barnum the Man, Barnum's Bridgeport and Showman to the World. A 5-minute introductory film is shown continuously. A 5,000-square-foot exhibitions wing houses two major shows a year. Rotating exhibits also are presented. Allow 1 hour minimum. Tues.-Sat. 10-4:30, Sun. noon-4:30; closed major holidays. Admission $5; over 65 and students with ID $4; ages 4-18, $3. Phone (203) 331-9881.

SAVE **BEARDSLEY ZOO,** in Beardsley Park, features 120 species of animals in North and South American outdoor habitats. The 35-acre zoo also features a children's zoo in a New England farm setting, an indoor rain forest and a seasonal carrousel. Food is available. Allow 2 hours minimum. Daily 9-4; closed Jan. 1, Thanksgiving and Dec. 25. Admission $5; over 61, physically impaired and ages 3-11, $3. Phone (203) 394-6565. *See color p. 24.*

THE DISCOVERY MUSEUM, 4450 Park Ave. in 90 Acres Park, contains art displays and interactive art and science exhibits, including the *Challenger* Learning Center and a planetarium. Live science shows are offered weekends; *Challenger* mini-missions are offered most weekends for ages 10 and older.

Museum open Mon.-Sat. 10-5, Sun. noon-5, July-Aug.; Tues.-Sat. 10-5, Sun. noon-5, rest of year. Planetarium shows Mon.-Fri. at 11 and 2, Sat.-Sun. at 1 and 3, July-Aug.; Tues.-Fri. at 1 and 3:30, Sat.-Sun. at 1 and 3, rest of year. Admission $6; over 64 and ages 3-17, $4. *Challenger* mini-missions $3. MC, VI. Phone (203) 372-3521. *See color ad p. 24.*

BRISTOL—*see Hartford p. 55.*

BROOKFIELD (C-2) pop. 14,100, elev. 285'

BROOKFIELD CRAFT CENTER, just s. of SR 7 and CR 25 at 286 Whisconier Rd., houses a craft school known for its innovative classes and workshops, including such specialized fields as boat and house building. An exhibition gallery presents the works of glassblowers, metalsmiths, weavers, potters and other artisans. Mon.-Sat. 10-5, Sun. noon-5; closed major holidays. Free. Phone (203) 775-4526.

CANTERBURY (B-5) pop. 4,500

THE PRUDENCE CRANDALL MUSEUM, on the Canterbury Green at SRs 14 and 169, occupies the 1805 house in which Prudence Crandall conducted an academy for young black women

STARRED ATTRACTIONS

Project Oceanology and the Lighthouse Program—Educational cruises let passengers learn how to identify fish, measure lobsters and test seawater, while tours of New London Harbor focus on the history of the area and its lighthouse. See Groton p. 44.

Stanley-Whitman House—Period furnishings decorate this well-preserved 18th-century example of the framed-overhang style with pendants. See Farmington p. 56.

Wadsworth Atheneum—The museum collection comprises nearly 50,000 works, including Hudson River School landscapes, Impressionist masterpieces, Colonial furniture, costumes and textures, and African-American artifacts. See Hartford p. 53.

Webb-Deane-Stevens Museum—The three historically significant 18th-century houses, furnished in the Colonial style, are restored on their original sites. See Wethersfield p. 60.

Yale University—Ivy-covered buildings, such as the 1752 Connecticut Hall, are among the appealing sights on the historic campus, which also features Gothic dormitories and a duplicate of the cathedral tower in Wrexham, Wales. See New Haven p. 68.

DID YOU KNOW?

During the Revolutionary War, Connecticut governor Jonathan Trumbull was the only Colonial governor to support America's battle for independence from Great Britain.

The New Haven District Telephone Company published the first telephone book in February 1878; it contained 50 names.

1833-34. An elaborate entrance doorway and a second floor Palladian window are among the Federal-style architectural features of the house.

Permanent and changing exhibits explore such themes as Prudence Crandall's life, women's history and local history. Allow 1 hour minimum. Wed.-Sun. 10-4:30, Feb. 1 to mid-Dec.; closed holidays. Admission $2; over 60 and ages 6-18, $1. Phone (860) 546-9916.

CANTON—*see Hartford p. 55.*

CENTRAL VILLAGE (B-6) pop. 1,600, elev. 185'

Founded about 1825 on the Moosup River, Central Village features several houses dating from the 18th century.

QUINEBAUG VALLEY HATCHERY, 1.7 mi. n.w. of I-395 exit 89 via SR 14, following signs, is one of the largest fish hatcheries east of the Mississippi and is the first to use round tanks. About 600,000 trout are raised annually; glass walls in the visitor center allow viewing into the hatchery. Informational exhibits also are displayed. A public fishing pond is open March 1 through Memorial Day weekend; reservations are required during March and part of April. Visitor center open daily 9:30-3:30. Free. Phone (860) 564-7542.

CLINTON (D-4) pop. 3,400, elev. 24'

Incorporated in 1838, Clinton was the home of Rev. Abraham Pierson, the first rector of Yale University, who taught the first students in his home. A monument on the green commemorates the early years of the university, known as Collegiate School 1701-07. The Tourist Center across the street from the chamber of commerce is open summer weekday afternoons.

Clinton Chamber of Commerce: 50 E. Main St., P.O. Box 334, Clinton, CT 06413; phone (860) 669-3889.

Shopping areas: Clinton Crossing Premium Outlets, on SR 81 just off I-95 exit 63, offers 70 discount outlets such as Anne Klein, Lenox, Spaulding and Waterford.

JOHN A. STANTON MEMORIAL (Stanton House), 63 E. Main St., was built in 1789 and houses local historical items, Colonial furnishings and a collection of antique American and Staffordshire china. Within is a restoration of the old Stanton country store. An outside well bears the date 1694. Allow 1 hour minimum. Tues.-Sun. 2-5, June-Sept. Donations. Phone (860) 669-2132.

COLLINSVILLE—*see Hartford p. 55.*

CORNWALL (B-2) pop. 1,400, elev. 437'

The Cornwalls—comprising Cornwall, Cornwall Bridge, Cornwall Center, Cornwall Hollow and West Cornwall—are in a series of upland bowls among steep, forested hills. The charming scenery has attracted many artists. The covered bridge in West Cornwall, built in 1841, spans the Housatonic River. It is one of two such bridges in the state that can be crossed by automobile traffic.

Litchfield Hills Travel Council: P.O. Box 968, Litchfield, CT 06759-0968; phone (860) 567-4506.

COS COB (E-1)

BUSH-HOLLEY HISTORIC SITE, I-95 exit 4 to 39 Strickland Rd., includes the Bush-Holley House, home of one of Connecticut's first art colonies, and a visitor center incorporating exhibition galleries in a renovated circa 1805 storehouse. Also featured are the Holley Barn and archives related to Greenwich history. The house contains Early American furniture reflecting the period of the 18th-century Bush family along with American Impressionist artwork of the area by artists who resided in the house at the turn of the 20th century.

Wed.-Fri. noon-4, Sat. 11-4, Sun. 1-4, Apr.-Dec.; Wed. noon-4, Sat. 11-4, Sun. 1-4, rest of year. Admission $6, over 64 and students with ID $4, under 12 free. Phone (203) 869-6899.

COVENTRY (B-5) pop. 10,100

First settled in 1700, Coventry was incorporated in 1711. From this rolling region issued livestock products for the West India trade, as well as the Morgan pacing horse that could make the 72-mile trip to Boston in 1 day and return the next.

Antique dolls are displayed at Special Joys Doll and Toy Museum at 41 N. River Rd. The museum's collection also includes Steiff animals and rare toys; phone (860) 742-6359.

[SAVE] **NATHAN HALE HOMESTEAD** is 4 mi. s. of SR 44 on South St., following signs. State hero Capt. Nathan Hale was born on this farm in 1755. The family rebuilt the house in 1776, the same year Hale was captured by the British and hanged as a spy. The house is restored and furnished with many Hale family possessions. Allow 30 minutes minimum. Daily 1-4, mid-May to mid-Oct. Admission $4; under 18, $1. Phone (860) 742-6917 or 247-8996.

DANBURY (C-1) pop. 65,600, elev. 371'

Founded by eight families in 1684, Danbury included the town of Bethel until 1855. Supplies were stored locally during the Revolution, and in 1777 Gen. William Tryon's British troops destroyed the stores and burned many of the buildings. Gen. David Wooster led a force in pursuit of the British; he was mortally wounded in one of the ensuing battles and was buried here.

For nearly two centuries, Danbury was the hat city of the world. Since the early 1950s, Danbury's economic base has undergone a dramatic transition and now comprises a broad range of corporate headquarters and businesses related to metal fabrication and high technology products, pharmaceuticals, bio-medical products, paper, publishing, energy and aerospace product development.

Pulitzer Prize-winning composer Charles Ives was born in Danbury; his birthplace is at 5 Mountainville Ave. Phone (203) 743-5200 or 778-3540 for more information. Musical and theatrical performances are presented each summer at Charles Ives Concert Park, and at other locations throughout the city.

Greater Danbury Chamber of Commerce: 72 West St., Danbury, CT 06810; phone (203) 743-5565.

DANBURY MUSEUM AND HISTORICAL SOCIETY (formerly the Scott-Fanton Museum and Historical Society), 43 Main St., consists of the restored 1785 John and Mary Rider House, which contains period furnishings, textile and historical exhibits; the 1790 Dodd Hat Shop with its exhibit about the hatting industry; the One Room Schoolhouse; gardens; and the Danbury Fair Mural. Huntington Hall houses the historical society's archives, a research library and gallery of changing exhibits.

Allow 1 hour minimum. Museum open Wed.-Fri. 2-5, Sat.-Sun. 2-4; closed holidays. Library by appointment. Donations. Phone (203) 743-5200.

[SAVE] **MILITARY MUSEUM OF SOUTHERN NEW ENGLAND** is at 125 Park Ave. Displayed outside are tanks, armored vehicles and artillery pieces from World War II and the Korean and Vietnam wars. Inside, life-size dioramas feature medals, photographs, uniforms, heavy fighting vehicles and artillery pieces. Allow 1 hour minimum. Tues.-Sat. 10-5, Sun. noon-5; closed Jan. 1, Easter, Labor Day, Thanksgiving and Dec. 25. Admission $4; over 61 and ages 6-18, $2. MC, VI. Phone (203) 790-9277.

DERBY (D-2) pop. 12,200, elev. 16'

OSBORNE HOMESTEAD MUSEUM is in Osbornedale State Park; go 1.7 mi. w. via SR 34, then n. on Cedric Ave. and w. on Hawthorne Ave. The homestead encompasses the estate of turn-of-the-20th-century industrialist Frances Osborne Kellogg. The Colonial Revival-style Kellogg residence, built in the early 1800s, contains American and European antiques, as well as a collection of delftware and local silverware.

Formal gardens, a rock garden, a rose garden and ornamental shrubs adorn the grounds. Also on the grounds is Kellogg Environmental Center, with exhibits, programs and nature trails (see Recreation Chart). Allow 1 hour minimum. Museum open Sat.-Sun. 10-4, Tues. and Thurs. 10-3, May 1 to mid-Dec.; grounds open daily 8-4. Donations. Phone (203) 922-7832 for the museum, or (203) 734-2513 for the environmental center.

EAST GRANBY—see Hartford p. 56.

EAST HADDAM (C-5) pop. 6,700

What is claimed to be the world's oldest church bell tolls from the tower of St. Stephen's Episcopal Church. Cast for a Spanish monastery in A.D. 815, the bell was salvaged after Napoleon's troops destroyed the monastery.

The bell arrived in New York on a 19th-century trading vessel as part of a shipload of metal. In 1834 William Pratt, a local resident and ships chandler, claimed the bell and shipped it to East Haddam. Also at St. Stephen's is the small schoolhouse where Nathan Hale taught 1773-74.

Goodspeed Opera House, a restored Victorian theater on the Connecticut River, offers nationally acclaimed musicals April through December; phone (860) 873-8664 for tickets and information.

Connecticut River Valley and Shoreline Visitors Council: 393 Main St., Middletown, CT 06457; phone (860) 347-0028 or (800) 486-3346.

★ **GILLETTE CASTLE STATE PARK** is 2.5 mi. s. off SR 82, then 1.7 mi. w., overlooking the Connecticut River. The park was the former estate of William Gillette, the American actor and playwright who was renowned for his portrayal of Sherlock Holmes. The castle, built 1914-19, is patterned after medieval castles in Germany. Its 24 rooms, 19 of which are open to the public, contain unusual furnishings and belongings of the actor.

Park open daily 8-dusk. Castle open Fri.-Sun. 10-5, Memorial Day-Labor Day. **Note:** The castle is under renovation and may close unexpectedly; phone ahead. Park free. Castle $4; ages 6-11, $2. Phone (860) 526-2336. See Recreation Chart.

EAST HAVEN (D-3) pop. 26,100, elev. 37′

Ironworks were established at the mouth of Lake Saltonstall in 1657, and the town of East

Haven was incorporated in 1785. A number of old buildings, a green where Marquis de Lafayette is said to have camped and a cemetery in use since 1707 have survived. Native son John Winthrop, Yale University's first student, graduated in 1704.

Greater New Haven Convention and Visitors Bureau: 59 Elm St., New Haven, CT 06510; phone (203) 777-8550 or (800) 332-7829.

SAVE **SHORE LINE TROLLEY MUSEUM** is at 17 River St. near the green; from I-95 take exit 51 northbound or exit 52 southbound, following signs. The museum contains a large collection of antique Canadian and U.S. streetcars, interurbans and rapid-transit cars. A 3-mile, round-trip trolley ride is offered. Picnicking is permitted. Allow 1 hour minimum.

Daily 11-5, Memorial Day-Labor Day; Sat.-Sun. and holidays 11-5, May 1-day before Memorial Day and day after Labor Day-Oct. 31; Sun. 11-5 in Apr. and Nov. Santa rides the trolley Sat.-Sun. 11-5, late Nov. to mid-Dec. Admission $5; over 62, $4; ages 2-11, $2. Phone (203) 467-6927.

EAST WINDSOR—*see Hartford p. 56.*

ESSEX (D-5) pop. 5,900, elev. 32'

Sea captains' houses still line Main Street, keeping Essex much the same as it was during the height of its shipbuilding prosperity about 1815. Among historic buildings are Hill's Academy, one of the earliest educational facilities in the region, and Pratt House, built by one of the earliest settlers. The first American warship, *Oliver Cromwell,* was built in Essex during the Revolutionary War.

CONNECTICUT RIVER MUSEUM, 67 Main St. on the Connecticut River, has exhibits relating to river steamboats, shipbuilding, archeology and the 1775 American *Turtle,* said to be the first submarine. A collection of boats built and used on the Connecticut River is displayed in the boat house. Changing exhibits are presented. Allow 30 minutes minimum. Tues.-Sun. 10-5; closed Labor Day, Thanksgiving and Dec. 25. Admission $4; over 60, $3; ages 6-12, $2. MC, VI. Phone (860) 767-8269.

SAVE **ESSEX STEAM TRAIN AND RIVERBOAT,** .2 mi. w. of SR 9 exit 3 on Railroad Ave., offers a 12-mile sightseeing trip through the Connecticut River Valley. Restored steam trains provide hour-long round trips; all except the last train of the

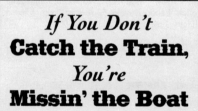

day connect with an optional 1.5-hour riverboat cruise on the Connecticut River. Thematic holiday trips also are available around Easter, Halloween and Christmas.

Trains depart every 90 minutes Mon.-Fri. 10:30-4:30, Sat.-Sun. and Labor Day 10:30-6, mid-June through Labor Day; Wed.-Sun. and Columbus Day 10:30-4:30, day after Labor Day-Columbus Day; Wed.-Fri. 1:30-3, Sat.-Sun. and Memorial Day noon-4:30, early May to mid-June. Train and riverboat $15; over 65, $13; ages 3-11, $7.50. Train only $10; over 65, $9; ages 3-11, $5. First class $3 extra. AE, MC, VI. Phone (860) 767-0103. *See ad.*

FAIRFIELD (E-2) pop. 53,400, elev. 52′

Known as Unquowa to the Pequot Indians, the land that is now Fairfield was purchased from them in 1639. During the Revolution, the town was looted and burned by the British under the command of Gen. William Tryon in 1779.

While only in his early 20s, Fairfield native Capt. Samuel Smedley, who had seized numerous prize ships by the end of the Revolution, inspired a British officer to remark upon capture, "There is little hope of conquering an enemy whose very schoolboys are capable of valor equaling that of trained veterans of naval warfare."

Coastal Fairfield County Convention & Visitors Bureau: 297 West Ave., Norwalk, CT 06850; phone (800) 866-7925.

CONNECTICUT AUDUBON CENTER AT FAIRFIELD, 2325 Burr St., includes 6 miles of boardwalk nature trails within a 160-acre wildlife sanctuary. The Birds of Prey Compound contains raptors such as an eagle, hawks and owls. A nature center is on the premises. Lectures, classes and walks are offered. Allow 1 hour, 30 minutes minimum. Sanctuary open daily dawn-dusk. Nature center open Tues.-Sat. 9-4:30, Sun. noon-4:30. Nature center building free. Sanctuary $2. Phone (203) 259-6305.

Birdcraft Museum and Sanctuary, 314 Unquowa Rd., contains hands-on exhibits, wildlife dioramas and a collection of dinosaur footprints. Tues.-Fri. 10-5, Sat.-Sun. noon-5. Admission $2. Phone (203) 259-0416.

FAIRFIELD HISTORICAL SOCIETY, 636 Old Post Rd. opposite the historic town green, features exhibits of area history, art and decorative arts. Walking tours and events also are offered. The library has local historical collections. Tues.-Sat. 10-4:30, Sun. 1-4:30; closed holidays. Admission $3; students with ID and under 12, $1. Phone (203) 259-1598.

OLD TOWN HALL, at 611 Old Post Rd. on the green, was rebuilt in 1791. The Old Town Hall contains land records and other documents dating from 1648. Mon.-Fri. 8:30-4:30, mid-June through Labor Day; 9-5, rest of year. Closed holidays. Free. Phone (203) 256-3000.

FARMINGTON—*see Hartford p. 56.*

GREENWICH (E-1) pop. 58,400, elev. 550′

Although Adriaen Block established the first settlement in Greenwich in 1614, a permanent community did not come about until about 1640, when the land was purchased from the original inhabitants for 25 coats. That land now is graced by large houses with commensurate price tags.

Putnam Cottage, 243 E. Putnam Ave., is where Gen. Israel Putnam escaped from the British in 1779. The cottage has been restored to the Colonial and Revolutionary appearance of its early Knapp Tavern days and contains 17th- and 18th-century furniture, decorative objects and Putnam memorabilia. Phone (203) 869-9697.

Coastal Fairfield County Convention & Visitors Bureau: 297 West Ave., Norwalk, CT 06850; phone (800) 866-7925.

AUDUBON CENTER IN GREENWICH, 8 mi. n. at jct. John St. and Riversville Rd., is a 522-acre nature preserve. Family programs are featured; nature trails are available. The nearby Audubon

Fairchild Garden offers more hiking trails. Center open daily 9-5; closed major holidays. Garden open daily dawn-dusk. Admission $3; over 54 and under 18, $1.50. Phone (203) 869-5272.

BRUCE MUSEUM, I-95 exit 3 following signs to 1 Museum Dr., is a multifaceted, family-oriented arts and science museum presenting hands-on activities and changing exhibits of artifacts and fine and decorative art. Permanent displays include an extensive mineral collection, a wildlife diorama, a marine touch tank, mounted birds and examples of American Indian culture. Tues.-Sat. 10-5, Sun. 1-5; closed major holidays. Admission $3.50; over 65 and ages 5-12, $2.50; free to all Tues. Phone (203) 869-0376.

GREENWICH LIBRARY, 101 W. Putnam Ave., contains a large art gallery with changing monthly exhibits and a free concert and lecture series. Mon.-Fri. 9-9, Sat. 9-5, Sun. 1-5, Oct.-Apr.; Mon.-Thurs. 9-9, Fri.-Sat. 9-5, rest of year. Free. Phone (203) 622-7900.

GROTON (D-6) pop. 45,100, elev. 47'

Groton is the home of the electric boat division of General Dynamics, the nation's largest submarine producer. General Dynamics built the USS *Nautilus*, the first atomic-powered submarine, which was launched Jan. 21, 1954, and now is permanently displayed. Groton also is a center for deep-sea fishing; numerous charters are available.

On the black granite, 60-foot-long Wall of Honor at Bridge and Thames streets are inscribed the names of the approximately 3,600 American submariners who died in the line of duty during World War II. There are monuments for each of the 52 boats lost.

Southeastern Connecticut Tourism: 470 Bank St., P.O. Box 89, New London, CT 06320; phone (860) 444-2206 or (800) 863-6569.

AVERY MEMORIAL is on Fort St. near the center of town. Erected by the descendants of Capt. James Avery, the memorial is on the site of his 1656 homestead. Descendant John D. Rockefeller helped fund the project.

FORT GRISWOLD STATE PARK, 17 acres off I-95 exit 87 at Monument St. and Park Ave., was the scene of a massacre in 1781 when British forces led by Benedict Arnold took the fort and burned New London and Groton. Also in the park is the 1750 Ebenezer Avery House to which the wounded were taken; the house contains period furnishings. Park daily 8-dusk. Free. Phone (860) 445-1729.

Groton Monument, on the hilltop in Fort Griswold, is 135 feet high. Dedicated in 1830 to victims of the massacre, the monument bears a tablet with their names. Daily 10-5, Memorial Day-Labor Day; Sat.-Sun. 10-5, day after Labor

GREENS

The green, also known as *the common,* is a distinctive feature of many New England towns. Lined with whitewashed Colonial-style structures, this well-manicured, grassy rectangle of public parkland usually contains a bandstand, gazebo or monument.

The green hasn't always been green, however. It wasn't until the early 19th century that New Englanders began restoring what a visitor described as "an uneven and barren sand waste, lying open to the public, traversed by vehicles in all directions."

Consisting of a few acres of common land, the green was a transplanted feature of the 17th-century English village, where common-field husbandry was practiced. With the help of their memories of the mother country—few professional urban planners were among the first settlers—and with the anonymous guide "The Ordering of Towns" in hand, New England colonists planned their towns to radiate outward from the meetinghouse and the meetinghouse lot, which would later be called the green.

Trampled by animals and neglected by the townspeople, who now sought profit instead of communal survival, the green didn't stay green for long. By 1654, few towns remained clustered around the meetinghouse lot, which meant the green was often a mudflat rutted by wagon wheels and strewn with rubbish; enterprising town officials would fence off the surviving patches of grass and rent them out as pasture, using the income to maintain the meetinghouse. Finally, the Revolutionary War didn't help matters, as at least one battle was fought over a green.

In the 1820s, a green green became fashionable again, so New Englanders began to fence the areas off and restore them. Soon, the town hall, country store, inn and stately houses were installed around the green, creating the impression of a typical "Colonial" New England town.

Day-Columbus Day. Free. Phone (860) 449-6877.

The Monument House contains relics of the Fort Griswold massacre and the whaling industry, as well as period furniture and china. Daily 10-5, Memorial Day-Labor Day; Sat.-Sun. 10-5, day after Labor Day-Columbus Day. Free. Phone (860) 449-6877.

HISTORIC SHIP *NAUTILUS*/**SUBMARINE FORCE MUSEUM**, off I-95 exit 86 and n. on SR 12 just outside the Naval Submarine Base, offers self-guiding tours of the world's first nuclear-powered submarine. Tours include the torpedo room, attack center, control room, officers' and crews' living quarters and dining areas. Allow 1 hour, 30 minutes minimum. Wed.-Mon. 9-5, Tues. 1-5, mid-May through Oct. 31; Wed.-Mon. 9-4, rest of year. Closed Jan. 1, Thanksgiving and Dec. 25. Phone to confirm maintenance schedule. Free. Phone (860) 694-3174 or (800) 343-0079.

The Museum, at the opposite end of the USS *Nautilus* pier, uses models, films and authentic equipment to trace the history and development of the U.S. submarine force. Highlights of the collection are a model of Capt. Nemo's *Nautilus* from Jules Verne's "20,000 Leagues Under the Sea," working periscopes, a submarine control room and submarines dating from the Revolutionary War to the present, including midget submarines from World War II.

Wed.-Mon. 9-5, Tues. 1-5, mid-May through Oct. 31; Wed.-Mon. 9-4, rest of year. Closed Jan. 1, Thanksgiving and Dec. 25. Phone to confirm maintenance schedule. Free. Phone (860) 694-3174.

⌷ ★ **PROJECT OCEANOLOGY AND THE LIGHTHOUSE PROGRAM,** departing from the University of Connecticut at Avery Point, offers 2.5-hour hands-on educational cruises aboard a 55-foot research vessel. On the *EnviroLab* cruises trained instructors teach passengers how to identify fish, measure lobsters and test seawater. Core samples from the ocean bottom also are taken and examined.

The Lighthouse Program cruises include a boat tour of New London Harbor during which instructors discuss its history from the days of privateering to the present. Instruction in the evolution of navigational aids is capped by a tour of the 1909 New London Ledge Lighthouse, from its foundation to the light four stories above. In addition, the Exploring the Bay cruise out of Narragansett Bay in Rhode Island is offered late July to late August, weather permitting; phone for schedules and fares.

EnviroLab cruises depart daily at 10 and 1, mid-June through Labor Day; Lighthouse Program cruises depart Tues., Thurs. and Sat.-Sun.

at 4. *EnviroLab* fare $17; ages 5-11, $12. Lighthouse fare $13; ages 6-11, $9. Reservations are strongly recommended. MC, VI. Phone (860) 445-9007, (800) 364-8472, or (401) 272-3540 for Exploring the Bay cruise information.

GUILFORD (D-4) pop. 19,800, elev. 14′

Settled by the Puritan congregation that followed Rev. Henry Whitfield from England in 1639, Guilford possibly was named for Guildford in Surrey. One distinguished citizen of the mid-18th century, Samuel Hill, who ran for office repeatedly from the time he was a young man, gave rise to the expression "run like Sam Hill." About 500 houses dating 1639-1876 are preserved; the shoreline has several striking promontories and bays.

Connecticut River Valley and Shoreline Visitors Council: 393 Main St., Middletown, CT 06457; phone (860) 347-0028 or (800) 486-3346.

SAVE **HENRY WHITFIELD STATE MUSEUM,** I-95 exit 58 then 1 mi. s. of US 1 via CR 77 to 248 Old Whitfield St., is housed in what is said to be the oldest building in Connecticut and the oldest stone house in New England. Built in 1639, the building was restored in the 1930s, incorporating what remained of the original structure. Visitors can view 17th- through 19th-century furnishings and stroll through a visitor's center.

Wed.-Sun. 10-4:30, Feb. 1-Dec. 14; by appointment rest of year. Closed Good Friday and Dec. 25. Admission $3; over 62 and ages 6-17, $1.50. Phone (203) 453-2457.

HYLAND HOUSE is 1 blk. e. of the green at 84 Boston St. An example of early saltbox construction, the 1660 house is furnished with period pieces and accessories. A 30-minute guided tour is available. Tues.-Sun. 10-4:30, early June-Labor Day; Sat.-Sun. 10-4:30, day after Labor Day-Columbus Day. Admission $2; over 54, $1.50; under 12 free with an adult. Phone (203) 453-9477.

THOMAS GRISWOLD HOUSE MUSEUM, 171 Boston St., is a classic Colonial saltbox house built in 1774. The house depicts a lifestyle of the early 1800s, when George Griswold and his family were in residence. Tues.-Sun. 11-4, mid-June to mid-Sept.; Sat.-Sun. 11-4, mid-Sept. through Nov. 30. Admission $2, under 12 free. Phone (203) 453-3176.

HADDAM (C-4) pop. 6,800, elev. 20′

Purchased from the Wangunk Indians and other tribes for the value of articles worth less than $100, Haddam was first homesteaded in 1662 by a group of young married men from older settlements up the Connecticut River, which bisects the town. Haddam retains the atmosphere of its early seafaring and fishing days.

CAMELOT CRUISES, departing from SR 82 across the Connecticut River from Goodspeed Opera House *(see East Haddam p. 40)*, offers a full-day excursion to Sag Harbor, N.Y.; a 3.5-hour Fall Foliage Cruise; and a 2.5-hour "Oldies But Goodies" cruise with live music from the '50s and '60s. Also offered are thematic dinner cruises, such as "Murder on the *Titanic*" and New Orleans Jazz.

Sag Harbor Cruise departs Tues.-Thurs. and Sat.-Sun. at 9 a.m., June 1-Labor Day. Sag Harbor cruise $22.50. Reservations are required for dinner and foliage cruises. AE, DS, MC, VI. Phone (860) 345-8591.

HADDAM NECK (C-4) pop. 300

One of Haddam Neck's most successful residents was born on a continent far from Connecticut. A black man named Broteer was born in Dukandara, Guinea, in 1728, the son of a king. He was kidnapped and sold into slavery, a time during which he became known as Venture Smith. After buying his freedom, this tall and formidable man, who reputedly could carry a barrel of molasses on each shoulder, acquired 100 acres of land, 20 ships and three houses.

HAMDEN (C-3) pop. 52,400, elev. 150′

ELI WHITNEY MUSEUM, 3 mi. s. of SR 15 exit 61 at 915 Whitney Ave., commemorates the inventor with permanent displays of Whitney memorabilia and working models of a cotton gin. The spirit of inventiveness is explored with various rotating hands-on exhibits. On the landscaped grounds are a covered bridge, a waterfall and a water learning lab, where valves and levers can be operated to alter the flow of water. Allow 30 minutes minimum. Daily 11-4, June 15-Sept. 1; Wed.-Fri. and Sun. noon-5, Sat. 10-3, rest of year. Admission $3, students with ID $2; additional fee for programs. Phone (203) 777-1833.

Hartford

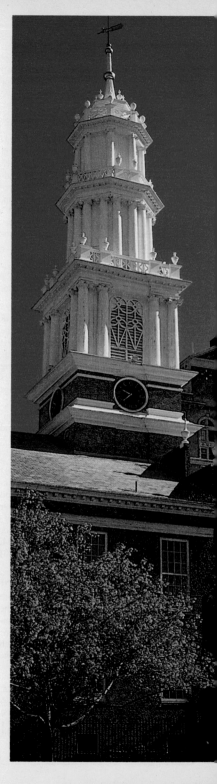

Contemporary Hartford is a dynamic blend of past and challenges to the future—its Ancient Burying Ground is only blocks away from the boat-shaped headquarters of Phoenix Mutual Life Insurance Co., the world's first two-sided building.

Although much of Hartford's reputation rests on the creation and collection of insurance premiums, this state capital can claim a boisterous history. Hartford grew from a Dutch trading post in 1633 into an English settlement founded 1636 by Rev. Thomas Hooker and Samuel Stone. Its name derives from Stone's birthplace in Hertford, England.

Hartford was the site of one of the first Colonial efforts to resist English rule. In 1687 Sir Edmund Andros, the English governor, demanded that Hartford's citizens relinquish a 25-year-old charter granted by King Charles II that gave the colony its independence; the colonists hid the charter in the trunk of a large oak tree for about 3 days. A round stone marker on Charter Oak Place marks the spot where the oak stood until 1856.

By the 1870s, Hartford had the highest per capita income in the country, and philanthropists and world literary figures made their homes here. Mark Twain and Harriet Beecher Stowe were neighbors in the lovely and exclusive Nook Farm area. The newspaper they read, *The Hartford Courant,* was founded in 1764 and today has the oldest continuous name and circulation of any newspaper in the country.

Hartford's path to insurance capital of the world began with the establishment of the Hartford Fire Insurance Co. in 1810; eventually, insurance companies expanded both in number and in scope of coverage until they formed today's multibillion-dollar industry. The Travelers Tower is one of the tallest structures in New England at 527 feet. A stunning example of insurance-company architecture is the green-tinted headquarters of the Phoenix Home Life Mutual Insurance Co. at Constitution Plaza.

In contrast, the past comes alive at the [SAVE] Butler-McCook Homestead nearby at 396 Main St. The house contains a collection of four generations of 18th- and 19th-century furnishings original to the 1782 house. A restored Victorian garden is behind the house; phone (860) 522-1806.

Education always has been important to Hartford. Founded in 1823, Trinity College, 300 Summit St., has some fine examples of collegiate Gothic architecture on its 96-acre campus. The interior of the chapel has many carvings in stone and wood. Free concerts are offered at the Plumb Memorial Carillon on Wednesday

evenings in the summer. The Austin Arts Center features changing exhibitions and theatrical and musical performances. The University of Connecticut School of Law is on 20 picturesque acres near Elizabeth Park. The University of Connecticut is nearby in Storrs.

Expert not just at innovating, Hartford also adopts and adapts. In a creative variation on Yankee Hospitality, the city has stationed in downtown the Hartford Guides, roving ambassadors of goodwill in red hats and khaki and white uniforms. Assisting visitors, workers and residents, these professionals offer insights into the city's history, information about its amenities, facilities and events, and can help in emergencies such as when keys are locked inside the vehicle. After more than 350 years, Hartford continues to stretch the envelope.

Approaches
By Car
Looking at a map, it almost seems as if all roads lead to Hartford. The major north-south highway into the city is I-91, while I-84 runs northeast-southwest. Signage is good with generally adequate warning for exit ramps. Avoid the 7-9 a.m. and 3-6 p.m. rush hours.

Getting Around
Street System
A good map is an absolute necessity for negotiating the Hartford vicinity. At some major intersections downtown traffic is stopped in all four directions and pedestrians may cross on the diagonal.

Parking
Parking downtown is readily available in the numerous garages and lots. Rates range from $10 per day in city-operated lots to $4 per hour in privately owned garages. On-street parking is nearly impossible to find.

What To See
ANCIENT BURYING GROUND, 60 Gold St., was the city's only cemetery until 1803. Still public property, it forms a green oasis in the middle of the glass-and-concrete jumble of downtown Hartford. The oldest gravestone dates from 1663. Buried here are many of the city's early founders.

The cemetery is on the north and west sides of the 1807 Center Church (the fourth meetinghouse), which traces its history to a meetinghouse established in 1636. The church, 675 Main St., contains six Tiffany windows that depict religious events. The U.S. Constitution was ratified inside the third meetinghouse. Tours of the church are available by appointment. Allow 30 minutes minimum. Cemetery open daily dawn-dusk. Free. Phone (860) 249-5631 only for Center Church tour information.

THE INFORMED TRAVELER

City Population: 133,100

Elevation: 100 ft.

Sales Tax: Connecticut sales tax is 6 percent. Lodging tax in the greater Hartford area is 12 percent. The car rental tax is 9.18 percent with an added $1 per day tourism tax.

WHOM TO CALL

Emergency: 911

Weather: (860) 246-1000

Hospitals: Hartford Hospital, (860) 545-5000; Saint Francis Hospital and Medical Center, (860) 714-4000; University of Connecticut Health Center, (860) 679-2000.

WHERE TO LOOK

Newspapers

Founded in 1764, *The Hartford Courant* is the morning daily newspaper.

Radio and TV

WCNN (680 AM) is an all-news/weather station; WPKT (90.5 FM) is a member of National Public Radio.

Major television channels include 3 (CBS), 8 (ABC), 24 (PBS) and 30 (NBC).

Visitor Information

Information can be obtained from the Greater Hartford Convention & Visitors Bureau, One Civic Center Plaza, Hartford, CT 06103-1592; phone (860) 728-6789. The welcome center in the Hartford Civic Center Mall is open daily; phone (860) 275-6456. Other welcome centers are in the Old State House at 800 Main St., and in the Connecticut State Capitol on Capitol Avenue. For events information phone (860) 522-6400.

WHAT TO WEAR

Summer in Hartford can be warm and humid, with daytime temperatures averaging in the low 80s and dropping into the 60s at night. Leaf peeping in fall, and blossom spotting in spring require sweaters or jackets. Temperatures fluctuate between 74 and 38.

Winter brings one or two snow storms a year, with January's temperatures ranging from 36 to 18 degrees.

BUSHNELL PARK adjoins the Capitol grounds on the north and contains the Spanish War Memorial, the Israel Putnam statue and the Pump House Gallery, which features art exhibits and noon concerts during the summer. Also in the 37-acre park is a working Stein and Goldstein 1914 carrousel with 48 horses, two chariots and a 1925 Wurlitzer band organ.

Park open daily 24 hours. Gallery open Tues.-Fri. 11-2. Carrousel operates Tues.-Sun. 11-5, mid-May through Aug. 31; Sat.-Sun. 11-5, mid-Apr. to mid-May and in Sept. Park free. Carrousel rides 50c. Phone (860) 246-7739 for the carrousel, or (860) 249-2201 for weather closures.

CATHEDRAL OF ST. JOSEPH (Catholic), 140 Farmington Ave., is a striking contemporary structure noted for the 26 huge stained-glass windows that line the nave. Tours are conducted by appointment. Allow 30 minutes minimum. Sun.-Fri. 7-1, Sat. 7-6. Free. Phone (860) 249-8431.

SAVE **CONNECTICUT HISTORICAL SOCIETY,** off I-84 exit 46 at 1 Elizabeth St., houses a museum with changing exhibits about Connecticut history. The museum also has permanent displays of 17th- through 19th-century Connecticut furniture and decorative arts.

Allow 1 hour minimum. Museum open Tues.-Sun. noon-5. Last admission 45 minutes before closing. Research library open Tues.-Sat. 10-5. Last admission is at 4:15. Closed holidays. Museum and library $6; senior citizens $5; students with ID and ages 6-18, $3. Museum free to all first Sat. of the month. Phone (860) 236-5621.

CONNECTICUT RESOURCES RECOVERY AUTHORITY VISITORS CENTER is e. of I-91 exit 27 (Brainard and Airport rds.) at 211 Murphy Rd. This 6,500-square-foot facility has exhibits about solid waste management and recycling. The Temple of Trash represents the old system of trash removal. Allow 1 hour minimum. Wed.-Fri. noon-4. Admission. Phone (860) 247-4280.

ELIZABETH PARK ROSE GARDENS, off I-84 exit 44 at 915 Prospect Ave., contains 15,000 plants of 750 varieties of roses. While the season of peak bloom for the rose, annual and perennial gardens is late June to early July, the gardens provide continuous color from spring through fall. Lawn bowling can be played in summer; ice skating is offered in winter. Park open daily dawn-dusk. Greenhouses open Mon.-Fri. 8-3. Free. Phone (860) 722-6541.

SAVE ★ **HARRIET BEECHER STOWE CENTER** is at 71 Forest St. near the Mark Twain House. The restored house contains assorted items belonging to the renowned author of "Uncle Tom's Cabin." Allow 1 hour minimum. Tours are given Mon.-Sat. 9:30-4, Sun. noon-4, day after Memorial Day-Dec. 31; Tues.-Sat. 9:30-4, Sun. noon-4, rest of year. Closed Jan. 1, Easter, Labor Day, Thanksgiving and Dec. 24-25. Admission $6.50;

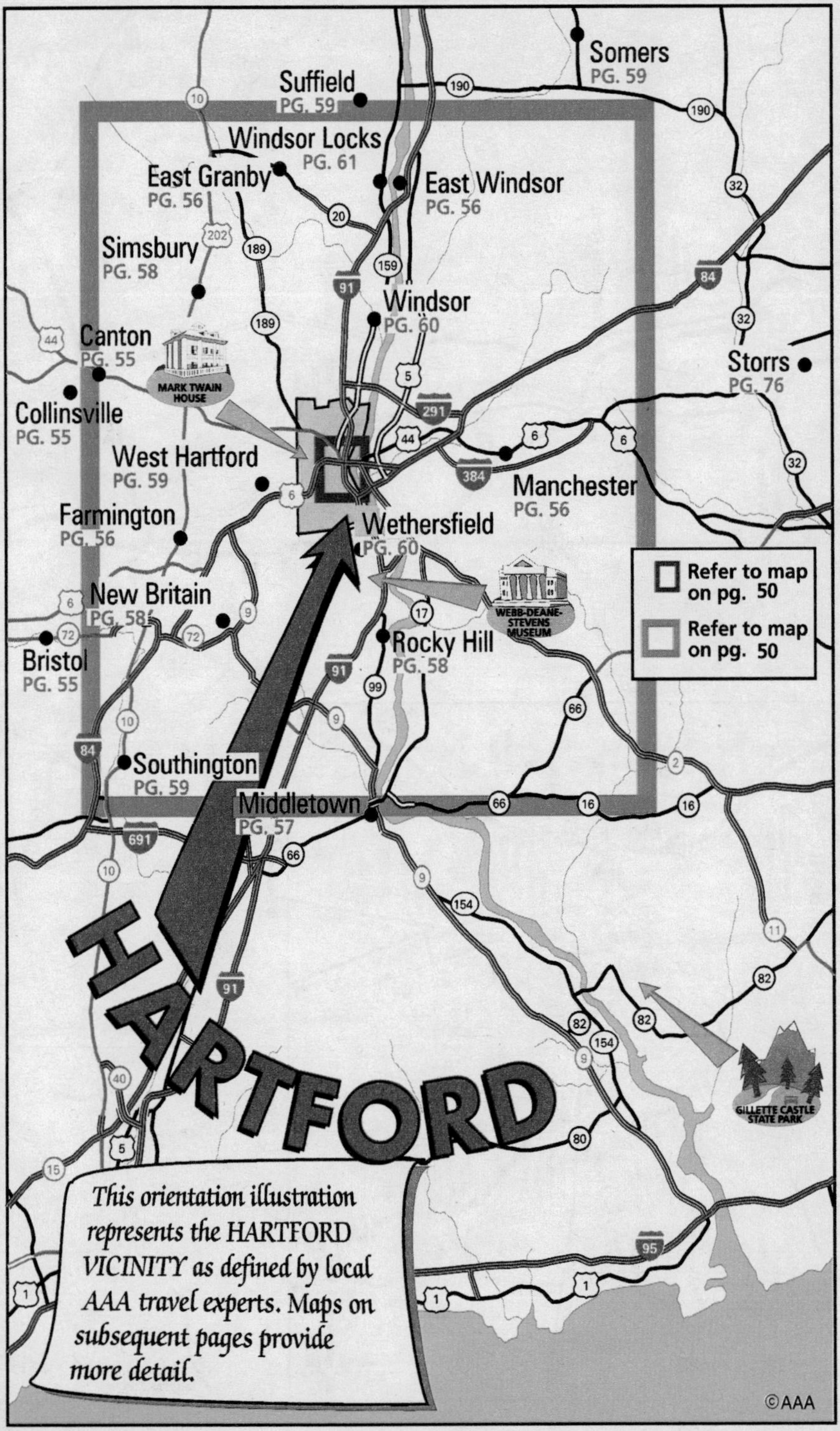

Somers
PG. 59

Suffield
PG. 59

Windsor Locks
PG. 61

East Granby
PG. 56

East Windsor
PG. 56

Simsbury
PG. 58

Storrs
PG. 76

Windsor
PG. 60

Canton
PG. 55

MARK TWAIN
HOUSE

Collinsville
PG. 55

West Hartford
PG. 59

Manchester
PG. 56

Farmington
PG. 56

Wethersfield
PG. 60

New Britain
PG. 58

WEBB-DEANE-
STEVENS
MUSEUM

Bristol
PG. 55

Rocky Hill
PG. 58

☐ Refer to map
   on pg. 50

☐ Refer to map
   on pg. 50

Southington
PG. 59

Middletown
PG. 57

HARTFORD

GILLETTE CASTLE
STATE PARK

*This orientation illustration
represents the HARTFORD
VICINITY as defined by local
AAA travel experts. Maps on
subsequent pages provide
more detail.*

©AAA

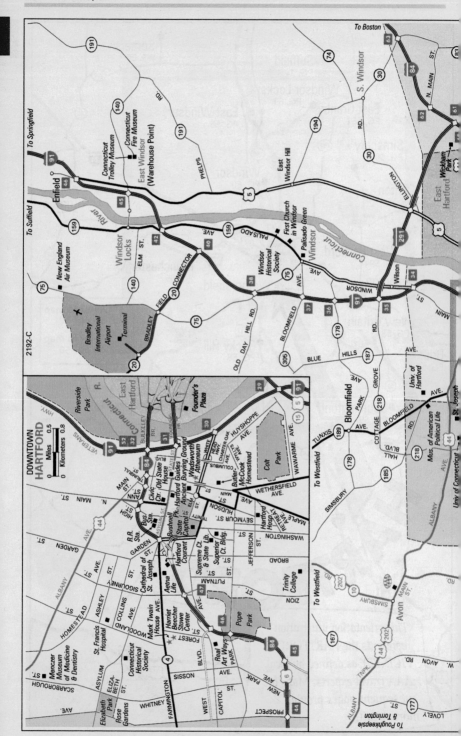

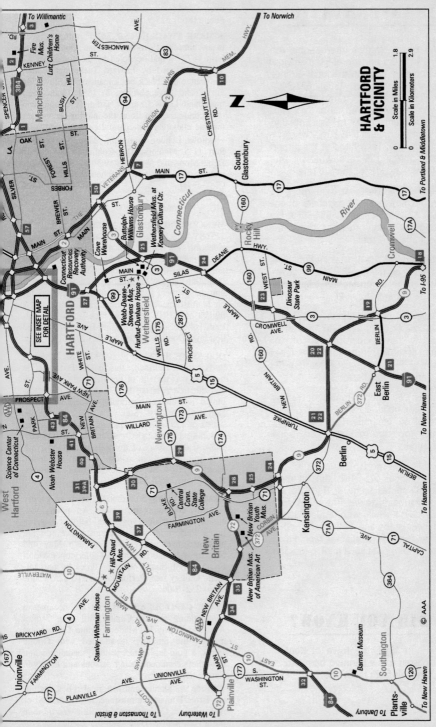

HARTFORD & VICINITY

Scale in Miles

Scale in Kilometers

To Portland & Middletown

© AAA

TRANSPORTATION

Air travel: Bradley International Airport, 12 miles north on I-91, is serviced by domestic and international airlines. Airport Connection, (860) 627-3400, provides scheduled transportation to downtown Mon.-Wed. until 8:45 p.m., Thurs.-Fri. until 7:30 p.m., Sat. until 5:45 p.m. and Sun. until 8:45 p.m.; the cost is $11 one-way. Taxis hired at the airport stand charge $28 to downtown; four persons may ride for the $28 rate.

Rental cars: Hertz, at the airport, offers discounts to AAA members; phone (860) 627-3850 or (800) 654-3080. For listings of other agencies check the telephone directory.

Rail service: The Amtrak station, (860) 727-1776 or (800) 872-7245, is downtown in the Union Station Transportation Center at 1 Union Pl.

Buses: Greyhound Lines Inc., (800) 231-2222 or (860) 522-9267, and other intercity buses operate out of the Union Station Transportation Center at 1 Union Pl. Taxis and CTTransit buses also are available here.

Taxis: Cab companies include Yellow, (860) 666-6666. Base fare is $2, with rate of $2 per mile. Base fare is the same for up to three additional passengers.

Public transport: The buses of CT-Transit, (860) 525-9181, run on more than 30 routes servicing Hartford and its surrounding towns. The buses operate 7 days a week, with reduced schedules weekends and holidays. Schedule information is available Mon.-Fri. 6 a.m.-11 p.m., Sat. 6 a.m.-9 p.m., Sun. 8-6.

DID YOU KNOW?

In 1993, the town of Kent passed a law banning barnyard animals from town sidewalks.

over 59, $6; ages 6-16, $2.75. AE, MC, VI. Phone (860) 525-9317.

★ **MARK TWAIN HOUSE,** 351 Farmington Ave., is an unusual 19-room Victorian Gothic house built 1873-74 and occupied by the author for 17 years. Designed by Edward Tuckerman Potter, the orange and black brick mansion has towering turrets and large porches. In 1881 Twain commissioned Louis Comfort Tiffany's design firm to decorate the first floor; the interior decorations include elaborate stencils and carved woodwork.

Allow 1 hour minimum. Mon.-Sat. 9:30-5, Sun. 11-5, Memorial Day-Columbus Day and in Dec.; Mon. and Wed.-Sat. 9:30-5, Sun. noon-5, rest of year. Last tour is 1 hour before closing. Closed Jan. 1, Easter, Thanksgiving and Dec. 24-25. Admission $9; over 59, $8; ages 6-12, $5. MC, VI. Phone (860) 493-6411.

MENCZER MUSEUM OF MEDICINE AND DENTISTRY, 230 Scarborough St. at Albany Ave., inside the Hartford Medical Society Building, traces the progress of medical and dental technology from the Revolutionary War through the mid-20th century. In addition to a collection of unusual medical and dental devices, displays include instruments, furnishings and paintings. A replica of a 1919 dentist's office is featured. Allow 1 hour minimum. Mon.-Fri. 10-4; closed holidays. Donations. Phone (860) 236-5613.

OLD STATE HOUSE is at 800 Main St. Designed by Charles Bulfinch, this 1796 Federal-style building was the site of the Hartford Convention and the first Amistad trial. Exhibits feature costumed interpreters portraying pivotal figures in Hartford's history. Steward's Museum, established in 1797, features paintings and curiosities including a two-headed calf and an 8.5-foot alligator. Guided tours of the state house are available by reservation. Allow 1 hour minimum. Mon.-Fri. 10-4, Sat. 11-4; closed major holidays. Free. Phone (860) 522-6766.

REAL ART WAYS, 56 Arbor St., is an art gallery featuring contemporary exhibits. Art, poetry, videotape and music events are held at varying times. Performing arts programs and events are presented evenings January through May and September to mid-December. Gallery open Mon.-Fri. 5-9, Sat.-Sun. 3-9; other times by appointment. Gallery free. Performances $10-$25. Phone (860) 232-1006.

STATE CAPITOL, off I-84 exit 48, occupies a commanding site on Capitol Hill near Capitol Ave. and Trinity St. Made of white Connecticut marble, the building is adorned with Gothic spires, a gold-leaf dome, statues, medallions and bas-reliefs commemorating persons and events in Connecticut history.

Inside are statues and historical relics, including Israel Putnam's tombstone, the figurehead of Adm. David G. Farragut's flagship *Hartford*, a statue of Nathan Hale and the battle flags of

Connecticut regiments in the Civil War. Also on the grounds is the "Petersburg Express," a mortar used by the 1st Connecticut Heavy Artillery.

Guided tours begin at the west entrance of the Legislative Office Building next to the Capitol building; free parking is in the garage. Allow 1 hour minimum. Tours hourly Mon.-Fri. 9:15-1:15, Sat. 10:15-2:15, Apr.-Oct.; Mon.-Fri. 9:15-1:15, rest of year. Building open Mon.-Fri. 7-5. Closed holidays. Free. Phone (860) 240-0222.

STATE LIBRARY AND SUPREME COURT BUILDING faces the Capitol grounds on the south. Within the building is the Museum of Connecticut History, which contains portraits of governors, an extensive Colt firearms collection and historic items. Library open Mon.-Fri. 9:30-5; museum open Mon.-Fri. 9:30-4. Closed state holidays. Free. Phone (860) 566-3056.

[SAVE] ★ **WADSWORTH ATHENEUM**, 600 Main St., was founded in 1842 and is said to be the nation's oldest continuously operated public art museum. Nearly 50,000 works are featured, including a large collection of Hudson River School landscape paintings, 16th- and 17th-century European paintings, Impressionist masterpieces, 20th-century art, decorative arts and Colonial furniture, two fully restored period rooms, a costume and textiles collection, European porcelain and two galleries of African-American art and artifacts. Food is available.

Allow 1 hour minimum. Tues.-Sun. 11-5 (also 5-8 first Thurs. of some months); closed Jan. 1, July 4, Thanksgiving and Dec. 25. Guided tours are given Wed.-Fri. at noon, Sat.-Sun. at 2:30 and the first Thurs. of the month at 5:30 and 7. Admission $7; over 59 and college students with ID $5; ages 6-17, $3; free to all on Thurs., and on Sat. 11-noon. Phone (860) 278-2670.

What To Do
Sightseeing

 Bus Tours

HERITAGE TRAILS SIGHTSEEING TOURS, which departs from Hartford hotels, offers narrated minibus tours of Hartford and a Colonial dinner tour of nearby Farmington. Tours that visit Amistad and Freedom Trail sites or ancient graveyards also are available. A self-guiding audio cassette driving tour of Hartford and of Farmington also is available for $12.95 (includes postage); write Heritage Trails, P.O. Box 138, Farmington, CT 06034. Two-hour tours depart daily at 9, 11, 1, 3 and 5; Colonial dinner tour departs at 5:30. Standard tour $15. Dinner tour $29.95. Reservations are required. Phone (860) 677-8867.

 Walking Tours

The 80-page guide "Hartford and Southern New England," published by the Greater Hart-

ford Convention & Visitors Bureau, includes a map for a walking tour of downtown Hartford; phone (860) 728-6789, or (800) 446-7811 out of Conn.

HARTFORD GUIDES leave from 101 Pearl St. which also houses the Police Museum. Narrated 2- to 2.5-hour walking tours of downtown Hartford are conducted by knowledgeable, professional guides who bring the people and events of Hartford's past to life and point out connections between the seemingly unrelated. Mon.-Fri. at 1, Apr.-Nov.; other times by appointment. Fee $5; over 59, $4; under 12 free with an adult. Phone (860) 522-0855 for reservations.

Sports and Recreation

American **Hockey** League contenders the Hartford Wolf Pack take to the ice October to mid-April at the Hartford Civic Center; phone (860) 246-7825. The Connecticut Pride CBA team roars down the court during **basketball** season; phone Ticketmaster at (860) 525-4500. **Collegiate athletics** hold court in nearby Storrs *(see place listing in the Vicinity section p. 76),* especially when the University of Connecticut's men's and women's basketball teams are on the court; phone (860) 486-2724.

When weather permits, Elizabeth Park is a good place to indulge in the region's winter pastime, **ice skating;** phone (860) 722-6514. Goodwin Park, 1130 Maple Ave., offers a driving

range and 27 holes of **golf,** a **swimming** pool, **tennis** courts, a fitness **trail** and other facilities; phone (860) 956-3601. The Hartford Parks and Recreation Department can be reached at (860) 722-6500.

Shopping

Downtown's Civic Center Mall at Trumbull and Asylum streets, off I-84 exit 49, offers 53 shops and restaurants. A skywalk connects the mall to historic Pratt Street and its shops and restaurants. Also downtown, at 855 Main St., is the outdoor Main Street Market which offers craft items, foods and locally grown seasonal produce Monday through Saturday from April through December.

In the Farmington area is West Farms on New Britain Avenue off I-84 exit 40 (SR 71); the mall contains Filene's, JCPenney, Lord & Taylor and Nordstrom. Buckland Hills Mall, I-84 exit 62 at 194 Buckland Hills Dr. in Manchester, contains more than 130 stores, including Filene's, JCPenney, Lord & Taylor and Sears, as well as a food court.

Old Wethersfield offers shops, restaurants and museums in preserved antebellum houses, warehouses, carriage houses and barns. Old Avon Village, on SR 44 in Avon, offers 50 shops and eateries. Riverdale Farms Shopping, off I-84 exit 39 in Avon, is on a restored and landscaped 19th-century dairy farm. The Marlborough Country Barn, in Marlborough on North Main Street off SR 2 exits 12 and 13, is a shopping village offering traditional wares, including reproduction lights and hardware.

Nearly 150 galleries, shops and boutiques can be visited at West Hartford Center, along Farmington Avenue in West Hartford.

BE AN EARLY BIRD!

START EARLY
to avoid traffic.

STOP EARLY
for the best selection
of accommodations.

Theater and Concerts

The Tony Award-winning Hartford Stage Company, (860) 527-5151, presents classics and contemporary experimental productions at 50 Church St. Producing Guild, (860) 528-2143, at 310 Prestige Park, and the TheaterWorks, (860) 527-7838, at 233 Pearl St., present off-Broadway type productions all year. In addition to presentations by local companies, the 1930s Art Deco Bushnell Memorial Hall's offerings include visiting orchestras, plays direct from or on their ways to Broadway, lectures, and performances by well-known entertainers; phone (860) 987-5900.

The musical arts are not neglected in Hartford. The Connecticut Opera, (860) 527-0713, the Hartford Ballet, (860) 525-9396, and the Hartford Symphony, (860) 244-2999, all have exciting seasons at Bushnell Memorial Hall. University of Connecticut's Jorgenson Auditorium in Storrs is host to professional dance, theater and music touring companies, as well as internationally known soloists and symphony orchestras October through May, and the UCONN Summer Fest June through August; for performance and ticket information phone (860) 486-4226. At the Meadows Music Theater, (860) 548-7370, offerings range from productions for children, to musicals to performances by superstars.

A variety of performances, lectures and workshops are held at Charter Oak Cultural Center, which is housed in what was once the state's first synagogue, built in 1876; phone (860) 249-1207. For a recorded, 24-hour events calendar for the Hartford area phone (860) 522-6400.

Special Events

Bushnell Park is the site of jazz concerts and other entertainment events in the spring and summer. Elizabeth Park, the nation's first municipally owned rose garden, also is the site of spring and summer concerts. Riverside Park is the site of warm-weather concerts. Residents take to the streets of New Britain during Main Street U.S.A., a community festival that takes place the second Saturday in June. In late June the professionals tee off at the River Highlands in nearby Cromwell for the PGA's Canon Greater Hartford Open.

The Podunk Bluegrass Music Festival is held on the green in East Hartford in July. New Britain's Italian Festival in late July offers arts and crafts, entertainment and food. Southington salutes local agriculture the first two weekends in October during the Apple Harvest Festival.

Middletown is host to a pair of fall events: the Head of the Connecticut Regatta in early October and the Wesleyan Potters Exhibit in late November and early December. Downtown's Constitution Plaza celebrates the holiday season with the Festival of Lights from late November through New Year's Day.

For a recorded, 24-hour events calendar phone (860) 522-6400.

The Hartford Vicinity

BRISTOL (C-3) pop. 60,600, elev. 332'

Bristol complements its manufacturing pursuits with several recreation areas, including Page Park in the Federal Hill section, which has facilities for swimming, tennis, basketball, baseball and skating, as well as a playground. Rockwell Park, west of the city, offers swimming and skating.

Bristol Chamber of Commerce: 17 Riverside Ave., Bristol, CT 06010-6395; phone (860) 584-4718.

⬛ **AMERICAN CLOCK AND WATCH MUSEUM,** 2 blks. s. off US 6 at 100 Maple St. in the 1801 Miles Lewis House, is supplemented by two modern wings and displays more than 3,000 clocks and watches dating from the 1590s. The exhibits include grandfather clocks, shelf clocks, novelties and church-tower clocks; many strike simultaneously on the hour.

A re-created 1825 clock shop area, an 1890 Victorian clock and watch store and a sundial garden are highlighted. Daily 10-5, Apr.-Nov.; closed Thanksgiving. Admission $3.50; over 60, $3; ages 8-15, $1.50; family rate $9. MC, VI. Phone (860) 583-6070.

HARRY BARNES MEMORIAL NATURE CENTER, .5 mi. e. of SR 69 at 175 Shrub Rd., comprises 70 acres of forest and field habitat with nature trails and an interpretive center housing living and preserved animals. Educational programs and displays designed for children also are featured. Allow 30 minutes minimum. Wed.-Fri. 2-5, Sat. 10-5, Sun. noon-5. Free. Phone (860) 585-8886.

LAKE COMPOUNCE THEME PARK is off I-84 exit 31, then 2 mi. n. on SR 229 following signs. This park, established in 1846, is said to be the oldest continuously operating amusement park in the nation. Rides and attractions include a steel roller coaster, a white-water raft ride, Kiddie Land and Splash Harbor Water Park. Among the more traditional features are a 1927 wooden roller coaster and a 1911 carrousel. *See color ad p. 24.*

Park opens daily at 11, Memorial Day weekend-late Sept. Closing times vary; phone ahead. Admission $21.95, over age 60 or under 52 inches tall $15.95, under age 4 free. DS, MC, VI. Phone (860) 583-3300.

⬛ **THE NEW ENGLAND CAROUSEL MUSEUM,** 95 Riverside Ave. (SR 72), displays hand-carved European and American carrousel pieces. Guided tours explore the history and development of the carrousel and allow visitors to watch the restoration process. Allow 1 hour minimum. Mon.-Sat. 10-5, Sun. noon-5, Apr.-Nov.; Thurs.-Sat. 10-5, Sun. noon-5, rest of year. Closed major holidays. Admission $4; over 62, $3.50; ages 4-14, $2.50. Phone (860) 585-5411.

CANTON (B-3) pop. 8,300, elev. 900'

Formerly a portion of Simsbury, Canton first was called Suffrage because of the hardships overcome by the early settlers in 1740. It separated from the parish of West Simsbury in 1806. The name of the town indicates the state's interest in the China trade at that time.

Local legend claims that the ghostly remains of a paymaster murdered at the Canton Tavern during the Revolution can be seen at night in the form of a galloping headless horseman.

Greater Hartford Tourism District: 234 Murphy Rd., Hartford, CT 06114; phone (860) 244-8181 or (800) 793-4480.

ROARING BROOK NATURE CENTER, 70 Gracey Rd., is 1.5 mi. n.e. of US 44; use Lawton Rd. n. from jct. US 44 and SR 177, following signs. The center has 6 miles of self-guiding trails and 115 acres of woodland. The interpretive building houses permanent and seasonal exhibits, including a small animal collection and a replica of an eastern woodland Indian longhouse.

Programs deal with the natural history of North America; folk concerts are offered weekend evenings in spring, fall and winter. Allow 1 hour, 30 minutes minimum. Mon.-Sat. and holidays 10-5, Sun. 1-5, July-Aug.; Tues.-Sat. 10-5, Sun. 1-5, rest of year. Closed Jan. 1, July 4, Thanksgiving and Dec. 25. Admission $3; over 61 and ages 2-12, $2. Phone (860) 693-0263

COLLINSVILLE (B-3) pop. 2,600, elev. 317'

On the east bank of the Farmington River, Collinsville is the site of one of the first ax factories in the world. In 1826 Samuel and David Collins and William Wells established the factory from which John Brown obtained pikes for his insurrection at Harper's Ferry.

CANTON HISTORICAL MUSEUM, 1 blk. off SR 179 at 11 Front St., occupies a building of the Collins Co., a tool manufacturer whose antique products are displayed within. Exhibits include Victorian memorabilia of the Canton area, as well as a general store, farm implements, machinery, a 19th-century transportation exhibit, a working 40- by 50-foot railroad diorama, a post office and reconstructed blacksmith and barber shops.

Also displayed are Victorian wedding gowns in a period parlor, antique tools and engines, a working nickelodeon and unusual toys and dolls. Allow 1 hour minimum. Wed.-Sun. 1-4 (also Thurs. 4-8), Apr.-Nov.; Sat.-Sun. 1-4, rest of year. Admission $3; over 64 and ages 2-15, $2. Phone (860) 693-2793.

EAST GRANBY (B-4) pop. 4,300

Divided by a mountain of traprock, East Granby was settled in 1710 in a region originally known as Turkey Hills. The country's first commercially successful silverplating process was perfected in 1845 by Asa Rogers for the Cowles Co. Rogers later moved to Hartford and established the Rogers Brothers trademark in 1847.

The Congregational Church, at SRs 20 and 187, was built in 1830 in the Gothic style and bears the distinctive features of a wooden belfry and pinnacles.

Connecticut's North Central Tourism Bureau: 111 Hazard Ave., Enfield, CT 06082; phone (860) 763-2578 or (800) 248-8283.

SAVE **OLD NEW-GATE PRISON AND COPPER MINE** is .7 mi. w. on SR 20, then 1 mi. n. on Newgate Rd. This Colonial copper mine served as a Revolutionary War prison and in 1776 became the first working state prison in the nation. It was abandoned in 1827. The old prison buildings and underground caverns can be visited; the guard house contains historical murals. Picnicking is permitted. Wed.-Sun. and holidays 10-4:30, mid-May through Oct. 31. Admission $3; over 61 and ages 6-17, $1.50. Phone (860) 566-3005.

EAST WINDSOR (B-4) pop. 1,900, elev. 69'

In 1636 William Pynchon built a warehouse at Warehouse Point to store cargo that could not be transported around Enfield Rapids. Goods were taken by oxcart to Thompsonville, where they were reloaded onto flatboats to complete the journey to Springfield.

Connecticut's North Central Tourism Bureau: 111 Hazard Ave., Enfield, CT 06082; phone (860) 763-2578 or (800) 248-8283.

CONNECTICUT FIRE MUSEUM is .5 mi. e. of I-91 exit 45 at 58 North Rd. (behind the Connecticut Trolley Museum). The museum houses a collection of antique fire equipment ranging from a circa 1894 fire sleigh to a 1955 Zabek pumper. Firetruck models and memorabilia also are displayed. Allow 1 hour minimum. Mon.-Fri. 10-4, Sat. 10-5, Sun. noon-5, July-Aug.; Sat.-Sun. noon-5, Apr.-June and Sept.-Oct. Admission $2; over 62 and ages 5-12, $1. Phone (860) 623-4732.

CONNECTICUT TROLLEY MUSEUM is .7 mi. e. of I-91 exit 45 at 58 North Rd. on SR 140. Displayed are operating trolleys and associated rail cars dating 1894-1947. A 3.7-mile ride on an antique trolley car is offered. The museum is host to events throughout the year. Tours and food are available.

Allow 1 hour, 30 minutes minimum. Mon.-Sat. 10-5, Sun. noon-5, Memorial Day-Labor Day; Sat. 10-5, Sun. noon-5, Mar. 1-day before Memorial Day and day after Labor Day-Thanksgiving; Mon.-Fri. 6 p.m.-9 p.m., Sat.-Sun. noon-4 and 5-9, Fri. after Thanksgiving-Dec. 31. Closed Thanksgiving and Dec. 24-25. Museum free. Unlimited trolley rides $6; over 62, $5; ages 5-12, $3. MC, VI ($10). Phone (860) 627-6540 or 627-6597.

FARMINGTON (B-3) pop. 20,600, elev. 245'

Farmington, an aristocratic old town, sits unchanged amid its wealth and culture. The long main street is laid out on a river terrace. To the east is wild hill country; to the west is a river plain.

Greater Hartford Tourism District: 234 Murphy Rd., Hartford, CT 06114; phone (860) 244-8181 or (800) 793-4480.

HERITAGE TRAILS SIGHTSEEING TOURS— *see Hartford p. 151.*

★ **HILL-STEAD MUSEUM**, 35 Mountain Rd., .2 mi. from the center of town by way of Farmington Ave. and Main St., displays etchings and paintings by Impressionists Mary Cassatt, Edgar Degas, Eduoard Manet, Claude Monet and James McNeill Whistler; Chinese porcelains of the Ming and Ching dynasties; and other art objects.

Set on 150 acres, which include a sunken garden designed by Beatrix Farrand, the Colonial-revival house was designed and built in 1901 by Theodate Pope, one of the first female architects in the country. Her father, industrialist Alfred Atmore Pope, used the house as a showplace for his art collection.

Hour-long guided tours are given every half-hour Tues.-Sun. 10-4, May-Oct.; 11-3, rest of year. Last tour departs 1 hour before closing. Admission $6; over 61 and students with ID $5; ages 6-12, $3. MC, VI. Phone (860) 677-4787.

SAVE ★ **STANLEY-WHITMAN HOUSE**, 37 High St., was built in the early 18th century. A well-preserved example of the framed-overhang style with pendants, the house contains period furnishings and other items. Herb and flower gardens are featured. Wed.-Sun. noon-4, May-Oct.; Sun. noon-4, rest of year. Closed holidays. Admission $5; over 64, $4; ages 6-12, $2. Phone (860) 677-9222.

MANCHESTER (B-4) pop. 51,600, elev. 117'

From a center of small industry in 1823, Manchester has grown into one of the state's major manufacturing cities, with several of its industries more than a century old. The town produced gunpowder that was used by the Continental Army during the Revolutionary War.

Prosperity skyrocketed after six grandsons of Timothy Cheney founded the Cheney Brothers Silk Co. in 1838; the Cheney Homestead is open to the public. The silk company made Manchester the nation's silk-producing capital and was responsible for the establishment of schools, local utilities and other public services before it went out of business after World War II.

Greater Hartford Tourism District: 234 Murphy Rd., Hartford, CT 06114; phone (860) 244-8181 or (800) 793-4480.

FIRE MUSEUM, 230 Pine St., is in a restored 1901 Manchester firehouse. Firefighting equipment and memorabilia include leather fire buckets used by Colonial settlers, an early motorized firetruck, a display about sprinkler evolution and a horse-drawn hose wagon. The extravagantly decorated four-wheel, hand-pulled hose reel reflects a time when fire departments provided protection and served as social centers. Guided tours are available. Fri.-Sat. 10-5, Sun. noon-5, mid-Apr. to mid-Nov. Donations. Phone (860) 649-9436.

LUTZ CHILDREN'S MUSEUM, 247 S. Main St., features changing participatory exhibits about such topics as art, history, science, nature and ethnology. There is a permanent collection of small native, domestic and exotic live animals. The nearby 53-acre Oak Grove Nature Center contains wildlife habitats. Allow 1 hour minimum. Tues.-Wed. 2-5, Thurs.-Fri. 9:30-5, Sat.-Sun. noon-5, Labor Day-July 4; Tues.-Wed. noon-5, rest of year. Closed holidays. Admission $3; ages 2-17, $2.50. Phone (860) 643-0949.

WICKHAM PARK is .5 mi. w. of I-84 exit 60 on US 6/US 44 to 1329 W. Middle Tpke. This 215-acre park has extensive manicured grounds which contain Oriental and lotus gardens as well as an aviary and a log cabin. Recreational facilities include play areas, tennis and volleyball courts, softball fields and walking and fitness trails. Picnicking is permitted. Daily 9:30-dusk, first Sat. in Apr.-last Sat. in Oct. Admission 3-day holiday weekends $3 per private vehicle; Fri.-Sun. $2 per private vehicle; Mon.-Thurs. $1 per private vehicle. Phone (860) 528-0856.

MIDDLETOWN (C-4) pop. 42,800, elev. 55'

From about 1750 until after the Revolution, Middletown was a great trading port and the largest and wealthiest city in Connecticut. Simeon North, the first official pistol maker for the government, built his factory in 1799. The city is now an important research and manufacturing center supporting diversified industries.

Capture the moment...

Tips for successful photographs

K now your camera, and be sure it's in good working order. Before going on a trip, shoot a roll of film so you won't have any surprises when it really counts. Use film best suited to your purpose; camera shop personnel can help you choose the right kind. Then, follow the instructions that come with it.

♦ *Compose your picture. Try framing it with a foreground feature (a fence or tree), making sure that parts of the subject are not being cut off. Get close enough so that your subject won't be dwarfed in an expanse of background.*

♦ *When taking close-ups of people, have them stand against a simple backdrop, and be sure they do something other than stare stiffly at the camera.*

♦ *Mid-morning and mid-afternoon, when the sun's angle creates definite but not overpowering shadows, are the best times for general photography. Pictures taken during the shadowless high noon hours tend to be flat.*

♦ *If the weather turns bad, take pictures anyway. Rain and fog can add a special magic to your efforts.*

Connecticut River Valley and Shoreline Visitors Council: 393 Main St., Middletown, CT 06457; phone (860) 347-0028 or (800) 486-3346.

CENTER FOR THE ARTS, on the Wesleyan University campus, features three performance halls and two galleries that present changing exhibits of contemporary and international art. The Davison Art Center focuses on printmaking and photography; the Zilkha Gallery often presents contemporary paintings and sculpture. Allow 30 minutes minimum. Both are open Tues.-Fri. noon-4, Sat.-Sun. 2-5, mid-Jan. to mid-June and early Sept.-early Dec.; closed holidays. Free. Phone (860) 685-2965, 685-2500 or 685-2695.

OLIN MEMORIAL LIBRARY, 252 Church St. on the Wesleyan University campus, opened in 1928. The library contains more than 1.4 million volumes and numerous portraits. Allow 30 minutes minimum. Mon.-Thurs. 8:30 a.m.-1 a.m., Sat. 10-10, Sun. 10 a.m.-1 a.m. Hours are limited during the summer and semester recess. Closed major holidays. Free. Phone (860) 685-2660.

NEW BRITAIN (B-4) pop. 72,400, elev. 199'

Metalworking industries are prevalent in New Britain, known as the "Hardware City." During the 19th and early 20th century, the city was at the forefront of industrial enterprise and urban development, as is visible in the Art Deco architecture downtown.

Those who like to wield the hardware known as golf clubs can play at the 27-hole municipal golf course in Stanley Quarter Park *(see Recreation Chart)* on Stanley Street north of Central Park. From April through September, the New Britain Rock Cats, the Class AA affiliate of the Minnesota Twins, entertain baseball fans at Beehive Field.

Central Connecticut Tourism District: 1 Grove St., Suite 310, New Britain, CT 06053; phone (860) 225-3901.

Self-guiding tours: The "Architectural Walking Tour" brochure is available at the tourism district office.

SAVE **NEW BRITAIN MUSEUM OF AMERICAN ART,** 56 Lexington St., contains a collection of permanent and changing exhibits, including more than 5,000 paintings, graphics and sculptures tracing the history of American art from 1740 to the present. Included are murals by Thomas Hart Benton and works by Mary Cassatt, John Singleton Copley, Winslow Homer, Gilbert Stuart, James McNeill Whistler and artists of the Hudson River School. Guided tours for the visually impaired are available by appointment.

Tues.-Fri. 1-5, Sat. 10-5, Sun. noon-5; closed holidays. Admission $3; over 62 and ages 12-18, $2; free to all Sat. 10-noon. Phone (860) 229-0257.

NEW BRITAIN YOUTH MUSEUM, 30 High St., contains children's artifacts and changing regional culture exhibits. Allow 1 hour minimum. Mon.-Fri. 1-5, July-Aug.; Tues.-Fri. 1-5, Sat. 10-4, rest of year. Closed holidays. Donations. Phone (860) 225-3020.

ROCKY HILL (C-4) pop. 16,600, elev. 46'

Giant prehistoric reptiles once roamed the Rocky Hill region, and their footprints and fossils still can be found. Millions of years after the dinosaurs' demise, the town was settled in 1650 as a suburb of Wethersfield. A change in the course of the Connecticut River caused Rocky Hill to become Wethersfield's chief port for a period of time; however, that function since has been relinquished.

Greater Hartford Tourism District: 234 Murphy Rd., Hartford, CT 06114; phone (860) 244-8181 or (800) 793-4480.

DINOSAUR STATE PARK is on West St., .5 mi. e. of I-91 exit 23. A geodesic dome exhibit center covers a sandstone layer in which more than 500 dinosaur footprints from the Lower Jurassic period have been preserved. Outside, casts can be made from actual dinosaur tracks; bring 10 pounds of plaster of Paris, a quarter-cup of cooking oil, a 5-gallon bucket and rags.

Park open daily 9-4:30, all year. Casting area open daily 9-3:30, May-Oct. Nature trails open daily 9-4. Exhibit center open Tues.-Sun. 9-4:30. Park and exhibit center closed Jan. 1, Thanksgiving and Dec. 25. Park free. Exhibit center admission $2; ages 6-17, $1. Phone (860) 529-8423 to verify prices.

SIMSBURY (B-3) pop. 22,000, elev. 164'

Simsbury, originally named Massacoe, was settled in 1640 by British emigrants from Symondsbury in Dorsetshire, England, who initially had settled in Windsor. The village was incorporated as the town of Simsbury in 1670.

Frightened by the depredations of King Phillip's War, the residents returned to their former town. Later, scouts reported that the village was left in ashes by the king's American Indian warriors. The discovery of copper at nearby East Granby stimulated economic recovery in the area, and Simsbury again flourished.

Panoramas of Farmington Valley to the west are offered by the Heublein Tower at Talcott Mountain State Park.

The International Skating Center of Connecticut, 1375 Hopmeadow St., lets visitors watch Olympic figure skating champions and Olympic hopefuls train and perform in shows; phone (860) 651-5400.

Greater Hartford Tourism District: 234 Murphy Rd., Hartford, CT 06114; phone (860) 244-8181 or (800) 793-4480.

SAVE **SIMSBURY HISTORICAL SOCIETY,** 800 Hopmeadow St., centers on an 18th-century house with period furniture and costumes. Especially interesting is the vaulted ceiling in the ballroom. Also featured are an 1840 one-room schoolhouse, an herb garden, a Victorian carriage house and a replica of a 1683 meetinghouse. The 1771 Phelps House was used as a tavern; the Hendricks Cottage houses weaving artifacts. Obsolete equipment used in making fuses is housed in a modern building.

Guided tours are available. Allow 1 hour, 30 minutes minimum. Daily 1-4, May-Oct.; closed holidays. Admission $6; over 60, $5; ages 5-18, $3.50. Phone (860) 658-2500.

SOMERS (A-4) pop. 9,100

Somers was named in 1734 after Lord John Somers, an adviser to King William III, and became part of Connecticut in 1749. Today the town is a residential and farming community producing apples and strawberries. Nearby Soapstone Mountain is topped by a weather radar installation and a platform offering a scenic view of the area.

Connecticut's North Central Tourism Bureau: 111 Hazard Ave., Enfield, CT 06082; phone (860) 763-2578 or (800) 248-8283.

SOMERS MOUNTAIN MUSEUM OF NATURAL HISTORY AND PRIMITIVE TECHNOLOGY is 1 mi. e. on SR 190, then 2 mi. n. on Turnpike Rd. This museum exhibits American Indian artifacts collected from across North America, with an emphasis on primitive technologies. Clothing, dolls, pottery, beadwork, peace pipes and stone tools are among the items displayed. A life-size tepee and a birch-bark canoe also are featured. Allow 30 minutes minimum. Wed.-Sun. 10-5, Apr.-Aug.; Sat.-Sun. 10-5, Sept.-Dec. Admission $2; over 64 and ages 6-16, 99c. Phone (860) 749-4129 to confirm schedule.

SOUTHINGTON (C-3) pop. 38,500, elev. 149'

Cement and hardware long have been the major industries in Southington, which was settled in 1696. Several historic houses, many with 18th-century doorways and trim, stand near the green.

Greater Southington Chamber of Commerce: 51 N. Main St., Southington, CT 06489; phone (860) 628-8036.

BARNES MUSEUM, 85 N. Main St., displays historic diaries, photographs, periodicals, clothing and other items dating from 1836. The house, framed in solid oak, has finely crafted woodwork, stairways and fireplaces. Allow 30 minutes minimum. Guided tours Mon.-Fri. 9-3; closed major holidays. Donations. Phone (860) 628-5426.

SUFFIELD (A-4) pop. 1,400, elev. 124'

In an area bought from the native inhabitants by John Pynchon in 1670, Suffield thrived on tobacco growing, which was learned from the former owners. As early as 1727 this crop was of such importance that it was legal tender; tobacco remains important.

Connecticut's North Central Tourism Bureau: 111 Hazard Ave., Enfield, CT 06082; phone (860) 763-2578 or (800) 248-8283.

SAVE **HATHEWAY HOUSE,** 55 S. Main St. (SR 75), reflects two 18th-century architectural styles. The original portion of the 1761 house is a typical Colonial house of the mid-1700s, while the north wing, added in 1794, is one of the first examples of the neoclassical style in the Connecticut Valley. It contains one of the few known signed and dated rooms; on its walls are four French hand-blocked wallpapers of the 1790s.

Allow 30 minutes minimum. Wed.-Sun. 1-4, July-Aug.; Wed. and Sat.-Sun. 1-4, mid-May through June 30 and Sept. 1 to mid-Oct. Admission $4; under 18, $1. Phone (860) 668-0055 or 247-8996.

WEST HARTFORD (B-3) pop. 60,100, elev. 146'

Noah Webster was born in West Hartford in 1758 and remained until 1798. His first small dictionary of the American language (as distinguished from the British) appeared in 1806; the large version in 1828. A 13.5-foot statue of the lexicographer sculpted by Korczak Ziolkowski stands on the town hall lawn.

A 1912 Pope-Hartford Model 28 Roadster is permanently displayed in the Automobile Club of Hartford's West Hartford office at 815 Farmington Ave.; phone (860) 236-3261. The display exemplifies the area's contribution to the advancement of automotive development in the early 1900s.

Greater Hartford Tourism District: 234 Murphy Rd., Hartford, CT 06114; phone (860) 244-8181 or (800) 793-4480.

MUSEUM OF AMERICAN POLITICAL LIFE, 200 Bloomfield Ave. on the University of Hartford campus, displays memorabilia relating to presidential campaigns, presidents and the electoral process. Permanent exhibits include "The Right to Vote," which traces the struggles of women and minorities to achieve political equality; "Perennial Political Issues," which examines three major, recurrent themes in presidential campaigns and "The History of Presidential Elections," which consists of a large display of historical objects and photographs covering an entire 70-foot-long wall of the museum.

Allow 1 hour minimum. Tues.-Fri. 11-4, Sat.-Sun. noon-4; closed national and university holidays. Donations. Phone (860) 768-4090.

SAVE **NOAH WEBSTER HOUSE/MUSEUM OF WEST HARTFORD HISTORY,** 227 S. Main St., was the 1758 birthplace of lexicographer Noah Webster, the author of the first American dictionary and of the "Blue-Backed Speller." The restored farmhouse and an adjoining museum contain period furnishings and changing exhibits; a videotape presentation commemorates Webster's life.

Allow 1 hour minimum. Costumed guides conduct tours Mon.-Tues. and Thurs.-Fri. 10-4, Sat.-Sun. 1-4, July-Aug.; Thurs.-Tues. 1-4, rest of year. Closed federal holidays and the first 5 weekdays in Jan. Admission $5; over 65, $4; students with ID $3; ages 6-12, $1. Phone (860) 521-5362.

SCIENCE CENTER OF CONNECTICUT, 950 Trout Brook Dr., a hands-on science, technology and nature museum, features a 30-foot walk-in kaleidoscope, a marine life touch tank, a miniature zoo, animal demonstrations, laser light and planetarium shows, a hands-on discovery room, the Kids Factory for preschoolers to explore, a computer center, national touring exhibits and a life-size replica of a sperm whale. Changing exhibits and events are presented throughout the year.

Tues.-Fri. 10-5 (also Thurs. 5-8), Sat. 10-5, Sun. noon-5; closed Easter, Thanksgiving and Dec. 25. Admission $6; over 60, students with ID and ages 3-15, $5. Planetarium and laser show $3; over 60, students with ID and ages 3-15, $2. Phone (860) 231-2824.

WETHERSFIELD (B-4) pop. 25,700, elev. 36'

Along with Windsor, Wethersfield claims to be the oldest permanent English settlement in Connecticut. One of the first Colonial uprisings against British authority occurred Apr. 11, 1640, when the townspeople held an illegal public election. As a result the Royal Court fined them 5 pounds, but the citizens refused to pay.

Wethersfield became the commercial center for towns along the Connecticut River; ships built, owned and manned by locals sailed along the coast and to the West Indies with goods produced by the rich valley soil. Many structures built prior to 1800 are marked with the date of construction and the names of the original owners. The original Colonial steeple and brickwork of the Meeting House, now the First Church of Christ, remain.

Greater Hartford Tourism District: 234 Murphy Rd., Hartford, CT 06114; phone (860) 244-8181 or (800) 793-4480.

SAVE **BUTTOLPH-WILLIAMS HOUSE,** Broad and Marsh sts., was built around 1710-20. Its hewn overhang and small casement windows give it a medieval appearance. Period furnishings help reflect the Colonial lifestyle. Allow 30 minutes

minimum. Wed.-Fri. and Mon. 10-4, May-Oct. Admission $3; under 16, $1. Phone (860) 529-0460.

COVE WAREHOUSE, n. end of Main St. in Cove Park, was one of several warehouses built in the 1600s; this warehouse is the only one left standing after a flood in 1692 that changed the course of the river. The warehouse displays maritime exhibits that depict the area's seafaring past. Thurs.-Sat. 10-4, Sun. 1-4, July 4-Labor Day; Sat. 10-4, Sun. 1-4, mid-May through July 3 and day after Labor Day to mid-Oct. Admission $1, under 16 free. Phone (860) 529-7656.

HURLBUT-DUNHAM HOUSE, 212 Main St., was built in the late 18th century and renovated in Italianate style in 1860. Guided tours take visitors through the house, which is furnished in Colonial revival. Thurs.-Sat. 10-4, Sun. 1-4, June-Oct.; Sat. 10-4, Sun. 1-4, Apr.-May and Nov.-Dec. Admission $3, under 16 free. Tickets are purchased at Keeney Cultural Center next door. Phone (860) 529-7656.

SAVE ★ **WEBB-DEANE-STEVENS MUSEUM,** .5 mi. w. of I-91 exit 26 at 211 Main St., comprises three 18th-century houses restored on their original sites and furnished to depict the Colonial home. George Washington and Comte de Rochambeau met in the Joseph Webb House in 1781 to plan the battle that led to the American victory at Yorktown. Murals commissioned in 1916 for the Webb House depict the Battle of Yorktown, from its conception to its conclusion.

Allow 1 hour minimum. Guided tours are given on the hour Wed.-Mon. 10-4, May-Oct.; Sat.-Sun. 10-4, rest of year. Last tour 1 hour before closing. Admission $8; over 60, $7; ages 6-18, $4. Phone (860) 529-0612.

WETHERSFIELD MUSEUM AT KEENEY CULTURAL CENTER, 200 Main St., was built in 1893 as a school. This center houses the Wethersfield Historical Society's museum which features a permanent exhibit about local history as well as displays of art and changing exhibits. Allow 30 minutes minimum. Tues.-Sat. 10-4, Sun. 1-4; closed major holidays. Admission $2, under 16 free. Phone (860) 529-7161 or 529-7656.

WINDSOR (B-4) pop. 27,800, elev. 54'

Windsor shares with Wethersfield a claim to being the oldest town in the state, a controversy that may never be settled. In 1639 Windsor united with Hartford and Wethersfield under the "Fundamental Orders" to form the Colony of Connecticut.

Connecticut's North Central Tourism Bureau: 111 Hazard Ave., Enfield, CT 06082: phone (860) 763-2578 or (800) 248-8283.

FIRST CHURCH IN WINDSOR (Congregational) is at 107 Palisado Ave. The present building was erected in 1794, but the organization, having begun in 1630, is among the oldest gathered congregations in North America. The adjoining cemetery contains tombstones dating from the 1600s. Allow 30 minutes minimum. Tours are available by appointment. Office open Mon.-Fri. 8-noon, July-Aug.; 8:30-3, rest of year. Free. Phone (860) 688-7229.

NORTHWEST PARK NATURE CENTER AND TOBACCO MUSEUM is off I-91N exit 38 or I-91S exit 38A, 1.5 mi. n. on SR 75, 1.2 mi. w. on Prospect Hill, then .5 mi. n. on Lang Rd. This 473-acre park includes more than 10 miles of trails for hiking, jogging and cross-country skiing. The nature center features hands-on displays in the Discovery Room; sheep, goats and chickens live in the adjacent animal barn. The Luddy/Taylor Connecticut Valley Tobacco Museum houses early and modern harvesting equipment in a former curing barn.

Allow 1 hour minimum. Park open daily dawn-dusk. Nature center open Mon.-Sat. 9-5. Tobacco museum open Tues.-Thurs. and Sat. noon-4, Mar. 1-Dec. 15. Free. Phone (860) 285-1886 for the nature center, or 285-1888 for the museum.

PALISADO GREEN, on Palisado Ave. (SR 159), occupies part of the site of the old stockade built during the 1637 Pequot War. The Founders Monument lists the English settlers who disembarked from the *Mary and John* in 1630. Adjacent is the Palisado Cemetery.

▣ **WINDSOR HISTORICAL SOCIETY,** 96 Palisado Ave. (SR 159), is the site of the 1640 Lt. Walter Fyler House and the 1765 Dr. Hezekiah Chaffe House. The museum contains a genealogical and historical research library and presents changing exhibits. Allow 1 hour minimum. Tues.-Sat. 10-4, Apr.-Oct.; Mon.-Fri. 10-4, rest of year. Closed major holidays. Admission $3; over 55, $2; students with ID and under 12 free. Phone (860) 688-3813.

WINDSOR LOCKS (A-4) pop. 12,400, elev. 49'

Connecticut's North Central Tourism Bureau: 111 Hazard Ave., Enfield, CT 06082: phone (860) 763-2578 or (800) 248-8283.

▣ **NEW ENGLAND AIR MUSEUM,** from I-91 exit 40, just off SR 75 and north of Bradley International Airport, displays vintage and modern aircraft as well as aviation memorabilia. Allow 1 hour minimum. Daily 10-5; closed Thanksgiving and Dec. 25. Admission $6.50; over 61, $6; ages 6-11, $3.50. AE, DS, MC, VI. Phone (860) 623-3305.

This ends listings for the Hartford Vicinity. The following page resumes the alphabetical listings of cities in Connecticut.

KENT (B-2) pop. 2,900, elev. 395'

Kent was incorporated in 1739 after lots were sold at public auction in Windham. Known as a center for winter sports and hiking, the town also is home to a large art colony. The Housatonic River has cut a gorge through the limestone, and geologists find excellent specimens of marble and schist in the area. Bull's Bridge, built circa 1842, spans the river. It is one of two covered bridges in the state that accommodate automobile traffic.

Litchfield Hills Travel Council: P.O. Box 968, Litchfield, CT 06759-0968; phone (860) 567-4506.

[SAVE] **THE SLOANE-STANLEY MUSEUM,** 1 mi. n. on US 7, houses Early American tools and paintings donated by artist and author Eric Sloane, who died in 1985. One wing houses a re-creation of Sloane's Warren studio. Next to the museum, a small structure depicts the austere conditions of an early frontier cabin. Below the museum are the ruins of a Kent iron furnace, which began producing pig iron in 1826 and continued for almost 70 years.

Wed.-Sun. and holidays 10-4, mid-May through Oct. 31. Admission $3; over 59 and ages 6-17, $1.50. Phone (860) 927-3849 or (860) 566-3005.

LAKEVILLE (A-1) elev. 975'

The Holley House Museum and Salisbury Cannon Museum, on the north side of US 44 in the Lakeville Historic District, feature hands-on exhibits and living-history tours about life in the 19th century and the contributions of the area's iron industry during the Revolutionary War. On the grounds are an ice house, a seven-hole outhouse, a maze and 19th-century heritage gardens. Phone (860) 435-2878 for museum hours and tour information.

Litchfield Hills Travel Council: P.O. Box 968, Litchfield, CT 06759-0968; phone (860) 567-4506.

Self-guiding tours: An audiotaped walking tour of the area's historic district is available at the Holley House Museum.

LIME ROCK PARK, 497 Lime Rock Rd., is one of America's oldest continuously operated sports car racing tracks and is host to amateur and professional racing events. The 1.5-mile track allows hillside viewing from the surrounding 325-acre Litchfield Hills. Food is available. Racing events are held early Apr. to mid-Oct.; major events take place holiday weekends. Admission $12-$75. Phone (860) 435-5000 or (800) 722-3577.

LEBANON (C-5) pop. 6,000, elev. 270'

Lebanon's tree-shaded streets, old houses, spacious lawns and green common give no indica-tion of the Revolutionary War activity that once took place. The town was a cultural center and home to the Trumbull family and its vast West India trade. When the Stamp Act was passed in 1770, trade was devastated and personal fortunes were lost. In April of the same year, local free-men drafted a declaration of rights and liberties that foreshadowed the Declaration of Independence.

JONATHAN TRUMBULL HOUSE, off SR 87 on Lebanon Green, was the home of the Revolutionary War governor of Connecticut, who is said to have been the only Colonial governor who supported the war. Trumbull served as a counselor to George Washington and housed a detachment of Comte de Rochambeau's army.

The 1735 house has a number of unusual design features and is furnished in period; behind it is the Wadsworth Stable. Also featured is the William Beaumont House, containing displays of surgical instruments of the "Father of Physiology." Trumbull House open Tues.-Sat. 1-5. Beaumont House open Sat. 1-4, May 15-Oct. 15. Admission $2, under 12 free. Phone (860) 642-7558.

LEDYARD (C-6)

Settled in 1653, the community became the parish of North Groton but later was renamed for Col. William Ledyard under whom townsmen fought during the American Revolution.

Southeastern Connecticut Tourism: 470 Bank St., P.O. Box 89, New London, CT 06320; phone (860) 444-2206 or (800) 863-6569.

 CASINOS

• **Foxwoods Resort Casino,** on SR 2, 7.3 mi. w. of I-95 exit 92; from I-395 exit 79A, s.e. 11 mi. on SR 2. Daily 24 hours. Phone (860) 885-3000 or (800) 752-9244.

LITCHFIELD (B-2) pop. 8,400, elev. 1,100'

First settled in 1719, Litchfield is noted for its many fine Colonial houses, including the birth-place of Harriet Beecher Stowe. The town also is the site of the first law school in the country, founded in 1784 by Judge Tapping Reeve. One of Reeve's first law students was his brother-in-law, Aaron Burr, who became Thomas Jefferson's vice president and killed Alexander Hamilton in a duel.

Litchfield Hills Travel Council: P.O. Box 968, Litchfield, CT 06759-0968; phone (860) 567-4506. *See color ad p. 63.*

LITCHFIELD HISTORICAL SOCIETY MUSEUM, jct. SRs 118 and 63, contains several galleries of paintings, furniture, decorative arts and costumes which tell the story of the town. A research library is available. Tues.-Sat. 11-5, Sun. 1-5, Apr.-Oct. Admission (with Tapping Reeve House and Law School) $5, senior citizens and students with ID $3, under 14 and law students free. Phone (860) 567-4501.

LOURDES IN LITCHFIELD, .5 mi. e. on SR 118, is a shrine modeled after the Shrine of Our Lady of Lourdes in France. Among the 35 acres are a grotto, the Stations of the Cross, several small shrines and Pilgrim Hall. Food is available. Picnicking is permitted. Tues.-Sun. dawn-dusk. Donations. Phone (860) 567-1041.

TAPPING REEVE HOUSE AND LAW SCHOOL is on South St. The renovated house and law school features an exhibition which tells the story of America's first school of law and the contributions of its many graduates to the development of politics, law, business and legal education in early 19th-century America. Tues.-Sat. 11-5, Sun. 1-5, May-Oct.; closed holidays. Admission (with Litchfield Historical Society Museum) $5, senior citizens and students with ID $3, under 14 and law students free. Phone (860) 567-4501.

TOPSMEAD STATE FOREST, 2 mi. e. on SR 118, right on E. Litchfield Rd., then right on Buell Rd., lies atop a 1,230-foot knoll. Once the summer home of Edith Morton Chase, the daughter of the founder of Chase Brass, the 511-acre forest contains her English Tudor-style cottage, which is furnished with 17th- and 18th-century antiques. Hiking, sledding and cross-country skiing are possible over several miles of trails, roads and open fields within the forest. Picnicking is permitted. Fires are not permitted.

Allow 30 minutes minimum. Park open daily 8-dusk; Chase House open Sat.-Sun. and holidays noon-5, second and fourth weekends of the month, June-Oct. Free. Phone (860) 567-5694. *See Recreation Chart.*

WHITE FLOWER FARM, 3.5 mi. s. on SR 63, contains 8 acres of display gardens, 20 acres of growing fields and a greenhouse with giant tuberous begonias. Peak blooming season is mid-June to mid-September. Daily 9-6, Apr.-Oct.; 10-5, rest of year. Free. Phone (860) 567-8789.

WHITE MEMORIAL FOUNDATION, 2 mi. s.w. on US 202, is a 4,000-acre wildlife sanctuary that includes about half the shoreline of Bantam Lake, the Bantam River, several streams and ponds, a milelong boardwalk and 35 miles of trails for cross-country skiing, hiking and horseback riding. Equipment rentals are not available. Camping facilities are available.

The White Memorial Conservation Center Museum, near the entrance, contains displays relating to the sanctuary's natural features and wildlife. Guided tours and nature programs are available upon request. Grounds open daily 24 hours. Center open Mon.-Sat. 9-5, Sun. noon-5,

Apr.-Oct.; Mon.-Sat. 8:30-4:30, Sun. noon-4, rest of year. Closed major holidays. Admission $4; ages 6-12, $2. Phone (860) 567-0857.

WINERIES

- **Haight Vineyard and Winery,** 1 mi. e. of the green on SR 118, then s. at wine trail sign onto Chestnut Hill Rd. Mon.-Sat. and holidays 10:30-5, Sun. noon-5; closed Jan. 1, Easter, Thanksgiving and Dec. 25. Phone (860) 567-4045, or (800) 325-9463 in Conn.

MADISON (D-4) pop. 15,500, elev. 30'

Madison is the site of Hammonasset Beach State Park *(see Recreation Chart),* Connecticut's largest waterfront park. The town's historic sites include the 1785 Allis-Bushnell House, which houses the Madison Historical Society and is open in summer as a museum of local history.

Connecticut River Valley and Shoreline Visitors Council: 393 Main St., Middletown, CT 06457; phone (860) 347-0028 or (800) 486-3346.

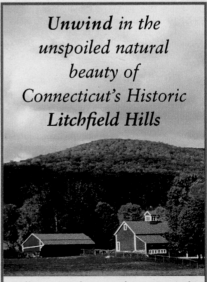

MANCHESTER—*see Hartford p. 56.*

MERIDEN (C-3) pop. 59,500, elev. 150′

Since the 19th century, Meriden has been a leader in the silverware industry. Ashbil Griswold made the first pewterware in 1808. In 1847 Asa Rogers invented electroplating. Meriden also is known for its vibrant daffodils.

Greater Meriden Chamber of Commerce: 5 Colony St., Meriden, CT 06451; phone (203) 235-7901.

HUBBARD PARK, about 2 mi. w. on I-691, is reached via W. Main St. This beautiful 900-acre park is in the Hanging Hills, which reach an elevation of 1,007 feet. Of interest are Castle Craig, a stone observation tower, and lovely Merimere Reservoir. Drives, paths, a nature trail and tennis courts are available. A highway leads to the top of West Peak, the highest elevation in the Hanging Hills. Daily dawn-dusk. Free. Phone (203) 630-4259.

MIDDLEBURY (C-2) pop. 6,100

SAVE **QUASSY AMUSEMENT PARK,** off I-84 exit 16E or 17W on SR 64, has rides, games, a beach and picnic facilities. Park open daily 7 a.m.-9 p.m. (extended hours weekends), Memorial Day-Labor Day. Rides operate daily 11-8, Memorial Day-Labor Day. Parking $3. Individual ride tickets $1.50. All-day ride pass (with beach) $11.95, under 42 inches tall $7.95. Beach only $2. Prices discounted after 5. Phone (203) 758-2913, or (800) 367-7275 in Conn.

MIDDLETOWN—*see Hartford p. 57.*

MOODUS (C-5) pop. 1,200

Moodus has been a center for twine production for more than a century, but an even older distinction is the strange subterranean rumblings associated with the area. American Indian legend claims the noises are the threats of evil spirits; early settlers believed the noises were the work of the devil.

Legend claims that in 1765 a Dr. Steele from Great Britain disappeared while researching the phenomenon, leaving word that the sounds were caused by two pearls he had discovered. He warned the residents that he had found others in miniature, that, when developed, would produce the same effect.

The "Moodus Noises" did not recur until 1791 when explosions and violent shocks that opened crevices in the earth again racked the area. Modern scientific opinion holds that the sounds are the result of movement along intersecting fractures in the Earth's crust.

SAVE **AMASA DAY HOUSE,** jct. SRs 149 and 151, dates from 1816. The house retains its original stenciled floors and is furnished with three generations of Day family heirlooms. The barn features a museum. Allow 30 minutes minimum. Fri.-Sun. 1-5, Memorial Day-Oct. 31. Admission $3, under 12 free. Phone (860) 873-8144.

MYSTIC (D-6) pop. 2,600, elev. 9′

The fastest clipper ships in the country were being built in Mystic by the middle of the 19th century. In 1861 the first regular ironclad vessel, the *Galena,* was built in the Mystic shipyards. Houses dating from those maritime days still stand.

Southeastern Connecticut Tourism: 470 Bank St., P.O. Box 89, New London, CT 06320; phone (860) 444-2206 or (800) 863-6569. *See color ad p. 65.*

Shopping areas: Olde Mistick Village, off I-95 exit 90 at Coogan Blvd., offers more than 60 specialty stores and restaurants set in a Colonial New England atmosphere, featuring gardens, a water wheel and duck pond. Across the street are the Mystic Factory Outlets, featuring Bass, Izod Lacoste, London Fog and Van Heusen.

CCINC. AUTO TAPE TOUR, available at the Mystic & Shoreline Visitor Information Center and Olde Mistick Village, lets you set your own pace; the tape runs 90 minutes. The history and romance of Mystic, New London and Stonington *(see place listings pp. 64, 69 and 75.)* are presented with voice, music and sound effects. To order the tape by mail write CCInc., P.O. Box 227, Allendale, NJ 07401. The tape costs $12.95, or $14.95 by mail (includes postage and handling). Phone (201) 236-1666.

DENISON HOMESTEAD, off I-95 exit 90, n. on SR 27, e. on Jerry Brown Rd., then s. on Pequotsepos Rd., dates from 1717 and illustrates home life in New England from the Colonial period to 1941. Heirlooms of 11 generations of Denisons represent five stylistic periods. Allow 1 hour minimum. Fri.-Mon. 10-4, mid-May to mid-Oct. Admission $4; over 60 and students with ID $3; under 12, $1. Phone (860) 536-9248.

SAVE **DENISON PEQUOTSEPOS NATURE CENTER** is n. of I-95 exit 90 on SR 27, e. on Jerry Brown Rd., then .5 mi. s. on Pequotsepos Rd. This nature center includes a 125-acre wildlife sanctuary with 7 miles of well-marked nature trails and a Trailside Interpretive Museum featuring both live and mounted animal specimens native to Connecticut. More than 150 species of birds have been identified within the sanctuary.

Allow 1 hour minimum. Mon.-Sat. 9-5, Sun. 1-5; closed Jan. 1, Thanksgiving and Dec. 25. Admission $4; over 60, $3; ages 6-12, $2. Phone (860) 536-1216.

MYSTIC ART ASSOCIATION GALLERY, 9 Water St. on the Mystic River, exhibits oils, watercolors, sculpture and etchings by popular local artists. There also are works by landscape painters who settled in the area in the early 20th century and created a thriving art colony. Allow 30 minutes minimum. Daily 11-5, June-Sept.; Tues.-Sun. 11-5, rest of year. Closed Thanksgiving and Dec. 25. Donations. Phone (860) 536-7601.

★ **MYSTIC MARINELIFE AQUARIUM** is off I-95 exit 90 and s. on SR 27. More than 3,500 living sea creatures are shown in 40 exhibits that include Seal Island, an outdoor area containing seals and sea lions, and Penguin Pavilion, an outdoor exhibit of African black-footed penguins. The 1,400-seat Marine Theater presents dolphin and whale demonstrations daily.

Allow 2 hours minimum. Daily 9-7, July 1-Labor Day; 9-5, rest of year. Last admission 1 hour before closing. Closed Jan. 1, Thanksgiving and Dec. 25. Admission $13; over 59, $12; ages 3-12, $8. AE, MC, VI. Phone (860) 572-5955.

★ **MYSTIC SEAPORT** is at 75 Greenmanville Ave., along the Mystic River on SR 27, .7 mi. s. of I-95 exit 90. Among its 17 acres are historic houses, shops and trade buildings that promote an understanding of life in a seaport during the mid-19th century. The last of the wooden whaling ships, the *Charles W. Morgan,* the 1882 training ship *Joseph Conrad* and the fishing schooner *L.A. Dunton* can be boarded by visitors; many other ships and boats are displayed.

Ships models, scrimshaw, figureheads, small boats and other relics trace the history of ships, shipbuilding and maritime activities. The R.J. Schaefer Building has changing exhibits of paintings and other items. There also is a children's museum where youngsters can play with toys, clothing and games popular in the 19th century. Events take place throughout the year.

The 1908 steamboat *Sabino* makes daytime and evening excursions on the Mystic River from May through October. Plum Pudding Tours and Lantern Light Tours also are available during the holiday season.

Allow 2 hours minimum. Museum open daily 9-6, July-Aug.; 9-5, Apr.-June and Sept.-Oct.; 10-4, rest of year. Closed Dec. 25. Admission $16; ages 6-12, $8. Reservations are required for cruises. AE, MC, VI. Phone (860) 572-0711 or 572-5315. *See color ad p. 24.*

SAVE **MYSTIC WHALER CRUISES,** 7 Holmes St., offers sightseeing excursions aboard an 83-foot schooner including a day cruise. A lobster dinner cruise also is available. Day cruises depart daily 9:45-3:30, May-Oct. Schedule may vary; phone ahead. Day cruise (includes lunch) $70; ages 5-10, $35. Reservations are required. AE, MC, VI. Phone (860) 536-4218 or (800) 697-8420.

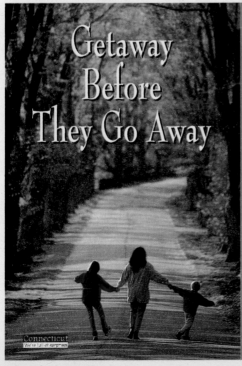

SAVE **VOYAGER CRUISES,** which leave from 73 Steamboat Wharf just s. of the drawbridge downtown, offers cruises aboard the schooner *Argia.* Half-day cruises depart daily at 10 and 2, sunset cruises at 6, May-Oct. Fare $32 (Sat.-Sun. $34); under 18, $22 (Sat.-Sun. $24). Phone for holiday weekend rates. Reservations are required. AE, MC, VI. Phone (860) 536-0416.

NEW BRITAIN—*see Hartford p. 58.*

NEW CANAAN (D-1) pop. 17,900, elev. 340'

Along SR 106 is the main area of the New Canaan Bird Sanctuary and Wildlife Preserve. Smaller areas of the preserve are on Cedar Lane and Wahackme Road; several nature trails are open for hiking daily during daylight hours.

Coastal Fairfield County Convention & Visitors Bureau: 297 West Ave., Norwalk, CT 06850; phone (800) 866-7925.

NEW CANAAN HISTORICAL SOCIETY, 2.5 mi. n. of Merritt Pkwy. exit 37 at SR 124, has five buildings housing museums, collections and a library. The Hanford-Silliman House Museum, completed in 1764, contains period furnishings. The John Rogers Studio and Museum houses sculptures by 19th-century artist John Rogers. The New Canaan Hand Press is a re-creation of 19th-century printing office with period machinery.

The Rock School, built in 1799, was one of New Canaan's early schoolhouses. The Tool Museum displays antique tools used by builders, cabinetmakers, shoemakers and other tradesmen, and farmers. The Town House includes the Costume Museum, with changing exhibits; the Cody Drug Store, containing materials and merchandise from the original store on Main Street; and a historical research and genealogical library. Guided tours are available.

Town House open Tues.-Sat. 9:30-4:30. Other buildings open Wed.-Thurs. and Sun. 2-4. Closed major holidays. Donations. Phone (203) 966-1776.

NEW CANAAN NATURE CENTER is 3 mi. n. from Merritt Pkwy. exit 37 at 144 Oenoke Ridge (off SR 124), .5-mi. from the town center. Native plants and animals inhabit the preserve's 40 acres of meadow, woodland, stream, pond and marsh habitats; gardens and displays adjoin nature trails. The Naturalist's Garden—Backyard New England offers environmental tips and exhibits about landscaping.

The Discovery Center offers hands-on exhibits; there also is a solar greenhouse. Events are held periodically. Mon.-Sat. 9-4. Trails open daily dawn-dusk. Donations. Phone (203) 966-9577.

SILVERMINE GUILD ARTS CENTER, off Merritt Pkwy. exit 38, is at 1037 Silvermine Rd. The guild maintains an art school and three galleries which offer exhibits throughout the year, including a holiday exhibit beginning in late November. Tues.-Sat. 11-5, Sun. 1-5; closed major holidays, Labor Day weekend and Dec. 25-31. Donations. Phone (203) 966-5617.

NEW HAVEN (D-3) pop. 130,500, elev. 33'

See map page 67.

If you've ever ridden a steamboat, fished with a steel fishhook, twisted a corkscrew or savored a lollipop, you might be interested to know that these four innovations were invented in New Haven. Termed the "Birthplace of the Nation's Hits," the Shubert Theatre on College Street is where many of the world's most popular actors, musicians and dancers made their debuts. Graced by the presence of Yale University, New Haven is a college town as well.

New Haven was laid out by the Puritans in 1638 in nine equal squares; the central square, or green, was reserved for the public. Today the green is lined with churches and offices. Historic buildings, such as the Gowie-Normand House, are scattered throughout the city. The Pardee House was burned during the Revolutionary War but was rebuilt in 1780 and has been restored and graced with furniture and decorative arts from the 17th through 19th centuries; phone (203) 562-4183 for details about its summer weekend schedule.

Sightseeing cruises off the coast of New Haven are available from Schooner Inc., which combines pleasure excursions with education aboard the *Quinnipiack,* a replica of a Biloxi freight schooner of the late 19th century. The two-masted ship serves as a floating classroom aboard which passengers can assist in its sailing and participate in science experiments; phone (203) 865-1737.

Greater New Haven Convention and Visitors Bureau: 59 Elm St., New Haven, CT 06510; phone (203) 777-8550 or (800) 332-7829.

EAST ROCK PARK, reached by Orange St. and East Rock Rd., encompasses 425 acres. The rock is 365 feet high and 1.5 miles long. The summit, accessible via Davis Rd., offers a panorama of Long Island Sound and the city of New Haven. The Civil War Soldiers and Sailors Monument, Indian Head Peak and the Pardee Rose Gardens are in the park. Events are scheduled throughout the year. Park open daily dawn-dusk. Summit open daily 8-dusk, Apr.-Oct.; Fri.-Sun. 8-dusk (weather permitting), rest of year. Free. Phone (203) 946-6086.

THE GREEN, covering 16 acres in the center of the city, remains as plotted by the original settlers. Three churches on Temple Street, built about 1815, are the only buildings remaining on the green.

First Church of Christ, 311 Temple St., is the fourth meeting place on this general site. The first services were held outdoors in 1638. The spire, Tiffany window and wall tablets are of interest. The church covers part of the old burial ground including 1,500 to 1,700 historic gravestones, the oldest dating from 1687. Guided tours are available Thurs. 11-1; crypt tours are available Sun. morning following 10 a.m. service, and by appointment. Free. Phone (203) 787-0121.

Trinity Church, Temple and Chapel sts., was founded in 1752 on Church St. The Episcopal congregation built the present church 1812-14. Mon.-Thurs. 10-2, Sat. 9-noon, Sun. 7:45-1. Free. Phone (203) 624-3101.

United Church-on-the-Green, 323 Temple St., was North Church, the second Congregational Church on the green. The church contains the first Hillebrand Tracker organ in the United States. In 1855 Henry Ward Beecher preached to Capt. Charles B. Line's anti-slavery company of 80 men starting out for Kansas. The sanctuary has been renovated to its original 1815 design.

Open by appointment. Free. Phone (203) 787-4195.

GROVE STREET CEMETERY, Grove St. between Prospect and Ashmun sts., contains the graves of Lyman Beecher, James D. Dana, Charles Goodyear, Roger Sherman, Noah Webster, Theodore Winthrop and Eli Whitney. Daily 8-3:45. Free. Phone (203) 787-1443.

LIGHTHOUSE POINT is off I-95 exit 50NB, then s. on Townsend Ave. to the end of Lighthouse Rd. The 90-foot light was built in 1840 and used 1845-77. The lighthouse is not open to the public, but boating, fishing and picnicking are permitted on the grounds; there also is a carrousel. Park area open daily 6 a.m.-dusk. Carrousel schedule varies; phone ahead. Park admission free. Carrousel fare 50c. Memorial Day-Labor Day parking $6. Phone (203) 946-8005.

MUSEUM OF THE NEW HAVEN COLONY HISTORICAL SOCIETY is at 114 Whitney Ave. near Trumbull St. (I-91 exit 3). Permanent and changing exhibits of furniture, paintings, maritime relics and inventions illustrate more than 350 years of New Haven history. The Whitney Library, a genealogical/historical library, also is available.

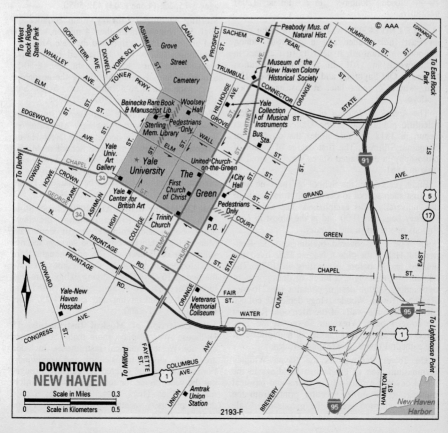

DOWNTOWN NEW HAVEN

Scale in Miles 0 0.3
Scale in Kilometers 0 0.5

2193-F

Allow 1 hour minimum. Museum open Tues.-Fri. 10-5, Sat.-Sun. 2-5. Library open Tues.-Fri. and occasional Sat. 1-5. Both are closed major holidays. Museum admission $2; senior citizens and students with ID $1.50; ages 6-16, $1. Library admission $2. Phone (203) 562-4183.

WEST ROCK RIDGE STATE PARK is off Merritt Pkwy. exit 60, s. on Dixwell Ave., w. on Benham St., s. on Main St., then s. on Wintergreen to park entrance. The park, a ridge rising 428 feet high and encompassing more than 1,500 acres, offers fishing, hiking and scenic views. The park drive is open seasonally; parking also is available at the West Rock Nature Center and at Lake Wintergreen. Of interest is Judges Cave, named for two Colonial judges hidden inside after they condemned Charles I to death. Daily 8-dusk. Free. Phone (203) 789-7498 for dates the gate to the drive is open.

West Rock Nature Center, just past West Rock Ridge State Park's entrance, contains native mammals, birds and reptiles. Injured wild animals are rehabilitated at the facility. The surrounding 40 acres of woods contain trails, ponds and meadows. Allow 1 hour minimum. Mon.-Fri. 10-4; closed holidays. Free. Phone (203) 946-8016.

★ **YALE UNIVERSITY** was named for Elihu Yale, an East India trader and a generous donor. Founded in Branford, it held its first classes in Killingworth in 1701. In 1707 the institution moved to Old Saybrook and in 1716 to New Haven, where 2 years later it was named Yale College.

The *American Journal of Science,* the oldest scientific publication in the United States, was begun in 1818 by Yale under the direction of Benjamin Silliman. The first degree of doctor of philosophy in the United States was conferred by Yale in 1861.

Eight years later, the School of The Fine Arts, the first such school to come within the scope of any university, was established. The School of Forestry began in 1900 and is the oldest in continuous operation in the country.

Of Yale's ivy-covered buildings, 1752 Connecticut Hall is the oldest. Nathan Hale lived and studied inside before graduating in 1773. The Memorial Quadrangle, a block of dormitories of outstanding Gothic design, contains the 216-foot Harkness Tower. Woodcarvings depicting college history adorn the walls of the Memorial Room at the tower's base. Wrexham Tower, at the York Street side of the quadrangle, is a duplicate of the cathedral tower in Wrexham, Wales.

On Tower Parkway is the Payne Whitney Gymnasium, one of the largest buildings in the world devoted exclusively to sports and physical training. About 1,000 sporting prints from the Garvan Collection are in the gymnasium. Yale Bowl and Athletic Fields are on Derby Ave.

Free guided tours of the campus start at the visitors center, 149 Elm St. The tours depart Mon.-Fri. at 10:30 and 2, Sat.-Sun. at 1:30. For further information phone (203) 432-2300 Mon.-Fri. 9-4:45, Sat.-Sun. 10-4.

Beinecke Rare Book and Manuscript Library, High and Wall sts., contains a Gutenberg Bible, books from the Yale Library of 1742, an Audubon "Birds of America" exhibit and changing exhibits of rare books and manuscripts. Allow 1 hour minimum. Mon.-Fri. 8:30-5, Sat. 10-5, Sept.-July; Mon.-Fri. 8:30-5, rest of year and during university vacations. Free. Phone (203) 432-2977.

⬛ **Peabody Museum of Natural History,** 170 Whitney Ave. at Sachem St., features collections of fossils of dinosaurs and prehistoric mammals, dioramas of North American habitat groups, birds of Connecticut and collections devoted to the Pacific Islands, the Plains Indians, ancient Egypt and Central and South America. Visitor parking is 1 block north at the south end of Yale lot No. 22.

Mon.-Sat. 10-5, Sun. noon-5; closed Jan. 1, Easter, July 4, Labor Day, Thanksgiving, Dec. 24-25 and Dec. 31. Admission $5; over 65 and ages 3-15, $3. Phone (203) 432-5050.

Sterling Memorial Library, main entrance on High St., contains more than 4 million volumes and historical manuscripts and the Yale Archives. Babylonian tablets may be viewed by appointment. Mon.-Thurs. 8:30-midnight, Fri. 8:30-5, Sat. 10-5, Sun. 1-midnight, during the academic year; Mon.-Fri. 8:30-5 (also Thurs. 5-10), Sat. 10-5, rest of year. Phone (203) 432-2798.

Woolsey Hall, College and Grove sts., seats 2,685 and contains the Newberry Memorial organ. The hall also is home to the New Haven Symphony Orchestra and Yale School of Music. Events are scheduled Sept.-May. The Friday edition of the *New Haven Register* has a listing of current events. A fee may be charged. Phone (203) 432-2310, 432-4157 or 776-1444.

Yale Center for British Art, 1080 Chapel St. at High St., displays British paintings, drawings, prints, books and sculpture. A gift from Paul Mellon, the extensive collection surveys the development of British art, life and thought from the Elizabethan period to the present, stressing the period 1697-1851. Changing exhibits are featured. Tues.-Sat. 10-5, Sun. noon-5; closed Jan. 1, July 4, Thanksgiving and Dec. 24-25. Free. Phone (203) 432-2800.

Yale Collection of Musical Instruments, 15 Hillhouse Ave., displays more than 150 Western and non-Western musical instruments. Included are historic violins, harpsichords and woodwinds. Formal concerts are offered periodically throughout the year; phone for schedule and ticket information. Tues.-Thurs. 1-4, Sept.-June; closed during university vacations. Admission $1. Phone (203) 432-0822.

Yale University Art Gallery, 1111 Chapel St. between York and High sts., is the oldest university art museum in the Western Hemisphere. Founded in 1832 with a gift of more than 100 paintings by patriot and artist John Trumbull, the gallery exhibits classical and contemporary pieces; highlights include paintings by Winslow Homer, Claude Monet, Pablo Picasso and Vincent Van Gogh. Tues.-Sat. 10-5, Sun. 1-6; closed Jan. 1, July 4, Thanksgiving and Dec. 25. Free. Phone (203) 432-0600.

NEW LONDON (C-6) pop. 28,500, elev. 27′

See map page below.

New London, founded in 1646 by a group of Puritan families under John Winthrop Jr., became the principal rendezvous of privateers during the Revolution. As such, the port was an important objective of Benedict Arnold's Tory force in 1781. The attackers, with the assistance of a 32-vessel fleet, burned wharves, houses and stores.

The whaling industry began in New London in 1784 and grew rapidly until it reached its height in the middle of the 19th century, when about 75 whaling vessels were based at the port. The industry declined in the late 1840s after whale populations were devastated and cheaper substitutes for whale products were found.

The downtown historic district includes Nathan Hale's Schoolhouse, the Captain's Walk and the Greek Revival houses of Whale Oil Row.

Boats remain an important resource. A ferry leaves from Ferry Street for Block Island, R.I., on a regular schedule from mid-June to mid-September; for ferry schedules and fares phone (860) 442-7891.

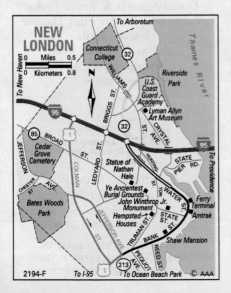

Southeastern Connecticut Tourism: 470 Bank St., P.O. Box 89, New London, CT 06320; phone (860) 444-2206 or (800) 863-6569.

CONNECTICUT COLLEGE ARBORETUM entrance is on William St. across the street from the campus. The arboretum, which is affiliated with the Connecticut College, contains more than 415 acres with 300 varieties of shrubs and trees native to eastern North America. A trail leads into Bolles Wood, a hemlock forest. Other hiking trails wind through the arboretum. Guided tours are available by arrangement Saturday and Sunday at 2, mid-May through Oct. 25. Daily dawn-dusk. Free. Phone (860) 439-5020.

⬛ **HEMPSTED HOUSES,** jct. of Hempsted, Jay and Truman sts., were built in 1678 and 1758 respectively and are furnished to represent several generations of Hempsted family life. Both contain many pieces of original furniture. The Nathaniel Hempsted House is an unusual example of New England stone construction.

Allow 1 hour minimum. Both houses are open Thurs.-Sun. noon-4, May 15-Oct. 31. Admission for both houses $4; under 18, $1. Phone (860) 443-7949 or 247-8996.

JOHN WINTHROP JR. MONUMENT, Buckley Pl. off Hempsted St., is a statue by Bela Lyon Pratt of the founder of New London, who governed the colony 1657-76.

LYMAN ALLYN ART MUSEUM, 625 Williams St., across from the Coast Guard Academy and adjacent to Connecticut College, has Colonial New England furniture, paintings and silver; master drawings and American and European paintings; toys and dollhouses; and Oriental, Greek and Roman art. Contemporary art by local artists also is displayed. Special exhibits are presented seasonally.

Tues.-Sat. 10-5, Sun. 1-5; closed holidays. Admission $4, senior citizens and students with ID $3, under 6 free. Phone (860) 443-2545.

MONTE CRISTO COTTAGE, 1.5 mi. s. of US 1 at 325 Pequot Ave., was the boyhood home of Eugene O'Neill, Nobel Prize winner and one of the nation's great dramatists. The setting for his play "Long Day's Journey into Night," the cottage contains O'Neill memorabilia; a short multimedia presentation introduces visitors to the playwright. Allow 1 hour minimum. Tues.-Sat. 10-5, Sun. 1-5, day after Memorial Day- day before Labor Day; schedule varies after Labor Day. Guided tours at 10, noon, 2 and 4. Closed major holidays. Admission $4, under 12 free. Phone (860) 443-0051 or 443-5378.

OCEAN BEACH PARK is off I-95 exit 83; take Colman St. 1.5 mi. s. to Bank St., then .2 mi. e. to Ocean Ave., then 3 mi. to end. This city-owned recreation area includes an Olympic-size pool, a playground, a video arcade, an 18-hole miniature golf course and waterslides. A boardwalk overlooks the beach and Long Island

Sound. A bathhouse with showers and lockers is available.

Park open daily 9 a.m.-10 p.m., Memorial Day-Labor Day; hours for individual facilities vary. Park admission per private vehicle is $5 Mon.-Thurs., $8 Fri.-Sun. and holidays. Walk-in admission $2; over 65 and ages 4-14, $1. Additional fees for individual facilities. Phone (860) 447-3031 or (800) 510-7263. *See color ad p. 24.*

PEQUOT AVENUE DRIVE leads from Bank St. to the New London Lighthouse and Ocean Beach, down the west bank of the Thames. New London Lighthouse, built in the 18th century and rebuilt in 1801, is one of the oldest in the United States. The present light was built in 1909.

SHAW MANSION, 11 Blinman St., dates from 1756 and was the home of ship owner Capt. Nathaniel Shaw Jr. and housed the Naval Office for Connecticut during the Revolution. Displays include antique furniture, silver, china and family portraits. Changing exhibits focus on New London County history. Flower gardens can be toured May through September. Allow 1 hour minimum. Wed.-Fri. 1-4, Sat. 10-4; closed holidays. Admission $4; over 65, $3; ages 5-12, $1. Phone (860) 443-1209.

STATUE OF NATHAN HALE, in Williams Park at the corner of Williams and Broad sts., is a duplicate of the one located in City Hall Park, New York City.

THE U.S. COAST GUARD ACADEMY, just off I-95 on Mohegan Ave. (SR 32), is on the west bank of the Thames River. The cadet corps passes in review most Friday afternoons at 4, April through May and September through October. The visitors' pavilion on Tampa Street shows a multimedia presentation depicting academy life.

A museum in Waesche Hall displays historical items. Allow 30 minutes minimum for each attraction. Pavilion open daily 10-5, May-Oct. Museum Mon.-Fri. 9-5, Sat. 10-5, Sun. noon-5. When in port, the training barque *Eagle* can be boarded weekends 1-dusk. All three are closed holidays. Free. Phone (860) 444-8270.

YE ANCIENTEST BURIAL GROUNDS, on Hempstead St., dates from 1653. From this point Benedict Arnold watched the burning of New London in 1781.

NEW PRESTON (B-2) pop. 1,200

Set in the Berkshire Hills, New Preston's main draw is Lake Waramaug, a haven for summer water activities. The top of nearby Pinnacle Mountain offers views of Massachusetts and New York.

Litchfield Hills Travel Council: P.O. Box 968, Litchfield, CT 06759-0968; phone (860) 567-4506.

WINERIES

• **Hopkins Vineyard** is off SR 45 on Hopkins Rd., on the northern side of Lake Waramaug. Mon.-Sat. 10-5, Sun. 11-5, May-Dec.; Wed.-Sat. 10-5, Sun. 11-5, Mar.-Apr.; Fri.-Sat. 10-5, Sun. 11-5, rest of year. Guided tours are given Sat.-Sun. at 2. Closed Jan. 1, Thanksgiving and Dec. 25. Phone (860) 868-7954.

NIANTIC (D-5) pop. 3,000, elev. 20′

⛨ **CHILDREN'S MUSEUM OF SOUTHEASTERN CONNECTICUT,** 409 Main St., is a hand-on museum which allows children through grade 5 to explore the arts, sciences, culture and history. Exhibits range from a scale-model Coast Guard cutter built of Legos® to child-oriented replicas of such everyday places as the supermarket. Allow 1 hour minimum. Mon.-Sat. 9:30-4:30 (also Fri. 4:30-8), Sun. noon-4, Memorial Day-Labor Day; Tues.-Sat. (and some Mon. school holidays), 9:30-4:30, Sun. noon-4, rest of year. Closed major holidays. Admission $3.50, under 2 free. Phone (860) 691-1111.

MILLSTONE INFORMATION AND SCIENCE CENTER, just w. of jct. SRs 156 and 161 at 278 Main St., has aquariums with touch tanks, a video theater and and hands-on exhibits that illustrate various forms and uses of energy, including basic electrical and nuclear. A nature trail is

on the center's grounds. Allow 1 hour minimum. Mon.-Fri. 9-4; hours may be extended in summer. Closed holidays. Free. Phone (860) 691-4670 or (800) 428-4234 in Conn. *See ad p. 70.*

THOMAS LEE HOUSE, about 3 mi. s.w. on SR 156, .2 mi. s.e. of I-95 exit 72, was built about 1660. An excellent example of early Colonial architecture, the house is furnished in period. Many articles date 1670-1800. It is said to be Connecticut's oldest frame house left in its original state. A Colonial herb garden is behind the house; next door is the well-preserved Little Boston School, dating from 1734. Tues.-Sun. 1-4, late June-Labor Day. Admission $2; ages 6-15, $1. Phone (860) 739-6070 or 739-5079.

NORWALK (E-2) pop. 78,300, elev. 39'

Today a suburb of New York, Norwalk was an agricultural town before the Revolution. In 1779 British soldiers seized the town and burned many buildings. By 1780 a kiln was built uptown, where the stoneware pottery for which Norwalk became recognized was produced. The Industrial Revolution prompted numerous companies to relocate to the area.

Norwalk's city hall complex, 3 blocks north of I-95 exit 16, contains an impressive collection of WPA murals commissioned expressly for the city. A self-guiding tour brochure is available inside city hall.

Coastal Fairfield County Convention & Visitors Bureau: 297 West Ave., Norwalk, CT 06850; phone (800) 866-7925.

SAVE **LOCKWOOD-MATHEWS MANSION MUSEUM,** 295 West Ave. via I-95 exit 14 or 15, was built by Civil War financier LeGrand Lockwood. The partially restored 60-room chateau contains stenciled walls, inlaid woodwork and a skylit rotunda. Displays include a collection of 19th-century music boxes.

Guided tours of the first and second floors are offered on the hour Tues.-Fri. 11-2, Sun. 1-4, mid-Mar. to mid-Dec.; closed holidays. Fee $5, senior citizens and students with ID $3, under 12 free with adult. Phone (203) 838-9799.

SAVE **THE MARITIME AQUARIUM AT NORWALK,** on the w. bank of the Norwalk River at 10 N. Water St., is a 5-acre restored 19th-century factory that features interactive exhibits about the maritime history and marine life of Long Island Sound. Highlights of the complex include an aquarium with more than 1,000 animals native to Long Island Sound; a touch tank; an IMAX® theater, which shows films on its six-story-high, 8-story-wide screen; and Maritime Hall, which displays boats and nautical relics. Changing exhibits and educational programs also are featured. Food is available.

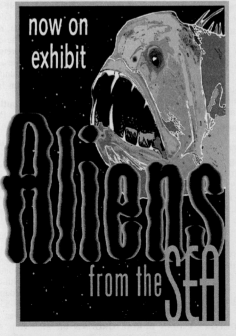

Allow 2 hours minimum. Daily 10-6, July 1-Labor Day; 10-5, rest of year. IMAX® theater shows are on the hour beginning at 11 and it is open for evening shows Fri.-Sat. Closed Thanksgiving and Dec. 25. Admission $7.75; over 62, $7; ages 2-12, $6.50. IMAX® theater $6.50; over 62, $5.50; ages 2-12, $4.75. Combination ticket $12; over 62, $10.50; ages 2-12, $9.50. Parking for 1 hour $1; 1-3 hours $2; 3-8 hours $3. Phone (203) 852-0700. *See color ad p. 24 and p. 71.*

SHEFFIELD ISLAND is the outermost of the Norwalk Islands and can be reached only by boat. The 60-passenger ferry departs from Hope Dock next to The Maritime Aquarium at Norwalk The boat offers a 40-minute scenic cruise through Norwalk harbor and past several other Long Island Sound islands en route to Sheffield. Passengers disembark to stroll through four landscaped acres and along the shore; there also is a guided tour of historic Sheffield Island Lighthouse. Clam bakes are held Thursdays in summer; reservations are required. Picnicking is permitted.

Ferry leaves Norwalk daily, late June-early Sept.; Sat.-Sun., late May-late June and early Sept.-late Sept. Phone for information and schedules. Fare (includes ferry, island visit and lighthouse tour) $10. Phone (203) 838-9444 or (888) 701-7785.

NORWICH (C-6) pop. 37,400, elev. 33′

Meeting House Rock, Norwichtown Green and the Old Burying Ground on Town Street served as the commons for Norwich's first settlers in the 17th century. Three miles north on what is now SR 12, one of the fiercest American Indian battles of the settlement period was fought. Uncas, chief of the Mohegans and friend of the colonists, defeated Miantonomoh, the Narragansett chief.

In more tranquil 1879, the Cathedral of St. Patrick, 213 Broadway, was built. It contains stained-glass windows, marble furnishings and a hand-carved baldachin.

Southeastern Connecticut Tourism: 470 Bank St., P.O. Box 89, New London, CT 06320; phone (860) 444-2206 or (800) 863-6569.

CHRISTOPHER LEFFINGWELL HOUSE MUSEUM, 348 Washington St. at SRs 2, 32 and 169 (I-95 exit 81E), was built in 1675 and converted to an inn in 1700 by Thomas Leffingwell. Because Christopher Leffingwell was a financier of the American Revolution and a member of the Committee of Correspondence, Continental officers, including George Washington, often stopped here. The restored building is furnished with 17th- and 18th-century pieces and displays a collection of Norwich silver. Tues.-Sun. 1-4, May 15-Oct. 15; by appointment rest of year. Closed major holidays. Admission $5; over 65 and ages 12-17, $3; under 12, $1. Phone (860) 889-9440.

MOHEGAN INDIAN BURIAL GROUND, off SR 32 near Sachem and Washington sts., was the burial place of rulers of the Mohegan Tribe. The cornerstone for a monument to Chief Uncas was laid in 1833 by Andrew Jackson; the granite shaft was erected in 1842.

MOHEGAN PARK AND MEMORIAL ROSE GARDEN, e. of SR 32 on Judd Rd., covers about 380 acres overlooking the city. The park contains the Memorial Rose Garden, which honors all war veterans and is in full bloom from late June to mid-July. There are nature trails as well as fishing and swimming in season. Picnicking is permitted. Daily dawn-dusk. Free. Phone (860) 823-3700, ext. 3759. *See Recreation Chart.*

NORWICHTOWN GREEN, to the n., was the center of the early settlement. The first church was built on this site in 1660.

SLATER MEMORIAL MUSEUM AND CONVERSE ART GALLERY of the Norwich Free Academy, off SR 2 at 108 Crescent St., has a Greek, Roman and Renaissance plaster cast collection; American art and furniture from the 17th through the 20th centuries, American Indian artifacts; and African, European, Oriental and American art. A separate section houses six galleries with rotating exhibits.

Tues.-Fri. 9-4, Sat.-Sun. 1-4, Sept.-June; Tues.-Sun. 1-4, rest of year. Closed major holidays. Admission $2, under 12 free. Phone (860) 887-2506 weekdays.

OLD LYME (D-5) pop. 6,500, elev. 14′

It has been said that at one time every house in Old Lyme was occupied by a sea captain, and the records indicate that 60 once lived here. These men of the sea brought their contact with foreign lands home in the form of treasures and tales. Today Old Lyme's treasure is its art community, which formed the nucleus of the American Impressionism movement in the early 1900s.

Southeastern Connecticut Tourism: 470 Bank St., P.O. Box 89, New London, CT 06320; phone (860) 444-2206 or (800) 863-6569.

FLORENCE GRISWOLD MUSEUM, .2 mi. n. of I-95 exit 70 at 96 Lyme St., is an American art and history museum with a collection of American Impressionist and Barbizon paintings displayed in a late Georgian mansion that housed an early 20th-century art colony. Period rooms offer a glimpse into the region's history through tools, toys, clothing and household items.

Changing gallery exhibits include American paintings, works on paper, sculpture, New England decorative arts and furniture. Herb and perennial gardens and Chadwick Studio, an early 20th-century artist's studio, also are on the grounds. Allow 30 minutes minimum. Tues.-Sat. 10-5, Sun. 1-5, June-Oct.; Wed.-Sun. 1-5, rest of year. Phone for schedule during Christmas season. Admission $4; over 62 and students with ID $3; under 12 free. Phone (860) 434-5542.

LYME ACADEMY OF FINE ARTS, 84 Lyme St., is in the 1817 Sill House, a restored Federal-style mansion. Two galleries feature the work of local artists and academy students; exhibits change every 6-8 weeks. An attached building houses studios and an art supply shop. Allow 30 minutes minimum. Tues.-Sat. 10-4, Sun. 1-4; other times by appointment. Closed major holidays. Donations. Phone (860) 434-5232.

LYME ART ASSOCIATION GALLERY is at US 1 and Lyme St., off I-95 exit 70. The gallery is headquarters for the Lyme Art Association, reputedly the nation's oldest art group to have held continuous exhibitions in its own gallery. The gallery features contemporary representational paintings and sculpture, as well as changing exhibitions. Tues.-Sat. noon-4:30, Sun. 1-4:30, Jan. 3-Dec. 22; otherwise varies. Closed holidays and between shows. Phone for winter exhibition schedule. Admission $4. Phone (860) 434-7802.

OLD SAYBROOK (D-4) pop. 9,600, elev. 24'

Pashbeshauke, "the place at the river's mouth," was the name American Indians gave to their settlement on the river they called Quonitocutt. Dutch traders lived in the region in the early 1600s, but in 1635 a group of English Puritans led by John Winthrop Jr. routed the Dutch and established a permanent colony. The colony was named Saybrook after Viscount Saye & Sele and Lord Brooke, heads of the settlers' Saybrook Co.

Years later, when the colony divided into seven communities, the original site became known as Old Saybrook. The first one-man submarine designed for battle, the *Turtle*, was invented in Old Saybrook. Constructed in 1776 by David Bushnell, the *Turtle* was used briefly during the American Revolution.

The General William Hart House, on SR 154 at 350 Main St., was built just a few years before the Revolution. It is typical of the residences of the well-to-do New Englanders of the period; phone (860) 388-2622.

Old Saybrook Chamber of Commerce: 146 Main St., P.O. Box 625, Old Saybrook, CT 06475; phone (860) 388-3266.

ONECO (B-6) pop. 700

SAVE **RIVER BEND MINING COMPANY** is in the River Bend Campground; from I-395 exit 88 go e. on SR 14A 5.5 mi. In this man-made cave, visitors can don miner's hats and dig for gems, minerals, fossils and shells. Those who would rather wet their hands than dirty them can pan for gemstones at the sluice. For an additional fee visitors may use the the campground facilities which include a picnic area, swimming pool, tennis court, fishing area, miniature golf course, playgrounds, and canoes, kayaks, paddle boats and aquacycles.

Daily 9-5, late Apr. to mid-Oct. Mine admission $6.50; under 12, $5.50. Gemstone panning and screening $3.50. Under 8 must be with an adult. Phone (860) 564-3440.

PAWCATUCK (C-6) pop. 5,300

MAPLE BREEZE PARK, 1 mi. e. on SR 2 (I-95 exit 92), is a small family amusement park with two waterslides, bumper boats, go-kart and children's tracks and a miniature golf course. Food is available. Allow 1 hour minimum. Daily 10-10 (bumper boats and children's track 10-9, waterslides 10-7), mid-June through Labor Day. Park free. Rides and activities $2-$6.50. Phone (860) 599-1232.

REDDING (D-2) pop. 7,900, elev. 410'

Redding first was secured for settlement in 1714 by John Read, a lawyer and land speculator who obtained a large grant from an American Indian chief named Chicken. The General Assembly had the land sold at auction, and in 1767 the area became incorporated as a town and was named for the speculator. The area is rich in mineral deposits, and a number of mines have prospered nearby.

PUTNAM MEMORIAL STATE PARK, n. at SRs 107 and 58, contains the 1778 winter quarters of Gen. Israel Putnam and his New England troops. The palisade and blockhouses have been restored; traces of other buildings can be seen. An interpretive trail winds through the area. The park offers hiking, fishing and ice skating. Picnic facilities are available. Daily 8-dusk. Free. Phone (203) 938-2285. *See Recreation Chart.*

RIDGEFIELD (D-1) pop. 20,900, elev. 725'

THE ALDRICH MUSEUM OF CONTEMPORARY ART, 258 Main St., offers changing exhibitions of contemporary painting, sculpture and photography. A 2-acre sculpture garden is featured. Allow 1 hour minimum. Tues.-Sun. noon-5 (also Fri. 5-8); guided tours are available Sun. at 2. Museum admission $5, senior citizens and students with ID $3, under 12 free. Sculpture garden free. Phone (203) 438-4519.

RIVERTON (A-3) pop. 500

Surrounded by hills, Riverton is in the northwestern corner of the state on the banks of the Farmington River. The town maintains its early 1800s appearance. Lambert Hitchcock, known as one of America's greatest chairmakers, built his mill in 1826. The Hitchcock Chair Co. reproduces most pieces from original designs.

Litchfield Hills Travel Council: P.O. Box 968, Litchfield, CT 06759-0968; phone (860) 567-4506.

ROCKY HILL—*see Hartford p. 58.*

SHARON (B-2) pop. 2,900

Litchfield Hills Travel Council: P.O. Box 968, Litchfield, CT 06759-0968; phone (860) 567-4506.

SHARON AUDUBON CENTER, 2.2 mi. s.e. on SR 4 and CR 41, is in the Clement R. Ford Home. The center holds nature exhibits, a children's discovery room and herb and wildflower gardens. Picnic facilities and 11 miles of hiking trails are available. Trails open daily dawn-dusk. Center open Mon.-Sat. 9-5, Sun. 1-5; closed major holidays. Admission $3; over 64 and under 16, $1.50. Phone (860) 364-0520.

SIMSBURY—*see Hartford p. 58.*

SOMERS—*see Hartford p. 59.*

SOUTHINGTON—*see Hartford p. 59.*

STAFFORD SPRINGS (A-5)

NORTHEAST STATES CIVILIAN CONSERVATION CORPS MUSEUM, 5.2 mi. w. on SR 190, displays photographs and other memorabilia of the Civilian Conservation Corps. Between 1933 and 1942 more than 3 million young men engaged in such conservation efforts as building roads, bridges and dams, planting trees and fighting forest fires. Allow 1 hour minimum. Daily noon-4, Memorial Day-Labor Day. Donations. Phone (860) 684-3430.

STAMFORD (E-2) pop. 108,100, elev. 34'

Siwanoys Indians sold the land now called Stamford to Nathaniel Turner, an agent for the New Haven Colony, in 1640; settlement began the following year. On a wide bay crossed by two tidal inlets, Stamford retains its New England charm despite its growth as a corporate center.

Coastal Fairfield County Convention & Visitors Bureau: 297 West Ave., Norwalk, CT 06850; phone (800) 866-7925.

THE BARTLETT ARBORETUM of the University of Connecticut is 1.5 mi. n. of Merritt Pkwy. exit 35 (High Ridge Rd.) at 151 Brookdale Rd. The arboretum contains collections of azaleas, rhododendrons, dwarf conifers and wildflowers. Also on its 63 acres are ecology trails, a swamp walk and a display greenhouse. Grounds open daily 8:30-dusk. Buildings open Mon.-Fri. 8:30-4. Free. Phone (203) 322-6971.

FIRST PRESBYTERIAN CHURCH, 1101 Bedford St., is a magnificent structure with a contemporary design inspired by an early Christian symbol, the fish. Of interest are the abstract colored-glass windows and the Visser-Rowland Opus 87 type organ. Outside, a walk of more than 100 stones depicts the history of religion from the time of Moses and Abraham.

Memorial Wall, fronting the church property, traces the history of Stamford. Carillon concerts are held on special days during the year; phone for schedule. Tour guides are available with 2 weeks' notice. Allow 30 minutes minimum. Mon.-Fri. 9-5, July-Aug.; Mon.-Fri. 9-3, rest of year. Free. Phone (203) 324-9522.

STAMFORD MUSEUM AND NATURE CENTER, High Ridge and Scofieldtown rds. on SR 137, is .7 mi. n. of Merritt Pkwy. exit 35. The center's 118 acres include nature trails and a boardwalk, a pond exhibit, a nature's playground and a 19th-century farm with animals. A lake with waterfowl, and a picnic area also are available. The museum contains six galleries, including an American Indian artifacts exhibit, an art gallery and Americana displays.

Museum open Mon.-Sat. and holidays 9-5, Sun. 1-5. A planetarium show is offered Sun. at 3. Observatory Visitors' Night is Fri. 8-10 p.m. (weather permitting). Closed Jan. 1, Thanksgiving and Dec. 25. Under 5 are not admitted to the planetarium show. Admission $5; over 61 and ages 5-13, $4. Planetarium show $2; ages 5-13, $1. Observatory $3; ages 5-13, $2. Phone (203) 322-1646, or 322-1647 weekends and holidays.

WHITNEY MUSEUM OF AMERICAN ART AT CHAMPION is off I-95 exit 7 or 8 at Atlantic St. and Tresser Blvd. in the Champion International Corp. building. A branch of the Whitney Museum of American Art in New York City, this museum sponsors approximately five major exhibitions a year and events that include lectures, concerts, films and educational programs. Allow 30 minutes minimum. Tues.-Sat. 11-5; closed Jan. 1, July 4, Thanksgiving and Dec. 25. Gallery talks are given Tues., Thurs. and Sat. at 12:30. Free. Phone (203) 358-7630 to verify schedule.

STONINGTON (D-6) pop. 1,100, elev. 7′

The Pequot Indians controlled the Stonington area until 1637, when an attack on their fort in nearby Mystic by Capt. John Mason opened the area for settlement. Conflict did not end, however. Both Massachusetts and Connecticut

claimed the Stonington region until 1662, and the town twice was attacked by the British, once during the Revolutionary War and again during the War of 1812.

With its favorable location as the last protected harbor in Long Island Sound, the town developed as a 19th-century center for sealing and whaling fleets and as a transportation hub; trains from Boston met steamboats from New York for 50 years. From Stonington, which became known as the "Nursery of Seamen," sailed men such as Capt. Nat Palmer who discovered Antarctica on a sealing trip in 1821. His clipper ship *Houqua* later broke the speed record to Hong Kong.

Visitors can learn more about the captain when they tour the 1852 Capt. Palmer House, a 16-room Victorian mansion on a hill overlooking Stonington Harbor. The building's octagonal cupola affords spectacular views of the area. Memorabilia pertaining to Palmer's discovery of Antarctica as well as period portraits, furnishings and relics are on display.

Southeastern Connecticut Tourism: 470 Bank St., P.O. Box 89, New London, CT 06320; phone (860) 444-2206 or (800) 863-6569.

OLD LIGHTHOUSE MUSEUM, 7 Water St., is housed in a stone lighthouse built in 1823. The building was moved from the shore in 1840 because of erosion and operated at its present site until 1889 when breakwaters were installed. The lighthouse contains ship models, whaling and naval battle gear, a China trade exhibit, oil portraits and a children's room, as well as early kitchen implements, stoneware and wooden tools. Feature exhibits change yearly.

A trip up the circular stone steps to the top of the tower provides views of three states. Daily 10-5, July-Aug.; Tues.-Sun. 10-5, May-June and Sept.-Oct.; by appointment rest of year. Admission $4; ages 6-12, $2. Phone (860) 535-1440.

STORRS (B-5) pop. 12,200, elev. 640'

Storrs is the home of the University of Connecticut, which was founded in 1881 as Storrs Agricultural College. It became the University of Connecticut in 1939. Scattered among the traditional turn-of-the-20th-century buildings are contemporary and modern structures that reflect the university's growth.

Maps are available in the Public Relations Building at 1266 Storrs Rd. Parking passes may be obtained at the Office of Parking Services, 1501 Storrs Rd., at the northeast end of campus. On campus are several greenhouses, animal barns and a dairy bar featuring the university's homemade ice cream.

Notable buildings include Atrium Gallery in the Fine Arts Building, William Benton State Museum of Art, State Museum of Natural History and Homer Babbidge Library. Jorgenson

Auditorium is host to professional touring companies such as dance, theater and music, as well as festivals and internationally known soloists and symphony orchestras; for performance and ticket information phone (860) 486-4226.

STRATFORD (D-3) pop. 49,400, elev. 21'

Established in 1639, Stratford adjoins Bridgeport *(see place listing p. 36)* on the Housatonic River. In its early years, Stratford was noted for its shipbuilding and oystering industries, which still exist.

Bridgeport Regional Business Council: P.O. Box 999, Bridgeport, CT 06601-0999; phone (203) 335-3800.

BOOTHE MEMORIAL PARK AND MUSEUM, s. off Merritt Pkwy. exit 53, 1 blk. s. on River Rd. (SR 110), then 1 blk s. on Main St., is the 32-acre former homestead of the Boothe family, who resided here 1663-1949. Ten of the 20 historic buildings have been restored; museum buildings display early farm, house and craft implements. The carriage house contains antique buggies and an award-winning rose garden.

Picnicking and playground facilities are available. Allow 2 hours minimum. Park open daily 9-5. Museum open Tues.-Fri. 11-1, Sat.-Sun. 1-4, June-Oct. Free. Phone (203) 381-2046 or 381-2068.

JUDSON HOUSE AND MUSEUM, 967 Academy Hill, is a good example of the clapboard-sheathed, post-and-beam construction that was typical of 18th-century New England. The 1750 house is furnished in period. The Mitchell Museum contains exhibits from periods of Stratford's history. Allow 1 hour, 30 minutes minimum. Wed. and Sat.-Sun. 11-4, mid-Apr. through Oct. 31; closed Easter and July 4. Admission $2, over 60 and students with ID $1. Phone (203) 378-0630.

SUFFIELD—see Hartford p. 59.

TERRYVILLE (B-2) pop. 5,400, elev. 609'

LOCK MUSEUM OF AMERICA, INC., .6 mi. w. of SR 72 at 230 Main St., displays more than 23,000 kinds of locks, including vault locks, door locks, padlocks, handcuffs, a cannon ball safe and early time locks. Three locks made by Stephen Bucknall in 1833 also are displayed. Separate rooms house locks and keys manufactured by nearly every lock company in the United States. Allow 1 hour minimum. Tues.-Sun. 1:30-4:30, May-Oct. Admission $3; over 50, $2.50; under 12 free. Phone (860) 589-6359.

TORRINGTON (B-2) pop. 33,700, elev. 593'

Settled in 1737, Torrington once was called Wolcottville for the factory established by Frederick and Guy Wolcott in 1813. After Israel Coe began making brass kettles in 1835, the town became an international producer and exporter of brass products. Brass manufacture was supplemented by the production of needles, ball bearings, machinery, roller skates and woolens. The town is still one of the state's largest commercial centers.

Litchfield Hills Travel Council: P.O. Box 968, Litchfield, CT 06759-0968; phone (860) 567-4506.

THE HOTCHKISS-FYLER HOUSE, 192 Main St., is a Victorian mansion containing family furnishings, glassware, porcelain, Oriental carpets and paintings by Connecticut artists. The house features elaborate woodwork with stenciled walls and murals. Visitors also may view a working machine shop. Displays in the adjacent museum reflect history and arts in Torrington. Allow 30 minutes minimum. Tues.-Fri. 10-4, Sat.-Sun. noon-4, Apr.-Oct.; closed legal holidays. The house also is open during Victorian Christmas; phone for hours. Admission $2, under 12 free. Phone (860) 482-8260.

UNCASVILLE (C-5) pop. 3,000

FORT SHANTOK STATE PARK, 167 acres on the west bank of the Thames River, is 4 mi. s. off SR 32. The remains of the old Mohegan Indian fort and burial ground can be seen. Daily 8-dusk. Free. Phone (860) 848-9876.

 CASINOS

- **Mohegan Sun Casino,** 1 mi. e. off I-395 exit 79A to 1 Mohegan Sun Blvd. Daily 24 hours. Phone (888) 226-7711.

WASHINGTON (C-2) elev. 478'

In a mountainous region scored by a gorge of the Shepaug River, Washington is noted for its scenery and the large number of country estates in the area.

Litchfield Hills Travel Council: P.O. Box 968, Litchfield, CT 06759-0968; phone (860) 567-4506.

THE GUNN MEMORIAL MUSEUM, on the town green at Wykeham Rd. and SR 47, is in the former Simeon-Mitchell House, built in 1781. The museum features period rooms and changing exhibits of local history. Allow 30 minutes minimum. Thurs.-Sun. noon-4; closed major holidays. Donations. Phone (860) 868-7756.

THE INSTITUTE FOR AMERICAN INDIAN STUDIES, 1.5 mi. s. on Curtis Rd. off SR 199, reconstructs the past 12,000 years of the area's cultural heritage through displays of American Indian artifacts and contemporary Native American art. A replica of a Northeastern Indian village, a nature trail, a simulated archeological site and changing exhibits highlight aspects of native life, including contemporary themes.

Films are shown Sat.-Sun. at 2:30; field trips and tours are available by appointment. Open Mon.-Sat. 10-5, Sun. noon-5, Apr.-Dec.; Wed.-Sat. 10-5, Sun. noon-5, rest of year. Closed major holidays. Admission $4; over 59, $3.50; ages 6-16, $2. Phone (860) 868-0518.

WATERBURY (C-3) pop. 109,000, elev. 280'

Two scouts reported in 1686 that the Waterbury townsite was so poor that it could accommodate no more than 30 families. Despite that grim assessment, Waterbury rose to become one of the world's major brass centers, supporting considerably more families than the initial estimate. Many of Waterbury's historic buildings and houses have been preserved and restored to their original appearances.

Greater Waterbury Chamber of Commerce: 83 Bank St., P.O. Box 1469, Waterbury, CT 06721; phone (203) 757-0701.

THE GREEN, W. Main St., contains the Soldiers' Monument, a Civil War memorial and a World Wars I and II veterans' memorial. Around this historic spot were clustered the 18- by 16-foot "mansion houses" of the original settlers. Also of interest are the 240-foot Republican American Tower, castlelike St. John's Episcopal Church, the Italian-Renaissance-style Church of the Immaculate Conception and the historic district.

MATTATUCK MUSEUM, 144 W. Main St., facing the green, is run by the Mattatuck Historical Society. The museum displays decorative arts and 18th- and 19th-century landscape and portrait paintings and sculpture by Connecticut artists. Local history exhibits, one of which highlights the industrial history of the area 1700-1950, also are presented. A second-floor gallery displays contemporary paintings by Connecticut artists. Of interest is Charles Goodyear's rubber desk. Allow 1 hour, 30 minutes minimum. Tues.-Sat. 10-5, Sun. noon-5, Sept.-June. Donations. Phone (203) 753-0381.

WATERFORD (D-5) pop. 2,900, elev. 48′

The settlements of Waterford and New London were Siamese twins both historically and geographically for 148 years. Founded in 1646, Waterford did not become a separate town until 1801. A nearby quarry was a source of millstones as early as 1737; the quarry's owner, the governor, eventually gave the lucrative property to his daughter for her dowry. Many of the estates built along the Niantic River by local wealthy families can be seen today.

Southeastern Connecticut Tourism: 470 Bank St., P.O. Box 89, New London, CT 06320; phone (860) 444-2206 or (800) 863-6569.

Shopping areas: Crystal Mall, I-95 exit 82 on SR 85, contains Filene's, JCPenney, Macy's and Sears.

HARKNESS MEMORIAL STATE PARK, Goshen Point off Great Neck Rd., comprises 125 acres and features the 42-room Harkness Mansion. Picnicking is permitted. Grounds open daily 8-dusk. Mansion open Sat.-Sun. and holidays 10-3, Memorial Day-Columbus Day. Admission Sat.-Sun. and holidays $5 per private vehicle (nonresidents $8), Mon.-Fri. $4 per private vehicle (non-residents $5), Memorial Day-Labor Day; free to all rest of year. Phone (860) 443-5725.

HISTORIC JORDAN GREEN, jct. SRs 156 and 213, is a village consisting of reconstructed and relocated 18th- and 19th-century buildings. A barn contains an extensive collection of farm implements, equipment and artifacts from Waterford's past. Other buildings include a 1740 schoolhouse, a blacksmith shop with working forge and an 1838 house with both Colonial and Victorian furnishings. Apple orchards and an herb garden also are on the grounds. Allow 30 minutes minimum. Wed.-Fri. 1-4, June 15-Sept. 15; closed July 4 and Labor Day. Donations. Phone (860) 442-2707.

WESTBROOK (D-4) pop. 2,100

Westbrook was founded in 1648 in an area known as Pochoug, an Indian name meaning "at the confluence of two rivers." Westbrook was the birthplace of David Bushnell, a Revolutionary War patriot who is recognized by the U.S. Navy as the inventor of the submarine.

Shopping areas: Westbrook Factory Stores, on SR 153 off I-95 exit 65, offers more than 65 discount outlets including J.Crew and Timberland. *See color ad.*

THE COMPANY OF MILITARY HISTORIANS is 1 mi. s. of I-95 exit 65 on N. Main St. This museum contains one of the largest collections of military uniforms in the United States. Exhibits devoted to medals and awards, women's uniforms and the instruments and uniforms of military bands are featured. Several vehicles used in military actions ranging from World War II to Operation Desert Storm also are displayed. A reference library is on the premises. Allow 30 minutes minimum. Tues.-Fri. 8-2:30; other times by appointment. Closed major holidays. Free. Phone (860) 399-9460.

WEST HARTFORD—*see Hartford p. 59.*

WESTPORT (E-2) pop. 24,400, elev. 26′

The "pedlar ships" that operated in the Westport harbor once brought an aura of romance to the local waters, similar to the effect steamboats had on the Mississippi. The town's scenic coves and hillocks attract artists, actors, writers and New York commuters.

Coastal Fairfield County Convention & Visitors Bureau: 297 West Ave., Norwalk, CT 06850; phone (800) 866-7925.

THE NATURE CENTER FOR ENVIRONMENTAL ACTIVITIES, about 1 mi. n. of US 1 at 10 Woodside Ln., is a 62-acre wildlife sanctuary which includes woods, fields, streams and wetlands, as well as a natural science museum, galleries, a children's discovery room, a hands-on aquarium tank and indoor/outdoor live animal exhibits. Mon.-Sat. 9-5, Sun. 1-4; closed major holidays. Admission $1; under 14, 50c. Phone (203) 227-7253.

WETHERSFIELD—*see Hartford p. 60.*

WILLIMANTIC (B-5) pop. 14,700, elev. 247′

⬛ **WINDHAM TEXTILE AND HISTORY MUSEUM,** 157 Union-Main St., is part of the Windham Mills and Heritage State Park project. This museum is dedicated to remembering the textile industry of southern New England as it was during the height of the Industrial Revolu-

tion. The museum occupies two 1877 buildings situated within the mill complex of the former Willimantic Linen Co. Dugan Mill depicts a late 19th-century factory setting, complete with overseer's office overlooking a fully equipped shop floor. Thread Mill Square II replicates an affluent mill owner's mansion and a worker's house.

The restored Dunham Hall Library contains books, manuscripts, photographs and a collection of architectural and engineering drawings. Changing exhibits are featured in the main building, which also has a company store. Allow 1 hour, 30 minutes minimum. Thurs.-Sun. 1-4, Memorial Day-Labor Day and by appointment; closed Jan. 1, Easter, July 4, Thanksgiving and Dec. 25. Admission $4; over 59 and ages 5-15, $2. MC, VI ($15). Phone (860) 456-2178.

WILTON (D-2) pop. 16,000, elev. 186′

Coastal Fairfield County Convention and Visitors Bureau: 297 West Ave., Norwalk, CT 06850; phone (800) 866-7925.

WEIR FARM NATIONAL HISTORIC SITE is .2 mi. w. on SR 102 past jct. US 7, then 1.4 mi. w. on Old Branchville Rd. to 735 Nod Hill Rd. Nearly 60 acres take visitors back to the time American Impressionist painter J. Alden Weir highlighted the area in his paintings. The visitor center displays historic photographs and a 20-minute videotape describing Weir's life and times on the property. Guided tours of two artist's studios on the site are available.

Self-guiding tours are available on mowed footpaths that cross the site, providing views of the landscapes and buildings Weir captured on canvas until his death in 1919. Picnicking is permitted. Allow 1 hour minimum. Grounds open

daily dawn-dusk. Visitors center Wed.-Sun. 8:30-5. Studio tour times vary; phone ahead. Free. Phone (203) 834-1896.

WINDSOR—*see Hartford p. 60.*

WINDSOR LOCKS—*see Hartford p. 61.*

WOODBURY (C-2) pop. 8,100, elev. 264'

Near the center of Woodbury a large boulder and a plaque honor Chief Pomperaug who once owned this territory. He was buried in 1650, and the town originally bore his name. In 1672 the Rev. Zechariah Walker and his congregation left Stratford after a church feud and settled in Woodbury.

The group established the First Congregational Church, the oldest in Litchfield County. In the south cemetery stands The Fathers' Monument, a granite slab honoring the church's first three pastors; together they served their congregations for 143 years. The ancestors of two Civil War generals, Ulysses S. Grant and William Tecumseh Sherman, also are buried at the site.

Litchfield Hills Travel Council: P.O. Box 968, Litchfield, CT 06759-0968; phone (860) 567-4506.

GLEBE HOUSE, on Hollow Rd., is an 18th-century, gambrel-roofed farmhouse where in 1783 Samuel Seabury was elected as the first American bishop of the Episcopal Church. His position as bishop illustrated the new nation's religious tolerance and the separation of church and state.

The house has regional period furnishings and is surrounded by gardens designed by Gertrude Jekyll. Changing exhibits are presented. Allow 30 minutes minimum. Wed.-Sun. 1-4, Apr.-Nov.; other times by appointment. Admission $4. Phone (203) 263-2855.

WOODSTOCK (B-5) pop. 6,000

Woodstock's land was purchased in 1686 by a company from Roxbury, Mass. The settlement became part of that state and was named for a town in Oxfordshire, England. Woodstock later was claimed by Connecticut under the Connecticut Charter; early residents included Rev. Jedidiah Morse, father of telegraph inventor Samuel F.B. Morse.

The town's first religious services were held in 1686; the minister preached from a boulder called "Pulpit Rock" to parishioners on the nearby hillside. The site is marked by a commemorative tablet.

SAVE **HENRY C. BOWEN HOUSE,** at 556 SR 169 facing Woodstock Common, is a Gothic Revival summer house built in 1846. Known as "Roseland Cottage" or "The Pink House," it contains much of its original furniture. Featured is one of New England's oldest known boxwood pattern gardens.

Highlights include the original icehouse, a garden house and a barn with one of the oldest indoor bowling alleys in the country. Allow 1 hour minimum. Guided tours on the hour Wed.-Sun. 11-5, June 1-Oct. 15. Last tour 1 hour before closing. Admission $4; over 65, $3.50; ages 5-12, $2. Phone (860) 928-4074.

Massachusetts

Path to Liberty

The Freedom Trail connects 16 sites important to the American Revolution

The Hills Are Alive

The Berkshire Hills roll through western Massachusetts under a verdant layer of forest

Quaint Seaside Villages

Waves lapping on the sand of Cape Cod calm the nerves of even the most frazzled visitors

Name Dropping

The homes of such well-known people as Norman Rockwell reveal lives touched by greatness

Pilgrims & Witches

Plymouth and Salem preserve a history marked by fortitude and marred by superstition

a great
place to hang
your hat

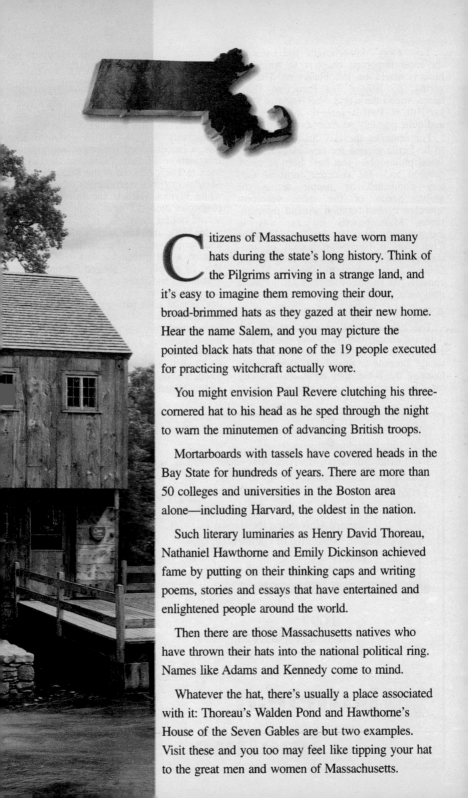

Citizens of Massachusetts have worn many hats during the state's long history. Think of the Pilgrims arriving in a strange land, and it's easy to imagine them removing their dour, broad-brimmed hats as they gazed at their new home. Hear the name Salem, and you may picture the pointed black hats that none of the 19 people executed for practicing witchcraft actually wore.

You might envision Paul Revere clutching his three-cornered hat to his head as he sped through the night to warn the minutemen of advancing British troops.

Mortarboards with tassels have covered heads in the Bay State for hundreds of years. There are more than 50 colleges and universities in the Boston area alone—including Harvard, the oldest in the nation.

Such literary luminaries as Henry David Thoreau, Nathaniel Hawthorne and Emily Dickinson achieved fame by putting on their thinking caps and writing poems, stories and essays that have entertained and enlightened people around the world.

Then there are those Massachusetts natives who have thrown their hats into the national political ring. Names like Adams and Kennedy come to mind.

Whatever the hat, there's usually a place associated with it: Thoreau's Walden Pond and Hawthorne's House of the Seven Gables are but two examples. Visit these and you too may feel like tipping your hat to the great men and women of Massachusetts.

Take away Massachusetts and some of the most important chapters in American history would be left blank: no Thanksgiving, no Boston Tea Party, no "shot heard 'round the world," no Battle of Bunker Hill, no Paul Revere, no John Hancock and quite possibly no American Revolution.

For centuries the Bay State has proven to be fertile ground for new ideas and political philosophies that have been admired, debated and—the sincerest form of flattery—duplicated by people across the globe. Scene of the most vehement speeches against taxation without representation, Massachusetts led the way to independence from Britain. And during the Civil War it became a hotbed of anti-slavery sentiment, producing many of the Union's most enthusiastic soldiers. Massachusetts has shaped America's destiny more than once.

A City on a Hill

The English Pilgrims who set sail for America aboard the *Mayflower* dreamed of establishing a religious community that would become a model for pious living. Quoting the Bible, they envisioned "a city on a hill" serving as a shining example to the world. Coincidentally, Massachusetts is an American Indian word meaning "at the great hill."

The Pilgrims settled at Plymouth in 1620 and celebrated the first Thanksgiving a year later. You don't need a time machine to see what everyday life was like for these early immigrants: With the aid of costumed actors, a reconstructed settlement and a little imagination, Plimoth Plantation takes you back to 1627. Moored at the State Pier, the *Mayflower II* is a reproduction of their ship, while Plymouth Rock, the Pilgrims' stepping-stone onto the new continent, is preserved not far away.

In 1692, the zeal with which Pilgrims and Puritans strove to create their idealistic city on a hill revealed a dark side. In Salem, 19 people were hanged for practicing witchcraft; five more of the accused died in jail, and another was tortured to death. Today several area museums vividly recount the hysteria that resulted in this tragedy.

By the time the infamous witch trials had begun, one Puritan city on *three* hills had surpassed all others to become the largest English settlement in Colonial America. Though founded just 10 years after Plymouth, Boston is more often associated

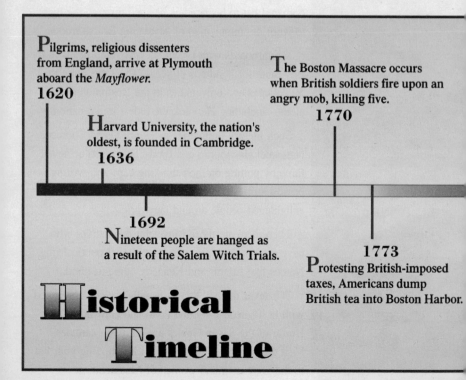

Pilgrims, religious dissenters from England, arrive at Plymouth aboard the *Mayflower*.
1620

The Boston Massacre occurs when British soldiers fire upon an angry mob, killing five.
1770

Harvard University, the nation's oldest, is founded in Cambridge.
1636

1692
Nineteen people are hanged as a result of the Salem Witch Trials.

1773
Protesting British-imposed taxes, Americans dump British tea into Boston Harbor.

Historical Timeline

with events of the following century. A lion's share of the path leading to independence from Britain—literally as well as figuratively—passes through downtown Boston. Known as the Freedom Trail, it connects more than a dozen historic sites.

Along this route you'll see the Boston Massacre site, where five colonists were killed by Redcoat troops in 1770, and Faneuil Hall, where Samuel Adams passionately called for American freedom. Stroll past Paul Revere's house and the Old North Church and recall his midnight ride to warn Colonial minutemen of approaching British forces. The trail includes Old Granary Burial Ground, the final resting place of Revere, Adams and Declaration of Independence signer John Hancock.

In nearby Lexington and Concord, Minute Man National Historical Park commemorates the first battle of the American Revolution. It was here, at the North Bridge, that "the shot heard 'round the world" was fired, beginning a running battle that ended at Boston's Bunker Hill.

More Fame to Claim

Past glories and patriotic struggles aren't the only reasons to celebrate Massachusetts. At Boston's New England Aquarium you'll *ooh* and *ahh* over giant tanks brimming with exotic sea life. Peruse a Picasso or marvel at a Monet inside the Museum of Fine Arts. Tickled by technology? You can tackle the city's Computer Museum in an afternoon.

Often eclipsed by its historical attractions, Massachusetts' natural beauty shouldn't be ignored. Outside of Beantown are Cape Cod, Nantucket and Martha's Vineyard, where beach communities, artists' colonies, lighthouses and sandy shores all but define the word "charm." In addition to the picturesque coast, the beautiful Berkshire Hills in western Massachusetts abound with parks and waterfalls. Here the Mohawk Trail connects quaint villages, covered bridges and vantage points offering lovely vistas. Visit in autumn and you'll be treated to the riot-of-color fall foliage display you'd expect in New England.

Visitors might wonder how so many historic landmarks, cultural sites and picture-postcard views could fit into such a small state. Somehow they do.

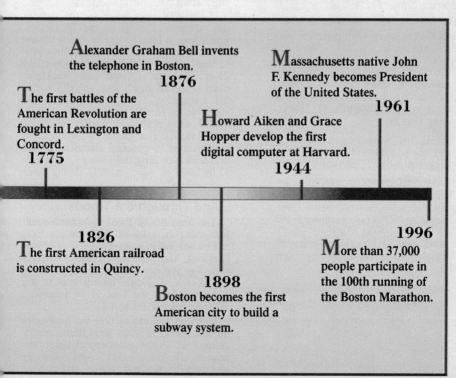

Alexander Graham Bell invents the telephone in Boston.
1876

Massachusetts native John F. Kennedy becomes President of the United States.
1961

The first battles of the American Revolution are fought in Lexington and Concord.
1775

Howard Aiken and Grace Hopper develop the first digital computer at Harvard.
1944

1826
The first American railroad is constructed in Quincy.

1898
Boston becomes the first American city to build a subway system.

1996
More than 37,000 people participate in the 100th running of the Boston Marathon.

FAST FACTS

POPULATION: 6,117,500.

AREA: 8,257 square miles; ranks 45th.

CAPITAL: Boston.

HIGHEST POINT: 3,491 ft., Mount Greylock.

LOWEST POINT: Sea level, Atlantic Ocean.

TIME ZONES: Eastern. DST.

MINIMUM AGE FOR DRIVERS: 18 (16½ with driver's education).

SEAT BELT/CHILD RESTRAINT LAWS: Seat belts required for driver and all passengers; child restraints required for under 12.

HELMETS FOR MOTORCYCLISTS: Required.

RADAR DETECTORS: Permitted.

FIREARMS LAWS: Vary by state and/or county. Contact the Massachusetts State Police, 1010 Commonwealth Ave., Boston, MA 02215; phone (617) 566-4500.

HOLIDAYS: Jan. 1; Martin Luther King Jr.'s Birthday, Jan. (3rd Mon.); Washington's Birthday, Feb. (3rd Mon.); Patriot's Day, April (3rd Mon.); Memorial Day, May (last Mon.); July 4; Labor Day, Sept. (1st Mon.); Columbus Day, Oct. (2nd Mon.); Veterans Day, Nov. 11; Thanksgiving; Dec. 25.

TAXES: The Massachusetts statewide sales tax is 5 percent. Lodging taxes range from 5.7 to 9.7 percent.

STATE INFORMATION CENTERS are maintained at the Massachusetts Turnpike at Lee (eastbound), Natick (eastbound) and Charlton (eastbound and westbound); I-95 at Mansfield (northbound); and SR 3 at Plymouth (southbound). State House center open daily 9-5.

Recreation

If you yearn to walk in the footsteps of our founding fathers, then you've come to the right place: Massachusetts is chock full of historic sites. But that's not all there is to the Bay State. Nature lovers have it good here, too. When all those famous names, dates and places start making your head swim, take a real dip—or a hike—in one of the state's numerous parks. This small state has one of the country's largest state park and forest systems.

Over the River...

Grab a paddle and head to Concord, where **canoeing** on the Concord River is especially pleasant. You'll pass beneath a replica of the Old North Bridge, where the first shots of the American Revolution were fired. Autumn is the best time to go with the flow here—there are fewer motorboats than in summer and dazzling fall foliage to boot.

Outside the concrete canyons of Boston, the Charles River flows through peaceful countryside. Drop your canoe in at Medfield and you're a far cry from the flotilla of racing sculls and sailboats just a few miles down river.

If you like your water on the frothier side, then head west to the Berkshires, which have a long history of luring urbanites from seacoast cities. Here **white-water rafting** is popular along the Deerfield River. Between Florida and Buckland, Class II and III rapids with colorful names like "Hangover Helper" are sure to get your blood racing. Farther upriver, the Monroe Bridge Dryway features Class III and IV rapids. This section of the Deerfield was diverted to generate electricity, but a deal with New England Power Co. ensures 32 releases of water, usually during summer weekends.

...And Through the Woods

The Appalachian Trail cuts a north-south path along the spine of the Berkshire Hills and passes within a stone's throw of Mount Greylock, Massachusetts' tallest peak. On a clear day you can see five states from this lofty perch. A 2-mile **hiking** trail to the summit ends at the base of an imposing, 100-foot-tall war memorial.

In winter you can explore the Berkshires on skis, thanks to many local cross-country **skiing** trails. A few miles east of Great Barrington, Butternut Ski Area features groomed Nordic and alpine trails. Near

Hancock, more downhill skiing is available at Jiminy Peak, which offers four trails and two lifts.

Travel to the state's extreme southwestern corner to hear the splish-splash of cascading water at Bash Bish Falls. Located within Mount Washington State Forest, the falls tumble through a series of gorges before plunging 60 feet into a crystal-clear pool. The surrounding forest offers hiking trails and wilderness **camping**.

On the opposite side of Massachusetts, Cape Cod is laced by so many trails that you could hike among the holly trees and salt marshes from one end (Cape Cod Canal) to the other (Provincetown). The Coskata-Coatue Wildlife Refuge on Nantucket Island boasts 10 miles of windswept shoreline along with tidal creeks, salt ponds and forests of pine, oak and holly. Terns, plovers, ducks and geese thrive along the crustacean-rich shallows.

Winding through scenery ranging from rural to suburban, the Minute Man Rail Trail near Boston is not only a good place for a workout, it's a perfect spot for a history lesson. The trail roughly parallels the route of Paul Revere's famed midnight ride. A great path for **biking**, **horseback riding** and **inline skating**, the Cape Cod Rail Trail stretches for 25 miles between the towns of Dennis and Wellfleet. You'll have several opportunities to reach the beach or grab a bite to eat along this former railway.

If you'd rather take a ride on the wild side, you can find numerous places for **mountain biking**, too. Off-roaders love the Holyoke Range of western Massachusetts. These mountains rise abruptly from the floor of the Connecticut Valley and offer fantastic views that have attracted tourists for more than a century. Stretching east-west for 9 miles, the range encompasses more than 45 miles of hiking and equestrian trails equally suitable for biking.

Recreational Activities

Throughout the TourBook, you may notice a Recreational Activities heading with bulleted listings of recreation-oriented establishments listed underneath. Since normal AAA inspection criteria cannot be applied, these establishments are presented for information only. Age, height and weight restrictions may apply. Reservations are often recommended and sometimes required. Visitors should phone or write the attraction for additional information, and the address and phone number are provided for this purpose.

FOR YOUR INFORMATION

FURTHER INFORMATION FOR VISITORS:
Massachusetts Office of Travel and Tourism
100 Cambridge St., 13th floor
Boston, MA 02202
(617) 727-3201 or (800) 447-6277

RECREATION INFORMATION:
Bureau of Recreation
Division of Parks and Forests
Department of Environmental Management
100 Cambridge St., Room 1905
Boston, MA 02202
(617) 727-3180

FISHING AND HUNTING REGULATIONS:
Division of Fisheries and Wildlife
100 Cambridge St., Room 1902
Boston, MA 02202
(617) 727-3151

DID YOU KNOW?

The longest geographical name in the country is the American Indian name for Webster Lake. They called it Lake Chargoggagoggmanchauggagoggchaubunagungamaugg.

The Constitution of Massachusetts is the oldest written document of its kind.

The first basketball game was played in Springfield and the first volleyball game was played in Holyoke.

The Pilgrims who settled at Plymouth had intended to settle in Virginia, which at the time included parts of what is now New York.

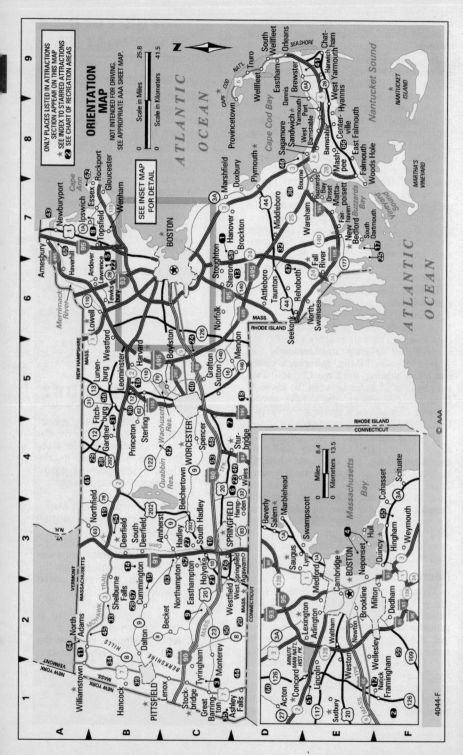

RECREATION AREAS

	MAP LOCATION	CAMPING	PICNICKING	HIKING TRAILS	BOATING	BOAT RAMP	BOAT RENTAL	FISHING	SWIMMING	PETS ON LEASH	BICYCLE TRAILS	WINTER SPORTS	VISITOR CENTER	LODGE/CABINS	FOOD SERVICE
NATIONAL SEASHORE															
Cape Cod National Seashore 28,000 acres. *(See place listing p. 145.)*			•	•				•	•		•	•	•		
STATE															
Ames Nowell (C-7) 607 acres n.w. of Abington via SR 123. Horse rental.	**1**		•	•	•			•		•		•			
Ashland (F-1) 47 acres 2 mi. s.w. of Ashland on SR 135.	**2**		•	•	•			•	•	•		•			
Beartown (C-1) 10,897 acres 3 mi. s.e. of Stockbridge on SR 23. Horse rental.	**3**	•	•	•	•			•	•	•		•			
Borderland (C-6) 1,772 acres on Massapoag Ave. in North Easton.	**13**		•	•				•				•	•		
Boston Harbor Islands (E-3) in Boston Harbor; head-quarters in Hingham off SR 228.	**4**														
Bumpkin Island		•	•	•	•			•		•					
Gallop's Island			•	•	•			•							

INDEX TO STARRED ATTRACTIONS
ATTRACTIONS AND PLACES OF EXCEPTIONAL INTEREST AND QUALITY

RECREATION AREAS

RECREATION AREAS	MAP LOCATION	CAMPING	PICNICKING	HIKING TRAILS	BOATING	BOAT RAMP	BOAT RENTAL	FISHING	SWIMMING	PETS ON LEASH	BICYCLE TRAILS	WINTER SPORTS	VISITOR CENTER	LODGE/CABINS	FOOD SERVICE
Georges Island Historic. (See Fort Warren p. 106.)			●	●	●			●							●
Grape Island		●	●	●	●			●		●					
Great Brewster Island		●	●	●	●			●		●					
Lovell's Island		●	●	●	●			●	●	●					
Peddock's Island		●	●	●	●			●		●					
Thompson's Island			●	●	●			●		●					●
Bradley Palmer (B-7) 721 acres s.w. of Topsfield off US 1.	5			●	●			●		●			●		
Brimfield (D-4) 3,250 acres 2 mi. s. of Brimfield off US 20. Horse rental.	6		●					●	●	●			●		
Buffumville (C-4) 400 acres 4 mi. s. of North Oxford of SR 12.	7		●		●	●		●	●	●					
Chester-Blandford (C-2) 2,308 acres 4 mi. s.e. of Chester on US 20.	9	●	●	●	●			●		●			●		
Chicopee (C-3) 574 acres on Burnett Rd. in Chicopee.	10							●	●	●	●	●	●		
Clarksburg (A-1) 3,431 acres 3 mi. n. of North Adams on SR 8.	11	●	●	●	●			●	●	●			●		
Cochituate (F-1) 1,126 acres 3 mi. e. of Framingham off SR 30.	12		●		●	●		●	●	●				●	●
Conway (B-3) 1,946 acres s. of Conway via SR 116. Horse rental.	14		●					●		●			●		
D.A.R. (B-3) 1,517 acres 3 mi. n. of Goshen off SR 9. Horse rental.	15	●	●	●	●			●	●	●			●		
Demarest Lloyd (F-7) 222 acres 3 mi. s. of Dartmouth off US 6 on Slocum Neck.	17		●					●	●	●					
Dighton Rock (D-6) 108 acres s. of Berkley on Bay View Rd.	47		●	●	●			●					●		
Douglas (D-5) 4,595 acres 2 mi. w. of Douglas off SR 16. Horse rental.	18		●	●	●	●		●	●	●			●		
Dunn Pond (B-4) 115 acres e. of Gardner on SR 101.	31		●					●	●			●	●		
Erving (B-3) 4,479 acres 2 mi. n.e. of Erving on SR 2A. Horse rental.	19	●	●	●	●			●	●	●		●			
Granville (D-2) 2,376 acres 1 mi. s.w. of West Granville off SR 57. Horse rental.	20	●	●	●				●	●	●			●		
Great Brook Farm (D-1) 934 acres on Lowell Rd. in Carlisle.	60		●	●	●			●		●					
Halibut Point (A-7) 56 acres n. of Rockport on SR 127.	62		●	●				●					●	●	
Hampton Ponds (C-2) 42 acres n.e. of Southampton off SR 10.	21		●	●	●	●	●	●	●	●					
Harold Parker (B-6) 3,500 acres 2 mi. n.w. of Middleton off SR 114. Horse rental.	22	●	●	●	●			●	●	●			●		
Holland Pond (D-4) 35 acres 2 mi. n. of Holland off SR 20. Horse rental.	23		●		●	●		●	●	●					
Hopkinton (C-5) 1,450 acres 3 mi. n. of Hopkinton on SR 85. Horse rental.	24		●	●	●			●	●	●			●		
Horseneck Beach (F-7) 537 acres 14 mi. s. of Fall River on SR 88 at Horseneck Beach.	25	●	●		●	●		●	●	●					●
J.A. Skinner (C-3) 390 acres 3 mi. n. on SR 47. Snow-mobiling; horse rental. (See South Hadley p. 169.)	27		●	●						●		●	●		
Kenneth M. Dubuque Memorial (B-2) 7,822 acres off SR 8A near Hawley. Backpack camping, horse rental.	28	●		●	●			●		●		●			
Lake Dennison (B-4) 4,221 acres 2 mi. n. of Baldwinsville on US 202.	29	●	●	●	●			●	●						
Leominster (B-5) 4,126 acres 7 mi. s. of Fitchburg on SR 31. Horse rental.	30	●	●	●				●	●	●		●			
Massasoit (D-7) 1,500 acres 3 mi. w. of Middleboro off SR 18. Horse rental.	32	●	●	●	●			●	●	●			●		
Maudslay (A-7) 476 acres on Curzon Mill Rd. in Newburyport.	65		●					●				●	●		
Mohawk Trail (B-2) 6,457 acres 3 mi. w. of Charlemont on SR 2.	33	●	●	●				●	●	●			●	●	
Mount Grace Forest (A-4) 1,689 acres off SR 78 in Warwick. Horse rental.	61		●	●					●			●			

RECREATION AREAS

	MAP LOCATION	CAMPING	PICNICKING	HIKING TRAILS	BOATING	BOAT RAMP	BOAT RENTAL	FISHING	SWIMMING	PETS ON LEASH	BICYCLE TRAILS	WINTER SPORTS	VISITOR CENTER	LODGE/CABINS	FOOD SERVICE
Mount Greylock (B-1) 12,500 acres s. of North Adams off SR 2. Horse rental.	34	•	•	•				•		•		•	•	•	•
Mount Tom (C-3) 1,800 acres e. of Easthampton on Reservation Rd.	52		•	•	•			•					•		
Mount Washington (C-1) 4,169 acres s.w. of South Egremont off SR 41 on Mount Washington Rd. Bash Bish Falls. Backpack camping; horse rental.	35	•		•				•	•	•					
Myles Standish (D-7) 14,651 acres 6 mi. w. of Plymouth off US 3. Horse rental.	36	•	•	•	•	•	•	•	•	•			•		
Natural Bridge (A-2) 47 acres on SR 8 in North Adams.	64		•	•				•							
October Mountain (C-2) 16,127 acres 3 mi. n. of Lee on a county road. Horse rental.	37	•	•	•	•			•	•	•					
Otter River (B-4) 12,788 acres 1 mi. n. of Baldwinsville on US 202.	38	•	•	•	•			•	•	•					
Pittsfield (B-1) 10,000 acres 4 mi. n.w. of Pittsfield. Horse rental.	39	•	•	•				•	•	•					
Quinsigamond (C-5) 51 acres 2 mi. e. of Worcester off SR 9.	40		•		•	•		•							
Robinson (C-3) 811 acres 3 mi. w. on SR 187 at Feeding Hills. Horse rental.	26		•	•				•	•	•					
Roland C. Nickerson (E-9) 1,955 acres 1 mi. e. of East Brewster off SR 6A. Horse rental.	41	•	•	•	•	•		•	•	•			•	•	•
Rutland (B-4) 396 acres 3 mi. s.w. of Rutland on SR 122A. Horse rental.	42		•	•	•			•	•	•					
Salisbury Beach (A-7) 520 acres 2 mi. e. of Salisbury off SR 1A.	43	•			•	•		•	•	•					•
Sandisfield (D-1) 7,785 acres 1 mi. w. of Sandisfield off SR 57. Backpack camping; horse rental.	44	•	•	•	•	•		•	•	•					
Savoy Mountain (B-2) 11,118 acres 6 mi. s.e. of North Adams off SR 2. Horse rental.	45	•	•	•	•			•	•	•			•		
Scusset Beach (D-8) 380 acres 3 mi. e. of Bournedale on Cape Cod Bay off US 6 and SR 3A.	46	•	•	•		•		•	•	•					•
South Cape Beach (E-8) 401 acres s. of Mashpee on Great Oak Rd.	66		•	•				•	•						
Spencer (C-4) 965 acres .5 mi. s. on SR 31. Historic. *(See Spencer p. 170.)*	48	•	•	•				•	•	•					
Streeter Point (D-4) 10 acres 1 mi. w. of Sturbridge off SR 20.	49			•	•	•		•							
Tolland (C-2) 4,893 acres 3 mi. n. of New Boston off SR 8. Horse rental.	50	•	•	•	•	•		•	•	•					
Wachusett Mountain (B-5) 2,842 acres s.w. of Shirley. Downhill skiing; horse rental.	16			•						•		•	•		•
Walden Pond (E-1) 304 acres .5 mi. s. on SR 126. Historic. *(See Concord p. 123.)*	51		•	•	•			•	•				•		
Wells (C-4) 1,470 acres 2 mi. n. of Sturbridge off SR 49N.	53	•						•					•		
Wendell (B-3) 7,900 acres e. of Farley off SR 2 on Wendell Rd. Horse rental.	54		•	•	•	•		•	•	•					
Willard Brook (B-5) 2,380 acres 3 mi. e. of Ashby off SR 119. Scenic. Horse rental.	56	•	•	•				•	•	•			•	•	
Windsor Forest (B-2) 1,743 acres off SR 116 in Windsor.	57	•	•	•	•			•	•	•					
Wompatuck (F-3) 3,500 acres off SR 228 s.e. of Hingham. Horse rental.	55	•						•			•	•			
OTHER															
D.W. Field Park (C-7) 700 acres in Brockton.	58		•						•		•				
Look Memorial Park (C-3) 200 acres on the Berkshire Trail (SR 9). Miniature railroad, petting zoo, tennis courts. *(See Northampton p. 164.)*	63		•		•	•	•	•	•						
Richard T. Crane Jr. Memorial Reservation (A-7) 1,399 acres 6 mi. e. of Ipswich via Argilla Rd.	8		•	•				•	•				•		
Rocky Woods Reservation (F-2) 490 acres 2 mi. n. of Medfield.	59		•	•									•	•	

STARRED ATTRACTIONS

Adams National Historic Site—Two American presidents share the name Adams and this site preserves their birthplaces, their home and the churchyard containing their graves. See Quincy p. 131.

American Textile History Museum—Displays of looms, spinning wheels, preserved fabrics and other items chronicle 3 centuries of American cloth making at this musuem. See Lowell p. 128.

Battleship Cove—Warships of the 20th century remain docked here including the Battleship *Massachusetts*, submarine *Lionfish*, destroyer *Joseph P. Kennedy Jr.*, two PT boats and a Russian-built missile corvette. See Fall River p. 156.

Boott Cotton Mills Museum—Mechanized looms in an 18th-century factory illustrate the workaday world during the Industrial Revolution. See Lowell p. 128.

Bunker Hill Monument—This 221-foot obelisk marks the site of the Battle of Bunker Hill, a critical early battle of the American Revolution. See Boston p. 103.

Cape Cod National Seashore—Wind-swept dunes, lighthouses, forests and 14 miles of protected shoreline distinguish this 44,000-acre national park. See place listing p. 145.

Concord Museum—A great place to start your visit to this historic town, the museum houses such Revolutionary War relics as the lantern used to signal Paul Revere. See Concord p. 122.

Cranberry World Visitors Center—Everything you ever wanted to know about this tart little fruit—from cultivating to cooking—is right here. See Plymouth p. 167.

Faneuil Hall—Stirring speeches and passionate pleas echoed within the walls of this famous building, ultimately leading to the American Revolution. See Boston p. 105.

Fruitlands Museums—Here you'll find several museums in one location including the Indian Museum, Picture Gallery, Shaker Museum and the Fruitlands Farmhouse. See Harvard p. 158.

Hancock Shaker Village—See what life was like in a 1790 Shaker community as you stroll among the 21 restored buildings and admire the simple, hand-crafted furnishings on display. See Pittsfield p. 166.

Harvard University—The epitome of Ivy-league prestige, Harvard's campus also exemplifies American architecture with buildings ranging from Colonial-style Massachusetts Hall to the ultramodern Carpenter Center. See Cambridge p. 119.

Continued on page 94

Points of Interest

ACTON—*see Boston p. 116.*

AGAWAM (D-3) pop. 27,300

A suburb of Springfield, Agawam was the hometown of Anne Sullivan, tutor and companion of Helen Keller. Robinson State Park is about 3 miles west on SR 187. *See Recreation Chart.*

Agawam Chamber of Commerce: P.O. Box 531, Agawam, MA 01001; phone (413) 787-1540.

SAVE ★ **RIVERSIDE AMUSEMENT PARK,** 1623 Main St., is said to be New England's largest amusement park. The park features a large assortment of rides, shows and amusements, including the Mind Eraser, a looping roller coaster on which passengers ride suspended below the track. Other roller coasters include the Black Widow, the Thunderbolt and the Cyclone. Riders on the Hellevator are carried to the top of a tower for a 20-story free fall. Aboard the Time War, passengers ride in pendulum-mounted gondolas that swing back and forth, ultimately turning upside down.

StarToon Studios is a movie-themed children's area featuring interactive exhibits. Island Kingdom Waterpark includes Hook's Lagoon, a children's play area with bridges, cargo nets, bubbling springs and waterfalls. A tidal pool, water toboggan, artificial river and water slides also are featured. Food is available.

Sun.-Thurs. 11-11, Fri.-Sat. 11 a.m.-midnight, July-Aug.; Mon.-Thurs. 10-6, Fri.-Sat. 11 a.m.-midnight, Sun. 11-11, in June; Sat.-Sun. 11-11, Fri. 10 a.m.-11 p.m., last weekend in Apr.-May 31; Sat.-Sun. 11-11, Fri. 5-11, Sept. 1-Nov. 1. Hours may vary; phone ahead. Admission $24.99; 36-48 inches tall $18.99; over age 54, $15.99. AE, DI, MC, VI. Phone (413) 786-9300 or (800) 370-7488.

AMESBURY—*see Boston p. 116.*

AMHERST (B-3) pop. 35,200, elev. 255'

Amherst was named for Lord Jeffrey Amherst, a British general in the French and Indian War. In the town's early years the residents made several efforts to industrialize but were most successful with cattle farming. In 1864 the livestock's prize-winning reputation led to the founding of Massachusetts Agricultural College, which later developed into the University of Massachusetts.

STARRED ATTRACTIONS

Harvard University Museums of Cultural and Natural History—Mayan artifacts, minerals, gemstones, fossils and representations of hundreds of plant species are just a small sampling of the range of exhibits at these four museums. See Cambridge p. 119.

Heritage Plantation—If variety is the spice of life then this 76-acre park is like a hot tamale. Enjoy gardens and nature trails or stay indoors to take in vintage automobiles, military miniatures, a restored carrousel and Early American crafts. See Sandwich p. 53.

Historic Deerfield—This complex of 12 historic houses built in the 18th and 19th centuries—each of which contains period decorative arts—also features a museum dedicated to early New England history. See Deerfield p. 154.

House of the Seven Gables Historic Site—Actually a collection of six historic houses that includes author Nathaniel Hawthorne's birthplace, the site is centered about the 1668 Turner-Ingersoll Mansion, a seven-gabled house that inspired Hawthorne's classic novel. See Salem p. 134.

Lexington—The Minute Man Statue looks out over the green where the American Revolution began in 1775. See place listing p. 126.

Longfellow's Wayside Inn of Sudbury— Made famous in a poem by Henry Wadsworth Longfellow, the inn—one of the country's oldest—encompasses a 13-room museum, a chapel, formal gardens, a barn and a carriage house. See Sudbury p. 138.

Lowell National Historical Park—Lowell was part of America's avant garde in the Industrial Revolution; this park commemorates the town's role in manufacturing and labor history. See Lowell p. 128.

Massachusetts Institute of Technology—Set along the Charles River, this hotbed of high-tech innovation features a museum with holography displays and other technology-centered exhibits along with the architecturally far-out MIT Chapel designed by Eero Saarinen. See Cambridge p. 119.

Mayflower II—Board this reproduction of the Pilgrims' ship and imagine the fortitude it took to make the 66-day voyage from Europe to North America. See Plymouth p. 167.

The Museum at the John Fitzgerald Kennedy Library—The life and legacy ofPresident Kennedy is portrayed here through exhibits, video presentations and period furnishings. See Boston p. 107.

Continued on next page

In 1821 Amherst College was founded and was dedicated to preparing young men for missionary work; in the mid-19th century more liberal educational aims were adopted. Among renowned graduates are Henry Ward Beecher and Calvin Coolidge. Also adding to the area's scholarly atmosphere were some of its residents: author Ray Stannard Baker (David Grayson) and poets Emily Dickinson, Robert Frost and Eugene Field.

The National Yiddish Book Center at 1021 W. St. on the campus of Hampshire College preserves more than 1.3 million books written in Yiddish. The center is housed in a building designed to look like a 19-century shtetl, a cluster of wooden buildings surrounding a synagogue. In addition to Yiddish texts the center houses educational exhibits.

The Emily Dickinson House, 280 Main St., offers guided tours of selected rooms; phone (413) 542-8161. Mead Art Museum, 1 block south of SR 9 on the Amherst College campus, contains changing displays of artifacts, paintings and sculpture from the 17th through the 20th century; phone (413) 542-2335.

Amherst Chamber of Commerce: 11 Spring St., Amherst, MA 01002; phone (413) 253-0700.

JONES LIBRARY, 43 Amity St., is a small public library arranged to resemble a luxurious private home. Several rooms, paneled in walnut and Philippine white mahogany, are decorated with Oriental rugs and paintings. The special collection section has research collections and individual rooms about Emily Dickinson, Robert Frost and others. Library open Mon.-Sat. 9-5:30 (also Tues. and Thurs. 5:30-9:30), Sept.-May. Special collections open Mon.-Fri. 10-5, Sat. 10-noon and 1-5. Free. Phone (413) 256-4090.

PRATT MUSEUM OF NATURAL HISTORY, on the Amherst College campus at the quadrangle, has collections of dinosaur and other fossils, skeletons of various vertebrates and invertebrates, minerals and crystals. Other exhibits examine such geologic processes as the formation of a mountain range and an oxbow lake. Allow 1 hour minimum. Mon.-Fri. 9-3:30, Sat. 10-4, Sun. noon-5, Sept. 1-June 15; Sat. 10-4, Sun. noon-5, rest of year. Closed holidays. Donations. Phone (413) 542-2165.

ANDOVER—see Boston p. 116.

ARLINGTON—see Boston p. 116.

ASHLEY FALLS (D-1) elev. 684'

BARTHOLOMEW'S COBBLE, .5 mi. w. on SR 7A to Weatogue Rd., is a 277-acre reservation on the Housatonic River with a wide variety of fern, wildflower and bird species. The nature preserve has a natural history museum, staffed by a naturalist, and hiking trails. Park open daily dawn-dusk. Museum open Wed.-Sun. 9-5, Apr.-Nov.; Tues.-Sat. 9-5, rest of year. Admission $3; ages 6-12, $1. Donations for hiking in off-season. Phone (413) 229-8600.

ATTLEBORO (D-6) pop. 38,400, elev. 133'

ATTLEBORO CAPRON PARK AND ZOO, 1 mi. w. on SR 123, contains a rain forest display of tropical flora and fauna. Educational programs are available. Park open daily dawn-dusk; zoo open daily 10-4. Closed Jan. 1, Thanksgiving and Dec. 25. Last admission 30 minutes before closing. Park free. Zoo $2.50; ages 6-12, $1. Phone (508) 222-3047.

ATTLEBORO MUSEUM FOR THE ARTS, 86 Park St., houses contemporary and historic art of regional interest. Tues.-Sat. 10-5 (also Wed. 5-8), Sun. noon-4; closed holidays. Free. Phone (508) 222-2644.

LA SALETTE SHRINE, 947 Park St. (SR 118), was opened by the Missionaries of Our Lady of La Salette. Within this Marian shrine are statuary gardens, chapels, a theater, retreat house and the Provincial House. Food is available. The shrine is open daily 9-8. Festival of Lights is presented daily 5-9, Thanksgiving-Jan. 1. Free. Phone (508) 222-5410.

BARNSTABLE—see Cape Cod p. 142.

BECKET (C-2) pop. 1,500, elev. 1,207'

Becket is a residential and recreational area in the Berkshire Hills. Nearby October Mountain State Forest (see Recreation Chart) offers year-round diversions.

Berkshire Visitors Bureau: Berkshire Common, Plaza Level, Pittsfield, MA 01201; phone (413) 443-9186 or (800) 237-5747.

BELCHERTOWN (C-4) pop. 10,600, elev. 476'

CHARLES L. MCLAUGHLIN TROUT HATCHERY is 3.75 mi. e. on SR 9, then .5 mi. s. to 90 East St. The hatchery, which raises rainbow, brown and brook trout, is part of the 1,000-acre Swift River Wildlife Management Area. Visitors can feed the fish with food pellets bought from machines in the hatchery; the machines accept only dimes. Daily 9-4. Free. Phone (413) 323-7671.

STARRED ATTRACTIONS

Museum of Fine Arts—This museum has all the Manets, Monets, Picassos, Rembrandts, Renoirs, Sargents and Whistlers you would expect to see at one of the country's premier art venues. See Boston p. 107.

Museum of Science—Scientist-wannabes and junior geniuses will have a field day at this museum, which features hands-on exhibits dealing with ecology, astronomy and optical illusions along with such displays as a skull of a large, meat-eating dinosaur. See Boston p. 107.

Nantucket Whaling Museum—A 16-foot lens from the Sankaty Lighthouse and a whale skeleton are just two of the whaling-related exhibits at this museum, housed in a former candleworks. See Nantucket Island p. 162.

New Bedford Whaling Museum—Here you can learn the history of Herman Melville's classic *Moby Dick*, scrutinize scrimshaw, view a fully-equipped whale boat or marvel at the size of a humpback whale skeleton. See New Bedford p. 163.

New England Aquarium—More than 2,000 species of exotic and home-grown fish stay wet at this Boston landmark. See Boston p. 108.

Norman Rockwell Museum at Stockbridge—Stockbridge was home to the famous illustrator for the last 25 years of his life, and this museum houses Rockwell's studio along with his personal collection of his work. See Stockbridge p. 172.

Old North Church—This is one of the oldest church buildings in Boston; a lantern in its steeple signaled the departure of British troops from the city in 1775. See Boston p. 108.

Old State House—The Boston Massacre occurred at the east front of this 1713 public building, and John Hancock was inaugurated here as the first governor of the commonwealth. See Boston p. 109.

Old Sturbridge Village—Rural New England life of the 1830s is re-created at this 200-acre living history museum. See Sturbridge p. 173.

Peabody Essex Museum—This eclectic museum boasts more than 400,000 art objects, is noted for its maritime art collection and comprises 11 historic houses. See Salem p. 134.

Peter Foulger Museum and Research Center—The history of Nantucket Island is depicted through a collection of furniture, baskets and portraits at this museum. See Nantucket Island p. 162.

Continued on next page

STARRED ATTRACTIONS

Pilgrim Hall Museum—Who were the Pilgrims? This museum answers that question with a collection of Pilgrim-era armor, furniture and decorative arts. See Plymouth p. 168.

Plimoth Plantation—Ask the costumed actors at this living-history museum what a transatlantic journey aboard the *Mayflower* was like, and they will tell you as if they lived through it themselves. See Plymouth p. 168.

Plymouth National Wax Museum—More than 180 wax figures strike a pose at this museum, which features more than 26 scenes of Pilgrim life. See Plymouth p. 168.

Plymouth Rock—In 1620, disembarking Pilgrims stepped onto this rock and into the earliest pages of American history. See Plymouth p. 168.

Riverside Amusement Park—The stress is on fun at this park which features enough roller coasters, thrill rides and water slides to satisfy even the most demanding amusment aficionados. See Agawam p. 92.

Saugus Iron Works National Historic Site—This restored 1646 water-powered ironworks was the first in North America to encompass all phases of iron production. See Saugus p. 137.

Springfield Library and Museums—Four museums make up this complex which contains—among many other items—European paintings, American sculpture, exhibits describing local history and science displays. See Springfield p. 171.

Stephen Phillips Memorial Trust House—Five generations of the Phillips family filled this Federal-style mansion with objects collected during their world travels, including Asian porcelain, rare Persian rugs and English furnishings. See Salem p. 137.

Sterling and Francine Clark Art Institute—This collection of art spans 6 centuries and includes works by Edgar Degas, Pierre Auguste Renoir, Auguste Rodin and John Singer Sargent. See Williamstown p. 175.

The USS Constitution—Nicknamed *Old Ironsides* during the War of 1812, this 1797 frigate has withstood British cannons and thwarted French privateers. See Boston p. 104.

Worcester Art Museum—Pick a year, any year, and odds are you will find an object of art from that date at the Worcester Art Museum, which includes everything from Egyptian antiquities to 20th-century pop art. See Worcester p. 176.

BERKSHIRES

In westernmost Massachusetts lies an area of rivers, lakes and hills known as the Berkshires. The serenity and separateness of the area shaped and influenced both settlers and visitors. For theologian Jonathan Edwards and Mother Lee's Shakers, this region served as part of their separate journeys to find and serve God. For writers Edith Wharton, Herman Melville and Nathaniel Hawthorne, the Berkshires nurtured great literary works, such as Melville's "Moby Dick," which he wrote while living in Pittsfield.

Strung along US 7, the major towns of the Berkshires offer a long procession of events, theater, dance, music, museums and historical sites. Recreational opportunities for downhill and cross-country skiing, bicycling, canoeing, fishing and hiking are abundant. Rounding out these offerings are the natural beauty of the fall foliage as well as numerous winter ski resorts and country inns.

Places and towns listed individually are Ashley Falls, Becket, Dalton, Great Barrington, Hancock, Lenox, North Adams, Pittsfield, Stockbridge, Tyringham and Williamstown.

Berkshire Visitors Bureau: Berkshire Common, Plaza Level, Pittsfield, MA 01201; phone (413) 443-9186 or (800) 237-5747.

BEVERLY—*see Boston p. 117*

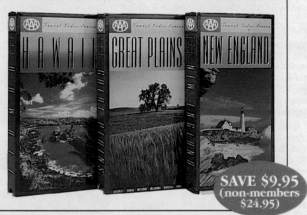

Boston

From the North End's tangle of narrow streets to the Prudential Center complex in Back Bay spans a distance of less than 3 miles and a history of more than 350 years. Herein lies much of Boston's appeal: It is eminently walkable and one of the nation's oldest cities.

Founded by Puritans in 1630, Boston soon became a major seaport and the largest British settlement on the continent. Part of an autonomous colony created by the Massachusetts Bay Co., the city came under the royal wing only after the company's charter was nullified in 1684. With this change of rule began years of mounting unrest and resistance to British authority—a story familiar to every American.

Growing animosity toward unpopular taxes brought military occupation to Boston in 1768, further fueling Colonial resentment of Crown rule. In 1770 British soldiers fired on a belligerent mob, killing five citizens in what has become known as the Boston Massacre. Three years later patriots loosely disguised as Indians dumped three shiploads of taxable tea into Boston Harbor. Furious, Parliament retaliated by closing the city's port.

Violent protests finally led to armed confrontation on nearby Lexington Green the morning after Paul Revere's famous midnight ride. "The shot heard 'round the world," fired in Concord later that day, sparked the American Revolution. Although defeated 3 months later at the bloody Battle of Breed's Hill, mistakenly called Bunker Hill, in neighboring Charlestown, the Colonials persevered. Patriots under the command of George Washington besieged Boston, and in March 1776 the British abandoned the city.

After the Revolution, Boston continued to prosper, growing rapidly during the 19th century. The hills were leveled and used for landfill, leaving only the modest hump of Beacon Hill. Stately avenues and the Public Garden rose from the former marshes and mudflats of Back Bay. As Boston's economy expanded, banking, investment and manufacturing surpassed maritime commerce in importance.

Along with this new vitality, Boston gained renown as a religious, educational and cultural center. Members of the social aristocracy (dubbed "Boston Brahmins" after the priestly caste of India) presided over the city's cultural life from the fashionable enclave of Beacon Hill, lending Boston an air of elegance and refinement as well as an unsurpassed reputation for snobbery.

In recent years Boston has embraced another revolution: high-technology. Tapping the formidable resources of the area's educational institutions—Harvard

University and the Massachusetts Institute of Technology in Cambridge head the list of more than 50 local universities and colleges—some 700 high-tech companies have settled nearby. Medical research and the city's role as state capital also contribute significantly to Boston's economy.

Although the surge of development that began in the 1960s continues to transform the face of the city, Boston manages to retain its historical appeal. But the past is not merely on display. The Common remains public ground in the truest sense. Orators still debate the issues of the day in Faneuil Hall. The 1713 Old State House holds its ground among the slick towers of the financial district, subway trains rumbling into the station beneath its floor.

Though adorned in places with gaslights, cobbled streets and brick sidewalks, the North End, Beacon Hill and Back Bay survive not simply as quaint relics but as vital and distinct communities. Icons of American history are inseparably woven within the fabric of the workaday city, a montage of glass, steel and stone rising from a matrix of red brick.

Comparing the city to Philadelphia in 1774, John Adams commented: "The Morals of our People are much better, their Manners are more polite, and agreeable . . . Our Language is better, our Persons are handsomer, our Spirit is greater, our Laws are wiser, our Religion is superior, our Education is better." Clearly, Bostonians have never suffered from a sense of inferiority.

Approaches
By Car

The major east-west highway into Boston is the Massachusetts Turnpike (I-90); this is paralleled by SR 9, a commercial route serving the suburbs. From the north I-93/US 1 leads to the Northeast Expressway, which enters the downtown area. I-93 and SR 3 (Southeast Expressway) enter Boston from the south. I-95/SR 128 encircles the metropolitan area, linking the main approaches to the city.

Getting Around
Street System

"We say the cows laid out Boston. Well, there are worse surveyors." But then Ralph Waldo Emerson never drove a car through the city. The rigors of driving in downtown Boston are legendary and should not be taken lightly.

The street system, a product of the city's piecemeal expansion, ranges from a bewildering tangle in the oldest part of the city to a relatively orderly grid of one-way streets in Back Bay (between Boylston Street and limited-access Storrow Drive, and between Massachusetts Avenue and the Public Garden). Fortunately, the central part of the city can be easily traversed on foot or by public transportation. Those who must drive should have a navigator at their side, armed with a map.

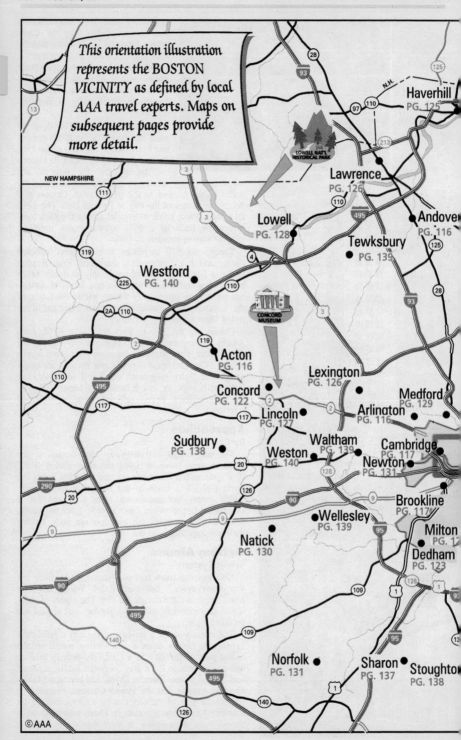

This orientation illustration represents the BOSTON VICINITY as defined by local AAA travel experts. Maps on subsequent pages provide more detail.

NEW HAMPSHIRE
N.H.

LOWELL NAT'L HISTORICAL PARK

CONCORD MUSEUM

Haverhill PG. 125

Lawrence PG. 126

Lowell PG. 128

Andover PG. 116

Tewksbury PG. 139

Westford PG. 140

Acton PG. 116

Lexington PG. 126

Medford PG. 129

Concord PG. 122

Lincoln PG. 127

Arlington PG. 116

Sudbury PG. 138

Waltham PG. 139

Cambridge PG. 117

Weston PG. 140

Newton PG. 131

Brookline PG. 117

Wellesley PG. 139

Milton PG. 1

Natick PG. 130

Dedham PG. 123

Norfolk PG. 131

Sharon PG. 137

Stoughto

© AAA

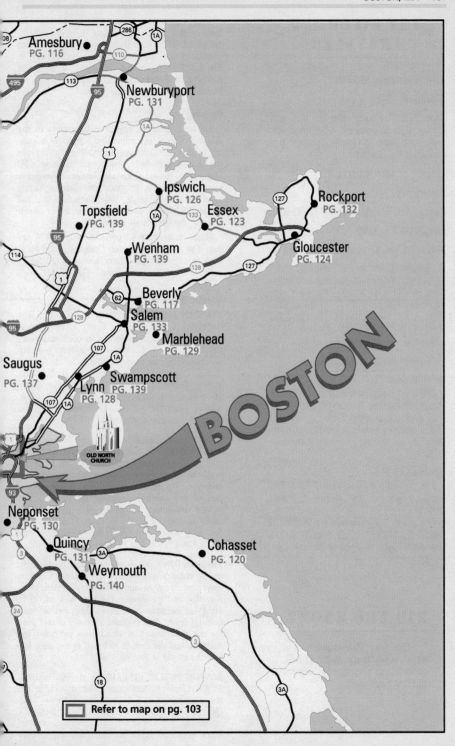

Amesbury
PG. 116

Newburyport
PG. 131

Ipswich
PG. 126

Topsfield
PG. 139

Essex
PG. 123

Rockport
PG. 132

Wenham
PG. 139

Gloucester
PG. 124

Beverly
PG. 117

Salem
PG. 133

Marblehead
PG. 129

Saugus
PG. 137

Swampscott
PG. 139

Lynn
PG. 128

BOSTON

OLD NORTH
CHURCH

Neponset
PG. 130

Quincy
PG. 131

Cohasset
PG. 120

Weymouth
PG. 140

Refer to map on pg. 103

THE INFORMED TRAVELER

City Population: 558,400

Elevation: 20 ft.

Sales Tax: The state sales tax in Massachusetts is 5 percent. Combined city and state taxes on hotel occupancy in Boston is 9.7 percent.

WHOM TO CALL

Emergency: 911

Police (non-emergency): (617) 343-4200

Fire: (617) 725-3550

Time and Temperature: (617) 637-1234

Hospitals: Beth Israel Hospital, (617) 667-2000; Boston Deaconess Medical Center, (617) 638-8000; Brigham and Women's Hospital, (617) 732-5500; Massachusetts General, (617) 726-2000; New England Medical Center, (617) 636-5000.

WHERE TO LOOK

Newspapers

The two daily newspapers published in Boston are the *Boston Herald* (morning) and the *Boston Globe* (morning). The *Christian Science Monitor* (morning) is published Monday through Friday.

Radio and TV

Boston radio station WBUR (90.9 FM) is programmed by National Public Radio.

The major TV channels are 2 (PBS), 7 (NBC), 5 (ABC), 4 (CBS) and 25 (FOX). Complete listings appear in the daily newspapers.

DID YOU KNOW?

The first Thanksgiving was eaten exclusively with knives, spoons and fingers; the Pilgrims did not have forks.

Unless otherwise posted, the speed limit on most streets is 30 mph. Right turns on red are permitted after a full stop, unless otherwise posted. Avoid rush-hour traffic—particularly in the tunnels and on the bridges—7-9 a.m. and 4-6:30 p.m. Be especially careful in outlying areas when crossing streetcar tracks.

Parking

On-street parking, regulated by meters in the downtown area, is limited and subject to a variety of posted restrictions. Centrally located parking garages include Auditorium Garage, 50 Dalton St.; Boston Common Garage, beneath the Common with an entrance on Charles Street; John Hancock Garage, 100 Clarendon St.; and Prudential Center Garage, with entrances on all sides of the Prudential Tower.

Rates range from $3 per half hour to $24 per day. The garages at Boston Common, John Hancock and Prudential Center are open 24 hours daily; times vary at Auditorium Garage.

What To See

AFRICAN MEETING HOUSE, 8 Smith Ct., was dedicated in 1806, and for nearly a century was the center for African-American community activities. It is said to be the oldest standing African-American church building in the United States. Changing exhibits are displayed in the gallery. Guided gallery tours are available. Daily 10-4, Memorial Day-Labor Day; Mon.-Fri. 10-4, rest of year. Closed Jan. 1, Thanksgiving and Dec. 25. Donations. Phone (617) 739-1200.

ARNOLD ARBORETUM is on the Arborway in Jamaica Plain (T: Forest Hills). The 265-acre park contains 4,000 kinds of trees—all from the northern temperate regions—grouped by family and type. The Hunnewell Building houses a herbarium and exhibits depicting the development of the arboretum. Grounds open daily dawn-dusk. Hunnewell Building open Mon.-Fri. 9-4, Sat.-Sun. noon-4; closed holidays. Free. Phone (617) 524-1718.

THE BOSTON COMMON, the oldest public park in the country, is bounded by Beacon, Charles, Boylston, Tremont and Park sts. (T: Arlington, Boylston or Park Street). The area was set off in 1634 for common use as a "cow pasture and training field." The Puritans kept stocks and pens for the punishment of those who profaned the Sabbath, and the British gathered in the park before the Battle of Bunker Hill.

BOSTON PUBLIC LIBRARY is at 700 Boylston St. (T: Copley). Permanent exhibits include the mural paintings of Edwin Austin Abbey's "The Quest of the Holy Grail," John Singer Sargent's "Judaism and Christianity" and the works of other American artists and sculptors. The library hosts many revolving exhibits throughout the year and also features an extensive collection of rare books and manuscripts.

The Research Building on Copley Square, designed in 1888, has an inner courtyard garden. Mon.-Thurs. 9-9, Fri.-Sat. 9-5, Sun. 1-5, Oct.-May; Mon.-Thurs. 9-9, Fri.-Sat. 9-5, rest of year. Closed holidays. Free. Phone (617) 536-5400.

THE BOSTON TEA PARTY SHIP AND MUSEUM is at the Congress Street Bridge on Harbor Walk (T: South Station). The notorious protest is recreated through museum exhibits and aboard the full-scale working replica of the tea party ship. Audiovisual presentations focus on the ship's voyage, the taxing of the tea and the actual dumping of the tea chests. Daily 9-5, Mar. 1-Dec. 1; closed Thanksgiving. Admission $7; over 55 and students with ID $5.50; ages 4-12, $3.50. Phone (617) 338-1773.

BULL & FINCH PUB ("CHEERS"), 84 Beacon St., is the Boston neighborhood bar which inspired the setting for the popular television series "Cheers." The front entrance of the bar was used for the opening scene on the series which aired from September 1982 for 11 seasons. This is the place where "everybody knows your name." Food is available. Daily 11 a.m.-2 a.m.; closed Dec. 25. Free. Phone (617) 227-9605.

★**BUNKER HILL MONUMENT,** in Monument Sq., is on Breed's Hill in Charlestown (T: Community College). The monument marks the site of the Battle of Bunker Hill, which took place June 17, 1775. The 221-foot granite obelisk contains a spiral staircase to the top. The lodge at the base of the monument contains dioramas and exhibits about the battle. Educational programs are offered. Monument open daily 9-4:30; lodge open daily 9-5. Free. Phone (617) 242-5641.

CHARLES RIVER is a reservation that extends along both sides of the Charles River from the dams at Boston and Cambridge to Newton Upper Falls near SRs 9 and 128. Within the 961-acre reservation are bicycle paths, six swimming pools, 12 tennis courts, a fitness course and other

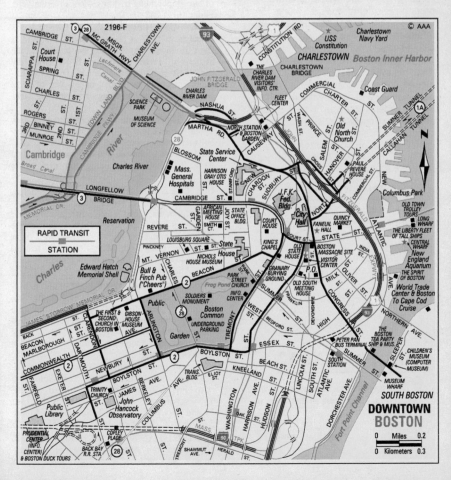

DOWNTOWN BOSTON

THE INFORMED TRAVELER

VISITOR INFORMATION

Information on Boston is available at the Greater Boston Convention & Visitors Bureau, Prudential Plaza, P.O. Box 490, Boston, MA 02199; phone (617) 536-4100 or (800) 888-5515.

Two information centers—one on the Tremont Street side of the Boston Common and the other at the Prudential Center near the Copley T—provide self-guiding tour maps, brochures and events information. The centers are open daily 9-5.

The National Park Service operates a visitor center on the Freedom Trail at 15 State St. An audiovisual orientation program is offered daily 9-5, June 15-Labor Day. The Park Service operates an information kiosk at Quincy Market daily 11-7.

Panorama, a biweekly publication, describes events and attractions in and around Boston. It is available at hotels, train stations and airline terminals. The *Boston Phoenix* is a weekly publication available at newsstands and bookstores. It contains detailed entertainment information. An events line also is available; phone (617) 536-4100 or (800) 858-0200.

WHAT TO WEAR

Seasons in Boston are distinct. Summers are humid, with temperatures in the 80s. In spring and fall the thermometer ranges from the 40s to the 60s. Winters tend to be cold and bitter although snow and sleet are not frequent.

DID YOU KNOW?

The sewing machine was invented by Elias Howe in Boston.

facilities. Hatch Memorial Shell offers free concerts from mid-April to mid-October. Canoeing, kayaking, sculling, sailing and windsurfing instruction and equipment are available for a fee. Phone (617) 727-5114.

THE CHARLES RIVER DAM VISITORS' INFORMATION CENTER is at Charles River Dam, 250 Warren Ave., at the end of Beverly St. (T: North Station). A 12-minute multimedia presentation explains the Charles River Dam operations, including flood control mechanisms, a fish ladder and boat locks. Guided tours are available. Mon.-Fri. 9-3. Free. Phone (617) 727-5114.

CHARLESTOWN NAVY YARD, off I-93 in Charlestown (T: Community College or North Station), is part of Boston National Historical Park. Built in 1800, it served as a repair and supply depot for 174 years. Such innovations as shiphouses and a ropewalk were among the yard's contributions. The Navy's first ship of the line, the USS *Independence*, was built and launched here in 1814. There are representatives of two shipbuilding traditions docked at the yard. Phone (617) 242-5601.

★**The USS *Constitution*,** at Pier 1, was launched in 1797 at Edmund Hartt's Shipyard, a short distance from its present berth, and was the nemesis of French privateers. It is purportedly the oldest commissioned ship in the world. Engagements with the British in the War of 1812 brought the vessel undying fame and the nickname *Old Ironsides*.

The 54-gun frigate was constructed of seasoned live oak and red cedar timbers secured by bolts and copper sheathing made by Paul Revere. Guided tours of the top two decks are conducted daily 9:30-3:50. Self-guiding top deck tours 3:50-dusk. Free. Phone (617) 242-5670.

USS *Constitution* Museum contains participatory exhibits that let visitors command *Old Ironsides* in battle, hoist a sail, fire a cannon or swing in a hammock. Model makers demonstrate the art of miniature shipbuilding. Allow 1 hour minimum. Daily 9-6, May-Oct.; 10-5, rest of year. Closed Jan. 1, Thanksgiving and Dec. 25. Free. AE, DS, MC, VI. Phone (617) 426-1812.

CHILDREN'S MUSEUM OF BOSTON is at Museum Wharf, 300 Congress St. (T: South Station). Designed for fun and education, the museum offers three floors of hands-on exhibits featuring boats and water play, giant building toys, raceways, bubbles, a climbing maze and a children's theater.

Allow 2 hours minimum. Daily 10-7 (also Fri. 7-9 p.m.), July 1-Labor Day; Tues.-Sun. 10-5 (also Fri. 5-9), rest of year. Closed Jan. 1, Thanksgiving and Dec. 25. Admission $7; over 59 and ages 2-15, $6; age 1, $2; all ages $1 Fri. 5-9. AE, MC, VI. Phone (617) 426-8855.

THE CHRISTIAN SCIENCE CHURCH CENTER, 175 Huntington Ave. (T: Prudential or Symphony), encompasses several buildings and is sponsored by The First Church of Christ, Scientist. Allow 2 hours minimum. Free. Phone (617) 450-3790.

The Mother Church is the world headquarters of the Christian Science Church. Romanesque in style, the original church is made of New Hampshire granite and contains stained-glass windows depicting Biblical events. A four-manual organ in the extension contains eight divisions of pipework, including 13,595 pipes, and occupies an area 75 feet wide, 10 feet deep and eight stories high. The church may be closed in 1999 for renovations; phone ahead. Tours are given Tues.-Sat. 10-4, Sun. at 11:30. Free. Phone (617) 450-3793.

Multimedia Bible Exhibit, 101 Belvidere St., offers a nondenominational presentation about the Bible. Included are a slide program, an interactive time line, a 400-volume resource center and a children's area. Tues.-Sat. 10-4, Sun. 11:15-4, Feb.-Dec. Free. Phone (617) 450-3732.

SAVE **COMPUTER MUSEUM,** on Museum Wharf at 300 Congress St. (T: South Station), uses more than 170 interactive exhibits to tell the story of the information revolution and its impact. The Walk-Thru Computer 2000 is a two-story-tall model of a personal computer. Other exhibits let visitors test drive the information highway and walk through "time tunnels" to observe milestones in computer and information technology. The Virtual Fishtank allows visitors to design computer-generated fish by selecting physical features and behavior patterns and then releasing their creation into a "tank" made up of 12 large projection screens.

The Best Software for Kids Gallery allows visitors to try out fully-functional versions of the 50 top-rated educational software for ages 2-12. Museum open daily 10-6, mid-June through Labor Day; Tues.-Sun. and Mon. holidays 10-5, rest of year. Closed holidays. Admission $7; over 65 and ages 3-18, $5; half-price to all Sun. 3-5. AE, MC, VI. Phone (617) 426-2800.

★**FANEUIL HALL**, at Faneuil Hall Sq., Merchants Row (T: State Street or Government Center). The 1742 building was given to the city by Peter Faneuil. It burned in 1761, was rebuilt in 1763 and was enlarged in 1805. The upper story served as a meeting hall, the scene of many stirring gatherings during the Revolutionary movement. British officers used the building as a theater during their occupation of the city. Known for its grasshopper weather vane, the hall contains a military museum and paintings of notable battles.

The Faneuil Hall Marketplace includes North and South Markets, Faneuil Hall and the adjacent Quincy Market, a renovated 19th-century complex containing more than 125 restaurants, boutiques, produce stands and retail pushcarts. Street performers entertain continuously.

TRANSPORTATION

Air travel: Most major airlines serve Logan International Airport. Combined bus and subway fare to downtown is about $1. Logan Express shuttles run daily 6 a.m.-11 p.m. between the airport and Framingham, Braintree and Woburn; phone (800) 235-6426. Taxi fare to downtown is about $20.

Rental cars: All major agencies have offices. Hertz, (617) 338-1512 or (800) 654-3080, offers discounts to AAA members. Arrangements should be made in advance; consult your AAA club for information.

Rail service: Amtrak, (800) 872-7245, provides service from South Station, Atlantic Avenue and Sumner Street, and Back Bay Station, 145 Dartmouth St.

Buses: Greyhound Lines Inc., (800) 231-2222, operates from South Station. From the same terminal Vermont Transit serves New England, New York City and Montréal; phone (802) 864-6811

Taxis: Cabs are metered and charge $1.50 for a pickup and $1.80 per mile. Companies include Checker, (617) 536-7000, and Independent Taxi Operators Association, (617) 426-8700.

Public transport: Massachusetts Bay Transportation Authority offers subway (or "T"), trolley and bus routes daily 5 a.m.-12:30 a.m.; phone (617) 722-3200. In-city subway fare is 85c; outbound fares are free and inbound fares are as much as $2. A token or exact change is required. Boston Passports provide unlimited passage on most routes. A 3-day pass is $9; 7-day pass $18; under 5 travel free. Buses provide crosstown and local service. The fare is 60c, and express buses are $1.50 and up. In the *What to See* section, attraction listings usually provide the subway or trolley stop (T).

Boats: The Water Shuttle offers 10-minute trips between the Logan dock and Rowes Wharf daily 6 a.m.-8 p.m. except on holidays (weather permitting). The fare is $7; phone (617) 439-3131.

Commuter boats also run to Quincy and Hingham from Rowes Wharf.

BOSTON NATIONAL HISTORICAL PARK

Boston National Historical Park consists of seven sites along the Freedom Trail as well as Dorchester Heights Monument in south Boston. Only two of these sites, Bunker Hill Monument and the Charlestown Navy Yard, are owned by the federal government. The others—Faneuil Hall, Old North Church, Old South Meeting House, Old State House and Paul Revere House—are owned privately or managed municipally.

Beginning with the information center on Boston Common and continuing through the center of downtown and the North End to Bunker Hill, the 3-mile Freedom Trail and the Boston National Historical Park encompass an abundance of American history.

The park's visitor center at 15 State St., across from the Old State House, gives an overview of Boston's Colonial history through an 8-minute slide show. The visitor center is open daily 9-6, June-Aug.; Mon.-Fri. 8-5, Sat.-Sun. 9-5, rest of year. Closed Jan. 1, Thanksgiving and Dec. 25.

Rangers conduct free 90-minute walking tours of the Freedom Trail daily on the half-hour 9:30-3, mid-June through Labor Day weekend. Guided tours are conducted daily on the hour 10-3, Memorial Day weekend-Columbus Day; Mon.-Fri. at 10 and 2, Sat.-Sun. at 10, 11, 1 and 2, mid-Apr. through Fri. before Memorial Day and day after Columbus Day-Thanksgiving weekend.

Information about the park also is available from the information center on the Common, at Charlestown Navy Yard and at the information desk in Faneuil Hall. Phone (617) 242-5642.

Rangers give talks every half-hour daily 9-5. Museum open Mon.-Fri. 10-5. Marketplace open Mon.-Sat. 10-9, Sun. noon-6. Closed Jan. 1, Thanksgiving and Dec. 25. Free. Phone (617) 523-1300 for information, or 338-2323 for marketplace schedules.

THE FIRST AND SECOND CHURCH IN BOSTON, 66 Marlborough St. (T: Arlington), was designed by Paul Rudolph in 1972, following a fire, around the Gothic steeple from the former 1868 edifice. The early congregation included Ralph Waldo Emerson, Paul Revere and Henry David Thoreau. Mon.-Fri. 9-5, Labor Day to mid-June; 9-3, rest of year. Free. Phone (617) 267-6730.

FORT WARREN, on Georges Island in Boston Harbor Islands State Park *(see Recreation Chart),* can be reached by ferry from Hewitt's Cove, Hingham and Long Wharf. Built 1834-60, the massive granite fort held Confederate prisoners during the Civil War and later served as a center for laying mines in Boston Harbor during the Spanish-American War and World Wars I and II. Rangers offer historic tours and environmental programs. Picnicking is permitted. Food is available. Daily 9-dusk, May 1-Oct. 12. Free. Phone (617) 727-5290.

SAVE **GIBSON HOUSE MUSEUM,** 137 Beacon St. (T: Arlington), is an 1859 Boston brownstone with Victorian furnishings. Guided tours are conducted Wed.-Sun. at 1, 2 and 3, May-Oct.; Sat.-Sun. at 1, 2 and 3, rest of year. Closed Jan. 1, Thanksgiving and Dec. 25. Admission $5. Phone (617) 267-6338.

GOVERNMENT CENTER, 60 acres on the site of old Scollay Sq. (T: Government Center or State Street), is an urban renewal project. The complex encompasses city, state and federal buildings, some of striking contemporary architecture as well as shops and stores.

GRANARY BURYING GROUND, Tremont St. (T: Park Street), at the head of Bromfield St., was established in 1660. Interred on the grounds are three signers of the Declaration of Independence—John Hancock, Samuel Adams and Robert Treat Paine—as well as Paul Revere, Peter Faneuil, Boston Massacre victims and Benjamin Franklin's parents. Daily 8-4:30. Free.

SAVE **HARRISON GRAY OTIS HOUSE,** 141 Cambridge St. (T: Charles, Bowdoin or Government Center), was designed by Charles Bulfinch for Harrison Gray Otis, lawyer, entrepreneur and Boston's third mayor. The 1796 house has been refurbished and decorated to reflect the style of the Federal period of the early 1800s. It now is headquarters of the Society for the Preservation of New England Antiquities.

Allow 1 hour minimum. Guided tours are conducted on the hour Wed.-Sun. 11-5. Last tour begins 1 hour before closing. Admission $4; over 64, $3.50; ages 6-12, $2. Phone (617) 227-3956.

INSTITUTE OF CONTEMPORARY ART, 955 Boylston St. (T: Hynes Convention Center-ICA), is in a restored 19th-century police station. The ICA was founded in 1936 as the first non-collecting contemporary art institution in the country. Exhibits feature cutting-edge contemporary photography, painting, sculpture, architecture, film and video. Wed.-Sun. noon-5 (also Thurs. 5-9). Admission $5.25; students with ID $3.25; over 65 and ages 5-16, $2.25; free to all Thurs. 5-9. AE, MC, VI. Phone (617) 266-5152.

ISABELLA STEWART GARDNER MUSEUM, 280 The Fenway (T: Museum), exhibits works by such artists as Titian, Rembrandt, James McNeill Whistler and John Singer Sargent in a Venetian palace-type setting reminiscent of the 15th century. An enclosed courtyard blooms year-round. Museum open Tues.-Sun. 11-5. Concerts are given Sat.-Sun. at 1:30, Sept.-May. Admission $10; over 65, $7; college students with ID $5; under 18 free. AE, MC, VI. Phone (617) 566-1401 for the museum, or 734-1359 for recorded concert information. See ad p. 109.

JOHN HANCOCK OBSERVATORY, St. James Ave. and Trinity Pl. (T: Copley), at 740 feet is said to be the highest vantage point in New England. The view encompasses the city and suburbs and extends as far as the mountains of southern New Hampshire. Historical exhibits and an audiovisual presentation also are offered. Daily 9 a.m.-11 p.m., Apr.-Oct.; Mon.-Sat. 9 a.m.-11 p.m., Sun. 9-6, rest of year. Closed Thanksgiving and Dec. 25. Admission $5; college students with ID $4; over 60 and ages 5-17, $3. AE, MC, VI. Phone (617) 572-6429. See ad p. 109.

KING'S CHAPEL, Tremont and School sts. (T: Government Center or Park Street), was built in 1749 by the Church of England. The interior is considered one of the finest examples of Georgian architecture in the U.S. The chapel can be toured Mon. and Thurs.-Sat. 9-4, Sun. 1-3, July-Aug.; Mon. and Fri.-Sat. 10-3, Apr.-June and Sept.-Oct.; Sat. 10-3, rest of year. Music recitals are held Tues. at 12:15. Donations. Phone (617) 523-1749.

King's Chapel Burying Ground was established in 1630 and is one of Boston's oldest burying grounds. It contains the graves of Gov. John Winthrop, Rev. John Cotton and John Davenport, founder of New Haven, Conn. Daily 9-4. Free.

LOUISBURG SQUARE, on Beacon Hill between Mount Vernon and Pinckney sts. (T: Charles), retains an English courtyard atmosphere.

MASSACHUSETTS HORTICULTURAL SOCIETY, 300 Massachusetts Ave. (T: Symphony), has a major horticultural library. Mon.-Fri. 8:30-4:30. Free. Phone (617) 536-9280.

★ THE MUSEUM AT THE JOHN FITZGERALD KENNEDY LIBRARY, on the campus of the University of Massachusetts, SR 3/I-93N exit 14 or I-93S exit 15 to Morrissey Blvd., following signs (T: JFK/UMASS), serves as a memorial to the 35th president of the United States. Exhibits include the president's Oval Office desk, documents, tape recordings and a 17-minute film about the life and times of John F. Kennedy; the last film begins at 3:50.

Allow 2 hours minimum. Daily 9-5; closed Jan. 1, Thanksgiving and Dec. 25. Admission $8; over 62 and students with ID $6; ages 13-17, $4. AE, DS, MC, VI. Phone (617) 929-4523. See ad p. 109.

★ MUSEUM OF FINE ARTS, BOSTON, 465 Huntington Ave. (T: Museum), contains nearly 200 galleries of Asiatic, Egyptian, Classical, European and American paintings and sculpture. Included in the museum's collection are 43 Claude Monet paintings as well as works by Edouard Manet, Pablo Picasso, Rembrandt, Pierre Auguste Renoir, John Singer Sargent and James McNeill Whistler. Among the items of Asian art displayed are paintings, carvings, silk textiles and ornate swords.

The west wing, opened in 1981, was designed by I.M. Pei and houses galleries for special exhibitions and contemporary art; it was constructed with granite from the quarry used for the museum's 1901 neoclassical building. The wing's design features glass walls, an atrium and vaulted skylights extending the length of the structure. Food is available.

Wed.-Fri. 10-9:45 (Only West Wing can be visited Thurs.-Fri. after 5), Sat.-Sun. 10-5:45, Mon.-Tues. 10-4:45. Closed Thanksgiving and Dec. 24-25. Admission $10, senior citizens and students with ID $8, under 18 free. Thurs.-Fri. after 5 p.m. $8, senior citizens and students with ID $6. Wed. after 4 p.m. by donation. Phone (617) 267-9300 for recorded events information. See ad p. 109.

★ MUSEUM OF SCIENCE, at Science Park (T: Science Park), features more than 600 interactive exhibits about natural history, physical science, medicine and astronomy. Daily 9-7 (also Fri. 7-9), July 5-Labor Day; 9-5 (also Fri. 5-9), rest of year. Closed Thanksgiving and Dec. 25. Admission $9; over 65 and ages 3-11, $7. Combination rate for any two facilities (museum, planetarium or theater) $14; over 65 and ages 3-11, $10. Combination rate for all three facilities $19; over 65 and ages 3-11, $15. AE, MC, VI. Phone (617) 723-2500. See ad p. 109.

The Charles Hayden Planetarium presents shows about the stars, planets and other phenomena of the universe, utilizing an interactive audience response system. Shows daily; phone for schedule. Closed Thanksgiving and Dec. 25. Admission $7.50; over 65 and ages 3-11, $5.50. For recorded schedule and reservation information phone (617) 723-2500.

The Mugar Omni Theater has a five-story, domed screen that creates a wraparound effect. Allow 1 hour minimum. Films shown daily; phone for schedule. Closed Thanksgiving and

CITYPASS

CityPass offers savings to those who plan visits to many Boston attractions. The pass covers the price of admission to six sites—Isabella Stewart Gardner Museum, The Museum at the John Fitzgerald Kennedy Library, John Hancock Observatory, Museum of Fine Arts, Museum of Science and New England Aquarium.

A pass, valid for 9 days once the first attraction is visited, is $26.50; over 64, $20.50; ages 12-17, $13.50. CityPass is available from visitor information centers, participating attractions and most major hotels.

DID YOU KNOW?

Before the Pilgrims hired the Mayflower to take them to America, the ship was used to transport wine between France and England.

The first public library in America was built in Boston.

Boston Common is the oldest public park in the country.

Harvard is the nation's oldest university.

Dec. 25. Admission $7.50; over 65 and ages 3-11, $5.50. Reservations are recommended 24 hours in advance. Phone (617) 723-2500.

MUSEUM OF THE NATIONAL CENTER OF AFRO-AMERICAN ARTISTS, off Columbus Ave. and Seaver St. at 300 Walnut Ave., offers changing exhibits of works in various media by African-American artists worldwide. The museum is housed in a neo-Gothic mansion of Roxbury puddingstone and Nova Scotia sandstone. Allow 30 minutes minimum. Tues.-Sun. 1-5. Admission $4; over 64 and ages 6-16, $3. Phone (617) 442-8614.

★**NEW ENGLAND AQUARIUM** is on the city's waterfront at Central Wharf off Atlantic Ave. (T: Aquarium). The aquarium displays more than 12,000 fish and aquatic animals ranging from piranhas to penguins. An outdoor seal exhibit, free to the public, features a raised tank for visitors to view the animals above and below the water's surface.

In the west wing, a 6,000-square-foot gallery highlights changing exhibits. Rising from the center of the building is a four-story, circular glass tank containing a coral reef, more than 180,000 gallons of water and hundreds of tropical fish and other marine life, including sharks, turtles and moray eels. A colony of penguins is on the ground level.

"Edge of the Sea" lets visitors handle tidepool animals. Sea lion performances are staged daily at Discovery, the adjacent floating pavilion. Whale-watch cruises and "Science at Sea" harbor tours are offered April 1 to mid-October for a fee. Food is available.

Allow 2 hours minimum. Mon.-Fri. 9-6 (also Wed.-Thurs. 6-8 p.m.), Sat.-Sun. and holidays 9-7, July 1-Labor Day; Mon.-Fri. 9-5, Sat.-Sun. and holidays 9-6, rest of year. Closed Jan. 1 until noon, Thanksgiving and Dec. 25. Admission $12.50; over 59, $11.50; ages 3-11, $6.50. Phone (617) 973-5200. *See ad p. 109.*

SAVE **NICHOLS HOUSE MUSEUM,** 55 Mount Vernon St. (T: Park Street), is a Federal-style house in the heart of Beacon Hill that was the former home of Rose Standish Nichols, a prominent Bostonian. The house preserves the Nichols' 16th-19th century furnishings, which reflect the wealth and privilege that were characteristic of Beacon Hill and Boston's upper class. Tues.-Sat. 12:15-4:15, May-Oct.; Mon., Wed. and Sat. 12:15-4:15, Feb.-Apr. and Nov.-Dec. Closed July 4, Labor Day, Thanksgiving and Dec. 25. Admission $5, under 12 free. Phone (617) 227-6993.

★**OLD NORTH CHURCH** (Christ Church), 193 Salem St. at the foot of Hull St. (T: Haymarket), was built in 1723 and is the oldest church building in Boston. The first peal (bells) on this continent, some of the oldest in the world, sounded from the church in 1744. On the evening of April 18, 1775, a sexton displayed two lanterns in the steeple to signal the departure of the British from Boston. The steeple has been destroyed and replaced twice following violent storms; the present steeple dates from 1954.

Housed in the church are box pews, large windows and the pulpit from which President Ford initiated the celebration of the nation's Bicentennial. Daily 9-5; Sun. services at 9, 11 and 4; closed Thanksgiving. Free. Phone (617) 523-6676.

OLD SOUTH MEETING HOUSE, 310 Washington St. (T: State or Washington), was built in 1729 as a Puritan church. It was the site of many town meetings preceding the Revolutionary War, including those concerning British-imposed taxes and the Boston Massacre. A photograph exhibit illustrates the renovation of the meeting house, and an audio program features re-enactments of the most dramatic moments in its history.

Allow 30 minutes minimum. Daily 9:30-5, Apr.-Oct.; 10-4, rest of year. Closed Jan. 1, Thanksgiving and Dec. 24-25. Admission $3; over 62 and students with ID $2.50; ages 6-18, $1. Phone (617) 482-6439.

★ **OLD STATE HOUSE** is at Washington St. at the head of State St. (T: State). The building is on the site of the old 1657 Town House. The present structure, built in 1713, is considered to be Boston's oldest public building. Royal governors and provincial representatives presided at the state house before the Revolution. The Boston Massacre occurred at the east front in 1770, and the Declaration of Independence was read to Bostonians on July 18, 1776 from the balcony. In 1780 John Hancock was inaugurated at the state house as first governor of the commonwealth.

The Bostonian Society maintains the building as a museum of Boston history. The collection of items dates from 1630 to the 20th century and includes tea from the Boston Tea Party, a coat that belonged to John Hancock, a model of the USS *Constitution*, paintings, prints and other artifacts. Daily 9-5; closed Jan. 1, Thanksgiving and Dec. 25. Admission $3; over 62 and students with ID $2; ages 6-18, $1. AE, MC, VI. Phone (617) 720-3290.

PARK STREET CHURCH, Park and Tremont sts. (T: Park Street), was built in 1809 and was the scene of William Lloyd Garrison's first antislavery address in 1829. Tues.-Sat. 9-3:30, July-Aug.; by appointment rest of year. Free. Phone (617) 523-3383.

PAUL REVERE HOUSE, 19 North Sq. (T: Haymarket), was built about 1680 and is the oldest house in downtown Boston. The restored home, which Paul Revere owned 1770-1800, contains 17th- and 18th-century furnishings and Revere memorabilia. A Colonial herb garden and Revere-made bell are on the grounds. Daily 9:30-5:15, Apr. 15-Oct. 31; daily 9:30-4:15, Nov.-Dec. and Apr. 1-14; Tues.-Sun. 9:30-4:15,

rest of year. Closed Jan. 1, Thanksgiving and Dec. 25. Admission $2.50; over 62 and college students with ID $2; ages 5-17, $1. Phone (617) 523-2338.

PRUDENTIAL CENTER, between Huntington Ave. and Boylston St. (T: Copley or Prudential), is Boston's first unified business, civic and residential development. The 52-story, 28-acre complex features shops, restaurants, plazas, covered walkways, a hotel and a 3,000-car parking garage.

Prudential Tower Skywalk, on the 50th floor, offers a panorama of the city and suburbs. Daily 10-10. Admission $4; over 62 and ages 5-10, $3. Phone (617) 859-0648.

PUBLIC GARDEN, bounded by Boylston, Charles, Beacon and Arlington sts. (T: Arlington), is landscaped and accented with statuary. Allow 30 minutes minimum. Garden open daily dawn-dusk. Swan boats operate daily (weather permitting) 10-5, late June-Labor Day; 10-4, mid-Apr. to mid-June and day after Labor Day to mid-Sept. Garden free. Swan boat fare $1.75; senior citizens $1.50; under 12, 95c. Phone (617) 522-1966.

SAVE **THE SHIRLEY-EUSTIS HOUSE,** .25 mi. s. of Massachusetts Ave. at 33 Shirley St., was built in 1747 in the Palladian style for Royal Colonial

Governor William Shirley. The house also served as the residence of former Massachusetts Governor William Eustis around the turn of the 19th century, when it was remodeled in the Federal style. The mansion has been restored to reflect the combination of Georgian and Federal architecture and furnishings during the Eustis occupancy. Some furnishings are original.

Allow 1 hour minimum. Thurs.-Sun. noon-4, June-Sept. Admission $5; over 60 and under 14, $3. Phone (617) 442-2275.

SOLDIERS' MONUMENT is on Dorchester Heights. By fortifying these heights, George Washington drove the British from Boston on March 17, 1776.

STATE HOUSE is on Beacon St. at the head of Park St. (T: Park Street). The original brick front section, designed by Charles Bulfinch and completed in 1798, remains almost unchanged. Statues, historical paintings, transparencies of battle flags and war relics are displayed inside. Across the street, Shaw Memorial, a bronze bas-relief of Col. Robert Gould Shaw by Augustus Saint-Gaudens, recalls the first black regiment to serve in the Civil War. Mon.-Sat. 9-5; closed Jan. 1, Thanksgiving and Dec. 25. Guided tours are given Mon.-Fri. 10-3:30. Free. Phone (617) 727-3676 for events information.

TRINITY CHURCH, Copley Sq. (T: Copley), was consecrated in 1877. Romanesque in style, the church is considered by many to be Henry Hobson Richardson's greatest architectural work. The interior artwork was created by John LaFarge. Daily 8-6; guided tours after Sun. morning service (approximately 12:15 p.m.) and by appointment. Organ concerts are given Fri. at 12:15 p.m., Sept.-June. Free. Phone (617) 536-0944.

★ **USS CONSTITUTION—**
see Charlestown Navy Yard p. 104.

USS CONSTITUTION MUSEUM—
see Charlestown Navy Yard p. 104.

"WHITES OF THEIR EYES" is in the Bunker Hill Pavilion on the Freedom Trail next to the USS *Constitution* in Charlestown (T: Community College or North Station). A multimedia re-enactment of the Battle of Bunker Hill using sound and visual effects creates the sensation of being in the midst of the battle. Daily 9:30-4:30, Apr.-Nov. Closed Thanksgiving. Admission $3; over 62, $2; ages 5-16, $1.50; family rate $8. Phone (617) 241-7575.

What To Do
Sightseeing

   Boat Tours

Sightseeing cruises of Boston Harbor and the Boston Harbor Islands are offered at Long Wharf throughout the summer by Boston Harbor Cruises; phone (617) 227-4321.

Skyline Cruises Inc. operates cruises along the Charles River. Boats depart from the dock behind the Museum of Science from mid-May to late September; phone (617) 523-2169.

BOSTON TO CAPE COD CRUISE offers one-way or round-trip transportation from Commonwealth Pier at the World Trade Center in Boston to MacMillan Wharf in Provincetown. The 3-hour cruise departs daily at 9 from Boston and at 3:30 from Provincetown, June 19-Sept. 10; Fri.-Mon. at 9 (Boston) and 3:30 (Provincetown), Memorial Day-June 18 and Sept. 11-Sept. 30. Round-trip fare $30; senior citizens $23; ages 3-12, $21. One-way fare $18; senior citizens $15, ages 3-12, $14. MC, VI. Phone (617) 457-1428.

THE LIBERTY FLEET OF TALL SHIPS sails from Boston Waterboat Marina on Long Wharf. Passengers aboard the 80-foot schooner *Liberty* can hoist sail, steer or simply enjoy the sights of Boston Harbor. "Shipwrecked!" is an on-board musical performance that takes a lighthearted look at Boston's maritime history and legends. A 3-hour Sunday brunch cruise on the 125-foot *Liberty Clipper* also is available. Allow 2 hours minimum. Cruises depart daily at noon, 3 and 6, Memorial Day weekend-Sept. 30. Fare $25-$60; under 13, $12.50-$25. Reservations are required. DS, MC, VI. Phone (617) 742-0333.

THE SPIRIT OF BOSTON, which departs from Commonwealth Pier on Northern Ave. at the World Trade Center, offers narrated lunch cruises of Boston Harbor. Lunch cruises depart daily at 11:30, Apr.-Oct. Dinner cruises depart daily at 6 p.m., Apr.-Sept. Closed holidays. Fare for lunch cruise $28-$45. Fare for dinner cruise $47-$73. Reservations are recommended. AE, CB, MC, VI. Phone (617) 457-1450.

Bus and Trolley Tours

Tours encompassing both the city and its environs are available. SAVE Gray Line of Boston, (617) 236-2148, provides a variety of excursions; especially popular is its Beantown Trolley, which makes 22 stops along the Freedom Trail and lets passengers get on and off at attractions along the way.

BOSTON DUCK TOURS depart from the Prudential Center, 101 Huntington Ave. (T: Copley or Prudential). Narrated tours of Boston landmarks are given inside renovated World War II amphibious landing vehicles, which splash into the Charles River for a waterside view of the city. Allow 1 hour, 30 minutes minimum. Tours are given daily every half-hour 9 a.m.-1 hour before dusk, Apr. 1-Nov. 28. Fare $21; over 62, military with ID $18; ages 4-12, $11; under 4, 25c. MC, VI. Phone (617) 723-3825.

BOSTON TOURS-FROM SUBURBAN HOTELS, which pick up passengers from nearly 50 hotels, offer narrated tours of historic Boston, Cambridge and Charlestown. The 6.5-hour tours travel along the Freedom Trail and offers views of Bunker Hill Monument, the waterfront, Copley Square, Beacon Hill, Victorian Back Bay and Harvard University. The 20-passenger vehicles visit Old North Church; Faneuil Hall; Quincy Market; and the Charlestown Navy Yard, where the USS *Constitution* is berthed. Tours depart daily, Apr. 6 to mid-Nov.; pickup times vary. Fare $40; ages 10-16, $10. Reservations are required. Phone (781) 899-1454.

JACK MAYFIELD TOURS, which make pickups at downtown and North Shore hotels, offer escorted excursions of Boston and nearby sights. The 6-hour tours, conducted in air-conditioned 13-passenger vehicles, examine the culture, architecture and history of the Back Bay area. Stops include John Hancock Observatory, Christian Science Mapparium, Faneuil Hall/Quincy Market Place, Paul Revere House, Old North Church and Bull and Finch Pub. The Freedom Trail, Charlestown, Beacon Hill, Cambridge and MIT areas also are covered. Daily 10-4. Fare $30. Phone (978) 921-0255.

OLD TOWN TROLLEY TOURS depart from Central Wharf or can be boarded at 16 stops along the route. The 1-hour, 40-minute narrated tours feature more than 100 points of interest including the Freedom Trail, Faneuil Hall, the Boston Tea Party Ship and Old North Church. Tours depart daily 9-dusk; closed Thanksgiving and Dec. 25. Fare $21; ages 4-12, $8. Phone (617) 269-7010.

 ### Walking Tours

From May through October, Boston By Foot offers various walking tours. Allow 1 hour, 30 minutes for each tour except the hour-long children's tour. Tours are given regardless of weather, and reservations are not required. Each tour is $8; ages 6-12, $6. Phone (617) 367-2345 or 367-3766 for information.

The Beacon Hill tour leaves from the foot of the State House steps Mon.-Fri. at 5:30 p.m., Sat. at 10 and Sun. at 2. Tours of Victorian Back Bay depart from the Trinity Church steps Fri.-Sat. at 10.

Tours starting at the statue of Samuel Adams in front of Faneuil Hall are the Heart of the Freedom Trail tour Tues.-Sat. at 10; the Waterfront tour Fri. at 5:30 and Sun. at 10; the North End tour Sat. at 2; Boston Underground on Sun. at 2; and Boston by Little Feet, a children's tour, Mon. and Sat. at 10 and Sun. at 2. Special tours are scheduled once a month.

Walking tour maps of the Black Heritage Trail can be obtained from the Afro-American Museum, the Freedom Trail Information Booth and

the National Park Service Visitor Center. Conducted tours are offered daily at 10, noon and 2, May 30-Labor Day. Phone (617) 742-5415.

A self-guiding walking tour, Harborwalk, focuses on Boston's cultural and maritime history. The 1-mile tour begins at the Old State House and ends at the Boston Tea Party Ship. Brochures outlining the tour are available at the Boston Common Visitor Center, New England Aquarium, Children's Museum and Boston Tea Party Ship.

Freedom Trail Walking Tour

The names of sites listed in detail in the Attractions section are printed in bold type. Even if you do not tour a listed site, reading the listing when you reach that point will make the tour more interesting.

Begin at the city's central park, **The Boston Common**, and look for the information kiosk in the center of the pedestrian mall on Tremont St. The Freedom Trail is directly north of this point. From the information kiosk cross the Common to the **State House**, recognizable by its gold dome. Return to the trail at Beacon St. and turn left. The red line will cross Beacon St. and follow the edge of the Common to **Park Street Church**.

Beyond the church is the **Granary Burying Ground**. Turn left when exiting the graveyard and continue north. Follow the stripe 1 block to the gray granite **King's Chapel**. Farther down School St. are the statue of Ben Franklin and Boston's old City Hall. At the end of School St. are the Old Corner Bookstore on the left corner and the **Old South Meeting House** diagonally across the street to the right.

Leaving the meetinghouse, turn right down Washington St. and go 2 blocks to the National Park Service Visitor Center and the **Old State House**. The trail resumes on the north side of the Old State House and runs to the intersection, where a circle of stones marks the site of the Boston Massacre.

Cross State St. and Congress St. and turn left to **Faneuil Hall**. Follow the stripe around the north corner of the building and across North St. Walk down Union St. and bear right down narrow Marshall St. just beyond the Union Oyster House. At the end of Marshall St. cross Blackstone St. and go through the pedestrian passageway beneath the elevated highway.

This section of the tour leads through the North End. Proceed across Cross St. and turn left at the corner of Hanover St. Walk 1 block and turn right onto Richmond St. At the next intersection turn left onto North St. and walk to the **Paul Revere House**, a half block down and on the left. Turn left on Prince St., which leads back to Hanover St., and turn right. Follow Hanover St. to St. Stephen's Church.

On the left are the equestrian statue of Paul Revere and the **Old North Church** directly behind it. Walk through the mall to enter the Old North Church. Cross Salem St. to resume the trail and walk directly ahead up Hull St. to Copp's Hill Burial Ground. Continue along Hull St. down the hill to Commercial St. and cross. Turn left and continue to the Charlestown Bridge.

Proceed across the bridge and turn right onto Chelsea St., then right onto Chamber St. (a gate and stairway provide access from the bridge to Paul Revere Landing Park and the **Charles River Dam Visitors' Information Center**). At the foot of the street cross Constitution Rd. and turn left to the **Charlestown Navy Yard** and the **USS *Constitution***.

Return along the same side of Constitution Rd. for 50 yards, then cross the street and go through the pedestrian underpass. Cross Chelsea St. and turn right. Bear left onto Chestnut St. and go 1 block. Turn left onto Adams St. and right on Winthrop St. This leads to **Bunker Hill Monument**. Return to the starting point by taking any bus marked "Downtown," found by walking down Monument to Main St.

Sports and Recreation

Boston is a mecca for spectator sports enthusiasts. The city's **baseball** team, the Boston Red Sox, (617) 267-1700, plays in Fenway Park. Its **football** team, the New England Patriots, plays at Foxboro Stadium, in Foxboro, (800) 543-1776. The Boston Bruins, (617) 624-1912, are the city's **hockey** team, and the Boston Celtics, (617) 523-6050, are perennial contenders on the **basketball** court; both teams play in FleetCenter, (617) 624-1050. From September through May, Boston's college and university teams supplement these professional activities.

Horse racing takes place at Suffolk Downs Racetrack in East Boston. Flat races are held all year; phone (617) 567-3900 for a schedule. **Dog racing** fans can watch the greyhounds throughout the year at Wonderland Dog Track, (781) 284-1300, in Revere and at Raynham Park, (508) 824-4071, in Raynham.

Note: Policies concerning admittance of children to pari-mutuel betting facilities vary. Phone for information.

Boating is popular on the Charles and Mystic rivers, in the harbor and bay and on inland lakes. Charter services for deep-sea **fishing** are along Atlantic Avenue. The Inland Fishing Guide is published by the Massachusetts Division of Fisheries and Wildlife. The Massachusetts Saltwater Fishing Guide can be obtained from the Massachusetts Commerce and Development Department, 100 Cambridge St., Boston, MA 02202; phone (617) 727-3221.

Golf is played on nine- and 18-hole public courses in the area. It is a popular sport on summer weekends, so plan to arrive early or phone in advance to reserve a tee time. **Tennis** can be played on several public courts in the city. **Ice**

© AAA

BOSTON
FREEDOM TRAIL
WALKING TOUR

P PUBLIC PARKING

RAPID TRANSIT
■ STATION

WARREN ST.
HIGH
Bunker
Hill
Monument
★

99

AUSTIN ST.

MONUMENT AVE.

MAIN ST.

WINTHROP ST.

ADAMS ST.

PARK ST.

CHESTNUT

Constitution
Museum ◆

93

RUTHERFORD AVE.

CHELSEA

MYSTIC RIVER BRIDGE

1

USS
Constitution
★

CONSTITUTION RD.
Whites of
Their Eyes ■

Charlestown
Navy Yard

WARREN AVE.

Charles
River
Dam
Visitors' Info.
Ctr. ■

Cambridge

River

CHARLESTOWN BRIDGE

JOHN

Scale in miles
0   0.2
Scale in Kilometers
0   0.3

Charles

CHARLES
RIVER
DAM

NASHUA

LEVERETT
CIRCLE

MARTHA RD.

28

CHARLES

COMMERCIAL

CHARTER ST.

HULL ST.

N. PRINCE

SHEAFE ST.

SNOWHILL ST.

Old North
Church

3

Fleet Center
Boston Garden
& North Sta.

F

WASHINGTON

Paul
Revere
Mall

Paul
Revere
Statue

CAUSEWAY ST.

PORTLAND ST.

MERRIMAC ST.

FITZGERALD

SALEM ST.

HANOVER ST.

FLEET ST.

Paul Revere
House

NEW ATLANTIC

STANIFORD ST.

State
Service
Center

CHARDON ST.

NEW

SUDBURY

CONGRESS ST.

Hay-
Market
Sq.

BLACKSTONE

RICHMOND ST.

Harrison
Gray Otis
House ■

P

J.F. Kennedy
Federal Building

MARSHALL ST.

UNION ST.

NORTH

EXPRESSWAY

Columbus
Park

CAMBRIDGE

BOWDOIN ST.

SOMERSET ST.

Boston
City
Hall

Faneuil
Hall ★

Quincy
Market

New England
Aquarium

Louisburg
Square

VERNON ST.

Pemberton
Sq.

King's
Chapel

Court
Sq.

COURT

BEN
FRANKLIN
STATUE &
OLD CITY
HALL

BOSTON
MASSACRE
SITE

STATE ST.

CENTRAL

MILK ST.

93

MT.
WILLOW ST.
WALNUT ST.

State
House

NAT'L PARK
SERVICE VISITOR
CTR.

OLD
STATE
HOUSE

KILBY ST.

MILK

PEARL

1

SPRUCE ST.

Granary
Burying
Ground

SCHOOL ST.

WATER

CHARLES
BEACON

Frog
Pond

PARK ST.

START
TOUR

Info
Kiosk

BROMFIELD ST.

PROVINCE ST.

OLD
CORNER
BOOK
STORE

MILK

OLD SOUTH
MEETING
HOUSE

ARCH ST.

P

CONGRESS ST.

PURCHASE ST.

3

Boston

TREMONT

WASHINGTON

TEMPLE PL.

Park Street
Church

FRANKLIN ST.

DEVONSHIRE ST.

TUNNEL

Common

P

Fort Point
Channel

2011-F

skating is available at the Public Garden as well as at many indoor rinks. For information on golf, tennis and ice skating facilities, phone the Metropolitan District Commission at (617) 727-5250.

Horseback riding opportunities are plentiful. Some of the longest and most scenic bridle paths are in the Blue Hills Reservation, where rates average $9-$10 an hour. Check a telephone directory for a complete listing of stables and riding academies in the Boston area.

Approximately 21 miles northwest in Tewksbury, licensed drivers can drive three-quarter-scale formula Grand Prix race cars on a one-third-mile track at the New England Grand Prix, 2087 Main St. (SR 38); phone (978) 658-4134.

Shopping

In the early 1800s New England was the cradle of American manufacturing, and Boston was its pre-eminent city. The harnessing of water power, the development of mills and the building of a fleet of ships to carry its goods throughout the world made Boston an industrial nexus. Stacked in its warehouses and shops were goods from the nearby mills, and lining its docks were silks, spices and porcelain brought from the other side of the world by the swift and graceful clipper ships.

The spectrum of goods that once made Boston the country's commercial center is still found in its marketplaces. Such modern markets as Copley Place and Quincy Market are symbol and substance of the city's vitality. Encompassing an entire block, Copley Place, Huntington Avenue and Dartmouth Street, is a delicate pink-marble hive of cosmopolitan elegance, with such stores as Gucci, Neiman-Marcus and Yves Saint Laurent setting the tone for this collection of shops, restaurants and hotels.

Unlike Copley Place's modern elegance, Quincy Market, Merchants Row and Clinton Street, reflects its New England origins with its classic granite facade. Vendors offer items displayed in pushcarts in the Bull Market, which flanks the North and South markets. In these two buildings, shops offer merchandise ranging from clothes to kitchen utensils.

A short walk from the marketplace is Boston's original shopping area, Downtown Crossing, a pedestrian mall extending along Washington Street from School to West and Bedford streets, and along Winter and Summer streets between Tremont and Chauncy. Anchored by Filene's Basement and Macy's and supplemented by specialty stores, the Crossing offers a variety of shopping opportunities.

At Filene's Basement, goods from the everyday to designer labels are marked down on a progressively lower scale the longer they remain on the racks. Of interest to collectors of original old advertising media is the Nostalgia Factory at 51 N. Margin St.; the store also features original movie posters dating from the silent movie era to the latest releases.

Across from the Public Garden are twin pillars of respectability, the Ritz-Carlton Hotel and Burberrys, gateways to fashionable Newbury Street. Specialty stores such as Brooks Brothers, F.A.O. Schwarz and Laura Ashley, as well as galleries and cafes, occupy the restored 19th-century townhouses lining the street. Louis, a haberdashery for men and women, and Shreve, Crump and Low, jewelers to the proper Bostonian, are two shopping landmarks on Boylston Street, which parallels Newbury Street.

Complementing the specialty and department stores of Back Bay is Antique Row, on Charles Street at the foot of Beacon Hill, where everything from bric-a-brac to fine Oriental antiques can be found. Beyond the central marketplaces are other areas: Chestnut Hill Mall in Newton, which contains Bloomingdales and numerous specialty shops; and Cambridge's Harvard Square, with renowned Harvard Cooperative Society, and CambridgeSide Galleria, with Lechmere and Filene's.

Boston also is known for such discount stores as Barnes & Noble Booksellers in Downtown Crossing, the Eastern Butcher Block, next to the Tea Party Museum, and John Barry on Kneeland Street.

Theater and Concerts

Boston offers musical performances excellent in quality and practically limitless in variety. Symphony Hall, at Huntington and Massachusetts avenues, is home to the Boston Pops and Boston Symphony orchestras. Regular season symphony performances are attended primarily by season subscribers, but seats usually are available for most concerts. Tickets, including those for open rehearsals, can be reserved in person at the box office or obtained up to 4 weeks in advance; phone (617) 266-1492.

The Boston Ballet Company offers tickets by subscription, but they can be obtained for individual performances 1 week prior to the performance; phone (617) 695-6950. Wang Center for the Performing Arts, 270 Tremont St., offers ballet and other types of performances; phone (617) 482-9393. The Boston Lyric Opera Company presents three productions each season at the Emerson Majestic Theatre, 219 Tremont St.; phone (617) 542-6772 for ticket and schedule information.

Spring heralds the "Pops" season in Boston. The Boston Pops Orchestra performs at Symphony Hall late April through late June. In July members of the Pops and the Boston Symphony join to present free open-air concerts in Hatch Memorial Shell on the Charles River. Concerts start at 8 p.m., but arrive early for the best seating on the grass.

Free chamber music concerts and individual recitals are given in palatial splendor at Isabella Stewart Gardner Museum *(see attraction listing p. 107)*. Also free are concerts, musicals and recitals by the students and teaching staff of the New England Conservatory of Music.

Area colleges and universities provide other sources of musical entertainment. Boston University has a fine opera department, MIT presents a chapel organ series, and Harvard and Radcliffe offer choral and band concerts. *(For attraction listings of Harvard and MIT, see Cambridge in the Vicinity section p. 117.)*

Throughout the year popular musical performers come to Boston for individual concerts. *Boston by Week*, a monthly publication, and the weekly *Phoenix* are good sources for schedules and prices.

Out-of-town tryouts for Broadway plays often mean runs in Boston's legitimate theaters. They include Colonial Theatre, (617) 426-9366, 100 Boylston St.; Shubert Theatre, (617) 482-9393, 265 Tremont St.; and the Wilbur, (617) 423-4008, 246 Tremont St.

Such repertory companies as Boston Repertory Theatre and Charles Playhouse offer a more experimental bill of fare. The long-running play "Shear Madness," a humorous murder mystery which differs every time it is presented, is featured at Charles Playhouse; phone (617) 426-5225. The Boston Center for the Arts presents plays and art exhibits. The Theatre Lobby,

216 Hanover St., presents musicals, plays and weekend cabarets; phone (617) 227-9872.

Universities and colleges in the area offer theater during the winter season. Of good caliber and often benefiting from the talents of notable visiting directors are Brandeis University's Spingold Theatre series and the Loeb Drama Festival, sponsored by Harvard. Tickets can be obtained at BosTix, the ticket booth next to Faneuil Hall, Mon.-Sat. 11-6, Sun. noon-6. Half-price tickets are available on the day of the performance.

Most cinemas in downtown Boston show single features, often on a reserved-seat basis, at an average price of $7. Classic, repertory and foreign films are offered at universities and neighborhood theaters, usually at a lower admission.

Special Events

Boston bases many of its annual celebrations on past events that shaped the character of the city as well as the nation. St. Patrick's Day on March 17 celebrates not only Boston's Irish heritage but also Evacuation Day, when the British troops left the city in 1776. The Battle of Bunker Hill Celebration is held on the anniversary of that June 17, 1775, battle.

Harborfest on July 4 commemorates the birth of the nation with a turnaround ceremony for the historic USS *Constitution*, which is physically turned around in the Charlestown Navy Yard to ensure equal weathering. Other activities surrounding this event include a Chowderfest competition between downtown restaurants and a concert by the Boston Pops on the Esplanade, followed by fireworks. At Old South Meeting House the Boston Tea Party is re-enacted by costumed patriots in mid-December.

Boston also is known for sports competition of impressive proportions. The Boston Marathon, held the third Monday in April, is one of the world's best-known foot races. Female runners pound the pavement around downtown Boston during the Tufts 10K on the Sunday of Columbus Day weekend. Head of the Charles Regatta, an internationally contested sculling event, draws hundreds of spectators to the banks of the Charles River on the third Sunday in October.

Noteworthy are the Italian Feasts that take place in the North End every weekend from the last weekend in June through the last weekend in August. Sponsored by the individual religious organizations dedicated to each saint, the feasts include street vendors, various types of foods, entertainment and a parade in which a plaster cast of each saint is carried on the shoulders of the faithful.

The New England Handbell Festival takes place in November at Faneuil Hall. Held outdoors, often in brisk temperatures, is Boston's First Night, a New Year's Eve celebration featuring more than 100 arts and entertainment groups and a children's parade.

The Boston Vicinity

ACTON (D-1) pop. 17,900

THE DISCOVERY MUSEUMS, 177 Main St., consist of two museums. The Children's Discovery Museum is a Victorian house with 10 theme rooms designed for preschoolers and toddlers. Presented are exhibits about dinosaurs, a water discovery area, a creative play space and a rainbow room. Also on the grounds are a climbable dinosaur mascot and picnic tables. Science Discovery Museum has 10 theme areas with more than 100 exhibits, inviting exploration and experimentation.

Tues.-Sun. 9-4:30, late June-early Sept.; Tues. and Thurs.-Fri. 1-4:30, Wed. 9-6, Sat.-Sun. 9-4:30, rest of year. Single-museum admission $6, senior citizens $5. Both museums (same day) $9, senior citizens $8. MC, VI. Phone (978) 264-4200, or TDD (978) 264-0030.

AMESBURY (A-6) pop. 15,000, elev. 26'

At the foot of Lake Gardner, Amesbury was once an important shipbuilding center. SAVE Mary Baker Eddy Historic House, 277 Main St., was the home of Eddy, the founder of Christian Science. Initially the Squire Bagley house, it contains original Bagley furnishings; phone (800) 277-8943.

Alliance for Amesbury: 5 Market Sq., Amesbury, MA 01913; phone (978) 388-3178.

SAVE **JOHN GREENLEAF WHITTIER HOME,** 86 Friend St., was the 1836-92 home of the abolitionist and author, whose works included "Snow-Bound" and "The Barefoot Boy." The house remains almost unchanged and contains original furnishings, portraits, engravings, manuscripts and a large portion of Whittier's library. Tues.-Sat. 10-4, May-Oct.; by appointment rest of year. Closed July 4, Thanksgiving and Dec. 25. Admission $3.50; under 18, $1. Phone (978) 388-1337.

 RECREATIONAL ACTIVITIES

Summer Activities

- **Amesbury Sports Park**, 12 Hunt Rd., Amesbury, MA 01913. Winter activities also are offered. Daily 10-10, Memorial Day-Labor Day; Tues.-Fri. 3-9:30, Sat.-Sun. and holidays 9 a.m-9:30 p.m., Oct.-Dec. Phone (978) 388-5788.

ANDOVER (B-6) pop. 29,200, elev. 89'

ADDISON GALLERY OF AMERICAN ART, off SR 28 on Chapel Ave. at Phillips Academy, contains a collection of ship models and American artwork from the 18th century to the present. Allow 30 minutes minimum. Tues.-Sat. 10-5, Sun. 1-5, Sept.-July; closed major holidays. Free. Phone (978) 749-4015.

ANDOVER HISTORICAL SOCIETY, 97 Main St., features period rooms, 18th- and 19th-century exhibits, a garden and an 1819 barn. Guided tours are available. Allow 1 hour minimum. Tues.-Sat. 9-5, Mon. by appointment; closed holidays. Admission $4; over 64 and under 17, $2. Phone (978) 475-2236.

ROBERT S. PEABODY MUSEUM OF ARCHEOLOGY, Phillips and Main sts., has changing and permanent exhibits about American Indian cultures including New England, the Southwest, the Southeast and Mexico. Tues.-Sat. noon-5, day after Labor Day-July 31; closed holidays. Free. Phone (978) 749-4490.

ARLINGTON (E-2) pop. 44,600, elev. 46'

The most significant event in Arlington's history occurred April 19, 1775, when British troops retreating from Concord and Lexington met Minutemen from at least 13 towns in several separate skirmishes. By the close of the day the British counted 40 men killed and 80 wounded, while the Americans lost at least 25, with 10 wounded and three captured.

The town's first industry, cotton manufacturing, began in the late 18th century. Wool cards, invented by resident Amos Whittemore, greatly improved the process of textile production. In the 1830s Gage, Hittinger Co. began cutting ice from Spy Pond and selling it to tropical countries, thus establishing a new industry. At the turn of the 20th century, when Boston's trolley line reached Arlington's boundaries, the town became a suburb of Boston.

Originally an abandoned railroad line, the Minuteman Bike Trail is popular with cyclists in summer and cross-country skiers in winter. The 11.2-mile trail begins in East Arlington and continues through Arlington, Lexington and Bedford.

Arlington Chamber of Commerce: 1 Whittemore Park, Arlington, MA 02474; phone (781) 643-4600.

JASON RUSSELL HOUSE AND GEORGE ABBOT SMITH HISTORY MUSEUM, 7 Jason St., was the scene of fierce hand-to-hand combat between British soldiers and Minutemen during the battle of April 19, 1775. The 1740 house contains some 18th-century furniture and artifacts. The adjacent Smith Museum features an exhibit about Arlington history. Tues.-Sat. 1-5, otherwise by appointment, Mar.-Dec.; closed holidays. Admission $2; ages 4-13, 50c. Phone (781) 648-4300.

JEFFERSON CUTTER HOUSE, jct. US 3 and SRs 60 and 2A (Massachusetts Ave.), is a restored 1832 home featuring displays about area history. A gallery presenting the works of sculptor Cyrus E. Dallin as well as works by local contemporary artists is featured. A visitor information center and the chamber of commerce also are on the site. Tours are offered by appointment. Daily noon-4; closed holidays. Donations. Phone (781) 641-0595.

OLD SCHWAMB MILL, 17 Mill Ln., is a living-history museum exhibiting a working collection of shaft- and pulley belt-driven antique wood-working machinery. Visitors can tour the mill and view the manufacturing process. Demonstrations of elliptical machinery and oval picture frame turning are given Tuesdays from 10 to 2. Allow 30 minutes minimum. Mon.-Fri. 10-2. Free. Phone (781) 643-0554.

BEVERLY (D-3) pop. 38,200, elev. 23′

Founded in 1626 as an extension of Salem, Beverly was named after a town in Yorkshire, England. In 1775 the local schooner *Hannah* was commissioned and armed by Gen. George Washington as the first ship in his Continental Navy. Beverly remained an important port during the first 2 years of the Revolutionary War.

North of Boston Convention and Visitors Bureau: 17 Peabody Sq., Peabody, MA 01960; phone (978) 977-7760 or (800) 742-5306.

BEVERLY HISTORICAL SOCIETY MUSEUMS, 117 Cabot St., is an umbrella organization managing three local historic homes: Balch House, Cabot House and Hale Farm. Phone (978) 922-1186.

Balch House, 448 Cabot St., stands on part of a land grant given to the "Old Planters" in 1635. Occupied by the Balch family until 1914, this 1636 frame house is one of the oldest in the country. Rooms are furnished in period. Guided tours are conducted Tues.-Sat. 11-4, Sun. 1-4, May 14-Oct. 18; closed holidays. Admission $2; over 64, $1.50; ages 6-12, $1. Combination ticket with Cabot and Hale houses $4. Phone (978) 922-1186.

SEDGWICK GARDENS AT LONG HILL RESERVATION is off SR 128N exit 18, then 1 mi. n. on SR 22 to 572 Essex St. This was the summer estate of Mr. and Mrs. Ellery Sedgwick, who built it in 1921 and modeled it after a Charleston home of the early 1800s. The surrounding fields, woods, wetlands and formal gardens have more than 1,500 varieties of trees, shrubs and flowers, many labeled. Nature trails traverse the grounds. A tour of the house and garden is offered by appointment. Grounds open daily 8-dusk. House and garden tour $5. Garden admission by donation. Phone (978) 921-1944.

BROOKLINE (E-2) pop. 54,700, elev. 43′

FREDERICK LAW OLMSTED NATIONAL HISTORIC SITE is 2 blks. s. of SR 9 at 99 Warren St. Frederick Law Olmsted, the designer of New York City's Central Park, worked and lived in the house from 1883 until his retirement a decade later. The estate reflects Olmsted's design principle that nature and buildings can exist in harmony. In the house and office are drawings, plans, photographs and models of the Boston park system. A 15-minute videotape introduces his life and work. Guided tours are available. Fri.-Sun. 10-4:30. Donations. Phone (617) 566-1689.

JOHN FITZGERALD KENNEDY NATIONAL HISTORIC SITE, 83 Beals St., was the birthplace of the 35th president of the United States. The house has been restored to its 1917 appearance and contains some original furnishings. Guided tours are given Wed.-Sun. at 10:45, 11:45, 1, 2, 3 and 4, mid-Mar. through last Sat. in Nov. Admission $2, under 16 free. Phone (617) 566-7937.

SAVE **MUSEUM OF TRANSPORTATION,** 15 Newton St. in Larz Anderson Park overlooking Boston, is in a historic carriage house. The museum has a collection of carriages, bicycles and antique and classic cars dating from 1899. Changing exhibits reflect the impact of the automobile on society. Guided tours are available by appointment. Museum open Tues.-Sun. 10-5; closed Thanksgiving and Dec. 25. Admission $5; over 65, students with ID and ages 4-17, $3. Phone (617) 522-6547.

CAMBRIDGE (E-3) pop. 95,800, elev. 48′

See map page 118.

Newtowne, as Cambridge first was known, began as an outpost for the government of the Massachusetts Bay Colony, but it became the pre-eminent center of learning with the founding of a college. The college's first major benefactor, John Harvard, left his library and half his estate to the new college. In his honor the General Court christened the college Harvard and also ordered that Newtowne be called Cambridge after the town where many Puritans had been educated.

Harvard played a major role in shaping the future of Cambridge as well as educating those who fashioned the future of the Colony and the country. Historians George Bancroft and John Fiske, poets Ralph Waldo Emerson and James Russell Lowell, Presidents John Adams and John F. Kennedy, and Supreme Court Justices Oliver Wendell Holmes and Louis Brandeis are among its graduates who left their imprints on the culture, history and institutions of this country.

Harvard graduates were not the only ones shaping history. On Cambridge Common, George Washington first took command of the Continental Army in 1775 and, from his headquarters on

Brattle Street, directed the siege of Boston. Four years later the first popularly elected constitutional convention met at the Cambridge meetinghouse and drew up the state constitution. This document became a model for the U.S. Constitution.

For the first 200 years Cambridge remained a quiet village of farms and a center of learning. However, by the mid-19th century it had incorporated major industrial areas, which thrived on trade with Boston. Such publishing houses as Little-Brown were founded, and Lever Bros. and other firms transformed Cambridge into a manufacturing center. The city's traditional industries have given way to firms specializing in research and development, consulting and high-technology.

Cambridge Office for Tourism: 18 Brattle St. #352, Cambridge, MA 02138; phone (617) 441-2884 or (800) 862-5678.

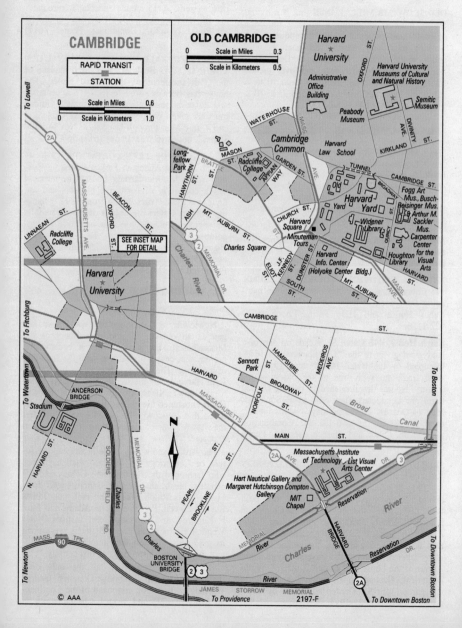

Self-guiding tours: Maps of Old Cambridge, which include historic sites in and around Harvard Square, are available for $2 from the information booth in Harvard Square.

★**HARVARD UNIVERSITY**, with an information center at 1350 Massachusetts Ave., is one of the oldest universities in the country, having been founded in 1636. In and around the historic "Yard" at Harvard Square, buildings represent the history of architecture in America. They range from Colonial-style Massachusetts Hall, built in 1720; the 19th-century work of Charles Bulfinch; University Hall; Henry Hobson Richardson's late 19th-century Sever Hall; and the contemporary style of Le Corbusier's Carpenter Center for the Visual Arts.

Guided tours leave the center Mon.-Sat. at 10, 11:15, 2 and 3:15, Sun. at 1:30 and 3, mid-June through Aug. 31; Mon.-Fri. at 10 and 2, Sat. at 2, mid-Sept. through May 31. Free. Phone (617) 495-1573.

Arthur M. Sackler Museum, 485 Broadway, contains Harvard's collections of Asian, Islamic and ancient art. Holdings include one of the world's finest collections of ancient Chinese jades, cave reliefs and bronzes as well as Japanese woodblock prints, Roman sculpture, Greek vases and Persian and Indian miniature paintings. Guided tours are available Wednesdays in July and August.

Mon.-Sat. 10-5, Sun. 1-5; closed holidays. Guided tours are given Mon.-Fri. at 2, Sept.-June; Wed. at 2, rest of year. Admission (including Busch-Reisinger Museum and Fogg Art Museum) $5; over 59, $4; college students with ID $3; under 18 free; free to all Wed. 10-5 and Sat. 10-noon. Phone (617) 495-9400.

Busch-Reisinger Museum, 32 Quincy St., reached via the second floor of Fogg Art Museum, features masterpieces of Central and Northern European art created 1880-1980, especially Vienna Succession art, German expressionism, 1920s abstraction, decorative arts and contemporary art.

Allow 30 minutes minimum. Mon.-Sat. 10-5, Sun. 1-5; closed holidays. Guided tours are given Mon.-Fri. at 1, Sept.-June; Wed. at 1, rest of year. Admission (including Arthur M. Sackler Museum and Fogg Art Museum) $5; over 59, $4; college students with ID $3; under 18 free; free to all Wed. 10-5 and Sat. 10-noon. Phone (617) 495-9400.

Carpenter Center for the Visual Arts, 24 Quincy St., was designed by Le Corbusier. The center exhibits contemporary art and video installations in the main floor lobby. Also housed in the building are the Department of Visual and Environmental Studies and the Harvard Film Archive, which screens films nightly. Mon.-Sat. 9 a.m.-11 p.m., Sun. noon-10. Center free. Films $6; senior citizens and students $5. Phone (617) 495-3251.

Fogg Art Museum, 32 Quincy St., houses sculpture, paintings, prints, drawings, photographs and decorative arts from Europe and North America, from the middle ages to the present. Open Mon.-Sat. 10-5, Sun. 1-5; closed holidays. Tours are given Mon.-Fri. at 11, Sept.-June; Wed. at 11, rest of year. Admission (including Busch-Reisinger Museum and Arthur M. Sackler Museum) $5; over 59, $4; college students with ID $3; under 18 free; free to all Wed. 10-5 and Sat. 10-noon. Phone (617) 495-9400.

★**Harvard University Museums of Cultural and Natural History**, with entrances at 26 Oxford St. and 11 Divinity Ave., houses four museums. Founded in 1866, Peabody Museum of Archeology and Ethnology has an extensive collection of Maya artifacts. Other areas covered include the Pacific Islands, Africa, South America and the Indians of North America.

Geological and Mineralogical Museum contains a large, systematically arranged collection of minerals, gemstones and agates. Glass representations of more than 800 plant species are shown in the Botanical Museum. The Museum of Comparative Zoology has exhibits ranging from the earliest fossil invertebrates and reptiles to modern fish and reptiles.

Mon.-Sat. 9-5, Sun. 1-5; closed Jan. 1, July 4, Thanksgiving and Dec. 25. Admission (includes all four museums) $5; over 65 and students with ID $4; ages 3-13, $3; free to all Sat. 9-noon. Phone (617) 495-3045.

Houghton Library, inside Harvard Yard, next to Widener Library, is a major rare book and manuscript library. Its more than 400,000 rare books and 5 million manuscripts support individual research, a lecture series and a variety of exhibitions during the year. Mon.-Fri. 9-5, Sat. 9-1. Free. Phone (617) 495-2440.

Semitic Museum, 6 Divinity Ave., features exhibits about the Sphinx and the Egyptian pyramids. More than 40,000 items from excavations in areas such as Cyprus and Mesopotamia are displayed. Allow 30 minutes minimum. Mon.-Fri. 10-4, Sun. 1-4; closed holidays. Free. Phone (617) 495-4631.

★**MASSACHUSETTS INSTITUTE OF TECHNOLOGY**, with its main building at 77 Massachusetts Ave., was founded by William Barton Rogers as a school where students could learn "exactly and thoroughly the fundamental principles of positive science with application to the industrial arts." It was chartered in 1861 and moved to this site in 1916.

The institute comprises the Schools of Architecture and Planning, Engineering, Humanities and Social Science, and Whitaker College of Health Science and Technology. MIT Museum, 265 Massachusetts Ave., features holography displays; phone (617) 253-4444. The institute's 135-acre campus extends more than a mile along the

Charles River Basin. Guided tours leave the Information Center in the lobby of the main building Mon.-Fri. at 10 and 2; closed holidays. Free. Phone (617) 253-4795.

Hart Nautical Gallery traces the development of marine engineering through ship models. Daily 9-8. Free. Phone (617) 253-5942.

List Visual Arts Center, in Wiesner Building at 20 Ames St., incorporates three galleries displaying the works of new and established contemporary artists. The center often mounts projects by artists-in-residence. Tues.-Sun. noon-6 (also Fri. 6-8 p.m.), Oct.-June; closed holidays. Free. Phone (617) 253-4680.

Margaret Hutchinson Compton Gallery, Building 10 at 77 Massachusetts Ave., contains changing exhibits that reflect a wide range of the institute's programs and activities. Mon.-Fri. 9-5. Free. Phone (617) 253-4444.

MIT Chapel, on the west campus, is a cylindrical brick structure designed by Eero Saarinen. The aluminum bell tower is by sculptor Theodore Roszak. A shallow moat surrounds the windowless building, and the bottom of the cylinder is penetrated by irregular arches through which light reflected from the moat plays on the interior walls. Daily dawn-dusk. Phone (617) 253-4444.

MINUTEMAN TOURS depart from Harvard Sq. or can be boarded at nine stops along the route. The 80-minute narrated tours of historic Cambridge and Boston include more than 100 points of interest. Tours depart on the hour Mon.-Fri. 9-4, Sat.-Sun. 9-5, Apr.-Oct. Fare (includes one full loop) $23; ages 4-12, $9. Phone (617) 269-7010.

MOUNT AUBURN CEMETERY, 580 Mount Auburn St., is purportedly the nation's first garden cemetery and contains an arboretum, outdoor sculptures and graves dating from 1831, including those of Mary Baker Eddy, Oliver Wendell Holmes, Julia Ward Howe, Henry Wadsworth Longfellow and James Russell Lowell. An audiotape driving tour is available. Daily 8-7, June-Aug.; 8-5, rest of year. Free. Phone (617) 547-7105.

OLD CAMBRIDGE encompasses several blocks around the perimeter of Harvard Square. The original town plan and many early buildings reflect Cambridge's history. Two buildings remain of those that once fronted the Common—Christ Church, built in 1761, and the 1753 Waterhouse House. Another major concentration of historic buildings is along Brattle Street, just east of Harvard Square. The most well-known mansion on the street is the Longfellow House. Phone (617) 497-1630.

CAPE ANN (A-7)

At the end of SR 128, Cape Ann consists of Gloucester *(see place listing in Boston p. 124)* and Rockport *(see place listing in Boston p. 132).* These communities are separated from the mainland by the tidal Annisquam River. Cape Ann also generally is considered to include the neighboring Essex *(see place listing in Boston p. 123)* and Manchester-by-the-Sea. Explored by Norsemen in the 11th century, the area first was settled in 1623 by Englishmen hoping to sell fish to Europe.

Cape Ann Chamber of Commerce: 33 Commercial St., Gloucester, MA 01930; phone (978) 283-1601 or (800) 321-0133. *See ad p. 121.*

COHASSET (F-4) pop. 7,100, elev. 24'

Capt. John Smith is said to have landed in Cohasset in 1614. For nearly 2 centuries the town was a fishing and farming community. Many residents now commute to work in Boston, and the town's bayside location attracts summer tourists.

About 2.5 miles offshore is Minot's Light; the 114-foot granite tower was built in 1860 to replace the original iron structure, destroyed in a storm. Moore's Rocks Reservation on Jerusalem Road provides a good view of the bay and light. Elm Street was known as "Ship Cove Lane" because it led to the shipyards and landing sites at Cohasset Harbor. It also was the street on which most of the shipbuilders and sea captains lived.

Capt. John Wilson House, built in 1810, is restored and furnished in period. Once a ship chandlery, Cohasset Maritime Museum contains model ships, nautical items, navigational equipment, Indian artifacts and a display depicting the building of Minot's Light.

Cohasset Chamber of Commerce: P.O. Box 336, Cohasset, MA 02025; phone (781) 383-1010.

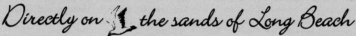 

CONCORD (D-1) pop. 17,100, elev. 130'

See map page below.

Concord was a driving force behind Massachusets' sudden literary renaissance in the 19th century. Ralph Waldo Emerson pursued the soul's relation to the infinite in his essays, poems and journals, and his friend and neighbor, Henry David Thoreau, wrote about the more finite world of nearby Walden Pond. Louisa May Alcott wrote "Little Women" about her childhood in Concord, and her father, Bronson Alcott, conducted his School of Philosophy, bringing together the leaders of American thought.

Joining these local writers was sculptor Daniel Chester French, who created his first, and probably most renowned sculpture—except for the Lincoln Memorial—"The Minute Man of Concord." More practical pursuits led Ephraim Bull to cultivate the Concord grape, which was the start of commercial production of table grapes in this country.

Concord maintains a stately New England elegance with its many fine homes and historic sites. As an alternative to a walking tour visitors can rent a canoe from the South Bridge boathouse on the Sudbury River on SR 62. The banks of the river, which feature a canopy of branches and gracious hillside houses, remain much as they were in the 1700s.

Concord is accessible by two scenic highways: SR 119, which travels northwest toward New Hampshire, and Lexington Road (SR 2A), which passes through Minute Man National Historical Park *(see place listing in Boston p. 130)* en route to Lexington.

Concord Chamber of Commerce: 2 Lexington Rd., Concord, MA 01742; phone (978) 369-3120. Its office is on Monument Square in Wright Tavern.

CONCORD ART ASSOCIATION, 37 Lexington Rd. (SR 2A), has changing exhibits of American contemporary arts and crafts. The 1720 house features a secret room and a garden with a waterfall. Tues.-Sat. 10-4:30, Sept.-July; closed holidays. Free. Phone (978) 369-2578.

CONCORD GUIDES departs from the front of St. Bernard's Church at Lexington Rd. and Bedford St. in Monument Square. These licensed guides conduct a historical walking tour of Concord and explain the town's importance in the American Revolution. Allow 2 hours minimum. Tours depart daily at 10, mid-June through Oct. 31; Sat.-Sun. at 10, mid-Apr. through early June. Fee $15; ages 11-18, $10; ages 6-10, $5. Phone (978) 287-0897.

SAVE ★ **CONCORD MUSEUM,** jct. Cambridge Tpke. and Lexington Rd., contains 19 period rooms and galleries. The introductory film "Exploring Concord" provides a historical overview, while the "Why Concord?" history galleries feature photographs, audiotapes and hands-on activities.

Collections include American Indian artifacts, relics from the Revolution, including the lantern that signaled Paul Revere's historic ride, the contents of Ralph Waldo Emerson's study, Henry David Thoreau's belongings used at Walden Pond, furniture and decorative arts. Guided tours are available by reservation.

Allow 1 hour minimum. Mon.-Sat. 9-5, Sun. noon-5, Apr.-Dec.; Mon.-Sat. 11-4, Sun. 1-4, rest of year. Closed Jan. 1, Easter, Thanksgiving and Dec. 25. Admission $6; over 61, $5; students with ID $4; ages 6-16, $3; family rate $12. MC, VI. Phone (978) 369-9609.

EMERSON HOUSE, Cambridge Tpke. and SR 2A, was the home of Ralph Waldo Emerson from 1835 until his death in 1882. The house contains original furnishings and Emerson memorabilia. Allow 30 minutes minimum. Tours are given Thurs.-Sat. 10-4:30, Sun. and holidays 2-4:30, mid-Apr. to late Oct. Admission $4.50; over 62 and ages 7-17, $3. Phone (978) 369-2236.

GREAT MEADOWS NATIONAL WILDLIFE REFUGE has two branches. The Concord Unit is 1.3 mi. e. on SR 62, then left on Monsen Rd. The Sudbury Unit is on Weir Hill Road in Sudbury *(see place listing in Boston p. 138).* The refuge includes nature and interpretive trails along the river marsh and refuge pools. Birdwatching is excellent during the spring and fall. Refuge is open daily dawn-dusk. Visitor center in Sudbury is open Mon.-Fri. 8-4. Free. Phone (978) 443-4661.

MINUTE MAN NATIONAL HISTORICAL PARK—*see place listing in Boston p. 130.*

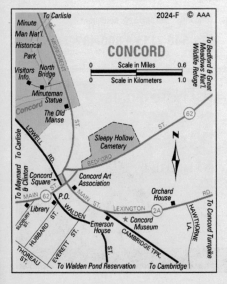

SAVE **THE OLD MANSE,** Monument St. next to the North Bridge, was built in 1770 by the grandfather of Ralph Waldo Emerson, who spent some of his boyhood at the home. Nathaniel Hawthorne occupied the house 1842-45 and gave the house its name. His "Mosses from an Old Manse" was written in the study. The home contains 18th- and 19th-century American furniture that belonged to the Emerson-Ripley family. Guided tours are given Mon.-Sat. 10-5, Sun. and holidays noon-5, mid-Apr. through Oct. 31. Last tour begins 30 minutes before closing. Admission $5.50; over 62 and students with ID $4; ages 6-12, $3.50; family rate $15. Phone (978) 369-3909.

SAVE **ORCHARD HOUSE,** 399 Lexington Rd., was the home of Louisa May Alcott and is where she wrote "Little Women." Mon.-Sat. 10-4:30, Sun. 1-4:30, Apr.-Oct.; Mon.-Fri. 11-3, Sat. 10-4:30, Sun. 1-4:30, rest of year. Closed Jan. 1-15, Easter, Thanksgiving and Dec. 25. Admission $5.50; over 62, $4.50; ages 6-17, $3.50; family rate $16. MC, VI. Phone (978) 369-4118.

SLEEPY HOLLOW CEMETERY, Bedford St., contains the graves of the Alcotts, Ralph Waldo Emerson, Daniel Chester French, Nathaniel Hawthorne and Henry David Thoreau. Daily 7-dusk. Free. Phone (978) 318-3233.

WALDEN POND RESERVATION, about 411 acres .25 mi. s. on SR 126, surrounds the 64-acre pond of Henry David Thoreau's "Walden." A sign on the north shore marks the site where Thoreau built his cabin in 1845. Fishing, swimming and boating are permitted. Daily dawn-dusk. Parking $2. Phone (978) 369-3254. *See Recreation Chart.*

DEDHAM (F-2) pop. 23,800, elev. 119′

DEDHAM HISTORICAL SOCIETY, 612 High St., houses a historical and genealogical research library and a history museum that includes Dedham and Chelsea pottery, paintings, artifacts, furniture from the 16th, 17th and 18th centuries, archives and exhibits. Museum open Tues.-Fri. noon-4, even-dated Sat. 1-4. Library open Tues.-Fri. 9-4. Museum admission $2; under 13, $1. Library $5. Phone (781) 326-1385.

FAIRBANKS HOUSE, 511 East St. at Eastern Ave., was built in 1636 and is one of the oldest wooden frame houses in North America. Inhabited by the Fairbanks family until the beginning of the 20th century, the house contains furniture, textiles and other objects that belonged to the family. Guided tours discuss life in New England during the first three centuries of European habitation.

Forty-five-minute tours are given Tues.-Sat. 10-5, Sun. 1-5, May-Oct. Last tour begins 1 hour before closing. Admission $5; under 13, $2. Phone (781) 326-1170.

ESSEX (B-7) pop. 3,300, elev. 26′

Founded as a shipbuilding center, Essex is home to the fishing schooner *Evelina M. Goulart*, one of some 4,000 schooners built in the area.

SAVE **ESSEX RIVER CRUISES AND CHARTERS,** 35 Dodge St., offers narrated journeys aboard the *Essex River Queen.* The 1.5-hour sightseeing cruise offers a glimpse into coastal life, including shipbuilding, fishing and clamming. Sightseeing cruise departs every 2 hours daily 11-7, May-Oct. Fare $16; over 62, $14 (Mon.-Fri. only); under 12, $7. DS, MC, VI. Phone (978) 768-6981 or (800) 748-3706.

ESSEX SHIPBUILDING MUSEUM, 66 Main St., is housed in an 1835 schoolhouse and a 1668 shipyard. Featuring antique shipbuilding tools, photographs and documents, the museum also displays artifacts portraying the shipbuilding industry. A videotape presentation and hands-on activities also are available. Allow 1 hour minimum. Mon.-Sat. 10-5, Sun. 1-5, May 1-Columbus Day; by appointment, rest of year. Admission $5; over 60, $4; ages 6-16, $3. AE, MC, VI. Phone (978) 768-7541.

FRAMINGHAM (F-1) pop. 65,000, elev. 180′

Settled in 1650, Framingham was named after Gov. Thomas Danforth's English hometown. By 1700 the town had grown to about 70 families. One resident, Crispus Attucks, was killed for inciting a mob against British soldiers March 5, 1770, an incident that later became known as the Boston Massacre. Attucks is considered the first African-American killed in the country's battle for independence.

In 1837 the waterpower of the Sudbury River led to the relocation of a textile company from Lowell to Framingham. Other industries followed. Framingham factories now produce sound systems, electronics, computer software, pharmaceuticals and biomedical products.

MetroWest Chamber of Commerce: 1671 Worcester Rd. #201, Framingham, MA 01701; phone (508) 879-5600.

DANFORTH MUSEUM OF ART, 123 Union Ave., is a fine arts museum with seven galleries, including a children's hands-on gallery. Changing exhibits of historic and contemporary American art are featured. Guided tours are available. Allow 1 hour minimum. Wed.-Sun. noon-5; closed holidays. Admission $3, over 64 and students with ID $2, under 13 free. Phone (508) 620-0050.

SAVE **GARDEN IN THE WOODS** is off SR 128 to SR 20W, then 8 mi. to Raymond Rd. S. and 1.3 mi. to Hemenway Rd. On display is one of the largest landscaped collections of wildflowers in the Northeast. There are 45 acres of wildflowers, ferns, shrubs and trees, including more than 1,600 species and varieties of native American plants and unusual flora from other countries. Guided tours are available.

Allow 1 hour, 30 minutes minimum. Daily 9-7, in May; daily 9-5, Apr. 15-30 and June 1-15; Tues.-Sun. 9-5, June 16-Oct. 31. Tours are given Mon.-Sat. at 10, Apr. 15-June 15; Tues.-Sat. at 10, June 16-Oct. 31. Last admission is 1 hour before closing. Admission $6; over 59, $5; ages 6-16, $3. MC, VI. Phone (508) 877-6574.

GLOUCESTER (B-8) pop. 28,700, elev. 52'

Gloucester, on Cape Ann, is a summer resort with a rocky coast and safe harbor. The town was settled in 1623 and has remained a fishing center. The harbor also bustles with traffic from sightseeing cruise ships and charter vessels.

East Gloucester encompasses Rocky Neck Art Colony, said to be the oldest art colony in the country. Within the colony, open May through October, are art galleries, shops and restaurants.

Cape Ann Chamber of Commerce: 33 Commercial St., Gloucester, MA 01930; phone (978) 283-1601 or (800) 321-0133.

SAVE **BEAUPORT** (Sleeper-McCann House) is off SR 128 via E. Gloucester to 75 Eastern Point Blvd. Built 1907-34 by interior decorator Henry Davis Sleeper, this 40-room house overlooking Gloucester Harbor contains 18th- and 19th-century American and European decorative arts and furnishings. Twenty-six rooms are open to the public. Guided tours are available on the hour.

Allow 1 hour minimum. Daily 10-4, mid-Sept. through Oct. 15; Mon.-Fri. 10-4, mid-May to mid-Sept. Closed holidays. Admission $6; senior citizens $5.50; students with ID and ages 6-12, $3. AE, DS, MC, VI. Phone (978) 283-0800.

CAPE ANN HISTORICAL MUSEUM, 27 Pleasant St., exhibits an extensive collection of paintings and drawings by Fitz Hugh Lane as well as works by other Cape Ann artists. The museum also displays American decorative arts, furnishings and exhibits about Cape Ann's fisheries and maritime history. The furnished home of Capt. Elias Davis is part of the museum complex. Allow 1 hour minimum. Tues.-Sat. 10-5, Mar.-Jan. Admission $4, senior citizens $3.50, students with ID $2.50, under 6 free with an adult. Phone (978) 283-0455.

SAVE **CAPE ANN WHALE WATCH,** 415 Main St. at Rose's Wharf, offers 3.5- to 4-hour whale-watch cruises, which include narratives by a naturalist from the Whale Conservation Institute, and sightseeing cruises from Gloucester to Provincetown.

Whale-watch cruises depart daily at 9 and 1:30, June 26-Labor Day; daily at 10 in Oct.; Mon.-Fri. at 10, Sat.-Sun. at 8:30 and 1:30, Apr. 22-June 25; Mon.-Fri. at 1:30, Sat.-Sun. at 8:30 and 1:30, day after Labor Day-Sept. 30. Round-trip Gloucester to Provincetown cruises depart Mon.-Fri. at 9, June 27-Labor Day. Whale-watch fare $23; over 60, $18; under 16, $14. Gloucester cruise $40; over 60, $35; ages 2-16, $20. Reservations are required. AE, DS, MC, VI. Phone (978) 283-5110 or (800) 877-5110. *See color ad.*

FIRST BAPTIST CHURCH, 38 Gloucester Ave., is a modern structure evocative of a ship and fortress. The interior features a pulpit reminiscent of the Mariner's Chapel in "Moby Dick." An 8-foot cross looms above the congregation. Allow 30 minutes minimum. Daily 9-noon. Free. Phone (978) 283-4808.

FISHERMEN'S MEMORIAL, on Western Ave., was erected in memory of Gloucester fishermen who have been lost at sea.

HAMMOND CASTLE MUSEUM is on Hesperus Ave. Built by inventor Dr. John Hay Hammond 1926-29, this medieval-type castle contains furniture and architectural pieces from dwellings and churches abroad as well as Roman, Medieval and Renaissance artifacts. An 8,200-pipe organ in the Great Hall is used for occasional concerts. Daily 10-4, Memorial Day-Labor Day; Sat.-Sun. 9-4, rest of year. Closed Jan. 1, Thanksgiving and Dec. 25. Admission $6; over 64 and students

with ID $5; ages 4-12, $4. Phone (978) 283-7673, or 283-2080 for a recorded message.

HARBOR TOURS INC., 9 Harborloop, offers a demonstration of lobstering. Trips depart daily at noon and 2:30, June 1-Labor Day. Departure times may vary; phone to confirm schedule. Fare $6; under 12, $3. Reservations are required. Phone (978) 283-5110.

NORTH SHORE ARTS ASSOCIATION is at the rear of 197 E. Main St. (Pirate Ln.). One of the earliest artist colonies in New England, the association contains paintings in several media, graphics and workshops. Demonstrations by artists are available. Two major exhibits are presented yearly. Allow 30 minutes minimum. Mon.-Sat. 10-6, Sun. noon-5, May-Oct. Free. Phone (978) 283-1857.

OUR LADY OF GOOD VOYAGE CHURCH, 142 Prospect St., is ornately decorated and has models of fishing vessels on its walls. A statue of Our Lady of Good Voyage stands between two steeples, guiding fishermen safely into port. Allow 30 minutes minimum. Mon.-Fri. 10-4. Free. Phone (978) 283-1490.

SARGENT HOUSE MUSEUM, 49 Middle St., is an 18th-century Georgian-style home built in 1782 for Judith Sargent Murray, who is known for her essays, poems and plays. The home is furnished in period. Allow 1 hour minimum for guided tours. Fri.-Mon. noon-4, Memorial Day-Columbus Day. Admission $3; over 64, $2; under 12 free. Phone (978) 281-2432.

SCHOONER _THOMAS E. LANNON_, departs from Seven Seas Wharf on Rogers St. at Gloucester House Restaurant. The schooner offers two-hour sightseeing cruises along the rocky shorelines near Gloucester and Salem. Passengers can see lighthouses, unspoiled islands, beaches and stately waterfront homes. Half-day excursions and dinner cruises are available. Cruises depart Mon. and Wed.-Fri. at 10, 1, 3:30 and 6; Tues. at 8:30, noon, 2, 4 and 6; Sat. at 8:30, 10:30, 1, 3:30 and 6; Sun. at 8:30, 10:30, 1 and 6, mid-

May through Nov. 1. Fare $25; over 59, $20; under 17, $15. Reservations are recommended. MC, VI. Phone (978) 281-6634.

SAVE **SEVEN SEAS WHALE WATCH** leaves from Seven Seas Wharf downtown. The 4-hour cruises feature lectures by an on-board naturalist. Sightings normally include Humpbacks and other species of whales and dolphins. If whales are not sighted, a raincheck is given. Food is available. Trips depart daily at 8:30 and 1:30, May 1 to mid-Oct. (weather permitting). Fare $24; over 60, $19; under 16, $15. Reservations are recommended. AE, DS, MC, VI. Phone (978) 283-1776, or (800) 238-1776 in Mass. _See color ad._

SAVE **YANKEE FLEET WHALE WATCH** cruises depart from Gloucester Harbor at 75 Essex Ave.; take SR 128 exit 14 to SR 133 (Essex Ave.). The 4-hour cruise offers commentaries by an on-board naturalist. Picnicking is permitted. Food is available. Trips depart daily at 8:30 and 1:30, May-Sept. (weather permitting); departures vary in Apr. and Oct. Fare $24; over 62, $19; under 16, $15. Reservations are recommended. MC, VI. Phone (978) 283-0313 or (800) 942-5464.

 CASINOS

- **Leisure Casino Cruises**, 6 Rowe Sq. Sun.-Thurs. noon-5 and 7-11:30; Fri.-Sat. noon-5 and 7 p.m.-12:30 a.m. Phone (978) 282-3330 or (877) 872-6287.

HAVERHILL (A-6) pop. 51,400, elev. 35'

Settled in 1640 on the site of the Indian village of Pentucket, Haverhill suffered frequent Indian raids. In 1697 Hannah Dustin was kidnapped; it is said she scalped 10 of her captors, escaped and reached home safely.

Greater Haverhill Chamber of Commerce: 87 Winter St., Haverhill, MA 01830; phone (978) 373-5663.

HAVERHILL HISTORICAL SOCIETY BUTTON-WOODS MUSEUM, 240 Water St., features the 1710 John Ward House, the 1815 Duncan House and Daniel Hunkins' 1850 shoe shop. Changing exhibits are offered. Daily 10-5, Memorial Day-Labor Day; Wed.-Thurs. and Sat.-Sun. 1-4:30, rest of year. Admission $5; ages 7-12, $3. Phone (978) 374-4626.

WHITTIER BIRTHPLACE is off I-495 exit 52, then 1 mi. e. on SR 110. This 1688 house is the birthplace and boyhood home of poet John Greenleaf Whittier. Furnished with original pieces, it remains as described in Whittier's poem "Snow-Bound." Tues.-Sat. 10-5, Sun. 1-5, May-Oct.; Tues.-Fri. and Sun. 1-5, Sat. 10-5, rest of year. Closed major holidays. Admission $2; over 65 and under 18, $1; family rate $5. Phone (978) 373-3979.

IPSWICH (A-7) pop. 11,900, elev. 26'

In 1633 Ipswich was settled by a group of 12 Colonists, among them several "proper gentlemen" who developed the town into a cultural center. Clothing industries, including shoemaking, lacemaking and machine knitting, later became the town's economic base. Tourism and the digging and marketing of clams are now a major source of income.

Richard T. Crane Jr. Memorial Reservation, 6 miles east on Argilla Road, offers 4 miles of shoreline and beaches on Ipswich Bay. The old Crane residence, called Great House, is the scene of weekend concerts and art lectures during the summer. *See Recreation Chart.*

Ipswich Visitor Information Center: 36 S. Main St., Ipswich, MA 01938; phone (978) 356-8540.

JOHN HEARD HOUSE MUSEUM is at 54 S. Main St. The 1800 homestead of a prominent China trade family, the museum contains American and Asian furnishings, decorative objects, an antique carriage collection and important works by artist Arthur Wesley Dow. Hourly guided tours are given Wed.-Sat. 10-4, Sun. 1-4, early May to mid-Oct. Last tour begins 1 hour before closing. Admission $5; ages 6-12, $2 (includes admission to John Whipple House Museum). Phone (978) 356-2811.

JOHN WHIPPLE HOUSE MUSEUM, 1 S. Village Green, was built around 1655 and contains 17th- and 18th-century furnishings and decorative arts. The garden has medicinal herbs and plants grown in the colony during the 17th century. Wed.-Sat. 10-4, Sun. 1-4, early May to mid-Oct. Admission $5; ages 6-12, $2 (includes admission to Heard House Museum). Phone (978) 356-2641.

LAWRENCE (B-6) pop. 70,200, elev. 65'

Lawrence was established in 1845 to support the growing number of industries along the Merrimack River. Through the efforts of the Lawrence brothers Great Stone Dam was built 1845-48 to generate electrical power. Constructed with hand-hewn granite blocks hauled by oxen and laid stone by stone on the river floor, the dam was considered an engineering triumph. The massive dam can be viewed from Falls Bridge.

Merrimack Valley Chamber of Commerce: 264 Essex St., Lawrence, MA 01840; phone (978) 686-0900.

LAWRENCE HERITAGE STATE PARK, 1 Jackson St., commemorates the history of this mill city. Lawrence's mills once produced 800 miles of cloth a day through the labor of thousands of immigrants, who made history during the Bread and Roses Strike of 1912. This strike sparked the American labor movement, bringing about national reforms of laws governing workers' rights. The visitor center, in a restored workers' boarding house, contains exhibits about the city's history, architecture and daily life. A gallery features changing art and historical exhibits. Park open daily dawn-dusk. Visitor center open daily 9-4. Free. Phone (978) 794-1655.

★ LEXINGTON (E-2) pop. 29,000, elev. 201'

See map page below.

Lexington is the site of the first conflict of the Revolutionary War, dramatized on the Lexington Battle Green during the Re-enactment of the Battle of Lexington in mid-April. Portions of Battle Road, the route used by British and American soldiers moving from Concord to Boston, now are covered by scenic SR 2A.

Lexington Visitors Center: 1875 Massachusetts Ave., Lexington, MA 02173; phone (781) 862-1450.

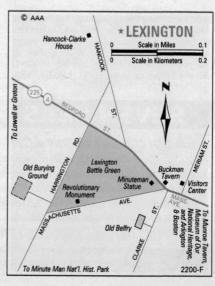

HISTORICAL SOCIETY HOUSES are open Mon.-Sat. 10-5, Sun. 1-5, Apr.-Oct. Last tour begins 30 minutes before closing. Admission (one building) $4; ages 6-16, $2. Combination tickets (three buildings) $10; ages 6-16, $4.

Buckman Tavern, 1 Bedford St., was built in 1709 and has furnishings of the Revolutionary War period. It was the headquarters of the Lexington Minutemen at the beginning of the Revolutionary War. Phone (781) 862-5598.

Hancock-Clarke House, 36 Hancock St., was built in 1698 and enlarged in 1734. Samuel Adams and John Hancock were at this site when Paul Revere brought the news of the British advance. The house includes period furniture and historical objects. Phone (781) 862-1703.

Munroe Tavern, 1332 Massachusetts Ave., served as the British headquarters and hospital during the Battle of Lexington. The 1695 building is restored. Phone (781) 862-1703.

LEXINGTON BATTLE GREEN, or Common, is at Massachusetts Ave. and Bedford St. The common was the site of the first skirmish of the Revolutionary War, April 19, 1775, between Minutemen and Concord-bound British troops. The line where the Minutemen stood is marked by a boulder inscribed with Capt. John Parker's courageous words: "Stand your ground; don't fire unless fired upon, but if they mean to have a war, let it begin here."

MINUTE MAN NATIONAL HISTORICAL PARK—see place listing p. 130.

MINUTEMAN STATUE, at the head of Battle Green on Massachusetts Ave., represents Capt. John Parker as he appeared on the morning of April 19, 1775, commanding the Minutemen gathered on the green. It faces the line of British approach.

MUSEUM OF OUR NATIONAL HERITAGE, 33 Marrett Rd., offers changing exhibits about American history and culture. Mon.-Sat. 10-4:45, Sun. noon-4:45; closed Jan. 1, Thanksgiving and Dec. 24-25 and 31. Free. Phone (781) 861-6559.

OLD BELFRY, off Clarke St., is near the Common. It is a reproduction of the original belfry whose bell sounded the alarm that assembled the Minutemen. The original was destroyed in 1909.

OLD BURYING GROUND is beyond the green, next to the Unitarian Church. Among the graves are those of Capt. John Parker, Gov. William Eustis and Rev. John Hancock. The oldest stone is dated 1690.

REVOLUTIONARY MONUMENT, on the Green, was dedicated in 1799 to the men killed in the first battle of the Revolutionary War. It is considered to be the first monument erected commemorating the American Revolution.

LINCOLN (E-1) pop. 7,700, elev. 208′

⬛ **CODMAN HOUSE** is on Codman Rd., .25 mi. e. of SR 126. The summer home of the Codman family for more than 200 years, Codman House was enlarged over the generations and represents several architectural styles, including Georgian, Federal, Victorian and Colonial Revival. The grounds include a perennial garden and a formal Italianate garden. Allow 1 hour minimum. Guided tours are given on the hour Wed.-Sun. 11-5, June 1-Oct. 15. Last tour begins 1 hour before closing. Admission $4; over 64, $3.50; ages 6-12, $2. Phone (781) 259-8843.

⬛ **THE DeCORDOVA MUSEUM AND SCULPTURE PARK** is on Sandy Pond Rd.; take Trapelo Rd. off SR 128/I-95 Lincoln exit 28 to intersection with Sandy Pond Rd. Surrounded by a 35-acre park, the 1880 castlelike structure is a cultural center for the visual and performing arts. The museum collects and exhibits significant examples of 20th-century American art, emphasizing the work of New England artists and expressionist painters.

Regional and national exhibitions, lectures and events are held. A sculpture park is on the grounds; outdoor concerts are performed July through September. Park open daily dawn-dusk. Museum open Tues.-Sun. 11-5; closed holidays. Admission $6; over 60, students with ID and ages 6-12, $4. Park admission free. Phone (781) 259-8355.

DRUMLIN FARM EDUCATION CENTER AND WILDLIFE SANCTUARY, on SR 117, .7 mi. e. of SR 126, has 252 acres of pastures, fields, woodlands and ponds. This center has animals representative of a New England farm including chickens, horses, mules, sheep, pigs, goats and cows as well as various species of such wildlife as deer, owls and pheasants. In the Burrowing Animal Building visitors go underground to see part of the dens or burrows of animals, including those of foxes, woodchucks and opossums.

Picnicking is permitted. Allow 1 hour minimum. Tues.-Sun. and Mon. holidays 9-5, Mar.-Oct.; 9-4, rest of year. Closed Jan. 1, Thanksgiving and Dec. 25. Admission $6; over 64 and ages 3-12, $4. MC, VI. Phone (781) 259-9807.

⬛ **GROPIUS HOUSE,** off SR 2, then s. on SR 126 to 68 Baker Bridge Rd., was built in 1938 by and for Walter Gropius, director of Germany's Bauhaus School and an innovative and influential architect of the 20th century. Using components ordered from catalogs and building supply stores, he produced a house that blends the Bauhaus principles of function and simplicity with New England traditions. The house has art and furnishings brought from Bauhaus workshops in Germany as well as pieces from the United States.

Tours are given on the hour Wed.-Sun. 11-4, June 1-Oct. 15; Sat.-Sun. 11-4, rest of year. Fee

$5; over 64, $4.50; students with ID and ages 6-12, $2.50. Phone (781) 259-8098.

LOWELL (B-6) pop. 103,400, elev. 104'

In 1813, after touring British textile factories, Boston merchant Francis Cabot Lowell supported the development of a power loom that shaped the history of the U.S. textile industry. Looking for a site to set up a factory, a group of investors called "The Boston Associates" discovered Lowell, at the confluence of the Concord and Merrimack rivers. They were impressed by the water power potential of the two rivers. Construction of textile mills and a series of power canals began in 1822.

In the following decades the town experienced economic prosperity at the cost of human needs. Reformer Sarah Bagley organized female workers to fight for better conditions. Due to the influx of unskilled immigrants beginning in 1850, protests were often futile. In the early 20th century, just as labor improvements were being realized, the industry began to collapse, forcing residents to leave. High-tech industry is beginning to revitalize the city.

Greater Merrimack Valley Convention and Visitors Bureau: 22 Shattuck St., Lowell, MA 01852; phone (978) 459-6150.

★**AMERICAN TEXTILE HISTORY MUSEUM,** off Lowell Connector exit 5B, following signs to 491 Dutton St., chronicles 300 years of American textile production with displays of a large assortment of hand-powered tools and equipment, fabrics and finished clothing. Spinning and weaving demonstrations are given periodically. Allow 1 hour, 30 minutes minimum. Tues.-Fri. 9-4, Sat.-Sun. and Mon. holidays 10-4; closed Jan. 1, Thanksgiving and Dec. 25. Admission $5; over 60 and ages 6-16, $3. AE, DS, MC, VI. Phone (978) 441-0400.

★**LOWELL NATIONAL HISTORICAL PARK,** off Lowell Connector exit 5B, following signs to 246 Market St., commemorates Lowell's pioneering role in the American Industrial Revolution. The park includes cotton textile mills, workers' housing, a 5.6-mile power canal system and industrial exhibits. The visitor center includes exhibits and a 20-minute multi-image video titled "Lowell: The Industrial Revelation."

Guided walking tours are given daily. Boat and trolley tours are offered several times daily in summer. Reproductions of 1901 electric trolley cars operate daily early March to late November.

Park open Mon.-Sat. 9-5, Sun. 10-5; closed Jan. 1, Thanksgiving and Dec. 25. Park admission free. Boat and trolley tours $4; over 61 and ages 6-16, $2. Reservations are suggested for tours. Phone (978) 970-5000, or TDD (978) 970-5002.

★**Boott Cotton Mills Museum,** 400 Foot of John St., is housed within the brick walls of a cotton mill built in 1873. Two floors of exhibits chronicle the age of Lowell's textile mills and the Industrial Revolution in general. On the first floor an orientation area gives way to a 1920s weave room containing 88 looms operating with the help of belts, shafts and pulleys.

Exhibits upstairs present Lowell's history from the preindustrial days to the present. A slide presentation traces the development of the industrial age, and mill workers present audiovisual histories of their work and times. An interactive exhibit explores the nature of work in the 21st century. Allow 1 hour minimum. Mon.-Sat. 9:30-5, Sun. 11-5; closed Jan. 1, Thanksgiving and Dec. 25. Admission $4; over 61 and ages 6-16, $2.

The Working People Exhibit is at the Patrick J. Mogan Cultural Center, 40 French St. Housed in a Boott Mill boardinghouse, this exhibit explores the story of the industrial revolution by concentrating on Lowell's working people. The histories of the "mill girl" and immigrant work forces are explored. Daily 1-5, Memorial Day-Labor Day; Sat.-Sun. 1-5, rest of year. Free.

NEW ENGLAND QUILT MUSEUM, 18 Shattuck St., presents changing exhibitions of both historic and contemporary quilts. Interpretation of each quilt is provided. Allow 30 minutes minimum. Tues.-Sat. 10-4, Sun. noon-4, May-Nov.; Tues.-Sat. 10-4, rest of year. Closed major holidays and between exhibitions. Admission $4; over 60 and ages 7-17, $3. MC, VI. Phone (978) 452-4207.

THE SPORTS MUSEUM OF NEW ENGLAND, 25 Shattuck St., traces the history of amateur and professional sports in New England. Interactive exhibits, artwork, memorabilia and videos highlight the area's sports history. Allow 1 hour minimum. Tues.-Sat. 10-5, Sun. noon-5. Admission $3; over 59 and ages 6-17, $2. AE, MC, VI. Phone (978) 452-6775.

WHISTLER HOUSE MUSEUM OF ART, 243 Worthen St., was the 1834 birthplace of James Abbott McNeill Whistler. Built in 1823, the house now contains a 19th- and 20th-century American art collection that includes etchings by Whistler. Wed.-Sat. 11-4, Sun. 1-4, Mar.-Dec.; closed holidays. Admission $3, senior citizens and students with ID $2, under 5 free. Phone (978) 452-7641.

LYNN (E-3) pop. 81,200, elev. 26'

Founded in 1629, Lynn is one of New England's oldest communities. Once a major shoe manufacturing center, the city is now home to a General Electric plant. Lynn Woods Reservation, a 2,200-acre municipal park, features mineral and glacial traces and offers hiking, rock climbing, picnicking and cross-country skiing. Spread over several hills, the Victorian-style Pine Grove Cemetery was founded in 1850 and offers a panorama of the area.

The Mary Baker Eddy Home at 12 Broad St. contains furnishings and articles relating to the life of the founder of the Church of Christ, Scientist. Tours are available; phone (617) 450-3790.

Lynn Area Chamber of Commerce: 23 Central Ave. #416, Lynn, MA 01901; phone (781) 592-2900.

LYNN HERITAGE STATE PARK VISITORS CENTER is at 590 Washington St. This downtown center, a separate part of the nearby waterfront state park, explores the history of Lynn and the people who built it. A 10-minute audiovisual presentation provides background information about the community, and exhibits depict important events in the city's industrial past, from its shoe manufacturing roots to its present day production of jet engines. Allow 1 hour minimum. Wed.-Sun. 9:30-4:30; closed Jan. 1, Thanksgiving and Dec. 25. Free. Phone (781) 598-1974.

LYNN MUSEUM, 125 Green St., is a 19th-century house with four period rooms and decorative arts from Lynn homes. A wing, added in 1929, contains changing exhibits. Mon.-Sat. 1-4. Admission $4; ages 6-16, $1. Phone (781) 592-2465.

MARBLEHEAD (D-3) pop. 20,000, elev. 32'

Founded in 1629, Marblehead flourished as a commercial fishing center and by the mid-18th century was port to hundreds of ships engaged in fishing and overseas trade. Today more than 200 houses built before the American Revolution and nearly 800 constructed during the 1800s still line the town's winding streets.

Views of the ocean, islands, harbor and Marblehead shoreline can be enjoyed from Crocker Park, off Front Street downtown, and Chandler Hovey Park, at the end of Harbor and Ocean avenues. The 1896 Marblehead light tower, closed to the public, is on the grounds of Chandler Hovey Park.

Marblehead Chamber of Commerce: 62 Pleasant St., P.O. Box 76, Marblehead, MA 01945; phone (781) 631-2868.

Self-guiding tours: Maps of a walking tour are available from the information booth on Pleasant Street, Memorial Day-October 31.

ABBOT HALL, Washington Sq., exhibits the 1684 deed recording the purchase of the peninsula from the Indians and the original *"Spirit of '76,"* painted in 1876 by A.M. Willard. Mon.-Tues. and Thurs. 8-5, Wed. 7:30-7:30, Fri. 8-1, Sat. 9-6, Sun. 11-6, June-Oct.; Mon.-Tues. and Thurs. 8-5, Wed. 7:30-7:30, Fri. 8-1, rest of year. Donations. Phone (781) 631-0000.

FORT SEWALL, at the n.e. end of Front St., offers views of the harbor and ocean. Built in 1742, the fort was manned through the Spanish-American War. Daily dawn-dusk. Free.

JEREMIAH LEE MANSION, 161 Washington St., was the 1768 Georgian home of a wealthy shipowner and patriot who helped finance the American revolt against King George. Its intricately carved interiors feature rare, original English wallpaper and early 18th- and 19th-century furnishings, paintings and artifacts. Mon.-Sat. 10-4, Sun. 1-4, mid-May through Oct. 31. Admission $4, over 60 and students with ID $3.50, under 10 free. Phone (781) 631-1768.

KING HOOPER MANSION, 8 Hooper St., is home to Marblehead Arts Association. The 1728 mansion was enlarged in 1747, at which time a facade was added, and contains a wine cellar and a ballroom. Artworks are exhibited. Guided tours are available. Mon.-Sat. 10-4, Sun. 1-5. Donations. Phone (781) 631-2608.

OLD BURIAL HILL, off Orne St., overlooks the harbor and hundreds of grave markers dating from the 1600s and 1700s.

POWDER HOUSE, at Green and Lattimer sts., was built in 1755. Muskets and powder were stored in this brick magazine during the French and Indian War, the American Revolution and the War of 1812. The building is not open to the public.

ST. MICHAEL'S CHURCH, 26 Pleasant St., was built in 1714 and remodelled in 1833 in Gothic Revival style. One of the oldest Episcopal churches in America, it still has an original, elaborate brass chandelier from England. The bell, rung at the news of the Declaration of Independence until it cracked, was recast by Paul Revere and is still used. Guided tours are available by appointment. Tues.-Fri. 9-2. Free. Phone (781) 631-0657.

MEDFORD (E-2) pop. 57,400

ROYALL HOUSE, George and Main sts., was built in 1637 and rebuilt 1732-37. The home is furnished in period. A nearby building, the original slave quarters, is the only structure of its kind remaining in New England. Tues.-Thurs. and Sat.-Sun. 2-5, May 1-Oct. 1. Admission $3, over 60 and students with ID $2, under 12 free. Phone (781) 396-9032.

MILTON (F-2) pop. 25,700, elev. 24'

BLUE HILLS RESERVATION is s. via Randolph Ave. (SR 28). This is a 7,000-acre Metropolitan District Commission reservation encompassing terrains from hills and meadows to forests and wetlands. Traversing this park are some 200 miles of hiking and horse trails. Other recreational facilities include tennis courts, ski slopes, cross-country ski trails, ice skating rinks, a beach and a golf course. Daily dawn-dusk. Free. Phone (617) 698-1802.

Blue Hills Trailside Museum, off SR 93/128 exit 2B to 1904 Canton Ave. (SR 138), offers an introduction to the wildlife and history of the Blue Hills. It contains displays about natural sciences, natural history and pioneer and American Indian life. Displays feature such native wildlife as otters, snakes, red foxes and honeybees. An exhibit hall displays natural science and history exhibits, including a wigwam, natural habitats and a viewing tower. Activities include storytelling, live animal programs and seasonal nature talks.

Tues.-Sun. and Mon. holidays 10-5; closed Jan. 1, Thanksgiving and Dec. 25. Admission $3; over 64, $2; ages 3-15, $1.50. Extra charge for events. MC, VI. Phone (617) 333-0690.

MINUTE MAN NATIONAL HISTORICAL PARK (D-2)

Encompassing lands in Concord, Lincoln and Lexington, Minute Man National Historical Park commemorates the opening battles of America's War for Independence. The majority of the park is a narrow strip of land on either side of Battle Road (SR 2A), with the Minute Man Visitor Center at one end, just off SR 128, and the North Bridge Visitor Center outside of Concord at the other. The events of April 19, 1775, were not one but many battles along a 20-mile stretch of hilly road between Boston and Concord.

Gen. Thomas Gage, head of the British forces occupying Boston, chose that day for a demonstration of force, ordering 700 redcoats to march to Concord and seize the rebel supplies of arms and ammunition. Drawing on the tenets of 18th-century warfare, Gage's intention was simply to overawe the Colonials, not to provoke a fight. However, once news of the British mobilization reached the patriots, hundreds of people materialized from the surrounding communities to contest the British march.

After a brief fight on Lexington Green, the British moved to Concord, where the militia drove three companies of redcoats from the North Bridge back to the main force in Concord. After a brief rest, the British began their return march to Boston and were soon met by the militia, who forced the British back to the city under steady gun fire.

A running battle continued back to Boston Harbor. The British sent out flankers to flush out the patriots and protect its column. As the day progressed an increasing number of colonists joined the fight.

Exhausted and near panic, the British column was met at Lexington by a relief force of 1,000 men, swelling the ranks to 1,700. Beyond Lexington the British column met fierce and bloody resistance in the towns of Menotomy, now Arlington, and Charlestown. At 6:30 p.m. the British finally reached the safety of Bunker Hill, which was under the guns of the British warship *Somerset*. In all, the British lost 73 men and the

patriots 49; many more were wounded or missing.

MINUTE MAN VISITOR CENTER, off SR 2A, serves as a starting point for most visitors. A 22-minute film details the events leading to the battle, and a multimedia presentation further recounts the events of April 19, 1775. Ranger programs chronicle the battle, and exhibits supplement these presentations. Maps are available for tours of the park. Daily 9-5, mid-Apr. through Nov. 1. Free. Phone (781) 862-7753.

THE NORTH BRIDGE, w. of Monument St., was the site of "the shot heard 'round the world"— the first major engagement of the Revolution—on April 19, 1775. Just across the bridge stands Daniel Chester French's Minuteman statue, which is engraved with a stanza from Ralph Waldo Emerson's "Concord Hymn." North Bridge Visitor Center is a short walk past the statue and up the hill.

NORTH BRIDGE VISITOR CENTER, 174 Liberty St., exhibits clothed mannequins, artifacts, muskets and a 12-minute film describing the North Bridge fight. A formal garden overlooks the North Bridge. Daily 9-5:30 (reduced hours in winter). Free. Phone (978) 369-6993.

THE WAYSIDE, 1 mi. e. of Concord on Lexington Rd., was the home of the muster master, or roll caller, of the Concord minutemen, and later the home of the Bronson Alcott family, the Nathaniel Hawthorne family and Margaret Sidney, an author of children's books during the late 19th century. Tours are given Fri.-Tues. 10:30-5, mid-May through Oct. 30. Last tour begins 1 hour before closing. Admission $4, under 16 free. Phone (978) 369-6975 or 369-6993.

NATICK (F-1) pop. 30,500, elev. 158'

BROADMOOR WILDLIFE SANCTUARY OF MASSACHUSETTS AUDUBON SOCIETY, 280 Eliot St. on SR 16, embraces 600 acres of marsh, ponds and meadows along the Charles River. Wildlife can be seen along the trails that wind through the sanctuary. The visitor center, in a restored barn, incorporates solar and other alternative systems to conserve energy and water. Sanctuary open Tues.-Sun. dawn-dusk. Center open Tues.-Fri. 9-5, Sat.-Sun. 10-5. Admission $3; over 65 and ages 3-12, $2. MC, VI. Phone (508) 655-2296 or (781) 235-3929.

NEPONSET (E-2)

PHILLIPS CANDY HOUSE, 818 Morrissey Blvd., offers guided tours of the old-fashioned candy house. The tours include a demonstration of each step in the candy-making process. Allow 30 minutes minimum. Tours are given Mon.-Thurs. 9-1; reservations are required. Free. Phone (617) 282-2090 or (800) 722-0905.

NEWBURYPORT (A-7) pop. 16,300, elev. 39'

Once a shipbuilding center, Newburyport is the birthplace of the U.S. Coast Guard. Built in the 1650s, SAVE the Coffin House, at 14 High Rd., reflects the many generations of residency by the Coffin family. Guided tours are given on weekends in summer; phone (978) 462-2634.

Greater Newburyport Chamber of Commerce: 29 State St., Newburyport, MA 01950; phone (978) 462-6680. An information kiosk is on Merrimac St.

Self-guiding tours: American architecture enthusiasts will appreciate a walking tour of High Street, where styles from the 17th through the 19th centuries, including several notable examples of the Federal period, are represented in the structures.

CUSTOM HOUSE MARITIME MUSEUM, 25 Water St., is a Classic Revival-style custom house built in 1835. Exhibits pertain to more than 300 years of maritime history, the China trade and shipbuilding on the Merrimac River. A 15-minute audiovisual program gives visitors an overview of Newburyport. Mon.-Sat. 10-4, Sun. 1-4, Apr. 1 to mid-Dec. Admission $3; over 59 and ages 5-15, $2. MC, VI. Phone (978) 462-8681.

HISTORICAL SOCIETY OF OLD NEWBURY (Cushing House Museum), 98 High St., has its headquarters in the 1808 Cushing House. The 21-room, Federal-style mansion contains period furnishings, portraits, paperweights, silver, china, needlework and toys. A French garden, carriage house and garden house are on the grounds. Tours are given Mon.-Sat. 10-3, mid-May through Oct. 31. Also open 1 week in Dec. for Christmas tours. Admission $4; ages 6-18, $1. Phone (978) 462-2681.

NEWBURYPORT WHALE WATCH departs from Hilton's Fishing Dock, 54 Merrimac St. The 4.5-hour excursions include a pre-cruise introduction and continuous narration by a marine biologist. A display featuring radar, sonar, Global Positioning System and Loran readings allows passengers to study navigation and whale activity. If whales are not sighted, a rain check is given.

Cruises depart daily at 8:30 and 1:30, July 1-Labor Day; Mon.-Fri. at 10, Sat.-Sun. at 8:30 and 1:30, in June; daily at 10, day after Labor Day-Sept. 30 (weather permitting). Call for departure times in May and Oct. Fare $24; senior citizens $20; ages 4-16, $17. Reservations are recommended. AE, DS, MC, VI. Phone (978) 465-9885 or (800) 848-1111.

PARKER RIVER NATIONAL WILDLIFE REFUGE, s.e. of Newburyport Center, encompasses the southern two-thirds of Plum Island and salt marshes west to the mainland. With headquarters at the old Coast Guard lighthouse at the north end of the island, the 4,662-acre refuge is an ex-

cellent birdwatching area. It has hiking trails, observation towers and 6.5 miles of beach. Surf fishing, nature study and cross-country skiing can be enjoyed.

Waterfowl hunting (in season), clamming and limited night surf fishing are available by permit only. Headquarters open Mon.-Fri. 8-4:30. Refuge open daily dawn-dusk; beach is closed Apr.-Aug. to protect nesting shorebirds. Admission $5 per private vehicle, or $2 per person arriving by bicycle or on foot. Phone (978) 465-5753.

NEWTON (E-2) pop. 82,600, elev. 33'

JACKSON HOMESTEAD, 527 Washington St., is a Federal-style farmhouse constructed in 1809. The homestead serves as a museum housing a permanent collection of historical artifacts and items that interpret Newton's history, including the role of Jackson Homestead as a stop on the underground railroad. A children's gallery and changing exhibits are featured.

Allow 1 hour minimum. Mon.-Thurs. noon-5, Sun. 2-5, Sept.-May; Mon.-Thurs. noon-5, rest of year. Closed holidays. Admission $2; over 65 and ages 6-17, $1. Phone (617) 552-7238.

NORFOLK (C-6) pop. 9,300, elev. 218'

STONY BROOK NATURE CENTER AND WILDLIFE SANCTUARY, 1 mi. s. on SR 115, is maintained by the Massachusetts Audubon Society. A 1-mile self-guiding nature trail, bounded by fields, wetlands and ponds, leads to a boardwalk over a marsh. Other features on the 241-acre site include a butterfly garden and interpretive exhibits in the nature center. Center open Tues.-Sat. 9-5, Sun. 10-4. Trails open daily dawn-dusk. Admission $3; over 65 and ages 3-16, $2. MC, VI. Phone (508) 528-3140.

QUINCY (F-3) pop. 85,000

As the birthplace of the constitution of Massachusetts—as well as of John and John Quincy Adams—Quincy has assured its prominence in American history. The city also was the birthplace of John Hancock, the president of the Continental Congress.

SAVE The Josiah Quincy House at 20 Muirhead St. was built in 1770 by the prominent lawyer and political leader. In addition to furniture and memorabilia from several generations of Quincy descendants, the house has period wall paneling and fireplaces surrounded by English tiles. Phone (617) 471-4508 for tour information.

★ **ADAMS NATIONAL HISTORIC SITE** includes a visitor center downtown at 1250 Hancock St.; the Old House; the birthplaces of John and John Quincy Adams; and the United First Parish Church. The visitor center is open daily 9-5, Apr. 19-Nov. 10. The visitor center is open all year.

Reservations must be made and tickets purchased at the visitor center. A trolley bus provides transportation to the historic site. Last tour leaves at 3. Admission (including all three houses) $2, under 17 free. Church $2 extra (including trolley service). Phone (617) 770-1175.

John Adams Birthplace was the 1735 birthplace and boyhood home of the second president. The salt box house was where he wrote his first letters to Abigail Smith, who later became his wife.

The John Quincy Adams Birthplace, 141 Franklin St., was the home of John and Abigail Adams until the end of the Revolution. The house was the 1767 birthplace of their son John Quincy, who became the sixth president. Of interest is the law office where the constitution of Massachusetts, which served as a model for the constitutions of other states and the United States, was drafted.

The Old House, 135 Adams St., was the home of the Adams family 1788-1927. The 1731 house has furnishings used by four generations, including two presidents, and a 14,000-volume library with books owned by the family. Outside is an 18th-century garden.

United First Parish Church is at 1306 Hancock St. Established in 1639, the congregation was an early proponent of religious freedom. The present church building, designed by noted architect Alexander Parris, was completed in 1828. John Adams donated most of the granite for its construction, and he, his son John Quincy Adams and their wives are buried here.

Allow 30 minutes minimum. Daily 9-5, Apr.19-Nov. 10. Admission $2, under 16 free. Phone (617) 773-0062.

QUINCY HISTORICAL SOCIETY MUSEUM, 8 Adams St., offers exhibits and a slide presentation relating the history of the area. Supplementing these exhibits are artifacts from the nation's first commercial railway as well as items pertaining to the local granite, glass and maritime industries. A reference and research library is on the premises. Mon.-Fri. 9-4. Donations. Phone (617) 773-1144.

THE QUINCY HOMESTEAD, 34 Butler Rd. at Hancock St., was built in 1686 and was the childhood home of Dorothy Quincy, wife of John Hancock. Guided tours are given Wed.-Sun. noon-4 or by appointment, May-Oct. Admission $3; under 12, $1. Phone (617) 472-5117.

ROCKPORT (A-8) pop. 7,500, elev. 62'

Rockport is the site of a well-known artists' colony on Cape Ann.

Rockport Chamber of Commerce: 3 Main St., P.O. Box 67, Rockport, MA 01966; phone (978) 546-6575 or (888) 726-3922.

JAMES BABSON COOPERAGE SHOP, 1.5 mi. s. on SR 127, is probably the oldest building on Cape Ann. Built in 1658, the shop displays early American tools and furniture. Allow 30 minutes minimum. Tues.-Sun. 2-5, July-Aug. Free. Phone (978) 546-2958.

PAPER HOUSE, .75 mi. off SR 127 via Curtis and Pigeon Hill sts. in Pigeon Cove, is built of 215 thicknesses of newspaper. The furniture, also made of newspaper, includes a desk made of papers concerning Charles Lindbergh's historic flight, a grandfather clock and a piano. Daily 10-5, Apr. 1 to mid-Oct. Admission $1.50; ages 6-14, $1. Phone (978) 546-2629.

ROCKPORT ART ASSOCIATION, 12 Main St., offers changing exhibits of paintings, photographs, graphics and sculpture. Events, including concerts, workshops and lectures, occasionally are scheduled. Mon.-Sat. 10-5, Sun. noon-5, June 1-Columbus Day; Tues.-Fri. 10-4, Sat. 10-5, Sun. noon-5, Feb.-May and day after Columbus Day-Dec. 24. Closed Thanksgiving. Free. Phone (978) 546-6604.

SANDY BAY HISTORICAL SOCIETY AND MUSEUM, 40 King St., contains early American and Victorian rooms, a marine room, children's room, military room, a library of genealogy and local history, fishing relics and full-rigged ship models. Also displayed are costumes, glass, ceramics, paintings and photographs. The Old Castle, nearby at Curtis and Granite sts., is a saltbox house built about 1715. Self-guiding tours of the house highlight historical items, including granite quarry tools.

Allow 1 hour minimum. Society and museum open daily 2-5 (also Mon. 9-1), mid-June to mid-Sept.; Mon. 9-1, rest of year. The Old Castle open Sat. 2-5, mid-June to mid-Sept. Admission (including The Old Castle) $3; over 65, $2; under 13 free. Phone (978) 546-9533.

SALEM (D-3) pop. 38,100, elev. 10'

See map page below.

Salem was capital of the Massachusetts Bay Colony from its founding 1626-30. During the witchcraft trials in 1692 the accusations of a group of children and women caused 19 people to be hanged and one to be crushed to death. Built in 1642, The Witch House, 310½ Essex St., was the home of Jonathan Corwin, one of the judges at the witchcraft trials, and was the site of the preliminary witchcraft examinations; phone (978) 744-0180.

By the end of the 18th century Salem was a prosperous shipping center. Ships from this port brought back rare and costly cargoes from around the world. Many handsome old houses are reminiscent of those seafaring days. The *Friendship*, a full-sized replica of a 1797 East Indian merchant ship, is at Central Wharf across from the Custom House on Derby St. Nathaniel Hawthorne, who wrote "The Scarlet Letter," was born in Salem in 1804. His birthplace may be viewed at House of the Seven Gables Historic Site *(see attraction listing).*

Salem Office of Tourism and Cultural Affairs: 10 Liberty St., Salem, MA 01970; phone (978) 741-3252. *See color ad p. 132.*

Self-guiding tours: Maps outlining walking tours are available at the National Park Service Visitor Information Center, 2 Liberty St.; phone (978) 740-1650.

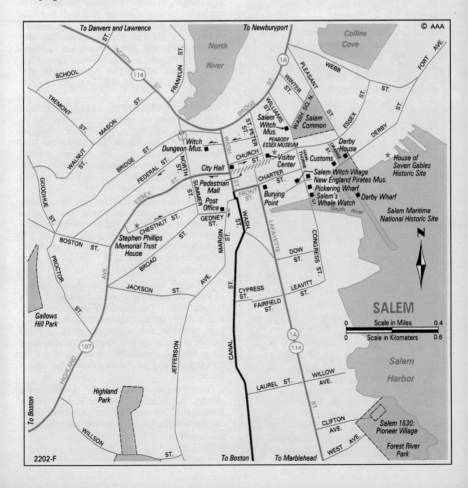

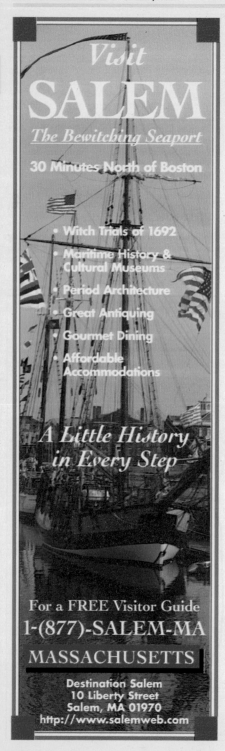

Shopping areas: Pickering Wharf, between the harbor and Derby Street, houses shops and restaurants in the character of 18th-century wharfside Salem.

CHARTER STREET BURYING POINT, on Charter St., was established 1637 and has the tombs of Gov. Simon Bradstreet, *Mayflower* passenger Richard More, Col. John Hathorne and many other notable Salem citizens. One of the stones is inscribed, "Mr. Nathaniel Mather, deceased Oct. 17, 1688, an aged person that had seen but nineteen Winters in the World." Nearby are the Broad Street and Howard Street burying grounds, which have the tombs of George Crowninshield and Col. Timothy Pickering.

CITY HALL, 93 Washington St., displays fine portraits and furnishings and contains the Indian deed to the town. Mon.-Fri. 8-4 (also Thurs. 4-7); closed holidays. Free. Phone (978) 745-9595.

NEW ENGLAND PIRATE MUSEUM, 274 Derby St., features exhibits recounting the history of marauding pirates who once plundered merchant ships off the New England Coast. The museum re-creates a colonial seaport, pirate ship and treasure-laden cave. Guided tours are available. Allow 30 minutes minimum. Daily 10-5, May-Oct.; Sat.-Sun. 10-5, in Nov. Admission $5; over 64, $4; ages 4-13, $3. MC, VI. Phone (978) 741-2800.

★**HOUSE OF THE SEVEN GABLES HISTORIC SITE,** 54 Turner St. (entrance to parking lot on Derby St.), was the inspiration for Nathaniel Hawthorne's novel. On the grounds are the 1682 Hathaway House, the 1658 Retire Beckett House, the Counting House, Nathaniel Hawthorne's 1804 birthplace, seaside period gardens and a panorama of Salem Harbor.

The guided tour includes an introductory audiovisual program; six rooms and a secret staircase in the Gables; and six rooms in Hawthorne's birthplace. Food is available. Mon.-Sat. 10-5, Sun. noon-5, May-Nov.; daily noon-5, rest of year. Admission $7; ages 6-17, $4. DI, MC, VI. Phone (978) 744-0991.

★**PEABODY ESSEX MUSEUM,** East India Sq., includes 30 galleries, a research library and 11 historic houses. The museum's international collection of art and culture consists of 400,000 objects, artifacts and works of art. Collections include maritime art and history, American decorative arts and architecture, Asian export art, the art of Japan and the Pacific Islands and natural history.

One of the best collections of its type in the country, the Maritime Art and History exhibit features maritime drawings and prints, rare nautical instruments, charts, maritime art, ship models, figureheads and decorative pieces.

Collections from Asia, Africa and the Pacific Rim include carvings, religious articles, textiles and other artifacts from China, Korea, India, Hawaii, Japan, Africa and New Guinea. The Asian Export Art collection features more than 13,000 pieces of porcelain, silver, furniture, textiles and works of art on paper produced from the 16th to the 20th centuries in China, Japan and India for export to the West. Natural history exhibits feature regional sea life and waterfowls.

American decorative arts exhibits include rare examples of furniture and decorative art from the multicultural American society from Colonial times to the early 20th century. The museum also contains an exhibit on the Salem witch trials.

Guided tours of historic houses are included in the admission. Tours are available for the Crowninshield-Bentley, Gardner-Pingree and John Ward houses. Food is available. Allow 2 hours minimum. Mon.-Sat. 10-5, Sun. noon-5, day after Memorial Day-Oct. 31; Tues.-Sat. 10-5, Sun. noon-5, rest of year. Closed Jan. 1, Thanksgiving and Dec. 25. Admission $7.50; ages 6-16, $5. AE, MC, VI. Phone (978) 745-9500 or (800) 745-4054. *See color ad.*

Crowninshield-Bentley House, 126 Essex St., was built in 1727 and contains 18th-century furnishings.

Gardner-Pingree House, 128 Essex St., contains the work of Salem master builder Samuel McIntire. The 1804-05 home is furnished in period.

John Ward House, a 1684 structure, depicts scenes from 17th-century domestic life. In the lean-to are an 1825 apothecary's shop, an 1840 Salem cent shop and a weaving room. In the neighboring gardens are Old Salem Meeting House, the 1830 Lye-Tapley Shoe Shop and the 1800 Derby Summer House.

SALEM MARITIME NATIONAL HISTORIC SITE, at 174 Derby St. on the waterfront, preserves wharves and buildings of the Port of Salem from 1670 to the early 1900s. Allow 2 hours minimum. Tours are given daily 9-5; closed Jan. 1, Thanksgiving and Dec. 25. Free. Tours $3; over 64 and ages 6-16, $2. Reservations are required and can be made at Central Wharf Warehouse Orientation Center. Phone (978) 740-1660.

Bonded Warehouse once was used to store cargoes awaiting re-export or claiming. This 1819 building now holds tea chests, rum barrels and original hoisting equipment.

Central Wharf Warehouse Orientation Center, Derby St. waterfront, offers exhibits and an audiovisual orientation program to Salem Maritime National Historic Site.

Custom House, known by its granite steps and large carved eagle, was built in 1819 and was used to conduct port business and collect tariffs. Nathaniel Hawthorne worked at this site for 3 years while acting as surveyor of the Port of Salem.

Derby House was built in 1762 for Elias Hasket Derby, a prominent merchant of the post-Revolutionary War period.

Derby Wharf was a base for privateers during the Revolutionary War. Between the Revolutionary War and the War of 1812, when foreign ports were opened to American trade, it was a shipping center. Daily dawn-dusk.

Narbonne-Hale House, 73 Essex St., was built in the 17th century and once was used as a home and a shop for various craftsmen and tradesmen.

Scale House, built in 1826, stored measuring devices to assess the value of imported cargoes. Equipment is still on display.

SALEM 1630: PIONEER VILLAGE, in Forest River Park at jct. SR 114/1A and West St., is a living-history museum comprised of gardens, animals, thatched cottages, workshops and wigwams. Guides in period costumes relate information about the people, conditions and politics of the time and perform period skills and chores. Allow 1 hour minimum. Mon.-Sat. 10-5, Sun. noon-5, mid-May through Oct. 31. Admission $5; over 62, $4; ages 6-17, $3. Phone (978) 744-0991. *See ad.*

SALEM TROLLEY offers a narrated sightseeing tour past the town's major attractions. The tour can be boarded at any stop. Allow 1 hour mini-

mum. Daily 10-5, Apr.-Oct.; Sat.-Sun. 10-5 in Nov. Fare $8; over 65, $7; ages 5-14, $4. Phone (978) 744-5469.

SALEM WITCH MUSEUM, Washington Sq., is opposite Salem Common on SR 1A. The museum depicts the witch trials of 1692. An audiovisual presentation is offered every half-hour. The "Do You Believe in Witches?" exhibit examines witch stereotypes, aspects of 17th-century witchcraft, modern witchcraft and the phenomenon of witch hunts. Allow 30 minutes minimum. Daily 10-7, July-Aug.; 10-5, rest of year. Closed Jan. 1, Thanksgiving and Dec. 25. Admission $5.50; over 62, $5; ages 6-14, $3.50. Phone (978) 744-1692. *See ad.*

SALEM WITCH VILLAGE, 282 Rear Derby St., features a labyrinth with scenes that depict myths associated with witchcraft and facts about present-day witchcraft. Daily 9-7, May-Oct.; 9-6, rest of year. Closed Easter, Thanksgiving and Dec. 25. Admission $4.50; ages 6-14, $2.75. DS, MC, VI. Phone (800) 298-2929.

SAVE **SALEM'S WHALE WATCH** cruises depart from Pickering Wharf, 197 Derby St. Naturalists provide commentary on whale behavior and offer facts and legends about historic Salem Harbor. Cruises depart daily at 9 and 2, July 1-Labor Day; Mon.-Fri. at 9, Sat.-Sun. at 9 and 2, day after Labor Day-Sept. 30; daily at 9, in June; daily

at 1, in Oct.; Sat.-Sun. at 11, in May. Fare $25; students with ID $23; senior citizens $20; ages 4-16, $16. AE, DS, MC, VI. Phone (978) 741-0434 or (800) 745-9594.

[SAVE] ★ **STEPHEN PHILLIPS MEMORIAL TRUST HOUSE**, 34 Chestnut St., is a Federal-style mansion with English and Early American furnishings, Chinese porcelains, rare rugs, paintings and memorabilia from the era of sailing ships. The carriage house contains period carriages and antique automobiles. Allow 30 minutes minimum. Mon.-Sat. 10-4:30, Memorial Day weekend-Oct. 31. Admission $3, senior citizens and students with ID $2, under 6 free. Phone (978) 744-0440.

WITCH DUNGEON MUSEUM, 16 Lynde St., is in a former 19th-century church. A scene from a 1692 witch trial is performed by professional actors. A guided tour of the re-created dungeon is included. Allow 30 minutes minimum. Daily 10-5, Apr.-Nov. Admission $5; over 64, $4; ages 4-13, $3. MC, VI. Phone (978) 741-3570. *See ad.*

SAUGUS (D-3) pop. 25,500, elev. 20'

The Saugus ironworks began in 1646 with an English investment totaling more than $165,000 by present standards. Its success gave the New World its first sustained production of cast and wrought iron and launched the American iron and steel industry.

Saugus Chamber of Commerce: 335 Central St., Saugus, MA 01906; phone (781) 233-8407.

★ **SAUGUS IRON WORKS NATIONAL HISTORIC SITE**, 244 Central St., has a reconstructed blast furnace, working water wheels, a forge and a rolling and slitting mill. This was America's first successfully integrated ironworks. The museum displays artifacts uncovered in excavation, including early ironworks products and a 500-pound hammer used in the original forge. A film is shown, and blacksmith demonstrations are presented. Picnicking is permitted.

Guided tours daily at 9:45, 11:15, 2:15 and 3:45, Apr.-Oct.; self-guiding tours 9-4, rest of year. Closed Jan. 1, Thanksgiving and Dec. 25. Free. Phone (781) 233-0050.

Iron Works House is a 17th-century house which contains early American furnishings and exhibits. Guided tours are available.

SHARON (C-6) pop. 15,500, elev. 234'

In an area once known as Massapoag, an Indian word meaning "great waters," Sharon is a residential community. Largemouth bass and pickerel inhabit Lake Massapoag, a popular fishing spot. Rockridge Cemetery contains the grave

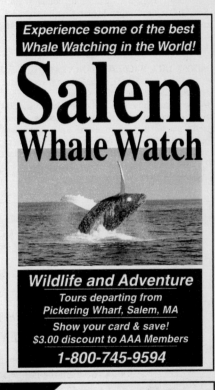

of and a memorial to Deborah Sampson Gannett, a woman who disguised herself as a man and fought in the Revolutionary War. When her gender was discovered by a physician in 1783, she was given an honorable discharge and a pension for her military service.

Metro South Chamber of Commerce: 60 School St., Brockton, MA 02301; phone (508) 586-0500.

KENDALL WHALING MUSEUM, 27 Everett St., contains international whaling-related items including paintings, scrimshaw, model ships and a whaleboat. Tues.-Sat. and Mon. holidays 10-5, Sun. 1-5; closed other holidays. Admission $4; over 65 and students with ID, $3; ages 6-16, $2.50; ages 5-15, $1; family rate $10. DS, MC, VI. Phone (781) 784-5642.

MOOSE HILL WILDLIFE SANCTUARY is .5 mi. e. of US 1 via SR 27, then 2 mi. s. on Moose Hill St. This is the oldest sanctuary maintained by the Massachusetts Audubon Society. Its 2,200 acres contain woods, meadows, marshes, a butterfly garden and 25 miles of trails. Sanctuary open daily dawn-dusk. Visitor center open Tues.-Sun. 9-5; closed Jan. 1, Thanksgiving and Dec. 25. Admission $3; over 65 and ages 3-12, $2. MC, VI. Phone (781) 784-5691.

STOUGHTON (C-6) pop. 26,800, elev. 239'

Stoughton was named for William Stoughton, an 18th-century Massachusetts lieutenant governor whose father once had owned the land. The 1868-70 [SAVE] Mary Baker Eddy Historic House, home of the founder of Christian Science, contains period furnishings and an 1840s shoemaking shop; phone (508) 586-0500.

Metro South Chamber of Commerce: 60 School St., Brockton, MA 02401; phone (508) 586-0500.

SUDBURY (E-1) pop. 14,400, elev. 201'

★**LONGFELLOW'S WAYSIDE INN OF SUDBURY** is .25 mi. w. off US 20, on Wayside Inn Rd. Made famous by Henry Wadsworth Longfellow's poem "Tales of a Wayside Inn," it is one of the country's oldest inns. Longfellow spent his summers at the inn during the mid-1800s. Refurbished by Henry Ford 1923-44, the inn features a 13-room museum, the Martha-Mary Chapel, formal gardens, a barn and carriage house, a stone bridge and a working gristmill.

Redstone Schoolhouse was attended by Mary E. Sawyer, the inspiration for the renowned nursery rhyme "Mary Had A Little Lamb." A self-guiding walking-tour brochure is provided. Food

is available. Inn open daily 8 a.m.-10 p.m.; closed July 4 and Dec. 25. Gristmill open daily 9:30-5, Apr.-Nov. (weather permitting). Schoolhouse open daily 11:30-5, May-Oct. Donations. Phone (978) 443-1776.

SWAMPSCOTT (E-3) pop. 13,700, elev. 38'

On Massachusetts Bay, Swampscott is one of the North Shore's popular summer resorts.

SAVE **THE MARY BAKER EDDY HISTORIC HOUSE** is at 23 Paradise Rd. (SR 1A). While living in the home for a brief period in 1866, Mrs. Eddy experienced the healing that led her to the discovery of Christian Science. The home is equipped with period furnishings, some of which belonged to Eddy. Allow 30 minutes minimum. Mon.-Sat. 10-5, Sun. 2-5, May-Oct.; Tues.-Sun. 1-4, Mar.-Apr. and Nov.-Jan. Closed holidays. Admission $3; senior citizens and students with ID $1.50, under 12 free. Phone (781) 599-1853.

TEWKSBURY (B-6) elev. 126'

Wamesit Indian Monument, on Main St., is a 7-foot-high cast bronze sculpture set on a 9-foot-high granite boulder. It was designed in honor of the peaceful American Indian by Mico Kaufman, a Tewksbury resident and world-class sculptor.

Kaufman also created the Water, Anne Sullivan-Helen Keller Monument, on Main St., depicting the turning point in Helen Keller's life. A young girl born deaf and blind feels water at the pump, and with three extended fingers understands sign language for the letter W and water. The monument is a tribute to her dedicated teacher Anne Sullivan, a long-time resident of Tewksbury.

TOPSFIELD (B-7) pop. 5,800, elev. 60'

IPSWICH RIVER WILDLIFE SANCTUARY is .5 mi. e. of US 1 on SR 97, s. on Perkins Row. This is the largest of the Massachusetts Audubon Society's sanctuaries, covering 2,800 acres of meadow, marsh and ponds as well as part of the Ipswich River. Ten miles of marked trails cross the sanctuary. Tues.-Fri. 9-4, Sat.-Sun. 9-5; closed Jan. 1, Thanksgiving and Dec. 24-25. Admission $3; over 65 and under 15, $2. Phone (978) 887-9264.

WALTHAM (E-2) pop. 57,900, elev. 79'

SAVE **CHARLES RIVER MUSEUM OF INDUSTRY** is at 154 Moody St. Exhibits, built around working machines, focus on the American Industrial Revolution and illustrate the innovation and development of successive manufacturing systems that affected American history and society. Mon.-Sat. 10-5. Admission $4; senior citizens and ages 6-15, $2. Phone (781) 893-5410.

SAVE **GORE PLACE**, 52 Gore St., is on SR 20 at the Waltham-Watertown line. Built in 1806 for Gov. Christopher Gore, the mansion is one of the oldest examples of Federal domestic architecture in New England. Set in a 40-acre park, the house features 22 rooms furnished in period. Tues.-Sat. 11-5, Sun. 1-5, Apr. 15-Nov. 15; closed holidays. Tours are given daily on the hour. Last tour begins 1 hour before closing. Admission $5; over 64 and students with ID $3; under 12, $2. MC, VI. Phone (781) 894-2798.

LYMAN ESTATE GREENHOUSES, .5 mi. n. of jct. US 20 at 185 Lyman St., offers a self-guiding tour through the 19th-century greenhouses which contain grapevines, camellia shrubs, orchids, tropical fruit trees and exotic plants. The camellias are in bloom November through April. The 1793 mansion (closed to the public) is surrounded by 30-acres of English-style gardens. Guided tours are available by appointment. Mon.-Sat. 9-4. Self-guiding tours by donation, guided tours $3. Phone (781) 891-4882, ext. 244.

ROSE ART MUSEUM, off South St. on the Brandeis University campus, presents changing exhibits of 20th-century American art, including works by Boston-area artists. Tues.-Sun. noon-5 (also Thurs. 5-9); closed holidays. Free. Phone (781) 736-3434.

WELLESLEY (F-2) pop. 26,600, elev. 140'

DAVIS MUSEUM AND CULTURAL CENTER, at Wellesley College, has a collection of some 5,000 paintings, prints, photographs, drawings and sculptures from classical through contemporary periods. Rotating exhibits are featured. Gallery talks are given; tours are available by request with 3 weeks notice. Tues.-Sat. 11-5 (also Wed.-Thurs. 5-8), Sun. 1-5 in Jan. and June-Aug.; Tues.-Sat. 11-5, Sun. 1-5, rest of year. Closed Jan. 1, July 4, Thanksgiving and Dec. 25. Free. Phone (781) 283-2051.

WENHAM (B-7) pop. 4,200, elev. 51'

Ellery Sedgwick, author and editor of the *Atlantic Monthly* 1909-38, spent many summers just outside Wenham. Long Hill, his home at 572 Essex St., contains a garden with more than 400 varieties of trees, shrubs, flowers and perennial herbs. The gardens and estate grounds are open to the public; phone (978) 921-1944.

North Shore Chamber of Commerce: 5 Cherry Hill Dr., Danvers, MA 01923; phone (978) 774-8565.

SAVE **WENHAM MUSEUM**, on SR 1A at 132 Main St., includes the 1660 Claflin-Richards House, with architecture and furnishings representing the 17th-19th centuries. The museum has a collection of more than 5,000 dolls, dollhouses and toys, and changing exhibit galleries, cultural and historical exhibits and interactive children's exhibits. A train room featues five operating HO layouts of various gauges and a display of railroad relics and antique trains. Allow 1 hour minimum. Mon.-Fri. 10-4, Sat.-Sun. 1-4; closed holidays. Admission $4; over 65, $3.50; ages 3-16, $2. Phone (978) 468-2377.

WESTFORD (B-5) pop. 16,400, elev. 406′

THE BUTTERFLY PLACE, 120 Tyngsboro Rd., near the Westford-Tyngsboro line, features a 3,100-square-foot glass atrium complete with winding paths and flowering plants and shrubs. Some 300 butterflies from 30 species can be seen. A 15-minute videotape presents the life cycle of butterflies. Picnicking is permitted. Allow 1 hour minimum. Daily 10-5, Apr. 1-Columbus Day. Last admission is 30 minutes before closing. Admission $7; over 65 and ages 3-12, $5. MC, VI. Phone (978) 392-0955.

WESTON (E-1) pop. 10,200, elev. 165′

SPELLMAN MUSEUM OF STAMPS AND POSTAL HISTORY, .5 mi. n. of jct. SR 30, next to the Regis College campus at 235 Wellesley St., features rare stamps, American and international collections and exhibits describing postal history and famous collectors. The Philatelic Research Library is open by appointment. Thurs.-Sun. noon-4; closed holidays. Admission $5, senior citizens and students with ID $3, under 16 free. Phone (781) 894-6735.

WEYMOUTH (F-3) pop. 54,100, elev. 30′

ABIGAIL ADAMS BIRTHPLACE is at North and Norton sts. Abigail Smith Adams, the wife of John Adams, the second U.S. president, and mother of John Quincy Adams, the sixth U.S. president, was born in the house Nov. 11, 1744. This restored 1685 home is furnished in period; some furnishings are original to the Smith family. Guided tours are available. Tues.-Sun. 1-4, July 1-Labor Day; by appointment in June and day after Labor Day-Oct. 15. Admission $1; under 13, 25c. Phone (781) 335-4205.

**This ends listings for the Boston Vicinity.
The following page resumes the alphabetical listings of
cities in Massachusetts.**

BOURNE—*see Cape Cod p. 142.*

BOYLSTON (C-5) pop. 950

SAVE **TOWER HILL BOTANIC GARDEN,** I-290 exit 24, then 3.25 mi. n. on Church St. to 11 French Dr., occupies 132 acres and includes an heirloom apple orchard; a cottage; secret, vegetable, lawn and wildlife gardens; and nature trails with views of Mount Wachusett and the Wachusett Reservoir. Special events are held throughout the year; phone for schedule. Food is available Sat.-Sun., May to mid-Oct.

Allow 1 hour minimum. Tues.-Sun. and Mon. holidays 10-5, Apr.-Dec.; Tues.-Fri. 10-5, rest of year. Closed Jan. 1, Thanksgiving and Dec. 24-25. Admission $7; over 65, $5; ages 6-18, $3. Phone (508) 869-6111.

BREWSTER—*see Cape Cod p. 143.*

BROCKTON (D-7) pop. 92,800, elev. 128′

Once a major shoe-manufacturing center, Brockton now supports more than 200 other industries. D.W. Field Park *(see Recreation Chart),* named after one of the city's shoe manufacturers, offers golfing, picnicking and bicycling in the park's 700 acres of woods, ponds and gardens.

Metro South Chamber of Commerce: 60 School St., Brockton, MA 02301-4087; phone (508) 586-0500.

Shopping areas: Westgate Mall, SR 24 at CR 27, has Macy's and Marshall's.

THE FULLER MUSEUM OF ART, 455 Oak St., situated on 22 acres overlooking Porter's Pond and houses a collection of 19th- and 20th-century American paintings, sculpture, photographs and decorative arts as well as contemporary crafts. The permanent collection is supplemented by changing exhibits. Children's programs and exhibits are offered. Allow 1 hour minimum. Tues.-Sun. noon-5; closed holidays. Admission $3, senior citizens and students with ID $2, under 18 free. Phone (508) 588-6000.

BROOKLINE—*see Boston p. 117.*

BUZZARDS BAY—*see Cape Cod p. 145.*

CAMBRIDGE—*see Boston p. 117.*

CAPE ANN—*see Boston p. 120.*

AAA Safety Poster Program

AAA Safety Poster Program promotes safety on the road and off...

each year hundreds of posters from around the U.S. and Canada flood to AAA to be judged and recognized for their distinguished achievement in executing a traffic safety message.

Through art education, the AAA Traffic Safety Poster Program encourages students to think about traffic safety practices, learn and have fun by doing.

Prizes totaling more than $17,000 in U.S. savings bonds are awarded each year.

Contact Traffic Safety Department...of the main office of your local AAA club for more information.

National Poster Program Headquarters at (407) 444-7916

Cape Cod

To architects, Cape Cod is a style; to gourmets, a cuisine; and to artists, changing moods and patterns of light, color and space. Summer visitors see the cape as beaches, shops, attractions, entertainment, country clubs and, often, a chance to rub elbows with celebrities. More basic is the Cape Cod of residents. Quiet and individualistic, they view the cape as a haven where life can proceed undisturbed, even by the annual influx of tourists.

US 6 curves northeast along the cape and allows access to the scrub oak-pitch pine covered sand dunes of the Cape Cod National Seashore *(see place listing p. 145)*. Beginning at Sagamore Bridge and ending in Provincetown, the route provides access to all of the towns on the cape. Another way to see the island is by traversing the 39-mile-long Cape Cod Bike Trail. Whether hiking or bicycling, the trail offers picturesque scenery and opportunities to explore the natural wonders of the island.

In November 1620 the *Mayflower* Pilgrims landed at the tip of the cape. By the end of the 17th century Cape Cod was a prosperous fishing and whaling center. During the 1800s wealthy sea captains built elaborate homes and furnished them with objects acquired on their world travels. Many homes have been restored as museums.

BARNSTABLE (E-8) pop. 40,900, elev. 72'

Settled in 1639 by pioneers whose livestock thrived in the salty hay marshes, Barnstable developed as a coastal trade center. Fish caught on the Grand Banks and maritime activities were economic mainstays. Sea captains of the village sailed on clipper ships to the Orient. The region now draws summer residents and is a popular seasonal resort.

TRAYSER MUSEUM COMPLEX, at the Old Customs House on SR 6A, was built in 1856 by the U.S. government. On display are ship models, nautical equipment, American Indian relics, Oriental memorabilia, farm and carpentry tools, an old wooden jail, and paintings. Tues.-Sun. 1:30-4:30, mid-June through Columbus Day. Donations. Phone (508) 362-2092.

BOURNE (E-7) pop. 16,100, elev. 19'

Bourne was named after Jonathan Bourne, the village's most prominent native son, a successful whaling merchant who set up offices in New Bedford.

Cape Cod Canal Region Chamber of Commerce: 70 Main St., Buzzards Bay, MA 02532; phone (508) 759-6000. *See color ads starting on p. 374.*

APTUCXET TRADING POST MUSEUM is on the s. side of the Bourne Canal Bridge, 1 mi. from jct. US 6 and SR 28 via Shore Rd. The museum is a replica of the trading post built on this site in 1627, perhaps the first such establishment on the continent. Exhibits include 17th-century furnishings and Pilgrim, Dutch and Indian relics. A runestone dates from about A.D. 1000.

President Grover Cleveland's private railroad station, an old windmill, saltworks and an herb garden are on the grounds. Picnicking is permitted. Guided tours are given Mon.-Sat. 10-5, Sun. 2-5, July-Aug.; Tues.-Sat. 10-5, Sun. 2-5, May-June and Sept. 1 to mid-Oct. Admission $2.50; grades 1-12, $1. Phone (508) 759-9487.

BREWSTER (D-9) pop. 8,400

Approximately at the geographic center of Cape Cod on SR 6A, Brewster is the setting of stately early 19th-century homes built by the sea captains who dominated the town's initial economy. The city offers antique shops, art galleries and museums that lure summer visitors to Cape Cod Bay. The Old Gristmill on Stoney Brook Road is one of the country's first gristmills.

BASSETT WILD ANIMAL FARM, 3 mi. n. of US 6 exit 10 at 620 Tubman Rd., features exotic and domestic animals in natural surroundings. A petting zoo and hayride also are available. Food is available. Picnicking is permitted. Allow 1 hour minimum. Daily 10-5, Memorial Day-Labor Day. Admission $6; ages 2-11, $4.25. Hayrides and pony rides 75c each. Phone (508) 896-3224.

CAPE COD MUSEUM OF NATURAL HISTORY, SR 6A, 2 mi. w. of SR 124, has two floors of exhibits, a library and art gallery, and nature trails along which native fauna and flora can be seen. Programs and nature trips are scheduled year-round. Allow 1 hour, 30 minutes minimum. Mon.-Sat. 9:30-4:30, Sun. 11-4:30; closed Jan. 1, Easter, Memorial Day, July 4, Labor Day, Thanksgiving and Dec. 25. Admission $5; senior citizens $4.50; ages 5-12, $2. DS, MC, VI. Phone (508) 896-3867.

NEW ENGLAND FIRE AND HISTORY MUSEUM, on SR 6A, .5 mi. w. of SR 137, includes five buildings on a 3-acre site. A collection of Early American firefighting equipment and memorabilia from the late 1700s to the early 1900s includes fire helmets and a reproduction of Benjamin Franklin's Union Firehouse. Also exhibited are an animated diorama of the Chicago fire of 1871; and a Victorian apothecary, herb garden and smithy. Short movies are shown daily in the video theater. Picnicking is permitted.

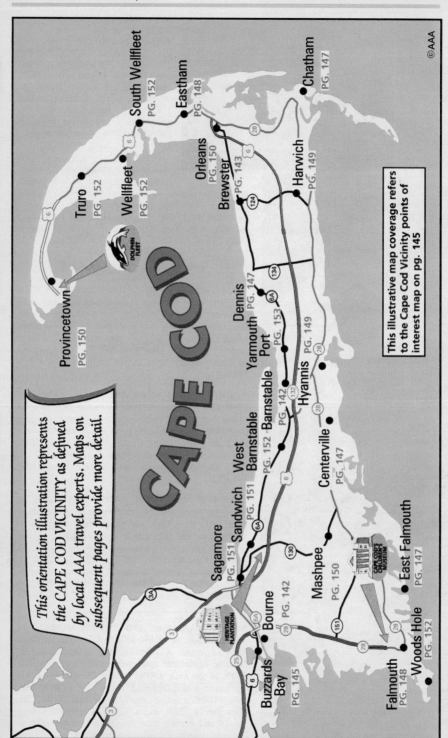

CAPE COD

This orientation illustration represents the CAPE COD VICINITY as defined by local AAA travel experts. Maps on subsequent pages provide more detail.

This illustrative map coverage refers to the Cape Cod Vicinity points of interest map on pg. 145

Provincetown PG. 150

DOLPHIN FLEET

Truro PG. 152

South Wellfleet PG. 152

Wellfleet PG. 152

Eastham PG. 148

Orleans PG. 150

Brewster PG. 143

Chatham PG. 147

Harwich PG. 149

Dennis PG. 147

Yarmouth Port PG. 153

Hyannis PG. 149

Barnstable PG. 142

West Barnstable PG. 152

Centerville PG. 147

Sagamore PG. 151

Sandwich PG. 151

HERITAGE PLANTATION

Bourne PG. 142

Buzzards Bay PG. 145

Mashpee PG. 150

CAPE COD CHILDREN'S MUSEUM

East Falmouth PG. 147

Falmouth PG. 148

Woods Hole PG. 152

© AAA

Guided tours are given Mon.-Fri. 10-4, Sat.-Sun. noon-4, Memorial Day to mid-Sept.; Sat.-Sun. noon-4, mid-Sept. through Columbus Day. Admission $5; over 62, $4.50; ages 5-12, $2.50; under 5, $1. Phone (508) 896-5711, or 432-2450 day after Columbus Day-day before Memorial Day.

BUZZARDS BAY (E-7)

CAPE COD CANAL, .25 mi. s. of Main St. on Academy Dr., is a 17.4-mile link between Buzzards Bay and Cape Cod Bay, designed to save an average of 135 miles of coastline travel around the tip of Cape Cod. Recreational facilities include paved walking and bicycling paths. Swimming is prohibited. A reception area in the field office on Academy Drive offers closed-circuit television and radar views of the canal and a scale model of the area. Recreational area open dawn-dusk. Field office open Mon.-Fri. 9-4. Phone (508) 759-5991 for recorded information, or 759-4431.

★CAPE COD NATIONAL SEASHORE (C-9)

Dunes constantly reshaped by storm and wind, 40 miles of coastline, marshland, glacial cliffs and dense forests accent the 44,000-acre Cape Cod National Seashore. Spared the scars of industrial buildup, the beaches, ponds and open fields remain protected in a natural state. The cape also is marked by weathered cottages, villages and lighthouses.

General Information and Activities

The National Seashore is open all year. Park headquarters is at the Marconi area in South Wellfleet. Near the headquarters are high cliffs that afford good views of the beach and ocean, and an inland nature trail traverses a white cedar swamp unusual to the cape. At Pilgrim Heights in North Truro is a spring thought to have been the Pilgrims' first source of fresh water. The spring is reached by a nature trail.

Guided walks and lectures are offered April through November. Interpretive shelters provide

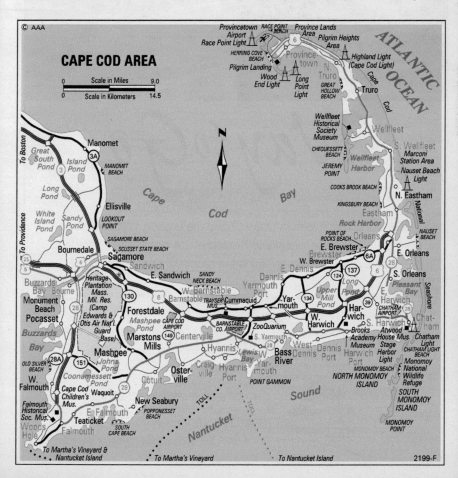

TO MARTHA'S VINEYARD & NANTUCKET

Way to Go

Enjoy smooth sailing and oceans of fun.
Take the Steamship from Cape Cod to the Islands, Woods Hole to
Martha's Vineyard or Hyannis to Nantucket. It's comfortable, affordable
and no passenger reservations are required. It's the way to go!

- frequent daily departures
- only year-round ferry service
- spacious indoor & outdoor decks
- food and beverage service

- No need for a car on
  the Islands. Taxi service,
  shuttle buses and bike rentals
  are readily available.

The Steamship

ASK FOR BROCHURE AND SCHEDULE.
www.islandferry.com
(508) 477-8600
TDD # (508) 540-1394 (for the hearing impaired)

historical exhibits. Self-guiding nature trails are open all year; trail leaflets are available at visitor centers and at the head of each trail.

There are four picnic areas, and picnicking is allowed on all beaches; a permit is required to build an open fire. Swimming is permitted on six beaches in the summer and lifeguards are on duty. No license is required for saltwater fishing, but a state license is required for freshwater fishing, and a town license is needed for shellfishing.

Hunting is permitted in season for upland game and migratory waterfowls; federal, state and local laws apply. Camping is prohibited in the seashore, except in privately owned campgrounds.

Three paved bicycle trails, originating near the visitor centers and at the head of the Meadow Beach parking lot, lead to beaches and picnic areas. Trail maps are available at the visitor centers. *See Recreation Chart.*

ADMISSION is free, but a parking fee of $5 is charged during summer at the beaches.

PETS must be physically restricted at all times; leashes are not to exceed 6 feet. Pets are not allowed in public buildings, picnic areas or on trails and are permitted on swimming beaches only during the off-season.

ADDRESS inquiries to the Superintendent, Cape Cod National Seashore, 99 Marconi Site Rd., Wellfleet, MA 02667; phone (508) 349-3785, ext. 200.

VISITOR CENTERS in Provincetown and Eastham provide information on the seashore. Both centers offer evening programs presented in adjacent amphitheaters in the summer; check locally for hours and schedules.

Province Lands Visitor Center, on Race Point Rd. in Provincetown, has an observation platform and offers movies and exhibits. Daily 9-5, mid-Apr. through late Nov. Phone (508) 487-1256.

Salt Pond Visitor Center, on US 6 in Eastham, offers movies and museum exhibits. Daily 9-5, early Feb.-Dec. 31; Sat.-Sun. 9-4:30, Jan. 1-early Feb. Closed Dec. 25. Phone (508) 255-3421.

CENTERVILLE (E-8)

With its maritime location on Nantucket Sound, Centerville was home to wealthy ship captains who built stately homes in the early 1800s. Craigville Beach offers boating, beachcombing and swimming in Nantucket Sound.

CENTERVILLE HISTORICAL SOCIETY MUSEUM, 513 Main St., is a 14-room museum housed in an 1840s home to which exhibition wings have been added. Exhibits include a Colonial revival kitchen, Victorian period rooms, gowns and accessories, marine and Civil War artifacts, farm tools, decorative arts and a research library. Wed.-Sat. 1:30-4:30, mid-June to mid-Sept. Last tour begins 30 minutes before closing. Admission $2.50; senior citizens $2; ages 6-17, $1. Phone (508) 775-0331.

CHATHAM (E-9) pop. 6,600, elev. 59'

With Nantucket Sound on one side and the Atlantic Ocean on the other, Chatham is a fine starting place for the saltwater angler in search of bass, bluefish and snapper. Commercial fishing boats unload their catches at the pier on Shore Road every afternoon. Chatham Light, which affords an excellent panorama of the Atlantic, is approximately 2 miles northeast off SR 28.

Chatham Chamber of Commerce: P.O. Box 793, Chatham, MA 02633; phone (508) 945-5199 or (800) 715-5567.

CHATHAM RAILROAD MUSEUM, on Depot St. in the passenger station of the former railroad company, contains artifacts, models of trains, the 1910 New York Central Caboose and a diorama of the Chatham railroad yard. Tues.-Sat. 10-4, mid-June to mid-Sept. Donations. Phone (508) 945-5199.

THE OLD ATWOOD HOUSE MUSEUM, .75 mi. s. at 347 Stage Harbor Rd., was built about 1752 for Joseph C. Atwood, a sea captain, and remained in the Atwood family for nearly 175 years. Fully restored, the two-story house is furnished in several periods, and additions and outbuildings contain historical items, a seashell collection, a portrait gallery and murals depicting the people of Chatham in the first half of the 20th century. A lighthouse turret and an herb garden are on the grounds. Allow 1 hour minimum. Tues.-Fri. 1-4, mid-June through Sept. 30. Admission $3; under 12, $1. Phone (508) 945-2493.

DENNIS (D-9) pop. 13,900, elev. 24'

Dennis, on SR 6A almost at the midpoint of the north shore of Cape Cod, is the site of graceful old homes, spacious summer residences, artists' studios and the famed Cape Playhouse. The method of cultivating cranberries in bogs originated in Dennis; commercial salt extraction from sea water was initiated in East Dennis in the late 18th century.

Established in 1927, the Cape Playhouse, off SR 6A, continues to offer first-rate theater every summer including plays, comedies, mysteries and musicals; phone (508) 385-3911. Cape Museum of Fine Arts displays the works of 20th-century Cape Cod artists year-round; phone (508) 385-4477.

EAST FALMOUTH (E-8) pop. 5,600

ASHUMET HOLLY & WILDLIFE SANCTUARY, 49 acres 4 mi. e. of jct. SRs 28 and 151, then left on Currier Rd. following signs, preserves the holly collection of Wilfred Wheeler. Well-marked trails wind through the bird and wildlife sanctuary. A barn swallow colony can be seen May through August. Daily dawn-dusk. Admission $3; over 65 and under 13, $2. Phone (508) 563-6390.

EASTHAM (D-9) elev. 32'

Eastham was settled in 1644 by Plymouth colonists. First Encounter Beach was the spot where Miles Standish and other *Mayflower* forefathers landed during their expedition from Provincetown. Naturalist Henry Beston, enchanted by the area's beauty in 1927, wrote "The Outermost House," a passionate novel about the winds, tides and wildlife of the beach. The hull of the World War II victory ship, the *Gen. James E. Longstreet*, was submerged in the bay for target practice by the Air Force more than 50 years ago. A visitor center for Cape Cod National Seashore *(see place listing)* is at Salt Pond, off scenic US 6.

Eastham Town Hall: 2500 State Hwy., Eastham, MA 02642; phone (508) 240-5900.

OLD EASTHAM WINDMILL, on US 6 opposite the town hall, is the oldest working windmill on Cape Cod. Occasionally corn is ground in the 1680 structure. Built in Plymouth by Thomas Paine, the mill was moved to Eastham in 1793. Mon.-Sat. 10-5, Sun. 1-5, July 1-Labor Day. Free. Phone (508) 240-5900.

THE OLD SCHOOLHOUSE MUSEUM, at jct. US 6 Nauset Rd. and Schoolhouse Rd., is a one-room schoolhouse built in 1869. Exhibits depict the area's history and include a model schoolroom, farming and household implements, shipwreck treasures, old paper currency, a coin collection and a 13-foot jawbone from a 65-foot finback whale. Allow 30 minutes minimum. Mon.-Fri. 1-4, July-Aug.; Sat. 1-4, in Sept. Free. Phone (508) 255-0788.

THE SWIFT-DALEY HOUSE, on US 6 next to the post office, was built in 1741. Eight furnished rooms feature clothing and artifacts from the Co-lonial to Victorian periods. Allow 1 hour minimum. Mon.-Fri. 1-4, July-Aug.; Sat. 1-4, in Sept. Free. Phone (508) 240-1247.

THE TOOL MUSEUM, on US 6 behind The Swift-Daley House, displays hundreds of tools and implements from the area, including a wooden crankshaft from the old saltworks, a foot-operated grindstone, cranberry sorters and doorposts from the First Eastham Meeting House. The Dill Beach Shack, which survived the storm of 1978 that ravaged the coast, also is on the grounds. Allow 30 minutes minimum. Mon.-Fri. 1-4, July-Aug.; Sat. 1-4 in Sept. Free. Phone (508) 240-1247.

FALMOUTH (E-8) pop. 28,000, elev. 44'

Falmouth was settled by Quakers in 1661 and was one of the first New England towns founded on the principles of religious tolerance. Originally a center for whaling, shipbuilding and agriculture, it later supported salt and glass industries. Falmouth is now a picturesque year-round beach resort centered on a historic village green. It also is a point of departure for ferries to Martha's Vineyard *(see place listing p. 160)* and seasonal connecting services to Nantucket *(see place listing p. 161).*

Falmouth Chamber of Commerce: 20 Academy Ln., P.O. Box 582, Falmouth, MA 02541; phone (508) 548-8500 or (800) 526-8532. *See color ad.*

CAPE COD CHILDREN'S MUSEUM, in Falmouth Mall, 1.75 mi. e. on SR 28, offers interactive and educational displays for children. Included are a medieval castle for toddlers, a 30-foot pirate ship, a puppet stage, a wooden train and a planetarium. Children under 13 must be accompanied by a parent. Allow 1 hour, 30 minutes minimum. Mon.-Sat. 10-5, Sun. noon-5; closed Easter, Thanksgiving and Dec. 25. Admission $3; over 59 and ages 1-4, $2. Phone (508) 457-4667.

FALMOUTH HISTORICAL SOCIETY MUSEUM is on Palmer Ave. off SR 28 at the Village Green. Two restored houses contain period

rooms, paintings, glass, china and a whaling exhibit. A barn houses period farm and kitchen equipment. Gardens are part of the complex. Guided tours are available by appointment. Mon.-Fri. 2-5, June 15-Sept. 15; closed holidays. Walking tours are given Tues. at 4. Admission $3; under 12, 50c. Phone (508) 548-4857.

HARWICH (E-9) pop. 10,300, elev. 70′

Harwich was named after the English village called "Happy-go-lucky Harwich" by Queen Elizabeth. At the elbow of Cape Cod, it is surrounded by the communities of North, South, East and West Harwich, Harwich Port and Pleasant Lake, all of which are known collectively as the Harwiches. Once a whaling and shipbuilding center, Harwich is now supported by the cranberry and tourism industries.

The town's population triples during the summer, as visitors arrive to enjoy nearby freshwater and saltwater beaches, fishing, scuba diving, sailing and bird watching. A 23-mile bicycle trail winds through woodlands and beaches.

Harwich Chamber of Commerce: P.O. Box 34, Harwich, MA 02646; phone (508) 432-1600 or (800) 441-3199.

BROOKS ACADEMY MUSEUM, 1 blk. s. of town center at 80 Parallel St., is housed in the original Pine Grove Seminary, built in 1844. The museum features historical displays, including one chronicling the local cranberry industry. Exhibits include maritime and textile displays, C.D. Cahoon paintings and sketches, manuscript collections, antique tools, housewares and toys. Research facilities are on the grounds. Allow 1 hour minimum. Wed.-Sat. 1-4, Memorial Day-Columbus Day; closed July 4. Donations. Phone (508) 432-8089.

BROOKS FREE LIBRARY, on Main St., contains 23 figurines by renowned sculptor John Rogers. Mon., Wed. and Fri.-Sat. 10-4, Tues. noon-8, Thurs. noon-4. Free. Phone (508) 430-7562.

HYANNIS (E-9) elev. 30′

Hyannis' nearby beaches—particularly Craigville Beach, the largest on the cape—are popular. The town's harbor is deep enough to accommodate oceangoing yachts. A memorial to John F. Kennedy on Ocean Street has a small pool and fountain with a circular fieldstone wall bearing the presidential seal.

Hyannis Area Chamber of Commerce: 1418 Rt. 132, Hyannis, MA 02601; phone (508) 362-5230.

Shopping areas: Cape Cod Mall, on SR 132, has Filene's Basement, Macy's and Sears. Hyannis Main Street Waterfront District offers more than 200 shops.

CAPE COD MELODY TENT, 21 W. Main St., presents theater-in-the-round concerts and comedy shows nightly at 8 and children's shows Wednesday at 11 a.m., late June-Labor Day. Evening performances $12.50-$47; children's shows $5.25. DS, MC, VI. Phone (508) 775-5630, or (781) 383-1400 day after Labor Day-late June.

THE CAPE COD SCENIC RAILROAD, 252 Main St., is a railway service from Hyannis to Cape Cod Canal via Sandwich. Trains, made of first-class parlor cars and restored coaches, pass cranberry bogs, the Great Salt Marsh, Cape Cod Bay, the Cape Cod Canal, Sandwich Glass Museum and Thornton Burgess Museum. A narrative is provided. An observation dome car also is available at an extra charge. Food is available on all trips; 3-hour dinner trips are scheduled throughout the year.

Trips depart Hyannis Tues.-Sun. at 10, 12:30 and 3, Sandwich Tues.-Sun. at 11:10 and 1:40, June-Oct. Trips also are scheduled Sat.-Sun. and holidays in May; phone for departure times. Round trip $11.50; over 65, $10.50; ages 3-12, $7.50. DS, MC, VI. Phone (508) 771-3788.

HYANNIS HARBOR TOURS, Pier 1 at Ocean St. Dock, offers 1-hour tours of Hyannis Harbor. A view of the Kennedy family's summer homes is included. Children must be with an adult. Hyannis Harbor Tours also operates Hy-Line Cruises *(see color ad p. 333)*. Round-trip daily cruises also run to Nantucket Island *(see place listing p. 161)* and Martha's Vineyard *(see place listing p. 160)*.

Harbor tours depart daily 9-8, June 1 to mid-Sept.; 10-2:30, Apr.-May and mid-Sept. through Oct. 31. Harbor tour fare $10; under 13, $5. Cruise fare $22; ages 4-12, $11. Phone (508) 778-2600.

HYANNIS WHALE WATCHER CRUISES departs from Millway Marina in Barnstable Harbor; from US 6 exit 6 take SR 132 1.5 mi. s., then 2.5 mi. n. via Phinneys Ln. and Millway. Sunset cruises are available in summer. Food is available. The narrated 4-hour whale-watching excursions depart daily Apr.-Oct. Fare $15-$25. Reservations are required. AE, DS, MC, VI. For departure times and reservations phone (508) 362-6088 or (888) 942-5392.

JOHN F. KENNEDY HYANNIS MUSEUM, downtown in the old Town Hall Building at 397 Main St., consists of photographs and oral histories dedicated to the times that Kennedy spent in the area with his family and friends. A 7-minute videotape reflects on the "Summer White House" and place of refuge for the 35th president. Exhibits are featured throughout the year. Mon.-Sat. 10-4, Sun. and holidays 1-4, Apr. 19-Oct. 12; Wed.-Sat. 10-4, Feb. 18-Apr. 18 and Oct. 13-Dec. 31. Last tour begins 30 minutes before closing. Admission $3, under 17 free. Phone (508) 790-3077.

MASHPEE (E-8) pop. 7,900

Descendants of the Mashpee Indians still gather cranberries from the many bogs in the Mashpee area. Old Indian Meeting House, the second Indian church on the cape, was erected in 1684; it stands in the old burying ground along SR 28 south of town.

ORLEANS (D-9) pop. 5,800, elev. 64'

Nestled between the beaches of the Atlantic Ocean and the coves and harbors of Cape Cod Bay, Orleans has a quaint town center surrounded by pristine shores and forests. The town was incorporated in 1797 and named after the Duke of Orleans, who visited the area that year while in exile after the French Revolution. Orleans residents have always relied heavily on the sea for their livelihoods. During the 19th century windmill-powered saltworks processed seawater into salt, deep-sea and shell fishing were major industries, and fields fertilized with nutrient-laden seaweed produced hearty crops.

The water is a recreational resource drawing tourists to beaches and fishing areas on both Cape Cod Bay and the ocean. A scenic portion of US 6 runs northward to Provincetown.

Orleans Chamber of Commerce: P.O. Box 153, Orleans, MA 02653; phone (508) 255-1386. An information booth is near the corner of SR 6A and Eldredge Parkway; phone (508) 240-2484.

PROVINCETOWN (D-8) pop. 3,400, elev. 32'

Provincetown was the site of the first landing of the Pilgrims. A monument stands on High Pole Hill commemorating the event. Isolated at the tip of Cape Cod, the settlement always depended upon the sea for its livelihood. Formerly a whaling port, the town is now an art colony and tourist mecca.

Miles of beaches line both sides of the peninsula. Bathhouse and parking facilities (fee $5 per vehicle or $3 per person arriving by bicycle or on foot) are at Herring Cove Beach. Along the "Back Shore," from Peaked Hill Bars to Race Point, surf casters catch striped bass from late May to mid-October. Dune tours are conducted daily. Charter boats also are available.

Provincetown is at the northern end of an especially scenic portion of US 6 that stretches through Cape Cod to Orleans.

Provincetown Chamber of Commerce: 307 Commercial St., P.O. Box 1017, Provincetown, MA 02657; phone (508) 487-3424.

[SAVE] **DOLPHIN FLEET,** at MacMillan Pier, offers 3- to 4-hour whale-watching trips accompanied by a scientist from the Center for Coastal Studies. Food is available. Trips depart daily, mid-Apr. to first weekend in Nov. Phone for schedule. Fare $18-$19; senior citizens $16-$17; ages 7-12, $15-$16. Reservations are required. MC, VI. Phone (800) 826-9300. *See color ad.*

PILGRIM MONUMENT & PROVINCETOWN MUSEUM, off SR 6 on High Pole Hill, is a 252-foot tower completed in 1910 to honor the first landing of the *Mayflower* Pilgrims. Stairs and ramps lead to the top of the tower, which affords views of the town and harbor. The museum relates the history of outer Cape Cod, with displays of ships models, whaling equipment and items salvaged from various nearby shipwrecks.

The Pilgrim Room has *Mayflower* memorabilia, as well as Colonial and Victorian china, pewter and silver. Daily 9-7, July-Aug.; 9-5, Apr.-June and Sept.-Nov. Last admission is 45 minutes before closing. Admission $5; ages 4-12, $3. MC, VI. Phone (508) 487-1310.

[SAVE] *PORTUGUESE PRINCESS* EXCURSIONS leaves from MacMillan Pier and offers 3.5-hour naturalist-conducted tours. Food is available. Tours depart daily, May 1 to late Oct.; phone for hours. Fare $18-$20; over 60 and ages 7-16, $15-$17. Reservations are required. AE, MC, VI. Phone (508) 487-2651 or (800) 442-3188.

PROVINCETOWN ART ASSOCIATION AND MUSEUM, 460 Commercial St., exhibits a collection of paintings by established and emerging artists. Daily noon-5 and 8-10 p.m., Memorial Day-Labor Day; daily noon-5 (also Fri.-Sat. 8-10 p.m.), in Oct.; Sat.-Sun. noon-4, rest of year. Hours may vary; phone ahead. Admission $3, senior citizens and children $1. Phone (508) 487-1750.

PROVINCETOWN HERITAGE MUSEUM, 356 Commercial St., contains one of the world's largest indoor models of a Grand Bank schooner. The museum, which depicts the history of Provincetown, features whaling and trapboat fishing displays as well as changing exhibitions. Daily 10-5:30, Memorial Day-Columbus Day. Admission $3, under 12 free. Phone (508) 487-7098.

PROVINCETOWN WHALE-WATCH INC. CRUISES ON *RANGER V,* at MacMillan Pier, offers 2.5-hour whale-watching trips. A naturalist provides commentary on local whale activity. Food is available. Cruises depart daily at 8:30, 11:30, 2:30 and 5:30, mid-June to mid-Sept.; at 11:30 and 2:30, early Apr. to mid-June and mid-Sept. to mid-Nov. Mid-June to mid-Sept. fare $18. Early Apr. to mid-June and mid-Sept to mid-Nov. fare $16. Phone (508) 487-3322 or (800) 992-9333.

SAGAMORE (D-8)

THE PAIRPOINT CRYSTAL, on SR 6A next to the Sagamore bridge, produces full lead crystal in the same manner used in 1837, the year the company's predecessor was founded. The glassmakers' art, practiced using a few simple tools, dexterous hands and years of knowledge, can be viewed from a glass wall in the shop or on the factory floor. Presentations are given upon request if staffing is available. Allow 30 minutes minimum. Glass blowing demonstrations are given Mon.-Fri. 9-4:30, May-Dec.; Mon.-Fri. 10-4:30, rest of year. Closed Dec. 25. Free. Phone (508) 888-2344 or (800) 899-0953.

SANDWICH (D-8) pop. 15,500, elev. 20'

One of the oldest towns on Cape Cod, Sandwich became the site of one of America's largest glass factories, an industry that flourished during the 19th century. The town also was the home of Thornton W. Burgess, naturalist and author of such children's stories as "Old Mother West Wind" and "Peter Cottontail." Green Briar Nature Center, 6 Discovery Hill Rd., promotes Burgess' interest in nature through its natural history exhibits and The Old Briar Patch Trail, a 1-mile, self-guiding nature trail.

Next to the center is Green Briar Jam Kitchen, about which Burgess wrote, "It is a wonderful thing to sweeten the world which is in a jam and needs preserving." The kitchen makes jams and jellies using the same methods it did at the turn of the 20th century. Free guided tours are offered.

Also in Sandwich, on SR 130, is First Church of Christ. Built in 1830, it has a spire designed by noted English architect Christopher Wren.

DEXTER'S GRISTMILL, Main St., built in 1654, is restored and grinds corn daily. Guides explain the history of the mill and its mechanical operation. Mon.-Sat. 10-4:45, Sun. 1-4:45, mid-June to early Oct. Admission $1.50; ages 12-16, 75c. Combination ticket with Hoxie House $2.50; ages 12-16, $1.

★ **HERITAGE PLANTATION** is at Grove and Pine sts. off SR 130. The plantation comprises 76 acres of landscaped grounds and several buildings with exhibits pertaining to Early American life. The arts building reveals the skill of American craftsmen and contains a restored carrousel; the military museum houses antique military miniatures, firearms and flags; and the Round Stone Barn displays restored automobiles dating from 1899. Gardens, nature trails and a mill are on the grounds. A small bus provides tours of the plantation. Picnicking is permitted. Food is available.

Daily 10-5, mid-May to late Oct. Last admission is 45 minutes before closing. Admission $9; over 60, $8; ages 6-18, $4.50. AE, DS, MC, VI. Phone (508) 888-3300. *See color ads starting on p. 374.*

HOXIE HOUSE, on Water St., is a restored 1675 saltbox house. Mon.-Sat. 10-5, Sun. 1-5, mid-June to early Oct. Admission $1.50; ages 12-16, 75c. Combination ticket with Dexter's Gristmill $2.50; ages 12-16, $1.

[SAVE] **SANDWICH GLASS MUSEUM,** 129 Main St. (SR 130), preserves and displays the kinds of glass manufactured in Sandwich during the 19th century. Exhibits of table and decorative glass are ordered chronologically and include pressed, lacy, colored, enameled, blown, engraved and cut glass. Daily 9:30-5, Apr.-Oct.; Wed.-Sun. 9:30-4, Feb.-Mar. and Nov.-Dec. Closed Thanksgiving and Dec. 25. Admission $3.50; ages 6-12, $1. MC, VI. Phone (508) 888-0251. *See color ads starting on p. 374.*

THORNTON W. BURGESS MUSEUM, 4 Water St., is a memorial to the well-known children's author and naturalist born in Sandwich in 1874. Housed in the restored 1756 Eldred House, the museum contains a large collection of Burgess' writings, original Harrison Cady illustrations of his animal characters and other mementos of Burgess' life and career. An herb garden is on the grounds. Mon.-Sat. and holidays 10-4, Sun. 1-4, Apr.-Oct. Donations. Phone (508) 888-6870.

WING FORT HOUSE is n. of SR 6A at 69 Spring Hill Rd. Built in 1641, the house was occupied continuously by members of the Wing family until it became a museum in 1942. Seven rooms are furnished with pieces from various periods. Guided tours are available. Tues.-Sat. 10-4, mid-June through mid-Sept.; closed July 4 and Labor Day. Admission $2; under 12, $1. Phone (508) 833-1540.

SAVE **YESTERYEARS DOLL AND MINIATURE MUSEUM,** River and Main sts., houses dolls, dollhouses and miniature shops. Mon.-Sat. 10-3:30, mid-May through Oct. 15. Admission $3.50; over 62 and students with ID $3; under 12, $1.50. Phone (508) 888-1711.

SOUTH WELLFLEET (D-9)

WELLFLEET BAY WILDLIFE SANCTUARY, off US 6, .5 mi. n. of the Eastham/Wellfleet town line, is a 1,000-acre nature preserve of the Massachusetts Audubon Society. Five miles of hiking trails through pine woods and fields lead to salt marsh, creeks, pond, heathland and beach. Natural history field walks, cruises and wildlife guided tours are conducted; for reservations write P.O. Box 236, South Wellfleet, MA 02663. Daily 8-8, June-Aug.; 8-dusk, rest of year. Admission $3; over 62 and ages 3-12, $2. MC, VI. Phone (508) 349-2615.

TRURO (D-9) pop. 1,600, elev. 20'

Near the tip of Cape Cod, Truro has long been a fishing center and is now a popular stop-off point along scenic US 6. Dune tours are available daily through local operators.

HIGHLAND LIGHT (Cape Cod Light) is 5 mi. n.e. off US 6. Although the 1795 lighthouse is not open to the public, its light is visible 20 miles out to sea (weather permitting).

WELLFLEET (D-9) pop. 2,500

An early whaling center, Wellfleet once was the leading oyster-producing port in New England. A town clock in the Congregational Church still strikes ship's time. The town, situated along the scenic Cape Cod segment of US 6, is a popular yet quiet summer retreat.

Wellfleet Chamber of Commerce: P.O. Box 571, Wellfleet, MA 02667; phone (508) 349-2510.

WELLFLEET HISTORICAL SOCIETY MUSEUM, on Main St., displays such area memorabilia as photographs, china, tools, scrimshaw, American

Indian artifacts, life-saving equipment, Sandwich glass and a 13-star American flag. Walking tours are available. Tues.-Sat. 2-5, late June-early Sept. Admission $1, under 12 free. Phone (508) 349-9157.

WEST BARNSTABLE (E-8) elev. 22'

WEST PARISH MEETINGHOUSE, SR 149 to US 6 exit 5, was built in 1717 and is reputedly the oldest Congregational church building in the country. It has a Revere bell cast in 1806 and an English weathercock dating from 1723. Daily 9-5, Memorial Day-Labor Day; by appointment rest of year. Free. Phone (508) 362-4445.

WEST YARMOUTH (E-9) pop. 5,400, elev. 20'

ZOOQUARIUM, 674 SR 28, is an animal center featuring a petting zoo, aquariums and hands-on demonstrations. Visitors can take a close look at both domesticated farm animals and wildlife from the forests of New England. A sea lion show is presented during regular hours. Allow 1 hour minimum. Mon.-Thurs. 9:30-8, Fri.-Sun. 9:30-6, late June-Labor Day; daily 9:30-5, Feb. 1 through mid-June and day after Labor Day-day after Thanksgiving. Admission $7.50; ages 2-9, $4.50. Phone (508) 775-8883.

WOODS HOLE (E-8) elev. 19'

On the southwest tip of Cape Cod, Woods Hole is chief port of the cape and a center for oceanographic research. Ferries to Martha's Vineyard operate year-round. Only limited on-street metered parking is available. A seasonal trolley service, the "WHOOSH," operates between Falmouth and Woods Hole.

Guided walking tours of the town are given Tuesdays at 4; they originate at Woods Hole Historical Museum & Collection (see attraction listing).

FISHERIES AQUARIUM, corner of Water and Albatross sts., is a major research center for marine science operated by the Northeast Fisheries Science Center of the National Marine Fisheries Service under the National Oceanic and Atmospheric Administration (NOAA). The aquarium contains exhibits about local and commercial species, a seal pool, hands-on tanks, a behind-the-scenes area and reserve tanks. Parking is limited. Daily 10-4, mid-June to mid-Sept.; Mon.-Fri. 10-4, rest of year. Free. Phone (508) 495-2001.

MARINE BIOLOGICAL LABORATORY, on Water St., was established in 1888 and is devoted to research and education in basic biology. Scientists and students use organisms found in surrounding waters as model systems. Guided tours consist of a videotape presentation, a visit to Marine Resources Center to look at marine animals used in research and a walk through MBL/WHOI (Marine Biological Laboratory/Woods Hole Oceanographic Institute) Library. Under age 10 admitted to videotape presentation only.

Allow 1 hour, 30 minutes minimum. Mon.-Sat. 10-4, June-Aug. Tours are given Mon.-Fri. at 1, 2 and 3, June-Aug. Free. Reservations are required at least 2 weeks in advance. Parking, which is limited, is on-street and metered. Phone (508) 289-7623.

WOODS HOLE HISTORICAL MUSEUM & COLLECTION, 573 Woods Hole Rd., depicts the history of Woods Hole through an audiovisual presentation, displays and dioramas. A scale model of the town as it was in 1895 is on display. A boat museum and a gentlemen's workshop of the 1890s also are on the grounds. Allow 30 minutes minimum. Tues.-Sat. 10-4, mid-June through Labor Day. Free. Parking, which is limited, is on-street and metered. Phone (508) 548-7270.

WOODS HOLE OCEANOGRAPHIC INSTITUTION'S EXHIBIT CENTER, 15 School St., offers displays about the oceanographic research conducted by the institution. Included are a full-size model of the interior of the *Alvin*, a research submersible; a video introduction to the institution's scientific work; and presentations about jellyfish, coastal science, research tools and deep-sea exploration.

Allow 30 minutes minimum. Mon.-Sat. 10-4:30, Sun. noon-4:30, Memorial Day-Labor Day; otherwise varies. Admission $2, under 10 free. Parking, which is limited, is on-street and metered. Phone (508) 289-222.

YARMOUTH PORT (D-8) pop. 4,300, elev. 54′

Incorporated in 1639 as part of the Plymouth Bay Colony, Yarmouth Port was chosen by many 19th-century sea captains as the site for their stately homes. Conservation areas and nature trails in the town spotlight wetlands, salt marshes and some of the Cape's most abundant foliage. The [SAVE] Winslow Crocker House, at 250 SR 6A, features collections of early American furniture, pewter, hooked rugs and ceramics.

Yarmouth Area Chamber of Commerce: 657 SR 28, West Yarmouth, MA 02673. Phone (508) 778-1008 or (800) 732-1008. *See color ad.*

This ends listings for Cape Code.
The following page resumes the alphabetical listings of cities in Massachusetts.

★ **CAPE COD NATIONAL SEASHORE**—see Cape Cod p. 145.

CENTERVILLE—see Cape Cod p. 147.

CHATHAM—see Cape Cod p. 147.

COHASSET—see Boston p. 120.

CONCORD—see Boston p. 122.

CUMMINGTON (B-2) pop. 800

WILLIAM CULLEN BRYANT HOMESTEAD is 1.5 mi. s. off SR 9 on SR 112. The poet and editor of the *New York Evening Post* was born in the home in 1794 and purchased it in 1865 to use as his summer residence. The homestead contains many of Bryant's personal effects as well as period furnishings and early farm implements.

A panorama of the Westfield River Valley can be seen from the site. A craft fair is held on the

grounds the third weekend in July. Guided tours are given Fri.-Sun. and holidays 1-5, last weekend in June-Labor Day; Sat.-Sun. and holidays 1-5, day after Labor Day-Columbus Day. Admission $5; under 12, $2.50. Phone (413) 634-2244.

DALTON (B-2) pop. 7,200, elev. 1,188′

CRANE MUSEUM OF PAPERMAKING is in Crane & Co.'s Old Stone Mill, w. on Housatonic St. on the grounds of Pioneer Mill off SRs 8 and 9. The museum traces the evolution of American papermaking. Allow 30 minutes minimum. Mon.-Fri. 2-5, June 1 to mid-Oct. Free. Phone (413) 684-2600.

WAHCONAH FALLS STATE PARK, 3 mi. n. off SR 9, contains a waterfall and scenic roads for hiking. Daily dawn-dusk. Free. Phone (413) 442-8992.

DEDHAM—see Boston p. 123.

DEERFIELD (B-3) pop. 5,000, elev. 204′

When settled in the 1660s, Deerfield was the northernmost outpost of English colonial civilization. Indian and French attacks on the town included the 1675 Bloody Brook Massacre and the great Deerfield Raid in 1704.

Franklin County Chamber of Commerce: 395 Main St., Box 790, Greenfield, MA 01302; phone (413) 773-5463.

Self-guiding tours: A booklet of a 2-mile walking tour that highlights 88 sites is available from Historic Deerfield.

★ HISTORIC DEERFIELD, off US 5 and SR 10, is a complex of 12 historic houses and other historic sites. Admission includes an orientation program and programs for families and children as well as a guided walking tour. Wine-tasting dinners are held periodically. The Flynt Center of Early New England Life features changing exhibitions and items from Historic Deerfield's collection of decorative arts and furniture. The information center in Hall Tavern is open daily 9:30-4:30; closed Thanksgiving and Dec. 24-25. Admission $12; ages 6-17, $6. MC, VI. Phone (413) 774-5581.

Allen House, built in 1720, contains American and English needlework and period furniture.

Ashley House, built in 1740, exhibits antique furnishings, fabrics, pewter and china in the home of a Tory parson.

Barnard Tavern, built in the early 1800s, served as an inn and stagecoach stop. The tavern features a ballroom with a vaulted ceiling.

Dwight House, built about 1725 in Springfield and moved to Deerfield in 1954, is noted for its paneled rooms and 18th-century doctor's office with period equipment.

rary House, built in the late 1700s and restored a 1890, chronicles Deerfield's role in both the rts and crafts and the antiquarian movements.

Helen Geier Flynt Textile Museum, behind the Henry Needham Flynt Silver and Metalware Collection, displays early coverlets, needlework, 8th-century attire and American and European extiles.

Henry Needham Flynt Silver and Metalware Collection exhibits more than 1,500 pieces of early American and English silver and pewter.

Hinsdale and Anna Williams House has been restored to its 1816-38 appearance using an inventory taken when Hinsdale Williams died.

Sheldon-Hawks House contains Queen Anne nd Chippendale furniture, original paneling and sewing room with 18th-century fabrics and early ceramics.

Stebbins House was the brick residence of a wealthy landowner. The home depicts the gracious living of the early 19th century. The paintings, hand-painted wall decorations, Federal-style furniture and ceramic displays are of interest.

Wells-Thorn House has a series of period rooms ating 1725-1850. These rooms portray the development of economic life and popular furnishings in the Connecticut River Valley.

Wright House, built in 1824, displays the Cluett Collection of American furniture and clocks as well as an extensive collection of Chinese porcelain.

MEMORIAL HALL MUSEUM, on Memorial St., is one of Deerfield's oldest museums. It is housed in a 1799 building that became Deerfield Academy. The museum contains the Sheldon Collection of Colonial, American Indian and military relics, a replica of a period schoolroom, collection of quilts and needlework and a pewter display. Daily 9:30-4:30, May-Oct. Admission 6; ages 6-12, $3. Phone (413) 774-7476.

DENNIS—*see Cape Cod p. 147.*

DUXBURY (D-8) pop. 13,900, elev. 31'

Around 1628 Pilgrims settled in Duxbury eeking room for their growing village and grazing lands for their cattle. Well-known residents ncluded Pilgrims John Alden and Miles Standish. Nearby an old burying ground contains ome of the pioneers' graves.

ALDEN HOUSE, 105 Alden St., was the last home of John and Priscilla Alden. Some interesting features of this 1653 building are the powdered clam-and-oyster-shell ceiling in the "great" room, the curved panels in the "best" oom and the gunstock beams found in the hambers. Mon.-Fri. 10-5, Sun. noon-5, mid-May

to mid-Oct.; by appointment rest of year. Admission $2.50; ages 6-12, $1. Phone (781) 934-9092.

THE ART COMPLEX AT DUXBURY, 189 Alden St., features contemporary regional art as well as works by Oriental, European and American artists. A collection of Shaker furniture also is displayed. Changing exhibits are presented. A Japanese tea ceremony is presented in a tea hut the last Sunday of the month, June through August. Allow 30 minutes minimum. Wed.-Sun. 1-4; closed holidays. Free. Phone (781) 934-6634.

KING CAESAR HOUSE, on King Caesar Rd. at Powder Point, was built in 1808 for shipping magnate Ezra Weston II ("King Caesar"). The house is an example of Federal architecture. Two front parlors feature French wallpaper, and a museum adjoining the house contains exhibits about maritime history. Wed.-Sun. 1-4, mid-June through Labor Day; Sat.-Sun. 1-4, day after Labor Day-Sept. 30. Admission $4; senior citizens and students with ID $3; ages 6-16, $1. Phone (781) 934-6106.

EAST FALMOUTH—*see Cape Cod p. 147.*

EASTHAM—*see Cape Cod p. 148.*

EASTHAMPTON (C-2) pop. 15,500, elev. 169'

MASSACHUSETTS AUDUBON SOCIETY AT ARCADIA is 1 mi. s. of I-91 exit 18 on SR 5, then 1 mi. w. on East St., following signs to Fort Hill Rd. Five miles of marked trails along the Mill River and marshes traverse the 650-acre sanctuary, a haven for native plants and wildlife. A visitor center offers trail maps and nature programs. Allow 2 hours minimum. Tues.-Sun. 9-3. Admission $3; over 65 and ages 3-15, $2. MC, VI. Phone (413) 584-3009.

EDGARTOWN—
see Martha's Vineyard p. 160.

ESSEX—*see Boston p. 123.*

FAIRHAVEN (E-7) pop. 16,100, elev. 17'

Across the harbor from New Bedford, Fairhaven shares a similar heritage, having developed and prospered from the whaling ships that once lined its docks. Reminders of that era survive in such historic buildings as the Weston-Howland Mansion or the public buildings donated by philanthropist Henry Huttleston Rogers.

Town of Fairhaven Visitors Center: 27 Center St., Fairhaven, MA 02719; phone (508) 979-4085.

FALL RIVER (E-6) pop. 92,700, elev. 121'

In the late 19th century America's need for cotton thread and cloth was met in Fall River, where an abundant supply of water power made the manufacturing process economical. By 1875 "Spindle City" was the leading textile producer, with more than 120 mills in operation. The Victorian mansions on the heights above the city act as reminders of the wealth made during this boom period. Manufacturers of finished clothing occupy the warehouses and offer bargains in many outlet stores.

Still standing in Fall River is Lizzie Borden House where, reputedly, "Lizzie Borden took an ax and gave her mother 40 whacks; when she saw what she had done, she gave her father 41." For the murders, which took place Aug. 4, 1892, Lizzie was accused, tried and acquitted. The house is now a bed and breakfast. Daily tours are available; phone (508) 675-7333.

Fall River Department of Tourism: One Government Center, Fall River, MA 02722; phone (508) 324-2620.

Shopping areas: Factory outlets are concentrated on Jefferson, Quequechan and Quarry streets off I-195.

★ **BATTLESHIP COVE**, off I-195 exit 5, harbors 20th-century vessels of the U.S. Navy, including a battleship, a destroyer, a submarine, a Russian-built missile corvette and two PT boats. A Bell Huey helicopter that served in Vietnam also is on display. Daily 9-5; closed Jan. 1, Thanksgiving and Dec. 25. Admission $9; over 65, $6.75; ages 6-14, $4.50. DS, MC, VI. Phone (508) 678-1100.

PT Boats 796 and 617 are two of the remaining operational torpedo boats of World War II.

USS Joseph P. Kennedy Jr., a destroyer, saw action in Korea, Vietnam and the Cuban Missile Crisis of 1962. Limited areas are open.

USS Lionfish, a World War II attack submarine, displays equipment and facilities.

USS Massachusetts (Big Mamie), a 680-foot battleship, survived 35 battles in both the Atlantic and Pacific during World War II. The main deck, gun turrets and bridge as well as the engine room and nine decks of the ship's interior may be visited. A PT boat museum and a scale model aircraft exhibit also are on board.

FALL RIVER CAROUSEL, off I-195 exit 5 in Battleship Cove, is a restored, 1920 Philadelphia Tobaggan Co. Carousel #54 with 48 hand-painted, hand-carved horses and two chariots. Each ride lasts 3 minutes. Daily 10-8, Memorial Day-Labor Day; hours vary rest of year, phone for schedule. Under 4 with adult $1; over 3, 75c; 10 rides $6. Phone (508) 324-4300.

FALL RIVER HERITAGE STATE PARK, off I-195 exit 5, is next to Battleship Cove. This 8-acre urban park has a visitor center with exhibits about Fall River's textile and nautical history. A video presentation documenting the city's role as a major cotton textile producer is available upon request. A boardwalk and esplanade follow the waterfront. Daily 10-4; closed Jan. 1 and Dec 25. Free. Phone (508) 675-5759.

FALL RIVER HISTORICAL SOCIETY, 451 Rock St., is a restored 19th-century mill owner's mansion and contains a Lizzie Borden display and memorabilia of Fall River steamships. Tues.-Fri. 9-4:30, Sat.-Sun. 1-5, June-Sept.; Tues.-Fri. 9-4:30, Apr.-May and Oct.-Dec. Tours are given Tues.-Fri. at 9, 10, 11, 1, 2 and 3, Sat.-Sun. at 1, 2, 3 and 4, June-Sept. Closed holidays. Admission $5; ages 6-14, $3. Phone (508) 679-1071.

MARINE MUSEUM, 70 Water St., relates the history of steam transportation through lithographs, paintings, photographs and scale-model ships. The *Titanic* exhibit features a 28-foot-long, 1-ton model of the transatlantic luxury liner. Mon.-Fri. 9-5, Sat. noon-5, Sun. and holidays noon-4. Admission $4; senior citizens $3.50; ages 5-12, $3. Phone (508) 674-3533.

OLD COLONY AND FALL RIVER RAILROAD MUSEUM, in Battleship Cove at Central and Water sts., is in a former railroad car with memorabilia of the Old Colony and Fall River Railroad, among others. Equipment includes a rail switch, two small trains children can operate, a caboose, a self-propelled diesel coach, a model steam engine and a boxcar containing a theater.

Sun.-Fri. noon-5, Sat. 10-5, July 1-Labor Day; Sat. noon-4, Sun. 10-2, Apr. 21-June 30 and day after Labor Day to first weekend in Dec. Admission $2; over 64, $1.50; ages 5-12, $1. Phone (508) 674-9340.

SAINT ANNE'S CHURCH AND SHRINE, opposite St. Anne's Hospital on S. Main St., is a stone, Roman Catholic Church built in 1906 by French Canadian emigrants. Features include the shrine of St. Anne (mother of Mary), a series of devotional areas to many saints and a Chapel of Perpetual Adoration in the lower church. The procession for the Feast of St. Anne is held July 26. Daily 24 hours. Free. Phone (508) 674-5651 or 678-5322.

FALMOUTH—see Cape Cod p. 148.

FITCHBURG (B-5) pop. 41,200, elev. 494'

FITCHBURG ART MUSEUM, 185 Elm St., contains permanent collections of American, European and Asian paintings, drawings, prints, sculpture and decorative arts, and antiquities from Mesoamerica, Egypt, Greece and Rome. Changing exhibits also are featured. Tues.-Sat. 11-4, Sun. 1-4; closed major holidays. Admission $3; over 62, $2; students with ID and children free. Phone (978) 345-4207.

FITCHBURG HISTORICAL SOCIETY MUSEUM, 0 Grove St., portrays the town's history through arious artifacts, a Victorian parlor, Colonial itchen and an archeological exhibit. Industrial ontributions to Fitchburg are chronicled. Allow hour minimum. Mon.-Thurs. 10-4. Admission 2. Phone (978) 345-1157.

FRAMINGHAM—see Boston p. 123.

GARDNER (B-4) pop. 20,100, elev. 1,030'

GARDNER HERITAGE STATE PARK VISITORS ENTER, SR 2 exit 23, following signs, displays cal history exhibits focusing on Gardner's air-making industry. Highlights are a 6-foot air and a Victorian gingerbread porch. Video-pe presentations illustrate the crafts of silver-nithing and chair-making. Tues.-Sat. 9-4, Sun.-lon. noon-4; closed Thanksgiving and Dec. 25. ee. Phone (978) 630-1497.

GLOUCESTER—see Boston p. 124.

GRAFTON (C-5) pop. 13,000

ILLARD HOUSE AND CLOCK MUSEUM INC. off I-90 exit 11, following signs. Built in 1718, is restored saltbox farmhouse is said to be the dest house in Grafton. The site includes the irthplace and original 1766 workshop of the Villard brothers, 18th-century clockmakers. Iore than 75 Willard clocks are displayed nong period furnishings, Oriental rugs, family ortraits and heirlooms. Tues.-Sat. 10-4, Sun. -5; closed holidays. Admission $5; over 60, $4; nder 12, $2. Phone (508) 839-3500.

GREAT BARRINGTON (C-1) pop. 7,700, elev. 726'

Resort and shopping center of the southern erkshires, historic Great Barrington was settled bout 1726. In August 1774, townspeople openly resisted British judicial rule by seizing the courthouse to prevent the king's court from holding session. Poet and journalist William Cullen Bryant made his home in Great Barrington 1816-25.

Two important firsts are part of Great Barrington's history. Dr. W.E.B. Du Bois, the first African-American to earn a Ph.D. from Harvard, was born in town in 1868. A park is named in his honor. In 1886 William Stanley pioneered the first commercial use of the electrical transformer and alternating current. Stanley's innovations gave Great Barrington the honor of being the first town in the world to have electric street lighting.

Southern Berkshire Chamber of Commerce: 362 Main St., Great Barrington, MA 01230; phone (413) 528-1510.

MONUMENT MOUNTAIN RESERVATION, 4 mi. n. on US 7, covers 503 acres. The 1,735-foot Monument Mountain, memorialized by poet William Cullen Bryant, provides a sweeping view. It is said that Nathaniel Hawthorne first met Herman Melville on a hike and picnic on Monument Mountain in 1850. Picnic facilities and hiking trails are available. Daily dawn-dusk. Free. Phone (413) 298-3239.

MOUNT EVERETT STATE RESERVATION, s.w. off SR 41 near South Egremont off Mount Washington Rd., is a 1,000-acre tract containing 2,624-foot Mount Everett and Guilder Pond. The upper parking area furnishes a panorama of three states and the Housatonic Valley. Daily dawn-dusk. Closed to vehicles from late Nov. to mid-Apr. Free. Phone (413) 528-0330.

HADLEY (C-3) pop. 4,200, elev. 125'

HADLEY FARM MUSEUM, next to the town hall at the intersection of SRs 9 and 47, is housed in a restored 1782 barn. Exhibits include a 15-seat stagecoach, an oxcart, a peddler's wagon, early broom-making machinery and household and farm implements. Children must be with an adult. Tues.-Sat. and holidays 10-4, Sun. 1-4, May 1-Columbus Day. Donations. Phone (413) 586-1812.

SAVE **PORTER-PHELPS-HUNTINGTON HISTORIC HOUSE MUSEUM** is at 130 River Dr., 2 mi. n. on SR 47. The 1752 Georgian-style house, unchanged structurally since 1799, contains the belongings of seven generations of the original owner's extended family. The activities of a wealthy and productive 18th-century household are interpreted through three generations of women. Guided tours are given Sat.-Wed. 1-4:30 and by appointment, May 15-Oct. 15; by appointment rest of year. Concerts are presented June-Aug. Admission $4; under 12, $1. An additional fee is charged for some concerts. Phone (413) 584-4699.

HAMPDEN (D-3) pop. 4,700

LAUGHING BROOK EDUCATION CENTER AND WILDLIFE SANCTUARY, 793 Main St., was the home of children's author Thornton W. Burgess. This is where he wrote many of his nature stories about Peter Cottontail, Reddy Fox and other animal characters. The 340-acre grounds contain 4 miles of walking trails. The Environmental Center houses natural history exhibits. Picnicking is permitted.

Center open Tues.-Sat. 10-4, Sun. 12:30-4; closed Jan. 1, Thanksgiving and Dec. 24-25. Trails open dawn-dusk. Admission $3; over 65 and ages 3-12, $2. Phone (413) 566-8034.

HANCOCK (B-1)

 RECREATIONAL ACTIVITIES

Skiing

• **Jiminy Peak, The Mountain Resort**, .5 mi. e. off SR 43. Write Jiminy Peak Mountain Resort, Corey Road, Hancock, MA 01237. Other activities are offered. Mon.-Fri. 9 a.m.-10:30 p.m., Sat.-Sun. and holidays 8:30 a.m.-10:30 p.m., early Nov. to mid-Apr. (weather permitting). Phone (413) 738-5500.

HANOVER (D-7) pop. 11,900, elev. 91′

STAR LAND RECREATION CENTER INC., off SR 3 exit 13, then 2.5 mi. s. on SR 53, is a 34-acre family recreation center. The center contains an 18-hole miniature golf course, double-deck driving range, softball and baseball batting cages, Go Karts, motorized bumper boats, carrousel, a video arcade and a playground. Picnicking is permitted. Food is available. Daily 10 a.m.-11 p.m., Apr. 15-Oct. 15; otherwise varies. Separate fees are charged for each activity. Phone (781) 826-3083.

HARVARD (B-5) pop. 12,300, elev. 286′

The first of two idealistic enterprises to organize in Harvard was a colony of the Shaker Society, founded in 1791; the second was Bronson Alcott's effort to found the settlement of New Eden at Fruitlands.

SAVE ★ **FRUITLANDS MUSEUMS** is .25 mi. s. of SR 2 on SR 110, then 2.25 mi. w. via Old Shirley and Prospect Hill rds. Fruitlands Farmhouse is where Bronson Alcott and leaders of the transcendentalist movement attempted a new social order in 1843; features include letters and memorabilia from the leaders. Shaker Museum is housed in an 18th-century building and contains Shaker furniture and artifacts.

Indian Museum displays dioramas and examples of North American Indian art and history. Picture Gallery includes portraits by early 19th-century itinerant artists and landscapes by members of the Hudson River School, the first formally recognized style of American painting. Programs for adults and hands-on children's activities are featured. The grounds offer nature trails and a picnic area. Food is available.

Grounds open daily 10-5. Museums open Tues.-Sun. and Mon. holidays 10-5, mid-May to mid-Oct. Admission $6; over 60, $5; students with ID $4; ages 4-17, $3. DS, MC, VI. Phone (978) 456-3924.

HARWICH—see Cape Cod p. 149.

HAVERHILL—see Boston p. 125.

HINGHAM (F-3) pop. 19,800, elev. 21′

THE OLD ORDINARY, 21 Lincoln St., was built in 1680 and enlarged in 1740. Of interest are 14 rooms featuring period furnishings, paintings, porcelain, glass, textiles, toys and tools. Tues.-Sat. 1:30-4:30, mid-June to mid-Sept. Admission $3; under 12, $1. Phone (781) 749-0013.

OLD SHIP MEETINGHOUSE, Main St., is one of the oldest continuously used wooden church structures in the country. The frame and walls stand as erected in 1681; the pulpit, pews and galleries date from 1755. Daily noon-4, July-Aug.; by appointment rest of year. Free. Phone (781) 749-1679.

HOLYOKE (C-3) pop. 43,700, elev. 115′

On the Connecticut River, the Pioneer Valley city of Holyoke was the first planned industrial center in the country. Volleyball, first known as mintonette, was invented in 1895 by W.G. Morgan, a physical education instructor at the local YMCA. On the Sunday following March 17, Holyoke holds one of the largest St. Patrick's Day parades in the country.

Greater Holyoke Chamber of Commerce: 177 High St., Holyoke, MA 01040; phone (413) 534-3376.

Shopping areas: Filene's, Filene's Basement, JCPenney, Lord and Taylor and Sears have stores in Holyoke Mall at Ingleside, off I-91 exit 15.

CHILDREN'S MUSEUM AT HOLYOKE, in the Heritage State Park Complex at 444 Dwight St., encourages visitors to become actively involved with exhibits. Permanent displays include a body playground featuring a two-story "Healthy Climber," an interactive building site, a cityscape, television station, papermaking exhibit, science discovery area and a tot lot as well as changing exhibits. Performances, workshops and programs also are offered. Tues.-Sat. 9:30-4:30, Sun. noon-5. Admission $4; over 62, $2.50; under 1 free. Phone (413) 536-5437.

HOLYOKE HERITAGE STATE PARK is in the Heritage State Park Complex at 444 Dwight St. The park offers cultural and recreational programs. A visitor center displays changing exhibits and presents "Holyoke's Visions," a multimedia program about the area. Guided tours, which can be tailored to visitors' interests, are available. A carrousel, volleyball hall of fame and railroad are featured. Park open daily 24 hours. Visitor center open Tues.-Sun. noon-4:30, July 4-Labor Day; otherwise varies. Park admission free. Fee for carrousel and train. Phone (413) 534-1723.

MOUNT TOM STATE RESERVATION is entered from US 5 n. of Holyoke. The reservation covers 1,800 acres on the western slope of Mount Tom, which rises 1,214 feet above the Connecticut Valley floor. The park's precipitous ridge is forested with pine, hemlock, hardwoods and spruce. Daily dawn-dusk. Admission $2 per private vehicle Sat.-Sun. and holidays, Memorial Day-Labor Day. Phone (413) 527-4805.

HULL (E-3) pop. 10,500, elev. 23'

PARAGON CAROUSEL, opposite Bernie King pavilion at 205 Nantasket Ave. (SR 228), is a 1928 wooden carrousel with 66 horses, 2 Roman chariots and a Wurlitzer 146 band organ. Daily 10-10, Memorial Day-Labor Day; Sat.-Sun. noon-6, May 1-day before Memorial Day and day after Labor Day to Columbus Day (weather permitting). Fare $1.50, 10 rides $13.50. Phone (781) 925-0472.

HULL LIFESAVING MUSEUM is at 1117 Nantasket Ave. Built in 1889 as a U.S. Life Saving Station, the building also served as a Coast Guard station 1915-69. Displays re-create life in a turn-of-the-20th-century lifesaving station and recount the rescue missions of Joshua James, a lifelong resident of Hull. The museum features photographs and stories of notable Boston harbor shipwrecks, lighthouse artifacts, exhibits of lifesaving equipment, a surf boat and a hands-on children's activity room.

Wed.-Sun. 10-5, late June-Labor Day; Fri.-Sun. and Mon. holidays 10-4, rest of year.

Closed Jan. 1, Thanksgiving and Dec. 25. Admission $2; senior citizens $1.50; ages 5-17, $1. Phone (781) 925-5433.

HYANNIS—*see Cape Cod p. 149.*

IPSWICH—*see Boston p. 126.*

LAWRENCE—*see Boston p. 126.*

LENOX (C-1) pop. 5,100, elev. 974'

Lenox is a Berkshire summer resort. A representative section of the Berkshires is preserved in Pleasant Valley Wildlife Sanctuary, 2 miles north of US 7/20 on West Dugway Road. Hiking trails traverse the area, and a museum contains exhibits about plants and wildlife.

Shakespeare & Company, whose alumni include Richard Dreyfuss and Sigourney Weaver, performs plays on four stages late May through late October; phone (413) 637-1199.

Lenox Chamber of Commerce: 75 Main St., Lenox, MA 01240; phone (413) 637-3646.

BERKSHIRE SCENIC RAILWAY MUSEUM, Lenox Station near Housatonic St. and Willow Creek Rd., offers short orientation train rides. A museum, housed in a restored 1902 depot, contains area railroading exhibits and three model train displays. Sat.-Sun. and holidays 10-4, Memorial Day weekend-Oct. 31. Train rides $1.50; children $1. Museum free. Phone (413) 637-2210.

THE MOUNT, at 2 Plunkett St. at the s. jct. of US 7 and SR 7A, was built in 1902 by writer Edith Wharton, the first woman novelist to win a Pulitzer Prize for fiction. Wharton and her niece, landscape architect Beatrix Farrand, designed the 50-acre estate, which includes lawns, woodlands and formal gardens. An ongoing restoration project, the home has several floors open for guided tours.

Allow 1 hour minimum. Daily 9-2, June-Oct.; Sat.-Sun. 9-2, in May. Admission $6; over 65, $5.50; ages 13-18, $4.50. Phone (413) 637-1899 for guided tour schedule.

TANGLEWOOD, summer home of the Boston Symphony Orchestra and the home of the Tanglewood Music Festival, is on a 550-acre estate on West St. Hawthorne Cottage, where Nathaniel Hawthorne wrote several books. Recitals, chamber music and larger works are held in Seiji Ozawa Hall. Concerts are presented May-Oct. The Tanglewood Music Festival takes place late June-early Sept. Concert prices range from $12-$65. Phone (413) 637-5165, (800) 274-8499, or (617) 266-1492 for festival schedule.

LEOMINSTER (B-5) pop. 38,100, elev. 400'

John Chapman, better known as Johnny Appleseed, was born in Leominster in 1774.

NATIONAL PLASTICS CENTER AND MUSEUM, 210 Lancaster St. (SR 117), is housed in a 1913 school building and is dedicated to the past, present and future of plastics. Features include hands-on activities, demonstrations on the chemistry of plastics, displays of historical artifacts, a discovery corner for children, a plastics in medicine exhibit and the Plastics Hall of Fame. Allow 1 hour minimum. Wed.-Sat. 11-4; closed major holidays. Admission $2; over 64 and under 12, $1. Phone (978) 537-9529.

★ **LEXINGTON**—*see Boston p. 126.*

LINCOLN—*see Boston p. 127.*

LOWELL—*see Boston p. 128.*

LUNENBURG (B-5) pop. 9,100, elev. 510'

WHALOM PARK is off SR 2 exit 32, then 3 mi. n. on SR 13. The park, on Lake Whalom, features 35 amusement rides, including a roller coaster, Ferris wheel, carrousel and the Prism, which offers an experience in color. Also on the grounds are puppet shows, a museum, a ballroom and miniature golf. The beach area offers waterslides, swimming, aquacycles and paddleboats. Picnicking is permitted. Food is available.

Allow 3 hours minimum. Sun.-Thurs. noon-9, Fri.-Sat. noon-10, July 1-Labor Day; Sat.-Sun. noon-6, Apr.-June. General park admission $5. Daytime admission (including rides) $13; nighttime admission (including rides) $5. Beach and waterslide admission $9.50. Combination ride/waterslide admission $15. Phone (978) 342-3707.

LYNN—*see Boston p. 128.*

MARBLEHEAD—*see Boston p. 129.*

MARSHFIELD (C-7) pop. 21,500, elev. 24'

HISTORIC WINSLOW HOUSE is on the corner of Webster and Careswell St. (SR 139). Built in 1699, this New England mansion has never been modernized. Also on the grounds are Daniel Webster's law office with memorabilia and a carriage house with three coaches. Wed.-Sun. 1-5, mid-June to mid-Oct. All-inclusive admission $3; under 12, 50c. Phone (781) 837-5753.

MARTHA'S VINEYARD (F-8)

Martha's Vineyard, like Nantucket, was an early refuge and supply point for the coastal ship traffic that regularly rounded Cape Cod. Vineyard Haven blossomed as a port for such traffic during the 18th and 19th centuries. Edgartown, the island's oldest European settlement, became an important whaling center. Such historic remnants as the Old Whaling Church in Edgartown, Mayhew Chapel and the Indian Burial Ground between West Tisbury and Vineyard Haven, and the Carpenter Gothic cottages of Oak Bluffs are part of Martha's Vineyard's charm.

Its quaint atmosphere, beaches and proximity to Cape Cod and the east coast make the island—and its six towns—a popular resort area. Edgartown and Vineyard Haven remain the island's principal commercial centers, supplemented in the summer by the bustle of Oak Bluffs' shopping district. The island's fishing heritage continues in the village of Menemsha, near the varicolored clay cliffs of Aquinnah.

Beaches are the island's most obvious recreational asset, providing opportunities for windsurfing and fishing. Four large harbors provide anchorage and departure points for sailing and charter fishing. Bicycling is the most common mode of transportation during the summer; shuttle bus service is available from mid-May to mid-October.

Car and passenger ferries operate daily from Woods Hole *(see Cape Cod p. 152)* to Vineyard Haven year-round and, in summer, to Oak Bluffs. Summer passenger service operates between Oak Bluffs and Falmouth *(see Cape Cod p. 148)* and Hyannis *(see Cape Cod p. 149)* on the south shore of Cape Cod and between Vineyard Haven and New Bedford *(see place listing p. 163).*

Martha's Vineyard Historical Island Tours provides 2.5-hour sightseeing tours of the island; phone (508) 693-1555, 693-0058 or 693-4681.

Martha's Vineyard Chamber of Commerce: P.O. Box 1698, Vineyard Haven, MA 02568; phone (508) 693-0085.

FELIX NECK WILDLIFE SANCTUARY, off Edgartown-Vineyard Haven Rd., encompasses 350 acres of beach, marsh, open fields and woodlands that harbor waterfowls. A visitor center features freshwater and saltwater tanks containing local species. Maps available at the center identify wildlife and guide visitors to trails and a reptile pond. Grounds open daily 8-7. Visitor center open daily 8-4, July-Aug.; Tues.-Sun. 9-4, rest of year. Admission $3; over 65 and ages 1-12, $2. Phone (508) 627-4850.

VINCENT HOUSE, Main and Church sts. in Edgartown, is considered the oldest house on the island. The unfurnished 1672 residence contains most of its original woodwork, brickwork, glass and hardware. During the home's renovation some of the walls were left exposed to demonstrate the type of construction used. Daily 11-2, late May to mid-Oct. Admission $3. Phone (508) 627-8017.

THE VINEYARD MUSEUM, 59 School St., includes Thomas Cooke House, Children's Gallery, Native American Gallery and Capt. Francis Pease House. The collections focus on whaling, fishing, farming and the commercial life of the island from the earliest Indian settlements to the present.

Allow 1 hour, 30 minutes minimum. Tues.-Sat. 10-5, June 12-Oct. 10; Wed.-Fri. 1-4, Sat. 10-4, Oct. 21-June 11. Closed holidays. Admission $6; ages 6-15, $4. Phone (508) 627-4441.

The Gale Huntington Library of History and Francis Foster Museum, Cooke St., contains reference material for historians and genealogists. An herb garden and boat shed are on the grounds. The shed contains a whaleboat, ship models, an 1854 fire engine and a peddler's cart. A reproduction of a whaling ship's tryworks— equipment used to create oil from whale blubber—and the lens that revolved on top of Gay Head Lighthouse 1854-1952 are of interest. Museum open same hours as The Vineyard Museum. Library open Wed.-Fri. 1-4, Sat. 10-4.

 WINERIES

• **Chicama Vineyards** is 1 mi. n. off Stoney Hill Rd. Tours are given on the hour Mon.-Sat. noon-4, Sun. 2-4, Memorial Day-Columbus Day. Tastings are offered Mon.-Sat. 11-5, Sun. 1-5, Memorial Day-Columbus Day; Sat.-Sun. 1-4, Nov. 15-Dec. 31; Sat. 1-4, Jan.1-day before Memorial Day. Closed July 4 and Labor Day. Phone (508) 693-0309.

MASHPEE—*see Cape Cod p. 150.*

MATTAPOISETT (E-7) pop. 5,900, elev. 18'

MATTAPOISETT HISTORICAL SOCIETY MUSEUM, 5 Church St., is in a former New England church built in 1821. The museum displays scrimshaw, whaling artifacts, period costumes and antiques. The Carriage House Museum contains carriages, an early firewagon, tools, an 1890 kitchen, a saltworks model and weaving equipment. Tues.-Sat. 1-4:30, July-Aug.; closed holidays. Admission $2; under 15, 50c. Phone (508) 758-2844.

MEDFORD—*see Boston p. 129.*

MENDON (C-5) pop. 4,000

SOUTHWICK'S ZOO, off SR 16, is one of New England's largest zoos dedicated to the preservation and breeding of rare and endangered species. Children's amusements, including a petting zoo, deer forest, playground and elephant and pony rides are offered. Food is available. Educational programs are offered. Allow 2 hours minimum. Daily 10-5, mid-Apr. to mid-Oct. Admission $8.75; over 65, $7.75; ages 3-12, $6.75. AE, DS, MC, VI. Phone (508) 883-9182 or (800) 258-9182.

MIDDLEBORO (D-7) pop. 6,800

THE MIDDLEBOROUGH HISTORICAL MUSEUM, off SR 105 and N. Main St., displays 19th-century costumes and wedding gowns, children's articles, Tom Thumb memorabilia, early vehicles and farm implements, an 18th-century law office, a firehouse and a carriage shed. Wed.-Sat. 1-4 (also Thurs. 4-8), July-Aug.; Sat.-Sun. 1-4, first 2 weekends of Sept. Admission $2, students with ID $1, under 6 free. Phone (508) 947-1969 or 947-2596.

MILTON—*see Boston p. 129.*

MINUTE MAN NATIONAL HISTORICAL PARK—*see Boston p. 130.*

MONTEREY (C-1)

THE BIDWELL HOUSE, n. on Tyringham Rd. from SR 23, then 1 mi. w. on Art School Rd., is a 1750 Georgian saltbox set on 190 acres of woodlands. The house, built for the first minister of Monterey, contains 18th- and early 19th-century furniture and decorative arts. Guided tours are available. Hiking trails are provided. Allow 30 minutes minimum. Tues.-Sun. 11-4, Memorial Day weekend-Oct. 15; by appointment rest of year. Admission $5; over 61 and students with ID $4; children $1. Phone (413) 528-6888.

NANTUCKET ISLAND (F-9)

Nantucket Island's history dates from 1659 when a group of colonists seeking economic opportunity and political and religious freedom formed a partnership with Thomas Mayhew of Martha's Vineyard to purchase Nantucket from the Indians for 30 British pounds and two beaver hats. Nantucket soon developed a successful whaling industry. During the 18th century a strong missionary-led Quaker movement took hold on the island.

Much of Nantucket's charm is associated with its cobblestone main street, small lanes, plain Quaker-style homes and handsome houses that date from the whaling days of the early 19th century. Thirty miles off the mainland, Nantucket is reached by air or boat. Daily ferry service is maintained from Hyannis (*see Cape Cod p. 149*) all year and from Martha's Vineyard *(see place listing p. 160)* from early May to late October.

Because streets are narrow, parking in Nantucket is limited. For those who choose not to walk, bicycles and mopeds are preferred modes of transportation. Cars can be parked at Hyannis. However, for those planning to take a car to Nantucket, a car ferry is available. Reservations for car transport are required; phone (508) 477-8600.

Nantucket is accessible by connecting flights worldwide. Hard-surfaced roads on the island connect the town with smaller hamlets.

The island supports an art colony; exhibitions are held in Artists' Association Gallery and outdoors throughout the year. Plays and concerts are presented all year.

Sailing and bicycling as well as fishing, particularly for bass and bluefish, are popular. The town maintains four bicycle paths: Milestone, a 6-mile hilly route between Milestone Rotary and Siasconset; Surfside, a 3-mile flat route from Surfside Beach to the junction of Atlantic Avenue and Vesper Lane; Cliff Road, which covers 2.5 rolling miles starting near Derrymore Road; and Madaket, a winding, 5-mile route beginning at the junction of Quaker and Madaket roads.

Nantucket Island Chamber of Commerce: 48 Main St., Nantucket, MA 02554; phone (508) 228-1700. Visitor kiosks are at Nantucket Memorial Airport, Steamboat Wharf and Straight Wharf.

Self-guiding tours: Information about downtown walking tours is available from Nantucket Historical Association, 5 Washington St., Nantucket, MA 02554-1016; phone (508) 228-1894.

MARIA MITCHELL BIRTHPLACE HOUSE, 1 Vestal St., is a restored traditional-style Nantucket house that was the birthplace of America's first woman astronomer. Exhibits depict the life of Mitchell, her discoveries and teachings. A summer lecture series is featured. Tues.-Sat. 10-4, mid-June through Aug. 31. Admission $3; over 55, $2; under 12, $1. Combination ticket with Aquarium and Hinchman House Natural History Museum $7; over 55, $5; under 14, $4. Phone (508) 228-2896.

Aquarium, 28 Washington St., displays marine life indigenous to Nantucket's salt marshes, harbors and nearshore waters. Outdoor excursions also are available. Allow 30 minutes minimum. Admission $1. Combination ticket with Maria Mitchell Birthplace House and Hinchman House Natural History Museum $7; over 55, $5; under 14, $4. Phone (508) 228-5387.

Hinchman House Natural History Museum, 7 Milk St., exhibits flowers and birds. Nature, birdwatching and marine ecology walks are offered daily. Admission $3; over 55, $2; under 12, $1. Combination ticket with Maria Mitchell Birthplace House and Aquarium $7; over 55, $5; under 14, $4. Phone (508) 228-0898.

NANTUCKET HISTORICAL ASSOCIATION maintains 11 properties. Daily 10-5, mid-June through Labor Day; 11-3, May 23 to mid-June and day after Labor Day-Oct. 31. Phone for schedule. Separate admissions are charged. Combination pass for all buildings except Research Center $10; ages 5-14, $5. Phone (508) 228-1894.

Fire Hose Cart House, 8 Gardner St., is the last example of the old neighborhood fire stations that were built following the Great Fire of 1846. A collection of 19th-century firefighting equipment is displayed. Allow 30 minutes minimum. Free.

Hadwen House, 96 Main St., is a Greek Revival-style home built in 1845 by Frederick Brown Coleman for William Hadwen, whale-oil merchant and candlemaker. The mansion's architecture and furnishings reflect the prosperity of Nantucket's whaling era. A garden is on the grounds. Allow 30 minutes minimum. Admission $3; ages 5-14, $2.

Macy-Christian House, 12 Liberty St., is a 1745 Colonial-style home restored and furnished in 18th- and 20th-century Colonial Revival pieces. Allow 30 minutes minimum. Admission $2; ages 5-14, $1.

★**Nantucket Whaling Museum,** Broad St., is housed in a former candleworks where whale oil once was refined. The museum contains ship models, tools, logbooks and a 16-foot lens from the Sankaty lighthouse. Also included are portraits of whaling masters, a whale skeleton and a large collection of scrimshaw. Allow 1 hour minimum. Daily 10-5, Memorial Day-Oct. 31; Sat.-Sun. 11-3, Nov.-Dec.; otherwise varies. Closed Dec. 25. Admission $5; ages 5-14, $3.

The Oldest House, on Sunset Hill, was built in the saltbox style in 1686 and is known as Horseshoe House and the Jethro Coffin House. Hit by lightning in 1987, the house underwent complete restoration. Daily 10-5, May 1-Labor Day; 11-3, day after Labor Day-Columbus Day. Admission $3; ages 5-14, $2.

The Old Gaol, on Vestal St., was built in 1805 and is representative of early New England penal institutions. Free.

Old Mill is on Mill Hill. Built of wood from shipwrecks in 1746, the mill contains its original intricate working machinery. Corn is ground and sold in season (weather permitting). Admission $2; ages 5-14, $1.

★**Peter Foulger Museum and Research Center,** on Broad St., depicts the history of Nantucket through furniture, baskets, portraits and other artifacts. Allow 1 hour minimum. Museum open daily 10-3; research center open Mon.-Fri. 10-5. Museum admission $4; ages 5-14, $3. Research Center $5.

Quaker Meetinghouse and Fair Street Museum, on Fair St., was built in 1838 and was used as a school and a church by the Wilburite

Friends. The adjoining museum features changing exhibits. Allow 30 minutes minimum. Meetinghouse free. Museum $3; ages 5-14, $2.

NANTUCKET: MESSAGES FROM A SMALL ISLAND, in the Performance Center of the Methodist Church on Centre St., is the title of a presentation depicting contemporary life on the island. Accompanied by music and commentary by native Nantucketers, the presentation lasts 40 minutes. Mon.-Sat. at 6:30 p.m. and 7:30 p.m., mid-June to mid-Sept. Admission $5; ages 3-12, $3. Phone (508) 228-3783.

NATICK—*see Boston p. 130.*

NEPONSET—*see Boston p. 130.*

NEW BEDFORD (E-7) pop. 99,900, elev. 52′

New Bedford, due to its position on Buzzards Bay, was once a great whaling port. Fishing and allied industries still contribute one-fifth of the city's income. A passenger ferry operates to Martha's Vineyard; for schedule phone Cape Island Express Lines at (508) 997-1688. Trips to Cuttyhunk Island aboard the MV *Alert II* depart from Fisherman's Wharf/Pier 3; phone (508) 992-1432.

The New Bedford Whaling National Historical Park is a 13-square-block area with cobblestone streets, period lighting and preserved buildings, some of which date back to the early 19th century. The New Bedford Public Library was one of the first public libraries in Massachusetts and is housed in a handsome, granite Greek Revival building downtown.

Bristol County Convention and Visitors Bureau: 70 N. Second St., Box 976, New Bedford, MA 02741; phone (508) 997-1250 or (800) 288-6263.

Self-guiding tours: Walking-tour maps of historical districts are available at the visitor information center at 33 William St.; phone (508) 991-6200.

NEW BEDFORD ART MUSEUM, 608 Pleasant St., displays paintings and prints created by local artists. Allow 1 hour minimum. Daily 10-5, Memorial Day-Labor Day; Wed.-Sun. noon-5, rest of year. Closed Jan. 1, Easter, July 4, Thanksgiving and Dec. 25. Admission $4, senior citizens $3, under 17 free. AE, CB, DS, MC, VI. Phone (508) 961-3072.

NEW BEDFORD FIRE MUSEUM is at 51 Bedford St. in a building adjacent to Old Station No. 4, which is still in use. The museum exhibits restored antique fire trucks and pieces of historic fire equipment. Upstairs are helmets, coats and boots for children to try on, a bell to ring and a 5-foot-long pole to slide down. Allow 30 minutes minimum. Daily 9-4, July 5-Sept. 1; by appointment rest of year. Admission $2; ages 6-16, $1. Phone (508) 992-2162.

SAVE ★ **NEW BEDFORD WHALING MUSEUM**, 18 Johnny Cake Hill, is one of the largest museums devoted to the history of whaling. The collection includes changing exhibits of prints, paintings, portraits, Pairpoint and New Bedford glass, logbooks, scrimshaw and a fully-equipped whaleboat as well as humpback whale and rare blue whale skeletons. The history of *Moby Dick*, the literary creation of Herman Melville, is the subject of a permanent exhibit. A whaling film also is shown.

Visitors can board a fully-rigged, 89-foot, half-scale replica of the whaling bark *Lagoda*. Daily 9-5; closed Jan. 1, Thanksgiving and Dec. 25. Admission $4.50; over 59, $3.50; ages 6-14, $3. Phone (508) 997-0046.

ROTCH-JONES-DUFF HOUSE AND GARDEN MUSEUM, 396 County St., is a 23-room Greek revival mansion designed by Richard Upjohn for William Rotch Jr., a prominent whaling merchant. Built in 1834, the house and its formal gardens were owned by three prominent families 1834-1981. Rooms display the decorative arts, furniture and belongings of the three families. The grounds encompass a rose garden, a wildflower walk and a formal cutting garden. Daily 10-4, June-Dec.; Tues.-Sun. 10-4, rest of year. Admission $4; over 65, $3; children $2. Phone (508) 997-1401.

SEAMEN'S BETHEL is in the Historic District at 15 Johnny Cake Hill. Dedicated in 1832 as a nondenominational whalemen's chapel, the building features a ship's bow pulpit and the Old Salt Box meeting room. In the novel "Moby Dick," Herman Melville described its cenotaphs—the stone tablets inscribed with the names of whalemen lost at sea since the 1840s. Allow 30 minutes minimum. Daily 10-4, June 1-Oct. 1; Sat. 10-4, Sun. 1-4, rest of year. Donations. Phone (508) 992-3295.

NEWBURYPORT—*see Boston p. 131.*

NEWTON—*see Boston p. 131.*

NORFOLK—*see Boston p. 131.*

NORTH ADAMS (A-2) pop. 16,800, elev. 706′

Once a thriving industrial and railroad center, North Adams is now a popular stop-off point along the scenic Mohawk Trail (SR 2), which winds through the Berkshire Mountains and follows the Deerfield River eastward to Greenfield. Williamstown *(see place listing p. 174)* is the western terminus of the route. Notch Road, off SR 2, leads to the 3,491-foot summit of Mount Greylock, the highest point in Massachusetts.

Northern Berkshire Chamber of Commerce: 40 Main St., North Adams, MA 01247; phone (413) 663-3735.

NATURAL BRIDGE, .5 mi. n. via SR 8 in Natural Bridge State Park, is a white-marble, water-eroded natural bridge and chasm that was formed at the end of the last ice age. Nathaniel Hawthorne described it in his "American Notebooks." A visitor center and an exhibit area are near the bridge. Picnic areas and 1-mile, self-guiding walking tours are available; interpretive programs are available by appointment. Allow 1 hour minimum. Mon.-Fri. 8:30-4:30, Sat.-Sun. and holidays 10-6, Memorial Day-Columbus Day. Admission $2 per private vehicle. Phone (413) 663-6392.

WESTERN GATEWAY HERITAGE STATE PARK, 9 Furnace St., just off the SR 8 bypass in the restored freight yard district, is a collection of six renovated buildings containing shops, a restaurant and exhibits. In the former Boston and Maine Freight House, the visitor center chronicles the cultural history of North Adams, 19th-century railroad and industrial history, and the building of the Hoosac Tunnel, an engineering feat that took 25 years and 196 lives.

Allow 1 hour, 30 minutes minimum. Visitor center open daily 10-5; closed Jan. 1, Easter, Thanksgiving and Dec. 25. Donations. Phone (413) 663-6312, or 663-8059 for a recorded message.

NORTHAMPTON (C-2) pop. 29,300, elev. 125'

Settled in 1654, Northampton was an isolated frontier village for its first 150 years. Puritan theologian Jonathan Edwards and President Calvin Coolidge both lived in this city. Northampton's educational center is Smith College, whose attractions include Lyman Plant House and Botanical Gardens.

Greater Northampton Chamber of Commerce: 62 State St., Northampton, MA 01060; phone (413) 584-1900.

LOOK MEMORIAL PARK, bordered by Mill River, lies on the Berkshire Trail (SR 9) on the n.w. edge of the city. Within its 200 acres are winding paths, tennis courts, picnic and paddle-boat facilities, a petting zoo, an amphitheater, a miniature railroad, miniature golf and bumper boats.

Park open daily dawn-dusk. Facilities open daily 11-7, Memorial Day-Labor Day; 1-6, day after Labor Day-Columbus Day. Admission $2

per private vehicle Sat.-Sun. and holidays, $1 Mon.-Fri. Additional charge for recreational facilities. Phone (413) 584-5457. *See Recreation Chart.*

SMITH COLLEGE MUSEUM OF ART, Elm St. at Bedford Terr., houses more than 24,000 works of art dating from antiquity, with emphasis on 19th- and 20th-century European and American painting. Guided tours, gallery talks, chamber music concerts, films and lectures are offered. Tues.-Wed. and Fri.-Sat. 9:30-4, Thurs. noon-8, Sun. noon-4, Sept.-June; Tues.-Sun. noon-4, rest of year. Hours may vary. Free. Phone (413) 585-2760.

NORTHFIELD (B-3) pop. 1,300

NORTHFIELD MOUNTAIN RECREATION AND ENVIRONMENTAL CENTER, 2 mi. n. of SR 2 on SR 63, is an underground, pumped-storage hydroelectric facility topped by a 320-acre reservoir filled by the Connecticut River. During peak electrical demand, water is released from the reservoir through pump turbines to generate electricity. Free bus tours are given May through October; phone for schedules. Children under 10 are not allowed on the power plant tour. Hiking, mountain biking, picnicking, camping, fishing, cross-country skiing and snowshoeing are permitted; fees may be charged.

The free fish-viewing area is open mid-May to mid-June. Center open Wed.-Sun. 9-5, Apr.-Oct.; daily for skiing mid-Dec. to mid-Mar. (weather permitting). Closed Easter, Patriot's Day, Thanksgiving week and Dec. 25. Free. Phone (413) 659-3714.

Quinnetukut II **Interpretive Riverboat Ride** departs from Riverview Picnic Area. The 1.5-hour Connecticut River cruise highlights local history and geography. Trips depart Wed.-Sun. at 11, 1:15 and 3, July-Aug.; otherwise varies, late May-June 30 and Sept.-Oct. Ninety-minute sunset music cruises and children's cruises are offered July-Aug. Departure times may vary; phone ahead. Interpretive ride fare $7; over 55, $6; under 15, $3. Reservations are required. Phone (413) 659-3714.

ONSET (E-8) elev. 24'

CAPE COD CANAL CRUISES depart from the Town Pier on Onset Bay. The narrated 2- and 3-hour scenic sightseeing cruises of Cape Cod Canal pass under the Bourne and Sagamore bridges and the vertical-lift railroad bridge. Music cruises also are offered.

Trips depart daily at 10 and 1:30, mid-May to mid-June and day after Labor Day to mid-Oct.; Mon.-Sat. at 10 and 1:30, Sun. at 10, mid-June through Labor Day; Sat.-Sun. at 10 and 1:30, late Apr. to mid-May. Three-hour sightseeing trip $8; ages 6-12, $4. Two-hour sightseeing trip $7; ages 6-12, $3.50. Phone (508) 295-3883.

ORLEANS—see Cape Cod p. 150.

PITTSFIELD (B-1) pop. 48,600, elev. 1,026'

Pittsfield, the county seat of Berkshire County, began as an agricultural community, but an abundance of natural resources established the city as an industrial center. During the late 19th and early 20th centuries immigrants came to Pittsfield in search of factory jobs, thus creating the diverse ethnic communities found throughout the area.

Cultural offerings in the area include the Berkshire Artisans, a municipal center for the visual arts. The center features a gallery and performance area, workshops, and artist's studios; phone (413) 499-9348. The Albany Berkshire Ballet performs classical and contemporary works year-round. Many of their productions are geared toward young children and their families. For information about performances and venues phone (413) 445-5382.

Recreational opportunities include hiking and camping in Pittsfield State Forest (see Recreation Chart and the AAA Northeastern CampBook) and at Onota and Pontoosuc lakes. Of interest is Canoe Meadows Wildlife Sanctuary, 3 miles south on US 7 and 2 miles northeast on Holmes Road, where hiking trails traverse woodlands, fields and marshes.

Pittsfield is credited with the creation of the country fair. Held on the village green in 1810, the fair was the brainchild of Elkanah Watson, a tireless promoter of agricultural progress and a friend of George Washington.

Berkshire Visitors Bureau: Berkshire Common, Plaza Level, Pittsfield, MA 01201; phone (413) 443-9186 or (800) 237-5747.

Self-guiding tours: Maps outlining historic sites and circle tours of the Berkshire region are available from the visitors bureau.

ARROWHEAD, home of Herman Melville, is 3.5 mi. s. on US 7/20, then 1.25 mi. n.e. on Holmes Rd. In 1851, during his 13-year residence, Melville completed "Moby Dick." Original inscriptions from the story "I and My Chimney" are on the mantelpiece. In addition, the 44-acre grounds contain a wildflower garden and nature trail. Daily 9:30-5, Memorial Day-Oct. 31; by appointment rest of year. Last tour begins 30 minutes before closing. Admission $5; senior citizens $4.50; ages 6-16, $3.50. Phone (413) 442-1793.

BERKSHIRE ATHENAEUM, 1 Wendell Ave., is the city's public library. A Herman Melville Memorial Room has works, photographs and personal items of the author. Mon.-Thurs. 9-9, Fri.

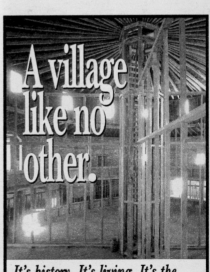

9-5, Sat. 10-5, Sept.-June; Mon.-Fri. 9-5 (also Tues. and Thurs. 5-9), Sat. 10-5, rest of year. Closed holidays. Free. Phone (413) 499-9480.

BERKSHIRE MUSEUM, 39 South St., displays 15th- to 20th-century paintings, including a collection of Hudson River School landscapes and portraits. An interactive aquarium features animals and fish representing 26 local and tropical ecosystems. Other exhibits detail ancient civilizations, natural history and Berkshire history. Films, concerts, children's programs and changing exhibits are presented.

Allow 1 hour minimum. Mon.-Sat. 10-5, Sun. 1-5, July-Aug.; Tues.-Sat. 10-5, Sun. 1-5, rest of year. Admission $6; over 60, $5; ages 3-18, $4. Phone (413) 443-7171.

SAVE ★ **HANCOCK SHAKER VILLAGE,** 5 mi. w. on US 20 at SR 41, is a 1,200-acre restoration of the Shaker community founded in 1790. The Shakers, dedicated to simplicity, celibacy and equality, lived at the Hancock village until 1960. The village includes 21 buildings with original Shaker furniture and artifacts, an unusual round, stone barn, a working farm, and an heirloom herb and vegetable garden. Hands-on activities are featured.

Staff demonstrate Shaker woodworking, weaving, oval box making and other 19th-century crafts. An evening tour and candlelight dinner is offered on most Saturdays from July through October. Guided tours are available by appointment in winter.

Allow 2 hours, 30 minutes minimum. Daily 9:30-5, Memorial Day weekend-late Oct.; 10-3, Apr. 1-day before Memorial Day weekend and late Oct.-Nov. 30. Closed Thanksgiving. Hours may vary. Ten-day village admission $13.50; ages 6-17, $5.50; family rate $33. Evening tour and dinner $38. AE, MC, VI. Phone (800) 817-1137. *See ad p. 165.*

SOUTH MOUNTAIN CONCERT HALL, 2 mi. s. on US 7, presents the South Mountain Concerts, which feature chamber music and recitals. Concerts are held Sun., late Aug.-early Oct. Tickets $20-$25. Phone (413) 442-2106.

PLYMOUTH (D-8) pop. 45,600, elev. 38'

It was on Plymouth Rock that the Pilgrims landed in December 1620 to found the first permanent European settlement on the North American continent north of Virginia. During the first winter, half of the 102 people brought by the *Mayflower* died of exposure, cold and hunger. Survivors John Alden, William Bradford, Elder Brewster, Miles Standish and Edward Winslow have been immortalized in poetry and history.

Brewster Gardens on Water Street is the location of the Pilgrims' first gardens, which were called "meersteads." The traditional Thanksgiving Day Celebration is held on Thanksgiving.

Plymouth Information Center: 130 Water St., Plymouth, MA 02360; phone (508) 747-7525 or (800) 872-1620.

Self-guiding tours: The Pilgrim Path features more than 20 sites. Brochures featuring a map of the path and descriptions of the sites are available from the information center.

Shopping areas: Cordage Park—The Ropewalk Marketplace is a factory-outlet center that occupies several restored turn-of-the-20th-century mill buildings on Court Street (CR 3A). Shoppers also enjoy Village Landing, a marketplace overlooking the harbor.

ANDY LYNN BOATS, which departs from Town Wharf, offers narrated 4-hour whale-watch

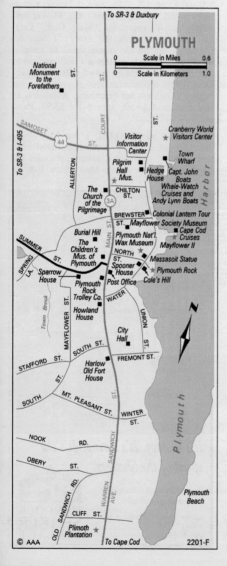

PLYMOUTH

To SR-3 & Duxbury

Scale in Miles
Scale in Kilometers

National Monument to the Forefathers

Cranberry World Visitors Center

Visitor Information Center

Town Wharf

Pilgrim Hall Mus.

Hedge House

Capt. John Boats

Whale-Watch Cruises and Andy Lynn Boats

The Church of the Pilgrimage

Colonial Lantern Tour

Mayflower Society Museum

Cape Cod Cruises

Burial Hill

Plymouth Nat'l. Wax Museum

The Children's Mus. of Plymouth

Mayflower II

Massasoit Statue

Spooner House

Plymouth Rock

Sparrow House

Post Office

Cole's Hill

Plymouth Rock Trolley Co.

Howland House

City Hall

Harlow Old Fort House

Plymouth Beach

Plimoth Plantation

© AAA

To Cape Cod

2201-F

cruises. Cruises depart Mon., Wed. and Fri.-Sun. at 2:30, June-Sept. Hours may vary; phone ahead. Fare $24; over 62, $20; under 12, $15. AE, MC, VI. Phone (508) 746-7776.

BURIAL HILL, at the head of Town Sq., was the site of a fort built 1622-23, a watchtower built in 1643 and the burial place of Gov. William Bradford. A replica of the powder house can be seen. At 6 p.m. each Friday in August, citizens dress in Pilgrim garb and walk from Plymouth Rock to Burial Hill to re-enact the church service attended by the 51 survivors of the winter of 1620-21. Free.

CAPE COD CRUISES departs from Mayflower II State Pier. Forty-minute harbor cruises depart on the hour daily 11-7, June-Sept. One-hour, 35-minute trips to Provincetown depart daily at 10, with return trips leaving Provincetown at 4:30, June 24-Sept. 2; Sat.-Sun., May 25-June 23 and Sept. 3-Sept. 29. Harbor trip $5; under 12, $3. Provincetown and return cruise $24; over 61, $19; under 12, $15. Reservations are recommended. MC, VI. Phone (508) 747-2400.

CAPTAIN JOHN BOATS WHALE-WATCH CRUISES, at Town Wharf, offers 4-hour whale-watching trips with commentary provided by a naturalist guide. Deep-sea fishing excursions, amphibious tours, lighthouse tours and harbor and dinner cruises also are offered. Food is available.

Trips depart daily at 9, 11 and 2, late June-early Sept. (also at 3:30, July-Aug.); Sat.-Sun. at 9, 11 and 2, Apr. 1-late June; Sat.-Sun. at 9 and 2, early Sept.-late Oct. Schedule may vary; phone ahead. Fare $24; over 62, $19; ages 2-12, $15. Reservations are recommended. DI, MC, VI. Phone (508) 746-2643. *See color ads starting on p. 412.*

THE CHILDREN'S MUSEUM OF PLYMOUTH is .5 mi. s. of jct. US 44 at 46-48 Main St. (SR 3A). Children learn through role playing as they explore child-size grocery stores and restaurants. Also available for inspection are the hull of a fishing boat, the front of a fire engine and computers in a schoolhouse. Allow 1 hour, 30 minutes minimum. Mon.-Sat. 10-6, Sun. noon-6; closed major holidays. Admission $4, under 1 free. Phone (508) 747-1234.

THE CHURCH OF THE PILGRIMAGE, 8 Town Sq., was built in 1840. A Roche pipe organ with three manuals, 55 ranks and 3,000 pipes is showcased. Mon.-Fri. 10-1, July-Sept. (weather permitting). Free concerts are given Tues. at 8 p.m., July-Aug. Free. Phone (508) 746-3026.

COLE'S HILL, Water St., was the burial place of Pilgrims who died during the first winter as well as the location of Cyrus Dallin's statue of the Indian chief Massasoit, who ratified the 1621 peace treaty. Free.

COLONIAL LANTERN TOUR departs from 98 Water St. (early tour) or from the lobby of John

Carver Inn (late tour). Participants carry punched-tin lanterns as they traverse the milelong route. The early tour focuses on Plymouth sites; the late tour reflects on the ghostly lore that colors the town's history. Tours depart nightly at 7:30 and 9, Apr.-Nov.; closed July 4. Fee $9; over 62, $8; ages 6-12, $7; family rate $6 per person. Reservations are recommended. VI. Phone (508) 747-4161 or (800) 698-5636. *See color ads starting on p. 412.*

★ **CRANBERRY WORLD VISITORS CENTER,** 225 Water St., has information on the history, cultivation and uses of the cranberry. Featured are outdoor working bogs, a scale model of a cranberry farm and antique harvesting tools. Cooking demonstrations are given throughout the day. Daily 9:30-5, May-Nov. Free. Phone (508) 747-2350.

HARLOW OLD FORT HOUSE, 119 Sandwich St., was built in 1677 and has period furnishings and articles illustrating the lives of the Plymouth colonists. Costumed interpreters demonstrate such skills as carding, spinning, weaving and candle dipping. Photographs are not permitted. Fri.-Sat. 10-4, July-Aug. and by appointment. Hours may vary. Admission $3; ages 6-12, 75c. Phone (508) 746-0012.

HEDGE HOUSE, 126 Water St., is a Federal-era building built in 1809. Once home to a merchant-shipowner, the house contains period furnishings and a changing exhibit gallery. Photography is not permitted. Thurs.-Sat. 10-4, July-Aug.; Thurs.-Sat. 10-3:30, in June and Sept. 1-Oct. 11. Hours may vary. Admission $3; ages 6-12, 75c. Phone (508) 746-0012.

HOWLAND HOUSE, 33 Sandwich St., is the 1666 house that was lived in by *Mayflower* passengers. Tours are given daily 10-4:30, Memorial Day weekend-Columbus Day; 10-3, Thanksgiving Day and Thanksgiving weekend. Admission $3.50; students with ID $3; ages 6-12, $1. Phone (508) 746-9590.

MAYFLOWER SOCIETY MUSEUM, 1 blk. w. of Plymouth Harbor at 4 Winslow St., is the headquarters of the General Society of *Mayflower* Descendants. The original home was built in 1754 by Edward Winslow, a Pilgrim descendant and great grandson of Gov. Edward Winslow of Massachusetts. The estate features a flying staircase, formal gardens and nine rooms with authentic furnishings of the 17th, 18th and 19th centuries.

Videotapes are not permitted. Allow 30 minutes minimum. Daily 10-4:15, July-Aug.; Fri.-Sun. 10-4:15, Memorial Day weekend-June 30 and Sept. 1 to mid-Oct. Admission $3; ages 6-12, 50c. Phone (508) 746-2590.

★ *MAYFLOWER II,* moored at State Pier, is a reproduction of the ship that brought the Pilgrims to the New World. An exhibition on the dock relates the story of their 66-day transatlantic voyage. On board the vessel artisans demonstrate wooden shipbuilding as they ready the ship for its next voyage at the turn of the 21st century. Allow 1 hour minimum. Daily 9-7, July-Aug.; 9-5, Apr.-June and Sept.-Nov. Admission $5.75; ages 6-17, $3.75. Combination rate with the Plimoth Plantation $18.50; ages 6-12, $11. AE, DS, MC, VI. Phone (508) 746-1622.

NATIONAL MONUMENT TO THE FOREFA-THERS, 1 blk. n. of US 44 on Allerton St., is a tribute to Plymouth's founding fathers. The 81-foot monument is one of largest statues in the United States. The names of the 102 *Mayflower* passengers are etched in granite. Daily 8:30-4:30, mid-May to mid-Oct. Free. Phone (508) 746-1620.

⛊ ★ **PILGRIM HALL MUSEUM,** Court and Chilton sts. (SR 3A), opened in 1824 and is one of the oldest public museums in America. The two-story museum houses a collection of Pilgrim furniture, armor, decorative arts, an Early American painting collection and the remains of *Sparrow Hawk,* a transatlantic ship dating from 1626. A historical treasure hunt for children is featured. Daily 9:30-4:30, Feb.-Dec.; closed Dec. 25. Admission $5; over 64, $4; ages 6-17, $2.50. AE, DS, MC, VI. Phone (508) 746-1620. *See color ads starting on p. 412.*

⛊ ★ **PLIMOTH PLANTATION** is 3 mi. s. on SR 3A; or take Plimoth Plantation Hwy., exit 4 off SR 3. In this living-history museum of 17th-century Plymouth, costumed interpreters portray residents of the colony. Program guides teach about the American Indian culture by showing how the natives cooked and made canoes and woven goods.

Seasonal activities include planting, house-building, harvesting, preparing and preserving foods and militia drills. Period tools are used by artisans to create 17th-century goods. Food is available. Allow 3 hours minimum. Daily 9-5, Apr.-Nov. Admission $15; ages 6-12, $9. Combination rate with the *Mayflower II* $18.50; ages 6-12, $11. AE, MC, VI. Phone (508) 746-1622. *See color ads starting on p. 412.*

⛊ ★ **PLYMOUTH NATIONAL WAX MUSEUM,** 16 Carver St., has more than 180 figures in 26 life-size scenes of Pilgrim life, including early Pilgrim struggles and the first Thanksgiving. A display depicts the settlers disembarking on Plymouth Rock. Each scene is enhanced by sound-and-light effects. Daily 9-9, July-Aug.; 9-7 in June and Sept.-Oct.; 9-5, Mar.-May and in Nov. Admission $5.50; ages 5-12, $2.25. AE, DS, MC, VI. Phone (508) 746-6468.

★ **PLYMOUTH ROCK,** on Water St., is the place where the Pilgrims first came ashore in December 1620. The rock is protected by a granite portico.

PLYMOUTH ROCK TROLLEY CO., 22 Main St., provides a narrated sightseeing tour past more than 40 historical sites. Passengers may disem-

bark at any stop and reboard later; trolleys pass each stop approximately every 20 minutes. Allow 30 minutes minimum. Daily 9:30-5, Memorial Day-Oct. 31; Sat.-Sun. 9:30-5, in Nov. All-day re-boarding pass $7; ages 3-12, $3. Phone (508) 747-3419.

SPARROW HOUSE, 42 Summer St., was built in 1640 and is considered to be the oldest house in Plymouth. An adjoining craft gallery features pottery that has been made on the premises since 1932. Regular exhibitions showcase the works of local artists. Thurs.-Tues. 10-5, Memorial Day weekend-Dec. 24. Admission $1.50, children 75c. MC, VI. Phone (508) 747-1240.

⛊ **THE SPOONER HOUSE,** 27 North St., was built in 1747 and owned by members of the Spooner family 1763-1954. The home contains family heirlooms that reflect the changes in taste, occupations and daily activities that have occurred in Plymouth since the mid-1700s. Photographs are not permitted.

Allow 30 minutes minimum. Thurs.-Sat. 10-4, July-Aug.; Thurs.-Sat. 10-3:30 in June and Sept. 1-Oct. 11. Hours may vary; phone ahead. Admission $3; ages 6-12, 75c. Phone (508) 746-0012.

WINERIES

- **Plymouth Colony Winery,** off SR 3 exit 6B, 3 mi. s.w. on US 44, then .5 mi. s. on Pinewood Rd. Mon.-Sat. 10-5, Sun. noon-5, May-Dec.; Sat. 10-4, Sun. noon-4, Feb.-Apr. Phone (508) 747-3334.

PRINCETON (B-4) pop. 3,200, elev. 957'

WACHUSETT MEADOW WILDLIFE SANCTUARY is .75 mi. w. on SR 62, then 1 mi. n. on Goodnow Rd. The 1,100-acre sanctuary incorporates landscapes ranging from gentle pastures to the rugged foothills of Mount Wachusett. Farm ponds are home to river otters, wood ducks and herons, and the meadows offer protection to more than 100 species of nesting birds.

Short walks lead to a 20-acre beaver pond, a glacial boulder and the Crocker Maple, a large North American sugar maple. Hiking trails cover 11 miles. Dogs are not allowed. Tues.-Sun. and Mon. holidays dawn-dusk. Closed Jan. 1, Thanksgiving and Dec. 24-25. Admission $3; over 60 and ages 4-15, $2. Phone (978) 464-2712.

PROVINCETOWN—*see Cape Cod p. 150.*

QUINCY—*see Boston p. 131.*

REHOBOTH (D-6) pop. 8,700

 RECREATIONAL ACTIVITIES

Canoeing
- ⛊ **Palmer River and Kayak,** 206 Wheeler St., Rehoboth, MA 02769. Daily 9-5, Apr.-Oct.

Phone (508) 336-2274, or (800) 689-7884 in Mass.

ROCKPORT—*see Boston p. 132.*

SAGAMORE—*see Cape Cod p. 151.*

SALEM—*see Boston p. 133.*

SANDWICH—*see Cape Cod p. 151.*

SAUGUS—*see Boston p. 137.*

SCITUATE (F-4) pop. 16,800, elev. 46'

Scituate Lighthouse is accessible from SR 3A to the harbor, then via Jericho Road. The 15- and 16-year-old daughters of the lighthouse keeper took fife and drum and frightened away British soldiers who planned to burn the town in the War of 1812.

Scituate Chamber of Commerce: P.O. Box 401, Scituate, MA 02066-0401; phone (781) 545-4000.

SEEKONK (D-6) pop. 13,000, elev. 50'

FANTASYLAND FAMILY ENTERTAINMENT CENTER, on US 6, .5 mi. s. of jct. SR 114A, features an outdoor area with 18-hole miniature golf and a mini-basketball court. An indoor children's area includes rides and amusements for all ages. Food is available.

Allow 1 hour, 30 minutes minimum. Indoor attractions daily 11-9 (also Fri.-Sat. 9-10 p.m.), early June-day before Labor Day weekend; Mon.-Thurs. 3-7, Fri. 3-9, Sat. and holidays 11-9, Sun. 11-8, rest of year. Outdoor attractions daily 10 a.m.-11 p.m. (also Fri.-Sat. 11 p.m.-midnight), early June-Labor Day weekend; daily 11-9 (also Fri.-Sat. 9-10 p.m.), Apr. 1-early June and day after Labor Day weekend-late Oct. Closed Thanksgiving and Dec. 24-25. Amusements are priced individually. Phone (508) 336-6262.

SHARON—*see Boston p. 137.*

SHELBURNE FALLS (B-2) pop. 2,000, elev. 252'

Interesting geological features around Shelburne Falls include some 50 glacial potholes formed several thousand years ago by Deerfield River.

BRIDGE OF FLOWERS, crossing Deerfield River between Shelburne Falls and Buckland, is a former trolley bridge. It is now a flower garden that provides displays of annuals and perennials. The bridge is illuminated until 10:30 p.m. in summer. Allow 30 minutes minimum. Daily 24 hours, May-Oct. Donations.

SOUTH DARTMOUTH (E-7)

[SAVE] **CHILDREN'S MUSEUM IN DARTMOUTH,** 276 Gulf Rd., contains two floors of hands-on exhibits about nature, science and cultural topics. The museum also has 60 acres of conservation land with nature trails and picnic areas. Tues.-Sat. and most Mon. holidays 10-5 (also first Fri. of each month 5-8), Sun. 1-5; closed Jan. 1, July 4, Thanksgiving and Dec. 25. Admission $3.75, under 1 free; free to all first Fri. of each month 5-8. Phone (508) 993-3361.

SOUTH DEERFIELD (B-3) pop. 1,900, elev. 208'

MOUNT SUGARLOAF STATE RESERVATION, e. on US 116, is on a forested mountain of red sandstone. A hiking trail and a road lead to the summit, where there is a view of Connecticut River Valley. Picnic facilities are available. Daily dawn-dusk, Memorial Day-day before Thanksgiving (weather permitting). Free. Phone (413) 665-2928 or 586-8706.

YANKEE CANDLE CO., on US 5, .25 mi. n. of I-91 exit 24, consists of a factory, candle store, museum and a Bavarian Christmas village. Costumed candlemakers create taper candles. The museum presents the history of candle-making with photographs and displays of past methods of production as well as artifacts and tools used by early chandlers. Visitors may dip their own candles; a fee is charged. Allow 1 hour minimum. Daily 9:30-8, Nov. 1-Dec. 23; 9:30-6, rest of year. Closed Thanksgiving and Dec. 25. Free. Phone (413) 665-8306.

Yankee Candle Car Museum, on US 5, .25 mi. n. of I-91 exit 24, focuses on the history of cars, both domestic and foreign. Among displays are a prototype of the first European car; gas-, steam- and diesel-powered vehicles; an amphibious car; and micro-cars, which were popular briefly in postwar Europe. Daily 9:30-8, Nov. 1-Dec. 23; 9:30-6, rest of year. Closed Thanksgiving and Dec. 25. Admission $5; ages 4-11, $2. AE, DS, MC, VI. Phone (413) 665-2020.

SOUTH HADLEY (C-3) pop. 16,700, elev. 126'

JOSEPH ALLEN SKINNER STATE PARK, on 954-foot Mount Holyoke, is 3 mi. n. on SR 47. A road into the park passes Titan's Piazza, a volcanic formation of overhanging rock columns, and Devil's Football, a magnetic boulder. The top of the mountain affords a 70-mile panorama of the Connecticut Valley. One of the oldest existing summit houses in New England is on the grounds.

Daily 10-7, Apr. 1 to mid-Nov. (weather permitting). Hours may vary. House tour by appointment only. Parking $2 per private vehicle Sat.-Sun. and holidays; free to all rest of week. Phone (413) 586-0350. *See Recreation Chart.*

MOUNT HOLYOKE COLLEGE ART MUSEUM, SR 116, on the campus of Mount Holyoke College, houses collections of 19th- and 20th-century paintings and drawings; Oriental, medieval and ancient art; and changing exhibitions. Tues.-Fri. 11-5, Sat.-Sun. 1-5; closed school vacations. Free. Phone (413) 538-2245.

SOUTH WELLFLEET—
see Cape Cod p. 152.

SPENCER (C-4) pop. 11,600

SPENCER STATE FOREST is .5 mi. s. on SR 31. The forest commemorates the Howe family. Elias Howe produced his first practical sewing machine in 1845. William Howe, inventor of the truss bridge, and Tyler Howe, inventor of the spring bed, were his uncles. Cross-country skiing, swimming, hiking and picnic facilities are available. *See Recreation Chart.*

SPRINGFIELD (C-3) pop. 157,000, elev. 101'

On the Connecticut River, Springfield was established as a trading post in 1636. Duryea Motor Wagon Co. of Springfield, one of the first motorcar corporations in the country, was established in 1895. That year in Chicago, a car made in Springfield won what is reputed to be the country's first automobile race.

The game of basketball originated on the Springfield College campus in 1892, a fact widely commemorated in Springfield. In late No-

vember the city plays host to the Basketball Hall of Fame Peach Basket Festival and Tip-Off Classic. The opening game of the collegiate basketball season at Springfield Civic Center is the highlight of this event. For more information contact the Basketball Hall of Fame *(see attraction listing).*

Greater Springfield Convention and Visitors Bureau: 1500 Main St., Springfield, MA 01115; phone (413) 787-1548 or (800) 723-1548.

Shopping areas: Filene's, JCPenney and Sears are at Eastfield Mall on Boston Road (US 20). Just outside the city limits is Fairfield Mall, on Memorial Drive via I-90 exit 5, which has Anderson Little, Bradlees and Caldors.

BASKETBALL HALL OF FAME, off I-91 exits 4 and 7 at 1150 W. Columbus Ave., is a state-of-the-art museum that features exhibits, basketball memorabilia, interactive videotape monitors and a movie theater. Visitors can shoot baskets and test their jumping skills. Allow 2 hours minimum. Daily 9-6 (also Wed. and Fri.-Sat. 6-8 p.m.); closed Jan. 1, Thanksgiving and Dec. 25. Admission $8; over 60 and ages 7-15, $5; full-time active military with ID and their dependents half price. AE, MC, VI. Phone (413) 781-6500.

FOREST PARK, on SR 83, is a 735-acre municipal park offering baseball fields, tennis courts, lawn bowling, a playground, picnic facilities, band concerts, a miniature train ride, paddleboats, an indoor ice rink and the Zoo at Forest Park.

Allow 2 hours minimum. Park open daily dawn-dusk. Zoo open daily 10-5, mid-Apr. to mid-Oct.; 10-3, rest of year (weather permitting). Park $2 per private vehicle Mon.-Fri., $3 per private vehicle Sat.-Sun. Ice rink $3; under 14, $2. Zoo $3; over 65 and ages 5-12, $2; under 5, 50c. Phone (413) 787-6461, 787-6438, and 733-2251 for zoo.

INDIAN MOTORCYCLE MUSEUM is off I-291 exit 4 via St. James Ave. at 33 Hendee St. The museum has a collection of American Indian motorcycles, the first gasoline-powered cycles

manufactured in the United States as well as collections of bicycles, toy motorcycles and other motor-powered items. Allow 1 hour minimum. Daily 10-4; closed Jan. 1, Thanksgiving and Dec. 25. Admission $3; ages 6-12, $1. Phone (413) 737-2624.

OLD FIRST CHURCH, Court Sq., was organized in 1636; the present building was constructed in 1819. The rooster weathervane is one of three shipped to the Colonies from England in 1749. There also is an art gallery with changing exhibits. Concerts are given Oct.-May. Allow 30 minutes minimum. Mon.-Fri. 9-4:30, Sun. 9-noon. Free. Phone (413) 737-1411.

SPRINGFIELD ARMORY NATIONAL HISTORIC SITE, adjoining the Springfield Technical Community College campus on Federal St., was commissioned by Gen. George Washington and was the first of two federal armories in the country. It houses one of the most extensive collections of firearms in the world, including Henry Wadsworth Longfellow's "Organ of Muskets," a collection of Civil War muskets. Daily 10-4:30. Hours may vary; phone ahead. Closed Jan. 1, Thanksgiving and Dec. 25. Free. Phone (413) 734-8551.

★**SPRINGFIELD LIBRARY AND MUSEUMS,** Chestnut and State sts. at the Quadrangle, includes several museums and exhibits. Allow 1 hour minimum per museum. Wed.-Sun. noon-4. Closed Jan. 1, Thanksgiving and Dec. 25. Admission $4; ages 6-18, $1. Phone (413) 263-6800.

The Connecticut Valley Historical Museum has galleries, a genealogy room and a research library. Changing exhibits highlight various aspects of Connecticut River Valley history since 1636.

George Walter Vincent Smith Art Museum contains collections of jade, bronzes, lacquer, porcelains, Islamic rugs, Oriental armor, American and European paintings and a classical sculpture cast gallery. Changing exhibits are featured.

Museum of Fine Arts contains more than 20 galleries of European and American paintings, graphics and sculpture. Works by Winslow Homer and Claude Monet are featured. Changing exhibits are featured.

Springfield Science Museum highlights dinosaur and African exhibit halls, displays about early aviation in Springfield, an exploration center with hands-on exhibits and a participatory investigation station. Also featured are an eco-center with live animals and an aquarium, a mineral hall, American Indian artifacts, interactive life-science exhibits and a planetarium. Planetarium shows Thurs.-Fri. at 3:30 (2:30, July-Aug.), Sat.-Sun. at 1, 2 and 3. Show times may vary; phone ahead. Planetarium $1.

THE TITANIC HISTORICAL SOCIETY MUSEUM, I-90 exit 7, .8 mi. s. on SR 21, then .9 mi. w. on SR 141 (Main St.) to 208 Main St., is the international headquarters of the Titanic Historical Society. Displays include artifacts from the ill-fated ship the *Titanic*. Allow 1 hour minimum. Mon.-Fri. 10-4, Sat. 10-3; closed holidays. Free. Under 7 are not permitted. Phone (413) 543-4770.

STERLING (B-5) elev. 502'

DAVIS' FARMLAND, 145 Redstone Hill Rd., features farming-related hands-on activities for children, a petting zoo, pony rides, hayrides and a rehabilitation area for endangered animals. Food is available. Allow 2 hours minimum. Daily 9:30-4:30, mid-Apr. through Labor Day; Thurs.-Sun. 9:30-4:30, day after Labor Day-Nov. 1 (weather permitting). Closed Jan. 1, Thanksgiving and Dec. 25. Admission $6.50; over 64, $6; under 2 free. DS, MC, VI. Phone (978) 422-6666.

STOCKBRIDGE (C-1) pop. 2,400, elev. 839'

A Berkshire town, Stockbridge was established as an American Indian mission in 1734. The Rev. John Sergeant taught and preached to the Stockbridge Indians in their language until his death in 1749. His successor, the Rev. Jonathan Edwards, later became the president of Princeton University. Field Chime Tower was erected in 1878 on the site of the mission; the tower's chimes were to be played "from apple blossom time 'til frost."

Guided tours of Stockbridge and Lenox *(see place listing p. 159)* are offered by Berkshire Tour Co. and include visits to Norman Rockwell Museum at Stockbridge *(see attraction listing),* "Berkshire Cottages," and the Village Cemetery, where the first slave to be legally freed in the United States is buried; phone (413) 738-5224.

Berkshire Visitors Bureau: Berkshire Common, Plaza Level, Pittsfield, MA 01201; phone (413) 443-9186 or (800) 237-5747.

Shopping areas: Main Street and Elm Street have quaint shops offering clothing, crafts and gifts.

SAVE **BERKSHIRE BOTANICAL GARDEN,** at SRs 102 and 183, contains herb gardens, annual and perennial beds, vegetable gardens, wooded trails, a pond garden, a primrose garden in May, cacti and succulent greenhouses, a sedum bed and passive solar greenhouses. Other floral exhibits are featured. Picnicking is permitted. Allow 1 hour minimum. Daily 10-5, May-Oct. Admission $5; over 60, $4; students with ID $3; under 12 free. Phone (413) 298-3926.

SAVE **CHESTERWOOD,** off SR 183, 1 mi. s. of SR 102, was the studio and summer residence of sculptor Daniel Chester French. Here he fashioned the statue of Abraham Lincoln for Lincoln Memorial in Washington, D.C. French also created the Minuteman statue in Concord *(see Boston p. 130)*. His plaster casts, bronze models, tools, drawings, books and belongings are displayed. An outdoor sculpture show is held July through October. A garden and woodland walk are open to the public. Allow 1 hour minimum. Daily 10-5, May-Oct. Admission $7.50; ages 13-18, $4; ages 6-12, $2. Phone (413) 298-3579.

INDIAN BURIAL GROUND, .5 mi. w. of the town hall on Main St., is a large mound with an obelisk inscribed "The Ancient Burial Place of the Stockbridge Indians, Friends of Our Fathers."

SAVE **MERWIN HOUSE,** 14 Main St., was built around 1825 and enlarged at the end of the century. The house has a collection of European and American furniture and decorative arts that was assembled at the turn of the 20th century. Allow 30 minutes minimum. Tues., Thurs. and Sat.-Sun. noon-4, June 1-Oct. 15. Admission $4; over 65, $3.50; ages 6-12, $2. Phone (413) 298-4703.

MISSION HOUSE, Main St., was built in 1739 and was the home of John Sergeant, the first missionary to the Stockbridge Indians. The house displays a collection of Early American furniture and American Indian artifacts. Gardens are on the grounds. Guided tours are available. Daily

10-5, Memorial Day weekend-Columbus Day. Admission $5; ages 6-12, $2.50. Phone (413) 298-3239.

NAUMKEAG, on Prospect Hill, is .5 mi. n. of US 7 and SR 102. Meaning "haven of peace," this was the summer estate of Joseph Choate, the ambassador to Britain 1899-1905. Designed by Stanford White, the house contains original furnishings and an extensive collection of Chinese porcelain. The grounds were landscaped in formal gardens, including fountain steps, an evergreen walk and rose and Chinese gardens. Guided tours of the house and self-guiding tours of the garden are available.

Daily 10-5, Memorial Day weekend-Columbus Day. Admission $7; ages 6-12, $2.50. Gardens only, $5. Phone (413) 298-3239.

★**NORMAN ROCKWELL MUSEUM AT STOCKBRIDGE,** I-90 exit 2, 7 mi. w. on SR 102, then .5 mi. s. on SR 183, is housed in a white clapboard building situated on 36 acres of rolling hills with views of the Housatonic River and the surrounding Berkshire Hills. The museum features what is said to be the largest collection of original artwork by illustrator Norman Rockwell.

The collection features some of Rockwell's most famous works including "Four Freedoms," "Stockbridge Main Street at Christmas," "Girl at Mirror" and "Triple Self-Portrait." Rockwell's Stockbridge studio has been relocated to the museum grounds and is open May through October.

Changing exhibits by other noted illustrators and contemporary outdoor sculptures by Peter Rockwell also are on display. Picnicking is permitted. Allow 2 hours minimum. Daily 10-5, May-Oct.; Mon.-Fri. 10-4, Sat.-Sun. and holidays 10-5, rest of year. Closed Jan. 1, Thanksgiving and Dec. 25. Admission $9; ages 6-18, $2. AE, MC, VI. Phone (413) 298-4100, or TDD (413) 298-4137. *See ad.*

STOCKBRIDGE LIBRARY ASSOCIATION, Main St., houses a museum exhibiting Stockbridge Indian artifacts, inventions by Anson Clark and memorabilia of Cyrus W. Field, financier and promoter of the first transatlantic telegraph cable. Library open Mon.-Fri. 9-5 (also Mon. and Fri. 7-9 p.m.), Sat. 9-4. Museum open Tues.-Fri. 9-5, Sat. 9-4. Donations. Phone (413) 298-5501.

STOUGHTON—*see Boston p. 138.*

STURBRIDGE (D-4) pop. 7,800

Settled in 1729, Sturbridge became an agricultural community. Orchards and sheep and dairy farms were the main source of income, along with water-powered saw- and gristmills. Textile mills eventually became prominent. The town's focus is now on its re-created village.

Tri-Community Area Chamber of Commerce: 380 Main St., Sturbridge, MA 01550; phone (508) 347-2761 or 347-2949.

★ **OLD STURBRIDGE VILLAGE,** on SR 20 W, .5 mi. w. of jct. I-84 exit 2 and I-90 exit 9, is a re-created New England rural village of the 1830s. This 200-acre living-history museum contains more than 40 restored buildings moved from various parts of New England. Throughout the village costumed staff demonstrate the daily life and work of early New Englanders. Around the Village Common are homes, a tin shop, a shoe shop, a printing office, a bank, a law office, a center meetinghouse and a general store.

Paths lead to a neighborhood where grist-, saw- and wool-carding mills operate by water power. Nearby is a blacksmith and cooper shop and a working historical farm. An exhibit area includes a seasonal herb garden with more than 400 plants. The visitor center offers changing exhibits, and J. Cheney Wells Clock Gallery features more then 100 clocks and timepieces. Picnic facilities and food are available. Boat rides are given.

Allow 3 hours minimum. Daily 9-5, late Mar.-early Nov.; 10-4, mid-Nov. to early Jan. and mid-Feb. to mid-Mar.; Sat.-Sun. 10-4, rest of year. Hours vary; phone to confirm schedule. Closed Dec. 25. Admission (valid for 2 consecutive days) $16; senior citizens $15; ages 6-15, $8. AE, DS, MC, VI. Phone (508) 347-3362, (800) 733-1830, or TDD (508) 347-5383.

SUDBURY—*see Boston p. 138.*

SUTTON (C-5) pop. 6,800, elev. 346′

PURGATORY CHASM STATE RESERVATION, about 4 mi. s.e., is .5 mi. n. on Purgatory Rd. off SR 146. The 188-acre reservation encompasses Purgatory Chasm, a fissure about .25 mile long. The chasm lies between great ledges and averages 40 feet in width and 48 to 70 feet in depth. Picnic facilities, hiking trails, a playground and a visitor center are available. Daily dawn-dusk. Free. Phone (508) 234-3733 or 234-9610.

SWAMPSCOTT—*see Boston p. 139.*

TAUNTON (D-6) pop. 49,800, elev. 47′

Founded in 1639 by Puritan Elizabeth Pole, Taunton is a major manufacturing center for clothing, tools, plastics, hardware and ceramic products.

Taunton Area Chamber of Commerce: 12 Taunton Green, Suite 201, Taunton, MA 02780; phone (508) 824-4068.

Self-guiding tours: A brochure outlining a historical walking tour of Taunton Green and the

Church Green is available from the chamber of commerce.

Shopping areas: Silver City Galleria, SRs 24 and 140, houses more than 160 stores including Filene's, JCPenney and Sears.

GERTRUDE M. BOYDEN WILDLIFE REFUGE, w. on US 44, s. on Joseph Warner Blvd., then w. to 1298 Cohannet St., features many varieties of plants and animals. Noteworthy are the native birds, ranging from the great blue herons of the marsh to the predatory red-tailed hawks. Allow 1 hour minimum. Daily 9-dusk. Free. Phone (508) 821-1676.

OLD COLONY HISTORICAL SOCIETY, 66 Church Green, is in a building designed by Richard Upjohn and built in 1852. It contains a museum of American decorative arts as well as a silver collection, military room and genealogical library. Guided tours are available. Allow 1 hour minimum. Tues.-Sat. 10-4; closed holidays and Sat. before Mon. holidays. Museum $2; over 64 and ages 12-18, $1. Library $5 per day. Phone (508) 822-1622.

TEWKSBURY—*see Boston p. 139.*

TOPSFIELD—*see Boston p. 139.*

TRURO—*see Cape Cod p. 152.*

TYRINGHAM (C-1) pop. 400

SANTARELLA, TYRINGHAM'S GINGERBREAD HOUSE is off I-90 exit 2; take SR 102 w. to Tyringham Rd. then s. to 75 Tyringham Rd. Santarella was the studio of Sir Henry Hudson Kitson, noted sculptor of the Minuteman statue at Lexington and the Pilgrim Maiden at Plymouth. Kitson designed this unusual residence, which has a roof that is actually an 80-ton sculpture of a thatched roof.

The building features exhibits about the construction of Santarella and the life and works of Kitson. Four gallery rooms contain changing works by local artists. A lily pond and woodland walks highlight the contemporary sculpture exhibited in gardens designed by Kitson. Daily 10-4:30, May-Oct. Admission $3.75, under 6 free. Phone (413) 243-3260.

WALES (D-4) pop. 1,600

NORCROSS WILDLIFE SANCTUARY, on Monson-Wales Rd., is w. off SR 19 or e. off SR 32. This 4,000-acre sanctuary contains rare wildflowers and indigenous flora and fauna. Two natural-history museums feature a collection of rocks, seashells, bird carvings and photographs of native plants. A self-guiding trail is on the grounds. Mon.-Sat. 9-4, Apr.-Dec.; Tues.-Sat. 9-4, rest of year. Closed holidays. Free. Phone (413) 267-9654.

WALTHAM—*see Boston p. 139.*

WAREHAM (E-7) pop. 19,200, elev. 19′

THE TREMONT NAIL CO., 8 Elm St., is one of the oldest nail companies in the world, having been established in 1819. The main mill building has been in operation since 1848. Visitors can view the production process through windows and doors; visitors are not permitted inside the mill. Tues.-Sat. 10-5, Sun. noon-5; closed holidays. Free. Phone (508) 291-7871.

WATER WIZZ WATER PARK, jct. of US 6 and SR 28, 1.5 mi. e. of SR 25, has more than 1,000 feet of water slides, including five serpentine slides, two speed slides, an enclosed free-fall body slide, a 503-foot tube ride and a swimming pool. A lazy river, a children's area and an 18-hole miniature golf course also are featured. Picnicking is permitted. Food is available.

Allow 4 hours minimum. Daily 10-6:30, mid-June through Labor Day; daily 10-5, Memorial Day to mid-June. All-day pass $20; over age 62 and under 48 inches tall, $12. After 4 p.m. $14; over age 62 and under 48 inches tall, $10. Phone (508) 295-3255.

WELLESLEY—*see Boston p. 139.*

WELLFLEET—*see Cape Cod p. 152.*

WENHAM—*see Boston p. 139.*

WEST BARNSTABLE—
see Cape Cod p. 152.

WEST SPRINGFIELD (D-3) pop. 27,500

Josiah Day House, 70 Park St., was built in 1754; it was occupied by the Day family until 1902. It is thought to be the oldest brick saltbox house in the nation. Furnishings depict lifestyles 1700-1900.

West Springfield Chamber of Commerce: P.O. Box 161, West Springfield, MA 01090; phone (413) 787-1550.

[SAVE] STORROWTON VILLAGE MUSEUM, 1 mi. w. of US 5 on SR 147, is on the exposition grounds. The restored Early American village comprises seven New England buildings dating

1767-1850. They were dismantled, moved and reassembled at Storrowton. Among them are a mansion, farmhouse, smithy, schoolhouse, tavern and church. Craft demonstrations and events also are featured; phone for schedule. Food is available.

Allow 1 hour, 30 minutes minimum. Guided tours are given Mon.-Fri. 11-3, June 15-Labor Day; by appointment rest of year. Museum $5; ages 6-16, $4. Grounds free. Phone (413) 787-0136.

WESTFIELD (C-2) pop. 38,400, elev. 155′

The westernmost town in the Massachusetts colony, Westfield began as an agricultural community but became an industrial center during the Industrial Revolution. Manufacturing, followed by wholesale and retail trade, is now Westfield's largest source of revenue.

Greater Westfield Chamber of Commerce: 166 Elm St., Westfield, MA 01085; phone (413) 568-1618 or 568-8731.

Self-guiding tours: Brochures outlining walking and driving tours of the historic area are available from the chamber of commerce.

STANLEY PARK AND CARILLON are at Western and Kensington aves. The 275-acre park includes floral, rose and Japanese gardens, a map of the United States and Canada made of inlaid slate, the International Bridge of Understanding, an arboretum and a wildlife sanctuary with trails. The 96-foot-high tower has 25 English and 61 Flemish "bells" and sculpted bronze doors. Concerts are given Thursday and Saturday evenings and Sunday afternoons during the summer. Allow 2 hours minimum. Daily 8-dusk, May 10-Columbus Day. Free. Phone (413) 568-9312.

WESTFIELD ATHENAEUM, Elm and Court sts., contains Jasper Rand Art Museum, which displays works by local artists. Allow 30 minutes minimum. Mon.-Thurs. 8:30-8, Fri. 8:30-5 (also Sat. 8:30-5, Sept.-June). Closed holidays. Free. Phone (413) 568-7833.

WESTFORD—*see Boston p. 140.*

WESTON—*see Boston p. 140.*

WEYMOUTH—*see Boston p. 140.*

WILLIAMSTOWN (A-1) pop. 8,200, elev. 603′

Williamstown is the western terminus of a scenic portion of SR 2, which follows sections of the Hoosic and Deerfield rivers and passes through Savoy Mountain State Forest *(see Recreation Chart).*

Williamstown Chamber of Commerce: P.O. Box 357, Williamstown, MA 01267; phone (413) 458-9077.

CHAPIN LIBRARY OF RARE BOOKS is .5 mi. e. of US 7 on SR 2 to Hopkins Hall Dr., on the campus of Williams College. The library contains original copies of the Constitution, Bill of Rights, Declaration of Independence and Articles of Confederation. Mon.-Fri. 10-noon and 1-5. Free. Phone (413) 597-2462.

★**STERLING AND FRANCINE CLARK ART INSTITUTE** is a complex at 225 South St., near the Williams College campus. It houses the collection of Robert Sterling Clark, with pieces dating from the 15th through 19th centuries. Among the paintings are works by Jean Baptiste Camille Corot, Edgar Degas, Jean Honoré Fragonard, Piero della Francesca, Thomas Gainsborough, Francisco José de Goya, Winslow Homer, Edouard Manet, Claude Monet, Pierre Auguste Renoir, John Singer Sargent and Gilbert Stuart. Sculptures include pieces by Auguste Rodin and Degas.

Fifteenth- to 20th-century drawings and prints range from Albrecht Dürer to Pablo Picasso. An antique silver collection also is featured. Tape tours are available. Picnicking is permitted. Allow 1 hour minimum. Daily 10-5 (also Tues. 5-8), July 1-Labor Day; Tues.-Sun. 10-5, rest of year. Closed Jan. 1, Thanksgiving and Dec. 25. Admission $5, July-Oct.; free, rest of year. Phone (413) 458-9545.

WILLIAMS COLLEGE MUSEUM OF ART, on Main St. between Spring and Water sts., has collections and changing exhibits focusing on American, modern, contemporary and non-Western art. Tues.-Sat. 10-5, Sun. 1-5; closed Jan. 1, Thanksgiving and Dec. 25. Free. Phone (413) 597-2429.

WOODS HOLE—*see Cape Cod p. 152.*

WORCESTER (C-4) pop. 169,800, elev. 473'

The "heart of the Commonwealth," Worcester not only is centrally located in the state but also serves as a commercial, industrial and cultural center. The town was known for its 19th-century dramatic, musical and civic events, which influenced educators to found several colleges. Mechanics Hall, 321 Main St., was built in 1857 and soon became an arena for concerts and other popular social events. A lecture tour of the restored Victorian-style building is offered once a week. Worcester Foothills Theatre carries on the cultural tradition October through May; phone (508) 755-7400.

Dr. Robert H. Goddard, the father of U.S. rocketry, was born in Worcester in 1882. Goddard received his doctorate at Clark University and later became a professor. He fired his first rocket in nearby Auburn.

Off I-290 exit 25 in nearby Berlin, Spookyworld is a horror theme park that comes to life nightly each October. A haunted hayride tour, scary special effects, animated movie sets and a haunted house are some of the ghoulish features; phone (978) 838-0200.

Worcester County Convention and Visitors Bureau: 33 Waldo St., Worcester, MA 01608; phone (508) 755-7400 or (800) 231-7557.

Shopping areas: Worcester Common Outlets, on Worcester Center Blvd., has some 100 stores, including Saks Clearinghouse.

AMERICAN ANTIQUARIAN SOCIETY, 185 Salisbury St. and Park Ave., is a research library of Early American history and culture. Allow 30 minutes minimum. Mon.-Fri. 9-5; closed holidays. Guided 1-hour tours are given Wed. at 2. Free. Phone (508) 755-5221.

BROAD MEADOW BROOK WILDLIFE SANCTUARY, 414 Massasoit Rd., is said to be the largest urban wildlife sanctuary in New England. Trails

and wooden walkways traverse 259 acres of oak woods, fields, streams and wetlands. A visitor center offers trail information and educational exhibits. Sanctuary open daily dawn-dusk. Visitor center open Tues.-Sat. 9-4, Sun. 12:30-4. Closed Jan. 1, Thanksgiving and Dec. 25. Admission $3; over 65 and ages 2-16, $2. MC, VI. Phone (508) 753-6087.

⟨SAVE⟩ ECOTARIUM, e. via SR 9 at 222 Harrington Way, is a 60-acre environmental exploration museum and wildlife center offering three floors of interactive exhibits, a planetarium, an observatory, a children's discovery room, aquariums, a telecommunications theater and a narrow-gauge railroad. Allow 2 hours minimum. Mon.-Sat. 10-5, Sun. noon-5; closed holidays. Admission $7; over 65 and ages 3-16, $5. Planetarium $3.50. Railroad $2.50. MC, VI. Phone (508) 929-2700.

GODDARD EXHIBITION, in Clark University's Goddard Library, contains displays of Dr. Robert Goddard's patents, notebooks, manuscripts and memorabilia of early rocketry. Allow 30 minutes minimum. Mon.-Fri. 9:30-4:30; closed holidays. Free. Phone (508) 793-7572.

⟨SAVE⟩ HIGGINS ARMORY MUSEUM, 100 Barber Ave., exhibits weapons and armor from medieval and Renaissance Europe, feudal Japan and ancient Greece and Rome in a Gothic castle setting. Also featured are interactive displays, arms and armor demonstrations, brass rubbings and sound-and-light shows. Tues.-Sat. 10-4, Sun. noon-4; closed holidays. Admission $5.75; over 60, $5; ages 6-16, $4.75. MC, VI. Phone (508) 853-6015.

SALISBURY MANSION, 40 Highland St., was built in 1772 by businessman and philanthropist Stephen Salisbury I. The mansion has been restored to its 1830s appearance. Exhibits trace Worcester's history from town to city. Allow 1 hour minimum. Thurs.-Sun. 1-4; closed major holidays. Admission $2, under 18 free. Phone (508) 753-8278.

★ WORCESTER ART MUSEUM, 55 Salisbury St., contains more than 35,000 objects representing some 5,000 years of art and culture from Egyptian antiquities and Roman mosaics to impressionist paintings and pop art. Included are works by Thomas Gainsborough, Claude Monet, Rembrandt, Pierre Auguste Renoir and John Singer Sargent. Food is available.

Wed.-Fri. and Sun. 11-5, Sat. 10-5; closed Easter, July 4, Thanksgiving and Dec. 25. Admission $8; over 64 and ages 13-18, $4; free to all Sat. 10-noon. AE, MC, VI. Phone (508) 799-4406.

Worcester Historical Museum, 30 Elm St., highlights the city's industrial accomplishments and community history through changing exhibits and programs. A research library also is featured. Allow 1 hour minimum. Museum open Tues.-Sat. 10-4, Sun. 1-4. Library open Tues.-Sat. 10-4; closed major holidays. Admission $2, under 18 free. Phone (508) 753-8278.

YARMOUTH PORT—
see Cape Cod p. 153.

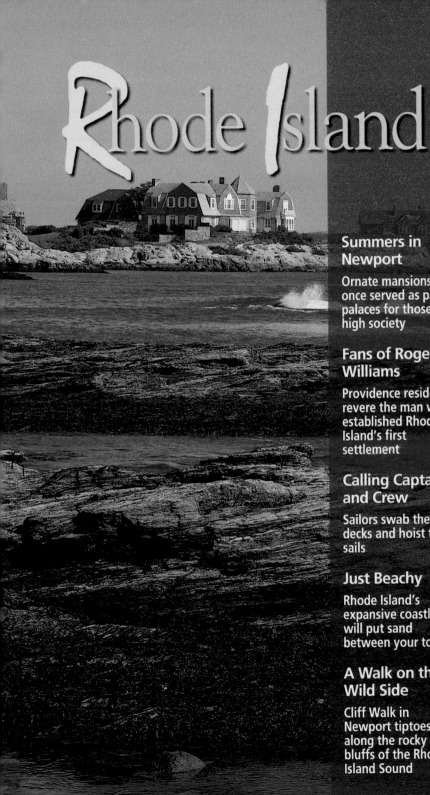

Rhode Island

Summers in Newport

Ornate mansions once served as party palaces for those in high society

Fans of Roger Williams

Providence residents revere the man who established Rhode Island's first settlement

Calling Captain and Crew

Sailors swab the decks and hoist the sails

Just Beachy

Rhode Island's expansive coastline will put sand between your toes

A Walk on the Wild Side

Cliff Walk in Newport tiptoes along the rocky bluffs of the Rhode Island Sound

a safe
harbor

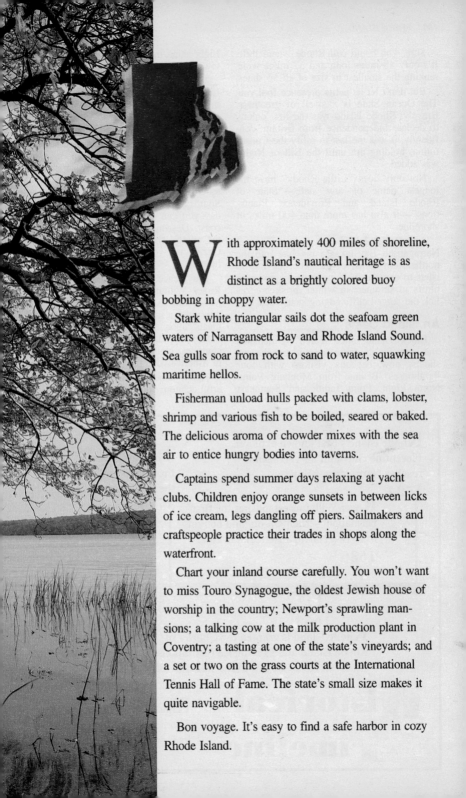

W ith approximately 400 miles of shoreline, Rhode Island's nautical heritage is as distinct as a brightly colored buoy bobbing in choppy water.

Stark white triangular sails dot the seafoam green waters of Narragansett Bay and Rhode Island Sound. Sea gulls soar from rock to sand to water, squawking maritime hellos.

Fisherman unload hulls packed with clams, lobster, shrimp and various fish to be boiled, seared or baked. The delicious aroma of chowder mixes with the sea air to entice hungry bodies into taverns.

Captains spend summer days relaxing at yacht clubs. Children enjoy orange sunsets in between licks of ice cream, legs dangling off piers. Sailmakers and craftspeople practice their trades in shops along the waterfront.

Chart your inland course carefully. You won't want to miss Touro Synagogue, the oldest Jewish house of worship in the country; Newport's sprawling mansions; a talking cow at the milk production plant in Coventry; a tasting at one of the state's vineyards; and a set or two on the grass courts at the International Tennis Hall of Fame. The state's small size makes it quite navigable.

Bon voyage. It's easy to find a safe harbor in cozy Rhode Island.

Sure, you could call Rhode Island little. It's only 48 miles long and 37 miles wide, ranking the smallest in size of all 50 states.

But don't let its petite presence fool you. The Ocean State is a swell of greatness. Bravely, Rhode Island was the first colony to declare independence from Britain; confidently, it was the last to ratify the Constitution, holding out until the Bill of Rights was added.

Not only does "Little Rhody" have the longest name of any state—"State of Rhode Island and Providence Plantations"—it also has more than 400 miles of shoreline.

And Rhode Island isn't just *one* island: Narragansett Bay takes a big bite into the northeastern corner of the state, leaving 35 islets to explore. Soft green grass grows on bluffs in summer; in winter, brisk breezes lick the jagged cliffs edging sandy beaches.

An Island Oasis

Block Island, once feared by captains and crew for its dense fog and treacherous shoals, now beckons visitors with four lighthouses. Beams from Montauk Point, North Light, Point Judith and Southeast Light shine the way to Block Island's only town, quaint Old Harbor.

Called Manisses (meaning "Island of the Little God") by the Narragansett Indians, this summer retreat is big on relaxation— just the place for barefoot beach strolling, window shopping and catching some rays.

For grand scenery, head to lush Mohegan Bluffs, a mile from downtown on the island's southeastern shore. From the top of these 200-foot-high cliffs you'll have an up-close view of the brick, Victorian-style Southeast Light, built in 1875. On a clear day you can even see the state's southern coast. Descend a cliff-clinging stairway to the craggy shore and search for seashells. Gazing up, you may feel a bit like a Lilliputian.

Providence, established by minister Roger Williams who was banished from Massachusetts due to his liberal theologies, grew into a major port but never forgot the ideals upon which it was founded. The town is populated with a number of historic churches, including the first Baptist church in America, also founded by Williams.

Aptly named, Providence boasts a powerful economy due to its location on skinny

Rhode Island's first known explorer, Florentine Giovanni da Verrazano, reaches Narragansett Bay.

1524

Roger Williams establishes the first permanent settlement on land bought from two Narragansett Indian chiefs.

1636

The state becomes the first to prohibit the importation of slaves.

1774

1663
Rhode Island is granted the Charter of Rhode Island and Providence Plantations, which serves as the law of the state for 180 years.

1776
Rhode Island preempts other colonies by 2 months in declaring its independence from British rule.

Historical Timeline

Providence Harbor. The watery band stretches almost 30 miles from downtown Providence to Narragansett Bay, where trading schooners once departed for the West Indies and Africa. Now the port is a major distribution point for oil and coal, and the city serves as the state's seat of government.

Lining Benefit Street are more than 200 restored buildings, which make up what locals call the "Mile of History." These houses, taverns, schools and shops, built by sea captains and shipbuilders, remind us how this and other struggling settlements in Rhode Island relied on ocean commerce for their big break.

Living Large

Newport is a nest for swarms of people who buzz in for summertime fun. In the late 1800s this town on yet another island in Narragansett Bay became *the* place to be for the ultra-rich. But you don't have to be a millionaire to share in its wealth.

Bellevue Avenue and Ocean Drive in Newport give new meaning to the word cottage. When the Astor, Vanderbilt and other families took summer holidays, they vacationed in style. Giant estates—called "cottages" by their aristocratic owners— overlook the cliffs of Rhode Island Sound.

The Breakers, a 70-room estate modeled after 16th-century *palazzos* in Genoa and Turin, is considered the most ornate of Newport's mansions. Built for Cornelius Vanderbilt II in 1893, one of its luxuries is a tub carved from a single slab of marble; four faucets dispense both rainwater and salt water, hot and cold.

The price tag on the Marble House, another in the Vanderbilt "collection," was $11 million in 1892; $7 million paid for the 500,000 cubic feet of marble used in its construction. The giant ballroom—sumptuous to some, gaudy to others—is swathed in golden decoration from top to bottom.

Home to numerous yacht clubs and the America's Cup Race 1930-83, Newport is synonymous with sailing. Bobbing on the bay's choppy waters are rusty lobster boats, cruisers, colorful sailboats and, of course, enormous yachts. The salty air agrees with Newporters, who stand steady on sea legs.

Try Rhode Island on for size. At first it may seem snug, but it'll grow on you.

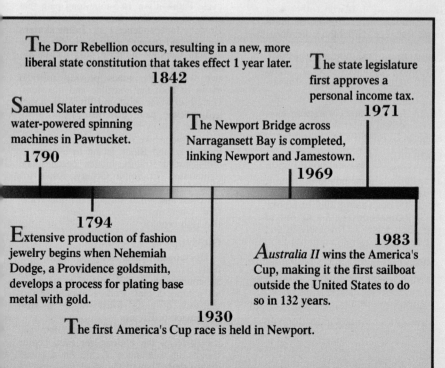

The Dorr Rebellion occurs, resulting in a new, more liberal state constitution that takes effect 1 year later.
1842

The state legislature first approves a personal income tax.
1971

Samuel Slater introduces water-powered spinning machines in Pawtucket.
1790

The Newport Bridge across Narragansett Bay is completed, linking Newport and Jamestown.
1969

1794
Extensive production of fashion jewelry begins when Nehemiah Dodge, a Providence goldsmith, develops a process for plating base metal with gold.

1983
Australia II wins the America's Cup, making it the first sailboat outside the United States to do so in 132 years.

1930
The first America's Cup race is held in Newport.

FAST FACTS

POPULATION: 987,400.

AREA: 1,214 square miles; ranks 50th.

CAPITAL: Providence.

HIGHEST POINT: 812 ft., Jerimoth Hill.

LOWEST POINT: Sea level, Atlantic Ocean.

TIME ZONE: Eastern. DST.

MINIMUM AGE FOR DRIVERS: 16.

SEAT BELT/CHILD RESTRAINT LAWS: Seat belts required for all passengers; child restraints required for under age 4.

HELMETS FOR MOTORCYCLISTS: Required for passenger.

RADAR DETECTORS: Permitted.

FIREARMS LAWS: Vary by state and/or county. Contact the Bureau of Criminal Identification, Attorney General's Office, 72 Pine St., Providence, RI 02903; phone (401) 421-5268.

HOLIDAYS: Jan. 1; Martin Luther King Jr.'s Birthday, Jan. (3rd Mon.); Presidents Day, Feb. (3rd Mon.); Memorial Day, May (last Mon.); July 4; Victory Day, Aug. (2nd Mon.); Labor Day, Sept. (1st Mon.); Columbus Day, Oct. (2nd Mon.); Veterans Day, Nov. 11; Thanksgiving; Dec. 25.

TAXES: Rhode Island's statewide sales tax is 7 percent, and there is a 5-percent lodgings tax.

STATE INFORMATION CENTERS: A welcome center that provides details about attractions, accommodations, historic sites, parks and events is on I-95 in Richmond. It is open daily 8:30-6:30, Memorial Day-Columbus Day; 8-4:30, rest of year. Closed Jan. 1, Thanksgiving and Dec. 25.

Recreation

From sparkling lakes to sailboat-packed Narragansett Bay to choppy Rhode Island Sound to the steel blue waves that meet the southern coast, water is Rhode Island's best feature.

With so many shores to choose from, **sunbathing, surfing, swimming** and simply **strolling** on the beach are favorite warm-weather pastimes. Surfing lessons are offered at Narragansett Town Beach in Narragansett during the summer. If waves are not your thing, bring a kite and catch some beach breezes.

Fish stories are as plentiful as the catches off Block Island. Tales that begin with "it was *this* big!" may just have merit—this **fishing** spot is said to be one of the best in the world due to the variety and abundance of fish as well as coastal accessibility. In Rhode Island Sound anglers can hook flounder, cod, swordfish, tuna and marlin. Inland waters are stocked with pike and bass. In winter, a cast into Rhode Island's many icy ponds may yield yellow perch, pike, and small- and large-mouth bass.

Like to Bike?

Rhode Island is the place for leisurely beachfront excursions. Try the East Bay Bicycle Path—it's a 14.5-mile-long path that stretches from Providence's India Point to Bristol's Independence Park. **Inline skaters** whoosh and **joggers** tread along this paved stretch. Curving Bellevue and Ocean avenues in Newport also are good places for two wheels; the roads provide splendid views of both the coastline and mansions. Get closer to the edge on Cliff Walk, a rugged **hiking** path that maneuvers along Newport's rocky bluffs.

Load your bike onto a ferry and pedal or **moped** around Block Island to explore its cliff-guarded strands, hidden beaches and lighthouses. In South County, Route 1A from Narragansett to North Kingstown hugs the coast and winds through historic Wickford, where many buildings date from the late 18th century.

Giddyup

Horseback riding along the beach or on trails across the state is another way to see the countryside. In fall, marvel at the colorful natural display from a prickly seat in the back of a hay-filled wagon in West Greenwich or Exeter.

And when snowflakes start falling and icicles form, the options get even cooler. Bundle up and enjoy a ride on a horse-drawn **sled.** Tighten the laces on some **ice** skates and hit frozen ponds at Goddards or Lincoln Woods state parks. Strap on a helmet and jump on a **snowmobile** to attack the trails at Colt or Lincoln Woods state parks.

Snap on the snow boots and head to Yawgoo Valley in Exeter, Rhode Island's only ski resort. Runs are usually open early December to late March; phone (401) 294-3802. Norman Bird Sanctuary in Middletown isn't just for the birds—**cross-country skiers** also flock to the area's trails.

Don't Forget Your Deck Shoes

With Newport home to the America's Cup Race, you're sure to spot first mates **sailing, boating** or **yachting** on Narragansett Bay. Charters and tours depart from Goat Island and Oldport marinas in the northern cove of Newport Harbor. **Sailboards** and **rowboats** also dot the waters surrounding Block Island.

Kayakers flirt with the waves of Narragansett Bay and Newport Harbor as well as those in New Harbor on Block Island; the season is late May through September. **Canoeists** head for the 45-mile-long Blackstone River, which heads south from the state's northern border to Narragansett Bay; put in at Woonsocket. And don't miss the Wood River in Exeter, Narrow River near Narragansett and Ninigret Pond, in Ninigret Park near Charlestown. When paddling on the pond, don't be surprised to encounter lots of feathered friends—the park is a saltwater refuge for many waterfowl species.

Near the Mohegan Bluffs on Block Island, **hang gliders** can be seen floating through the air. **Parasailing** also is popular on Block Island. Brave souls can **sky dive** in Lincoln; the Providence-Boston Sky Diving Company schedules jumps April through November; you must be 18. And **climbers** have their choice of clinging to rocks at Lincoln Woods, Snake Den or Fort Wetherill state parks.

Recreational Activities

Throughout the TourBook, you may notice a Recreational Activities heading with bulleted listings of recreation-oriented establishments listed underneath. Since normal AAA inspection criteria cannot be applied, these establishments are presented for information only. Age, height and weight restrictions may apply. Reservations are often recommended and sometimes required. Visitors should phone or write the attraction for additional information, and the address and phone number are provided for this purpose.

FOR YOUR INFORMATION

FURTHER INFORMATION FOR VISITORS:
Rhode Island Tourism Division
1 W. Exchange St.
Providence, RI 02903
(401) 277-2601 or (800) 556-2484

FISHING AND HUNTING REGULATIONS:
Department of Environmental Management
83 Park St.
Providence, RI 02903
(401) 277-3075

NATIONAL FOREST INFORMATION:
Rhode Island Division of Environmental Management
Forest Division Headquarters
1037 Hartford Pike
North Scituate, RI 02857
(401) 647-3367
(877) 444-6777 (reservations)

DID YOU KNOW?

President John F. Kennedy and Jacqueline Bouvier were married at St. Mary's Church in Newport; the reception followed at Hammersmith Farm.

The smallest state has the longest name—its official title is "State of Rhode Island and Providence Plantations."

The first speeding ticket was given in Newport in 1904.

Rhode Island has no county government.

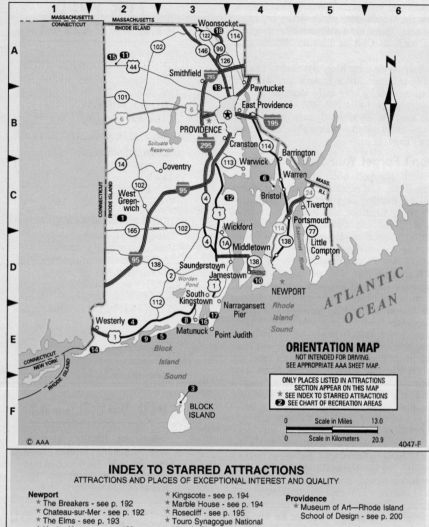

4047-F

ORIENTATION MAP
NOT INTENDED FOR DRIVING.
SEE APPROPRIATE AAA SHEET MAP.

ONLY PLACES LISTED IN ATTRACTIONS
SECTION APPEAR ON THIS MAP
★ SEE INDEX TO STARRED ATTRACTIONS
❷ SEE CHART OF RECREATION AREAS

| 0 | Scale in Miles | 13.0 |
| 0 | Scale in Kilometers | 20.9 |

INDEX TO STARRED ATTRACTIONS
ATTRACTIONS AND PLACES OF EXCEPTIONAL INTEREST AND QUALITY

Newport
★ The Breakers - see p. 192
★ Chateau-sur-Mer - see p. 192
★ The Elms - see p. 193
★ Hunter House - see p. 193

★ Kingscote - see p. 194
★ Marble House - see p. 194
★ Rosecliff - see p. 195
★ Touro Synagogue National
   Historic Site - see p. 196

Providence
★ Museum of Art—Rhode Island
   School of Design - see p. 200

RECREATION AREAS

	MAP LOCATION	CAMPING	PICNICKING	HIKING TRAILS	BOATING	BOAT RAMP	BOAT RENTAL	FISHING	SWIMMING	PETS ON LEASH	BICYCLE TRAILS	WINTER SPORTS	VISITOR CENTER	LODGE/CABINS	FOOD SERVICE
STATE															
Arcadia (C-2) 14,000 acres at Arcadia off SR 165.	1		•	•	•			•	•						
Block Island Beach (F-3) 18 acres on Block Island. *(See Block Island p. 186)*	3		•					•	•						•
Burlingame (E-2) 2,100 acres 5 mi. w. of Charlestown off US 1.	4	•	•	•	•	•		•	•						
Charlestown Breachway (E-3) 62 acres 5 mi. s. of Charlestown via US 1 and Charlestown Breach Rd.	5	•						•	•						
Colt (C-4) 455 acres 2 mi. w. of Bristol on Narragansett Bay. Historic. Nature program. Horse trails.	6		•	•	•	•		•	•	•	•		•		•
East Matunuck (E-3) 102 acres 3 mi. s.e. of Perryville off US 1.	8		•					•	•						
Fort Adams (D-4) 105 acres in w. Newport adjoining Narragansett Bay. Historic. *(See Newport p. 191)*	10		•			•		•	•	•			•		•
George Washington (A-2) 100 acres 2 mi. e. of West Glocester on US 44.	11	•		•	•	•		•	•				•		
Goddard (C-4) 472 acres e. of East Greenwich on Ives Rd. Golf; horse trails. *(See Warwick p. 203)*	12		•	•	•	•		•	•	•		•			•
Lincoln Woods (B-3) 627 acres 5 mi. n. of Providence on SR 146. Horse rental, horse trails.	13		•	•	•	•		•	•	•		•			
Misquamicut Beach (E-2) 57 acres 5 mi. s. of Westerly off SR 1A. Surfing.	14		•					•	•						
Ninigret (E-2) 174 acres in Charlestown off US 1.	9	•	•	•				•	•			•			
Pulaski Memorial (A-2) 100 acres 3 mi. n. of West Glocester off US 44. Cross-country skiing.	15		•	•				•	•			•			
Roger W. Wheeler Beach (E-3) 27 acres e. of Galilee via Sand Hill Cove Rd.	16		•					•	•						•
Scarborough Beach (E-3) 33 acres 2 mi. n. of Point Judith on Ocean Rd. Surfing.	17		•					•	•						•
World War II Memorial (A-3) 15 acres in Woonsocket off Pond Rd. Tennis.	18		•						•				•		

HEAD FOR THE HILLS!

And the mountains, plains and forests with the help of AAA CampBooks, TourBooks and maps.

STARRED ATTRACTIONS

The Breakers—This 70-room cottage was once the summer home of Cornelius Vanderbilt II. Built in 1895 in the European Renaissance style, the interior boasts imported stone and marble, ornate ceiling paintings and mosaics. Coaches and carriages can be found in the stable. See Newport p. 192.

Chateau-sur-Mer—The name says it all: This French "Castle by the Sea" features intricate woodwork, a French-style ballroom and a stained-glass skylight that illuminates a three-story central hall. See Newport p. 192.

The Elms—Highlights of this neoclassical mansion, modeled after an 18th-century chateau near Paris, include a conservatory mimicking the Hall of Mirrors at Versailles and a Louis XIV drawing room. The grounds display statuary, fountains and terraces. See Newport p. 193.

Hunter House—The restored Colonial-style house contains 18th-century furniture crafted in Newport, period paintings and a Colonial garden. See Newport p. 193.

DID YOU KNOW?

Rhode Island was the first colony to break from Britain, yet the last to sign the Constitution.

Built in 1763, Newport's Touro Synagogue is the oldest surviving synagogue in North America.

Continued on page 188

Points of Interest

BARRINGTON (B-4) pop. 15,800, elev. 24'

In 1653 the land that is now Barrington was purchased from the Wampanoag Indians and divided among Gov. William Bradford, Capt. Miles Standish and others of the Plymouth colony. One of the first settlers was Rev. John Myles, who in 1649 founded the first Baptist church in the Massachusetts Bay Colony. Many estates are nearby, particularly at Nayatt Point and Rumstick Point on Narragansett Bay.

BARRINGTON TOWN HALL, on SR 114, was built 1887-88. The medieval-style building features a steep-flank gable roof and two circular corner turrets. Glacial rocks and other unusual stones are among the boulders used in the construction of the ground level. The weathervane features a replica of the *Mayflower*. Allow 30 minutes minimum. Mon.-Fri. 8:30-4:30. Free. Phone (401) 247-1900.

BLOCK ISLAND (F-3) elev. 22'

Previously called Manisses ("Island of the Little God") by the Narragansett Indians, Claudia by explorer Giovanni da Verrazano, Adriaen's Eylant by Dutch trader Adriaen Block and the Town of New Shoreham by the Rhode Island assembly, Block Island is a popular family vacation resort. Its only town, Old Harbor, has the look and feel of vintage New England, with white clapboard Victorian buildings lining its waterfront street.

Sixteen families seeking religious and political freedom bought the 11-square-mile island in 1661 and established it as a democratic settlement.

Block Island features the 18-acre Block Island Beach Recreation Area *(see Recreation Chart)* and many nature, bicycling and hiking trails as well as wildlife sanctuaries. Popular nature trails include the Clayhead Trails, 2 miles north off Corn Neck Road, and the Greenway Trails, a half-mile west off Center Road. There are more than 40 rare and endangered wildlife species on the island; phone The Nature Conservancy at (401) 466-2129.

Mohegan Bluffs, rising to 200 feet along the southeast shore, affords an excellent view of the southern coast of Rhode Island. Southeast Light, a restored lighthouse built in 1875, still stands. Its lantern, 240 feet above sea level, sends light 35 miles out to sea. The Block Island Historical Society, Old Town Road and Ocean Avenue, provides archival information about the island; phone (401) 466-2481.

Passenger ferries run 2-hour crossings from Newport and 4-hour crossings from Providence mid-June through Labor Day; phone (401) 783-4613. A 1-hour crossing aboard an automobile ferry is offered all year from Point Judith; phone (401) 783-4613 a month in advance for reservations. Additional ferry service is available from Montauk, Long Island, N.Y. Crossing time is approximately 2 hours; phone (516) 668-5700.

Scheduled air transportation is available from Westerly, while charters are available from Providence. Phone New England Airlines at (401) 596-2460, or (800) 243-2460 out of R.I.

Block Island Chamber of Commerce: Drawer D, Block Island, RI 02807; phone (401) 466-2982 or (800) 383-2474. *See ad.*

Shopping areas: The New Harbor and the Old Harbor areas contain restaurants, specialty shops and galleries.

THE NORTH LIGHT is 4 mi. from the ferry dock to Settlers' Rock (via taxi or bicycle or moped rental), then a .25-mi. walk n. along a stony beach. The 1867 granite lighthouse is now a maritime interpretive center. The tower is closed for restoration, but a museum on the first floor features displays about lifesaving and renovation efforts as well as historic photographs and the original French Fresnel light. Guided tours are available.

Allow 1 hour minimum. Mon.-Fri. 10-4, June 20-Sept. 14; Fri.-Sun. 10-4, Sept. 15-Columbus Day (weather permitting). Hours may vary; phone ahead. Admission $2, under 12 free. Phone 1 day in advance to arrange transportation for the physically impaired. Phone (401) 466-2982 Mon.-Sat. 10-3, or (800) 383-2474.

SETTLERS' ROCK, at Cow Cove, bears the names of the town's first settlers, who landed at the spot in 1661.

 RECREATIONAL ACTIVITIES
Horseback Riding
• **Rustic Rides Farm**, West Side Rd. Write P.O. Box 842, Block Island, RI 02807. Daily 9-6. Phone (401) 466-5060.

BRISTOL (C-4) pop. 21,600, elev. 42′

The Wampanoag chieftain King Philip established his stronghold in the swamp at the foot of Mount Hope; he later was killed there. In its early days Bristol was a port for trading vessels, but its harbor now shelters mainly pleasure craft.

After the Revolutionary War the triangular trade—the transfer of rum, slaves and molasses among Africa, the Caribbean and New England—made Bristol a prosperous community. The result of that wealth still is evident in the fine 18th- and 19th-century homes that grace the town's waterfront.

Herreshoff Manufacturing Co. designed and built eight defenders of the America's Cup 1893-1934. The shipyard also built the nation's first torpedo boat in 1876. The tradition of boat building continues in Bristol—local companies have built recent America's Cup contenders and winners.

Bristol Historical and Preservation Society, 48 Court St., chronicles more than 300 years of Bristol history; phone (401) 253-7223. Coggeshall Farm Museum, off SR 114, portrays the lifestyles and work of a 1790s coastal farm; phone (401) 253-9062.

Bristol Art Museum on Wardwell Street presents changing exhibits by local and national artists during summer.

Ferry service to Prudence and Hog islands is offered all year on a frequent schedule. Trips depart from the Church Street wharf; phone (401) 253-9808 for schedule and fee information.

⌷ **BLITHEWOLD MANSION & GARDENS,** 1.5 mi. s. via SR 114 on Ferry Rd., was the summer residence of Pennsylvania coal magnate Augustus Van Wickle. The 45-room 1908 mansion, styled after a 19th-century English country manor, is surrounded by 33 acres of landscaped grounds, gardens and exotic plants. Of interest is a 90-foot giant sequoia, native to California. A pamphlet identifies the many tree species along a self-guiding trail. Events are scheduled year-round. Picnicking is permitted.

STARRED
ATTRACTIONS

Kingscote—On the facade of the 1839 wooden Gothic Revival-style house are towers, gables, eaves and arches. A Tiffany glass wall is in the dining room. See Newport p. 194.

Marble House—Every room of this gold and marble structure is furnished in period. White columns grace the exterior, which resembles an 18th-century French castle. See Newport p. 194.

Museum of Art—Rhode Island School of Design—Among the art in the collection are ancient Greek and Roman pieces, porcelains, American paintings and sculpture as well as works from India and China. See Providence p. 200.

Rosecliff—The house, featured in the 1974 film "The Great Gatsby," contains a heart-shaped staircase, a giant ballroom and numerous antique furnishings. See Newport p. 195.

Touro Synagogue National Historic Site—The oldest Jewish house of worship in the country, the synagogue boasts interior columns and hand-carved paneling. See Newport p. 196.

DID YOU KNOW?

Encompassing only 45 square miles, Rhode Island is the smallest state in the country.

The Flying Horse Carousel in Westerly is America's oldest.

Aptly named the "Ocean State," Rhode Island has more than 400 miles of coastline.

Allow 1 hour, 30 minutes minimum. Guided tours of the mansion and grounds are given every 45 minutes Tues.-Sun. and Mon. holidays 10-4, Apr. 15-Sept. 30. Holiday exhibits and hours are available in Dec. Hours may vary; phone ahead. Mansion closed July 4 and Dec. 25. Self-guiding grounds tours daily 10-5. Mansion and grounds $7.50; ages 6-12, $2.50; family rate (two adults and children under 12) $17.50. Grounds $5; ages 6-12, $1; family rate (two adults and children under 12) $12. Phone (401) 253-2707.

SAVE **HAFFENREFFER MUSEUM OF ANTHROPOLOGY, BROWN UNIVERSITY,** near jct. Metacom Ave. (SR 136) and Tower Rd., contains worldwide ethnographic and archeological items. The museum's 375 acres of woodland include important Wampanoag Indian sites. Allow 1 hour minimum. Tues.-Sun. 11-5, June-Aug.; Sat.-Sun. 11-5 or by appointment, rest of year. Admission $2; over 65 and ages 2-12, $1. Phone (401) 253-8388.

HERRESHOFF MARINE MUSEUM, SR 114 at jct. Burnside and Hope sts., contains the America's Cup Hall of Fame as well as 40 original sailing and power yachts designed and built by the Herreshoff family 1859-1947, including the 1859 *Sprite* and the 1914 *Aria.* Also displayed are steam engines and photographs chronicling the role of Herreshoff Manufacturing Co. during the "Golden Age of Yachting." A videotape depicts shipbuilding, America's Cup races and Herreshoff family history.

Allow 1 hour minimum. Daily 10-4, June 16-Oct. 31; Mon.-Fri. 1-4, Sat.-Sun. 11-4, May 1-June 15. Admission $3; over 65, $2; under 18, $1; family rate $5. MC, VI. Phone (401) 253-5000.

SAVE **LINDEN PLACE,** 500 Hope St., is an 1810 Federal mansion built for Gen. George DeWolf. The house later was occupied by the general's descendents, including the prominent Colt family and theatrical scions Ethel, Lionel and John Drew Barrymore. Numerous dignitaries, among them four U.S. presidents, were entertained at the antique-furnished home. The 1.8-acre site also features a ballroom, carriage barn, summer house, bronze sculptures and rose arbors.

Allow 30 minutes minimum. Thurs.-Sat. 10-4, Sun. noon-4, May 1-Columbus Day; daily noon-8 in Dec. Closed July 4 and Dec. 24-25. Admission $5; ages 6-12, $2.50. MC, VI. Phone (401) 253-0390.

COVENTRY (C-3) pop. 31,100

GENERAL NATHANAEL GREENE HOMESTEAD, 50 Taft St., was built overlooking the river in 1770 by Greene, the Quaker general second in command to George Washington. Each of the two main floors has four rooms, two on either side of a central hall. Every room has a paneled fireplace and large double-hung windows. Period furnishings and Greene family memorabilia complete the ambience. On the grounds are a veterans' garden and a Revolutionary War field-artillery cannon. Allow 30 minutes minimum. Wed. and Sat. 10-5, Sun. 1-5, Apr.-Oct. Admission $3; ages 5-18, $1. Phone (401) 821-8630.

CRANSTON (B-4) pop. 76,100, elev. 40'

NATURE'S BEST DAIRY WORLD is on SR 14, .7 mi. w. of I-295, exit 4. Tours include a display describing a day in the life of a cow, a videotape showing how milk is processed, a 1913 Ford Model T delivery truck and a glimpse of the processing plant in action. It is best to visit in the morning, when the plant is more likely to be operating. Allow 30 minutes minimum. Mon.-Fri. 9:30-4, Sat. 10-4; closed holidays. Admission $1, under 6 free. MC, VI. Phone (401) 946-1122 or (888) 315-8687.

EAST PROVIDENCE (B-4) pop. 50,400, elev. 59'

LOOFF CAROUSEL AT CRESCENT PARK is in Riverside at Bullocks Point Ave. The 1895 carrousel, designed by Charles Looff, features 66 hand-carved figures. The park's pavilion has an onion-dome roof and stained-glass windows that project colored lights onto the mirrored carrousel frame. Crescent Park overlooks Narragansett Bay. Food is available. Wed.-Sun. and holidays noon-8, late June-Labor Day; Sat.-Sun. and holidays noon-8, Easter-late June and day after Labor Day-Columbus Day. Fare 50c; 5 rides $2. Phone (401) 433-2828.

JAMESTOWN (D-3) pop. 5,000

Historic Jamestown, on Conanicut Island, is accessible by bridges from Newport on the east and from the mainland on the west. Burned by the British in 1775, Jamestown still boasts several old houses.

The original Beavertail Lighthouse at the southern tip of the island was established in 1749; the site is one of the oldest lighthouse locations in the country. A 1938 hurricane uncovered the lighthouse's original base, exposing a fine example of Colonial stonework. The present lighthouse, closed to visitors, was built in 1856. A pictorial display at the assistant lightkeeper's house chronicles the history of lighthouses.

In addition to historic houses and the lighthouse, the island town is represented by attractions of military and agricultural interest. Three U.S. forts guard the entrance to Narragansett Bay.

Jamestown Museum, housed in a 19th-century schoolhouse at 92 Narragansett Ave., displays temporary exhibits and memorabilia from ferries; phone (401) 423-0937 or 423-0784.

SAVE WATSON FARM is off SR 138 Helm St. exit, then s. to 455 North Rd. Operating since the late 18th century, this 285-acre working historical farm produces lamb, beef, custom-spun yarns and free-range eggs. A 2-mile self-guiding tour goes through the barnyard, past the windmill and fields, along Narragansett Bay and the edge of the swamp, by the old orchard, then back to the barnyard. Picnicking is permitted. Allow 1 hour minimum. Tues., Thurs. and Sun. 1-5, June 1-Oct. 15. Admission $3. Pets are not permitted. Phone (401) 423-0005.

LITTLE COMPTON (D-5) pop. 3,300

Little Compton has several churches and an old burying ground containing the graves of many original settlers. Among the graves is that of Elizabeth Alden Pabodie, daughter of John and Priscilla Alden. In nearby Adamsville a Rhode Island Red hen monument stands to honor the breed developed in Little Compton.

WILBOR HOUSE, 1 mi. s. on SR 77 at 548 W. Main Rd., was built in 1690 and contains furnishings that date 1680-1850. Antique farming and household equipment as well as carriages and sleighs are displayed in an adjoining barn, which was built about 1860. Also on the grounds are an early schoolhouse and an artist's studio. Allow 1 hour minimum. Thurs.-Mon. 2-5, mid-June to mid-Sept. Admission $5; under 12, $1. Phone (401) 635-4143 or 635-4035.

WINERIES

• **Sakonnet Vineyards**, 162 W. Main Rd. Tours are given daily on the hour 11-5, Memorial Day-Columbus Day; 11-4, rest of year. Phone (401) 635-8486.

MATUNUCK (E-3)

THEATRE-BY-THE-SEA is 1.5 mi. s. of US 1N on Matunuck Beach Rd., then w. to 364 Card's Pond Rd. Summer theater is presented in a restored, converted 1929 barn. Since the theater opened in 1933, it has presented shows featuring such stars as Marlon Brando, Helen Reddy, Jessica Tandy and Mae West. For tickets write Theatre-by-the-Sea, 364 Card's Pond Rd., Matunuck, RI 02879.

Allow 3 hours minimum. Performances are given Tues.-Fri. at 8 p.m. (also Thurs. at 2), Sat. at 5 and 9 p.m., Sun. at 7 p.m., late May-late Sept. Children's theater Fri. at 10 and noon, July-Aug. Hours may vary; phone ahead. Tickets $25-$28; children's theater $6. MC, VI. Phone (401) 782-8587.

MIDDLETOWN (D-4) pop. 19,500, elev. 34'

During the almost 3 years of British occupation of Newport in the Revolutionary War, Middletown accommodated British Green End Fort and served as the eastern terminus of the British Newport defense lines. A plaque describing the fort's history is all that remains of the site on Vernon Avenue.

Purgatory Chasm, a narrow cleft between the rock ledges of Easton Point off Purgatory Road, has a scenic overlook.

NORMAN BIRD SANCTUARY, Third Beach Rd., features 7 miles of trails through a refuge of fields, swamp woodlands and rocky ridge cliff overlooks. A museum displays mounted birds and other natural-history exhibits. Programs, field walks and workshops are scheduled year-round.

Daily 9-5, June-Aug.; Tues.-Sun. 9-5, rest of year. Closed Thanksgiving and Dec. 25. Free 1-hour bird walks are given Sun. mornings, Apr.-June and Sept.-Dec. Admission $4; over 65, $3; ages 3-12, $1. Phone (401) 846-2577.

PRESCOTT FARM, 2.5 mi. n. of jct. SRs 114 and 138 to windmill and sign on e. side of road, provides a glimpse of early New England. During the Revolutionary War, Gen. Richard Prescott, commander of the British forces in Rhode Island, was captured here. Farm sights include a four-story, 1811 windmill still used to grind grain, a 1715 country store with period farm implements and the 1730 guardhouse where Prescott was held; it now is a museum furnished in period. The grounds include a medicinal- and culinary-herb and edible flower garden. Geese, ducks and rabbits run free on the farm.

Guided tours are available. Allow 30 minutes minimum. Daily 10-4, Apr.-Nov. Admission (includes mill, store and museum) $2; ages 2-11, $1. Phone (401) 847-6230.

WHITEHALL MUSEUM HOUSE, near Green End Ave. at 311 Berkeley Ave., was built in 1729 by Bishop George Berkeley, noted British philosopher and educator. Furnishings date from the late 17th and early 18th centuries; a small herb garden is on the grounds. Tues.-Sun. 10-5, July-Aug.; by appointment rest of year. Admission $3; ages 6-12, $1. Phone (401) 846-3116 July-Aug., or 847-7951 rest of year.

WINERIES

- **Newport Vineyards and Winery**, 909 E. Main Rd. (SR 138). Mon.-Sat. 10-5, Sun. noon-5; closed Thanksgiving and Dec. 25. Phone (401) 848-5161.

NARRAGANSETT PIER (E-4)
pop. 3,700

Narragansett Pier occupies a narrow strip of land between the Pettaquamscutt River and Narragansett Bay. Its sandy beaches and lush inland woods appealed to wealthy Victorians, who

transformed the area into an exclusive resort by building hotels, Narragansett Pier and the renowned Towers Casino. Built in 1883, the casino has been restored fully and now houses the local chamber of commerce.

Although the 1938 hurricane washed away the pier, locals still refer to the downtown area as "the pier." Area beaches attract many visitors.

Narragansett Chamber of Commerce: 36 Ocean Rd., Box 742, Narragansett, RI 02882; phone (401) 783-7121.

CANONCHET MEMORIAL, at the corner of Beach St. and Ocean Rd. (SR 1A), opposite the Narragansett town beach at Gazebo Park, is a 6,000-pound limestone sculpture of the historical Narragansett Indian chief. Daily dawn-dusk. Free.

NARRAGANSETT INDIAN MONUMENT, Kingstown Rd. and Strathmore St., is a 23-foot-high sculpture carved from a single Douglas fir tree by artist Peter Toth. The monument honors the American Indian. Daily dawn-dusk. Free.

SAVE **SOUTH COUNTY MUSEUM**, n. of the post office on SR 1A at Canonchet Farm across from Narragansett town beach, exhibits nearly 20,000 items relating to early Rhode Island life. A working letterpress print shop is of interest. On the grounds are a historic cemetery, a general store, a one-room schoolhouse, a smithy, nature trails and several farm buildings. A carriage collection also is featured. Guided tours are available.

Allow 1 hour minimum. Wed.-Sun. 11-4, May-Oct. Admission $3.50; ages 6-16, $1.75; family rate $10. Phone (401) 783-5400.

NEWPORT (D-4) pop. 28,200, elev. 6'

See map page 191.

Settled in 1639, Newport was a shipbuilding center as early as 1646; it rivaled Boston and New York as a seaport before the Revolution. The Colonial seaport atmosphere remains to this day, particularly on the waterfront off Thames Street at Bowen's Wharf, an area of restored 18th- and 19th-century commercial shops.

French Gen. Count de Rochambeau greeted George Washington at the 1739 Old Colony House on Washington Square. The building is said to be the nation's second-oldest Capitol; the first Catholic masses celebrated in the state were held here 1780-81. The Declaration of Independence was read from its balcony, and the Federal Constitution was ratified in the building in 1790. Dwight David Eisenhower, Andrew Jackson, Thomas Jefferson and George Washington were said to have been entertained here.

Two residents of Newport embodied the town's seafaring heritage. Oliver Hazard Perry's exploits in the War of 1812 included securing the British surrender in the Battle of Lake Erie. His report of the event was, "We have met the enemy and they are ours." The opening of Japan in 1854—considered one of America's most successful naval diplomatic quests—capped younger brother Matthew Perry's illustrious naval career.

Newport was the site of the Naval Academy during the Civil War; the Naval Training Station and the Naval War College were established in the 1880s. In the early 1900s Narragansett Bay was the principal anchorage for the Atlantic Fleet, which was protected by Fort Adams, one of the largest bastioned forts in the nation and guardian of the bay 1799-1945.

The fortifications still can be seen in Fort Adams State Park off Harrison Avenue. A reproduction of the ship *Providence*, the first authorized ship of the Continental Navy and the first command of John Paul Jones, also is at Fort Adams. *See Recreation Chart.*

Modern Newport continues to be a center for U.S. Navy activities with the Naval Underwater Warfare Center and numerous other schools that make up the Naval Education and Training Center. Visitors should enter at Gate 4, Connel Highway.

Newport's best-known feature is its resort section of magnificent estates. Bailey's Beach is th private beach of the elite; another semi-private Hazard's Beach. Public beaches include Goose berry Beach and Easton's Beach in Newport, an Sachuest Beach and Third Beach in Middletow. The Cliff Walk skirts the surrounding bluffs for miles between the public Easton Beach an Bailey's Beach, affording beautiful vistas.

Note: Portions of the Cliff Walk path are nar row at cliffside or directly on boulders at the wa ter's edge. Wear good walking shoes and us caution.

Two-mile-long Claiborne Pell Bridge connect Newport with Jamestown and charges $2 to cros in either direction. Ferry service to Newport de parts the port area on India Street in Providence Leaving Newport, ferry service continues t Block Island *(see place listing p. 186).*

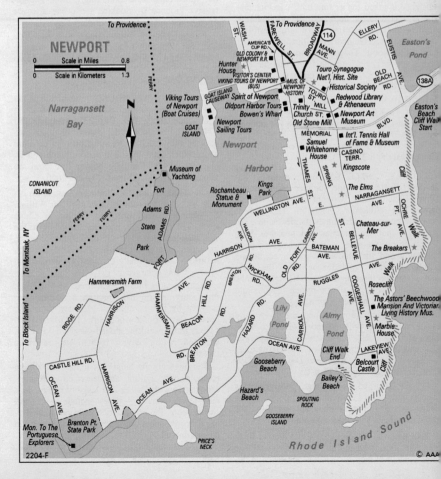

Newport Jai Alai, 150 Admiral Kalbfus Rd. (SR 138), offers jai alai entertainment year-round; phone (401) 849-5000.

Note: Policies concerning admittance of children to pari-mutuel betting facilities vary. Phone for information.

Newport County Convention and Visitors Bureau: 23 America's Cup Ave., Newport, RI 02840; phone (401) 849-8048, or (800) 326-6030 out of R.I.

Self-guiding tours: The Newport Information Center offers an auto-tape tour of Ocean Drive as well as maps and brochures of a walking tour of historic Newport.

Shopping areas: The Brick Marketplace, America's Cup and Bellevue aves., and Spring and Thames sts., offers specialty shops.

SAVE **THE ASTORS' BEECHWOOD MANSION AND VICTORIAN LIVING HISTORY MUSEUM,** 580 Bellevue Ave., was completed in 1857 and is one of Newport's oldest "summer cottages." The residence is noted for its fine Italian architecture. The present mansion duplicates the original 1852 Andrew Jackson Downing structure, destroyed by fire in 1855. Guided living-history tours feature Beechwood Theater Company actors in period dress. The 45-minute tour visits the ballroom, bedrooms, servants' quarters, a dining room and the kitchen.

Daily 10-5, May-Oct.; daily 10-4, Nov.-Dec.; Fri.-Sun. 10-4, Feb.-Apr. Hours may vary; phone ahead. Last tour at closing. Tour $8.75; students with ID $7.25; over 65 and ages 6-12, $6.75; family rate (two adults and all children) $25. Phone (401) 846-3772.

BELCOURT CASTLE, 657 Bellevue Ave., was designed in 1891 as the summer residence for Oliver Hazard Perry Belmont and his wife, the former Mrs. William K. Vanderbilt. The castle is now the home of the Tinney family, whose art collection includes antiques and treasures from 33 countries. Of note is the fine stained-glass collection and the renowned golden coronation coach. A 1-hour guided tour visits the main rooms of the French Louis XIII-style castle. Events are scheduled year-round. Candlelight tours are offered by reservation.

Allow 1 hour minimum. Tours are given daily every hour 9:30-4:30, Memorial Day to mid-Oct.; at 11, 1 and 2, Apr. 1-day before Memorial Day and mid-Oct. through Nov. 30. Ghost tours are given Thurs. at 5, Memorial Day to mid-Oct. Closed Thanksgiving and Dec. 25.

Fee $8; over 65 and college undergraduates $6.50; ages 13-18, $5.50; ages 6-12, $3.50. Ghost tour $14. Reservations are suggested for ghost tour. MC, VI. Phone (401) 846-0669.

★ **THE BREAKERS,** on Ochre Point Ave. at Ruggles Ave., was built in 1895 and is probably the most opulent of Newport's mansions. Though designed by American architect Richard Morris Hunt, this 70-room summer cottage of Cornelius Vanderbilt II appears more the product of the European High Renaissance. Many original furnishings and decorative details were inspired by French and Italian designs of that period.

The Vanderbilt's great wealth was reflected in the extensive use of imported French and Italian stone, marble and alabaster as well as the mansion's wooden trim, ceiling paintings, mosaics and gilded plaster. The most spectacular room is the dining room, lavishly decorated with red alabaster, bronze and gilt. Particularly noteworthy are the 18th-century reception room—a gift from Marie Antoinette to her goddaughter—and the great hall, which is more than two stories high and arrayed with marble columns, pilasters, cornices and plaques.

The first floor and a portion of the second are open to the public. In addition, the stable has a collection of coaches, carriages and riding equipment. "All Aboard the New York Central with the Vanderbilts" is a continuing exhibit. The extensive grounds overlooking the ocean also are open to the public.

Allow 1 hour minimum. Daily 10-5, Apr.-Oct. (also Sat. 5-6, July 1-Labor Day). Admission, including stables, $10; students with ID $6; ages 6-11, $4. Stables $3.50, ages 6-11 free. AE, DS, MC, VI. Phone (401) 847-1000.

CCINC. AUTO TAPE TOURS are available at the convention and visitors bureau or by contacting Auto Tape Tours, P.O. Box 227, Allendale, NJ 07401. The audiotapes let drivers set their own pace as they listen to Newport history. Tape are about 90 minutes long and can be purchased by mail for $14.95 (includes postage) or from the bureau for $12.95. Phone (201) 236-1666.

★ **CHATEAU-SUR-MER,** Bellevue Ave., is an ornate Victorian mansion built in 1852 for William S. Wetmore, who made his fortune in China trade. The house, with property extending to the sea, was modeled after a French chateau, hence its name, "Castle by the Sea." Although it was luxurious and unusually spacious for its day, the structure was enlarged in 1872.

Light streams into the galleried, 45-foot-high, three-story central hall through a stained-glass skylight by Luigi Fullini of Florence, who also created the intricate woodwork. The grand staircase is illuminated by stained-glass windows and accented with canvas painted to resemble tapestry.

The huge granite building's library and dining room, also by Fullini, are decorated in Renaissance style with leather and lavishly carved walnut. Other notable features include a Turkish sitting room, the French-style ballroom with sliding mirrored doors and a Chinese "moongate" in the south wall.

Allow 1 hour minimum. Daily 10-5, May-Sept.; Sat.-Sun. 10-5 in Apr. and Oct.; Sat.-Sun.

10-4, rest of year. Admission $8; students with ID $5; ages 6-11, $3.50. AE, DS, MC, VI. Phone (401) 847-1000.

★ THE ELMS, Bellevue Ave., is a neoclassical mansion designed by American architect Horace Trumbauer and built in 1901 as a summer residence for Edward J. Berwind, the king of America's coal industry. The mansion, based on the 18th-century Château d'Asnières near Paris, is a museum of lavish 18th-century French antique furniture and art, some of which were original to the house.

The large proportions of the rooms, especially the entrance hall and ballroom, are awe-inspiring, yet logical considering they were modeled after rooms in French palaces. For instance, the Hall of Mirrors at Versailles was the inspiration for the conservatory. Noteworthy are the Louis XVI drawing room and the breakfast room, with lacquered panels that date from the K'an Hsi period. Windows open onto the terraces off the 80-foot by 40-foot ballroom.

Bronze and marble statuary, fountains, terraces and gazebos embellish the well-tended grounds; rare trees and shrubs are labeled. The formal sunken gardens are reminiscent of 18th-century France. Daily 10-5, May-Oct.; Sat.-Sun. 10-4, rest of year. Admission $8; students with ID $5; ages 6-11, $3.50. AE, DS, MC, VI. Phone (401) 847-1000.

SAVE HAMMERSMITH FARM, on Ocean Dr., is a 28-room mansion built in 1887 for John W. Auchincloss on what is said to be Newport's oldest working farm. The childhood home of Jacqueline Bouvier, whose stepfather was Hugh Auchincloss, Hammersmith Farm was the summer residence of the Auchincloss family for four generations. The farm was the site of the 1953 wedding reception for Jacqueline Bouvier and John F. Kennedy. The mansion, which served as the "summer White House" 1961-63, contains original furnishings.

Tours are given daily 10-5, Apr. 1-Nov. 7. Holiday tours are given on weekends, late Nov. through late Dec. Admission $8.50; ages 6-12, $3.50. Phone (401) 846-7346.

★ HUNTER HOUSE, 54 Washington St., was built in 1748 by Jonathan Nichols, deputy governor of Rhode Island, and served as the headquarters of the Chevalier de Ternay, admiral over the French naval forces during the American Revolution. The restored house, an outstanding example of Colonial architecture, features fine 18th-century Newport-crafted Goddard-Townsend furniture. Period paintings, paneling and silver as well as a Colonial garden grace the estate.

Allow 1 hour minimum. Daily 10-5, May-Sept.; Sat.-Sun. and holidays 10-5 in Apr. and Oct. Admission $8; students with ID $5; ages 6-11, $3.50. AE, DS, MC, VI. Phone (401) 847-1000.

COMBINATION TICKETS

Many Newport mansions offer both individual admission and combination tickets. Included in the combination ticket are The Breakers, Chateau-sur Mer, The Elms, Hunter House, Kingscote, Marble House and Rosecliff, all in Newport; and Green Animals, in Portsmouth (see place listings beginning on p. 190 and 197).

Two properties $14; students with ID $8.50; ages 6-11, $5.50. Three $19; students with ID $11.50; ages 6-11, $7.50 Four $24; students with ID $14.50; ages 6-11, $9.50. Five $27; students with ID $16; ages 6-11, $10.50. Six $30; student with ID $18; ages 6-11, $11. Seven $33 students with ID $20; ages 6-11, $13 Eight $35.50; students with ID $21; ages 6-11, $14. Combination tickets are available at the mansions. Phone (401 847-1000.

DID YOU KNOW?

America's first water-powered cotton mill was created in Pawtucket in 1790.

Italian navigator Giovanni da Verazzano's exploration trip to Narragansett Bay was extended for 2 weeks and is reputed to be the first paid vacation.

SAVE **INTERNATIONAL TENNIS HALL OF FAME AND MUSEUM,** 194 Bellevue Ave., is in the 1880 Newport Casino, an architectural masterpiece. The casino was host to the United States National Lawn Tennis Championships, now the U.S. Open, 1881-1914. The site includes 13 grass tennis courts, which are open for public play. The facility presents tennis history and memorabilia of tennis greats. Interactive videodisc presentations let visitors test their tennis savvy. A professional tournament takes place in July.

Allow 30 minutes minimum. Daily 9:30-5; closed Thanksgiving and Dec. 25. During tournaments, the museum is open only to tournament ticket holders. Admission $8; over 65, military with ID or students with ID $6; under 17, $4; family rate $20. AE, MC, VI. Phone (401) 849-3990. *See ad.*

★ **KINGSCOTE,** Bellevue Ave., is one of the most modest of the Newport mansions. The 1839 Gothic Revival-style house, designed for planter George Noble Jones of Savannah, Ga., was the first summer residence to be built in this section of Newport. William Henry King bought the house in 1864 and commissioned Stanford White to design additions to it in 1881.

The wooden house, which has interesting towers, gables, eaves and arches, also features a cork ceiling, in what is believed to be the first use of

cork for acoustical purposes. Although the interior is somber, light spilling through a Tiffany glass wall illuminates the cherry and mahogany dining room. In addition to heavy Victorian furniture, Kingscote contains fine Oriental paintings, rugs and porcelain as well as Goddard-Townsend furniture.

Allow 1 hour minimum. Daily 10-5, May-Sept.; Sat.-Sun. 10-5 in Apr. and Oct. Admission $8; students with ID $5; ages 6-11, $3.50. Phone (401) 847-1000.

★ **MARBLE HOUSE,** Bellevue Ave., was built in 1892 for William K. Vanderbilt and is one of the most sumptuous of Newport's mansions. The house cost $2 million to build and $9 million to furnish. Designed by Richard Morris Hunt, the columned white mansion recalls 17th- and 18th-century French castles and employs features of the Grand and Petit Trianons of Versailles. Every room is in period.

The most elaborate room of this gold and marble edifice is the gold ballroom, with its carved and gilded woodwork, chandeliers and large ceiling mural. Also of interest are the grand staircase and the Gothic Room. The Harold S. Vanderbilt Memorial Room features yachting trophies and memorabilia. On the grounds is a restored 1913 Chinese teahouse.

Allow 1 hour minimum. Daily 10-5, Apr.-Oct.; Sat.-Sun. 10-4, rest of year. Admission $8; students with ID $5; ages 6-11, $3.50. Phone (401) 847-1000.

THE MUSEUM OF NEWPORT HISTORY, 127 Thames St., is housed in the restored 1762 Brick Market building. Decorative arts, artifacts, graphics, audiovisual programs and hundreds of historic photographs depict the city's story. Among exhibits are model ships, paintings, Colonial silver, a rifle from the Battle of Lexington and the printing press Ben Franklin's brother brought from England.

Allow 1 hour minimum. Mon. and Wed.-Sat. 10-5, Sun. 1-5; closed Easter, Thanksgiving and Dec. 25. Admission $5; over 65, $4; ages 6-16, $3. Phone (401) 841-8770.

SAVE **MUSEUM OF YACHTING,** in Fort Adams State Park, features four galleries: Mansions and Yachts Gallery, which is focused on the yachting style of the late 1800s; Small Craft Gallery, which displays wooden sail and power boats; America's Cup Gallery, which features photographs, models and artifacts related to America's Cup races; and Single-Handed Sailors Hall of Fame, which honors those who have accomplished either transatlantic or around the world solo feats.

Classic yachts are located in an adjacent boat basin; included in the display is the flagship *Courageous,* a two-time winner of the America's Cup. A slide show also is presented. Allow 1 hour minimum. Daily 10-5, May 15-Oct. 31; by appointment rest of year. Admission $3; over 62, $2.50; under 12 free; family rate $6. Phone (401) 847-1018.

MV *SPIRIT OF NEWPORT*, Newport Harbor Hotel and Marina at 49 America's Cup Ave., offers 1-hour narrated tours on Narragansett Bay and Newport Harbor. Food is available. Cruises depart every 90 minutes daily 11-6:30, June 19-Labor Day; Mon.-Fri. at 11 and 2, Sat.-Sun. at 11, 12:30, 2 and 3:30, May 8-June 18 and day after Labor Day-Oct. 11. Fare $7.50; over 62, $6.50; ages 5-12, $3.50. Phone (401) 849-3575.

NAVAL WAR COLLEGE MUSEUM is in Founders Hall on Coasters Harbor Island; access is through Gate 1 of the Naval Education and Training Center. Founders Hall, built in 1820, is the original site of the U.S. Naval War College, established in 1884. The college was the first of such colleges in the world. Exhibits focus on the history of naval warfare and the naval heritage of Narragansett Bay. Allow 30 minutes minimum. Mon.-Fri. 10-4 (also Sat.-Sun. noon-4, June-Sept.); closed holidays. Free. Phone (401) 841-4052 or 841-1317.

NEWPORT ART MUSEUM, 76 Bellevue Ave., is home to a collection including works by Winslow Homer, George Inness, Fitzhugh Lane and William Trost Richards. Events are held year-round. Allow 1 hour minimum. Daily 10-5, July-Aug.; Mon.-Tues. and Thurs.-Sat. 10-4, Sun. noon-4, rest of year. Closed holidays. Admission $4; over 64, $3; students with ID $2; under 6 free; admission by donation Sat. 10-noon. Phone (401) 848-8200.

NEWPORT HISTORICAL SOCIETY MUSEUM AND LIBRARY, 82 Touro St., has changing exhibits, manuscript archives and a library. Guided 90-minute walking tours of historic Newport are available. Tues.-Fri. 9:30-4:30, Sat. 9:30-noon (also Sat. noon-4:30, mid-June through Aug. 31). Newport walking tours are given Fri.-Sat. at 10, mid-June through Oct. 15. Museum exhibits free. Newport walking tour $7, under 12 free. Phone (401) 846-0813.

NEWPORT SAILING TOURS depart from Goat Island Marina, off Washington St. at Dock A5. Narrated tours sail through Newport Harbor and Narragansett Bay. Passengers may take the helm. Daily 10-8, May-Oct. One-hour tour $15. Two-hour tour $25. Reduced rates for children under 10 are available. The maximum number of passengers is six. Phone (401) 848-2266 May-Oct., or 246-1595 year-round.

OCEAN DRIVE is a 9.5-mile circuit offering panoramas of the rugged Atlantic coastline. Large summer houses border the drive.

OLD COLONY & NEWPORT RAILROAD, America's Cup Ave. and Bridge St., journeys along Narragansett Bay. Train departs Thurs. and Sat. at 11, 12:30 and 2, Sun. and holidays at 12:30, late June-late Sept.; Sun. and holidays at 12:30, May 1-late June; Sun. at 12:30, late Sept. to mid-Nov. Round-trip fare $6.50; over 60, $5; ages 3-17, $4; family rate $17 (Sun. only); first-class seat $10. Phone (401) 849-0546 or 624-6951.

OLDPORT HARBOR TOURS depart from Oldport Marina at Newport Yachting Center on America's Cup Ave. The *Amazing Grace* offers 1-hour narrated cruises in the harbor and on Narragansett Bay, past Newport's mansions, Fort Adams, Brenton Cove, Goat and Rose islands, Jamestown and Clingstone.

Cruises depart daily every 90 minutes noon-7:30, mid-June through Labor Day; Mon.-Fri. at 2, Sat.-Sun. at noon, 1:30 and 3, mid-May to mid-June and day after Labor Day to mid-Oct. Fare $7.50; over 55, $7; ages 4-11, $5.50. Reservations are recommended for the 7:30 cruise. MC, VI. Phone (401) 847-9109.

OLD STONE MILL, in Touro Park at Bellevue Ave. and Mill St., is a Newport landmark. It is believed by some to have been built by Norsemen long before Columbus' voyage; others claim it dates from the mid-17th century.

REDWOOD LIBRARY AND ATHENAEUM, 50 Bellevue Ave., was built 1748-50 and contains many valuable books. A fine collection of early 18th- and 19th-century portraits includes six by Gilbert Stuart. The 250th anniversary of the library will be celebrated with special events through 2000. Allow 30 minutes minimum. Mon.-Sat. 9:30-5:30; closed holidays. Donations. Phone (401) 847-0292.

ROCHAMBEAU STATUE AND MONUMENT, in King's Park, commemorates the landing of the French allies in America on July 10, 1780. A fine view can be seen of Newport Harbor and Lime Rock Lighthouse, now the Ida Lewis Yacht Club.

★ **ROSECLIFF,** Bellevue Ave., was built in 1902 for Mrs. Hermann Oelrichs, whose wealthy Irish immigrant father discovered the Comstock Lode in Nevada. Designed by Stanford White after Marie Antoinette's Grand Trianon at Versailles, the terra-cotta mansion replaced a less opulent one. The estate was named for its many rose beds. Sculptor Augustus Saint-Gaudens provided the garden ornamentation, including the Court of Love.

"The Great Gatsby" was filmed at Rosecliff in 1974; "True Lies" was filmed here in 1994. The mansion boasts a 40-foot by 80-foot ballroom with windows opening onto terraces, a heart-shaped staircase considered to be one of White's finest works, a Caen Stone carved fireplace, exquisite antique furnishings, hand-painted washbasins and 18th- and 19th-century sculptures. Allow 1 hour minimum. Daily 10-5, Apr.-Oct. Admission $8; students with ID $5; ages 6-11, $3.50. AE, DS, MC, VI. Phone (401) 847-1000.

SAMUEL WHITEHORNE HOUSE, 416 Thames St., is an example of Federal-period architecture. Notable are the collection of 18th-century Goddard-Townsend furniture and silver and pewter by local craftsmen. A garden is behind the house. Allow 30 minutes minimum. Sat.-Mon. and holidays 10-4, Tues.-Thurs. by appointment, Fri. 1-4, May-Oct. Admission $5, by appointment $6. Phone (401) 847-2448 or 849-7300.

★ **TOURO SYNAGOGUE NATIONAL HISTORIC SITE** is at 85 Touro St. Built in 1763, the oldest Jewish house of worship in the nation—and the only one to survive from Colonial times—is considered an architectural masterpiece. Designed by Peter Harrison, the Georgian structure has a simple, almost austere exterior that contrasts with a graceful interior adorned with massive brass candelabra, hand-carved paneling, balustrades and 12 Ionic and Corinthian columns.

Tours are given every 30 minutes Sun.-Fri. 10-4, July 4-Labor Day; Mon.-Fri. 1-3, Sun. 11-3, Memorial Day-July 3 and day after Labor Day-Columbus Day; Sun. 1-3, Mon.-Fri. by appointment rest of year. Closed Jewish holidays. Last tour is 30 minutes before closing. Donations. Admission is only by guided tour, and proper dress is required. Phone (401) 847-4794.

TRINITY CHURCH, Queen Anne Sq., has been in continuous use since it was built by Richard Munday in 1726. It is modeled on Old North Church in Boston. A three-tiered wineglass pulpit, Tiffany windows and a 1733 organ tested by George Frideric Handel grace the interior. The original chandeliers, once lowered so the candles could be lit, hang from the rafters by ropes, Colonial-style. Concert and choral performances are scheduled during summer and fall.

Allow 30 minutes minimum. Daily 10-4, July 4-Labor Day; Mon.-Fri. 10-4, day after Labor Day-Columbus Day; by appointment rest of year. Donations. Phone (401) 846-0660.

[SAVE] **VIKING TOURS OF NEWPORT** depart from the convention and visitors bureau information center at 23 America's Cup Ave. Boat cruises depart from Goat Island Marina off Washington Street. Bus excursions pass Newport's historic homes and mansions. Cruises of Narragansett Bay and Newport Harbor are offered.

Bus tours depart daily every 90 minutes 9:30-2, mid-June through Labor Day; daily every 2 hours 9:30-1:30, day after Labor Day-Oct. 31; daily at 9:30 and 1:30 (also Sat. at 11:30), Apr. 1 to mid-June; Sat. at 11:30, rest of year. Cruises depart daily every 90 minutes 10-4 and at 5:15, mid-June through Labor Day; at 11:30, 1 and 2:30, mid-May to mid-June and day after Labor Day to mid-Oct.

Ninety-minute bus tour $14; ages 5-11, $8. Three-hour tour $22; ages 5-11, $11. Four-hour tour $27; ages 5-11, $14. One-hour cruise $8; ages 5-11, $3. Phone (401) 847-6921.

PAWTUCKET (A-4) pop. 72,600, elev. 86'

Thick forests, rocky land and untamed rivers discouraged Roger Williams from settling the area north of Providence in the 1630s. Called the "place by the waterfall," Pawtucket is where the Blackstone River—designated an American Heritage River by President Clinton—forms Pawtucket Falls as it tumbles into the Pawtucket River.

With its abundant water power and timber for fuel, Pawtucket soon enticed blacksmiths to set up shop. Despite a setback in 1676 when the town virtually was destroyed in King Philip's War, Pawtucket grew quickly as an innovative manufacturing center, emerging as the birthplace of America's Industrial Revolution. In 1793 Samuel Slater started North America's first successful cotton-manufacturing mill, which was operated by water power.

Pawtucket is part of the Blackstone River Valley, through which the Blackstone River flows for 48 miles. Established by the U.S. Congress in 1986 as a national historic region, the Blackstone River Valley National Heritage Corridor helps preserve the history of the American Industrial Revolution. The area spans nine Rhode Island towns and covers 250,000 acres from Worcester, Mass., to Providence. Among the Blackstone River Valley towns listed individually are East Providence, Smithfield and Woonsocket *(see place listings p. 189, 201 and 204).*

A popular recreation area is Slater Memorial Park on Newport Avenue (US 1A). The park offers recreational facilities and attractions, including an 1895 Looff carrousel and paddleboats.

The Pawtucket Red Sox, the AAA International Baseball League affiliate of the Boston Red Sox, play at McCoy Stadium; phone (401) 724-7300 for Pawtucket Red Sox information.

Blackstone Valley Tourism Council and Visitor Center: 171 Main St., Pawtucket, RI 02860; phone (401) 724-2200.

Self-guiding tours: Maps and brochures for walking, fall foliage, canoe and driving tours are available at the visitor center.

RHODE ISLAND WATERCOLOR SOCIETY, in a restored historic building at Slater Memorial Park, has changing monthly displays of watercolors. Tues.-Sat. 10-4, Sun. 1-5; closed holidays. Free. Phone (401) 726-1876.

[SAVE] **SLATER MILL HISTORIC SITE,** downtown at 67 Roosevelt Ave., has been restored to its early 1800s appearance to depict the development of factory production and life in a 19th-century industrial village. Guided tours include visits to the 1758 Sylvanus Brown House, where handspinning and weaving are demonstrated, and the 1793 Slater Mill. An 8-ton water wheel powers the 1810 Wilkinson Mill. A 15-minute multimedia show about Pawtucket and the Industrial Revolution also is offered.

Allow 1 hour, 30 minutes minimum. Mon.-Sat. 10-5, Sun. 1-5, June-Oct.; Sat.-Sun. 1-5, Mar.-May and Nov. 1 to mid-Dec. Tours are given at 1 and 3 (also Mon.-Sat. at 10:30, June-Oct.). Closed Jan. 1, Easter, Thanksgiving and Dec. 25. Admission $6.50; over 65, $5.50; ages 6-12, $5. Phone (401) 725-8638.

POINT JUDITH (E-3)

FRANCES FLEET WHALE WATCHING departs from 2 State St. in Port Galilee. Six-hour ocean cruises provide views of finback, humpback, minke and right whales. Other sightings include sharks, dolphins, sea turtles and various sea birds. Allow a full day. Trips depart Mon.-Sat. at 1, July 1-Labor Day. Boarding begins approximately one hour prior to departure. Fare $30; over 62, $27; ages 5-12, $20. Reservations are suggested. DS, MC, VI. Phone (401) 783-4988 or (800) 662-2824.

PORTSMOUTH (C-5) pop. 16,900, elev. 36'

Portsmouth, once the most populous town in the colony, was settled in 1638. The first settlers, among them free-speech advocate Anne Hutchinson, landed at Founders' Brook on Boyd's Lane. On Pudding Rock is a bronze tablet inscribed with a copy of the Portsmouth Compact. At Butts Hill Fort off Sprague Street, Portsmouth later witnessed Rhode Island's only major land battle of the Revolution. Founders Memorial Grove, across from Founders Brook, permits picnicking daily until dusk.

GREEN ANIMALS, .7 mi. w. off SR 114 on Cory's Ln., is a topiary garden started by Thomas Brayton about 1880. Boxwood-lined ornamental gardens surround 80 pieces of topiary, including a lion, a dinosaur and a giraffe, sculpted in privet and yew, as well as boxwood and privet geometric forms and ornamental designs. Formal, rose, fruit and vegetable gardens are featured. Ten rooms in the main estate contain period furnishings, Brayton memorabilia and Victorian toy collections.

Picnicking is permitted. Allow 1 hour minimum. Daily 10-5, May-Oct. Admission $8; students with ID $5; ages 6-11, $3.50. AE, DS, MC, VI. Phone (401) 847-1000.

PROVIDENCE (B-3) pop. 160,700, elev. 80'

See map page 198.

Founded in 1636 by Roger Williams, who was banished from Massachusetts for his religious views, Providence was named in gratitude "for God's merciful providence unto me in my distress." A monument on Gano Street between Power and William streets marks the site where Williams first stepped ashore. A statue in Prospect Terrace, at Congdon and Cushing streets, marks his grave.

In its early days Providence was a shipping and shipbuilding town. Its ships ran the triangular trade route with rum, slaves and molasses to Africa, the West Indies and the Colonies. A thriving trade with East India and China developed in the area immediately following the Revolutionary War.

Today, the city is Rhode Island's capital as well as an educational, arts and medical center. Products manufactured in Providence include fashion jewelry, silverware, plastics, electronic equipment, hardware, machine tools and oil and rubber goods.

The port of Providence is at the head of navigation on Narragansett Bay, 27 miles from the open sea. One of the most important distributing ports on the Atlantic seaboard for oil, coal, lumber and other products, it has a 600-foot state pier and a 3,000-foot municipal quay, as well as many private wharves.

Educational facilities also influence the city's economic and cultural base. The city is home to Brown University (see attraction listing), Johnson and Wales University, Providence College and the Rhode Island School of Design, near which the art community of the College Hill-Benefit Street area thrives.

Along Benefit Street, restorations of 18th-century mansions have been in progress for many years. The "Mile of History" is a concentration of original Colonial homes along Benefit Street with fine examples of early Federal and 19th-century architecture. Edgar Allan Poe once courted Helen Whitman at Providence Athenaeum, 251 Benefit St.; the site is among the nation's oldest libraries and cultural centers.

Waterplace Park, on the site of the 1848 Cove Basin, is a 4-acre urban park focused on a 240-foot-diameter basin, on which gondola rides are offered. Joining it to the east is Providence Riverwalk, with Venetian-style footbridges, more than a mile of cobblestone and brick walkways and 7 acres of parkland. Kennedy Plaza contains an ice skating rink.

One of the nation's finest acting companies, Trinity Square Repertory Players, regularly offers performances at Trinity Repertory Theatre; phone (401) 351-4242. Providence Civic Center, on Sabin Street at La Salle Square, is the scene of frequent sporting events, concerts and conventions; phone (401) 331-0700.

The Providence Bruins, the farm team of the Boston Bruins, play hockey at Providence Civic Center; phone (401) 273-5000.

Greater Providence Convention and Visitors Bureau: 1 W. Exchange St., Providence, RI

02903; phone (401) 751-1177, or (800) 233-1636 out of R.I.

Self-guiding tours: A map indicating the location of landmark attractions is available from the bureau.

Shopping areas: Dating from 1828, The Arcade on Westminster and Weybosset streets is a Greek Revival structure and a forerunner of enclosed shopping malls. This 1828 landmark has been updated with specialty stores and restaurants. Renovated commercial buildings on South Main Street, along the Providence River, now house restaurants, offices and shops. Weyland Square1360, on the eastern side on the city, offers diverse shops in an early 20th-century neighborhood.

BENEFICENT CONGREGATIONAL CHURCH (ROUND TOP CHURCH) is at 300 Weybosset St. Opened in 1810, the structure is one of the earliest examples of Classical Revival architecture in the country. The interior, patterned after the New England-style meetinghouse, contains an Austrian-crystal chandelier and a gallery clock that has been in continuous service since 1826. The exterior dome is modeled after the Custom House Building in Dublin, Ireland. Allow 30 minutes minimum. Mon.-Fri. 8:30-3:30, Sat. by appointment, Sun. 9-1; closed holidays. Donations. Phone (401) 331-9844.

BROWN UNIVERSITY is on College Hill at the end of College St. Brown began in 1764 as Rhode Island College in Warren and was relocated to Providence in 1770. The Admissions Office provides information about guided tours; it is open Mon.-Fri. 8:30-5, during the academic year; 8-4, rest of year. Phone (401) 863-2378.

Annmary Brown Memorial, 21 Brown St., contains European and American paintings from the Renaissance through the early 20th century. Mon.-Fri. 1-5. Free. Phone (401) 863-1994.

John Carter Brown Library, corner of George and Brown sts., is a 1904 Beaux-Arts building considered the classical gem of the university. The library contains one of the finest collections

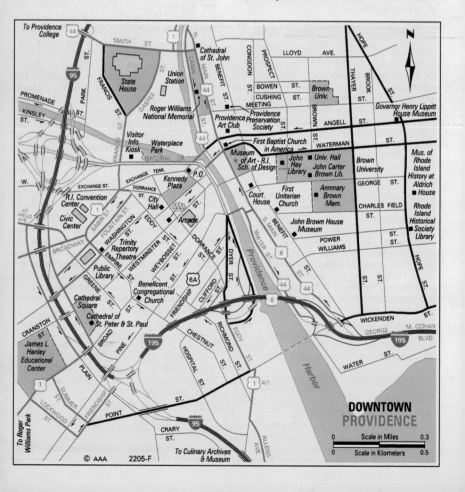

DOWNTOWN
PROVIDENCE

Scale in Miles   0   0.3
Scale in Kilometers   0   0.5

© AAA   2205-F

of Americana printed before 1825. Other exhibits and maps are devoted to the exploration and settlement of America. Mon.-Fri. 8:30-5, Sat. 9-noon during the academic year; otherwise varies. Closed holidays. Free. Phone (401) 863-2725.

John Hay Library, 20 Prospect St., contains the writings of John Hay, assistant private secretary to President Abraham Lincoln and secretary of state 1898-1905. Also shown are the Harris Collection of American Poetry and Plays, the McLellan Lincoln Collection and the Anne S.K. Brown Military Collection. Mon.-Fri. 9-5. Free. Phone (401) 863-2146.

University Hall, on the main green, now houses administrative offices. The structure was built in 1770 and served as a barracks and hospital for Colonial troops during the American Revolution. Mon.-Fri. 8:30-5, during the academic year; 8-4, rest of year. Free. Phone (401) 863-2378.

CATHEDRAL OF ST. JOHN is at 271 N. Main St. Built in 1810, the cathedral is the oldest Episcopal church in the city and one of four original Colonial parishes of Rhode Island. There is an 1851 refurbished Hook organ and a 17th-century altar table. Many of Providence's early settlers are buried in an adjoining graveyard. Guided tours of the cathedral are available on request. Mon.-Fri. 9-4. Free. Phone (401) 331-4622.

CATHEDRAL OF ST. PETER AND ST. PAUL, on Cathedral Sq., dates from the late 19th century. Renovated in the neo-Gothic style, the Catholic church contains a rare 6,330-pipe Cassavant organ, with pipes ranging in size from 6 inches to 32 feet. Mon.-Fri. 7:30-4:30, Sat. 11-6, Sun. 8-7, holidays 7:30-11. Donations. Phone (401) 331-2434.

CULINARY ARCHIVES & MUSEUM, 315 Harborside Blvd. at Johnson & Wales University, features more than 300,000 culinary- and hospitality-related items. Exhibits reflect food history from ancient times to the present. Displays include cooking tools, antique kitchen appliances, 19th- and 20th-century stoves, graphic prints of chef's uniforms, cookbooks, menus and food-related correspondence signed by emperors, kings and U.S. presidents. Guided 1-hour tours are available.

Mon.-Fri. 9-5, Sat. 10-4; closed holidays. Admission $5; over 65 and students with ID $2; ages 5-18, $1. Phone (401) 598-2805.

FIRST BAPTIST CHURCH IN AMERICA, 75 N. Main St. at Waterman St., was established by Roger Williams in 1638 and is the oldest Baptist church in America. Faithfully restored, the 1775 structure boasts a Waterford crystal chandelier dating from 1792. Mon.-Fri. 9-3:30. Guided tours are given Sun. at 12:15, following the 11 a.m. service, Sept.-June; at 11:15, following the 10 a.m. service, rest of year. Closed holidays. Donations. Phone (401) 454-3418.

FIRST UNITARIAN CHURCH OF PROVIDENCE, Benefit and Benevolent sts., combines elements of classical and Gothic architecture. Built in 1816, it has the largest bell ever cast in the foundry of Paul Revere. Guided tours are given Mon.-Fri. 9-5. Free. Reservations are required. Phone (401) 421-7970.

GOVERNOR HENRY LIPPITT HOUSE MUSEUM, 199 Hope St., is a Renaissance revival mansion built in 1865. The interior features brass chandeliers, stenciling, hand-carved woodwork, faux marble, stained- and etched-glass windows, paintings, family china and period furnishings. Allow 30 minutes minimum. Guided tours are given on the hour Tues.-Fri. 11-3, Sat.-Sun. by appointment, Apr.-Dec.; by appointment rest of year. Tour $4; over 65 and ages 7-18, $2. Phone (401) 453-0688.

JOHN BROWN HOUSE MUSEUM, 52 Power St., was built in 1786 by the wealthy China trade merchant John Brown. This restored three-story Georgian-style house is furnished with fine examples of Colonial antiques, decorative arts and pewter and silver collections. Guided tours are available. Tues.-Sat. 10-5, Sun. noon-4, Mar.-Dec.; by appointment rest of year. Holiday hours may vary; phone ahead. Admission $6; over 62 and students with ID $3.50; ages 7-17, $3; family rate $15. Phone (401) 331-8575.

★ **MUSEUM OF ART—RHODE ISLAND SCHOOL OF DESIGN,** 224 Benefit St., is home to more than 65,000 works of art. The diverse collection features ancient Greek and Roman art; 18th-century European porcelains; American and European paintings and sculpture; contemporary pieces and American furniture. Also featured are holdings of works from China, India, Latin America, France and Egypt. Pendleton House, which features American furniture and decorative arts, is closed for renovations.

Braille gallery guides are available. Wed.-Sun. 10-5 (also Fri. 5-8). Closed Jan. 1, July 4, Thanksgiving and Dec. 25. Admission $5; over 60, $4; college students with ID $2; ages 5-18, $1; by donation on Sat. Phone (401) 454-6500.

MUSEUM OF RHODE ISLAND HISTORY AT ALDRICH HOUSE, 110 Benevolent St., is an 1822 Federal-style mansion with changing exhibits about Rhode Island history, architecture and decorative arts. Allow 30 minutes minimum. Tues.-Fri. 9-5, Sun. noon-4. Holiday hours may vary; phone ahead. Admission $2; over 62, $1.50; under 18, $1; family rate $6. Phone (401) 331-8575.

PROVIDENCE ART CLUB, 11 Thomas St., is in two houses dating 1786-91. Changing exhibits are featured. Mon.-Fri. 10-4, Sat. noon-3, Sun. 3-5, Sept.-June; Mon.-Fri. 10-3, rest of year. Closed holidays. Free. Phone (401) 331-1114.

RHODE ISLAND HISTORICAL SOCIETY LIBRARY, 121 Hope St., has genealogy, graphics and manuscript collections pertaining to Rhode Island history. Tues.-Sat. 9-5, Sun. noon-4. Free. Phone (401) 331-8575.

ROGER WILLIAMS NATIONAL MEMORIAL, 282 N. Main St., is the site of the original 1636 Providence settlement. A visitor center offers displays and a 3-minute videotape describing the life of the city's founder. Daily 9-4:30; closed Jan. 1, Thanksgiving and Dec. 25. Free. Phone (401) 521-7266.

ROGER WILLIAMS PARK can be reached from I-95S exit 17 or I-95N exit 16 to Elmwood Ave., following signs. The 435-acre area has a chain of 10 lakes, extensive flower gardens and 9 miles of winding drives. The William E. Benedict Memorial to Music amphitheater is a stage for concerts and outdoor productions. Also on the grounds are greenhouses and Betsy Williams Cottage, built in 1773. Carousel Village features bumper boats, miniature golf, a replica of a Victorian carrousel and other children's amusements.

Park open daily 9-9. Greenhouses and Carousel Village daily 11-5; extended hours in summer. Park admission free. Amusement rides $1. Phone (401) 785-9450.

Roger Williams Park Museum of Natural History features wildlife displays, interactive exhibits, a model of Narragansett Bay and artifacts of various cultures. The museum also contains Cormack Planetarium, which offers shows on weekends. Daily 10-5; closed Jan. 1, Thanksgiving and Dec. 25. Museum $2; under 8, $1. Planetarium and museum $3; ages 5-8, $2. Under 5 are not permitted in the planetarium. Reservations are required for the planetarium. Phone (401) 785-9457.

Roger Williams Park Zoo features animal exhibits including the Plains of Africa natural habitat; the Tropical Rainforest building; and the Marco Polo Trail, which traces the explorer's journey through Asia. Mon.-Fri. 9-5, Sat.-Sun. and holidays 9-6, during daylight-saving time; daily 9-4, rest of year. Last admission is 30 minutes before closing. Closed Dec. 25. Admission $6; senior citizens and ages 3-12, $3.50. Phone (401) 785-3510. *See color ad.*

STATE HOUSE, on Smith St. between Francis and Gaspee sts., overlooks the city. Outside the senate chambers is the original Parchment Charter of 1663, granted by King Charles II. There also are relics and noteworthy paintings, including a Gilbert Stuart portrait of George Washington. A large marble dome—the first unsupported dome built in the United States—caps the building. A gilded bronze statue, "Independent Man," stands atop the dome. Guided tours are available.

Allow 1 hour minimum. Mon.-Fri. 8:30-4:30; closed holidays. Reservations are required for guided tours. Free. Phone (401) 277-2357.

SAUNDERSTOWN (D-3)

A Scottish emigrant and his wife established Saunderstown, site of the first snuff mill in the 13 original colonies, on the Mettatuxet River in 1751. The snuff-grinder's son, Gilbert Stuart, became a renowned portrait painter.

[SAVE] **CASEY FARM** is 1 mi. s. of SR 138 at 2325 Boston Neck Rd. (SR 1A). This 300-acre historic farm, once an 18th-century plantation, is now a community-supported organic vegetable farm. Visitors may take a guided tour of the house, then explore the farm, family graveyard and hiking trails. Tues., Thurs. and Sat. 1-5, June 1-Oct. 15. Admission $3; over 54, $2.50; ages 5-12, $1.50. MC, VI. Phone (401) 295-1030.

GILBERT STUART BIRTHPLACE, 1 mi. e. of US 1 on Gilbert Stuart Rd., dates from 1750. Stuart, one of America's foremost portrait painters who was especially noted for his series of George Washington, was born in 1755. Period furnishings, a water wheel and a snuff mill are featured. Allow 30 minutes minimum. Thurs.-Mon. 11-4, Apr.-Oct. Admission $3; ages 6-12, $1. Phone (401) 294-3001.

SMITHFIELD (A-3) pop. 19,200

AUDUBON SOCIETY OF RHODE ISLAND, 12 Sanderson Rd., manages more than 8,000 acres of natural wildlife habitats in the state. The office, which includes Hathaway Library of Natural History, is surrounded by the 75-acre Powder Mill Ledges Wildlife Refuge, with 2.5 miles of nature trails. Five-mile trails include the George B. Parker Woodland in Coventry and the Fisherville Brook Wildlife Refuge in Exeter.

Additional refuges with trails are in Charleston, North Kingstown, North Smithfield, Tiverton and Warren. Self-guiding trail brochures and naturalist programs are available. Office open Mon.-Fri. 9-5, Sat. noon-4; closed holidays. Refuge trails open daily dawn-dusk. Donations. Phone (401) 949-5454.

SOUTH KINGSTOWN (E-3) pop. 24,600

Near the observation tower in South Kingstown is a rock that is at the heart of a tragic love story. In 1765 Hannah Robinson, the lovely young daughter of a prominent local citizen, fell in love with her French tutor. Hannah's father disapproved of the courtship, and the couple was forced to meet secretly, often at a large rock more than a mile from her house. They eventually eloped, resulting in Hannah's disinheritance. Her new husband soon deserted her, and Hannah,

in declining health, was brought home to die, for the last time passing the rock where she and her beloved had met in happier times.

The University of Rhode Island, established in 1892, is on 1,200 acres in Kingston Village. The village's main street, SR 138, retains its 18th-century charm.

OBSERVATION TOWER AT HANNAH ROBIN-SON PARK is at jct. US 1 and SR 138, overlooking Bonnet Shores. The 100-foot-high wooden tower, which sits atop a natural, wooded hill overlooking flowering plants and trees, provides a panorama of Narragansett Bay, the Atlantic Ocean and the rocky, uneven shoreline of Rhode Island. Picnicking is permitted. Daily dawn-dusk. Free.

TIVERTON (C-5) pop. 7,300, elev. 50′

A popular resort on the shores of Narragansett Bay and the Sakonnet River, Tiverton was part of the Plymouth Colony. A royal decree in 1746 deemed that Tiverton be included within Rhode Island's boundaries, a ruling disregarded by Massachusetts, which reclaimed part of the town in 1862. Present-day Tiverton is one of the few towns in the state where farming provides the main livelihood.

Fort Barton, on Highland Road, was a Revolutionary redoubt, where British troops practiced their invasion of Aquidneck Island and Newport. More than 3 miles of nature trails mark the site of the fort overlooking the Sakonnet River.

WARREN (C-4) pop. 11,400

BAY QUEEN CRUISES, 461 Water St., Gate 4, offers sightseeing luncheon cruises with narration about Newport Harbor aboard a 114-foot, 350-passenger vessel, *Vista Jubilee.* Lighthouse cruises explore the beacons of Narragansett Bay; phone for cruise dates. Brunch, dinner and dinner/dance cruises as well as thematic excursions also are available. Four-hour luncheon cruises depart Wed.-Fri. at 11, June-Oct. Fare $21-$32.50; ages 4-12, $15.50-$19. Reservations are required. AE, DS, MC, VI. Phone (401) 245-1350 or (800) 439-1350.

WARWICK (C-4) pop. 85,400

Samuel Gorton, Warwick's founder, was one of early Rhode Island's most colorful characters. An extreme individualist who did not believe in civic or religious authority, Gorton was exiled successively from Plymouth Colony and Portsmouth. Even Roger Williams, also an exile, banished Gorton from Providence. Seeking to avoid persecution, Gorton and several followers purchased lands at Shawomet from the Narragansett Indians in 1643.

Disputing Gorton's claim at Shawomet, the Massachusetts Bay Colony arraigned Gorton and his fellow purchasers before a tribunal, which condemned the men to prison for blasphemy. Upon his release, Gorton went to England to gain protection from Massachusetts. Promised protection by the Earl of Warwick, an important member of Parliament, Gorton confidently returned to Shawomet and renamed it after the earl.

About the beginning of the 19th century, Warwick developed as a confederation of villages built around textile mills along the Pawtuxet River. Now a major retail center and suburban area, Warwick is second in size only to Providence.

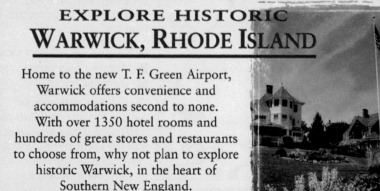

Although rapid industrial and commercial expansion erased most vestiges of Warwick's early history, progress has left the 39 miles of coastline along Narragansett and Greenwich bays untouched. Each summer Warwick's beaches and shoreline attract boaters and inland residents.

Warwick City Park on Asylum Road features beach and recreational facilities on 170 acres. Oakland Beach, south from SR 117 on Oakland Beach Avenue, and Conimicut Point, east off SR 117, offer swimming, fishing and scenic views. At low tide, beachcombers search the shore for clams, locally known as quahogs.

Goddard Memorial State Park, which occupies more than 472 acres off SR 1 on Ives Rd., was planted more than 100 years ago with an unusual selection of trees. Considered a fine example of private forestry, the main portion of the park is open from April through September, with limited access the rest of the year. In addition to swimming, hiking, picnicking and a public golf course, the park offers summer concerts in a restored carrousel building near the beach. *See Recreation Chart.*

Regional art is featured year-round at Warwick Museum in Kentish Artillery Armory, 3259 Post Rd.; phone (401) 737-0010.

Warwick Department of Economic Development: Tourism Office, 3275 Post Rd., Warwick, RI 02886; phone (401) 738-2000, ext. 6403, (800) 492-7942 or TDD (401) 739-9150. *See color ad p. 202.*

Shopping areas: Major malls include Rhode Island Mall, I-295 exit 1 at the junction of SRs 2 and 113, which features Cherry & Webb and Sears; and Warwick Mall, I-295 exit 2 at the junction of SRs 2 and 5, which is anchored by Filene's, JCPenney and Macy's.

WESTERLY (E-2) pop. 16,500, elev. 34′

The first permanent European settlers of Westerly, so named for its westerly position in the state, supposedly were John and Mary Babcock, who eloped in 1648. They were joined more than a decade later by residents from Newport, Providence and Warwick, who bought shares from a Newport company that claimed title to the Misquamicut tract, as this region was called.

Border disputes between Connecticut and Rhode Island plagued the region for more than 50 years until the boundary line officially was drawn in 1728. Throughout the Revolutionary War the coast around Westerly was besieged by marauding British expeditions. Nearby Watch Hill, now a quiet resort town, was established as a lookout for British privateers. Shipbuilding, agriculture and trade sustained the village throughout the 18th century.

Prosperity reigned in the late 19th century, a result of textile manufacturing and granite quarrying. Westerly is a supply center for nearby seaside resorts. There are many public beaches with bathhouse facilities between Weekapaug and Watch Hill, including Misquamicut State Beach *(see Recreation Chart)*. Eighteen-acre Wilcox Park, on High Street, includes collections of day lilies and dwarf conifers, a garden of senses, a library and a display about the granite industry; phone (401) 596-8590.

Greater Westerly-Pawcatuck Area Chamber of Commerce: 74 Post Rd., Westerly, RI 02891; phone (401) 596-7761 or (800) 732-7636.

FLYING HORSE CAROUSEL, Watch Hill Beach at Bay St., was built in 1870. Each horse is carved from a single piece of wood and has a real horsehair tail and mane, agate eyes and a leather saddle. Allow 30 minutes minimum. Daily 1-9, mid-June through Labor Day. Fare $1. Open only to children whose feet do not touch the ground when astride a horse. Phone (401) 596-7761.

WEST GREENWICH (C-2) elev. 327′

RECREATIONAL ACTIVITIES
Horseback Riding

• **Stepping Stone Ranch**, 201 Escoheag Hill Rd., West Greenwich, RI 02817. Wed.-Sun. 9-4, Mar.-Dec.; closed holidays. Reservations are recommended. Phone (401) 397-3725.

WICKFORD (C-4) elev. 90′

Settled in 1707, Wickford was a key port for shipping produce from the rich plantations of South County to the bustling markets of Newport. Commerce came to a halt during the Revolutionary War, but Wickford's economy rebounded with a shipping boom 1780-1830. Many houses from this period still stand.

OLD NARRAGANSETT CHURCH, Church Ln. off Main St., was built in 1707 and was moved to its present site in 1800. Among the oldest Episcopal churches in the country, the church is one of the state's four original Colonial parishes. Of interest are the box pews, wineglass pulpit and slave gallery. The church organ dates from 1660. Communion silver donated by Queen Anne still is used for services the first Sunday in August, designated Queen Anne Sunday. Guided tours are given Fri.-Sun. 11-4, July-Aug. Free. Phone (401) 294-4357.

SMITH'S CASTLE, 1.5 mi. n. on US 1 to 55 Richard Smith Dr., is a plantation house built in 1678 by Richard Smith Jr. Members of the prominent Updike family, which later laid out Wickford, lent prestige to the plantation when they inherited much of the property in 1692. The family's guests included Benjamin Franklin,

Marquis de Lafayette and Gen. Nathanael Greene. Costumed interpreters conduct guided tours of the grounds and restored house, which is furnished with 18th-century antiques.

Guided tours are given Thurs.-Mon. noon-4, June-Aug.; Fri.-Sun. noon-4 in May and Sept.; by appointment rest of year. Admission $3; over 62 and students with ID $2; under 12, $1. Phone (401) 294-3521.

WOONSOCKET (A-3) pop. 43,900, elev. 162'

SAVE **MUSEUM OF WORK AND CULTURE**, from SR 146, 2 mi. n. on SR 104/Providence St./Main St. to 42 S. Main St. Exhibits housed in a former textile mill tell the stories of French Canadian immigrants who left their Quebec agricultural backgrounds to work in the mills in Woonsocket prior to World War I. Displays trace difficulties due to low-paying jobs; grim factory conditions; the establishment of organized labor; and ultimate successes of the workers as they acclimated to American life. Hands-on displays, films and walk-through sets are included.

Mon.-Fri. 9:30-4, Sat. 10-5, Sun. 1-5; closed Easter, Thanksgiving and Dec. 25. Admission $5; students and over 64, $3; under 10 free. MC, VI. Phone (401) 769-9675.

Connecticut

AVON—See Hartford p. 225.

BETHEL—18,150

LODGINGS

BEST WESTERN BERKSHIRE MOTOR INN Rates Subject to Change Phone: (203)744-3200
(AAA) All Year [CP] 1P: $80- 120 2P/1B: $85- 125 2P/2B: $85- 125 XP: $8-15 F12
◆◆ **Location:** Just e of I-84, exit 8 on US 6. 11 Stony Hill Rd 06801 (Rt 6, Box 325). Fax: 203/744-3979.
Motel **Facility:** 69 rooms. Solarium breakfast area. 3 stories; interior corridors. **All Rooms:** extended cable TV.
Some Rooms: whirlpools. **Cards:** AE, CB, DI, DS, MC, VI. *(See ad p 209)*

BEST WESTERN STONY HILL INN Rates Subject to Change Phone: (203)743-5533
(AAA) All Year [CP] 1P: $80- 120 2P/1B: $85- 125 2P/2B: $85- 125 XP: $8-15 F12
◆◆ **Location:** Between exits 8 & 9 at I-84, on US 6E. 46 Stony Hill Rd US Rte 6 06801. Fax: 203/743-4958.
Motor Inn **Facility:** 36 rooms. Cozy rooms on 40 acres around pond. 4 efficiencies, $10 extra charge; 1 story; exterior
corridors; playground. Fee: driving range. **Dining:** Restaurant; 11:30 am-2:30 & 5:30-9:30 pm, Fri & Sat-10
pm, Sun 10:30 am-2:30 pm; $10-$20; cocktails. **All Rooms:** extended cable TV. **Cards:** AE, CB, DI, DS,
MC, VI. *(See ad p 209)*

BOZRAH—2,850

LODGINGS

BLUEBERRY INN Guaranteed Rates Phone: (860)889-3618
◆◆◆ All Year [BP] 1P: $85- 135 2P/1B: $85- 135 XP: $15 F10
Bed & **Location:** From SR 2 exit 23, just n on SR 163; 1 mi w on Fitchville Rd & 0.5 mi s. 40 Bashon Hill Rd
Breakfast 06334. Fax: 860/892-0046. **Terms:** Age restrictions may apply; reserv deposit; 2 night min stay, 5/25-10/31.
Facility: 3 rooms. Modern home on extensive grounds in quiet country setting; conveniently located to nearby
casino. 2 stories; interior corridors; smoke free premises. **All Rooms:** combo or shower baths. **Cards:** MC, VI.

FITCH CLAREMONT HOUSE Rates Subject to Change Phone: (860)889-0260
◆◆◆ Fri-Sun [BP] 2P/1B: $110- 150 2P/2B: $110- 150
Bed & Mon-Thurs [BP] 2P/1B: $85- 95 2P/2B: $85- 95
Breakfast **Location:** From SR 2 westbound exit 24, 0.4 mi e; eastbound exit 23, just n, then 1.7 mi e. 83 Fitchville Rd
06334. **Terms:** Age restrictions may apply; reserv deposit, 5 day notice; 2 night min stay, weekends.
Facility: 4 rooms. Nestled in a working vineyard, the original home dates from 1790. Individually furnished rooms with fireplace; conveniently located to casino. 2 stories; interior corridors; smoke free premises. **Cards:** AE, DS, MC, VI.

BRANFORD—27,600 (See map p. 245; index p. 243)

LODGINGS

ADVANCED MOTEL Phone: (203)481-4528 ④
(AAA) [SAVE] 5/1-10/31 1P: $45- 65 2P/1B: $50- 70 2P/2B: $50- 70 XP: $5 F9
11/1-4/30 1P: $35- 65 2P/1B: $40- 65 2P/2B: $40- 65 XP: $5 F9
◆◆ **Location:** I-95 exit 56, just s. 81 Leetes Island Rd 06405. Fax: 203/483-6885. **Terms:** Reserv deposit, 3 day
Motel notice; handling fee imposed; weekly rates. **Facility:** 32 rooms. 3 whirlpool rms, extra charge; 2 stories; exterior corridors. **Some Rooms:** 16 efficiencies. **Cards:** AE, CB, DI, DS, JC, MC, VI. **Special Amenities:**
Early check-in/late check-out and free room upgrade (subject to availability with advanced reservations).

DAYS INN & CONFERENCE CENTER Phone: (203)488-8314 ②
(AAA) [SAVE] 5/1-9/30 [CP] 1P: $55- 65 2P/2B: $75- 99 XP: $5 F16
10/1-4/30 [CP] 1P: $50- 55 2P/2B: $60- 70 XP: $5 F16
◆◆ **Location:** On US 1, just n of I-95, exit 53. 375 E Main St 06405. Fax: 203/483-6885. **Terms:** Weekly rates.
Motel **Facility:** 74 rooms. Variety of accommodations. 2 suites, $75-$150; 2 stories; interior/exterior corridors.
Dining: Restaurant nearby. **All Rooms:** extended cable TV. **Some Rooms:** 2 kitchens, whirlpools.
Cards: AE, DI, DS, MC, VI. **Special Amenities: Free breakfast and free local telephone calls.**

MACDONALD'S MOTEL Phone: 203/488-4381 ③
(AAA) [SAVE] All Year 1P: $40- 65 2P/1B: $45- 70 2P/2B: $45- 75 XP: $5 D10
◆◆ **Location:** On US 1, 0.4 mi w of I-95 exit 56. 565 E Main St 06405. Fax: 203/488-4568. **Terms:** Reserv
Motel deposit, 3 day notice; handling fee imposed; weekly rates. **Facility:** 22 rooms. Modestly equipped rooms.
Whirlpool rm, extra charge; 1 story; exterior corridors. **Dining:** Restaurant nearby. **All Rooms:** extended
cable TV. **Cards:** AE, DI, DS, MC, VI.

MOTEL 6 - 1279 Guaranteed Rates Phone: 203/483-5828 ⑥
(AAA) All Year 1P: $49 2P/1B: $59 2P/2B: $59 XP: $6 F17
◆◆ **Location:** I-95 exit 55, 0.3 mi s on US 1. 320 E Main St (US 1) 06405. Fax: 203/488-4579. **Terms:** Pets.
Motel **Facility:** 99 rooms. 2 stories; interior corridors. **Dining:** Restaurant nearby. **All Rooms:** combo or shower
baths, extended cable TV. **Cards:** AE, CB, DI, DS, MC, VI.

**Look For The Lodging Signs
Backed By A 100%
Satisfaction Guarantee**

HOW TO RUN A HOTEL.℠

Free local calls and in-room coffee makes Quality the perfect place for today's traveler. For over 50 years, Quality has been making everything just right.

It's more than a room. It's Comfort.℠

You always enjoy extra amenities when you stay at Comfort Inn & Comfort Suites. Like our Free Breakfast to help you start the day off right.

Upgrade your room, not your rate.℠

At Clarion, you'll find everything you expect at an upscale hotel. Well, everything except the high rates. And AAA members save 20% at most Clarions.

In a class by itself.℠

With low rates and state-of-the-art rooms, it's no wonder Sleep Inn is rated among the best hotels for satisfaction, service and value.

Stay longer for less.℠

The reasonably-priced option for travelers who are looking for a comfortable extended-stay hotel. A great place for visits that last a night, a week, or more.

For Reservations Call
1-800-228-1AAA
Or Contact Your Local AAA Club.

 TourBookMark
Lodging Listing Symbols

Member Values
- SAVE Official Appointment lodging providing minimum 10% discount
- SAVE SYC&S chain partners offering member benefits
- AAA Official Appointment
- ASK May offer discounts to members upon request
- SD Senior Discount

Member Services
- Transportation to Airport
- Pets Allowed
- Cocktail Lounge
- Restaurant on Premises
- Restaurant off Premises (walking distance)
- 24 Hour Room Service
- Night Club
- Entertainment

Room Amenities
- Coffee Maker in Room
- Honor Bar
- Data Port/Modem Line
- No Cable TV
- Movies
- VCR
- Radio
- Non-Smoking Rooms
- Microwaves
- Refrigerator
- No Air Conditoner
- No Telephones

Safety Features
- Safe

Special Features
- Child Care
- Business Services
- Laundry Service
- Fully Accessible
- Semi-Accessible
- Roll-in Showers
- Hearing Impaired
- Valet Parking

Sports/Recreation
- Pool
- Fitness Center
- Recreation Facilities

Call property for detailed information about fees & restrictions relating to the lodging listing symbols.

CHOICE HOTELS
INTERNATIONAL

HOW TO RUN A HOTEL.℠

It's more than a room. It's Comfort.℠

Upgrade your room, not your rate.℠

In a class by itself.℠

Stay longer for less.℠

For Reservations Call
1-800-228-1AAA
Or Contact Your Local AAA Club.

(king of the road)

Don't hit the road without enrolling in the **AT&T One Rate® Calling Card Plan.** Unlike some other calling card plans that have a hidden service charge for every call, this plan has just a flat $1 monthly fee. Plus a low per minute rate for domestic AT&T Calling Card calls. Just call **1 800 378-8562 x62549** for this outstanding travel value.

It's all within your reach.

(See map p. 245)

RAMADA LIMITED   Rates Subject to Change   **Phone:** (203)488-4991   ❶
◆◆   Fri & Sat 7/1-10/31 [CP]   1P: $90- 100   2P/1B: $90- 100   2P/2B: $90- 100   XP: $10   F18
Motel   Fri & Sat 6/1-6/30 &
      Sun-Thurs 7/1-9/6 [CP]   1P: $80- 110   2P/1B: $80- 110   2P/2B: $80- 100   XP: $10   F18
      Fri & Sat 5/1-5/31, Sun-Thurs
      6/1-6/30 & 9/7-10/31 [CP]   1P: $70- 90   2P/1B: $70- 90   2P/2B: $70- 90   XP: $10   F18
      Sun-Thurs 5/1-5/31 &
      11/1-4/30 [CP]   1P: $60- 80   2P/1B: $60- 80   2P/2B: $60- 80   XP: $10   F18
Location: Just n of I-95, exit 56. 3 Business Park Dr 06405. **Fax:** 203/488-6508. **Facility:** 85 rooms. 30 efficiency units, $75-$85; 2 stories; interior corridors. **Cards:** AE, CB, DI, DS, JC, MC, VI. *(See color ad inside front cover)*

RESTAURANTS

CAFE BELLE VITA   **Lunch:** $6-$12   **Dinner:** $15-$20   **Phone:** 203/483-5639   ②
◆◆◆   **Location:** From jct US 1 & SR 146, 1.3 mi e. 2 E Main St 06405. **Hours:** 11:30 am-2:30 & 5:30-9:30 pm,
Steak and   Sat from 5:30 pm. Closed major holidays & Sun. **Reservations:** suggested. **Features:** casual dress; health
Seafood   conscious menu items; cocktails. Upscale bistro with seasonal menus featuring fish, beef, pasta & veal ;
     in-house dessert & bread. Smoke free premises. **Cards:** AE, DS, MC, VI.

PASTI COSI   **Lunch:** $5-$10   **Dinner:** $9-$17   **Phone:** 203/483-9397   ④
◆   **Location:** From center, 2.5 me e on SR 146. 202 S Montowese Ave 06405. **Hours:** 11 am-9 pm, Fri &
Italian   Sat-10 pm. Closed major holidays, Sun & Mon. **Reservations:** suggested. **Features:** casual dress; children's
     menu; health conscious menu items; carryout. Surprisingly ambitious food with specialty ravioli, fresh made
pasta & sauce; also beef & chicken. Smoke free premises.

USS CHOWDER POT III   **Lunch:** $6-$10   **Dinner:** $10-$20   **Phone:** 203/481-2356   ①
◆◆   **Location:** N of I-95, exit 56 on US 1. 560 E Main St 06405. **Hours:** 11:30 am-10 pm, Fri & Sat-11 pm, Sun
Seafood   noon-9 pm; 10/1-5/31 Sat-10 pm, Sun-8 pm. Closed: 11/25 & 12/25. **Reservations:** accepted; for 7 or more.
     Features: casual dress; children's menu; early bird specials; cocktails & lounge; entertainment. Generous
portions of extensive fresh seafood. Prime rib also featured. Buffet 5 pm-6:30 pm. **Cards:** AE, DS, MC, VI.

BRIDGEPORT—141,700

LODGING

BRIDGEPORT HOLIDAY INN   **Phone:** (203)334-1234
Ⓐ SAVE   All Year   1P: $99- 139   2P/1B: $99- 139   2P/2B: $99- 139   XP: $10   F19
     Location: From SR 8, exit 2 northbound, 0.7 mi se; southbound, just s then e. 1070 Main St 06604.
◆◆◆   **Fax:** 203/367-1985. **Terms:** Small pets only. **Facility:** 234 rooms. Large modern lobby with sunken restaurant
Hotel   area. Voice mail avail. 9 stories; interior corridors; small heated indoor/outdoor pool. **Dining:** Restaurant;
     6:30 am-10 pm; $7-$18; cocktails. **Cards:** AE, CB, DI, DS, JC, MC, VI. **Special Amenities:** Free
newspaper and free room upgrade (subject to availability with advanced reservations).

RESTAURANT

AMERICAN STEAK HOUSE   **Lunch:** $4-$7   **Dinner:** $7-$10   **Phone:** 203/576-9989
◆   **Location:** SR 8 exit 5; 0.5 mi s. 210 Boston Ave 06606. **Hours:** 11:30 am-9:30 pm, Fri & Sat-10 pm.
Steakhouse   Closed: 11/25 & 12/25. **Features:** casual dress; children's menu; senior's menu; carryout; salad bar; beer &
     wine only. Cafeteria-style family dining. **Cards:** MC, VI.

BRISTOL—See Hartford p. 225.

BROOKFIELD—14,100

LODGING

TWIN TREE INN   Rates Subject to Change   **Phone:** (203)775-0220
◆◆   5/1-10/31   1P: $70- 80   2P/1B: $85- 95   2P/2B: $85- 95   XP: $15   F13
Motel   11/1-4/30   1P: $65- 75   2P/1B: $80- 90   2P/2B: $80- 90   XP: $15   F13
     Location: From jct SR 25 & US 202, 1 mi n. 1030 Federal Rd (Rts 7 & 202) 06804. **Fax:** 203/775-6415.
Facility: 47 rooms. 1-2 stories; interior/exterior corridors. **All Rooms:** combo or shower baths. **Cards:** AE, CB, DI, DS, MC, VI.

CHESHIRE—25,000   (See map p. 245; index p. 244)

LODGING

CHESHIRE WELCOME INN   **Phone:** (203)272-3244   ④④
Ⓐ SAVE   All Year   1P: $55   2P/1B: $55   2P/2B: $60   XP: $5
     Location: On SR 10, 0.5 mi s of jct SR 42W. 1106 S Main St 06410. **Fax:** 203/699-8053. **Terms:** Reserv
◆◆   deposit. **Facility:** 25 rooms. Very well maintained with beautiful landscaping. 2 stories; exterior corridors.
Motel   **All Rooms:** extended cable TV. **Some Rooms:** whirlpools. **Cards:** AE, CB, DI, JC, MC, VI.

CLINTON—3,400

LODGING

CLINTON MOTEL   Phone: (860)669-8850

5/1-9/6		2P/1B:	$58-	72	2P/2B:	$68-	89
9/7-10/31		2P/1B:	$52-	62	2P/2B:	$62-	72
4/1-4/30		2P/1B:	$42-	48	2P/2B:	$52-	62
11/1-3/31		2P/1B:	$42-	48	2P/2B:	$48-	52

Motel

Location: At jct US 1 & SR 145, 1.9 mi s of I-95 exit 64. 163 E Main St 06413. Fax: 860/669-3849.
Terms: Reserv deposit. **Facility:** 15 rooms. Rates for up to 4 persons; 1 story; exterior corridors. **All Rooms:** combo or shower baths, extended cable TV. **Cards:** AE, DS, MC, VI. **Special Amenities:** Free local telephone calls.

COVENTRY—9,900

LODGING

SPECIAL JOYS BED & BREAKFAST   Guaranteed Rates   Phone: (860)742-6359
All Year [BP]   1P: $47   2P/1B: $62   2P/2B: $62   XP: $10

Bed & Breakfast

Location: From jct US 44, 1.1 mi s on SR 31, then just e. 41 North River Rd 06238. **Terms:** Age restrictions may apply; reserv deposit. **Facility:** 2 rooms. Solarium breakfast/common room. Lovely gardens. 2 stories; interior corridors; smoke free premises. **All Rooms:** shower baths. **Cards:** DS, MC, VI.

CROMWELL—See Hartford p. 225.

DANBURY—65,600

LODGINGS

DANBURY HILTON & TOWERS   Rates Subject to Change   Phone: 203/794-0600
Hotel

Mon-Thurs	1P: $145- 185	2P/1B: $145- 185	2P/2B: $145- 185	XP: $15	F18
Fri-Sun	1P: $99- 139	2P/1B: $99- 139	2P/2B: $99- 139	XP: $15	F18

Location: I-84 eastbound exit 2, westbound exit 2A. 18 Old Ridgebury Rd 06810. Fax: 203/798-2709.
Facility: 242 rooms. Luxurious public area, large well equipped guest rooms. 10 stories; interior corridors; heated indoor pool; 2 lighted tennis courts. **Services:** giftshop; area transportation. **Cards:** AE, CB, DI, DS, MC, VI. *(See color ad p 37)*

DAYS INN   Phone: (203)743-6701

5/1-10/31 [CP]	1P: $70- 90	2P/1B: $70- 90	2P/2B: $75- 90	XP: $12	F16
11/1-4/30 [CP]	1P: $61- 80	2P/1B: $61- 80	2P/2B: $70- 80	XP: $12	F16

Motel

Location: I-84 exit 7 (US 7N), 0.5 mi n to exit 11 (Federal Rd), 1 mi e. 78 Federal Rd 06810.
Fax: 203/743-1825. **Terms:** Weekly rates. **Facility:** 72 rooms. Modestly equipped rooms. 3 stories, no elevator; interior corridors. **Dining:** Restaurant nearby. **All Rooms:** extended cable TV. **Cards:** AE, CB, DI, DS, MC, VI. **Special Amenities:** Free breakfast and free local telephone calls.

ETHAN ALLEN INN   Guaranteed Rates   Phone: (203)744-1776

1/1-4/30	1P: $110	2P/1B: $120	2P/2B: $120	XP: $10	F17
5/1-12/31	1P: $105	2P/1B: $115	2P/2B: $115	XP: $10	F17

Motor Inn

Location: I-84 exit 4, 0.3 mi w on US 6 & 202. 21 Lake Ave Extension 06811. Fax: 203/791-9673.
Facility: 195 rooms. Ethan Allen furniture in rooms with separate seating area. 2-6 stories; interior corridors; racquetball court.
Cards: AE, CB, DI, DS, MC, VI.

HOLIDAY INN   Phone: (203)792-4000
All Year   1P: $111- 124   2P/1B: $111- 124   2P/2B: $111- 124   XP: $10   F18

Motor Inn

Location: I-84 exit 8, 0.5 mi s on US 6W. 80 Newtown Rd 06810. **Terms:** BP avail; package plans; pets. **Facility:** 114 rooms. In retail area. Well-equipped rooms. 4 stories; interior corridors.
Dining: Restaurant; 6:30 am-midnight; $8-$14; cocktails. **Services:** area transportation, transportation depot.
Cards: AE, CB, DI, DS, JC, MC, VI.

QUALITY INN OF DANBURY
                                                                      Phone: (203)748-6677
🅰🅰🅰 SAVE   All Year [CP]   1P: $85- 104   2P/1B: $85- 108 2P/2B: $85- 108 XP: $10   F18
◆◆   **Location:** I-84 exit 8, just s on US 6W. Rt 6, Newtown Rd 06810. Fax: 203/744-0891. **Facility:** 120 rooms. 4
Motel   stories; interior corridors. **All Rooms:** extended cable TV. **Cards:** AE, CB, DI, DS, MC, VI.
           Special Amenities: Free breakfast and free local telephone calls. *(See color ad p 208)*

🄯 🄯 🄯 🄯 🄯 🄯 🄯

RAMADA INN
                                                                      Phone: (203)792-3800
🅰🅰🅰 SAVE   All Year   1P: $69- 105   2P/1B: $69- 105 2P/2B: $69- 115 XP: $10   F18
◆◆   **Location:** I-84 exit 8 (Newtown Rd), ne corner. 116 Newtown Rd 06810. Fax: 203/730-1899.
Motor Inn **Terms:** Package plans; pets. **Facility:** 181 rooms. 10 suites, $115-$130; 2-5 stories; interior corridors; heated
           indoor pool. **Dining:** Restaurant; 7-10:30 am, 11:30-2:30 & 4:30-11 pm, Sat & Sun 7 am-midnight; $6-$13;
           cocktails. **All Rooms:** extended cable TV. **Some Rooms:** 6 efficiencies. **Cards:** AE, CB, DI, DS, JC, MC, VI.
Special Amenities: Free breakfast and free local telephone calls. *(See color ad inside front cover)*

🄯 🄯 🄯 🄯 🄯 🄯 🄯 🄯 🄯 🄯 🄯 🄯 🄯 🄯 🄯

RESIDENCE INN BY MARRIOTT   Rates Subject to Change   Phone: 203/797-1256
FYI   Mon-Thurs 11/1-4/30   1P: $129- 139   2P/1B: $129- 139 2P/2B: $139- 149
           Mon-Thurs 5/1-10/31   1P: $109- 119   2P/1B: $109- 119 2P/2B: $129- 139
Motel   Fri-Sun 5/1-10/31   1P: $99- 109   2P/1B: $109- 119
           Fri-Sun 11/1-4/30   1P: $79- 89   2P/1B: $89- 99   2P/2B: $89- 109
Too new to rate. **Location:** I-84 exit 4. 22 Segar St 06810. Fax: 203/797-1268. **Terms:** Reserv deposit. **Facility:** 78 rooms.
Scheduled to open January, 1999. **Cards:** AE, CB, DI, DS, JC, MC, VI.

ASK 🄯 🄯

RESTAURANTS

CHUCK'S STEAK HOUSE   **Lunch:** $7-$10   **Dinner:** $10-$25   **Phone:** 203/792-5555
🅰🅰🅰   **Location:** I-84 eastbound exit 4, bottom of ramp, thru light 100 yards; I-84 westbound exit 4, 1st left under
◆◆   hwy & 1st right. 20 Segar St 06810. **Hours:** 11:30 am-3 & 4:30-10 pm, Fri & Sat-10:30 pm, Sun 4 pm-10
Steak and pm. Closed: 11/25 & 12/25. **Features:** casual dress; children's menu; health conscious menu items; salad
Seafood   bar; cocktails & lounge; a la carte. Sprawling roadside family restaurant with rustic decor. Some fireplace &
           solarium seating. Fresh fish, hearty steak & crispy vegetable salad bar. Early bird 4:30-6 pm Mon-Fri.
           Cards: AE, DI, DS, MC, VI.   🄯

CIAO! CAFE & WINE BAR   **Lunch:** $9-$17   **Dinner:** $9-$17   **Phone:** 203/791-0404
🅰🅰🅰   **Location:** Just e on White St & just s. 2B Ives St 06810. **Hours:** 11:30 am-10 pm. Closed major holidays.
◆◆   **Reservations:** accepted. **Features:** casual dress; Sunday brunch; carryout; cocktails; fee for parking; a la
Italian   carte. Innovative Italian cuisine in casual atmosphere. **Cards:** AE, MC, VI.   🄯

D & J'S KOZY KITCHEN   **Lunch:** $7-$9   **Phone:** 203/794-0900
◆◆   **Location:** I-84, exit 5 (Main St) 1.2 mi e. 135 Main St 06810. **Hours:** 11:30 am-2 & 5-9 pm, Tues-2 pm, Sat
American   8 am-2 & 5-9:30 pm, Sun 8 am-1:30 pm. Closed: Mon. **Features:** casual dress; children's menu; carryout;
& cake. Friendly, comfortable service. Smoke free premises. **Cards:** MC, VI. beer & wine only. Real, honest, made-from-scratch food. A variety to please anyone. Homemade bread, pies
                                                                                     🄯

TWO STEPS DOWNTOWN GRILLE   **Lunch:** $6-$15   **Dinner:** $6-$15   **Phone:** 203/794-0032
🅰🅰🅰   **Location:** Just e on White St off Main St & just s. 5 Ives St 06810. **Hours:** 11:30 am-11 pm, Fri &
◆◆   Sat-midnight, Sun from 10 am. Closed: 9/6 & 12/25. **Reservations:** accepted. **Features:** casual dress;
Southwest Sunday brunch; children's menu; carryout; cocktails & lounge; fee for parking; a la carte. Historic firehouse
American   with fun atmosphere. **Cards:** AE, MC, VI.   🄯

DARIEN—17,300   (See map p. 212; index p. 211)

LODGING

HOWARD JOHNSON LODGE   Rates Subject to Change   **Phone:** (203)655-3933   27
◆◆   All Year   1P: $94- 104   2P/1B: $99- 109 2P/2B: $99- 109 XP: $99-109 F18
Motel   **Location:** I-95, exit 11; just n. 150 Ledge Rd 06820. Fax: 203/655-3084. **Facility:** 72 rooms. 8 whirlpool rms,
           extra charge; 2 stories; interior corridors. **Cards:** AE, CB, DI, DS, MC, VI.

ASK 🄯 🄯 🄯 🄯 🄯 🄯 🄯 🄯

EAST HARTFORD—See Hartford p. 226.

EAST HAVEN—26,100

LODGING

HOLIDAY INN EXPRESS   **Phone:** (203)469-5321
AAA SAVE   5/1-10/31 [CP]   1P: $89- 109   2P/1B: $99- 139   2P/2B: $99- 139   XP: $10   D18
◆◆   11/1-4/30 [CP]   1P: $69- 89   2P/1B: $79- 109   2P/2B: $89- 119   XP: $10   D18
Motel   **Location:** I-95 exit 51, eastbound 0.5 mi e of ramp; westbound 0.8 mi w on N Frontage Rd to overpass, 0.8
mi e. 30 Frontage Rd 06512. Fax: 203/469-2544. **Facility:** 82 rooms. 2 stories; interior/exterior corridors.
Dining: Restaurant nearby. **Services:** area transportation, within 5 mi. **All Rooms:** extended cable TV.
Some Rooms: whirlpools. **Cards:** AE, CB, DI, DS, JC, MC, VI. **Special Amenities:** Free breakfast and free local
telephone calls.

EAST WINDSOR—See Hartford p. 226.

ENFIELD—See Hartford p. 227.

ESSEX—5,900

LODGING

GRISWOLD INN   Rates Subject to Change   **Phone:** 860/767-1776
◆◆◆   All Year [CP]   1P: $90- 115   2P/1B: $90- 115   2P/2B: $90- 115   XP: $10
Historic   **Facility:** 30 rooms. Restored Colonial inn in continuous operation since 1776. Suites, some with fireplace,
Country Inn $135-$185; 3 stories; interior corridors; designated smoking area. **All Rooms:** combo or shower baths.
Cards: AE, MC, VI.

RESTAURANT

GRISWOLD INN   Country Inn   **Lunch:** $6-$12   **Dinner:** $16-$23   **Phone:** 860/767-1776
◆◆   **Location:** 2.3 mi e of SR 9, exit 3; in Griswold Inn. 36 Main St 06426. **Hours:** 11:45 am-3 & 5:30-9 pm,
American   Fri-10 pm, Sat 11:30 am-3 & 5-10 pm, Sun 11 am-2:30 & 4:30-9 pm. Closed: 12/24 for dinner & 12/25.
Reservations: suggested. **Features:** casual dress; Sunday brunch; children's menu; cocktails & lounge;
entertainment. New England fare served in historic rustic country inn. 250 year-old Tap Room lounge. Sun Hunt breakfast 11
am-2:30 pm, $12.95. Traditional entertainment nightly in the Tap Room. Smoke free premises. **Cards:** AE, MC, VI.

FARMINGTON—See Hartford p. 227.

GLASTONBURY—See Hartford p. 228.

GREENWICH
pop. 58,400

This index helps you "spot" where approved accommodations are located on the detailed maps that follow. Rate ranges are for comparison only and show the property's high season. Turn to the listing page for more detailed rate information and consult display ads for special promotions. Restaurant rate range is for dinner, unless only lunch (L) is served.

Spotter/Map Pg.Number	OA	GREENWICH - Lodgings	Rating	Rate	Listing Page
❶ / p. 212		Howard Johnson Hotel	◆◆	$89-129	213
❷ / p. 212		Hyatt Regency Greenwich	◆◆◆	$264-300	213
		GREENWICH - Restaurant			
⑤ / p. 212		Manero's	◆	$13-22	213

Nearby Accommodations

Spotter/Map Pg.Number	OA	NORWALK - Lodgings	Rating	Rate	Listing Page
❻ / p. 212		Club Hotel by Doubletree Norwalk	◆◆◆	$179	249
❼ / p. 212		Four Points Hotel Norwalk	◆◆◆	$161	249
❾ / p. 212	⏣	**The Silvermine Tavern**	◆◆◆	$99-175 [SAVE]	249
❿ / p. 212		Courtyard by Marriott	◆◆◆	$154	249
		NORWALK - Restaurant			
⑨ / p. 212		The Silvermine Tavern	◆◆	$15-25	249
		STAMFORD - Lodgings			
⓭ / p. 212		Grand Chalet Inn & Suites	◆◆◆	$90-120	255
⓮ / p. 212		Stamford Suites Hotel	◆◆	$229-269	255
⓯ / p. 212		Holiday Inn Select	◆◆◆	$89-170	255
⓰ / p. 212		Sheraton Stamford Hotel - see color ad p 255	◆◆◆	$195-219	255
⓱ / p. 212		Stamford Marriott Hotel	◆◆◆	$169	255
		STAMFORD - Restaurants			
⑮ / p. 212	⏣	**Amadeus**	◆◆◆	$19-27	256
⑯ / p. 212		Il Falco	◆◆◆	$12-22	256
		WESTPORT - Lodgings			
㉒ / p. 212		The Westport Inn - see color ad p 260	◆◆◆	$120-164	260
㉓ / p. 212	⏣	**The Inn at National Hall**	◆◆◆◆◆	$200-600 [SAVE]	260
		WESTPORT - Restaurant			
⑲ / p. 212		The Restaurant At National Hall	◆◆◆◆	$18-27	261
		DARIEN - Lodgings			
㉗ / p. 212		Howard Johnson Lodge	◆◆	$99-109	209
		NEW CANAAN - Restaurant			
⑳ / p. 212		The Roger Sherman Inn	◆◆◆	$20-32	242
		SOUTH NORWALK - Restaurant			
㉓ / p. 212		Rattlesnake Southwestern Grill	◆◆	$8-15	254

QUESTIONS, QUESTIONS!

Bridge tolls? Ferry schedules?
Fishing and hunting seasons? Your local AAA office
can answer these queries and many more.

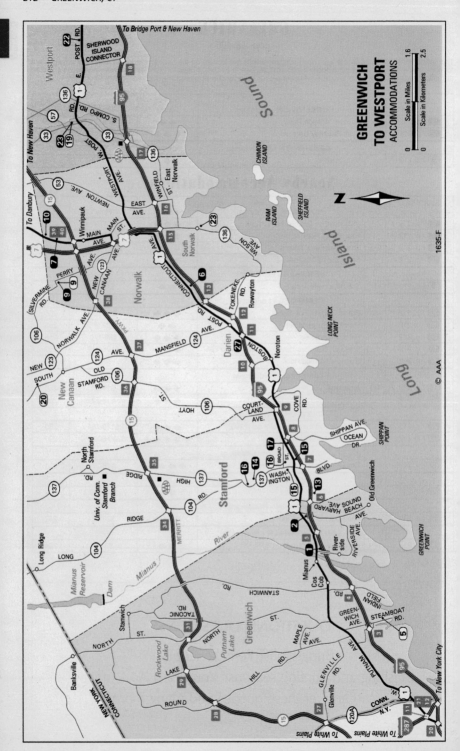

GREENWICH—58,400   (See map p. 212; index p. 211)

LODGINGS

HOWARD JOHNSON HOTEL
◆◆
Motel
JC, MC, VI.

Rates Subject to Change

All Year [CP]   1P: $79- 99   2P/1B: $89- 109   2P/2B: $89- 129   XP: $10   F18

Phone: 203/637-3691 ①

Location: I-95 exit 5, just s on US 1 (Boston Post Rd). 1114 Boston Post Rd 06878. Fax: 203/637-0661. **Facility:** 104 rooms. 2-3 stories; exterior corridors. **All Rooms:** combo or shower baths. **Cards:** AE, DI, DS,

HYATT REGENCY GREENWICH
◆◆◆
Hotel
Services: giftshop; area transportation.

Rates Subject to Change

All Year   1P: $239- 275   2P/1B: $264- 300   2P/2B: $264- 300   XP: $25   F18

Phone: (203)637-1234 ②

Location: I-95 exit 5, 0.5 mi n on US 1; in Old Greenwich. 1800 E Putnam Ave 06870. Fax: 203/637-2940. **Facility:** 374 rooms. Whirlpool rm, $675-$875; 4 stories; interior corridors; small heated indoor pool. **All Rooms:** combo or shower baths. **Cards:** AE, CB, DI, DS, JC, MC, VI.

RESTAURANT

MANERO'S
◆
American
MC, VI.

Lunch: $7-$11   **Dinner:** $13-$22   **Phone:** 203/869-0049 ⑤

Location: Just e of I-95, exit 3, then s. 559 Steamboat Rd 06830. **Hours:** noon-10 pm, Sat-11 pm, Sun-9 pm. Closed: 11/25 & 12/25. **Features:** casual dress; children's menu; senior's menu; carryout; cocktails. Informal family atmosphere. Complete dinners with retail meat market & deli section. **Cards:** AE, CB, DI,

GROTON—45,100

LODGINGS

CLARION INN
🅰🅰🅰 SAVE
Motor Inn

Phone: (860)446-0660

5/1-9/5	1P:	$79- 129	2P/1B:	$99- 159	2P/2B:	$89- 139	XP: $10 F16
9/6-10/30	1P:	$69- 129	2P/1B:	$89- 159	2P/2B:	$79- 139	XP: $10 F16
10/31-4/30	1P:	$49- 109	2P/1B:	$69- 139	2P/2B:	$59- 119	XP: $10 F16

Location: On SR 184; 0.3 mi ne of jct I-95 exit 86. 156 Kings Hwy 06340. Fax: 860/445-4082. **Terms:** Reserv deposit. **Facility:** 69 rooms. Very attractive public areas. 30 efficiencies, $135 in season for up to 2 persons; 3 stories; interior corridors; heated indoor pool, saunas, whirlpool. **Dining:** G. Williker's, see separate listing. **Recreation:** game room. **All Rooms:** extended cable TV. **Some Rooms:** whirlpools. **Cards:** AE, CB, DI, DS, MC, VI. **Special Amenities:** Free newspaper and free room upgrade (subject to availability with advanced reservations).

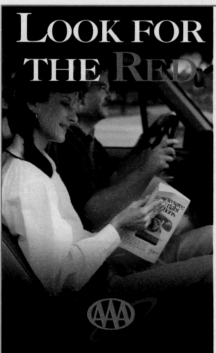

GROTON INN & SUITES

Phone: (860)445-9784

AAA SAVE

◆◆ Motor Inn

5/11-10/30	1P: $113- 189	2P/1B: $113- 189	2P/2B: $113- 189	XP: $10	F18
5/1-5/10 & 10/31-4/30	1P: $84- 114	2P/1B: $84- 114	2P/2B: $84- 114	XP: $10	F18

Location: On SR 184; 0.3 mi ne of jct I-95 exit 86. 99 Gold Star Hwy 06340 (PO Box 807). **Fax:** 860/445-2664. **Terms:** Weekly/monthly rates; BP avail; package plans; 2 night min stay. **Facility:** 115 rooms. In several buildings. 20 two-bedroom units. 2 stories; interior/exterior corridors. **Dining:** Restaurant; 5:30 am-9 pm, Fri-10 pm, Sat 7 am-10 pm, Sun 7 am-9 pm; $12-$21; cocktails. **All Rooms:** extended cable TV. **Some Rooms:** 4 efficiencies, 41 kitchens. **Cards:** AE, DI, MC, VI. **Special Amenities:** Early check-in/late check-out and free room upgrade (subject to availability with advanced reservations). (See color ad p 240)

MORGAN INN & SUITES

Phone: (860)448-3000

AAA SAVE

◆◆◆ Suite Motor Inn

5/1-9/7	1P: $75- 100	2P/1B: $90- 165	XP: $15	F12
9/8-11/9	1P: $85	2P/1B: $95- 145	XP: $15	F12
11/10-4/30	1P: $49	2P/1B: $59- 109	XP: $15	F12

Location: I-95 exit 86, 0.5 mi ne on SR 184. 135 Gold Star Hwy 06340. **Fax:** 860/445-1152. **Terms:** Pets, in limited rooms. **Facility:** 56 rooms. Many suites avail, convenient to Naval Base. 7 two-bedroom units. 8 three-bedroom suites, $109-$165; 4 stories; interior corridors. **All Rooms:** extended cable TV. **Some Rooms:** 37 kitchens, whirlpools. **Cards:** AE, DS, MC, VI. **Special Amenities:** Free breakfast and free local telephone calls. (See color ad below)

QUALITY INN

Phone: (860)445-8141

AAA SAVE

◆◆ Motor Inn

Fri & Sat 5/1-10/31 [CP]	1P: $120- 160	2P/1B: $120- 160	2P/2B: $120- 160	XP: $10-20	F18
Sun-Thurs 7/1-8/31 [CP]	1P: $95- 110	2P/1B: $95- 110	2P/2B: $95- 100	XP: $10-20	F18
Sun-Thurs 5/1-6/30, 9/1-4/30 & 11/1-4/30 [CP]	1P: $55- 75	2P/1B: $55- 75	2P/2B: $55- 75	XP: $10-20	F18

Location: 0.7 mi e of I-95 exit 85 northbound, exit 86 southbound. 404 Bridge St 06340. **Fax:** 860/445-8141. **Terms:** Reserv deposit. **Facility:** 95 rooms. 2 stories; exterior corridors; wading pool. **Dining:** Restaurant; 5 pm-9 pm, 5/15-9/12, noon-midnight; $8-$15; cocktails. **All Rooms:** extended cable TV. **Cards:** AE, CB, DI, DS, JC, MC, VI. **Special Amenities:** Free breakfast and free local telephone calls.

RESTAURANT

G. WILLIKER'S

AAA

◆◆ American

Lunch: $5-$17   **Dinner:** $7-$17   **Phone:** 860/445-8043

Location: On SR 184; 0.3 mi ne of jct I-95, exit 86; in Clarion Inn. 156 Kings Hwy 06340. **Hours:** 6:30 am-10 pm. **Closed:** 11/25 & 12/25. **Reservations:** accepted. **Features:** casual dress; children's menu; carryout; cocktails. Casual atmosphere. Steak, seafood, burgers, Italian & Mexican dishes. **Cards:** AE, DS, MC, VI.

For smooth starting and stopping:

Start with Triple-A

— TourBooks, TripTik maps, sheet maps.

Stop with Triple-A

— at approved lodgings and restaurants.

GUILFORD—19,800

LODGINGS

GUILFORD SUITES HOTEL Phone: (203)453-0123
🔺🔺 SAVE 5/1-5/14 & 9/21-4/30 1P: $85- 108 2P/1B: $85- 108 2P/2B: $85- 108 XP: $10
◆◆◆ 5/15-9/20 1P: $99 2P/1B: $99 2P/2B: $99 XP: $10
Suite Motel **Location:** On US 1; 1 mi w if jct I-95 exit 57. 2300 Boston Post (US 1) Rd 06437. Fax: 203/458-1244.
Terms: Monthly rates; BP avail; 2 night min stay, weekends 5/1-9/30. **Facility:** 32 rooms. Rural setting. Large
units with separate living & bedroom. 2 stories; exterior corridors. **All Rooms:** efficiencies, utensils extra
charge, extended cable TV. **Cards:** AE, CB, DI, DS, JC, VI. **Special Amenities:** Free breakfast and free local telephone
calls. *(See ad below)* 🈺 ⬜ 🖨 🎁 ✕

TOWER SUITES MOTEL Rates Subject to Change Phone: 203/453-9069
◆◆ 5/1-12/31 1P: $61- 66 2P/1B: $66- 69 2P/2B: $66- 69 XP: $10 F16
Motel 1/1-4/30 1P: $59- 61 2P/1B: $61- 66 2P/2B: $61- 66 XP: $10 F16
Location: I-95 exit 59, 0.5 mi e on US 1. 320 Boston Post Rd 06437. **Terms:** Reserv deposit, 7 day notice.
Facility: 13 rooms. Early American. 1 story. **All Rooms:** kitchens. **Cards:** AE, MC, VI. 🈯 🆒 🐾 💻 🖨 🎁 ✕

RESTAURANTS

THE BISTRO ON THE GREEN **Lunch:** $6-$10 **Dinner:** $10-$20 Phone: 203/458-9059
◆◆ **Location:** I-95, exit 58, 0.8 e on SR 77. 25 Whitfield St 06437. **Hours:** 11 am-10 pm, Sat from 8 am, Sun 8
American am-9 pm. Closed: 12/25. **Reservations:** suggested. **Features:** casual dress; carryout; cocktails. Overlooking
Guilford Green. Specialties include rack of lamb, yellow fin tuna, or beef fillet which is grilled & treated to
international sauces. Smoke free premises. **Cards:** AE, MC, VI. ✕

GUILFORD TAVERN **Lunch:** $5-$11 **Dinner:** $10-$17 Phone: 203/453-2216
◆◆ **Location:** I-95, exit 57 & 1.5 mi w on US 1. 2455 Boston Post Rd 06437. **Hours:** 11:30 am-4:30 & 5-10 pm,
American Fri & Sat-11 pm, Sun 11 am-9 pm. Closed: 12/25. **Reservations:** suggested. **Features:** casual dress;
Sunday brunch; cocktails & lounge. On site of a foundry; elegant country atmosphere. **Cards:** AE, CB, DI,
DS, MC, VI.

SACHEM COUNTRY HOUSE **Dinner:** $9-$17 Phone: 203/453-5261
◆◆ **Location:** N side of I-95, exit 59. 111 Goose Ln 06437. **Hours:** 4 pm-9 pm, Sat 5 pm-10 pm, Sun 11
American am-2:30 & 3-8 pm. Closed: Mon. **Reservations:** suggested; weekends. **Features:** casual dress; Sunday
brunch; children's menu; carryout; salad bar; cocktails & lounge. Colonial atmosphere. **Cards:** AE, MC, VI. ✕

STONE HOUSE SEASIDE RESTAURANT **Dinner:** $9-$21 Phone: 203/458-2526
◆◆ **Location:** From I-95 exit 58, 2.2 mi s on SR 77. 506 Whitfield St 06437. **Hours:** 4 pm-9:30 pm, Fri & Sat-10
Steak and pm; 3 pm-11 pm 6/1-9/30. Closed: 12/25. **Reservations:** accepted. **Features:** casual dress; children's menu;
Seafood early bird specials; carryout; cocktails & lounge. **Cards:** AE, DS, MC, VI. ✕

HAMDEN—52,400 (See map p. 245; index p. 243)

LODGING

DAYS INN Phone: (203)288-2505 🔟
🔺🔺 SAVE All Year [CP] 1P: $55- 65 2P/1B: $65- 70 2P/2B: $70- 80 XP: $10 F15
◆◆ **Location:** On SR 10, 1.3 mi n of jct SR 40. 3400 Whitney Ave 06518. Fax: 203/230-1090. **Terms:** Reserv
Motel deposit, 4 day notice. **Facility:** 34 rooms. Variety of room sizes. 1 story; exterior corridors.
Dining: Restaurant nearby. **All Rooms:** combo or shower baths, extended cable TV.
Some Rooms: whirlpools. **Cards:** AE, CB, DI, DS, JC, MC, VI. 🆒 🈺 🛗 🐾 ⬜ 🎁 ✕

RESTAURANT

J.B. WINBERIE RESTAURANT AND BAR **Lunch:** $5-$7 **Dinner:** $7-$10 Phone: 203/288-6608 ㉓
◆◆ **Location:** On SR 10, 0.3 mi n of jct SR 15. 2323 Whitney Ave 06518. **Hours:** 11:30 am-10 pm, Fri & Sat-11
American pm, Sun 10:30 am-9 pm. Closed: 11/25 & 12/25. **Reservations:** accepted. **Features:** casual dress; Sunday
brunch; children's menu; health conscious menu; carryout; cocktails & lounge; a la carte. **Cards:** AE, CB, DI,
DS, MC, VI. ✕

HARTFORD—See Hartford p. 222.

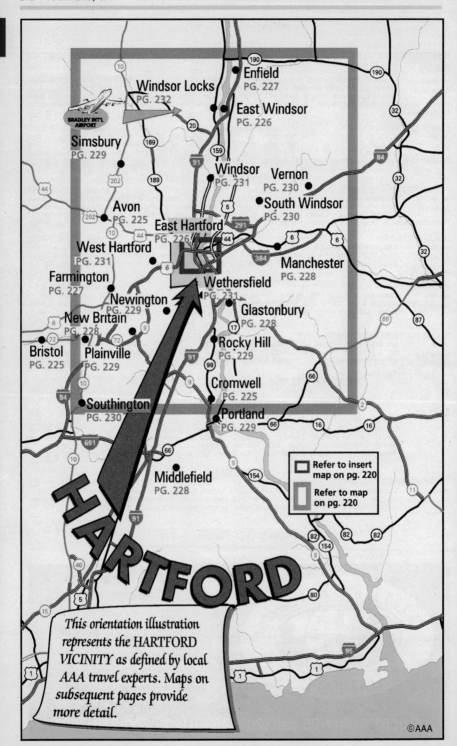

Enfield
PG. 227

Windsor Locks
PG. 232

East Windsor
PG. 226

BRADLEY INT'L
AIRPORT

Simsbury
PG. 229

Windsor
PG. 231

Vernon
PG. 230

Avon
PG. 225

South Windsor
PG. 230

East Hartford
PG. 226

West Hartford
PG. 231

Manchester
PG. 228

Farmington
PG. 227

Wethersfield
PG. 231

Newington
PG. 229

Glastonbury
PG. 228

New Britain
PG. 228

Rocky Hill
PG. 229

Bristol
PG. 225

Plainville
PG. 229

Cromwell
PG. 225

Southington
PG. 230

Portland
PG. 229

Middlefield
PG. 228

Refer to insert
map on pg. 220

Refer to map
on pg. 220

HARTFORD

This orientation illustration
represents the HARTFORD
VICINITY as defined by local
AAA travel experts. Maps on
subsequent pages provide
more detail.

©AAA

Hartford

pop. 139,700

This index helps you "spot" where approved accommodations are located on the detailed maps that follow. Rate ranges are for comparison only and show the property's high season. Turn to the listing page for more detailed rate information and consult display ads for special promotions. Restaurant rate range is for dinner, unless only lunch (L) is served.

Spotter/Map Pg.Number	OA	HARTFORD - Lodgings	Rating	Rate	Listing Page
25 / p. 220		Grand Chalet Inn & Suites	◆◆	$75-95	222
26 / p. 220		Super 8 Motel	◆◆	$57-62	224
27 / p. 220	AAA	**Red Roof Inn**	◆◆	$61-86 SAVE	224
28 / p. 220	AAA	**The Hilton Hartford - see color ad p 223**	◆◆◆	$119-239 SAVE	223
31 / p. 220	AAA	**Goodwin Hotel**	◆◆◆	$299-499 SAVE	222
		HARTFORD - Restaurants			
13 / p. 220		Costa Del Sol Restaurant	◆◆◆	$12-22	224
14 / p. 220		Gaetano's Ristorante	◆◆	$15-22	224
15 / p. 220	AAA	**Carbone's Restaurant**	◆◆	$13-25	224
16 / p. 220		Casa Lisboa	◆◆	$13-15	224
17 / p. 220		Pierpont's	◆◆◆	$15-25	225
18 / p. 220		Max Downtown	◆◆◆	$13-23	224
19 / p. 220		Civic Cafe on Trumbull	◆◆	$18-25	224
20 / p. 220		Oasis Diner & Pancho's Tex Mex	◆◆	$5-11	224

Hartford Vicinity

Spotter/Map Pg.Number	OA	AVON - Lodgings	Rating	Rate	Listing Page
1 / p. 220		Avon Old Farms Hotel	◆◆◆	$119-179	225
		AVON - Restaurants			
1 / p. 220	AAA	**Avon Old Farms Inn Restaurant**	◆◆◆	$14-25	225
2 / p. 220		Seasons Restaurant	◆◆◆	$14-24	225
		CROMWELL - Lodgings			
5 / p. 220	AAA	**Comfort Inn**	◆◆◆	$79-109 SAVE	225
6 / p. 220		Radisson Hotel and Conference Center Cromwell	◆◆◆	$125	225
7 / p. 220	AAA	**Holiday Inn**	◆◆◆	$107-116 SAVE	225
8 / p. 220		Super 8 Motel	◆◆	$58-64	225
		CROMWELL - Restaurant			
5 / p. 220		Cromwell Diner	◆	$5-12	226
		EAST HARTFORD - Lodgings			
11 / p. 220	AAA	**Wellesley Inn - see color ad p 224**	◆◆◆	$60-85 SAVE	226
12 / p. 220		Ramada Inn - see color ad inside front cover	◆◆	$99-109	226
13 / p. 220		Holiday Inn - see color ad p 226	◆◆◆	$89	226
		EAST WINDSOR - Lodgings			
15 / p. 220	AAA	**Holiday Inn Express**	◆◆◆	$115-125 SAVE	226
16 / p. 220	AAA	**Best Western Colonial Inn**	◆◆◆	$115 SAVE	226
		EAST WINDSOR - Restaurant			
8 / p. 220		The Eatery Restaurant & Banquet Facility	◆◆	$14-23	226
		FARMINGTON - Lodgings			
19 / p. 220		The Farmington Inn	◆◆◆	$119-139	227
20 / p. 220		Centennial Inn Suites - see color ad p 227	◆◆◆	$169	227
21 / p. 220		Marriott Hotel-Farmington	◆◆◆	$99-139	227
		FARMINGTON - Restaurants			
10 / p. 220		Apricots	◆◆◆	$16-28	228
11 / p. 220		Piccolo Aranco	◆◆	$12-22	228
		GLASTONBURY - Lodgings			
24 / p. 220		Butternut Farm	◆◆◆	$75-95	228

Spotter/Map Pg.Number	OA	GLASTONBURY - Restaurant	Rating	Rate	Listing Page
⑫ / p. 220		Max Amore	◆◆	$10-20	228
		MANCHESTER - Lodgings			
㊱ / p. 220	⚑	**Connecticut Motor Lodge**	◆	$55	228
		MANCHESTER - Restaurants			
㉑ / p. 220		Cavey's Restaurant-Italian	◆◆◆	$13-21	228
㉒ / p. 220		Shady Glen Dairy Stores	◆	$3-8	228
		PLAINVILLE - Lodgings			
㊶ / p. 220		Howard Johnson Hotel	◆◆	$49-59	229
		PLAINVILLE - Restaurant			
㉔ / p. 220		J Timothy's Taverne	◆◆	$10-15	229
		ROCKY HILL - Lodgings			
㊹ / p. 220	⚑	**Traveler's Motor Lodge**	◆◆	$60-75 [SAVE]	229
㊺ / p. 220		Hartford Marriott Rocky Hill	◆◆◆	$69-164	229
		SOUTHINGTON - Lodgings			
㊾ / p. 220	⚑	**Holiday Inn Express**	◆◆◆	$84-104	230
		SOUTHINGTON - Restaurants			
㉕ / p. 220		Patton Brook Restaurant & Pizza	◆	$6-15	230
㉖ / p. 220		Branningan's	◆◆	$10-15	230
		WEST HARTFORD - Lodgings			
㊾ / p. 220	⚑	**West Hartford Inn**	◆◆	$70-85 [SAVE]	231
		WEST HARTFORD - Restaurant			
㉘ / p. 220		Maharaja	◆◆	$8-15	231
		WETHERSFIELD - Lodgings			
㊹ / p. 220		Terra Motel	◆	$47	231
㊺ / p. 220		Chester Bulkley House	◆◆◆	$75-85	231
		WINDSOR - Lodgings			
㊾ / p. 220		Courtyard by Marriott - see color ad p 222	◆◆◆	$119-129	231
㊿ / p. 220		The Residence Inn by Marriott Hartford-Windsor	◆◆◆	$169	231
		WINDSOR LOCKS - Lodgings			
㊻ / p. 220		Baymont Inn & Suites-Hartford/Airport - see color ad p 223	◆◆◆	$69-74	232
㊼ / p. 220		Fairfield Inn by Marriott	◆◆◆	$60-76	232
㊺ / p. 220	⚑	**Days Inn Bradley International Airport**	◆◆◆	$71-109 [SAVE]	232
㊹ / p. 220		Sheraton Hotel At Bradley International Airport	◆◆◆	$115	233
㊳ / p. 220		Homewood Suites Hartford-Windsor Locks	◆◆◆	$130	233
㊴ / p. 220	⚑	**DoubleTree Hotel Bradley International Airport - see color ad p 232**	◆◆◆	$62-92 [SAVE]	232
		WINDSOR LOCKS - Restaurant			
㉞ / p. 220		Alberts Restaurant	◆◆	$9-19	233
		ENFIELD - Lodgings			
㊵ / p. 220		Harley Hotel of Hartford-Springfield - see ad p 222	◆◆◆	$124-144	227
㊶ / p. 220		Red Roof Inn	◆◆	$46-61	227
㊷ / p. 220	⚑	**Super 8 Motel-Enfield**	◆◆	$69-79 [SAVE]	227
		SIMSBURY - Lodgings			
㊸ / p. 220	⚑	**The Ironhorse Inn**	◆◆	$83 [SAVE]	229
㊾ / p. 220		Simsbury Inn	◆◆◆	$149-275	229
		SIMSBURY - Restaurants			
㉟ / p. 220		Lily's of the Valley	◆◆	$7-21	229
㊲ / p. 220		METRO bis	◆◆	$11-22	230
㊴ / p. 220		Murasaki Japanese Restaurant	◆◆◆	$13-28	230
		SOUTH WINDSOR - Restaurant			
㊷ / p. 220		The Mill on the River	◆◆	$12-19	230

Spotter/Map Pg.Number	OA	NEW BRITAIN - Restaurants	Rating	Rate	Listing Page
㊹ / p. 220		Great Taste Restaurant	◆◆◆	$8-17	228
㊺ / p. 220		Paradise Pizza Restaurant	◆	$5-14	228
		NEWINGTON - Restaurant			
㊾ / p. 220		Carringtons Restaurant	◆	$9-13	229

What the Icons Mean

Member Services

🍸 Cocktail Lounge

🍽 Restaurant on Premises

🍽 Restaurant off Premises
(walking distance)

🕛 24 Hour Room Service

🎵 Nightclub

🎭 Entertainment

✈ Transportation to Airport

🐾 Pets Allowed

Special Features

👶 Child Care

💼 Business Services

🧺 Laundry Service

♿ Fully Accessible

♿ Semi-Accessible

🚿 Roll-in Showers

👂 Hearing Impaired

🅿 Valet Parking

Room Amenities

☕ Coffee Maker in Room

🍾 Honor Bar

🖥 Data Port/Modem Line

📺 No Cable TV

🎬 Movies

📼 VCR

📻 Radio

🚭 Non-Smoking Rooms

📱 Microwaves

🧊 Refrigerator

❄ No Air Conditioning

☎ No Telephones

Sports/Recreation

🏊 Pool

🏋 Fitness Center

🎾 Recreation Facilities

Safety Features

Ⓢ Sprinklers

Ⓓ Smoke Detectors

🔒 Safe

Meal plans, if any, are indicated after the effective dates:

[AP] American Plan (three meals)   [BP] Breakfast Plan (full breakfast)

[MAP] Modified American Plan (two meals)   [CP] Continental Plan (pastry and beverage)

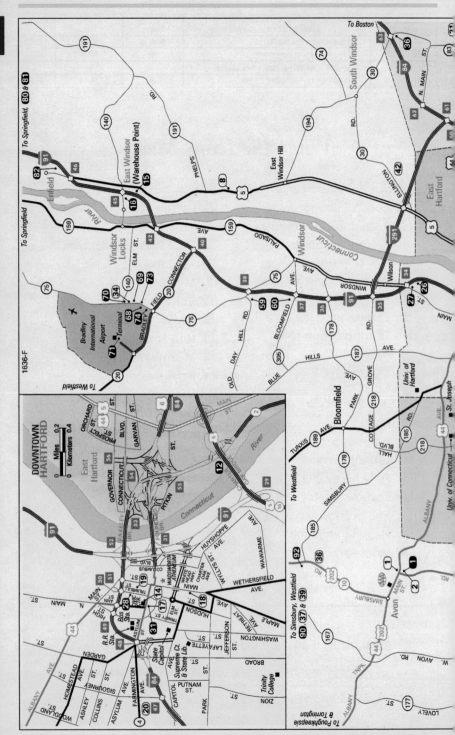

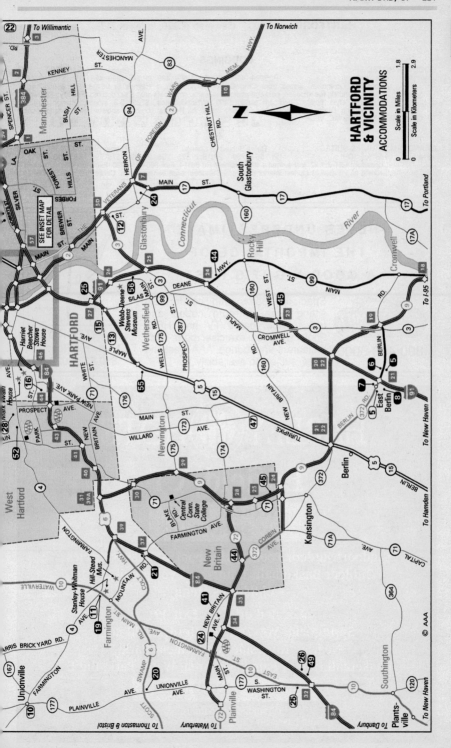

HARTFORD & VICINITY
ACCOMMODATIONS

Scale in Miles
Scale in Kilometers

© AAA

HARTFORD—139,700   (See map p. 220; index p. 217)

LODGINGS

GOODWIN HOTEL   **Phone:** (860)246-7500   **31**
AAA SAVE   All Year   1P: $299- 499   2P/1B: $299- 499   2P/2B: $299- 499   XP: $15   F17
◆◆◆   **Location:** Downtown, across from Civic Center (Asylum St). 1 Haynes St 06103. Fax: 860/247-4576.
Hotel   **Terms:** Handling fee imposed; package plans, weekends; small pets only, $300 dep req. **Facility:** 124 rooms.
                  European style hotel. 2-bedroom suite, $499. Whirlpool rms, $725; 5-6 stories; interior corridors.
                  Fee: parking. **Dining:** Pierpont's, see separate listing. **All Rooms:** combo or shower baths, extended cable
TV. **Cards:** AE, CB, DI, DS, MC, VI.

GRAND CHALET INN & SUITES   Rates Subject to Change   **Phone:** (860)525-9306   **25**
◆◆   All Year [CP]   1P: $69- 89   2P/1B: $75- 95   2P/2B: $75- 95   XP: $10   F17
Motel   **Location:** I-91 exit 27, just e, then s. 185 Brainard Rd 06114. Fax: 860/525-2990. **Facility:** 130 rooms. Iron &
VI.   ironing board avail. 3 stories; interior corridors. **Services:** area transportation. **Cards:** AE, CB, DI, DS, MC,

(See map p. 220)

THE HILTON HARTFORD
All Year   1P: $99- 219   2P/1B: $119- 239   2P/2B: $119- 239   XP: $20   **Phone:** (860)728-5151   28   F18
Location: Downtown; at Civic Center Plaza. 315 Trumbull St 06103. Fax: 860/240-7247. **Terms:** Reserv deposit; BP, CP avail; package plans. **Facility:** 388 rooms. Connected by sky bridge to shopping mall. 22 stories; interior corridors; heated indoor pool, saunas, whirlpool. Fee: parking. **Dining:** Restaurant, cafeteria; 6:30 am-2 & 5-10 pm; $7-$19; cocktails. **Cards:** AE, CB, DI, DS, JC, MC, VI. **Special Amenities:** Early check-in/late check-out and free newspaper. (See color ad p 37 and below)
Hotel

(See map p. 220)

RED ROOF INN **Phone:** (860)724-0222 🄻

AAA SAVE

6/1-10/31	1P:	$51-	71	2P/1B:	$56-	76	2P/2B:	$61- 86 XP: $10	F18
5/1-5/31 & 11/1-4/30	1P:	$46-	66	2P/1B:	$51-	71	2P/2B:	$51- 71 XP: $10	F18

Motel

Location: Just w of jct I-91 exit 33. 100 Weston St 06120. Fax: 860/724-0433. **Terms:** Small pets only. **Facility:** 115 rooms. Hacienda design. 2 stories; exterior corridors. **Dining:** Restaurant nearby. **All Rooms:** combo or shower baths. **Cards:** AE, CB, DI, DS, MC, VI. **Special Amenities:** Free local telephone calls.

SUPER 8 MOTEL Rates Subject to Change **Phone:** (860)246-8888 🄻

All Year 1P: $49- 54 2P/1B: $53- 58 2P/2B: $57- 62 XP: $4-8 F12

Motel

Location: 0.8 mi se of I-91, exit 33. 57 W Service Rd 06120. Fax: 860/246-8887. **Facility:** 100 rooms. Modestly equipped rooms in tudor style building. 2 stories; interior corridors. **Cards:** AE, CB, DI, DS, JC, MC, VI.

RESTAURANTS

CARBONE'S RESTAURANT **Lunch:** $8-$13 **Dinner:** $13-$25 **Phone:** 860/296-9646 🄻

AAA

Italian

Location: I-91, exit 27; 0.6 mi w on Airport Rd/Brown St, 0.4 mi s. 588 Franklin Ave 06114. **Hours:** 11:30 am-2 & 5-10 pm, Sat from 5 pm. Closed major holidays & Sun. **Reservations:** suggested. **Features:** casual dress; cocktails & lounge. American & Italian specialties, casual atmosphere. **Cards:** AE, DI, MC, VI.

CASA LISBOA **Lunch:** $4-$8 **Dinner:** $13-$15 **Phone:** 860/233-3184 🄻

Portuguese

Location: From I-84 exit 44, 0.5 mi n on Prospect, then just e. 1911 Park St 06106. **Hours:** 11:30 am-3 & 5-9 pm, Thurs & Fri-10 pm, Sat from 5 pm, noon-9 pm. Closed: 11/25, 12/25, Mon & 8/23-8/29. **Reservations:** accepted. **Features:** dressy casual; senior's menu; carryout; cocktails & lounge; a la carte. **Cards:** AE, DI, MC, VI.

CIVIC CAFE ON TRUMBULL **Lunch:** $7-$16 **Dinner:** $18-$25 **Phone:** 860/493-7412 🄻

American

Location: Downtown; I-91 exit 32B; I-84 eastbound exit 50, westbound exit 52. 150 Trumbull St 06103. **Hours:** 11 am-2:30 pm & 5-10 pm. Closed major holidays. **Features:** dressy casual; children's menu; cocktails & lounge; a la carte. Eclectic menu in stylish dining room with fusion dining experience. **Cards:** AE, DI, DS, MC, VI.

COSTA DEL SOL RESTAURANT **Lunch:** $7-$10 **Dinner:** $12-$22 **Phone:** 860/296-1714 🄻

Ethnic

Location: I-91 exit 27, 0.5 mi w on Airport Rd & 0.5 mi s. 901 Wethersfield Ave 06114. **Hours:** 11:30 am-2 & 5:30-10 pm, Sat from 5 pm, Sun 4 pm-9 pm. Closed major holidays & Mon. **Reservations:** suggested. **Features:** casual dress; carryout; cocktails. Featuring Spanish seafood dishes & other entrees. **Cards:** AE, DI, MC, VI.

GAETANO'S RISTORANTE **Lunch:** $8-$10 **Dinner:** $15-$22 **Phone:** 860/249-1629 🄻

Italian

Location: In Civic Center, 2nd level. 1 Civic Center Plaza 06103. **Hours:** 11:30 am-2 & 5-10 pm, Sat from 5 pm. Closed major holidays & Sun. **Reservations:** suggested. **Features:** casual dress; children's menu; carryout; cocktails & lounge; a la carte, buffet. Northern Italian cuisine. Some seating overlooking the street. **Cards:** AE, DI, MC, VI.

MAX DOWNTOWN **Lunch:** $8-$15 **Dinner:** $13-$23 **Phone:** 860/522-2530 🄻

Italian

Location: Downtown. 185 Asylum St 06103. **Hours:** 11:30 am-2:30 & 5-10:30 pm, Fri-11:30 pm, Sat 5 pm-11:30 pm. Closed major holidays. **Reservations:** suggested. **Features:** cocktails; a la carte. Contemporary American cuisine in a metropolitan style atmosphere. Smoke free premises. **Cards:** AE, DI, MC, VI.

OASIS DINER & PANCHO'S TEX MEX **Lunch:** $5-$11 **Dinner:** $5-$11 **Phone:** 860/241-8200 🄻

American

Location: I-84 eastbound exit 48A, 0.5 mi w; westbound exit 47, just n, then w. 267 Farmington Ave 06105. **Hours:** 11:30 am-midnight, Fri & Sat-1 am. Closed major holidays. **Reservations:** accepted. **Features:** casual dress; Sunday brunch; children's menu; carryout; cocktails; minimum charge-evenings. Art deco embossed stainless steel diner with black tile & pink enamel interior; serving pot pie & extra thick chocolate malteds, 90's style fried calamari & chicken caesar salad. **Cards:** AE, DS, MC, VI.

(See map p. 220)

PIERPONT'S
◆◆◆
Continental
DI, DS, MC, VI.

Lunch: $6-$13   **Dinner:** $15-$25   **Phone:** 860/246-7500   ⑰
Location: Downtown, across from Civic Center (Asylum St); in Goodwin Hotel. 1 Haynes St 06103.
Hours: 6:30-10:30 am, 11:30-2 & 5:30-10:30 pm. **Reservations:** suggested. **Features:** dressy casual;
cocktails & lounge; valet parking; a la carte, buffet. Formal service. Sun brunch 11 am-2 pm. **Cards:** AE, CB,

The Hartford Vicinity

AVON—14,700   (See map p. 220; index p. 217)

LODGING

AVON OLD FARMS HOTEL
◆◆◆
Motor Inn

	Rates Subject to Change			**Phone:** 279/677-1651 ❶
5/1-6/30 & 9/1-10/31	1P: $119- 179	2P/1B: $119- 179	2P/2B: $119- 179	
7/1-8/31, 11/1-12/31 & 3/1-4/30	1P: $109- 169	2P/1B: $109- 169	2P/2B: $109- 169	
1/1-2/29	1P: $99- 149	2P/1B: $99- 149	2P/2B: $99- 149	

Location: Jct US 44 & SR 10. 279 Avon Mountain Rd 06001 (PO Box 1295). Fax: 860/677-0364. **Facility:** 160 rooms. 2 suites,
$140-$225; 2-3 stories; interior/exterior corridors. **Cards:** AE, DI, DS, MC, VI.

RESTAURANTS

AVON OLD FARMS INN RESTAURANT   Historical   **Lunch:** $6-$12   **Dinner:** $14-$25   **Phone:** 860/677-2818   ①
◆◆◆
Regional
American

Location: At jct US 44 & SR 10. 1 Nod Rd 06001. **Hours:** 11:30 am-9:30 pm, Fri-10 pm, Sat-10:30 pm, Sun
10 am-2:30 & 3:30-8:30 pm. Closed: 7/4 & 12/25. **Reservations:** suggested. **Features:** casual dress;
Sunday brunch; children's menu; health conscious menu; cocktails & lounge; entertainment; buffet. Colonial
inn operating since 1757. Charming dining rooms; unique old forge room for cocktails & dining. **Cards:** AE,
CB, DI, DS, MC, VI.

SEASONS RESTAURANT   **Lunch:** $6-$9   **Dinner:** $14-$24   **Phone:** 860/677-6352   ②
◆◆◆
Continental

Location: Jct US 44 & SR 10; in Avon Old Farms Hotel. 279 Avon Mountain Rd 06001. **Hours:** 6:30-10 am,
11:30-2 & 5-9 pm, Sat 7 am-11 & 5-9 pm, Sun 7 am-1 pm. **Reservations:** suggested. **Features:** children's
menu; cocktails & lounge; a la carte. Elegant dining room overlooking tree lit stream. Sun brunch 9 am-1 pm.
Casual dining avail in The Pub. Smoke free premises. **Cards:** AE, CB, DI, DS, MC, VI.

BRISTOL—60,600

LODGING

RADISSON INN BRISTOL
◆◆◆
Motor Inn

			Phone: (860)589-7766
All Year	1P: $94	2P/1B: $104	2P/2B: $104 XP: $10 F17

Location: Exit 31, I-84, 3 mi n on SR 229; in Technology Park. 42 Century Dr 06010. Fax: 860/585-0707.
Terms: BP avail; package plans. **Facility:** 120 rooms. All rooms with iron & ironing board. 6 stories; interior
corridors; heated indoor pool, sauna. **Dining:** Dining room; 6:30 am-2 & 5-10 pm, Sat & Sun from 7 am;
$8-$17; cocktails. **Services:** giftshop. **Cards:** AE, CB, DI, DS, JC, MC, VI. **Special Amenities:** Free local
telephone calls and free newspaper.

CROMWELL—12,300   (See map p. 220; index p. 217)

LODGINGS

COMFORT INN
◆◆◆
Motel

				Phone: (860)635-4100 ❺
5/1-10/31 & 4/1-4/30 [CP]	1P: $71- 94	2P/1B: $79- 99	2P/2B: $79- 109 XP: $5-10	F18
11/1-3/31 [EP]	1P: $69- 84	2P/1B: $74- 89	2P/2B: $74- 89 XP: $5-10	F18

Location: Just e on SR 372; I-91 exit 21. 111 Berlin Rd (Rt 372) 06416. Fax: 860/632-9546.
Terms: Weekly/monthly rates; pets, $15 extra charge. **Facility:** 77 rooms. Spacious rooms. 4 stories; interior
corridors. **Dining:** Restaurant nearby. **All Rooms:** extended cable TV. **Cards:** AE, CB, DI, DS, MC, VI.

HOLIDAY INN
◆◆◆
Motor Inn

				Phone: (860)635-1001 ❼
All Year	1P: $107- 116	2P/1B: $107- 116	2P/2B: $107- 116	

Location: Just w of I-91, exit 21. 4 Sebethe Dr 06416. Fax: 860/635-0684. **Terms:** AP avail. **Facility:** 145
rooms. Contemporary lobby, well equipped rooms. 41 whirlpool rms, extra charge; 3 stories; interior corridors;
heated indoor pool, saunas. **Dining:** Restaurant; 6:30-11 am, 11:30-2 & 5-10 pm, Sat & Sun from 7 am;
$10-$16; cocktails. **All Rooms:** extended cable TV. **Cards:** AE, CB, DI, DS, JC, MC, VI.

**RADISSON HOTEL AND CONFERENCE
CENTER CROMWELL**
◆◆◆
Hotel

	Rates Subject to Change			**Phone:** (860)635-2000 ❻
All Year	1P: $115	2P/1B: $125	2P/2B: $125 XP: $10	F17

Location: SR 372, just e of I-91, exit 21. 100 Berlin Rd 06416. Fax: 860/635-6970. **Facility:** 211 rooms. Large
elegant lobby with trees, sunken seating area. 4 stories; interior corridors; heated indoor pool.
Services: giftshop. **Cards:** AE, CB, DI, DS, JC, MC, VI.

SUPER 8 MOTEL
◆◆
Motel

	Rates Subject to Change			**Phone:** (860)632-8888 ❽
All Year	1P: $50- 56	2P/1B: $54- 60	2P/2B: $58- 64 XP: $4-8	F12

Location: I-91 exit 21, just w. 1 Industrial Park Rd 06416. Fax: 860/632-8889. **Facility:** 116 rooms. Modestly
equipped rooms in tudor style building. 3 stories; interior corridors. **Cards:** AE, CB, DI, DS, JC, MC, VI.

(See map p. 220)

RESTAURANT

CROMWELL DINER   **Lunch:** $5-$12   **Dinner:** $5-$12   **Phone:** 860/635-7112   ⑤
◆   **Location:** 0.3 mi w on SR 372; I-91, exit 21. 135 Berlin Rd (SR 372) Rd 06416. **Hours:** 24 hours. Closed:
American   12/25. **Features:** casual dress; children's menu; beer & wine only. Bright, modern decor. Also Greek, Italian
     & Jewish style dishes avail. Breakfast served all day. **Cards:** AE, MC, VI.   ⊠

EAST HARTFORD—50,400   (See map p. 220; index p. 217)

LODGINGS

HOLIDAY INN   Rates Subject to Change   **Phone:** (860)528-9611   ⑬
◆◆◆   Mon-Thurs   1P: $89   2P/1B: $89   2P/2B: $89
Motor Inn   Fri-Sun 5/1-12/31 & 4/1-4/30   1P: $79   2P/1B: $79   2P/2B: $79
     Fri-Sun 1/1-3/31   1P: $59   2P/1B: $59   2P/2B: $59
Location: I-84 exit 58, then w. 363 Roberts St 06108. Fax: 860/289-0270. **Facility:** 130 rooms. Rates are for up to 4 persons;
5 stories; interior corridors; heated indoor pool. **Cards:** AE, CB, DI, DS, MC, VI. *(See color ad below)*

⟨ASK⟩ ⟨S⟩ 🕭 🖥 🛰 ⚓ ¶ 🛆 🌇 🎿 💻 🖨 🎧 ⊠ 🗀

RAMADA INN   Rates Subject to Change   **Phone:** 860/528-9703   ⑫
◆◆   All Year   1P: $99- 109   2P/1B: $99- 109   2P/2B: $99- 109   XP: $10   F18
Motor Inn   **Location:** From SR 2 exit 4, 1 mi w. 100 E River Dr 06108. Fax: 860/289-4728. **Facility:** 198 rooms. 8 stories;
     interior corridors; heated indoor pool. **Services:** area transportation. **Cards:** AE, CB, DI, DS, MC, VI.
(See color ad inside front cover)

🕭 🛰 🖥 🛆 ¶ 🍴 🕂 🛆 🎿 💻 🖨 🎧 ⊠

WELLESLEY INN   **Phone:** (860)289-4950   ⑪
⟨AAA⟩ ⟨SAVE⟩   All Year [CP]   1P: $50- 75   2P/1B: $50- 85   2P/2B: $60- 85   XP: $10   F18
     Location: I-84, exit 58; then w. 333 Roberts St 06108. Fax: 860/289-9258. **Terms:** Pets, $5 extra charge.
◆◆◆   **Facility:** 103 rooms. Well-equipped small to medium rooms. 4 stories; interior corridors. **All Rooms:** combo
Motel   or shower baths. **Cards:** AE, CB, DI, DS, MC, VI. **Special Amenities:** Free breakfast and free local
     telephone calls. *(See color ad p 224)*   ⟨S⟩ 🕭 🖥 🛆 🕂 🎿 💻 🖨 🎧 ⊠

EAST WINDSOR—9,200   (See map p. 220; index p. 217)

LODGINGS

BEST WESTERN COLONIAL INN   **Phone:** (860)623-9411   ⑯
⟨AAA⟩ ⟨SAVE⟩   9/1-11/15 [CP]   1P: $95   2P/2B: $115   XP: $10   F16
     5/1-8/31 [CP]   1P: $89   2P/2B: $99   XP: $10   F16
◆◆◆   11/16-4/30 [CP]   1P: $69   2P/2B: $69   XP: $10   F16
Motor Inn   **Location:** On SR 140; just w of I-91 exit 45. 161 Bridge St 06088. Fax: 860/623-2145. **Terms:** Package
     plans; pets, $25 dep req. **Facility:** 121 rooms. 2 stories; interior corridors. **Dining:** Restaurant; 6:30 am-2 &
     5-9 pm; $6-$15; cocktails. **All Rooms:** combo or shower baths. **Some Rooms:** whirlpools. **Cards:** AE, DI, DS, MC, VI.
Special Amenities: Free breakfast and free local telephone calls.

⟨S⟩ 🕭 🛰 🖥 🛆 ¶ 🕂 🛆 🌇 🎿 💻 🖨 🗀 ⊠

HOLIDAY INN EXPRESS   **Phone:** (860)627-6585   ⑮
⟨AAA⟩ ⟨SAVE⟩   All Year [CP]   1P: $105- 115   2P/1B: $115- 125   2P/2B: $115- 125   XP: $10   F17
     Location: Jct US 5 & I-91, exit 44. 260 Main St 06088. Fax: 860/292-1391. **Terms:** Reserv deposit; handling
◆◆◆   fee imposed. **Facility:** 115 rooms. Rooms range from standard to corporate executive. 2 stories; interior corri-
Motel   dors. **Services:** area transportation, local restaurants. **All Rooms:** extended cable TV. **Cards:** AE, CB, DI,
     DS, JC, MC, VI. **Special Amenities:** Free breakfast and free local telephone calls.

⟨S⟩ 🖥 🛰 🕂 🛆 🌇 🎿 💻 🖨 🎧 🗀 ⊠ 🗀

RESTAURANT

THE EATERY RESTAURANT & BANQUET FACILITY   **Lunch:** $4-$10   **Dinner:** $14-$23   **Phone:** 860/627-7094   ⑧
◆◆   **Location:** Off I-91 exit 35, 2.8 mi e on I-291, 4.8 mi n on US 5. 297 S Main St 06088. **Hours:** 11:30 am-2:30
Continental   & 5-8 pm, Fri & Sat-10 pm. Closed: Sun. **Reservations:** required. **Features:** cocktails; a la carte, buffet.
     American continental menu, served in uniquely themed dining rooms. **Cards:** AE, DI, MC, VI.   ⊠

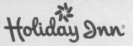

ENFIELD—42,700 (See map p. 220; index p. 218)

LODGINGS

HARLEY HOTEL OF HARTFORD-SPRINGFIELD   Rates Subject to Change   **Phone:** 860/741-2211   80
◆◆◆   All Year   1P: $104- 124   2P/1B: $124- 144   2P/2B: $114- 134   XP: $10   F18
Hotel   **Location:** Just se of jct I-91, exit 49 on Service Rd. 1 Bright Meadow Blvd 06082. Fax: 860/741-6917.
Facility: 181 rooms. On extensive grounds. Ambassador's Row rooms-$139; 6 stories; interior corridors; heated indoor pool; 2 lighted tennis courts. **Services:** area transportation. **All Rooms:** combo or shower baths. **Cards:** AE, CB, DI, DS, JC, MC, VI. *(See ad p 222)*

RED ROOF INN   Rates Subject to Change   **Phone:** (860)741-2571   81
◆◆   5/1-10/31   1P: $41- 56   2P/1B: $46- 61   2P/2B: $46- 61   XP: $7   F18
Motel   11/1-4/30   1P: $36- 51   2P/1B: $41- 56   2P/2B: $41- 56   XP: $7   F18
Location: At jct SR 190 & I-91, exit 47E. 5 Hazard Ave 06082. Fax: 860/741-2576. **Facility:** 108 rooms. 2 stories; exterior corridors. **Cards:** AE, CB, DI, DS, MC, VI.

SUPER 8 MOTEL-ENFIELD   **Phone:** (860)741-3636   82
[AAA] [SAVE]   Fri & Sat 9/1-9/30 [CP]   1P: $64- 69   2P/1B: $64- 74   2P/2B: $69- 79   XP: $5   F12
    Fri & Sat 5/1-8/31, Sun-Thurs
◆◆   9/1-9/30 & Fri & Sat
Motel   10/1-10/31 [CP]   1P: $59- 64   2P/1B: $64- 69   2P/2B: $64- 74   XP: $5   F12
    Sun-Thurs 5/1-8/31,
    10/1-10/31 & 4/1-4/30 [CP]   1P: $54- 59   2P/1B: $59- 64   2P/2B: $59- 69   XP: $5   F12
    11/1-3/31 [CP]   1P: $45- 55   2P/1B: $50- 55   2P/2B: $52- 62   XP: $5   F12
Location: I-91, exit 46; 0.3 mi n on US 5. 1543 King St 06082. Fax: 860/741-3497. **Terms:** Weekly rates; pets, $10 extra charge. **Facility:** 64 rooms. 1-2 stories; exterior corridors. **Dining:** Restaurant nearby. **All Rooms:** extended cable TV. **Some Rooms:** 4 efficiencies. **Cards:** AE, CB, DI, DS, MC, VI. **Special Amenities:** Free breakfast and free local telephone calls.

FARMINGTON—20,600 (See map p. 220; index p. 217)

LODGINGS

CENTENNIAL INN SUITES   Rates Subject to Change   **Phone:** (860)677-4647   20
◆◆◆   All Year   1P: $119   2P/1B: $119   2P/2B: $169
Suite Motel   **Location:** From US 6, 0.3 mi e of jct SR 177. 5 Spring Ln 06032. Fax: 860/676-0685. **Terms:** Reserv deposit. **Facility:** 112 rooms. Charming suites with fireplace. All the comforts & conveniences of home, in lovely wooded setting. 14 two-rm suites, $170-$210; 2 stories; interior/exterior corridors. **All Rooms:** kitchens, combo or shower baths. **Cards:** AE, CB, DI, DS, MC, VI. *(See color ad below)*

THE FARMINGTON INN   Rates Subject to Change   **Phone:** (860)677-2821   19
◆◆◆   5/1-6/30 & 9/1-10/31 [CP]   1P: $119- 139   2P/1B: $119- 139   XP: $10   F14
Motor Inn   7/1-8/31 & 11/1-4/30 [CP]   1P: $109- 129   2P/1B: $109- 129   XP: $10   F14
   Location: On SR 4, 1.8 mi w of I-84, exit 39. 827 Farmington Ave (SR 4) 06032-2382. Fax: 860/677-8332. **Facility:** 72 rooms. Medium to large rooms in a country decor. 13 suites $129-$149 for up to 2 persons; 2 stories; interior corridors. **Cards:** AE, CB, DI, DS, MC, VI.

MARRIOTT HOTEL-FARMINGTON   Rates Subject to Change   **Phone:** 860/678-1000   21
◆◆◆   9/1-11/17   1P: $89- 129   2P/1B: $89- 129   2P/2B: $99- 139
Hotel   5/1-8/31   1P: $69- 119   2P/1B: $69- 119   2P/2B: $79- 129
    11/18-4/30   1P: $59- 109   2P/1B: $59- 109   2P/2B: $69- 119
Location: I-84 exit 37; in Farm Springs Executive Park. 15 Farm Springs Rd 06032. Fax: 860/677-8849. **Terms:** Check-in 4 pm. **Facility:** 381 rooms. Modern lobby with sunken seating area. 3-4 stories; interior corridors; heated indoor pool; 2 lighted tennis courts. **Services:** giftshop; area transportation. **Recreation:** jogging. **All Rooms:** combo or shower baths. **Cards:** AE, DI, DS, MC, VI.

(See map p. 220)

RESTAURANTS

APRICOTS
♦♦♦
American
Lunch: $8-$13   Dinner: $16-$28   Phone: 860/673-5405   ⑩
Location: On SR 4; 4.5 mi w of I-84, exit 39. 1593 Farmington Ave 06032. **Hours:** 11:30 am-2:30 & 6-10 pm, Sun 11:30 am-2:30 & 5:30-9 pm. Closed: 1/1, 7/4 & 12/25. **Reservations:** suggested. **Features:** Sunday brunch; cocktails & lounge; a la carte. Eclectic dining overlooking river. Also light menu in pub, 2:30 pm-closing. Patio dining 11:30 am-4 pm weather permitting. **Cards:** AE, CB, DI, DS, MC, VI.
⊗

PICCOLO ARANCO
♦♦
Italian
Lunch: $6-$9   Dinner: $12-$22   Phone: 860/674-1224   ⑪
Location: On SR 4, 1.8 mi w of I-84, exit 39; at The Framington Inn. 819 Farmington Ave 06032. **Hours:** 11:30 am-2:30 & 5-10 pm, Fri & Sat-11 pm. Closed major holidays & Sun. **Reservations:** suggested. **Features:** cocktails & lounge; a la carte. Contemporary, informal dining. **Cards:** AE, DI, MC, VI.
♿ ⊗

GLASTONBURY—27,400   (See map p. 220; index p. 217)

LODGING

BUTTERNUT FARM
♦♦♦
Historic Bed & Breakfast
Rates Subject to Change   Phone: 860/633-7197   ㉔
All Year [BP]   1P: $75- 95   2P/1B: $75- 95   2P/2B: $75- 95   XP: $15-20   D21
Location: From SR 2 exit 8, 0.5 mi w. 1.6 mi s. 1654 Main St 06033. Fax: 860/659-1758. **Terms:** Reserv deposit, 10 day notice; handling fee imposed. **Facility:** 4 rooms. Charming 18th century Colonial home & cozy barn apartment with extensive antique collection; a small farm-like setting with assorted animals. 2 stories; interior/exterior corridors; smoke free premises. **All Rooms:** combo or shower baths. **Some Rooms:** kitchen, color TV. **Cards:** AE.
🄿 📺 🖥 🛎 🖨 ⊗

RESTAURANT

MAX AMORE
♦♦
Northern Italian
Lunch: $7-$11   Dinner: $10-$20   Phone: 860/659-2819   ⑫
Location: From SR 3 Main St exit; in Shops at Somerset Square shopping arcade. 140 Glastonbury Blvd 06033. **Hours:** 11:30 am-10:00 pm, Fri & Sat-11:00 pm. Closed major holidays. **Reservations:** suggested. **Features:** casual dress; carryout; cocktails & lounge. Open kitchen sends aromas of roasted garlic, grilled seafood into a stylish dining room with a European flair. **Cards:** AE, CB, DI, DS, MC, VI.
⊗

MANCHESTER—51,600   (See map p. 220; index p. 218)

LODGING

CONNECTICUT MOTOR LODGE
ⒶⒶⒶ
♦
Motel
Guaranteed Rates   Phone: 860/643-1555   ㊱
All Year   1P: $40   2P/1B: $45   2P/2B: $55   XP: $5   F12
Location: I-84 exit 63, 0.3 mi w. 400 Tolland Tpk 06040. Fax: 860/643-1881. **Facility:** 31 rooms. 1 story; exterior corridors. **Dining:** Restaurant nearby. **Services:** winter plug-ins. **All Rooms:** shower baths, extended cable TV. **Cards:** AE, CB, DI, DS, JC, MC, VI.
🆚 🍴 ⊗

RESTAURANTS

CAVEY'S RESTAURANT-ITALIAN
♦♦♦
Northern Italian
Lunch: $9-$13   Dinner: $13-$21   Phone: 860/643-2751   ㉑
Location: Downtown on US 6 & 44, just e of jct SR 83. 45 E Center St 06040. **Hours:** 11:30 am-2:30 & 5:30-9:30 pm, Fri-10 pm, Sat 5:30 pm-10 pm. Closed major holidays, Sun, Mon & 7/4-9/1 for lunch. **Reservations:** suggested. **Features:** cocktails & lounge; a la carte. Inviting dining, country decor. Smoking permitted in lounge only. **Cards:** AE, MC, VI.
⊗

SHADY GLEN DAIRY STORES
♦
American
Lunch: $3-$8   Dinner: $3-$8   Phone: 860/649-4245   ㉒
Location: On US 6 & 44, 1 mi w of jct SR 85. 840 E Middle Tpk 06040. **Hours:** 7 am-11:30 pm, Sun-from 10:30 am. Closed: 11/25 & 12/25. **Features:** casual dress; children's menu; carryout. Smoke free premises.
⊗

MIDDLEFIELD—1,300

LODGING

BEST WAY INN
ⒶⒶⒶ 🅂🄰🅅🄴
♦
Motel
   Phone: 860/347-6955
5/1-12/31 & 4/1-4/30   1P: $45   2P/1B: $50   2P/2B: $55- 60   XP: $10   F
1/1-3/31   1P: $40   2P/1B: $45   2P/2B: $50   XP: $5   F
Location: SR 66, 0.5 mi e of jct SR 217. 31 Meriden Rd 06455. Fax: 860/347-6956. **Terms:** Weekly rates. **Facility:** 25 rooms. Well maintained rooms, convenient to I-91. 1 story; exterior corridors. **All Rooms:** combo or shower baths, extended cable TV. **Cards:** AE, DS, MC, VI.
🆚 🛎 ⊗

NEW BRITAIN—72,400   (See map p. 220; index p. 219)

RESTAURANTS

GREAT TASTE RESTAURANT
♦♦♦
Chinese
Lunch: $6-$8   Dinner: $8-$17   Phone: 860/229-7373   ㊹
Location: From SR 72 exit 7, just n, then just e. 597 W Main St 06053. **Hours:** 11 am-10 pm, Fri & Sat-11 pm. Closed: 11/25. **Reservations:** suggested. **Features:** casual dress; health conscious menu; carryout; cocktails; a la carte. Casual yet simple elegance; excellent variety includes fresh seafood & meat; noted specialty Peking Duck. **Cards:** AE, DI, MC, VI.
⊗

PARADISE PIZZA RESTAURANT
♦
Italian
Lunch: $5-$8   Dinner: $5-$14   Phone: 860/827-8123   ㊺
Location: SR 9 exit 24; 0.5 mi w, then exit 71N; 0.3 mi n, then 0.5 mi e. 10 East St 06051. **Hours:** 11 am-midnight. Closed: 11/25, 12/25 & Easter. **Reservations:** accepted; 6 or more. **Features:** casual dress; senior's menu; carryout; cocktails. Excellent seafood, beef, chicken & veal entrees offered in a casual setting.
⊗

NEWINGTON—28,400   (See map p. 220; index p. 219)

RESTAURANT

CARRINGTONS RESTAURANT   **Lunch:** $5-$7   **Dinner:** $9-$13   **Phone:** 860/667-1122   [47]
◆   **Location:** On US 5 & SR 15, just s of jct SR 173. 3237 Berlin Tpk 06111. **Hours:** 11:30 am-9 pm, Fri &
American   Sat-10 pm. **Closed:** 11/25 & 12/25. **Reservations:** suggested. **Features:** casual dress; children's menu; early
                     bird specials; senior's menu; carryout; cocktails & lounge. Good selection of beef, pasta, chicken & seafood.
Cards: AE, DS, MC, VI.   [X]

PLAINVILLE—17,200   (See map p. 220; index p. 218)

LODGING

HOWARD JOHNSON HOTEL   Rates Subject to Change   **Phone:** 860/747-6876   [41]
◆◆   All Year   1P: $49- 59 2P/1B: $64   2P/2B: $54   XP: $10   F16
Motel   **Location:** On SR 72, nw of I-84, exit 34. 400 New Britain Ave 06062. Fax: 860/747-9747. **Facility:** 105 rooms.
                  4 stories; interior corridors. **Cards:** AE, DI, DS, MC, VI.

[icons]

RESTAURANT

J TIMOTHY'S TAVERNE   **Lunch:** $10-$15   **Dinner:** $10-$15   **Phone:** 860/747-6813   [24]
◆◆   **Location:** On SR 372, 0.6 mi e of jct SR 10. 143 New Britain Ave 06062. **Hours:** 11:30 am-2 & 5-10 pm,
American   Sun noon-8 pm. **Closed:** 5/30, 5/31, 9/5, 9/6 & 12/25. **Reservations:** accepted; 6 or more. **Features:** No
                A/C; casual dress; children's menu; early bird specials; carryout; cocktails & lounge. Historic 1789 tavern in
comfortable, relaxed atmosphere; pub with continuous service. **Cards:** AE, CB, DI, DS, MC, VI.   [icons]

PORTLAND—8,400

LODGING

RIVERDALE MOTEL   Guaranteed Rates   **Phone:** (860)342-3498
[AAA]   All Year   1P: $45- 54 2P/1B: $45- 59 2P/2B: $49- 59 XP: $10   F16
◆◆   **Location:** On SR 66; 1.5 mi w of jct SR 151. 1503 Portland Cobalt Rd 06480. Fax: 860/342-0624.
Motel   **Terms:** Reserv deposit; weekly rates. **Facility:** 39 rooms. Rural location; mostly large rooms. 1-2 stories;
                  interior/exterior corridors. **Services:** winter plug-ins. **All Rooms:** combo or shower baths, extended cable TV.
                  Some Rooms: 4 kitchens. **Cards:** AE, DI, DS, MC, VI.   [icons]

ROCKY HILL—16,600   (See map p. 220; index p. 218)

LODGINGS

HARTFORD MARRIOTT ROCKY HILL   Rates Subject to Change   **Phone:** (860)257-6000   [45]
◆◆◆   All Year   1P: $69- 164 2P/1B: $69- 164 2P/2B: $69- 164
Hotel   **Location:** 0.3 mi e of I-91, exit 23. 100 Capital Blvd 06067. Fax: 860/257-6060. **Terms:** Check-in 4 pm.
                  Facility: 251 rooms. Located at entrance to business park. Rates for up to 4 persons; 4 stories; interior corri-
dors; heated indoor pool. **Services:** giftshop. **Cards:** AE, CB, DI, DS, JC, MC, VI.

[icons]

TRAVELER'S MOTOR LODGE   **Phone:** 860/529-3341   [44]
[AAA] [SAVE]   All Year   1P: $45- 52 2P/1B: $45- 55 2P/2B: $60- 75 XP: $10   F10
◆◆   **Location:** On SR 99, just e of I-91 exit 24. 1760 Silas Deane Hwy 06067. Fax: 860/529-3341.
Motel   **Terms:** Weekly rates. **Facility:** 33 rooms. 2 stories; exterior corridors. **Dining:** Restaurant nearby.
                  All Rooms: extended cable TV. **Cards:** AE, DI, DS, MC, VI.   [icons]

SIMSBURY—22,000   (See map p. 220; index p. 218)

LODGINGS

THE IRONHORSE INN   **Phone:** (860)658-2216   [90]
[AAA] [SAVE]   All Year [CP]   1P: $73   2P/1B: $73   2P/2B: $83   XP: $10
◆◆   **Location:** On US 202 & SR 10. 969 Hopmeadow St 06070. Fax: 860/651-0822. **Terms:** Weekly/monthly
Motel   rates; pets, $10 extra charge. **Facility:** 27 rooms. 1 two-bedroom unit. 3 stories, no elevator; interior corridors;
                  sauna. **All Rooms:** extended cable TV. **Some Rooms:** 8 efficiencies. **Cards:** AE, MC, VI.
                  Special Amenities: Free breakfast and preferred room **(subject to availability with advanced
reservations).**   [icons]

SIMSBURY INN   Rates Subject to Change   **Phone:** (860)651-5700   [92]
◆◆◆   All Year [CP]   1P: $149- 275 2P/1B: $149- 275 2P/2B: $149- 275
Hotel   **Location:** On US 202 & SR 10, 0.4 mi n of SR 185. 397 Hopmeadow St 06070. Fax: 860/651-8024.
                  Facility: 97 rooms. Contemporary, upscale public areas. Charming country decor in guest rooms. 1 two-
bedroom unit. Rates for up to 4 persons; 4 stories; interior corridors; heated indoor pool; 1 tennis court. **Services:** area
transportation. **Recreation:** jogging. **Cards:** AE, DI, DS, JC, MC, VI.

[icons]

RESTAURANTS

LILY'S OF THE VALLEY   **Lunch:** $3-$10   **Dinner:** $7-$21   **Phone:** 860/651-3676   [35]
◆◆   **Location:** On US 202 & SR 10, 1.1 mi s of jct SR 185. 142 Hopmeadow St 06070. **Hours:** 11:30 am-9 pm,
American   Mon-2:30 pm, Fri-10 pm, Sat 9 am-10 pm, Sun 9 am-9 pm. **Closed:** 11/25 & 12/25. **Reservations:** accepted;
                6 or more. **Features:** casual dress; Sunday brunch; children's menu; health conscious menu items; carryout;
cocktails & lounge. Fun & friendly farmhouse with farm animal inspired accents. Features 4 meatless entrees, duckling, filet
mignon, homemade muffins & smoked chicken breast. **Cards:** AE, MC, VI.   [X]

(See map p. 220)

METRO BIS
◆◆
French

Lunch: $6-$12   **Dinner:** $11-$22   **Phone:** 860/651-1908   ㊲
Location: Center, in Simsburytown S.H.O.P.S. shopping arcade. 928 Hopmeadow St 06070. **Hours:** 11 am-2 & 5:30-9 pm, Fri & Sat-10 pm, Sun 9 am-2 & 5-8 pm. Closed: Mon. **Reservations:** accepted. **Features:** casual dress; Sunday brunch; carryout; cocktails. Decorated with Parisian subway artifacts & oil paintings. Features include vichyssoise, beef tournedos & several types of crepes. Smoke free premises. **Cards:** MC, VI.
⊠

MURASAKI JAPANESE RESTAURANT   **Lunch:** $8-$13   **Dinner:** $13-$28   **Phone:** 860/651-7929   ㊴
◆◆◆
Japanese
Location: Center, SR 10 & 202. 10 Wilcox St 06070. **Hours:** 11:45 am-2 & 5-9:30 pm. Closed: 1/1, 11/25, 12/25 & Mon. **Reservations:** suggested; weekends. **Features:** casual dress; children's menu; carryout; beer & wine only. Excellent variety includes sushi & sashimi, noodle & rice dishes; also meat & seafood. Smoke free premises. **Cards:** AE, DI, DS, MC, VI.
⊠

SOUTHINGTON—38,500   (See map p. 220; index p. 218)

LODGING

HOLIDAY INN EXPRESS
🅰🅰🅰
◆◆◆
Motel

Rates Subject to Change   **Phone:** (860)276-0736   ㊾

5/1-10/31 [CP]	1P:	$74- 94	2P/1B:	$84- 104	2P/2B:	$84- 104	XP: $10	F18
11/1-4/30 [CP]	1P:	$64- 84	2P/1B:	$74- 94	2P/2B:	$74- 94	XP: $10	F18

Location: Just s of jct I-84, exit 32 & SR 10, then just e. 120 Laning St 06489. Fax: 860/276-9405. **Facility:** 122 rooms. A few small rooms. 3 stories; interior corridors. **Dining:** Restaurant nearby. **Some Rooms:** whirlpools. **Cards:** AE, CB, DI, DS, MC, VI.

RESTAURANTS

BRANNINGAN'S
◆◆
American

Lunch: $6-$11   **Dinner:** $10-$15   **Phone:** 860/621-9311   ㉖
Location: Just e of I-84, exit 32. 176 Laning St 06489. **Hours:** 11:30 am-9:30 pm, Fri & Sat-10 pm, Sun-9 pm. Closed major holidays. **Reservations:** accepted. **Features:** casual dress; children's menu; early bird specials; health conscious menu; cocktails & lounge. Relaxed dining. House specialty is barbecue ribs. Sun brunch 11 am-2:30 pm; also fresh seafood, poultry & choice beef. **Cards:** AE, DI, MC, VI.
⊠

PATTON BROOK RESTAURANT & PIZZA   **Lunch:** $5-$15   **Dinner:** $6-$15   **Phone:** 860/621-2554   ㉕
◆
American

Location: On SR 10; 1.7 mi n of I-84, exit 32. 966 Queen St 06489. **Hours:** 6 am-9 pm, Fri & Sat-11 pm. Closed: 12/25. **Reservations:** suggested; Fri & Sat. **Features:** casual dress; children's menu; early bird specials; senior's menu; carryout; cocktails. Also serving beef & seafood specialities. Inviting combinations to choose from in a relaxed, informal atmosphere. **Cards:** AE, DI, MC, VI.
⊠

SOUTH WINDSOR—22,000   (See map p. 220; index p. 218)

RESTAURANT

THE MILL ON THE RIVER
◆◆
American

Lunch: $5-$10   **Dinner:** $12-$19   **Phone:** 860/289-7929   ㊷
Location: 2 mi s on SR 30. 989 Ellington Rd (SR 30) 06074. **Hours:** 11:30 am-2:30 & 5-9:30 pm, Fri-10 pm, Sat 5 pm-10 pm, Sun 11 am-2:30 & 3-8 pm. **Reservations:** suggested. **Features:** Sunday brunch; cocktails; a la carte. Restored mill in park setting overlooking river with dam. Fresh seafood & pasta specialties. Patio dining avail. **Cards:** AE, DI, MC, VI.
⊠

VERNON—28,300

LODGINGS

COMFORT INN
🅰🅰🅰 SAVE
◆◆◆
Motel

                                                       Phone: (860)871-2432
All Year   1P: $69- 117   2P/1B: $77- 117   2P/2B: $77- 117   XP: $10   F18
Location: Just n of I-84, exit 65. 425 Hartford Tpk (SR 30) 06066. Fax: 860/871-2432. **Facility:** 69 rooms. Adjacent to small shopping area. 2 stories; interior corridors. **Dining:** Restaurant nearby. **All Rooms:** extended cable TV. **Cards:** AE, CB, DI, DS, JC, MC, VI. **Special Amenities:** Free breakfast and free local telephone calls.

HOWARD JOHNSON LODGE
◆◆ Rates Subject to Change Phone: (860)875-0781
Motel All Year 1P: $50- 60 2P/1B: $55- 65 2P/2B: $60- 75 XP: $8 F18
Location: On SR 30; just n of jct I-84 exit 65. 451 Hartford Tpk (SR 30) 06066. Fax: 860/872-8449.
Facility: 64 rooms. Studio room, $70-75; 2 stories; interior corridors. **Cards:** AE, CB, DI, DS, MC, VI.
(See ad p 230)

QUALITY INN & CONFERENCE CENTER
Phone: (860)646-5700
All Year [CP] 1P: $80- 160 2P/1B: $90- 160 2P/2B: $90- 160 XP: $10 F18
◆◆◆ **Location:** Just w on SR 30, then 0.8 mi s on SR 30 & 83; from I-84 exit 64. 51 Hartford Tpk (SR 83) 06066.
Motor Inn Fax: 860/646-0202. **Terms:** Package plans. **Facility:** 127 rooms. 2 suites, $125-$150; 2 stories; interior corri-
dors; miniature golf. **Dining:** Restaurant; 11:30 am-10 pm, Fri & Sat-11 pm, Sun noon-9 pm; $11-$18;
cocktails. **All Rooms:** extended cable TV. **Cards:** AE, CB, DI, DS, JC, MC, VI. **Special Amenities: Free**
breakfast and free local telephone calls.

RESTAURANT

REIN'S NEW YORK STYLE DELI-RESTAURANT **Lunch:** $3-$9 **Dinner:** $3-$9 **Phone:** 860/875-1344
◆◆ **Location:** On SR 30; 0.3 mi n of I-84, exit 65. 435A Hartford Tpk (SR 30) 06066. **Hours:** 7 am-midnight.
American Closed: 11/25, 12/31 & 12/25 for dinner. **Features:** children's menu; carryout; cocktails & lounge; a la carte.
Informal family dining. Deli sandwiches, omelets & dinner entrees. Breakfast always served. Small bakery on
site.

WEST HARTFORD—60,100 (See map p. 220; index p. 218)

LODGING

WEST HARTFORD INN
Phone: (860)236-3221 [52]
All Year [CP] 1P: $70- 85 2P/1B: $70- 85 2P/2B: $70- 85 XP: $10 F16
◆◆ **Location:** I-84 exit 43, just e, then 0.6 mi n, just e. 900 Farmington Ave 06119. Fax: 860/236-3445.
Hotel **Facility:** 50 rooms. Small to medium well equipped rooms. 5 stories; interior corridors. **Dining:** Restaurant
nearby. **All Rooms:** combo or shower baths, extended cable TV. **Cards:** AE, DI, MC, VI. **Special Amenities:**
Free breakfast and free newspaper.

RESTAURANT

MAHARAJA **Lunch:** $5-$7 **Dinner:** $8-$15 **Phone:** 860/233-7184 [28]
◆◆ **Location:** Center. 964 Farmington Ave 06107. **Hours:** 11:30 am-3:00 & 4:30-10:30 pm. Closed: 11/25.
Indian **Reservations:** accepted. **Features:** casual dress; Sunday brunch; children's menu; senior's menu; health
conscious menu; carryout; cocktails. Indian food featuring vegetarian favorites baked eggplant or cheese &
spinach. Specialties include lemon-soaked rainbow trout or lamb stew. **Cards:** AE, CB, DI, DS, MC, VI.

WETHERSFIELD—25,700 (See map p. 220; index p. 218)

LODGINGS

CHESTER BULKLEY HOUSE Guaranteed Rates Phone: (860)563-4236 [56]
◆◆◆ All Year 1P: $75- 85 2P/1B: $75- 85 2P/2B: $75- 85 XP: $5
Historic Bed **Location:** In the center of The Old Village. 184 Main St 06109. Fax: 860/257-8266. **Terms:** Check-in 4 pm;
& Breakfast reserv deposit, 7 day notice. **Facility:** 5 rooms. Restored 1830 private residence on Main St of historical dis-
trict. 2 stories; interior corridors; smoke free premises. **Recreation:** bicycles. **Cards:** AE, DS, MC, VI.

TERRA MOTEL Guaranteed Rates Phone: (860)529-6804 [55]
◆ All Year 1P: $37 2P/1B: $42 2P/2B: $47 XP: $5 F10
Motel **Location:** On US 5/SR 15, 0.5 mi n of jct SR 175. 1809 Berlin Tpk 06109. Fax: 860/721-1038.
Terms: Reserv deposit. **Facility:** 12 rooms. 1 story; exterior corridors. **All Rooms:** shower baths.
Cards: AE, DI, MC, VI.

WINDSOR—27,800 (See map p. 220; index p. 218)

LODGINGS

COURTYARD BY MARRIOTT Rates Subject to Change Phone: 860/683-0022 [59]
◆◆◆ Sun-Thurs 1P: $119- 129 2P/1B: $119- 129 2P/2B: $119- 129
Motor Inn Fri & Sat 6/1-12/31 1P: $74 2P/1B: $84 2P/2B: $84
Fri & Sat 5/1-5/31 & 1/1-4/30 1P: $64 2P/1B: $69 2P/2B: $69
Location: Jct SR 75 & I-91 exit 38; southbound exit 38B. 1 Day Hill Rd 06095. Fax: 860/683-1072. **Facility:** 149 rooms. Rates
for up to 4 persons; 2-3 stories; interior corridors; heated indoor pool. **Cards:** AE, DI, DS, MC, VI. *(See color ad p 222)*

THE RESIDENCE INN BY MARRIOTT HARTFORD-WINDSOR Rates Subject to Change
Phone: (860)688-7474 [60]
◆◆◆ 5/1-12/31 [CP] 1P: $139 2P/1B: $139 2P/2B: $169
Apartment 1/1-4/30 [CP] 1P: $135 2P/1B: $135 2P/2B: $165
Location: From I-91 exit 37 (Windsor-Bloomfield Ave), just w on SR 305 to Dunfey Ln, 0.3 mi n. 100 Dunfey
Ln 06095. Fax: 860/683-8457. **Facility:** 96 rooms. Complimentary beverages & hors d'oeuvres Mon-Thurs. 24 Penthouses
avail for up to 5 persons; 2 stories; exterior corridors; small pool. **Recreation:** sports court. **All Rooms:** kitchens.
Cards: AE, CB, DI, DS, JC, MC, VI.

WINDSOR LOCKS—12,400 (See map p. 220; index p. 218)

✈ Airport Accommodations

Spotter/Map Pg. Number	OA	WINDSOR LOCKS	Rating	Rate	Listing Page
68 / p. 220		Baymont Inn & Suites-Hartford/Airport, 1.3 mi e of airport	◆◆◆	$69-74	232
70 / p. 220	🚗	**Days Inn Bradley International Airport, 1 mi e of airport**	◆◆◆	$71-109 SAVE	232
74 / p. 220	🚗	**DoubleTree Hotel Bradley International Airport, 1.5 mi e of airport**	◆◆◆	$62-92 SAVE	232
69 / p. 220		Fairfield Inn by Marriott, 1 mi e of airport	◆◆◆	$60-76	232
73 / p. 220		Homewood Suites Hartford-Windsor Locks, 1.3 mi e of airport	◆◆◆	$130	233
71 / p. 220		Sheraton Hotel At Bradley International Airport, inside airport	◆◆◆	$115	233

LODGINGS

BAYMONT INN & SUITES-HARTFORD/AIRPORT Rates Subject to Change **Phone:** 860/623-3336 68
◆◆◆ All Year [CP] 1P: $57- 72 2P/1B: $64- 79 2P/2B: $69- 74 XP: $7
Motel **Location:** On SR 75, just n of jct SR 20. 64 Ella T Grasso Tpk 06096. Fax: 860/627-6641. **Facility:** 107 rooms. Located on commercial strip. 4 stories; interior corridors. **Some Rooms:** kitchen. **Cards:** AE, CB, DI, DS, MC, VI. *(See color ad p 223)* [ASK] 🛎 📶 📺 🎬 🍴 ✈ 🛝 🐾 💻 🖨 🛗 👤 ✕

DAYS INN BRADLEY INTERNATIONAL AIRPORT **Phone:** (860)623-9417 70
🚗 SAVE All Year 1P: $67- 109 2P/1B: $71- 109 2P/2B: $71- 109 XP: $10 D12
◆◆◆ **Location:** On SR 75, 1 mi n of jct SR 20. 185 Ella T Grasso Tpk (Rt 75) 06096. Fax: 860/623-5268.
Motel **Terms:** Package plans. **Facility:** 100 rooms. 2 stories; interior corridors. **Dining:** Restaurant nearby. **All Rooms:** extended cable TV. **Cards:** AE, DI, DS, MC, VI. **Special Amenities: Free local telephone calls and free room upgrade (subject to availability with advanced reservations).**
🛝 🎬 📺 🍴 🍴 ✈ 🛝 🖨 🖨 🛗 ✕

DOUBLETREE HOTEL BRADLEY INTERNATIONAL AIRPORT **Phone:** (860)627-5171 74
🚗 SAVE All Year [BP] 1P: $62- 92 2P/1B: $62- 92 2P/2B: $62- 92 XP: $10 F18
◆◆◆ **Location:** On SR 75, at jct SR 20. 16 Ella T Grasso Tpk 06096. Fax: 860/627-7029. **Facility:** 200 rooms. Art
Hotel deco exterior. Nicely furnished rooms, hair dryer, iron & ironing board. 5 stories; interior corridors; small heated indoor pool. **Dining:** Dining room; 6 am-11 pm; $15-$20; cocktails. **Services:** area transportation, within 5 mi. **Cards:** AE, CB, DI, DS, JC, MC, VI. **Special Amenities: Free breakfast.** *(See color ad below)*
🛝 🎬 📺 🏊 🍴 ✈ 🛝 🐾 💻 🖨 🖨 🛗 👤 ✕ 🈺

FAIRFIELD INN BY MARRIOTT Rates Subject to Change **Phone:** 860/627-9333 69
◆◆◆ All Year [CP] 1P: $50- 66 2P/1B: $60- 73 2P/2B: $60- 76
Motel **Location:** On SR 75, 0.5 mi n of jct SR 20. 2 Loten Dr 06096. Fax: 860/627-9333. **Facility:** 135 rooms. 3 stories; interior/exterior corridors; heated pool. **Cards:** AE, CB, DI, DS, MC, VI.
📺 🛝 ✈ 🛝 🐾 🖨 ✕ 🈺

(See map p. 220)

HOMEWOOD SUITES HARTFORD-WINDSOR LOCKS   Rates Subject to Change   **Phone:** 860/627-8463   🎫73
◆◆◆   All Year [CP]   1P: $130   2P/1B: $130   XP: $10   F18
Suite Motel   **Location:** On SR 75, 0.3 mi n of jct SR 20. 65 Ella T Grasso Tpk 06096. Fax: 860/627-9313. **Facility:** 132 rooms. 24 suites with fireplace, $10 extra charge. 8 two-bedroom suites, $160; 3 stories; interior/exterior corridors. **Services:** giftshop; area transportation. **Recreation:** sports court. **All Rooms:** kitchens. **Cards:** AE, DI, DS, MC, VI.

🛏️ 🍽️ 🎦 ⊃ 🔌 ⛱️ ✕ 🌐 🍸 [VCR] ▣ ▢ 🖨️ 🔒 ✕ 🐾

SHERATON HOTEL AT BRADLEY
INTERNATIONAL AIRPORT   Rates Subject to Change   **Phone:** 860/627-5311   🎫71
◆◆◆   Sun-Thurs   1P: $115   2P/1B: $115   2P/2B: $115   XP: $15   F12
Hotel   Fri & Sat   1P: $89   2P/1B: $89   2P/2B: $89   XP: $15   F12
Location: At Bradley International Airport terminal. 1 Bradley Int'l Airport 06096-1045. Fax: 860/627-9348.
Terms: Reserv deposit. **Facility:** 237 rooms. 8 stories; interior corridors; heated indoor pool. **Cards:** AE, CB, DI, DS, MC, VI.

🛏️ 🍽️ 🎦 ⊃ 🍴 🍸 🌐 ⛱️ 🌐 🍸 ▣ 🖨️ 🔒 ✕ 🐾

RESTAURANT

ALBERTS RESTAURANT   **Dinner:** $9-$19   **Phone:** 860/292-6801   🎫34
◆◆   **Location:** 0.5 mi n on SR 75 from jct SR 20, 1 mi e of airport. 159 Ella Grasso Tpk (SR 75) 06096.
Steakhouse   **Hours:** 4 pm-10 pm, Sun noon-9 pm. Closed: 11/25 & 12/25. **Reservations:** suggested. **Features:** dressy casual; children's menu; senior's menu; salad bar; cocktails & lounge; a la carte. Contemporary decor, prime rib specialty. **Cards:** AE, DI, DS, MC, VI.   ✕

This ends listings for the Hartford Vicinity.
The following page resumes the alphabetical listings of
cities in Connecticut.

IVORYTON—2,300

RESTAURANT

COPPER BEECH INN   Country Inn   **Dinner:** $21-$26   Phone: 860/767-0330
◆◆◆◆   **Location:** 1.5 mi w of SR 9, exit 3. 46 Main St 06442. **Hours:** 5:30 pm-8 pm, Sat-9 pm, Sun 1 pm-8 pm.
French   Closed: 1/1, 12/24, 12/25 & Mon; also Tues 1/6-3/24. **Reservations:** suggested. **Features:** dressy casual;
cocktails; also prix fixe. Fine candlelight dining in an elegant setting with innovative food preparations &
international flair. Smoke free premises. **Cards:** AE, CB, DI, MC, VI.   ⊠

KENT—2,900

LODGING

FIFE 'N DRUM   **Phone:** 860/927-3509
(AAA) [SAVE]   Fri-Sun 5/1-10/31 & 4/1-4/30 1P: $110   2P/1B: $110   2P/2B: $110   XP: $13
Mon-Thurs 5/1-10/31, Fri-Sun
◆◆◆   11/1-3/31 & Mon-Thurs
Motor Inn   4/1-4/30   1P: $95   2P/1B: $95   2P/2B: $95   XP: $13
Mon-Thurs 11/1-3/31   1P: $85   2P/1B: $85   2P/2B: $85   XP: $13
Location: 0.3 mi n on US 7. 53 N Main St (US 7) 06757. **Fax:** 860/927-4595. **Terms:** Reserv deposit, 10 day notice;
handling fee imposed. **Facility:** 8 rooms. Rooms furnished with some antiques. Closed Tues by prior arrangement.
Railroad tracks behind the inn. 2 stories; interior/exterior corridors; designated smoking area. **Dining:** Restaurant, see
separate listing. **Services:** giftshop. **All Rooms:** combo or shower baths, extended cable TV. **Cards:** AE, MC, VI.
                                                                                            📶 💻 🖨 ⊠

RESTAURANTS

BULL'S BRIDGE INN   **Dinner:** $11-$22   Phone: 860/927-1617
(AAA)   **Location:** 4 mi s. 333 US 7 06757. **Hours:** 5 pm-9:30 pm, Fri & Sat-10 pm, Sun 4 pm-9 pm. Closed: 11/25
◆◆   & 12/25. **Features:** casual dress; early bird specials; carryout; salad bar; cocktails & lounge. Seasonal cozy
Continental   fireplace dining or porch dining. **Cards:** AE, DS, MC, VI.   ⊠

FIFE 'N DRUM   **Lunch:** $5-$9   **Dinner:** $14-$23   Phone: 860/927-3509
(AAA)   **Location:** 0.3 mi n on US 7; in Fife 'n Drum. 53 N Main St (US 7) 06757. **Hours:** 11:30 am-3 & 5:30-9:30
◆◆   pm, Fri-10 pm, Sat-10:30 pm, Sun 3 pm-9 pm. Closed: 12/25 & Tues. **Reservations:** suggested.
Continental   **Features:** casual dress; Sunday brunch; carryout; cocktails & lounge; entertainment; a la carte. Warm tavern
atmosphere. Sun brunch 11:30 am-3 pm. Piano concert every evening by owner. A 25-year tradition.
Cards: AE, MC, VI.   ⊠

LAKEVILLE—1,900

LODGINGS

INN AT IRON MASTERS   **Phone:** (860)435-9844
(AAA) [SAVE]   5/1-10/31 & 4/1-4/30 [CP]   1P: $85- 125   2P/1B: $95- 135 2P/2B: $95- 135 XP: $15-25   F12
11/1-3/31 [CP]   1P: $75- 85   2P/1B: $85- 95 2P/2B: $85- 95 XP: $15-25   F12
◆◆◆   **Location:** 0.5 mi ne on US 44 & SR 41. 229 Main St 06039 (PO Box 690). Fax: 860/435-2254. **Terms:** Pets,
Motor Inn   in limited rooms. **Facility:** 27 rooms. 1 story; exterior corridors. **Dining:** Cocktails. **All Rooms:** extended
cable TV. **Cards:** AE, MC, VI. **Special Amenities:** Free breakfast and preferred room (subject to
availability with advanced reservations).   🐾 🛄 🛢 🖵 🔒 ⊠

INTERLAKEN INN RESORT AND CONFERENCE CENTER   Guaranteed Rates   **Phone:** (860)435-9878
◆◆◆   Fri & Sat 5/1-10/31   1P: $149- 189   2P/1B: $149- 189 2P/2B: $149- 189
Complex   Sun-Thurs 5/1-10/31   1P: $119- 129   2P/1B: $119- 129 2P/2B: $119- 129 XP: $10   F17
11/1-4/30   1P: $109   2P/1B: $109   2P/2B: $109   XP: $10   F17
Location: On SR 112, 0.5 mi w of jct SR 41. 74 Interlaken Rd 06039 (RFD Rt 112). Fax: 860/435-2980. **Terms:** Reserv
deposit, 7 day notice; 2 night min stay, weekends 5/1-10/31. **Facility:** 82 rooms. Varied room styles & configurations, most are
large & offer patio or balcony. 7 one-bedroom townhouse suites with fireplace & kitchen, $272; 11/1-4/30, $180; 2 stories; interior corridors; heated pool; racquetball court, 2 tennis courts; boat dock. **Services:** giftshop. Fee: massage.
Recreation: swimming, boating, canoeing, fishing, paddleboats; bicycles, hiking trails. **Cards:** AE, MC, VI.
                                        🐾 🚵 🛄 🍴 △ ⊠ ➕ [VCR] 💻 🖨 🔒 ⊠ 🏌

LEDYARD—15,000

LODGINGS

GRAND PEQUOT TOWER   **Phone:** (860)312-3000
(AAA) [SAVE]   6/25-9/5   1P: $280   2P/1B: $280   2P/2B: $280
5/1-6/24, 9/6-11/27 &
[FYI]   3/30-4/30   1P: $240   2P/1B: $240   2P/2B: $240
11/28-3/29   1P: $195   2P/1B: $195   2P/2B: $195
Hotel   Too new to rate. **Location:** On SR 2 at jct SR 214. Rt 2 06339 (PO Box 3777). Fax: 860/312-7474.
Facility: 825 rooms. 19 stories; interior corridors; heated indoor pool, saunas, steamrooms, whirlpools.
Dining: 5 restaurants, 4 cafeterias, 2 coffee shops, deli; 24 hrs; $10-$25; health conscious menu items; cocktails.
Services: giftshop. Fee: massage. **All Rooms:** extended cable TV. **Some Rooms:** whirlpools. **Cards:** AE, DI, DS, MC, VI.
Special Amenities: Free local telephone calls and free newspaper.
                        🌊 🚴 🚵 🍴 🍸 🎿 🎣 🚤 △ ➕ [VCR] 💻 🖨 🔒 🅾 ⚙ ⊠ 🏌

EXPERIENCE THE WONDER OF FOXWOODS.

Nestled in the beautiful New England countryside, you'll find the world's favorite casino. Foxwoods Resort Casino, now even more breathtaking than ever. Inside our magnificent new Grand Pequot Tower, you'll find a world class hotel, with 800 luxurious rooms and suites. With gourmet restaurants, and more table games, slot machines and chances to win.

Our new hotel is the perfect complement to our 312-room AAA rated four diamond Great Cedar Hotel, and our quaint Two Trees Inn, with 280 charming rooms.

Foxwoods is fine dining with 24 fabulous restaurants. And room service is available 24 hours a day, for your convenience. Foxwoods is five different gaming environments, with over

5,750 Slot Machines, Blackjack, Craps, Roulette and Baccarat,including a Smoke-Free casino.

Foxwoods is High Stakes Bingo, Keno, a Poker Room and the Ultimate Race Book.

Foxwoods is entertainment. With stars like Diana Ross, Julio Iglesias, Paul Anka and Bill Cosby. It's two challenging golf courses. It's Championship Boxing. It's Cinetropolis, with the 1,500-seat Fox Theater. It's a Turbo Ride, Cinedrome, and our Dance Club. With its Hotels, Restaurants, Gaming and Entertainment, it's no wonder that Foxwoods has become the hottest entertainment destination in the country.

FOXWOODS
RESORT · CASINO

EXPERIENCE THE WONDER OF THE CONNECTICUT WOODS.
Call 1-800-PLAY-BIG. Conveniently located in Mashantucket. Exit 92 off I-95 in southeastern CT.
Visit our website at www.foxwoods.com

Mashantucket Pequot Tribal Nation

GREAT CEDAR HOTEL
Phone: (860)312-3000

(AAA) (SAVE)

◆◆◆◆

Hotel

	6/25-9/5 5/1-6/24, 9/6-11/27 &	1P: $245	2P/1B: $245	2P/2B: $245
	4/1-4/30	1P: $210	2P/1B: $210	2P/2B: $210
	11/28-3/31	1P: $170	2P/1B: $170	2P/2B: $170

Location: On SR 2, at jct SR 214. SR 2 06339. Fax: 860/312-4040. **Terms:** Package plans. **Facility:** 312 rooms. Striking modern resort decorated with Native American artifacts has extensive casino & entertainment facilities. Bright, inviting very comfortably furnished rooms & suites. 11 two-bedroom units. 8 stories; interior corridors; heated indoor pool, saunas, whirlpools. **Dining:** 5 restaurants, 4 cafeterias, 2 coffee shops, deli; 24 hours; $10-$25; health conscious menu items; cocktails. **Services:** giftshop. Fee: massage. **Recreation:** salon. **All Rooms:** extended cable TV. **Some Rooms:** whirlpools. **Cards:** AE, DI, DS, MC, VI. **Special Amenities:** Free local telephone calls and free newspaper. (See color ad p 235)

THE MARE'S INN B & B
Phone: 860/572-7556

◆◆

Bed & Breakfast

Rates Subject to Change

	Fri & Sat	1P: $125- 175	2P/1B: $125- 175	2P/2B: $125- 175
	Sun-Thurs	1P: $95- 125	2P/1B: $95- 125	2P/2B: $95- 125

Location: I-95 exit 89, 1 mi n to Gold Star Hwy, 0.6 mi w then 0.7 mi n. 333 Colonel Ledyard Hwy 06372. Fax: 860/572-2976. **Terms:** Age restrictions may apply; reserv deposit, 14 day notice; handling fee imposed; 2 night min stay, weekends in season. **Facility:** 5 rooms. Country Cape style home on well kept grounds in quiet rural location. Comfortable rooms are individually furnished. 2 stories; interior corridors; smoke free premises. **Some Rooms:** kitchen. **Cards:** AE, DS, MC, VI.

TWO TREES INN AT FOXWOODS
Phone: (860)312-3000

(AAA) (SAVE)

◆◆◆

Motor Inn

	6/25-9/5 5/1-6/24, 9/6-11/27 &	1P: $195	2P/1B: $195	2P/2B: $195
	3/26-4/30	1P: $160	2P/1B: $160	2P/2B: $160
	11/28-3/25	1P: $135	2P/1B: $135	2P/2B: $135

Location: On SR 214; just sw of jct SR 2. Adjacent to Foxwoods Resort Casino. 240 Lantern Hill Rd 06339. Fax: 860/312-4050. **Terms:** Handling fee imposed; package plans. **Facility:** 280 rooms. Very inviting country inn ambiance. Rooms & 60 one-bedroom suites. Rates for up to 4 persons. Suites, $165-$220; 3 stories; interior corridors; heated indoor pool, whirlpool. **Dining:** Restaurant; 6:30 am-11 pm, Fri & Sat-midnight; $9-$15; cocktails. **Services:** giftshop; area transportation, casino. **Recreation:** facilities of Foxwoods Resort Casino avail to guests. **All Rooms:** extended cable TV. **Cards:** AE, DI, DS, MC, VI. **Special Amenities:** Free local telephone calls and free newspaper. (See color ad p 235)

LITCHFIELD—8,400

LODGING

LITCHFIELD INN
Phone: (860)567-4503

(AAA) (SAVE)

◆◆

Country Inn

All Year [CP]   1P: $100- 180   2P/1B: $110- 190   2P/2B: $110- 190   XP: $10   F15
Location: 1.5 mi w on SR 202. 432 Bantam Rd 06759. Fax: 860/567-5358. **Terms:** Reserv deposit, 3 day notice; package plans. **Facility:** 32 rooms. Theme rooms avail; 2 stories; interior corridors. **Dining:** Restaurant; 11:30-9:30 pm, Fri & Sat-10 pm; $12-$21; cocktails. **Cards:** AE, DI, MC, VI. **Special Amenities:** Free breakfast and free local telephone calls.

MANCHESTER—See Hartford p. 228.

MANSFIELD DEPOT—400

RESTAURANT

THE DEPOT RESTAURANT
Lunch: $4-$9   **Dinner:** $9-$24   **Phone:** 860/429-3663

◆◆

American

Location: On US 44, 0.5 mi w of jct SR 32. 57 Middle Tpk (Rt 44) 06251. **Hours:** 11:30 am-11 pm, Fri & Sat to midnight, Sun 11 am-11 pm. Closed: 12/24 & 12/25. **Reservations:** suggested. **Features:** casual dress; Sunday brunch; children's menu; senior's menu; carryout; cocktails & lounge; a la carte. Converted railroad station, excellent dessert. **Cards:** AE, DI, MC, VI.

MERIDEN—59,500

LODGINGS

RAMADA PLAZA HOTEL
Phone: (203)238-2380

(AAA) (SAVE)

◆◆◆

Hotel

All Year   1P: $89- 129   2P/1B: $89- 129   2P/2B: $89- 129   XP: $10   F18
Location: I-91 exit 17 southbound, exit 16 northbound, 0.5 mi e, then s. 275 Research Pkwy 06450. Fax: 203/238-3172. **Terms:** Weekly rates; small pets only. **Facility:** 150 rooms. 6 stories; interior corridors; heated indoor pool, sauna. **Dining:** Dining room; 6:30 am-11 pm; $8-$18; cocktails. **Services:** area transportation, within 12 mi. **All Rooms:** extended cable TV. **Cards:** AE, CB, DI, DS, JC, MC, VI. **Special Amenities:** Free breakfast and free local telephone calls. (See color ad inside front cover)

RESIDENCE INN BY MARRIOTT
Phone: 203/634-7770

◆◆◆

Suite Motel

Rates Subject to Change

All Year [CP]   1P: $79- 129   2P/1B: $79- 129   2P/2B: $99- 149
Location: From I-91 northbound exit 16, southbound exit 17, just e. 390 Bee St 06450. Fax: 203/238-4081. **Terms:** Reserv deposit. **Facility:** 106 rooms. 25 two-bedroom units. Some rooms with fireplace; 3 stories; interior/exterior corridors; heated pool. **Recreation:** sports court. **All Rooms:** kitchens. **Cards:** AE, DI, DS, MC, VI.

RESTAURANT

AMERICAN STEAK HOUSE
Lunch: $4-$6   **Dinner:** $5-$9   **Phone:** 203/634-9994

◆

American

Location: 0.3 mi e on Main St from I-91, exit 16; 0.5 mi e on Main St from I-91, exit 17. 1170 E Main St 06457. **Hours:** 11 am-9 pm, Fri & Sat-10 pm. Closed: 11/25 & 12/25. **Features:** casual dress; cafeteria, buffet. Cafeteria style family dining. **Cards:** MC, VI.

MIDDLEFIELD—See Hartford p. 228.

MILFORD—51,000   (See map p. 245; index p. 243)

LODGINGS

HAMPTON INN   Phone: (203)874-4400   **12**
⚫ SAVE   All Year [CP]   1P: $75- 89 2P/1B: $85- 99 2P/2B: $85- 99
◆◆◆   **Location:** I-95 exit 36. 129 Plains Rd 06460. Fax: 203/874-5348. **Facility:** 148 rooms. Traditional rooms with
Motel   pleasant decor. 3 stories; interior corridors. **Cards:** AE, DI, DS, MC, VI. **Special Amenities: Free breakfast
           and free local telephone calls.**

HOWARD JOHNSON LODGE   Rates Subject to Change   Phone: 203/878-4611   **10**
◆◆   All Year   1P: $45- 85 2P/1B: $50- 90 2P/2B: $50- 90 XP: $10   F18
Motor Inn **Location:** On US 1 at I-95, exit 39A. 1052 Boston Post Rd 06460. Fax: 203/877-6224. **Facility:** 165 rooms.
           Some rooms with balcony or patio. 4 stories; interior/exterior corridors; heated indoor pool; playground.
Fee: miniature golf. **Cards:** AE, CB, DI, DS, MC, VI.

RED ROOF INN   Rates Subject to Change   Phone: (203)877-6060   **15**
◆◆   5/1-11/15   1P: $56- 76 2P/1B: $61- 81 2P/2B: $66- 86 XP: $7   F18
Motel   4/1-4/30   1P: $56- 76 2P/1B: $61- 81 2P/2B: $66- 81 XP: $7   F18
           11/16-3/31   1P: $46- 66 2P/1B: $51- 71 2P/2B: $56- 71 XP: $7   F18
Location: Just nw of I-95, exit 35. 10 Rowe Ave 06460. Fax: 203/874-3287. **Facility:** 110 rooms. 3 stories; exterior corridors.
All Rooms: combo or shower baths. **Cards:** AE, CB, DI, DS, MC, VI.

RESTAURANTS

THE GATHERING   **Lunch:** $9-$12   **Dinner:** $12-$19   Phone: 203/878-6537   **5**
◆◆   **Location:** On US 1, 0.3 mi w of I-95, exit 39A. 989 Boston Post Rd 06460. **Hours:** noon-3 & 4:30-9 pm,
American   Fri-10 pm, Sat noon-3 & 4-10 pm, Sun noon-8 pm. Closed: 12/25. **Reservations:** suggested.
           Features: casual dress; children's menu; early bird specials; salad bar; cocktails & lounge; a la carte.
Informal atmosphere. Menu features beef, chicken & fresh fish. **Cards:** AE, MC, VI.

GUSTO'S RESTAURANT   **Lunch:** $6-$11   **Dinner:** $10-$20   Phone: 203/876-7464   **8**
◆◆   **Location:** I-95, exit 36; just s on Plains Rd. 255 Boston Post Rd 06460. **Hours:** 11:30 am-10 pm, Fri-11 pm,
Italian   Sat 4 pm-11 pm, Sun 1 pm-10 pm. Closed: 12/25. **Reservations:** accepted. **Features:** casual dress; early
           bird specials; carryout; cocktails. Lively atmosphere with creative Italian cuisine. **Cards:** AE, CB, DI, DS, MC,
VI.

SCRIBNER'S   **Lunch:** $5-$9   **Dinner:** $14-$24   Phone: 203/878-7019   **6**
⚫   **Location:** I-95 exit 41, 2.3 mi s; via e on Marsh Hill Rd, s on Merwin Ave, e on Chapel St, then just s via
           Kings. 31 Village Rd 06460. **Hours:** 11:30 am-2:30 & 5-9:30 pm, Fri-10:30 pm, Sat 5 pm-10:30 pm, Sun 5
◆◆   pm-9 pm. Closed major holidays. **Reservations:** suggested. **Features:** casual dress; early bird specials;
Seafood   cocktails. Creative menu. Nautical atmosphere. Smoke free premises. **Cards:** AE, MC, VI.

MILLDALE—800

LODGING

DAYS INN   Rates Subject to Change   Phone: (860)621-9181
◆◆   5/1-9/30 [CP]   1P: $65- 99 2P/1B: $65- 99 2P/2B: $75- 149 XP: $10   F12
Motel   10/1-4/30 [CP]   1P: $40- 65 2P/1B: $40- 65 2P/2B: $50- 80 XP: $10   F12
Terms: Reserv deposit. **Facility:** 60 rooms. 2 whirlpool rms, $80; 3 stories; interior corridors. **Some Rooms:** efficiency.
Cards: AE, CB, DI, DS, MC, VI.

MORRIS—2,000

RESTAURANT

DEER ISLAND GATE RESTAURANT   **Dinner:** $13-$21   Phone: 860/567-4622
⚫   **Location:** 3 mi n on SR 209. 174 Bantam Lake Rd 06763. **Hours:** 5 pm-9 pm, Sun 1 pm-7 pm. Closed:
           Mon, Tues, 12/24, 12/25, also Wed & Thurs 1/2-1/31; 2/1-2/28. **Reservations:** suggested. **Features:** casual
◆   dress; Sunday brunch; early bird specials; cocktails; a la carte. Casual, family atmosphere overlooking
German   Bantam Lake. Sunday German buffet 1 pm-7 pm with piano music. **Cards:** MC, VI.

MYSTIC—2,600

LODGINGS

THE ADAMS HOUSE   Guaranteed Rates   Phone: 860/572-9551
◆◆   All Year [BP]   1P: $85- 145 2P/1B: $95- 175 2P/2B: $95- 175 XP: $25   F3
Historic Bed **Location:** 0.5 mi n of jct I-95 exit 89. 382 Cow Hill Rd 06355. **Terms:** Reserv deposit, 7 day notice; handling
& Breakfast   fee imposed; 2 night min stay, weekends in season. **Facility:** 7 rooms. Restored 1749 colonial home has cozy
           rooms with period furnishings in the main house, 2 rooms with fireplace. Cottage suite with sauna & kitchen-
           ette, $125-$175; 2 stories; interior/exterior corridors; smoke free premises. **All Rooms:** combo or shower baths.
Some Rooms: color TV. **Cards:** MC, VI.

BEST WESTERN SOVEREIGN HOTEL-MYSTIC

| | | Guaranteed Rates | | Phone: (860)536-4281 |

AAA

◆◆◆

Motor Inn

6/1-10/31	1P: $70- 140	2P/1B: $70- 140	2P/2B: $70- 140	XP: $10	F18
5/1-5/31	1P: $50- 75	2P/1B: $50- 75	2P/2B: $50- 75	XP: $10	F18
11/1-4/30	1P: $55- 70	2P/1B: $55- 70	2P/2B: $55- 70	XP: $10	F18

Location: On SR 27, Just n of jct I-95, exit 90. 9 Whitehall Ave 06355. Fax: 860/536-4802. **Terms:** Reserv deposit. **Facility:** 150 rooms. 2 stories; interior corridors; heated indoor pool, sauna; playground. **Dining:** Restaurant; Comedy club Fri & Sat; 6:30 am-10:30 & 5-9 pm, Fri & Sat-10:30 pm, Sat & Sun from 7 am-11 am; $8-$16; cocktails. **Services:** Fee: area transportation, Mystic trolly & casino. **All Rooms:** extended cable TV. **Some Rooms:** whirlpools. **Cards:** AE, CB, DI, DS, MC, VI.

COMFORT INN OF MYSTIC

Phone: (860)572-8531

AAA SAVE

◆◆◆

Motel

All Year [CP]   1P: $49- 159   2P/1B: $49- 159   2P/2B: $49- 159   XP: $5-25

Location: I-95 exit 90, just n, on SR 27. 48 Whitehall Ave 06355. Fax: 860/572-9358. **Facility:** 120 rooms. 2 stories; interior corridors. **Dining:** Restaurant nearby. **Services:** Fee: area transportation, casino. **All Rooms:** extended cable TV. **Cards:** AE, DI, DS, JC, MC, VI. **Special Amenities: Free breakfast and free local telephone calls.** *(See ad below)*

DAYS INN OF MYSTIC

Phone: (860)572-0574

AAA SAVE

◆◆◆

Motor Inn

All Year [CP]   1P: $49- 159   2P/1B: $49- 159   2P/2B: $49- 159   XP: $5-25   F

Location: Just n of I-95, exit 90. 55 Whitehall Ave (SR 27) 06355. Fax: 860/572-1164. **Facility:** 122 rooms. 2 stories; interior corridors; playground. **Dining:** Restaurant; 6 am-2 & 5-9 pm, Fri & Sat-10 pm; $9-$12; wine/beer only. **Services:** Fee: area transportation, to Foxwoods casino. **All Rooms:** extended cable TV. **Some Rooms:** whirlpools. **Cards:** AE, DI, DS, JC, MC, VI. **Special Amenities: Free local telephone calls and preferred room (subject to availability with advanced reservations).** *(See ad below)*

THE INN AT MYSTIC

| | | Rates Subject to Change | | Phone: (860)536-9604 |

AAA

◆◆◆

Motor Inn

8/27-10/23	1P: $125- 265	2P/1B: $125- 265	2P/2B: $125- 265	XP: $10	F18
5/14-6/17	1P: $115- 265	2P/1B: $115- 265	2P/2B: $115- 265	XP: $10	F18
6/18-8/26	1P: $140- 265	2P/1B: $140- 625	2P/2B: $104- 175	XP: $10	F18
5/1-5/13 & 10/24-4/30	1P: $90- 235	2P/1B: $90- 235	2P/2B: $85- 135	XP: $10	F18

Location: On US 1 at jct SR 27. 3 Williams Ave 06355 (PO Box 216). Fax: 860/572-1635. **Terms:** Reserv deposit; MAP avail; package plans; 2 night min stay, weekends. **Facility:** 67 rooms. On 15 landscaped acres overlooking the water. Charming rooms, few with patio or balcony. Also, 9 rooms in 1904 mansion & gatehouse building. 17 whirlpool & fireplace rms $150-$250; $135-$235 off season. 2 night min stay in luxury rms; 1-2 stories; interior/exterior corridors; heated pool, whirlpool; 1 tennis court. **Dining:** Flood Tide Restaurant, see separate listing. **Services:** Fee: area transportation, Mystic trolly stop. **Recreation:** boating, canoeing, fishing. **All Rooms:** extended cable TV. **Cards:** AE, DI, DS, MC, VI. *(See ad p 239)*

RESIDENCE INN BY MARRIOTT
Phone: (860)536-5150

(AAA) (SAVE)

◆◆◆
Apartment

	5/16-9/5 [CP]	1P: $169- 199	2P/1B: $169- 199
	5/1-5/15 & 9/6-10/30 [CP]	1P: $139- 199	2P/1B: $139- 199
	10/31-4/30 [CP]	1P: $119- 199	2P/1B: $119- 199

Location: On SR 27, just n of I-95 exit 90. 40 Whitehall Ave 06355. Fax: 860/572-4724. **Terms:** Weekly/monthly rates; 2 night min stay, weekends in season. **Facility:** 128 rooms. 18 two-bedroom suites, $179-$325; 3 stories; interior corridors; heated indoor pool, whirlpool. **Services:** Fee: area transportation, casino. **Recreation:** sports court, weekly barbecue. **All Rooms:** combo or shower baths, extended cable TV. **Some Rooms:** 110 efficiencies, 18 kitchens, whirlpools. **Cards:** AE, CB, DI, DS, JC, MC, VI. **Special Amenities:** Free breakfast and free newspaper.

SEAPORT MOTOR INN
Phone: 860/536-2621

(AAA)

◆◆
Motor Inn

Rates Subject to Change

	6/25-9/5	1P: $98- 128	2P/1B: $98- 128	2P/2B: $98- 128	XP: $10
	5/1-6/24	1P: $48- 118	2P/1B: $48- 118	2P/2B: $48- 118	XP: $10
	9/6-10/30	1P: $58- 118	2P/1B: $58- 118	2P/2B: $58- 118	XP: $10
	10/31-4/30	1P: $42- 75	2P/1B: $42- 75	2P/2B: $42- 75	XP: $10

Location: Just s on SR 27 from jct I-95 exit 90; then e. Opposite the Mystic Marinelife Aquarium. Coogan Blvd 06355 (PO Box 135). Fax: 860/536-4493. **Terms:** Reserv deposit. **Facility:** 118 rooms. 4 two-bedroom units. 2 stories; exterior corridors. **Dining:** Jamms Restaurant, see separate listing. **All Rooms:** extended cable TV. **Cards:** AE, DS, MC, VI. *(See color ad p 240)*

SIX BROADWAY INN   Rates Subject to Change   **Phone:** 860/536-6010
◆◆◆   5/1-10/31 [BP]   2P/1B: $150- 225   XP: $25
Bed &   11/1-1/2 [BP]   2P/1B: $130- 195   XP: $25
Breakfast   1/3-4/30 [CP]   2P/1B: $90- 190   XP: $25
    Location: 0.3 mi w on US 1, from jct SR 27, then just n. 6 Broadway Ave 06355. Fax: 860/536-6010.
Terms: Age restrictions may apply; reserv deposit, 7 day notice; handling fee imposed. **Facility:** 5 rooms. 2 stories; interior corridors; smoke free premises. **Services:** area transportation. **All Rooms:** combo or shower baths. **Cards:** AE, DS, MC, VI.

STEAMBOAT INN
◆◆◆
Bed &
Breakfast

Rates Subject to Change

Phone: (860)536-8300

5/21-9/12		2P/1B:	$180- 275	2P/2B:	$180- 225	XP:	$35	F15
9/13-11/28		2P/1B:	$165- 275	2P/2B:	$165- 205	XP:	$35	F15
5/1-5/20 & 3/3-4/30		2P/1B:	$130- 225	2P/2B:	$130- 170	XP:	$35	F15
11/29-3/2		2P/1B:	$110- 195	2P/2B:	$110- 150	XP:	$35	F15

Location: In center along wharf, on US 1. 73 Steamboat Wharf 06355. **Fax:** 860/536-9528. **Terms:** Reserv deposit, 5 day notice; 2 night min stay, weekends. **Facility:** 10 rooms. Most units with water view. 2 stories; interior/exterior corridors; smoke free premises. **Cards:** AE, DS, MC, VI. *(See color ad below)*

TABER INNE & SUITES
(AAA) [SAVE]
◆◆◆
Motel

Phone: 860/536-4904

5/1-10/31	1P:	$95- 185	2P/1B:	$95- 210	2P/2B:	$110- 210	XP: $15	D12
11/1-4/30	1P:	$65- 150	2P/1B:	$85- 185	2P/2B:	$95- 210	XP: $15	D12

Location: On US 1, 0.4 mi e of jct SR 27. 66 Williams Ave 06355. **Fax:** 860/572-9140. **Terms:** Reserv deposit, 3 day notice; handling fee imposed; 2 night min stay, weekends 5/1-10/31. **Facility:** 26 rooms. Inviting motel with rooms ranging from standard to 2-bedroom townhouse. 2-bedroom water view townhouse with fireplace & whirlpool, $295-$325; $265-310 off season; 1-2 stories; exterior corridors. **Dining:** Restaurant nearby. **All Rooms:** extended cable TV. **Some Rooms:** whirlpools. **Cards:** AE, MC, VI. *(See ad below)*

WHALER'S INN
◆◆◆
Motel

Rates Subject to Change

Phone: 860/536-1506

5/8-9/6		2P/1B:	$109- 145	2P/2B:	$119- 135	XP:	$10	F15
9/7-11/28		2P/1B:	$89- 139	2P/2B:	$109- 125	XP:	$10	F15
5/1-5/7 & 3/27-4/30		2P/1B:	$85- 129	2P/2B:	$103- 119	XP:	$10	F15
11/29-3/26		2P/1B:	$69- 105	2P/2B:	$79- 95	XP:	$10	F15

Location: On US 1, 0.5 mi w of jct SR 27. 20 E Main St 06355. **Fax:** 860/572-1250. **Terms:** Reserv deposit, 4 day notice; 2 night min stay, weekends in season. **Facility:** 41 rooms. Large suite, $125-$210; 2-3 stories, no elevator; interior/exterior corridors. **All Rooms:** combo or shower baths. **Cards:** AE, MC, VI. *(See color ad below)*

WHITEHALL MANSION
◆◆◆
Historic Bed
& Breakfast

	Rates Subject to Change		
7/1-9/2 [CP]	1P: $179- 250	2P/1B: $179- 250	
5/1-6/30, 9/3-12/31 &			
4/1-4/30 [CP]	1P: $119- 250	2P/1B: $119- 250	
1/1-3/31 [CP]	1P: $79- 169	2P/1B: $79- 169	

Phone: 860/572-7280

Location: On SR 27, just n of jct I-95 exit 90. 42 Whitehall Ave 06355. **Fax:** 860/572-9358. **Facility:** 5 rooms. Built in 1771. Beautifully restored, all rooms have antique period furnishings, fireplace & modern bath. Interior corridors; smoke free premises. **Services:** Fee: area transportation. **Cards:** AE, CB, DI, DS, MC, VI.

RESTAURANTS

BRAVO BRAVO
◆◆◆
Nouvelle Italian
Lunch: $6-$12   **Dinner:** $12-$23   **Phone:** 860/536-3228
Location: On US 1, 0.5 mi w of jct SR 27; in Whaler's Inn. 20 E Main St 06355. **Hours:** 11:30 am-2:30 & 5-9 pm, Fri & Sat-10 pm, Sun 5 pm-9 pm. Closed major holidays & Mon. **Reservations:** suggested. **Features:** dressy casual; carryout; cocktails; street parking. Bistro atmosphere. Outside terrace dining, in season. Smoke free premises. **Cards:** AE, DI, DS, MC, VI.

CAPTAIN DANIEL PACKER INNE
◆◆
American
Lunch: $6-$11   **Dinner:** $15-$22   **Phone:** 860/536-3555
Location: 0.7 mi e on SR 215, from jct US 1. 32 Water St 06355. **Hours:** 11 am-4 & 5-10 pm, Sun 11 am-10 pm. **Reservations:** suggested. **Features:** casual dress; children's menu; cocktails & lounge; a la carte. Restored 1754 inn with pub. **Cards:** AE, MC, VI.

FLOOD TIDE RESTAURANT
◆◆◆
Continental
Lunch: $7-$15   **Dinner:** $17-$30   **Phone:** 860/536-8140
Location: On US 1 at jct SR 27; in The Inn at Mystic. 06355. **Hours:** 7-10:30 am, 11:30-2 & 5:30-9:30 pm, Fri & Sat-10 pm. Closed for dinner. **Reservations:** suggested. **Features:** dressy casual; children's menu; cocktails & lounge; a la carte. Overlooking Mystic River. Inviting dining atmosphere. Sun brunch 11 am-2 pm. Afternoon tea 4 pm-5 pm. **Cards:** AE, DI, DS, MC, VI. *(See ad p 239)*

JAMMS RESTAURANT
◆◆
American
Lunch: $5-$9   **Dinner:** $12-$18   **Phone:** 860/536-2683
Location: Just s on SR 27 from jct I-95 exit 90, then e; in Seaport Motor Inn. Coogan Blvd 06355. **Hours:** 11:30 am-midnight; 8 am-10:30 & 11:30-midnight 5/1-10/31. Closed: 11/25, 12/24 & 12/25. **Features:** casual dress; children's menu; carryout; cocktails & lounge. Relaxing atmosphere. Menu features steak, fresh seafood & pasta. **Cards:** AE, DI, MC, VI.

SEAMEN'S INNE RESTAURANT AND PUB
◆◆◆
Regional
American
Lunch: $6-$10   **Dinner:** $14-$22   **Phone:** 860/572-5303
Location: On SR 27; 0.8 mi s of I-95, exit 90. 105 Greenmanville Ave 06355. **Hours:** 11 am-3 & 4:30-9 pm, Fri & Sat 11 am-10 pm. Closed: 12/24 for dinner & 12/25. **Reservations:** suggested. **Features:** children's menu; cocktails & lounge. Built as a replica of a sea captain's home. Pleasant dining featuring New England fare, Inne's specialties include roast prime rib, baked stuffed lobster & seafood pot pie. Famous Dixieland country breakfast buffet every Sunday 10:30 am-2. **Cards:** AE, DI, DS, MC, VI.

STEAK LOFT
◆◆
American
Lunch: $5-$12   **Dinner:** $12-$23   **Phone:** 860/536-2661
Location: Just s of I-95 exit 90. Olde Mistick Village 06355. **Hours:** 11:30 am-11 pm, Fri & Sat-midnight. Closed: 11/25, 12/24 & 12/25. **Features:** casual dress; children's menu; salad bar; cocktails & lounge. In New England farmhouse replica. **Cards:** AE, DI, DS, MC, VI.

NEW BRITAIN—See Hartford p. 228.

NEW CANAAN—17,900   (See map p. 212; index p. 211)

RESTAURANT

THE ROGER SHERMAN INN   Country Inn   **Lunch:** $11-$21   **Dinner:** $20-$32   **Phone:** 203/966-4541   20
◆◆◆
French
Location: 3 mi n of exit 37 of Merritt Pkwy on CR 124. 195 Oenoke Ridge 06840. **Hours:** noon-2 & 6-9:30 pm, Fri & Sat-10 pm, Sun 11:30 am-2 & 6-8 pm. Closed: 7/4 & 12/25. **Reservations:** suggested. **Features:** dressy casual; health conscious menu; cocktails & lounge; a la carte. Traditional dining room & terrace dining. Sun brunch 11:30 am-2 pm, $22.75. **Cards:** AE, DI, MC, VI.

NEW HAVEN
pop. 130,500

This index helps you "spot" where approved accommodations are located on the detailed maps that follow. Rate ranges are for comparison only and show the property's high season. Turn to the listing page for more detailed rate information and consult display ads for special promotions. Restaurant rate range is for dinner, unless only lunch (L) is served.

Spotter/Map Pg.Number	OA	NEW HAVEN - Lodgings	Rating	Rate	Listing Page
20 / p. 245		The Colony - see ad p 246	◆◆◆	$109	246
22 / p. 245		Holiday Inn at Yale - see color ad p 246	◆◆	$105	246
23 / p. 245		Residence Inn by Marriott	◆◆◆	$140-189	246
24 / p. 245	🌐	Quality Inn Conference Center	◆◆	$99-159 SAVE	246
/ p. 0		Grand Chalet Inn and Suites	◆◆	$79-99	246
		NEW HAVEN - Restaurants			
11 / p. 245		India Palace	◆◆	$7-10	247
13 / p. 245		Chavoya's	◆◆	$8-15	247

Nearby Accommodations

Spotter/Map Pg.Number	OA	BRANFORD - Lodgings	Rating	Rate	Listing Page
1 / p. 245		Ramada Limited - see color ad inside front cover	◆◆	$90-110	207
2 / p. 245	🌐	Days Inn & Conference Center	◆◆	$75-99 SAVE	206
3 / p. 245	🌐	MacDonald's Motel	◆◆	$45-75 SAVE	206
4 / p. 245	🌐	Advanced Motel	◆◆	$50-70 SAVE	206
6 / p. 245	🌐	Motel 6 - 1279	◆◆	$59	206
		BRANFORD - Restaurants			
1 / p. 245		USS Chowder Pot III	◆◆	$10-20	207
2 / p. 245		Cafe Belle Vita	◆◆◆	$15-20	207
4 / p. 245		Pasti Cosi	◆	$9-17	207
		MILFORD - Lodgings			
10 / p. 245		Howard Johnson Lodge	◆◆	$50-90	237
12 / p. 245	🌐	Hampton Inn	◆◆◆	$85-99 SAVE	237
15 / p. 245		Red Roof Inn	◆◆	$66-86	237
		MILFORD - Restaurants			
5 / p. 245		The Gathering	◆◆	$12-19	237
6 / p. 245	🌐	Scribner's	◆◆	$14-24	237
8 / p. 245		Gusto's Restaurant	◆◆	$10-20	237
		NORTH HAVEN - Lodgings			
30 / p. 245	🌐	Holiday Inn	◆◆◆	$79-109 SAVE	249
		WALLINGFORD - Lodgings			
34 / p. 245		Susse Chalet Inn - see ad p 223	◆◆	$68-74	257
35 / p. 245		Courtyard by Marriott - see color ad p 257	◆◆◆	$109	257
		WALLINGFORD - Restaurant			
16 / p. 245		Thaddeus J Peppercorn's Ltd	◆◆	$10-12	257
		WEST HAVEN - Lodgings			
38 / p. 245		Days Hotel New Haven/West Haven	◆◆	$89-125	259
		WEST HAVEN - Restaurants			
18 / p. 245		Jimmies	◆◆	$6-18	259
19 / p. 245		American Steak House	◆	$6-10	259
		HAMDEN - Lodgings			
40 / p. 245	🌐	Days Inn	◆◆	$70-80 SAVE	215
		HAMDEN - Restaurant			
23 / p. 245		J.B. Winberie Restaurant and Bar	◆◆	$7-10	215

Spotter/Map Pg.Number	OA	CHESHIRE - Lodgings	Rating	Rate	Listing Page
44 / p. 245	AAA	Cheshire Welcome Inn	◆◆	$60 SAVE	207
		SEYMOUR - Lodgings			
47 / p. 245		The Inn at Villa Bianca	◆◆	$95	253

Affordable Adventure

Make your next vacation an adventure - at a price that won't make paying the bill adventuresome. Travel consultants will help you plan a vacation that will meet all your needs. From a quiet getaway to a family gathering, AAA can arrange for the most economical or the most extravagant use of your vacation dollar. Come to your local AAA Travel Agency for the vacation adventure you can afford to enjoy.

Travel With Someone You Trust®

BUSY, BUSY, BUSY!
Restaurant listings note when reservations
are advised or required.

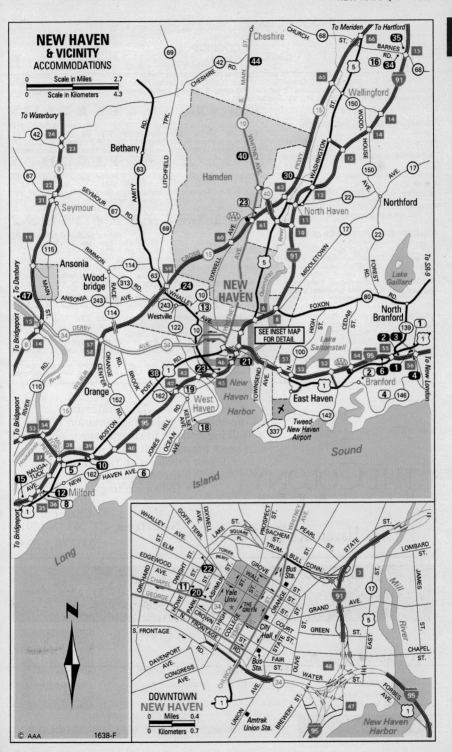

NEW HAVEN
& VICINITY
ACCOMMODATIONS

Scale in Miles 0 — 2.7
Scale in Kilometers 0 — 4.3

DOWNTOWN
NEW HAVEN

Miles 0 — 0.4
Kilometers 0 — 0.7

© AAA

1638-F

NEW HAVEN—130,500 (See map p. 245; index p. 243)

LODGINGS

THE COLONY — Rates Subject to Change — Phone: 203/776-1234 **20**
◆◆◆ All Year — 1P: $99 — 2P/1B: $109 — 2P/2B: $109 — XP: $10 — F12
Hotel — **Location:** Downtown; SR 34 exit 2, 0.3 mi w (N Frontage Rd), then 0.4 mi n (York St), just w; from I-95, exit 47; I-91, exit 1. 1157 Chapel St 06511. Fax: 203/772-3929. **Terms:** Reserv deposit. **Facility:** 86 rooms. Small intimate hotel with European ambiance. 2 two-bedroom units. 5 stories; interior corridors. Fee: parking. **Services:** area transportation. **Cards:** AE, CB, DI, MC, VI. *(See ad below)*

⟦ASK⟧ ⟦🔊⟧ ⟦📶⟧ ⟦3☞⟧ ⟦📶⟧ ⟦📺⟧ ⟦🍽⟧ ⟦❌⟧ ⟦🛄⟧ ⟦♿⟧ ⟦VCR⟧ ⟦🖥⟧ ⟦□⟧ ⟦🖨⟧ ⟦☎⟧ ⟦✖⟧

GRAND CHALET INN AND SUITES — Rates Subject to Change — Phone: (203)562-1111
◆◆ All Year — 1P: $79- 99 — 2P/1B: $79- 99 — 2P/2B: $79- 99 — XP: $10 — F17
Motel — **Location:** I-95 exit 46, northbound, 0.4 mi n, then just w. 400 Sargent Dr 06511 (PO Box 657, WILTON, NH, 03086). Fax: 203/865-7440. **Facility:** 153 rooms. 8 stories; interior corridors. **Services:** area transportation.
All Rooms: combo or shower baths. **Cards:** AE, CB, DI, DS, MC, VI. ⟦📶⟧ ⟦🛄⟧ ⟦❌⟧ ⟦🛄⟧ ⟦📶⟧ ⟦♿⟧ ⟦VCR⟧ ⟦□⟧ ⟦☎⟧ ⟦♿⟧ ⟦✖⟧

HOLIDAY INN AT YALE — Rates Subject to Change — Phone: 203/777-6221 **22**
◆◆ All Year — 1P: $105 — 2P/1B: $105 — 2P/2B: $105
Motor Inn — **Location:** Downtown; SR 34 exit 2, 0.5 mi w (N Frontage Rd), then 0.8 mi n (Howe); from I-95 exit 47; I-91, exit 1. 30 Whalley Ave 06511. Fax: 203/772-1089. **Facility:** 160 rooms. Attractive public areas, some covered parking. Rates for up to 4 persons; 8 stories; interior corridors. **Services:** area transportation. **Cards:** AE, CB, DI, DS, JC, MC, VI. *(See color ad below)* ⟦🔊⟧ ⟦📶⟧ ⟦3☞⟧ ⟦🛄⟧ ⟦📶⟧ ⟦🍽⟧ ⟦❌⟧ ⟦🛄⟧ ⟦📶⟧ ⟦📺⟧ ⟦VCR⟧ ⟦🖥⟧ ⟦□⟧ ⟦🖨⟧ ⟦☎⟧ ⟦✖⟧ ⟦📶⟧

QUALITY INN CONFERENCE CENTER — Phone: (203)387-6651 **24**
Ⓐ Ⓐ Ⓐ ⟦SAVE⟧ — 5/1-10/31 [CP] — 1P: $89- 149 — 2P/1B: $99- 159 — 2P/2B: $99- 159 — XP: $10 — F18
11/1-4/30 [CP] — 1P: $69- 129 — 2P/1B: $79- 139 — 2P/2B: $79- 139 — XP: $10 — F18
◆◆ **Location:** Just ne of jct SR 66 & 15 (Wilbur Cross Pkwy) exit 59. 100 Pond Lily Ave 06525.
Motel — Fax: 203/387-6651. **Terms:** Pets. **Facility:** 122 rooms. 1-2 stories; interior/exterior corridors; heated indoor pool, sauna, whirlpool. **Dining:** Restaurant nearby. **Services:** area transportation, downtown.
All Rooms: combo or shower baths, extended cable TV. **Some Rooms:** whirlpools. **Cards:** AE, CB, DI, DS, JC, MC, VI.
Special Amenities: Free breakfast and free local telephone calls. ⟦🔊⟧ ⟦🛏⟧ ⟦📶⟧ ⟦3☞⟧ ⟦🛄⟧ ⟦🍽⟧ ⟦❌⟧ ⟦🛄⟧ ⟦📶⟧ ⟦VCR⟧ ⟦🖥⟧ ⟦□⟧ ⟦🖨⟧ ⟦☎⟧ ⟦✖⟧

RESIDENCE INN BY MARRIOTT — Rates Subject to Change — Phone: 203/777-5337 **23**
◆◆◆ 5/1-12/5 & 2/16-4/30 [CP] — 1P: $140- 189 — 2P/1B: $140- 189 — 2P/2B: $140- 189
Apartment — 12/6-2/15 [CP] — 1P: $119- 159 — 2P/1B: $119- 159 — 2P/2B: $119- 159
Location: 0.6 mi nw of I-95, exit 46. 3 Long Wharf Dr 06511. Fax: 203/777-5337. **Facility:** 112 rooms. In cluster buildings, studio & 1-bedroom units; all with fireplace. 2 stories; exterior corridors. **Services:** area transportation.
Recreation: sports court. **All Rooms:** kitchens. **Cards:** AE, DI, DS, MC, VI. ⟦🛏⟧ ⟦📶⟧ ⟦3☞⟧ ⟦🛄⟧ ⟦❌⟧ ⟦🛄⟧ ⟦✖⟧ ⟦📶⟧ ⟦📺⟧ ⟦🖥⟧ ⟦□⟧ ⟦🖨⟧ ⟦☎⟧ ⟦✖⟧ ⟦📶⟧

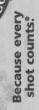

YOUR PICTURES...ON YOUR COMPUTER!

MYSTIC PC PHOTOS ON Kodak PhotoNet online

- See and work with your photos on your computer.
- No special software needed and no programs to install!
- Available from 35mm and APS 24mm color print film.
- Your choice of floppy disk, CD ROM or Internet delivery.

With Mystic PC Photos, you'll be up and running in no time. You don't need any special software. You still get all of your regular prints and negatives, plus you'll get your pictures digitized and delivered to you either on a 3 1/2" floppy disk, CD ROM or over the Internet. When you order Mystic PC Photos on floppy or CD ROM, you'll also get a convenient index print showing your entire roll of shots in thumbnail size.

Minimum System Requirements:

Floppy disk and Internet: 386 processor, 4MB of RAM, 16 bit operating system, 256 colors. Windows 3.1 or higher. Mac or Power Mac system 7.5.5 or higher, 4MB of RAM. Additional for Internet: Internet access and 28.8K modem.

CD ROM: CD ROM drive required, 486-33 MHz processor, 8MB of RAM, 16 bit operating system, 640 x 480 screen display. SVGA video card, 10MB free hard disk space plus additional 30MB hard drive space for film rolls. Windows 3.1 or higher. Limited capabilities for Mac and Power Mac.

(See map p. 245)

RESTAURANTS

CHAVOYA'S
◆◆
Mexican

Lunch: $4-$8   **Dinner:** $8-$15   **Phone:** 203/389-4730   ⑬
Location: On SR 63, 1.5 mi s of SR 15 (Merit Pkwy), exit 59. 883 Whalley Ave 06515. **Hours:** 11:30 am-2:30 & 5-10 pm, Fri & Sat-10:30 pm, Sun 4 pm-10 pm. Closed: 11/25, 12/24 & 12/25. **Features:** casual dress; children's menu; carryout; cocktails; a la carte. Cheerful atmosphere, parking in rear. **Cards:** AE, DS, MC, VI.
☒

INDIA PALACE
◆◆
Ethnic

Lunch: $5-$6   **Dinner:** $7-$10   **Phone:** 203/776-9010   ⑪
Location: W on N Frontage Rd, n on Howe St; SR 34, exit 3. 65 Howe St 06511. **Hours:** 11:30 am-10:30 pm. Closed: 12/25. **Reservations:** suggested. **Features:** casual dress; carryout; beer & wine only; a la carte. North Indian cuisine in casual atmosphere. Lunch buffet 11:30 am-3 pm $5.95. Parking in rear. **Cards:** DI, DS, MC, VI.
☒

NEWINGTON—See Hartford p. 229.

NEW LONDON—28,500

LODGINGS

HOLIDAY INN
🅰 SAVE
◆◆◆
Motor Inn

All Year   1P: $72- 144   2P/1B: $82- 154   2P/2B: $82- 154   XP: $10   F18
Phone: (860)442-0631
Location: I-95 northbound exit 82A, 0.8 mi n, then just w, then 0.6 mi s; southbound exit 83, 0.6 mi s. 380 Bayonet St 06320. Fax: 860/442-0130. **Terms:** Weekly/monthly rates. **Facility:** 136 rooms. Near many shopping centers. 2 stories; interior corridors. **Dining:** Restaurant; 6:30 am-10 pm, Sat & Sun from 7 am; $12-$20; cocktails. **Services:** area transportation, casinos. **All Rooms:** extended cable TV.
Some Rooms: whirlpools. **Cards:** AE, CB, DI, DS, JC, MC, VI. **Special Amenities:** Free newspaper.
🆑 🕭 ⌛ ➷ 🍽 🎾 💻 ▢ 🖨 🎁 ☒ 🕗

THE RADISSON HOTEL
◆◆
Hotel

Rates Subject to Change   **Phone:** 860/443-7000
7/1-10/31   1P: $99- 219   2P/1B: $109- 219   2P/2B: $149- 219   XP: $10   F18
5/1-6/30   1P: $99- 189   2P/1B: $109- 189   2P/2B: $129- 189   XP: $10   F18
11/1-4/30   1P: $69- 189   2P/1B: $79- 189   2P/2B: $119- 189   XP: $10   F18
Location: I-95 northbound exit 83, southbound exit 84, 0.5 mi s to downtown. 35 Governor Winthrop Blvd 06320. Fax: 860/443-1239. **Facility:** 120 rooms. 5 stories; interior corridors; heated indoor pool. **Services:** area transportation. **Cards:** AE, CB, DI, DS, MC, VI. *(See ad p 240)*
🕭 ⌛ ➷ 🍽 🍸 ➷ 🎾 💻 ▢ 🖨 🎁 ☒

RED ROOF INN
🅰 SAVE
◆◆
Motel

7/1-8/31   1P: $61- 81   2P/1B: $66- 86   2P/2B: $71- 91   XP: $10   F18
5/1-6/30 & 9/1-10/31   1P: $56- 76   2P/1B: $61- 81   2P/2B: $66- 86   XP: $10   F18
11/1-4/30   1P: $41- 61   2P/1B: $46- 66   2P/2B: $51- 71   XP: $10   F18
Phone: (860)444-0001
Location: I-95 northbound exit 82A, southbound 83, just n. 707 Colman St 06320. Fax: 860/443-7154. **Terms:** Weekly rates; pets. **Facility:** 108 rooms. Small to medium size rooms, moderately equipped. 2 stories; exterior corridors. **All Rooms:** extended cable TV. **Cards:** AE, CB, DI, DS, MC, VI. **Special Amenities:** Free local telephone calls.
🖭 🕭 🎾 🖨 ☒ 🕗

RESTAURANT

GRIDLOCK GRILLE
🅰
◆
American

Lunch: $4-$8   **Dinner:** $8-$16   **Phone:** 860/442-7146
Location: I-95, northbound exit 82A, southbound exit 83; 0.3 mi s on US 1. 566 Colman St 06320. **Hours:** 7:30 am-10 pm. Closed: 11/25 & 12/25. **Reservations:** accepted; 8 or more. **Features:** casual dress; children's menu; health conscious menu; carryout; salad bar; cocktails & lounge. Family atmosphere. Fresh seafood, live lobster, prime rib. **Cards:** AE, CB, DI, DS, MC, VI. *(See ad p 242)*
☒

NEW MILFORD—23,400

LODGINGS

THE HERITAGE INN OF LITCHFIELD COUNTY
🅰 SAVE
◆◆
Historic Bed
& Breakfast

All Year [BP]   1P: $75- 85   2P/1B: $85- 100   2P/2B: $90- 100   XP: $15   F6
Phone: (860)354-8883
Location: Center. 34 Bridge St 06776. Fax: 860/350-5543. **Terms:** Pets. **Facility:** 20 rooms. Converted 1800's tobacco warehouse. 2 stories; interior corridors. **All Rooms:** combo or shower baths. **Cards:** AE, DI, DS, MC, VI.
🆑 🐾 🖨

THE HOMESTEAD INN
🅰
◆◆◆
Historic Bed
& Breakfast

Rates Subject to Change   **Phone:** (860)354-4080
All Year [CP]   1P: $72- 95   2P/1B: $80- 105   2P/2B: $80- 105   XP: $10   D11
Location: In Village Center; 100 yds e of the green off Main St. 5 Elm St 06776. Fax: 860/354-7046. **Terms:** Reserv deposit; 2 night min stay, 5/1-10/31 weekends; dog on premises. **Facility:** 15 rooms. Victorian inn & 6 motel rooms. Inn was built in 1853. 3 stories; interior/exterior corridors; designated smoking area. **Dining:** Breakfast 6:30-9 am, Sat & Sun 8-10 am. **All Rooms:** combo or shower baths, extended cable TV. **Cards:** AE, CB, DI, DS, MC, VI.
🎁 ☒

RESTAURANTS

ADRIENNE-FINE AMERICAN DINING
◆◆◆
American

Dinner: $14-$25   **Phone:** 860/354-6001
Location: 1.5 mi n on US 7. 218 Kent Rd 06776. **Hours:** Open 5/1-2/15 & 3/7-4/30; 5:30 pm-10 pm, Sun 11:30 am-3:30 pm. Closed: Mon. **Reservations:** suggested. **Features:** casual dress; cocktails; a la carte. Sophisticated preparation of beef, game, seafood & duck served in a quiet atmosphere. Located in a 19th century home with fireplaces & plank floors. Dining room is entirely non-smoking on weekends. **Cards:** AE, DI, MC, VI.

THE BISTRO CAFE
◆◆
American

Lunch: $7-$10   **Dinner:** $13-$20   **Phone:** 860/355-3266
Location: Just w off town green. 31 Bank St 06776. **Hours:** 11 am-3 & 5:30-10 pm. Closed major holidays. **Reservations:** suggested. **Features:** casual dress; Sunday brunch; children's menu; carryout; cocktails; a la carte. Excellent food presentation. Lively bistro atmosphere. **Cards:** AE, MC, VI.
☒

THE COOKHOUSE
◆
American

Lunch: $9-$15   **Dinner:** $11-$25   **Phone:** 860/355-4111
Location: Just s on US 202/SR 7. 31 Danbury Rd 06776. **Hours:** Noon-10 pm, Fri & Sat-11 pm, Sun-9 pm, Mon 5 pm-10 pm. Closed major holidays. **Reservations:** suggested; 6 or more. **Features:** casual dress; Sunday brunch; children's menu; carryout; cocktails & lounge; a la carte. Authentic smoked barbecue chicken, pork, ribs, brisket, burgers, steak & seafood. Barn wood & rafters country ambiance. Pasta & daily fish specials also avail. **Cards:** AE, MC, VI.   [icons]

JOEY'S RESTAURANT
◆ ◆
Seafood

Dinner: $10-$24   **Phone:** 860/355-2255
Location: 1.8 mi s of jct of US 7 & 202. 188 Danbury Rd (US 7) 06776. **Hours:** 5 pm-9 pm, Fri-10 pm, Sat 5 pm-10 pm. Closed: 11/25, 12/25 & Mon. **Reservations:** suggested. **Features:** casual dress; a la carte. Seafood & pasta specialties with some chicken & steak entrees. **Cards:** AE, DI, MC, VI.   [X]

NIANTIC—3,000

LODGINGS

BEST WESTERN HILL TOP INN
◆ ◆ ◆
Motel

	Rates Subject to Change							**Phone:** 860/739-3951
Fri & Sat 5/16-10/31 [CP]			2P/1B:	$125- 140	2P/2B:	$125- 140	XP: $10	F17
Sun-Thurs 5/16-10/31 [CP]			2P/1B:	$89- 99	2P/2B:	$89- 99	XP: $10	F17
5/1-5/15 & 11/1-4/30 [CP]	1P:	$59	2P/1B:	$69	2P/2B:	$69	XP: $10	F17

Location: On US 161, 0.5 mi se of I-95, exit 74. 239 Flanders Rd 06357. **Fax:** 860/739-3517. **Terms:** Reserv deposit; 2 night min stay, Fri & Sat 5/16-10/22. **Facility:** 90 rooms. Attractive rooms. Hillside location. 2 stories; interior corridors. **Cards:** AE, CB, DI, DS, MC, VI. (See color ad p 238)   [icons]

DAYS INN
◆ ◆
Motel

	Rates Subject to Change						**Phone:** (860)739-6921
Fri & Sat 6/1-10/31	1P: $115	2P/1B:	$115	2P/2B:	$115	XP: $10	F17
Sun-Thurs 6/1-10/31	1P: $95	2P/1B:	$95	2P/2B:	$95	XP: $10	F17
Fri & Sat 5/1-5/31 & 11/1-4/30	1P: $70	2P/1B:	$70	2P/2B:	$70	XP: $10	F17
Sun-Thurs 5/1-5/31 & 11/1-4/30	1P: $55	2P/1B:	$55	2P/2B:	$55	XP: $10	F17

Location: On US 161, just se of I-95, exit 74. 265 Flanders Rd 06357. **Fax:** 860/739-9491. **Terms:** Reserv deposit, 7 day notice. **Facility:** 93 rooms. Hilltop location, convenient to shore. 2 stories; interior corridors. **Cards:** AE, CB, DI, DS, JC, MC, VI.   [icons]

THE INN AT HARBOR HILL MARINA
◆ ◆ ◆
Bed & Breakfast

	Rates Subject to Change						**Phone:** 860/739-0331
5/1-11/1 [CP]	1P: $140- 165	2P/1B:	$140- 165	2P/2B:	$140- 165		
11/2-4/30 [CP]	1P: $85- 125	2P/1B:	$85- 125	2P/2B:	$85- 125	XP: $10	

Fax: 860/691-3078. **Terms:** Age restrictions may apply; reserv deposit, 10 day notice; handling fee imposed; 2 night min stay, 5/1-10/31 weekends. **Facility:** 8 rooms. Overlooking the marina docks & picturesque Niantic river. All rooms with water view. 2 waterfront rms with balcony; 3 stories, no elevator; interior corridors; smoke free premises; marina. **Recreation:** fishing. **All Rooms:** shower baths. **Some Rooms:** color TV. **Cards:** AE, MC, VI.   [icons]

Location: From jct SR 156, just n on SR 161, then 0.3 mi e. 60 Grand St 06357 (PO Box 452).

RESTAURANT

CONSTANTINE'S RESTAURANT
[AAA]
◆ ◆
Steakhouse

Lunch: $4-$12   **Dinner:** $7-$18   **Phone:** 860/739-2848
Location: On SR 156, just w of jct SR 161. 252 Main St 06357. **Hours:** 11:30 am-9 pm, Fri & Sat-10 pm. Closed: 11/25, 12/25 & Mon. **Reservations:** required; 5 or more. **Features:** casual dress; children's menu; carryout; cocktails & lounge; a la carte. Family oriented popular establishment, since 1929. Extended summer hours. **Cards:** AE, DS, MC, VI.   [X]

NOANK—1,500

LODGING

THE PALMER INN
◆ ◆ ◆
Historic Bed & Breakfast

Guaranteed Rates   **Phone:** 860/572-9000
All Year [CP]   1P: $115- 175   2P/1B: $115- 225   2P/2B: $115- 195
Location: Town center, just w of Main St. 25 Church St 06340. **Terms:** Reserv deposit, 14 day notice; handling fee imposed; 2 night min stay, weekends. **Facility:** 6 rooms. Historic turn-of-the-century home graciously restored, in quiet village setting. Rooms are individually furnished with antiques & the owners personal touches. Advance reservation weekends; 3 stories, no elevator; interior corridors; smoke free premises. **All Rooms:** combo or shower baths. **Cards:** AE, DS, MC, VI. (See ad p 239)   [icons]

RESTAURANT

ABBOTT'S LOBSTER IN THE ROUGH
[AAA]
◆
Seafood

Lunch: $4-$20   **Dinner:** $4-$20   **Phone:** 860/536-7719
Location: On waterfront, 0.6 mi e of center from Main St. 117 Pearl St 06340. **Hours:** Open 5/1-10/11; noon-9 pm; 9/4-10/8 Fri-Sun only, noon-7 pm. **Features:** No A/C; casual dress; children's menu. Outstanding fresh seafood featuring lobster. Informal, self service. Indoor & outdoor dining on Noank Harbour. Experience a tantalizing New England seafood feast. **Cards:** AE, MC, VI.   [X]

NORFOLK—2,250

LODGINGS

BLACKBERRY RIVER INN
◆ ◆
Bed & Breakfast

	Rates Subject to Change				**Phone:** 860/542-5100
All Year [BP]		2P/1B: $100- 110	2P/2B:	$100- 110	XP: $20

Location: On US 44, 3 mi w of jct SR 272. 536 Greenwoods Rd W 06058. **Fax:** 860/542-1763. **Terms:** Reserv deposit, 14 day notice; handling fee imposed; 2 night min stay, 05/1-10/31 weekends. **Facility:** 15 rooms. 3 two-bedroom units. 2 stories; interior corridors; smoke free premises; heated pool. **Some Rooms:** color TV. **Cards:** AE, MC, VI.   [icons]

MANOR HOUSE
◆◆◆   All Year [BP]   Rates Subject to Change   **Phone: 860/542-5690**
Historic Bed   1P: $85- 250   2P/1B: $95- 300 2P/2B: $125- 300   XP: $25-75   D
& Breakfast   **Location:** Jct SR 272, just e on US 44, 0.3 mi n. 69 Maple Ave 06058. Fax: 860/542-5690. **Terms:** Age
restrictions may apply; reserv deposit, 10 day notice; handling fee imposed; 2 night min stay, weekends.
Facility: 9 rooms. 1898 Victorian Tudor estate built by Charles Spofford. 1 two-bedroom unit. 3 stories, no el-
evator; interior corridors; smoke free premises. **All Rooms:** combo or shower baths. **Cards:** DS, MC, VI.

NORTH HAVEN—22,600   (See map p. 245; index p. 243)

LODGING

HOLIDAY INN   **Phone: (203)239-4225**   30
AAA SAVE   All Year   1P: $79- 99   2P/1B: $79- 109 2P/2B: $79- 109   XP: $10   F18
◆◆◆   **Location:** On US 5; at I-91, exit 12. 201 Washington Ave 06473. Fax: 203/234-1247. **Terms:** Pets.
Motor Inn   **Facility:** 140 rooms. 2 stories; interior corridors; heated indoor pool, saunas. **Dining:** Restaurant; 6:30 am-2
& 5-10 pm; $8-$16; cocktails. **All Rooms:** extended cable TV. **Cards:** AE, CB, DI, DS, MC, VI.

NORTH STONINGTON—5,250—See also STONINGTON.

LODGING

ANTIQUES AND ACCOMMODATIONS   Guaranteed Rates   **Phone: (860)535-1736**
◆◆◆   5/1-1/14   1P: $129- 189   2P/1B: $129- 199
Historic Bed   1/15-4/30   1P: $99- 129   2P/1B: $99- 189
& Breakfast   **Location:** I-95 exit 92, 2.5 mi nw on SR 2, 0.3 mi n. 32 Main St 06359. Fax: 860/535-2613. **Terms:** Reserv
deposit, 10 day notice; 2 night min stay, weekends. **Facility:** 5 rooms. Beautifully restored Victorian home on
landscaped grounds in quiet historical village. Candlelight breakfasts. 1 two-bedroom unit, 1 three-bedroom unit. 2 stories; interior corridors; smoke free premises. **All Rooms:** combo or shower baths. **Some Rooms:** kitchen, color TV. **Cards:** MC, VI.

NORWALK—78,300   (See map p. 212; index p. 211)

LODGINGS

CLUB HOTEL BY DOUBLETREE NORWALK   Rates Subject to Change   **Phone: (203)853-3477**   6
◆◆◆   All Year   1P: $179   2P/1B: $179   2P/2B: $179   XP: $18   F18
Motor Inn   **Location:** On US 1, 0.3 mi e of tpk exit 13, I-95. 789 Connecticut Ave 06854. Fax: 203/855-9404.
Facility: 268 rooms. 8 stories; interior corridors; heated indoor pool. **All Rooms:** combo or shower baths.
Cards: AE, CB, DI, DS, JC, MC, VI.

COURTYARD BY MARRIOTT   Rates Subject to Change   **Phone: 203/849-9111**   10
◆◆◆   Sun-Thurs   1P: $154   2P/1B: $154   2P/2B: $154
Motor Inn   Fri & Sat   1P: $94   2P/1B: $104   2P/2B: $104
Location: On US 7, 0.5 mi n of exit 40B of Merritt Pkwy; 3.5 mi n of exit 15 of I-95; just se. 474 Main Ave
06851. Fax: 203/849-8144. **Facility:** 145 rooms. Weekend rates for up to 4 persons. Suites, $199; 4 stories; interior corridors;
heated indoor pool. **Cards:** AE, DI, DS, MC, VI.

FOUR POINTS HOTEL NORWALK   Rates Subject to Change   **Phone: 203/849-9828**   7
◆◆◆   All Year   1P: $161   2P/1B: $161   2P/2B: $161   XP: $10   F17
Motor Inn   **Location:** 0.3 mi n of exit 40B of Merritt Pkwy (US 15); 3 mi n of exit 15 I-95 via US 7, 0.5 mi s. 426 Main
Ave 06851. Fax: 203/846-6925. **Terms:** Reserv deposit. **Facility:** 127 rooms. Suites avail; 4 stories; interior
corridors. **Cards:** AE, CB, DI, DS, MC, VI.

THE SILVERMINE TAVERN   **Phone: (203)847-4558**   9
AAA SAVE   All Year [CP]   1P: $75- 99   2P/1B: $99- 175 2P/2B: $99- 125   XP: $18
◆◆◆   **Location:** Merrit Pkwy exit 40A, 0.5 mi s on Main Ave, 2 mi nw. 194 Perry Ave 06850. Fax: 203/847-9171.
Historic   **Terms:** Reserv deposit, 3 day notice; handling fee imposed; package plans, winter months. **Facility:** 11 rooms.
Country Inn   Colonial guest rooms above 200 year-old inn & above adjacent country store. Early American decor. Closed
Tues 9/3-5/27. No single rates weekends. One bedroom suite avail; 2 stories; interior corridors; smoke free
premises. **Dining:** Restaurant, see separate listing. **Recreation:** walking tour. **All Rooms:** combo or tub
baths. **Some Rooms:** kitchen. **Cards:** AE, CB, DI, MC, VI. **Special Amenities:** Free breakfast.

RESTAURANT

THE SILVERMINE TAVERN   Country Inn   **Lunch:** $7-$12   **Dinner:** $15-$25   **Phone:** 203/847-4558   9
◆◆   **Location:** Merritt Pkwy exit 40A, 0.5 mi s on Main Ave, 2 mi nw; in The Silvermine Tavern. 194 Perry Ave
American   06850. **Hours:** noon-3 & 6-9 pm, Fri-10 pm, Sat noon-4 & 6-10 pm, Sun 11 am-2:30 & 3:30-9 pm. Closed:
12/25 & Tues. **Reservations:** suggested. **Features:** casual dress; Sunday brunch; children's menu; cocktails
& lounge; minimum charge-$7; a la carte. Attractive country inn on Silvermine River. Colonial dining rooms; terrace dining in
summer. **Cards:** AE, CB, DI, MC, VI.

NORWICH—37,400

LODGINGS

COURTYARD MARRIOTT   Rates Subject to Change   **Phone: (860)886-2600**
◆◆◆   Fri & Sat 5/1-10/31   1P: $149- 159   2P/1B: $149- 159 2P/2B: $149- 159   XP: $10   F
Motor Inn   Sun-Thurs 5/1-10/31 & Fri &
Sat 4/1-4/30   1P: $109- 119   2P/1B: $109- 119 2P/2B: $109- 119   XP: $10   F
11/1-3/31   1P: $99- 109   2P/1B: $99- 109 2P/2B: $99- 109   XP: $10   F
Sun-Thurs 4/1-4/30   1P: $89- 99   2P/1B: $89- 99 2P/2B: $89- 99   XP: $10   F
Location: I-395 exit 82, just w. 181 W Town St 06360. Fax: 860/889-2001. **Facility:** 120 rooms. 4 stories; interior corridors;
heated indoor pool. **Services:** area transportation. **All Rooms:** combo or shower baths. **Cards:** AE, DI, DS, MC, VI.

RAMADA HOTEL NORWICH/MYSTIC   Phone: (860)889-5201

	7/2-10/31	1P:	$79- 145	2P/1B:	$89- 155	2P/2B:	$89- 155	XP: $10	F18
	5/28-7/1	1P:	$69- 145	2P/1B:	$79- 155	2P/2B:	$79- 155	XP: $10	F18
◆◆◆	5/1-5/27 & 11/1-4/30	1P:	$59- 135	2P/1B:	$59- 145	2P/2B:	$59- 145	XP: $10	F18

Hotel **Location:** On SR 82; 0.3 mi w of I-395 southbound exit 80, northbound exit 80W. 10 Laura Blvd 06360. Fax: 860/889-1767. **Terms:** Reserv deposit; package plans. **Facility:** 127 rooms. Some rooms with balcony. 6 stories; interior corridors; heated indoor pool. **Dining:** Restaurant; 6:30-11 am, 11:30-2 & 5:30-9 pm; $10-$18; cocktails. **Services:** area transportation, to casino only. **All Rooms:** extended cable TV. **Cards:** AE, DI, DS, MC, VI. **Special Amenities:** Free newspaper and free room upgrade (subject to availability with advanced reservations). *(See color ad inside front cover)*

RESTAURANTS

AMERICUS ON THE WHARF   **Lunch:** $7-$11   **Dinner:** $7-$20   **Phone:** 860/887-8555
◆◆   **Location:** Downtown on waterfront. 1 American Wharf 06360. **Hours:** 11:30 am-11 pm. Closed: 10/2-3/31.
South Italian **Reservations:** suggested; weekends. **Features:** casual dress; Sunday brunch; children's menu; senior's menu; health conscious menu; carryout; salad bar; cocktails & lounge. Nautical theme in casual atmosphere. Outside dining weather permitting. **Cards:** AE, MC, VI.

PRINCE OF WALES RESTAURANT   **Lunch:** $8-$12   **Dinner:** $17-$27   **Phone:** 860/886-2401
◆◆◆   **Location:** From I-395, exit 79A; 0.5 mi e on SR 2A & 1.3 mi n on SR 32; in the Norwich Inn & Spa. 607 W
Regional Thames St 06360. **Hours:** 7 am-10, noon-2 & 6-9 pm, Fri 6 pm-10:30 pm, Sat 7 am-10:30, noon-3 &
American 6-10:30 pm, Sun 7 am-10:30, 11:30-3 & 6-9 pm. **Reservations:** suggested. **Features:** casual dress; Sunday brunch; health conscious menu; carryout; cocktails & lounge. Comfortable relaxed atmosphere. Terrace dining weather permitting. Smoke free premises. **Cards:** AE, DI, MC, VI.

OLD LYME—6,500

LODGINGS

BEE & THISTLE INN   Rates Subject to Change   **Phone:** (860)434-1667
◆◆◆   1P: $75- 210   2P/1B: $95- 210   2P/2B: $75- 140   XP: $15
Historic **Location:** I-95 southbound, exit 70, just n on US 1; from I-95 northbound, exit 70, just w on SR 156, then
Country Inn 1.2 mi n on US 1. 100 Lyme St 06371. Fax: 860/434-3402. **Terms:** Age restrictions may apply; reserv deposit, 10 day notice; handling fee imposed. **Facility:** 12 rooms. A clapboard Dutch Colonial built in 1756. Located on the Lieutenant River in the Historic District of Old Lyme. No single person rate on weekends. Cottage, $210. Closed 2 weeks in January; 3 stories, no elevator; interior corridors; designated smoking area. **All Rooms:** combo or shower baths. **Some Rooms:** kitchen, color TV. **Cards:** AE, DI, DS, MC, VI.

OLD LYME INN   Rates Subject to Change   **Phone:** (860)434-2600
	5/1-12/31 [CP]	1P:	$86- 140	2P/1B:	$99- 175	2P/2B:	$99- 175	XP: $50	F12
	1/1-4/30 [CP]	1P:	$86- 140	2P/1B:	$99- 165	2P/2B:	$99- 165	XP: $50	F12

◆◆◆ **Location:** From I-95 southbound, at exit 70; from I-95 northbound, exit 70, n on SR 156, right on US 1 for
Historic 0.5 mi then left. 85 Lyme St 06371 (PO Box 787). Fax: 860/434-5352. **Terms:** Reserv deposit; pets.
Country Inn **Facility:** 13 rooms. Restored charming 1850 house. 2 stories; interior corridors. **Dining:** Restaurant, see separate listing. **All Rooms:** combo or shower baths, extended cable TV. **Cards:** AE, CB, DI, DS, MC, VI.

RESTAURANTS

BEE & THISTLE INN Country Inn   **Lunch:** $8-$12   **Dinner:** $18-$27   **Phone:** 860/434-1667
◆◆◆   **Location:** I-95 southbound, exit 70 just n on US 1; from I-95 northbound, exit 70, just w on SR 156, then 1.2
American mi n on US 1. 100 Lyme St 06371. **Hours:** 11:30 am-2 & 6-9 pm, Sat-9:30 pm, Sun 11 am-2 & 5:30-9 pm.
Closed: 1/1, 12/24, 12/25, Tues & 2 weeks in Jan. **Reservations:** suggested. **Features:** dressy casual; Sunday brunch; cocktails. Charming country inn. Sophisticated New England cuisine. Dress code weekends. Age restrictions apply. Smoke free premises. **Cards:** AE, DI, MC, VI.

HIDEAWAY RESTAURANT & PUB   **Lunch:** $6-$9   **Dinner:** $11-$18   **Phone:** 860/434-3335
◆◆   **Location:** I-95 exit 70, 0.5 mi s, on US 1; in Old Lyme shopping center. 19 Halls Rd 06371. **Hours:** 11
American am-10 pm. Closed: 11/25 & 12/25. **Reservations:** accepted. **Features:** casual dress; children's menu; health conscious menu; carryout; cocktails & lounge. **Cards:** AE, MC, VI.

OLD LYME INN Country Inn   **Lunch:** $7-$11   **Dinner:** $15-$29   **Phone:** 860/434-2600
◆◆◆   **Location:** From I-95 southbound, at exit 70; from I-95 northbound, exit 70, n on SR 156, right on US 1 for
American 0.5 mi then left; in Old Lyme Inn. 85 Lyme St 06371. **Hours:** noon-2 & 6-9 pm, Sun 11 am-3 & 4-9 pm. **Reservations:** suggested. **Features:** casual dress; health conscious menu; cocktails & lounge; a la carte. Innovative cuisine served in elegant atmosphere. Sun brunch 11 am-3 pm. **Cards:** AE, DI, DS, MC, VI.

OLD MYSTIC—600

LODGING

THE OLD MYSTIC INN   Rates Subject to Change   **Phone:** (860)572-9422
◆◆◆   All Year   2P/1B: $125- 155
Historic Bed **Location:** I-95 exit 90, 1.3 mi n. 52 Main St 06372-0634 (PO Box 634, 06372). **Terms:** Reserv deposit;
& Breakfast handling fee imposed; 2 night min stay, weekends in season. **Facility:** 8 rooms. Restored 1784 house & carriage house with country decor; some rooms with fireplace. 2 stories; interior/exterior corridors; designated smoking area. **Cards:** AE, MC, VI.

RESTAURANT

J. P. DANIELS   **Dinner:** $6-$17   **Phone:** 860/572-9564
◆◆◆   **Location:** On SR 184, 0.5 mi e of jct SR 27. **Hours:** 5 pm-9 pm, Fri & Sat-9:30 pm, Sun 11 am-2 & 5-9 pm.
Continental Closed: 12/24 & 12/25. **Reservations:** suggested. **Features:** Sunday brunch; children's menu; cocktails & lounge; a la carte. Intimate dining in a relaxed country setting. Smoke free premises. **Cards:** AE, DS, MC, VI.

OLD SAYBROOK—9,600

LODGINGS

COMFORT INN   Rates Subject to Change   **Phone:** (860)395-1414

5/1-10/31 [CP]	1P:	$95- 115	2P/1B:	$95- 115	2P/2B:	$90- 130	XP: $10	F18
11/1-4/30 [CP]	1P:	$60- 75	2P/1B:	$60- 75	2P/2B:	$55- 85	XP: $10	F18

◆ ◆ ◆
Motel

Location: At jct SR 9, exit 2 & I-95, exit 69. 100 Essex Rd 06475. Fax: 860/388-9578. **Terms:** Weekly rates. **Facility:** 120 rooms. Large rooms. Whirlpool rm, extra charge; 3 stories; interior corridors; heated indoor pool, saunas. **Dining:** Restaurant nearby. **Some Rooms:** 8 efficiencies. **Cards:** AE, CB, DI, DS, JC, MC, VI.

(See color ad below)

DAYS INN   Rates Subject to Change   **Phone:** (860)388-3453

◆ ◆
Motel

5/22-9/5 & 9/6-10/23 [CP]	1P:	$59- 118	2P/1B:	$68- 118	2P/2B:	$68- 118	XP: $10	F18
5/22-9/5 [CP]	1P:	$58- 118	2P/1B:	$58- 118	2P/2B:	$58- 118	XP: $10	F18
5/1-5/21 & 10/24-4/30 [CP]	1P:	$49- 59	2P/1B:	$59	2P/2B:	$59	XP: $10	F18

Location: I-95 exit 66, 0.3 mi e on SR 166, then 0.5 mi n on US 1. 1430 Boston Post Rd 06475. Fax: 860/395-0209. **Facility:** 47 rooms. 3 whirlpool rms, extra charge; 2 stories; exterior corridors; heated indoor pool. **Cards:** AE, CB, DI, DS, MC, VI.

HERITAGE MOTOR INN   Rates Subject to Change   **Phone:** 860/388-3743

◆ ◆
Motel

All Year	1P: $95	2P/1B: $95	2P/2B: $95	XP: $5	F10

Location: On US 1, 0.4 mi n of jct SR 166; from I-95 exit 66. 1500 Boston Post Rd 06475. **Terms:** Reserv deposit, 10 day notice, in season; 2 night min stay, weekends 5/28-10/11. **Facility:** 12 rooms. Early American decor rooms attached to 1755 Nathaniel Bushnell House. 1 story; exterior corridors. **All Rooms:** combo or shower baths. **Cards:** AE, DS, MC, VI.

LIBERTY INN   Rates Subject to Change   **Phone:** 860/388-1777

◆ ◆
Motel

Fri & Sat 5/24-9/30	1P:	$88- 98	2P/1B:	$88- 98	2P/2B:	$88- 98	XP: $10
Sun-Thurs 5/24-9/30	1P:	$68- 78	2P/1B:	$68- 78	2P/2B:	$68- 78	XP: $10
5/1-5/23 & Fri & Sat 10/1-4/30	1P:	$58- 68	2P/1B:	$58- 68	2P/2B:	$58- 68	XP: $10
Sun-Thurs 10/1-4/30	1P:	$48- 58	2P/1B:	$48- 58	2P/2B:	$48- 58	XP: $10

Location: I-95S exit 68; I-95N, exit 67, 0.9 mi n on US 1, then w. 55 Springbrook Rd 06475. Fax: 860/395-4705. **Terms:** Reserv deposit, 10 day notice. **Facility:** 21 rooms. 2 stories; exterior corridors. **Cards:** AE, DS, MC, VI.

SANDPIPER INN
(AAA) (SAVE)
◆ ◆
Motel

Phone: (860)399-7973

		1P:		2P/1B:		2P/2B:		XP:	
5/16-9/9 [CP]		$75- 100		$75- 125		$85- 135		$10	F12
5/1-5/15, 9/10-11/1 &									
4/11-4/30 [EP]		$62- 85		$65- 95		$65- 95		$6	F12
11/2-4/10 [EP]		$52- 59		$65- 85		$65- 85		$6	F12

Location: On US 1, just s of jct SR 166; I-95 exit 66. 1750 Boston Post Rd 06475. Fax: 860/399-7387. **Terms:** Weekly/monthly rates; pets, $10 extra charge, limited rms. **Facility:** 45 rooms. Variety of choice accommodations, serene & relaxing setting. 2-3 stories; interior/exterior corridors; small pool. **Dining:** Restaurant nearby. **All Rooms:** extended cable TV. **Cards:** AE, CB, DI, DS, JC, MC, VI. **Special Amenities:** Early check-in/late check-out and free breakfast.

SAYBROOK POINT INN & SPA
(AAA) (SAVE)
◆ ◆ ◆ ◆
Motor Inn

Phone: (860)395-2000

		1P:		2P/1B:		2P/2B:		XP:	
Fri & Sat 5/1-11/30 &									
3/1-4/30		$189- 395		$189- 395		$189- 395		$25	F12
Sun-Thurs 5/1-11/30 &									
3/1-4/30		$179- 375		$179- 375		$179- 375		$25	F12
Fri & Sat 12/1-2/29		$155- 345		$155- 345		$155- 345		$25	F12
Sun-Thurs 12/1-2/29		$145- 335		$145- 335		$145- 335		$25	F12

Location: On SR 154; 2.2 mi s of jct US 1 at Saybrook Point. 2 Bridge St 06475-2502. Fax: 860/388-1504. **Terms:** Reserv deposit, 30 day notice; package plans; 2 night min stay, weekends in season. **Facility:** 63 rooms. Overlooking Connecticut River & Long Island Sound. Large rooms most with fireplace & many with balcony. 1 two-bedroom unit. 3 stories; interior corridors; oceanfront; heated indoor pool, steamroom, whirlpool; marina. Fee: beach pass. **Dining:** Terra Mar Grille, see separate listing. **Services:** area transportation, train station. Fee: massage. **Recreation:** Fee: pamper spa, tennis & country club privileges. **All Rooms:** extended cable TV. **Some Rooms:** whirlpools. **Cards:** AE, DI, DS, MC, VI. *(See color ad p 251)*

SUPER 8 MOTEL
(AAA) (SAVE)
◆
Motel

Phone: (860)399-6273

		1P:		2P/1B:		2P/2B:		XP:	
5/1-10/31 [CP]		$59- 120		$65- 130		$75- 150		$7-20	F16
11/1-4/30 [CP]		$35- 60		$35- 60		$45- 65		$5-20	F16

Location: On SR 166, just s of jct I-95 exit 66. 37 Spencer Plaine Rd 06475. Fax: 860/399-2525. **Terms:** Reserv deposit; handling fee imposed; weekly rates. **Facility:** 44 rooms. Rates for up to 4 persons; 2 stories; exterior corridors. **All Rooms:** extended cable TV. **Cards:** AE, DI, DS, MC, VI. **Special Amenities:** Early check-in/late check-out and free breakfast.

RESTAURANTS

THE DOCK & DINE
◆ ◆
Seafood

Lunch: $5-$13   Dinner: $12-$21   Phone: 860/388-4665
Location: 2 mi s of US 1 on SR 154, via Main St. 145 College St 06475. **Hours:** 11:30 am-10 pm; to 9 pm off season. Closed: Mon & Tues 10/14-4/12. **Features:** casual dress; children's menu; salad bar; cocktails & lounge. On the waterfront. Entertainment weekends, in season. **Cards:** AE, DI, DS, MC, VI.

TERRA MAR GRILLE
◆ ◆ ◆
Continental

Lunch: $8-$12   Dinner: $15-$29   Phone: 860/388-1111
Location: On SR 154; 2.2 mi s of jct US 1 at Saybrook Point; in Saybrook Point Inn & Spa. 2 Bridge St 06475. **Hours:** 7-10 am, 11:30-2 & 6-9 pm, Fri & Sat-10 pm. **Reservations:** suggested. **Features:** semi-formal attire; children's menu; health conscious menu items; cocktails & lounge. Overlooking Long Island Sound. Sun brunch 11 am-2 pm, $24. Smoking permitted in lounge. Smoke free premises. **Cards:** AE, CB, DI, DS, MC, VI. *(See color ad p 251)*

PLAINVILLE—*See Hartford p. 229.*

PORTLAND—*See Hartford p. 229.*

REDDING RIDGE—600

RESTAURANT

THE SPINNING WHEEL INN
◆ ◆ ◆
Regional American

Dinner: $14-$19   Phone: 203/938-2511
Location: SR 58 exit 45, 9 mi n of Merritt Pkwy. 107 Bladerock Tpk (SR 58) 06876. **Hours:** 5:30 pm-9:30 pm, Fri & Sat-10 pm, Sun 11 am-2:30 & 4:30-7 pm. Closed: Mon. **Reservations:** suggested. **Features:** dressy casual; Sunday brunch; cocktails; a la carte. Rural setting. Smoke free premises. **Cards:** AE, CB, DI, MC, VI.

RIDGEFIELD—20,900

LODGING

WEST LANE INN
◆ ◆ ◆
Historic Bed & Breakfast

Rates Subject to Change   Phone: 203/438-7323

		1P:		2P/1B:		2P/2B:		XP:	
6/1-7/15		$155		$165		$165		$10	
5/1-5/31, 7/16-9/14 &									
11/1-4/30		$120		$135		$135		$10	
9/15-10/31		$140		$155		$10			

Location: On SR 35, w of jct SR 33, 12 mi e of I-684 exit 6, SR 35. 22 West Ln 06877. Fax: 203/438-7325. **Terms:** Reserv deposit, 10 day notice. **Facility:** 18 rooms. Gracious & comfortably elegant converted home, built in 1849, also newer, slightly more modest cottage building. 2 rooms with fireplace, $175; 2-3 stories, no elevator; interior corridors. **Some Rooms:** 4 efficiencies. **Cards:** AE, CB, DI, MC, VI.

RESTAURANTS

THE INN AT RIDGEFIELD   Country Inn
◆ ◆ ◆
Continental
Pianist on weekends.

Lunch: $10-$23   Dinner: $18-$32   Phone: 203/438-8282
Location: Jct Rt 35 & 33 on Rt 35. 20 West Ln 06877. **Hours:** noon-2 & 6-9:30 pm, Fri & Sat-10:30 pm, Sun noon-8 pm. Closed major holidays. **Reservations:** suggested. **Features:** casual dress; cocktails & lounge; a la carte. Prix fixe menu, $49. Sun brunch noon-3 pm, $23. Elegant, formal lunches & dinners. Chef-owned. **Cards:** AE, DI, MC, VI.

STONEHENGE INN   Country Inn   **Dinner:** $18-$34   **Phone:** 203/438-6511
◆◆◆◆   **Location:** On US 7, 1 mi s of jct SR 35; in Stonehenge Inn. 35 Stonehenge Rd 06877. **Hours:** 6 pm-9 pm;
French   weekends 6 pm-9:30 pm, Sun seatings at noon-2:30 pm & 4-8 pm. Closed: Mon. **Reservations:** suggested.
           Features: dressy casual; cocktails; valet parking; a la carte. Rack of lamb, escallop of veal. Sunday brunch
$28. Jackets appropriate, especially weekends. Smoke free premises. **Cards:** AE, MC, VI.   ⊠

RIVERTON—600

LODGING

OLD RIVERTON INN   Rates Subject to Change   **Phone:** 860/379-8678
◆◆   All Year [BP]   1P: $45- 115   2P/1B: $80- 115 2P/2B: $115   XP: $15   F12
Historic   **Location:** Center. SR 20 06065. Fax: 860/379-1006. **Terms:** Reserv deposit, 10 day notice; handling fee
Country Inn imposed. **Facility:** 12 rooms. Built in 1796 as a Stagecoach stop. 1 room with fireplace, $170; 3 stories; inte-
           rior corridors. **All Rooms:** combo or shower baths. **Cards:** AE, CB, DI, DS, MC, VI.

🛏 🐟 🍴 🅾 🖨 🛗 ⊠

RESTAURANT

OLD RIVERTON INN   Country Inn   **Lunch:** $7-$13   **Dinner:** $13-$20   **Phone:** 860/379-8678
◆◆   **Location:** Center; in Old Riverton Inn. SR 20 06065. **Hours:** noon-2:30 & 5-8:30 pm, Sat-9 pm, Sun noon-8
American   pm. Closed: Mon & Tues. **Reservations:** suggested. **Features:** casual dress; children's menu; early bird
           specials; health conscious menu; cocktails & lounge. Atmosphere of an old stagecoach stop. Smoke free
premises. **Cards:** AE, CB, DI, DS, MC, VI.   ⊠

ROCKY HILL—See Hartford p. 229.

SEYMOUR—14,300   (See map p. 245; index p. 244)

LODGING

THE INN AT VILLA BIANCA   Rates Subject to Change   **Phone:** 203/735-4883   **47**
◆◆   All Year [CP]   1P: $85   2P/1B: $95   2P/2B: $95   XP: $10   F16
Motel   **Location:** On SR 34, 4.6 mi w of SR 8, exit 15. 312 Roosevelt Dr 06483. Fax: 203/732-3959. **Facility:** 12
rooms. 3 stories, no elevator; interior corridors. **Services:** Fee: area transportation. **Cards:** AE, CB, DI.

🐟 🛆 🎾 📼 🖨 ⊠

SHARON—2,900

LODGING

SHARON MOTOR LODGE   Rates Subject to Change   **Phone:** 860/364-0036
◆◆   Thurs-Sat 5/1-10/31   2P/2B: $115- 125 XP: $10   F12
Motel   Sun-Wed 5/1-10/31 & Fri &
           Sat 11/1-4/30   2P/2B: $69- 79 XP: $10   F12
           Sun-Thurs 11/1-4/30   2P/2B: $62- 72 XP: $10   F12
Location: 0.8 mi n on SR 41. Rt 41 06069 (PO Box 1772). Fax: 860/364-0462. **Terms:** Reserv deposit, 15 day notice;
handling fee imposed; 2 night min stay, weekends 5/1-10/31. **Facility:** 22 rooms. Quiet small town location. 1 story; exterior
corridors. **All Rooms:** combo or shower baths. **Cards:** AE, DI, MC, VI.   🏊 🍴 🖨 🛗 ⊠

SHELTON—36,800

LODGINGS

AMERISUITES   **Phone:** (203)925-5900
⌂⌂⌂ SAVE   All Year [CP]   1P: $154- 169 2P/1B: $154- 169 2P/2B: $154- 175 XP: $10
           Too new to rate. **Location:** From SR 8 exit 12, 0.5 mi w, then just s. 695 Bridgeport Ave 06484.
FYI   Fax: 203/944-9180. **Facility:** 128 rooms. Scheduled to open November 1998; 4 stories; interior corridors;
           heated indoor pool. **Cards:** AE, CB, DI, DS, MC, VI. **Special Amenities:** Free breakfast and free local
Motel   telephone calls.   🐾 🛆 ✚ 💻 ⬜ 🖨 🛗

RAMADA PLAZA HOTEL   **Phone:** (203)929-1500
⌂⌂⌂ SAVE   All Year   1P: $89- 194 2P/1B: $89- 214 2P/2B: $89- 214 XP: $20   F18
           Location: 0.8 mi sw SR 8, exit 12. 780 Bridgeport Ave 06484. Fax: 203/929-6711. **Terms:** Weekly/monthly
◆◆◆   rates; BP avail; package plans; weekend rates avail; small pets only. **Facility:** 155 rooms. Art deco lobby decor.
Hotel   7 stories; interior corridors; heated indoor pool, sauna. **Dining:** Restaurant; 6:30 am-10 pm, Sat & Sun from
           7 am; $9-$15; cocktails. **Some Rooms:** whirlpools. **Cards:** AE, CB, DI, DS, JC, MC, VI. **Special Amenities:**
Free breakfast and free local telephone calls. *(See color ad inside front cover)*

🅢 🐾 🛆 🐟 ⤢ ✚ 🛆 ✚ 🎾 💻 ⬜ 🖨 🛗 ⊠

RESIDENCE INN BY MARRIOTT   Rates Subject to Change   **Phone:** 203/926-9000
◆◆◆   All Year [BP]   1P: $159- 189 2P/1B: $159- 189 2P/2B: $169- 199
Apartment **Location:** 0.3 sw of SR 8, exit 11. 1001 Bridgeport Ave 06484. Fax: 203/929-7663. **Facility:** 96 rooms. Large
           apartment rooms, some with lofts. 24 two-bedroom units. 2 stories; exterior corridors. **Recreation:** sports
court. **All Rooms:** kitchens. **Cards:** AE, CB, DI, DS, MC, VI.

🛏 🐟 🅾 🛆 🛆 ✕ ✚ 🎾 💻 ⬜ 🖨 🛗 🍽 ⊠

SIMSBURY—See Hartford p. 229.

SOUTHBURY—17,000

LODGINGS

HERITAGE INN   Rates Subject to Change   Phone: (203)264-8200
All Year   1P: $129- 139   2P/1B: $129- 139 2P/2B: $129- 139 XP: $20   F14
Location: 0.4 mi n on SR 67, then 1 mi w; from I-84, exit 15. Heritage Rd 06488. Fax: 203/264-5035.
Motor Inn   **Terms:** Check-in 4 pm; reserv deposit; MAP avail; package plans. **Facility:** 163 rooms. Quiet, rustic & intimate setting. 3 stories; interior corridors; heated indoor pool, saunas, steamrooms, whirlpool; racquetball courts, 3 tennis courts (2 lighted). Fee: 9 holes golf. **Dining:** Dining room; 7 am-10, noon-2 & 6-10 pm; Sun brunch 11 am-2:30 pm; $10-$21; cocktails. **Services:** giftshop; area transportation, within 5 mi. Fee: massage. **Recreation:** Fee: fishing; bicycles. **All Rooms:** combo or shower baths, extended cable TV. **Some Rooms:** whirlpools. **Cards:** AE, CB, DI, DS, MC, VI. *(See color ad below)*

SOUTHBURY HILTON   Guaranteed Rates   Phone: (203)598-7600
All Year   1P: $125   2P/1B: $140   2P/2B: $140   XP: $15   F18
Hotel   **Location:** Exit 16 of I-84. 1284 Strongtown Rd 06488. Fax: 203/598-7541. **Facility:** 198 rooms. 9 suites; $120-$235. 2 whirlpool rms, extra charge; 3 stories; interior corridors; heated indoor pool. **Services:** area transportation. **Cards:** AE, DI, DS, JC, MC, VI. *(See color ad p 37 & below)*

SOUTHINGTON—See Hartford p. 230.

SOUTH NORWALK   (See map p. 212; index p. 211)

RESTAURANT

RATTLESNAKE SOUTHWESTERN GRILL   Lunch: $8-$15   Dinner: $8-$15   Phone: 203/852-1716   (23)
Southwest American   **Location:** Downtown; jct W Washington St. 2 S Main St 06854. **Hours:** 11:30 am-10 pm, Weds & Thurs-11 pm, Fri & Sat-midnight, Sun noon-10 pm. Closed: 11/25 & 12/25. **Reservations:** required; 6 or more. **Features:** casual dress; children's menu; health conscious menu items; carryout; cocktails & lounge; fee for parking; a la carte. Upbeat casual fun eatery. Extensive menu. Free parking after 5 pm. **Cards:** AE, DI, MC, VI.

SOUTH WINDSOR—See Hartford p. 230.

SOUTH WOODSTOCK—1,100

LODGING

INN AT WOODSTOCK HILL
◆◆◆   All Year [CP]   Rates Subject to Change   1P: $90- 145   2P/1B: $90- 155   2P/2B: $100- 150   XP: $12   Phone: 860/928-0528
Historic
Country Inn   **Location:** 0.8 mi n on SR 169. 94 Plaine Hill Rd 06267 (PO Box 98). Fax: 860/928-3236. **Terms:** Reserv deposit, 3 day notice. **Facility:** 22 rooms. Early 19th-century Christopher Wren style country estate. Some rooms with fireplace. 3 stories, no elevator; interior corridors. **All Rooms:** combo or shower baths.
Cards: DS, MC, VI.

RESTAURANT

INN AT WOODSTOCK HILL   Country Inn   **Lunch:** $5-$13   **Dinner:** $15-$28   Phone: 860/928-0528
◆◆◆
Continental   **Location:** 0.8 mi n on SR 169; in Inn at Woodstock Hill. 94 Plaine Hill Rd 06267. **Hours:** 11 am-2 & 5:30-9 pm, Sun 11 am-2 & 3:30-7 pm. Closed: Mon for lunch. **Reservations:** suggested. **Features:** Sunday brunch; cocktails & lounge. Romantic country setting. Smoke free premises. **Cards:** DS, MC, VI.

STAMFORD—108,100   (See map p. 212; index p. 211)

LODGINGS

GRAND CHALET INN & SUITES   Rates Subject to Change   Phone: 203/357-7100   **13**
◆◆◆   All Year [CP]   1P: $90- 120   2P/1B: $90- 120   2P/2B: $90- 120   XP: $5
Motor Inn   **Location:** I-95 exit 6 (Harvard Ave). 135 Harvard Ave 06902. Fax: 203/358-9332. **Facility:** 158 rooms. 8 stories; interior corridors; heated indoor pool. **Services:** area transportation. **All Rooms:** combo or shower baths. **Cards:** AE, CB, DI, DS, MC, VI.

HOLIDAY INN SELECT   Rates Subject to Change   Phone: (203)358-8400   **15**
◆◆◆   All Year   1P: $89- 170   2P/1B: $89- 170   2P/2B: $89- 170
Motor Inn   **Location:** Downtown; southbound 95 exit 8, then w; northbound 95 exit 7, just w, then n. 700 Main St 06901. Fax: 203/358-8872. **Facility:** 383 rooms. Spacious atrium multi-level lobby, restaurant & pool areas. 2 two-bedroom units. 10 stories; interior corridors; small heated indoor pool. Fee: parking. **Services:** giftshop.
All Rooms: combo or shower baths. **Cards:** AE, DI, DS, MC, VI.

SHERATON STAMFORD HOTEL   Rates Subject to Change   Phone: (203)359-1300   **16**
◆◆◆   8/30-12/31   1P: $195- 215   2P/1B: $195- 215   2P/2B: $195- 219   XP: $15   F17
Hotel   5/1-8/29 & 4/5-4/30   1P: $185- 205   2P/1B: $185- 205   2P/2B: $185- 205   XP: $15-25   F17
    1/1-4/4   1P: $175- 195   2P/1B: $175- 195   2P/2B: $175- 195   XP: $15-25   F17
Location: 2.5 mi s of Merrit Pkwy, exit 34 Long Ridge Rd; I-95 northbound exit 8, Atlantic St & Bedford; I-95 southbound, exit 7 North St, n on Atlantic St & Bedford. 2701 Summer St 06905. Fax: 203/348-7937. **Facility:** 445 rooms. Atrium lobby. 5 stories; interior corridors; heated indoor pool. **Cards:** AE, CB, DI, DS, JC, MC, VI. *(See color ad below)*

STAMFORD MARRIOTT HOTEL   Rates Subject to Change   Phone: 203/357-9555   **17**
◆◆◆   Sun-Thurs   1P: $169   2P/1B: $169   2P/2B: $169   XP: $20   F16
Hotel   Fri & Sat   1P: $99   2P/1B: $99   2P/2B: $99   XP: $20   F16
Location: At northbound I-95 exit 8, n under viaduct & n on Tresser Blvd; southbound exit 8. Two Stamford Forum 06901. Fax: 203/324-6897. **Terms:** Reserv deposit. **Facility:** 506 rooms. 17 stories; interior corridors; heated indoor/outdoor pool. Fee: parking; racquetball courts. **Services:** giftshop; area transportation. **Recreation:** jogging.
Cards: AE, CB, DI, DS, MC, VI.

STAMFORD SUITES HOTEL   Rates Subject to Change   Phone: (203)359-7300   **14**
◆◆   11/20-12/30   1P: $195- 229   2P/1B: $195- 229
Suite Motel   5/1-11/19 & 12/31-4/30   1P: $229- 269   2P/1B: $229- 269
Location: 1 mi n of I-95, exit 8; via Atlantic & Bedford sts. 720 Bedford St 06901. Fax: 203/359-7304.
Terms: Reserv deposit. **Facility:** 42 rooms. Residential, apartment style atmosphere with spacious 1 bedroom suites & sleeper sofa. 7 stories; interior corridors. **All Rooms:** kitchens. **Cards:** AE, DI, DS, MC, VI.

(See map p. 212)

RESTAURANTS

AMADEUS   **Lunch:** $10-$16   **Dinner:** $19-$27   **Phone:** 203/348-7775   ⑮
🅰🅰🅰   **Location:** Downtown; jct Broad St, just s. 201 Summer St 06901. **Hours:** 11:45 am-2:30 & 5:30-9:30 pm,
◆◆◆   Fri-10 pm; Sat 5 pm-11 pm; Sun 5 pm-9 pm. Closed major holidays. **Reservations:** suggested.
Continental   **Features:** dressy casual; cocktails; entertainment; fee for parking; a la carte. Viennese specialties. Elegant,
    romantic Old World charm. Prix fixe lunch $19.97, dinner $35. Parking fee validated. **Cards:** AE, DI, DS, MC,
    VI.   ⊗

IL FALCO   **Lunch:** $10-$19   **Dinner:** $12-$22   **Phone:** 203/327-0002   ⑯
◆◆◆   **Location:** Downtown; between Summer St & Washington Blvd. 59 Broad St 06901. **Hours:** noon-3 &
Northern   5:30-10:30 pm, Fri-11 pm, Sat 5:30 pm-11 pm. Closed major holidays & Sun. **Reservations:** suggested.
Italian   **Features:** dressy casual; cocktails; a la carte. Upscale casual dress. Softly elegant, intimate dining room.
    Local favorite for creative entrees. **Cards:** AE, DI, DS, MC, VI.   ⊗

STONINGTON—16,900—See also NORTH STONINGTON.

LODGING

SEA BREEZE MOTEL   Rates Subject to Change   **Phone:** 860/535-2843
◆◆   6/20-9/7   1P: $45- 95   2P/1B: $45- 95   2P/2B: $55- 105
Motel   5/1-6/19, 9/8-10/31 &
    4/1-4/30   1P: $30- 85   2P/1B: $30- 85   2P/2B: $40- 95
    11/1-3/31   1P: $30- 50   2P/1B: $35- 55   2P/2B: $35- 75
Location: On US 1, 2.9 mi se of I-95, exit 91. 812 Stonington Rd 06378. **Terms:** Reserv deposit; handling fee imposed.
Facility: 30 rooms. Large rooms & quiet location. 2 two-bedroom units. 2 room suite, $45-$135; 2 stories; interior/exterior corridors. **All Rooms:** combo or shower baths. **Cards:** MC, VI.   ▢⊘🖨⊗

STRATFORD—49,400

LODGING

RAMADA INN STRATFORD   Guaranteed Rates   **Phone:** (203)375-8866
◆◆   5/1-2/29   1P: $89- 99   2P/1B: $99- 100   2P/2B: $89- 99   XP: $10   F17
Motor Inn   3/1-4/30   1P: $79- 89   2P/1B: $89- 99   2P/2B: $89- 99   XP: $10   F17
    Location: S of I-95, exit 30. 225 Lordship Blvd 06497. Fax: 203/375-2482. **Facility:** 145 rooms. 6 stories; interior corridors; small heated indoor pool. **Services:** area transportation. **Cards:** AE, CB, DI, DS, JC, MC, VI.
(See color ad inside front cover)   🄰🅂🄺 🆂🄰 🐾 🐕 🔟 🏊 ¶¶ ✈ ⚓ ♿ 🌣 💻 🖥 🖨 🔟 ⊗

THOMPSON—9,400

RESTAURANT

THE WHITE HORSE INN AT VERNON STILES   **Lunch:** $6-$10   **Dinner:** $13-$21   **Phone:** 860/923-9571
◆◆   **Location:** On SR 193, at jct SR 200; 0.7 mi e of I-395 exit 99. 351 SR 193 06277. **Hours:** 11 am-2 & 5-9
American   pm, Fri & Sat-10 pm, Sun 11 am-2 & 4-8 pm. Closed: 12/25 & Mon. **Features:** dressy casual; Sunday
    brunch; cocktails. Colonial atmosphere. Smoke free premises. **Cards:** AE, DI, DS, MC, VI.   ⊗

TOLLAND—11,500

LODGING

THE TOLLAND INN   Rates Subject to Change   **Phone:** 860/872-0800
◆◆◆   All Year [BP]   1P: $60- 120   2P/1B: $70- 130   2P/2B: $80
Bed &   **Location:** 0.8 mi nw on SR 195 & 74, I-84 exit 68. 63 Tolland Green 06084-0717. Fax: 860/870-7958.
Breakfast   **Terms:** Age restrictions may apply; check-in 4 pm; reserv deposit, 14 day notice; handling fee imposed.
    Facility: 7 rooms. Restored 1800 Colonial house. 2 night min stay, weekends 5/1-5/31 & 10/1-10/31. Whirlpool
rm with fireplace, $110-$130; 2 stories; interior corridors; smoke free premises. **All Rooms:** combo or shower baths.
Some Rooms: color TV. **Cards:** AE, CB, DI, DS, MC, VI.   ▢⊘🖨⊗

TORRINGTON—33,700

LODGINGS

SUPER 8 MOTEL   **Phone:** (860)496-0811
◆◆   All Year   1P: $51- 63   2P/1B: $56- 68   2P/2B: $56- 68   XP: $5   F12
Motel   **Location:** 1 mi e on US 202; SR 8 exit 44. 492 E Main St 06790. Fax: 860/482-6796. **Facility:** 51 rooms. 3
    stories; interior/exterior corridors. **Cards:** AE, CB, DI, DS, JC, MC, VI.   🄰🅂🄺 ♿ 🆅🄲🅁 ▢ 🖥 🖨 ⊗

YANKEE PEDLAR INN HOTEL   **Phone:** (860)489-9226
🅰🅰🅰 🆂🄰🆅🄴   All Year [CP]   1P: $99- 139   2P/1B: $99- 139   2P/2B: $99- 139   XP: $15
    Location: Downtown. 93 Main St 06790. Fax: 860/482-7851. **Facility:** 60 rooms. Authentic 1891 Inn with
◆◆   Hitchcock furnishing. 3 stories; interior corridors. **Dining:** Dining room; noon-2:30 & 5-10 pm; $10-$20;
Historic Hotel   cocktails. **All Rooms:** extended cable TV. **Cards:** AE, DI, MC, VI. **Special Amenities:** Free breakfast and
    free newspaper.   ♿ 🔟 ¶¶ ♿ ✚ ♿ 🆅🄲🅁 💻 ▢ 🖥 🖨 ⊗

TRUMBULL—32,000

LODGING

TRUMBULL MARRIOTT
◆◆◆
Hotel

Rates Subject to Change   Phone: 203/378-1400
Sun-Thurs   1P: $169- 189   2P/1B: $189- 209   2P/2B: $189- 209   XP: $20   F17
Fri & Sat   1P: $119- 139   2P/1B: $119- 139   2P/2B: $119- 139   XP: $20   F17
Location: 0.7 mi se of jct SR 108 & 8, exit 8. 180 Hawley Ln 06611. Fax: 203/378-4958. **Terms:** Check-in 4 pm. **Facility:** 323 rooms. 5 stories; interior corridors; heated indoor pool. **Services:** giftshop. Fee: area transportation. **Cards:** AE, CB, DI, DS, MC, VI.

UNION—650

RESTAURANT

TRAVELER'S FOOD & BOOKS
◆
American

Lunch: $6-$9   **Dinner:** $6-$9   Phone: 860/684-4920
Location: I-84 at exit 74, just e. 1257 Buckley Hwy 06076. **Hours:** 7 am-9 pm. Closed: 11/25 & 12/25.
Features: casual dress; children's menu; carryout; cocktails. Traveler's reprive. Wholesome family dining; free book with each meal. Used book cellar & adjacent Traveler's collectible shop. **Cards:** AE, MC, VI.

VERNON—See Hartford p. 230.

WALLINGFORD—41,800   (See map p. 245; index p. 243)

LODGINGS

COURTYARD BY MARRIOTT
◆◆◆
Motor Inn

Rates Subject to Change   Phone: 203/284-9400   **35**
Sun-Thurs   1P: $109   2P/1B: $109   2P/2B: $109
Fri & Sat   1P: $64   2P/2B: $74
Location: SR 68, just w of I-91, exit 15. 600 Northrup Rd 06492. Fax: m03/294-1163. **Facility:** 149 rooms. Contemporary setting; all rooms with hair dryer, iron & ironing board. 3 stories; interior corridors; heated indoor pool. **Cards:** AE, DI, DS, MC, VI. *(See color ad below)*

SUSSE CHALET INN
◆◆
Motel

Rates Subject to Change   Phone: (203)284-0001   **34**
All Year [CP]   1P: $54- 64   2P/1B: $61- 71   2P/2B: $68- 74   XP: $3   F17
Location: SR 68; just w of jct I-91, exit 15. 100 Chalet Dr 06492. Fax: 203/265-4703. **Facility:** 119 rooms. Very comfortable rooms. 4 stories; interior corridors. **Cards:** AE, CB, DI, DS, MC, VI. *(See ad p 223)*

RESTAURANT

THADDEUS J PEPPERCORN'S LTD
◆◆
American

Lunch: $10-$12   **Dinner:** $10-$12   Phone: 203/265-0222   **16**
Location: I-91 exit 15, 2.2 mi w. 101 N Plains Industrial Rd 06492. **Hours:** 11:30 am-10 pm, Fri & Sat-11 pm, Sun 11:30 am-9 pm; 7/1-10/4 Sat 4 pm-11 pm, Sun 4 pm-9 pm. Closed major holidays. **Reservations:** accepted; Mon-Thurs. **Features:** casual dress; children's menu; carryout; cocktails & lounge. Popular & buzzing casual dining, with extensive menu selection. **Cards:** AE, DS, MC, VI.

WASHINGTON—4,100

LODGING

THE MAYFLOWER INN
(AAA)
◆◆◆◆
Historic
Country Inn

Guaranteed Rates   Phone: (860)868-9466
All Year   2P/1B: $280- 720   XP: $50
Location: 0.3 mi s on SR 47. 118 Woodbury Rd 06793 (PO Box 1288). Fax: 860/868-1497. **Terms:** Age restrictions may apply; 2 night min stay, weekends. **Facility:** 25 rooms. Secluded wooded location set on 28 acres of rolling hills, stately maples, running streams & formal gardens. Spacious & impeccably appointed rooms & suites with sumptuous feather beds. 1 two-bedroom unit. 2-3 stories; interior corridors; smoke free premises; heated pool, saunas, steamrooms; 1 tennis court. **Dining:** Dining room, see separate listing. **Services:** giftshop. Fee: massage. **Recreation:** joggling board, country club privileges, hammocks, spa facilities. **Some Rooms:** kitchen, whirlpools. **Cards:** AE, MC, VI.

RESTAURANT

THE MAYFLOWER INN DINING ROOM   Country Inn   **Lunch:** $10-$14   **Dinner:** $17-$30   **Phone:** 860/868-9466
◆◆◆◆   **Location:** 0.3 mi s on SR 47; in The Mayflower Inn. 118 Woodbury Rd (Rt 47) 06793. **Hours:** 7:30 am-10,
Regional   noon-2 & 6-9 pm. **Reservations:** suggested. **Features:** casual dress; cocktails & lounge; valet parking; a la
American   carte. Fine dining in a relaxed, resort-casual setting. Innovative food preparation incorporate the freshest
             regional ingredients & international influences. Smoke free premises. **Cards:** AE, MC, VI.

WATERBURY—109,000

LODGINGS

COURTYARD BY MARRIOTT, WATERBURY CT   Rates Subject to Change   **Phone:** (203)596-1000
◆◆◆   Sun-Thurs   1P: $99   2P/1B: $99   2P/2B: $99
Hotel   Fri & Sat   1P: $80   2P/1B: $80   2P/2B: $80
          Location: I-84 exit 22, then n. 63 Grand St 06702. Fax: 203/753-6276. **Facility:** 200 rooms. Downtown. Ex-
tended stay suites w/kitchens avail; 11 stories; interior corridors; heated indoor pool. **Some Rooms:** 11 kitchens. **Cards:** AE,
DS, MC, VI.

HOUSE ON THE HILL   Guaranteed Rates   **Phone:** (203)757-9901
◆◆◆   5/1-12/15 & 1/15-4/30 [BP]   1P: $100- 150   2P/1B: $100- 150   XP: $15   F5
Historic Bed   **Location:** I-84 exit 21, 0.6 mi n on Meadow & Willow sts, 0.4 mi ne on Pine St. 92 Woodlawn Terr
& Breakfast   06710-1929. **Terms:** Open 5/1-12/15 & 1/15-4/30; age restrictions may apply; reserv deposit, 7 day notice;
handling fee imposed. **Facility:** 4 rooms. In quiet residential neighborhood. 1888 Victorian House. 3 stories;
interior corridors; smoke free premises. **All Rooms:** combo or tub baths.

SHERATON WATERBURY HOTEL   Rates Subject to Change   **Phone:** (203)573-1000
◆◆◆   All Year   1P: $95   2P/1B: $95   2P/2B: $95
Hotel   **Location:** I-84; westbound exit 26, eastbound exit 25A; 1st left & 1st right. 3580 E Main St 06705.
Fax: 203/573-1349. **Facility:** 279 rooms. Large central atrium with lounge, many plants & waterfall. Medium to
large well-equipped rooms. 2 suites; 4 stories; interior corridors; heated indoor pool; racquetball court. **Services:** giftshop.
Cards: AE, CB, DI, DS, MC, VI. *(See ad below)*

RESTAURANTS

AMERICAN STEAK HOUSE   **Lunch:** $5-$8   **Dinner:** $6-$10   **Phone:** 203/756-7529
◆   **Location:** On SR 69; 2.5 mi n of jct I-84, exit 23. 1011 Wolcott St 06705. **Hours:** 11 am-9 pm, Fri & Sat-10
Steak and pm. Closed: 11/25, 12/25 & 12/24 for dinner. **Features:** casual dress; children's menu; senior's menu; salad
Seafood   bar; beer & wine only. Cafeteria-style dining offering a varied selection of beef, seafood & chicken entrees
           with salad bar. **Cards:** MC, VI.

BACCO'S RESTAURANT   **Lunch:** $6-$9   **Dinner:** $6-$15   **Phone:** 203/755-1173
ⓐⓐⓐ   **Location:** SR 8, exit 36; 0.3 mi e on Huntingdon Ave & 0.3 mi s. 1230 Thomaston Ave 06704. **Hours:** 11:30
◆◆   am-10 pm, Fri-11 pm, Sat 4 pm-11 pm, Sun noon-8:30 pm. Closed major holidays & Mon.
Italian   **Reservations:** suggested. **Features:** casual dress; children's menu; carryout; cocktails; a la carte. Family
           atmosphere. **Cards:** AE, MC, VI.

DIORIO   **Lunch:** $8-$12   **Dinner:** $15-$23   **Phone:** 203/754-5111
◆◆◆   **Location:** Downtown. 231 Bank St 06702. **Hours:** 11:30 am-2:30 & 5:30-10 pm, Sat from 5:30 pm. Closed
Northern   major holidays & Sun. **Reservations:** suggested; weekends. **Features:** casual dress; carryout; cocktails &
Italian   lounge; a la carte. Historic restaurant originally opened 1927. Fresh pasta & daily specials. Valet parking
           Thurs-Sat evening. **Cards:** AE, DI, MC, VI.

TEQUILA'S   **Lunch:** $6-$8   **Dinner:** $8-$19   **Phone:** 203/755-4806
ⓐⓐⓐ   **Location:** Jct Wolcott St, just n. 733 Lakewood Rd 06704. **Hours:** 11 am-11 pm, Fri & Sat-midnight. Closed:
◆◆   12/25. **Features:** casual dress; children's menu; carryout; cocktails & lounge; a la carte. Creative entrees
Mexican   plus standard fare done well; a best of Connecticut award winner in a reader's poll. **Cards:** AE, DI, DS, MC,
           VI.

WATERFORD—2,900

LODGINGS

FAIRFIELD SUITES
♦♦♦
Motel

Rates Subject to Change | | | | Phone: 860/439-0151

6/1-8/31 [CP]	2P/1B:	$99-	139	2P/2B:	$99-	139	XP: $10	F18
9/1-10/31 [CP]	2P/1B:	$99-	109	2P/2B:	$99-	109	XP: $10	F18
5/1-5/31 & 4/1-4/30 [CP]	2P/1B:	$89-	109	2P/2B:	$89-	109	XP: $10	F18
11/1-3/31 [CP]	2P/1B:	$79-	99	2P/2B:	$79-	99	XP: $10	F18

Location: I-95 northbound, exit 82A, 0.8 mi n, then just w, then 0.8 mi s; southbound exit 83, 0.9 mi s. 401 N Frontage Rd 06385. Fax: 860/440-0809. **Terms:** 2 night min stay, weekends 6/1-8/31. **Facility:** 80 rooms. 3 stories; interior corridors. **Services:** area transportation. **Cards:** AE, CB, DI, DS, MC, VI.

LAMPLIGHTER MOTEL
Ⓐ
♦♦
Motel

Rates Subject to Change | | | | Phone: (860)442-7227

5/1-11/1	1P:	$55-	135	2P/1B:	$65-	135	2P/2B: $65- 135	XP: $10	F12
11/2-4/30	1P:	$55-	85	2P/1B:	$55-	85	2P/2B: $55- 85	XP: $10	F12

Location: I-95 exit 81, then s. 211 Waterford Pkwy North 06385. Fax: 860/442-7227. **Terms:** Reserv deposit; small pets only, $50 dep req. **Facility:** 38 rooms. 16 efficiencies; 2 stories; exterior corridors. **All Rooms:** extended cable TV. **Cards:** AE, CB, DI, DS, MC, VI.

OAKDELL MOTEL
Ⓐ
♦♦
Motel

Rates Subject to Change | | | | Phone: (860)442-9446

7/1-10/16	1P:	$50-	85	2P/1B:	$55-	85	2P/2B: $60- 95	XP: $5	F12
5/1-6/30	1P:	$45-	60	2P/1B:	$50-	75	2P/2B: $55- 85	XP: $5	F12
10/17-4/30	1P:	$45-	60	2P/1B:	$50-	75	2P/2B: $55- 85	XP: $5	F12

Location: On SR 85; 2 mi n of I-95, exit 82. 983 Hartford Rd 06385. **Terms:** 2 night min stay, weekends in season. **Facility:** 22 rooms. 2 stories; interior/exterior corridors. **All Rooms:** combo or shower baths. **Cards:** AE, DI, DS, MC, VI. *(See color ad p 239)*

WESTBROOK—2,100

LODGING

MAPLES MOTEL
Ⓐ [SAVE]
♦♦
Motel

Phone: 860/399-9345

5/15-10/15	1P:	$55	2P/1B:	$55- 75	2P/2B:	$75	XP: $5	F18
5/1-5/14, 10/16-12/15 & 4/2-4/30	1P:	$45	2P/1B:	$45	2P/2B:	$55	XP: $5	F18
12/16-4/1	1P:	$40	2P/1B:	$40	2P/2B:	$50	XP: $5	F18

Location: On US 1, 1.5 mi e of jct SR 153; I-95, exit 65. 1935 Boston Post Rd 06498. **Terms:** Reserv deposit, 5 day notice; weekly rates; 2 night min stay, summer weekends; pets. **Facility:** 18 rooms. Short walk to private beach. 1 two-bedroom unit. 1 story; exterior corridors. **All Rooms:** combo or shower baths. **Some Rooms:** 8 efficiencies. **Cards:** AE, MC, VI.

WEST HARTFORD—*See Hartford p. 231.*

WEST HAVEN—56,200   (See map p. 245; index p. 243)

LODGING

DAYS HOTEL NEW HAVEN/WEST HAVEN
♦♦
Motel

Rates Subject to Change | Phone: (203)933-0344 | 🔟38

All Year	1P:	$79- 109	2P/1B:	$79- 109	2P/2B:	$89- 125	XP: $10	F16

Location: On SR 162, 0.3 mi w of jct I-95, exit 42. 490 Sawmill Rd 06516. Fax: 203/937-1678. **Facility:** 102 rooms. 7 stories; interior corridors; heated indoor pool. **Cards:** AE, DI, MC, VI.

RESTAURANTS

AMERICAN STEAK HOUSE
♦
Steak and
Seafood

Lunch: $2-$5   **Dinner:** $6-$10   **Phone:** 203/937-7818   🔟19

Location: On SR 162, just n of I-95, exit 42. 354 Saw Mill Rd 06516. **Hours:** 11:30 am-9 pm, Fri & Sat-10 pm. Closed: 11/25 & 12/25. **Features:** casual dress; children's menu; senior's menu; carryout; salad bar; beer & wine only; minimum charge-after 1 pm. Cafeteria-style dining offering a varied selection of beef, seafood & chicken entrees with salad bar. **Cards:** MC, VI.

JIMMIES
♦♦
Seafood
VI.

Lunch: $5-$8   **Dinner:** $6-$18   **Phone:** 203/934-3212   🔟18

Location: At Savin Rock; I-95 exit 42, 2 mi e on Saw Mill Rd & Kelsey Ave. 5 Rock St 06516. **Hours:** 11 am-10 pm, Fri & Sat-11 pm. Closed: 11/25 & 12/25. **Features:** children's menu; early bird specials; cocktails & lounge. Hearty portions. Informal atmosphere. Setting looks out over Long Island Sound. **Cards:** DS, MC,

WESTON—12,500

RESTAURANT

COBB'S MILL BY THE WATERFALL Country Inn   **Lunch:** $8-$15   **Dinner:** $21-$30   **Phone:** 203/227-7221
♦♦♦
Continental

Location: Merritt Pkwy, exit 42; 4 mi n, just w on Old Mill Rd. 12 Old Mill Rd 06883. **Hours:** 11:30 am-2:30 & 5-9 pm, Mon from 5 pm, Fri & Sat 6 pm-10 pm, Sun 11 am-3 & 5-9 pm. Closed: 12/25. **Reservations:** suggested. **Features:** semi-formal attire; Sunday brunch; early bird specials; cocktails & lounge; a la carte. Converted pre-Revolutionary mill in picturesque setting. Charming rustic dining rooms. Valet parking for dinner. Early bird Mon-Thurs 5 pm-6:30pm. **Cards:** AE, DI, DS, MC, VI.

LODGINGS

THE INN AT NATIONAL HALL
Phone: (203)221-1351   [23]
All Year [CP]   1P: $200- 600   2P/1B: $200- 600   XP: $15   F
Location: I-95 exit 17, 1.5 mi n on SR 33. Two Post Rd W 06880. Fax: 203/221-0276. **Terms:** Reserv deposit, 7 day notice. **Facility:** 15 rooms. Historic luxurious property on the Saugatuck River. Individual room theme decor. Trompe L'oeil & stencil whimsy complement antiques & rich furnishings. A member of Relais & Chateaux. 3 stories; interior corridors; smoke free premises. **Dining:** The Restaurant At National Hall, see separate listing. **Recreation:** YMCA privileges nearby. **All Rooms:** extended cable TV. **Some Rooms:** whirlpools. **Cards:** AE, DI, MC, VI. **Special Amenities: Free breakfast and free newspaper.**

Historic Country Inn

THE WESTPORT INN
Rates Subject to Change   Phone: (203)259-5236   [22]
All Year   1P: $110- 154   2P/1B: $120- 164   2P/2B: $120- 164   XP: $10   F18
Location: Northbound I-95 exit 18, n to US 1; 1.5 mi e on US 1; southbound exit 19, 1 mi w. 1595 Post Rd E 06880. Fax: 203/254-8439. **Facility:** 116 rooms. 1-bedroom suite, $210; 2-bedroom suite, $255; 2 whirlpool rms, extra charge; 2 stories; interior/exterior corridors; heated indoor pool. **Cards:** AE, CB, DI, DS, MC, VI.
(See color ad below)

Motel

RED ALERT!

receive from AAA members. They are telling you they're willing to go the extra mile to get your business. Some even offer special amenities designed just for you.

And don't forget to look for the establishments that display the familiar SAVE icon to receive discounts.

So, when you turn to the AAA TourBook to make your travel plans, be on the look out for the establishments that will give you the special treatment you deserve.

Whenever you pick up a AAA TourBook®, be alert for the establishments that display a bright red AAA logo beside their listing. These establishments place a high value on the patronage they

(See map p. 212)

RESTAURANT

THE RESTAURANT AT NATIONAL HALL   **Lunch:** $10-$14   **Dinner:** $18-$27   **Phone:** 203/221-7572   ⑲
◆◆◆◆   **Location:** I-95 exit 17, 1.5 mi n on SR 33; in The Inn at National Hall. Two Post Rd W 06880.
Regional   **Hours:** noon-2 & 6-10 pm; Sun noon-3 pm. **Reservations:** suggested. **Features:** casual dress; Sunday
American   brunch; health conscious menu items; cocktails & lounge; a la carte. Contemporary & continental influences
with an award-winning wine list. Refined, warm decor. Gracious service. Seasonal ala carte & prixe fixe
menus with innovative daily chef specials. Outdoor patio dining in summer. Smoke free premises. **Cards:** AE, DI, MC, VI.
☒

WETHERSFIELD—See Hartford p. 231.

WILLINGTON—6,000

LODGING

SLEEP INN   **Phone:** (860)684-1400
🅰🅰🅰 [SAVE]   5/1-10/31 Wkly [CP]   1P: $63- 72   2P/1B: $72- 81   2P/2B: $68- 75   XP: $10   F18
                     11/1-4/30 Wkly [CP]   1P: $50- 59   2P/1B: $59- 63   2P/2B: $54- 58   XP: $10   F18
◆◆   **Location:** On SR 320, just s of I-84, exit 71. 327 Ruby Rd 06279. Fax: 860/684-1400. **Facility:** 62 rooms. Ad-
Motel   jacent to Travel Park Rest Area. Free fax, local telephone call service & voice mail. 3 stories; interior corridors.
      Dining: Restaurant nearby. **All Rooms:** combo or shower baths. **Cards:** AE, CB, DI, DS, JC, MC, VI.
**Special Amenities: Early check-in/late check-out and free room upgrade (subject to availability with advanced
reservations).** (See color ad p 424)

WINDSOR—See Hartford p. 231.

WINDSOR LOCKS—See Hartford p. 232.

WOODBURY—8,100

RESTAURANTS

CURTIS HOUSE   Country Inn   **Lunch:** $8-$13   **Dinner:** $14-$20   **Phone:** 203-263-2101
◆   **Location:** From I-84 exit 15, 5 mi n on US 6. 506 Main St S (SR 6) 06798. **Hours:** noon-2 & 5-8:30 pm, Fri
American   & Sat-9 pm, Sun noon-8 pm. Closed: 12/25 & Mon for lunch. **Features:** casual dress; cocktails & lounge.
      Complete dinners. Colonial decor tavern. Traditional American cuisine such as Yankee pot roast. **Cards:** DS,
MC, VI.
☒

GOOD NEWS CAFE   **Lunch:** $8-$14   **Dinner:** $13-$24   **Phone:** 203/266-4663
◆◆◆   **Location:** At Rt 6 & 64. 694 Main St S 06798. **Hours:** 11:30 am-2:30 & 5-10 pm, Fri & Sat-10:30 pm, Sun
American   noon-3 & 5-10 pm. Closed major holidays & Tues. **Reservations:** suggested. **Features:** dressy casual;
      health conscious menu items; carryout; cocktails & lounge; a la carte. Whimsical atmosphere with artwork &
sculpture; dining on patio. Menu features onion bundle, wok-seared shrimp & whipped yucca. Desserts include lemon
shortcake, peach tarts & chocolate cupcakes. Asian & French entree choices. **Cards:** AE, DI, MC, VI.
☒

Meal Plan Indicators

CP = Continental Plan of pastry, juice and another beverage or may offer
expanded breakfast items

BP = Breakfast Plan of full hot breakfast

AP = American Plan of three meals daily

MAP = Modified American Plan of two meals daily

EP = European Plan, where rate includes only room

Family Plan Indicators

The establishment may limit the number of children to whom the family plan applies.

F17 = children 17 and under stay free (age displayed will reflect property's policy)

D17 = discount for children 17 and under

F = children stay free

D = discounts for children

Use Your AAA Membership Card to SAVE BIG!

Whenever you see the Show Your Card & Save* symbol at thousands of participating businesses, show your AAA membership card for exclusive discounts. Save big on hotel rooms, theme park tickets, car rentals, and more — just for being a AAA member! For more information, call your local AAA office. Have your membership card handy when calling.

The Show Your Card & Save program is the official discount program of AAA and CAA. Valid AAA membership card required. Various restrictions apply. Not valid with other discounts. Good at participating locations only. Offers subject to change without notice. Offers expire 12/31/99.

Massachusetts

ACTON—See Boston p. 291.

AMESBURY—See Boston p. 291.

AMHERST—35,200

LODGINGS

ALLEN HOUSE VICTORIAN BED & BREAKFAST INN   Rates Subject to Change   **Phone:** 413/253-5000
5/1-11/15 & 4/1-4/30 [BP]   1P: $65- 105   2P/1B: $75- 125   2P/2B: $85- 135   XP: $10-20
11/16-3/31 [BP]   1P: $45- 85   2P/1B: $55- 105   2P/2B: $65- 115   XP: $10-20
Location: Center, 0.8 mi e. 599 Main St 01002. **Terms:** Reserv deposit, 14 day notice; weekly rates; EP
avail. **Facility:** 7 rooms. Vintage 1886 Queen Anne stick style Victorian home, with its unique charm & char-
Historic Bed & Breakfast   acter carefully preserved. 2 stories; interior corridors. **Dining:** Afternoon tea. **All Rooms:** shower or tub
baths. **Cards:** DS, MC, VI.

UNIVERSITY LODGE   Rates Subject to Change   **Phone:** (413)256-8111
All Year   1P: $55- 95   2P/1B: $65- 95   2P/2B: $65- 95   XP: $10   F17
Motel   **Location:** 0.9 mi n of center. 345 N Pleasant St 01002. **Facility:** 20 rooms. 2 stories; exterior corridors.
Cards: AE, MC, VI. *(See color ad below)*

ANDOVER—See Boston p. 291.

AUBURN—15,000

LODGINGS

BAYMONT INN & SUITES-WORCESTER   Rates Subject to Change   **Phone:** 508/832-7000
Fri & Sat 5/28-10/30   1P: $68- 84   2P/1B: $78- 94   2P/2B: $84- 89
Motel   5/1-5/27, Sun-Thurs
5/28-10/30 & 10/31-4/30   1P: $63- 79   2P/1B: $73- 89   2P/2B: $79- 84
Location: From I-90 (Massachusetts Tpk) exit 10, 1 mi n on SR 12; from I-290, exit 9 to SR 12, then s. 444 Southbridge St
01501. Fax: 508/832-5790. **Facility:** 102 rooms. 3 stories; interior corridors. **Cards:** AE, CB, DI, DS, MC, VI.
(See color ad p 435)

DAYS INN-AUBURN
◆◆◆   5/1-11/15 [CP]
Motel   11/16-4/30 [CP]

Rates Subject to Change
1P: $68- 115 2P/1B: $74- 126 2P/2B: $74- 126 XP: $10   F18
1P: $70- 77 2P/1B: $78- 86 2P/2B: $78- 86 XP: $10   F18

Phone: 508/832-8300

Location: From I-90 (Massachusetts Tpk) exit 10, 1 mi n on SR 12; from I-290 exit 9 to SR 12. 426 Southbridge St 01501. Fax: 508/832-4579. **Facility:** 70 rooms. Across from shopping mall. 3 whirlpool rms, $125-$138; 3 stories; interior corridors. **Cards:** AE, CB, DI, DS, MC, VI.

RAMADA INN-WORCESTER/AUBURN
(AAA)   All Year
◆◆◆
Motor Inn

Rates Subject to Change
1P: $90   2P/1B: $90   2P/2B: $100   XP: $10   F17

Phone: (508)832-3221

Location: On SR 12 at I-90 (Massachusetts Tpk) exit 10, SR 12 north ramp; from I-290 exit 8 to SR 12S. 624 Southbridge St 01501. Fax: 508/832-8366. **Terms:** Package plans. **Facility:** 161 rooms. Colonial decor. 8 suites with refrigerator, $125; 2-3 stories; interior corridors; heated indoor pool, sauna, whirlpool. **Dining:** Restaurant; 6 am-10 pm, Sun-9 pm; $12-$16; cocktails. **Services:** area transportation. **Cards:** AE, CB, DI, DS, JC, MC, VI. *(See color ad inside front cover & p 435)*

RESTAURANT

PICCADILLY PUB   **Lunch:** $4-$10   **Dinner:** $6-$12   Phone: 508/832-4762
◆◆
American

Location: On SR 12; just s of I-90 exit 10; from I-290 exit to SR 12S. 602 Southbridge St 01501-1912. **Hours:** 11:30 am-1 am, Sun noon-10 pm. Closed: 11/25 & 12/25. **Features:** casual dress; children's menu; carryout; cocktails & lounge. Informal relaxed atmosphere. Ample portions. Burgers, sandwiches, Angus beef, poultry & seafood. Friendly service. **Cards:** AE, CB, DI, DS, MC, VI.

BARNSTABLE—*See Cape Cod p. 333.*

BARRE—4,500

LODGING

JENKINS INN   Phone: (978)355-6444
(AAA) SAVE   All Year [BP]   1P: $95- 135 2P/1B: $95- 135 2P/2B: $95- 135 XP: $25
◆◆◆
Historic
Country Inn

Location: Ne end of town green on SR 122 & 32. 7 West St 01005 (PO Box 779). **Terms:** Age restrictions may apply; reserv deposit, 14 day notice; handling fee imposed; 2 night min stay, weekends 5/1-10/31; pets, $5 extra charge. **Facility:** 5 rooms. 1834 house on town green with English gardens. 2 stories; interior corridors; smoke free premises. **Dining:** Dining room; noon-2:30 & 5-8 pm, Fri & Sat-9:30 pm. Closed Mon & Tues; $10-$16; cocktails. **Cards:** AE, CB, DI, DS, MC, VI. **Special Amenities:** Free breakfast and free local telephone calls.

BEDFORD—*See Boston p. 292.*

BEVERLY—*See Boston p. 292.*

24-HOUR SERVICE

Is a requirement for all AAA establishments
with overnight accommodations.
It is not necessary for the office to be open
24 hours, but a responsible attendant
must be available on the premises at all times.

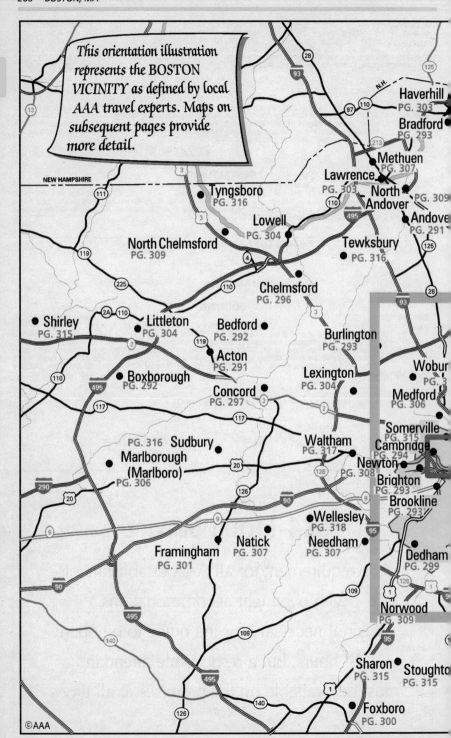

This orientation illustration represents the BOSTON VICINITY as defined by local AAA travel experts. Maps on subsequent pages provide more detail.

NEW HAMPSHIRE

Haverhill
PG. 303

Bradford
PG. 293

Methuen
PG. 307

Lawrence
PG. 303

North Andover
PG. 309

Andover
PG. 291

Tyngsboro
PG. 316

Lowell
PG. 304

Tewksbury
PG. 316

North Chelmsford
PG. 309

Chelmsford
PG. 296

Shirley
PG. 315

Littleton
PG. 304

Bedford
PG. 292

Burlington
PG. 293

Wobur
PG. 3

Acton
PG. 291

Lexington
PG. 304

Medford
PG. 306

Boxborough
PG. 292

Concord
PG. 297

Somerville
PG. 315

Cambridge
PG. 294

PG. 316 Sudbury

Waltham
PG. 317

Newton
PG. 308

Marlborough
(Marlboro)
PG. 306

Brighton
PG. 293

Brookline
PG. 293

Wellesley
PG. 318

Natick
PG. 307

Needham
PG. 307

Dedham
PG. 299

Framingham
PG. 301

Norwood
PG. 309

Sharon
PG. 315

Stoughto
PG. 315

Foxboro
PG. 300

©AAA

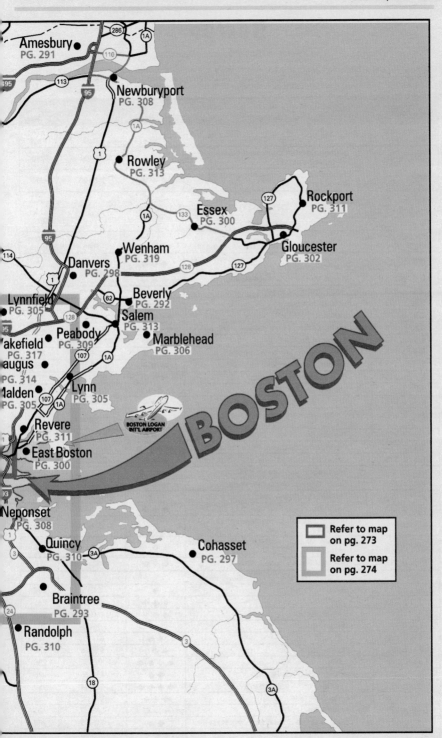

Amesbury
PG. 291

Newburyport
PG. 308

Rowley
PG. 313

Rockport
PG. 311

Essex
PG. 300

Wenham
PG. 319

Gloucester
PG. 302

Danvers
PG. 298

Lynnfield
PG. 305

Beverly
PG. 292

Salem
PG. 313

Peabody
PG. 309

akefield
PG. 317

augus
PG. 314

Marblehead
PG. 306

Lynn
PG. 305

Malden
PG. 305

BOSTON LOGAN
INT'L AIRPORT

BOSTON

Revere
PG. 311

East Boston
PG. 300

Neponset
PG. 308

Quincy
PG. 310

Cohasset
PG. 297

Braintree
PG. 293

Randolph
PG. 310

Refer to map
on pg. 273

Refer to map
on pg. 274

Boston

pop. 574,300

This index helps you "spot" where approved accommodations are located on the detailed maps that follow. Rate ranges are for comparison only and show the property's high season. Turn to the listing page for more detailed rate information and consult display ads for special promotions. Restaurant rate range is for dinner, unless only lunch (L) is served.

✈ Airport Accommodations

Spotter/Map Pg. Number	OA	BOSTON	Rating	Rate	Listing Page
122 / p. 274	⊕	Harborside Hyatt Conference Center and Hotel, at the airport	◆◆◆	$325-400 [SAVE]	290
140 / p. 274		Holiday Inn Boston-Logan Airport, 1.5 mi n of airport terminal	◆◆◆	$189-209	300

DOWNTOWN BOSTON

Spotter/Map Pg.Number	OA	DOWNTOWN BOSTON - Lodgings	Rating	Rate	Listing Page
1 / p. 273		Holiday Inn Select-Boston Government Center - see color ad p 275	◆◆◆	$116-260	279
2 / p. 273		Boston Marriott Long Wharf Hotel	◆◆◆	$335-365	276
3 / p. 273	⊕	Regal Bostonian Hotel	◆◆◆	$289 [SAVE]	283
4 / p. 273		Hotel Le Meridien	◆◆◆◆	$345-440	279
5 / p. 273		Boston Harbor Hotel	◆◆◆◆	$235-510	276
7 / p. 273		Fairmont Copley Plaza - see ad p 278	◆◆◆◆	$289-309	279
8 / p. 273	⊕	Swissotel Boston	◆◆◆	$260-290 [SAVE]	283
9 / p. 273		Tremont Hotel - see color ad p 284	◆◆◆	$209-299	284
10 / p. 273		Newbury Guest House	◆◆◆	$125-155	282
12 / p. 273	⊕	Four Seasons Hotel Boston	◆◆◆◆◆	$550-705	279
13 / p. 273	⊕	The Ritz-Carlton, Boston	◆◆◆◆	$335-425	283
15 / p. 273		Harborside Inn of Boston	◆◆◆	$145-185	279
16 / p. 273		Boston Park Plaza Hotel & Towers - see ad p 277	◆◆◆	$319	277
17 / p. 273		The Eliot Suite Hotel	◆◆◆	$275-395	278
19 / p. 273		The Westin Hotel,Copley Place Boston	◆◆◆◆	$219-365	284
20 / p. 273		Copley Square Hotel - see ad p 277	◆◆◆	$215-245	278
21 / p. 273	⊕	The Lenox Hotel - see ad p 282	◆◆◆◆	$298-498	282
22 / p. 273		Boston Marriott Hotel Copley Place	◆◆◆	$189-329	276
23 / p. 273	⊕	The Midtown Hotel - see color ad p 283	◆◆	$119-229 [SAVE]	282
24 / p. 273		Boston Back Bay Hilton - see color ad p 37	◆◆◆	$210-250	276
25 / p. 273	⊕	Howard Johnson Lodge Fenway - see color ad p 281	◆	$115-199 [SAVE]	280
26 / p. 273	⊕	Howard Johnson Hotel-Kenmore - see color ad p 281	◆	$135-235 [SAVE]	280
27 / p. 273	⊕	Sheraton-Boston Hotel & Towers	◆◆◆	$314	283
		DOWNTOWN BOSTON - Restaurants			
1 / p. 273		No Name Restaurant	◆	$8-15	286
2 / p. 273		Clio	◆◆◆	$20-34	285
4 / p. 273		Mamma Maria	◆◆◆	$19-28	286
5 / p. 273	⊕	Durgin Park	◆	$6-20	285
6 / p. 273		Lala Rokh	◆◆	$14-16	286
7 / p. 273		Maison Robert	◆◆◆	$18-30	286
9 / p. 273		Julien	◆◆◆◆	$35-50	286
10 / p. 273		Jimmy's Harborside Restaurant	◆◆	$16-25	286
12 / p. 273		The Oak Room - see ad p 278	◆◆◆◆	$23-34	286
13 / p. 273		Locke-Ober Cafe	◆◆◆	$19-40	286
15 / p. 273	⊕	Aujourd'hui	◆◆◆◆◆	$32-39	285
16 / p. 273		Legal Seafoods at the Boston Park Plaza	◆◆	$15-25	286
17 / p. 273		Biba	◆◆◆	$25-35	285

Spotter/Map Pg.Number	OA	DOWNTOWN BOSTON - Restaurants (contd.)	Rating	Rate	Listing Page
⑱ / p. 273		The Ritz-Carlton Dining Room	◆◆◆◆	$32-43	287
⑲ / p. 273		Small Planet Bar & Grill	◆◆	$10-16	287
㉑ / p. 273	AAA	**The Cafe Budapest**	◆◆◆	$20-33	285
㉒ / p. 273	AAA	**The Capital Grille**	◆◆◆	$22-35	285
㉓ / p. 273		Top of the Hub	◆◆◆	$19-30	287
㉔ / p. 273		L'Espalier	◆◆◆◆	$65-82	286
㉖ / p. 273		Ristorante Davide	◆◆◆	$18-30	287
㉗ / p. 273		Eastern Pier Chinese Restaurant	◆	$7-12	285
㉘ / p. 273		Anago	◆◆◆	$20-30	285
㉜ / p. 273		Pignoli	◆◆◆	$20-35	287
㉝ / p. 273		Rowes Wharf Restaurant	◆◆◆◆	$26-31	287
㉞ / p. 273		Red Herring	◆◆	$21-27	287
㊱ / p. 273		Ambrosia on Huntington	◆◆◆	$15-35	285
㊲ / p. 273		Cottonwood Restaurant & Cafe	◆◆	$13-22	285
㊳ / p. 273		Davio's	◆◆◆	$15-29	285
㊴ / p. 273		Grill 23 & Bar	◆◆◆	$19-35	286
㊵ / p. 273		Legal SeaFoods Restaurant	◆◆	$14-25	286
㊶ / p. 273		Icarus	◆◆◆	$20-30	286
㊷ / p. 273		Galleria Italiana	◆◆◆	$17-22	285
㊸ / p. 273		Omonia Greek Restaurant	◆◆	$12-19	286
㊹ / p. 273		Sonsie	◆◆	$12-27	287

BOSTON

Spotter/Map Pg.Number	OA	BOSTON - Lodgings	Rating	Rate	Listing Page
(125) / p. 274		Daystop-Boston	◆◆	$109	287
(124) / p. 274		Days Inn-Boston	◆◆	$109-129	287
(123) / p. 274	AAA	**Best Western Boston-The Inn at Longwood Medical - see color ad p 280**	◆◆◆	$129-209	287
(121) / p. 274		Doubletree Guest Suites-Boston/Cambridge - see color ad p 290	◆◆◆	$159-259	289
(122) / p. 274	AAA	**Harborside Hyatt Conference Center and Hotel**	◆◆◆	$325-400 SAVE	290
		BOSTON - Restaurants			
(132) / p. 274		Harborside Grill	◆◆	$21-26	290
(133) / p. 274		Hamersley's Bistro	◆◆◆	$20-30	290

Boston Vicinity

Spotter/Map Pg.Number	OA	CAMBRIDGE - Lodgings	Rating	Rate	Listing Page
㉘ / p. 273		Royal Sonesta Hotel Boston	◆◆◆	$149-319	296
㉙ / p. 273		Boston Marriott Cambridge	◆◆◆	$179-279	295
㊻ / p. 274	AAA	**Best Western Homestead Inn - see color ad p 295**	◆◆◆	$149-229	295
㊼ / p. 274		Harvard Square Hotel	◆◆	$189-199	295
㊽ / p. 274		A Cambridge House Bed & Breakfast Inn - see ad p 284	◆◆◆	$129-250	294
㊾ / p. 274		The Inn at Harvard	◆◆◆	$229	295
㊿ / p. 274		Sheraton Commander Hotel	◆◆◆	$299	296
(51) / p. 274		Hyatt Regency Cambridge	◆◆◆	$325-350	295
(52) / p. 274	AAA	**Howard Johnson Hotel Cambridge - see color ad p 281**	◆	$135-245 SAVE	295
(53) / p. 274		The Charles Hotel in Harvard Square	◆◆◆	$185	295
(55) / p. 274		Irving House at Harvard	◆	$115-165	296
		CAMBRIDGE - Restaurants			
㊺ / p. 273		Legal Sea Foods	◆◆	$15-25	296
㊻ / p. 273		Salamander	◆◆◆	$19-29	296

Spotter/Map Pg.Number	OA	CAMBRIDGE - Restaurants (contd.)	Rating	Rate	Listing Page
61 / p. 274		Sandrine's Bistro	◆◆◆	$18-29	296
62 / p. 274		Bisuteki Japanese Steak House	◆◆	$15-20	296
63 / p. 274		Cottonwood Cafe	◆◆	$13-18	296
64 / p. 274		Rialto	◆◆◆	$20-34	296
		BEDFORD - Lodgings			
30 / p. 274		Renaissance Bedford Hotel	◆◆◆	$179	292
31 / p. 274		Travelodge-Bedford	◆	$79-89	292
32 / p. 274	⚋	Ramada Inn-Bedford/Boston - see color ad inside front cover	◆◆◆	$89-119 ⬛	292
		BEDFORD - Restaurants			
49 / p. 274		Dalya's Restaurant	◆◆	$10-23	292
50 / p. 274		Havilland's Grill	◆◆◆	$14-30	292
		BROOKLINE - Lodgings			
37 / p. 274		Holiday Inn Boston Brookline - see color ad p 275	◆◆◆	$199-259	293
		BURLINGTON - Lodgings			
40 / p. 274		Summerfield Suites Hotel	◆◆◆	$209-289	293
42 / p. 274		Boston Marriott Hotel Burlington	◆◆◆	$159-229	293
43 / p. 274		Wyndham Garden Hotel - see color ad p 294	◆◆◆	$134-143	294
		BURLINGTON - Restaurants			
55 / p. 274		Victoria Station-Burlington	◆	$12-21	294
56 / p. 274		Johnny Rockets Restaurant	◆	$3-6	294
57 / p. 274		The Dandelion Green	◆◆	$14-22	294
58 / p. 274		Legal Sea Foods	◆◆	$14-22	294
59 / p. 274		Cafe Escadrille	◆◆◆	$17-23	294
		DEDHAM - Lodgings			
56 / p. 274	⚋	Holiday Inn-Dedham - see color ad p 275, p 299	◆◆	$99-129 ⬛	300
57 / p. 274		Hilton at Dedham Place - see color ad p 37	◆◆◆	$150-205	299
58 / p. 274	⚋	Comfort Inn-Dedham	◆◆	$102-122 ⬛	299
60 / p. 274	⚋	Residence Inn by Marriott	◆◆◆	$135-165	300
		NEPONSET - Lodgings			
62 / p. 274	⚋	Susse Chalet Boston Lodge - see ad p 289	◆◆	$120-145 ⬛	308
63 / p. 274	⚋	Susse Chalet Boston Inn - see ad p 289 & color ad p 284	◆◆◆	$135-175 ⬛	308
		NEPONSET - Restaurant			
75 / p. 274	⚋	Phillips Old Colony House	◆◆◆	$14-19	308
		LEXINGTON - Lodgings			
65 / p. 274		Sheraton Lexington Inn	◆◆◆	$250	304
66 / p. 274		Battle Green Motor Inn - see ad p 289	◆	$95-99	304
		MALDEN - Lodgings			
68 / p. 274	⚋	New Englander Motor Court	◆	$89-99 ⬛	305
		NEWTON - Lodgings			
70 / p. 274		Sheraton Newton Hotel	◆◆◆	$89-199	308
71 / p. 274		Boston Marriott Hotel Newton	◆◆◆	$189	308
72 / p. 274		Susse Chalet Inn - see ad p 289	◆◆	$97-120	308
73 / p. 274		Holiday Inn - see color ad p 275	◆◆◆	$119-159	308
		NEWTON - Restaurant			
80 / p. 274		Pillar House	◆◆◆	$17-30	309
		NORWOOD - Lodgings			
75 / p. 274		Sheraton Four Points	◆◆	$109-145	309
76 / p. 274		Courtyard by Marriott-Norwood - see color ad p 280	◆◆◆	$139	309
		NORWOOD - Restaurants			
86 / p. 274		Spaghetti Freddy's	◆◆	$8-12	309
87 / p. 274		Franco's	◆◆◆	$12-24	309

Spotter/Map Pg.Number	OA	PEABODY - Lodgings	Rating	Rate	Listing Page
79 / p. 274		Holiday Inn - see color ad p 275	◆◆	$129	309
80 / p. 274		Boston Marriott Peabody	◆◆◆	$129-159	309
		PEABODY - Restaurants			
91 / p. 274		Bugaboo Creek Steak House	◆◆	$8-17	310
93 / p. 274		Legal Sea Foods	◆◆	$7-18	310
		REVERE - Lodgings			
83 / p. 274		Comfort Inn-Revere - see color ad p 311	◆◆◆	$88-169	311
84 / p. 274		Howard Johnson Hotel	◆◆	$99-139	311
		SAUGUS - Lodgings			
86 / p. 274	⚛	**Days Inn-Saugus/Logan Airport - see color ad p 278**	◆◆◆	$109-199 🈂	314
		SAUGUS - Restaurants			
98 / p. 274		Kelly's World Famous Roast Beef & Seafood	◆	$4-12	314
100 / p. 274	⚛	**The Continental Restaurant**	◆◆	$14-20	314
101 / p. 274		Spud's Restaurant & Pub	◆	$5-9	314
103 / p. 274		Ristorante Donatello	◆◆◆	$13-20	314
		WAKEFIELD - Lodgings			
87 / p. 274	⚛	**Best Western Lord Wakefield Hotel**	◆◆	$69-109	317
88 / p. 274		Colonial Hilton and Resort - see color ad p 37	◆◆◆	$189	317
		WALTHAM - Lodgings			
90 / p. 274		Home Suites Inn of Boston-Waltham - see color ad p 288	◆◆◆	$95-160	317
91 / p. 274		Best Western TLC Hotel		$99-175	317
92 / p. 274		Susse Chalet Inn-Waltham/Boston - see ad p 289	◆◆	$85-107	318
93 / p. 274		The Westin Hotel,Waltham	◆◆◆◆	$99-255	318
94 / p. 274		Doubletree Guest Suites Boston/Waltham - see color ad p 290, p 317	◆◆◆	$175	317
95 / p. 274		Wyndham Garden Hotel - see color ad p 318	◆◆◆	$134-143	318
96 / p. 274		Summerfield Suites Hotel	◆◆◆	$169-299	318
		WALTHAM - Restaurants			
115 / p. 274		Tuscan Grill	◆◆◆	$14-18	318
116 / p. 274		Erawan of Siam	◆◆	$15-20	318
117 / p. 274		Il Capriccio	◆◆◆	$19-27	318
		WOBURN - Lodgings			
99 / p. 274		Sierra Suites Hotel	◆◆◆	$145	320
100 / p. 274		Courtyard By Marriott-Woburn - see color ad p 280	◆◆◆	$119-169	319
101 / p. 274		Crowne Plaza Boston/Woburn	◆◆◆	$189	319
102 / p. 274		Susse Chalet Inn - see ad p 289	◆◆	$77-97	320
103 / p. 274		Howard Johnson Hotel-Woburn	◆◆	$89-135	319
104 / p. 274		Ramada Inn Hotel - see color ad inside front cover	◆◆	$129	319
105 / p. 274	⚛	**Red Roof Inn Woburn**	◆◆	$86-116 🈂	320
106 / p. 274		Hampton Inn Boston-Woburn	◆◆	$149-159	319
		WOBURN - Restaurants			
120 / p. 274		Spud's Restaurant & Pub	◆	$7-11	320
121 / p. 274		J C Hillary's, Ltd	◆◆	$12-18	320
		NEEDHAM - Lodgings			
108 / p. 274		Sheraton Needham Hotel	◆◆◆	$179-400	307
		RANDOLPH - Lodgings			
110 / p. 274		Holiday Inn-Randolph - see color ad p 275	◆◆◆	$149	310
		RANDOLPH - Restaurant			
124 / p. 274		Caffe Bella	◆◆◆	$16-20	310
		STOUGHTON - Lodgings			
112 / p. 274		Courtyard by Marriott-Stoughton - see color ad p 280	◆◆◆	$124-139	315

Spotter/Map Pg.Number	OA	LYNN - Lodgings	Rating	Rate	Listing Page
114 / p. 274		The Red Maple Bed & Breakfast	◆◆	$120-140	305
116 / p. 274		Diamond District Bed & Breakfast Inn - see color ad p 305	◆◆◆	$110-245	305
		BRAINTREE - Lodgings			
118 / p. 274	ⓐⓐⓐ	**Days Inn-Braintree**	◆◆	$100-110 🆂🅰🆅🅴	293
120 / p. 274		Sheraton Braintree Hotel	◆◆	$234	293
		BRAINTREE - Restaurant			
127 / p. 274		Hilltop Steak House	◆	$10-20	293
		BRIGHTON - Lodgings			
127 / p. 274	ⓐⓐⓐ	**Best Western-Terrace Inn - see ad p 279**	◆◆	$109-149 🆂🅰🆅🅴	293
		SOMERVILLE - Lodgings			
130 / p. 274	ⓐⓐⓐ	**Holiday Inn-Boston/Somerville - see color ad p 275**	◆◆◆	$190 🆂🅰🆅🅴	315
		SOMERVILLE - Restaurant			
138 / p. 274		Dali Restaurant & Tapas Bar	◆◆	$14-21	315
		QUINCY - Lodgings			
135 / p. 274		Presidents' City Inn	◆	$79-85	310
		QUINCY - Restaurants			
141 / p. 274		The Fours Restaurant & Sports Bar	◆◆	$7-14	310
144 / p. 274		Mando's Italian Bistro	◆◆	$10-16	310
		EAST BOSTON - Lodgings			
140 / p. 274		Holiday Inn Boston-Logan Airport - see color ad p 275	◆◆◆	$189-209	300
		LYNNFIELD - Restaurants			
147 / p. 274		Weathervane Seafood Restaurant	◆	$5-18	305
148 / p. 274	ⓐⓐⓐ	**The Kernwood At Lynnfield**	◆◆	$11-20	305
		WELLESLEY - Restaurant			
150 / p. 274		Amarin	◆◆	$9-15	318

Want to stay close to **the stadium?**

The ocean? The convention center?

Spotting maps of selected major metropolitan

and resort areas will help you choose the best location.

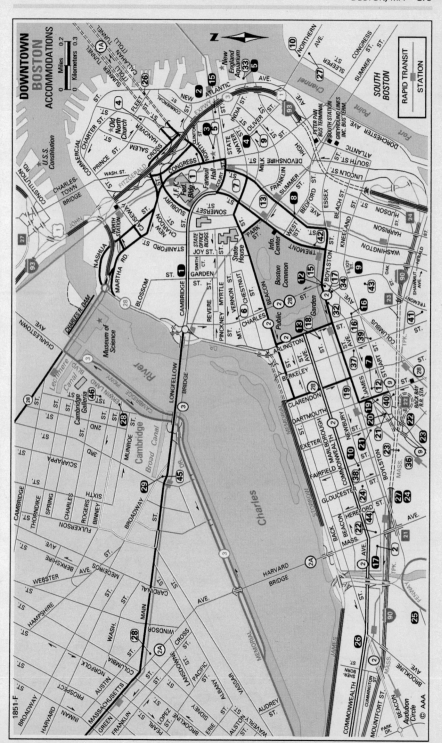

DOWNTOWN BOSTON ACCOMMODATIONS

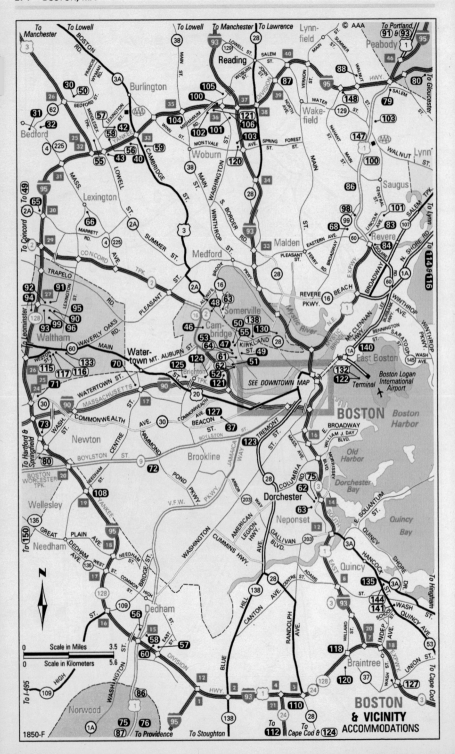

BOSTON & VICINITY ACCOMMODATIONS

You're always close to a great stay in the Boston Area.

As you travel through Boston, there's always a Holiday Inn® hotel nearby. Now better than ever with brand new renovations, a great stay is always on the way.

Holiday Inn
www.holiday-inn.com

Call 1-800-HOLIDAY or these hotels directly for AAA Rates in the Boston Area.

Show this ad and receive $10.00 off the AAA Rate:*

1 Boxborough
(I-495 Exit 28)
242 Adams Place
Boxborough, MA
(978) 263-8701

2 Brookline
1200 Beacon St.
Brookline, MA
(617) 277-1200

3 Dedham Hotel &
Conference Center
55 Ariadne Road
Dedham, MA
(781) 329-1000

4 Logan Airport
225 McClellan Hwy.
Boston, MA
(617) 569-5250

5 Mansfield–
Foxboro Area
31 Hampshire St.
Mansfield, MA
(508) 339-2200

6 Metro South/
Brockton
195 Westgate Drive
Brockton, MA
(508) 588-6300

7 Newton (I-95)
399 Grove Street
Newton, MA
(617) 969-5300

8 Peabody
1 Newbury Street
Peabody, MA
(978) 535-4600

9 Randolph
(Quincy–Braintree Area)
1374 N. Main Street
Randolph, MA
(781) 961-1000

10 Somerville
30 Washington Street
Somerville, MA
(617) 628-1000

11 Tewksbury–Andover
4 Highwood Drive
Tewksbury, MA
(978) 640-9000

12 Worcester
500 Lincoln Street
Worcester, MA
(508) 852-4000

Holiday Inn SELECT

13 Government Center
5 Blossom Street
Boston, MA
(617) 742-7630

Boston Area

DOWNTOWN BOSTON　(See map p. 273; index p. 268)

LODGINGS

BOSTON BACK BAY HILTON
◆◆◆
Hotel

Rates Subject to Change

9/1-11/30	1P: $275- 295	2P/1B: $295- 315	2P/2B: $295- 315	XP: $20	F18
5/1-8/31 & 4/1-4/30	1P: $255- 275	2P/1B: $275- 295	2P/2B: $275- 295	XP: $20	F18
12/1-12/31	1P: $170- 235	2P/1B: $190- 255	2P/2B: $190- 255	XP: $20	F18
1/1-3/31	1P: $150- 215	2P/1B: $170- 235	2P/2B: $170- 235	XP: $20	F18

Phone: 617/236-1100 🔟24

Location: Adjacent to Copley Place at Dalton & Belvedere sts. 40 Dalton St 02115. Fax: 617/867-6104. **Facility:** 385 rooms. 26 stories; interior corridors; heated indoor pool. Fee: parking. **Services:** giftshop. **Cards:** AE, CB, DI, DS, JC, MC, VI. *(See color ad p 37)*

🅂🄰🅅🄴 🏨 📶 📺 🈁 🏊 🍽 ⓥ ⊕ 🛁 ⛑ 🎥 💻 📠 🔋 🅿 ✕ 📶

BOSTON HARBOR HOTEL
◆◆◆◆
Hotel

Rates Subject to Change

1P: $235- 510　2P/1B: $235- 510　2P/2B: $235- 510　XP: $50

Phone: 617/439-7000 🔟5

All Year　　　　　　　　　　　　　　　　　　　　　　　　　　　　F16

Location: At Rowes Wharf. 70 Rowes Wharf 02110. Fax: 617/330-9450. **Terms:** Reserv deposit. **Facility:** 230 rooms. Luxury hotel overlooking harbor. Gracious hospitality. Suites, $350-$1600; 16 stories; interior corridors; heated indoor pool. Fee: parking; boat dock. **Services:** giftshop; area transportation. Fee: massage. **Cards:** AE, CB, DI, DS, MC, VI. A Preferred Hotel.

🏨 📶 📺 🈁 🍽 🍸 ⊕ 🛁 🏊 ✕ ⛑ 🎥 🍴 📠 ✕ 📶

BOSTON MARRIOTT HOTEL COPLEY PLACE
◆◆◆
Hotel

Rates Subject to Change

1P: $189- 329　2P/1B: $189- 329　2P/2B: $189- 329

Phone: (617)236-5800 🔟22

All Year

Location: At Copley Place, just s of Copley Sq. 110 Huntington Ave 02116. Fax: 617/236-5885. **Terms:** Check-in 4 pm. **Facility:** 1139 rooms. Rates for up to 5 persons; 38 stories; interior corridors; heated indoor pool. Fee: parking. **Services:** giftshop. Fee: massage. **Cards:** AE, CB, DI, DS, JC, MC, VI.

🄰🅂🄺 🅂🄳 📶 📺 🈁 🍽 🍸 🈁 🍴 ⊕ 🛁 🏊 ⛑ 🎥 💻 📠 🔋 🅿 ✕ 📶

BOSTON MARRIOTT LONG WHARF HOTEL
◆◆◆
Hotel

Rates Subject to Change

9/1-10/31	1P: $335- 365	2P/1B: $335- 365	2P/2B: $335- 365
5/1-8/31	1P: $300- 335	2P/1B: $300- 335	2P/2B: $300- 335
11/1-4/30	1P: $205- 295	2P/1B: $205- 295	2P/2B: $205- 295

Phone: 617/227-0800 🔟2

Location: On historic Long Wharf adjacent to the New England Aquarium. 296 State St 02109. Fax: 617/227-2867. **Terms:** Check-in 4 pm. **Facility:** 402 rooms. Overlooking Boston Harbors. Rates for up to 4 persons; 7 stories; interior corridors; heated indoor pool. **Services:** giftshop. **All Rooms:** combo or shower baths. **Cards:** AE, CB, DI, DS, MC, VI.

📶 📺 🈁 🍽 🍸 🍴 🛁 🏊 ⛑ 🎥 🍴 📠 🔋 🅿 🐕 ✕ 📶

(See map p. 273)

BOSTON PARK PLAZA HOTEL & TOWERS		Rates Subject to Change			Phone: (617)426-2000	16
◆◆◆	9/7-11/20	1P: $299	2P/1B: $319	2P/2B: $319	XP: $20	F18
Historic Hotel	5/1-6/30 & 4/1-4/30	1P: $269	2P/1B: $289	2P/2B: $289	XP: $20	F18
	7/1-9/6 & 3/1-3/31	1P: $259	2P/1B: $279	2P/2B: $279	XP: $20	F18
	11/21-2/29	1P: $129	2P/1B: $129	2P/2B: $129	XP: $20	F18

Location: Just s of Boston Common & Public Garden. 64 Arlington St/Park Plaza 02116. Fax: 617/426-5545. **Terms:** Reserv deposit. **Facility:** 905 rooms. Compact, to excellent rooms. On the National Register of Historic Places. 15 stories; interior corridors. Fee: parking. **Services:** giftshop. **All Rooms:** combo or shower baths. **Cards:** AE, CB, DI, DS, JC,

(See map p. 273)

MC, VI. *(See ad p 277)*

COPLEY SQUARE HOTEL	Rates Subject to Change			Phone: (617)536-9000	**20**
◆◆◆ 9/1-10/31	1P: $215- 225	2P/1B: $245	2P/2B: $245	XP: $20	F17
Historic Hotel 5/1-8/31	1P: $195- 215	2P/1B: $215- 225	2P/2B: $225	XP: $20	F17
1/1-4/30	1P: $195	2P/1B: $195- 215	2P/2B: $215- 225		
11/1-12/31	1P: $195	2P/1B: $195	2P/2B: $225	XP: $20	F17

Location: Jct I-90 tpk exit 22, Copley Sq. 47 Huntington Ave 02116. Fax: 617/267-3547. **Facility:** 143 rooms. Boston's oldest continuously operating hotel. Rooms vary in size. Gourmet restaurant & sports saloon. 12 two-bedroom units. 11 two-bedroom units, $325 for up to 4 persons; 7 stories; interior corridors. Fee: parking. **All Rooms:** combo or shower baths. **Cards:** AE, CB, DI, DS, JC, MC, VI. *(See ad p 277)*

THE ELIOT SUITE HOTEL	Rates Subject to Change			Phone: (617)267-1607	**17**
◆◆◆ All Year	1P: $255- 305	2P/1B: $275- 395	2P/2B: $275- 395	XP: $20	F18

Historic Hotel   **Location:** Corner Commonwealth (SR 2) & Massachusetts (SR 2A) aves. 370 Commonwealth Ave 02215. Fax: 617/536-9114. **Terms:** Reserv deposit. **Facility:** 95 rooms. Intimate European style hotel with emphasis on personalized service. 9 stories; interior corridors. **All Rooms:** combo or shower baths. **Cards:** AE, DI, MC, VI.

(See map p. 273)

FAIRMONT COPLEY PLAZA
◆◆◆◆
Historic Hotel

	Rates Subject to Change			Phone: (617)267-5300	7
9/8-11/20	1P: $259- 279	2P/1B: $259- 279	2P/2B: $289- 309	XP: $30	F18
5/1-9/7 & 3/1-4/30	1P: $239- 259	2P/1B: $239- 259	2P/2B: $269- 289	XP: $30	F18
11/21-2/29	1P: $179- 199	2P/1B: $179- 199	2P/2B: $209- 229	XP: $30	F18

Location: At Copley Sq. 138 St. James Ave 02116. Fax: 617/375-9648. **Terms:** Reserv deposit. **Facility:** 379 rooms. Guest rooms vary in size. Elegant public areas with Old World charm. 6 stories; interior corridors. **Services:** giftshop. **All Rooms:** combo or shower baths. **Cards:** AE, CB, DI, DS, JC, MC, VI. *(See ad p 278)*

FIFTEEN BEACON
[FYI]
Hotel

	Rates Subject to Change		Phone: (617)670-1500
All Year	1P: $275- 700	2P/1B: $300- 750	

Too new to rate. **Location:** Center. Just e of the State House; just ne of the Boston Common. 15 Beacon St 02108. Fax: 617/670-2525. **Facility:** 63 rooms. Rooms & mini-suites with canopy bed, fax machine, speaker phone & cell phone. Scheduled to open Spring, 1999. 9 stories; interior corridors. **All Rooms:** combo or shower baths. **Cards:** MC, VI.

FOUR SEASONS HOTEL BOSTON
(AAA)
◆◆◆◆◆
Hotel

	Rates Subject to Change			Phone: 617/338-4400	12
All Year	1P: $470- 625	2P/1B: $510- 665	2P/2B: $550- 705	XP: $40	F18

Location: At Boylston St & Park Sq. 200 Boylston St 02116. Fax: 617/423-0154. **Terms:** Package plans; weekend rates avail; small pets only. **Facility:** 288 rooms. Luxury hotel overlooking the Public Gardens. Elegant guest rooms. 16 stories; interior corridors; heated indoor pool, saunas, whirlpool. **Dining:** Afternoon tea; also, Aujourd'hui, see separate listing. **Services:** giftshop. Fee: massage. **All Rooms:** combo or shower baths. **Cards:** AE, DI, DS, MC, VI.

HARBORSIDE INN OF BOSTON
◆◆◆
Motel

	Rates Subject to Change			Phone: 617/723-7500	15
5/1-11/30 [CP]	1P: $135- 175	2P/1B: $145- 185		XP: $10	F3
12/1-4/30 [CP]	1P: $110- 140	2P/1B: $120- 150		XP: $10	F3

Location: State St & Atlantic Ave. 185 State St 02109. Fax: 617/670-2010. **Facility:** 54 rooms. In the heart of downtown Boston, close to Quincy Market Place. Off site garage parking only for a fee. 8 stories; interior corridors. **Cards:** AE, CB, DI, DS, MC, VI.

HOLIDAY INN SELECT-BOSTON GOVERNMENT CENTER Rates Subject to Change **Phone:** (617)742-7630 1
◆◆◆
Hotel

All Year	1P: $116- 260	2P/1B: $116- 260	2P/2B: $116- 260	XP: $20	F19

Location: From center, at Cambridge & Blossom sts; in the Beacon Hill District. 5 Blossom St 02114. Fax: 617/742-4192. **Terms:** Check-in 4 pm. **Facility:** 303 rooms. Some rooms have panoramic views of city. 14 stories; interior corridors; heated pool. Fee: parking. **All Rooms:** combo or shower baths. **Cards:** AE, DI, DS, JC, MC, VI. *(See color ad p 275)*

HOTEL LE MERIDIEN
◆◆◆◆
Hotel

	Rates Subject to Change			Phone: 617/451-1900	4
9/8-11/20 & 12/1-12/31	1P: $385- 635	2P/1B: $415- 665	2P/2B: $445- 695	XP: $30	F12
5/1-6/25	1P: $365- 625	2P/1B: $395- 660	2P/2B: $425- 690	XP: $30	F12
6/26-9/7, 11/21-11/30 & 1/1-4/30	1P: $325- 575	2P/1B: $355- 605	2P/2B: $385- 635	XP: $30	F12

Location: Center on Post Office Sq. 250 Franklin St 02110. Fax: 617/423-2844. **Terms:** Reserv deposit, 14 day notice; handling fee imposed; weekend rates avail. **Facility:** 326 rooms. Luxury hotel in European style; in historic building. 9 stories; interior corridors; heated indoor pool. Fee: parking. **Services:** giftshop; area transportation. Fee: massage. **All Rooms:** combo or shower baths. **Cards:** AE, CB, DI, DS, MC, VI.

(See map p. 273)

HOWARD JOHNSON HOTEL-KENMORE
Phone: (617)267-3100 [26]
All Year   1P: $125- 195   2P/1B: $135- 235 2P/2B: $135- 235 XP: $15   F17
Location: Just w of Kenmore Sq, 2 blks n of Fenway Park. 575 Commonwealth Ave 02215.
Fax: 617/424-1045. **Terms:** Pets. **Facility:** 180 rooms. Some small rooms. 8 stories; interior corridors; small
heated indoor pool. **Dining:** Restaurant; 7 am-1 am; $8-$14; cocktails. **Services:** area transportation, local
hospitals. **All Rooms:** extended cable TV. **Cards:** AE, CB, DI, DS, JC, MC, VI. **Special Amenities: Free
newspaper and preferred room (subject to availability with advanced reservations).** *(See color ad p 281)*
Hotel

HOWARD JOHNSON LODGE FENWAY
Phone: (617)267-8300 [25]
All Year   1P: $105- 179   2P/1B: $115- 199 2P/2B: $115- 199 XP: $15   F17
Location: Backing on to Fenway Park. 1271 Boylston St 02215. Fax: 617/267-2763. **Terms:** Pets.
Facility: 94 rooms. 2 stories; interior corridors; small pool. **Dining:** Restaurant; 7-11 am continental breakfast
only & 5 pm-10 pm; $9-$18; cocktails. **Services:** area transportation, local hospitals. **All Rooms:** extended
cable TV. **Cards:** AE, CB, DI, DS, JC, MC, VI. **Special Amenities: Free newspaper and preferred room
(subject to availability with advanced reservations).** *(See color ad p 281)*
Motor Inn

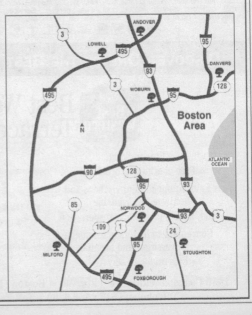

(See map p. 273)

THE LENOX HOTEL   Rates Subject to Change   Phone: (617)536-5300   21
5/1-6/30, 9/1-11/15 &
3/9-4/30   1P: $298- 498   2P/1B: $298- 498   2P/2B: $298- 498   XP: $40   F16
7/1-8/31 & 11/16-3/8   1P: $278- 398   2P/1B: $278- 398   2P/2B: $278- 398   XP: $40   F16
Historic Hotel   **Location:** Adjacent to Prudential Center & Copley Pl, tpk exit 22. 710 Boylston St 02116.
Fax: 617/267-1237. **Terms:** Package plans, seasonal. **Facility:** 212 rooms. Attractive guest rooms & public
areas. Some units with in-room fax. 11 stories; interior corridors. Fee: parking. **Dining:** 2 restaurants; 7 am-midnight;
$11-$19; cocktails; also, Anago, see separate listing. **Cards:** AE, CB, DI, DS, JC, MC, VI. *(See ad below)*

THE MIDTOWN HOTEL   Phone: 617/262-1000   23
All Year   1P: $109- 199   2P/1B: $119- 229   2P/2B: $119- 229   XP: $15   F18
Location: 3 blks sw of Copley Pl, opposite Prudential Center. Just n of Symphony Hall & jct Massachusetts
Motel   Ave. 220 Huntington Ave 02115. Fax: 617/262-8739. **Terms:** Reserv deposit; handling fee imposed; weekend
rates avail. **Facility:** 159 rooms. Located in busy downtown area. 2 stories; interior corridors; heated pool 5/24-
9/1. **Dining:** Restaurant; 7 am-11 pm; $12-$18. **Cards:** AE, DI, DS, MC, VI. *(See color ad p 283)*

NEWBURY GUEST HOUSE   Rates Subject to Change   Phone: (617)437-7666   10
5/1-12/15 & 3/9-4/30 [CP]   1P: $110- 140   2P/1B: $125- 155   2P/2B: $125- 155
Historic Bed   12/16-3/8 [CP]   1P: $100- 130   2P/1B: $115- 145
& Breakfast   **Location:** Between Fairfield & Gloucester sts; in Back Bay area. 261 Newbury St 02116. Fax: 617/262-4243.
Terms: 2 night min stay, weekends. **Facility:** 32 rooms. Late 19th-century converted townhouse. Attractive
guest rooms. Very convenient downtown location. 4 stories; interior corridors. Fee: parking. **All Rooms:** combo or shower
baths. **Cards:** AE, CB, DI, MC.

(See map p. 273)

REGAL BOSTONIAN HOTEL
Phone: (617)523-3600 **3**

11/15-4/30	1P: $249	2P/1B: $249	2P/2B: $249	XP: $20 F17
5/1-11/14	1P: $289	2P/1B: $289		XP: $20 F17

♦♦♦
Hotel
Location: Faneuil Hall Marketplace 02109-1503. Fax: 617/523-2454. **Terms:** Reserv deposit; handling fee imposed; package plans; weekend rates avail; small pets only. **Facility:** 163 rooms. In the heart of downtown Boston & next door to the Quincy Market Place. Attractive & cozy guest rooms, top floor rooms with view of city skyline. 7 stories; interior corridors. Fee: parking. **Dining:** Restaurant; 6:30 am-2 & 5-10 pm, Fri-11 pm, Sat 5 pm-11 pm; $28-$55; cocktails. **All Rooms:** combo or shower baths. **Some Rooms:** whirlpools. **Cards:** AE, CB, DI, DS, MC, VI.
Special Amenities: Free newspaper and free room upgrade (subject to availability with advanced reservations).

THE RITZ-CARLTON, BOSTON
Rates Subject to Change   Phone: (617)536-5700 **13**
All Year   1P: $295- 385   2P/1B: $335- 425   2P/2B: $335- 425   XP: $20 F12
♦♦♦♦
Hotel
Location: Overlooking the Public Gardens; Arlington & Newbury sts. 15 Arlington St 02117. Fax: 617/536-1335. **Terms:** Package plans; pets, $75 dep req. **Facility:** 275 rooms. Distinguished, traditionally formal hotel. Gracious guest services. Old World charm & elegance. 44 suites with working fireplace, $340-$670; 17 stories; interior corridors; sauna. Fee: parking. **Dining:** Restaurant; 6:30 am-midnight. Open air rooftop dining & dancing Thurs-Sat, in season. Sun brunch in season; $13-$26; health conscious menu items; cocktails; afternoon tea; dining room, see separate listing. **Services:** giftshop; area transportation, financial district. Fee: massage. **Cards:** AE, CB, DI, DS, MC, VI.

SHERATON-BOSTON HOTEL & TOWERS
Guaranteed Rates   Phone: (617)236-2000 **27**

9/5-12/17	1P: $314	2P/1B: $314	2P/2B: $314	XP: $20 F17
5/1-9/4	1P: $301	2P/1B: $301	2P/2B: $301	XP: $20 F17
12/18-12/31	1P: $215	2P/1B: $215	2P/2B: $215	XP: $20 F17

♦♦♦
Hotel
Location: Prudential Center, tpk exit 22. 39 Dalton St 02199. Fax: 617/236-1702. **Terms:** Open 5/1-12/31; package plans; pets. **Facility:** 1181 rooms. 29 stories; interior corridors; heated indoor/outdoor pool, sauna, whirlpool. Fee: parking. **Dining:** Restaurant; 6:30 am-2 am; $12-$25; cocktails. **Services:** giftshop. Fee: area transportation. **All Rooms:** combo or shower baths. **Cards:** AE, CB, DI, DS, JC, MC, VI.

SWISSOTEL BOSTON
Phone: (617)451-2600 **8**
All Year   1P: $235- 275   2P/1B: $260- 290   2P/2B: $260- 290   XP: $25 F16
♦♦♦
Hotel
Location: Center; just e of Boston Common at Lafayette Pl. One Ave de Lafayette 02111. Fax: 617/451-2198. **Terms:** Package plans; weekend rates avail; pets, signed waiver. **Facility:** 500 rooms. A unique atrium-like setting on several of the guest room floors. Guest rooms are average size, but very comfortable. Located in the heart of downtown Boston. 21 stories; interior corridors; heated indoor pool, saunas. Fee: parking. **Dining:** Restaurant; 7 am-3 & 6-11 pm; $11-$20; cocktails. **Services:** giftshop. **Some Rooms:** whirlpools. **Cards:** AE, CB, DI, DS, MC, VI. **Special Amenities: Early check-in/late check-out.**

(See map p. 273)

TREMONT HOTEL
◆◆◆ Historic Hotel

Rates Subject to Change					Phone: (617)426-1400	9
9/3-11/25	1P: $189- 279	2P/1B: $209- 299	2P/2B: $209- 299	XP: $20		F17
5/1-9/2	1P: $159- 259	2P/1B: $179- 279	2P/2B: $179- 279	XP: $20		F17
11/26-4/30	1P: $149- 199	2P/1B: $169- 219	2P/2B: $169- 219	XP: $20		F17

Location: Adjacent to Shubert Theatre. 275 Tremont St 02116. Fax: 617/482-6730. **Terms:** Reserv deposit. **Facility:** 322 rooms. Built in 1924 with dramatic neo-classic room decor. Many small guest rooms. 15 stories; interior corridors. **Services:** giftshop. **All Rooms:** combo or shower baths. **Cards:** AE, DI, DS, MC, VI. *(See color ad below)*

THE WESTIN HOTEL,COPLEY PLACE BOSTON
◆◆◆◆ Hotel

Rates Subject to Change					Phone: 617/262-9600	19
9/8-12/14	1P: $219- 340	2P/1B: $219- 365	2P/2B: $219- 365	XP: $25		F18
5/1-9/7 & 3/7-4/30	1P: $189- 330	2P/1B: $189- 355	2P/2B: $189- 355	XP: $25		F18
12/15-3/6	1P: $149- 265	2P/1B: $149- 290	2P/2B: $149- 290	XP: $25		F18

Location: Exit 22 of I-90 (Tpk) at Copley Sq. 10 Huntington Ave 02116. Fax: 617/424-7483. **Facility:** 800 rooms. Inviting, spacious lobby with marble accents. In the heart of a large upscale shopping district. 53 rooms with in-room fax machines. 36 stories; interior corridors; heated indoor pool. **Services:** giftshop. Fee: massage. **All Rooms:** combo or shower baths. **Cards:** AE, CB, DI, DS, MC, VI.

(See map p. 273)

RESTAURANTS

AMBROSIA ON HUNTINGTON Lunch: $8-$16 Dinner: $15-$35 Phone: 617/247-2400 ㊱
◆◆◆ **Location:** On Huntington Ave at Garrison. 116 Huntington Ave 02116. **Hours:** 11:30 am-2 & 5:30-10 pm, Sat
French 5 pm-11 pm, Sun 5 pm-10 pm. Closed major holidays. **Reservations:** suggested; for dinner.
Features: semi-formal attire; cocktails & lounge; fee for valet parking; a la carte. Creative French cuisine
with Asian influence served in eclectic casual elegance. Chef-owner. Smoke free premises. **Cards:** AE, DI, MC, VI. ⊠

ANAGO Lunch: $8-$14 Dinner: $20-$30 Phone: 617/266-6222 ㉘
◆◆◆ **Location:** Adjacent to Prudential Center & Copley Pl, tpk exit 22; in The Lenox Hotel. 65 Exeter St 02116.
Regional **Hours:** 11:30 am-2 & 5-10 pm, Sat-10:30 pm, Sun 11 am-2:30 & 5-10 pm. **Reservations:** suggested.
American **Features:** dressy casual; Sunday brunch; health conscious menu; cocktails; fee for parking & valet parking;
a la carte. Innovative cuisine with French overtones. Clean contemporary lines, intimate atmosphere. Smoke
free premises. **Cards:** AE, DI, DS, MC, VI. 🅰 ⊠

AUJOURD'HUI Lunch: $17-$19 Dinner: $32-$39 Phone: 617/338-4400 ⑮
🄰🄰 **Location:** At Boylston St & Park Sq; in Four Seasons Hotel Boston. 200 Boylston St 02116. **Hours:** 6:30
am-11, 11:30-2:30 & 5:30-10:30 pm. Closed: Sat for lunch. **Reservations:** suggested. **Features:** semi-formal
◆◆◆◆◆ attire; Sunday brunch; children's menu; health conscious menu; cocktails & lounge; fee for valet parking; a la
American carte. Contemporary haute cuisine. Gracious, formal dining room overlooking the Public Gardens.
Cards: AE, CB, DI, DS, MC, VI. 🅰 ⊠

BIBA Lunch: $13-$17 Dinner: $25-$35 Phone: 617/426-7878 ⑰
◆◆◆ **Location:** At Hadassah Way, across from Public Gardens. 272 Boylston St 02116. **Hours:** 11:30 am-2:30 &
American 5:30-10 pm, Fri-11 pm, Sat 5:30 pm-11 pm, Sun 11:30 am-3 & 5:30-10 pm. Closed major holidays.
Reservations: suggested. **Features:** casual dress; Sunday brunch; cocktails & lounge; fee for valet parking;
a la carte. Seasonal menu of bistro cuisine served in art deco, primitive, Mediterranean decor overlooking Public Gardens.
Cigar smoking permitted in bar. **Cards:** AE, CB, DI, DS, MC, VI. ⊠

THE CAFE BUDAPEST Lunch: $9-$24 Dinner: $20-$33 Phone: 617/266-1979 ㉑
🄰🄰 **Location:** Jct I-90, tpk exit 22, Copley Sq; in Copley Square Hotel. 90 Exeter St 02116. **Hours:** noon-3 &
5-10:30 pm, Fri & Sat-11:30 pm, Sun 1 pm-10:30 pm. Closed: 1/1, 12/25 & 1st week in July.
◆◆◆ **Reservations:** suggested. **Features:** formal attire; cocktails & lounge; entertainment; a la carte. Elegant,
Ethnic romantic Hungarian restaurant. **Cards:** AE, CB, DI, DS, MC, VI.

THE CAPITAL GRILLE Dinner: $22-$35 Phone: 617/262-8900 ㉒
🄰🄰 **Location:** At jct of SR 2A, Massachusetts Ave & Newbury St. 359 Newbury St 02115. **Hours:** 5 pm-10 pm,
Thurs-Sat-11 pm. Closed: 11/25 & 12/25. **Reservations:** suggested. **Features:** semi-formal attire; cocktails &
◆◆◆ lounge; fee for valet parking; a la carte. Upscale dining amidst fine antiques. Specializing in dry-aged beef &
Steak and fresh seafood. Extensive wine list. **Cards:** AE, DI, DS, MC, VI. ⊠
Seafood

CLIO Dinner: $20-$34 Phone: 617/536-7200 ②
◆◆◆ **Location:** In the Eliot Suite Hotel at corner of Massachusettes & Commonwealth aves. 370A Commonwealth
American Ave 02215. **Hours:** 6:30 am-10:30 & 5:30-10 pm, Fri & Sat 7 am-11 & 5:30-10:30 pm, Sun 7 am-2 &
5:30-10:30 pm. **Reservations:** suggested. **Features:** semi-formal attire; Sunday brunch; health conscious
menu items; cocktails; fee for valet parking; a la carte. Popular. Locally acclaimed rising star. Contemporary decor, relaxed
service & exceptional food. Save room for dessert. Chef's tasting menu $95/person. Some vegetarian items. Smoke free
premises. **Cards:** AE, DI, MC, VI. 🅰 ⊠

COTTONWOOD RESTAURANT & CAFE Lunch: $6-$11 Dinner: $13-$22 Phone: 617/247-2225 ㊲
◆◆ **Location:** Corner of Berkeley St at St James. 222 Berkeley St 02116. **Hours:** 11:30 am-2:30 & 5:30-10 pm,
Southwest Fri & Sat-11 pm, Sun 11 am-2:30 & 5:30-9 pm, Thurs-Sat cafe menu to 11 pm, closing hour may vary.
American Closed major holidays. **Reservations:** suggested. **Features:** casual dress; health conscious menu; carryout;
cocktails & lounge; fee for parking; a la carte. Contemporary, Southwest decor. Casual dining. Creative
cuisine. Sat & Sun brunch. Outdoor heated patio dining weather permitting. Valet parking Tues-Sat & 2-hour validated
parking all week; dinner only. **Cards:** AE, DI, DS, MC, VI. ⊠

DAVIO'S Dinner: $15-$29 Phone: 617/262-4810 ㊳
◆◆◆ **Location:** On Newbury St between Fairfield & Gloucester sts; in Back Bay area. 269 Newbury St 02116.
Northern **Hours:** 5 pm-10 pm, Fri & Sat-11 pm. Closed: 11/25 & 12/25. **Reservations:** suggested.
Italian **Features:** semi-formal attire; cocktails & lounge; street parking. Leisurely dining in lower level of converted
brownstone. Casual fare upstairs. Patio dining in season. Valet parking for dinner. Lunch in upstairs cafe
from 11:30 am. Smoke free premises. **Cards:** AE, DI, DS, MC, VI. ⊠

DURGIN PARK Lunch: $4-$15 Dinner: $6-$20 Phone: 617/227-2038 ⑤
🄰🄰 **Location:** 340 Faneuil Hall Marketplace 02109. **Hours:** 11:30 am-10 pm, Fri & Sat-10:30 pm, Sun 11:30
am-9 pm. Closed: 12/25. **Features:** No A/C; casual dress; carryout; cocktails & lounge; fee for parking; a la
◆ carte. Generous portions of traditional New England fare including fresh seafood served at family-style
Regional tables, in 2nd floor dining rooms. Homemade dessert. Popular. Informal service style. Smoking in lounge
American only. Smoke free premises. **Cards:** AE, DI, DS, MC, VI. ⊠

EASTERN PIER CHINESE RESTAURANT Lunch: $5-$12 Dinner: $7-$12 Phone: 617/423-7756 ㉗
◆ **Location:** Just e of World Trade Center, opposite Boston Fish Pier. 237 Northern Ave 02210. **Hours:** 11:30
Chinese am-10:30 pm, Fri & Sat-11:30 pm, Sun noon-10:30 pm. Closed: 11/25. **Features:** casual dress; carryout;
cocktails; a la carte. Lively, cozy ambiance. Featuring Hong Kong & Szechuan cuisine with many seafood
entrees. Full menu avail for take-out. Metered street parking. Smoke free premises. **Cards:** AE, DI, DS, MC, VI. ⊠

GALLERIA ITALIANA Dinner: $17-$22 Phone: 617/423-2092 ㊷
◆◆◆ **Location:** On Tremont St, opposite Boston Commons. 177 Tremont St 02111. **Hours:** 7 am-3:30 & 5-10:30
Regional pm, Sat 5 pm-10:30 pm, Sun 4 pm-9 pm. Closed: 7/4, 11/25, 12/25 & Mon for dinner.
Italian **Reservations:** suggested. **Features:** casual dress; beer & wine only; minimum charge-$20; a la carte.
Creative regional Italian cuisine served in a contemporary Italian trattoria ambiance. Cafeteria-style breakfast
& lunch with assorted pasta specialities. Credit cards at dinner only. **Cards:** AE, DI, MC, VI. ⊠

(See map p. 273)

GRILL 23 & BAR — **Dinner:** $19-$35 — **Phone:** 617/542-2255 — ㊴
◆◆◆ **Location:** On the corner of Berkeley & Stuart sts. 161 Berkeley St 02116. **Hours:** 5:30 pm-10:30 pm, Fri &
American — Sat-11 pm, Sun-10 pm. Closed major holidays. **Reservations:** suggested. **Features:** semi-formal attire;
cocktails; fee for valet parking; a la carte. Specializing in grilled meat & seafood. On the former trading floor
of the old Salada Tea Building dating from 1923. **Cards:** AE, CB, DI, DS, MC, VI.

ICARUS — **Dinner:** $20-$30 — **Phone:** 617/426-1790 — ㊶
◆◆◆ **Location:** Just w off Tremont St. 3 Appleton St 02116. **Hours:** 6 pm-10 pm, Sat 5:30 pm-10:30 pm, Sun
American — 5:30 pm-9:30 pm. Closed major holidays. **Reservations:** suggested. **Features:** casual dress; cocktails &
lounge; street parking & fee for valet parking; a la carte. Creative American cuisine served in upscale casual
contemporary decor. Smoke free premises. **Cards:** AE, DI, MC, VI.

JIMMY'S HARBORSIDE RESTAURANT — **Lunch:** $14-$19 — **Dinner:** $16-$25 — **Phone:** 617/423-1000 — ㉾
◆◆ **Location:** Harborfront at the Boston Fish Pier. 242-248 Northern Ave 02210. **Hours:** noon-9:30 pm, Fri &
Seafood — Sat-10 pm, Sun 4 pm-9:30 pm. Closed: 12/25. **Reservations:** suggested; for dinner. **Features:** casual dress;
carryout; cocktails & lounge; fee for parking & valet parking; a la carte. Popular long-established dining spot
overlooking water. Also some beef & poultry. A dining tradition since 1924. 3-tiered dining room with a nautical ambiance.
Boat bar. **Cards:** AE, CB, DI, JC, MC, VI.

JULIEN — **Lunch:** $17-$21 — **Dinner:** $35-$50 — **Phone:** 617/451-1900 — ⑨
◆◆◆◆ **Location:** Center on Post Office Sq; in Hotel Le Meridien. 250 Franklin St 02110. **Hours:** noon-2 & 6-10:30
French — pm, Sat 6 pm-11 pm. Closed: Sat for lunch, Sun & 7/1-7/7. **Reservations:** suggested. **Features:** formal
attire; cocktails & lounge; fee for valet parking; a la carte. Creative cuisine. Intimate, elegant dining room was
formerly the Members Court of the Federal Reserve Bank. **Cards:** AE, CB, DI, DS, MC, VI.

LALA ROKH — **Dinner:** $14-$16 — **Phone:** 617/720-5511 — ⑥
◆◆ **Location:** Just e of Charles St. 97 Mt Vernon St 02108. **Hours:** 5:30 pm-10 pm. **Reservations:** accepted.
Ethnic — **Features:** casual dress; carryout; beer & wine only. Classic Persian specialties served by well informed,
cordial staff. Casual upscale dining rooms decorated with Persian family artwork & maps dating from 1620.
Cards: AE, DI, MC, VI.

LEGAL SEAFOODS AT THE BOSTON PARK PLAZA — **Lunch:** $8-$13 — **Dinner:** $15-$25 — **Phone:** 617/426-4444 — ⑯
◆◆ **Location:** Just s of Boston Common & Public Garden; in Boston Park Plaza Hotel & Towers. 35 Columbus
Seafood — Ave 02116. **Hours:** 11 am-2:30 & 5-10 pm, Fri-11 pm, Sat noon-11 pm, Sun noon-10 pm. Closed: 11/25 &
12/25. **Reservations:** accepted. **Features:** casual dress; children's menu; carryout; cocktails & lounge; fee
for parking; a la carte. Extensive menu of grilled, broiled, fried & Cajun-style fresh seafood; also Shandong Chinese specials
& Kappo style Japanese appetizers. **Cards:** AE, DI, DS, JC, MC, VI.

LEGAL SEAFOODS RESTAURANT — **Lunch:** $8-$15 — **Dinner:** $14-$25 — **Phone:** 617/266-7775 — ㊵
◆◆ **Location:** Near Darmouth St entrance; in Copley Place Galleria. 100 Huntington Ave 02116. **Hours:** 11
Seafood — am-10 pm, Sat-10:30 pm, Sun noon-9 pm. Closed: 11/25 & 12/25. **Reservations:** accepted.
Features: casual dress; children's menu; carryout; cocktails; fee for parking. Grilled, broiled, fried &
Cajun-style fresh seafood. Contemporary informal dining room. **Cards:** AE, CB, DI, DS, MC, VI.

L'ESPALIER — **Dinner:** $65-$82 — **Phone:** 617/262-3023 — ㉔
◆◆◆◆ **Location:** 30 Gloucester St 02115. **Hours:** 6 pm-10 pm. Closed major holidays & Sun.
French — **Reservations:** required. **Features:** semi-formal attire; cocktails; fee for valet parking. Modern french cuisine
with sauce reductions & changes of menu. Intimate dining rooms in restored brownstone. Prix fixe; also
degustation menu on request, including a vegetarian tasting menu. Smoke free premises. **Cards:** AE, DI, DS, MC, VI.

LOCKE-OBER CAFE — Historical — **Lunch:** $7-$18 — **Dinner:** $19-$40 — **Phone:** 617/542-1340 — ⑬
◆◆◆ **Location:** Between Washington & Tremont sts, off Winter St. 3-4 Winter Pl 02108. **Hours:** 11:30 am-10 pm,
Continental — Fri-10:30 pm, Sat 5:30 pm-10:30 pm. Closed major holidays. **Reservations:** suggested.
Features: semi-formal attire; cocktails & lounge; a la carte. Gracious, Old World dining rooms; established in
1875. Valet parking at dinner. **Cards:** AE, DI, DS, MC, VI.

MAISON ROBERT — **Lunch:** $10-$22 — **Dinner:** $18-$30 — **Phone:** 617/227-3370 — ⑦
◆◆◆ **Location:** Old City Hall. 45 School St 02108. **Hours:** 11:30 am-2:30 & 5:30-10 pm, Sat 5:30 pm-10:30 pm.
French — Closed major holidays & Sun. **Reservations:** suggested. **Features:** semi-formal attire; cocktails & lounge; a
la carte. Modern intimate dining rooms, cafe with outdoor terrace in lower level. Valet parking Wed-Sat 6
pm-10 pm. Open some Sun in spring & fall. **Cards:** AE, CB, DI, MC, VI.

MAMMA MARIA — **Dinner:** $19-$28 — **Phone:** 617/523-0077 — ④
◆◆◆ **Location:** In the north end. 3 North Square 02113. **Hours:** 5-10 pm, Fri & Sat-11 pm. Closed major holidays.
Northern — **Reservations:** suggested. **Features:** casual dress; cocktails; street parking & fee for valet parking; a la
Italian — carte. Converted townhouse, overlooking North Square. Smoke free premises. **Cards:** AE, DI, DS, MC, VI.

NO NAME RESTAURANT — **Lunch:** $6-$9 — **Dinner:** $8-$15 — **Phone:** 617/423-2705 — ①
◆ **Location:** Harborfront on "Boston Fish Pier", just e of World Trade Center. 17 Fish Pier 02210. **Hours:** 11
Seafood — am-10 pm. Closed: 11/25 & 12/25. **Reservations:** accepted. **Features:** casual dress; carryout; beer & wine
only. Originally built as a restaurant for fisherman. Family owned & operated for over 78 years. Very casual &
rustic atmosphere overlooking fishing boats. Ample portions of broiled & fried seafood. Smoke free premises.

THE OAK ROOM — **Dinner:** $23-$34 — **Phone:** 617/267-5300 — ⑫
◆◆◆◆ **Location:** At Copley Sq; in Fairmont Copley Plaza. 138 St James Ave 02116. **Hours:** 5:30 pm-10 pm, Fri &
Steakhouse — Sat-11 pm. **Reservations:** suggested. **Features:** semi-formal attire; cocktails & lounge; fee for valet parking.
An elegant dining room with "Old World" charm specializing in steak & seafood. Smoke free premises.
Cards: AE, CB, DI, DS, MC, VI. *(See ad p 278)*

OMONIA GREEK RESTAURANT — **Lunch:** $6-$13 — **Dinner:** $12-$19 — **Phone:** 617/426-4310 — ㊸
◆◆ **Location:** On Charles St, just off Stuart St. 75 S Charles St 02116. **Hours:** 11:30 am-10 pm, Sat & Sun from
Greek — 3 pm. Closed: 12/25 & Mon. **Reservations:** suggested; for dinner. **Features:** semi-formal attire; carryout;
beer & wine only; fee for parking. Bright & airy decor reminiscent of the Greek countryside & serving
authentic cuisine. In theatre district. Informal atmosphere. Discounted parking at specific garage. **Cards:** AE, DI, MC, VI.

(See map p. 273)

PIGNOLI — Lunch: $12-$14 — Dinner: $20-$35 — Phone: 617/338-7500 ㉜
♦♦♦
Italian — **Location:** In Park Square, between Charles & Arlington sts. 79 Park Plaza 02116. **Hours:** 11:30 am-2:30 & 5:30-10 pm, Fri & Sat-11 pm, Sun 5:30 pm-10 pm. Closed major holidays. **Reservations:** suggested. **Features:** semi-formal attire; cocktails & lounge; fee for valet parking; a la carte. Eclectic meals are multiple courses of small portions. The menu is a concise collection of antipasta, pasta, meat, fish & wildgame dishes. Expressive ambiance. Outdoor dining in season. Late night menu Wed-Sat until 1 am. **Cards:** AE, DI, DS, MC, VI. ✕

RED HERRING — Lunch: $5-$8 — Dinner: $21-$27 — Phone: 617/225-2121 ㉞
♦♦
Ethnic — **Location:** In the Statler Office Bldg. One Columbus Ave 02116. **Hours:** 11 am-10 pm, Sat from 5 pm. Closed major holidays & Sun. **Features:** casual dress; beer & wine only. Unique tapas-style dishes with Southeast Asian influence served in casual bustling contemporary atmosphere. Smoke free premises. **Cards:** DI, DS, MC, VI. ✕

RISTORANTE DAVIDE — Lunch: $5-$12 — Dinner: $18-$30 — Phone: 617/227-5745 ㉖
♦♦♦
Northern
Italian — **Location:** Just n of Faneuil Hall Marketplace, facing Union Wharf. 326 Commercial St 02109. **Hours:** 11:30 am-3 & 5-11 pm, Sat & Sun from 5 pm. Closed: 1/1, 11/25 & 12/25. **Reservations:** suggested; req Fri & Sat. **Features:** dressy casual; cocktails; fee for valet parking; a la carte. European ambiance & service. Finely prepared cuisine. Extensive wine list. **Cards:** AE, MC, VI. ✕

THE RITZ-CARLTON DINING ROOM — Dinner: $32-$43 — Phone: 617/536-5700 ⑱
♦♦♦♦
French — **Location:** Overlooking the Public Gardens; Arlington & Newbury sts; in The Ritz-Carlton-Boston. 15 Arlington St 02117. **Hours:** 5:30 pm-10 pm, Fri & Sat-11 pm, Sun 10:45 am-2:30 & 5:30-10 pm. **Reservations:** suggested. **Features:** formal attire; Sunday brunch; children's menu; health conscious menu items; cocktails & lounge; entertainment; fee for valet parking; a la carte. Gracious, formal dining in an elegant setting overlooking the Public Gardens. Featuring traditional New England entrees. Sun brunch 10:45 am-2:30 pm. Smoke free premises. **Cards:** AE, CB, DI, DS, MC, VI. ♿ ✕

ROWES WHARF RESTAURANT — Lunch: $11-$17 — Dinner: $26-$31 — Phone: 617/439-3995 �33
♦♦♦♦
Regional
American — **Location:** At Rowes Wharf; in Boston Harbor Hotel. 70 Rowes Wharf 02110. **Hours:** 6:30-11 am, 11:30-2:30 & 5:30-9 pm, Sat-11 pm, Sun 6:30-9 am, 10:30-2 & 5:30-9 pm. **Reservations:** suggested. **Features:** formal attire; Sunday brunch; children's menu; health conscious menu items; cocktails & lounge; fee for valet parking; a la carte. An elegant harborfront setting with Old World charm featuring creative New England cuisine. **Cards:** AE, CB, DI, DS, MC, VI. ♿ ✕

SMALL PLANET BAR & GRILL — Lunch: $7-$11 — Dinner: $10-$16 — Phone: 617/536-4477 ⑲
♦♦
Ethnic — **Location:** On n side of Copley Sq. 565 Boylston St 02116. **Hours:** 11:30 am-midnight, Mon from 5 pm. Closed: 11/25 & 12/25. **Features:** casual dress; Sunday brunch; carryout; cocktails; street parking; a la carte. Sidewalk cafe in summer. Global cuisine. Informal & almost clamorous atmosphere. **Cards:** AE, DI, DS, MC, VI. ✕

SONSIE — Lunch: $7-$11 — Dinner: $12-$27 — Phone: 617/351-2500 ㊹
♦♦
Ethnic — **Location:** Just s of jct of SR 2A, Massachusetts Ave. 327 Newbury St 02115. **Hours:** 11:30 am-2:30 & 6-11 pm, Thurs-Sat to midnight. Closed: 12/25. **Reservations:** suggested. **Features:** casual dress; carryout; cocktails; minimum charge-$10, lunch & dinner; a la carte. Asian & Italian influences on menu casually served in bustling trendy decor. Also Sat & Sun brunch 11:30 am-3 pm & lite fare daily 2:30 pm-6 pm. Continental breakfast 7-11:30 am. Valet parking $9 from 6 pm. **Cards:** AE, DI, MC, VI. ✕

TOP OF THE HUB — Lunch: $9-$18 — Dinner: $19-$30 — Phone: 617/536-1775 ㉓
♦♦♦
American — **Location:** On 52nd floor of Prudential Tower. 800 Boylston St 02199. **Hours:** 11:30 am-2:30 & 5:30-10 pm, Fri-11 pm, Sat noon-3 & 5:30-11 pm, Sun 10 am-2:30 & 5-10 pm. Closed: 12/25. **Reservations:** suggested. **Features:** semi-formal attire; Sunday brunch; health conscious menu; cocktails & lounge; a la carte. Spectacular panoramic view of city. Overlooking the scenic Charles River. Also, 5 or 7 course tasting menu changes daily. Smoke free premises. **Cards:** AE, DI, DS, MC, VI. ♿ ✕

BOSTON—574,300 (See map p. 274; index p. 269)

LODGINGS

BEST WESTERN BOSTON-THE INN AT LONGWOOD MEDICAL
Rates Subject to Change — Phone: (617)731-4700 ⓭
Ⓐ — All Year — 1P: $129- 199 — 2P/1B: $129- 209 — 2P/2B: $129- 209 — XP: $15 — F17
♦♦♦ — **Location:** Adjoining Children's Hospital at Brookline Ave. 342 Longwood Ave 02115. Fax: 617/731-6273.
Hotel — **Facility:** 155 rooms. Attached to the Galleria & food court. 6 stories; interior corridors. Fee: parking. **Dining:** Restaurant; 7 am-10 pm, Sun 8 am-9 pm; $7-$12; cocktails. **Recreation:** Fee: health club privileges. **All Rooms:** combo or shower baths. **Some Rooms:** 14 efficiencies, no utensils. **Cards:** AE, CB, DI, DS, MC, VI. *(See color ad p 280)*

DAYS INN-BOSTON
Rates Subject to Change — Phone: 617/254-1234 ⓬
♦♦ — 5/1-10/31 & 4/1-4/30 — 1P: $99- 109 — 2P/1B: $109- 119 — 2P/2B: $109- 129 — XP: $10 — F18
Motor Inn — 11/1-3/31 — 1P: $79- 89 — 2P/1B: $89- 99 — 2P/2B: $89- 109 — XP: $10 — F18
Location: On s side of river, 1.3 mi e of jct US 20. 1234 Soldiers Field Rd 02135. Fax: 617/254-1234. **Facility:** 113 rooms. Across from the Charles River. 3-5 stories; interior corridors. **Cards:** AE, CB, DI, DS, MC, VI.

DAYSTOP-BOSTON
Rates Subject to Change — Phone: 617/254-0200 ⓭
♦♦ — All Year [CP] — 1P: $89 — 2P/1B: $99 — 2P/2B: $109 — XP: $10 — F18
Motel — **Location:** On s side of river, 0.3 mi e of jct US 20. 1800 Soldiers Field Rd 02135. Fax: 617/782-8001. **Facility:** 54 rooms. Large rooms. 2 stories; interior corridors. **Cards:** AE, CB, DI, DS, MC, VI.

GOING UP? Expect elevators in establishments of three or more stories. We tell you in the listings if there are none.

(See map p. 274)

DOUBLETREE GUEST SUITES-BOSTON/ CAMBRIDGE
◆◆◆ Suite Hotel
Rates Subject to Change
Phone: (617)783-0090 [121]
All Year 1P: $139- 259 2P/1B: $139- 259 2P/2B: $159- 259 XP:$10-15 F10
Location: I-90/Massachusetts Tpk, exit 20 westbound or exit 18 eastbound. 400 Soldiers Field Rd 02134. Fax: 617/783-0897. Facility: 310 rooms. 1-bedroom units with living room. Overlooking Charles River. 16 stories; interior corridors; heated indoor pool. Fee: parking. Services: giftshop; area transportation. Cards: AE, CB, DI, DS, MC, VI. (See color ad p 290)

(See map p. 274)

HARBORSIDE HYATT CONFERENCE CENTER AND HOTEL   Phone: (617)568-1234   122

(AAA)(SAVE)	6/1-12/5	1P: $300- 375	2P/1B: $325- 400	2P/2B: $325- 400	XP: $25	F18
	5/1-5/31	1P: $255- 330	2P/1B: $280- 355	2P/2B: $280- 355	XP: $25	F18
◆◆◆	12/6-4/30	1P: $255- 330	2P/1B: $280- 355	2P/2B: $280- 330	XP: $25	F18

Hotel   **Location:** On the Boston Harborfront, SR 1A or I-93 to harbor tunnels. 101 Harborside Dr 02128. **Fax:** 617/567-8856. **Terms:** Weekend rates avail. **Facility:** 270 rooms. Panoramic view of Boston skyline. Elegantly-appointed contemporary units. Junior or conference suites, $425-$550; 14 stories; interior corridors; heated indoor pool, sauna, whirlpool. Fee: parking. **Dining:** Harborside Grill, see separate listing. **Recreation:** jogging. Fee: water shuttle to downtown. **All Rooms:** combo or shower baths. **Cards:** AE, CB, DI, DS, JC, MC, VI.

SEAPORT HOTEL   Rates Subject to Change   Phone: 617/385-4000

FYI	8/1-11/30	1P: $310- 345	2P/1B: $310- 345	2P/2B: $310- 345
	5/1-7/31 & 12/1-4/30	1P: $225- 255	2P/1B: $225- 255	2P/2B: $225- 255

Hotel   Too new to rate. **Location:** At World Trade Center/Commonwealth Pier. 1 Seaport Ln 02210. **Fax:** 617/385-4010. **Terms:** $2 service charge. **Facility:** 427 rooms. Recently opened. A no-tipping hotel. 18 stories; interior corridors; smoke free premises. **Services:** giftshop; area transportation. Fee: massage. **All Rooms:** combo or shower baths. **Cards:** AE, DI, DS, MC, VI.

RESTAURANTS

HAMERSLEY'S BISTRO   **Dinner:** $20-$30   Phone: 617/423-2700   133
◆◆◆   **Location:** On Tremont St at Clarendon. 553 Tremont St 02116. **Hours:** 6 pm-10 pm, Sat 5:30 pm-10:30 pm,
American   Sun 5:30 pm-9:30 pm. Closed major holidays & 1st week of Jan & July. **Reservations:** suggested.
Features: dressy casual; cocktails; fee for valet parking; a la carte. American contemporary bistro cuisine with French country & bistro influences served leisurely in a former piano factory infused with soft lighting & simple elegance. Smoke free premises. **Cards:** AE, DI, DS, MC, VI.

HARBORSIDE GRILL   **Lunch:** $9-$17   **Dinner:** $21-$26   Phone: 617/568-6060   132
◆◆   **Location:** On the Boston Harborfront, SR 1A or I-93 to harbor tunnels; in Harborside Hyatt Conference
American   Center and Hotel. 101 Harborside Dr 02128. **Hours:** 6 am-11 pm. **Reservations:** suggested; at dinner.
Features: casual dress; children's menu; health conscious menu items; carryout; cocktails & lounge; fee for valet parking; area transportation; a la carte. Panoramic view of the Boston Harbor & downtown skyline. An open kitchen featuring New England seafood specialties & grilled entrees. A relaxed ambiance. Water shuttle from downtown. **Cards:** AE, CB, DI, DS, JC, MC, VI.

The Boston Vicinity

ACTON—17,900

RESTAURANT

SCUPPERJACK'S   **Lunch:** $6-$11   **Dinner:** $13-$17   **Phone:** 978/263-8327
◆◆   **Location:** On SR 2A & 119, 2 mi w of SR 27; 4 mi se of I-495, exit 30 or 31; in Nagog Park Shopping Mall.
American   3 Nagog Park 01720. **Hours:** 11:30 am-2:30 & 5-9:30 pm, Sat 5 pm-10 pm, Sun 4 pm-9 pm. Closed: Sat &
Sun for lunch & 12/25. **Reservations:** suggested. **Features:** casual dress; children's menu; early bird
specials; carryout; salad bar; cocktails & lounge; a la carte. Inviting restaurant overlooking pond. Outdoor dining in season.
Cards: AE, DS, MC, VI.   ⊠

AMESBURY—15,000

LODGING

SUSSE CHALET INN   Rates Subject to Change   **Phone:** (978)388-3400
◆◆   7/2-9/5 [CP]   1P: $65- 85   2P/1B: $69- 89 2P/2B: $79- 89 XP: $3   F17
Motel   9/6-10/16 [CP]   1P: $56- 84   2P/1B: $59- 88 2P/2B: $69- 88 XP: $3   F17
              5/1-7/1 & 10/17-4/30 [CP] 1P: $46- 66   2P/1B: $54- 74 2P/2B: $59- 74 XP: $3   F17
Location: Jct I-95 & SR 110; southbound exit 58 or northbound exit 58B; 0.5 mi e of I-495 northbound exit 55. 35 Clarke Rd
01913. Fax: 978/388-9850. **Facility:** 104 rooms. 4 stories; interior corridors. **Cards:** AE, CB, DI, DS, MC, VI.
(See ad p 289)   🎦 🛌 🍴 🕹 🐾 🖨 ⊠

ANDOVER—29,200

LODGINGS

ANDOVER INN   Rates Subject to Change   **Phone:** (978)475-5903
◆◆   All Year   1P: $95   2P/1B: $110   XP: $10   F12
Country Inn   **Location:** 2.3 mi s of I-495, exit 41A via SR 28, at Phillips Academy Campus. 1 Chapel Ave 01810.
Fax: 978/475-1053. **Terms:** Check-in 4 pm. **Facility:** 29 rooms. A charming nostalgic 1930's Inn on the beau-
tifully landscaped grounds of Phillips Academy. A few cozy rooms with twin beds. 6 one-bedroom suites, $120-$170; 3 stories;
interior corridors. **Cards:** AE, CB, DI, DS, MC, VI.   🐾 🖥 🍴 🕹 🕹 🐾 🐾 🖨 ⊠

BOSTON MARRIOTT ANDOVER   Rates Subject to Change   **Phone:** (978)975-3600
◆◆◆   Sun-Thurs   1P: $159   2P/1B: $159   2P/2B: $159
Hotel   Fri & Sat   1P: $109   2P/1B: $109   2P/2B: $109
Location: 4.5 mi w at jct I-93 & River Rd; just e of I-495, exit 45; behind office park. 123 Old River Rd 01810.
Fax: 978/975-2664. **Terms:** Check-in 4 pm. **Facility:** 293 rooms. Spacious inviting lobby with marble & brass accents. Some
units with private balcony or patio. 5 stories; interior corridors; heated indoor pool. **Cards:** AE, CB, DI, DS, MC, VI.
🐾 🖥 🎦 🛌 🍴 🍸 🕹 🐾 🐾 🖨 🔒 🕹 ⊠ 🖨

COURTYARD BY MARRIOTT   Rates Subject to Change   **Phone:** (978)794-0700
◆◆◆   5/1-12/17   1P: $99- 129   2P/1B: $99- 129 2P/2B: $99- 129
Motor Inn   12/18-4/30   1P: $49- 119   2P/1B: $49- 119 2P/2B: $49- 119
              Location: Just e of I-93, exit 45 (River Rd); 2 mi n of jct I-495/93; in Riverbend Business Park. 10
Campanelli Dr 01810. Fax: 978/794-9558. **Facility:** 146 rooms. Many units with patio or balcony. Rates for up to 5 persons; 3
stories; interior corridors; heated indoor pool. **All Rooms:** combo or shower baths. **Cards:** AE, DI, DS, MC, VI.
(See color ad p 280)   🍴 🖥 🎦 🛌 🍴 🕹 🐾 🐾 🐾 🖥 🖨 🔒 🕹 🕹 ⊠

ROLLING GREEN INN AND CONFERENCE CENTER/RAMADA Rates Subject to Change **Phone:** (978)475-5400
◆◆   9/12-11/1   1P: $119   2P/1B: $89- 129 2P/2B: $129   XP: $10   F17
Motor Inn   5/1-9/11 & 11/2-12/31   1P: $115   2P/1B: $125   2P/2B: $125   XP: $10   F17
              1/1-4/30   1P: $109   2P/1B: $119   2P/2B: $119   XP: $10   F17
Location: On SR 133 just e of jct I-93, exit 43A; 1.3 mi s of I-495 exit 40A. 311 Lowell St 01810. Fax: 978/470-1108.
Facility: 178 rooms. 1-2 stories; interior corridors; heated indoor pool; 6 indoor tennis courts. **Services:** area transportation.
Cards: AE, CB, DI, DS, JC, MC, VI. *(See color ad inside front cover)*
(ASK) 🍴 🐾 🖥 🎦 🛌 🍴 🍸 🕹 🐾 🕹 🐾 🐾 🖥 🖨 🔒 ⊠

TAGE INN   Guaranteed Rates   **Phone:** (978)685-6200
(AAA)   All Year [CP]   1P: $65- 75   2P/1B: $73- 83 2P/2B: $78   XP: $8   F12
              Location: At I-93 exit 45; 2 mi n of I-495 exit 40B. 131 River Rd 01810. Fax: 978/794-9626. **Facility:** 180
◆◆◆   rooms. 2-3 stories; interior corridors; heated indoor pool, whirlpool; 2 lighted tennis courts. **Dining:** Limited
Motor Inn   pub fare, 5 pm-10 pm. **Some Rooms:** whirlpools. **Cards:** AE, DI, DS, MC, VI.
🖥 🎦 🛌 🍸 🕹 🐾 🐾 🐾 🐾 🖥 🖨 🔒 ⊠

RESTAURANT

ANDOVER INN DINING ROOM   **Lunch:** $10-$13   **Dinner:** $19-$23   **Phone:** 978/475-5903
◆◆◆   **Location:** 2.3 mi s of I-495, exit 41A via SR 28, at Phillips Academy Campus; in Andover Inn. Chapel Ave
Continental   01810. **Hours:** 11:30 am-2:45 & 5:30-9:45 pm, Sun 9/10-6/30, 11 am-2 & 5-8:45 pm. Closed: 12/25.
Reservations: suggested. **Features:** semi-formal attire; cocktails & lounge; a la carte. Gracious dining
atmosphere. International cuisine. Sun evening Indonesian Rijsttafel. Sunday Brunch except 7/1-9/5. Breakfast 7:30 am-9:45
am. Smoke free premises. **Cards:** AE, CB, DI, DS, MC, VI.   ⊠

BEDFORD—13,000   (See map p. 274; index p. 270)

LODGINGS

RAMADA INN-BEDFORD/BOSTON   Phone: (781)275-6700   **32**
(AAA) [SAVE]   5/1-10/31 [BP]   1P: $89- 119   2P/1B: $89- 119   2P/2B: $89- 119   XP: $10   F18
              11/1-4/30 [BP]   1P: $79- 109   2P/1B: $79- 109   2P/2B: $79- 109   XP: $10   F18
♦♦♦   **Location:** 0.8 mi se of Bedford on SR 4 & 225; 1.3 mi nw of SR 128 & I-95 exit 31B. 340 Great Rd 01730.
Motor Inn   **Fax:** 781/275-3011. **Terms:** Reserv deposit; handling fee imposed. **Facility:** 100 rooms. Many rooms overlook
an attractive contemporary garden atrium. 3 stories; interior corridors; heated indoor pool.
Dining: Restaurant; 6:30 am-9 pm, Sat 7 am-noon & 5-9 pm, Sun 7 am-noon; $11-$18; cocktails. **Cards:** AE, CB, DI, DS,
MC, VI. **Special Amenities:** Free breakfast and free newspaper. *(See color ad inside front cover)*
[icons]

RENAISSANCE BEDFORD HOTEL   Rates Subject to Change   Phone: (781)275-5500   **30**
♦♦♦   9/5-11/20   1P: $179   2P/1B: $179   2P/2B: $179
Hotel   5/1-9/4, 11/21-12/31 &
             3/1-4/30   1P: $159   2P/1B: $159   2P/2B: $159
             1/1-2/29   1P: $149   2P/1B: $149   2P/2B: $149
Location: 2.5 mi n of I-95 (SR 128), exit 32B via Middlesex Tpk. 44 Middlesex Tpk 01730. Fax: 781/275-3042. **Facility:** 285
rooms. Buildings set into rolling grounds with very attractive landscaping. A few cozy rooms with 2 beds. Many spacious
king-bed units. 3 stories; interior corridors; heated indoor pool. Fee: 4 tennis courts (2 indoor, 4 lighted). **Services:** giftshop;
area transportation. **Recreation:** jogging. **Cards:** AE, CB, DI, DS, MC, VI.
[icons]

TRAVELODGE-BEDFORD   Rates Subject to Change   Phone: 781/275-6120   **31**
♦   6/1-10/31   1P: $59- 69   2P/1B: $69- 79   2P/2B: $79- 89   XP: $6-10   F14
Motel   5/1-5/31 & 11/1-4/30   1P: $49- 59   2P/1B: $49- 59   2P/2B: $54- 64   XP: $6   F14
             Location: 0.3 mi se; on SR 4 & 225; 1.8 mi nw of I-95 & SR 128 exit 31B. 285 Great Rd 01730.
Fax: 781/275-6120. **Facility:** 42 rooms. 2 stories; interior/exterior corridors; small pool. **All Rooms:** combo or shower baths.
Cards: AE, DI, DS, MC, VI.
[icons]

RESTAURANTS

DALYA'S RESTAURANT   **Lunch:** $5-$13   **Dinner:** $10-$23   Phone: 781/275-0700   **49**
♦♦   **Location:** On SR 4, just n of jct 225 & 62W; at Bedford Farms. 20 North Rd 01730. **Hours:** 11:30 am-2 &
American   5:30-9 pm. Closed major holidays, Sun & Sat for lunch. **Reservations:** suggested. **Features:** dressy casual;
carryout; cocktails. American & Mediterranean cuisines served in European farmhouse atmosphere with
fireplace & antiques. Menu changes seasonally. Smoke free premises. **Cards:** AE, CB, DI, DS, MC, VI.   [X]

HAVILLAND'S GRILL   **Lunch:** $7-$16   **Dinner:** $14-$30   Phone: 781/275-5500   **50**
♦♦♦   **Location:** 2.5 mi n of I-95 (SR 128), exit 32B via Middlesex Tpk; in Renaissance Bedford Hotel. 44
Continental Middlesex Tpk 01730. **Hours:** 6:30 am-10 pm, Sat & Sun from 7:30 am. Closed: 12/25.
             Reservations: suggested. **Features:** semi-formal attire; children's menu; cocktails & lounge; entertainment;
a la carte. Charming, comfortable dining room. Fresh seafood specialties. Mediterranean influenced cuisine. Daily breakfast
buffet. Fri evening seafest special. Smoke free premises. **Cards:** AE, CB, DI, DS, JC, MC, VI.   [X]

BEVERLY—38,200

LODGING

LAKEVIEW MOTOR LODGE   Phone: (978)922-7535
(AAA) [SAVE]   6/1-10/31   1P: $73- 83   2P/1B: $83- 95   2P/2B: $83- 95   XP: $10   D18
              5/1-5/31 & 11/1-4/30   1P: $59- 69   2P/1B: $69- 83   2P/2B: $69- 83   XP: $10   D18
♦♦   **Location:** On SR 1A, 0.8 mi n of jct SR 128 exit 20A. 5 Lakeview Ave 01915. Fax: 978/922-7535.
Motel   **Terms:** Reserv deposit, 7 day notice; handling fee imposed; weekly rates, monthly rates in winter.
Facility: 20 rooms. Some units with living room. Few rooms on lower level have small windows. 2 stories;
interior/exterior corridors. **Dining:** Restaurant nearby. **All Rooms:** combo or shower baths. **Some Rooms:** 19 kitchens,
utensil deposit. **Cards:** AE, DS, MC, VI.
[icons]

RESTAURANTS

THE BEVERLY DEPOT   Country Inn   **Dinner:** $12-$20   Phone: 978/927-5402
♦♦   **Location:** Just w of SR 1A facing the post office; 0.5 mi s of jct SR 62, at the RR station. 10 Park St 01915.
Steak and   **Hours:** 5 pm-10 pm, Fri & Sat-11 pm, Sun 4 pm-9 pm. Closed major holidays & 12/24.
Seafood   **Reservations:** accepted; 5 or more. **Features:** casual dress; children's menu; health conscious menu items;
carryout; salad bar; cocktails & lounge; a la carte. Bustling, informal dining in converted train station.
Cards: AE, DI, DS, MC, VI.   [X]

THE COMMODORE RESTAURANT   **Lunch:** $6-$10   **Dinner:** $8-$17   Phone: 978/922-5590
(AAA)   **Location:** On SR 1A; 1 mi n of jct SR 128, exit 20A. 45 Enon St 01915. **Hours:** 11:30 am-9 pm, Fri &
             Sat-10 pm, Sun noon-9 pm. Closed: 1/1, 7/4 & 12/25. **Reservations:** accepted. **Features:** casual dress;
♦♦   children's menu; early bird specials; carryout; cocktails & lounge; entertainment; a la carte. Well established.
American   Attractive dining rooms & pub. **Cards:** AE, DI, DS, MC, VI.   [X]

BOXBOROUGH—3,300

LODGING

HOLIDAY INN BOXBOROUGH WOODS   Rates Subject to Change   Phone: 978/263-8701
♦♦♦   All Year   1P: $129- 139   2P/1B: $139- 149   2P/2B: $139- 149   XP: $10   F17
Motor Inn   **Location:** I-495 exit 28, just e. 242 Adams Pl 01719. Fax: 978/263-0518. **Terms:** Reserv deposit.
             Facility: 143 rooms. 11 suites, $179-$199 rates for up to 2 persons; 3 stories, no elevator; interior corridors;
heated indoor pool. **Cards:** AE, DI, DS, MC, VI. *(See color ad p 275)*
[icons]

BRADFORD

RESTAURANT

THE ROMA RESTAURANT   **Lunch:** $5-$7   **Dinner:** $9-$14   **Phone:** 978/374-8001
♦♦   **Location:** From I-495 exit 48, 1 mi e, then 2.5 mi n on SR 125, just w of SR 125. 29 Middlesex St 01835.
Italian   **Hours:** 11 am-9 pm, Fri & Sat-10 pm. Closed: 12/25. **Features:** casual dress; children's menu; carryout; cocktails & lounge. Family oriented for over 20 years. Along Merrimac River with outdoor patio dining in season. Featuring homemade pasta & local seafood. Very popular. **Cards:** AE, DS, MC, VI.   ☒

BRAINTREE—33,800   (See map p. 274; index p. 272)

LODGINGS

DAYS INN-BRAINTREE   **Phone:** (781)848-1260   **118**

ⒶⒶⒶ ⒮ⒶⓋⒺ	5/1-10/31 & 4/1-4/30 [EP]	1P: $100- 110	2P/1B: $100- 110	2P/2B: $110	XP: $5	F16
	1/1-3/31 [EP]	1P: $78	2P/1B: $83	2P/2B: $83	XP: $5	F16
♦♦	11/1-12/31 [CP]	1P: $78	2P/1B: $83	2P/2B: $83	XP: $5	F16

Motel   **Location:** Just n of jct I-93 & SR 128 on SR 37; 0.5 mi w. 190 Wood Rd 02184. Fax: 781/848-9799.
Terms: Pets, $6 extra charge. **Facility:** 104 rooms. 3 stories; interior corridors. **Cards:** AE, DI, DS, MC, VI.
Special Amenities: Free breakfast and free room upgrade (subject to availability with advanced reservations).

SHERATON BRAINTREE HOTEL   Rates Subject to Change   **Phone:** 781/848-0600   **120**

♦♦	9/13-11/21	1P: $234	2P/1B: $234	2P/2B: $234	XP: $15	F
Hotel	5/1-9/12	1P: $210	2P/1B: $210	2P/2B: $210	XP: $15	F
	3/7-4/30	1P: $189	2P/1B: $189	2P/2B: $189	XP: $15	F
	11/22-3/6	1P: $169	2P/1B: $169	2P/2B: $169	XP: $15	F

Location: Just n of jct I-93 & SR 128 on SR 37, just w of exit. 37 Forbes Rd 02184. Fax: 781/843-9492. **Facility:** 376 rooms.
Tudor style exterior. Across from a shopping mall. Rates for up to 4 persons; 6 stories; interior corridors; heated indoor pool.
Fee: racquetball court. **Services:** giftshop; area transportation. **Cards:** AE, CB, DI, DS, MC, VI.

RESTAURANT

HILLTOP STEAK HOUSE   **Lunch:** $7-$16   **Dinner:** $10-$20   **Phone:** 781/848-3363   **127**
♦   **Location:** At jct SR 3, exit 17 & Union St. 210 Union St 02184. **Hours:** 11 am-10 pm, Fri & Sat-11 pm, Sun
Steakhouse   11:30 am-10 pm. Closed: 11/25 & 12/25. **Features:** casual dress; children's menu; carryout; cocktails & lounge. Casual family dining in a very popular rustic atmosphere. All entrees cooked to order. Generous portions. **Cards:** AE, DS, MC, VI.   ☒

BRIGHTON   (See map p. 274; index p. 272)

LODGING

BEST WESTERN-TERRACE INN   **Phone:** (617)566-6260   **127**

ⒶⒶⒶ ⒮ⒶⓋⒺ	5/1-10/31 [CP]	1P: $99- 129	2P/1B: $109- 139	2P/2B: $109- 149	XP: $10	F18
	11/1-4/30 [CP]	1P: $89- 99	2P/1B: $99- 109	2P/2B: $99- 119	XP: $10	F18

♦♦   **Location:** Just s of SR 30 (Commonwealth Ave), just w of jct Washington St at Mt Hood Rd. 1650
Motel   Commonwealth Ave 02135. Fax: 617/731-3543. **Terms:** Reserv deposit; weekly rates. **Facility:** 72 rooms. Built into hillside in residential area. 6 one-bedroom suites $149-$169; $139 off season; 2 stories; exterior corridors.
Some Rooms: 59 efficiencies. **Cards:** AE, CB, DI, DS, JC, MC, VI. **Special Amenities: Free breakfast and free room upgrade (subject to availability with advanced reservations).** (See ad p 279)

BROOKLINE—54,700   (See map p. 274; index p. 270)

LODGING

HOLIDAY INN BOSTON BROOKLINE   Rates Subject to Change   **Phone:** 617/277-1200   **37**

♦♦♦	5/1-11/6	1P: $189- 249	2P/1B: $199- 259	2P/2B: $199- 259	XP: $10	F18
Motor Inn	11/7-11/20	1P: $179- 249	2P/1B: $189- 259	2P/2B: $189- 259	XP: $10	F18
	12/19-4/30	1P: $129- 249	2P/1B: $139- 259	2P/2B: $139- 259	XP: $10	F18
	11/21-12/18	1P: $159- 249	2P/1B: $169- 259	2P/2B: $169- 259	XP: $10	F18

Location: 1 mi sw of Kenmore Square at Beacon & St Paul sts. 1200 Beacon St 02146. Fax: 617/734-6991. **Facility:** 225
rooms. Max of 4 persons per room. 18 suites with wet bar, microwave & refrigerator, $299 for up to 2 persons; 2-6 stories; interior corridors; small heated indoor pool. Fee: parking. **All Rooms:** combo or shower baths. **Cards:** AE, CB, DI, DS, JC, MC, VI. (See color ad p 275)

BURLINGTON—23,300   (See map p. 274; index p. 270)

LODGINGS

BOSTON MARRIOTT HOTEL BURLINGTON   Rates Subject to Change   **Phone:** (781)229-6565   **42**
♦♦♦   All Year   1P: $159- 229   2P/1B: $159- 229   2P/2B: $159- 229
Hotel   **Location:** Jct SR 3A & I-95/SR 128, exit 33B. 1 Mall Rd 01803. Fax: 781/229-7973. **Terms:** Check-in 4
pm; reserv deposit. **Facility:** 419 rooms. 4 suites, $350. Rates for up to 5 persons; 9 stories; interior corridors;
heated indoor pool. **Services:** giftshop; area transportation. Fee: massage. **All Rooms:** combo or shower baths. **Cards:** AE, CB, DI, DS, JC, MC, VI.

SUMMERFIELD SUITES HOTEL   Rates Subject to Change   **Phone:** (781)270-0800   **40**
♦♦♦   All Year   1P: $209- 289   2P/1B: $209   2P/2B: $289
Suite Motel   **Location:** I-95 exit 33, just s on US 3, then 0.5 mi w on Wayside Rd. 2 Van de Graaf Dr 01803.
Fax: 781/270-5554. **Terms:** Check-in 4 pm; reserv deposit; handling fee imposed. **Facility:** 151 rooms. Attractive, relaxing suites. 38 two-bedroom rms, $249; $179 off seasson; 3 stories; interior corridors; heated pool. **Services:** area transportation. **Recreation:** sports court. **Some Rooms:** 7 efficiencies, 144 kitchens. **Cards:** AE, CB, DI, DS, JC, MC, VI.

(See map p. 274)

WYNDHAM GARDEN HOTEL		Rates Subject to Change	Phone: (781)272-8800	**43**

WYNDHAM GARDEN HOTEL
◆◆◆   Fri & Sat   Rates Subject to Change   **Phone: (781)272-8800**   **43**
Motor Inn   Fri & Sat   1P: $79- 104   XP: $10-20   F18
    Sun-Thurs   1P: $134- 143   XP: $10-20   F18
     Location: S of I-95 & SR 128 exit 32B, Middlesex Tpk. 30 Wheeler Rd 01803. Fax: 781/221-4605.
Facility: 180 rooms. Upscale public areas. 4 stories; interior corridors; heated indoor pool. **Services:** area transportation.
All Rooms: combo or shower baths. **Cards:** AE, CB, DI, DS, JC, MC, VI. *(See color ad below)*

RESTAURANTS

CAFE ESCADRILLE   **Lunch:** $10-$17   **Dinner:** $17-$23   **Phone:** 781/273-1916   **59**
◆◆◆   **Location:** On SR 3A, 0.3 mi s of I-95 & SR 128, exit 33A. 26 Cambridge St 01803. **Hours:** 11:30 am-10 pm,
Continental   Fri & Sat-11 pm. Closed: 1/1, 12/25 & Sun (except 5/12). **Reservations:** accepted; except Sat.
     Features: semi-formal attire; carryout; cocktails & lounge. Creative gourmet entrees in an elegant, candlelit
ambiance. Also a lively garden atrium. Very popular. Family operated for over 25 years. Lighter fare avail to midnight in cafe
or lounge area. **Cards:** AE, DI, MC, VI.

THE DANDELION GREEN   **Lunch:** $9-$12   **Dinner:** $14-$22   **Phone:** 781/273-1616   **57**
◆◆   **Location:** SR 128 southbound, 1 mi w of exit 33B; from SR 128 northbound exit 32B, follow past Burlington
American   Mall, 0.5 mi e on Mall Rd; in Marketplace Shopping Ctr. 90 Mall Rd 01803. **Hours:** 11:30 am-2:30 & 5-10
     pm; Sat from 5 pm, Sun 5 pm-9 pm; 10/19-6/21 Sun noon-8:30 pm. Closed major holidays & 12/24 after 6
pm. **Reservations:** suggested. **Features:** casual dress; children's menu; carryout; salad bar; cocktails & lounge. Lively,
candlelit dining in a contemporary setting amidst abundant greenery & natural woods. Featuring steak, chops & seafood.
Also, lite fare pub menu. Lounge open Sat for lunch at noon. **Cards:** AE, CB, DI, DS, MC, VI.

JOHNNY ROCKETS RESTAURANT   **Lunch:** $3-$6   **Dinner:** $3-$6   **Phone:** 781/273-2727   **56**
◆   **Location:** In Burlington Mall, ne entrance from I-95 & SR 128, exit 32B. 1 Burlington Mall Rd 01803.
American   **Hours:** 11:30 am-10 pm, Fri & Sat-11 pm, Sun-8 pm. Closed: 11/25, 12/25 & Easter. **Features:** casual dress;
     carryout; a la carte. A fun, lively, meticulously clean, rock "n" roll eatery. Open kitchen counter features lean
burgers, chili, fries & fountain drinks. Nickel wall-style jukebox. Smoke free premises.

LEGAL SEA FOODS   **Lunch:** $8-$15   **Dinner:** $14-$22   **Phone:** 781/270-9700   **58**
◆◆   **Location:** In Burlington Mall; ne entrance from I-95 & SR 128, exit 32B. 1310 Burlington Mall 01803.
Seafood   **Hours:** 11 am-10 pm, Sun noon-9 pm. Closed: 11/25 & 12/25. **Features:** casual dress; children's menu;
     health conscious menu items; cocktails & lounge; a la carte. Bustling, popular, contemporary dining room.
Extensive menu of grilled, broiled, fried, steamed & Cajun-style fresh seafood. Smoke free premises. **Cards:** AE, DI, DS,
MC, VI.

VICTORIA STATION-BURLINGTON   **Lunch:** $6-$10   **Dinner:** $12-$21   **Phone:** 781/273-2230   **55**
◆   **Location:** 0.3 mi n of SR 128, exit 32B. 128 Middlesex Tpk 01803. **Hours:** 11:30 am-10 pm, Sun noon-9
Steak and   pm. Closed: 12/25. **Reservations:** suggested; weekends. **Features:** casual dress; children's menu; early
Seafood   bird specials; carryout; cocktails & lounge. Dining in railroad boxcars. Specializing in prime rib; daily fresh
seafood specials. Popular with families for over 25 years. **Cards:** AE, DI, DS, MC, VI.

CAMBRIDGE—95,800   (See map p. 274; index p. 269)

LODGINGS

A CAMBRIDGE HOUSE BED & BREAKFAST INN   Rates Subject to Change   **Phone:** 617/491-6300
◆◆◆   9/1-10/31 [BP]   1P: $119- 185   2P/1B: $129- 250   2P/2B: $129- 250   XP: $35
Historic Bed   5/1-8/31 [BP]   1P: $109- 175   2P/1B: $129- 209   2P/2B: $129- 209   XP: $35
& Breakfast   11/1-4/30 [BP]   1P: $89- 155   2P/1B: $109- 179   2P/2B: $109- 179   XP: $35
     Location: On SR 2A; 0.8 mi s of SR 16. 2218 Massachusetts Ave 02140. Fax: 617/868-2848. **Terms:** Age
restrictions may apply; handling fee imposed. **Facility:** 16 rooms. 1892 Victorian home. Many rooms have canopy beds and/or
a functional fireplace. 3 stories, no elevator; interior corridors; smoke free premises. **Cards:** AE, DI, DS, MC, VI.
(See ad p 284)

(See map p. 274)

BEST WESTERN HOMESTEAD INN — Rates Subject to Change — Phone: (617)491-8000
All Year [CP]   1P: $129- 199 2P/1B: $129- 209 2P/2B: $149- 229 XP: $10-25 F17
Location: At jct SR 2, 3 & 16 in N Cambridge; from I-90 (MA Tpk), Cambridge/Allston exit to Rt 2W, Fresh Pond Pkwy. 220 Alewife Brook Pkwy 02138-1102. Fax: 617/491-4932. **Terms:** Reserv deposit; package plans. **Facility:** 69 rooms. Charming guest rooms with traditional or contemporary furnishings. Inviting homey lobby with carved mahogany fireplace. 4 stories; interior corridors; heated indoor pool, whirlpool.
Dining: Restaurant nearby. **Cards:** AE, DI, DS, MC, VI. *(See color ad below)*
Motel

BOSTON MARRIOTT CAMBRIDGE — Rates Subject to Change — Phone: 617/494-6600
All Year   1P: $179- 279 2P/1B: $179- 279 2P/2B: $179- 279 XP: $15 F18
Location: Corner Broadway & Third sts. 2 Cambridge Center 02142. Fax: 617/494-0036. **Terms:** Check-in 4 pm; weekend rates avail. **Facility:** 431 rooms. 26 stories; interior corridors; heated indoor pool. Fee: parking.
Services: giftshop. **All Rooms:** combo or shower baths. **Cards:** AE, CB, DI, DS, JC, MC, VI.
Hotel

THE CHARLES HOTEL IN HARVARD SQUARE — Rates Subject to Change — Phone: (617)864-1200
5/1-6/30, 9/1-12/31 &
4/1-4/30   1P: $185 2P/1B: $185 2P/2B: $185
7/1-8/31 & 1/1-3/31 1P: $165 2P/1B: $165 2P/2B: $165 XP: $20 F18
Location: Just s from Harvard Square; corner Eliot & Bennett sts. 1 Bennett St 02138. Fax: 617/864-5715. **Facility:** 293 rooms. Charming & cozy country style room decor. 10 stories; interior corridors; heated indoor pool. Fee: parking.
Services: giftshop. Fee: massage. **All Rooms:** combo or shower baths. **Cards:** AE, CB, JC, MC, VI. A Preferred Hotel.
Hotel

HARVARD SQUARE HOTEL — Rates Subject to Change — Phone: 617/864-5200
5/1-12/15   1P: $189- 199 2P/1B: $189 2P/2B: $199
12/16-4/30 1P: $139 2P/1B: $139 2P/2B: $139
Location: Harvard Square at Mt Auburn & Eliot sts. 110 Mt Auburn St 02138. Fax: 617/864-2409. **Facility:** 73 rooms. Conveniently close to Harvard University. Property offers clean, average size guest rooms with some rooms overlooking Harvard Square. 5 stories; interior corridors. Fee: parking. **Cards:** AE, CB, DI, DS, MC, VI.
Motel

HOWARD JOHNSON HOTEL CAMBRIDGE — Phone: (617)492-7777
All Year   1P: $125- 210 2P/1B: $135- 245 2P/2B: $135- 245 XP: $15 F17
Location: On US 3 & SR 2; 3 blks from tpk & I-90 exit 18, via River St Bridge. 777 Memorial Dr 02139. Fax: 617/492-6038. **Terms:** Pets. **Facility:** 205 rooms. Overlooking Charles River. 16 stories; interior corridors; small heated indoor pool. **Dining:** Restaurant; cocktails; also, Bisuteki Japanese Steak House, see separate listing. **All Rooms:** extended cable TV. **Cards:** AE, CB, DI, DS, JC, MC, VI. **Special Amenities:** Free newspaper and preferred room **(subject to availability with advanced reservations).** *(See color ad p 281)*
Hotel

HYATT REGENCY CAMBRIDGE — Rates Subject to Change — Phone: (617)492-1234
All Year   1P: $300- 325 2P/1B: $325- 350 2P/2B: $325- 350 XP: $25 F18
Terms: Check-in 4 pm. **Facility:** 469 rooms. Some rooms have extensive riverview. 16 stories; interior corridors; heated indoor pool. Fee: parking. **Services:** giftshop; area transportation. Rental: bicycles. **All Rooms:** combo or shower baths. **Cards:** AE, CB, DI, DS, JC, MC, VI.
Hotel

THE INN AT HARVARD — Rates Subject to Change — Phone: 617/491-2222
5/1-12/15   1P: $209 2P/1B: $209 2P/2B: $229 XP: $10 F18
12/16-4/30 1P: $189 2P/1B: $189 2P/2B: $209 XP: $10 F18
Location: Opposite Harvard Yard, at jct of Quincy, Bow & Harvard sts. 1201 Massachusetts Ave 02138. Fax: 617/520-3711. **Facility:** 113 rooms. Charming, traditional style inn with an elegant glass enclosed atrium. Fine antiques & custom furnishings. Warm hospitality. 4 stories; interior corridors. Fee: parking. **All Rooms:** combo or shower baths. **Cards:** AE, DI, DS, JC, MC, VI.
Motor Inn

(See map p. 274)

IRVING HOUSE AT HARVARD   Rates Subject to Change   Phone: 617/547-4600
◆
Motel

9/1-11/30 & 3/1-4/30 [CP]		1P: $85- 150		2P/1B: $115- 165		XP: $15-25	D17
6/1-8/31 [CP]		1P: $80- 140		2P/1B: $110- 155		XP: $15-25	D17
12/1-2/29 [CP]		1P: $70- 110		2P/1B: $95- 120		XP: $15-25	D17
5/1-5/31 [CP]		1P: $75- 140		2P/1B: $100- 155		XP: $15	D17

Location: Between Kirkland & Cambridge sts. 24 Irving St 02138. Fax: 617/576-2814. **Facility:** 44 rooms. In the heart of Harvard University campus. Guest rooms are clean but very basic & a few rooms are quite small. Limited guest parking. 4 stories, no elevator; interior corridors; designated smoking area. Fee: parking. **Some Rooms:** combo or shower baths, shared bathrooms, color TV. **Cards:** AE, DI, DS, MC, VI. 🖨 ✕

ROYAL SONESTA HOTEL BOSTON   Rates Subject to Change   **Phone: 617/806-4200**   [28]
◆◆◆   All Year   1P: $149- 319 2P/1B: $149- 319 2P/2B: $149- 319 XP: $25   F17
Hotel   **Location:** Corner Kinney & Edwin Land Blvd. 5 Cambridge Pkwy 02142. Fax: 617/806-4232. **Terms:** Weekend rates avail. **Facility:** 400 rooms. 10 stories; interior corridors; heated indoor pool. Fee: parking. **Recreation:** bicycles. **All Rooms:** combo or shower baths. **Some Rooms:** 16 efficiencies. **Cards:** AE, CB, DI, DS, JC, MC, VI.   🅢 🕮 🛋 🍴 🍽 🖥 🛏 🌊 🗙 🛅 🐾 📼 🛏 🖨 🖥 🎧 ✕

SHERATON COMMANDER HOTEL   Rates Subject to Change   **Phone: 617/547-4800**
◆◆◆

		1P:		2P/1B:		2P/2B:		XP:	
9/16-11/23		1P: $279		2P/1B: $299		2P/2B: $299		XP: $20	F16
5/1-9/15 & 4/1-4/30		1P: $259		2P/1B: $279		2P/2B: $279		XP: $20	F16
11/24-3/31		1P: $179		2P/1B: $199		2P/2B: $199		XP: $20	F16

Hotel   **Location:** Just n of Harvard Square on Cambridge Common. 16 Garden St 02138. Fax: 617/868-8322. **Facility:** 175 rooms. Attractively appointed rooms in elegant, traditional style hotel. Gracious public areas. Hotel was constructed in 1927. 4 two-bedroom units. 7 stories; interior corridors. **Services:** giftshop. **Cards:** AE, CB, DI, DS, MC, VI.

🅢 🕮 🍴 🍽 🛫 🖥 🛋 🌊 🐾 🖥 🛏 🖨 🎧 ✕ 🎵

RESTAURANTS

BISUTEKI JAPANESE STEAK HOUSE   Dinner: $15-$20   Phone: 617/492-7777   [62]
◆◆   **Location:** On US 3 & SR 2; 3 blks from tpk & I-90 exit 18, via River St Bridge; in Howard Johnson Hotel
Ethnic   Cambridge. 777 Memorial Dr 02139. **Hours:** 5 pm-10 pm, Fri & Sat-11 pm, Sun 4 pm-10 pm. Closed: 1/1, 11/25, 12/24 & 12/25. **Reservations:** suggested. **Features:** casual dress; children's menu; cocktails & lounge. Food prepared hibachi style at tables of 8. Menu features steak, seafood, chicken & sushi. Smoke free premises. **Cards:** AE, DI, DS, MC, VI.   ✕

COTTONWOOD CAFE   Lunch: $4-$8   Dinner: $13-$18   Phone: 617/661-7440   [63]
◆◆   **Location:** On SR 2A; in Cambridge at Porter Square. 1815 Massachusetts Ave 02140. **Hours:** 11:45 am-3 &
Southwest   5-9 pm, Fri & Sat-10:30 pm, Sun 10:30 am-2:45 & 5-9 pm. Closed major holidays. Contemporary,
American   **Reservations:** suggested. **Features:** casual dress; carryout; cocktails & lounge; a la carte. Contemporary, southwest decor, casual dining. Creative cuisine. Sat & Sun brunch. **Cards:** AE, DI, DS, MC, VI.   🖥 ✕

LEGAL SEA FOODS   Lunch: $8-$14   Dinner: $15-$25   Phone: 617/864-3400   [45]
◆◆   **Location:** At Kendall Square adjacent to Marriott Hotel. 5 Cambridge Center 02142. **Hours:** 11 am-10 pm,
Seafood   Fri-10:30, Sat noon-10:30 pm, Sun noon-9 pm. Closed: 11/25 & 12/25. **Reservations:** accepted. **Features:** casual dress; children's menu; carryout; cocktails & lounge; fee for parking; a la carte. Grilled, broiled, fried & Cajun-style fresh seafood. Contemporary, informal dining room. Smoke free premises. **Cards:** AE, DI, DS, MC, VI.   ✕

RIALTO   Dinner: $20-$34   Phone: 617/661-5050   [64]
◆◆◆   **Location:** Just s from Harvard Square; corner Eliot & Bennett sts; in The Charles Hotel in Harvard Square. 1
Regional   Bennett St 02138. **Hours:** 5:30 pm-11 pm. Closed: 1/1, 11/25 & 12/25. **Reservations:** required.
Continental   **Features:** dressy casual; cocktails & lounge; fee for parking & valet parking; a la carte. Mediterranean cuisine with French, Spanish & Italian influence served in contemporary upscale casual elegance. Smoke free premises. **Cards:** AE, CB, DI, JC, MC, VI.   ✕

SALAMANDER   Lunch: $4-$7   Dinner: $19-$29   Phone: 617/225-2121   [46]
◆◆◆   **Location:** Corner of First St; in the Riverview Bldg. 1 Athenaeum St 02142. **Hours:** 11:30 am-3:30 & 6-10
Ethnic   pm, Sat from 6 pm. Closed: 11/25, 12/25 & Sun. **Reservations:** suggested. **Features:** semi-formal attire; carryout; cocktails; fee for parking. Eclectic Asian-influenced cuisine & live fire cooking. Leisurely dining in contemporary atmosphere. Smoke free premises. **Cards:** AE, DI, DS, MC, VI.   ✕

SANDRINE'S BISTRO   Lunch: $7-$15   Dinner: $18-$29   Phone: 617/497-5300   [61]
◆◆◆   **Location:** Adjacent to Holyoke Center; in Harvard Square. 8 Holyoke St 02138. **Hours:** 11:30 am-2:30 &
Ethnic   5:30-10 pm, Thurs-Sat until 10:30 pm. Closed major holidays. **Reservations:** suggested. **Features:** casual dress; beer & wine only; street parking; a la carte. French Alsatian Bistro. Authentic Alsatian cuisine. Menu changes seasonally. Chef/owner operated. Smoke free premises. **Cards:** AE, DI, MC, VI.   ✕

CHELMSFORD—32,400

LODGINGS

BEST WESTERN CHELMSFORD INN   Rates Subject to Change   **Phone: (978)256-7511**
◆◆   All Year   1P: $85- 95 2P/1B: $95- 105 2P/2B: $95- 105 XP: $6   F16
Motor Inn   **Location:** On SR 110 at jct I-495, exit 34. 187 Chelmsford St 01824. Fax: 978/250-1401. **Terms:** Check-in 4 pm. **Facility:** 117 rooms. Large rooms in tower section. 2-5 stories; interior corridors. **Cards:** AE, CB, DI, DS, MC, VI.

🅐🅢🅚 🅢 🛋 🅢 🕮 🅢 🛋 🍴 🍽 🛫 🛋 🐾 🖥 🖨 🖥 ✕

RADISSON HERITAGE HOTEL   Rates Subject to Change   **Phone: (978)256-0800**
◆◆◆   All Year   1P: $69- 89 2P/1B: $79- 99 2P/2B: $69- 99 XP: $15   F17
Hotel   **Location:** 0.3 mi s on SR 110, Parlmont Plaza; I-495, exit 34. 10 Independence Dr 01824. Fax: 978/256-0750. **Terms:** Reserv deposit, 7 day notice; handling fee imposed. **Facility:** 214 rooms. Traditional decor. Some large deluxe suites. Suites, $105; $75-$85 off season. Rates for up to 4 persons; 5 stories; interior corridors; heated indoor pool. **Services:** giftshop. **Cards:** AE, DI, DS, MC, VI.

🅐🅢🅚 🅢 🛋 🕮 🛋 🍴 🍽 🛫 🛋 🐾 🖥 🖨 🖥 🗆 🖨 🖨 ✕

CHESTNUT HILL

RESTAURANT

LEGAL SEAFOODS
◆◆
Seafood
Lunch: $7-$12   **Dinner:** $12-$20   **Phone:** 617/277-7300
Location: On SR 9, in Chestnut Hill Shopping Center. 43 Boylston St 02167. **Hours:** 11 am-10 pm, Fri & Sat-11 pm, Sun noon-10 pm. Closed: 11/25 & 12/25. **Features:** casual dress; children's menu; carryout; cocktails & lounge; a la carte. Bustling, popular, friendly dining room. Extensive menu of grilled, broiled, fried, steamed & Cajun-style fresh seafood. Smoke free premises. **Cards:** AE, DI, DS, MC, VI.

COHASSET—7,100

LODGING

KIMBALLS BY-THE-SEA
◆◆◆
Motor Inn

		Rates Subject to Change			**Phone:** 781/383-6650	
5/1-10/31	1P:	$89- 119	2P/1B:	$109- 139	2P/2B: $109- 139	XP: $10	F12
11/1-4/30	1P:	$65- 80	2P/1B:	$70- 90	2P/2B: $70- 90	XP: $10	F12

Location: At Cohasset Harbor. 124 Elm St 02025. Fax: 781/383-2872. **Facility:** 55 rooms. Bayside location. Most rooms with balcony. 3 stories; interior corridors; heated indoor pool. **Cards:** AE, CB, DI, DS, MC, VI.

RESTAURANT

THE RED LION INN
◆
American
Lunch: $4-$7   **Dinner:** $9-$16   **Phone:** 781/383-1704
Location: Center. 71 S Main St 02025. **Hours:** Open 6/1-4/30; 11:30 am-9 pm, Fri & Sat-10 pm, Sun noon-9 pm. Closed: 12/25. **Reservations:** accepted; weekends. **Features:** casual dress; children's menu; carryout; cocktails & lounge. Historic restaurant. Original building dates to 1704. Regional American & Continental cuisine served in casual atmosphere. **Cards:** AE, MC, VI.

CONCORD—17,100

LODGINGS

BEST WESTERN AT HISTORIC CONCORD
◆◆
Motel

| | | Rates Subject to Change | | | **Phone:** (978)369-6100 | |
| All Year [CP] | 1P: | $74- 114 | 2P/1B: | $79- 119 | 2P/2B: $84- 124 | XP: $10 | F12 |

Location: 1.8 mi w just off SR 2 & 2A. 740 Elm St 01742. Fax: 978/371-1656. **Facility:** 106 rooms. 2 stories; interior corridors. **Cards:** AE, CB, DI, DS, JC, MC, VI.

THE COLONIAL INN
🅰🅰🅰 [SAVE]
◆◆◆
Country Inn

		Phone: (978)369-9200	
5/1-10/31 & 4/1-4/30	1P: $159- 195	2P/1B: $159- 195	
11/1-3/31	1P: $135- 155	2P/1B: $135- 155	

Location: On the green; center of SR 2A & 62. 48 Monument Sq 01742. Fax: 978/371-1533. **Terms:** Package plans. **Facility:** 49 rooms. Country inn-type decor in rooms & public areas. Original section built in early 1700's & is on the National Register of Historic Places. 2 two-bedroom units. 2 housekeeping apartments, $205-$295 for 2 persons; 2 stories; interior corridors. **Dining:** Afternoon tea; dining room, see separate listing. **Services:** giftshop. **All Rooms:** combo or shower baths. **Cards:** AE, CB, DI, DS, JC, MC, VI. **Special Amenities:** Free local telephone calls and free newspaper. *(See color ad below)*

THE HAWTHORNE INN
◆◆◆
Bed & Breakfast

		Rates Subject to Change			**Phone:** (978)369-5610	
5/1-12/31 & 4/1-4/30 [BP]	1P:	$125- 185	2P/1B:	$175- 225	2P/2B: $175- 195	XP: $15-25	D10
1/1-3/31 [BP]	1P:	$95- 125	2P/1B:	$140- 175	2P/2B: $140- 175	XP: $15-25	D10

Location: 0.8 mi e of town square. 462 Lexington Rd 01742. Fax: 978/287-4949. **Terms:** Reserv deposit, 14 day notice; handling fee imposed. **Facility:** 7 rooms. 1870 colonial-style home. Inviting rooms decorated with antiques & owner's artwork. Expanded continental breakfast. 2 stories; interior corridors; smoke free premises. **Services:** area transportation. **All Rooms:** combo or shower baths. **Cards:** AE, DS, MC, VI.

RESTAURANTS

AIGO BISTRO
◆◆◆
French
Lunch: $8-$15   **Dinner:** $15-$25   **Phone:** 978/371-1333
Location: Upstairs in The Concord Depot; 0.7 mi s of town square. 84 Thoreau St 01742. **Hours:** 11:30 am-2:30 & 5:30-9 pm, Fri & Sat-10 pm. Closed major holidays. **Reservations:** suggested. **Features:** casual dress; Sunday brunch; carryout; cocktails & lounge; a la carte. Mediterranean style French cuisine served in casual atmosphere upstairs in former train station. Smoke free premises. **Cards:** AE, DI, MC, VI.

THE COLONIAL INN DINING ROOM   Country Inn   **Lunch:** $8-$15   **Dinner:** $12-$28   **Phone:** 978/369-2373
◆◆   **Location:** On the green; center of SR 2A & 62, in The Colonial Inn. 48 Monument Sq 01742. **Hours:** 7
Regional   am-9:30 pm, Sun-8:30 pm. **Reservations:** suggested. **Features:** semi-formal attire; Sunday brunch;
American   children's menu; carryout; cocktails & lounge; entertainment; a la carte. Traditional New England cuisine.
Continental specials. Warm, colonial-style decor. **Cards:** AE, CB, DI, DS, MC, VI.   ⊠

DANVERS—24,200

LODGINGS

COMFORT INN DANVERS   **Phone:** (978)777-1700
(AAA) [SAVE]   9/10-11/1   1P: $99- 130   2P/1B: $109- 145   2P/2B: $109- 145   XP: $10   F18
             6/4-9/9   1P: $99- 126   2P/1B: $109- 136   2P/2B: $109- 136   XP: $10   F18
◆◆◆   5/1-6/3   1P: $89- 119   2P/1B: $89- 129   2P/2B: $89- 129   XP: $10   F18
Motel   11/2-4/30   1P: $79- 109   2P/1B: $79- 119   2P/2B: $79- 119   XP: $10   F18
Location: Just w of US 1, 0.8 mi n of jct SR 114, northbound Center St exit, w under US 1; southbound
Dayton St exit. 50 Dayton St 01923. Fax: 978/777-4647. **Terms:** Weekly/monthly rates; package plans. **Facility:** 136 rooms.
5 stories; interior corridors; heated indoor pool. **Dining:** Restaurant nearby. **Cards:** AE, CB, DI, DS, MC, VI.
**Special Amenities: Early check-in/late check-out and free room upgrade (subject to availability with advanced
reservations).** *(See color ad p 313)*

COURTYARD BY MARRIOTT-DANVERS   Rates Subject to Change   **Phone:** 978/777-8630
◆◆◆   All Year   1P: $119- 144   2P/1B: $119- 144   2P/2B: $119- 144
Motel   **Location:** From SR 128, exit 24; behind Liberty Tree Mall. 275 Independence Way 01923.
Fax: 978/777-7341. **Facility:** 122 rooms. A charming Colonial style brick building. Contemporary room decors
& traditional furnishings. Quiet location. 3 stories; interior corridors; heated pool. **Cards:** AE, DI, DS, MC, VI.
(See color ad p 280)

QUALITY INN KING'S GRANT INN   **Phone:** (978)774-6800
(AAA) [SAVE]   9/1-10/31   1P: $119- 159   2P/1B: $119- 159   2P/2B: $119- 159   XP: $10   F18
             5/1-8/31 & 11/1-4/30   1P: $109- 149   2P/1B: $109- 149   2P/2B: $109- 149   XP: $10   F18
◆◆   **Location:** On SR 128, at Trask Ln, exit 21N eastbound, exit 22 westbound. Rt 128 at Trask Ln 01923 (PO
Motor Inn   Box 274). Fax: 978/774-6502. **Terms:** Package plans. **Facility:** 125 rooms. Some rooms with balcony. Indoor
tropical garden. Some deluxe rooms. 2 stories; interior corridors; heated indoor pool, whirlpool.
Dining: Lion's Head Tavern, see separate listing. **Services:** giftshop. **Cards:** AE, CB, DI, DS, JC, MC, VI.
Special Amenities: Free local telephone calls and free newspaper. *(See ad below)*

RESIDENCE INN BY MARRIOTT
◆◆◆ All Year [CP]
Suite Motel
Rates Subject to Change
1P: $200   2P/1B: $200   2P/2B: $227
Phone: 978/777-7171

Location: On US 1 northbound; just s of jct SR 114; entrance via T.G.I. Friday's parking lot. 51 Newbury St (Rt 1) 01923. Fax: 978/774-7195. **Facility:** 96 rooms. Residential style accommodations. 24 two-bedroom units. 2 stories; exterior corridors; heated pool. **Recreation:** sports court. **All Rooms:** kitchens. **Cards:** AE, CB, DI, DS, MC, VI.

SHERATON FERNCROFT RESORT
◆◆◆ All Year
Hotel
Rates Subject to Change
1P: $109- 149   2P/1B: $109- 149   2P/2B: $109- 149   XP: $15   F16
Phone: 978/777-2500

Location: Jct I-95 & US 1; from I-95 southbound, exit 50 to US 1S; from I-95 northbound, exit 50 follow signs for US 1S to Ferncroft Village. 50 Ferncroft Rd 01923. Fax: 978/750-7959. **Facility:** 367 rooms. Contemporary, spacious accommodations. 8 stories; interior corridors; putting green; heated indoor pool. Fee: 27 holes golf; racquetball courts, 8 lighted tennis courts. **Services:** giftshop. Fee: massage. **Recreation:** jogging. Fee: cross country skiing. **Cards:** AE, CB, DI, DS, MC, VI. *(See color ad p 298)*

SUPER 8 MOTEL
◆◆ All Year [CP]
Motel
Rates Subject to Change
1P: $61- 69   2P/1B: $61   2P/2B: $69
Phone: 978/774-6500

Location: US 1 northbound, 1.4 mi n of SR 114, just s of SR 62 (no access from US 1 southbound). 225 Newbury St 01923. Fax: 978/762-6491. **Facility:** 77 rooms. 2 stories; exterior corridors. **All Rooms:** combo or shower baths. **Some Rooms:** 11 efficiencies. **Cards:** AE, CB, DI, DS, MC, VI.

RESTAURANTS

THE HARDCOVER
ⒶⒶⒶ
◆◆
American
Dinner: $12-$20
Phone: 978/774-1223

Location: On US 1 (northbound); just s of jct SR 114; 2.2 mi n of jct I-95 exit 44 (no access from US 1 southbound). 15A Newbury St 01923. **Hours:** 5 pm-10 pm, Fri & Sat-11 pm, Sun 4 pm-9:30 pm. Closed major holidays. **Features:** casual dress; children's menu; health conscious menu items; salad bar; cocktails & lounge; a la carte. Pleasant contemporary dining rooms. A library setting where the hardcover classics surround you. Smoke free premises. **Cards:** AE, DI, DS, MC, VI.

LION'S HEAD TAVERN
◆◆
Regional
American

(See ad p 298)
Lunch: $5-$10   Dinner: $11-$20   Phone: 978/774-6800

Location: On SR 128, at Trask Ln, exit 21N; in Quality Inn King's Grant. SR 128 at Trask Ln 01923. **Hours:** 7 am-10 pm, Sun 8 am-9 pm. Closed: 12/25 & 12/24 for lunch & dinner. **Reservations:** accepted. **Features:** casual dress; Sunday brunch; children's menu; early bird specials; carryout; cocktails & lounge; entertainment; a la carte. Hearty New England fare. Old English style decor. **Cards:** AE, DI, DS, MC, VI.

SPUD'S RESTAURANT & PUB
◆
American
Lunch: $4-$9   Dinner: $6-$10   Phone: 978/774-7786

Location: SR 128 exit 24; at Endicott Plaza. 139 Endicott St 01923. **Hours:** 11 am-11 pm, Fri & Sat-midnight, Sun & Mon-10 pm. Closed: 7/4, 11/25 & 12/25. **Features:** casual dress; children's menu; health conscious menu items; carryout; cocktails & lounge; a la carte. Popular family dining in a rustic ambiance. **Cards:** AE, DS, MC, VI.

DEDHAM—23,800   (See map p. 274; index p. 270)

LODGINGS

COMFORT INN-DEDHAM
ⒶⒶⒶ (SAVE)
◆◆
Motel
5/1-11/15 [CP]   1P: $97- 99   2P/1B: $97- 109   2P/2B: $102- 122   XP: $10   F17
11/16-4/30 [CP]   1P: $82- 86   2P/1B: $82- 96   2P/2B: $86- 106   XP: $10   F17
Phone: (781)326-6700   58

Location: From I-95 & SR 128, exit 15A, 0.3 mi n on US 1, 0.3 mi e. 235 Elm St 02026. Fax: 781/326-9264. **Facility:** 159 rooms. 8 suites, $85-$135; 3 stories; interior/exterior corridors; heated pool. **Dining:** Restaurant nearby. **Some Rooms:** 8 efficiencies. **Cards:** AE, CB, DI, DS, JC, MC, VI. **Special Amenities:** Free breakfast and free local telephone calls.

HILTON AT DEDHAM PLACE
◆◆◆
Hotel
5/1-11/17 & 4/1-4/30   1P: $135- 179   2P/1B: $135- 179   2P/2B: $150- 205   XP: $10-20   F18
11/18-3/31   1P: $129- 159   2P/1B: $129- 159   2P/2B: $144- 179   XP: $10-20   F18
Phone: (781)329-7900   57

Location: Just e of jct I-95 & SR 128, exit 14. 25 Allied Dr 02026. Fax: 781/329-5552. **Terms:** 2 night min stay, weekends in fall; weekend rates avail. **Facility:** 249 rooms. Quiet location adjacent to conservation area. Elegant public areas & attractively landscaped grounds. 4 stories; interior corridors; heated indoor pool. Fee: racquetball courts, 2 lighted tennis courts. **Services:** giftshop; area transportation. Fee: massage. **Recreation:** jogging. **Some Rooms:** color TV. **Cards:** AE, CB, DI, DS, JC, MC, VI. *(See color ad p 37)*

(See map p. 274)

HOLIDAY INN-DEDHAM Phone: (781)329-1000 🔲56
🔺🔺🔺 SAVE All Year 1P: $99- 119   2P/1B: $99- 129   2P/2B: $99- 129   XP: $10 F18
Motor Inn **Location:** On US 1; at jct I-95 & SR 128, exit 15A. 55 Ariadne Rd 02026. Fax: 781/329-0903.
◆ ◆ **Terms:** Monthly rates; BP avail. **Facility:** 203 rooms. 2-8 stories; interior corridors; heated pool.
Dining: Dining room; 6:30 am-2 & 5-10 pm, Sat & Sun from 7 am; $12-$20; cocktails. **Services:** area
transportation, within 10 mi. **Cards:** AE, CB, DI, DS, JC, MC, VI. *(See color ad p 275 & p 299)*

RESIDENCE INN BY MARRIOTT Rates Subject to Change Phone: (781)407-0999 🔲60
🔺🔺🔺 9/12-3/13 [EP] 1P: $135- 165   2P/1B: $135- 165
◆◆◆ 5/1-9/11 & 3/14-4/30 [CP] 1P: $135- 155   2P/1B: $135- 155
Apartment **Location:** I-95 & SR 128 exit 15A, 0.3 mi n on US 1, then 0.4 mi e. 259 Elm St 02026. Fax: 781/407-0752.
Motel **Terms:** Reserv deposit. **Facility:** 81 rooms. 6 two-bedroom units. Rates for up to 4 persons in one-bedroom,
5 persons in two-person rms. Shopping service avail; 3 stories; interior corridors; heated pool, whirlpool.
Dining: Restaurant nearby. **All Rooms:** combo or shower baths. **Some Rooms:** 75 efficiencies, 6 kitchens.
Cards: AE, DI, DS, MC, VI.

EAST BOSTON (See map p. 274; index p. 272)

LODGING

HOLIDAY INN BOSTON-LOGAN AIRPORT Rates Subject to Change Phone: 617/569-5250 🔲140
◆◆◆ 9/1-11/30 1P: $179- 199   2P/1B: $189- 209   2P/2B: $189- 209   XP: $10 F18
Hotel 5/1-8/31 1P: $149- 169   2P/1B: $159- 179   2P/2B: $159- 179   XP: $10 F18
3/1-4/30 1P: $109- 149   2P/1B: $119- 159   2P/2B: $119- 159   XP: $10 F18
12/1-2/29 1P: $89- 119   2P/1B: $99- 129   2P/2B: $99- 129   XP: $10 F18
Location: On SR 1A; 1.5 mi n of Logan International Airport Terminal. 225 McClellan Hwy 02128. Fax: 617/569-5159.
Facility: 351 rooms. 12 stories; interior corridors. **Services:** giftshop. **All Rooms:** combo or shower baths. **Cards:** AE, CB,
DI, DS, MC, VI. *(See color ad p 275)*

ESSEX—3,300

LODGING

GEORGE FULLER HOUSE Rates Subject to Change Phone: 978/768-7766
◆◆◆ 5/24-10/31 [BP] 1P: $90- 115   2P/1B: $100- 125   2P/2B: $125   XP: $15 F6
Historic Bed 5/1-5/23 & 11/1-4/30 [BP] 1P: $80- 110   2P/1B: $90- 115   2P/2B: $115   XP: $15 F6
& Breakfast **Location:** 0.5 mi e on SR 133; 3 mi w of jct SR 128, exit 14. 148 Main St 01929. Fax: 978/768-6178.
Terms: Reserv deposit, 14 day notice; 2 night min stay, weekends in summer. **Facility:** 7 rooms. Victorian late
Federalist home circa 1830. 4 rooms with functional fireplace. 1 two-bedroom unit. 2 suites, $145-$155; 3 stories, no elevator;
interior corridors; designated smoking area. **All Rooms:** combo or shower baths. **Cards:** AE, CB, DI, DS, MC, VI.

RESTAURANT

JERRY PELONZI'S HEARTHSIDE RESTAURANT Historical Lunch: $6-$10 Dinner: $13-$17 Phone: 978/768-6002
🔺🔺🔺 **Location:** On SR 133; 2.2 mi nw of SR 128, exit 14. 109 Eastern Ave 01929. **Hours:** 11:30 am-9 pm, Fri,
Sat & 6/15-9/2-10 pm. **Closed:** 12/25 & 12/24 for dinner. **Reservations:** accepted; weekends.
◆ ◆ **Features:** casual dress; children's menu; early bird specials; health conscious menu; carryout; cocktails.
Continental Popular dining in the warmth of a rustic New England farmhouse circa 1680. Generous portions. Fresh
seafood specialties. **Cards:** AE, MC, VI.

FOXBORO—14,600

LODGINGS

COURTYARD BY MARRIOTT Rates Subject to Change Phone: 508/543-5222
◆◆◆ Sun-Thurs 5/1-11/17 &
Motel 4/8-4/30 1P: $110- 145   2P/1B: $110- 145   2P/2B: $110- 145
Fri & Sat 5/1-11/17, 11/18-4/7
& Fri & Sat 4/8-4/30 1P: $69- 109   2P/1B: $69- 109   2P/2B: $69- 109
Location: 0.5 mi s of I-95 exit 7A; 1.3 mi n of jct I-495, just off SR 140 exit 12; in Foxborough Business Park. 35 Foxboro
Blvd 02035. Fax: 508/543-0445. **Terms:** Reserv deposit. **Facility:** 149 rooms. Modern brick building in a quiet park setting. In-
viting guest rooms with mahogany furnishings. Many units with patio or balcony overlooking professionally landscaped court-
yard. Marble, brass & greenery accent the lobby. 3 stories; interior corridors; heated indoor pool. **Cards:** AE, DI, DS, MC, VI.
(See color ad p 280)

END-ZONE MOTOR INN Rates Subject to Change Phone: 508/543-4000
◆ All Year 1P: $50- 60   2P/1B: $55- 58 2P/2B: $60   XP: $5 F12
Motel **Location:** On US 1, 0.5 mi n of jct SR 140, 0.5 mi s of Foxboro Stadium. 105 Washington St 02035.
Fax: 508/543-4000. **Facility:** 48 rooms. Features a large display of authentic sports memorabilia. 2 stories; in-
terior corridors. **Some Rooms:** 14 efficiencies. **Cards:** AE, CB, DI, DS, MC, VI.

Checkout time is noted in the listing if the
required time is before 10 a.m.

RESTAURANT

LAFAYETTE HOUSE   Historical   **Lunch:** $7-$10   **Dinner:** $16-$23   **Phone:** 508/543-5344
◆◆   **Location:** On US 1; 0.5 mi n of jct SR 140. 109 Washington St, Rt 1 02035. **Hours:** 11:45 am-3 & 5-9 pm,
Continental   Fri & Sat-10 pm, Sun 11:45 am-9 pm. Closed: 1/1, 12/24 for dinner & 12/25. **Reservations:** suggested.
          Features: semi-formal attire; Sunday brunch; cocktails & lounge. Inviting, cozy, Colonial-style dining rooms in
a stately, restored carriage house built in 1784. A local tradition. Gracious service. Smoking permitted in lounge. Smoke free
premises. **Cards:** AE, CB, DI, DS, MC, VI.   ⊠

FRAMINGHAM—65,000

LODGINGS

ECONO LODGE   **Phone:** (508)879-1510

		1P:		2P/1B:		2P/2B:		XP:		F16
AAA SAVE	5/1-10/31	1P:	$75- 89	2P/1B:	$75- 89	2P/2B:	$75- 89	XP:	$6	F16
◆	11/1-4/30	1P:	$50- 65	2P/1B:	$50- 65	2P/2B:	$50- 65	XP:	$6	F16

Motel   **Location:** On SR 9E; 1 mi e from MA Tpk, exit 12. 1186 Worcester Rd 01701. Fax: 508/875-2686.
          Facility: 33 rooms. 2 stories; interior/exterior corridors. **Cards:** AE, DI, DS, MC, VI. **Special Amenities: Free
local telephone calls and free room upgrade (subject to availability with advanced reservations).**

🅢 🞲 ⊠

MOTEL 6 - 1249   Rates Subject to Change   **Phone:** 508/620-0500
AAA   All Year   1P: $59   2P/2B: $69   XP: $3   F17
◆◆   **Location:** On SR 9 at tpk exit 12, follow signs to SR 9W. 1668 Worcester Rd 01702. Fax: 508/820-0868.
Motel   **Terms:** Pets. **Facility:** 105 rooms. Good size rooms. 4 stories; interior corridors. **Dining:** Restaurant nearby.
          All Rooms: combo or shower baths. **Cards:** AE, CB, DI, DS, MC, VI.

🖭 🍽 🖾 📶 🞲 🖴 🖥 🕹 ⊠

RED ROOF INN   **Phone:** (508)872-4499

		1P:		2P/1B:		2P/2B:		XP:		F18
AAA SAVE	5/1-10/31	1P:	$61- 86	2P/1B:	$71- 96	2P/2B:	$71- 96	XP:	$8	F18
◆◆	11/1-4/30	1P:	$51- 71	2P/1B:	$61- 81	2P/2B:	$61- 81	XP:	$8	F18

Motel   **Location:** On SR 30 at jct I-90 (MA Tpk), exit 13; from SR 9 in Natick, 0.8 mi n on Speen St, then w on SR
          30, following signs for MA Tpk. 650 Cochituate Rd 01701. Fax: 508/872-2579. **Terms:** Small pets only.
          Facility: 170 rooms. 2 stories; exterior corridors. **Dining:** Restaurant nearby. **Cards:** AE, CB, DI, DS, MC,
VI. **Special Amenities: Free local telephone calls.**

🖭 🍽 📶 🞲 🖥 🖴 📀 🖥 🕹 ⊠

SHERATON-FRAMINGHAM   Rates Subject to Change   **Phone:** 508/879-7200

		1P:		2P/1B:		2P/2B:		XP:		F18
◆◆◆	9/1-11/21	1P:	$149	2P/1B:	$149	2P/2B:	$149	XP:	$15	F18
Hotel	5/1-8/31	1P:	$135	2P/1B:	$135	2P/2B:	$135	XP:	$15	F18
	1/1-4/30	1P:	$120	2P/1B:	$120	2P/2B:	$120	XP:	$15	F18
	11/22-12/31	1P:	$119	2P/1B:	$119	2P/2B:	$119	XP:	$15	F18

Location: On SR 9 at tpk exit 12, follow signs to SR 9W. 1657 Worcester Rd 01701. Fax: 508/875-7593. **Facility:** 373 rooms.
Attractive Tudor castle design; landscaped grounds. 6 stories; interior corridors; heated indoor pool. **Services:** giftshop; area
transportation. Fee: massage. **Cards:** AE, DI, DS, MC, VI.

🅢 🞲 🈲 🍽 🞲 🈁 🖾 🞲 🖥 🖴 📀 🖥 🖴 ⊠ 🗐

RESTAURANTS

BUGABOO CREEK STEAK HOUSE   **Dinner:** $9-$17   **Phone:** 508/879-1555
◆◆   **Location:** 0.5 mi off SR 9; just off SR 30 (behind Caldor's). 345 Cochituate Rd 01701. **Hours:** 11:30 am-10
Steakhouse   pm, Fri & Sat-10:30 pm. Closed: 11/25 & 12/25. **Reservations:** suggested. **Features:** casual dress;
          children's menu; cocktails & lounge. Friendly service in a mythical Canadian Rockies Ski lodge with a north
country gothic decor & "talking" mooseheads. Very popular, well worth the wait. Featuring dry-aged beef specialties &
burgers. **Cards:** AE, DI, DS, MC, VI.   🚹 ⊠

KEN'S STEAK HOUSE   **Lunch:** $6-$12   **Dinner:** $10-$21   **Phone:** 508/875-4455
◆◆   **Location:** 1.5 mi e on SR 9; 1 mi w of tpk exit 13. 95 Worcester Rd 01701. **Hours:** 11:30 am-10 pm,
American   Sat-10:30 pm, Sun 1 pm-9 pm. Closed: 7/4 & 12/25. **Reservations:** accepted. **Features:** semi-formal attire;
          children's menu; early bird specials; carryout; cocktails & lounge. Popular suburban restaurant. Proper
business attire requested at dinner. **Cards:** AE, DI, DS, MC, VI.   ⊠

GLOUCESTER—28,700

LODGINGS

BEST WESTERN BASS ROCKS OCEAN INN

Phone: (978)283-7600

AAA SAVE	6/25-9/5 [CP]	1P: $125- 170	2P/1B: $125- 170	2P/2B: $125- 170	XP: $8		F12
	5/28-6/24 & 9/6-10/31 [CP]	1P: $120- 160	2P/1B: $120- 160	2P/2B: $120- 160	XP: $8		F12
◆ ◆	5/1-5/27 [CP]	1P: $105- 135	2P/1B: $105- 135	2P/2B: $105- 135	XP: $8		F12

Motel   **Location:** At terminus SR 128, left on Bass Ave 0.5 mi, then right 0.8 mi. 107 Atlantic Rd 01930. Fax: 978/281-6489. **Terms:** Open 5/1-10/31; reserv deposit, 7 day notice; 3 night min stay, weekends in season. **Facility:** 48 rooms. Patio or balcony. Large widow's walk/sundeck on main building roof overlooks picturesque rocky shore. Afternoon cookies & beverages. 2 stories; exterior corridors; oceanview; golf & tennis privileges; heated pool. **Recreation:** bicycles, billiard room. **All Rooms:** extended cable TV. **Cards:** AE, CB, DI, DS, MC, VI. **Special Amenities:** Free breakfast.

CAPE ANN MOTOR INN

Rates Subject to Change   **Phone: 978/281-2900**

AAA	6/11-9/6	1P: $108- 123	2P/1B: $108- 123	2P/2B: $108- 123	XP: $10	F5
	5/7-6/10 & 9/7-10/11	1P: $78- 93	2P/1B: $78- 93	2P/2B: $78- 93	XP: $10	F5
◆ ◆	5/1-5/6 & 4/1-4/30	1P: $62- 77	2P/1B: $62- 77	2P/2B: $62- 77	XP: $10	F5
Motel	10/12-3/31	1P: $58- 73	2P/1B: $58- 73	2P/2B: $58- 73	XP: $10	F5

Location: 2 mi n of SR 128 via SR 127A. 33 Rockport Rd 01930. Fax: 978/281-1359. **Terms:** Reserv deposit, 7 day notice; weekly rates, in winter; 2 night min stay, weekends in season; pets. **Facility:** 31 rooms. All rooms have balcony. Efficiency units, $10 extra charge; 3 stories, no elevator; exterior corridors; oceanfront; beach. **Recreation:** swimming. **Some Rooms:** 16 efficiencies, whirlpools. **Cards:** AE, DS, MC, VI. *(See ad p 121)*

THE MANOR INN

Phone: 978/283-0614

AAA SAVE	6/25-9/5 [CP]	1P: $64- 100	2P/1B: $69- 105	2P/2B: $69- 105	XP: $5	F13
	5/21-6/24 & 9/6-10/17 [CP]	1P: $59- 84	2P/1B: $64- 89	2P/2B: $64- 89	XP: $5	F13
◆	5/1-5/20 & 10/18-10/31 [EP]	1P: $45- 75	2P/1B: $49- 79	2P/2B: $49- 79	XP: $5	F13

Complex   **Location:** On SR 133, 2.3 mi e of exit 14, SR 128. 141 Essex Ave 01930. **Terms:** Open 5/1-10/31; reserv deposit; pets, $5 extra charge. **Facility:** 27 rooms. Motel units & 11 rooms in Victorian mansion. 1-3 stories, no elevator; interior/exterior corridors. **Cards:** AE, DS, MC, VI.

OCEAN VIEW INN

Phone: (978)283-6200

AAA SAVE	5/1-10/31	1P: $69- 180	2P/1B: $69- 180	2P/2B: $69- 180	
	11/1-4/30	1P: $69- 120	2P/1B: $69- 120	2P/2B: $69- 120	

◆ ◆   Motor Inn   **Location:** At terminus SR 128, left on Bass Ave & right on Atlantic Rd. 171 Atlantic Rd, On the Ocean 01930. Fax: 978/283-1852. **Terms:** Reserv deposit, 7 day notice; package plans. **Facility:** 63 rooms. 8 buildings on spacious, tastefully landscaped grounds just across the road from ocean shoreline. Many units with bay windows looking out over the Atlantic. Main Tudor-style manor built circa 1907. Rates for up to 4 persons; 3 stories, no elevator; interior/exterior corridors; oceanview; heated pool. **Dining:** Dining room; 7 am-9:30 pm, Fri & Sat-10 pm; $19-$28; cocktails. **Recreation:** volleyball. **All Rooms:** extended cable TV. **Cards:** AE, DI, DS, MC, VI. **Special Amenities:** Early check-in/late check-out and free newspaper. *(See ad below)*

SEA LION MOTOR INN

Rates Subject to Change   **Phone: 978/283-7300**

◆	6/25-9/6	1P: $76	2P/1B: $76	2P/2B: $82	XP: $5	
	9/7-10/18	1P: $58	2P/1B: $58	2P/2B: $62	XP: $5	
Motel	5/8-6/24	1P: $48	2P/1B: $48	2P/2B: $52	XP: $5	

Location: On SR 127, 0.5 mi n of jct SR 128, exit 10. 138 Eastern Ave 01930. **Terms:** Open 5/8-10/18; reserv deposit; 2 night min stay, weekends in season. **Facility:** 21 rooms. 2 stories; exterior corridors; heated pool. **Cards:** AE, MC, VI.

RESTAURANTS

THE GLOUCESTER HOUSE RESTAURANT

Lunch: $6-$10   Dinner: $10-$19   **Phone: 978/283-1812**

AAA ◆ Seafood   **Location:** On waterfront; on SR 127, 0.8 mi s of SR 128, exit 10. Seven Seas Wharf 01930. **Hours:** 11:30 am-10 pm, Fri & Sat-11 pm, 11/1-4/1 to 8 pm, Fri & Sat-9 pm. Closed: 11/25 & 12/25. **Reservations:** suggested; in season, Fall. **Features:** casual dress; children's menu; health conscious menu items; carryout; cocktails & lounge; minimum charge-$5 dinner; a la carte. Casual dining rooms overlooking harbor & fishing fleet. Outdoor cafe. **Cards:** AE, CB, DI, DS, MC, VI.

WINDJAMMER RESTAURANT Lunch: $4-$9 Dinner: $7-$14 Phone: 978/281-7212
Location: 0.4 mi e of jct end SR 128 & 127A. 116 E Main 01930. **Hours:** 11:30 am-9 pm, Fri & Sat-10 pm.
Closed: 11/25 & 12/25. **Reservations:** suggested; weekends. **Features:** casual dress; children's menu; early
bird specials; carryout; cocktails & lounge. Casual, cozy family dining with nautical decor. Fresh seafood
American   specialties, also Italian. **Cards:** AE, DI, DS, MC, VI.

HAVERHILL—51,400

LODGINGS

BEST WESTERN MERRIMACK VALLEY LODGE Phone: (978)373-1511
6/1-10/31 [CP] 1P: $79- 129 2P/1B: $79- 129 2P/2B: $79- 129
5/1-5/31 & 11/1-4/30 [CP] 1P: $69- 99 2P/1B: $69- 99 2P/2B: $69- 99
Location: At jct I-495, exit 49 & SR 110. 401 Lowell Ave 01832. **Facility:** 126 rooms. Va-
Motel   riety of rooms with some small, older-style units. Rates for up to 4 persons; 2-3 stories; interior corridors;
heated indoor pool, whirlpool. **Dining:** Restaurant nearby. **Cards:** AE, CB, DI, DS, MC, VI.
Special Amenities: Free breakfast and free local telephone calls. *(See color ad below)*

COMFORT SUITES Phone: (978)374-7755
6/4-10/23 [CP] 1P: $99- 109 2P/1B: $105- 115 2P/2B: $115- 125 XP: $10 F18
10/24-11/6 [CP] 1P: $89- 99 2P/1B: $95- 105 2P/2B: $105- 115 XP: $10 F18
5/1-6/3 & 11/7-4/30 [CP] 1P: $75- 85 2P/1B: $79- 89 2P/2B: $89- 99 XP: $10 F18
Location: At I-495 exit 49, entrance road 0.5 mi s of I-495 on SR 110. 106 Bank Rd 01832.
Fax: 978/521-1894. **Terms:** Weekly/monthly rates. **Facility:** 131 rooms. Vibrant modern room decor with tradi-
Motel   tional furnishings. 4 stories; interior corridors; whirlpool. **Cards:** AE, CB, DI, DS, MC, VI. **Special Amenities:** Early
check-in/late check-out and free room upgrade (subject to availability with advanced reservations).
(See color ad p 93 & p 272)

RESTAURANT

RALPH'S RESTAURANT Lunch: $6-$9 Dinner: $10-$17 Phone: 978/372-0991
Location: I-495 exit 48, 0.8 mi s on Rt 125. 8 Knipe Rd, Rt 125 01835. **Hours:** 11:30 am-9:30 pm, Fri &
American   Sat-10:30 pm, Sun noon-9 pm. Closed: 11/25, 12/25 & Mon. **Reservations:** suggested; weekends.
Features: casual dress; children's menu; early bird specials; carryout; cocktails & lounge; minimum
charge-$5 for charges. Cozy, popular, rustic ambiance. Specializing in veal, seafood & Italian entrees. **Cards:** AE, MC, VI.

LAWRENCE—70,200

LODGING

HAMPTON INN BOSTON/NORTH ANDOVER Rates Subject to Change Phone: 978/975-4050
8/31-11/3 [CP] 1P: $99 2P/1B: $99 2P/2B: $109
5/1-8/30 [CP] 1P: $89 2P/1B: $89 2P/2B: $99
11/4-4/30 [CP] 1P: $79 2P/1B: $79 2P/2B: $89
Location: At jct I-495, exit 42A & SR 114. 224 Winthrop Ave 01843. Fax: 978/687-7122. **Facility:** 126 rooms. Max 4 persons
per room; 5 stories; interior corridors. **Cards:** AE, CB, DI, DS, MC, VI.

RESTAURANT

BISHOP'S RESTAURANT Lunch: $5-$8 Dinner: $12-$21 Phone: 978/683-7143
Location: Just e of SR 28, 0.3 mi n of river. 99 Hampshire St 01840. **Hours:** 11:30 am-9 pm, Fri-10 pm, Sat
Ethnic   4 pm-10 pm, Sun 4 pm-9 pm 7/5-9/6 & 2 pm-9 pm 9/7-7/4. Closed: 11/25 & 12/25.
Reservations: suggested. **Features:** casual dress; cocktails & lounge. Popular, informal restaurant with
Middle Eastern flair. Also Arabic specialties, lamb, roast beef, steak & seafood entrees. Generous portions. **Cards:** AE, CB,
DI, DS, MC, VI.

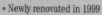

LEXINGTON—29,000   (See map p. 274; index p. 270)

LODGINGS

BATTLE GREEN MOTOR INN	Rates Subject to Change			Phone: (781)862-6100	66

◆
BATTLE GREEN MOTOR INN
Motel

| | 5/1-11/15 [CP] | 1P: $95- 99 | 2P/1B: $99 | 2P/2B: $109 | XP: $5 | F18 |
| | 11/16-4/30 [EP] | 1P: $75- 79 | 2P/1B: $79 | 2P/2B: $82 | XP: $5 | F18 |

Location: Center on SR 4 & 225, 2 mi s of I-95 & SR 128, exit 31A. 1720 Massachusetts Ave 02173. Fax: 781/861-9485. **Facility:** 96 rooms. 2 stories; interior corridors; heated indoor pool. **All Rooms:** comb, shower or tub baths. **Cards:** AE, DI, DS, MC, VI. *(See ad p 289)*

🛏️ 📶 🏊 🍴 ⛱️ 🐾 VCR 🖥️ 📠 🔒 ✕

SHERATON LEXINGTON INN	Rates Subject to Change			Phone: 781/862-8700	65

◆◆◆
Motor Inn

| | Sun-Thurs | 1P: $250 | 2P/1B: $250 | 2P/2B: $250 | XP: $10 | F18 |
| | Fri & Sat | 1P: $139 | 2P/1B: $139 | 2P/2B: $139 | XP: $10 | F18 |

Location: Jct I-95 & SR 128, exit 30B & SR 2A. 727 Marrett Rd 02173. Fax: 781/863-0404. **Terms:** Handling fee imposed. **Facility:** 119 rooms. 3 stories, no elevator; interior corridors. **Cards:** AE, CB, DI, DS, MC, VI.

ASK 📶 📶 🐾 🏊 🍴 ⛱️ 🐾 🖥️ 📠 🔒 ✕

LITTLETON—2,900

RESTAURANT

KEN'S AMERICAN CAFE	Lunch: $3-$11	Dinner: $6-$17	Phone: 978/952-6700

◆◆
American

Location: I-495 exit 31, on SR 110 just ne of jct SR 119. 529 King St 01460. **Hours:** 8 am-9 pm, Fri & Sat-10 pm, Sun-8:30 pm. Closed: 12/25. **Reservations:** suggested; weekends. **Features:** casual dress; children's menu; carryout; cocktails & lounge. Friendly, folksy service. Regionally eclectic menu with many New England specialties. **Cards:** AE, CB, DI, DS, MC, VI.

✕

LOWELL—103,400

LODGINGS

COURTYARD BY MARRIOTT-LOWELL	Rates Subject to Change		Phone: 978/458-7575

◆◆◆
Motel

| | All Year | 1P: $119 | 2P/1B: $119 | 2P/2B: $119 |

Location: From I-495 exit 36 to Lowell connector, then exit 3. 30 Industrial Ave E 01852. Fax: 978/458-1302. **Facility:** 120 rooms. Very attractive, traditionally furnished rooms. Lovely public areas. Rates for up to 5 persons; 3 stories; interior corridors. **Services:** area transportation. **Cards:** AE, CB, DI, DS, JC, MC, VI. *(See color ad p 280)*

📶 📶 🐾 🍴 ⛱️ 🐾 🖥️ 🖥️ 📠 🔒 ✕ 🍽️

DOUBLETREE HOTEL, LOWELL	Rates Subject to Change			Phone: (978)452-1200	

AAA
◆◆◆
Hotel

| | 6/1-10/31 | 1P: $99- 129 | 2P/1B: $99- 129 | 2P/2B: $99- 129 | XP: $15 | F17 |
| | 5/1-5/31 & 11/1-4/30 | 1P: $79- 99 | 2P/1B: $79- 99 | 2P/2B: $79- 99 | XP: $15 | F17 |

Location: Center; 0.5 mi from end of Lowell connector; exit 36 from I-495 via Gorham & Church sts, following signs. 50 Warren St 01852. Fax: 978/453-4674. **Terms:** Monthly rates. **Facility:** 252 rooms. Overlooks Pawtucket Canal & Concord River. 9 stories; interior corridors; heated indoor pool, wading pool, sauna, whirlpool. **Dining:** Dining room; 6:30 am-10 pm; $13-$17; cocktails. **Services:** area transportation, within 5 mi, limited hrs. **Cards:** AE, CB, DI, DS, MC, VI. *(See color ad below)*

ASK 📶 📶 🐾 🏊 🍴 ⛱️ 🐾 🖥️ 🖥️ 📠 🔒 ✕ 🍽️

KNOW THE ZERO HOUR. Confirm the checkout time with the front desk employee before planning your departure time.

LYNN—81,200   (See map p. 274; index p. 272)

LODGINGS

DIAMOND DISTRICT BED & BREAKFAST INN   Rates Subject to Change   **Phone:** (781)599-5122   **116**
◆◆◆   All Year [BP]   1P: $110- 245   2P/1B: $110- 245   2P/2B: $110- 245   XP: $20
Historic Bed   **Location:** Just off ocean; 0.8 mi s of SR 129 (Eastern Ave) via Wolcott St. 142 Ocean St 01902-2007.
& Breakfast   **Fax:** 781/599-4470. **Terms:** Reserv deposit, 16 day notice; handling fee imposed; 2 night min stay, weekends 6/1-10/31. **Facility:** 11 rooms. 2 units with fireplace. 1911 Georgian-style house was the private estate of P J Harney, a Lynn shoe manufacturer. 3 stories, no elevator; interior/exterior corridors; smoke free premises. **Cards:** AE, CB, DI, DS, MC, VI. *(See color ad below)*

THE RED MAPLE BED & BREAKFAST   Guaranteed Rates   **Phone:** (781)581-3671   **114**
◆◆   All Year [BP]   1P: $85- 95   2P/1B: $110- 130   2P/2B: $120- 140   XP: $20   F16
Bed &   **Location:** 0.3 mi n of Lynnfield St (SR 129). 210 Broadway 01904. **Fax:** 781/593-1320. **Terms:** Reserv
Breakfast   deposit, 7 day notice. **Facility:** 4 rooms. 3 stories, no elevator; interior corridors; designated smoking area.

LYNNFIELD—11,300   (See map p. 274; index p. 272)

RESTAURANTS

THE KERNWOOD AT LYNNFIELD   **Lunch:** $6-$10   **Dinner:** $11-$20   **Phone:** 781/245-4011   **148**
AAA   **Location:** 0.5 mi e of SR 128, I-95 exit 42. 55 Salem St 01940. **Hours:** 11 am-10 pm, Sun & Mon-9 pm.
◆◆   Closed: 7/4 & 12/25. **Reservations:** suggested. **Features:** casual dress; children's menu; health conscious
Regional   menu items; cocktails & lounge; a la carte. Traditional New England cuisine. Casual, popular dining in a
American   rustic setting with open hearth cooking area. **Cards:** AE, CB, DI, MC, VI.

WEATHERVANE SEAFOOD RESTAURANT   **Lunch:** $5-$10   **Dinner:** $5-$18   **Phone:** 781/592-2428   **147**
◆   **Location:** On US 1 southbound, 1.5 mi s of jct I-95 & SR 128. 2428 Broadway 01940. **Hours:** 11 am-9 pm.
Seafood   Closed: 11/25, 12/24 & 12/25. **Features:** casual dress; children's menu; carryout; cocktails; a la carte.
Casual family dining. Nice prints of sailing ships. **Cards:** MC, VI.

MALDEN—53,900   (See map p. 274; index p. 270)

LODGING

NEW ENGLANDER MOTOR COURT   **Phone:** (781)321-0505   **68**
AAA SAVE   5/1-11/1 [CP]   1P: $65- 79   2P/1B: $79- 89   2P/2B: $89- 99   XP: $10   F17
◆   11/2-4/30 [CP]   1P: $49- 59   2P/1B: $59- 69   2P/2B: $69- 79   XP: $10   F17
Motel   **Location:** On SR 99; 1.5 mi ne of Malden. 551 Broadway 02148. **Fax:** 781/321-2514. **Terms:** Reserv
deposit; weekly rates, off season; pets, attended. **Facility:** 21 rooms. 2 stories; exterior corridors. **Cards:** AE,
DS, MC, VI. **Special Amenities:** Free breakfast and free local telephone calls.

MANCHESTER—5,300

RESTAURANT

7 CENTRAL PUBLICK HOUSE   **Lunch:** $6-$10   **Dinner:** $8-$16   **Phone:** 978/526-7494
◆◆   **Location:** Center. 7 Central St 01944. **Hours:** 11:30 am-10 pm; Fri & Sat-10:30 pm. Closed: 12/24 & 12/25.
American   **Features:** casual dress; Sunday brunch; children's menu; cocktails & lounge; street parking. Pub
atmosphere. Menu offers wide variety of seafood & some beef entrees. Some Cajun seafood dishes
available. **Cards:** AE, DI, DS, MC, VI.

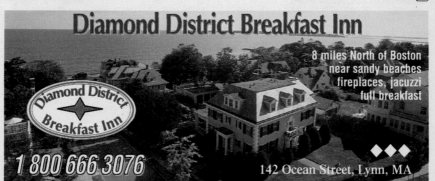

MARBLEHEAD—20,000

LODGING

SPRAY CLIFF ON THE OCEAN
Guaranteed Rates   **Phone:** (781)631-6789
◆◆◆   All Year [CP]   1P: $150- 210   2P/1B: $150- 210   XP: $25
Bed &   **Location:** Just s on Atlantic Ave (SR 129W) to Clifton Ave, just e. 25 Spray Ave 01945. Fax: 781/639-4563.
Breakfast   **Terms:** Age restrictions may apply; reserv deposit, 7 day notice; handling fee imposed; 2 night min stay, most weekends. **Facility:** 7 rooms. Overlooking the Atlantic with bright & airy contemporary decor. 3 rooms with fireplace. Sandy public beach adjacent. 3 stories, no elevator; interior corridors; smoke free premises. **Recreation:** bicycles.
All Rooms: combo or shower baths. **Cards:** AE, MC, VI.   ⊠ 📺 🅩 🅚 🖨 ⊠

MARLBOROUGH—31,800

LODGINGS

BEST WESTERN ROYAL PLAZA HOTEL & TRADE CENTER   Rates Subject to Change   **Phone:** 508/460-0700
◆◆   All Year   2P/1B: $115- 139   2P/2B: $115- 139   XP: $10   F18
Motor Inn   **Location:** On US 20; 1 mi w of jct I-495, exit 24B. 181 Boston Post Rd W 01752. Fax: 508/480-8218.
Terms: Reserv deposit. **Facility:** 430 rooms. Suites $175; 6 stories; interior corridors; heated indoor pool.
Services: giftshop; area transportation. **Cards:** AE, CB, DI, DS, MC, VI.
🅢 🅟 🖇 🍽 🍸 🅚 🛆 🎇 🅧 🖥 🖵 🖨 🔋 🅕 ⊠ 🅐

EMBASSY SUITES BOSTON MARLBOROUGH   Rates Subject to Change   **Phone:** (508)485-5900
◆◆◆   All Year [BP]   1P: $95- 140   2P/1B: $95- 140   2P/2B: $95- 174   XP: $10   F12
Suite Motel   **Location:** Just off US 20, 0.5 mi w of I-495 exit 24B. 123 Boston Post Rd W 01752. Fax: 508/481-3110.
Terms: Reserv deposit. **Facility:** 229 rooms. 3 two-bedroom units. 6 stories; interior corridors; heated indoor pool. **Services:** giftshop; area transportation. **All Rooms:** combo or shower baths. **Some Rooms:** 26 kitchens. **Cards:** AE, DI, DS, MC, VI.
🅐🅢🅚 🅢 🖇 🅢 🍽 🍸 🅚 🛆 🎇 🅧 🖥 🖵 🖨 🔋 🅕 ⊠ 🅐

HOLIDAY INN HOTEL & SUITES   **Phone:** (508)481-3000
🅐🅐🅐 🆂🅰🆅🅴   All Year   1P: $129   2P/1B: $139   2P/2B: $139   XP: $10   F19
◆◆◆   **Location:** On US 20, jct I-495, exit 24A. 265 Lakeside Ave 01752. Fax: 508/480-8530. **Terms:** BP avail.
Motor Inn   **Facility:** 174 rooms. 20 suites with microwave, refrigerator & full breakfast, $165 for 2 persons; 4 stories; interior corridors; heated indoor pool. **Dining:** Dining room; 6:30 am-2 & 5-10 pm; $10-$22; cocktails.
Services: giftshop; area transportation, within 10 mi. **All Rooms:** combo or shower baths. **Cards:** AE, CB, DI, DS, JC, MC, VI. **Special Amenities:** Free newspaper and free room upgrade (subject to availability with advanced reservations).
🅢 🅟 🖇 🍽 🍸 🅚 🛆 🎇 🅧 🖥 🖵 🖨 🔋 🅵 ♿ ⊠ 🅐

RADISSON INN MARLBOROUGH   Rates Subject to Change   **Phone:** 508/480-0015
◆◆◆   All Year   1P: $144   2P/1B: $154   2P/2B: $154   XP: $10   F18
Motor Inn   **Location:** Just off US 20; just w of jct I-495 exit 24B. 75 Felton St 01752. Fax: 508/485-2242.
Terms: Reserv deposit, Mon.-Wed. **Facility:** 206 rooms. 2 suites $195-$325; 5 stories; interior corridors; heated indoor pool. Fee: racquetball courts. **Services:** giftshop; area transportation. **Cards:** AE, CB, DI, DS, JC, MC, VI.
🅢 🅟 🖇 🍽 🍸 🅚 🛆 🅧 🎇 🅧 🖥 🖵 🖨 🔋 🅕 ⊠ 🅐

SUPER 8-MARLBORO   **Phone:** 508/460-1000
🅐🅐🅐 🆂🅰🆅🅴   All Year [CP]   1P: $54- 64   2P/1B: $59- 70   2P/2B: $59- 70   XP: $5-20   F12
◆◆   **Location:** I-290 at exit 25B. 880 Donald J Lynch Blvd 01752. Fax: 508/460-9103. **Terms:** Pets. **Facility:** 64
Motel   rooms. 2 stories; interior corridors. **Cards:** AE, DI, DS, MC, VI.
🅢 🖇 🅟 🛆 📺 🎇 🖵 🖨 🅕 ⊠ 🅐

RESTAURANT

DONACESCA   Lunch: $5-$9   **Dinner:** $11-$19   **Phone:** 508/460-6778
◆◆   **Location:** On SR 85 at US 20. 26 S Bolton St 01754. **Hours:** 11:30 am-4 & 4:30-10 pm. Closed: 11/25,
Italian   12/25 & Sun for lunch. **Reservations:** suggested. **Features:** casual dress; carryout; cocktails. Well prepared Italian cuisine from old family recipes, served in casually elegant atmosphere. Piano bar Fri & Sat. Family owned & operated. **Cards:** AE, DI, DS, MC, VI.   ⊠

MEDFORD—57,400   (See map p. 274)

LODGING

AMERISUITES-BOSTON/MEDFORD   **Phone:** (781)395-8500
🅐🅐🅐 🆂🅰🆅🅴   5/1-10/31 [CP]   1P: $189   2P/1B: $199   2P/2B: $199   XP: $10   F
🅵🅨I   11/1-4/30 [CP]   1P: $159   2P/1B: $169   2P/2B: $169   XP: $10   F
   Too new to rate. **Location:** Just sw of I-93, exit 32 via SR 60, River St & Riverside Ave. 116 Riverside Ave
Suite Motel   NE 02155. Fax: 781/395-0077. **Facility:** 158 rooms. Scheduled to open October, 1998. 8 stories; interior corridors; heated indoor pool. **Dining:** Restaurant nearby. **All Rooms:** combo or shower baths, extended cable TV. **Cards:** AE, CB, DI, DS, JC, MC, VI. **Special Amenities:** Free breakfast and free local telephone
calls.   🅢 🅢 🅟 🖇 🍽 🛆 🎇 🅧 🆅🅲🆁 🖥 🖵 🖨 🔋 🅕 🅕 ⊠ 🅐

METHUEN—40,000

LODGING

DAYS INN   **Phone: (978)686-2971**
(AAA) (SAVE)
◆◆
Motor Inn

10/1-10/31 [CP]	1P: $65- 90	2P/1B: $65- 90	2P/2B: $85- 100	XP: $8	F18
5/1-9/30 & 11/1-4/30 [CP]	1P: $60- 80	2P/1B: $60- 80	2P/2B: $70- 90	XP: $8	F18

Location: Just w of I-93 exit 47. 159A Pelham St 01844. Fax: 978/681-8903. **Facility:** 68 rooms. 2 stories; interior corridors. **Dining:** Dining room; 11:30 am-midnight; closed Sun; $7-$13. **Cards:** AE, CB, DI, DS, JC, MC, VI. **Special Amenities:** Free breakfast. *(See color ad below)*

NATICK—30,500

LODGINGS

CROWNE PLAZA BOSTON-NATICK   **Phone: (508)653-8800**
(AAA) (SAVE)
◆◆◆
Hotel

Sun-Thurs 9/7-4/30	1P: $179- 220	2P/1B: $179- 250	2P/2B: $179- 250	XP: $20-25	F12
Sun-Thurs 5/1-9/6	1P: $169- 210	2P/1B: $169- 240	2P/2B: $169- 240	XP: $20-25	F12
Fri & Sat	1P: $109- 199	2P/1B: $109- 199	2P/2B: $109- 199	XP: $20-25	F12

Location: On SR 9, 4 mi e of Framingham Center; 0.5 mi w of tpk I-90 exit 13; opposite Natick Mall. 1360 Worcester Rd 01760. Fax: 508/653-1708. **Facility:** 251 rooms. 7 stories; interior corridors. **Dining:** Dining room; 6 am-midnight; $14-$24; cocktails. **Services:** giftshop; area transportation, within 1 mi. **Cards:** AE, CB, DI, DS, JC, MC, VI. **Special Amenities:** Free newspaper and preferred room (subject to availability with advanced reservations).

HAMPTON INN BOSTON-NATICK   Rates Subject to Change   **Phone: 508/653-5000**
◆◆◆
Motel

All Year [CP]	1P: $99	2P/1B: $99	2P/2B: $99

Location: Off SR 9, 0.5 mi se of tpk, I-90 exit 13. 319 Speen St 01760. Fax: 508/651-9733. **Facility:** 190 rooms. Large rooms. Adjacent to large shopping mall. Rates for up to 4 persons; 7 stories; interior corridors. **All Rooms:** combo or shower baths. **Cards:** AE, CB, DI, DS, MC, VI. *(See color ad p 289)*

NATICK TRAVELODGE   **Phone: (508)655-2222**
(AAA) (SAVE)
◆◆
Motel

7/1-10/31 [CP]	1P: $89- 94	2P/1B: $94- 99	2P/2B: $104- 109	XP: $5	F18
5/1-6/30 [CP]	1P: $84- 89	2P/1B: $89- 94	2P/2B: $99- 104	XP: $5	F18
11/1-4/30 [CP]	1P: $69- 74	2P/1B: $74- 79	2P/2B: $84- 89	XP: $5	F18

Location: On SR 9, 4 mi e of Framingham Center; 0.5 mi w of tpk I-90 exit 13; opposite Natick Mall. 1350 Worcester Rd 01760. Fax: 508/655-7953. **Facility:** 68 rooms. Cozy units; deluxe furnishings in first level rooms. Daily tours to Boston in summer season. 2 two-bedroom units. 2 stories; exterior corridors. **Dining:** Restaurant nearby. **All Rooms:** combo or shower baths. **Cards:** AE, CB, DI, DS, MC, VI. **Special Amenities:** Free breakfast and free local telephone calls.

RESTAURANT

LEGAL SEAFOODS   **Lunch:** $7-$25   **Dinner:** $14-$25   **Phone:** 508/820-1115
◆◆
Seafood

Location: On SR 9; 1 mi w of tpk exit 13; in Milton's Shopping Plaza w end. 1400 Worcester Rd, Rt 9 01760. **Hours:** 11:30 am-10 pm, Fri-10:30 pm, Sat noon-10:30 pm, Sun noon-9:30 pm. Closed: 11/25 & 12/25. **Reservations:** accepted; Sun-Thurs. **Features:** casual dress; children's menu; carryout; cocktails. Contemporary decor. Bustling, busy atmosphere. Extensive menu of grilled broiled, fried, steamed & Cajun-style fresh seafood. Smoke free premises. **Cards:** AE, DI, DS, MC, VI.

NEEDHAM—27,600   (See map p. 274; index p. 271)

LODGING

SHERATON NEEDHAM HOTEL   Rates Subject to Change   **Phone: (781)444-1110**   [108]
◆◆◆
Hotel

1/1-4/10	1P: $139- 239	2P/1B: $139- 239	XP: $15	F18
5/1-9/11 & 4/11-4/30	1P: $159- 269	2P/1B: $159- 269	XP: $15	F18
11/21-12/31	1P: $149- 239	2P/1B: $149- 239	XP: $15	F18
9/12-11/20	1P: $179- 400	2P/1B: $179- 400	XP: $15	F18

Location: Just e of jct I-95 & SR 128, exit 19A. 100 Cabot St 02194. Fax: 781/449-3945. **Terms:** Reserv deposit; weekend rates avail. **Facility:** 247 rooms. Set atop a rolling hill. 5 stories; interior corridors; small heated indoor pool. **Services:** giftshop; area transportation. **Cards:** AE, CB, DI, DS, MC, VI.

NEPONSET (See map p. 274; index p. 270)

LODGINGS

SUSSE CHALET BOSTON INN   **Phone:** (617)287-9200   63
AAA SAVE   All Year   1P: $125- 165   2P/2B: $135- 175
◆◆◆   **Location:** From I-93 & SR 3, 0.5 mi sw northbound use exit 13, southbound exit 12 follow signs to Morrissey
Motel   Blvd. 900 Morrissey Blvd 02122. Fax: 617/282-2365. **Terms:** Pets, with restrictions. **Facility:** 133 rooms. 5 sto-
ries; interior corridors. **Dining:** Restaurant nearby. **Services:** area transportation, subway & hospitals.
All Rooms: combo or shower baths. **Cards:** AE, DI, DS, MC, VI. **Special Amenities:** Free local telephone
calls. *(See ad p 289 & color ad p 284)*

SUSSE CHALET BOSTON LODGE   **Phone:** (617)287-9100   62
AAA SAVE   All Year   1P: $95- 125   2P/2B: $120- 145
◆◆   **Location:** From I-93 & SR 3, 0.5 mi sw; northbound use exit 13, southbound exit 12, follow signs to
Motel   Morrissey Blvd. 800 Morrissey Blvd 02122. Fax: 617/265-9287. **Terms:** Weekend rates avail; pets, with
restrictions. **Facility:** 175 rooms. Some rooms overlook Dorchester Bay. 2-3 stories; interior/exterior corridors.
Dining: Restaurant nearby. **Services:** area transportation, designated locations. **Cards:** AE, DI, DS, MC, VI.
Special Amenities: Free local telephone calls. *(See ad p 289)*

RESTAURANT

PHILLIPS OLD COLONY HOUSE   **Lunch:** $6-$10   **Dinner:** $14-$19   **Phone:** 617/282-7700   75
AAA   **Location:** From I-93 & SR 3, 0.5 mi sw; northbound exit 13, southbound exit 12; follow signs to Morrissey
◆◆◆   Blvd. 780 Morrissey Blvd 02122. **Hours:** 11:30 am-10 pm, Fri & Sat-10:30 pm, Sun 10:30 am-10 pm.
Continental   Closed: 12/25. **Reservations:** suggested; weekends. **Features:** casual dress; children's menu; health
conscious menu items; carryout; cocktails & lounge. Upscale dining in a charming traditional setting.
MC, VI.   Specializing in American & New England fare. Sunday brunch buffet, 10:30 am-2:30 pm. **Cards:** AE, CB, DI,

NEWBURYPORT—16,300

LODGING

GARRISON INN   Rates Subject to Change   **Phone:** 978/499-8500   6
◆◆   All Year [CP]   1P: $98- 165 2P/1B: $98- 165 2P/2B: $98- 165 XP: $10   F16
Motel   **Location:** I-95 exit 57, 2.6 mi e on SR 1A, just n on Green St, just w of I-90 exit 1, then just s. 11 Brown
Sq 01950. Fax: 978/499-8555. **Facility:** 24 rooms. Modern units in an historic building dating to 1809. 1 two-
bedroom unit. 4 stories; interior corridors. **Cards:** AE, MC, VI.

RESTAURANT

SCANDIA   **Lunch:** $5-$8   **Dinner:** $11-$18   **Phone:** 978/462-6271
◆◆◆   **Location:** Center. 25 State St 01950. **Hours:** 11:30 am-3 & 4:30-10 pm, Sun 11 am-10 pm. Closed: 11/25 &
American   12/25. **Reservations:** suggested. **Features:** casual dress; Sunday brunch; early bird specials; carryout;
cocktails; street parking; a la carte. Romantic Victorian atmosphere, very small & quaint. Combination of
French & American novelle cuisine. Smoke free premises. **Cards:** AE, DI, DS, MC, VI.

NEWTON—82,600 (See map p. 274; index p. 270)

LODGINGS

BOSTON MARRIOTT HOTEL NEWTON   Rates Subject to Change   **Phone:** 617/969-1000   71
◆◆◆   5/1-11/21 & 3/9-4/30   1P: $189   2P/1B: $189   2P/2B: $189
Hotel   11/22-3/8   1P: $159   2P/1B: $159   2P/2B: $159
Location: On SR 30, e of I-95, SR 128 exit 24; from I-90 (MA Tpk) exit 14 eastbound, exit 15 westbound.
2345 Commonwealth Ave 02166. Fax: 617/527-6914. **Terms:** Check-in 4 pm. **Facility:** 430 rooms. Graciously appointed public
areas. Some rooms overlooking Charles River with patio or balcony. An inviting park-like setting. Rates for up to 5 persons; 7
stories; interior/exterior corridors; heated indoor pool. **Services:** giftshop. **Recreation:** Fee: bicycles. **All Rooms:** combo or
shower baths. **Cards:** AE, CB, DI, DS, MC, VI.

HOLIDAY INN   Rates Subject to Change   **Phone:** 617/969-5300   73
◆◆◆   5/1-11/21 & 3/16-4/30   1P: $119- 159 2P/1B: $119- 159 2P/2B: $119- 159
Motor Inn   11/22-3/15   1P: $99- 119 2P/1B: $99- 119 2P/2B: $99- 119
Location: Just e of jct I-95, exit 22; 0.3 mi s of I-90 (MA Tpk). 399 Grove St 02162. Fax: 617/965-4280.
Facility: 192 rooms. 7 stories; interior corridors; heated pool. **All Rooms:** combo or shower baths. **Cards:** AE, CB, DI, DS,
JC, MC, VI. *(See color ad p 275)*

SHERATON NEWTON HOTEL   Rates Subject to Change   **Phone:** 617/969-3010   70
◆◆◆   All Year   1P: $89- 199 2P/1B: $89- 199 2P/2B: $89- 199 XP: $15
Hotel   **Location:** At I-90 (MA Tpk) exit 17 & jct SR 16. 320 Washington St 02158. Fax: 617/244-5894. **Facility:** 272
rooms. 28 wirlpool rms, extra charge; 12 stories; interior corridors; small heated indoor pool.
Services: giftshop. **Cards:** AE, CB, DI, DS, MC, VI.

SUSSE CHALET INN   Rates Subject to Change   **Phone:** (617)527-9000   72
◆◆   7/2-11/6 [CP]   1P: $90- 120 2P/1B: $90- 120 2P/2B: $97- 120 XP: $3   F17
Motel   5/1-7/1 & 11/7-4/30 [CP] 1P: $70- 90 2P/1B: $80- 99 2P/2B: $88- 99 XP: $3   F17
Location: On SR 9, 3 mi e of jct SR 128 exit 20A. 160 Boylston St 02167. Fax: 617/527-4994. **Facility:** 144
rooms. Multiple buildings across from Chestnut Hill Mall. 3-6 stories; interior/exterior corridors. **Services:** area transportation.
All Rooms: combo or shower baths. **Cards:** AE, CB, DI, DS, MC, VI. *(See ad p 289)*

(See map p. 274)

RESTAURANT

PILLAR HOUSE   **Dinner:** $17-$30   **Phone:** 617/969-6500   80
◆◆◆   **Location:** On SR 16 at jct I-95 & SR 128, exit 21 northbound; 21 A southbound; 0.5 mi s of I-90 (MA Tpk).
American   26 Quinobequin Rd 02162. **Hours:** 5 pm-9:30 pm, Fri-10 pm. **Closed:** 9/6, 12/25, Sat, Sun & 7/1-7/14 may
vary. **Reservations:** suggested. **Features:** semi-formal attire; cocktails & lounge; a la carte. In restored 1828
residence. International & New England cuisine also featured. Smoke free premises. **Cards:** AE, DI, DS, MC, VI.   ⊠

NORTH ANDOVER—22,800

RESTAURANT

CHINA BLOSSOM   **Lunch:** $5-$14   **Dinner:** $7-$14   **Phone:** 978/682-2242
ⒶⒶⒶ   **Location:** On SR 125 & 133, 4 mi ne of jct 114, opposite Lawrence Airport. 946 Osgood St 01845.
   Hours: 11:30 am-10 pm, Fri & Sat-midnight, Sun noon-9:30 pm. **Closed:** 11/25. **Reservations:** accepted.
◆◆   **Features:** casual dress; health conscious menu items; carryout; cocktails & lounge; a la carte, buffet.
Chinese   Cantonese, Hunan & Szechuan dishes. Generous portions. Smoke free premises. **Cards:** AE, CB, DI, DS,
MC, VI.   ⊠

NORTH CHELMSFORD

RESTAURANT

BAINBRIDGE'S RESTAURANT AT THE MILL   **Lunch:** $7-$17   **Dinner:** $7-$17   **Phone:** 978/251-8670
◆◆   **Location:** On SR 3A; from SR 3, exit 32 follow 0.8 mi n on SR 4N, 0.5 mi n on SR 3A. 75 Princeton St
American   01863. **Hours:** 11:30 am-10 pm, Fri & Sat-11 pm, Sun 10:30 am-10 pm. **Closed:** 7/4 & 12/25.
Reservations: suggested; for dinner. **Features:** casual dress; Sunday brunch; children's menu; carryout;
cocktails & lounge. Tranquil setting along Stoney Brook. Leisurely dining in a restored turn-of-the-century woolen mill
featuring fresh seafood, steak & pasta. Comedy acts on Sat nights. Large authentic water wheel accents the grounds.
Cards: AE, DS, MC, VI.   ⊠

NORWOOD—28,700   (See map p. 274; index p. 270)

LODGINGS

COURTYARD BY MARRIOTT-NORWOOD   Rates Subject to Change   **Phone:** 781/762-4700   76
◆◆◆   9/1-12/31   1P: $139   2P/1B: $139   2P/2B: $139
Motor Inn   5/1-8/31 & 3/1-4/30   1P: $130   2P/1B: $130   2P/2B: $130
   1/1-2/29   1P: $115   2P/1B: $115   2P/2B: $115
Location: On US 1, 4 mi s of jct I-95 & SR 128 exit 15B, in River Ridge Office Park. 300 River Ridge Dr 02062.
Fax: 781/762-9459. **Facility:** 148 rooms. Some units with patio or balcony overlooking professionally landscaped courtyard with gazebo & sun deck. Suites, $129-$149. Max 5 persons per room; 2-3 stories; interior corridors;
heated indoor pool. **Cards:** AE, DS, MC, VI. *(See color ad p 280)*

SHERATON FOUR POINTS   Rates Subject to Change   **Phone:** (781)769-7900   75
◆◆   Sun-Thurs [BP]   1P: $99- 135   2P/1B: $99- 135   2P/2B: $109- 145   XP: $10   F18
Motor Inn   Fri & Sat [EP]   1P: $79- 99   2P/1B: $79- 99   2P/2B: $89- 109   XP: $10   F18
   Location: On US 1, 4 mi s of jct I-95 & SR 128, exit 15B. 1151 Boston-Providence Tpk 02062.
Fax: 781/551-3552. **Terms:** Reserv deposit. **Facility:** 123 rooms. 5 stories; interior corridors; heated pool. **Cards:** AE, CB,
DI, DS, JC, MC, VI.

RESTAURANTS

FRANCO'S   **Lunch:** $5-$12   **Dinner:** $12-$24   **Phone:** 781/769-7795   87
◆◆◆   **Location:** On US 1, 4.8 mi s of jct I-95 & SR 128, exit 15B. 1381 Providence Hwy 02062. **Hours:** 11:30
Northern   am-10 pm, Sat-10:30 pm, Sun noon-9 pm. **Closed:** 12/25. **Features:** semi-formal attire; children's menu;
Italian   carryout; cocktails & lounge; minimum charge-$5 lunch; $8 dinner. Some American & Continental entrees,
also hardwood grilled items. **Cards:** AE, CB, DI, MC, VI.   ⊠

SPAGHETTI FREDDY'S   **Lunch:** $5-$8   **Dinner:** $8-$12   **Phone:** 781/255-1898   86
◆◆   **Location:** On US 1, 2.3 mi s of I-95 & SR 128, exit 15B. 404 Providence Hwy 02062. **Hours:** 11:15
Italian   am-10:30 pm, Fri & Sat-11 pm, Sat 11:15 am-10:30 pm, Sun noon-9:30 pm. **Closed:** 11/25, 12/24 for dinner
& 12/25. **Features:** casual dress; children's menu; health conscious menu items; carryout; cocktails &
lounge. Very popular, lively & fun family dining amidst early Americana collectibles. Homemade sauces & famous
breadsticks. Generous portions. All-you-can eat buffet Sun-Thurs during lunch & early dinner. **Cards:** AE, MC, VI.   ⊠

PEABODY—47,000   (See map p. 274; index p. 271)

LODGINGS

BOSTON MARRIOTT PEABODY   Rates Subject to Change   **Phone:** 978/977-9700   80
◆◆◆   All Year   1P: $129- 159   2P/1B: $129- 159   2P/2B: $129- 159
Hotel   **Location:** In Centennial Office Park, from SR 128 exit 28, then s. 8A Centennial Dr 01960.
Fax: 978/977-0297. **Terms:** Check-in 4 pm. **Facility:** 256 rooms. Rates for up to 4 persons; 6 stories; interior
corridors; small heated indoor pool. **Services:** giftshop. **Cards:** AE, CB, DI, DS, MC, VI.

HOLIDAY INN   Rates Subject to Change   **Phone:** 978/535-4600   79
◆◆   All Year   1P: $119   2P/1B: $129   2P/2B: $129   XP: $10   F18
Hotel   **Location:** On US 1 just s of jct SR 128; exit 44, follow signs to reverse direction. 1 Newbury St, Rt 1N
01960. Fax: 978/535-8238. **Terms:** Reserv deposit. **Facility:** 204 rooms. 4 stories; interior corridors.
Services: giftshop. **Cards:** AE, CB, DI, DS, MC, VI. *(See color ad p 275)*

(See map p. 274)

MAINSTAY SUITES

(AAA) [SAVE]   All Year   1P: $49- 109   2P/1B: $49- 109 2P/2B: $49- 109
[FYI]   Too new to rate. **Location:** SR 128, exit 28, just s to Centenial Dr, w to the end, n to Jubilee Dr, then 1.1 mi
                 e. 200 Jubilee Dr 01960. **Facility:** 96 rooms. Scheduled to open April, 1999. **All Rooms:** efficiencies.
Motor Inn   **Cards:** AE, CB, DI, DS, JC, MC, VI. **Special Amenities:** Early check-in/late check-out and free room
                 upgrade (subject to availability with advanced reservations). *(See color ad p 276)*

RESTAURANTS

BUGABOO CREEK STEAK HOUSE   **Lunch:** $5-$12   **Dinner:** $8-$17   **Phone:** 978/538-0100   (91)
◆ ◆   **Location:** On SR 114, 0.3 mi w of jct SR 128, exit 25B; at the main entrance of North Shore Mall. Rt 114,
Steakhouse   North Shore Mall 01960. **Hours:** 11:30 am-10 pm, Fri & Sat-10:30 pm, Sat noon-11 pm, Sun noon-9 pm.
                 Closed: 11/25 & 12/25. **Features:** casual dress; children's menu; carryout; cocktails & lounge. Friendly
service in a mythical Canadian Rockies ski lodge with a North Country Gothic decor & "talking" mooseheads. Very popular.
Featuring dry-aged beef & lumberjack pie. **Cards:** AE, DI, DS, MC, VI.   [&] [X]

LEGAL SEA FOODS   **Lunch:** $5-$17   **Dinner:** $7-$18   **Phone:** 978/532-4500   (93)
◆ ◆   **Location:** In the North Shore Mall, n entrance; on SR 114, 0.3 mi w of jct SR 128, exit 25B. North Shore
Seafood   Mall 01960. **Hours:** 11:30 am-10 pm, Fri & Sat-10:30 pm, Sun-9 pm. Closed: 11/25, 12/24 for dinner &
                 12/25. **Reservations:** accepted. **Features:** casual dress; children's menu; health conscious menu items;
carryout; cocktails & lounge; a la carte. Bustling, popular, contemporary dining room. Extensive menu of grilled, broiled, fried,
steamed, & Cajun-style fresh seafood. Smoke free premises. **Cards:** AE, DI, DS, MC, VI.   [X]

QUINCY—85,000   (See map p. 274; index p. 272)

LODGING

PRESIDENTS' CITY INN   Rates Subject to Change   **Phone:** 617/479-6500   (135)
◆   5/1-10/31   1P: $79- 85   2P/1B: $79- 85 2P/2B: $79- 85 XP: $5   F18
Motel   11/1-4/30   1P: $65- 75   2P/1B: $65- 75 2P/2B: $65- 75 XP: $5   F18
                 Location: From I-93, exit 12 (Quincy) to Hancock St, then 3 mi se. 845 Hancock St 02170.
Fax: 617/479-6500. **Facility:** 36 rooms. Park right at the guest doors. Guest rooms are comfortable with a pleasant decor. 2
story section offers the larger rooms. Quiet park-like area. 2 stories; exterior corridors. **All Rooms:** shower baths.
Cards: AE, MC, VI.   [X]

RESTAURANTS

THE FOURS RESTAURANT & SPORTS BAR   **Lunch:** $5-$9   **Dinner:** $7-$14   **Phone:** 617/471-4447   (141)
◆ ◆   **Location:** Center, opposite Norfolk County Courthouse. 15 Cottage Ave 02169. **Hours:** 11 am-midnight.
American   Closed: 12/25. **Features:** casual dress; children's menu; early bird specials; carryout; cocktails & lounge.
                 Sports themed pub with memorabilia from Boston area teams. Originally named for the number worn by
Bobby Orr. Soup, chili, salads, burgers, pasta, sea food & steak. Large portions. **Cards:** AE, CB, DI, DS, MC, VI. [&] [X]

MANDO'S ITALIAN BISTRO   **Lunch:** $6-$9   **Dinner:** $10-$16   **Phone:** 617/773-5300   (144)
◆ ◆   **Location:** In Quincy Center at corner of Maple St. 1388 Hancock St 02169. **Hours:** 11:30 am-9 pm, Fri &
Italian   Sat-10:30 pm, Sun 4 pm-9 pm. Closed: 11/25, 12/25 & Easter. **Features:** casual dress; children's menu;
                 carryout; cocktails & lounge; street parking; a la carte. Modern, upbeat relaxing decor. European, Italian &
Mediterranean cuisines. Colorful presentations. **Cards:** AE, DI, MC, VI.   [&] [X]

RANDOLPH—30,100   (See map p. 274; index p. 271)

LODGING

HOLIDAY INN-RANDOLPH   Rates Subject to Change   **Phone:** (781)961-1000   (110)
◆ ◆ ◆   9/7-11/15 & 3/31-4/30   1P: $139   2P/1B: $149   2P/2B: $149
Motor Inn   5/1-9/6 & 11/16-3/30   1P: $129   2P/1B: $139   2P/2B: $139
                 Location: On SR 28 at jct I-93 & SR 128, exit 5A. 1374 N Main St 02368. Fax: 781/963-0089. **Facility:** 158
rooms. 4 stories; interior corridors. **Services:** area transportation. **Cards:** AE, CB, DI, DS, JC, MC, VI.
(See color ad p 275)

RESTAURANT

CAFFE BELLA   **Dinner:** $16-$20   **Phone:** 781/961-7729   (124)
◆ ◆ ◆   **Location:** On SR 139 at SR 28; 1.5 mi e of jct SR 24 exit 20A; in Randolph Village Shopping Plaza. 19
Northern   Warren St 02368. **Hours:** 5 pm-10 pm. Closed major holidays, 12/24 & Sun. **Features:** casual dress;
Italian   cocktails & lounge; minimum charge-$13.50; a la carte. Creative rustic Italian cuisine, emphasizing healthfull
                 eating, with homemade bread, pasta & dessert. Served in casually elegant atmosphere. Menu changes
frequently. Generous portions. Smoke free premises. **Cards:** AE, CB, DI, MC, VI.   [X]

Most AAA offices will cash a personal check for up
to **$100** for a visiting member **with membership
card and other required identification.**

REVERE—42,800 (See map p. 274; index p. 271)

LODGINGS

COMFORT INN-REVERE
◆◆◆
Motor Inn
Rates Subject to Change
All Year [CP]   1P: $78- 169   2P/1B: $88- 169   2P/2B: $88- 169   XP: $10
Phone: 781/324-1900 83 F18
Location: On US 1; 1.5 mi n of jct SR 60. 100 Morris St 02151. Fax: 781/321-9018. **Facility:** 118 rooms. 5 stories; interior corridors. **Cards:** AE, CB, DI, DS, MC, VI. *(See color ad below)*

〔SAVE〕🚭 🎦 📶 🍽 ➡ 🛋 🏋 🖨 🛗 ✕ 🐾

HOWARD JOHNSON HOTEL
◆◆
Motor Inn
Rates Subject to Change
6/1-11/1 [CP]   1P: $89- 139   2P/1B: $99- 139   2P/2B: $99- 139   XP: $10   F18
5/1-5/31 & 11/2-4/30 [CP]   1P: $69- 109   2P/1B: $79- 109   2P/2B: $79- 109   XP: $10   F18
Phone: 781/284-7200 84
Location: On SR 60 & jct US 1. 407 Squire Rd 02151. Fax: 781/289-3176. **Facility:** 107 rooms. Attractively landscaped center courtyard with fenced pool. 4 stories, no elevator; interior corridors. **Services:** area transportation. **All Rooms:** combo or shower baths. **Cards:** AE, CB, DI, DS, MC, VI.

🐕 🚭 🎦 ➡ 📶 🍽 ➡ 🛋 🏋 🖥 🖨 🔲 🎧 ✕ 🐾

ROCKPORT—7,500

LODGINGS

ADDISON CHOATE INN
◆◆◆
Bed & Breakfast
Rates Subject to Change
5/1-9/20 [BP]   1P: $85- 115   2P/1B: $110- 140   XP: $25
9/21-4/30 [BP]   1P: $70   2P/1B: $95- 120   XP: $25
Phone: (978)546-7543
Location: 0.3 mi w on SR 127A. 49 Broadway 01966. Fax: 978/546-7638. **Terms:** Age restrictions may apply; reserv deposit, 10 day notice; 2 night min stay, weekends in summer. **Facility:** 8 rooms. Mid-19th century Greek Revival architecture. 2 one-bedroom apartments with kitchen, $800 weekly for up to 4 persons. Suite $130-$155, $115-$140 off season for up to 3 persons; 3 stories, no elevator; interior/exterior corridors; smoke free premises. **All Rooms:** combo or shower baths. **Some Rooms:** 2 kitchens, color TV. **Cards:** DS, MC, VI.

🛥 🎧 🖨 🔒 ✕

THE INN ON COVE HILL
◆◆◆
Historic Bed & Breakfast
Guaranteed Rates
5/28-10/17 [CP]   1P: $65- 115   2P/1B: $65- 115   2P/2B: $109   XP: $25
5/1-5/27 & 4/16-4/30 [CP]   1P: $60- 92   2P/1B: $60- 92   2P/2B: $85   XP: $25
Phone: 978/546-2701
Location: Just s on SR 127A. 37 Mt Pleasant St 01966. **Terms:** Open 5/1-10/17 & 4/16-4/30; reserv deposit, 10 day notice; 2 night min stay, wkends summer & fall. **Facility:** 11 rooms. Colonial home built in 1791. 2 rooms with shared bath, $48 for 2 persons; 3 stories, no elevator; interior/exterior corridors; designated smoking area. **Cards:** MC, VI.

📶 🎧 ✕

LINDEN TREE INN
◆◆◆
Bed & Breakfast
Guaranteed Rates
6/1-11/1   1P: $70- 87   2P/1B: $97- 105   2P/2B: $97- 105   XP: $15
Sun-Thurs 5/1-5/31 &
3/1-4/30   1P: $50- 70   2P/1B: $77- 79   XP: $15
Fri & Sat 5/1-5/31 & 3/1-4/30 1P: $60- 80   2P/1B: $88- 89
Phone: 978/546-2494
Location: Just e of SR 127. 26 King St 01966. Fax: 978/546-3297. **Terms:** Open 5/1-11/1 & 3/1-4/30; reserv deposit, 14 day notice; 2 night min stay, in season. **Facility:** 19 rooms. An early Victorian in quiet residential location with spacious lawn & gardens behind the Carriage House. 2 two-bedroom units. 4 one-bedroom efficiency units, $109 for up to 2 persons; $80 off season; 3 stories, no elevator; interior/exterior corridors; smoke free premises. **All Rooms:** combo or shower baths. **Some Rooms:** 4 efficiencies, color TV. **Cards:** MC, VI.

🖥 🎧 🖨 🔒 ✕

OLD FARM INN
◆◆◆
Bed & Breakfast
Rates Subject to Change
5/1-6/30 [CP]   1P: $78- 88   2P/1B: $78- 88   2P/2B: $88- 125   XP: $15
7/1-10/31 [CP]   1P: $88- 110   2P/1B: $88- 110   2P/2B: $111- 125   XP: $15
Phone: 978/546-3237
Location: 2 mi nw on SR 127. 291 Granite St 01966. **Terms:** Open 5/1-10/31; age restrictions may apply; reserv deposit, 14 day notice; 2 night min stay, weekends. **Facility:** 10 rooms. 8 units have telephones with outgoing capability only. 2 two-bedroom units. 1 two-bedroom cottage $1050 weekly in season, $135 daily off season for 2 persons; 2 stories; interior/exterior corridors; designated smoking area. **All Rooms:** combo or shower baths. **Some Rooms:** 2 kitchens. **Cards:** AE, MC, VI.

🖥 🖨 🔒 ✕

RALPH WALDO EMERSON INN
◆◆
Country Inn

Rates Subject to Change   **Phone:** (978)546-6321

5/7-10/25 [BP]	1P:	$85- 150	2P/1B:	$115- 165	2P/2B:	$135- 175	XP: $15
5/1-5/6 & 10/26-4/30 [CP]	1P:	$55- 120	2P/1B:	$85- 135	2P/2B:	$105- 135	XP: $15

Location: Just e of SR 127. 1 Cathedral Ave 01966 (PO Box 2369). Fax: 978/546-7043. **Terms:** Reserv deposit, 14 day notice; 2 night min stay, weekends. **Facility:** 34 rooms. Inn constructed in 1840 & 1912 with private baths added in the 1950's. 1 two-bedroom unit. 4 stories, no elevator; interior corridors; oceanview. **Services:** area transportation. Fee: massage. **All Rooms:** combo or shower baths. **Cards:** AE, CB, DI, DS, MC, VI.

ROCKY SHORES INN & COTTAGES
◆◆
Country Inn

Guaranteed Rates   **Phone:** 978/546-2823

6/25-9/5	1P:	$89- 125	2P/1B:	$92- 128	2P/2B:	$118- 128	XP: $10
9/6-10/23	1P:	$83- 102	2P/1B:	$86- 105	2P/2B:	$99- 105	XP: $10
5/1-6/24	1P:	$79- 96	2P/1B:	$82- 99	2P/2B:	$93- 99	XP: $10

Location: 1.3 mi s via SR 127A, 0.8 mi via Eden Rd. 65 Eden Rd 01966. **Terms:** Open 5/1-10/23; reserv deposit, 14 day notice; handling fee imposed; 2 night min stay, in season. **Facility:** 22 rooms. Charming 11-room Victorian Mansion, circa 1905. Panoramic views overlooking the twin lighthouses of Thacher Island & the open sea beyond. 11 two- & three-bedroom housekeeping cottages, $850-$1055 weekly; $655-$850 off season for 2 persons; 2 stories; interior/exterior corridors; designated smoking area; oceanview. **All Rooms:** combo or shower baths. **Cards:** AE, MC.

SANDY BAY MOTOR INN
AAA
◆◆
Motel

Rates Subject to Change   **Phone:** (978)546-7155

6/11-9/5	1P:	$100- 144	2P/1B:	$100- 144	2P/2B:	$100- 144	XP: $10	D12
9/6-10/31 & 3/31-4/30	1P:	$79- 118	2P/1B:	$83- 118	2P/2B:	$83- 118	XP: $10	D12
5/1-6/10	1P:	$76- 114	2P/1B:	$80- 114	2P/2B:	$80- 114	XP: $10	D12
11/1-3/30	1P:	$68- 101	2P/1B:	$72- 101	2P/2B:	$72- 101	XP: $10	D12

Location: 0.5 mi s on SR 127. 173 Main St 01966. Fax: 978/546-9131. **Terms:** Reserv deposit, 7 day notice; 2 night min stay, weekends in season; pets, $50 dep req in designated rooms. **Facility:** 79 rooms. Nicely landscaped grounds, excellent recreational facilities. 6 bi-level units with skylight. 6 two-bedroom units, $168; $116 off season for up to 4 persons; 2 stories; interior/exterior corridors; putting green; heated indoor pool, saunas, whirlpool; 2 tennis courts. **Dining:** Coffee shop; 7-11 am, Sat & Sun-noon. **All Rooms:** extended cable TV. **Some Rooms:** 25 efficiencies, whirlpools. **Cards:** AE, MC, VI. *(See ad p 121)*

SEAWARD INN
AAA
◆◆
Country Inn

Rates Subject to Change   **Phone:** (978)546-3471

5/1-12/31 & 4/15-4/30 [BP]	1P:	$100- 200	2P/1B:	$125- 300	2P/2B:	$125- 300	XP: $20-40 D10

Location: 0.8 mi e on SR 127A, 0.5 mi n. 44 Marmion Way 01966. Fax: 978/546-7661. **Terms:** Open 5/1-12/31 & 4/15-4/30; reserv deposit, 14 day notice; handling fee imposed; weekly/monthly rates; 2 night min stay, weekends. **Facility:** 38 rooms. Rooms in main lodge, individual & multiple units, some with living room & some studio-type. 10 two-bedroom units. 2 stories; interior/exterior corridors; smoke free premises; oceanview. **Dining:** Sea Garden Restaurant in Seward Inn, see separate listing. **Recreation:** swimming; wild bird sanctuary. **All Rooms:** combo or shower baths, extended cable TV. **Some Rooms:** 6 efficiencies. **Cards:** AE, DI, DS, MC, VI.

SEVEN SOUTH STREET-THE INN
◆◆
Bed & Breakfast

Rates Subject to Change   **Phone:** 978/546-6708

6/6-11/15 [CP]	2P/1B: $75- 90	XP: $10

Location: 0.5 mi s on SR 127A. 7 South St 01966. **Terms:** Open 6/6-11/15; age restrictions may apply; reserv deposit, 7 day notice; 2 night min stay, weekends. **Facility:** 9 rooms. Main building circa 1750. 1 efficiency, 1-bedroom cottage & 1-bedroom suite with kitchen $550-$700 weekly; 2 stories; interior/exterior corridors; designated smoking area. **Some Rooms:** color TV. **Cards:** MC, VI.

TURK'S HEAD MOTOR INN
AAA SAVE
◆◆
Motel

Phone: (978)546-3436

6/18-9/7 [EP]	1P:	$89	2P/1B:	$95	2P/2B:	$95	XP: $6 F12
5/22-6/17 & 9/8-10/16 [EP]	1P:	$75	2P/1B:	$81	2P/2B:	$81	XP: $6 F12
5/1-5/21 [EP]	1P:	$69	2P/1B:	$75	2P/2B:	$75	XP: $6 F12
4/7-4/30 [CP]	1P:	$55	2P/1B:	$60	2P/2B:	$60	XP: $6 F12

Location: 1.8 mi s, on SR 127A. 151 South St 01966. **Terms:** Open 5/1-10/16 & 4/7-4/30; reserv deposit, 7 day notice; handling fee imposed; weekly/monthly rates. **Facility:** 29 rooms. Quiet residential location. 1 efficiency, $109-$129; 2 stories; interior corridors; heated indoor pool, heated indoor pool open 5/1-10/15. **Dining:** Coffee shop; 6:30-noon. **All Rooms:** extended cable TV. **Cards:** AE, DS, MC, VI. **Special Amenities:** Free local telephone calls.

YANKEE CLIPPER INN
AAA
◆◆◆
Historic Country Inn

Rates Subject to Change   **Phone:** (978)546-3407

5/24-10/19 [BP]	2P/1B: $109- 269	2P/2B: $109- 269	XP: $26
Fri & Sat 5/1-5/23, 10/20-12/15 & 3/1-4/30 [CP]	2P/1B: $115- 157	2P/2B: $115- 157	XP: $26
Sun-Thurs 5/1-5/23, 10/20-12/15 & 3/1-4/30 [CP]	2P/1B: $83- 115	2P/2B: $83- 115	XP: $26

Location: 0.8 mi nw on SR 127. 96 Granite St 01966 (PO Box 2399). Fax: 978/546-9730. **Terms:** Open 5/1-12/15 & 3/1-4/30; reserv deposit, 14 day notice; EP, MAP avail; package plans; 2 night min stay, weekends. **Facility:** 26 rooms. Ocean views from many rooms. Some rooms with porch or sunroom. Charming rooms in several builldings, 1 circa 1840, another 1929. 1 three-bedroom unit, 2 two-bedroom units. 1 three-bedroom housekeeping villa, $2400 weekly in season for up to 6 persons; 3 stories, no elevator; interior/exterior corridors; smoke free premises; heated saltwater pool. **Dining:** Dining room; 7:30 am-10:30 & 5:30-9 pm, 5/15-10/31; 6-9 pm Fri & Sat 3/1-5/14 & 11/1-11/30; $12-$24. **Services:** giftshop; area transportation. **All Rooms:** combo or shower baths, extended cable TV. **Some Rooms:** kitchen, whirlpools. **Cards:** AE, DS, MC, VI.

RESTAURANTS

PEG LEG RESTAURANT
AAA
◆◆
American

Dinner: $9-$15   **Phone:** 978/546-3038

Location: At King & Beach sts. 18 Beach St 01966. **Hours:** Open 5/1-10/20; 5:30 pm-9 pm, off season-8:30 pm, Sun noon-8:30 pm, off season-8 pm. **Reservations:** suggested. **Features:** No A/C; casual dress; children's menu; health conscious menu items; minimum charge-$7 dinner; a la carte. Cozy, comfortable dining in a beautiful seacoast setting. Fresh seafood specialties. A local favorite. **Cards:** AE, CB, DI, MC, VI.

SEA GARDEN RESTAURANT IN SEWARD INN   Country Inn
◆◆
Regional American

Phone: 978/546-3471

Location: 0.8 mi e on SR 127A, 0.5 mi n; in Seaward Inn. 44 Marmion Way 01966. **Hours:** Open 5/1-10/31 & 4/1-4/30; 8 am-9:30 & 5:30-9 pm. Closed: Mon, 6/15-9/1; Mon-Wed, rest of year. **Reservations:** suggested. **Features:** No A/C; casual dress; children's menu; prix fixe. Creative American cuisine specializing in New England seafood. Overlooking ocean & gardens. Menu changes weekly. Smoke free premises. **Cards:** AE, MC, VI.

ROWLEY—4,500

LODGING

COUNTRY GARDEN INN & MOTEL
AAA SAVE All Year   1P: $65- 145 2P/1B: $75- 145 2P/2B: $80- 150 XP: $10-15   F12
♦♦ **Location:** On SR 1A, 0.3 mi n of jct SR 133. 101 Main St (Rt 1A) 01969 (PO Box 726). **Fax:** 978/948-7947.
Complex **Terms:** Weekly rates; pet on premises. **Facility:** 19 rooms. Picturesque country setting. Some cozy rooms. Homey decor. 4 units with working fireplace & whirlpool. 2 stories; interior/exterior corridors; whirlpool. **Recreation:** chipping greens. **All Rooms:** extended cable TV. **Cards:** AE, DS, MC, VI. **Special Amenities:**
Early check-in/late check-out and free local telephone calls.   **Phone:** (978)948-7773

RESTAURANT

SPUD'S RESTAURANT & PUB **Lunch:** $5-$11 **Dinner:** $5-$11 **Phone:** 978/948-7551
♦ **Location:** On US 1, 0.3 mi n of jct SR 133. 255 Newburyport Tpk 01969. **Hours:** 11 am-10 pm, Sun from
American 11:30 am. Closed: 7/4, 11/25 & 12/25. **Features:** casual dress; children's menu; carryout; cocktails & lounge; a la carte. Popular, friendly dining in a rustic setting. A local favorite. **Cards:** AE, DS, MC, VI.

SALEM—38,100

LODGINGS

HAWTHORNE HOTEL Rates Subject to Change **Phone:** 978/744-4080
♦♦♦ All Year   1P: $92- 172 2P/1B: $107- 187 2P/2B: $107- 187 XP: $15   F16
Historic Hotel **Location:** On SR 1A, adjoining the historical district & facing the Salem Witch Museum. 18 Washington Sq W 01970. **Fax:** 978/745-9842. **Facility:** 89 rooms. Circa 1925, facing Salem Common. Some smaller rooms. 6 stories; interior corridors. **Services:** giftshop. **All Rooms:** combo or shower baths. **Cards:** AE, CB, DI, DS, MC, VI.
(See ad below)

THE SALEM INN **Phone:** (978)741-0680
AAA SAVE 10/1-11/2 [CP]   1P: $160- 290 2P/1B: $160- 290 2P/2B: $160-290 XP: $25
5/1-9/30 & 4/15-4/30 [CP] 1P: $129- 239 2P/1B: $129- 239 2P/2B: $149- 239 XP: $15
♦♦♦ 11/3-4/14 [CP]   1P: $119- 239 2P/1B: $119- 239 2P/2B: $149-239 XP: $15
Historic Bed **Location:** On SR 114 at jct Essex St; 3 mi e of jct SR 128, exit 25A. 7 Summer St 01970.
& Breakfast **Fax:** 978/744-8924. **Terms:** Reserv deposit, 7 day notice; handling fee imposed; 2 night min stay, weekends 10/1-10/31; pets. **Facility:** 39 rooms. Converted, 1834 & 1854 townhouses. Additional units in 2 converted historic buildings. 1 two-bedroom unit. 4 stories, no elevator; interior corridors. **Dining:** Restaurant nearby. **All Rooms:** combo or shower baths, extended cable TV. **Some Rooms:** 16 kitchens, whirlpools. **Cards:** AE, DI, DS, JC, MC, VI. **Special Amenities: Free breakfast and free local telephone calls.**

RESTAURANTS

NATHANIEL'S   **Lunch:** $9-$14   **Dinner:** $14-$21   **Phone:** 978/825-4311
◆◆◆   **Location:** On SR 1A, adjoining the historical district & facing the Salem Witch Museum; in Hawthorne Hotel.
American   18 Washington Square West 01970. **Hours:** 6:30-11 am, 11:30-2 & 5-10 pm, Sat 7 am-10:30 & 5-10 pm,
Sun 7-10:30 am, 11-2 & 5-10 pm. **Reservations:** suggested. **Features:** casual dress; Sunday brunch;
children's menu; cocktails; a la carte. Casually elegant dining in contemporary atmosphere. Creative menu items. Smoke
free premises. **Cards:** AE, DI, DS, MC, VI. *(See ad p 313)*   ⊠

ROOSEVELT'S RESTAURANT & SALOON   **Lunch:** $5-$10   **Dinner:** $10-$19   **Phone:** 978/745-1133
◆◆   **Location:** 0.3 mi sw on SR 1A. 300 Derby St 01970. **Hours:** 11:30 am-1 am. Closed: 7/4, 12/24 for dinner &
Steak and   12/25. **Reservations:** accepted. **Features:** casual dress; children's menu; early bird specials; salad bar;
Seafood   cocktails & lounge; entertainment; street parking. Informal 2nd floor themed dining rooms. **Cards:** AE, DS,
MC, VI.   ⊠

VICTORIA STATION   **Lunch:** $6-$10   **Dinner:** $11-$21   **Phone:** 978/745-3400
◆◆   **Location:** Center. Pickering Wharf 01970. **Hours:** 11:30 am-9 pm, Fri & Sat-10 pm; 5/1-10/31 to 10 pm, Fri
Steak and   & Sat-11 pm. Closed: 12/25. **Reservations:** suggested. **Features:** casual dress; children's menu; salad bar;
Seafood   cocktails & lounge; street parking; a la carte. Attractive informal restaurant overlooking water. Deck dining in
summer. Prime rib specialties. **Cards:** AE, CB, DI, DS, MC, VI.   ⊠

SALISBURY—6,900

LODGING

BEACHWAY MOTEL   **Phone:** 978/465-0336
(AAA) [SAVE]

Fri & Sat	1P:	$59- 99	2P/1B:	$59- 99	2P/2B:	$79- 109	XP:	$10
Sun-Thurs	1P:	$49- 79	2P/1B:	$49- 79	2P/2B:	$59- 79	XP:	$10

◆
Motel   **Location:** From I-495, exit 55; 3 mi e on SR 110, 1 mi n on SR 1A. 82 Beach Rd 01952 (Rt 1A).
Fax: 978/465-0336. **Terms:** Reserv deposit, 7 day notice; handling fee imposed; weekly rates. **Facility:** 30
rooms. Compact rooms. Attractive grounds with a picnic area. Limited number of units open in winter. 1 efficiency unit, $89-$129 daily, $500-$600 weekly, in season; for up to 6 persons; 1 story; exterior corridors. **All Rooms:** combo
or shower baths, extended cable TV. **Cards:** AE, DS, MC, VI.   ⊇ ⊠ ▤

SAUGUS—25,500   (See map p. 274; index p. 271)

LODGING

DAYS INN-SAUGUS/LOGAN AIRPORT   **Phone:** (781)233-1800   86
(AAA) [SAVE]

5/1-10/31 [CP]	1P:	$99- 199	2P/1B:	$109- 199	2P/2B:	$109- 199	XP:	$10	F17
11/1-4/30 [CP]	1P:	$89- 129	2P/1B:	$89- 139	2P/2B:	$89- 139	XP:	$10	F17

◆◆◆   **Location:** On US 1, 3.4 mi s of jct SR 128. 999 Broadway 01906. Fax: 781/233-1814. **Terms:** Package
Motel   plans. **Facility:** 148 rooms. 4 stories; interior corridors. **Cards:** AE, DI, DS, MC, VI. **Special Amenities:** Free
breakfast and free newspaper. *(See color ad p 278)*   🅂🄰 🄲 ⊕ ⊠ 🄷 🄵 🄰 ⊠ 🄰

RESTAURANTS

THE CONTINENTAL RESTAURANT   **Lunch:** $6-$11   **Dinner:** $14-$20   **Phone:** 781/233-2587   100
(AAA)   **Location:** On US 1; 3.3 mi s of jct SR 128. 266 Broadway 01906. **Hours:** 11:30 am-10 pm, Fri & Sat-11 pm,
◆◆   Sun noon-10 pm. Closed: 12/25. **Reservations:** suggested. **Features:** semi-formal attire; children's menu;
American   early bird specials; health conscious menu items; cocktails & lounge; a la carte. Pleasant club atmosphere,
serves generous portions. Minimum charge $3.50 lunch; $5 dinner. **Cards:** AE, DS, MC, VI.   ⊠

KELLY'S WORLD FAMOUS ROAST BEEF & SEAFOOD **Lunch:** $4-$12 **Dinner:** $4-$12 **Phone:** 781/233-5000   98
◆   **Location:** On US 1, 2.7 mi s of I-95 exit 44. 595 Broadway 01906. **Hours:** 10 am-1 am. Closed: 11/25 &
American   12/25. **Features:** casual dress; carryout; a la carte. Upscale fast food style of service. Very popular. Ample
portions. A family owned & operated business since 1951. Smoke free premises.   🄵 ⊠

RISTORANTE DONATELLO   **Lunch:** $6-$10   **Dinner:** $13-$20   **Phone:** 781/233-9975   103
◆◆◆   **Location:** On US 1, 2 mi s of jct SR 128, exit 44. 44 Broadway, (US 1) 01906. **Hours:** 11 am-10 pm, Fri &
Regional   Sat-11 pm, Sun 4 pm-10 pm. Closed: 1/1, 11/25 & 12/25. **Reservations:** required; weekends.
Italian   **Features:** semi-formal attire; health conscious menu items; cocktails & lounge. Bright, contemporary, formal
dining rooms. Wide selection of finely-prepared entrees & wood-grilled selections. Valet parking at dinner.
Cards: AE, CB, DI, MC, VI.   ⊠

SPUD'S RESTAURANT & PUB   **Lunch:** $4-$9   **Dinner:** $5-$9   **Phone:** 781/233-2757   101
◆   **Location:** Off US 1, Essex St exit, 1 mi e to rotary, 1.5 mi n. 22 Lincoln Ave 01906. **Hours:** 11 am-10 pm,
American   Fri & Sat-11 pm. Closed: 7/4, 11/25 & 12/25. **Features:** casual dress; children's menu; health conscious
menu items; carryout; cocktails & lounge; a la carte. Popular, casual family dining. **Cards:** AE, DS, MC, VI.   ⊠

SHARON—15,500

LODGINGS

SHARON INN
Rates Subject to Change
Phone: (781)784-5800
All Year   1P: $74- 79   2P/1B: $74- 79   2P/2B: $84- 89   XP: $5   F12
Location: On US 1 at jct I-95 exit 9. 775 Providence Hwy 02067. Fax: 781/784-4862. **Terms:** Reserv deposit, 3 day notice. **Facility:** 51 rooms. Third generation family operation. Several buildings with many ground-level entries; surrounded by mature trees. 1-2 stories; exterior corridors. **Dining:** Restaurant nearby. **Cards:** AE, CB, DI, DS, MC, VI. *(See color ad below)*
Motel

SUPER 8 MOTEL
Rates Subject to Change
Phone: 781/784-1000
All Year [CP]   1P: $63   2P/1B: $71   2P/2B: $71   XP: $8   F12
Motel
Location: On US 1, 0.5 mi s of jct I-95, exit 9. 395 Old Post Rd 02067. Fax: 781/784-1242. **Facility:** 95 rooms. A brick & stucco Tudor-style building. 2 stories; interior corridors. **Cards:** AE, CB, DI, DS, MC, VI.

SHIRLEY—6,100

RESTAURANT

BULL RUN RESTAURANT Historical   Lunch: $5-$9   Dinner: $10-$17   Phone: 978/425-4311
American
Location: SR 2, exit 36, 1 mi n on Shirley Rd, just e on Main St, 3 mi n on Center Rd, 1 mi n on Parker Rd, just e on SR 2A. SR 2A, Mohawk Tr 01464. **Hours:** 11 am-9 pm, Fri & Sat-10 pm, Sun 10 am-9 pm. **Reservations:** suggested. **Features:** casual dress; Sunday brunch; children's menu; early bird specials; cocktails; a la carte. 1740 colonial tavern. **Cards:** AE, DI, DS, MC, VI.

SOMERVILLE—76,200   (See map p. 274; index p. 272)

LODGING

HOLIDAY INN-BOSTON/SOMERVILLE
Phone: (617)628-1000   130
9/7-11/13   1P: $170   2P/1B: $190   2P/2B: $190   XP: $20   F13
5/1-9/6   1P: $150   2P/1B: $170   2P/2B: $170   XP: $20   F13
11/14-4/30   1P: $110   2P/1B: $130   2P/2B: $130   XP: $20   F13
Hotel
Location: From I-93 southbound, exit Sullivan Square, northbound, Cambridge/Somerville exit 26, then follow signs for SR 28N to Washington St eastbound. 30 Washington St 02143. Fax: 617/628-0143. **Facility:** 184 rooms. Very attractive public areas. 9 stories; interior corridors; heated indoor pool, saunas, whirlpool. **Dining:** Restaurant; 6:30 am-11:30 & 5-10 pm; lunch noon-2 pm in "Night Games" lounge; $11-$19; cocktails. **Services:** area transportation, designated areas. **Cards:** AE, DI, DS, JC, MC, VI. **Special Amenities:** Early check-in/late check-out and free newspaper. *(See color ad p 275)*

RESTAURANT

DALI RESTAURANT & TAPAS BAR   Dinner: $14-$21   Phone: 617/661-3254   138
Ethnic
Location: On the Somerville-Cambridge line at the corner of Beacon & Washington sts. 415 Washington St 02143. **Hours:** 5:30 pm-10:30 pm. Closed: 1/1, 11/25, 12/24 & 12/31. **Features:** casual dress; cocktail lounge; beer & wine only; street parking; a la carte. Offerings from all regions of Spain. Over 40 Tapas (appetizer size) selections. The small portions provide a lot of variety & taste delights. A very social & fun dining experience. **Cards:** AE, DI, MC, VI.

STOUGHTON—26,800   (See map p. 274; index p. 271)

LODGING

COURTYARD BY MARRIOTT-STOUGHTON   Rates Subject to Change   Phone: 781/297-7000   112
Sun-Thurs   1P: $124- 139   2P/1B: $124- 139   2P/2B: $124- 139
Fri & Sat   1P: $69- 139   2P/1B: $69- 139   2P/2B: $79- 139
Motor Inn
Location: On SR 139 at Randolph town line; just e of jct SR 24, exit 20A. 200 Technology Center Dr 02072. Fax: 781/297-7025. **Terms:** Reserv deposit. **Facility:** 152 rooms. Some rooms with balcony or patio. Rates for up to 4 persons; 4 stories; interior corridors; heated indoor pool. **Cards:** AE, DI, DS, MC, VI. *(See color ad p 280)*

SUDBURY—14,400

LODGINGS

CLARION CARRIAGE HOUSE INN — Rates Subject to Change — Phone: 978/443-2223
◆◆◆ All Year [BP]   1P: $98- 128   2P/1B: $103- 133   2P/2B: $103-133   XP: $5   F18
Motel   **Location:** On US 20; 7.3 mi e of I-495, exit 24A. 738 Boston Post Rd 01776. **Fax:** 978/443-5830. **Facility:** 37 rooms. Charming country inn type decor & atmosphere. Spacious rooms. 3 stories, no elevator; interior corridors. **Cards:** AE, CB, DI, DS, MC, VI. 🖫 🕭 🛰 🖳 🍽 🅥🅒🅡 ☎ 🖵 🚪 🖬 ⊠

LONGFELLOW'S WAYSIDE INN — Rates Subject to Change — Phone: 978/443-1776
◆◆ 9/1-12/31 [BP]   1P: $95- 105   2P/1B: $120- 130   2P/2B: $120-130   XP: $15   F12
Historic   5/1-8/31 & 4/1-4/30 [BP]   1P: $80- 85   2P/1B: $100- 110   2P/2B: $100-110   XP: $15   F12
Country Inn   1/1-3/31 [BP]   1P: $65- 75   2P/1B: $80- 100   2P/2B: $80-100   XP: $15   F12
   Location: 6.5 mi e of I-495, exit 24A; off US 20, following signs. 24 Wayside Inn Rd 01776. **Fax:** 978/443-8041. **Terms:** Reserv deposit. **Facility:** 10 rooms. A charming early 17th-century inn. Amidst formal gardens, working grist mill & an old stone bridge. Closed 12/25. 2 stories; interior corridors. **Services:** giftshop. **All Rooms:** combo or shower baths. **Cards:** AE, CB, DI, DS, MC, VI. 🛰 🖳 🍽 🅟🅥

RESTAURANT

LONGFELLOW'S WAYSIDE INN   Historical   Lunch: $8-$11   Dinner: $17-$22   Phone: 978/443-1776
◆◆   **Location:** 6.5 mi e of I-495, exit 24A; off US 20, following signs; in Longfellow's Wayside Inn. Wayside Inn
Regional   Rd 01776. **Hours:** 11:30 am-3 & 5-9 pm, Sun noon-8 pm. Closed: 7/4, 12/24 & 12/25.
American   **Reservations:** suggested. **Features:** casual dress; children's menu; cocktails & lounge; minimum charge-$5; a la carte. 17th-century inn. Fine hospitality by staff in Colonial day costumes. A working grist mill provides flour for homemade bread. Smoke free premises. **Cards:** AE, CB, DI, DS, MC, VI. ⊠

TEWKSBURY—27,300

LODGINGS

HOLIDAY INN TEWKSBURY/ANDOVER — Rates Subject to Change — Phone: (978)640-9000
◆◆◆ 9/1-10/31   1P: $129- 139   2P/1B: $129- 139   2P/2B: $129- 139
Hotel   5/1-8/31 & 4/1-4/30   1P: $109- 119   2P/1B: $109- 119   2P/2B: $109- 119
   11/1-3/31   1P: $99- 109   2P/1B: $99- 109   2P/2B: $99- 109
Location: On SR 133, just w of I-495, exit 39; in Highwood Office Park. 4 Highwood Dr 01876-1138. **Fax:** 978/640-0623. **Facility:** 237 rooms. A quiet rural setting. Elegant public areas. Spacious guest rooms. Rates for up to 4 persons; 5 stories; interior corridors; heated indoor pool. **Services:** area transportation. **Cards:** AE, CB, DI, DS, JC, MC, VI. *(See color ad p 275)* 🅐🅢🅚 🕭 🛰 🖳 🛌 🍽 🍴 ⊞ ✦ 🛆 🖢 🚿 🖳 🖵 🖬 🖬 ⊠ 🖉

RESIDENCE INN BY MARRIOTT-BOSTON/TEWKSBURY — Rates Subject to Change — Phone: 978/640-1003
◆◆◆ All Year [CP]   1P: $135   2P/1B: $135   2P/2B: $165
Suite Motel   **Location:** On SR 133; from I-495 exit 39, 0.3 mi w. 1775 Andover St 01876. **Fax:** 978/851-5780. **Facility:** 130 rooms. A quiet rural setting with 11 New England style buildings. Spacious units; some with fireplace. 33 two-bedroom units. 1 bedroom up to 4 persons, 2 bedroom up to 6 persons; 3 stories; exterior corridors; heated pool. **Recreation:** sports court. **All Rooms:** kitchens, combo or shower baths. **Cards:** AE, CB, DI, DS, MC. 🐾 🕭 🛰 🖳 🛌 🖳 🍽 🛆 🚿 ✦ 🖳 🖵 🖬 🖬 ⚄ 🚪 ⊠ 🖉

SUSSE CHALET INN — Rates Subject to Change — Phone: (978)640-0700
◆◆ All Year [CP]   1P: $57- 69   2P/1B: $64- 76   2P/2B: $66- 75   XP: $3   F17
Motel   **Location:** On SR 133; 0.3 mi w of I-495 exit 39. 1695 Andover St 01876. **Fax:** 978/640-1175. **Facility:** 133 rooms. Quiet setting. 5 stories; interior corridors. **Cards:** AE, CB, DI, DS, MC, VI. *(See ad p 289)* 🖳 🛌 ✦ 🛆 🖵 🖬 🖬 ⊠

TYNGSBORO—8,600

LODGING

STONEHEDGE INN — Rates Subject to Change — Phone: (978)649-4400
◆◆◆◆ 5/1-9/30   1P: $185- 235   2P/1B: $185- 235   2P/2B: $185-235   XP: $50   F12
Country Inn   10/1-4/30   1P: $185- 225   2P/1B: $185- 225   2P/2B: $185-225   XP: $50   F12
   Location: On SR 113; 2 mi se of jct SR 3A. 160 Pawtucket Blvd 01879. **Fax:** 978/649-9256. **Facility:** 30 rooms. Country style manor with large comfortably appointed rooms. On 30 acres. Many units with balcony. Spacious grounds & pastures with thoroughbred horses. Gracious hospitality. 7 fireplace units; 2 adults per room max; 2 stories; interior corridors; heated indoor pool; 1 lighted tennis court. **Services:** Fee: massage. **Cards:** AE, CB, DI, DS, JC, MC, VI. 🅐🅢🅚 🕭 🛰 🖳 🛌 🍽 🍴 ✦ 🎁 🛆 🛆 🚿 ✦ 🖳 🅥🅒🅡 🖭 🖵 ⊠ 🖉

RESTAURANTS

THE FIREHOUSE RESTAURANT   Lunch: $5-$14   Dinner: $8-$15   Phone: 978/649-4118
◆   **Location:** On SR 3A; 1.5 mi se of US 3, exit 34; at South Bridge Square shopping plaza. 130 Middlesex Rd
American   01879. **Hours:** 11:30 am-9 pm, Thurs-Sat to 11 pm. Closed: 11/25 & 12/25. **Features:** casual dress; children's menu; carryout; cocktails & lounge; a la carte. Popular family dining with firehouse memorabilia. Also lite fare. Extensive collection of fire department patches. **Cards:** AE, DI, DS, MC, VI. ⊠

SILKS   Country Inn   Lunch: $11-$16   Dinner: $22-$30   Phone: 978/649-4400
◆◆◆◆   **Location:** On SR 113; 2 mi se of jct SR 3A; in Stonehedge Inn. 160 Pawtucket Blvd 01879. **Hours:** 7-10
Provincial   am, 11:30-3 & 6-9 pm, Wed-Thurs to 10 pm, Fri 5:30 pm-10 pm; Sat 7-11 am, 11:30-3 & 5:30-10 pm, Sun 7
French   am-2 & 5:30-9 pm. Closed: 12/25 & Mon for dinner to the public. **Reservations:** suggested. **Features:** semi-formal attire; Sunday brunch; cocktails & lounge; valet parking; a la carte. Intimate dining in an elegant setting with an equestrian theme. Creative gourmet presentations. Extensive wine list. 100% non-smoking Sat & holidays. **Cards:** AE, CB, DI, DS, JC, MC, VI. ♿ ⊠

WAKEFIELD—24,800 (See map p. 274; index p. 271)

LODGINGS

BEST WESTERN LORD WAKEFIELD HOTEL   Rates Subject to Change   **Phone:** (781)245-6100   87
(AAA)
All Year   1P: $69- 99 2P/1B: $69- 109 2P/2B: $69- 109 XP: $5-10   F16
◆ ◆
Motor Inn
Location: At I-95 & SR 128 exit 39. 595 North Ave 01880-1685. Fax: 781/245-2904. **Terms:** Monthly rates.
Facility: 89 rooms. Brick Colonial-style building along scenic Lake Quannapowitt. Many larger size lakefront
rooms. 2 stories; interior corridors. **Dining:** Dining room; 7 am-11 pm, Sun & Mon-10 pm; $8-$13; cocktails.
Recreation: access to 3 1/4 mi walking trail around lake. **Cards:** AE, CB, DI, DS, JC, MC, VI.

(ASK) (S₀) (⌂) (3⁰) (⌇) (¶) (Y) (⊀) (⌂) (☂) (▢) (Ø) (✕)

SHERATON COLONIAL & GOLF CLUB BOSTON NORTH   Rates Subject to Change   **Phone:** 781/245-9300   88
◆◆◆
Resort
9/12-11/11	1P: $150	2P/1B: $150	2P/2B: $150	XP: $15	F18
5/1-9/11 & 4/11-4/30	1P: $131	2P/1B: $131	2P/2B: $131	XP: $15	F18
11/12-12/31 & 1/1-4/10	1P: $113	2P/1B: $113	2P/2B: $113	XP: $15	F18
11/22-3/7	1P: $119	2P/1B: $119	2P/2B: $119	XP: $15	F

Location: N side of I-95 & SR 128, between exits 42 & 43. 427 Walnut St 01880. Fax: 781/245-0842. **Facility:** 280 rooms. On
220 acres of rolling countryside. Excellent guest services. 2-11 stories; interior corridors; heated indoor pool. Fee: 18 holes
golf; racquetball courts, 12 tennis courts (4 indoor, 12 lighted). **Services:** Fee: massage. **All Rooms:** combo or shower
baths. **Cards:** AE, CB, DI, DS, MC, VI. *(See color ad p 37)*

(SAVE) (⌂) (3⁰) (⌇) (¶) (Y) (⊀) (⌂) (✕) (☂) (▢) (☎) (Ø) (⌂) (✕) (⌇)

WALTHAM—57,900 (See map p. 274; index p. 271)

LODGINGS

BEST WESTERN TLC HOTEL   Rates Subject to Change   **Phone:** (781)890-7800   91
(FYI)
5/1-11/13	1P: $99- 165	2P/1B: $99- 175	2P/2B: $99- 175	XP: $10	F12
11/14-4/30	1P: $89- 139	2P/1B: $99- 149	2P/2B: $99- 149	XP: $10	F12

Motor Inn   Under major renovation. **Location:** At exit 27A of I-95 & SR 128. 477 Totten Pond Rd 02154.
Fax: 781/890-4937. **Facility:** 100 rooms. Under major renovation, scheduled for completion, late Spring/early
Summer 1999. 6 stories; interior corridors; heated indoor pool. **Cards:** AE, CB, DI, DS, MC, VI.

(ASK) (S₀) (⌂) (3⁰) (⌇) (¶) (Y) (⊀) (⌂) (☂) (☏) (☂) (▢) (⌂) (☎) (Ø) (✕)

DOUBLETREE GUEST SUITES BOSTON/WALTHAM   Rates Subject to Change   **Phone:** (781)890-6767   94
◆◆◆
Suite Hotel
Sun-Thurs	1P: $175	2P/1B: $175	2P/2B: $175	XP: $15	F18
Fri & Sat 9/9-11/15	1P: $164	2P/1B: $164	2P/2B: $164	XP: $15	F18
Fri & Sat 5/1-9/8	1P: $144	2P/1B: $144	2P/2B: $144	XP: $15	F18
Fri & Sat 11/16-4/30	1P: $114	2P/1B: $114	2P/2B: $114	XP: $15	F18

Location: Just w of I-95 & SR 128 exit 27B. 550 Winter St 02154. Fax: 781/890-8917. **Facility:** 275 rooms. One bedroom units
with living room overlooking an inviting indoor atrium lobby with mahogany woods & greenery. 8 stories; interior corridors;
heated indoor pool. **Services:** giftshop; area transportation. **Cards:** AE, CB, DI, DS, MC, VI. *(See color ad p 290)*

(ASK) (⌂) (3⁰) (⌇) (¶) (Y) (⊀) (⌂) (☂) (⌂) (VCR) (☂) (▢) (⌂) (☎) (Ø) (⌂) (✕) (⌇)

HOMESTEAD VILLAGE   Rates Subject to Change   **Phone:** 781/890-1333
(FYI)
Sun-Thurs	1P: $89- 99	2P/1B: $89- 99	2P/2B: $89- 99	XP: $5	F
Fri & Sat	1P: $59- 69	2P/1B: $59- 69	2P/2B: $59- 69	XP: $5	F

Extended Stay   Too new to rate. **Location:** Just se of I-95 & SR 128, exit 27A (behind the Westin Hotel). 52 Fourth Ave
Motel   02254. Fax: 781/890-1901. **Facility:** 139 rooms. Scheduled to open fall 1998. Daily maid service, $10; 3 sto-
ries; interior corridors. **All Rooms:** efficiencies, combo or shower baths. **Cards:** AE, DI, DS, MC, VI.

(⌇) (3⁰) (⊪) (⌂) (☂) (⌂) (☂) (▢) (⌂) (☎) (⌂) (✕)

HOME SUITES INN OF BOSTON-WALTHAM   Rates Subject to Change   **Phone:** 781/890-3000   90
◆◆◆
Motel
Sun-Thurs	1P: $105- 140	2P/1B: $105- 140	2P/2B: $105- 140	XP: $10	
Fri & Sat	1P: $79- 99	2P/1B: $79- 99	2P/2B: $79- 99	XP: $10	

Location: At exit 27A of I-95 & SR 128. 455 Totten Pond Rd 02154. Fax: 781/890-0233. **Facility:** 100 rooms.
Some deluxe units with cherrywood furnishings & contemporary appointments. 2-room, 2-bath suites; $139-$169; 2 stories; interior corridors. **Cards:** AE, CB, DI, DS, MC, VI. *(See color ad p 288)*

(⌂) (3⁰) (⌇) (⊪) (Y) (⊀) (⌂) (☂) (⌂) (VCR) (☂) (▢) (⌂) (Ø) (✕)

SIERRA SUITES   **Phone:** 781/938-3737
(FYI)
Under construction. **Location:** Just se of I-95 & SR 128, exit 27A. 42 4th Ave 02154. Fax: 781/622-3939.
Facility: 130 rooms. Scheduled to open spring 1999.

(See map p. 274)

SUMMERFIELD SUITES HOTEL   Rates Subject to Change   **Phone:** 781/290-0026 96
◆◆◆   5/1-11/15 [BP]   1P: $149- 219   2P/1B: $149- 219   2P/2B: $169- 299
Suite Motel   11/16-4/30 [BP]   1P: $99- 169   2P/1B: $99- 169   2P/2B: $119- 249
    Location: Just e of I-95 & SR 128 exit 27A; behind the Westin Hotel. 54 Fourth Ave 02154.
Fax: 781/290-0037. **Terms:** Check-in 4 pm. **Facility:** 136 rooms. Wonderfully large guest rooms all fully self contained. 51 two-bedroom units. 3 stories; interior corridors; heated pool. **Services:** giftshop. **All Rooms:** kitchens. **Cards:** AE, DI, DS, JC, MC, VI.

SUSSE CHALET INN-WALTHAM/BOSTON   Rates Subject to Change   **Phone:** 781/890-2800 92
◆◆   All Year [CP]   1P: $71- 89   2P/1B: $80- 98   2P/2B: $85- 107   XP: F18
Motel   **Location:** Just ne of I-95 & SR 128 exit 27A. 385 Winter St 02154. Fax: 781/890-1021. **Facility:** 149 rooms.
    Updated property featuring some nicely decorated guest rooms. Some rooms offer parking near the door. 2 stories; interior/exterior corridors. **All Rooms:** combo or shower baths. **Cards:** AE, DI, DS, MC, VI. *(See ad p 289)*

THE WESTIN HOTEL,WALTHAM   Rates Subject to Change   **Phone:** 781/290-5600 93
◆◆◆◆   Sun-Thurs   1P: $99- 255   2P/1B: $99- 255   2P/2B: $99- 255   XP: $20   F18
Hotel   Fri & Sat   1P: $89- 119   2P/1B: $89- 119   2P/2B: $89- 119   XP: $20   F18
    Location: Just se of jct I-95 & SR 128, exit 27A. 70 Third Ave 02154. Fax: 781/290-5626. **Facility:** 346 rooms.
Impressive blue reflective glass lodging on a hillside overlooking the Cambridge Reservoir. Elegant public areas. 8 stories; interior corridors; heated indoor pool. **Services:** giftshop; area transportation. **All Rooms:** combo or shower baths. **Cards:** AE, CB, DI, JC, MC, VI.

WYNDHAM GARDEN HOTEL   Rates Subject to Change   **Phone:** (781)890-0100 95
◆◆◆   Sun-Thurs   1P: $134- 143   XP: $10-20   F18
Motor Inn   Fri & Sat   1P: $84- 114   XP: $10-20   F18
    Location: Just e of I-95 & SR 128 exit 27A. 420 Totten Pond Rd 02154. Fax: 781/890-4777. **Facility:** 148 rooms. Elegantly appointed public areas. 6 stories; interior corridors; heated indoor pool. **Services:** area transportation. **Cards:** AE, CB, DI, DS, JC, MC, VI. *(See color ad below)*

RESTAURANTS

ERAWAN OF SIAM   **Lunch:** $6-$15   **Dinner:** $15-$20   **Phone:** 781/899-3399 116
◆◆   **Location:** Downtown, 0.5 mi s of jct US 20. 469 Moody St 02154. **Hours:** 11:30 am-3 & 5-10 pm, Sat & Sun
Ethnic   from 5 pm. Closed major holidays. **Reservations:** accepted. **Features:** casual dress; carryout; cocktails; a la carte. Very attractive dining room. Featuring fine Thai cuisine with exotic herbs. **Cards:** AE, DS, MC, VI.

IL CAPRICCIO   **Dinner:** $19-$27   **Phone:** 781/894-2234 117
◆◆◆   **Location:** 1.1 mi e of I-95/SR 128 exit 26, on US 20. 888 Main St 02154. **Hours:** 5-10 pm. Closed major
Northern   holidays & Sun. **Reservations:** suggested. **Features:** semi-formal attire; cocktails. Northern Italian cuisine
Italian   with French & German influences, served in upscale casual contemporary Florentine ambiance. Smoke free premises. **Cards:** AE, CB, DI, DS, MC, VI.

TUSCAN GRILL   **Dinner:** $14-$18   **Phone:** 781/891-5486 115
◆◆◆   **Location:** Downtown, 0.5 mi s of jct US 20. 361 Moody St 02154. **Hours:** 5:30 pm-10 pm, Fri & Sat-10 pm,
Regional   Sun 5 pm-9 pm. Closed: 11/25, 12/24, 12/25 & Easter. **Reservations:** suggested. **Features:** casual dress;
Italian   cocktails; a la carte. Lively trattoria featuring the cuisine of Tuscany. Smoke free premises. **Cards:** DS, MC, VI.

WELLESLEY—26,600   (See map p. 274; index p. 272)

RESTAURANT

AMARIN   **Lunch:** $8-$10   **Dinner:** $9-$15   **Phone:** 781/239-1350 150
◆◆   **Location:** Just w of SR 135 & 61, just s of the square. 27 Grove St 02181. **Hours:** 11:30 am-9:15 pm, Fri &
Thai   Sat-10:15, Sun 4:30 pm-9:15 pm. Closed: 7/4, 11/25 & 12/25. **Reservations:** suggested; weekends.
    Features: casual dress; carryout; beer & wine only; street parking. Regionally eclectic menu. Traditional Thai spicing. Friendly service. Smoke free premises. **Cards:** AE, CB, DI, MC, VI.

WENHAM—4,200

RESTAURANT

THE WENHAM TEA HOUSE & SHOPS
◆
American
Lunch: $5-$10
Phone: 978/468-1398
Location: Center; just w of SR 1A, 2.5 mi n of jct SR 128, exit 20A. 4 Monument St 01984. **Hours:** 9:30 am-4:30 pm. Closed major holidays & Sun. **Reservations:** suggested; for lunch. **Features:** casual dress; salad bar; street parking. Seatings at 11:30 am, 12:30 pm & 1:30 pm for lunch. Afternoon tea 3:15-4:30 pm. Coffee & pastries 9:30-10:30 am. Dining rooms located behind the gift/gourmet shop. Smoke free premises. **Cards:** DS, MC, VI. ⊠

WOBURN—36,000   (See map p. 274; index p. 271)

LODGINGS

COURTYARD BY MARRIOTT-WOBURN
◆◆◆
Motel

Sun-Thurs	1P: $169	2P/1B: $169	2P/2B: $169	XP: $10	F16
Fri & Sat	1P: $119- 169	2P/1B: $119- 169	2P/2B: $119- 169	XP: $10	F16

Rates Subject to Change   **Phone:** 781/932-3200 ⑩⓪
Location: N side of I-95 & SR 128, exit 36, southbound 0.3 mi w of exit; northbound just n, 0.5 mi w. 240 Mishawum Rd 01801. Fax: 781/935-6163. **Facility:** 120 rooms. Very attractive traditionally furnished rooms. A charming Colonial ambiance. 3 stories; interior corridors; heated pool. **Cards:** AE, DI, DS, MC, VI. *(See color ad p 280)*

CROWNE PLAZA BOSTON/WOBURN
◆◆◆
Hotel
All Year   1P: $189   2P/1B: $189   2P/2B: $189
Rates Subject to Change   **Phone:** 781/932-0999 ⑩①
Location: 0.5 mi s of jct I-95 & SR 128; exit 36 via Washington St, e at Getty Station, jct of Cedar St & Forbes Rd. 2 Forbes Rd 01801. Fax: 781/932-0903. **Facility:** 345 rooms. A striking modernistic structure with an interior glass elevator. Many rooms with balcony overlooking a spectacular garden atrium. 7 stories; interior corridors; heated indoor pool. **Services:** giftshop; area transportation. **Cards:** AE, CB, DI, DS, JC, MC, VI.

HAMPTON INN BOSTON-WOBURN
◆◆
Motor Inn

9/1-10/31 [EP]	1P: $149- 159	2P/1B: $149- 159	2P/2B: $149- 159
7/2-8/31 [CP]	1P: $139	2P/1B: $139	2P/2B: $139
5/1-7/1 [EP]	1P: $129- 139	2P/1B: $129- 139	2P/2B: $129- 139
11/1-4/30 [EP]	1P: $119- 129	2P/1B: $119- 129	2P/2B: $119- 129

Rates Subject to Change   **Phone:** 781/935-7666 ⑩⑥
Location: N side of I-95 & SR 128, exit 36, southbound at exit, northbound just n, just w; opposite Woburn Mall. 315 Mishawum Rd 01801. Fax: 781/933-6899. **Facility:** 99 rooms. Rates for up to 4 persons; 5 stories; interior corridors. **All Rooms:** combo or shower baths. **Cards:** AE, CB, DI, DS, JC, MC, VI.

HOWARD JOHNSON HOTEL-WOBURN
◆◆
Motor Inn

5/1-10/31 [CP]	1P: $89- 135	2P/1B: $89- 135	2P/2B: $89- 135	XP: $10	F17
11/1-4/30 [CP]	1P: $79- 129	2P/1B: $79- 129	2P/2B: $79- 129	XP: $10	F17

Rates Subject to Change   **Phone:** 781/935-8160 ⑩③
Location: Just e of I-93, exit 36. 1 Mack Rd 01801. Fax: 781/932-9623. **Facility:** 100 rooms. 5 stories; interior corridors; heated indoor pool. **Services:** area transportation. **Cards:** AE, DI, DS, MC, VI.

RAMADA INN HOTEL
◆◆
Motor Inn
All Year   1P: $119   2P/1B: $129   2P/2B: $129   XP: $10   F12
Rates Subject to Change   **Phone:** 781/935-8760 ⑩④
Location: S of exit 35 of I-95 & SR 128 via SR 38. 15 Middlesex Canal Park Rd 01801. Fax: 781/938-1790. **Facility:** 195 rooms. 4 stories; interior corridors; heated indoor pool. **Services:** area transportation. **Cards:** AE, DI, DS, MC, VI. *(See color ad inside front cover)*

(See map p. 274)

RED ROOF INN WOBURN   **Phone:** (781)935-7110   ⓐ⓪⑤

5/1-5/31 & 7/1-10/31	1P:	$76-	96	2P/1B:	$86-	106	2P/2B:	$86-	116	XP: $6-10	F18
6/1-6/30 & 4/1-4/30	1P:	$66-	86	2P/1B:	$71-	91	2P/2B:	$76-	96	XP: $6-10	F18
11/1-3/31	1P:	$61-	81	2P/1B:	$66-	86	2P/2B:	$71-	91	XP: $6-10	F18

Motel   **Location:** N side of I-95 & SR 128, exit 36, southbound at exit; northbound just n, just w on Mishawum Rd to Commerce Way. 19 Commerce Way 01801. Fax: 781/932-0657. **Facility:** 159 rooms. 5 stories; interior corridors; heated indoor pool, whirlpool. **All Rooms:** combo or shower baths. **Cards:** AE, CB, DI, DS, MC, VI. **Special Amenities:** Free local telephone calls.

SIERRA SUITES HOTEL   Rates Subject to Change   **Phone:** 781/938-3737   ⑨⑨
All Year   1P: $145   2P/1B: $145   2P/2B: $145
Suite Motel   **Location:** On SR 38; just n of I-95, exit 35. 831 Main St 01801. Fax: 781/938-0838. **Facility:** 101 rooms. 3 stories; interior corridors; heated pool. **All Rooms:** combo or shower baths. **Cards:** AE, CB, DI, DS, JC, MC.

SUSSE CHALET INN   Rates Subject to Change   **Phone:** 781/938-7575   ⓐ⓪②

5/1-10/30 [CP]	1P:	$70-	90	2P/1B:	$77-	97	2P/2B:	$77-	97	XP:	$6	F17
10/31-4/30 [CP]	1P:	$55-	70	2P/1B:	$62-	77	2P/2B:	$62-	77	XP:	$3	F17

Motel   **Location:** N side of I-95 & SR 128 exit 36, southbound 0.3 mi w of exit, northbound just n, 0.5 mi w. 285 Mishawum Rd 01801. Fax: 781/937-0623. **Facility:** 129 rooms. 5 stories; interior corridors. **Cards:** AE, CB, DI, DS, MC, VI. *(See ad p 289)*

RESTAURANTS

J C HILLARY'S, LTD   **Lunch:** $7-$13   **Dinner:** $12-$18   **Phone:** 781/935-7200   ⓐ②①
American   **Location:** N side of I-95 & SR 128, exit 36, southbound at exit, northbound just n, just w; opposite Woburn Mall; in Comfort Inn. 311 Mishawum Rd 01801. **Hours:** 11:30 am-10:30 pm, Fri & Sat-11 pm. Closed: 12/25. **Reservations:** suggested. **Features:** casual dress; children's menu; carryout; cocktails & lounge. Upscale, lively dining in an authentic 1890's country tavern with mahogany woods, brass rails & etched glass. Sat & Sun brunch 11:30 am-3:30 pm. Large portions. **Cards:** AE, DS, MC, VI.

SPUD'S RESTAURANT & PUB   **Lunch:** $5-$11   **Dinner:** $7-$11   **Phone:** 781/937-0304   ①②⓪
American   **Location:** At I-93, Montvale Ave exit 36. 1 Mack Rd 01801. **Hours:** 11 am-11 pm, Sat & Sun from 8 am. Closed: 7/4, 11/25, 12/24 for dinner & 12/25. **Reservations:** accepted. **Features:** casual dress; children's menu; carryout; cocktails & lounge; a la carte. Popular, family dining in a rustic ambiance. **Cards:** AE, DS, MC, VI.

This ends listings for the Boston Vicinity.
The following page resumes the alphabetical listings of
cities in Massachusetts.

BOURNE—See Cape Cod p. 334.

BOXBOROUGH—See Boston p. 292.

BRADFORD—See Boston p. 293.

BRAINTREE—See Boston p. 293.

BREWSTER—See Cape Cod p. 334.

BRIGHTON—See Boston p. 293.

BRIMFIELD—3,000

LODGING

NEW ENGLAND MOTEL
AAA ◆ Motel
Rates Subject to Change
5/1-11/1   1P: $40   2P/1B: $45   2P/2B: $45- 55   XP: $10   F12
Phone: 413/245-3348
Location: 8 mi w on US 20, I-84, exit 3B. 30 Palmer Rd (Rt 20) 01010. **Fax:** 413/245-7024. **Terms:** Open 5/1-11/1; weekly rates. **Facility:** 8 rooms. Quiet, small town location. 1 story; exterior corridors. **Cards:** AE, DS, MC, VI.

BROCKTON—92,800

LODGINGS

CARLTON HOUSE MOTOR INN
AAA SAVE ◆ Motel
All Year   1P: $55- 85   2P/1B: $65- 95   2P/2B: $70- 100 XP: $10
Phone: (508)588-3333
Location: On SR 123; just e of SR 24, exit 17A. 1005 Belmont St 02401. **Fax:** 508/588-3333. **Terms:** Reserv deposit; handling fee imposed. **Facility:** 65 rooms. 2 whirlpool rms, $100-$150 for up to 2 persons; 2 stories; interior corridors. **Dining:** Dining room; 11:30 am-9 pm, Fri-10 pm, Sat 4 pm-10 pm, Closed Sun; $10-$15. **Cards:** AE, CB, DI, DS, JC, MC, VI.

HOLIDAY INN METRO SOUTH/BROCKTON
AAA SAVE ◆◆◆ Motor Inn
All Year   1P: $90- 109 2P/1B: $90- 109 2P/2B: $90- 109 XP: $10   F17
Phone: (508)588-6300
Location: On SR 27, 0.3 mi e of jct SR 24 exit 18A; w side of Westgate Mall. 195 Westgate Dr 02401. **Fax:** 508/580-4384. **Terms:** Monthly rates; package plans. **Facility:** 185 rooms. 3 suites, $145-$250; 3 stories; interior corridors; heated indoor pool, sauna, whirlpool. **Dining:** Restaurant; 6:30 am-2 & 5-10 pm; $10-$15; cocktails. **Cards:** AE, DI, DS, JC, MC, VI. **Special Amenities:** Early check-in/late check-out and free room upgrade (subject to availability with advanced reservations).** *(See color ad p 275)*

SUPER 8 MOTEL-BROCKTON
◆◆ Motel
Rates Subject to Change
All Year [CP]   1P: $64- 69   2P/1B: $69- 74   2P/2B: $69- 74   XP: $10   F12
Phone: 508/588-8887
Location: On SR 27, 0.3 mi e of SR 24 exit 18A, w side of Westgate Mall. 385 Westgate Dr 02401. **Fax:** 508/588-8899. **Facility:** 57 rooms. Inviting lobby & bright atrium breakfast area. 6 whirlpool rms, $109; 2 stories; interior corridors. **All Rooms:** combo or shower baths. **Cards:** AE, DI, DS, MC, VI.

BROOKLINE—See Boston p. 293.

BURLINGTON—See Boston p. 293.

BUZZARDS BAY—See Cape Cod p. 336.

CAMBRIDGE—See Boston p. 294.

DIAMONDS tell the story—read The AAA Diamonds.

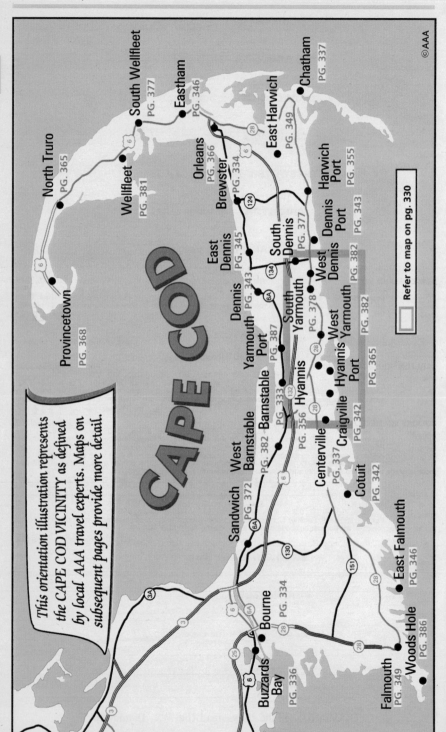

© AAA

This orientation illustration represents the CAPE COD VICINITY as defined by local AAA travel experts. Maps on subsequent pages provide more detail.

CAPE COD

Refer to map on pg. 330

Provincetown PG. 368

North Truro PG. 365

South Wellfleet PG. 377

Eastham PG. 346

Chatham PG. 337

Wellfleet PG. 381

Orleans PG. 366

Brewster PG. 334

East Harwich PG. 349

Harwich Port PG. 355

East Dennis PG. 345

South Dennis PG. 377

Dennis Port PG. 343

Dennis PG. 343

West Dennis PG. 382

Yarmouth Port PG. 387

South Yarmouth PG. 378

West Yarmouth PG. 382

Hyannis Port PG. 365

Barnstable PG. 333

Hyannis PG. 356

Craigville PG. 342

West Barnstable PG. 382

Sandwich PG. 372

Centerville PG. 337

Cotuit PG. 342

East Falmouth PG. 346

Bourne PG. 334

Buzzards Bay PG. 336

Falmouth PG. 349

Woods Hole PG. 386

Cape Cod

This index helps you "spot" where approved accommodations are located on the detailed maps that follow. Rate ranges are for comparison only and show the property's high season. Turn to the listing page for more detailed rate information and consult display ads for special promotions. Restaurant rate range is for dinner, unless only lunch (L) is served.

Nearby Accommodations

Spotter/Map Pg.Number	OA	HYANNIS - Lodgings	Rating	Rate	Listing Page
1 / p. 332	⊕	Anchor-In Motel - see color ad p 357	◆◆◆	$90-150	356
2 / p. 332	⊕	The Breakwaters - see color ad p 356	◆◆	$950-1800	358
3 / p. 332		Four Points Hyannis Sheraton - see color ad p 360	◆◆◆	$109-139	359
4 / p. 332	⊕	Captain Gosnold Village - see color ad p 358	◆◆	$106-270	358
5 / p. 332	⊕	The Country Lake Lodge	◆	$59-89 🕮	358
6 / p. 332	⊕	SeaCoast on the Towne - see color ad p 363	◆◆	$68-98	363
8 / p. 332	⊕	Hyannis Motel-Budget Host Inn - see color ad p 264, p 362	◆◆	$75-95	360
10 / p. 332	⊕	Hyannis Travel Inn - see color ad p 362	◆◆	$70-99	361
11 / p. 332		Cape Cod Hyannis Hotel - see color ad p 358	◆◆	$89-169	358
12 / p. 332	⊕	Hyannis Inn Motel - see color ad p 357	◆◆	$81-139 🕮	360
13 / p. 332	⊕	Heritage House Hotel - see color ad p 360	◆◆	$109-160	359
14 / p. 332	⊕	Sheraton Hyannis Resort - see color ad p 360	◆◆◆	$189-219	363
15 / p. 332	⊕	Days Inn - see color ad p 359	◆◆◆	$85-250 🕮	359
16 / p. 332		Ramada Inn Regency - see color ad inside front cover, p 363	◆◆	$99-169	363
17 / p. 332	⊕	Craigville Motel - see color ad p 359	◆◆	$55-85	359
18 / p. 332	⊕	Radisson Inn	◆◆◆	$109-149 🕮	362
19 / p. 332		Quality Inn	◆◆	$109-139	361
③ / p. 332		HYANNIS - Restaurants			
③ / p. 332		Hearth 'n Kettle Restaurant	◆	$9-15	364
④ / p. 332		Penguins Sea Grill	◆◆	$16-22	364
⑥ / p. 332	⊕	The Paddock	◆◆◆	$15-23	364
⑦ / p. 332		Sam Diego's Mexican Cookery & Bar	◆◆	$8-12	364
⑧ / p. 332	⊕	Mildred's Chowder House	◆◆	$10-15	364
⑨ / p. 332	⊕	The Original Gourmet Brunch	◆	$4-8(L)	364
⑩ / p. 332	⊕	Alberto's Ristorante	◆◆◆	$13-26	363
⑪ / p. 332		Main Street Seafood & Grill	◆◆	$9-13	364
⑫ / p. 332		Barbyann's Restaurant	◆◆	$7-13	364
⑬ / p. 332		Tugboats	◆◆	$9-15	364
⑭ / p. 332		Roadhouse Cafe	◆◆	$15-24	364
⑮ / p. 332		Dragon Lite Restaurant	◆	$5-13	364
⑯ / p. 332	⊕	The Egg & I	◆	varies	364
⑰ / p. 332		The Black Cat	◆◆◆	$14-22	364
		CRAIGVILLE - Lodgings			
21 / p. 332	⊕	Trade Winds Inn - see color ad p 342	◆◆◆	$99-169	342
		SOUTH YARMOUTH - Lodgings			
23 / p. 332	⊕	All Seasons Motor Inn - see color ad p 333, p 384	◆◆◆	$99-125	378
24 / p. 332	⊕	Motel 6 - 4042 - see color ad p 380	◆◆	$65-95 🕮	379
25 / p. 332	⊕	Beach 'N Towne Motel	◆◆	$60-67 🕮	378
26 / p. 332	⊕	Best Western Blue Waters on The Ocean - see color ad p 379	◆◆◆	$170-280	379
27 / p. 332	⊕	Best Western Blue Rock Inn - see color ad p 379	◆◆◆	$115-170	379
28 / p. 332	⊕	The Ocean Club on Smugglers Beach - see color ad p 384	◆◆◆	$230 🕮	380
29 / p. 332	⊕	Ocean Mist Resort - see color ad p 333	◆◆◆	$164-274	380
30 / p. 332	⊕	Red Jacket Beach Motor Inn - see color ad p 361	◆◆◆	$165-245	380

Spotter/Map Pg.Number	OA	**SOUTH YARMOUTH** - Lodgings (contd.)	Rating	Rate	Listing Page
31 / p. 332	⊕	Red Mill Motel	◆◆	$65-85 SAVE	381
32 / p. 332	⊕	Riviera Beach Resort - see color ad p 380	◆◆◆	$150-255	381
33 / p. 332	⊕	Surfcomber on the Ocean - see color ad p 381	◆◆◆	$140-160	381
		SOUTH YARMOUTH - Restaurants			
⑳ / p. 332		The Skipper Restaurant	◆◆	$9-18	381
㉑ / p. 332		Hearth'n Kettle Family Restaurant	◆	$6-15	381
㉓ / p. 332	⊕	Riverway Lobster House	◆◆	$9-23	381
		WEST YARMOUTH - Lodgings			
35 / p. 332	⊕	Americana Holiday Motel - see color ad p 333 , p 382	◆◆	$60-69	382
36 / p. 332	⊕	Tidewater Motor Lodge - see color ad p 357	◆◆◆	$87-109	385
38 / p. 332	⊕	The Cape Point - see color ad p 385	◆◆◆	$89-129	383
39 / p. 332		Olde Schoolhouse Bed & Breakfast	◆◆◆	$98-155	385
40 / p. 332		The Manor House B&B - see ad p 343	◆◆◆	$98-128	385
41 / p. 332	⊕	The Cove at Yarmouth - see color ad p 384	◆◆	$130-165 SAVE	384
42 / p. 332	⊕	Bayside Resort Park Inn - see color ad p 383	◆◆◆	$99-179 SAVE	383
43 / p. 332	⊕	Green Harbor on the Ocean - see color ad p 361	◆◆◆	$190-425	384
44 / p. 332	⊕	Hunters Green Motel	◆	$56-66	384
45 / p. 332	⊕	The Mariner Motor Lodge - see color ad p 385	◆◆	$72-109	385
47 / p. 332	⊕	The Cape Sojourn Motor Lodge - see color ad p 383	◆◆	$58-78	383
		WEST YARMOUTH - Restaurants			
㉖ / p. 332		Clancy's	◆◆	$9-16	386
㉗ / p. 332	⊕	Yarmouth House Restaurant	◆◆	$11-24	386
㉘ / p. 332		Captain Parker's	◆◆	$9-16	386
		DENNIS PORT - Lodgings			
49 / p. 332	⊕	The Rose Petal Bed & Breakfast	◆◆◆	$69-98	345
50 / p. 332	⊕	Colonial Village Motel	◆◆	$94-129 SAVE	343
52 / p. 332	⊕	Corsair & Cross Rip Resort Motels - see color ad p 344	◆◆	$145-225	344
53 / p. 332	⊕	Edgewater Beach Resort - see color ad p 344	◆◆	$95-200	344
54 / p. 332	⊕	Holiday Hill Motor Inn - see ad p 345	◆◆	$59-89	345
56 / p. 332		Spouter Whale Motor Inn	◆◆	$100-162	345
		DENNIS PORT - Restaurants			
㉚ / p. 332		Captain William's House	◆◆	$13-19	345
㉛ / p. 332		Clancy's	◆◆	$10-17	345
		WEST DENNIS - Lodgings			
60 / p. 332	⊕	Dennis West Motor Lodge	◆	$63-75	382
61 / p. 332	⊕	The Huntsman Motor Lodge	◆◆	$79-89 SAVE	382
		SOUTH DENNIS - Lodgings			
66 / p. 332	⊕	Captain Nickerson Inn	◆◆	$82-95	377
		BARNSTABLE - Lodgings			
68 / p. 330		Ashley Manor Inn	◆◆◆	$130-180	334
69 / p. 330		Beechwood Inn - see ad p 333	◆◆◆	$135-170	334
70 / p. 330		The Acworth Inn	◆◆◆	$115-185	333
		HYANNIS PORT - Lodgings			
68 / p. 332	⊕	Harbor Village	◆◆	$140-1550 SAVE	365
		WOODS HOLE - Lodgings			
71 / p. 330	⊕	Sands of Time Motor Inn - see color ad p 354	◆◆◆	$100-170	386
72 / p. 330	⊕	Sleepy Hollow Motor Inn	◆◆	$105-135	386
73 / p. 330		Nautilus Motor Inn - see color ad p 386	◆◆	$98-152	386
74 / p. 330	⊕	The Marlborough	◆◆◆	$95-165	386

Spotter/Map Pg.Number	OA	FALMOUTH - Lodgings	Rating	Rate	Listing Page
75 / p. 330		The Capewind - see color ad p 349	◆	$85-125	350
76 / p. 330	⊕	**The Moorings Lodge**	◆ ◆	$95-139 SAVE	352
79 / p. 330		The Inn at One Main Street	◆ ◆ ◆	$115-130	352
80 / p. 330	⊕	**Falmouth Heights Motor Lodge - see ad p 351**	◆ ◆	$95-130	351
83 / p. 330	⊕	**Mariner Motel - see color ad p 353**	◆ ◆	$79-119	352
84 / p. 330	⊕	**Red Horse Inn - see color ad p 352**	◆ ◆ ◆	$135-150	354
86 / p. 330	⊕	**Grafton Inn - see color ad p 353**	◆ ◆ ◆	$139-179	351
87 / p. 330	⊕	**Ocean View Motel**	◆	$75-140 SAVE	353
88 / p. 330		Woods Hole Passage Bed & Breakfast	◆ ◆ ◆	$125-145	355
89 / p. 330		Ramada Inn on the Square - see color ad inside front cover, p 354	◆ ◆ ◆	$129-199	354
90 / p. 330		The Beach House at Falmouth Heights	◆ ◆	$129-159	349
91 / p. 330		Village Green Inn	◆ ◆ ◆	$120-160	354
93 / p. 330	⊕	**Capt Tom Lawrence House - see color ad p 351**	◆ ◆ ◆	$145-190 SAVE	351
94 / p. 330		Wildflower Inn	◆ ◆ ◆	$120-175	355
97 / p. 330		Holiday Inn-Falmouth Cape Cod	◆ ◆	$159-209	351
98 / p. 330	⊕	**The Palmer House Inn - see color ad p 352**	◆ ◆ ◆	$130-145 SAVE	353
99 / p. 330	⊕	**The Admiralty Inn - see color ad p 350**	◆ ◆	$100-175 SAVE	349
100 / p. 330	⊕	**Best Western-Marina/Trade Winds - see color ad p 350**	◆ ◆	$135-215	349
		FALMOUTH - Restaurants			
50 / p. 330		Hearth'n Kettle Family Restaurant	◆	$10-14	355
51 / p. 330		The Regatta of Falmouth by the Sea	◆ ◆ ◆	$21-30	355
52 / p. 330		Coonamessett Inn Cahoon Dining Room	◆ ◆ ◆	$16-30	355
54 / p. 330		The Golden Swan	◆ ◆	$15-22	355
55 / p. 330	⊕	**Winston's Restaurant**	◆	$7-14	355
		SOUTH HARWICH - Lodgings			
113 / p. 330		Handkerchief Shoals Motel	◆ ◆	$72-78	377
		CHATHAM - Lodgings			
120 / p. 330	⊕	**Carriage House Inn**	◆ ◆ ◆	$155-180 SAVE	338
121 / p. 330	⊕	**Chatham Town House Inn - see color ad p 339**	◆ ◆ ◆	$225-295	339
122 / p. 330		The Cranberry Inn at Chatham	◆ ◆ ◆	$175-255	340
123 / p. 330	⊕	**Cyrus Kent House Inn**	◆ ◆ ◆	$135-250 SAVE	340
124 / p. 330	⊕	**The Dolphin of Chatham Inn & Motel**	◆ ◆ ◆	$144-275	340
125 / p. 330	⊕	**Port Fortune Inn**	◆ ◆ ◆	$130-170	340
127 / p. 330		Hawthorne Motel	◆ ◆	$130-160	340
128 / p. 330	⊕	**Moses Nickerson House Inn**	◆ ◆ ◆	$129-179	340
129 / p. 330	⊕	**The Old Harbor Inn**	◆ ◆ ◆	$139-239 SAVE	340
130 / p. 330	⊕	**Pleasant Bay Village**	◆ ◆ ◆	$195-265 SAVE	340
131 / p. 330	⊕	**Chatham Wayside Inn - see color ad p 339**	◆ ◆ ◆	$205-375	339
133 / p. 330	⊕	**The Bradford of Chatham - see color ad p 338**	◆ ◆ ◆	$155-285	337
134 / p. 330	⊕	**Captain's House Inn of Chatham**	◆ ◆ ◆ ◆	$165-350	337
135 / p. 330		Chatham Highlander	◆ ◆	$104-124	338
136 / p. 330	⊕	**Chatham Motel - see color ad p 338**	◆ ◆	$115-175 SAVE	338
139 / p. 330	⊕	**The Seafarer of Chatham - see color ad p 341**	◆ ◆	$125-150 SAVE	341
		CHATHAM - Restaurants			
59 / p. 330		Christian's	◆ ◆ ◆	$8-22	342
60 / p. 330		The Main Dining Room of the Chatham Bars Inn	◆ ◆ ◆	$25-34	342
61 / p. 330		Pate's	◆ ◆	$14-21	342
62 / p. 330		Campari's Italian Bistro & Bennedetto's	◆ ◆	$17-24	341
64 / p. 330		The Impudent Oyster	◆ ◆	$14-25	342
		EAST HARWICH - Lodgings			
145 / p. 330	⊕	**Wequassett Inn - see ad p 341**	◆ ◆ ◆	$275-510	349

Spotter/Map Pg.Number	OA	EAST HARWICH - Restaurant	Rating	Rate	Listing Page
67 / p. 330	⚉	Wequassett Inn Main Dining Room	◆◆◆	$19-24	349
		SANDWICH - Lodgings			
148 / p. 330		Whaleback Hill Cottages	◆	$65-80	373
150 / p. 330		The Dan'l Webster Inn - see color ad starting on p 374	◆◆◆	$149-345	372
151 / p. 330		Isaiah Jones Homestead	◆◆◆	$115-140	372
152 / p. 330		The Earl of Sandwich Motor Manor - see color ad starting on p 374	◆◆	$89-109	372
153 / p. 330		Old Colony Motel - see color ad starting on p 374	◆◆	$75-89	373
154 / p. 330	⚉	Sandwich Lodge & Resort	◆	$109-196 ⛊	373
156 / p. 330		Sandy Neck Motel - see color ad starting on p 374	◆◆	$79-89	373
157 / p. 330		Shady Nook Inn & Motel - see color ad starting on p 374	◆◆◆	$95-125	373
158 / p. 330	⚉	Spring Garden Inn & Motel - see color ad starting on p 374	◆◆	$83-99	373
159 / p. 330	⚉	Spring Hill Motor Lodge - see color ad starting on p 374	◆◆◆	$95-115	373
160 / p. 330		The Captain Ezra Nye House	◆◆	$100-110	372
161 / p. 330	⚉	Bay Beach - see color ad starting on p 374	◆◆◆◆	$175-345	372
162 / p. 330		Country Acres Motel - see color ad starting on p 374	◆◆	$89-99	372
		SANDWICH - Restaurants			
70 / p. 330		The Bee-Hive Tavern	◆◆	$9-16	373
72 / p. 330		Aqua Grill	◆◆◆	$10-20	373
73 / p. 330	⚉	Horizon's on Cape Cod Bay	◆◆	$11-14	376
76 / p. 330		Barney's Grill & Fare	◆	$6-18	373
78 / p. 330		The Dan'l Webster Inn	◆◆◆	$17-25	376
		CENTERVILLE - Lodgings			
169 / p. 330		Adam's Terrace Gardens Inn	◆◆	$75-110	337
170 / p. 330	⚉	Centerville Corners Motor Lodge - see color ad p 337	◆◆	$110-130	337
		CENTERVILLE - Restaurant			
80 / p. 330		Hearth'n Kettle Restaurant & Bakery	◆	$4-11	337
		YARMOUTH PORT - Lodgings			
174 / p. 330		The Inn at Cape Cod	◆◆◆	$120-185	387
175 / p. 330		One Centre Street Inn	◆◆◆	$95-130	387
		YARMOUTH PORT - Restaurant			
82 / p. 330		Abbicci	◆◆◆	$15-25	387
		DENNIS - Lodgings			
180 / p. 330	⚉	Isaiah Hall B & B Inn - see ad p 343	◆◆◆	$107-156	343
		DENNIS - Restaurant			
84 / p. 330		Gina's	◆◆	$10-18	343
		EAST DENNIS - Lodgings			
185 / p. 330	⚉	Sesuit Harbor Motel	◆◆	$88-110 ⛊	345
		BREWSTER - Lodgings			
190 / p. 330		Ocean Edge Resort & Golf Club	◆◆◆	$235-475	335
191 / p. 330	⚉	The Ruddy Turnstone Bed & Breakfast	◆◆◆	$99-160	336
192 / p. 330	⚉	Candleberry Inn	◆◆◆	$125-145	335
193 / p. 330	⚉	Brewster Farmhouse Inn - see ad p 334	◆◆◆	$115-190	334
194 / p. 330	⚉	Isaiah Clark House	◆◆◆	$98-130 ⛊	335
196 / p. 330		The Bramble Inn	◆◆◆	$105-135	334
197 / p. 330		The Captain Freeman Inn - see color ad p 335	◆◆◆	$125-250	335
198 / p. 330		The Inn at the Egg	◆◆◆	$95-150	335
199 / p. 330		The Old Manse Inn	◆◆	$115-125	335
200 / p. 330	⚉	Old Sea Pines Inn	◆◆◆	$55-155	336
202 / p. 330		Pepper House Inn	◆◆◆	$109-139	336

Spotter/Map Pg.Number	OA	**BREWSTER** - Restaurants	Rating	Rate	Listing Page
89 / p. 330		The Brewster Fish House	◆◆	$14-20	336
90 / p. 330		Old Manse Inn Dining Room	◆◆	$16-28	336
91 / p. 330		The Bramble Inn Dining Room	◆◆◆	$42-52	336
93 / p. 330		High Brewster Dining Room	◆◆◆	$36-55	336
		ORLEANS - Lodgings			
210 / p. 330	⊕	The Cove - see ad p 366	◆◆◆	$124-134	366
212 / p. 330		Nauset Knoll Motor Lodge	◆◆	$135	367
213 / p. 330	⊕	Olde Tavern Motel & Inn - see color ad p 367	◆◆◆	$79-110	367
218 / p. 330	⊕	Skaket Beach Motel - see color ad p 367	◆◆◆	$78-163	368
219 / p. 330	⊕	Ridgewood Motel & Cottages - see ad p 367	◆◆	$69-80	368
221 / p. 330		The Barley Neck Inn & Lodge	◆◆	$95-125	366
		ORLEANS - Restaurants			
96 / p. 330		Old Jailhouse Tavern	◆◆	$15-20	368
97 / p. 330		The Barley Neck Inn	◆◆◆	$13-20	368
98 / p. 330		The Arbor Restaurant	◆◆	$14-22	368
99 / p. 330	⊕	Lobster Claw Restaurant	◆	$8-16	368
100 / p. 330		Nauset Beach Club	◆◆	$12-19	368
		EASTHAM - Lodgings			
225 / p. 330	⊕	Eagle Wing Motel	◆◆	$89-102	347
226 / p. 330	⊕	Viking Shores Motor Lodge - see color ad p 348	◆◆	$85-93	348
227 / p. 330	⊕	Anchorage On The Cove	◆◆	$1300-1600	346
228 / p. 330	⊕	Aspinet Cottages & Motel Efficiencies	◆	$79-95	346
230 / p. 330		Captain's Quarters Motel - see color ad p 346	◆◆	$96-126	346
231 / p. 330	⊕	Cranberry Cottages	◆◆	$80-85	347
232 / p. 330	⊕	Ocean View Motel	◆◆	$78-86	347
233 / p. 330	⊕	Midway Motel & Cottages	◆◆	$80-86	347
234 / p. 330	⊕	Penny House Inn - see color ad p 346	◆◆◆	$165-230 ⟨SAVE⟩	348
235 / p. 330		Four Points Hotel by Sheraton - see color ad p 347	◆◆◆	$173	347
236 / p. 330	⊕	Town Crier Motel	◆◆	$69-109 ⟨SAVE⟩	348
237 / p. 330	⊕	Gull Cottages	◆◆	$650	347
238 / p. 330	⊕	Whalewalk Inn	◆◆◆	$150-250	348
		EASTHAM - Restaurant			
103 / p. 330	⊕	Arnold's Lobster & Clam Bar	◆	$7-17	348
		SOUTH WELLFLEET - Lodgings			
245 / p. 330	⊕	The Even'tide Motel - see color ad p 377	◆◆	$85-112	377
247 / p. 330	⊕	Southfleet Motor Inn - see ad p 377	◆◆◆	$99-120	378
248 / p. 330	⊕	Wellfleet Motel and Lodge - see color ad p 378	◆◆◆	$76-150	378
		SOUTH WELLFLEET - Restaurant			
105 / p. 330	⊕	Van Rensselaer's Restaurant	◆◆	$12-22	378
		PROVINCETOWN - Lodgings			
254 / p. 330		White Wind Inn	◆◆	$115-200	371
255 / p. 330	⊕	Best Western Tides Beachfront - see color ad p 369	◆◆◆	$169-219	369
256 / p. 330	⊕	Best Western Chateau Motor Inn - see color ad p 369	◆◆◆	$139-169	368
257 / p. 330	⊕	Cape Colony Inn	◆	$106 ⟨SAVE⟩	369
258 / p. 330		Bayshore	◆◆◆	$795-1595	368
259 / p. 330		Holiday Inn	◆◆◆	$129-160	369
260 / p. 330		The Masthead - see ad p 370	◆◆◆	$145-322 ⟨SAVE⟩	370
261 / p. 330	⊕	The Shamrock	◆	$130-170 ⟨SAVE⟩	370
262 / p. 330	⊕	Somerset House	◆◆◆	$80-130	370
263 / p. 330	⊕	Surfside Inn - see color ad p 371	◆◆	$89-169	371

Spotter/Map Pg.Number	OA	PROVINCETOWN - Restaurants	Rating	Rate	Listing Page
110 / p. 330	⊕	Gallerani's Cafe	◆◆	$12-25	372
112 / p. 330		The Mews	◆◆	$18-25	372
113 / p. 330	⊕	Pepe's Wharf	◆◆◆	$15-26	372
114 / p. 330	⊕	The Martin House	◆◆	$14-28	372
		NORTH TRURO - Lodgings			
271 / p. 330		White Sands Motel - see color ad p 371	◆	$109-250	366
272 / p. 330	⊕	Blue Sea Motor Inn - see color ad p 370	◆◆	$117-147 🗎	365
273 / p. 330	⊕	Coral Sands Motel	◆	$85-125	365
274 / p. 330		Crows Nest Motel	◆◆	$82-85	365
275 / p. 330	⊕	Sea Gull Motel - see color ad p 371	◆◆	$78-110 🗎	365
276 / p. 330		Seaside Village Motel	◆◆	$82-104	366
277 / p. 330	⊕	East Harbour Motel & Cottages	◆◆	$95-110	365
		NORTH TRURO - Restaurants			
120 / p. 330		Adrian's	◆◆	$10-19	366
121 / p. 330		The Whitman House Restaurant	◆◆◆	$9-25	366
		PLYMOUTH - Lodgings			
285 / p. 330	⊕	Pilgrim Sands Motel - see color ad starting on p 412	◆◆	$98-130	415
286 / p. 330	⊕	Cold Spring Motel - see color ad starting on p 412	◆◆	$79-99	411
287 / p. 330	⊕	Blue Spruce Motel & Townhouses - see color ad starting on p 412	◆◆	$64-82	411
288 / p. 330	⊕	The Governor Bradford on the Harbour - see color ad starting on p 412	◆◆	$79-119 🗎	411
289 / p. 330	⊕	John Carver Inn At Town Brook - see color ad starting on p 412	◆◆	$99-179 🗎	411
290 / p. 330		Sheraton Inn Plymouth - see color ad starting on p 412	◆◆◆	$120-140	416
291 / p. 330	⊕	The Sleepy Pilgrim Motel		$79-109	416
		PLYMOUTH - Restaurants			
124 / p. 330		Isaac's on the Waterfront	◆◆	$10-15	417
125 / p. 330		Mamma Mia's Restaurant on the Waterfront	◆	$5-13	417
127 / p. 330	⊕	McGrath's Seafood Grille	◆◆	$10-15	417
131 / p. 330		Iguana's Mexican/Southwestern Restaurant & Bar	◆◆	$6-15	416
132 / p. 330		Run of the Mill Tavern	◆	$6-12	417
135 / p. 330		Ernie's Restaurant	◆	$9-14	416
136 / p. 330		Hearth 'n Kettle Restaurant & Tavern	◆	$8-14	416
		EAST WAREHAM - Lodgings			
299 / p. 330	⊕	Atlantic Motel	◆	$89-109 🗎	390
		HARWICH PORT - Lodgings			
301 / p. 330		Wychmere Village - see color ad p 356	◆◆	$89-139	356
303 / p. 330		Augustus Snow House - see ad p 333	◆◆◆	$145-160	355
304 / p. 330		Dunscroft By-The-Sea B & B Inn	◆◆◆	$155-235	355
305 / p. 330		Coachman Motor Inn	◆◆	$80-98	355
		HARWICH PORT - Restaurants			
141 / p. 330		L'Alouette Restaurant	◆◆	$17-25	356
142 / p. 330		Country Inn	◆◆	$15-25	356
		BUZZARDS BAY - Lodgings			
308 / p. 330	⊕	Bay Motor Inn	◆	$89-99 🗎	336
		BUZZARDS BAY - Restaurant			
144 / p. 330		Lindsey's Family Restaurant	◆◆	$8-19	336
		BOURNE - Lodgings			
310 / p. 330		Best Western Bridge-Bourne Hotel	◆◆	$119-149	334
		WEST BARNSTABLE - Lodgings			
315 / p. 330		Honeysuckle Hill Bed & Breakfast	◆◆◆	$95-185	382

Spotter/Map Pg.Number	OA	WELLFLEET - Restaurants	Rating	Rate	Listing Page
(150) / p. 330	⟨AAA⟩	Moby Dick's Family Restuarant	◆	$8-13	382
(152) / p. 330		Aesop's Tables	◆◆◆	$14-26	381
		SOUTH CARVER - Restaurant			
(165) / p. 330		Crane Brook Restaurant & Tea Room	◆◆◆	$18-28	421
		COTUIT - Restaurant			
(170) / p. 330		The Regatta of Cotuit at the Crocker House	◆◆◆	$19-28	342
		NORTH FALMOUTH - Restaurant			
(175) / p. 330	⟨AAA⟩	Silver Lounge Restaurant	◆◆	$11-15	365

Your AAA club magazine provides timely articles about safety, car maintenance, travel resources, legislation affecting motorists, automotive engineering, special trip opportunities and more.

Capture the moment...

Tips for successful photographs

Know your camera, and be sure it's in good working order. Before going on a trip, shoot a roll of film so you won't have any surprises when it really counts. Use film best suited to your purpose; camera shop personnel can help you choose the right kind. Then, follow the instructions that come with it.

♦ Compose your picture. Try framing it with a foreground feature (a fence or tree), making sure that parts of the subject are not being cut off. Get close enough so that your subject won't be dwarfed in an expanse of background.

♦ When taking close-ups of people, have them stand against a simple backdrop, and be sure they do something other than stare stiffly at the camera.

♦ Mid-morning and mid-afternoon, when the sun's angle creates definite but not overpowering shadows, are the best times for general photography. Pictures taken during the shadowless high noon hours tend to be flat.

♦ If the weather turns bad, take pictures anyway. Rain and fog can add a special magic to your efforts.

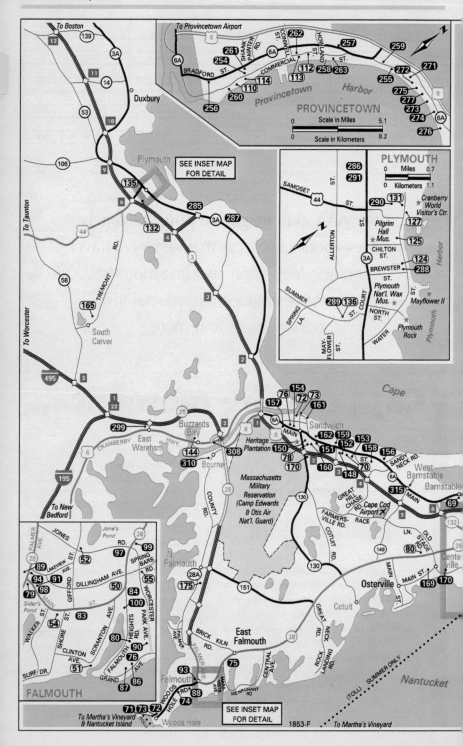

To Boston

12
139

3A

11
14

Duxbury

53

10

106

Plymouth

135

To Taunton

6

285

44

132

4

3A
287

58

3

165

To Worcester

South Carver

3

2

495

2

22

299

Buzzards Bay

25

2

East Wareham

CRANBERRY HWY.

6

195

144

310

Bourne

308

Heritage Plantation

150

78
170

To New Bedford

Massachusetts Military Reservation (Camp Edwards & Otis Air Nat'l. Guard)

COUNTY RD.

28

N. Falmouth

28A

175

151

130

130

Cape

Sandwich

6A

MAIN

162 159
151 152
160
148

153
158
156

70

SANDY NECK RD.

West Barnstable

6A

Barnstable

315

MAIN

6

69

132

GREAT HILL CHASE

FARMERS-VILLE RD.

Cape Cod Airport

RACE

5

COTUIT RD.

149

80

Osterville

MAIN ST.

LN.

OLD STAGE RD.

MAIN ST.

169 170

Centerville

28

Cotuit

GREAT NECK RD.

ROCK LANDING RD.

East Falmouth

BRICK KILN RD.

PALMER AVE.

CENTRAL AVE.

75

MENAUHANT RD.

SUMMER ONLY

(TOLL)

Nantucket

Falmouth

93

WOODS HOLE RD.

74
88

To Martha's Vineyard & Nantucket Island

71 73
72

(TOLL)

Woods Hole

SEE INSET MAP FOR DETAIL

1853-F

To Martha's Vineyard

Provincetown Inset

To Provincetown Airport

6

262

CONWELL ST.

COMMERCIAL ST.

BRADFORD ST.

6A

261
254

SHANK PAINTER RD.

112
258 263

257

259

272 271

255

275

277
273
274

276

114
113

110

256
260

Provincetown Harbor

PROVINCETOWN

Scale in Miles   5.1

Scale in Kilometers   8.2

6

6A

Plymouth Inset

PLYMOUTH

Miles   0.7

Kilometers   1.1

SAMOSET ST.

44

286
291

290
131

Cranberry World Visitor's Ctr.

Pilgrim Hall Mus.

127

125

CHILTON ST.

124
288

3A

BREWSTER ST.

Plymouth Nat'l. Wax Mus.

Mayflower II

289 136

NORTH ST.

WATER ST.

Plymouth Rock

SPRING LA.

MAY-FLOWER ST.

SUMMER ST.

ALLERTON ST.

COURT ST.

Harbor

Plymouth

Falmouth Inset

FALMOUTH

JONES RD.

Jone's Pond

28

PALMER AVE.

LAKEVIEW AVE.

89
94 91
98
79

Sider's Pond

52

97

99

SPRING BARS RD.

55

DILLINGHAM AVE.

50

GIFFORD ST.

84
100

WORCESTER AVE.

WALKER ST.

83

SHORE ST.

54

CLINTON AVE.

SCRANTON AVE.

PARK AVE.

80

FALMOUTH HEIGHTS RD.

90
76

GRAND AVE.

86
87

SURF DR.

51

MAIN ST.

Falmouth

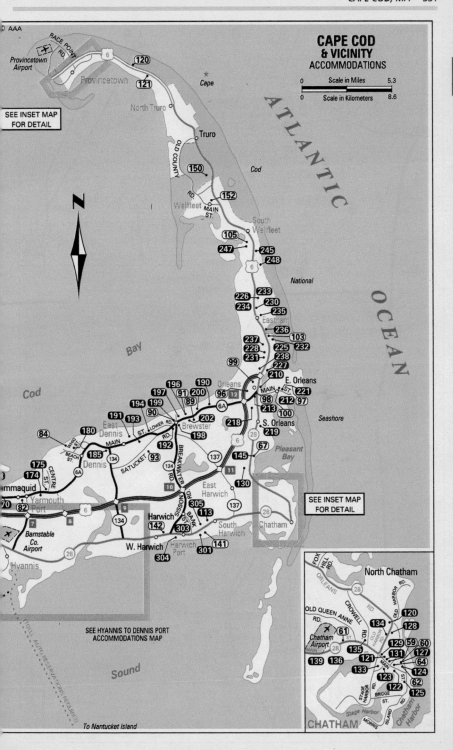

© AAA

CAPE COD & VICINITY
ACCOMMODATIONS

Scale in Miles
0   5.3
Scale in Kilometers
0   8.6

RACE POINT RD.
Provincetown Airport
120
121
Provincetown
North Truro
Cape
Truro
Cod

SEE INSET MAP FOR DETAIL

ATLANTIC OCEAN

OLD COUNTY RD.
150
152
Wellfleet
MAIN ST.
South Wellfleet
105
247
245
248

National

226
234
233
230
235
Eastham
236
237
228
231
225
238
227
103
232
99

Bay

Cod

Orleans
196
190
197
91
200
199
89
194
90
202
191
193
East Dennis
180
LOWER RD.
Brewster
198
84
185
Dennis
192
93
BREAKWATER RD.
175
174
6A
SATUCKET
CROWELL RD.
124
BANK ST.
Yarmouth Port
82
70
7
8
134
9
305
113
Harwich
142
303
W. Harwich
304
Harwich Port
301
141
South Harwich

96
12
Main St.
210
98
212
221
97
213
100
E. Orleans
S. Orleans
218
219
67
Seashore
145
137
11
130
137

Pleasant Bay

Chatham
28

SEE INSET MAP FOR DETAIL

East Harwich

Barnstable Co. Airport

Hyannis

SEE HYANNIS TO DENNIS PORT
ACCOMMODATIONS MAP

Sound

To Nantucket Island

CHATHAM

North Chatham
FOX HILL RD.
ORLEANS RD.
28
CROWELL RD.
OLD HARBOR RD.
120
128
OLD QUEEN ANNE RD.
134
Chatham Airport
61
129
59
60
127
135
131
64
124
139
136
121
133
123
62
125
122
STAGE HARBOR RD.
BRIDGE ST.
MAIN ST.
Chatham Harbor
MORRIS ISLAND RD.
Stage Harbor

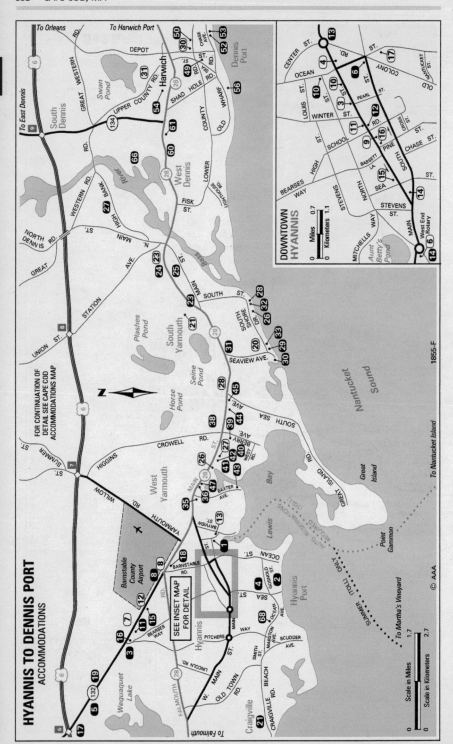

HYANNIS TO DENNIS PORT
ACCOMMODATIONS

FOR CONTINUATION OF DETAIL SEE CAPE COD ACCOMMODATIONS MAP

SEE INSET MAP FOR DETAIL

DOWNTOWN HYANNIS

© AAA

1855-F

Scale in Miles

Scale in Kilometers

CAPE COD   (See map p. 330; index p. 323)

BARNSTABLE—40,900   (See map p. 330; index p. 324)

LODGINGS

THE ACWORTH INN

◆◆◆   5/1-10/31 [BP]

Historic Bed & Breakfast   11/1-4/30 [BP]

	Guaranteed Rates	
1P: $115- 185	2P/1B: $115- 185	
1P: $95- 185	2P/1B: $95- 185	

Phone: 508/362-3330   **70**

XP: $25
XP: $25

Location: 0.5 mi w of jct Willow St, exit 7 from US 6. 4352 Old Kings Hwy, SR 6A 02637 (PO Box 256, CUMMAQUID). Fax: 508/375-0304. **Terms:** Age restrictions may apply; reserv deposit, 15 day notice; handling fee imposed; 2 night min stay, weekends in season. **Facility:** 5 rooms. 2-room suite with fireplace. Light & airy country decor with hand-painted weathered furniture. A classic 19th-century house. 2 stories, no elevator; interior corridors; designated smoking area. **Recreation:** bicycles. **All Rooms:** combo or shower baths. **Some Rooms:** color TV. **Cards:** AE, DS, MC, VI.

(See map p. 330)

ASHLEY MANOR INN   Rates Subject to Change   Phone: (508)362-8044   68
◆◆◆   All Year [BP]   1P: $130- 180   2P/1B: $130- 180   2P/2B: $130- 180   XP: $40
Historic Bed   **Location:** 0.8 mi e on SR 6A. 3660 Olde Kings Hwy, SR 6A 02630 (PO Box 856). Fax: 508/362-9927.
& Breakfast   **Terms:** Age restrictions may apply; reserv deposit, 15 day notice. **Facility:** 6 rooms. Elegant inn built in mid-1700's on beautiful grounds. Individually decorated rooms with antiques; all but 1 have a working fireplace. 2 stories; interior/exterior corridors; designated smoking area; 1 tennis court. **Recreation:** bicycles. **Cards:** DI, DS, JC, MC, VI.

BEECHWOOD INN   Guaranteed Rates   Phone: (508)362-6618   69
◆◆◆   5/1-10/31 [BP]   1P: $135- 170   2P/1B: $135- 170   2P/2B: $135- 170   XP: $25
Historic Bed   11/1-4/30 [BP]   1P: $95- 130   2P/1B: $95- 130   2P/2B: $95- 130   XP: $25
& Breakfast   **Location:** 0.8 mi w on SR 6A. 2839 Main St 02630. Fax: 508/362-0298. **Terms:** Age restrictions may apply; reserv deposit, 15 day notice; handling fee imposed; 2 night min stay, weekends in season. **Facility:** 6 rooms. Authentically restored Queen Anne style home, furnished with lovely antiques. 2 units with fireplace. 3 stories; interior/exterior corridors; smoke free premises. **Recreation:** bicycles. **All Rooms:** combo or shower baths. **Cards:** AE, DS, MC, VI.
(See ad p 333)

BOURNE—16,100   (See map p. 330; index p. 328)

LODGING

BEST WESTERN BRIDGE-BOURNE HOTEL   Rates Subject to Change   Phone: 508/759-0800   310
◆◆   Fri & Sat 5/22-9/26   1P: $119- 149   2P/1B: $119- 149   2P/2B: $119- 149   XP: $10   F16
Motel   Fri & Sat 5/1-5/21, Sun-Thurs
5/22-9/26 & Fri & Sat
9/27-10/24   1P: $90- 126   2P/1B: $90- 126   2P/2B: $90- 126   XP: $10   F16
Sun-Thurs 5/1-5/21,
9/27-4/30 & 10/25-4/30   1P: $54- 95   2P/1B: $54- 95   2P/2B: $54- 95   XP: $10   F16
Location: On SR 28, just w of the rotary on Cape Cod side of bridge. 100 Trowbridge Rd 02532. Fax: 508/759-4575. **Terms:** Reserv deposit, in season. **Facility:** 43 rooms. Some deluxe units with patio overlooking Cape Cod Canal. Rates for up to 4 persons; 2 stories; interior corridors; heated indoor pool. **Cards:** AE, DI, DS, MC, VI.

BREWSTER—8,400   (See map p. 330; index p. 326)

LODGINGS

THE BRAMBLE INN   Rates Subject to Change   Phone: 508/896-7644   196
◆◆◆   5/1-12/31 [BP]   2P/1B: $105- 135   2P/2B: $105- 135   XP: $20
Historic   **Location:** On SR 6A; 0.3 mi e of jct SR 124. 2019 Main St 02631 (PO Box 807). Fax: 508/896-9332.
Country Inn   **Terms:** Open 5/1-12/31; age restrictions may apply; reserv deposit, 14 day notice; handling fee imposed; 2 night min stay, weekends. **Facility:** 8 rooms. Charmingly restored rooms in 2 buildings. Main inn circa 1861 & an 1849 house. 2 stories; interior corridors; designated smoking area. **All Rooms:** combo or shower baths. **Some Rooms:** color TV. **Cards:** AE, DS, MC, VI.

BREWSTER FARMHOUSE INN   Rates Subject to Change   Phone: (508)896-3910   193
ⓐⓐⓐ   5/29-10/11 [BP]   2P/1B: $115- 190   XP: $35
◆◆◆   5/1-5/28 & 10/12-4/30 [BP]   2P/1B: $100- 160   XP: $35
Bed &   **Location:** 2 mi w on Main St (SR 6A). 716 Main St 02631. Fax: 508/896-4232. **Terms:** Age restrictions may
Breakfast   apply; reserv deposit, 15 day notice; handling fee imposed; 2 night min stay, in season. **Facility:** 5 rooms. Farmhouse circa 1850. Beautifully decorated rooms & common areas. Peaceful, landscaped deck & pool area. 2 stories; interior corridors; smoke free premises; heated pool, whirlpool. **Dining:** Afternoon tea. **Recreation:** bicycles. **All Rooms:** extended cable TV. **Cards:** AE, CB, DI, DS, MC, VI. *(See ad below)*

(See map p. 330)

CANDLEBERRY INN
Rates Subject to Change
Phone: 508/896-3300 `192`

	1P:	2P/1B:	2P/2B:	XP:
6/15-9/15	$95- 195	$95- 195	$125- 145	$20
5/1-6/14 & 9/16-10/31	$90- 165	$90- 165	$110- 135	$20
11/1-4/30	$80- 145	$80- 145	$100- 120	$20

Historic Bed
& Breakfast
◆◆◆
Location: On SR 6A, 0.3 mi w of jct SR 124. 1882 Main St 02631. Fax: 508/896-4016. **Terms:** Age restrictions may apply; reserv deposit, 14 day notice; 2 night min stay, in season. **Facility:** 9 rooms. Federal style home, circa 1800. Spacious, attractive guest rooms furnished with antiques; 3 with fireplace. 2 stories; interior corridors; designated smoking area. **Recreation:** croquet, horseshoes. **All Rooms:** combo or shower baths, extended cable TV. **Some Rooms:** color TV, whirlpools. **Cards:** AE, DS, MC, VI.

THE CAPTAIN FREEMAN INN
Guaranteed Rates
Phone: (508)896-7481 `197`

	1P:	2P/1B:	2P/2B:	XP:
5/1-10/31 [BP]	$125- 250	$125- 250		$30-35
11/1-4/30 [BP]	$110- 225	$110- 225		$30-35

◆◆◆
Historic Bed
& Breakfast
Location: On SR 6A; just e of jct SR 124. 15 Breakwater Rd 02631. Fax: 508/896-5618. **Terms:** Age restrictions may apply; reserv deposit, 14 day notice; handling fee imposed; 2 night min stay, in season. **Facility:** 12 rooms. Restored sea captain's mansion circa 1860. 5 units with working fireplace. 3 stories, no elevator; interior corridors; smoke free premises; heated pool. **Recreation:** bicycles. **Some Rooms:** color TV. **Cards:** AE, MC, VI.
(See color ad below)

THE INN AT THE EGG
Rates Subject to Change
Phone: 508/896-3123 `198`

	2P/1B:	2P/2B:	XP:
6/1-10/15 [BP]	$95- 150	$150	$25
5/1-5/31 & 10/16-4/30 [BP]	$75- 120	$120	$25

◆◆◆
Bed &
Breakfast
Location: On SR 6A at jct SR 124. 1944 Old King's Hwy 02631 (PO Box 453). Fax: 508/896-6821. **Terms:** Age restrictions may apply; reserv deposit, 14 day notice; handling fee imposed; 2 night min stay, 6/15-10/15. **Facility:** 5 rooms. Contemporary accommodation on Brewsters Historic Green. Extensive grounds. 2 stories; interior/exterior corridors; smoke free premises. **Cards:** AE, MC, VI.

ISAIAH CLARK HOUSE
Phone: (508)896-2223 `194`

	1P:	2P/1B:	2P/2B:	XP:
5/1-10/31 [BP]	$88- 120	$98- 130	$98- 130	$25
11/1-4/30 [BP]	$68- 98	$78- 108	$78- 108	$25

◆◆◆
Historic Bed
& Breakfast
Location: 1.5 mi w of SR 124 on SR 6A. 1187 Main St 02631. Fax: 508/896-2138. **Terms:** Age restrictions may apply; reserv deposit, 10 day notice; handling fee imposed; weekly rates; 2 night min stay, weekends in season. **Facility:** 7 rooms. Sea captains estate. Modern comforts with colonial motifs. 3 rooms with working fireplace. 2 stories; interior corridors; smoke free premises. **Dining:** Afternoon tea. **All Rooms:** extended cable TV. **Some Rooms:** color TV. **Cards:** AE, DS, MC, VI. **Special Amenities:** Free breakfast and free room upgrade (subject to availability with advanced reservations).

OCEAN EDGE RESORT & GOLF CLUB
Rates Subject to Change
Phone: 508/896-9000 `190`

	2P/1B:	2P/2B:
6/20-8/31	$235- 475	$235- 475
5/16-6/19 & 9/1-11/1	$165- 475	$165- 475
5/1-5/15, 11/2-12/1 & 4/4-4/30	$95- 305	$95- 305
12/2-4/3	$95- 225	$95- 225

◆◆◆
Resort
Location: On SR 6A, 2.3 mi e of SR 124. 2907 Main St 02631. Fax: 508/896-9123. **Terms:** Check-in 4 pm; reserv deposit, 30 day notice, in villas; handling fee imposed; 2 night min stay, weekends. **Facility:** 258 rooms. Large hotel rooms & 1, 2 & 3 bedroom villas located on manicured 1200 acre resort. Some units with view of Cape Cod Bay. 18 two-bedroom units, 24 three-bedroom units. 1-3 bedroom villas $1400-$4700 weekly in season, daily rates avail; 2 stories; interior corridors; putting green; heated indoor pool; playground. Fee: 18 holes golf; 11 tennis courts. **Services:** giftshop; area transportation. Fee: massage. **Recreation:** Fee: bicycles. **Some Rooms:** 157 kitchens. **Cards:** AE, DI, DS, MC, VI.

THE OLD MANSE INN
Rates Subject to Change
Phone: 508/896-3149 `199`

	1P:	2P/1B:	2P/2B:	XP:
All Year [BP]	$105	$115- 125	$125	$20

◆◆
Historic Bed
& Breakfast
Location: On SR 6A; 0.3 mi w of jct SR 124. 1861 Main St 02631 (PO Box 745). **Terms:** Age restrictions may apply. **Facility:** 8 rooms. Restored sea captain's home circa 1800. 4 rooms with canopy bed. 3 stories, no elevator; interior corridors; designated smoking area. **All Rooms:** combo or shower baths.
Some Rooms: color TV.

(See map p. 330)

OLD SEA PINES INN　　　　Rates Subject to Change　　　　**Phone:** (508)896-6114　　20
(AAA)　　All Year [BP]　　　1P: $55- 155　2P/1B: $55- 155　2P/2B: $55- 155　XP: $5-20　　F
◆◆◆　　**Location:** On SR 6A, 1.3 mi e of jct SR 124. 2553 Main St 02631 (PO Box 1070). Fax: 508/896-738
Historic Bed　　**Terms:** Age restrictions may apply; reserv deposit, 14 day notice; handling fee imposed; weekly rates;
& Breakfast　　night min stay, weekends 7/1-8/30. **Facility:** 23 rooms. Former girls finishing school with atmosphere of 1930
　　summer home. Some rooms in outlying buildings. 2 two-bedroom units. 1 one-bedroom garden suite with fire
　　place, $150; 2 standard rooms with working fireplace, $110 off season; 3 stories, no elevator; interior/exterio
corridors; smoke free premises. **Dining:** Dinner theater Sun evening $38 per person; cocktails. **Recreation:** croque
All Rooms: extended cable TV. **Some Rooms:** color TV. **Cards:** AE, CB, DI, DS, MC, VI.　　　☎ ⊳

PEPPER HOUSE INN　　　　Rates Subject to Change　　　　**Phone:** (508)896-4389　　20
◆◆◆　　5/21-10/12 [BP]　　　　2P/1B: $109- 139　　　　XP: $20
Historic Bed　5/1-5/20 & 10/13-4/30 [EP]　2P/1B: $89- 119
& Breakfast　　**Location:** 0.4 mi e of jct SR 124. 2062 Main Street, Rt 6A 02631 (PO Box 2085). Fax: 508/896-5012
　　Terms: Age restrictions may apply; reserv deposit, 10 day notice; handling fee imposed; 2 night min stay
weekends in season. **Facility:** 4 rooms. Federal Colonial style built in 1793 by Captain Bangs Pepper. 2 stories, no elevato
interior corridors; designated smoking area. **All Rooms:** combo or shower baths. **Cards:** AE, MC, VI.　🎥 ☎ ⊳

THE RUDDY TURNSTONE BED & BREAKFAST　　Guaranteed Rates　　**Phone:** (508)385-9871　　19
(AAA)　　6/15-10/15　　　1P: $99- 160　2P/1B: $99- 160　2P/2B: $99- 160
◆◆◆　　5/1-6/14 & 10/16-4/30　1P: $85- 130　2P/1B: $85- 130　2P/2B: $80- 130
Bed &　　**Location:** On SR 6A, 1.5 mi e of SR 134, 2.5 mi w of SR 124. 463 Main St 02631. Fax: 508/385-569
Breakfast　　**Terms:** Age restrictions may apply; reserv deposit, 14 day notice; handling fee imposed; 2 night min stay
　　weekends. **Facility:** 5 rooms. Expansive grounds overlooking Cape Cod Bay. Cozy to large rooms with
　　couple of rooms in the adjacent Carriage House. 1 two-bedroom unit. 2 stories; interior corridors; smoke fre
premises. **Recreation:** badminton, horseshoes. **All Rooms:** combo or shower baths, extended cable TV
Some Rooms: color TV. **Cards:** MC, VI.　　　　☎ 📠 ⊳

RESTAURANTS

THE BRAMBLE INN DINING ROOM　Country Inn　　**Dinner:** $42-$52　　**Phone:** 508/896-7644　　9
◆◆◆　　**Location:** On SR 6A; 0.3 mi e of jct SR 124; in The Bramble Inn. 2019 Main St 02631. **Hours:** Ope
Continental　5/1-12/31; 6 pm-9 pm. **Closed:** Mon 9/1-9/30, Mon-Wed 10/1-12/31. **Reservations:** suggeste
　　Features: semi-formal attire; cocktails; prix fixe. 4-course table d'hote menu, $42-$52. Gracious dining
restored 1861 house. Chef/Owner. Smoke free premises. **Cards:** AE, DS, MC, VI.　　　⊳

THE BREWSTER FISH HOUSE　**Lunch:** $7-$10　　**Dinner:** $14-$20　　**Phone:** 508/896-7867　　8
◆◆　　**Location:** 0.5 mi e of SR 124, on SR 6A. 2208 Main St, Rt 6A 02631. **Hours:** Open 5/1-12/22 & 4/4-4/3
Seafood　　11:30 am-3 & 5-10 pm, Sun noon-3 & 5-9:30 pm. **Closed:** Mon 4/4-5/30 & 9/1-12/22. **Features:** casu
　　dress; cocktails; a la carte. Friendly & casual. Fresh quality seafood. **Cards:** MC, VI.　　⊳

HIGH BREWSTER DINING ROOM　Country Inn　　**Dinner:** $36-$55　　**Phone:** 508/896-3636　　9
◆◆◆　　**Location:** 0.8 mi n on SR 6A from jct SR 137; 0.8 mi sw via Stoneybrook & Satucket rds. 964 Satucket F
Regional　　02631. **Hours:** 5:30 pm-8:30 pm. **Closed:** Mon & Tues 1/1-3/31, call to verify. **Reservations:** require
American　　**Features:** casual dress; beer & wine only. Leisurely elegant dining in historic 1730's house. 4-course pr
　　fixe menu. Tues tasting menu only. Smoke free premises. **Cards:** AE, MC, VI.　　⊳

OLD MANSE INN DINING ROOM　Country Inn　　**Dinner:** $16-$28　　**Phone:** 508/896-3149　　9
◆◆　　**Location:** On SR 6A; 0.3 mi w of jct SR 124; in The Old Manse Inn. 1861 Main St 02631. **Hours:** Ope
Continental　5/1-12/31 & 4/1-4/30; 5:30 pm-10 pm. **Closed:** 12/24, 12/25, Sun & Mon. **Features:** casual dress; cocktail
　　Creative Bistro dining with emphasis on local seafood. Menu changes every 6 weeks. Smoke free premise
Cards: AE, DS, MC, VI.　　⊳

BUZZARDS BAY—3,300　　(See map p. 330; index p. 328)

LODGING

BAY MOTOR INN　　　　　　　　　　　**Phone:** (508)759-3989　　30
(AAA) [SAVE]　Fri & Sat 6/4-10/3　　　2P/1B: $79- 89　2P/2B: $89- 99　XP: $10　　F
　　Sun-Thurs 6/4-10/3　　　2P/1B: $72- 79　2P/2B: $82- 89　XP: $10　　F
◆　　Fri & Sat 5/1-6/3, 10/4-11/15
Motel　　& 4/1-4/30　　　　　2P/1B: $56- 72　2P/2B: $56- 72　XP: $10　　F
　　Sun-Thurs 5/1-6/3,
　　10/4-11/15 & 4/1-4/30　2P/1B: $46- 62　2P/2B: $46- 62　XP: $10　　F
Location: 0.5 mi w of the Bourne Rotary, exit 2 from SR 25. 223 Main St 02532. Fax: 508/759-3199. **Terms:** Ope
5/1-11/15 & 4/1-4/30; reserv deposit, 14 day notice; handling fee imposed; weekly rates; pets, must be attended. **Facility:** 1
rooms. Cottage style & motel units. 2 two-room efficiencies, $98-$110 in season for up to 2 persons & 1 studio efficienc
$85-$95 in season for up to 2 persons; 1 story; exterior corridors. **All Rooms:** combo or shower baths, extended cable T
Some Rooms: 3 efficiencies. **Cards:** AE, DS, MC, VI. **Special Amenities:** Free local telephone calls and preferred roo
(subject to availability with advanced reservations).　　🅢 🐾 🛁 🎥 ▣

RESTAURANT

LINDSEY'S FAMILY RESTAURANT　**Lunch:** $5-$11　　**Dinner:** $8-$19　　**Phone:** 508/759-5544　　14
◆◆　　**Location:** 1 mi w on US 6 & SR 28; 2 mi nw of Bourne rotary. 3138 Cranberry Hwy 02532. **Hours:** 11:3
American　　am-9 pm. **Closed:** 12/25. **Features:** casual dress; children's menu; carryout; cocktails & lounge. A loc
　　favorite since 1948. Old-fashioned, homestyle cooking featuring fresh local seafood. **Cards:** AE, DS, MC, VI
　　⊳

CENTERVILLE—9,200   (See map p. 330; index p. 326)

LODGINGS

ADAM'S TERRACE GARDENS INN   Rates Subject to Change   Phone: (508)775-4707   169
      5/21-9/15 [BP]   1P: $50- 90   2P/1B: $75- 110 2P/2B: $75- 110 XP: $5-20   F10
◆◆   5/1-5/20 & 9/16-4/30 [BP]   1P: $40- 70   2P/1B: $60- 90 2P/2B: $60- 90 XP: $5-20   F10
Bed &   **Location:** 0.9 mi s of SR 28. 539 Main St 02632. Fax: 508/775-4707. **Terms:** Reserv deposit, 14 day notice;
Breakfast   handling fee imposed. **Facility:** 8 rooms. Originally built in 1830 for Captain John Baker. 2 stories; interior corridors; smoke free premises; street parking only. **Cards:** AE, DS, MC, VI.   ☎ 🐾 ✕

CENTERVILLE CORNERS MOTOR LODGE   Guaranteed Rates   Phone: (508)775-7223   170
🅰🅰   7/23-8/22 [CP]   1P: $110- 130   2P/1B: $110- 130 2P/2B: $110- 130 XP: $15   F14
   7/1-7/22 & 8/23-9/5 [CP]   1P: $105- 120   2P/1B: $105- 120 2P/2B: $105- 120 XP: $15   F14
◆◆   5/14-6/30 & 9/6-10/10 [EP]   1P: $60- 80   2P/1B: $60- 80 2P/2B: $60- 80 XP: $15   F14
Motel   5/1-5/13, 10/11-10/30 &
   4/15-4/30 [EP]   1P: $42- 48   2P/1B: $42- 48 2P/2B: $42- 48 XP: $10-15   F14
Location: 1 mi s of SR 28 at jct S Main St & Craigville Beach Rd. 369 S Main St 02632 (PO Box 507). Fax: 508/775-4147.
Terms: Open 5/1-10/30 & 4/15-4/30; reserv deposit, 7 day notice; weekly rates; package plans, off season; 2 night min stay,
weekends 5/15-10/15; pets, $5 extra charge. **Facility:** 48 rooms. Village setting. Most units with 2 double beds. 1 one-room
efficiency, $120-$140 in season for up to 5 persons; 1 two-room efficiency, $130-$150 in season for up to 5 persons; 2 stories;
exterior corridors; heated indoor pool, saunas. **All Rooms:** extended cable TV. **Some Rooms:** 2 efficiencies. **Cards:** AE,
DS, MC, VI. *(See color ad below)*   🐾 🛄 🖥 📠 🅗 ✕

RESTAURANT

HEARTH'N KETTLE RESTAURANT & BAKERY   **Lunch:** $5-$8   **Dinner:** $4-$11   **Phone:** 508/775-8878   80
◆   **Location:** On SR 28 behind Bell Tower Mall; 4 mi s of jct SR 149 & 28. 23 Richardson Rd 02632. **Hours:** 6
American   am-9 pm. Closed: 12/25. **Features:** casual dress; children's menu; health conscious menu; carryout; beer &
   wine only. Very popular; cozy, friendly family dining. Breakfast avail all day. Fine homemade bread & pastry.
Cards: AE, DS, MC, VI.   ✕

CHATHAM—6,600   (See map p. 330; index p. 325)

LODGINGS

THE BRADFORD OF CHATHAM   Guaranteed Rates   Phone: (508)945-1030   133
🅰🅰   6/25-9/6 [CP]   1P: $155- 285   2P/1B: $155- 285 2P/2B: $155- 285 XP: $25
   9/7-10/11 [CP]   1P: $115- 245   2P/1B: $115- 245 2P/2B: $115- 245 XP: $25
◆◆◆   10/12-1/3 [CP]   1P: $95- 205   2P/1B: $95- 205 2P/2B: $95- 205 XP: $25
Complex   **Location:** Center; just off Main St. 26 Cross St 02633 (PO Box 750). Fax: 508/945-9652. **Terms:** Open
6/25-1/3; age restrictions may apply; check-in 4 pm; reserv deposit, 14 day notice, 21 day 6/1-9/30; handling
fee imposed; package plans. **Facility:** 35 rooms. Inviting inn & motel rooms on nicely landscaped grounds. Some rooms with
fireplace. One-bedroom suites avail; 1-2 stories; interior corridors; heated pool. **Dining:** Restaurant; breakfast avail 8-11 am.
All Rooms: combo or shower baths, extended cable TV. **Some Rooms:** whirlpools. **Cards:** AE, DS, MC, VI.
(See color ad p 338)   🍳 🕒 🛄 🍴 VCR 📠 ✕

CAPTAIN'S HOUSE INN OF CHATHAM   Rates Subject to Change   Phone: (508)945-0127   134
🅰🅰   5/1-10/31 [BP]   2P/1B: $165- 350
   11/1-4/30 [EP]   2P/1B: $145- 300
◆◆◆◆   **Location:** 0.8 mi n of the rotary on SR 28. 369 Old Harbor Rd 02633. Fax: 508/945-0866. **Terms:** Age
restrictions may apply; reserv deposit, 14 day notice; 3 night min stay, 7/1-9/30. **Facility:** 19 rooms. Elegantly
Bed &   furnished, spacious rooms with fine antiques. Circa 1839. 13 units with fireplace. 2 stories; interior/exterior cor-
Breakfast   ridors; smoke free premises. **Dining:** Afternoon tea. **Recreation:** bicycles, croquet. **All Rooms:** combo or
shower baths, extended cable TV. **Some Rooms:** color TV, whirlpools. **Cards:** AE, DS, MC, VI.
                    ✕ VCR 🖥 📠 🅗 ✕

(See map p. 330)

CARRIAGE HOUSE INN   Phone: (508)945-4688 120

AAA SAVE
◆◆◆
Bed &
Breakfast

5/1-6/24 & 9/7-10/28 [BP]	2P/1B:	$130- 155	
6/25-9/6 [BP]	2P/1B:	$155- 180	
10/29-4/30 [BP]	2P/1B:	$95- 120	

Location: 1 mi n of the rotary on SR 28S. 407 Old Harbor Rd 02633. Fax: 508/945-8909. **Terms:** Age restrictions may apply; reserv deposit, 14 day notice; handling fee imposed; 2 night min stay, 5/1-10/31. **Facility:** 6 rooms. Circa 1860. Comfortably decorated rooms with some antiques or reproductions. 2 rooms with canopy bed & 3 rooms with working fireplace. 2 stories; interior/exterior corridors; designated smoking area. **Dining:** Afternoon refreshments avail. **All Rooms:** combo or shower baths. **Cards:** AE, DS, MC, VI. 📺 🚭 🖨 🎁 ✕

CHATHAM HIGHLANDER   Rates Subject to Change   Phone: 508/945-9038 135

◆◆
Motel

6/18-9/6	1P: $104	2P/1B: $104- 124	2P/2B: $104- 114	XP: $10-20	D14
9/7-10/11	1P: $79	2P/1B: $79- 94	2P/2B: $79- 89	XP: $10-20	D14
5/21-6/17 & 10/12-11/30	1P: $69	2P/1B: $69- 84	2P/2B: $69- 89	XP: $10-15	D14
5/1-5/20 & 4/1-4/30	1P: $58	2P/1B: $58- 73	2P/2B: $58- 68	XP: $10-15	D14

Location: 0.5 mi w of the rotary on SR 28. 946 Main St 02633 (PO Box 326). Fax: 508/945-5731. **Terms:** Open 5/1-11/30 & 4/1-4/30; reserv deposit, 10 day notice; handling fee imposed; 2 night min stay, in season & weekends. **Facility:** 27 rooms. Nicely kept. 1 story; exterior corridors. **Some Rooms:** 2 efficiencies. **Cards:** DS, MC, VI. 🏊 🎁 ✕

CHATHAM MOTEL   Phone: (508)945-2630 136

AAA SAVE
◆◆
Motel

7/1-9/10	1P: $110- 150	2P/1B: $115- 160	2P/2B: $115- 175
5/1-6/30 & 9/11-10/31	1P: $70- 120	2P/1B: $75- 120	2P/2B: $75- 120

Location: 1.8 mi w of the rotary, on SR 28. 1487 Main St 02633. **Terms:** Open 5/1-10/31; reserv deposit, 14 day notice; 2 night min stay, weekends in season. **Facility:** 32 rooms. Back from highway in pine grove & landscaped grounds. 1 story; exterior corridors; playground. **Recreation:** grills, shuffleboard. **Cards:** MC, VI.
Special Amenities: Free local telephone calls. *(See color ad below)* 🏊 ✕ 🎥 🖨 🎁 ✕

(See map p. 330)

CHATHAM TOWN HOUSE INN
AAA
◆◆◆
Country Inn

	Guaranteed Rates			Phone: (508)945-2180		121
6/25-9/6 [BP]	1P: $195- 310	2P/1B: $195- 310	2P/2B: $225- 295	XP: $25		
5/21-6/24 & 9/7-10/31 [BP]	1P: $145- 285	2P/1B: $145- 285	2P/2B: $195- 285	XP: $25		
5/1-5/20 & 11/1-4/30 [BP]	1P: $115- 275	2P/1B: $115- 275	2P/2B: $165- 275	XP: $25		

Location: Center; just e of the rotary. 11 Library Ln 02633. Fax: 508/945-3990. **Terms:** Age restrictions may apply; reserv deposit, 21 day notice, 60 day for cottages; handling fee imposed; 3 night min stay, in season. **Facility:** 25 rooms. 1880's sea captain house with eclectic decor. 2 two-bedroom units. 2 housekeeping cottages with fireplace & laundry, $2625 weekly in season for up to 4 persons; 2 stories; interior/exterior corridors; designated smoking area; heated pool, whirlpool. **Dining:** Restaurant; 8 am-10 & 5-9 pm; 11/1-4/30 to 10 am; snacks served at pool bar 11:30 am-6 pm in summer.; $16-$25; cocktails; Reservations suggested; afternoon tea. **All Rooms:** combo or shower baths. **Cards:** AE, CB, DI, DS, JC, MC, VI. (See color ad below)

CHATHAM WAYSIDE INN
AAA
◆◆◆
Complex

	Guaranteed Rates			Phone: (508)945-5550		131
6/25-9/6	1P: $165- 375	2P/1B: $165- 375	2P/2B: $205- 375	XP: $20		F12
5/21-6/24 & 9/7-10/11	1P: $135- 285	2P/1B: $135- 285	2P/2B: $165- 285	XP: $20		F12
5/1-5/20, 10/12-1/4 &						
1/16-4/30	1P: $95- 230	2P/1B: $95- 230	2P/2B: $120- 230	XP: $20		F12

Location: 0.3 mi e of the rotary. 512 Main St 02633 (PO Box 685). Fax: 508/945-3407. **Terms:** Open 5/1-1/4 & 1/16-4/30; check-in 4 pm; reserv deposit, 14 day notice; handling fee imposed; 2 night min stay, in season. **Facility:** 56 rooms. Restored 1860 inn. Variety of room types & styles, some with fireplace. 3 stories; interior corridors; heated pool. **Dining:** Restaurant; 8 am-9 pm; $12-$22; cocktails. **Services:** giftshop. **All Rooms:** combo or shower baths, extended cable TV. **Some Rooms:** whirlpools. **Cards:** AE, DS, MC, VI. (See color ad below)

Check out our **bold** listings!

(See map p. 330)

THE CRANBERRY INN AT CHATHAM   Rates Subject to Change   **Phone:** (508)945-9232   122
◆◆◆   6/25-9/7 [BP]   1P: $165- 255   2P/1B: $165- 255   2P/2B: $175- 255   XP: $30
Bed &   5/14-6/24 & 9/8-10/30 [BP]   1P: $120- 235   2P/1B: $120- 235   2P/2B: $130- 235   XP: $30
Breakfast   5/1-5/13 & 10/31-4/30 [BP]   1P: $85- 175   2P/1B: $85- 175   2P/2B: $89- 175   XP: $30
Location: 0.5 mi e of the rotary. 359 Main St 02633. Fax: 508/945-3769. **Terms:** Age restrictions may apply; reserv deposit, 14 day notice; handling fee imposed; 3 night min stay, weekends 5/15-11/30. **Facility:** 18 rooms. Restored circa 1830 structure. 1 two-bedroom unit. 8 rooms with fireplace, 4 with deck; 2 stories; interior corridors; designated smoking area. **All Rooms:** combo or shower baths. **Cards:** AE, DS, MC, VI.

CYRUS KENT HOUSE INN   **Phone:** (508)945-9104   123
AAA SAVE   6/15-10/14 [CP]   2P/1B: $135- 250   2P/2B: $135- 250   XP: $20   F
   5/1-6/14 & 4/15-4/30 [CP]   2P/1B: $110- 200   2P/2B: $110- 200   XP: $20   F
◆◆◆   10/15-4/14 [CP]   2P/1B: $95- 180   2P/2B: $95- 180   XP: $20   F
Bed &   **Location:** Center, just off Main St. 63 Cross St 02633. Fax: 508/945-9104. **Terms:** Age restrictions may
Breakfast   apply; reserv deposit, 10 day notice. **Facility:** 10 rooms. Captain's house built in 1877. Nicely landscaped. 2 stories; interior/exterior corridors; designated smoking area. **All Rooms:** combo or shower baths, extended cable TV. **Cards:** AE, MC, VI. **Special Amenities: Free breakfast and free room upgrade (subject to availability with advanced reservations).**

THE DOLPHIN OF CHATHAM INN & MOTEL   Rates Subject to Change   **Phone:** (508)945-0070   124
AAA   Fri & Sat 5/14-10/18   1P: $144- 204   2P/1B: $144- 204   2P/2B: $144- 275   XP: $20
   Sun-Thurs 5/14-10/18   1P: $110- 154   2P/1B: $110- 154   2P/2B: $110- 209   XP: $20
◆◆◆   5/1-5/13 & 10/19-4/30   1P: $84- 124   2P/1B: $84- 124   2P/2B: $94- 169   XP: $20
Complex   **Location:** 0.5 mi e of the rotary. 352 Main St 02633. Fax: 508/945-5945. **Terms:** Age restrictions may apply; reserv deposit, 14 day notice; handling fee imposed; package plans, off season. **Facility:** 36 rooms. Motel & inn rooms, some located in 1805 sea captain's home. 3 two-bedroom housekeeping cottages, $950-$1500 weekly up to 4 persons; 3-night min stay in 3 efficiencies, $84-$154; 1-2 stories; interior/exterior corridors; heated pool, whirlpool. **Dining:** Breakfast buffet, poolside lunch. **All Rooms:** combo or shower baths, extended cable TV. **Some Rooms:** whirlpools. **Cards:** AE, DI, DS, MC, VI.

HAWTHORNE MOTEL   Rates Subject to Change   **Phone:** 508/945-0372   127
◆◆   6/25-9/6   1P: $130- 160   2P/1B: $130- 160   2P/2B: $130- 160   XP: $15-20   D
Motel   5/14-6/24 & 9/7-10/12   1P: $100- 130   2P/1B: $100- 130   2P/2B: $100- 130   XP: $15-20   D
Location: 0.8 mi e of the rotary via Main St, 0.5 mi n. 196 Shore Rd 02633. **Terms:** Open 5/14-10/12; age restrictions may apply; reserv deposit, 14 day notice; handling fee imposed. **Facility:** 27 rooms. Landscaped lawns overlooking ocean. 4-night min stay in motel & efficiencies, 7-night min stay for 2-bedroom housekeeping cottage, $275 for up to 2 persons, $20 extra person; 1 story; exterior corridors. **Recreation:** swimming, fishing. **Some Rooms:** 10 efficiencies, kitchen. **Cards:** AE, MC, VI.

MOSES NICKERSON HOUSE INN   Rates Subject to Change   **Phone:** (508)945-5859   128
AAA   5/21-10/12   1P: $129- 179   2P/1B: $129- 179   XP: $25
◆◆◆   5/1-5/20 & 10/13-4/30   1P: $95- 139   2P/1B: $95- 139
Bed &   **Location:** 0.8 mi n of the rotary on SR 28S. 364 Old Harbor Rd 02633. Fax: 508/945-7087. **Terms:** Age
Breakfast   restrictions may apply; reserv deposit, 14 day notice; handling fee imposed; 2 night min stay, in season. **Facility:** 7 rooms. A former sea captain's house furnished with many antiques & reproductions. 3 units with working fireplace. 2 stories; interior corridors; smoke free premises. **Recreation:** bocci ball, croquet. **All Rooms:** combo or shower baths, extended cable TV. **Cards:** AE, DS, MC, VI.

THE OLD HARBOR INN   Rates Subject to Change   **Phone:** (508)945-4434   129
AAA SAVE   6/15-9/13 [CP]   1P: $139- 239   2P/1B: $139- 239   2P/2B: $139- 239   XP: $25
   5/1-6/14 & 9/14-11/1 [CP]   1P: $129- 189   2P/1B: $129- 189   2P/2B: $129- 189   XP: $25
◆◆◆   11/2-4/30 [CP]   1P: $99- 169   2P/1B: $99- 169   2P/2B: $99- 169   XP: $25
Bed &   **Location:** On SR 28 just n of rotary. 22 Old Harbor Rd 02633. Fax: 508/945-7665. **Terms:** Age restrictions
Breakfast   may apply; reserv deposit, 14 day notice; handling fee imposed; weekly rates; 2 night min stay, in season & weekends. **Facility:** 8 rooms. English country decor with some antiques. Located in a quiet residential area. 2 units with working fireplace. 1-bedroom suite; 2 stories; interior corridors; smoke free premises. **All Rooms:** extended cable TV. **Cards:** AE, CB, DI, DS, MC, VI. **Special Amenities: Early check-in/late check-out and free local telephone calls.**

PLEASANT BAY VILLAGE   **Phone:** (508)945-1133   130
AAA SAVE   8/1-9/6   1P: $155- 265   2P/1B: $155- 255   2P/2B: $195- 265   XP: $15-20
   6/26-7/31   1P: $125- 215   2P/1B: $125- 205   2P/2B: $155- 215   XP: $20
◆◆◆   5/1-6/25 & 9/7-10/31   1P: $115- 185   2P/1B: $115- 155   2P/2B: $135- 185   XP: $20
Motel   **Location:** 3 mi n on SR 28. 1191 Orleans Rd 02633 (PO Box 772). Fax: 508/945-9701. **Terms:** Open 5/1-10/31; handling fee imposed; weekly rates; 2 night min stay, weekends in season. **Facility:** 58 rooms. Quiet, beautiful grounds with unique landscaping. Meticulously maintained motel rooms, efficiencies & studio apartments. 8 two-bedroom suites with living room, $395-$415 for up to 4 persons in season; 1 story; exterior corridors; designated smoking area; heated pool; playground. **Dining:** Breakfast room 8-11 am, poolside lunch 7/1-8/31, noon-2 & 6-9 pm. **Recreation:** shuffleboard. **All Rooms:** combo or shower baths, extended cable TV. **Cards:** AE, MC, VI. **Special Amenities: Free local telephone calls and free newspaper.**

PORT FORTUNE INN   Rates Subject to Change   **Phone:** (508)945-0792   125
AAA   6/11-9/11 [CP]   1P: $130- 170   2P/1B: $130- 170   2P/2B: $150   XP: $20
◆◆◆   5/1-6/10 & 9/12-10/31 [CP]   1P: $110- 155   2P/1B: $110- 155   2P/2B: $130   XP: $20
Bed &   11/1-4/30 [CP]   1P: $85- 115   2P/1B: $85- 115   2P/2B: $105   XP: $20
Breakfast   **Location:** 0.9 mi e of rotary, just s at Shore Rd. 201 Main St 02633. Fax: 508/945-0792. **Terms:** Age restrictions may apply; reserv deposit, 10 day notice; handling fee imposed; 2 night min stay, weekends in season. **Facility:** 13 rooms. Charming country decor. 2 stories; interior/exterior corridors; designated smoking area. **All Rooms:** combo or shower baths. **Some Rooms:** color TV. **Cards:** AE, MC, VI.

(See map p. 330)

THE SEAFARER OF CHATHAM
Phone: 508/432-1739   139

	7/16-9/6	2P/1B:	$125- 150	2P/2B:	$125- 150	XP: $10-15
	6/18-7/15 & 9/7-9/23	2P/1B:	$95- 125	2P/2B:	$95- 125	XP: $10-15
	5/14-6/17 & 9/24-10/10	2P/1B:	$65- 95	2P/2B:	$65- 95	XP: $10-15
Motel	5/1-5/13, 10/11-1/3 &					
	3/1-4/30	2P/1B:	$55- 95	2P/2B:	$55- 95	XP: $10-15

Location: 2.8 mi w of the rotary on SR 28. Rt 28 & Ridgevale Rd 02633-1020. **Terms:** Open 5/1-1/3 & 3/1-4/30; reserv deposit, 15 day notice; handling fee imposed; 2 night min stay, or 3 in season. **Facility:** 20 rooms. Quiet country setting. Attractive hand-stenciled rooms. 4 night min stay for 7 efficiencies, 3 night off season; 1 story; exterior corridors. **All Rooms:** extended cable TV. **Cards:** AE, MC, VI. *(See color ad below)*

RESTAURANTS

CAMPARI'S ITALIAN BISTRO & BENNEDETTO'S
Dinner: $17-$24
Phone: 508/945-9123   62

Italian
Location: On SR 28, 4.3 mi s of jct SR 39. 323 Orleans Rd 02650. **Hours:** 11:30 am-3 & 5-9 pm, in summer to 10 pm. Closed: 12/25. **Reservations:** suggested. **Features:** casual dress; cocktails & lounge; a la carte. Innovative dishes, served in a casual atmosphere. Also family styled restaurant featuring pizza, burgers & pasta from $7-15. Smoke free premises. **Cards:** AE, MC, VI.

(See map p. 330)

CHRISTIAN'S
◆◆◆
Continental
Dinner: $8-$22   **Phone:** 508/945-3362 ⑤⑨
Location: Center, 0.7 mi n of rotary. 443 Main St 02633. **Hours:** 4 pm-10 pm; piano bar 8 pm-midnight. Closed: 12/25. **Reservations:** suggested. **Features:** casual dress; cocktails & lounge; entertainment; a la carte. Casual upstairs with bar. Local seafood specialties. **Cards:** AE, DS, MC, VI. ⊠

THE IMPUDENT OYSTER
◆◆
American
Lunch: $6-$12   **Dinner:** $14-$25   **Phone:** 508/945-3545 ⑥④
Location: Off Main St; 0.3 mi e of rotary. 15 Chatham Bars Ave 02633. **Hours:** 11:30 am-3 & 5-10 pm, Sun noon-3 pm; closing hours may vary Mon-Sat. Closed: 11/25, 12/24 for dinner & 12/25. **Reservations:** suggested. **Features:** casual dress; children's menu; carryout; cocktails & lounge; minimum charge-$15 in summer; a la carte. Casual, popular restaurant. Specializing in uniquely prepared local seafood & cuisine with an international flavor. Smoke free premises. **Cards:** AE, MC, VI. ⊠

THE MAIN DINING ROOM OF THE CHATHAM BARS INN   **Dinner:** $25-$34   **Phone:** 508/945-0096 ⑥⓪
◆◆◆
Regional
American
Location: 0.8 mi e of the rotary thru Main St & 0.8 mi n. 297 Shore Rd 02633. **Hours:** Open 5/1-11/12 & 4/4-4/30; 7:30 am-11 & 6-10 pm. **Reservations:** suggested. **Features:** semi-formal attire; children's menu; cocktails & lounge. Creative Regional American cuisine served in formal dining room overlooking Nantucket Sound. 17% service charge added to the check. Sun evening buffet 7/1-8/31 $45 per person. Smoke free premises. **Cards:** AE, DI, MC, VI. ⊠

PATE'S
◆◆
Steak and
Seafood
Dinner: $14-$21   **Phone:** 508/945-9777 ⑥①
Location: 1.3 mi w of the rotary, on SR 28. 1260 Main St 02633. **Hours:** Open 5/1-1/15 & 4/26-4/30; 5:30 pm-10 pm; Sun-Thurs 9/7-1/15 to 9 pm. Closed: 11/25, 12/24 & 12/25. **Features:** casual dress; children's menu; cocktails & lounge; a la carte. Popular, casual restaurant. Open-hearth grilled items. **Cards:** AE, CB, DI, DS, MC, VI. ⊠

COTUIT—2,400   (See map p. 330; index p. 329)

RESTAURANT

THE REGATTA OF COTUIT AT THE CROCKER HOUSE   Historical **Dinner:** $19-$28 **Phone:** 508/428-5715 ⑰⓪
◆◆◆
American
Location: Just ne of jct SR 130. 4631 Falmouth Rd, Rt 28 02635. **Hours:** 5:30 pm-10 pm. **Reservations:** suggested. **Features:** semi-formal attire; cocktails & lounge. Intimate dining in a 200-year old stagecoach inn with excellent service. Extensive menus feature local seafood & some continental cuisine. **Cards:** AE, MC, VI. ⊠

CRAIGVILLE—100   (See map p. 332; index p. 323)

LODGING

TRADE WINDS INN   Rates Subject to Change   **Phone:** (508)775-0365 ㉑
Ⓐ
◆◆◆
Motel
6/13-9/2 [CP]   2P/1B: $99- 169 2P/2B: $99- 169 XP: $10
5/1-6/12 & 9/3-10/26 [EP]   2P/1B: $85- 110 2P/2B: $85- 110 XP: $10
Location: At Craigville Beach. 780 Craigville Beach Rd 02636 (PO Box 477, CENTERVILLE, 02632). **Terms:** Open 5/1-10/26; reserv deposit, 15 day notice; handling fee imposed; weekly rates. **Facility:** 35 rooms. Quiet hillside setting on attractive grounds overlooking the ocean & beach. Many rooms with balcony or patio. 3 efficiencies $150-$225 for up to 2 persons; $95-$150 off season; 2 stories; exterior corridors; putting green; beach. **All Rooms:** combo or shower baths, extended cable TV. **Some Rooms:** 3 efficiencies. **Cards:** AE, MC, VI. 🅱⊠🖨🔒
(See color ad below)

For **guaranteed** rates, you MUST show your membership card.

DENNIS—13,900   (See map p. 330; index p. 326)

LODGING

ISAIAH HALL B & B INN
🔶🔶🔶

Historic Bed & Breakfast

	Guaranteed Rates			Phone: (508)385-9928	180
6/11-9/6 [CP]	1P: $83- 118	2P/1B: $107- 156	2P/2B: $107- 156	XP: $15	F12
9/7-10/16 [CP]	1P: $79- 118	2P/1B: $102- 149	2P/2B: $102- 149	XP: $15	F12
5/1-6/10 [CP]	1P: $75- 112	2P/1B: $98- 142	2P/2B: $98- 142	XP: $15	F12

Location: Center, 0.5 mi ne of SR 6A via Hope Ln & Whig St. 152 Whig St 02638 (PO Box 1007). **Fax:** 508/385-5879. **Terms:** Open 5/1-10/16; age restrictions may apply; reserv deposit, 14 day notice; weekly rates. **Facility:** 10 rooms. Original farmhouse built 1857 in Greek Revival style & located in quiet residential area. Cozy, charming rooms decorated in old New England style. 1 one-bedroom suite, $156 in season; 1 fireplace unit, $122. 2-3 night min stay weekends; 2 stories; interior corridors; smoke free premises. **All Rooms:** combo or shower baths, extended cable TV. **Cards:** AE, MC, VI. *(See ad below)*

[VCR] [☎] [🖨] [X]

RESTAURANT

GINA'S
🔶🔶
Italian

Lunch: $6-$8	Dinner: $10-$18	Phone: 508-385-3213	84

Location: 2 mi nw of SR 6A & center, via New Boston Rd & Beach St, follow signs. 134 Taunton Ave 02638. **Hours:** Open 5/1-11/30 & 4/1-4/30; 11:30 am-3 & 5-10 pm, Sat & Sun from 5 pm. Closed: Mon-Wed, 4/1-5/30 & 10/1-11/30. **Features:** No A/C; casual dress; children's menu; carryout; cocktails & lounge; a la carte. Casual beach house; quality seafood, summer patio. **Cards:** AE, MC, VI.

[X]

DENNIS PORT—2,800   (See map p. 332; index p. 324)

LODGINGS

COLONIAL VILLAGE MOTEL
🔶🔶🔶 [SAVE]

🔶🔶
Motel

	Phone: 508-398-2071	50

	1P	2P/1B	2P/2B	XP
7/17-8/22	1P: $94- 129	2P/1B: $94- 129	2P/2B: $94- 129	XP: $10
7/3-7/16 & 8/23-9/6	1P: $85- 110	2P/1B: $85- 110	2P/2B: $85- 110	XP: $10
6/19-7/2	1P: $70- 100	2P/1B: $70- 100	2P/2B: $70- 100	XP: $10
5/14-6/18 & 9/7-10/14	1P: $59- 75	2P/1B: $59- 75	2P/2B: $59- 75	XP: $10

Location: From jct SR 28, 0.5 mi s on Depot St, just e. 426 Lower County Rd 02639 (PO Box 521). **Fax:** 508/398-2071. **Terms:** Open 5/14-10/14; reserv deposit, 14 day notice; package plans; 7 night min stay, in cottages. **Facility:** 59 rooms. In pine grove & on landscaped grounds. Motel rooms & cottages with fireplace. 29 kitchenettes. 11 two-bedroom units. Cottages, $630-$750 weekly, $350-$500 weekly off season; 2 stories; exterior corridors; heated indoor pool, sauna, whirlpool. **Dining:** Restaurant nearby. **All Rooms:** combo or shower baths, extended cable TV. **Some Rooms:** 10 kitchens. **Cards:** AE, DS, MC, VI.

[🐕] [🏊] [🍴] [📺] [🖨] [X]

(See map p. 332)

CORSAIR & CROSS RIP RESORT MOTELS   Guaranteed Rates   Phone: (508)398-2279   52

6/25-8/28	1P: $115- 130	2P/1B: $115- 130	2P/2B: $145- 225	XP: $10-25
6/11-6/24 & 8/29-9/11	1P: $75- 89	2P/1B: $75- 89	2P/2B: $95- 165	XP: $10-25
5/1-6/10, 9/12-10/24 & 4/1-4/30	1P: $54- 62	2P/1B: $54- 62	2P/2B: $68- 145	XP: $10-25

Motel

Location: 1 mi se of jct SR 28 via Depot St, on the ocean. 41 Chase Ave 02639. Fax: 508/760-6681.
Terms: Open 5/1-10/24 & 4/1-4/30; reserv deposit, 14 day notice; handling fee imposed; weekly rates; 4 night min stay, in season. **Facility:** 47 rooms. Beachfront, side by side motels. 2 stories; exterior corridors; beach, heated pool, whirlpool, indoor heated pool across the street. **Recreation:** swimming. **All Rooms:** extended cable TV. **Some Rooms:** 40 efficiencies. **Cards:** AE, MC, VI. *(See color ad below)*

EDGEWATER BEACH RESORT   Rates Subject to Change   Phone: 508/398-6922   53

6/18-9/5	1P: $95	2P/1B: $95- 200	2P/2B: $250	XP: $15	D
5/12-6/17 & 9/6-10/11	1P: $70- 130	2P/1B: $70- 130	2P/2B: $165	XP: $10	D
5/1-5/11, 10/12-11/13 & 3/9-4/30	1P: $42- 95	2P/1B: $42- 95	2P/2B: $115	XP: $10	D

Motel

Location: 1.3 mi s of SR 28 via Belmont Ave, on the ocean. 95 Chase Ave 02639 (PO Box 68). Fax: 508/760-3447. **Terms:** Open 5/11-11/13 & 3/9-4/30; reserv deposit, 14 day notice; handling fee imposed; package plans, off season; 3 night min stay, in season. **Facility:** 88 rooms. Beachfront, many rooms with balcony. 14 units with Murphy beds in 1-story building across hwy. 2 two-bedroom units. 2 two-bedroom units with kitchen, $230 in season for up to 4 persons; 2 stories; exterior corridors; putting green; beach, heated indoor/outdoor pool, sauna, whirlpool. **Recreation:** swimming; Shuffle board. **All Rooms:** combo or shower baths, extended cable TV. **Some Rooms:** 65 efficiencies. **Cards:** AE, DS, MC, VI. *(See color ad below)*

Look for the AAA in our listings!

(See map p. 332)

HOLIDAY HILL MOTOR INN   Rates Subject to Change   Phone: 508/394-5577   **54**

	6/25-8/28	1P:	$59- 89	2P/1B:	$59- 89	2P/2B:	$59- 89	XP:	$8
	8/29-9/5	1P:	$49- 69	2P/1B:	$49- 69	2P/2B:	$49- 69	XP:	$8
	6/18-6/24	1P:	$45- 69	2P/1B:	$45- 69	2P/2B:	$45- 69	XP:	$8
Motel	5/1-6/17 & 9/6-10/11	1P:	$30- 49	2P/1B:	$30- 49	2P/2B:	$30- 49	XP:	$8

Location: On SR 28, 0.8 mi e of jct SR 134. 352 Main St 02639. **Terms:** Open 5/1-10/11; reserv deposit, 7 day notice. **Facility:** 56 rooms. Large rooms. 2 stories; exterior corridors; heated pool. Fee: miniature golf. **Dining:** Restaurant nearby. **Services:** giftshop. **Recreation:** game room. **All Rooms:** extended cable TV. **Cards:** AE, DI, DS, MC, VI. *(See ad below)*   🛎 ▥ VCR 🔌 ✕

THE ROSE PETAL BED & BREAKFAST   Rates Subject to Change   Phone: (508)398-8470   **49**

	6/18-9/19 [BP]	1P:	$69- 98	2P/1B:	$69- 98	2P/2B:	$69- 98	XP:	$10-12	F3
	5/1-6/17, 9/20-10/24 &									
	4/3-4/30 [BP]	1P:	$65- 89	2P/1B:	$65- 89	2P/2B:	$65- 89	XP:	$10-12	F3
Bed &	10/25-4/2 [BP]	1P:	$62- 75	2P/1B:	$62- 75	2P/2B:	$62- 75	XP:	$10	F3
Breakfast										

Location: 0.5 mi s of SR 28; 1 mi e of SR 134. 152 Sea St 02639 (PO Box 974). **Terms:** Reserv deposit, 14 day notice; handling fee imposed; weekly rates. **Facility:** 3 rooms. All rooms located on the 2nd floor of this 1872 home. Beautiful rose gardens around white picket fence. Early American motif with contemporary baths. Walk to beach. 2 stories; interior/exterior corridors; smoke free premises. **Dining:** Restaurant nearby. **Cards:** AE, MC, VI.   🛎 CTV ▥ 🔌 ✕

SPOUTER WHALE MOTOR INN   Rates Subject to Change   Phone: 508/398-8010   **56**

	7/3-8/23		2P/2B:	$100- 162	XP: $15
Motel	6/15-7/2 & 8/24-9/20		2P/2B:	$65- 95	XP: $10
	6/1-6/14 & 9/21-9/26		2P/2B:	$40- 75	XP: $10
	5/1-5/31, 9/27-10/23 &				
	4/3-4/30		2P/2B:	$38- 60	XP: $10

Location: 0.8 mi s of SR 28 via Depot St, on the ocean. 405 Old Wharf Rd 02639 (PO Box 127). **Terms:** Open 5/1-10/23 & 4/8-4/30; reserv deposit, 14 day notice; handling fee imposed; 2 night min stay, weekends in season. **Facility:** 38 rooms. Exceptionally well-kept, telephones for outgoing calls only. 6 efficiencies, $130-$155; $45-$60 off season, for up to 2 persons; 2 stories; exterior corridors; designated smoking area; oceanfront; heated pool.   🛎 🔌 ✕

RESTAURANTS

CAPTAIN WILLIAM'S HOUSE   **Dinner:** $13-$19   Phone: 508/398-3910   **30**

American   **Location:** 0.5 mi s of SR 28. 106 Depot St 02639. **Hours:** Open 5/1-11/28 & 4/1-4/30; 4:30 pm-10 pm. Closed: Mon & Tues 4/1-4/30 & 11/1-11/28. **Reservations:** suggested. **Features:** casual dress; children's menu; early bird specials; cocktails; a la carte. Several cozy dining rooms in restored sea captain's home. Lobster also featured. **Cards:** AE, DI, DS, MC, VI.   ✕

CLANCY'S   **Lunch:** $5-$10   **Dinner:** $10-$17   Phone: 508/394-6661   **31**

American   **Location:** 0.8 mi n of SR 28; just n on Depot Rd, 0.5 mi nw. 8 Upper County Rd 02639. **Hours:** 11:30 am-10 pm, Fri & Sat 6/15-9/1 to midnight. Closed: 11/25 & 12/25. **Features:** casual dress; Sunday brunch; children's menu; carryout; cocktails & lounge; a la carte. Dining rooms & open air deck overlook river & marsh. Natural woods, brass & etched glass highlight dining room decor. Generous portions. **Cards:** AE, DI, MC, VI.   ✕

EAST DENNIS—2,600   (See map p. 330; index p. 326)

LODGING

SESUIT HARBOR MOTEL   Phone: (508)385-3326   **185**

	6/15-9/14			2P/1B:	$80- 105	2P/2B:	$88- 110	XP: $6-12	D12
	5/1-6/14, 9/15-10/31 &								
	4/15-4/30			2P/1B:	$67- 87	2P/2B:	$74- 92	XP: $9	D12
Motel	11/1-4/14	1P:	$55	2P/1B:	$60	2P/2B:	$60- 65	XP: $6	D12

Location: On SR 6A, 0.3 mi w of jct SR 134. 1421 Main St, Rt 6A 02639 (PO Box D). Fax: 508/385-3326. **Terms:** Reserv deposit, 14 day notice, 30 day for housekeeping units; weekly rates. **Facility:** 19 rooms. Back from hwy. Exceptionally well-kept. 5 housekeeping units, $650-$890 weekly. Check-out 10 am in housekeeping units; 2 stories; exterior corridors. **All Rooms:** combo or shower baths, extended cable TV. **Cards:** MC, VI.   🛎 🔌 ✕

EAST FALMOUTH—5,600

RESTAURANT

IGUANA'S MEXICAN/SOUTHWESTERN RESTAURANT & BAR **Lunch:** $8-$14 **Dinner:** $8-$14 **Phone:** 508/540-6000
◆◆ **Location:** 1 mi e on SR 28 in Tataket Square. 31 Teaticket Hwy 02536. **Hours:** 11:30 am-10 pm; to
American midnight, 5/22-9/30. Closed: 12/25. **Features:** casual dress; children's menu; carryout; cocktails & lounge.
Casual southwestern style atmosphere. **Cards:** AE, MC, VI. ⊠

EASTHAM—1,100 (See map p. 330; index p. 327)

LODGINGS

ANCHORAGE ON THE COVE Guaranteed Rates **Phone:** 508/255-1442 `227`
Ⓐ 6/26-10/30 Wkly 2P/2B:$1300-1600 XP: $70 D
◆◆ 5/1-6/25 Wkly 2P/2B: $700- 900 XP: $70 D
Cottage **Location:** 0.3 mi n of Eastham/Orleans Rotary. 450 State Hwy, US 6 02642 (PO Box 474, ORLEANS,
02653). **Terms:** Open 5/1-10/30; reserv deposit, 30 day notice; handling fee imposed. **Facility:** 4 rooms.
2-bedroom housekeeping cottages with fireplace, overlooking town cove waterfront, weekly rentals only. Rates
for up to 4 persons in season; 2 persons off season; 1-2 stories; exterior corridors; boat dock. **Recreation:** fishing;
badminton, croquet. Rental: boats. **All Rooms:** shower baths, extended cable TV. 🖭⊠🖳🎦🖨

ASPINET COTTAGES & MOTEL EFFICIENCIES Rates Subject to Change **Phone:** 508/255-2835 `228`
Ⓐ All Year 1P: $61- 89 2P/1B: $61- 89 2P/2B: $79- 95 XP: $12
◆ **Location:** 0.8 mi n of Eastham/Orleans Rotary. 995 State Hwy, Rt 6 02642 (PO Box 505). **Terms:** Reserv
Complex deposit, 30 day notice; weekly rates; 2 night min stay, weekends. **Facility:** 10 rooms. Motel efficiencies,
1-bedroom housekeeping cottages on shaded grounds. Some units with rustic wood interior. 1 two-bedroom
unit. 4 housekeeping cottages, $495-$550 weekly in season; 1 deluxe cottage, $610-$640 weekly in season,
charge for linen in cottage units; 1 story; exterior corridors. **Recreation:** outdoor grill. **All Rooms:** combo or shower baths,
extended cable TV. **Some Rooms:** 5 kitchens. **Cards:** MC, VI. 🖳🞐🎦

CAPTAIN'S QUARTERS MOTEL Rates Subject to Change **Phone:** (508)255-5686 `230`
◆◆ 6/25-9/5 1P: $96- 126 2P/1B: $96- 126 2P/2B: $96- 126 XP: $12 F12
Motel 5/1-6/24, 9/6-11/15 &
4/1-4/30 1P: $60- 96 2P/1B: $60- 96 2P/2B: $60- 96 XP: $6 F12
Location: 2.3 mi n of National Seashore Visitor's Center. SR 6 02651 (PO Box 1896, NORTH EASTHAM).
Fax: 508/240-0280. **Terms:** Open 5/1-11/15 & 4/1-4/30; reserv deposit. **Facility:** 75 rooms. Large rooms. On spacious
grounds. 1 story; exterior corridors; heated pool; 2 tennis courts. **Services:** area transportation. **Recreation:** bicycles.
Cards: AE, CB, DI, DS, MC, VI. *(See color ad below)* 🕭🛆🞐⊠🖨🞐⊠

(See map p. 330)

CRANBERRY COTTAGES

◇◇◇◇

Cottage

Phone: 508/255-0602 **231**

Rates Subject to Change

	1P:		2P/1B:		2P/2B:		XP:	
7/1-9/6	1P: $80-	85	2P/1B:	$80	2P/2B:	$85	XP:	$10
6/1-6/30	1P: $60-	62	2P/1B:	$60	2P/2B:	$62	XP:	$10
9/7-10/2	1P: $54-	56	2P/1B:	$54	2P/2B:	$56	XP:	$10
10/3-11/30	1P: $42-	46	2P/1B:	$42-	46	2P/2B:	$46	XP:	$10

Location: 0.8 mi n of Eastham/Orleans Rotary. 785 State Hwy, US 6 02642. **Terms:** Open 6/1-11/30; reserv deposit, 14 day notice; handling fee imposed; weekly rates; 2 night min stay, weekends in season. **Facility:** 7 rooms. Cozy cottages in a quiet, wooded setting. A charming old Cape Cod ambiance. 1 story; exterior corridors. **All Rooms:** shower baths, extended cable TV. **Cards:** DI, MC, VI.

EAGLE WING MOTEL

◇◇◇◇

◇◇

Motel

Phone: 508/240-5656 **225**

Rates Subject to Change

	1P:		2P/1B:		2P/2B:		XP:	
6/25-9/5	1P: $80-	100	2P/1B:	$89-	102	2P/2B:	$89-	102	XP:	$12
5/14-6/24 & 9/6-10/12	1P: $52-	72	2P/1B:	$59-	79	2P/2B:	$59-	79	XP:	$8

Location: 0.8 mi n of Eastham/Orleans rotary. 960 Route 6 02642. **Terms:** Open 5/14-10/12; reserv deposit, 14 day notice; handling fee imposed. **Facility:** 19 rooms. Quaint guest units with honey enhancements. Adjacent to late 18th century home. 1 story; exterior corridors; smoke free premises. **All Rooms:** extended cable TV. **Cards:** DS, MC, VI.

FOUR POINTS HOTEL BY SHERATON

◇◇◇

Motor Inn

Phone: (508)255-5000 **235**

Rates Subject to Change

	1P:	2P/1B:	2P/2B:	XP:	
6/20-9/5 [BP]	1P: $173	2P/1B: $173	2P/2B: $173	XP: $10	F17
1/1-4/30 [EP]	1P: $119	2P/1B: $119	2P/2B: $119	XP: $10	F17
5/1-6/19 & 9/6-12/31 [BP]	1P: $101	2P/1B: $101	2P/2B: $101	XP: $10	F17

Location: 1 mi n of National Seashore Visitor's Center. 3800 Rt 6 02642. Fax: 508/240-1870. **Terms:** Reserv deposit; 2 night min stay, weekends off season. **Facility:** 107 rooms. Some units with private balcony. 2 stories; interior corridors; heated indoor pool; 2 lighted tennis courts. **Cards:** AE, DI, DS, MC, VI. *(See color ad below)*

GULL COTTAGES

◇◇◇◇

◇◇

Cottage

Phone: 508/255-4644 **237**

Rates Subject to Change

	1P:	2P/1B:	2P/2B:
6/12-8/27 Wkly		2P/1B: $525	2P/2B: $650
5/1-6/11 & 8/28-10/29 Dly	1P: $80		2P/2B: $95
10/30-4/30 Dly		2P/1B: $70	2P/2B: $85

Location: On US 6, 1 mi n of Eastham/Orleans Rotary. 885 State Hwy 02642. **Terms:** Reserv deposit, 30 day notice; weekly rates; 2 night min stay. **Facility:** 4 rooms. 2 cottages with fireplace. 3 two-bedroom housekeeping units, $625 weekly in season for up to 4 persons. 1 one-bedroom housekeeping unit, $510 in season for 2 persons; 1 story; exterior corridors. **All Rooms:** kitchens, combo or shower baths, extended cable TV.

MIDWAY MOTEL & COTTAGES

◇◇◇◇

◇◇

Motel

Phone: 508/255-3117 **233**

Guaranteed Rates

	1P:		2P/1B:		2P/2B:		XP:	
6/25-9/5	1P: $78-	84	2P/1B:	$78-	84	2P/2B:	$80-	86	XP:	$7	F16
6/11-6/24	1P: $58-	62	2P/1B:	$58		2P/2B:	$66	XP:	$7	F16
5/1-6/10, 9/6-10/30 &									
2/1-4/30	1P: $46-	50	2P/1B:	$46-	50	2P/2B:	$48-	54	XP:	$7	F16

Location: 2.5 mi n of National Seashore Center. 5460 State Hwy (US 6) 02651 (PO Box 1859, NORTH EASTHAM). Fax: 508/255-4235. **Terms:** Open 5/1-10/30 & 2/1-4/30; reserv deposit, 10 day notice; package plans; 2 night min stay, in season. **Facility:** 11 rooms. Carefully kept units in peaceful wooded setting. Complimentary coffee in common area. 1 two-bedroom unit, 1 three-bedroom unit. 1 efficiency, $600 weekly; 2 housekeeping cottages, $655-$780 weekly, in season. 2-bedroom motel room, $122 in season. Check-out 10 am in housekeeping units; 1 story; exterior corridors; playground. **Recreation:** badminton, horseshoes, paved bike trail, shuffleboard. Fee: bicycles. **All Rooms:** extended cable TV. **Cards:** AE, CB, DI, DS, MC, VI.

OCEAN VIEW MOTEL

◇◇◇◇

◇◇

Motel

Phone: 508/255-1600 **232**

Rates Subject to Change

	1P:		2P/1B:		2P/2B:		XP:	
6/25-9/6	1P: $78-	86	2P/1B:	$78-	86	2P/2B:	$84	XP:	$10	F12
5/1-6/24, 9/7-10/24 &									
2/11-4/30			2P/1B:	$47-	59	2P/2B:	$54-	59	XP:	$5	F12

Location: 2.5 mi n of Eastham/Orleans Rotary. 2470 Rt 6 02642 (Rt 6, Box 428). Fax: 508/240-7104. **Terms:** Open 5/1-10/24 & 2/11-4/30; reserv deposit, 7 day notice; handling fee imposed. **Facility:** 31 rooms. Tastefully landscaped grounds with sundeck. 4 units with patio. Some at-door parking. Family owned & operated. 2 night min stay in season & weekends off season. 1 two-bedroom unit, $124 in season for up to 4 persons; 2 stories; exterior corridors; heated pool. **All Rooms:** extended cable TV. **Cards:** AE, CB, DI, JC, MC, VI.

(See map p. 330)

PENNY HOUSE INN Phone: (508)255-6632 234
(AAA) (SAVE) 6/18-9/18 1P: $125- 175 2P/1B: $135- 195 2P/2B: $165- 230 XP: $35
5/1-6/17 & 9/19-4/30 1P: $115- 175 2P/1B: $135- 155 2P/2B: $155- 195 XP: $35
◆◆◆ **Location:** 2 mi n of National Seashore Visitor's Center. 4885 Rt 6 02651 (Box 238, NORTH EASTHAM).
Historic Bed **Fax:** 508/255-4893. **Terms:** Age restrictions may apply; reserv deposit, 14 day notice; 2 night min stay, in
& Breakfast season. **Facility:** 11 rooms. Charming former sea captain's home, circa 1751. 2 stories; interior corridors;
smoke free premises. **Dining:** Afternoon tea. **All Rooms:** combo or shower baths. **Cards:** AE, DS, MC, VI.
Special Amenities: Free local telephone calls and free newspaper. *(See color ad p 346)* (S) (P) (PV) (⊟) (∎) (X)

TOWN CRIER MOTEL Phone: (508)255-4000 236
(AAA) (SAVE) 6/25-9/6 1P: $69- 109 2P/1B: $69- 109 2P/2B: $69- 109 XP: $10-15 F12
5/1-6/24 & 9/7-4/30 1P: $49- 79 2P/1B: $49- 79 2P/2B: $49- 79 XP: $5-10 F12
◆◆ **Location:** 0.8 mi n of National Seashore Visitor's Center. 3620 Rt 6 02642 (PO Box 457).
Motel **Fax:** 508/255-7491. **Terms:** Reserv deposit, 7 day notice; handling fee imposed; package plans; 2 night min
shop; 7-11 am 5/1-10/31. **Recreation:** game room. **All Rooms:** extended cable TV. **Cards:** AE, CB, DI, DS, MC, VI.
stay, in season. **Facility:** 33 rooms. 1 story; exterior corridors; heated indoor pool 5/15-10/12. **Dining:** Coffee
Special Amenities: Free room upgrade and preferred room (each subject to availability with advanced reservations).
(≋) (¶) (☂) (⊟) (∎) (X)

VIKING SHORES MOTOR LODGE Rates Subject to Change Phone: (508)255-3200 226
(AAA) 6/26-9/7 [CP] 1P: $84- 89 2P/1B: $84- 89 2P/2B: $85- 93 XP: $8 F12
5/1-6/25 & 9/8-10/31 [CP] 1P: $43- 55 2P/1B: $43- 55 2P/2B: $46- 59 XP: $8 F12
◆◆ **Location:** 2.3 mi n of National Seashore Visitor's Center. 5200 Rt 6 02651 (PO Box 1899).
Motel **Fax:** 508/240-0205. **Terms:** Open 5/1-10/31; reserv deposit, 7 day notice; weekly rates; 2 night min stay, in
season. **Facility:** 40 rooms. Attractive, peaceful country setting with picnic grounds. 1 story; exterior corridors;
heated pool; 2 tennis courts. **Recreation:** Fee: bicycles. **All Rooms:** extended cable TV. **Cards:** AE, DS, MC, VI.
(See color ad below) (≋) (X) (☂) (∎)

WHALEWALK INN Rates Subject to Change Phone: (508)255-0617 238
(AAA) 5/28-10/11 [BP] 1P: $150- 250 2P/1B: $150- 250 2P/2B: $150- 250 XP: $30
5/1-5/27, 10/12-11/28 &
◆◆◆ 4/1-4/30 [BP] 1P: $130- 200 2P/1B: $130- 200 2P/2B: $130- 200 XP: $30
Historic Bed **Location:** 0.8 mi w of Orleans Rotary; Rock Harbor Rd exit. 220 Bridge Rd 02642. **Fax:** 508/240-0017.
& Breakfast **Terms:** Open 5/1-11/28 & 4/1-4/30; age restrictions may apply; reserv deposit, 14 day notice; handling fee
imposed; package plans; 2 night min stay, in season & weekends. **Facility:** 16 rooms. 1830's home converted
into charming inn; quiet setting. 13 units with working fireplace. 2 stories; interior/exterior corridors; smoke free premises.
Recreation: bicycles. **All Rooms:** combo or shower baths. **Some Rooms:** 5 kitchens, color TV, whirlpools. **Cards:** MC, VI.
(X) (PV) (⊒) (Z) (⊟) (∎) (X)

RESTAURANT

ARNOLD'S LOBSTER & CLAM BAR Lunch: $7-$17 Dinner: $7-$17 Phone: 508/255-2575 103
(AAA) **Location:** 0.7 mi n of National Seashore Visitor's Center. Rt 6 & Orchard Rd 02642. **Hours:** Open 5/15-9/13;
◆ 11 am-10 pm; to 8 pm 5/15-6/18. **Features:** No A/C; casual dress; carryout; beer & wine only. Very informal
Seafood dining in old Cape Cod tradition with paper plates & plastic utensils. Fresh Cape Cod lobster, steamers,
oysters & mussels. Fried & baked entrees. (X)

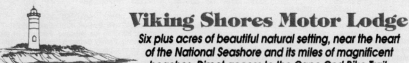
IT COULD HAPPEN. Some lodgings require advance payment when you check in, and if your trip is cut short a refund may be impossible.

EAST HARWICH—3,800 (See map p. 330; index p. 325)

LODGING

WEQUASSETT INN   Rates Subject to Change   **Phone:** (508)432-5400   145

6/26-9/6	2P/1B:	$275- 510	2P/2B:	$275- 510	XP: $25			F11
5/22-6/25 & 9/7-10/11	2P/1B:	$225- 400	2P/2B:	$255- 400	XP: $25			F11
5/1-5/21 & 10/12-10/31	2P/1B:	$175- 375	2P/2B:	$175- 375	XP: $20			F11
11/1-11/16 & 4/15-4/30	2P/1B:	$100- 225	2P/2B:	$100- 225	XP: $25			F11

Resort   **Location:** 4.5 mi n of Chatham rotary on SR 28S, from US 6, exit 11, first left to Pleasant Bay Rd, 2.5 mi e. 273 Orleans Rd 02645 (Rt 28 at Pleasant Bay, CHATHAM, 02633). Fax: 508/432-1915. **Terms:** Open 5/1-11/16 & 4/15-4/30; reserv deposit, 15 day notice; AP, MAP avail; 2 night min stay, weekends. **Facility:** 104 rooms. Spacious grounds overlooking harbor. Luxuriously appointed rooms in the New England tradition. Multiple unit cottages nestled in 25 acres of pine & oak trees. 1 two-bedroom unit. 9 units with fireplace, $300-$495; 1-2 stories; exterior corridors; putting green; beach, heated pool; boat dock. Fee: 18 holes golf; 4 tennis courts, tennis instruction. **Dining:** Dining room, see separate listing. **Services:** giftshop; area transportation. **Recreation:** swimming; croquet, volleyball. Fee: sailboating, windsurfing; launch to Outer Beach. Rental: boats. **All Rooms:** extended cable TV. **Some Rooms:** kitchen. **Cards:** AE, DI, DS, MC, VI. A Preferred Hotel. *(See ad p 341)*

RESTAURANT

WEQUASSETT INN MAIN DINING ROOM   **Lunch:** $8-$14   **Dinner:** $19-$24   **Phone:** 508/432-5400   67

Location: 4.5 mi n of Chatham rotary on SR 28S, from US 6, exit 11, first left to Pleasant Bay Rd, 2.5 mi e; in Wequassett Inn. 273 Orleans Rd 02645. **Hours:** Open 5/1-11/5 & 4/15-4/30; 7 am-10 pm.
Regional   **Reservations:** suggested. **Features:** dressy casual; children's menu; cocktails & lounge; entertainment; a la
American   carte. Fine dining in a 19th-century sea captain's mansion overlooking Pleasant Bay. Seafood specialties featured. Alfresco garden terrace. Smoke free premises. **Cards:** AE, CB, DI, DS, MC, VI.

FALMOUTH—4,000 (See map p. 330; index p. 325)

LODGINGS

THE ADMIRALTY INN   **Phone:** (508)548-4240   99

6/25-10/10	1P: $100- 175	2P/1B:	$100- 175	2P/2B:	$100- 175	XP: $10	F16
5/1-6/24	1P: $55- 150	2P/1B:	$55- 150	2P/2B:	$55- 150	XP: $10	F16
10/11-4/30	1P: $60- 120	2P/1B:	$60- 120	2P/2B:	$60- 120	XP: $10	F16

Motor Inn   **Location:** 1.5 mi e on SR 28. 53 Teaticket Hwy 02540 (PO Box 606). Fax: 508/457-0535. **Terms:** Reserv deposit, 15 day notice; handling fee imposed; BP, MAP avail; package plans; 2 night min stay, weekends. **Facility:** 98 rooms. Large contemporary rooms around courtyard pool. 28 bi-level townhouse units $150, $80 off season; 8 whirlpool rms, $20 extra charge; 3 stories; interior/exterior corridors; heated indoor pool, whirlpool. **Dining:** Restaurant; 6 pm-10 pm, Sat & Sun also 7:30-11:30 am; $8-$16; cocktails. **Services:** area transportation, season. **All Rooms:** extended cable TV. **Some Rooms:** whirlpools. **Cards:** AE, CB, DI, DS, MC, VI. *(See color ad p 350)*

THE BEACH HOUSE AT FALMOUTH HEIGHTS   Rates Subject to Change   **Phone:** 508/457-0310   90

All Year [CP]   2P/1B: $129- 159   2P/2B: $129- 159   XP: $20

Bed &   **Location:** 0.8 mi e of SR 28. 10 Worcester Ct 02540. Fax: 508/548-7895. **Terms:** Age restrictions may
Breakfast   apply; reserv deposit, 14 day notice; handling fee imposed; 2 night min stay, weekends 7/1-8/31. **Facility:** 8 rooms. Whimsical colorful decor accented by fanciful handcrafted furnishings & hand painted murals by New England artists. 2 stories; exterior corridors; designated smoking area. **All Rooms:** combo or shower baths. **Cards:** MC, VI.

BEST WESTERN-MARINA/TRADE WINDS   Rates Subject to Change   **Phone:** (508)548-4300   100

6/18-9/5 [CP]	1P: $135- 215	2P/1B:	$135- 215	2P/2B:	$135- 215	XP: $10	F12
5/1-6/17 & 9/6-10/10 [CP]	1P: $80- 165	2P/1B:	$80- 165	2P/2B:	$80- 165	XP: $10	F12
10/11-10/30 & 4/7-4/30 [CP]	1P: $70- 150	2P/1B:	$70- 150	2P/2B:	$70- 150	XP: $10	F12

Motel   **Location:** 0.8 mi e via SR 28, just s on Falmouth Heights Rd. 26 Robbins Rd 02540 (PO Box 337, 02541). Fax: 508/548-6787. **Terms:** Open 5/1-10/30 & 4/7-4/30; reserv deposit, 7 day notice; 2 night min stay, weekends. **Facility:** 63 rooms. Overlooking harbor. 1 two-bedroom unit. 7 kitchens, 5 efficiencies, $140-$170; $85-$115 off season; 2 stories; exterior corridors. **All Rooms:** extended cable TV. **Cards:** AE, CB, DI, DS, MC, VI. *(See color ad p 350)*

(See map p. 330)

THE CAPEWIND		Guaranteed Rates				Phone: 508/548-3400	75
◆	7/1-9/6	1P: $85- 125	2P/1B:	$85- 125	2P/2B:	$85- 125 XP: $10	F15
Motel	5/1-6/30 & 9/7-10/31	1P: $65- 95	2P/1B:	$65- 95	2P/2B:	$65- 95 XP: $10	F15
	11/1-4/30	1P: $40- 60	2P/1B:	$40- 60	2P/2B:	$40- 60 XP: $10	F15

Location: 2.2 mi e via SR 28, then just s following signs. 34 Maravista Extension 02536. **Fax:** 508/495-0316. **Terms:** Reserv deposit, 7 day notice. **Facility:** 32 rooms. Secluded location on spacious grounds overlooking salt water pond. 1 story; exterior corridors; heated pool; boat dock. **Recreation:** boating, canoeing. **All Rooms:** combo or shower baths. **Some Rooms:** 12 efficiencies. **Cards:** DS, MC, VI. *(See color ad p 349)*

DON'T WAIT FOR THE BIG CHILL.
Check the blanket supply in your room when you arrive;
you might not be able to get extras during the night.

(See map p. 330)

CAPT TOM LAWRENCE HOUSE   **Phone: 508/540-1445**   93

AAA [SAVE]

5/28-10/12 [BP]	1P: $110- 145	2P/1B: $135- 160	2P/2B: $145- 190	XP: $30	F
5/1-5/27, 10/13-12/31 &					
2/1-4/30 [BP]	1P: $98- 140	2P/1B: $105- 150	2P/2B: $120- 150	XP: $30	F

Historic Bed & Breakfast

Location: 0.3 mi s of SR 28 on the road to Woodshole. 75 Locust St 02540. Fax: 508/457-1790. **Terms:** Open 5/1-12/31 & 2/1-4/30; reserv deposit, 14 day notice; handling fee imposed; weekly rates, off season; 2 night min stay, weekends in season. **Facility:** 7 rooms. An 1861 sea captain's home. Lovely rooms feature 4-poster canopy bed. 1 efficiency, $150 in season for up to 3 persons; 2 stories; interior corridors; designated smoking area. **All Rooms:** shower baths, extended cable TV. **Some Rooms:** efficiency. **Cards:** MC, VI. *(See color ad below)*

[icons]

FALMOUTH HEIGHTS MOTOR LODGE   Rates Subject to Change   **Phone: (508)548-3623**   80

AAA

6/25-9/6	1P: $79- 109	2P/1B: $79- 109	2P/2B: $95- 130	XP: $10	D
6/11-6/24 & 9/7-9/26	1P: $69- 80	2P/1B: $69- 89	2P/2B: $79- 100	XP: $10	D
5/1-6/10 & 9/27-10/24	1P: $55- 79	2P/1B: $55- 79	2P/2B: $69- 89	XP: $10	D

Motel

Location: 0.8 mi e on SR 28, 0.5 mi s. 146 Falmouth Heights Rd 02540. Fax: 508/548-8186. **Terms:** Open 5/1-10/24; reserv deposit, 14 day notice; handling fee imposed. **Facility:** 24 rooms. 3 acres of landscaped grounds. Friendly staff. Short walk to ferry & beach. Complimentary morning coffee in lobby. Nicely decorated rooms. Extremely well-kept. 7 night min stay 6/26-9/6 for efficiencies, $100-$135 for 2 persons; $69-$110 off season; 2 stories; interior/exterior corridors; playground. **Dining:** Restaurant nearby. **Recreation:** gas grills, glider swings, picnic grove, shuffleboard. **All Rooms:** combo or shower baths, extended cable TV. **Cards:** MC, VI. *(See ad below)*

[icons]

GRAFTON INN   Rates Subject to Change   **Phone: 508/540-8688**   86

AAA

5/14-10/24 [BP]	2P/1B: $139- 179	XP: $35	
5/1-5/13 & 10/25-4/30 [BP]	2P/1B: $95- 149	XP: $35	

Bed & Breakfast

Location: 0.8 mi e on SR 28, 1.3 mi se via Falmouth Heights Rd & Grand Ave S. 261 Grand Ave S 02540. Fax: 508/540-1861. **Terms:** Age restrictions may apply; reserv deposit, 15 day notice; handling fee imposed. **Facility:** 10 rooms. Queen Anne style restored Victorian home. 3 stories, no elevator; interior corridors; smoke free premises; oceanfront; beach chairs, umbrellas & towels. **Recreation:** swimming. **All Rooms:** shower baths, extended cable TV. **Cards:** AE, MC, VI. *(See color ad p 353)*

[icons]

HOLIDAY INN-FALMOUTH CAPE COD   Rates Subject to Change   **Phone: 508/540-2000**   97

6/25-9/2	1P: $159- 209	2P/1B: $159- 209	2P/2B: $159- 209	XP: $10	F18
9/3-10/23	1P: $129- 149	2P/1B: $129- 149	2P/2B: $129- 149	XP: $10	F18
5/28-6/24	1P: $109- 129	2P/1B: $109- 129	2P/2B: $109- 129	XP: $10	F18
5/1-5/27 & 10/24-4/30	1P: $65- 79	2P/1B: $65- 79	2P/2B: $65- 79	XP: $10	F18

Motor Inn

Location: 0.5 mi e of SR 28 on Jones Rd, just e of jct Jones & Gillford sts. 291 Jones Rd 02540. Fax: 508/548-2712. **Terms:** 2 night min stay, most summer weekends. **Facility:** 98 rooms. In the process of total renovation to be completed by May, 1999. 3 stories, no elevator; interior corridors; heated indoor pool. **Cards:** AE, CB, DI, DS, JC, MC, VI.

[icons]

(See map p. 330)

THE INN AT ONE MAIN STREET
♦♦♦
Bed &
Breakfast

Rates Subject to Change

5/31-10/31 [BP]	1P:	$85- 95	2P/1B:	$95- 115	2P/2B:	$115- 130	XP: $25-35
5/1-5/30 & 11/1-4/30 [BP]	1P:	$75- 85	2P/1B:	$85- 105	2P/2B:	$95- 115	XP: $25-35

Phone: (508)540-7469 79

Location: On the corner of Main St (SR 28) & Woods Hole Rd. One Main St 02540. **Terms:** Age restrictions may apply; reserv deposit, 14 day notice; 2 night min stay, weekends in season. **Facility:** 6 rooms. A 1892 Victorian style home complete with decorative shingles & a two-story turret. Designated smoking area. **All Rooms:** shower baths. **Cards:** AE, DS, MC, VI.

MARINER MOTEL
[AAA]
♦♦
Motel

Rates Subject to Change

6/25-8/21	1P:	$79- 119	2P/1B:	$79- 119	2P/2B:	$79- 119	XP: $10	D18
6/18-6/24 & 8/22-9/5	1P:	$69- 99	2P/1B:	$69- 99	2P/2B:	$69- 99	XP: $10	D18
5/28-6/17 & 9/6-10/10	1P:	$59- 89	2P/1B:	$59- 89	2P/2B:	$59- 89	XP: $10	D18
5/1-5/27 & 10/11-4/30	1P:	$49- 79	2P/1B:	$49- 79	2P/2B:	$49- 79	XP: $10	D18

Phone: 508-548-1331 83

Location: 0.5 mi e on SR 28. 555 Main St 02540. **Terms:** Reserv deposit, 14 day notice; handling fee imposed; weekly rates; pets, $5 extra charge, 1 dog only. **Facility:** 30 rooms. 1 story; exterior corridors; smoke free premises; heated pool; playground. **Dining:** Restaurant nearby. **Recreation:** picnic tables. **All Rooms:** combo or shower baths. **Cards:** AE, CB, DI, DS, MC, VI. *(See color ad p 353)*

THE MOORINGS LODGE
[AAA] [SAVE]
♦♦
Bed &
Breakfast

6/16-9/14 [BP]	1P:	$85- 110	2P/1B:	$95- 139	2P/2B:	$95- 139	XP: $15	D12
5/15-6/15 [BP]	1P:	$75- 95	2P/1B:	$85- 120	2P/2B:	$85- 120	XP: $15	D12
9/15-10/15 [BP]	1P:	$75- 95	2P/1B:	$85- 120	2P/2B:	$85- 120	

Phone: (508)540-2370 76

Location: 0.8 mi e on SR 28, then 1.8 mi se via Falmouth Heights Rd & Grand Ave. 207 Grand Ave S 02540. Fax: 508/457-6074. **Terms:** Open 5/15-10/15; reserv deposit, 10 day notice; handling fee imposed; weekly rates. **Facility:** 8 rooms. Opposite beach. 3 stories; interior corridors; smoke free premises. **Recreation:** TV avail on request. **All Rooms:** combo or shower baths. **Cards:** MC, VI. **Special Amenities:** Early check-in/late check-out and preferred room (subject to availability with advanced reservations).

(See map p. 330)

OCEAN VIEW MOTEL   Phone: (508)540-4120 [87]

AAA SAVE
Motel

6/12-9/9		2P/1B:	$75- 140	2P/2B:	$75- 140
5/15-6/11 & 9/10-9/30		2P/1B:	$55- 65	2P/2B:	$55- 105
10/1-10/14		2P/1B:	$50- 60	2P/2B:	$65- 95

Location: 0.8 mi e on SR 28, 1.3 mi se via Falmouth Heights Rd & Grand Ave. 263 Grand Ave 02540.
Fax: 508/540-7154. **Terms:** Open 5/15-10/14; reserv deposit, 7 day notice; handling fee imposed;
weekly/monthly rates; 2 night min stay, weekends in season; pets, $25 fee, $50 extra charge. **Facility:** 17 rooms. Rates for up
to 5 persons; 2 stories; exterior corridors; oceanview; beach. **Dining:** Restaurant nearby. **Recreation:** swimming.
All Rooms: combo or shower baths, extended cable TV. **Some Rooms:** 9 efficiencies. **Cards:** AE, DS, MC, VI.
Special Amenities: Early check-in/late check-out and free local telephone calls.

THE PALMER HOUSE INN   Phone: (508)548-1230 [98]

AAA SAVE
◆◆◆
Historic Bed
& Breakfast

6/18-10/10 [BP]	1P:	$95- 175	2P/1B:	$105- 175	2P/2B:	$130- 145	XP:	$30
5/1-6/17 & 10/11-10/31 [BP]	1P:	$80- 175	2P/1B:	$90- 175	2P/2B:	$120- 135	XP:	$25
11/1-4/30 [BP]	1P:	$70- 150	2P/1B:	$80- 150	2P/2B:	$95- 110	XP:	$20

Location: 0.5 mi nw on SR 28, in the historic district. 81 Palmer Ave 02540. Fax: 508/540-1878. **Terms:** Age
restrictions may apply; reserv deposit, 14 day notice; handling fee imposed; package plans; 2 night min stay,
weekends in season. **Facility:** 13 rooms. Queen Anne Victorian home of 1901. Period antique furnishings.
Suite, $150-$199; 1-3 stories, no elevator; interior/exterior corridors; smoke free premises. **Dining:** Afternoon & evening
refreshments. **Services:** area transportation, pick up at bus station. **Recreation:** bicycles. **All Rooms:** combo or shower
baths, extended cable TV. **Some Rooms:** color TV, whirlpools. **Cards:** AE, CB, DI, DS, MC, VI. **Special Amenities:** Free
breakfast and free local telephone calls. *(See color ad p 352)*

With your AAA membership card and exclusive Hertz discount card,
you are recognized all over the world as a special customer.

(See map p. 330)

RAMADA INN ON THE SQUARE
◆◆◆
Motor Inn

| | Rates Subject to Change | | | Phone: 508/457-0606 | 89 |

Fri & Sat 5/21-10/12 — 2P/1B: $129- 199 — 2P/2B: $129- 199 — XP: $10 — F16
Sun-Thurs 5/21-10/12 — 2P/1B: $99- 129 — 2P/2B: $99- 129 — XP: $10 — F16
5/1-5/20 & 10/13-4/30 — 2P/1B: $79- 109 — 2P/2B: $79- 109 — XP: $10 — F16

Location: On SR 28, just n of jct Woods Hole Rd, 0.8 mi s of Jones Rd. 40 N Main St 02540. Fax: 508/457-9694. **Facility:** 72 rooms. 3 two-room whirlpool suites, $109-$239; max of 5 persons per room; 2 stories; interior/exterior corridors; heated indoor pool. **Cards:** AE, CB, DI, DS, MC, VI. *(See color ad inside front cover & below)*

RED HORSE INN
◇◇◇
◆◆◆
Motel

| | Rates Subject to Change | | | Phone: 508/548-0053 | 84 |

6/25-9/6 — 2P/1B: $116- 130 — 2P/2B: $135- 150 — XP: $20 — D
5/15-6/24 & 9/7-10/31 — 2P/1B: $89- 98 — 2P/2B: $104- 120 — XP: $20 — D

Location: 0.8 mi e on SR 28, just s. 28 Falmouth Heights Rd 02540. Fax: 508/540-6563. **Terms:** Open 5/15-10/31; reserv deposit, 14 day notice; handling fee imposed; 2 night min stay, weekends in season. **Facility:** 22 rooms. Charming, individually-decorated rooms, some cozy units. Beautifully landscaped grounds. A short walk to island ferries. 2 stories; exterior corridors. **Cards:** AE, MC, VI. *(See color ad p 352)*

VILLAGE GREEN INN
◆◆◆
Bed & Breakfast

| | Guaranteed Rates | | Phone: 508/548-5621 | 91 |

5/28-10/31 [BP] — 2P/1B: $120- 160 — XP: $25
1/1-4/30 [BP] — 2P/1B: $90- 130 — XP: $25
5/1-5/27 & 11/1-12/31 [BP] — 2P/1B: $85- 130 — XP: $25

Location: On the Village Green. 40 Main St 02540. Fax: 508/457-5051. **Terms:** Age restrictions may apply; reserv deposit, 14 day notice. **Facility:** 5 rooms. 19th century Victorian inn. On the register of historical places. Some rooms with fireplace, 2 working, 2 decorative. 2 night min stay weekends, 3 night min stay weekends, in season; 3 stories, no elevator; interior corridors; designated smoking area. **All Rooms:** combo or shower baths. **Cards:** AE, MC, VI.

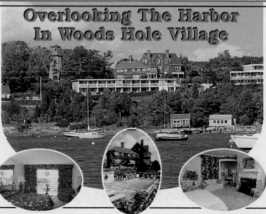

(See map p. 330)

WILDFLOWER INN Rates Subject to Change **Phone:** (508)548-9524 94
◆◆◆ 5/1-10/31 [BP] 2P/1B: $120- 175 XP: $20
Bed & 11/1-4/30 [BP] 2P/1B: $80- 125
Breakfast **Location:** On SR 28, 0.3 mi n of jct Woods Hole Rd; or 0.5 mi s of jct Jones Rd. 167 Palmer Ave 02540.
Fax: 508/548-9524. **Terms:** Age restrictions may apply; reserv deposit, 15 day notice; handling fee imposed;
2 night min stay, weekends. **Facility:** 6 rooms. Restored home, built prior to 1898, with each room having its own theme. Complimentary refreshments offered 24 hrs. Complimentary bicycles avail. 1-bedroom loft kitchen unit, $800 weekly in season, for
up to 3 persons, breakfast extra charge; 3 stories; interior/exterior corridors; designated smoking area. **All Rooms:** combo
or shower baths. **Some Rooms:** kitchen, color TV. **Cards:** AE, MC, VI.

WOODS HOLE PASSAGE BED & BREAKFAST Rates Subject to Change **Phone:** 508/548-9575 88
◆◆◆ 5/1-10/31 [BP] 1P: $120- 140 2P/1B: $125- 145 2P/2B: $125-145 XP: $20
Bed & 11/1-4/30 [BP] 1P: $80- 100 2P/1B: $85- 105 2P/2B: $85-105 XP: $20
Breakfast **Location:** 1.5 mi s. 186 Woods Hole Rd 02540. Fax: 508/540-4771. **Terms:** Age restrictions may apply;
reserv deposit, 14 day notice; handling fee imposed; 2 night min stay, in season. **Facility:** 5 rooms. Charming
restored carriage house; quiet setting. 2 stories; interior corridors; smoke free premises. **All Rooms:** shower baths.
Cards: AE, DI, DS, MC, VI.

RESTAURANTS

COONAMESSETT INN CAHOON
DINING ROOM Country Inn **Lunch:** $8-$14 **Dinner:** $16-$30 **Phone:** 508/548-2300 52
◆◆◆ **Location:** 0.8 mi n of SR 28. 311 Gifford St 02541. **Hours:** 11:30 am-10 pm. **Reservations:** suggested.
Regional **Features:** semi-formal attire; Sunday brunch; cocktails & lounge. Elegant fine dining in a traditional New
American England country inn surrounded by rolling grounds & attractive gardens. Gracious hospitality. Fresh local
seafood & creative Regional recipes. Lighter fare & dining room menu avail. **Cards:** AE, MC, VI.

THE GOLDEN SWAN **Dinner:** $15-$22 **Phone:** 508/540-6580 54
◆◆ **Location:** On SR 28, center of town. 323 Main St 02540. **Hours:** 5 pm-10 pm. Closed major holidays.
Continental **Reservations:** suggested. **Features:** casual dress; children's menu; early bird specials; carryout; cocktails &
lounge; minimum charge-$6; street parking. Intimate, relaxed atmosphere with a touch of Europe.
Cards: AE, DS, MC, VI.

HEARTH'N KETTLE FAMILY RESTAURANT **Lunch:** $5-$10 **Dinner:** $10-$14 **Phone:** 508/548-6115 50
◆ **Location:** 0.8 mi e on SR 28, opposite Falmouth Plaza. 874 Main St 02540. **Hours:** 7 am-10 pm, Fri &
American Sat-11 pm; to 9 pm 10/15-5/15; Fri & Sat-10 pm. Closed: 12/25. **Features:** casual dress; children's menu;
early bird specials; carryout; cocktails; a la carte. Very popular, cheerful, family dining in a charming colonial
day ambiance. Staff in period costumes. **Cards:** AE, DS, MC, VI.

THE REGATTA OF FALMOUTH BY THE SEA **Dinner:** $21-$30 **Phone:** 508/548-5400 51
◆◆◆ **Location:** At the mouth of Falmouth Harbor, 0.8 mi s of SR 28, via Scranton Ave. 217 Clinton Ave 02540.
American **Hours:** Open 5/21-9/19; 4:30 pm-9 pm. **Reservations:** suggested. **Features:** dressy casual; early bird
specials; wine only; entertainment. Innovative cuisine; strong on local seafood & French finish. Overlooking
entrance to Falmouth Harbor. Valet parking weekends. Smoke free premises. **Cards:** AE, MC, VI.

WINSTON'S RESTAURANT **Lunch:** $4-$8 **Dinner:** $7-$14 **Phone:** 508/548-0590 55
🅰🅰🅰 **Location:** 0.5 mi e of SR 28, in Falmouth Trade Center. 97 Spring Bars Rd 02540. **Hours:** 11:30 am-10 pm,
Sun from noon. Closed: 11/25 & 12/25. **Features:** casual dress; children's menu; carryout; cocktails &
◆ lounge; a la carte. Also, sandwiches & luncheon specials. Very casual pub atmosphere. **Cards:** AE, CB, DI,
American DS, MC, VI.

HARWICH PORT—1,000 (See map p. 330; index p. 328)

LODGINGS

AUGUSTUS SNOW HOUSE Rates Subject to Change **Phone:** 508/430-0528 303
◆◆◆ 5/22-10/15 [BP] 2P/1B: $145- 160 XP: $20
Bed & 5/1-5/21, 10/16-12/1 &
Breakfast 4/16-4/30 [BP] 2P/1B: $135- 150 XP: $20
12/2-4/15 [BP] 2P/1B: $135- 150 XP: $20
Location: Center. 528 Main St 02646. Fax: 508/432-7995. **Terms:** Age restrictions may apply; reserv deposit, 15 day notice;
handling fee imposed; 2 night min stay, weekends in season. **Facility:** 5 rooms. A 1901 Queen Anne Victorian with spacious
back lawn. All units with working fireplace. 3 stories; interior/exterior corridors; designated smoking area. **Cards:** AE, DS,
MC, VI. *(See ad p 333)*

COACHMAN MOTOR INN Rates Subject to Change **Phone:** 508/432-0707 305
◆◆ 6/21-9/15 2P/2B: $80- 98 XP: $10 F10
Motor Inn 5/1-6/20 & 9/16-10/31 2P/2B: $60- 75 XP: $10 F10
Location: 1 mi e on SR 28. 774 Main St 02646. Fax: 508/432-7951. **Terms:** Open 5/1-10/31; reserv deposit,
15 day notice; handling fee imposed; 2 night min stay, in season. **Facility:** 26 rooms. German is spoken here. 1 two-bedroom
unit. 1 story; exterior corridors. **Some Rooms:** kitchen. **Cards:** AE, DI, MC, VI.

DUNSCROFT BY-THE-SEA B & B INN Guaranteed Rates **Phone:** (508)432-0810 304
◆◆◆ 7/16-8/28 [BP] 2P/1B: $155- 235 2P/2B: $155- 235 XP: $35
Bed & 6/18-7/15 & 8/29-10/16 [BP] 2P/1B: $125- 210 2P/2B: $125- 210 XP: $35
Breakfast 5/1-6/17 & 10/17-11/1 [BP] 2P/1B: $115- 210 2P/2B: $115- 210 XP: $35
Location: 0.3 mi s of SR 28. 24 Pilgrim Rd 02646. Fax: 508/432-5134. **Terms:** Open 5/1-11/1; age
restrictions may apply; reserv deposit, 14 day notice; handling fee imposed. **Facility:** 8 rooms. Charming, quiet property in exclusive residential area. 1-bedroom cottage with fireplace & whirlpool; 2 stories; interior/exterior corridors; smoke free premises. **All Rooms:** combo or shower baths. **Some Rooms:** color TV. **Cards:** AE, MC, VI.

(See map p. 330)

WYCHMERE VILLAGE	Guaranteed Rates			Phone: (508)432-1434	301

◆◆   6/18-9/20   1P: $89- 139   2P/1B: $89- 139   2P/2B: $89- 139
Motel   5/1-6/17, 9/21-11/30 &
       4/1-4/30   1P: $45- 95   2P/1B: $45- 95   2P/2B: $45- 95
Location: 2 mi e of SR 39 & 124 on SR 28. 767 Main St 02646. Fax: 508/432-8904. **Terms:** Open 5/1-11/30 & 4/1-4/30.
Facility: 24 rooms. Attractively landscaped grounds. Gas grill & picnic area. 5 two-bedroom units. 4 two-bedroom units, $139;
$95 off season. 1 two-bedroom cottage, $850 weekly; $750 weekly off season; 1 story; exterior corridors; heated pool.
All Rooms: combo or shower baths. **Some Rooms:** 11 efficiencies, kitchen. **Cards:** AE, DS, MC, VI.
(See color ad below)

ASK ⬛ ⬛ ⬛ ⬛ ⬛ ⬛ ⬛ ⬛

RESTAURANTS

COUNTRY INN Country Inn	Dinner: $15-$25	Phone: 508/432-2769	142

◆◆   **Location:** 0.3 mi n of jct SR 28. 86 Sisson Rd (SR 39) 02646. **Hours:** 5 pm-9 pm. Closed: 12/24, 12/25 &
American   Tues 10/15-5/30. **Reservations:** suggested. **Features:** No A/C; dressy casual; early bird specials; cocktails
& lounge; minimum charge-$10. Homey inn-style dining room with country decor. Homemade bread &
dessert. Call for off season hours. Dancing Fri & Sat. **Cards:** AE, MC, VI.   ⬛

L'ALOUETTE RESTAURANT	Dinner: $17-$25	Phone: 508/430-0405	141

◆◆   **Location:** 1 mi e on SR 28. 787 Main St 02646. **Hours:** 5 pm-9 pm, Fri & Sat-2:30
French   & 5-9 pm except 7/1-8/31. Closed: Mon & 2/1-2/28. **Reservations:** required. **Features:** casual dress;
cocktails; minimum charge-$13; a la carte. Fine dining in a casual atmosphere. **Cards:** AE, DS, MC, VI. ⬛

HYANNIS—10,000   (See map p. 332; index p. 323)

LODGINGS

ANCHOR-IN MOTEL	Guaranteed Rates			Phone: 508/775-0357	1

AAA   6/11-9/11   1P: $90- 150   2P/1B: $90- 150   2P/2B: $90- 150   XP: $10   F10
   5/1-6/10 & 9/12-10/23   1P: $49- 125   2P/1B: $49- 125   2P/2B: $49- 125   XP: $10   F10
◆◆◆   10/24-4/30   1P: $39- 85   2P/1B: $39- 85   2P/2B: $39- 85   XP: $10   F10
Motel   **Location:** 0.5 mi se overlooking Lewis Bay. 1 South St 02601. Fax: 508/775-1313. **Terms:** Reserv deposit, 7
day notice; handling fee imposed; weekly rates. **Facility:** 43 rooms. Most units with balcony overlooking harbor.
Enclosed sun deck. Family owned & operated. Executive waterfront rooms avail; 2 stories; interior/exterior corridors.
All Rooms: combo or shower baths. **Some Rooms:** 2 efficiencies. **Cards:** AE, DS, MC, VI. *(See color ad p 357)*

⬛ ⬛ ⬛ ⬛ ⬛ ⬛ ⬛

(See map p. 332)

THE BREAKWATERS

		Rates Subject to Change			Phone: 508/775-6831	2
AAA	6/27-8/28 Wkly	1P: $950-1800	2P/1B: $950-1800	2P/2B: $950-1800		
◆◆	6/12-6/26 Wkly	1P: $650-1000	2P/1B: $650-1000	2P/2B: $650-1000		
Cottage	8/29-9/18 Wkly	1P: $525-1000	2P/1B: $525-1000	2P/2B: $525-1000		
	5/11-6/11 & 9/19-10/12 Wkly	1P: $475- 850	2P/1B: $475- 850	2P/2B: $475- 850		

Location: 1 mi s of Main St via Sea St. 432 Sea St 02601 (PO Box 118). Fax: 508/775-6831. **Terms:** Open 5/11-10/12; reserv deposit, 30 day notice. **Facility:** 18 rooms. Adjacent to public beach. 1- to 3-bedroom housekeeping units in duplex or triplex condominium cottages. 5 two-bedroom units. Max rates for up to 6 persons; 2 stories; exterior corridors; heated pool. **All Rooms:** kitchens, combo or shower baths, extended cable TV. *(See color ad p 356)*

⤳ 💻 🖥 🚫 🖨

CAPE COD HYANNIS HOTEL

		Rates Subject to Change			Phone: (508)775-6600	11
◆◆	5/1-10/31	1P: $79- 159	2P/1B: $89- 169	2P/2B: $89- 169 XP: $10		F
Motor Inn	11/1-4/30	1P: $59- 129	2P/1B: $59- 129	2P/2B: $69- 139 XP: $10		F

Location: 0.3 mi nw of jct SR 28; adjacent to mall. 707 Rt 132 02601. Fax: 508/790-0119. **Terms:** Handling fee imposed. **Facility:** 120 rooms. 2 stories; interior corridors; heated indoor pool; 1 tennis court. **Cards:** AE, CB, DI, DS, JC, MC, VI. *(See color ad below)*

ASK 🔒 🐕 🖥 ⤳ 🍴 🍸 🚗 🚫 VCR 🖨 📶 ✖

CAPTAIN GOSNOLD VILLAGE

		Rates Subject to Change			Phone: 508/775-9111	4
AAA	6/18-9/6	1P: $75- 95	2P/1B: $75- 95	2P/2B: $106- 270 XP: $10		F5
	5/1-6/17, 9/7-11/15 &					
◆◆	4/15-4/30	1P: $45		2P/2B: $150 XP: $15		F5
Cottage						

Location: 1 mi s via Old Colony Rd. 230 Gosnold St 02601. **Terms:** Open 5/1-11/15 & 4/15-4/30; reserv deposit, 30 day notice; handling fee imposed. **Facility:** 33 rooms. Motel & housekeeping units, all with gas grill. 4 two-bedroom units, 4 three-bedroom units. 3 night min stay in housekeeping units, 2 nights for motel units in season. Air-conditioned units, $8 extra charge; 1 story; interior/exterior corridors; heated pool; playground. **All Rooms:** combo or shower baths, extended cable TV. **Some Rooms:** 8 efficiencies, 18 kitchens. **Cards:** MC, VI. *(See color ad below)*

⤳ 🚫 VCR 💻 🖨 📶

THE COUNTRY LAKE LODGE

					Phone: (508)362-6455	5
AAA SAVE	6/20-9/7	1P: $59- 69	2P/1B: $59- 79	2P/2B: $59- 89 XP: $4-10		F16
	5/1-6/19, 9/8-10/31 &					
◆	4/1-4/30	1P: $39- 49	2P/1B: $39- 54	2P/2B: $39- 59 XP: $4		F16
Motel						

Location: US 6, exit 6, 1 mi se on SR 132, on Shallow Pond. 1545 Rt 132 02601. Fax: 508/362-8050. **Terms:** Open 5/1-10/31 & 4/1-4/30; reserv deposit, 14 day notice; handling fee imposed. **Facility:** 20 rooms. All units on attractively landscaped, sloping grounds overlooking lake. Peaceful setting. 5 efficiencies, $79-$89; $49-$79 off season. Max 4 persons per room; 1 story; exterior corridors; heated pool; playground. **Recreation:** swimming, boating, fishing; shuffleboard. **Cards:** AE, DS, MC, VI.

🔒 ⤳ 🚫 📶 ✖

(See map p. 332)

CRAIGVILLE MOTEL ⒄ F15

Rates Subject to Change

Phone: (508)362-3401

6/26-9/6 [CP]	1P: $55- 85	2P/1B: $55- 85	2P/2B: $55- 85	XP: $10			F15
5/1-6/25, 9/7-12/6 & 4/1-4/30 [CP]	1P: $36- 59	2P/1B: $36- 59	2P/2B: $36- 59	XP: $10			F15

Motel **Location:** S of US 6 & SR 132, at interchange eastbound exit 6. 8 Shoot Flying Hill Rd 02632. Fax: 508/362-5426. **Terms:** Open 5/1-12/6 & 4/1-4/30; reserv deposit, 3 day notice. **Facility:** 39 rooms. A quiet, rural setting. 1 story; exterior corridors. **All Rooms:** extended cable TV. **Cards:** AE, DS, MC, VI. *(See color ad below)*

DAYS INN ⒂

Phone: (508)771-6100

6/25-9/18 [CP]	1P: $85- 250	2P/1B: $85- 250	2P/2B: $85- 250	XP: $8	F18
5/1-6/24 [CP]	1P: $65- 200	2P/1B: $65- 200	2P/2B: $65- 200	XP: $8	F18
9/19-11/28 [CP]	1P: $60- 160	2P/1B: $60- 160	2P/2B: $60- 160	XP: $8	F18
2/11-4/30 [CP]	1P: $50- 150	2P/1B: $50- 150	2P/2B: $50- 150	XP: $8	F18

Motel **Location:** 0.5 mi nw of jct SR 28; adjacent to Cape Cod Mall. 867 Iyanough Rd, Rt 132 02601. Fax: 508/775-3011. **Terms:** Open 5/1-11/28 & 2/11-4/30. **Facility:** 99 rooms. Vibrant room decors. Some units with balcony. 2 stories; interior corridors; heated indoor pool, whirlpool. **All Rooms:** extended cable TV. **Cards:** AE, CB, DI, DS, JC, MC, VI. **Special Amenities: Free breakfast and preferred room (subject to availability with advanced reservations).** *(See color ad below)*

FOUR POINTS HYANNIS SHERATON ❸

Rates Subject to Change

Phone: 508/771-3000

6/1-10/31	1P: $109- 139	2P/1B: $109- 139	2P/2B: $109- 139	XP: $15	F17
5/1-5/31 & 4/1-4/30	1P: $99- 109	2P/1B: $99- 109	2P/2B: $99- 109	XP: $15	F17
11/1-3/31	1P: $69- 99	2P/1B: $69- 99	2P/2B: $69- 99	XP: $15	F17

Motor Inn **Location:** Exit 6 off SR 6, 2 mi w. Rt 132 & Bearse's Way 02601. Fax: 508/771-6564. **Terms:** Check-in 4 pm. **Facility:** 261 rooms. Attractively landscaped grounds. 6 bi-level suites, $145-$210. 1 presidential suite, $195-$310; 2 stories; interior corridors; heated indoor pool; 1 tennis court; playground. **Services:** giftshop. Fee: massage. **Cards:** AE, CB, DI, DS, MC, VI. *(See color ad p 360)*

HERITAGE HOUSE HOTEL ⒀

Rates Subject to Change

Phone: (508)775-7000

7/1-9/15	1P: $109- 160	2P/1B: $109- 160	2P/2B: $109- 160	XP: $12	F16
5/1-6/30, 9/16-11/30 & 2/10-4/30	1P: $50- 100	2P/1B: $50- 100	2P/2B: $50- 100	XP: $12	F16

Motel **Location:** 0.3 mi e. 259 Main St 02601. Fax: 508/778-5687. **Terms:** Open 5/1-11/30 & 2/10-4/30; reserv deposit, 14 day notice, 7 day off season; package plans; 2 night min stay, weekends in summer. **Facility:** 143 rooms. 2-3 stories; interior corridors; heated indoor pool, saunas, whirlpool. **Dining:** Restaurant; 7 am-noon. **All Rooms:** extended cable TV. **Cards:** AE, CB, DI, DS, MC, VI. *(See color ad p 360)*

(See map p. 332)

HYANNIS INN MOTEL   Phone: 508/775-0255   [12]

AAA SAVE
6/28-8/22	2P/1B:	$81- 139	2P/2B:	$81- 139	XP: $10	F12
8/23-9/26	2P/1B:	$71- 129	2P/2B:	$71- 129	XP: $10	F12
6/1-6/27	2P/1B:	$50- 129	2P/2B:	$50- 129	XP: $10	F12
5/1-5/31, 9/27-11/15 &						
2/1-4/30	2P/1B:	$40- 90	2P/2B:	$40- 90	XP: $10	F12

◆ ◆

Motel

Location: Center. 473 Main St 02601. Fax: 508/771-0456. **Terms:** Open 5/1-11/15 & 2/1-4/30; reserv deposit, 7 day notice; handling fee imposed. **Facility:** 77 rooms. Family operated since 1954. 2 stories; exterior corridors; heated indoor pool, saunas. **Dining:** Coffee shop; 6:30 am-noon. **All Rooms:** combo or shower baths, extended cable TV. **Some Rooms:** whirlpools. **Cards:** AE, DS, MC, VI. *(See color ad p 357)*

HYANNIS MOTEL-BUDGET HOST INN   Rates Subject to Change   Phone: 508/775-8910   [8]

AAA
6/20-9/5 [EP]	2P/1B:	$69- 95	2P/2B:	$75- 95	XP: $10	F17
5/1-6/19 & 9/6-10/30 [CP]	2P/1B:	$49- 65	2P/2B:	$49- 65	XP: $5	F17
10/31-4/30 [CP]	2P/1B:	$45- 55	2P/2B:	$49- 55	XP: $5	F17

◆ ◆

Motel

Location: On SR 132, 0.3 mi nw of jct SR 28. 614 Rt 132 02601. Fax: 508/775-6476. **Terms:** Reserv deposit, 7 day notice; weekly/monthly rates. **Facility:** 43 rooms. 8 efficiencies $75, $55 off season; 2 stories; exterior corridors. **Cards:** AE, DI, DS, MC, VI. *(See color ad p 264 & p 362)*

(See map p. 332)

HYANNIS TRAVEL INN
| | | Rates Subject to Change | | | | Phone: (508)775-8200 | **10** |

6/26-9/6 [CP] — 2P/1B: $50- 70 2P/2B: $70- 99 XP: $10 — F15
5/1-6/25, 9/7-11/29 &
2/4-4/30 [CP] — 2P/1B: $36- 55 2P/2B: $45- 69 XP: $10 — F15
Motel

Location: Just n of Main St. 18 North St 02601 (PO Box 1300). Fax: 508/775-8200. **Terms:** Open 5/1-11/29 & 2/4-4/30; reserv deposit, 7 day notice; package plans. **Facility:** 83 rooms. Many rooms with balcony or patio. Entries to all levels of rooms via stairway. 3 stories, no elevator; interior corridors; heated indoor pool, sauna, whirlpool. **All Rooms:** combo or shower baths, extended cable TV. **Cards:** AE, DS, MC, VI. *(See color ad p 362)*

QUALITY INN
| | | Rates Subject to Change | | | | Phone: 508/771-4804 | **19** |

6/30-9/4 [CP] — 1P: $98- 129 2P/1B: $109- 139 2P/2B: $109- 139 XP: $10 — F18
Motel — 5/1-6/29, 9/5-10/10 &
4/1-4/30 [CP] — 1P: $69- 89 2P/1B: $79- 99 2P/2B: $79- 99 XP: $10 — F18
10/11-3/31 [CP] — 1P: $49- 69 2P/1B: $59- 79 2P/2B: $59- 79 XP: $10 — F18

Location: US 6, exit 6, 1.3 mi se on SR 132. 1470 Rt 132 02601. Fax: 508/790-2336. **Facility:** 104 rooms. A quiet, natural hillside location. Vibrant room decors. Rates for up to 5 persons; 2-3 stories, no elevator; interior/exterior corridors; heated indoor pool. **Cards:** AE, CB, DI, DS, MC, VI.

(See map p. 332)

RADISSON INN

	7/2-9/2	1P:	$109- 149	2P/1B:	$109- 149	2P/2B:	$109- 149	XP: $10	F18
	9/3-10/28	1P:	$89- 129	2P/1B:	$89- 129	2P/2B:	$89- 129	XP: $10	F18
	5/28-7/1	1P:	$99- 119	2P/1B:	$99- 119	2P/2B:	$99- 119	XP: $10	F18
Motor Inn	5/1-5/27 & 10/29-4/30	1P:	$59- 109	2P/1B:	$59- 109	2P/2B:	$59- 109	XP: $10	F18

Phone: (508)771-1700

Location: On SR 28, 0.3 mi se of jct SR 132. 287 Iyanough Rd (Rt 28) 02601. Fax: 508/771-5156. **Terms:** Reserv deposit, 3 day notice; handling fee imposed; MAP avail; package plans; 2 night min stay, weekends in summer. **Facility:** 160 rooms. Contemporary style rooms. 10 two-person whirlpool rms, $169-$189; 2 stories; interior corridors; heated indoor pool, sauna, steamroom. **Dining:** Restaurant; 6:30-10 am, 11-1:30 & 5-10 pm, Sat & Sun 7 am-1:30 & 5-10 pm; $10-$18. **Cards:** AE, CB, DI, DS, JC, MC, VI.

FIND THE HIDDEN MONEY!
Read TourBook advertisements carefully;
some offer special discounts for AAA members.

(See map p. 332)

RAMADA INN REGENCY
◆◆   7/1-8/31
Motor Inn   9/1-10/12
   5/1-6/30
   10/13-4/30

	Rates Subject to Change				
1P: $99- 169	2P/1B:	$99- 169	2P/2B:	$99- 169	XP: $10	F18
1P: $89- 149	2P/1B:	$89- 149	2P/2B:	$89- 149	XP: $10	F18
1P: $79- 129	2P/1B:	$79- 129	2P/2B:	$79- 129	XP: $10	F18
1P: $59- 99	2P/1B:	$59- 99	2P/2B:	$59- 99	XP: $10	F18

Phone: (508)775-1153 🔟6

Location: US 6 exit 6, 2.3 mi se. 1127 Rt 132 02601. Fax: 508/771-9118. **Terms:** Reserv deposit, in season; handling fee imposed. **Facility:** 196 rooms. 16 efficiency loft suites, $89-$149 for 2 persons in season; 2 stories; interior corridors; heated indoor pool. **Cards:** AE, CB, DI, DS, MC, VI. *(See color ad inside front cover & below)*

SEACOAST ON THE TOWNE
Ⓐ
   6/25-9/5 [CP]
   5/1-6/24 & 9/6-10/31 [CP]
◆◆
Motel

	Rates Subject to Change				
1P: $54- 78	2P/1B:	$64- 88	2P/2B:	$68- 98	
1P: $42- 58	2P/1B:	$42- 68	2P/2B:	$44- 74	XP: $10	F12

Phone: (508)775-3828 🔟6

Location: Just s of Main St, at corner of Ocean/South St. 33 Ocean St 02601. Fax: 508/771-2179. **Terms:** Open 5/1-10/31. **Facility:** 26 rooms. Cheerful, homey rooms. 2 stories; interior corridors; whirlpool. **All Rooms:** extended cable TV. **Some Rooms:** 25 efficiencies. **Cards:** AE, DS, MC, VI.

(See color ad below)

SHERATON HYANNIS RESORT
◆◆◆   7/2-9/1
Hotel   5/1-7/1 & 9/2-11/1
   11/2-4/30

	Rates Subject to Change				
1P: $189- 219	2P/1B:	$189- 219	2P/2B:	$189- 219	XP: $15	F12
1P: $129- 199	2P/1B:	$129- 199	2P/2B:	$129- 199	XP: $15	F12
1P: $89- 129	2P/1B:	$89- 129	2P/2B:	$89- 129	XP: $15	F12

Phone: 508/775-7775 🔟4

Location: 1 mi w at Main St & Scudder Ave. West End Cir 02601. Fax: 508/778-6423. **Terms:** Reserv deposit, 3 day notice. **Facility:** 232 rooms. All rooms with patio or balcony. Elegant public areas & excellent guest services. Beautifully landscaped. 2 stories; interior corridors; 18 holes golf, putting green; heated indoor pool; 2 lighted tennis courts. **Services:** giftshop; area transportation. Fee: massage. **Cards:** AE, CB, DI, DS, MC, VI. *(See color ad p 360)*

RESTAURANTS

ALBERTO'S RISTORANTE
Ⓐ
◆◆◆
Northern
Italian

Lunch: $6-$13   **Dinner:** $13-$26   **Phone:** 508/778-1770 🔟0
Location: Downtown, just w of jct Barnstable Rd & Main St. 360 Main St 02601. **Hours:** 3 pm-10 pm, Sun from noon. Closed: 11/25, 12/24 & 12/25. **Reservations:** required; in season. **Features:** casual dress; early bird specials; cocktails & lounge; a la carte. Romantic candlelit ambiance with brass & etched glass touches. Several dining rooms. Featuring homemade pasta & veal specialties. **Cards:** AE, CB, DI, DS, MC, VI.

(See map p. 332)

BARBYANN'S RESTAURANT   **Lunch:** $4-$8   **Dinner:** $7-$13   **Phone:** 508/775-9795   ⑫
◆◆   **Location:** 0.5 mi n of jct SR 28 & 132. 120 Airport Rd 02601. **Hours:** 11:30 am-11 pm, Sun 11 am-10 pm.
American   **Closed:** 11/25, 12/24 & 12/25. **Features:** casual dress; Sunday brunch; children's menu; carryout; cocktails &
lounge. Bustling, family dining in a rustic setting. Specializing in prime rib & variety of seafood. **Cards:** AE,
DI, DS, MC, VI.

THE BLACK CAT   **Lunch:** $6-$13   **Dinner:** $14-$22   **Phone:** 508/778-1233   ⑰
◆◆◆   **Location:** 0.8 mi s overlooking harbor. 165 Ocean St 02601. **Hours:** 11:30 am-10 pm, Fri & Sat-11 pm;
American   hours may vary. **Closed:** 11/25, 12/25, 1/1-1/31 & 2/1-2/14. **Reservations:** accepted. **Features:** semi-formal
attire; Sunday brunch; children's menu; cocktails & lounge. Comfortable atmosphere across from harbor.
Tavern menu of lighter fare served from 3 pm. Patio dining in season. Valet parking for dinner in season. **Cards:** AE, DI,
MC, VI.

DRAGON LITE RESTAURANT   **Lunch:** $4-$7   **Dinner:** $5-$13   **Phone:** 508/775-9494   ⑮
◆   **Location:** Downtown, at corner of Main & Sea sts. 620 Main St 02601. **Hours:** 11:30 am-1 am, Sun &
Chinese   holidays noon-1 am; to 10 pm in winter; call to verify hours. **Closed:** 11/25. **Reservations:** accepted.
Features: casual dress; carryout; cocktails & lounge; minimum charge-$10; a la carte. Features authentic
Chinese recipes with Szechuan, Mandarin, Cantonese & Hunan cuisine. **Cards:** AE, DI, MC, VI.

THE EGG & I   **Phone:** 508/771-1596   ⑯
Ⓐ   **Location:** Downtown, between High School Rd & Pine St. 521 Main St 02601. **Hours:** Open 5/1-11/30 &
◆   3/1-4/30; 6 am-1 & 11-3 am; Fri 11 pm-3 am, Sat 6 am-1 & 11-3 am, Sun 6 am-1 pm 11/1-11/30. **Closed:**
American   12/1-2/29 & weekdays 11/1-11/30. **Features:** casual dress; children's menu; senior's menu; street parking. A
landmark restaurant since 1971 serving breakfast all night long $3-$6. Specialty omelettes. Few sandwiches.
Cards: AE, CB, DI, DS, MC, VI.

HEARTH 'N KETTLE RESTAURANT   **Lunch:** $4-$7   **Dinner:** $9-$15   **Phone:** 508/771-3737   ③
◆   **Location:** Center. 412 Main St 02601. **Hours:** 7 am-9 pm; 7/4-9/3 to 10 pm. **Closed:** 12/25.
American   **Features:** casual dress; children's menu; early bird specials; health conscious menu items; carryout;
cocktails. Relaxed, family dining in a charming colonial day ambiance. Delightful staff. **Cards:** AE, DS, MC,
VI.

MAIN STREET SEAFOOD & GRILL   **Lunch:** $5-$8   **Dinner:** $9-$13   **Phone:** 508/771-8585   ⑪
◆◆   **Location:** Center. 462 Main St 02601. **Hours:** Open 5/1-12/31 & 3/1-4/30; 11:30 am-10 pm. **Closed:** 12/25.
American   **Reservations:** suggested; on weekends. **Features:** casual dress; Sunday brunch; children's menu; health
conscious menu items; carryout; cocktails & lounge. Friendly, downtown dining in a nautical setting. Fresh
seafood specialties. Family-operated. **Cards:** AE, DS, MC, VI.

MILDRED'S CHOWDER HOUSE   **Lunch:** $5-$15   **Dinner:** $10-$15   **Phone:** 508/775-1045   ⑧
Ⓐ   **Location:** 0.3 mi se of jct SR 132. 290 Iyanough Rd, Rt 28 02601. **Hours:** 11 am-10 pm, from 7 am,
◆◆   5/26-9/1. **Closed:** 11/25 & 12/25. **Features:** casual dress; children's menu; carryout; cocktails & lounge.
Seafood   Home of Cape Cod's original clam chowder for over 40 years. Lobster specials. Early bird specials Mon-Fri.
Cards: AE, MC, VI.

THE ORIGINAL GOURMET BRUNCH   **Lunch:** $4-$8   **Phone:** 508/771-2558   ⑨
Ⓐ   **Location:** Center; set back s of Main St, just w of High School Rd. 517 Main St 02601. **Hours:** 7 am-3 pm.
◆   **Closed:** 11/25 & 12/25. **Features:** casual dress; children's menu; carryout; beer & wine only; street parking.
American   Popular, cozy & unpretentious with friendly staff. Owner operated. Excellent food, specialty omelettes,
quiche, sandwiches, salad & dessert.

THE PADDOCK   **Lunch:** $5-$10   **Dinner:** $15-$23   **Phone:** 508/775-7677   ⑥
Ⓐ   **Location:** 1 mi w at Main St Rotary. W Main St Rotary 02601. **Hours:** Open 5/1-11/8 & 4/1-4/30; 11:30
◆◆◆   am-2:30 & 5-10 pm, Sun noon-9 pm. **Reservations:** suggested. **Features:** casual dress; children's menu;
American   cocktails & lounge; entertainment; valet parking; a la carte. Elegant Victorian candlelit ambiance. Delightful
garden room setting for lunch. A local favorite. **Cards:** AE, CB, DI, MC, VI.

PENGUINS SEA GRILL   **Dinner:** $16-$22   **Phone:** 508/775-2023   ④
◆◆   **Location:** Downtown, at jct Ocean & Main sts. 331 Main St 02601. **Hours:** 5 pm-10 pm, 7/4-9/7 to 11 pm.
Seafood   **Closed:** 1/1, 11/25 & 12/25. **Reservations:** suggested; dinner. **Features:** casual dress; children's menu;
early bird specials; carryout; cocktails & lounge; street parking; a la carte. Upscale bistro featuring local &
exotic seafood creations. Wood grilled meat & some pasta, also lobster. Extensive wine list. **Cards:** AE, DS, MC, VI.

ROADHOUSE CAFE   **Dinner:** $15-$24   **Phone:** 508/775-2386   ⑭
◆◆   **Location:** Downtown; just s of Main St at jct of South & Sea sts. 488 South St 02601. **Hours:** 4 pm-11 pm,
Italian   Fri & Sat-midnight, off season hours may vary. **Closed:** 11/25, 12/24 & 12/25. **Reservations:** suggested; for
dinner. **Features:** casual dress; early bird specials; carryout; cocktails; entertainment; valet parking; a la
carte. Charming, casual ambiance. Specializing in veal & fresh seafood entrees. Light fare avail. Homemade dessert &
piano bar. **Cards:** AE, DI, DS, MC, VI.

SAM DIEGO'S MEXICAN COOKERY & BAR   **Lunch:** $5-$10   **Dinner:** $8-$12   **Phone:** 508/771-8816   ⑦
◆◆   **Location:** On SR 132. 950 Iyanough Rd 02601. **Hours:** 11:30 am-midnight. **Closed:** 3/30, 11/25, & 12/25.
Mexican   **Features:** casual dress; children's menu; cocktails & lounge; a la carte. Lively contemporary dining room
with southwestern decor. Generous portions. Very popular. Outdoor patio in season. Smoke free dining
room. **Cards:** AE, DS, MC, VI.

TUGBOATS   **Lunch:** $5-$10   **Dinner:** $9-$15   **Phone:** 508/775-6433   ⑬
◆◆   **Location:** At the Hyannis Marina. 21 Arlington St 02601. **Hours:** Open 5/1-9/25 & 4/15-4/30; 11:30 am-10
American   pm. **Closed:** Mon, 4/15-5/25 & 9/14-10/25. **Reservations:** accepted; off season. **Features:** casual dress;
children's menu; carryout; cocktails & lounge; a la carte. Relaxed dining overlooking Hyannis harbor &
marina. Fresh seafood specialties. Open patio deck dining in season. **Cards:** AE, DI, DS, MC, VI.

HYANNIS PORT—1,200   (See map p. 332; index p. 324)

LODGING

HARBOR VILLAGE   Phone: (508)775-7581   68
AAA SAVE   6/26-9/4   1P:$1100   2P/1B: $1350   2P/2B:$1550   XP: $50
                                        5/1-6/25, 9/5-11/1 & 4/1-4/30 1P: $100- 120 2P/1B: $110- 140 2P/2B: $140- 155 XP: $35
◆◆   **Location:** From Hyannis, 1 mi w on Main St, 0.3 mi sw on Scudder Ave, 0.5 mi s on Greenwood Ave. 160
Cottage   Marstons Ave 02647 (PO Box 635). **Terms:** Open 5/1-11/1 & 4/1-4/30; check-in 3:30 pm; reserv deposit, 30
day notice; pets, $100 weekly extra charge. **Facility:** 14 rooms. Wooded setting along Tidal River & adjacent
to ocean. 1- to 3-bedroom cottages with living room, kitchen & fireplace. 9 two-bedroom units, 3 three-bedroom units. 3-night
min stay off season. 1 four-bedroom cottage, $1450 weekly in season for up to 8 persons, $25 extra person; 1 story; exterior
corridors; beach. **Recreation:** swimming. **All Rooms:** kitchens, combo or shower baths, extended cable TV.

NORTH FALMOUTH—2,600   (See map p. 330; index p. 329)

RESTAURANT

SILVER LOUNGE RESTAURANT   **Lunch:** $4-$11   **Dinner:** $11-$15   **Phone:** 508/563-2410   175
AAA   **Location:** 0.5 mi s of jct SR 151 & 28A. Rt 28A 02556. **Hours:** 11:30 am-1 am. Closed: 11/25 & 12/25.
◆◆   **Features:** casual dress; carryout; cocktails & lounge; a la carte. Very popular, established, friendly, rustic pub
Steak and with antique marine artifacts, ship models, fishing nets in main dining room & a restored railroad caboose.
Seafood   Wide variety of entrees & sandwiches. **Cards:** AE, DS, MC, VI.

NORTH TRURO—1,000   (See map p. 330; index p. 328)

LODGINGS

BLUE SEA MOTOR INN   Phone: 508/487-1041   272
AAA SAVE   5/21-5/23 & 6/25-9/5 [CP]   1P: $117- 147   2P/1B: $117- 147   2P/2B: $117- 147
           5/1-5/20, 5/24-6/24 &
◆◆   9/6-10/17 [CP]   1P: $61- 92   2P/1B: $61- 92   2P/2B: $61- 92
Motel   **Location:** On SR 6A, 7.5 mi n of Truro Center. 696 Shore Rd 02657 (PO Box 537, PROVINCETOWN).
           Terms: Open 5/1-10/17; reserv deposit, 7 day notice, in writing, 30 day efficiencies; handling fee imposed.
Facility: 45 rooms. 2 night min stay, motel units in season. 11 efficiencies, $650-$920 weekly for up to 5 persons; $75-$110
daily off season for up to 5 persons; 1-2 stories; exterior corridors; beachfront; beach, heated indoor pool, whirlpool.
Recreation: swimming, fishing. **All Rooms:** combo or shower baths, extended cable TV. **Cards:** MC, VI.
(See color ad p 370)

CORAL SANDS MOTEL   Rates Subject to Change   **Phone:** (508)487-1410   273
AAA   2P/1B: $65- 125   2P/2B: $85- 125   XP:$8-20   D12
                                               2P/1B: $40- 60   2P/2B: $50- 75   XP:$5-10   D12
◆   7/1-9/6
Motel   5/14-6/30 & 9/7-10/12
           Location: 6.8 mi n of Truro Center. 535 Shore Rd, Rt 6A 02652 (PO Box 523, PROVINCETOWN, 02657).
           Terms: Open 5/14-10/12; reserv deposit, 14 day notice; handling fee imposed. **Facility:** 33 rooms. Most rooms
with balcony or patio. 10 efficiencies, $110 in season, $650-$700 weekly; 3 rooms beachfront with queen bed,
$95 in season; all for up to 2 persons; 2 stories; exterior corridors; oceanfront; beach. **Recreation:** swimming, fishing.
All Rooms: combo or shower baths, extended cable TV. **Cards:** MC, VI.

CROWS NEST MOTEL   Rates Subject to Change   **Phone:** 508/487-9031   274
◆◆   6/25-9/7   1P: $80   2P/1B: $80   2P/2B: $82- 85   XP: $10
Motel   5/1-6/24, 9/8-12/1 & 4/1-4/30 1P: $50   2P/1B: $50   2P/2B: $54- 56   XP: $7
           Location: On SR 6A, 6.5 mi n of Truro Center. 496 Shore Rd 02652 (PO Box 177). **Terms:** Open 5/1-12/1 &
4/1-4/30; reserv deposit, 14 day notice; handling fee imposed; 3 night min stay, in season. **Facility:** 33 rooms. 1 two-bedroom
unit. 2 stories; exterior corridors; oceanfront. **Recreation:** swimming, fishing. **All Rooms:** efficiencies. **Cards:** DS, MC, VI.

EAST HARBOUR MOTEL & COTTAGES   Rates Subject to Change   **Phone:** 508/487-0505   277
AAA   7/5-9/7   2P/2B: $95- 110   XP: $15   D14
           6/19-7/4   2P/2B: $74- 92   XP: $15   D14
◆◆   9/8-10/25   2P/2B: $52- 75   XP: $15   D14
Complex   5/1-6/18 & 4/15-4/30   2P/2B: $52- 72   XP: $15   D14
           Location: SR 6A, 7.3 mi n of Truro Center. 618 Shore Rd 02652 (PO Box 183). Fax: 508/487-6693.
Terms: Open 5/1-10/25 & 4/15-4/30; reserv deposit, 7 day notice, 30 day in cottages; handling fee imposed; weekly rates; 2
night min stay, in season. **Facility:** 17 rooms. 7 two-bedroom units. 7 two-bedroom cottages $800-$900 weekly for 2 persons,
extra person $100-$200, off season rates avail; 1 story; exterior corridors; beach. **Recreation:** swimming, fishing; bird
watching. **All Rooms:** combo or shower baths, extended cable TV. **Some Rooms:** 8 kitchens. **Cards:** AE, DS, MC, VI.

SEA GULL MOTEL   Phone: (508)487-9070   275
AAA SAVE   6/26-9/5   2P/2B: $78- 110   XP: $10
           5/1-6/25 & 9/6-10/17   2P/2B: $48- 70   XP: $10
◆◆   **Location:** On SR 6A, 7.3 mi n of Truro Center. 654 Shore Rd 02652 (PO Box 126). Fax: 508/487-9070.
Motel   **Terms:** Open 5/1-10/17; reserv deposit, 7 day notice, 30 day for housekeeping units. **Facility:** 26 rooms. Family owned & operated. Boardwalk to the beach area with small covered deck. 1 studio
efficiency, $670 weekly for up to 2 persons & 4 housekeeping apartments $820 weekly in season for up to 4 persons; 1 story;
exterior corridors; beachfront; beach. **Recreation:** swimming, fishing. **Cards:** AE, DS, MC, VI. **Special Amenities:** Free
local telephone calls and preferred room (subject to availability with advanced reservations). *(See color ad p 371)*

(See map p. 330)

SEASIDE VILLAGE MOTEL   Rates Subject to Change   Phone: 508/487-1215   `276`
◆◆   6/18-9/6   1P: $82- 104   2P/1B: $82- 104   2P/2B: $82- 104   XP: $10
Motel   5/14-6/17 & 9/7-10/17   1P: $52- 85   2P/1B: $52- 85   2P/2B: $52- 85   XP: $10
     Location: 6.5 mi n of Truro Center. 482 Shore Rd, Rt 6A 02652 (Dept A, PO Box 275). Fax: 508/487-1215.
Terms: Open 5/14-10/17; reserv deposit, 14 day notice, 30 day for cottages & efficiences. **Facility:** 32 rooms. 11 two-bedroom units. 2-two bedroom cottages & 13 housekeeping cottages & efficiencies, $575-$900 weekly, $50-$80 daily off season; 2 stories; exterior corridors; oceanfront. **Recreation:** swimming, fishing. **All Rooms:** combo or shower baths. **Some Rooms:** 2 kitchens. **Cards:** AE, MC, VI.

WHITE SANDS MOTEL   Rates Subject to Change   Phone: (508)487-0244   `271`
◆   6/25-9/9 [CP]   1P: $99- 199   2P/1B: $99- 159   2P/2B: $109- 250   XP: $50   F16
Motel   5/1-6/24, 9/10-11/30 &
     4/1-4/30 [EP]   1P: $55- 95   2P/1B: $55- 95   2P/2B: $55-175   XP: $15   F16
Location: On SR 6A, 7.5 mi n of Truro Center at the Provincetown line. 706 Shore Rd 02652 (PO Box 611, PROVINCETOWN, 02657). Fax: 508/487-0291. **Terms:** Open 5/1-11/30 & 4/1-4/30; reserv deposit, 7 day notice; handling fee imposed; 3 night min stay, weekends in season. **Facility:** 51 rooms. 1 two-bedroom unit. 1-2 stories; exterior corridors; heated indoor pool. **Recreation:** swimming. **All Rooms:** combo or shower baths. **Some Rooms:** 11 efficiencies. **Cards:** AE, MC, VI. *(See color ad p 371)*

RESTAURANTS

ADRIAN'S   **Dinner:** $10-$19   Phone: 508/487-4360   `120`
◆◆   **Location:** 5.3 mi ne of Truro Center. 535 Route 6 02652. **Hours:** Open 5/15-10/12; 8 am-noon & 5:30-10
Italian   pm. Closed: Tues & Wed 5/15-6/18 & 9/5-10/12. **Features:** No A/C; casual dress; carryout; cocktails & lounge; a la carte. Open, airy casual decor. Serving a variety of regional Italian dishes. Featuring gourmet breakfast. Deck dining in season. Smoking permitted in the lounge. Smoke free premises. **Cards:** AE, MC, VI.

THE WHITMAN HOUSE RESTAURANT   **Dinner:** $9-$25   Phone: 508/487-1740   `121`
◆◆◆   **Location:** 2 mi ne of Truro Center. Rt 6 02666. **Hours:** Open 5/1-12/31 & 4/1-4/30; 5 pm-9 pm. Closed:
American   12/25. **Reservations:** suggested. **Features:** casual dress; children's menu; early bird specials; cocktails & lounge; minimum charge-$4 per person. Charming, fine dining in traditional "Early American" decor. Featuring fresh seafood & prime rib. Family operated for over 30 years. **Cards:** AE, DI, DS, MC, VI.

ORLEANS—5,800   (See map p. 330; index p. 327)

LODGINGS

THE BARLEY NECK INN & LODGE   Rates Subject to Change   Phone: 508/255-8484   `221`
◆◆   6/15-9/15 [CP]   2P/1B: $95- 125   2P/2B: $95- 125   XP: $15   F12
Motor Inn   5/1-6/14 & 9/16-4/30 [EP]   2P/1B: $59- 75   2P/2B: $59- 75   XP: $10   F12
     Location: 1.5 mi e of SR 6A via Main St. 5 Beach Rd 02643 (PO Box 486, EAST ORLEANS).
Fax: 508/255-3626. **Terms:** Reserv deposit, 15 day notice; handling fee imposed; 2 night min stay, weekends in season. **Facility:** 18 rooms. 2 stories; exterior corridors. **Cards:** AE, MC, VI.

THE COVE   Rates Subject to Change   Phone: (508)255-1203   `210`
Ⓐ   6/25-9/6   1P: $99- 179   2P/1B: $99- 179   2P/2B: $124- 134   XP: $10   F17
    Fri & Sat 5/1-6/12, 6/13-6/24
◆◆◆   & 9/7-10/11   1P: $79- 128   2P/1B: $79- 128   2P/2B: $83- 93   XP: $10   F17
Motel   Sun-Thurs 5/1-6/12 &
    10/12-4/30   1P: $59- 89   2P/1B: $59- 89   2P/2B: $62- 67   XP: $10   F17
Location: Just s of jct SR 6A. 13 Rt 28 02653 (PO Box 279). Fax: 508/255-7736. **Terms:** Reserv deposit, 14 day notice; handling fee imposed; 2 night min stay, in season. **Facility:** 47 rooms. 7-room, 100 year old inn in a converted residence along with several motel sections on sloping landscaped grounds overlooking town cove. 5 kitchens & 3 efficiencies, $152-$179 for up to 4 persons in season; 2 stories; interior/exterior corridors; heated pool. **Recreation:** floatboat tours 5/15-10/15. **All Rooms:** combo or shower baths, extended cable TV. **Cards:** AE, CB, DI, DS, MC, VI. *(See ad below)*

(See map p. 330)

NAUSET KNOLL MOTOR LODGE   Rates Subject to Change   Phone: 508/255-2364   212

◆◆   6/18-9/6   1P: $135   2P/1B: $135   2P/2B: $135   XP: $10   F6
Motel   5/28-6/17 & 9/7-10/24   1P: $95   2P/1B: $95   2P/2B: $95   XP: $5   F6
    5/1-5/27 & 4/15-4/30   1P: $75   2P/1B: $75   2P/2B: $75   XP: $5   F6

Location: 3 mi e via Main St & Beach Rd, at Nauset Beach. 237 Beach Rd 02643 (PO Box 642, EAST ORLEANS). **Terms:** Open 5/1-10/24 & 4/15-4/30; reserv deposit, 4 day notice; 2 night min stay, weekends in season. **Facility:** 12 rooms. On hilltop overlooking Nauset Beach. 1 story; exterior corridors; oceanview. **Recreation:** swimming. **All Rooms:** shower baths. **Cards:** MC, VI.

OLDE TAVERN MOTEL & INN   Rates Subject to Change   Phone: 508/255-1565   213

AAA   6/18-9/6   2P/1B: $79- 110 2P/2B: $79- 110 XP: $9
    5/7-6/17 & 9/7-11/28   2P/1B: $52- 89 2P/2B: $56- 89 XP: $6-9
◆◆◆   5/1-5/6 & 3/31-4/30   2P/1B: $49- 79 2P/2B: $49- 79 XP: $6-9
Motel   **Location:** 0.5 mi e of jct US 6, exit 12, 0.8 mi w of jct US 6, exit 13 (Orleans rotary). 151 Rt 6A 02653 (PO Box 943). **Terms:** Open 5/1-11/28 & 3/31-4/30; reserv deposit, 7 day notice; 2 night min stay, in season.

Facility: 28 rooms. 1790's stagecoach tavern public building, with modern motel rooms adjoining. Back from highway. 1 story; exterior corridors; heated pool. **Cards:** AE, DS, MC, VI. *(See color ad below)*

(See map p. 330)

RIDGEWOOD MOTEL & COTTAGES　　　Rates Subject to Change　　　　**Phone: 508/255-0473**　🄻🄸🄾

⚛	6/18-9/6	1P:	$69- 80	2P/1B:	$69- 80	2P/2B:	$69- 80	
	5/14-6/17 & 9/7-10/11	1P:	$48- 56	2P/1B:	$48- 56	2P/2B:	$48- 56	
◆◆	5/1-5/13 & 10/12-10/31	1P:	$42- 45	2P/1B:	$42- 45	2P/2B:	$42- 45	

Complex　　**Location:** At jct SR 28 & 39. 10 Quanset Rd 02662 (PO Box 82, SOUTH ORLEANS). **Terms:** Open 5/1-10/31; reserv deposit, 30 day for cottages; handling fee imposed. **Facility:** 18 rooms. Woodsy setting. Check-in 3 pm & check-out 10 am for cottages. 2 two-bedroom units. Housekeeping cottages $490-$600 weekly; $280-$440 off season. Rates for up to 3-5 persons motel; rates for up to 4-6 persons cottages; 1 story; exterior corridors; playground. **Recreation:** badminton, basketball, horseshoes, volleyball. **All Rooms:** shower baths. **Some Rooms:** 6 kitchens. **Cards:** MC, VI. *(See ad p 367)*　　　　　　🔊 ⊠ 🖭 🄩 🔒 ⊠

SKAKET BEACH MOTEL　　　Rates Subject to Change　　　　**Phone: 508/255-1020**　🄻🄸🄴

⚛	6/25-9/5 [CP]	1P:	$78- 163	2P/1B:	$78- 163	2P/2B:	$78- 163	XP: $8-11
	5/21-6/24 & 9/6-10/11 [CP]	1P:	$54- 134	2P/1B:	$54- 134	2P/2B:	$54- 134	XP: $8-11
◆◆◆	5/1-5/20, 10/12-11/27 &							
Motel	4/2-4/30 [CP]	1P:	$50- 102	2P/1B:	$50- 102	2P/2B:	$50- 102	XP: $8-11

　　Location: At jct US 6, exit 12. 203 Cranberry Hwy, Rt 6A 02653. Fax: 508/255-6487. **Terms:** Open 5/1-11/27 & 4/2-4/30; reserv deposit, 10 day notice; handling fee imposed; 2 night min stay, weekends in summer; pets, off season, $9 extra charge. **Facility:** 46 rooms. 1 two-bedroom unit. 5 efficiencies, $99-$113 for up to 2 persons & 1 apartment, $156 for up to 4 persons; 2 stories; exterior corridors; heated pool. **Dining:** Restaurant nearby. **Recreation:** croquet, horseshoes. **All Rooms:** combo or shower baths, extended cable TV. **Cards:** AE, DI, DS, MC, VI. *(See color ad p 367)*

🛒 🕽 🔊 🍴 🅰 🐾 🖭 🖵 🖥 🔒 ⊠

RESTAURANTS

THE ARBOR RESTAURANT　　　　**Dinner:** $14-$22　　　　**Phone: 508/255-4847**　🄥
◆◆　　**Location:** On SR 28; 0.3 mi s of jct SR 6A. 20 S Orleans Rd 02653. **Hours:** 5 pm-10 pm. Closed: 11/25,
Continental　12/25 & Mon-Thur 10/14-5/1. **Reservations:** suggested. **Features:** casual dress; children's menu; early bird specials; carryout; cocktails & lounge. Small dining rooms, casual atmosphere. Classical cuisine with a creative flair. For a more casual experience, try the Binnacle Tavern downstairs, featuring gourmet pizza, pasta & local seafood. Open until 11 pm for pizza. Smoke free premises. **Cards:** AE, MC, VI.　　　　　　　　⊠

THE BARLEY NECK INN　　　　**Dinner:** $13-$20　　　　**Phone: 508/255-0212**　🄦
◆◆◆　　**Location:** In East Orleans; 1.5 mi e of SR 6A via Main St. 5 Beach Rd 02643. **Hours:** 5 pm-10 pm.
French　　**Reservations:** suggested. **Features:** cocktails & lounge; entertainment. Converted 1857 farmhouse serving contemporary French cuisine in a casually elegant atmosphere. Brasserie menu served in casual grille. **Cards:** AE, DI, MC, VI.　　　　　　　　　　　⊠

LOBSTER CLAW RESTAURANT　　**Lunch:** $4-$12　　**Dinner:** $8-$16　　**Phone: 508/255-1800**　🄦
⚛　　**Location:** At jct SR 28. 42 Route 6A 02653. **Hours:** Open 5/1-10/30 & 4/1-4/30; 11:30 am-9 pm.
　　Features: casual dress; children's menu; early bird specials; senior's menu; carryout; cocktails & lounge.
◆　　Bustling family dining room; hearty portions. **Cards:** AE, DI, DS, MC, VI.　　　　　⊠
Seafood

NAUSET BEACH CLUB　　　　**Dinner:** $12-$19　　　　**Phone: 508/255-8547**　🄡🄞🄞
◆◆　　**Location:** In East Orleans; 1.5 mi e of SR 6A via Main St. 222 Main St 02643. **Hours:** 5:30 pm-9:30 pm;
Italian　　10/14-5/21 to 9 pm. Closed: 1/1, 11/25, 12/25, Sun & Mon 10/15-5/22. **Features:** casual dress; cocktails; a la carte. Popular, cozy, casual dining in converted residence. Very innovative cuisine. Good wine list with selection of premium glass wine. Entree minimum per person. Smoke free premises. **Cards:** AE, CB, DI, DS, MC, VI.　⊠

OLD JAILHOUSE TAVERN　　　**Lunch:** $5-$8　　　**Dinner:** $15-$20　　**Phone: 508/255-5245**　🄦
◆◆　　**Location:** 0.3 mi n of jct SR 6A, near Skaket Corners Shopping Center. 28 West Rd 02653. **Hours:** 11:30
American　　am-midnight, Sun from 11 am. Closed: 11/25 & 12/25. **Features:** casual dress; Sunday brunch; carryout; cocktails & lounge. Casual family dining in a contemporary atmosphere with Victorian accents. **Cards:** AE, DS, MC, VI.　　　　　　　　　　　　　　　　　　　　　⊠

PROVINCETOWN—3,400　(See map p. 330; index p. 327)

LODGINGS

BAYSHORE　　　　Rates Subject to Change　　　　**Phone: (508)487-9133**　🄴

◆◆◆	6/19-9/11 Wkly	1P:	$795-1595	2P/1B:	$795-1595	2P/2B:	$795-1595	XP: $60
Motel	5/1-6/18 & 9/12-11/1 Dly	1P:	$85- 175	2P/1B:	$85- 175	2P/2B:	$85- 175	XP: $10
	11/2-4/30 Dly	1P:	$75- 145	2P/1B:	$75- 145	2P/2B:	$75- 145	XP: $10

Location: 0.8 mi e of Town Hall. 493 Commercial St 02657. Fax: 508/487-9133. **Terms:** Reserv deposit, 90 day notice; handling fee imposed; 2 night min stay, weekends off season. **Facility:** 19 rooms. Studios, 1- & 2-bedroom suites with living room & kitchen. On bay & across street. Delightful unique units, some with private deck & patio. 3 units with fireplace. Rates for up to 4 persons; 2-3 stories, no elevator; exterior corridors. **Recreation:** swimming, fishing. **All Rooms:** combo or shower baths. **Cards:** AE, DS, MC, VI.　　　　　　🍴 ⊠ 🖭 🖨 🔒

BEST WESTERN CHATEAU MOTOR INN　Rates Subject to Change　**Phone: (508)487-1286**　🄴

⚛	6/25-9/5 [CP]	2P/1B:	$139- 169	2P/2B:	$139- 169	XP: $20-50	F18
	Fri & Sat 5/1-6/24 &						
◆◆◆	9/6-10/17 [CP]	2P/1B:	$89- 139	2P/2B:	$89- 139	XP: $20-50	F18
Motel	Sun-Thurs 5/1-6/24 &						
	9/6-10/17 [CP]	2P/1B:	$79- 139	2P/2B:	$79- 139	XP: $20-50	F18

Location: On SR 6A, 0.8 mi w of Town Hall. 105 Bradford St W 02657 (PO Box 558). Fax: 508/487-3557. **Terms:** Open 5/1-10/17; reserv deposit, 7 day notice; handling fee imposed; 2 night min stay, weekends in season. **Facility:** 54 rooms. Hilltop location with panoramic views of bay & dunes. Variety of rooms in a quiet, restful ambiance. 1-2 stories; exterior corridors; heated pool. **All Rooms:** extended cable TV. **Cards:** AE, CB, DI, DS, MC, VI. *(See color ad p 369)*

🅢 🕽 🔊 🐾 🖭 🖨 🔒 🅄 ⊠ ✍

(See map p. 330)

BEST WESTERN TIDES BEACHFRONT
Motel

	Rates Subject to Change		Phone: (508)487-1045	255
6/25-9/5	2P/1B: $129- 199	2P/2B: $169- 219	XP: $20-50	F18
Fri & Sat 5/14-6/24 & 9/6-10/17	2P/1B: $89- 129	2P/2B: $99- 139	XP: $20-50	F18
Sun-Thurs 5/14-6/24 & 9/6-10/17	2P/1B: $79- 129	2P/2B: $89- 139	XP: $20-50	F18

Location: 2.3 mi se on SR 6A, 0.5 mi s of jct Snail Rd & SR 6A. 837 Commercial St 02657 (PO Box 617). Fax: 508/487-1621. **Terms:** Open 5/14-10/17; reserv deposit, 7 day notice; handling fee imposed; 2 night min stay, weekends in season. **Facility:** 64 rooms. Many units with patio or balcony & panoramic harbor views. Family owned & operated. 2 two-bedroom units. 1-2 stories; exterior corridors; beachfront; beach, heated pool. **Dining:** Coffee shop; 7 am-2 pm; to 4 pm in summer. **Recreation:** swimming, fishing; shuffleboard. **All Rooms:** combo or shower baths, extended cable TV. **Cards:** AE, CB, DI, DS, MC, VI. *(See color ad below)*

CAPE COLONY INN
Motel

	Phone: 508/487-1755			257
8/1-9/1	2P/1B: $106	2P/2B: $103	XP: $20	F12
6/27-7/31	2P/1B: $97	2P/2B: $95	XP: $20	F12
5/1-6/26 & 9/2-10/22	2P/1B: $87	2P/2B: $64	XP: $10	F12

Location: On SR 6A; 1 mi e of Town Hall. 280 Bradford St 02657. **Terms:** Open 5/1-10/22; reserv deposit, 7 day notice; handling fee imposed; 2 night min stay, in season. **Facility:** 54 rooms. 8 two-bedroom units, $144 in season for up to 4 persons; 2 stories; exterior corridors; heated pool. **Recreation:** picnic tables & grills, shuffleboard, volleyball. **All Rooms:** combo or shower baths, extended cable TV. **Cards:** DS, MC, VI.

HOLIDAY INN
Motor Inn

	Rates Subject to Change		Phone: 508/487-1711	259
6/26-9/6		2P/2B: $129- 160	XP: $10	F18
5/1-6/25 & 9/7-11/1		2P/2B: $89- 150	XP: $10	F18

Location: 1.5 mi se on SR 6A. 698 Commercial St 02657 (PO Box 392). Fax: 508/487-3929. **Terms:** Open 5/1-11/1; reserv deposit, 3 day notice; 2 night min stay, weekends 6/19-9/12. **Facility:** 78 rooms. Across from the bay. 2 stories; exterior corridors. **Services:** area transportation. **Cards:** AE, CB, DI, DS, JC, MC, VI.

AAA has it covered!
We publish 23 TourBooks annually,
covering North America from Florida to Alaska and all of Canada.

(See map p. 330)

THE MASTHEAD   Phone: (508)487-0523   [260]

(AAA) (SAVE)

Cottage

7/1-9/7	1P:	$81- 322	2P/1B:	$81- 322	2P/2B: $145- 322	XP: $20-50	F12
6/1-6/30 & 9/8-9/20	1P:	$76- 317	2P/1B:	$76- 317	2P/2B: $140- 317	XP: $20-50	F12
Fri-Sun 5/1-5/31 & 9/21-4/30	1P:	$63- 168	2P/1B:	$63- 168	2P/2B: $99- 168	XP: $20-50	F12
Mon-Thurs 5/1-5/31 & 9/21-4/30	1P:	$63- 122	2P/1B:	$63- 122	2P/2B: $86- 122	XP: $20-50	F12

Location: 0.8 mi w of Town Hall, on the ocean. 31-41 Commercial St 2657 (PO Box 577, 02657-0577). Fax: 508/487-9251. **Terms:** Check-in 4 pm; reserv deposit, 90 day notice; handling fee imposed; weekly/monthly rates; package plans. **Facility:** 20 rooms. Waterfront grounds. Unique rooms & 1- to 3-bedroom cottages with living room, kitchen & dining area. Boat moorings & launch service. 7 motel rooms, $134-$154 in season for 2 persons. Rates in cottages & apartments for up to 4 persons. Check-out 10 am in cottages & apartments; 1-2 stories; exterior corridors; off site parking only; beach. **Dining:** Restaurant nearby. **Recreation:** swimming, fishing. **All Rooms:** combo or shower baths, extended cable TV. **Some Rooms:** 2 efficiencies. **Cards:** AE, CB, DI, DS, MC, VI. **Special Amenities:** Free newspaper and free room upgrade (subject to availability with advanced reservations). *(See ad below)*

THE SHAMROCK   Phone: (508)487-1133   [261]

(AAA) (SAVE)

◆

Complex

5/21-5/26 & 6/27-9/9 [CP]	2P/1B:	$130- 170	2P/2B: $130- 170	XP: $20	F14
5/27-6/26, 9/10-11/1 & 12/31-1/4 [CP]	2P/1B:	$80- 90	2P/2B: $80- 90	XP: $20	F14
5/1-5/20, 11/2-12/30 & 1/5-4/30 [CP]	2P/1B:	$65- 85	2P/2B: $65- 85	XP: $20	F14

Location: On SR 6A, 0.3 mi w of Town Hall. 49 Bradford St 02657. **Terms:** Reserv deposit, 15 day notice; handling fee imposed; weekly rates. **Facility:** 14 rooms. 5 two-bedroom units. 3 one- & two-bedroom cottages, $850-$895 weekly for 2 persons, 3 two-bedroom apartments $995 weekly for 2 persons. 1 week im cottages & apts, in season; 3 stories, no elevator; exterior corridors; whirlpool. **Dining:** Restaurant nearby. **All Rooms:** combo or shower baths, extended cable TV. **Some Rooms:** 6 kitchens. **Cards:** AE, DS, MC, VI. **Special Amenities:** Free local telephone calls and free newspaper.

SOMERSET HOUSE   Phone: 508/487-0383   [262]

(AAA)

◆◆◆

Bed & Breakfast

Rates Subject to Change

6/18-9/12 [CP]	1P: $80- 130	2P/1B: $80- 130	2P/2B: $80- 130	XP: $20
5/1-6/17 & 9/13-10/31 [CP]	1P: $65- 120	2P/1B: $65- 120	2P/2B: $65- 120	XP: $20
11/1-4/30 [CP]	1P: $60- 95	2P/1B: $60- 95	2P/2B: $60- 95	XP: $20

Location: 0.6 e of Town Hall. 378 Commercial St 02657. Fax: 508/487-4746. **Terms:** Age restrictions may apply; reserv deposit, 14 day notice; handling fee imposed; 4 night min stay, in season. **Facility:** 12 rooms. Circa 1850. Garden patio. Attractive gardens & elegant, comfortable public areas. 1 two-bedroom apartment, $1250 weekly in season, for up to 4 persons; 3 stories, no elevator; interior corridors; designated smoking area. **All Rooms:** extended cable TV. **Some Rooms:** kitchen. **Cards:** DS, MC, VI.

(See map p. 330)

SURFSIDE INN   Rates Subject to Change   Phone: (508)487-1726   263

AAA
◆ ◆
Motel

	6/4-9/5	1P:	$89- 169	2P/1B:	$89- 169	2P/2B:	$89- 169
	9/6-11/7 & 4/20-4/30	1P:	$69- 149	2P/1B:	$69- 149	2P/2B:	$69- 149
	5/1-6/3	1P:	$69- 129	2P/1B:	$69- 129	2P/2B:	$69- 129

Location: 1 mi e of Town Hall. 543 Commercial St 02657. Fax: 508/487-1726. **Terms:** Open 5/1-11/7 & 4/20-4/30; reserv deposit, 14 day notice; handling fee imposed; weekly rates. **Facility:** 86 rooms. 1 two-bedroom unit. 3 night min stay, waterfront rooms, in season; 3-4 stories; interior/exterior corridors; oceanfront; beach, heated pool. **Dining:** Coffee shop; 6:30 am-5 pm. **Recreation:** swimming, fishing. **All Rooms:** extended cable TV. **Some Rooms:** 2 kitchens. **Cards:** AE, DS, MC, VI. *(See color ad below)*

ASK 🛎 🍴 ✕ 🛗 □ 🔒

WHITE WIND INN   Rates Subject to Change   Phone: (508)487-1526   254

◆ ◆
Bed &
Breakfast

	6/12-9/27 [CP]	2P/1B:	$115- 200	XP: $35
	5/1-6/11 & 9/28-12/7 [CP]	2P/1B:	$100- 160	XP: $30
	12/8-4/30 [CP]	2P/1B:	$85- 140	XP: $25

Location: Just w of town hall. 174 Commercial St 02657 (PO Box 1307). Fax: 508/487-3985. **Terms:** Reserv deposit, 21 day notice; handling fee imposed; 5 night min stay, in season. **Facility:** 11 rooms. An 1845 Victorian. 2 units with working fireplace & some with balcony. 2 stories; interior corridors; designated smoking area. **All Rooms:** combo or shower baths. **Cards:** DS, MC, VI.

🍴 🍴 ⚡ VCR 🖥 □ 🖨 🔒 ✕

(See map p. 330)

RESTAURANTS

GALLERANI'S CAFE   Dinner: $12-$25   Phone: 508/487-4433   (110)
◆◆
Continental
Location: 0.5 mi w of Town Hall. 133 Commerical St 02657. **Hours:** 6 pm-10:30 pm, Fri & Sat-11 pm, 10/1-5/15 5:30 pm-9:30 pm, Fri & Sat-10 pm. Closed: 12/1-12/31; Mon & Tues 10/1-5/31. **Reservations:** accepted; 5 or more. **Features:** casual dress; carryout; cocktails; minimum charge-$10 in season. Emphasis on Northern Italian cuisine served in casual atmosphere. Lower priced entrees off season. **Cards:** DS, MC, VI.   ☒

THE MARTIN HOUSE   Historical   Dinner: $14-$28   Phone: 508/487-1327   (114)
◆◆
American
Location: 0.3 mi w of Town Hall. 157 Commercial St 02657. **Hours:** 6 pm-10 pm, Fri & Sat-11 pm. Closed: Tues & Wed 11/1-3/31 & 12/11-12/25. **Reservations:** required; 8/1-8/31. **Features:** No A/C; casual dress; cocktails; street parking; a la carte. Eclectic creative American cuisine with international flair, served in colonial dining rooms dating from 1750's. Artwork from various periods by local artists. **Cards:** AE, CB, DI, DS, MC, VI.   ☒

THE MEWS   Lunch: $8-$15   Dinner: $18-$25   Phone: 508/487-1500   (112)
◆◆
Continental
Location: 0.5 mi e of Town Hall. 429 Commercial St 02657. **Hours:** Open 5/1-12/15 & 1/15-4/30; 11 am-2:30 & 5:30-10:30 pm; 9/15-12/15 & 1/14-5/15 Thurs-Mon dinner only; call for hours on 12/31. Closed: 12/25. **Reservations:** suggested. **Features:** casual dress; cocktails & lounge; street parking. Relaxed atmosphere, dining rooms overlooking harbor & bay. Coffee house with entertainment Mon off season. Lighter American menu in cafe only. Sat & Sun brunch. **Cards:** AE, CB, DI, DS, MC, VI.   ☒

PEPE'S WHARF   Lunch: $7-$13   Dinner: $15-$26   Phone: 508/487-0670   (113)
◆◆◆
Continental
Location: Just e of Town Hall. 371 Commercial St 02657. **Hours:** Open 5/15-10/14; 11:30 am-10 pm. **Reservations:** suggested. **Features:** No A/C; casual dress; children's menu; early bird specials; cocktails & lounge; street parking. Overlooking the bay & harbor. Informal lunch served on open deck in season. Creative entrees featuring fresh local seafood & bistro selections. **Cards:** MC, VI.   ☒

SANDWICH—15,500   (See map p. 330; index p. 326)

LODGINGS

BAY BEACH   Rates Subject to Change   Phone: 508/888-8813   (161)
◆◆◆◆
Bed & Breakfast
5/1-10/31 [BP]   1P: $175- 345   2P/1B: $175- 345   2P/2B: $175- 345   XP: $50
Location: At Bay Beach, 1.3 mi n of SR 6A via Tupper & Town Neck rds & Freeman Ave, follow signs for town beach. One Bay Beach Ln 02563 (PO Box 151). Fax: 508/888-5416. **Terms:** Open 5/1-10/31; age restrictions may apply; reserv deposit, 21 day notice; handling fee imposed. **Facility:** 7 rooms. Spacious & luxurious rooms in private & quiet contemporary beach house on Cape Cod Bay. 2-3 stories, no elevator; interior corridors; smoke free premises; oceanfront; beach. **Recreation:** swimming. **All Rooms:** extended cable TV. **Some Rooms:** whirlpools. **Cards:** MC, VI. (See color ad starting on p 374)   ☒ ⊕ ⊕ ⊟ ⊟ ☒

THE CAPTAIN EZRA NYE HOUSE   Rates Subject to Change   Phone: (508)888-6142   (160)
◆◆
Historic Bed & Breakfast
5/16-10/31   1P: $90- 100   2P/1B: $100- 110
5/1-5/15 & 11/1-4/30   1P: $75- 90   2P/1B: $85- 100
Location: SR 6, exit 2, 1.5 mi n. 152 Main St 02563. Fax: 508/833-2897. **Terms:** Age restrictions may apply; handling fee imposed; 2 night min stay, weekends in season. **Facility:** 6 rooms. 1829 vintage captain's house. Comfortable Early American ambiance. 1 unit with working fireplace. 2 stories; interior/exterior corridors; smoke free premises. **All Rooms:** combo or shower baths. **Some Rooms:** color TV. **Cards:** AE, DS, JC, MC, VI.   ⊗ ⊠ ⊟ ☒

COUNTRY ACRES MOTEL   Rates Subject to Change   Phone: 508/888-2878   (162)
◆◆
Motel
6/25-9/5   2P/1B: $79- 89   2P/2B: $89- 99   XP: $8
5/1-6/24 & 9/6-10/31   2P/1B: $65- 75   2P/2B: $75- 85   XP: $8
11/1-4/30   2P/1B: $50- 60   2P/2B: $50- 60   XP: $8
Location: 0.8 mi e of jct SR 6A & Jarvis St. 187 Rt 6A 02563 (PO Box 307). Fax: 508/888-8511. **Terms:** Reserv deposit, 7 day notice. **Facility:** 18 rooms. On 8 acres adjoining the Great Salt Marsh. 1 one-bedroom housekeeping cottage, $475 weekly in season for up to 2 persons; 1 story; exterior corridors. **All Rooms:** combo or shower baths. **Cards:** AE, CB, DI, DS, MC, VI. (See color ad starting on p 374)   ⊇ ⊟ ⊟

THE DAN'L WEBSTER INN   Guaranteed Rates   Phone: 508/888-3622   (150)
◆◆◆
Country Inn
5/1-5/27 & 4/7-4/30   1P: $129- 295   2P/1B: $129- 295   2P/2B: $129- 295   XP: $10   F12
10/26-4/6   1P: $109- 280   2P/1B: $109- 280   2P/2B: $109- 280   XP: $10   F12
5/28-10/25   1P: $149- 345   2P/1B: $149- 219   2P/2B: $149- 219   XP: $10   F12
Location: Center, 2 mi n of US 6, exit 2. 149 Main St 02563. Fax: 508/888-5156. **Terms:** 2 night min stay, weekends. **Facility:** 47 rooms. A unique Colonial style motor inn featuring a range of rooms & styles including rooms with a whirlpool bath or working fireplace. 2 stories; interior/exterior corridors. **Services:** giftshop. **All Rooms:** combo or shower baths. **Cards:** AE. (See color ad starting on p 374)   ⊞ ⊞ ⊇ ⊟ ⊞ ⊞ ⊞ ⊞ ☒ ⊞

THE EARL OF SANDWICH MOTOR MANOR   Guaranteed Rates   Phone: (508)888-1415   (152)
◆◆
Motel
6/25-9/5 [CP]   2P/1B: $85- 105   2P/2B: $89- 109   XP: $10   F12
5/1-6/24 & 9/6-10/30 [CP]   2P/1B: $65- 85   2P/2B: $69- 89   XP: $10   F12
10/31-4/30 [CP]   2P/1B: $55- 65   2P/2B: $59- 69   XP: $10   F12
Location: MM 5.1. 378 Rt 6A 02537-1442. Fax: 508/833-1039. **Terms:** Reserv deposit, 7 day notice. **Facility:** 23 rooms. Tudor theme rooms around peaceful duck pond, nicely landscaped grounds. 1 story; exterior corridors; playground. **Cards:** AE, CB, DI, DS, MC, VI. (See color ad starting on p 374)   ⊟ ☒ ⊟ ⊟

ISAIAH JONES HOMESTEAD   Rates Subject to Change   Phone: (508)888-9115   (151)
◆◆◆
Bed & Breakfast
5/21-11/1 [BP]   1P: $95- 155   2P/1B: $95- 155   2P/2B: $115- 140   XP: $25
5/1-5/20 & 11/2-4/30 [BP]   1P: $75- 155   2P/1B: $75- 155   2P/2B: $75- 140   XP: $25
Location: Center, 2 mi n of US 6, exit 2. 165 Main St 02563. Fax: 508/888-9648. **Terms:** Age restrictions may apply; reserv deposit, 14 day notice; handling fee imposed; 2 night min stay, weekends in season. **Facility:** 5 rooms. Built 1849, furnished with many antiques & reproductions. Three rooms with working fireplace. 2 stories; interior corridors; designated smoking area. **All Rooms:** combo or shower baths. **Cards:** AE, DS, MC, VI.   ⊞ ⊗ ⊠ ⊟ ☒

(See map p. 330)

OLD COLONY MOTEL   Rates Subject to Change   Phone: (508)888-9716   [153]
◆◆   6/18-9/6 [CP]   1P: $75- 89   2P/1B: $75- 89   2P/2B: $75- 89   XP: $8   F6
Motel   5/1-6/17 & 9/7-10/30 [CP]   1P: $54- 69   2P/1B: $54- 69   2P/2B: $54- 69   XP: $8   F6
    10/31-4/30 [CP]   1P: $50- 60   2P/1B: $50- 60   2P/2B: $50- 60   XP: $8   F6
Location: 3 mi e. 436 Rt 6A 02537 (PO Box 429, EAST SANDWICH). **Terms:** Reserv deposit, 7 day notice. **Facility:** 10 rooms. 1 story; exterior corridors. **Cards:** AE, DS, MC, VI. *(See color ad starting on p 374)*

SANDWICH LODGE & RESORT   Phone: (508)888-2275   [154]
[AAA] [SAVE]   7/3-9/19   2P/2B: $109- 196
◆   5/1-7/2 & 4/1-4/30   2P/2B: $89- 159
Motel   9/20-3/31   2P/2B: $69- 152
    Location: 1 mi w. 54 Rt 6A 02563 (PO Box 1038). Fax: 508/888-8102. **Terms:** Weekly rates; pets, $15 extra charge. **Facility:** 68 rooms. 2 honeymoon suites, &179, $125 off season; 2 stories; interior/exterior corridors; heated indoor pool, whirlpool. **Dining:** Restaurant nearby. **Recreation:** game room, shuffleboard, horseshoes. **Some Rooms:** whirlpools. **Cards:** AE, CB, JC, MC, VI. **Special Amenities: Early check-in/late check-out and free breakfast.**

SANDY NECK MOTEL   Rates Subject to Change   Phone: 508/362-3992   [156]
◆◆   6/11-9/6   1P: $79- 89   2P/1B: $79   2P/2B: $89   XP: $10
Motel   9/7-11/1   1P: $65- 75   2P/1B: $65- 75   2P/2B: $65- 75   XP: $10
    5/1-6/10 & 4/15-4/30   1P: $55- 65   2P/1B: $55- 65   2P/2B: $55- 65   XP: $10
Location: 5.3 mi e on SR 6A at entrance road to Sandy Neck Beach. 669 Rt 6A 02537. Fax: 508/362-5170. **Terms:** Open 5/1-11/1 & 4/15-4/30; reserv deposit, 7 day notice. **Facility:** 12 rooms. 1 efficiency $75-$115 for 2 persons, $125-$194 with the connected room for 4 persons in season; 1 story; exterior corridors. **All Rooms:** combo or shower baths. **Cards:** AE, CB, DI, MC, VI. *(See color ad starting on p 374)*

SHADY NOOK INN & MOTEL   Rates Subject to Change   Phone: 508/888-0409   [157]
◆◆◆   6/12-9/6   2P/2B: $95- 125   XP: $10   F12
Motel   9/7-10/31   2P/2B: $75- 95   XP: $10   F12
    5/1-6/11 & 4/1-4/30   2P/2B: $65- 85   XP: $10   F12
    11/1-3/31   2P/2B: $55- 75   XP: $10   F12
Location: 1.5 mi w on SR 6A. 14 Old Kings Hwy (SR 6A) 02563 (PO Box 402). Fax: 508/888-4039. **Terms:** Reserv deposit, 10 day notice; handling fee imposed; 2 night min stay, weekends in season. **Facility:** 30 rooms. Spacious, attractive rooms on shaded landscaped grounds. 2 units on second floor. 1 two-bedroom unit, $150, 7 efficiencies with microwave, $110; 1 story; exterior corridors; heated pool. **All Rooms:** combo or shower baths. **Cards:** AE, CB, DI, DS, MC, VI. *(See color ad starting on p 374)*

SPRING GARDEN INN & MOTEL   Rates Subject to Change   Phone: (508)888-0710   [158]
[AAA]   6/18-9/6 [CP]   1P: $83- 99   2P/1B: $83- 99   2P/2B: $83- 99   XP: $10   F12
    5/21-6/17 & 9/7-10/22 [CP]   1P: $69- 79   2P/1B: $69- 79   2P/2B: $69- 79   XP: $10   F12
◆◆   5/1-5/20, 10/23-11/22 &
Motel   4/9-4/30 [CP]   1P: $59- 69   2P/1B: $59- 69   2P/2B: $59- 69   XP: $6   F12
Location: 4.5 mi e. 578 Rt 6A 02537 (PO Box 867, EAST SANDWICH). Fax: 508/833-2849. **Terms:** Open 5/1-11/22 & 4/9-4/30; reserv deposit. **Facility:** 11 rooms. A really charming, mature property featuring clean, cozy guest rooms overlooking a unique salt marsh & tidal creek. Fruit trees on property & guests are invited to take some home when fruits in season. 2 efficiencies, $10 extra charge; 2 stories; exterior corridors. **All Rooms:** combo or shower baths, extended cable TV. **Cards:** AE, DS, MC, VI. *(See color ad starting on p 374)*

SPRING HILL MOTOR LODGE   Rates Subject to Change   Phone: 508/888-1456   [159]
[AAA]   6/4-9/5   2P/1B: $89- 105   2P/2B: $95- 115   XP: $10
    9/6-10/31   2P/1B: $75- 85   2P/2B: $75- 95   XP: $10
◆◆◆   5/1-6/3 & 4/1-4/30   2P/1B: $75- 85   2P/2B: $75- 85   XP: $10
Motel   11/1-3/31   2P/1B: $65- 75   2P/2B: $65- 75   XP: $10
    Location: 2.5 mi e. 351 Rt 6A 02537. Fax: 508/833-1556. **Terms:** Reserv deposit, 7 day notice. **Facility:** 28 rooms. Modern rooms. Nicely landscaped grounds, pool & tennis area. 3 two-bedroom units. 2 two-bedroom efficiencies, $925 weekly in season for up to 2 persons. 4 cottages $1100-$1400 weekly, for up to 2 persons in season; 1 story; exterior corridors; heated pool; 1 lighted tennis court. **All Rooms:** combo or shower baths, extended cable TV. **Cards:** AE, DI, DS, MC, VI. *(See color ad starting on p 374)*

WHALEBACK HILL COTTAGES   Rates Subject to Change   Phone: 508/888-0338   [148]
◆   6/28-9/6   2P/1B: $65- 80   2P/2B: $65- 80   XP: $5
Cottage   5/1-6/27, 9/7-11/1 & 4/1-4/30   2P/1B: $45- 50   2P/2B: $45- 50   XP: $5
Location: At MM 5.1. 376 Rt 6A 02537 (PO Box 482). **Terms:** Open 5/1-11/1 & 4/1-4/30; reserv deposit, 10 day notice; handling fee imposed. **Facility:** 14 rooms. 1 story; exterior corridors. **All Rooms:** shower baths. **Some Rooms:** 4 efficiencies, 2 kitchens. **Cards:** DS, MC, VI.

RESTAURANTS

AQUA GRILL   **Lunch:** $5-$10   **Dinner:** $10-$20   Phone: 508/888-8889   [72]
◆◆◆   **Location:** 1.5 mi n of SR 6A via Tupper, Town Neck & Gallo rds; adjacent to Sandwich Marina. 14 Gallo Rd
American   02563. **Hours:** Open 5/1-10/31 & 4/2-4/30; 11:30 am-9 pm, Fri-9:30 pm, Sat noon-9:30 pm, Sun noon-9 pm.
    Closed: 11/1-4/1. **Reservations:** suggested. **Features:** casual dress; children's menu; carryout; cocktails & lounge; entertainment; a la carte. Casual dining. Some outdoor dining, weather permitting. Overlooking marina & Cape Cod Canal. Piano bar entertainment Thurs-Sat 7 pm. Hrs vary in off season. **Cards:** AE, MC, VI.

BARNEY'S GRILL & FARE   **Lunch:** $6-$14   **Dinner:** $6-$18   Phone: 508/888-4344   [76]
◆   **Location:** 1.3 mi w. 46 Rt 6A 02563. **Hours:** 11 am-11 pm. Closed: 12/25. **Features:** casual dress; Sunday
American   brunch; children's menu; carryout; cocktails & lounge; a la carte. Including a good selection of sandwiches, pasta & pizza. **Cards:** AE, DS, MC, VI.

THE BEE-HIVE TAVERN   **Lunch:** $5-$9   **Dinner:** $9-$16   Phone: 508/833-1184   [70]
◆◆   **Location:** 3 mi e. 406 Rt 6A 02537. **Hours:** 11:30 am-9 pm, Sun from 8 am, Sat 5/23-9/6 from 8 am.
American   Closed: 12/25. **Features:** casual dress; children's menu; cocktails & lounge; a la carte. Casual Colonial tavern. Smoking permitted in lounge only. **Cards:** MC, VI.

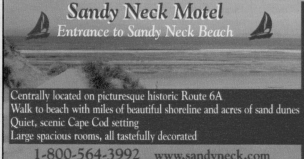

(See map p. 330)

THE DAN'L WEBSTER INN   Country Inn   **Lunch:** $8-$12   **Dinner:** $17-$25   **Phone:** 508/888-3623   ⑦⑧
◆◆◆   **Location:** Center, 2 mi n of US 6, exit 2; in The Dan'l Webster Inn. 149 Main St 02563. **Hours:** 8 am-9 pm,
American   Fri & Sat-10 pm. Closed: 12/25. **Reservations:** suggested. **Features:** dressy casual; Sunday brunch;
children's menu; early bird specials; carryout; cocktails; a la carte. A proud inn with a sun-filled conservatory
& intimate dining rooms. Wonderful wine list. Casual tavern grille menu. **Cards:** AE, CB, DI, DS, MC, VI.   ✕

HORIZON'S ON CAPE COD BAY   **Lunch:** $5-$7   **Dinner:** $11-$14   **Phone:** 508/888-6166   ⑦③
⚫⚫⚫   **Location:** On Cape Cod Bay at Town Neck Beach; 0.5 mi s of SR 6A via Tupper & Town Neck rds. 98 Town
◆◆   Neck Rd 02563. **Hours:** Open 5/1-11/1 & 4/1-4/30; 11:30 am-9 pm. **Features:** No A/C; casual dress;
Seafood   children's menu; cocktails & lounge; a la carte. Casual dining overlooking Cape Cod Bay. Informal pub/sports
bar atmosphere. Limited deck dining also avail. **Cards:** AE, DS, MC, VI.

SAVE = AAA/CAA member discounts

SOUTH DENNIS—3,600   (See map p. 332; index p. 324)

LODGING

CAPTAIN NICKERSON INN	Rates Subject to Change			Phone: 508/398-5966	66
◆◆ 5/28-10/15	1P: $77- 90	2P/1B:	$82- 95	XP: $12	D10
Historic Bed 5/1-5/27, 10/16-12/21 &					
& Breakfast 3/1-4/30	1P: $60- 65	2P/1B:	$70- 75	XP: $10	D10

Location: US 6, exit 9; 0.8 mi s on SR 134, 0.3 mi w on Upper County Rd, 0.3 mi s. 333 Main St 02660. Fax: 508/398-5966. **Terms:** Open 5/1-12/21 & 3/1-4/30; reserv deposit, 14 day notice; 2 night min stay, weekends in season. **Facility:** 5 rooms. 1879 Queen Anne sea captain's home. Comfortable, cozy rooms. 3 stories, no elevator; interior corridors; designated smoking area. **Recreation:** bicycles. **Cards:** DS, MC, VI.   [ASK] [🅢🅐] [X] [PTV] [Z] [🖨] [X]

SOUTH HARWICH—900   (See map p. 330; index p. 325)

LODGING

HANDKERCHIEF SHOALS MOTEL	Rates Subject to Change		Phone: 508/432-2200	113
◆◆ 6/25-9/7	2P/1B: $70	2P/2B: $72- 78	XP: $8	
Motel 5/1-6/24, 9/8-10/11 &				
4/15-4/30	2P/1B: $45	2P/2B: $47- 52	XP: $5	

Location: 0.3 mi w on SR 28. 888 Main St (Rt 28) 02661 (PO Box 306). **Terms:** Open 5/1-10/11 & 4/15-4/30; reserv deposit, 10 day notice. **Facility:** 26 rooms. 1 story; exterior corridors. **All Rooms:** combo or shower baths. **Cards:** DS, MC, VI.   [🏊] [□] [X] [🛗]

SOUTH WELLFLEET—2,400   (See map p. 330; index p. 327)

LODGINGS

THE EVEN'TIDE MOTEL	Guaranteed Rates		Phone: 508/349-3410	245
◍ 6/11-9/6	2P/1B: $82- 99	2P/2B: $85- 112	XP: $7-10	D18
9/7-10/10	2P/1B: $55	2P/2B: $58- 62	XP: $7-10	D18
◆◆ 5/1-6/10, 10/11-10/30 &				
Motel 4/7-4/30	2P/1B: $46	2P/2B: $49- 53	XP: $7-10	D18

Location: US 6, 4.5 mi n of National Seashore Visitor's Center. 650 Rt 6 02663 (PO Box 41). Fax: 508/349-7804. **Terms:** Open 5/1-10/30 & 4/7-4/30; reserv deposit, 14 day notice; handling fee imposed; weekly rates; 2 night min stay, in season. **Facility:** 31 rooms. On wooded grounds. Family owned & operated. 3 studio housekeeping apartments, $115 for 2 persons in season, 3 night min stay; 2 stories; exterior corridors; heated indoor pool; playground. **Recreation:** adjacent to Cape Cod rail bicycle trail. **All Rooms:** combo or shower baths, extended cable TV. **Some Rooms:** 3 efficiencies. **Cards:** AE, CB, DI, DS, MC, VI. *(See color ad below)*   [🏊] [🅐] [X] [🖥] [□] [🖨] [🛗] [X]

(See map p. 330)

SOUTHFLEET MOTOR INN
Phone: 508/349-3580 **247**
Rates Subject to Change
🔺🔺🔺
6/25-9/6   1P: $99- 110   2P/1B: $99- 110   2P/2B: $99- 120   XP: $10   F12
5/1-6/24 & 9/7-4/30   1P: $71- 85   2P/1B: $71- 85   2P/2B: $71- 85   XP: $5   F12
Motel
◆◆◆   **Location:** On US 6; 5.3 mi n of National Seashore Visitor's Center. Rt 6 (PO Box 217, 02663).
Fax: 508/349-0250. **Terms:** Reserv deposit, 14 day notice; handling fee imposed; weekly rates; package plans; 2 night min stay, in season. **Facility:** 30 rooms. Across from the Cape Cod Bike Trail. 1-2 stories; exterior corridors; heated indoor pool, sauna, whirlpool. **Dining:** Restaurant nearby. **Recreation:** video game room basketball hoop. Fee: bicycles. **All Rooms:** extended cable TV. **Cards:** AE, CB, DI, DS, MC, VI. *(See ad p 377)*

🅢 🚭 📶 ⊗ 🍸 🖨 🖥 ✕

WELLFLEET MOTEL AND LODGE
Phone: 508/349-3535 **248**
Rates Subject to Change
🔺🔺🔺
6/11-9/6   1P: $70- 150   2P/1B: $76- 150   2P/2B: $70- 190   XP: $10
5/1-6/10 & 9/7-4/30   1P: $60- 90   2P/1B: $60- 90   2P/2B: $60- 120   XP: $10
Motel
◆◆◆   **Location:** 3.5 mi n of National Seashore Visitor's Center. 170 US 6 02663 (PO Box 606).
Fax: 508/349-1192. **Terms:** Check-in 3:30 pm; reserv deposit, 14 day notice; package plans, off season; 2 night min stay, in season. **Facility:** 65 rooms. Variety of room types & styles. Adjacent to Cape Cod Rail Trail. 4 night min stay weekends; 1-2 stories; exterior corridors; heated indoor pool, whirlpool. **Dining:** Coffee shop; 7 am-noon 5/23-10/12, weekends 4/1-5/22 & 10/13-10/31,; cocktail lounge in season. **All Rooms:** extended cable TV. **Cards:** AE, CB, DI, MC, VI. *(See color ad below)*

🅢 🚭 📶 🍸 🖨 🔲 🖥 🖥 ✕

RESTAURANT

VAN RENSSELAER'S RESTAURANT
Dinner: $12-$22   Phone: 508/349-2127   **105**
🔺🔺🔺
Location: 5.3 mi n of National Seashore Visitor's Center. 1019 Rt 6 02663. **Hours:** Open 5/1-11/29 & 4/10-4/30; 8 am-noon & 4:30-9 pm 5/23-10/12. Call for off-season hours. **Reservations:** accepted.
◆◆
American   **Features:** casual dress; children's menu; early bird specials; carryout; salad bar; cocktails & lounge.
Comfortable, cheerful dining. Featuring fresh seafood, lobster, prime rib & creative pasta entrees. Family owned & operated. Screened porch dining in season. Smoke free premises. **Cards:** AE, CB, DI, DS, JC,
MC, VI.

🅑 ✕

SOUTH YARMOUTH—10,400   (See map p. 332; index p. 323)

LODGINGS

ALL SEASONS MOTOR INN
Phone: 508/394-7600 **23**
Guaranteed Rates
🔺🔺🔺
6/25-9/5   1P: $99- 125   2P/1B: $99- 125   2P/2B: $99- 125   XP: $5   D12
Fri & Sat 5/1-6/24, 9/6-10/31 & 4/11-4/30   1P: $65- 99   2P/1B: $65- 99   2P/2B: $65- 99   XP: $5   D12
Motel
Sun-Thurs 5/1-6/24, 9/6-10/31 & 11/1-4/10   1P: $59- 75   2P/1B: $59- 75   2P/2B: $59- 75   XP: $5   D12
Sun-Thurs 11/1-4/10   1P: $39- 59   2P/1B: $39- 59   2P/2B: $39- 59   XP: $5   D12
Location: On SR 28, 0.5 mi w of Bass River Bridge. 1199 Main St, Rt 28 02664. **Fax:** 508/398-7160. **Terms:** Reserv deposit, 7 day notice. **Facility:** 114 rooms. Vibrant, modern room decors. Many units with balcony or patio overlook secluded garden courtyard. 2 stories; interior corridors; heated indoor pool, saunas, whirlpool; playground. **Dining:** Coffee shop; 7:30-11 am; 6/30-9/4 also noon-2:30 pm. **Recreation:** video game room. **All Rooms:** extended cable TV. **Cards:** AE, CB, DI, DS, MC, VI. *(See color ad p 333 & p 384)*

🅢 🈺 🚭 📶 🛆 ⊗ 🍽 🍸 📼 🖨 🖥 🅗 ✕

BEACH 'N TOWNE MOTEL
Phone: (508)398-2311 **25**
🔺🔺🔺 (SAVE)
6/25-8/28   1P: $60- 67   2P/1B: $60- 67   2P/2B: $60- 67   XP: $7   F12
6/3-6/24 & 8/29-9/9   1P: $44- 54   2P/1B: $44- 54   2P/2B: $44- 54   XP: $7   F12
Motel
5/1-6/2, 9/10-11/28 & 2/4-4/30   1P: $36- 54   2P/1B: $36- 54   2P/2B: $36- 54   XP: $7   F12
Location: 0.5 mi w of Bass River Bridge. 1261 Rt 28 02664. **Terms:** Open 5/1-11/28 & 2/4-4/30; reserv deposit, 10 day notice; handling fee imposed. **Facility:** 21 rooms. Cozy units in quiet setting. 1 story; exterior corridors; playground. **Recreation:** basketball, ping pong, shuffleboard. **All Rooms:** combo or shower baths, extended cable TV. **Cards:** AE, DS, MC, VI. **Special Amenities:** Free local telephone calls and preferred room (subject to availability with advanced reservations).

🚭 ⊗ 🖥 ✕

(See map p. 332)

BEST WESTERN BLUE ROCK INN
Rates Subject to Change   Phone: (508)398-6962   **27**

AAA

6/25-9/5	1P: $115- 170	2P/1B: $115- 170	2P/2B: $115- 170	XP: $10	F12
Fri & Sat 5/1-6/24 & 9/6-10/10	1P: $105- 170	2P/1B: $105- 170	2P/2B: $105- 170	XP: $5	F12
Sun-Thurs 5/1-6/24, 9/6-10/10, 10/11-10/31 & 4/7-4/30	1P: $89- 165	2P/1B: $89- 165	2P/2B: $89- 165	XP: $5	F12
Sun-Thurs 10/11-10/31 & 4/7-4/30	1P: $65- 125	2P/1B: $65- 125	2P/2B: $65- 125	XP: $5	F12

Motel

Location: Jct SR 28, 1 mi ne via N Main St & High Bank Rd, 0.5 mi n on Country Club Dr following signs. 39 Todd Rd 02664 (PO Box 419). Fax: 508/398-1830. **Terms:** Open 5/1-10/31 & 4/7-4/30; reserv deposit, 14 day notice; handling fee imposed; BP avail; package plans; 2 night min stay, weekends. **Facility:** 45 rooms. Adjacent to golf course. 1 one-bedroom apartment for 2-4 persons, $160 in season; 2 stories; exterior corridors; heated pool, whirlpool; 1 tennis court. Fee: 18 hole par 3, executive golf course. **Dining:** Coffee shop; 7 am-2:30 pm. **Recreation:** shuffleboard. **All Rooms:** extended cable TV. **Some Rooms:** whirlpools. **Cards:** AE, CB, DI, DS, MC, VI. (See color ad below)

BEST WESTERN BLUE WATERS ON THE OCEAN
Rates Subject to Change   Phone: (508)398-2288   **26**

AAA

6/25-9/5	1P: $170- 280	2P/1B: $170- 280	2P/2B: $170- 280	XP: $10	F12
5/21-6/24 & 9/6-10/10	1P: $122- 225	2P/1B: $122- 225	2P/2B: $122- 225	XP: $5	F12
5/1-5/20, 10/11-10/31 & 4/15-4/30	1P: $90- 140	2P/1B: $90- 140	2P/2B: $90- 140	XP: $5	F12

Motor Inn

Location: 1 mi s off SR 28 on the ocean. 291 South Shore Dr 02664 (PO Box 276, 02664-0276). Fax: 508/398-1010. **Terms:** Open 5/1-10/31 & 4/15-4/30; reserv deposit, 10 day notice; handling fee imposed; BP, MAP avail; package plans; 2 night min stay, weekends. **Facility:** 110 rooms. Variety of rooms, some with balcony. 9 two-bedroom units. 3 stories, no elevator; interior/exterior corridors; beachfront; putting green; beach, heated indoor pool, saunas, whirlpool; 1 tennis court. **Dining:** Restaurant, coffee shop; 7:30 am-11 & noon-2 pm, Fri & Sat 6:30 pm-9 pm; closed for dinner 6/26-9/10; $11-$16; cocktails. **All Rooms:** extended cable TV. **Some Rooms:** 26 kitchens, whirlpools. **Cards:** AE, DI, DS, MC, VI. (See color ad below)

MOTEL 6 - 4042
Phone: (508)394-4000   **24**

AAA SAVE

6/25-9/6	1P: $65- 95	2P/1B: $65- 95	2P/2B: $65- 95	XP: $10	F16
5/1-6/24 & 9/7-10/10	1P: $40- 70	2P/1B: $40- 70	2P/2B: $40- 70	XP: $10	F16
10/11-4/30	1P: $40- 60	2P/1B: $40- 60	2P/2B: $40- 60	XP: $10	F16

Motel

Location: 0.3 mi w of Bass River Bridge. 1314 Rt 28 02664 (PO Box 777). Fax: 508/394-8319. **Terms:** Reserv deposit; BP avail; package plans; 2 night min stay, weekends; small pets only, 1 per rm, must be attended. **Facility:** 89 rooms. Open weekends only 10/25-4/30, except school vacations. 2 two-bedroom units. 2 two-bedroom units, $95 in season; 2 stories; interior corridors; heated indoor pool, sauna, whirlpool. **Dining:** Coffee shop; 7 am-10 am; 7/4-10/14. **Recreation:** video game room. **All Rooms:** extended cable TV. **Cards:** AE, CB, DI, DS, MC, VI. **Special Amenities:** Free local telephone calls. (See color ad p 380)

(See map p. 332)

THE OCEAN CLUB ON SMUGGLERS BEACH   Phone: (508)398-6955   28

(AAA) SAVE

◆◆◆
Motel

7/2-9/9	1P: $230	2P/1B: $230	
5/14-7/1 & 9/10-10/14	1P: $130	2P/1B: $130	
5/1-5/13 & 10/15-1/7	1P: $110	2P/1B: $110	
1/8-4/30	1P: $120	2P/1B: $120	

Location: 1 mi s off SR 28 on the ocean. 329 South Shore Dr 02664. Fax: 508/394-3788. **Terms:** Check-in 4 pm; reserv deposit; weekly rates; 2 night min stay, weekends. **Facility:** 60 rooms. Scenic beachfront location. All charming rooms with ocean view, whirlpool & fireplace. Many rooms with small balcony & patio. Rates for up to 4 persons & higher on weekends. 2 two-bedroom units $285 in season; 2 stories; interior corridors; beach, heated indoor pool, sauna, whirlpool. **Recreation:** activity center. **All Rooms:** extended cable TV. **Some Rooms:** 11 efficiencies. **Cards:** AE, MC, VI.

⛱ 🏊 🖥 VCR 🖨 📺 📠 🕽 📷

OCEAN MIST RESORT   Rates Subject to Change   Phone: (508)398-2633   29

(AAA)

◆◆◆
Motel

7/2-9/5	1P: $164- 274	2P/1B: $164- 274	2P/2B: $164- 274	XP: $10	F15
5/28-7/1 & 9/6-11/13	1P: $124- 204	2P/1B: $124- 204	2P/2B: $124- 204	XP: $10	F15
5/1-5/27, 11/14-1/2 &				
2/4-4/30	1P: $89- 159	2P/1B: $89- 159	2P/2B: $89- 159	XP: $10	F15

Location: 1 mi s off SR 28 on the ocean. 97 South Shore Dr 02664. Fax: 508/760-3151. **Terms:** Open 5/1-1/2 & 2/4-4/30; 2 night min stay, weekends in season. **Facility:** 63 rooms. Attractive contemporary decor. 32 bi-level loft suites with balcony on second floor. 2 two-bedroom units. Some deluxe units, $240-$250; 2 stories; interior/exterior corridors; oceanfront; beach, heated indoor pool, saunas, whirlpool; 1 tennis court; boat dock; playground. **Dining:** Coffee shop; 5/23-10/12, 7:30-10:30 am; weekends only off season. **All Rooms:** extended cable TV. **Some Rooms:** 21 efficiencies. **Cards:** AE, DS, MC, VI. *(See color ad p 333)*

⛱ 🍴 🏊 VCR 📺 🕽

RED JACKET BEACH MOTOR INN   Rates Subject to Change   Phone: (508)398-6941   30

(AAA)

◆◆◆
Motor Inn

6/27-9/5	1P: $165- 245	2P/1B: $165- 245	2P/2B: $165- 245	XP: $20	F4
5/21-6/26, 9/6-10/10 &				
4/9-4/30	1P: $95- 165	2P/1B: $95- 165	2P/2B: $95- 165	XP: $10	F4
5/1-5/20 & 10/11-10/31	1P: $85- 140	2P/1B: $85- 140	2P/2B: $85- 140	XP: $10	F4

Location: 2 mi s off SR 28; on the ocean. 1 South Shore Dr 02664 (PO Box 88). Fax: 508/398-1214. **Terms:** Open 5/1-10/31 & 4/9-4/30; reserv deposit, 14 day notice; handling fee imposed; BP avail, off season; package plans. **Facility:** 150 rooms. On landscaped beachfront grounds. Patio or balcony. Oceanview or riverside rooms. 2 stories; interior/exterior corridors; putting green; beach, heated indoor pool, saunas, whirlpool; 1 tennis court; boat dock; playground. **Dining:** Restaurant; 7:30 am-11, noon-3 & 5:30-9:30 pm, off season 7:30 am-11 & noon-2 pm; $9-$18; cocktails. **Services:** giftshop. **Recreation:** fishing; badminton, basketball, horseshoes, jet boat rentals, shuffleboard, volleyball. **Fee:** sailboating, parasailing, kayaks, trimaran cruises. **Rental:** boats, paddleboats. **All Rooms:** extended cable TV. **Some Rooms:** whirlpools. **Cards:** AE, MC, VI. *(See color ad p 361)*

🅿 ⛱ 🍴 🎣 🎿 🏊 ✕ 🖥 📠 🕽 ✕ 📷

(See map p. 332)

RED MILL MOTEL
AAA SAVE
6/23-9/7 [CP]
5/1-6/22, 9/8-1/31 & 3/1-4/30
◆◆ [CP]
Motel
Phone: (508)398-5583 31
2P/2B: $65- 85 XP: $10 F14

2P/2B: $38- 55 XP: $10 F14
Location: On SR 28, 2 mi w of jct SR 134. 793 Main St 02664. Fax: 508/398-5470. **Terms:** Open 5/1-1/31 & 3/1-4/30; reserv deposit, 4 day notice; handling fee imposed; 2 night min stay, weekends in season. **Facility:** 18 rooms. Owner operated. 4 Efficiencies $65-$79 for 2 persons in season; 2 stories, no elevator; interior corridors. **Recreation:** picnic area. **All Rooms:** extended cable TV. **Some Rooms:** 4 efficiencies. **Cards:** AE, DS, MC, VI. **Special Amenities: Free breakfast.**

⊇ ▢ ▤ ✕

RIVIERA BEACH RESORT
AAA
6/25-9/5
6/11-6/24
9/6-10/11
5/14-6/10
◆◆◆
Motel

Rates Subject to Change

				Phone: (508)398-2273 32
1P: $150- 255	2P/1B: $150- 255	2P/2B: $150- 255	XP: $10	F8
1P: $115- 190	2P/1B: $115- 190	2P/2B: $115- 190	XP: $5	F8
1P: $93- 175	2P/1B: $93- 175	2P/2B: $93- 175	XP: $5	F8
1P: $75- 150	2P/1B: $75- 150	2P/2B: $75- 150	XP: $5	F8

Location: 1 mi s off SR 28 on the ocean. 327 South Shore Dr 02664. Fax: 508/398-1202. **Terms:** Open 5/14-10/11; reserv deposit, 10 day notice; handling fee imposed; BP avail; 2 night min stay, weekends. **Facility:** 125 rooms. Nicely landscaped grounds. Variety of rooms with deck or patio. 2 family kitchen units, $275 in season for up to 4 persons; 2 stories; interior/exterior corridors; oceanfront; beach, heated indoor pool, whirlpool. **Dining:** Coffee shop; 7:30 am-11 & noon-2 pm 6/27-9/7, to 12:30 pm off season. **Recreation:** aquatrike, kayak rental; shuffleboard. Fee: sailboats 6/26-9/7. **All Rooms:** extended cable TV. **Some Rooms:** 4 efficiencies, 2 kitchens, whirlpools. **Cards:** AE, MC, VI. *(See color ad p 380)*

$O ⊇ Ⓨ ✕ VCR ▢ ▤ ▢ ▤ ▤ ✕ ⓕ

SURFCOMBER ON THE OCEAN
AAA
6/25-8/28
6/11-6/24 & 8/29-9/11
◆◆◆
5/21-6/10 & 9/12-10/12
Motel

Guaranteed Rates

Phone: 508/398-9228 33
2P/2B: $140- 160
2P/2B: $85- 135
2P/2B: $80- 110
Location: 1 mi s off SR 28, on the ocean. 107 South Shore Dr 02664. Fax: 508/398-1002. **Terms:** Open 5/21-10/12; reserv deposit, 14 day notice; handling fee imposed; 3 night min stay, weekends in season. **Facility:** 33 rooms. Some rooms with balcony or patio. Rooms overlook an attractive courtyard. Many with ocean views. 2 two-bedroom units. 15 efficiencies, $100-$240; $90-$145 off season for up to 2 persons; 2 stories; exterior corridors; beachfront; beach, heated pool. **Recreation:** swimming; Shuffleboard. **All Rooms:** combo or shower baths, extended cable TV. **Cards:** MC, VI. *(See color ad below)*

⊇ ✕ ▢ ▤ ▤

RESTAURANTS

HEARTH'N KETTLE FAMILY RESTAURANT   **Lunch:** $4-$10   **Dinner:** $6-$15   **Phone:** 508/394-2252 21
◆
American
Location: 0.8 mi w of Bass River Bridge. 1196 Main St, Rt 28 02664. **Hours:** 7 am-9 pm; 7/4-9/4 to 10 pm. Closed: 12/25. **Features:** casual dress; children's menu; early bird specials; carryout; cocktails; a la carte. Relaxed, family dining in a charming Colonial day ambiance. Delightful staff in period costume. Overlooking James Pond. **Cards:** AE, DS, MC, VI.

✕

RIVERWAY LOBSTER HOUSE   **Dinner:** $9-$23   **Phone:** 508/398-2172 23
AAA
◆◆
American
Location: At jct N Main St; just w of Bass River Bridge. 1328 Rt 28 02664. **Hours:** 4:30 pm-10 pm, Sun noon-9 pm. Closed: 12/25 & Mon 10/13-4/15. **Reservations:** suggested. **Features:** casual dress; Sunday brunch; children's menu; early bird specials; carryout; cocktails & lounge; a la carte. Very popular, lively family dining in a charming ambiance. Serving fine foods since 1943. Ocean fresh lobster, pasta & prime rib featured. Many seafood entrees. **Cards:** AE, DI, DS, MC, VI.

✕

THE SKIPPER RESTAURANT   **Lunch:** $4-$10   **Dinner:** $9-$18   **Phone:** 508/394-7406 20
◆◆
American
Location: 1.5 mi s of SR 28; across from the ocean. 152 South Shore Dr 02664. **Hours:** Open 5/1-9/21 & 4/14-4/30; 11:30 am-10 pm, Sun from 8 am. **Features:** No A/C; casual dress; children's menu; early bird specials; carryout; cocktails & lounge; a la carte. Nautical atmosphere, light menu served in 2nd floor Lookout Lounge. Seafood featured. Very popular. **Cards:** AE, DI, DS, MC, VI.

✕

WELLFLEET—2,500   (See map p. 330; index p. 329)

RESTAURANTS

AESOP'S TABLES   Historical   **Dinner:** $14-$26   **Phone:** 508/349-6450 152
◆◆◆
American
Location: Center, 0.5 mi w of jct SR 6N. 316 Main St 02667. **Hours:** Open 5/11-10/13; 5:30 pm-9:30 pm; 7/1-9/6 to 10 pm. Closed: Tues & Wed 5/11-6/15 & 9/15-10/13. **Reservations:** suggested. **Features:** No A/C; dressy casual; children's menu; cocktails & lounge; a la carte. Gracious dining in restored 1805 Govenor's summer mansion. Featuring New American cuisine. Smoke free premises. **Cards:** AE, CB, DI, MC, VI.

✕

(See map p. 330)

MOBY DICK'S FAMILY RESTUARANT   **Lunch:** $8-$13   **Dinner:** $8-$13   **Phone:** 508/349-9795   [150]
Ⓐ   **Location:** In Wellfleet Center, Opposite Gull Pond Rd. US 6 02667. **Hours:** Open 5/8-10/1; 11:30 am-9 pm;
◆   6/19-9/7 to 10 pm. **Features:** No A/C; casual dress; children's menu; carryout; a la carte. Very informal
Seafood   dining in old Cape Cod tradition with paper plates & plastic utensils. Fresh Cape Cod lobster, clambakes,
    steamers & mussels. Fried & broiled entrees. Screened picnic area. Smoke free premises.   ☒

WEST BARNSTABLE   (See map p. 330; index p. 328)

LODGING

HONEYSUCKLE HILL BED & BREAKFAST   Rates Subject to Change   **Phone:** 508/362-8418   [315]
◆◆◆   All Year [BP]   1P: $95- 135 2P/1B: $95- 185
Historic Bed   **Location:** 0.7 mi w of jct SR149. 591 Old Kings Highway, Rt 6A 02668. **Terms:** Age restrictions may apply;
& Breakfast   reserv deposit, 14 day notice; handling fee imposed; 2 night min stay, weekends. **Facility:** 4 rooms. An 1810
    Victorian Farmhouse, all rooms with featherbeds. 1 two-bedroom unit. 2 stories; interior corridors; designated
smoking area. **All Rooms:** shower baths. **Cards:** AE, DS, MC, VI.   ⊠ ☎ 🖨 ☒

WEST DENNIS—2,300   (See map p. 332; index p. 324)

LODGINGS

DENNIS WEST MOTOR LODGE   Rates Subject to Change   **Phone:** 508/394-7434   [60]
Ⓐ   Fri & Sat 6/25-9/6   1P: $58- 70 2P/1B: $63- 75 2P/2B: $63- 75 XP: $10   F12
    Sun-Thurs 6/25-9/6   1P: $52- 60 2P/1B: $55- 65 2P/2B: $55- 65 XP: $7   F12
◆   5/1-6/24, 9/7-11/29 &
Motel   2/12-4/30   1P: $36- 45 2P/1B: $36- 50 2P/2B: $38- 50 XP: $7   F12
    Location: 0.5 mi w of jct SR 134. 691 Main St (Rt 28) 02670. **Terms:** Open 5/1-11/29 & 2/12-4/30; reserv
deposit, 7 day notice; handling fee imposed; 2 night min stay, weekends in summer. **Facility:** 22 rooms. 2 stories; exterior corridors. **Recreation:** picnic area. **All Rooms:** extended cable TV. **Cards:** AE, DS, MC, VI.   🏊 ▢ 🖨 ☒

THE HUNTSMAN MOTOR LODGE   **Phone:** (508)394-5415   [61]
Ⓐ SAVE   6/25-8/31   2P/1B: $79- 89 2P/2B: $79- 89
◆◆   Fri & Sat 5/1-6/24 & 9/1-4/30   2P/1B: $49- 69 2P/2B: $49- 69
Motel   Sun-Thurs 5/1-6/24 &
    9/1-4/30   2P/1B: $39- 59 2P/2B: $39- 59
    Location: On SR 28, 0.3 mi w of jct SR 134. 829 Main St 02670. Fax: 508/398-7852. **Terms:** Reserv
deposit, 7 day notice, 14 day for efficiencies; handling fee imposed; package plans. **Facility:** 27 rooms. Quiet accommoda-
tions. 9 efficiencies $89, $59 off season; 2 stories; exterior corridors. **Recreation:** shuffleboard & picnic area with grills.
All Rooms: extended cable TV. **Cards:** MC, VI. **Special Amenities:** Early check-in/late check-out and free room
upgrade (subject to availability with advanced reservations).   🅢 🏊 🖨

WEST YARMOUTH—5,400   (See map p. 332; index p. 324)

LODGINGS

AMERICANA HOLIDAY MOTEL   Guaranteed Rates   **Phone:** 508/775-5511   [35]
Ⓐ   6/27-9/5 [EP]   1P: $60- 69 2P/1B: $60- 69 2P/2B: $60- 69 XP: $5   F12
◆◆   5/1-6/26, 9/6-10/30 &
    3/26-4/30 [CP]   1P: $30- 36 2P/1B: $30- 36 2P/2B: $30- 36 XP: $5   F12
Motel   **Location:** 0.3 mi e of Hyannis on SR 28. 99 Main St 02673. Fax: 508/790-0597. **Terms:** Open 5/1-10/30 &
3/26-4/30; reserv deposit, 7 day notice. **Facility:** 153 rooms. 5 buildings on expansive grounds. Family-
oriented. 4 two-bedroom units. 4 persons per room max. 4 two-bedroom suites, $104 in season for up to 4 persons; 2 stories;
exterior corridors; putting green; heated indoor pool, sauna, whirlpool; playground. **Dining:** 7-10:30 am; breakfast room.
Recreation: shuffleboard, video game room. **All Rooms:** extended cable TV. **Cards:** AE, CB, DI, DS, MC, VI.
(See color ad p 333 & below)   🎮 🏊 ☒ 🖨 🖥 ☒

(See map p. 332)

BAYSIDE RESORT PARK INN   **Phone:** (508)775-5669   42

	6/18-9/5 [CP]	1P:	$99- 179	2P/1B:	$99- 179	2P/2B:	$99- 179	XP: $10	F12
	9/6-10/30 [CP]	1P:	$59- 129	2P/1B:	$59- 129	2P/2B:	$59- 129	XP: $10	F12
	5/1-6/17 & 10/31-4/30 [CP]	1P:	$49- 119	2P/1B:	$49- 119	2P/2B:	$49- 119	XP: $10	F12

Motel   **Location:** 1.8 mi e Hyannis. 225 Route 28 02673. Fax: 508/775-8862. **Terms:** Reserv deposit, 3 day notice; weekly rates; package plans; 2 night min stay, weekends in season. **Facility:** 128 rooms. 8 whirlpool rms, $99-$169 for up to 2 persons; 2 stories; interior corridors; heated indoor pool, saunas, whirlpool. **Recreation:** video game room, volleyball. **All Rooms:** combo or shower baths, extended cable TV. **Cards:** AE, DI, MC, VI. **Special Amenities:** Early check-in/late check-out and free breakfast. *(See color ad below)*

THE CAPE POINT   Rates Subject to Change   **Phone:** (508)778-1500   38

6/1-8/31	1P:	$89- 129	2P/1B:	$89- 129	2P/2B:	$89- 129	XP: $10
5/1-5/31 & 1/1-4/30	1P:	$39- 89	2P/1B:	$39- 89	2P/2B:	$39- 89	XP: $10
9/1-10/31	1P:	$49- 79	2P/1B:	$49- 79	2P/2B:	$49- 79	XP: $10
11/1-12/31	1P:	$34- 69	2P/1B:	$34- 69	2P/2B:	$34- 69	XP: $10

Motel   **Location:** On SR 28, just e of Higgins Crowell Rd. 476 Main St 02673. Fax: 508/778-5516. **Terms:** Reserv deposit, 3 day notice; 2 night min stay. **Facility:** 116 rooms. Hotel style public facilities. 4 two-bedroom units. Max of 5 persons per room. Family suites, $69-$149; 2 stories; interior corridors; heated indoor pool, wading pool, saunas, whirlpool. **Dining:** 7-11 am; cocktails. **Recreation:** video game room. **All Rooms:** extended cable TV. **Cards:** AE, DS, MC, VI. *(See color ad p 385)*

THE CAPE SOJOURN MOTOR LODGE   Rates Subject to Change   **Phone:** 508/775-3825   47

7/9-8/28 [CP]	1P:	$56- 70	2P/1B:	$58- 78	2P/2B:	$58- 78
6/18-7/8 & 8/29-9/18 [CP]	1P:	$40- 58	2P/1B:	$44- 62	2P/2B:	$44- 68
5/1-6/17, 9/19-10/30 &						
4/15-4/30 [CP]	1P:	$30- 40	2P/1B:	$30- 56	2P/2B:	$30- 62

Motel   **Location:** 0.9 mi e of jct SR 132. 149 Main St, Rt 28 02673. Fax: 508/778-2870. **Terms:** Open 5/1-10/30 & 4/15-4/30; reserv deposit, 7 day notice; handling fee imposed; weekly rates; package plans; 2 night min stay, weekends in summer. **Facility:** 68 rooms. Limit of 2 adults per room. 9 units with patio. 8 king rooms, for up to 4 persons; 2 stories; exterior corridors; heated indoor pool, whirlpool; playground. **Recreation:** picnic area, video game room. **All Rooms:** combo or shower baths, extended cable TV. **Cards:** DS, MC, VI. *(See color ad below)*

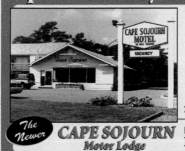
**AAA CampBooks—valuable additions for
members who enjoy outdoor vacations.**

(See map p. 332)

THE COVE AT YARMOUTH   Phone: (508)771-3666   **41**

(AAA) (SAVE)

6/25-9/6		2P/2B:	$130- 165
5/14-6/24 & 9/7-10/14		2P/2B:	$90- 110
5/1-5/13 & 10/15-4/30		2P/2B:	$75- 90

◆◆

Condominium **Location:** On SR 28; 1 mi e of jct SR 132. 183 Main St 02673. Fax: 508/771-9410. **Terms:** Check-in 4 pm; reserv deposit, 48 day notice; weekly rates; package plans; 2 night min stay, weekends. **Facility:** 229 rooms. Attractively furnished suites & townhouse units. Extensive recreational facilities. An interval ownership property. Rates for up to 5 persons; 2 stories; interior corridors; heated indoor pool, saunas, steamrooms, whirlpool; racquetball courts, 5 tennis courts (3 indoor, 5 lighted). **Dining:** Restaurant nearby. **Recreation:** squash 1-court. **All Rooms:** extended cable TV. **Some Rooms:** whirlpools. **Cards:** AE, CB, DI, MC, VI. *(See color ad below)*

GREEN HARBOR ON THE OCEAN   Guaranteed Rates   Phone: (508)771-1126   **43**

(AAA)

7/17-8/27		2P/2B:	$190- 425 XP: $5
6/18-7/16 & 8/28-9/5		2P/2B:	$135- 425 XP: $5
5/14-6/17 & 9/6-10/12		2P/2B:	$70- 250 XP: $5

◆◆◆

Complex **Location:** 0.5 mi e of SR 132 on SR 28, 0.8 mi s. 182 Baxter Ave 02673 (PO Box 746). Fax: 508/771-0701. **Terms:** Open 5/14-10/12; reserv deposit, 30 day notice; handling fee imposed; weekly rates. **Facility:** 51 rooms. Spacious landscaped grounds, overlooking Nantucket Sound. All units with sun deck or balcony with ocean views. Very attractive, peaceful setting. 22 two-bedroom units, 7 three-bedroom units. 1-to 4-bedroom housekeeping cottages in season, $1250-$2750 weekly for up to 8 persons; 1-2 stories; exterior corridors; miniature golf; beach, heated pool; boat dock; playground. **Recreation:** fishing; basketball, shuffleboard. Fee: canoeing; bicycles. Rental: boats. **All Rooms:** combo or shower baths, extended cable TV. **Some Rooms:** 14 efficiencies, 37 kitchens. **Cards:** MC, VI. *(See color ad p 361)*

HUNTERS GREEN MOTEL   Rates Subject to Change   Phone: 508/771-1169   **44**

(AAA)

6/26-8/22 & 9/4-9/6	1P: $56- 66	2P/1B: $54- 64	2P/2B: $54- 64	XP: $6	F12
6/19-6/25 & 8/23-9/3	1P: $44- 60	2P/1B: $44- 54	2P/2B: $44- 54	XP: $5	F12
5/1-6/18, 9/7-10/25 &					
4/16-4/30	1P: $34- 48	2P/1B: $34- 45	2P/2B: $34- 45	XP: $5	F12

◆

Motel **Location:** 2.8 mi e of Hyannis on SR 28. 553 Main St, Rt 28 02673. **Terms:** Open 5/1-10/25 & 4/16-4/30; reserv deposit, 5 day notice. **Facility:** 74 rooms. Family operated. 2 night min stay weekends, 3 night in season; 2 stories; exterior corridors; heated indoor/outdoor pool, whirlpool. **Recreation:** shuffleboard. **All Rooms:** extended cable TV. **Cards:** AE, DS, MC, VI.

See the Sample Lodging Listing.

(See map p. 332)

THE MANOR HOUSE B&B
◆◆◆
Bed & Breakfast

	Guaranteed Rates					Phone: (508)771-3433	40
5/15-10/31 [BP]	1P:	$88- 118	2P/1B:	$98- 128	2P/2B:	$98- 128	XP: $20
5/1-5/14 & 11/1-4/30 [BP]	1P:	$58- 88	2P/1B:	$68- 98	2P/2B:	$68- 98	XP: $20

Location: 0.8 mi s of SR 28 via Berry Ave & Broadway. 57 Maine Ave 02673. Fax: 508/790-1186. **Terms:** Age restrictions may apply; reserv deposit, 14 day notice; handling fee imposed. **Facility:** 7 rooms. A 1920's Dutch Colonial with individually decorated guest rooms. A 2 minute walk to beaches on Lewis Bay. 2-night min stay may be req; 2 stories; interior corridors; smoke free premises. **Services:** Fee: massage. **All Rooms:** combo or shower baths. **Cards:** AE, MC, VI. *(See ad p 343)*

THE MARINER MOTOR LODGE
(AAA)
◆◆
Motel

	Rates Subject to Change					Phone: (508)771-7887	45
7/2-8/28	1P:	$72- 109	2P/1B:	$72- 109	2P/2B:	$72- 109	XP: $10	F18
6/20-7/1 & 8/29-9/9	1P:	$45- 75	2P/1B:	$45- 75	2P/2B:	$45- 75	XP: $10	F18
Fri & Sat 5/1-6/19 & 9/10-4/30	1P:	$45- 70	2P/1B:	$45- 70	2P/2B:	$45- 70	XP: $10	F18
Sun-Thurs 5/1-6/19 & 9/10-4/30	1P:	$32- 49	2P/1B:	$32- 49	2P/2B:	$32- 49	XP: $10	F18

Location: 2.8 mi e of Hyannis. 573 Main St, Rt 28 02673. Fax: 508/771-2811. **Terms:** CP avail, off season; 2 night min stay, Sat arrivals. **Facility:** 100 rooms. All rooms have interior access to indoor pool for off season use. 2 stories; interior corridors; heated indoor pool, saunas, whirlpool. Fee: miniature golf. **Dining:** Restaurant nearby. **Recreation:** video game room. **All Rooms:** extended cable TV. **Cards:** AE, DS, MC, VI. *(See color ad below)*

OLDE SCHOOLHOUSE BED & BREAKFAST
◆◆◆
Bed & Breakfast

	Guaranteed Rates			Phone: (508)778-9468	39
5/15-10/15 [BP]	2P/1B:	$98- 155		XP: $20
5/1-5/14 & 10/16-4/30 [BP]	2P/1B:	$88- 135		XP: $20

Location: Just s of SR 28, 0.2 mi w of Higgins Crowell Rd. 22 Lewis Rd 02673. Fax: 508/790-7091. **Terms:** Age restrictions may apply; reserv deposit, 10 day notice; handling fee imposed; 2 night min stay, weekends in season. **Facility:** 5 rooms. Pleasant rooms with high ceilings in a converted historic school house. 2 stories; interior corridors. **Cards:** AE, MC, VI.

TIDEWATER MOTOR LODGE
(AAA)
◆◆◆
Motel

	Rates Subject to Change					Phone: 508/775-6322	36
7/2-9/5	1P:	$87- 109	2P/1B:	$87- 109	2P/2B:	$87- 109	XP: $6	F12
6/6-7/1 & 9/6-10/23	1P:	$44- 79	2P/1B:	$44- 79	2P/2B:	$44- 79	XP: $6	F12
5/1-6/5 & 10/24-4/30	1P:	$37- 75	2P/1B:	$37- 75	2P/2B:	$37- 75	XP: $6	F12

Location: On SR 28; 0.8 mi e of jct SR 132. 135 Main St 02673. Fax: 508/778-5105. **Terms:** Reserv deposit, 3 day notice; BP avail; 2 night min stay, weekends in season. **Facility:** 101 rooms. Quiet setting on 4 landscaped acres with wooden glider swings. Some units with balcony overlooking Mill Pond, others with sundeck. Fri & Sat rates higher. 4 whirlpool rms, $149 7/3-8/29 for up to 2 persons; $89-$119 off season; 2 stories; interior/exterior corridors; heated indoor pool, sauna, whirlpool; playground. **Dining:** Coffee shop; 7-11 am; to 10 am off season. **All Rooms:** extended cable TV. **Some Rooms:** whirlpools. **Cards:** AE, DS, MC, VI. *(See color ad p 357)*

(See map p. 332)

RESTAURANTS

CAPTAIN PARKER'S   Lunch: $5-$13   Dinner: $9-$16   Phone: 508/771-4266   [28]
◆◆
American   **Location:** 3.3 mi e of Hyannis. 668 Route 28 02673. **Hours:** 11:30 am-11 pm. Closed: 11/25 & 12/25. **Features:** casual dress; Sunday brunch; children's menu; carryout; cocktails & lounge. Casual dining with emphasis on seafood. **Cards:** AE, CB, DI, MC, VI. ⊗

CLANCY'S   Lunch: $5-$10   Dinner: $9-$16   Phone: 508/775-3332   [26]
◆◆
American   **Location:** 1 mi e of Hyannis. 175 Main St; Rt 28 02673. **Hours:** 11:30 am-10 pm, light pub menu avail to midnight, Sun from 11 am. Closed: 11/25 & 12/25. **Features:** casual dress; Sunday brunch; children's menu; carryout; cocktails & lounge. Lively, popular dining in a county tavern. Generous portions. Variety of entrees, burgers & sandwiches. **Cards:** AE, MC, VI. ⊗

YARMOUTH HOUSE RESTAURANT   Lunch: $5-$11   Dinner: $11-$24   Phone: 508/771-5154   [27]
(AAA)
◆◆
American   **Location:** 2 mi e of Hyannis. 335 Main St, Rt 28 02673. **Hours:** 11:30 am-11 pm, off season-10 pm. Closed: 12/25. **Reservations:** suggested. **Features:** casual dress; Sunday brunch; children's menu; early bird specials; carryout; cocktails & lounge. Inviting rooms & a garden atrium with a waterwheel. Wide variety of entrees featuring sauteed dishes & fresh lobster. Candlelit dinners. **Cards:** AE, CB, DI, DS, MC, VI. ⊗

WOODS HOLE—1,200   (See map p. 330; index p. 324)

LODGINGS

THE MARLBOROUGH
(AAA)
◆◆◆
Bed &
Breakfast

	Rates Subject to Change		Phone: (508)548-6218 [74]
5/28-10/12 [BP]	1P: $95- 165	2P/1B: $95- 165	XP: $20
10/13-11/30 [BP]	1P: $95- 165	2P/1B: $95- 165	XP: $20
12/1-4/30 [BP]	1P: $85- 155	2P/1B: $85- 155	XP: $20
5/1-5/27 [BP]	1P: $95- 145	2P/1B: $95- 145	XP: $20

Location: 2 mi n on Woods Hole Rd, 2 mi s of SR 28. 320 Woods Hole Rd 02543 (PO Box 238). Fax: 508/457-7519. **Terms:** Age restrictions may apply; reserv deposit, 14 day notice; handling fee imposed; 2 night min stay, weekends in season. **Facility:** 6 rooms. Country cottage style inn. 1 cottage avail in season, $135 for up to 2 persons; 2 stories; interior corridors; smoke free premises. **Dining:** Afternoon tea. **Services:** complimentary evening beverages. **Recreation:** English paddle tennis. **All Rooms:** combo or shower baths, extended cable TV. **Some Rooms:** color TV. **Cards:** AE, MC, VI. ⊇ ⊗

NAUTILUS MOTOR INN
◆◆
Motel

	Rates Subject to Change			Phone: (508)548-1525 [73]
6/11-9/25	1P: $98- 152	2P/1B: $98- 152	2P/2B: $98- 152	XP: $6
5/21-6/10 & 9/26-10/31	1P: $78- 146	2P/1B: $78- 146	2P/2B: $78- 146	XP: $4
4/1-4/30	1P: $60- 130	2P/1B: $60- 130	2P/2B: $60- 130	XP: $4
5/1-5/20	1P: $58- 130	2P/1B: $58- 130	2P/2B: $58- 130	XP: $4

Location: 0.3 mi n, 3.8 mi s of SR 28. 539 Woods Hole Rd 02543 (PO Box 147). Fax: 508/457-9674. **Terms:** Open 5/1-10/31 & 4/1-4/30; reserv deposit. **Facility:** 54 rooms. Many rooms with harbor view. 2 stories; exterior corridors; 2 tennis courts. **Cards:** AE, DI, DS, MC, VI. *(See color ad below)* 🆒 ▨ ⊇ ⊪ ⊗ 🍴

SANDS OF TIME MOTOR INN
(AAA)
◆◆◆
Motel

	Rates Subject to Change		Phone: 508/548-6300 [71]
6/1-9/30		2P/2B: $100- 170	XP: $8 D
5/1-5/31 & 10/1-11/15		2P/2B: $85- 120	XP: $8 D
4/1-4/30		2P/2B: $75- 100	XP: $8 D

Location: 0.3 mi n, 3.8 mi s of SR 28. 549 Woods Hole Rd 02543 (PO Box 106). Fax: 508/457-0160. **Terms:** Open 5/1-11/15 & 4/1-4/30; reserv deposit, 7 day notice; handling fee imposed; package plans, off season. **Facility:** 30 rooms. Overlooking harbor. 20 motel units with country inn decor, 10 rooms in 1870's home with 5 wood-burning fireplaces. 2 kitchen units, $150 in season for up to 2 persons; 3 stories; interior/exterior corridors. **Dining:** Restaurant nearby. **All Rooms:** combo or shower baths, extended cable TV. **Cards:** AE, CB, DI, DS, MC, VI. *(See color ad p 354)* 📷 ⊇ ⊪ 🖨

SLEEPY HOLLOW MOTOR INN
(AAA)
◆◆
Motel

	Rates Subject to Change		Phone: 508/548-1986 [72]
6/18-9/13		2P/1B: $95	2P/2B: $105- 135 XP: $10
5/1-6/17 & 9/14-10/25		2P/1B: $75	2P/2B: $85- 115 XP: $10

Location: 0.3 mi n on Woods Hole Rd, 3.5 mi s of SR 28. 527 Woods Hole Rd 02543. Fax: 508/548-5932. **Terms:** Open 5/1-10/25; reserv deposit, 7 day notice; handling fee imposed. **Facility:** 24 rooms. Attractive grounds. 2 stories; exterior corridors. **All Rooms:** combo or shower baths, extended cable TV. **Cards:** AE, CB, DI, MC, VI. ⊇ 🍴 🖥 🖨

YARMOUTH PORT—4,300   (See map p. 330; index p. 326)

LODGINGS

THE INN AT CAPE COD
◆◆◆
Historic Bed
& Breakfast

Rates Subject to Change
6/1-10/31 [BP]   2P/1B: $120- 185
5/1-5/31, 11/1-11/30 &
2/1-4/30 [EP]   2P/1B: $100- 150

Phone: 508/375-0590   [174]

Location: Rt 6 exit 7 (Willow St/Yarmouth Port), 1 mi n on Willow St then 0.5 mi e, corner 6A & Summer St. 4 Summer St 02675 (PO BOX 96). Fax: 508/362-9520. **Terms:** Open 5/1-11/30 & 2/1-4/30; age restrictions may apply; reserv deposit, 14 day notice; handling fee imposed. **Facility:** 8 rooms. Colonial building with an impressive exterior featuring a large column front porch area. 3 stories, no elevator; interior corridors; designated smoking area. **All Rooms:** combo or shower baths. **Cards:** AE, MC, VI.   [VCR] [X]

ONE CENTRE STREET INN
◆◆◆
Historic Bed
& Breakfast

Guaranteed Rates
5/15-10/15   1P: $95- 130 2P/1B: $95- 130 2P/2B: $95- 130 XP: $25-35   D
5/1-5/14 & 10/16-4/30   1P: $85- 130 2P/1B: $85- 130 2P/2B: $85- 130 XP: $25-35   D

Phone: (508)362-8910   [175]

Location: 1 mi e on SR 6A, just w of jct Union St. One Centre St 02675. **Terms:** Age restrictions may apply; reserv deposit, 14 day notice; handling fee imposed; 2 night min stay, weekends 7/1-8/31. **Facility:** 6 rooms. In restored 1824 home. Family ambiance. 1 room with fireplace. 3 stories, no elevator; designated smoking area. **Some Rooms:** color TV. **Cards:** DS, MC, VI.   [☎] [🍴] [🖨] [X]

RESTAURANT

ABBICCI
◆◆◆
Italian

Lunch: $7-11   Dinner: $15-$25   Phone: 508/362-3501   [82]

Location: 0.8 mi w on SR 6A; 0.3 mi w of jct Willow St. 43 Main St & Rt 6A 02675. **Hours:** 11:30 am-2:30 & 5-10 pm. **Reservations:** suggested. **Features:** casual dress; cocktails; a la carte. Authentic contemporary cuisine. Creative entrees & rudiments. Valet parking for dinner in season. **Cards:** AE, DI, DS, MC, VI.   [X]

This ends listings for Cape Cod.
The following page resumes the alphabetical listings of
cities in Massachusetts.

CENTERVILLE—See Cape Cod p. 337.

CHARLEMONT—1,200

LODGING

THE OXBOW RESORT MOTEL   Guaranteed Rates   **Phone:** 413/625-6011
◆◆   5/20-10/20   1P: $49   2P/1B: $59   2P/2B: $69   XP: $10   F16
Motel   5/1-5/19 & 10/21-4/30   1P: $44   2P/1B: $49   2P/2B: $59
          Location: On SR 2, 2.8 mi w of jct SR 112 S. Rt 2 Mohawk Tr 01339 (PO Box 669). Fax: 413/625-6457.
Facility: 24 rooms. Scenic location overlooking the Deerfield River; extensive exercise equipment. 1 story; exterior corridors;
2 tennis courts; playground. **Services:** winter plug-ins. **All Rooms:** combo or shower baths. **Cards:** MC, VI.

CHATHAM—See Cape Cod p. 337.

CHELMSFORD—See Boston p. 296.

CHESTNUT HILL—See Boston p. 297.

CHICOPEE—56,600

LODGINGS

BEST WESTERN-CHICOPEE MOTOR LODGE   **Phone:** (413)592-6171
(AAA) [SAVE]   Fri & Sat   1P: $49   2P/1B: $49   2P/2B: $49   XP: $8   F18
                Sun-Thurs   1P: $39- 49   2P/1B: $49   2P/2B: $39   XP: $8   F18
◆◆   **Location:** At I-90, MA Tpk exit 5. 463 Memorial Dr (Rt 33) 01020. Fax: 413/598-8351. **Terms:** Reserv
Motel   deposit, 10 day notice; pets, no exotic pets. **Facility:** 106 rooms. Medium size rooms with traditional decor. 2
                stories; interior corridors. **Dining:** Restaurant nearby. **Cards:** AE, CB, DI, DS, MC, VI. **Special Amenities:**
Early check-in/late check-out and free local telephone calls.

PLANTATION INN OF NEW ENGLAND   Rates Subject to Change   **Phone:** 413/592-8200
◆◆   All Year [CP]   1P: $40- 55   2P/1B: $45- 60   2P/2B: $50- 65   XP: $5   F9
Motel   **Location:** Just n of I-90, exit 6. 295 Burnett Rd 01020. Fax: 413/592-9671. **Facility:** 184 rooms. 2 stories; in-
          terior corridors. **Cards:** AE, DS, MC, VI.

RESTAURANT

ADMIRAL D W'S   **Lunch:** $4-$9   **Dinner:** $6-$20   **Phone:** 413/594-2124
◆◆   **Location:** On SR 33; just s of I-90 (MA Tpk), exit 5. 345 Memorial Dr 01020. **Hours:** 11 am-9 pm, Fri &
Seafood   Sat-10 pm, Sun noon-8 pm. **Closed:** 11/25, 12/24 & 12/25. **Reservations:** accepted; 8 or more.
          Features: children's menu; early bird specials; carryout; cocktails & lounge. Nautical atmosphere for casual
family dining. **Cards:** AE, MC, VI.

CLINTON—13,200

LODGING

CLINTON MOTOR INN   Rates Subject to Change   **Phone:** 978/368-8133
◆   All Year   1P: $35- 40   2P/1B: $40- 45   2P/2B: $45- 50   XP: $5   F9
Motel   **Location:** 1 mi sw. 146 Main St (SR 110) 01510. **Facility:** 20 rooms. 2 stories; exterior corridors.
          Some Rooms: 6 efficiencies. **Cards:** AE, DS, MC, VI.

COHASSET—See Boston p. 297.

CONCORD—See Boston p. 297.

COTUIT—See Cape Cod p. 342.

CRAIGVILLE—See Cape Cod p. 342.

DALTON—7,200

LODGING

THE DALTON HOUSE
◆◆◆
Bed & Breakfast

								Phone: 413/684-3854
6/16-9/15 [CP]	1P:	$95- 125	2P/1B:	$95- 125	2P/2B:	$95- 125	XP: $15	
9/16-11/1 [CP]	1P:	$78- 105	2P/1B:	$78- 105	2P/2B:	$78- 105		
5/1-6/15 [CP]	1P:	$78- 105	2P/1B:	$78- 105	2P/2B:	$78- 105		
11/2-4/30 [CP]	1P:	$68- 95	2P/1B:	$68- 95	2P/2B:	$68- 95		

Rates Subject to Change

Location: 1 mi se on SR 8. 955 Main St 01226. Fax: 413/684-0203. **Terms:** Age restrictions may apply; reserv deposit, 14 day notice, in season; 2 night min stay, weekends in season. **Facility:** 11 rooms. Quaint & cozy inn. Beautifully landscaped grounds. 1-2 stories; interior corridors; smoke free premises; small pool. **All Rooms:** shower baths. **Cards:** AE, MC, VI.

DANVERS—See Boston p. 298.

DEDHAM—See Boston p. 299.

DEERFIELD—5,000—See also SOUTH DEERFIELD.

LODGING

DEERFIELD INN
◆◆◆
Historic Country Inn

					Phone: (413)774-5587	
9/15-10/31 [BP]	1P: $206	2P/2B: $241	XP: $72	F6
5/1-9/14 [BP]	1P: $151	2P/2B: $186	XP: $65	F6
Fri & Sat 11/1-4/30 [BP]	1P: $139	2P/2B: $176	XP: $65	F6
Sun-Thurs 11/1-4/30 [BP]	1P: $127	2P/2B: $147	XP: $45	F6

Rates Subject to Change

Location: Center. 81 Old Main St 01342 (PO Box 305). Fax: 413/773-8712. **Terms:** Reserv deposit, 7 day notice; handling fee imposed; 10% service charge. **Facility:** 23 rooms. Handsome 1884 New England country inn; rooms with local decor. 2 stories; interior corridors; smoke free premises. **Cards:** AE, DI, MC, VI.

RESTAURANT

DEERFIELD INN DINING ROOM Country Inn **Lunch:** $8-$11 **Dinner:** $18-$23 **Phone:** 413/774-5587
◆◆◆
Continental **Location:** Center; in Deerfield Inn. 81 Old Main St 01342. **Hours:** 7:30-9 am, noon-2 & 6-9 pm, Sat & Sun 7:30-10 am, noon-2 & 6-9 pm. **Closed:** 12/24 & 12/25. **Reservations:** suggested. **Features:** children's menu; cocktails & lounge; a la carte. Charming dining room in traditional New England inn circa 1884. Light lunches served on terrace cafe, noon-2 pm. Smoke free premises. **Cards:** AE, DI, MC, VI.

DENNIS—See Cape Cod p. 343.

DENNIS PORT—See Cape Cod p. 343.

EAST BOSTON—See Boston p. 300.

EAST DENNIS—See Cape Cod p. 345.

EAST FALMOUTH—See Cape Cod p. 346.

EASTHAM—See Cape Cod p. 346.

EAST HARWICH—See Cape Cod p. 349.

AAA Plus® provides you extended services, such as up to 100 miles of free towing.

EAST WAREHAM—1,600   (See map p. 330; index p. 328)

LODGING

ATLANTIC MOTEL   Phone: (508)295-0210   [299]

AAA SAVE

◆

Motel

Fri & Sat 6/19-9/5	1P:	$79-	99	2P/1B:	$79-	99	2P/2B:	$89- 109	XP: $10	F12
Sun-Thurs 6/19-9/5	1P:	$67-	78	2P/1B:	$67-	78	2P/2B:	$78- 89	XP: $8-10	F12
5/1-6/18 & 9/6-10/4	1P:	$56-	79	2P/1B:	$56-	79	2P/2B:	$67- 89	XP: $6-8	F12
10/5-4/30	1P:	$49-	66	2P/1B:	$49-	66	2P/2B:	$56- 69	XP: $6	F12

Location: Between east- & westbound lanes of US 6/SR 28, at jct SR 25. 2859 Cranberry Hwy 02538. **Fax:** 508/295-0210. **Terms:** Reserv deposit, 7 day notice; handling fee imposed; 2 night min stay, summer weekends. **Facility:** 24 rooms. 2 stories; exterior corridors; Seasonal pool. **All Rooms:** extended cable TV. **Cards:** AE, DS, MC, VI. **Special Amenities:** Early check-in/late check-out and preferred room (subject to availability with advanced reservations).

⊇ ▥ ▢ 🔒 ✕

ESSEX—See Boston p. 300.

FAIRHAVEN—16,100

LODGINGS

EDGEWATER BED & BREAKFAST   Rates Subject to Change   Phone: 508/997-5512

◆◆   All Year   1P: $70- 95   2P/1B: $75- 90   2P/2B: $100

Bed & Breakfast

Location: From I-195 exit 18, s on SR 240 to US 6; 1.5 mi w to Main St 0.4 mi n, then just 0.3 mi w to the harbor. 2 Oxford St 02719. **Fax:** 508/997-5784. **Terms:** Age restrictions may apply; reserv deposit, 3 day notice. **Facility:** 5 rooms. Colonial/Victorian dating from 1760 & 1880. On water's edge at Acushnet River & New Bedford Harbor. 2 units with working fireplace. 2-3 stories, no elevator; interior/exterior corridors; smoke free premises. **All Rooms:** comb, shower or tub baths. **Some Rooms:** efficiency. **Cards:** AE, DS, MC, VI.

▤ ② 🐴 🔒 ✕

HAMPTON INN   Rates Subject to Change   Phone: 508/990-8500

◆◆◆   6/23-9/7 [CP]   1P: $84- 92   2P/1B: $89- 99   2P/2B: $89- 99

Motel   5/1-6/22, 9/8-10/26 &

4/15-4/30 [CP]   1P: $79   2P/1B: $84   2P/2B: $84

10/27-4/14 [CP]   1P: $67   2P/1B: $72   2P/2B: $72

Location: 0.5 mi s of I-95, exit 18 via SR 240, Bridge St & Alden Rd. 1 Hampton Way 02719. **Fax:** 508/990-0183. **Terms:** Reserv deposit. **Facility:** 77 rooms. Tastefully appointed lobby and rooms. 6 rooms with refrigerator, microwave & coffeemaker $104-$114 for 2 persons in-season; 3 stories; interior corridors. **All Rooms:** combo or shower baths. **Cards:** AE, CB, DI, DS, MC, VI.

🐴 🎬 ⊇ 🍴 △ 🕭 ▥ 🖨 🎿 🐟 ✕

RESTAURANTS

HUTTLESTON HOUSE RESTAURANT   Lunch: $5-$9   Dinner: $10-$18   Phone: 508/999-1791

◆◆◆   **Location:** 1 mi w on US 6 from jct SR 240. 111 Huttleston Ave, Rt 6 02719. **Hours:** 11:30 am-10 pm.

Continental   Closed: 1/1, 11/25 & 12/25. **Reservations:** accepted. **Features:** casual dress; carryout; cocktails & lounge. Warm, cheerful & intimate dining in a cozy, rustic dining room. Lobster & veal specialties & extensive fresh local seafood entrees. **Cards:** AE, MC, VI.

✕

MIKE'S RESTAURANT   Lunch: $3-$6   Dinner: $7-$20   Phone: 508/996-9810

◆   **Location:** US 6, 1.8 mi e of jct SR 240. 390 Huttleston Ave 02719. **Hours:** 11:30 am-10 pm, Sun from noon.

American   Closed: 11/25, 12/24 for dinner & 12/25. **Features:** casual dress; children's menu; carryout; cocktails & lounge. Casual family dining. Specialities lobster & prime rib.

✕

FALL RIVER—92,700

LODGING

BEST WESTERN FALL RIVER   Rates Subject to Change   Phone: (508)672-0011

◆◆   5/1-10/15 [CP]   1P: $55- 89   2P/1B: $64- 99   2P/2B: $64- 99   XP: $8   F12

Motel   10/16-4/30 [CP]   1P: $55- 69   2P/1B: $55- 69   2P/2B: $55- 79   XP: $8   F12

Location: Exit 8 of SR 79 & SR 24; at Fall River Airport. 360 Airport Rd 02720. **Fax:** 508/676-6251. **Terms:** Reserv deposit, weekends, handling fee imposed. **Facility:** 82 rooms. Set back from highway in an industrial park. 4 stories; interior corridors; heated indoor pool. **Cards:** AE, CB, DI, DS, JC, MC, VI. *(See color ad p 391)*

ASK 🍸 🐴 🎬 ⊇ △ 🕭 ▥ 🖨 🔒 ✕

RESTAURANTS

THE EAGLE RESTAURANT   Lunch: $4-$8   Dinner: $7-$15   Phone: 508/677-3788

◆◆   **Location:** Downtown, just n of Government Center. 35 N Main St 02720. **Hours:** 11 am-10 pm; Fri &

American   Sat-midnight. Closed: 1/1, 7/4 & 12/25. **Reservations:** suggested. **Features:** casual dress; children's menu; early bird specials; carryout; cocktails & lounge; entertainment. Featuring fresh local seafood, steak & seafood pasta dishes. Second-level dining amidst elegant arches, cornices & stained glass windows. **Cards:** AE, DS, MC, VI.

✕

Choose an establishment with

the AAA next to its listing!

LE PAGE'S SEAFOOD & GRILLE   **Lunch:** $5-$14   **Dinner:** $8-$20   **Phone:** 508/677-2180
◆◆   **Location:** US 6, 0.8 mi w of I-195, exit 9 eastbound following signs to US 6 w, at Fall River/Westport line.
Seafood   439 Martine St 02723. **Hours:** 11 am-9 pm; Fri & Sat-10 pm. Closed: 11/25 & 12/25.
        Reservations: accepted. **Features:** casual dress; children's menu; carryout; cocktails & lounge. Overlooking
scenic Watuppa Pond. Generous portions. Fresh local seafood, pasta, steak, chops & chicken. Outdoor dining in season.
Cards: AE, DS, MC, VI.   ✕

T A RESTAURANT   **Lunch:** $7-$13   **Dinner:** $7-$13   **Phone:** 508/673-5890
◆   **Location:** Downtown; 0.5 mi s of I-195, exit 5. 408 S Main St 02721. **Hours:** 11 am-10 pm, Sun noon-9 pm.
Ethnic   Closed major holidays. **Features:** casual dress; children's menu; carryout; cocktails & lounge; a la carte.
        Popular dining featuring authentic Portuguese cuisine. Sandwiches & some American food avail. **Cards:** AE,
CB, DI, DS, MC, VI.   ✕

FALMOUTH—*See Cape Cod p. 349.*

FITCHBURG—41,200

LODGING

BEST WESTERN ROYAL PLAZA HOTEL & TRADE CENTER   **Phone:** (978)342-7100
Fri & Sat [CP]   1P: $95- 110   2P/1B: $100- 120   2P/2B: $100- 120   XP: $10   F16
Sun-Thurs [CP]   1P: $85- 105   2P/1B: $95- 110   2P/2B: $95- 115   XP: $10   F16
Motor Inn   **Location:** Just s on SR 31; SR 2, exit 28. 150 Royal Plaza Dr 01420. Fax: 978/343-7376. **Terms:** Package
plans; pets. **Facility:** 245 rooms. Large luxurious lobby with raised seating area. Adjacent to trade center. 6
stories; interior corridors; heated indoor pool, sauna, whirlpool. **Dining:** Restaurant; 6:30-10:30 am, 11:30-2
& 5-10 pm; $10-$17; cocktails. **Services:** giftshop. **Cards:** AE, CB, DI, DS, JC, MC, VI. **Special Amenities:** Early
check-in/late check-out and free newspaper.

FLORIDA—750

LODGING

WHITCOMB SUMMIT MOTEL   Rates Subject to Change   **Phone:** 413/662-2625
◆◆   9/17-10/20   1P: $65- 75   2P/1B: $70- 80   2P/2B: $80- 90   XP: $10   F12
Motor Inn   5/20-9/16   1P: $50- 65   2P/1B: $55- 70   2P/2B: $70- 80   XP: $10   F12
        Location: 1 mi e on SR 2. 229 Mohawk Tr 01247. Fax: 413/664-8373. **Terms:** Open 5/20-10/20; reserv
deposit. **Facility:** 18 rooms. Panoramic view. 2 two-bedroom units. 3 cabins avail; 2 stories; exterior corridors; mountain view.
Cards: AE, DS, MC, VI.

FOXBORO—*See Boston p. 300.*

FRAMINGHAM—*See Boston p. 301.*

GARDNER—20,100

LODGINGS

COLONIAL BED & BREAKFAST   Rates Subject to Change   **Phone:** 978/630-2500
◆◆◆   All Year [MAP]   1P: $70- 90   2P/1B: $80- 100   2P/2B: $89- 99   XP: $10   F12
Motor Inn   **Location:** 1 mi n on SR 140, 0.5 mi w on Betty Spring Rd; SR 2, eastbound exit 24, westbound 24B. c25
Betty Spring Rd 01440. Fax: 978/632-0913. **Terms:** Reserv deposit. **Facility:** 109 rooms. 3 suites $110-$250;
2 stories; interior corridors; heated indoor pool. **Cards:** AE, DS, MC, VI. *(See color ad p 282)*

SUPER 8 MOTEL
◆◆   9/1-10/31 [CP]   Rates Subject to Change   Phone: 978/630-2888
Motel   9/1-10/31 [CP]   1P: $41- 44   2P/1B: $51- 55   2P/2B: $51- 55   XP: $5   F12
        5/1-8/31 & 11/1-4/30 [CP]   1P: $37   2P/1B: $42   2P/2B: $42   XP: $5   F12
        Location: Just n of SR 2, exit 23. 22 Pearson Blvd 01440. Fax: 978/630-1716. **Facility:** 48 rooms. 2 stories;
interior corridors. **Cards:** AE, CB, DI, DS, MC, VI.

GLOUCESTER—See Boston p. 302.

GREAT BARRINGTON—7,700

LODGINGS

BARRINGTON COURT MOTEL
        All Year   Rates Subject to Change   Phone: 413/528-2340
        All Year   1P: $50- 125   2P/1B: $50- 125   2P/2B: $50- 125   XP: $5   F12
◆◆   **Location:** On US 7, 1.2 mi s of jct SR 183. 400 Stockbridge Rd 01230. **Terms:** Reserv deposit, 7 day
Motel   notice; weekly/monthly rates; 2 night min stay, weekends in season. **Facility:** 23 rooms. Exceptional house-
        keeping. Well maintained grounds. 2 one-bedroom luxury suites, $100-$200 in season; 2 stories; exterior cor-
        ridors. **Recreation:** bocci ball court. **All Rooms:** combo or shower baths. **Some Rooms:** 2 efficiencies.
Cards: AE, DS, MC, VI.

LANTERN HOUSE MOTEL
        Thurs-Sun 6/25-8/31 & Fri &   Rates Subject to Change   Phone: 413/528-2350
          Sat 9/17-10/31   1P: $80- 90   2P/1B: $85- 95   2P/2B: $90- 105   XP: $10   D6
◆◆   Mon-Wed 6/25-8/31   1P: $60- 70   2P/1B: $65- 75   2P/2B: $70- 85   XP: $10   D6
Motel   Fri & Sat 5/1-6/24, 9/1-9/16 &
          11/1-4/30   1P: $55- 65   2P/1B: $60- 70   2P/2B: $65- 75   XP: $5   D6
        Sun-Thurs 5/1-6/24 &
          9/1-4/30   1P: $50- 60   2P/1B: $55- 65   2P/2B: $60- 70   XP: $5   D6
Location: On US 7, 1.2 mi s of jct SR 183. Stockbridge Rd 01230 (PO Box 97). Fax: 413/528-0435. **Terms:** Reserv deposit,
7 day notice; handling fee imposed; 3 night min stay, weekends 7/1-9/5. **Facility:** 14 rooms. 1 story; exterior corridors; heated
pool. **Dining:** Restaurant nearby. **All Rooms:** extended cable TV. **Cards:** DS, MC, VI.

MONUMENT MOUNTAIN MOTEL
        Thurs-Sun 6/26-9/6 & Fri &   Rates Subject to Change   Phone: 413/528-3272
          Sat 9/7-10/31
        Mon-Wed 6/26-9/6   2P/1B: $100- 105   2P/2B: $105- 115   XP: $10
◆◆   Fri-Sun 5/1-6/25 & 11/1-4/30   2P/1B: $65- 80   2P/2B: $80- 90   XP: $5
Motel   Sun-Thurs 5/1-6/25,   2P/1B: $50- 70   2P/2B: $60- 80   XP: $5
          9/7-10/31 & 11/1-4/30   2P/1B: $55- 65   2P/2B: $55- 70   XP: $5
Location: On US 7, 1.2 mi s of jct SR 183. 249 Stockbridge (US 7) Rd 01230. Fax: 413/528-3132. **Terms:** Reserv deposit,
14 day notice; handling fee imposed; weekly rates; package plans; 3 night min stay, weekends in summer. **Facility:** 18 rooms.
Small to large rooms on extensive, landscaped grounds. 1 story; exterior corridors; 1 lighted tennis court; playground.
Services: winter plug-ins. **Recreation:** badminton. **All Rooms:** combo or shower baths, extended cable TV. **Cards:** AE, CB,
DI, DS, MC, VI.

WINDFLOWER INN
◆◆◆   All Year [BP]   2P/1B: $110- 180   2P/2B: $110- 180   XP: $25
Bed &   **Location:** On SR 23, 3 mi w of jct US 7. 684 S Egremont Rd 01230. Fax: 413/528-5147. **Terms:** Reserv
Breakfast deposit, 21 day notice; handling fee imposed; 2 night min stay, weekends. **Facility:** 13 rooms. Late 1800's
        federal-style inn. 2 stories; interior corridors; designated smoking area. **All Rooms:** combo or shower baths.
Cards: AE.

GREENFIELD—18,700

LODGINGS

THE BRANDT HOUSE
◆◆◆   5/1-11/1 [CP]   Rates Subject to Change   Phone: 413/774-3329
Historic Bed 5/1-11/1 [CP]   2P/1B: $125- 195   2P/2B: $195- 300   XP: $20
& Breakfast 11/2-4/30 [CP]   2P/1B: $95- 150   2P/2B: $150- 300   XP: $20
        Location: From I-91, exit 26, 1.8 mi e on SR 2A, & se via Cresent St. 29 Highland Ave 01301-3605.
        Fax: 413/772-2908. **Terms:** Reserv deposit. **Facility:** 7 rooms. Turn-of-the-century colonial revival mansion
with wraparound porch in quiet neighborhood. 3 stories, no elevator; interior corridors; smoke free premises; 1 tennis court.
Cards: AE, DS, MC, VI.

SUPER 8 MOTEL
◆◆   10/1-10/31 [CP]   Rates Subject to Change   Phone: 413/774-5578
Motel   10/1-10/31 [CP]   1P: $56   2P/1B: $67   2P/2B: $67   XP: $5   F12
        5/1-9/30 & 11/1-4/30 [CP] 1P: $42- 47   2P/1B: $50- 57   2P/2B: $50- 57   XP: $5   F12
        Location: Just n of SR 2W; at jct I-91 exit 26 & SR 2. 21 Colrain Rd 01301. Fax: 413/774-4383. **Facility:** 60
rooms. Modern guest rooms in Tudor style motel. 2 stories; interior corridors. **Cards:** AE, CB, DI, DS, MC, VI.

RESTAURANT

FAMOUS BILL'S   **Lunch:** $4-$10   **Dinner:** $6-$14   Phone: 413/773-9230
        Location: On US 5 & SR 10; 1 mi e of I-91, exit 26. 30 Federal St 01301. **Hours:** 11 am-9 pm, Sat & Mon
◆   from 4 pm. **Reservations:** suggested. **Features:** casual dress; children's menu; senior's menu; carryout;
American   cocktails & lounge; a la carte. Popular family-style restaurant. Lite menu avail. **Cards:** MC, VI.

HADLEY—4,200

LODGINGS

ECONO LODGE
(AAA) [SAVE]
◆◆
Motel
calls.

Phone: (413)584-9816
All Year   1P: $66- 76 2P/1B: $76- 86 2P/2B: $86   XP:$5-25   F
Location: I-91, northbound exit 19; southbound exit 20; 3 mi e on SR 9. 237 Russell St (SR 9) 01035.
Fax: 413/586-7512. **Terms:** Check-in 4 pm; weekly rates. **Facility:** 60 rooms. 1-2 stories; interior/exterior corridors; small pool. **All Rooms:** combo or shower baths, extended cable TV. **Some Rooms:** 12 efficiencies, no utensils. **Cards:** AE, DI, DS, MC, VI. **Special Amenities:** Free breakfast and free local telephone

HOWARD JOHNSON
◆◆◆
Motel

Rates Subject to Change   Phone: (413)586-0114
All Year [CP]   1P: $65- 115 2P/1B: $75- 115 2P/2B: $75- 115 XP: $10   F17
Location: On SR 9 at jct SR 116N. 401 Russell St 01035. Fax: 413/584-7163. **Facility:** 100 rooms. 2-3 stories; interior corridors. **Cards:** AE, DI, DS, MC, VI. (See color ad p 264)

RESTAURANTS

CARMELINAS AT THE COMMONS
◆◆
Italian

MC, VI.

Dinner: $8-$19   Phone: 413/584-8000
Location: On SR 9, 1.5 mi e of I-91 exit 19. 96 Russell St 01035. **Hours:** 5 pm-9:30 pm, Fri & Sat 4:30 pm-10 pm. Closed: 7/4, 11/25, 12/24 & 12/25. **Reservations:** suggested. **Features:** carryout; cocktails & lounge; a la carte. Informal atmosphere, very popular. Large variety of excellent & unique dishes. **Cards:** AE,

CASA ANTONIO
(AAA)
◆
Italian

Lunch: $4-$13   Dinner: $8-$13   Phone: 413/586-3880
Location: 0.5 mi n on SR 9 from SR 47. 206 Russell St (SR 9) 01035. **Hours:** 11 am-10 pm, Fri & Sat-11 pm. **Features:** casual dress; children's menu; carryout; cocktails & lounge. Family restaurant & pizzeria. Also feature American cuisine. Delivery service. **Cards:** AE, CB, DI, DS, MC, VI.

HANCOCK—600

LODGINGS

THE COUNTRY INN AT JIMINY PEAK
(AAA) [SAVE]
◆◆◆
Resort

Phone: (413)738-5500
All Year   1P: $95- 229 2P/1B: $95- 229 2P/2B: $95- 229 XP: $15   F12
Location: From US 7, 3 mi w on Brodie Mountain Rd. Corey Rd 01237. Fax: 413/738-5513.
Terms: Check-in 4 pm; reserv deposit, 14 day notice; handling fee imposed; weekly/monthly rates; package plans; 2 night min stay, seasonal weekends. **Facility:** 145 rooms. Situated on 800 wooded acres at the base of Jiminy Peak Ski Resort; many condo units have deck & fireplace. 2- & 3-bedroom condos, $175-$305; 3 stories; interior/exterior corridors; miniature golf; heated pool, saunas, whirlpools; 5 tennis courts; playground. **Dining:** Restaurant; 7:30 am-10:30 & 5-9 pm, Fri & Sat-10 pm, $9-$18; cocktails. **Recreation:** fishing; ice skating; hiking trails, laser trap shooting, mountain bike trails & Alpine slide. Fee: downhill skiing. **All Rooms:** kitchens. **Some Rooms:** whirlpools. **Cards:** AE, DI, DS, MC, VI. **Special Amenities:** Free local telephone calls and free newspaper. (See ad p 165)

JERICHO VALLEY INN
(AAA) [SAVE]
◆◆◆
Motel

Phone: (413)458-9511
All Year [CP]   1P: $78- 108 2P/1B: $78- 108 2P/2B: $78- 108 XP: $10   F16
Location: On SR 43, 5 mi s of jct US 7. 2541 Hancock Rd 01267. Fax: 413/458-9515. **Terms:** Reserv deposit, 14 day notice, 30 day for cottages & suites; handling fee imposed; 2 night min stay, weekends in season; pets, in cottages only. **Facility:** 24 rooms. Quiet, mountain setting with lovely view. Newly decorated motel rooms & cottages with some luxury amenities. Cottages with original knotty pine walls. Secluded wooded environment. 2 two-bedroom units, 2 three-bedroom units. 14 one- to three-bedroom suites & housekeeping cottages, some with wood-burning fireplace, $138-$258; 1-2 stories; interior/exterior corridors; heated pool. **Dining:** Breakfast room 7:30-10 am. **Recreation:** hiking trails. **Some Rooms:** 14 kitchens. **Cards:** AE, MC, VI. **Special Amenities:** Free breakfast and free local telephone calls. (See ad p 432)

HANOVER—11,900

RESTAURANT

PAPA RAZZI
◆◆
Northern
Italian

Lunch: $7-$13   Dinner: $10-$24   Phone: 781/982-2800
Location: On SR 53, 0.5 mi n of SR 3 exit 13. 2087 Washington St 02339. **Hours:** 11:30 am-10 pm, Fri-Sat-11 pm. Closed: 11/25 & 12/25. **Reservations:** accepted. **Features:** casual dress; Sunday brunch; children's menu; carryout; cocktails & lounge; a la carte. Family dining in upscale rustic atmosphere in converted 18th century building. Ample portions. **Cards:** AE, DI, DS, MC, VI.

HARWICH PORT—See Cape Cod p. 355.

HAVERHILL—See Boston p. 303.

HINGHAM—19,800

RESTAURANTS

NINO'S STEAK & CHOP HOUSE
◆◆
Steakhouse

Dinner: $8-$18   Phone: 781/340-7300
Location: On SR 53, 1.3 mi n of jct SR 228; from SR 3 exit 15, 2 mi ne via Cushing St. 415 Whiting St (Rt 53) 02043. **Hours:** 5 pm-9 pm, Fri & Sat-10 pm. Closed: 1/1, 12/24, 12/25 & Mon. **Features:** casual dress; cocktails & lounge. A converted abandoned granite foundry overlooking a quarry. Also serving Italian entrees. Smoke free premises. **Cards:** AE, DI, DS, MC, VI.

TOSCA
◆◆◆
Regional
Italian

Dinner: $18-$27   **Phone:** 781/740-0080
Location: Just w of SR 3A, just n of the Rotary. 14 North St 02043. **Hours:** 5 pm-10 pm, Fri & Sat-11 pm, Sun 2 pm-10 pm. Closed: Mon 11/1-4/30, 12/24 & 12/25. **Reservations:** suggested. **Features:** casual dress; cocktails & lounge. Regional Italian dishes in casually elegant rustic Italian atmosphere. Menu changes 6 times a year. **Cards:** AE, DI, DS, MC, VI.   ⊠

HOLYOKE—43,700

LODGINGS

HOLIDAY INN-HOLIDOME & CONVENTION CENTER   Rates Subject to Change   **Phone:** 413/534-3311
◆◆◆   All Year   1P: $81- 135   2P/1B: $81- 135   2P/2B: $81- 135
Motor Inn   **Location:** At jct I-91 exit 15. 245 Whiting Farms Rd 01040. **Fax:** 413/533-8443. **Terms:** Reserv deposit. **Facility:** 219 rooms. Short distance to Holyoke Mall. All rooms with iron & ironing board. 4 stories; interior corridors; heated indoor pool. **All Rooms:** combo or shower baths. **Cards:** AE, CB, DI, DS, MC, VI.

SUPER 8 MOTEL   **Phone:** (413)536-1980
ⒶⒶⒶ SAVE   5/1-10/31   1P: $50- 150   2P/1B: $60- 160   2P/2B: $60- 160 XP: $6-10   F12
          11/1-4/30   1P: $40- 90   2P/1B: $40- 110   2P/2B: $45-145 XP: $5-10   F12
◆ ◆
Motel   **Location:** Just n on US 5, from I-91 exit 17 southbound; exit 17A northbound. 1515 Northampton St 01040. **Fax:** 413/533-2775. **Terms:** Reserv deposit, 3 day notice. **Facility:** 52 rooms. 2-3 stories; interior/exterior corridors. **Cards:** AE, CB, DI, DS, JC, MC, VI. **Special Amenities:** Free breakfast and free local telephone calls.

RESTAURANTS

THE DELANEY HOUSE   **Dinner:** $13-$24   **Phone:** 413/532-1800
ⒶⒶⒶ   **Location:** US 5, 2.8 mi s of I-91, exit 18. US 5 at Smith's Ferry 01040. **Hours:** 5 pm-9:30 pm, Fri & Sat-10 pm, Sun 1 pm-7:30 pm. Closed: 1/1, 7/4 & 12/25. **Reservations:** suggested. **Features:** children's menu;
◆◆◆   cocktails & lounge; a la carte. 1880 house with 4 uniquely decorated dining rooms. Smoke free premises.
American   **Cards:** AE, CB, DI, DS, MC, VI.   ⊠

YANKEE PEDLAR INN "OYSTER BAR & GRILL ROOM"   **Lunch:** $7-$11   **Dinner:** $16-$20   **Phone:** 413/532-9494
◆◆◆   **Location:** Jct US 5 & 202; 0.3 mi e of I-91, exit 16. 1866 Northampton St 01040. **Hours:** 11:30 am-2 & 5-10
Regional   pm, Sat 11:30 am-10 pm, Sun 2 pm-8 pm. Closed: 12/25 & Mon. **Reservations:** suggested.
American   **Features:** dressy casual; children's menu; cocktails & lounge; entertainment; a la carte. Colonial style dining rooms, New England cuisine. Victorian lounge & oyster bar. Smoke free premises. **Cards:** AE, DS, MC, VI.   ⊠

HULL—10,500

RESTAURANT

SAPORITO'S FLORENCE CLUB CAFE   **Dinner:** $15-$19   **Phone:** 781/925-3023
◆◆◆   **Location:** Between SR 228 & George Washington Blvd, just sw of Horizons condominiums. 11 Rockland Cir
Regional   02045. **Hours:** 5 pm-9 pm, Fri & Sat-10 pm. Closed major holidays, Mon 5/24-9/6 & Tues 9/7-5/23.
Italian   **Reservations:** suggested. **Features:** casual dress; cocktails; a la carte. Delicious specialties. Seasonal menu changes. Quaint, informal dining room. Very popular. Call for detailed directions. **Cards:** DS, MC, VI.   ⊠

HYANNIS—See Cape Cod p. 356.

HYANNIS PORT—See Cape Cod p. 365.

KINGSTON—9,000

LODGING

THE INN AT PLYMOUTH BAY   **Phone:** (781)585-3831
ⒶⒶⒶ SAVE   6/25-9/6   1P: $69- 99   2P/1B: $69- 99   2P/2B: $89- 125 XP: $10   F18
          5/1-6/24 & 9/7-10/11   1P: $69- 79   2P/1B: $69- 89   2P/2B: $79- 114 XP: $10   F18
◆ ◆   10/12-4/30   1P: $59- 69   2P/1B: $69- 79   2P/2B: $79- 99 XP: $10   F18
Motel   **Location:** On SR 3A at jct SR 3, exit 9; 3.5 mi n of jct US 44/SR 3A. 149 Main St 02364. **Fax:** 781/585-7928. **Terms:** Pets. **Facility:** 66 rooms. All units with patio or balcony. 2 stories; interior corridors; heated indoor pool, sauna, whirlpool. **Dining:** Restaurant nearby. **All Rooms:** combo or shower baths. **Cards:** AE, CB, DI, DS, MC, VI. **Special Amenities:** Early check-in/late check-out and free room upgrade (subject to availability with advanced reservations). *(See color ad starting on p 412)*

LANESBORO—3,000

LODGINGS

MT VIEW MOTEL   **Phone:** (413)442-1009
ⒶⒶⒶ SAVE   7/1-8/31   1P: $80- 105   2P/1B: $85- 125   2P/2B: $95- 125
          5/1-6/30 & 9/1-4/30   1P: $35- 55   2P/1B: $38- 80   2P/2B: $42- 85
◆
Motel   **Location:** 1 mi s on US 7. 499 S Main St 01237 (PO Box 1859). **Fax:** 413/499-4568. **Terms:** Reserv deposit, 3 day notice; handling fee imposed; weekly rates; small pets only, in limited rooms. **Facility:** 13 rooms. Modest facilities, some small cottages. 1 story; exterior corridors. **All Rooms:** combo or shower baths, extended cable TV. **Some Rooms:** 3 efficiencies. **Cards:** AE, DS, MC, VI.

THE WEATHERVANE MOTEL

Phone: (413)443-3230

AAA SAVE

	1P:		2P/1B:		2P/2B:		XP:	
7/1-8/31	1P: $42-	75	2P/1B: $42-	95	2P/2B: $48-	98	XP: $5	F18
5/1-6/30 & 1/1-4/30	1P: $32-	35	2P/1B: $35		2P/2B: $35-	42	XP: $5	F18
9/1-12/31	1P: $32-	35	2P/1B: $35		2P/2B: $35		XP: $5	F18

◆
Motel

Location: 1.3 mi s on US 7. 475 S Main St 01237. **Terms:** Weekly/monthly rates; pets, $5 extra charge. **Facility:** 14 rooms. Modestly equipped small to average sized rooms. 1 story; exterior corridors. **All Rooms:** extended cable TV. **Some Rooms:** 4 efficiencies. **Cards:** AE, DI, DS, MC, VI. **Special Amenities:** Early check-in/late check-out and free local telephone calls.

LAWRENCE—See Boston p. 303.

LEE—5,800—See also SOUTH LEE.

LODGINGS

APPLEGATE-A BED N' BREAKFAST

Rates Subject to Change   **Phone:** 413/243-4451

◆◆◆

6/1-8/31 [CP]	1P: $120-	230	2P/1B: $120-	230	XP: $30	
9/1-10/31 [CP]	1P: $100-	230	2P/1B: $100-	230	XP: $30	
5/1-5/31 & 11/1-4/30 [CP]	1P: $95-	195	2P/1B: $95-	195	XP: $30	

Bed &
Breakfast

Location: From center 0.8 mi w. 279 W Park St 01238 (RR 1, Box 576). **Terms:** Age restrictions may apply; reserv deposit, 14 day notice; handling fee imposed; 3 night min stay, weekends 7/1-8/31. **Facility:** 6 rooms. Georgian colonial home on 6 well landscaped grounds. 2 night min stay 6/1-6/30, 9/1-9/30 & 10/1-10/31 weekends; 2 stories; interior corridors; smoke free premises; small pool. **Recreation:** bicycles. **All Rooms:** combo or shower baths. **Cards:** MC, VI.

BEST WESTERN BLACK SWAN INN

Rates Subject to Change   **Phone:** (413)243-2700

AAA

	1P:		2P/1B:		2P/2B:		XP:	
6/25-9/8	1P: $95-	220	2P/1B: $95-	220	2P/2B: $95-	220	XP: $10	F12
9/9-10/26	1P: $90-	175	2P/1B: $90-	175	2P/2B: $90-	175	XP: $10	F12
5/21-6/24	1P: $90-	140	2P/1B: $90-	140	2P/2B: $90-	140	XP: $10	F12
5/1-5/20 & 10/27-4/30	1P: $80-	120	2P/1B: $80-	120	2P/2B: $80-	120	XP: $10	F12

◆◆◆
Motor Inn

Location: On Us 20, 2 mi w of I-90 exit 2. 435 Laurel St 01238. Fax: 413/243-2700. **Terms:** Reserv deposit, 14 day notice, 3 day off season; handling fee imposed; 2 night min stay, weekends in season. **Facility:** 52 rooms. Some with fireplace & balcony overlooking lake. Interior corridors; sauna; boat dock. **Dining:** Cygnets Lakeside Restaurant, see separate listing. **Recreation:** fishing. Fee: pontoon boats. Rental: boats, paddleboats. **All Rooms:** extended cable TV. **Some Rooms:** whirlpools. **Cards:** AE, CB, DI, DS, MC, VI.

CHAMBERY INN

Rates Subject to Change   **Phone:** 413/243-2221

AAA
◆◆◆
Historic Bed
& Breakfast

		2P/1B:		2P/2B:		XP:	
Thurs-Sun 7/1-9/6 & Fri-Sun 10/1-10/31 [CP]		2P/1B: $125-	265	2P/2B: $250		XP: $25	
Fri-Sun 6/17-6/30 & 9/7-9/30 [CP]		2P/1B: $125-	220	2P/2B: $195		XP: $25	
5/1-6/16, Mon-Thurs 6/17-6/30, 9/7-9/30 & 11/1-4/30 [CP]		2P/1B: $75-	220	2P/2B: $110-	169	XP: $25	
Mon-Wed 7/1-9/6 & Mon-Thurs 10/1-10/31 [CP]		2P/1B: $99-	175	2P/2B: $135		XP: $25	

Location: On US 20, 1 mi n of I-90 exit 2. 199 Main St 01238. Fax: 413/243-3600. **Terms:** Age restrictions may apply; reserv deposit, 14 day notice; weekly/monthly rates; 3 night min stay in season. **Facility:** 9 rooms. 1885 schoolhouse with 8 fireplace rooms. 2 night min stay off season. Double-spa suite $150-$265; 2 stories; interior corridors; smoke free premises. **Dining:** Restaurant nearby. **All Rooms:** extended cable TV. **Some Rooms:** whirlpools. **Cards:** AE, DS, MC, VI. *(See color ad below)*

Our **bold type** listings have a special interest in serving you!

DAYS INN
Phone: (413)243-0501

AAA SAVE

◆◆ Motel

Fri & Sat 6/20-9/5 & 10/7-10/31 [CP]	1P:	$99- 145	2P/1B:	$99- 145	2P/2B:	$99- 145	XP:	$5	F12
Sun-Thurs 6/20-9/5, 9/6-10/6 & Sun-Thurs 10/7-10/31 [CP]	1P:	$55- 85	2P/1B:	$55- 85	2P/2B:	$65- 95	XP:	$5	F12
5/1-6/19 [CP]	1P:	$45- 65	2P/1B:	$45- 65	2P/2B:	$55- 85	XP:	$5	F12
11/1-4/30 [CP]	1P:	$30- 55	2P/1B:	$30- 55	2P/2B:	$40- 65	XP:	$5	F12

Location: On SR 102, 1.8 mi w of I-90 exit 2. Pleasant St 1238 (PO Box 426). Fax: 413/243-0370. **Terms:** Reserv deposit, 7 day notice; 2 night min stay, weekends in season. **Facility:** 26 rooms. Traditional decor rooms. Whirlpool rm, extra charge; 2 stories; exterior corridors. **All Rooms:** extended cable TV. **Cards:** AE, DI, DS, MC, VI. **Special Amenities: Free breakfast and free local telephone calls.** ⊠

THE PILGRIM INN
Phone: (413)243-1328

AAA SAVE

◆◆ Motel

Fri & Sat 7/1-9/4 [CP]	1P:	$145- 175	2P/1B:	$165- 195	2P/2B:	$165- 195	
Sun-Thurs 7/1-9/4 [CP]	1P:	$85- 155	2P/1B:	$105- 175	2P/2B:	$105- 175	
9/5-10/31 [CP]	1P:	$65- 155	2P/1B:	$65- 175	2P/2B:	$65- 175	
5/1-6/30 & 11/1-4/30 [CP]	1P:	$45- 105	2P/1B:	$55- 115	2P/2B:	$55- 115	

Location: On US 20; 0.3 mi n of I-90, exit 2. 165 Housatonic St 01238. Fax: 413/243-2339. **Terms:** Handling fee imposed; CP avail; 2 night min stay, weekends in season. **Facility:** 34 rooms. Whirlpool rm, $95-$185; 2 stories; interior/exterior corridors. **All Rooms:** combo or shower baths, extended cable TV. **Cards:** AE, CB, DI, DS, MC, VI. **Special Amenities: Free breakfast and free local telephone calls.** 🅢🄳 ⊇ 🖨 □ 🔒 ⊠

RESTAURANTS

CORK 'N HEARTH
Dinner: $13-$19
Phone: 413/243-0535

◆◆ American

Location: On US 20, 1.3 mi s of jct US 7. US 20 01238. **Hours:** 5 pm-9 pm, Fri & Sat-9:30 pm, Sun 4 pm-9 pm. **Closed:** 11/25, 12/24, 12/25 & Mon. **Reservations:** suggested. **Features:** casual dress; children's menu; cocktails & lounge; minimum charge-$9 in season; a la carte. Overlooking Laurel Lake. Featuring fresh seafood, steak, veal, chicken & pork. Smoke free premises. **Cards:** AE, MC, VI. ⊠

CYGNETS LAKESIDE RESTAURANT
Dinner: $13-$22
Phone: 413/243-2700

◆◆◆ American

Location: On US 20, 2 mi w of I-90 exit 2; in Best Western Black Swan Inn. Laurel Lake 01238. **Hours:** 5:30 pm-8 pm; in season 7 am-10:30 & 5:30-9 pm, Sat & Sun 8 am-11 & 5:30-9 pm. **Reservations:** suggested. **Features:** cocktails; a la carte. Continental American cuisine. Atrium seating ovelooking Laurel Lake. Smoke free premises. **Cards:** AE, CB, DI, DS, MC, VI. ⊠

LEICESTER—10,200

RESTAURANT

THE CASTLE RESTAURANT
Lunch: $5-$8
Dinner: $22-$35
Phone: 508/892-9090

◆◆◆ Continental

Location: West side on SR 9. 1230 Main St 01524. **Hours:** 11:30 am-9:30 pm, Sun 2 pm-9 pm. **Closed:** 1/1, 11/25, 12/25, Mon & Tues-Thurs 7/12-8/23. **Reservations:** suggested; required Sat. **Features:** dressy casual; children's menu; carryout; cocktails & lounge; a la carte. Castle-like atmosphere. Terrace dining in summer. Extensive wine list. **Cards:** AE, CB, DI, DS, MC, VI. ⊠

LENOX—5,100

LODGINGS

BROOK FARM INN
Rates Subject to Change
Phone: 413/637-3013

◆◆◆ Historic Bed & Breakfast

6/15-9/6 [BP]	1P:	$115- 200	2P/1B:	$115- 200	2P/2B:	$115- 200	XP: $20
9/15-10/31 [BP]	1P:	$95- 155	2P/1B:	$95- 155	2P/2B:	$95- 155	XP: $20
5/1-6/14, 9/7-9/14 & 11/1-4/30 [BP]	1P:	$80- 130	2P/1B:	$80- 130	2P/2B:	$80- 130	XP: $20

Location: 1 mi s on SR 183, 0.3 mi s on Old Stockbridge Rd & 0.1 mi w. 15 Hawthorne St 01240. Fax: 413/637-4751. **Terms:** Age restrictions may apply; reserv deposit, 15 day notice; handling fee imposed. **Facility:** 12 rooms. 1850 farmhouse in quiet residential area. 2-3 night min stay weekends; 3 stories, no elevator; interior corridors; smoke free premises. **All Rooms:** combo or shower baths. **Cards:** MC, VI. 🄸🄿 ⊇ 🄿🅅 🖨 ⊠

CRANWELL RESORT & GOLF CLUB
Rates Subject to Change
Phone: (413)637-1364

AAA

◆◆◆ Resort

7/1-9/6	2P/1B:	$199- 439	XP: $20	F16
9/7-11/14	2P/1B:	$129- 359	XP: $20	F16
5/1-6/30	2P/1B:	$129- 359	XP: $20	F16
11/15-4/30	2P/1B:	$89- 229	XP: $20	F16

Location: On US 7/20, 3.5 mi n of I-90 exit 2. 55 Lee Rd 01240. Fax: 413/637-4364. **Terms:** Reserv deposit, 14 day notice; handling fee imposed; monthly rates; CP avail; package plans; 3 night min stay, weekends 6/18-8/31. **Facility:** 95 rooms. 100 year-old Tudor mansion with carriage house & out buildings. Elegant public areas; guest rooms have many luxury appointments. 2-bedroom suites avail; 2-3 stories, no elevator; interior/exterior corridors; driving range, indoor golf center; heated pool; 2 tennis courts. Fee: 18 holes golf. **Dining:** Dining room, restaurant, 2 coffee shops; 7 am-11 pm, Sunday brunch 11:30 am-2:30 pm, limited hours in winter; $16-$27; cocktails. **Services:** giftshop; area transportation, within 10 mi. Fee: massage. **Recreation:** cross country skiing; hiking trails. Fee: bicycles. **All Rooms:** combo or shower baths. **Some Rooms:** 10 efficiencies. **Cards:** AE, CB, DI, DS, JC, MC, VI. 🄰🅂🄺 🅢🄳 🄲 🅹 ⊇ 🍴 🍸 🄵 🖾 🐾 🍹 🄿 □ 🖨 🔒 ⊠

THE GABLES INN
Guaranteed Rates
Phone: 413/637-3416

◆◆◆ Historic Bed & Breakfast

5/25-10/30	1P:	$90- 210	2P/1B:	$90- 210	2P/2B:	$90- 210	XP: $20
5/1-5/24 & 10/31-4/30	1P:	$80- 160	2P/1B:	$80- 160	2P/2B:	$80- 160	XP: $20

Location: Center; on Rt 183. 81 Walker St 01240. **Terms:** Age restrictions may apply; reserv deposit, 14 day notice; 3 night min stay, weekends 6/25-9/7. **Facility:** 17 rooms. Handsome Victorian home; residence of novelist Edith Wharton. Some rooms with fireplace. 2 night min stay 9/8-10/31; 3 stories, no elevator; interior corridors; designated smoking area; 1 tennis court. **All Rooms:** combo or shower baths. **Cards:** DS, MC, VI. ⊇ ⊠ 🄩 🖨 🔒 ⊠

HOWARD JOHNSON

Phone: (413)442-4000

⏣	7/1-8/31 [CP]	1P:	$75- 165	2P/1B:	$89- 185	2P/2B:	$89- 185	XP: $5	F18
	9/1-10/31 [CP]	1P:	$48- 125	2P/1B:	$58- 135	2P/2B:	$65- 135	XP: $5	F18
◆◆◆	5/1-6/30 & 11/1-4/30 [CP]	1P:	$48- 65	2P/1B:	$58- 75	2P/2B:	$58- 75	XP: $5	F18

Motel **Location:** 3.5 mi n on US 7 & 20. 462 Pittsfield Rd 01240 (PO BOX 116). Fax: 413/443-7954. **Terms:** Reserv deposit, 14 day notice; handling fee imposed. **Facility:** 44 rooms. 5 whirlpool suites, $98-$195; 1 room with sauna; 2 stories; exterior corridors. **Services:** winter plug-ins. **All Rooms:** combo or shower baths, extended cable TV. **Cards:** AE, DI, DS, JC, MC, VI. **Special Amenities:** Free breakfast and free local telephone calls. *(See color ad p 398)*

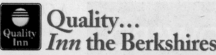

THE KEMBLE INN

Rates Subject to Change

Phone: 413/637-4113

◆◆◆	6/16-9/1 [CP]	1P: $160- 275	2P/1B: $160- 275	2P/2B: $205			XP: $25
Historic Bed	9/2-10/31 [CP]	1P: $135- 225	2P/1B: $135- 225	2P/2B: $160			XP: $25
& Breakfast	5/1-6/15 & 11/1-4/30 [CP]	1P: $110- 195	2P/1B: $110- 195	2P/2B: $135			XP: $25

Location: Corner of SR 183 & US 7A. 2 Kemble St 01240. **Terms:** Age restrictions may apply; reserv deposit, 14 day notice; handling fee imposed; 3 night min stay, Thurs-Sun 7/1-8/31. **Facility:** 15 rooms. 1881 Georgian mansion. 3 stories, no elevator; interior corridors; smoke free premises; mountain view. **All Rooms:** combo or shower baths. **Cards:** MC, VI.

THE LENOX MOTEL

Rates Subject to Change

Phone: 413/499-0324

⏣	6/1-10/31	2P/1B: $60- 135	2P/2B: $60- 135	XP: $7	F12
◆◆	5/1-5/31 & 11/1-4/30	2P/1B: $35- 60	2P/2B: $35- 60	XP: $7	F12

Motel **Location:** 4 mi n on US 7/20. 525 Pittsfield-Lenox Rd 01240 (PO Box 713). Fax: 413/499-5618. **Terms:** Reserv deposit, 10 day notice; handling fee imposed; weekly rates, off season; 2 night min stay, weekends 7/1-9/4. **Facility:** 17 rooms. 1 story; exterior corridors. **Dining:** Restaurant nearby. **All Rooms:** extended cable TV. **Cards:** AE, CB, DI, DS, MC, VI.

MAYFLOWER MOTOR INN

Rates Subject to Change

Phone: 413/443-4468

⏣	Fri & Sat 7/1-10/31	2P/1B: $110- 139	2P/2B: $139	XP: $6	F12
◆◆	Sun-Thurs 7/1-10/31	2P/1B: $58- 98	2P/2B: $65- 98	XP: $6	F12
	5/1-6/30 & 11/1-4/30	2P/1B: $45- 68	2P/2B: $52- 68	XP: $6	F12

Motel **Location:** 3.5 mi n on US 7/20. 474 Pittsfield-Lenox Rd 01240 (PO Box 952). Fax: 413/443-8748. **Terms:** Reserv deposit, 10 day notice; weekly rates; 2 night min stay, Fri-Sun 7/1-8/31. **Facility:** 20 rooms. 1-2 stories; interior/exterior corridors; heated pool. **Dining:** Restaurant nearby. **All Rooms:** combo or shower baths, extended cable TV. **Cards:** AE, DI, DS, MC, VI.

QUALITY INN
Phone: (413)637-4244

	7/2-9/5 [CP]	1P:	$95- 179	2P/1B:	$95- 179	2P/2B:	$95- 179	XP:	$5
	9/6-10/16 [CP]	1P:	$59- 129	2P/1B:	$59- 129	2P/2B:	$59- 129	XP:	$5
	5/1-7/1 [CP]	1P:	$59- 79	2P/1B:	$59- 79	2P/2B:	$59- 79	XP:	$5
Motor Inn	10/17-4/30 [CP]	1P:	$59- 69	2P/1B:	$59- 69	2P/2B:	$59- 69	XP:	$5

Location: On US 7/20, 2 min n of jct. 130 Pittsfield Rd 01240 (PO Box 755). Fax: 413/637-1969. **Terms:** Reserv deposit, 7 day notice; 2 night min stay, weekends 7/1-8/31. **Facility:** 120 rooms. 2 stories; exterior corridors; 2 lighted tennis courts. **Services:** winter plug-ins. **All Rooms:** extended cable TV. **Cards:** AE, CB, DI, DS, JC, MC, VI. **Special Amenities:** Free breakfast and free local telephone calls. *(See color ad p 397)*

SEVEN HILLS COUNTRY INN & RESTAURANT   Rates Subject to Change   Phone: (413)637-0060

◆◆◆	6/20-9/10 & 9/25-10/19 [CP]	1P:	$65- 250	2P/1B:	$85- 275	2P/2B:	$85- 275	XP:	$26	F6
Historic	10/20-4/30 [CP]	1P:	$55- 150	2P/1B:	$65-1050	2P/2B:	$65- 150	XP:	$10-26	F6
Country Inn									

Location: From jct US 7 & 20, 0.6 mi e on US 20, then 0.8 mi s. 40 Plunkett St 01240. Fax: 413/637-3651. **Terms:** Reserv deposit, 30 day notice; handling fee imposed; 3 night min stay, summer weekends. **Facility:** 52 rooms. Original Berkshire cottage & 38 recently renovated motel units on 27 acres. Secluded. 2 stories; interior/exterior corridors; smoke free premises; 2 tennis courts. **All Rooms:** combo or shower baths. **Cards:** AE, CB, DI, DS, JC, MC, VI.

THE VILLAGE INN   Guaranteed Rates   Phone: 413/637-0020

◆◆	6/25-8/31	1P:	$100- 245	2P/1B:	$100- 245	2P/2B:	$245	XP:	$20
Historic	9/1-10/31	1P:	$80- 200	2P/1B:	$80- 200	2P/2B:	$200	XP:	$15
Country Inn	11/1-4/30	1P:	$65- 175	2P/1B:	$65- 175	2P/2B:	$175	XP:	$10
	5/1-6/24	1P:	$50- 145	2P/1B:	$50- 145	2P/2B:	$145	XP:	$5

Location: Just n of SR 183. 16 Church St 01240 (PO Box 1810). Fax: 413/637-9756. **Terms:** Age restrictions may apply; reserv deposit, 30 day notice; 2 night min stay, weekends. **Facility:** 32 rooms. A historic farm home close to other historic properties nestled in downtown Lenox. 1 two-bedroom unit. Midweek rates, 10/26-6/24. 2-bedroom suite with kitchen & living room, $240-$395 for 4 persons. 3 night min stay weekends in summer; 3 stories; interior corridors. **All Rooms:** combo or shower baths. **Some Rooms:** efficiency. **Cards:** AE, DS, MC, VI.

WAGON WHEEL MOTEL   Rates Subject to Change   Phone: 413/445-4532

ⒶⒶⒶ	Fri & Sat 6/21-10/31	1P:	$110- 135	2P/1B:	$110- 135	2P/2B:	$110- 135	XP: $5-10	F10
◆◆	Sun-Thurs 6/21-10/31	1P:	$45- 65	2P/1B:	$45- 65	2P/2B:	$45- 65	XP: $5-10	F10
Motel	5/1-6/20 & 11/1-4/30	1P:	$30- 45	2P/1B:	$30- 55	2P/2B:	$35- 55	XP: $5-10	F10

Location: On US 7/20, 3.5 mi n of jct. 484 Pittsfield-Lenox Rd 01240 (PO Box 808). Fax: 413/499-3508. **Terms:** Reserv deposit; handling fee imposed; weekly rates; 2 night min stay, weekends in summer. **Facility:** 18 rooms. Whirlpool suite, $85-$175; 1 story; exterior corridors. **Dining:** Restaurant nearby. **All Rooms:** combo or shower baths, extended cable TV. **Cards:** AE, DS, MC, VI.

THE YANKEE-HOME COMFORT
Rates Subject to Change
Phone: 413/499-3700

7/1-8/31 [CP]	1P:	$78- 199	2P/1B:	$78- 199	2P/2B:	$92- 199
9/1-10/17 [CP]	1P:	$78- 199	2P/1B:	$78- 199	2P/2B:	$92- 199
5/1-6/30 [CP]	1P:	$78- 125	2P/1B:	$78- 125	2P/2B:	$92- 125
10/18-4/30 [CP]	1P:	$69- 125	2P/1B:	$69- 125	2P/2B:	$79- 125

Motel   **Location:** 3.5 mi n on US 7/20. 461 Pittsfield Rd 01240 (PO Box 829). Fax: 413/499-3634. **Terms:** Reserv deposit, 14 day notice, 7/1-10/31; weekly/monthly rates; 3 night min stay, Thurs-Sun 7/1-8/31. **Facility:** 61 rooms. Quality accommodations ranging from budget to deluxe. 12 units with fireplace, $111-$173. Rates for up to 4 persons; 1-2 stories; exterior corridors; heated pool. **All Rooms:** combo or shower baths. **Some Rooms:** 4 efficiencies. **Cards:** AE, CB, DI, DS, MC, VI. *(See color ad p 398)*

RESTAURANTS

BLANTYRE MAIN DINING ROOM   Country Inn   **Lunch:** $38   **Dinner:** $70   **Phone:** 413/637-3556
French   **Location:** 1 mi s on US 20 from jct SR 183. Blantyre St 01240. **Hours:** Open 5/15-11/1; 6 pm-8:45 pm; 7/1-8/31 12:30 pm-1:45 pm. Closed: Mon. **Reservations:** required. **Features:** semi-formal attire; cocktails; entertainment; prix fixe. Replica of Grand Scottish Manor. 1902 Tudor-style mansion. 18% service charge. Smoke free premises. **Cards:** AE, CB, DI, MC, VI.

THE CANDLELIGHT INN RESTAURANT   **Lunch:** $7-$10   **Dinner:** $15-$22   **Phone:** 413/637-1555
American   **Location:** On SR 7A & 183. 35 Walker St 01240. **Hours:** 6 pm-9:30 pm; noon-2:30 pm in summer & weekends. Closed: Tues (off season). **Reservations:** suggested. **Features:** casual dress; cocktails & lounge; minimum charge-$15 dinner in summer; a la carte. Attractive intimate dining rooms. Smoke free premises. **Cards:** AE, MC, VI.

GATEWAYS INN   Country Inn   **Dinner:** $15-$23   **Phone:** 413/637-2532
Continental   **Location:** Center, on SR 183. 51 Walker St 01240. **Hours:** 5:15 pm-9:30 pm 6/1-8/31; 6 pm-9 pm 9/1-5/31. Closed: Mon. **Reservations:** required. **Features:** casual dress; Sunday brunch; cocktail lounge. Relaxed dining in a Victorian Inn; an excellent variety of entrees featuring fresh seafood, prime beef, lamb & game. Smoke free premises. **Cards:** AE, CB, DI, DS, MC, VI.

LENOX HOUSE   **Lunch:** $6-$11   **Dinner:** $10-$18   **Phone:** 413/637-1341
American   **Location:** On US 7 & 20, 2 mi n. 55 Pittsfield-Lenox Rd 01240. **Hours:** 11:30 am-9:30 pm. **Reservations:** suggested. **Features:** children's menu; health conscious menu; cocktails & lounge. Inviting country dining room known for excellent service & popovers. Continental cuisine. Smoke free premises. **Cards:** AE, DS, MC, VI.

LENOX 218   **Lunch:** $6-$9   **Dinner:** $11-$20   **Phone:** 413/637-4218
      Location: 0.8 mi n on SR 7A. 218 Main St SR 7A 01240. **Hours:** 11:30 am-2:30 & 5-10 pm. **Reservations:** suggested. **Features:** casual dress; children's menu; carryout; cocktails & lounge; a la carte. Contemporary casual atmosphere. Lite fare avail in fireplace lounge & dining room. Smoking in lounge only.
Northern Italian   **Cards:** AE, CB, DI, DS, MC, VI.

WHEATLEIGH   Historical   **Lunch:** $10-$18   **Dinner:** $75-$95   **Phone:** 413/637-0610
French   **Location:** 1.8 mi s on SR 183, 1 mi e. Hawthorne Rd 01240. **Hours:** 6 pm-9 pm; Fri & Sat-9:30 pm; noon-1:30 & 5-9 pm 7/1-8/31. Closed: Tue & Wed 9/1-9/30 & 11/1-3/31. **Reservations:** required. **Features:** dressy casual; health conscious menu items; cocktails; valet parking; prix fixe. Prix fixe 4-course dinners, $75. Gracious dining in restored 1893 summer mansion. International haute cuisine. Extensive wine list. Smoke free premises. **Cards:** AE, CB, DI, MC, VI.

LEOMINSTER—38,100

LODGINGS

FOUR POINTS HOTEL
Rates Subject to Change
Phone: (978)534-9000

5/1-11/15	1P:	$84- 140	2P/1B:	$84- 140	XP: $10	F18
11/16-4/30	1P:	$82- 135	2P/1B:	$82- 135	XP: $10	F18

Motor Inn   **Location:** Jct SR 2 & 12. 99 Erdman Way 01453. Fax: 978/534-0891. **Facility:** 187 rooms. 22 executive rms, $115-$145. 22 whirlpool rms, extra charge; 7 stories; interior corridors; heated indoor pool. **Cards:** AE, CB, DI, DS, MC, VI.

SUPER 8 MOTEL
Rates Subject to Change
Phone: 978/537-2800

9/1-10/31 [CP]	1P:	$44	2P/1B:	$50	2P/2B:	$50	XP: $6	F12
5/1-8/31 & 11/1-4/30 [CP]	1P:	$41	2P/1B:	$47	2P/2B:	$47	XP: $6	F12

Motel   **Location:** On SR 12, just n of SR 2, exit 31B. 482 N Main St 01453. Fax: 978/840-4367. **Facility:** 101 rooms. 4 stories; interior corridors. **Cards:** AE, CB, DI, DS, MC, VI.

RESTAURANTS

E.J. MARRONE'S RESTAURANT & GOOD TIME LOUNGE   **Lunch:** $5-$12   **Dinner:** $5-$12   **Phone:** 978/537-6029
American   **Location:** On SR 12; 3.1 mi s of SR 2, exit 31; 4 mi n of I-190, exit 6. 700 Central St 01453. **Hours:** 11 am-11 pm, Wed-Sat-midnight, Sun-10 pm. Closed: 11/25 & 12/25. **Features:** casual dress; children's menu; early bird specials; carryout; cocktails & lounge. Fresh daily seafood. Also, steak, chicken, veal & pasta. Presidential Lounge with JFK memorabilia. **Cards:** AE, DS, MC, VI.

WEATHERVANE SEAFOOD RESTAURANT   **Lunch:** $5-$13   **Dinner:** $5-$13   **Phone:** 978/345-2877
Seafood   **Location:** SR 2 exit 32, 2 mi n on SR 13. 1290 Main St (SR 13) 01453. **Hours:** 11 am-9 pm. Closed: 11/25, 12/24 & 12/25. **Features:** casual dress; children's menu; carryout; cocktails & lounge. Casual family dining. **Cards:** MC, VI.

LEXINGTON—See Boston p. 304.

LITTLETON—See Boston p. 304.

LOWELL—See Boston p. 304.

LYNN—See Boston p. 305.

LYNNFIELD—See Boston p. 305.

MALDEN—See Boston p. 305.

MANCHESTER—See Boston p. 305.

MANSFIELD—16,600

LODGINGS

HOLIDAY INN MANSFIELD
◆◆◆
Motor Inn
Rates Subject to Change
All Year   1P: $89- 159 2P/1B: $99- 169 2P/2B: $99- 169 XP: $10   F18
Phone: 508/339-2200
Location: From I-95 exit 7A, 0.5 mi s on SR 140, 1 mi w on Forbes Rd; from I-495 exit 12, 2 mi n on SR 140, then w on Forbes Rd; in I-95 Industrial Center. 31 Hampshire St 02048. Fax: 508/339-1040.
Facility: 202 rooms. 2-3 stories; interior corridors; heated indoor pool. Fee: racquetball courts, 2 lighted tennis courts.
Cards: AE, CB, DI, DS, MC, VI. *(See color ad p 275)*
🐕 🛎 🛍 🍴 🍽 🅿 ⚹ 📶 🛗 💻 📠 🖥 ⊗

MOTEL 6 - 1248
ⓐⓐⓐ
◆ ◆
Motel
Rates Subject to Change
All Year   1P: $59   2P/1B: $69
Phone: 508/339-2323
XP: $6   F17
Location: From I-95 exit 7A, 1.3 mi n of jct I-495 exit 12, just off SR 140; in Cabot Business Park. 60 Forbes Blvd 02048. Fax: 508/337-6733. **Terms:** Small pets only, one per room. **Facility:** 126 rooms. 5 stories; interior corridors. **All Rooms:** combo or shower baths. **Cards:** AE, CB, DI, DS, MC, VI.
🐕 🛍 🅿 📶 🛗 ⊗

MARBLEHEAD—See Boston p. 306.

MARLBOROUGH—See Boston p. 306.

MARSHFIELD—21,500

RESTAURANT

THE FIELDSTON
◆◆◆
Continental
Dinner: $11-$19
Phone: 781/834-2909
Location: 6 mi e of SR 3, exit 12. 882 Ocean St (Rt 139) 02050. **Hours:** 5 pm-10 pm. Closed: Mon & Tues.
Reservations: accepted. **Features:** casual dress; cocktails & lounge; a la carte. A sweet Victorian decor of lace curtains, rich mosaic wallpaper, smoked glass lighting fixtures & candlelit tables dressed in linens. A romantic yet casual "touch of class" dining ambiance. Menu changes seasonally. Smoke free premises. **Cards:** AE, DS, MC, VI.
⊗

MARTHA'S VINEYARD (ISLAND)

LODGINGS

ASHLEY INN
◆◆
Bed &
Breakfast
Rates Subject to Change
6/11-9/19 [CP]   1P: $135- 275 2P/1B: $135- 275 2P/2B: $195   XP: $20
5/1-6/10 & 9/20-4/30 [CP] 1P: $100- 200 2P/1B: $100- 200 2P/2B: $155 XP: $20
Phone: 508/627-9655
Location: 2 blks w. 129 Main St 02539 (PO Box 650, EDGARTOWN). Fax: 508/627-6629. **Terms:** Age restrictions may apply; reserv deposit, 14 day notice; handling fee imposed; 3 night min stay, weekends in season. **Facility:** 10 rooms. 1800's sea captain's home. Some rooms with canopy bed, 1 with fireplace. 3 stories; interior corridors; designated smoking area. **All Rooms:** combo or shower baths. **Cards:** AE, DS, MC, VI.
📠 🖥 ⊗

CAPTAIN DEXTER HOUSE
◆◆
Bed &
Breakfast
Rates Subject to Change
6/1-9/7 [CP]   1P: $110- 225 2P/1B: $110- 225   XP: $20   D12
9/8-10/31 [CP]   1P: $100- 200 2P/1B: $100- 200   XP: $20   D12
5/1-5/31 & 11/1-4/30 [CP] 1P: $95- 165 2P/1B: $95- 165 XP: $20   D12
Phone: (508)693-6564
Location: Center, just n of ferry dock. 92 Main St 02568 (PO Box 2457, VINEYARD HAVEN).
Fax: 508/693-8448. **Terms:** Age restrictions may apply; reserv deposit, 14 day notice; 3 night min stay, weekends in season. **Facility:** 8 rooms. Former sea captain's home built in 1843. 2 rooms with fireplace. 1-bedroom suite, $175; off season $155 for up to 2 persons. 2 night min stay weekends off season; 3 stories, no elevator; interior corridors; designated smoking area.
All Rooms: comb, shower or tub baths. **Cards:** AE, MC, VI.
ⒶⓈⓀ 🅢 🛗 📶 🅩 📠 ⊗

CAPTAIN DEXTER HOUSE OF EDGARTOWN

◆◆◆ Bed & Breakfast

Rates Subject to Change   Phone: (508)627-7289

	1P:	2P/1B:	2P/2B:	XP:	
6/1-9/7 [CP]	$125- 225	$125- 225	$125- 225	$20	F12
5/1-5/31, 9/8-10/31 & 4/15-4/30 [EP]	$95- 165	$95- 165	$95- 162	$20	F12

Location: Just w of Main St. 35 Pease's Point Way 02539 (PO Box 2798, EDGARTOWN).
Fax: 508/627-3328. **Terms:** Open 5/1-10/31 & 4/15-4/30; reserv deposit, 14 day notice; handling fee imposed; 3 night min stay, 7/1-8/31. **Facility:** 11 rooms. A restored 1840's house. 2 stories; interior/exterior corridors; smoke free premises. **All Rooms:** combo or shower baths. **Cards:** AE, MC, VI.

(ASK) (S□) (♻) (☎) (🖨) (✕)

COLONIAL INN OF MARTHA'S VINEYARD

Ⓐ

Historic Country Inn

Guaranteed Rates   Phone: (508)627-4711

	1P:	2P/1B:	2P/2B:	XP:	
5/28-9/25 [CP]	$152- 255	$152- 255	$173- 255	$15	F16
9/26-10/31 [CP]	$115- 185	$115- 185	$130- 185	$15	F16
5/1-5/27 & 4/1-4/30 [CP]	$99- 156	$99- 156	$109- 156	$15	F16
11/1-12/1 [CP]	$77- 152	$77- 152	$87- 152	$15	F16

Location: Main St, just n. 38 N Water St 02539 (PO Box 68, EDGARTOWN). Fax: 508/627-5904. **Terms:** Open 5/1-12/1 & 4/1-4/30; reserv deposit, 14 day notice; weekly rates; 2 night min stay. **Facility:** 43 rooms. Operated continuously as an inn since 1911. Small covered deck off 4th floor overlooks harbor. Handicap/wheelchair lift between ground & 2nd floor. 4 stories, no elevator; interior corridors; oceanview. **Dining:** Restaurant; 5:30 pm-11 pm; $16-$25; cocktails. **Services:** giftshop. **All Rooms:** combo or shower baths, extended cable TV. **Some Rooms:** 2 kitchens. **Cards:** AE, MC, VI.

(♿) (▨) (¶¶) (♉) (△) (VCR) (☎) (🖨) (🔒) (✕)

DAGGETT HOUSE

Ⓐ (SAVE)

◆◆◆ Historic Country Inn

Phone: 508/627-4600

	1P:	2P/1B:
5/1-10/17	$155- 550	$155- 550
10/18-4/30	$85- 275	$85- 275

Location: Just n on Water St. 59 N Water St 02539 (P O Box 1333, EDGARTOWN). Fax: 508/627-4611. **Terms:** Reserv deposit, 14 day notice; handling fee imposed. **Facility:** 25 rooms. 3 buildings, main building built in 1660. 2 night min stay in season, weekends off season. 1- & 2-bedroom suites, $395; 2 stories; interior/exterior corridors; smoke free premises; oceanview. **Dining:** Dining room; 7:30 am-11 & 5:30-9 pm in season; call for hrs off season & Sun brunch 8 am-1 pm; $22-$25; cocktails. **All Rooms:** combo or shower baths, extended cable TV. **Some Rooms:** 2 efficiencies, 3 kitchens, whirlpools. **Cards:** AE, DS, MC, VI.

(¶¶) (✕)

THE DOCKSIDE INN

Ⓐ

◆◆◆ Bed & Breakfast

Rates Subject to Change   Phone: (508)693-2966

	1P:	2P/1B:	2P/2B:
6/11-9/19 [CP]	$130- 175	$130- 175	$150- 350
9/20-10/24 [CP]	$115- 155	$115- 155	$135- 295
5/1-6/10 [CP]	$95- 145	$95- 145	$120- 225
4/2-4/30 [CP]	$80- 110	$80- 110	$90- 195

Location: Town center; opposite passenger ferry dock. Circuit Ave Ext 02557 (PO Box 1206, OAK BLUFFS). Fax: 508/696-7293. **Terms:** Open 5/1-10/24 & 4/2-4/30; reserv deposit, 21 day notice; package plans; 3 night min stay, in summer; dog on premises. **Facility:** 22 rooms. Victorian inn. Some small rooms. 3 suites with kitchen, $240-$275 in season for up to 9 persons; 3 stories, no elevator; exterior corridors; designated smoking area. **Dining:** Restaurant nearby. **Recreation:** recreation room. **All Rooms:** combo or shower baths, extended cable TV. **Some Rooms:** whirlpools. **Cards:** AE, DS, MC, VI. (See ad below)

(¶↧) (🖨) (✕)

GREENWOOD HOUSE B & B

Ⓐ

◆◆◆ Bed & Breakfast

Rates Subject to Change   Phone: (508)693-6150

	1P:	2P/1B:	2P/2B:
6/15-10/15 [CP]	$179- 269	$179- 269	$179- 269
5/1-6/14 & 10/16-4/30 [CP]	$109- 199	$109- 199	$109- 199

Location: 4 blks n of the Vineyard Haven ferry. 40 Greenwood Ave 02568-2734 (PO Box 2734, VINEYARD HAVEN). Fax: 508/696-8113. **Terms:** Reserv deposit, 21 day notice; handling fee imposed; 3 night min stay, weekends in season. **Facility:** 4 rooms. Rooms & suites in a large home in residential area. 3 stories; interior corridors; smoke free premises. **Recreation:** croquet. **All Rooms:** combo or shower baths, extended cable TV. **Cards:** AE, CB, DI, MC, VI.

(🖨) (🔒) (✕)

THE HANOVER HOUSE

Ⓐ

◆◆◆ Bed & Breakfast

Rates Subject to Change   Phone: (508)693-1066

	2P/1B:	2P/2B:	XP:
6/1-9/30 [CP]	$145- 195	$175- 205	$20
5/1-5/31, 10/1-11/30 & 3/1-4/30 [CP]	$118- 188	$138- 198	$20

Location: 0.5 mi sw of ferry dock in Vineyard Haven on the road to Edgartown. 28 Edgartown Rd 02568 (PO Box 2107, VINEYARD HAVEN). Fax: 508/696-6099. **Terms:** Open 5/1-11/30 & 3/1-4/30; age restrictions may apply; reserv deposit, 15 day notice; handling fee imposed; 3 night min stay, weekends in season. **Facility:** 15 rooms. Cozy country decor. Some units with patio or deck. 2 one-bedroom housekeeping units, for up to 2 persons in season; 1-bedroom suite, for up to 2 persons in season; 2 stories; interior/exterior corridors; smoke free premises. **All Rooms:** combo or shower baths, extended cable TV. **Some Rooms:** 2 kitchens. **Cards:** AE, DS, MC, VI. (See ad p 402)

(☎) (🖨) (✕)

HARBOR VIEW HOTEL
◆◆◆
Hotel

	Rates Subject to Change			Phone: (508)627-7000	
6/11-9/18		2P/1B: $185- 475	2P/2B: $280- 295	XP: $20	F15
5/1-6/10, 9/19-11/7 &					
4/23-4/30		2P/1B: $175- 295	2P/2B: $175	XP: $20	F15
11/8-4/22		2P/1B: $115- 195	2P/2B: $100	XP: $20	F15

Location: 0.3 mi n center. 131 N Water St 02539 (PO Box 7, EDGARTOWN). Fax: 508/627-8417. **Terms:** Reserv deposit, 14 day notice; 2 night min stay, weekends in season. **Facility:** 124 rooms. Some units with patio or balcony. 4 stories; interior/exterior corridors; oceanview; heated pool; 2 tennis courts. Fee: boat dock. **Recreation:** swimming, fishing. Fee: bicycles. **Some Rooms:** 9 kitchens. **Cards:** AE, DI, JC, VI.

KELLEY HOUSE
◆◆◆
Country Inn

	Rates Subject to Change		Phone: (508)627-7900	
6/11-9/18	2P/1B: $255- 295	2P/2B: $245	XP: $20	F15
5/10-6/10 & 9/19-11/1	2P/1B: $155- 185	2P/2B: $140	XP: $20	F15

Location: Historic district center on Kelly St at Water St. 23 Kelly St 02539 (PO Box 37, EDGARTOWN). Fax: 508/627-8142. **Terms:** Open 5/10-11/1; reserv deposit, 14 day notice; 2 night min stay, weekends in season. **Facility:** 53 rooms. Complex of 5 buildings with the earliest opened in 1742. Rooms, 1- & 2-bedroom suites & townhouse units with harbor view. 5 two-bedroom units. 4 two-bedroom townhouse or apartment units w/kitchen, $575 up to 4 persons; $350 off season; 1 kitchen unit, $435. Suites, $255-$675; 3 stories, no elevator; interior corridors. **Cards:** AE, DI, MC, VI.

MARTHA'S VINEYARD CLARION-EDGARTON HERITAGE HOTEL
Ⓐ SAVE
◆◆
Motel

			Phone: (508)627-5161	
6/18-9/11 [CP]	1P: $170	2P/1B: $185	2P/2B: $185	XP: $15	F18
5/7-6/17 & 9/12-10/23 [CP]	1P: $120	2P/1B: $135	2P/2B: $135	XP: $15	F18
5/1-5/6 & 10/24-4/30 [CP]	1P: $80	2P/1B: $95	2P/2B: $95	XP: $15	F18

Location: 0.8 mi nw. 227 Upper Main St 02539 (PO Box 1808, EDGARTOWN). Fax: 508/627-3444. **Terms:** Reserv deposit, 14 day notice; handling fee imposed; 2 night min stay, weekends 5/1-10/31. **Facility:** 34 rooms. 2 stories; interior corridors. **Dining:** Restaurant; noon-3 & 5-9 pm; $10-$17; cocktails. **All Rooms:** extended cable TV. **Cards:** AE, CB, DI, DS, JC, MC, VI. *(See color ad below)*

THE OAK HOUSE
Ⓐ
◆◆◆
Bed & Breakfast

	Rates Subject to Change			Phone: (508)693-4187
6/11-9/19 [CP]	1P: $160- 200	2P/1B: $160- 200	2P/2B: $250	
9/20-10/17 [CP]	1P: $125- 170	2P/1B: $125- 170	2P/2B: $200	
5/6-6/10 [CP]	1P: $120- 140	2P/1B: $120- 140	2P/2B: $180	

Location: 0.3 mi se. Corner of Seaview & Pequot Aves 02557 (PO Box 299, OAK BLUFFS). Fax: 508/696-7385. **Terms:** Open 5/6-10/17; age restrictions may apply; reserv deposit, 21 day notice; handling fee imposed; 3 night min stay, weekends in season; dog on premises. **Facility:** 10 rooms. An 1876 Victorian mansion & former governor's summer home with the sun porch added in 1902. 1 two-bedroom unit. 1 two-bedroom suite, $250 & 1 one-bedroom suite, $245; 3 stories, no elevator; interior corridors; designated smoking area; oceanview; street parking only. **Dining:** Afternoon tea. **Recreation:** barbecue grill. **All Rooms:** combo or shower baths, extended cable TV. **Cards:** AE, DS, MC, VI. *(See ad p 401)*

1720 HOUSE
◆◆
Historic Bed
& Breakfast

Rates Subject to Change
5/22-10/11 [CP] 1P: $110- 135 2P/1B: $135- 150 2P/2B: $110- 135
5/1-5/21 & 10/12-4/30 [CP] 1P: $75- 110 2P/1B: $95- 110 2P/2B: $75- 110

Phone: 508/693-6407

Location: 0.5 mi n of town center & ferry dock. 130 Main St 02568 (PO Box 1193, VINEYARD HAVEN). Fax: 508/696-0034. **Terms:** Age restrictions may apply; reserv deposit, 14 day notice; handling fee imposed; 2 night min stay, weekends in season. **Facility:** 6 rooms. Shotgun style Colonial built in 1720. Basic stark accommodations. 2 stories; interior corridors; designated smoking area. **Recreation:** bicycles. **Some Rooms:** color TV. **Cards:** MC, VI.

⊠ ☎ ✕

THORNCROFT INN
Ⓐ

◆◆◆◆
Bed &
Breakfast

Guaranteed Rates
6/18-9/6 [BP] 2P/1B: $275- 450
5/1-6/17 & 9/7-11/8 [BP] 2P/1B: $250- 425
11/9-4/30 [BP] 2P/1B: $225- 375

Phone: (508)693-3333

Location: 1 mi n of ferry dock. 460 Main St 02568 (PO Box 1022, VINEYARD HAVEN). Fax: 508/693-5419. **Terms:** Age restrictions may apply; reserv deposit, 21 day notice. **Facility:** 14 rooms. Rooms furnished with antiques. Tranquil setting on 3 1/2 acres. 8 units with fireplace. 2 rooms with hot tub & a fireplace. 2 stories; interior/exterior corridors; smoke free premises. **Dining:** Afternoon tea. **All Rooms:** combo or shower baths. **Some Rooms:** whirlpools. **Cards:** AE, CB, DI, DS, MC, VI.

3P VCR 📶 🖨 🔒 ✕

TUCKERMAN HOUSE
Ⓐ

◆◆◆
Bed &
Breakfast

Guaranteed Rates
5/1-6/20 [BP] 1P: $165- 295 2P/1B: $165- 295
6/21-9/30 [BP] 1P: $195- 295 2P/1B: $195- 295
10/1-4/30 [BP] 1P: $140- 300 2P/1B: $140- 300

Phone: (508)693-0417

Location: Corner of William & Camp sts, 0.5 mi w of Vineyard Haven Ferry. 45 William St 02568 (PO Box 194, VINEYARD HAVEN). Fax: 508/693-7654. **Terms:** Reserv deposit, 21 day notice; handling fee imposed. **Facility:** 5 rooms. 2 units with fireplace. 1836 sea captain's home. 2 stories; interior/exterior corridors; smoke free premises. **All Rooms:** combo or shower baths, extended cable TV. **Some Rooms:** color TV. **Cards:** AE, CB, DI, DS, MC, VI.

☎ 🖨 ✕

TUSCANY INN
◆◆◆
Bed &
Breakfast

Rates Subject to Change
6/18-9/6 [BP] 2P/1B: $325- 375 2P/2B: $200 XP: $35
5/14-6/17 & 9/7-10/24 [BP] 2P/1B: $245- 280 2P/2B: $150 XP: $35
5/1-5/13, 10/25-12/31 &
4/1-4/30 [CP] 2P/1B: $145- 175 2P/2B: $90 XP: $35

Phone: (508)627-5999

Location: In historic distric center, just n of Main St. 22 N Water St 02539-2428 (PO Box 2428, EDGARTOWN, 02539). Fax: 508/627-6605. **Terms:** Open 5/1-12/31 & 4/1-4/30; age restrictions may apply; reserv deposit, 15 day notice; handling fee imposed; 3 night min stay, weekends in season. **Facility:** 8 rooms. Italianate Victorian setting & decor. 3 stories, no elevator; interior corridors; smoke free premises. **All Rooms:** comb, shower or tub baths. **Cards:** AE, DI, DS, MC, VI.

☎ ✕

RESTAURANTS

BLACK DOG TAVERN & BAKERY
◆◆
American

Lunch: $5-$15 **Dinner:** $11-$25 **Phone:** 508/693-9223
Location: On the harbor, 1st wharf s of the Steamship Authority ferry wharf. Beach St Extension, Vineyard Haven 02568. **Hours:** 7 am-11, noon-2:30 & 5-9 pm; 7/1-9/30 to 10 pm, Sun 7 am-1 & 5-9:30 pm. Closed: 11/25 & 12/25. **Features:** No A/C; casual dress; Sunday brunch; children's menu; carryout; street parking; a la carte. Rustic, very popular harbor front restaurant. Eclectic, changing menu. Winter hours may vary. An island tradition. Featuring fresh local seafood, homemade bread & tempting pastry. Smoke free premises. **Cards:** AE, DS, MC, VI.

✕

DAVID RYANS
◆◆
American

Lunch: $6-$14 **Dinner:** $13-$23 **Phone:** 508/627-4100
Location: Just n of Main St, just off harbor. 11 N Water St 02539. **Hours:** 11:30 am-10 pm, Fri & Sat-11 pm. Closed: 1/1-1/31. **Features:** casual dress; children's menu; carryout; cocktails & lounge; street parking; a la carte. Informal, lively atmosphere. Cheery, contemporary decor. **Cards:** MC, VI.

✕

LE GRENIER
◆◆◆
French

Dinner: $19-$29 **Phone:** 508/693-4906
Location: Just n of ferry dock. 96 Main St (Vineyard Haven) 02568. **Hours:** 6 pm-10 pm. **Reservations:** suggested. **Features:** casual dress; a la carte. A bustling bistro, relaxed candlelight dining. Guests are welcome to bring their own alcoholic beverages. Setups avail for a nominal charge. Smoke free premises. **Cards:** AE, DS, MC, VI.

LOLA'S
◆◆
South Seafood

Dinner: $20-$26 **Phone:** 508/693-5007
Location: 1.3 mi se. Beach Rd 02557. **Hours:** 5 pm-10 pm; pub menu available to midnight. Closed: 12/25. **Reservations:** suggested; for dinner. **Features:** No A/C; casual dress; Sunday brunch; children's menu; carryout; cocktails & lounge. Casual dining overlooking golf course. Featuring southern style seafood. Smoking permitted only at the bar. Smoke free premises. **Cards:** DI, MC, VI.

✕

LOUIS' TISBURY CAFE
Ⓐ

◆◆
Italian

Dinner: $13-$21 **Phone:** 508/693-3255
Location: 0.8 mi w of ferry dock. 350 State Rd 02568. **Hours:** 5:30 pm-9 pm, Fri & Sat-9:30 pm; off season to 8:30 pm, Fri & Sat-9 pm; 11 am-5:30 pm for takeout, sit down space avail. Closed major holidays. **Features:** casual dress; children's menu; carryout; salad bar. Cozy, bustling dining room. Homemade rolls, pasta & dessert. Also, some American entrees. Many vegetarian dishes. Complete line of pizza, subs & daily specials at deli case for carry out. Smoke free premises. **Cards:** AE, DS, MC, VI.

SAVOIR FARE
◆◆◆
American

Dinner: $24-$33 **Phone:** 508/627-9864
Location: In old Court House Square opposite town hall, behind court house. 14 Church St, Edgartown 02539. **Hours:** Open 5/1-11/1 & 4/3-4/30; 5:30 pm-10 pm, from 6 pm off season. Closed: Mon & Tues 4/3-4/30 & 10/15-11/1. **Reservations:** suggested. **Features:** No A/C; casual dress; beer & wine only; a la carte. Compact & cute. Exciting inventive menu. Some al fresco dining. Smoke free premises. **Cards:** AE, MC, VI.

✕

THE SQUARE RIGGER RESTAURANT
◆◆
Seafood

Dinner: $15-$22 **Phone:** 508/627-9968
Location: In Edgartown; 1.3 mi w, on upper Main St at jct Beach & Edgartown rds, at the Point of "The Triangle". 235 State Rd Egartown 02539. **Hours:** 5 pm-10 pm, off season-9 pm. Closed: 12/24, 12/25 & Mon 12/1-3/31. **Reservations:** suggested. **Features:** casual dress; children's menu; health conscious menu; carryout; cocktails. Charbroiled entrees, seafood, pasta specials & an open hearth. Casual nautical atmosphere. Smoke free premises. **Cards:** AE, MC, VI.

✕

STRIPERS ON-THE-WATER
◆◆◆
Regional
American
Dinner: $20-$27 **Phone:** 508/693-8383
Location: 0.5 mi s of Vineyard Haven Ferry on the road to Oak Bluffs. 52 Beach Rd 02568. **Hours:** Open 5/1-10/15; 5:30 pm-10 pm; off season to 9 pm. Closed: Tues 9/15-10/15 & Tues & Wed 5/1-6/14.
Features: No A/C; casual dress; Sunday brunch; children's menu; carryout; a la carte. Eclectic New American Cuisine specializing in seafood & served in casual upscale atmosphere overlooking Vineyard Haven Harbor. Outdoor seating avail. Smoke free premises. **Cards:** DI, MC, VI. ⊠

MEDFORD—See Boston p. 306.

METHUEN—See Boston p. 307.

MIDDLEBORO—6,800

LODGINGS

DAYS INN-PLYMOUTH/MIDDLEBORO **Phone:** (508)946-4400
◆◆
Motel

5/28-9/6 [CP]	1P:	$80-	90	2P/1B:	$85- 95	2P/2B:	$85- 95	XP: $6	F19
5/1-5/27 & 9/7-10/11 [CP]	1P:	$75-	85	2P/1B:	$80- 90	2P/2B:	$80- 90	XP: $6	F19
10/12-4/30 [CP]	1P:	$70-	80	2P/1B:	$75- 85	2P/2B:	$75- 85	XP: $6	F19

Location: I-495 exit 4, at SR 105. 30 E Clark St 02346. Fax: 508/946-0966. **Facility:** 113 rooms. Large, tastefully appointed guest rooms. 2 stories; interior corridors; heated pool. **All Rooms:** combo or shower baths. **Cards:** AE, CB, DI, DS, JC, MC, VI. *(See color ad p 416)* 🛢 🆘 🚗 🐕 🖆 🅰 ➡ 🍴 📺 □ 🖥 🔒 ♿ ⊠

SUSSE CHALET INN **Phone:** (508)946-4000
◆◆
Motel

7/2-9/5 [CP]	1P:	$60-	85	2P/1B:	$70- 90	2P/2B:	$70- 85	XP: $3	F17
5/1-7/1 & 9/6-10/16 [CP]	1P:	$50-	79	2P/1B:	$55- 84	2P/2B:	$55- 80	XP: $3	F17
10/17-4/30 [CP]	1P:	$50-	60	2P/1B:	$55- 65	2P/2B:	$55- 60	XP: $3	F17

Location: On US 44; 0.3 mi w of jct I-495, exit 6. 4 Chalet Rd 02346. Fax: 508/478-4234. **Facility:** 105 rooms. 4 stories; interior corridors. **Cards:** AE, CB, DI, DS, MC, VI. *(See ad p 289)* 🔟 ➡ 🅰 🍴 📺 □ 🖥 🔒 ⊠

RESTAURANT

LORENZO'S ITALIAN RESTAURANT **Lunch:** $4-$12 **Dinner:** $5-$12 **Phone:** 508/947-3000
◆◆
Italian
Location: On SR 28; 0.3 mi s of jct SR 18, 28 & US 44. 500 W Grove St 02346. **Hours:** 11 am-10 pm; 9/2-6/17 to 9 pm, Fri & Sat-10 pm. Closed: 11/25 & 12/25. **Features:** casual dress; children's menu; health conscious menu; carryout; cocktails & lounge; a la carte. Relaxed family setting. Also sandwiches, pizza & seafood specials. Patio dining & outdoor barbecue grilled items in season. **Cards:** AE, MC, VI. ⊠

MILFORD—25,400

LODGINGS

COURTYARD BY MARRIOTT **Phone:** 508/634-9500
◆◆◆
Motel
All Year 1P: $109 2P/2B: $109
Location: 0.3 mi s on SR 85, I-495, exit 20. 10 Fortune Blvd 01757. Fax: 508/634-9694. **Facility:** 152 rooms. Rates for up to 4 persons; 4 stories; interior corridors; heated indoor pool. **Cards:** AE, DI, DS, MC, VI.
(See color ad p 280) 🎿 🔟 ➡ 🅰 🅰 🖆 🍴 📺 □ 🖥 🔒 ⊠

RADISSON HOTEL MILFORD **Phone:** (508)478-7010
◆◆◆
Hotel

9/15-11/15	1P:	$89- 129	2P/1B:	$99- 139	2P/2B:	$99- 139	XP: $10	F17
5/1-9/14	1P:	$79- 119	2P/1B:	$89- 129	2P/2B:	$89- 129	XP: $10	F17
11/16-4/30	1P:	$69- 119	2P/1B:	$79- 129	2P/2B:	$79- 129	XP: $10	F17

Location: I-495 exit 19, at jct Rt 109. 11 Beaver St 01757. Fax: 508/478-5600. **Facility:** 173 rooms. 5 stories; interior corridors; heated indoor pool. **All Rooms:** combo or shower baths. **Cards:** AE, DI, DS, MC, VI. 🅰🆂🅺 🆘 🐕 🔟 ➡ 🍴 🅰 🖆 🍴 📺 □ 🖥 🔒 ♿ ⊠ 🎯

THE TAGE INN **Phone:** (508)478-8243
◆◆◆
Motel
All Year [CP] 1P: $60- 87 2P/1B: $68- 95 2P/2B: $72 XP: $8 F12
Location: Just w of jct SR 109 & I-495, exit 19. 24 Beaver St 01757. Fax: 508/634-9936. **Facility:** 93 rooms. 4 king waterbeds $74-$82. 1 suite, $87-$95; 5 stories; interior corridors. **Cards:** AE, DI, MC, VI. 🐕 🔟 🖆 🅰 🍴 💻 🖥 🔒 ⊠

NANTUCKET ISLAND—6,000

LODGINGS

THE CARRIAGE HOUSE **Phone:** (508)228-0326
◆◆
Bed &
Breakfast

6/14-10/16 [CP]	1P:	$120- 150	2P/1B:	$140- 160	2P/2B:	$140- 160	XP: $10	D
5/1-6/13 & 10/17-4/30 [CP]	1P:	$70- 110	2P/1B:	$80- 120	2P/2B:	$80- 120	XP: $10	D

Location: Just s of Main St via Fair St. 5 Ray's Ct 02554. **Terms:** Reserv deposit, 15 day notice; handling fee imposed; 3 night min stay, weekends in season. **Facility:** 7 rooms. Cozy rooms in converted carriage house built circa 1865. A quiet setting along a crushed clamshell lane. 2 stories; interior corridors; smoke free premises; street parking only. **All Rooms:** shower baths. 📺 🆓 🅺 ⊠

NANTUCKET INN & CONFERENCE CENTER · Rates Subject to Change · **Phone:** (508)228-6900

◆◆◆	6/18-9/7	1P: $190- 210	2P/1B: $190- 210	2P/2B: $190- 210	XP: $12	F18
Motor Inn	5/21-6/17 & 9/8-10/4	1P: $160- 180	2P/1B: $160- 180	2P/2B: $160- 180	XP: $12	F18
	5/1-5/20, 10/5-10/23 &					
	4/15-4/30	1P: $110- 130	2P/1B: $110- 130	2P/2B: $110- 130	XP: $12	F18

Location: Opposite Nantucket Memorial Airport; 0.3 mi w of airport terminal. 27 Macy's Ln 02554. Fax: 508/228-9861.
Terms: Open 5/1-10/23 & 4/15-4/30; check-in 4 pm; reserv deposit, 3 day notice; handling fee imposed. **Facility:** 100 rooms.
6 units with fireplace. 2 stories; exterior corridors; heated indoor pool; 2 lighted tennis courts. **Cards:** AE, DI, DS, MC, VI.
(See color ad below)

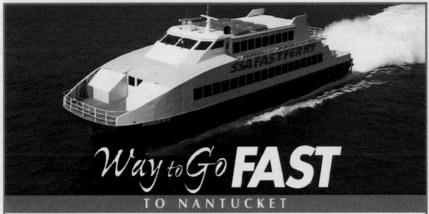

Going to the Caribbean?
Ask for the AAA Caribbean TravelBook, Including Bermuda.

SEVEN SEA STREET INN   Rates Subject to Change   Phone: 508/228-3577
  (AAA)
6/25-9/11 [CP]	2P/1B:	$155- 195	2P/2B:	$235- 265	XP: $20
5/21-6/24 & 9/12-10/16 [CP]	2P/1B:	$125- 155	2P/2B:	$195- 235	XP: $20
5/1-5/20 & 10/17-12/31 [CP]	2P/1B:	$105- 125	2P/2B:	$165- 195	XP: $20
1/1-4/30 [CP]	2P/1B:	$75- 95	2P/2B:	$125- 165	XP: $20

Bed &
Breakfast

Location: Center, in historic district. 7 Sea St 02554. Fax: 508/228-3578. **Terms:** Age restrictions may apply; reserv deposit, 14 day notice; handling fee imposed; package plans, off season; 3 night min stay, weekends in season. **Facility:** 11 rooms. Early American style furnishings, combined with modern comforts & conveniences. Widow's walk on roof. Suite, $235-$265 in season; $125-$195 off season; 3 stories, no elevator; interior corridors; smoke free premises; whirlpool. **All Rooms:** combo or shower baths, extended cable TV. **Some Rooms:** kitchen. **Cards:** AE, DS, MC, VI.
(See color ad below)

SHERBURNE INN   Rates Subject to Change   Phone: 508/228-4425
◆◆◆
5/27-10/12 [CP]	1P: $135- 225	2P/1B:	$135- 225		XP: $25
10/13-12/31 [CP]	1P: $75- 175	2P/1B:	$75- 175		
5/1-5/26 & 1/1-4/30 [CP]	1P: $65- 125	2P/1B:	$65- 125		

Historic Bed
& Breakfast

Location: 0.5 w of Steamboat Wharf. 10 Gay St 02554. Fax: 508/228-8114. **Terms:** Age restrictions may apply; reserv deposit, 15 day notice; handling fee imposed; 3 night min stay, weekends in season. **Facility:** 8 rooms. Built in 1835 as headquarters for the Atlantic Silk Company & converted to a guest house in 1872. 1 room with working fireplace. Furnished with antiques & reproductions. 3 stories, no elevator; interior corridors; smoke free premises; street parking only. **Services:** Fee: massage. **All Rooms:** combo or shower baths. **Some Rooms:** color TV. **Cards:** AE, DS, MC, VI.
(See color ad below)

TUCKERNUCK INN   Rates Subject to Change   Phone: (508)228-4886
◆◆
6/11-9/25 [EP]	1P: $180- 250	2P/1B: $180- 250	2P/2B: $180- 250	XP: $20

Country Inn
5/1-6/10, 9/26-10/30 & 4/21-4/30 [EP]	1P: $130- 180	2P/1B: $130- 180	2P/2B: $130- 220	XP: $20
10/31-4/20 [CP]	1P: $80- 125	2P/1B: $80- 125	2P/2B: $80- 125	XP: $20

Location: 0.5 e of Main St. 60 Union St 02554. Fax: 508/228-4890. **Terms:** Age restrictions may apply; reserv deposit, 15 day notice; handling fee imposed; 3 night min stay, weekends in season. **Facility:** 19 rooms. Widow's walk on roof, small library. Wood burning fireplace in dining room. 1 two-bedroom unit, $250 up to 4 persons. 1 one-bedroom housekeeping unit, $225 up to 2 persons; 2 stories; interior/exterior corridors; smoke free premises. **Some Rooms:** kitchen, combo or shower baths, shared bathrooms. **Cards:** AE, MC, VI. *(See color ad p 407)*

THE WHARF COTTAGES   Rates Subject to Change   Phone: 508/228-4620
◆◆
6/12-9/26	1P: $295- 425	2P/1B: $295- 425	2P/2B: $325- 495	XP: $20 F16
5/25-6/11	1P: $250- 295	2P/1B: $250- 259	2P/2B: $275- 350	XP: $20 F16

Cottage

Location: On the harborfront at Swain's Wharf & Old South Wharf. New Whale St 02554 (PO Box 1139). Fax: 508/325-1378. **Terms:** Open 5/25-9/26; reserv deposit, 14 day notice; handling fee imposed. **Facility:** 25 rooms. Along marina docks. Studio & 1- to 3-bedroom cottages with private deck overlooking the harbor. 10 two-bedroom units, 3 three-bedroom units. 1-2 stories; exterior corridors; oceanfront; street parking only. Fee: marina. **Services:** area transportation. **All Rooms:** kitchens. **Cards:** AE, CB, DI, DS, JC, MC, VI.

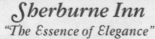

RESTAURANTS

AMERICAN BOUNTY RESTAURANT   **Dinner:** $14-$25   **Phone:** 508/228-3886
◆◆◆   **Location:** 0.5 e of Main St; in Tuckernuck Inn. 60 Union St 02554. **Hours:** Open 5/1-10/31 & 4/23-4/30; 8
Regional   am-11 & 6-9:30 pm. Closed: Call for days closed. **Reservations:** suggested. **Features:** semi-formal attire;
American   beer & wine only; a la carte. Creative cuisine served in intimate garden-like setting. Half orders on all entrees
avail. Vegetarian entrees. Casual attire in summer. Smoke free premises. **Cards:** AE, MC, VI.
(See color ad below)

THE CHANTICLEER Country Inn   **Lunch:** $20-$25   **Dinner:** $30-$40   **Phone:** 508/257-6231
◆◆◆◆   **Location:** On New St; in Siasconset. 9 New St 02554. **Hours:** Open 5/9-10/24; noon-2 & 6:30-10 pm.
Provincial   Closed: Mon. **Reservations:** suggested. **Features:** formal attire; cocktails & lounge; a la carte. Gracious
French   dining room. Prix fixe dinner, $65. Extensive wine list. Garden courtyard setting for lunch service. **Cards:** AE,
MC, VI.

JARED'S Country Inn   **Dinner:** $18-$24   **Phone:** 508/228-2400
◆◆◆   **Location:** Village edge. 29 Broad St 02554. **Hours:** Open 5/1-10/31 & 11/22-1/1; 7:30-10:30 am & 5-9 pm.
Regional   **Reservations:** suggested. **Features:** dressy casual; Sunday brunch; children's menu; cocktails; a la carte.
American   Inviting, historic dining atmosphere; lunch served year round in cozy Taproom, also on patio in summer.
Traditional entrees with a creative flair. Smoke free premises. **Cards:** AE, DI, DS, MC, VI.

OBADIAH'S NATIVE SEAFOOD RESTAURANT   **Lunch:** $7-$13   **Dinner:** $15-$25   **Phone:** 508/228-4430
◆◆   **Location:** Center. 2 India St 02554. **Hours:** Open 6/24-10/11; 11:30 am-2:30 & 5:30-10 pm.
Seafood   **Reservations:** suggested. **Features:** casual dress; children's menu; carryout; cocktails. Intimate rustic dining
room. Patio dining weather permitting. Entrees prepared with Nantucket native spicing. Homemade dessert.
Fresh lobster & shellfish. Smoke free premises. **Cards:** AE, CB, DI, MC, VI.

TOPPER'S AT THE WAUWINET   **Lunch:** $20-$27   **Dinner:** $35-$40   **Phone:** 508/228-8768
◆◆◆◆   **Location:** 8 mi e, adjacent to Coatue Wildlife Refuge. 120 Wauwinet Rd 02554. **Hours:** Open 5/3-11/1;
American   noon-2 & 6-9:30 pm, Sun 11 am-2 & 6-9:30 pm. **Reservations:** required; for dinner. **Features:** formal attire;
Sunday brunch; cocktails & lounge; minimum charge-brunch $36; a la carte. New American cuisine served in
gracious dining rooms. View of Nantucket Bay. Complimentary jitney from Nantucket town. Complimentary water taxi from
Strait Wharf in season. Smoke free premises. **Cards:** AE, DI, MC, VI.

THE WOODBOX INN Historical   **Dinner:** $19-$29   **Phone:** 508/228-0587
◆◆◆   **Location:** 29 Fair St 02554. **Hours:** Open 6/1-1/2; 8:30 am-10:30 & 6:30-9 pm. Closed: Mon.
Continental   **Reservations:** suggested. **Features:** No A/C; dressy casual; children's menu; beer & wine only; a la carte.
Built in 1709. Fine dining in a romantic setting. Smoke free premises.

NATICK—*See Boston p. 307.*

NEEDHAM—*See Boston p. 307.*

NEPONSET—*See Boston p. 308.*

NEW ASHFORD—100

LODGING

ECONO LODGE SPRINGS MOTEL   **Phone:** (413)458-5945
Ⓐ ⓈⒶⓋⒺ   Fri & Sat 7/1-9/4   1P: $97- 120   2P/1B: $97- 120 2P/2B: $97- 120 XP: $10   F17
5/1-6/30, Sun-Thurs 7/1-9/4
◆◆   & 9/5-4/30   1P: $50- 99   2P/1B: $68- 99 2P/2B: $68- 99 XP: $10   F17
Motor Inn   **Location:** 5.3 mi s of jct SR 43. 94 US 7 01237. **Terms:** Reserv deposit, 10 day notice; weekly/monthly
rates. **Facility:** 42 rooms. Rural setting with mountain view. 2 two-bedroom units. 2 chalets with fireplace, $120-
$240 for up to 4 persons; 2 stories; exterior corridors; heated pool. Fee: 1 tennis court. **Dining:** Restaurant, coffee shop;
7-11:30 am; also, The Springs, see separate listing. **Services:** giftshop; winter plug-ins. **Some Rooms:** 2 kitchens, no
utensils. **Cards:** AE, CB, DI, DS, MC, VI.

RESTAURANTS

MILL ON THE FLOSS
◆◆◆
Continental
Dinner: $20-$26   **Phone:** 413/458-9123
Location: On US 7, 4.1 mi s of jct SR 43. Rt 7 01237. **Hours:** open from 5 pm. Closed: Mon. **Reservations:** suggested. **Features:** casual dress; cocktails & lounge; a la carte. Country atmosphere with open kitchen; sweetbread entree specialties. **Cards:** AE, MC, VI.

THE SPRINGS
AAA
◆◆
American
Lunch: $5-$15   **Dinner:** $10-$20   **Phone:** 413/458-3465
Location: 5.3 mi s of jct SR 43; in Econo Lodge Springs Motel. US 7 01237. **Hours:** 11:30 am-9:30 pm, Sat-10 pm, Sun 10 am-9pm. Closed: 12/25. **Reservations:** suggested. **Features:** casual dress; Sunday brunch; children's menu; cocktails & lounge; a la carte. Attractive mountain setting. Italian specials Tues & Wed. **Cards:** AE, DI, DS, MC, VI.

NEW BEDFORD—99,900

LODGING

DAYS INN-NEW BEDFORD
◆◆
Motor Inn
Rates Subject to Change   **Phone:** 508/997-1231

		1P:		2P/1B:		2P/2B:	
Fri & Sat 5/1-10/31		$79-	99	$79-	99	$79-	99
Sun-Thurs 5/1-10/31 & 3/1-4/30		$69-	89	$69-	89	$69-	89
11/1-2/29		$59		$59		$59-	79

Location: Just w of jct I-95, exit 13B & SR 140, exit 3. 500 Hathaway Rd 02740. **Fax:** 508/984-7977. **Terms:** Reserv deposit. **Facility:** 153 rooms. Whirlpool rm, extra charge; 2-3 stories, no elevator; interior/exterior corridors; heated indoor pool.
Cards: AE, DI, DS, MC, VI.

RESTAURANTS

ANTONIO'S RESTAURANT & CAFE
◆
Portuguese
Lunch: $4-$11   **Dinner:** $6-$12   **Phone:** 508/990-3636
Location: At jct of Coggeshall & N Front sts; From I-195, eastbound exit 16 via Washburn St; westbound exit 17, Coggeshall St, then 0.3 mi w. 267 Coggeshall St 02746. **Hours:** 11:30 am-9:30 pm, Fri & Sat-10 pm. Closed: 7/4, 11/25 & 12/25. **Features:** casual dress; carryout; cocktails & lounge. Cozy, lively family dining featuring Portuguese & West Mediterranean cuisine, fresh local seafood entrees & stew. Generous portions.

DAVY'S LOCKER INC
◆◆
Seafood
Lunch: $5-$11   **Dinner:** $8-$18   **Phone:** 508/992-7359
Location: I-195 exit 15, 2.7 mi s on SR 18, then 0.9 mi e (at 4th light). Adjacent to the ferry dock. 1480 E Rodney French Blvd 02744. **Hours:** 11 am-10 pm, Fri & Sat-11 pm, off season Mon-Thurs until 9 pm. **Reservations:** accepted. **Features:** casual dress; children's menu; health conscious menu items; carryout; cocktails & lounge. Overlooking New Bedford harbor. Patio dining in summer. In addition to seafood, steak, chicken & ribs. **Cards:** AE, DI, DS, MC, VI.

FREESTONE'S CITY GRILL
AAA
◆◆
American
Lunch: $6-$16   **Dinner:** $6-$16   **Phone:** 508/993-7477
Location: In downtown historic district, at corner William & 2nd sts. 41 William St 02740. **Hours:** 11 am-11 pm, Fri & Sat-midnight, Sun noon-10 pm. Closed: 9/6, 11/25 & 12/25. **Features:** casual dress; children's menu; carryout; cocktails & lounge. Upscale dining surrounded by marble, brass & mahogany in a restored 1877 bank building. Features fresh local seafoods. **Cards:** AE, DI, MC, VI.

NEWBURYPORT—See Boston p. 308.

NEWTON—See Boston p. 308.

NORTH ADAMS—16,800

LODGING

HOLIDAY INN BERKSHIRES
AAA SAVE
◆◆◆
Hotel
Phone: (413)663-6500
All Year   1P: $99- 109   2P/1B: $99- 109   2P/2B: $99- 109   XP: $10   F18
Location: Downtown, at jct of SR 8. 40 Main St 02147. **Fax:** 413/663-6380. **Terms:** AP avail; package plans. **Facility:** 87 rooms. Downtown location. 7 stories; interior corridors; heated indoor pool, sauna, steamroom, whirlpool. **Dining:** Restaurant; 6:30-11 am, 11:30-2:30 & 5-9:30 pm; $8-$17; cocktails. **Services:** Fee: massage. **Cards:** AE, CB, DI, DS, JC, MC, VI. **Special Amenities:** Early check-in/late check-out and free room upgrade (subject to availability with advanced reservations).

RESTAURANTS

THE FREIGHT YARD RESTAURANT & PUB
AAA
◆
American
Lunch: $5-$12   **Dinner:** $5-$12   **Phone:** 413/663-6547
Location: On SR 8 just s of Main St & SR 2. Follow the signs to Heritage Park. Heritage St Park Bldg 3 01247. **Hours:** 11:30 am-11 pm. Closed: 12/25. **Reservations:** suggested. **Features:** casual dress; children's menu; carryout; cocktails & lounge. In restored railroad station area. Lunch buffet Mon-Fri, 11:30 am-2 pm. **Cards:** AE, MC, VI.

LA VERANDA RISTORANTE
◆
Italian
Dinner: $9-$15   **Phone:** 413/663-3321
Location: 2.5 mi w on SR 2. 896 State Rd 01247. **Hours:** 4 pm-9 pm. Closed major holidays & Sun. **Reservations:** suggested. **Features:** casual dress; children's menu; carryout; cocktails; a la carte. Warm family atmosphere. **Cards:** AE, MC, VI.

NORTHAMPTON—29,300

LODGINGS

AUTUMN INN
◆◆◆
Motel

Rates Subject to Change

5/1-12/1   1P: $72- 82   2P/1B: $100- 108   2P/2B: $100- 108   XP: $12-16
12/2-4/30   1P: $68- 72   2P/1B: $96- 104

Phone: 413/584-7660

Location: On SR 9; 1 mi w of jct SR 5. 259 Elm (SR 9) St 01060. **Fax:** 413/586-4808. **Terms:** 2 night min stay, weekends in season. **Facility:** 30 rooms. Quiet residential area. 2 suites, $110-$120; 2 stories; interior/exterior corridors. **Some Rooms:** 2 efficiencies. **Cards:** AE, CB, DI, MC, VI.

HOTEL NORTHAMPTON
◆◆◆
Historic Hotel

Rates Subject to Change

9/1-11/30 [CP]   1P: $113- 162   2P/1B: $125- 174   2P/2B: $131- 275   XP: $12   F16
5/1-8/31 & 4/1-4/30 [CP]   1P: $103- 152   2P/1B: $115- 164   2P/2B: $121- 265   XP: $12   F16
12/1-3/31 [CP]   1P: $93- 142   2P/1B: $105- 154   2P/2B: $111- 255   XP: $12   F16

Phone: (413)584-3100

Location: Center; at jct US 5 & SR 9. 36 King St 01060. **Fax:** 413/584-9455. **Facility:** 80 rooms. Restored 1927 hotel. 4 suites, $225-$285; 5 stories; interior/exterior corridors. **Some Rooms:** 2 efficiencies. **Cards:** AE, DI, DS, MC, VI.

THE INN AT NORTHAMPTON
◆◆◆
Motor Inn

Rates Subject to Change

Fri & Sat 5/1-10/31   1P: $109- 149   2P/1B: $109- 149   2P/2B: $109- 149   XP: $10   F18
Sun-Thurs 5/1-10/31 &
11/1-4/30   1P: $80- 149   2P/1B: $80- 149   2P/2B: $80- 149   XP: $10   F18

Phone: (413)586-1211

Location: On US 5, just s of I-91 exit 18. 1 Atwood Dr 01060. **Fax:** 413/586-0630. **Terms:** Reserv deposit, 24 day notice; 2 night min stay, weekends 5/1-10/31. **Facility:** 124 rooms. Poolside & balcony rooms. 2 stories; interior corridors; heated indoor pool; 2 lighted tennis courts. **Services:** massage. **All Rooms:** combo or shower baths. **Cards:** AE, CB, DI, DS, MC, VI.
(See color ad below)

RESTAURANTS

LA CAZUELA
◆◆
Mexican

Dinner: $6-$12

Phone: 413/586-0400

Location: Just s of Rt 9. 7 Old South St 01060. **Hours:** 5 pm-9 pm, Fri-10 pm. Closed major holidays. **Reservations:** suggested; 6 or more. **Features:** casual dress; children's menu; health conscious menu items; cocktails & lounge. Mexican & American southwest cuisine, specializing in health conscious & vegetarian specialties, as well as standard Mexican fare. Smoke free premises. **Cards:** AE, DS, MC, VI.

SPAGHETTI FREDDY'S AT THE DEPOT
◆◆
American

Lunch: $5-$8   **Dinner: $7-$13**   **Phone: 413/586-5366**

Location: I-91 exit 18, 0.8 mi n on US 5. 125A Pleasant St (US 50) 01060. **Hours:** 11:30 am-9:30 pm, Fri & Sat-10:30 pm, Sun 10:30 am-1:30 & 4-9 pm. **Closed:** 7/4 & 12/25. **Reservations:** accepted. **Features:** casual dress; Sunday brunch; children's menu; early bird specials; senior's menu; health conscious menu; cocktails. Restored train station. Spaghetti Freddy's offers Italian & American cuisine. Smoke free premises. **Cards:** AE, MC, VI.

WIGGINS TAVERN   Historical
◆◆◆
American

Dinner: $15-$25   **Phone: 413/584-3100**

Location: Jct US 5 & SR 9; in Hotel Northampton. 36 King St 01060. **Hours:** 5:30 pm-10 pm, Sun 10:30 am-2 & 4:30-9 pm. **Closed:** Mon. **Reservations:** suggested. **Features:** casual dress; children's menu; cocktails; a la carte. New England cuisine in 200 year old tavern. Sun brunch $13.95. Smoke free premises. **Cards:** AE, DI, DS, MC, VI.

NORTH ANDOVER—*See Boston p. 309.*

NORTH CHELMSFORD—*See Boston p. 309.*

NORTH DARTMOUTH—8,100

LODGING

COMFORT INN   Rates Subject to Change   Phone: 508/996-0800
◆◆   5/21-10/12 [CP]   1P: $64- 89 2P/1B: $74- 99 2P/2B: $74- 99 XP: $10   F18
Motel   5/1-5/20 & 10/13-4/30 [CP]   1P: $60- 75 2P/1B: $60- 85 2P/2B: $60- 85 XP: $10   F18
Location: I-195, westbound exit 12A; eastbound exit 12, then s. 171 Faunce Corner Rd 02747.
Fax: 508/996-0800. **Facility:** 85 rooms. Peaceful setting. Meticulously clean guest rooms with oakwod furnishings. Near large shopping malls. 2 stories; interior corridors. **Cards:** AE, CB, DI, DS, MC, VI.

NORTH FALMOUTH—*See Cape Cod p. 365.*

NORTH SCITUATE—*See SCITUATE.*

NORTH TRURO—*See Cape Cod p. 365.*

NORWELL—9,300

RESTAURANT

STRAWBERRY FAIR RESTAURANT   **Lunch:** $5-$12   **Dinner:** $5-$12   **Phone:** 781/878-7878
◆◆   **Location:** On SR 228 just s of jct SR 53. 14 Pond St 02061. **Hours:** 7:30 am-9 pm, Sun 8:30 am-2 pm,
American   Mon 11 am-3 pm. Closed: 7/4, 11/25 & 12/25. **Features:** casual dress; Sunday brunch; children's menu;
early bird specials; carryout; cocktails. Homespun New England cuisine in quaint ambiance. Smoke free premises. **Cards:** AE, MC, VI.

NORWOOD—*See Boston p. 309.*

ORANGE—7,300

LODGING

BALD EAGLE MOTEL   Phone: (978)544-8864
(AAA) SAVE   All Year   1P: $35- 55 2P/1B: $35- 55 2P/2B: $40- 70 XP: $7   F10
Location: US 202, just n of jct SR 2, exit 16. 110 Daniel Shay Hwy 01364. Fax: 978/544-3179.
◆◆   **Terms:** Reserv deposit, 7 day notice; pets, $7 extra charge, $7 dep req. **Facility:** 27 rooms. Rooms furnished
Motel   with old and new contemporary appointments. 1 story; interior/exterior corridors. **All Rooms:** combo or
shower baths, extended cable TV. **Cards:** AE, CB, DI, JC, MC, VI. **Special Amenities:** Free breakfast and
free local telephone calls.

ORLEANS—*See Cape Cod p. 366.*

PEABODY—*See Boston p. 309.*

PEMBROKE—14,500

RESTAURANT

CAFE CHRISTINA   **Lunch:** $7-$10   **Dinner:** $13-$19   **Phone:** 781/829-9001
◆◆   **Location:** On SR 53, 0.3 mi n of jct SR 139 & SR 53 in the Pembroke Crossing Shopping Plaza; 2 mi w of
Italian   SR 3. 15 Columbia Rd (Rt 53) 02359. **Hours:** 11:30 am-9:30 pm, Fri & Sat-10 pm, Sun 4 pm-9 pm. Closed:
11/25, 12/24 & 12/25. **Reservations:** accepted. **Features:** casual dress; carryout; cocktails & lounge; a la
carte. Casual & elegant. Homemade pasta & dessert. Brick oven pizza. Veal, chicken & fish dishes are offered. Smoke free premises. **Cards:** AE, DI, MC, VI.

PITTSFIELD—48,600

LODGINGS

COMFORT INN   Phone: (413)443-4714
(AAA) SAVE   Fri & Sat 7/1-8/31 [BP]   1P: $180- 190 2P/1B: $180- 190 2P/2B: $180- 190 XP: $10   F18
Fri & Sat 9/1-10/17 [BP]   1P: $120- 130 2P/1B: $120- 130 2P/2B: $120- 130 XP: $10   F18
Fri & Sat 5/1-6/30 &
◆◆   10/18-4/30 [BP]   1P: $85- 95 2P/1B: $85- 95 2P/2B: $85- 95 XP: $10   F18
Motel   Sun-Thurs [BP]   1P: $65- 75 2P/1B: $65- 75 2P/2B: $65- 75 XP: $10   F18
Location: ON US 7 & 20, 3 mi s. 1055 South St 01201. Fax: 413/445-7400. **Terms:** 2 night min stay, weekends 7/1-8/31.
Facility: 59 rooms. 3 stories; interior corridors. **Dining:** Restaurant nearby. **All Rooms:** extended cable TV. **Cards:** AE, DI,
DS, JC, MC, VI. **Special Amenities:** Free breakfast and free newspaper. *(See color ad p 397)*

CROWNE PLAZA PITTSFIELD BERKSHIRES
♦♦♦
Hotel

6/20-9/6	1P: $140- 210	2P/1B: $140- 210	2P/2B: $140- 210	XP: $15	F17
9/19-10/23	1P: $119- 159	2P/1B: $119- 159	2P/2B: $119- 159	XP: $15	F17
5/1-6/19, 9/7-9/18 & 10/24-4/30	1P: $119- 139	2P/1B: $119- 139	2P/2B: $119- 139	XP: $15	F17

Rates Subject to Change   Phone: 413/499-2000

Location: Center; at Berkshire Common. 1 West St, Berkshire Common 01201. **Fax:** 413/442-0449. **Terms:** Reserv deposit, 14 day notice; 2 night min stay, weekends in summer. **Facility:** 179 rooms. 13 stories; interior corridors; heated indoor pool. **Services:** giftshop; area transportation. **All Rooms:** combo or shower baths. **Cards:** AE, CB, DI, DS, MC, VI.

PITTSFIELD CITY MOTEL
🅐🅐🅐 SAVE
♦♦
Motel

Phone: (413)443-3000

7/1-9/10 [CP]	1P: $85- 139	2P/1B: $85- 139	2P/2B: $85- 139	XP: $10	F
5/27-6/30 [CP]	1P: $85- 95	2P/1B: $85- 95	2P/2B: $85- 95	XP: $10	F
5/1-5/26 & 9/11-4/30 [CP]	1P: $45- 65	2P/1B: $45- 65	2P/2B: $45- 65	XP: $10	F

Location: On US 20, 0.4 mi w from jct US 7. 150 W Housatonic St 01201. **Fax:** 413/443-3549. **Terms:** Reserv deposit, 14 day notice; weekly rates. **Facility:** 38 rooms. 1 story; exterior corridors. **All Rooms:** combo or shower baths. **Cards:** AE, MC, VI. **Special Amenities: Free breakfast and free local telephone calls.**

RESTAURANTS

DAKOTA
🅐🅐🅐
♦♦
American

Dinner: $9-$21   Phone: 413/499-7900

Location: 3 mi s on US 7 & 20. 1035 South St 01201. **Hours:** 5 pm-10 pm, Fri-11 pm, Sat 4 pm-11 pm, Sun 10 am-2 & 4-10 pm. **Closed:** 11/25 & 12/25. **Reservations:** suggested. **Features:** casual dress; children's menu; health conscious menu; carryout; salad bar; cocktails & lounge; a la carte. Relaxed, rustic lodge atmosphere. Sun brunch 10 am-2 pm. Smoke free premises. **Cards:** AE, CB, DI, DS, MC, VI.

GIOVANNI'S RISTORANTE
♦♦
Italian

Lunch: $6-$10   Dinner: $8-$20   Phone: 413/443-2441

Location: On US 7, 1.6 mi n of jct SR 9e. 1331 North St 01201. **Hours:** noon-3 & 4:30-9 pm, Fri & Sat-10 pm, Sun noon-9 pm. **Closed:** 7/4 & 12/25. **Reservations:** accepted; 6 or more. **Features:** casual dress; children's menu; health conscious menu; carryout; cocktails & lounge; a la carte. Warm, relaxed atmosphere. **Cards:** AE, DI, MC, VI.

PLYMOUTH—45,600   (See map p. 330; index p. 328)

LODGINGS

BLUE SPRUCE MOTEL & TOWNHOUSES   Rates Subject to Change   Phone: 508/224-3990   287
🅐🅐🅐
♦♦
Motel

5/1-11/30	1P: $58	2P/1B: $58- 64	2P/2B: $64- 82	XP: $6
12/1-4/30	1P: $52	2P/1B: $52- 58	2P/2B: $58- 70	XP: $6

Location: 6.5 mi s on SR 3A. 710 State Rd 02360. **Fax:** 508/224-2279. **Terms:** Reserv deposit, 7 day in townhouses & cottages; package plans. **Facility:** 29 rooms. Cozy units with patio. Picturesque sloping grounds. Family operated. 1 two-bedroom unit. 4 one-bedroom townhouses, $167 for up to 4 persons & two-bedroom cottage, $150 for up to 4 persons; 1 story; exterior corridors; heated pool. **Recreation:** shuffleboard. **All Rooms:** combo or shower baths, extended cable TV. **Some Rooms:** kitchen. **Cards:** AE, CB, DI, DS, MC, VI.
(See color ad starting on p 412)

COLD SPRING MOTEL   Rates Subject to Change   Phone: 508/746-2222   286
🅐🅐🅐
♦♦
Motel

Fri & Sat 6/25-10/23 [CP]	1P: $79- 99	2P/1B: $79- 99	2P/2B: $79- 99	XP: $10	F12
Fri & Sat 5/1-6/24 & Sun-Thurs 6/25-10/23 [CP]	1P: $69- 89	2P/1B: $69- 89	2P/2B: $69- 89	XP: $10	F12
Sun-Thurs 5/1-6/24, 10/24-11/28 & 4/2-4/30 [EP]	1P: $59- 79	2P/1B: $59- 79	2P/2B: $59- 79	XP: $10	F12

Location: 0.5 mi n on SR 3A from jct US 44. 188 Court St 02360. **Fax:** 508/746-2744. **Terms:** Open 5/1-11/28 & 4/2-4/30; reserv deposit; package plans. **Facility:** 31 rooms. A beautifully landscaped hillside setting. Cozy rooms with charming New England decor. 12 larger deluxe units. Family operated. 2 two-bedroom cottages, $89-$109 for up to 4 persons in season; 2 stories; exterior corridors. **All Rooms:** combo or shower baths, extended cable TV. **Cards:** AE, DS, MC, VI.
(See color ad starting on p 412)

THE GOVERNOR BRADFORD ON THE HARBOUR   Phone: (508)746-6200   288
🅐🅐🅐 SAVE
♦♦
Motel

6/26-8/29	1P: $79- 119	2P/1B: $79- 119	2P/2B: $79- 119	XP: $10	F16
5/1-6/25 & 8/30-10/17	1P: $69- 105	2P/1B: $69- 105	2P/2B: $69- 105	XP: $10	F16
10/18-4/30	1P: $52- 65	2P/1B: $52- 65	2P/2B: $52- 65	XP: $10	F16

Location: Overlooking waterfront at Water & Brewster sts, opposite scenic Plymouth Harbor. 98 Water St 02360. **Fax:** 508/747-3032. **Terms:** Reserv deposit; package plans. **Facility:** 94 rooms. A 20 year tradition. Many waterfront or harbor view units. Majority of rooms with 2 double beds. 3 stories, no elevator; exterior corridors; small heated pool. **Dining:** Restaurant nearby. **All Rooms:** combo or shower baths, extended cable TV. **Cards:** AE, CB, DI, DS, MC, VI. **Special Amenities: Free local telephone calls.** *(See color ad starting on p 412)*

JOHN CARVER INN AT TOWN BROOK   Phone: (508)746-7100   289
🅐🅐🅐 SAVE
♦♦
Motor Inn

6/11-10/16	1P: $99- 179	2P/2B: $99- 179	XP: $10	F18
10/17-11/27 & 4/15-4/30	1P: $89- 169	2P/2B: $89- 169	XP: $10	F18
5/1-6/10	1P: $79- 159	2P/2B: $79- 159	XP: $10	F18
11/28-4/14	1P: $69- 149	2P/2B: $69- 149	XP: $10	F18

Location: Historic town center. 25 Summer St 02360. **Fax:** 508/746-8299. **Terms:** MAP avail; package plans. **Facility:** 79 rooms. An inviting, charming colonial-style inn. Spacious rooms with traditional furnishings. Some deluxe king units. Gracious hospitality. 3 stories; interior corridors; golf privileges. **Dining:** Health conscious menu items; also, Hearth 'n Kettle Restaurant & Tavern, see separate listing. **Services:** giftshop. **All Rooms:** extended cable TV. **Cards:** AE, CB, DI, DS, MC, VI. **Special Amenities: Early check-in/late check-out and preferred room (subject to availability with advanced reservations).** *(See color ad starting on p 412)*

(See map p. 330)

PILGRIM SANDS MOTEL

		Rates Subject to Change			Phone: 508/747-0900	285
	6/18-9/5	1P: $98- 130	2P/1B: $98- 130	2P/2B: $98- 130	XP: $8	
	5/7-6/17 & 9/6-10/23	1P: $85- 110	2P/1B: $85- 110	2P/2B: $85- 110	XP: $6	
	5/1-5/6, 10/24-11/27 &					
	4/1-4/30	1P: $65- 85	2P/1B: $65- 85	2P/2B: $65- 85	XP: $6	
Motel	11/28-3/31	1P: $55- 75	2P/1B: $55- 75	2P/2B: $55- 75	XP: $6	

Location: 3 mi s on SR 3A, on Cape Cod Bay. 150 Warren, Rt3A Ave 02360. Fax: 508/746-8066. **Terms:** Package plans. **Facility:** 64 rooms. A panoramic oceanfront location with spacious sun deck. Many rooms overlook ocean beach or Plymouth Plantation. 6 units with balcony. 2 two-bedroom units. 2 stories; interior/exterior corridors; beach, heated indoor pool, whirlpool. **Dining:** Breakfast room 7-11 am. **All Rooms:** extended cable TV. **Some Rooms:** 2 efficiencies, 2 kitchens. **Cards:** AE, CB, DI, DS, JC, MC, VI. *(See color ad starting on p 412)*

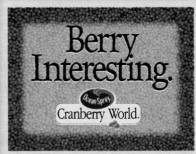

(See map p. 330)

SHERATON INN PLYMOUTH
◆◆◆
Hotel

	Rates Subject to Change					
6/11-10/23	1P: $120- 140	2P/1B: $120- 140	2P/2B: $120- 140	XP: $15		F18
3/31-4/30	1P: $110- 130	2P/1B: $110- 130	2P/2B: $110- 130	XP: $15		F18
5/1-6/10 & 10/24-11/26	1P: $100- 120	2P/1B: $100- 120	2P/2B: $100- 120	XP: $15		F18
11/27-3/30	1P: $95- 115	2P/1B: $95- 115	2P/2B: $95- 115	XP: $15		F18

Phone: (508)747-4900   [290]

Location: Center, just e of SR 3A, following signs. 180 Water St 02360. **Fax:** 508/746-2609. **Facility:** 175 rooms. Spacious, elegant public areas. Traditional furnishings. Some units with small balcony. 4 stories; interior corridors; heated indoor pool. **Cards:** AE, CB, DI, DS, JC, MC, VI. *(See color ad starting on p 412)*

THE SLEEPY PILGRIM MOTEL
ⒶⒶⒶ
[FYI]
Motel

	Rates Subject to Change				
6/18-10/17 [CP]	1P: $59- 79	2P/1B: $69- 79	2P/2B: $79- 109	XP: $5-10
5/1-6/17 & 10/18-4/30 [EP]	1P: $49- 69	2P/1B: $49- 69	2P/2B: $59- 79	XP: $5-10

Phone: (508)746-1962   [291]

Under major renovation. **Location:** 0.5 mi n on SR 3A from jct US 44. 182 Court St 02360. **Fax:** 508/746-0203. **Terms:** Reserv deposit. **Facility:** 16 rooms. Charming, cozy, well-kept units, 4 with carport. Relaxing tree-shaded grounds. 1 story; exterior corridors. **All Rooms:** combo or shower baths. **Cards:** AE, DS, MC, VI.

RESTAURANTS

ERNIE'S RESTAURANT   **Lunch:** $4-$10   **Dinner:** $9-$14   **Phone:** 508/746-3444   [135]
◆
American
Location: On SR 3A, 1.5 mi n of jct US 44/SR 3A. 330 Court St 02360. **Hours:** 11 am-10 pm. Closed: 11/25, 12/25 & Wed. **Features:** casual dress; children's menu; early bird specials; carryout; cocktails & lounge. Very popular, friendly family dining since 1946. Featuring fresh seafood & Italian dishes. Smoke free premises. **Cards:** AE, CB, DI, DS, MC, VI.

HEARTH 'N KETTLE RESTAURANT & TAVERN   **Lunch:** $5-$8   **Dinner:** $8-$14   **Phone:** 508/747-7405   [136]
◆
Regional
American
Location: Historic town center; in John Carver Inn At Town Brook. 25 Summer St 02360. **Hours:** 7 am-10 pm. Closed: 12/25 & 12/24 for dinner. **Features:** casual dress; children's menu; early bird specials; health conscious menu; carryout; cocktails & lounge; a la carte. Relaxed, family dining in a charming Colonial day ambiance. Delightful staff in period costume. Traditional Cape Cod recipes. Generous portions. **Cards:** AE, CB, DI, DS, MC, VI.

IGUANA'S MEXICAN/SOUTHWESTERN RESTAURANT & BAR   **Lunch:** $6-$15   **Dinner:** $6-$15
◆◆
American
Phone: 508/747-4000   [131]
Location: Across from Plymouth Harbor at Town Wharf. 170 Water St 02360. **Hours:** 11:30 am-midnight, Sun from noon. Closed: 12/25. **Features:** casual dress; children's menu; carryout; cocktails & lounge. Casual southwestern style atmosphere. Ocean view from second floor. Outdoor patio in season. **Cards:** AE, MC, VI.

(See map p. 330)

ISAAC'S ON THE WATERFRONT   **Lunch:** $6-$10   **Dinner:** $10-$15   **Phone:** 508/830-0001   [124]
◆◆   **Location:** Opposite harbor. 114 Water St 02360. **Hours:** 11:30 am-11 pm, Sun from 11 am. Closed: 12/24
Seafood   for dinner & 12/25. **Reservations:** suggested. **Features:** casual dress; children's menu; carryout; cocktails &
lounge; valet parking; a la carte. Upscale contemporary dining room with panoramic view. Outdoor patio
dining in season. Valet parking at dinner. Well worth the wait. **Cards:** AE, CB, DI, DS, MC, VI.   [⊗]

MAMMA MIA'S RESTAURANT ON THE WATERFRONT **Lunch:** $4-$7 **Dinner:** $5-$13 **Phone:** 508/747-4670   [125]
◆   **Location:** Opposite harbor. 122 Water St 02360. **Hours:** 11 am-10 pm; 5/1-10/31 to 11 pm, Sun 11
Italian   am-10:30 pm. Closed: 11/25, 12/25 & Easter. **Reservations:** accepted. **Features:** casual dress; children's
menu; carryout; cocktails & lounge; fee for parking. Bustling, popular dining room with harbor view. Authentic
recipes featuring homemade pasta, also pizza & subs. **Cards:** AE, MC, VI.   [⊗]

MCGRATH'S SEAFOOD GRILLE   **Lunch:** $5-$13   **Dinner:** $10-$15   **Phone:** 508/746-9751   [127]
Ⓐ   **Location:** On Plymouth Harbor at Town Wharf. Water St 02360. **Hours:** 11 am-10 pm; 1/2-3/31 to 8 pm.
Closed: 12/25. **Reservations:** suggested. **Features:** casual dress; children's menu; carryout; cocktails &
◆◆   lounge. Family dining in popular harborfront atmosphere. Dining room menu served in lounge for smoking
Seafood   guests. Smoke free premises. **Cards:** AE, DI, DS, MC, VI.   [🏠] [⊗]

RUN OF THE MILL TAVERN   **Lunch:** $4-$7   **Dinner:** $6-$12   **Phone:** 508/830-1262   [132]
◆   **Location:** Historic town center at Jenney Grist Mill & Town Brook. 6 Spring Ln 02360. **Hours:** 11:30 am-10
American   pm, Fri & Sat-11 pm, Sun noon-10 pm. Closed: 11/25, 12/24 for dinner, 12/25 & Easter. **Features:** casual
dress; children's menu; carryout; cocktails; a la carte. Jovial, rustic pinewood turn-of-the-century tavern in a
park-like setting with an operating waterwheel. Very popular. Patio dining in season. **Cards:** AE, MC, VI.   [⊗]

PRINCETON—3,200

RESTAURANT

MOUNTAIN BARN   **Lunch:** $4-$7   **Dinner:** $5-$14   **Phone:** 978/464-2044
◆◆   **Location:** 1.8 mi s on SR 31. 174 Worcester Rd 01541-0327. **Hours:** 4:30 pm-9 pm, Fri & Sat-10 pm, Sun
American   noon-9 pm. Closed: 12/24, 12/25 & Mon-Wed. **Features:** casual dress; children's menu; cocktails & lounge;
a la carte. Country decor with pine paneling in scenic rural location.   [⊗]

PROVINCETOWN—See Cape Cod p. 368.

QUINCY—See Boston p. 310.

RANDOLPH—See Boston p. 310.

RAYNHAM—9,900

LODGING

DAYS INN TAUNTON   Rates Subject to Change   **Phone:** 508/824-8647
◆◆   5/15-10/31 [CP]   1P: $65- 70   2P/1B: $69   2P/2B: $74   XP: $5   F17
Motel   5/1-5/14 & 11/1-4/30 [CP]   1P: $53- 55   2P/1B: $57   2P/2B: $59   XP: $5   F17
Location: On US 44, 0.8 mi w of SR 24, exit 13B. 164 New State Hwy 02767. Fax: 508/824-8647.
Facility: 70 rooms. 2 stories; interior/exterior corridors. **All Rooms:** combo or shower baths. **Cards:** AE, CB, DI, DS, MC,
VI.   [SAVE] [🛒] [📶] [🏊] [🍴] [📺] [♿] [⊗]

REHOBOTH—8,700

LODGINGS

FIVE BRIDGE INN BED & BREAKFAST   Guaranteed Rates   **Phone:** (508)252-3190
Ⓐ   All Year [BP]   1P: $78   2P/1B: $88   XP: $15   F12
Location: 1.6 mi n of US 44, 3.3 mi w of jct SR 118. From US 44 n on Blanding, e on Broad, n on Salisbury,
◆◆◆   then w. 154 Pine St 02769. Fax: 508/252-3190. **Terms:** Reserv deposit, 14 day notice; handling fee
Bed &   imposed; weekly/monthly rates; small pets only. **Facility:** 5 rooms. Georgian colonial style on 60 acres in se-
Breakfast   cluded area. Bridal suite with fireplace, $125; 3 stories, no elevator; interior corridors; designated smoking area;
1 tennis court. **Some Rooms:** color TV. **Cards:** CB, DS, MC, VI.

[ASK] [🛏] [🛒] [🏊] [⊗] [📺] [💻] [🖥] [🍽] [🔌] [⊗]

PERRYVILLE INN BED & BREAKFAST   Guaranteed Rates   **Phone:** 508/252-9239
◆◆◆   All Year [CP]   1P: $55- 85   2P/1B: $65- 95   XP: $10
Historic Bed   **Location:** 1.5 mi w of SR 118, 0.5 mi n of jct US 44; opposite Rehoboth Country Club. 157 Perryville Rd
& Breakfast   02769. Fax: 508/252-9054. **Terms:** Reserv deposit, 14 day notice. **Facility:** 4 rooms. Peaceful, rural setting.
Large country farmhouse built between 1820-1897 on 4 1/2 acres with stone walls, shaded paths & a quiet
brook. Across from 18-hole public golf course. 1 two-bedroom unit. 2 stories; interior corridors; designated smoking area.
Recreation: bicycles. **All Rooms:** combo or shower baths. **Cards:** AE, DS, MC, VI.   [⊗] [📺] [🅿] [🍽] [⊗]

REVERE—See Boston p. 311.

RICHMOND—1,700

LODGING

THE INN AT RICHMOND — Rates Subject to Change — Phone: 413/698-2566
◆◆◆   5/28-10/31 [BP]   1P: $155- 250   2P/1B: $155- 250   XP: $25
5/1-5/27 & 11/1-4/30 [BP]   1P: $110- 195   2P/1B: $110- 195   XP: $25
Historic Bed & Breakfast   **Location:** On SR 41, 2.5 mi s of jct US 20. 802 State Rd (SR 41) 01254. Fax: 413/698-2100. **Terms:** Age restrictions may apply; reserv deposit, 15 day notice; 3 night min stay, summer weekends. **Facility:** 8 rooms. 18th-century restored farm house on 27 acres, surrounded by gardens & reflecting pool. Some suites with fireplace. Cottage & carriage house avail at weekly rates; 2 stories; interior/exterior corridors; smoke free premises. **Recreation:** cross country skiing; hiking trails. **All Rooms:** combo or shower baths. **Some Rooms:** 2 kitchens. **Cards:** AE, MC, VI.

ROCKLAND—16,100

LODGINGS

DAYS INN-ROCKLAND/HINGHAM — Rates Subject to Change — Phone: 781/982-1000
◆◆   5/1-10/31 [CP]   2P/1B: $89- 104   2P/2B: $89- 104   XP: $10   F17
Motel   11/1-4/30 [CP]   2P/1B: $72- 79   2P/2B: $72- 79   XP: $10   F17
Location: On SR 228; 0.5 mi sw of jct SR 3, exit 14. 850 Hingham St 02370. Fax: 781/982-9935. **Facility:** 101 rooms. Cozy colonial style living room public areas. 3 stories; interior corridors. **Cards:** AE, CB, DI, DS, MC, VI.

HOLIDAY INN EXPRESS-BOSTON/ROCKLAND — Rates Subject to Change — Phone: (781)871-5660
◆◆   5/1-10/31   1P: $125   2P/1B: $125   2P/2B: $125
Motel   11/1-4/30   1P: $99   2P/1B: $99   2P/2B: $99
Location: On SR 228, 0.3 mi sw of SR 3, exit 14. 909 Hingham St 02370. Fax: 781/871-7255. **Facility:** 76 rooms. 2 stories; interior/exterior corridors. **Cards:** AE, DS, MC, VI.

RAMADA INN-ROCKLAND — Rates Subject to Change — Phone: (781)871-0545
◆◆◆   All Year   1P: $129- 169   2P/1B: $139- 179   2P/2B: $139- 179   XP: $10   F17
Motor Inn   **Location:** On SR 228, 0.3 mi sw of SR 3, exit 14. 929 Hingham St 02370. Fax: 781/871-0545. **Facility:** 127 rooms. 10 whirlpool rms, $169 for up to 2 persons; 5 stories; interior corridors; heated pool. **Cards:** AE, CB, DS, JC, MC, VI. *(See color ad inside front cover)*

RESTAURANTS

BELLA'S — **Lunch:** $5-$10 — **Dinner:** $12-$26 — Phone: 781/871-5789
◆◆   **Location:** On SR 228, 0.3 mi sw of jct SR 3, exit 14. 933 Hingham St 02370. **Hours:** 11:30 am-10 pm,
Italian   Mon-9 pm, Sat 4 pm-10 pm, Sun 4 pm-9 pm. Closed: 7/4, 11/25, 12/24 & 12/25. **Reservations:** suggested. **Features:** casual dress; children's menu; early bird specials; carryout; cocktails & lounge. **Cards:** AE, MC, VI.

NOT JUST SEAFOOD RESTAURANT — **Lunch:** $6-$15 — **Dinner:** $12-$16 — Phone: 781/871-4466
◆◆   **Location:** In Rockland Center, opposite the public library. 371 Union St 02370. **Hours:** 11 am-2:30 & 5-9
Seafood   pm, Fri & Sat-10 pm, Sun 11:30 am-8 pm, Mon 5 pm-9 pm. Closed: 11/25 & 12/25. **Reservations:** suggested; weekends. **Features:** casual dress; Sunday brunch; carryout; cocktails; a la carte. Intimate upscale bistro featuring over 50 gourmet entrees. Specializing in French, Italian & Cajun style cuisine. Chef/owner. **Cards:** DS, MC, VI.

ROCKPORT—See Boston p. 311.

ROWLEY—See Boston p. 313.

SALEM—See Boston p. 313.

SALISBURY—See Boston p. 314.

SANDWICH—See Cape Cod p. 372.

SAUGUS—See Boston p. 314.

SCITUATE—16,800—See also NORTH SCITUATE.

LODGING

THE ALLEN HOUSE
Rates Subject to Change
Phone: (781)545-8221

Fri & Sat 5/1-10/30 [BP]	1P: $139- 199	2P/1B: $139- 199	XP: $30
Sun-Thurs 5/1-10/30 [BP]	1P: $119- 159	2P/1B: $119- 159	XP: $30
Fri & Sat 11/22-3/12 [BP]	1P: $89- 159	2P/1B: $89- 159	XP: $30
Sun-Thurs 11/22-3/12 [BP]	1P: $69- 119	2P/1B: $69- 119	XP: $30

Bed &
Breakfast
Location: Just w of Front St at Situate Harbor. 1818 Allen Pl 02066-1302. Fax: 781/545-8221. **Terms:** Open 5/1-10/30 & 11/22-3/12; age restrictions may apply; check-in 4 pm; reserv deposit, 10 day notice; handling fee imposed; weekly rates. **Facility:** 6 rooms. Overlooking Scituate Harbor. Genuine English hospitality. 3 stories, no elevator; interior/exterior corridors; designated smoking area. **Dining:** Afternoon tea. **All Rooms:** combo or shower baths. **Some Rooms:** color TV, whirlpools. **Cards:** AE, DS, MC, VI.

RESTAURANT

CHESTER'S AT THE MILL WHARF   **Lunch:** $7-$13   **Dinner:** $12-$18   **Phone:** 781/545-3999
Nouvelle
American
Location: Front St on Scituate Harbor; behind Welsh Company. 150 R Front St 02066. **Hours:** 11:30 am-10 pm, Sun from 10:30 am; 10/15-4/15 11:30 am-9 pm, Fri & Sat-10 pm. Closed: 12/25. **Reservations:** accepted. **Features:** casual dress; Sunday brunch; children's menu; carryout; cocktails & lounge. Overlooking Scituate Harbor. Wood grilled or wood roasted specialties. Pub menu available in lounge to 10 pm. Smoking permitted in lounge. Smoke free premises. **Cards:** AE, DI, DS, MC, VI.

SEEKONK—13,000   (See map p. 457; index p. 455)

LODGINGS

HISTORIC JACOB HILL FARM BED & BREAKFAST/INN   Rates Subject to Change   **Phone:** 508/336-9165   **14**
All Year [BP]   1P: $95- 175   2P/1B: $110- 250 2P/2B: $120- 180 XP: $25
Historic Bed
& Breakfast
Location: 0.5 mi n on Jacob St off US 44, 1.7 mi e of jct SR 114A & US 44. 120 Jacob St 02771. Fax: 508/336-0951. **Terms:** Age restrictions may apply; reserv deposit, 14 day notice; handling fee imposed. **Facility:** 5 rooms. Built in 1722 as a Fox Hunt Club. Situated in quiet residential area on 5 acres. 3 units with working fireplace; 1 with wood stove. 2 two-bedroom units. 3 stories, no elevator; interior corridors; designated smoking area; seasonal pool; 1 tennis court. **All Rooms:** extended cable TV. **Some Rooms:** color TV, whirlpools. **Cards:** AE, DS, MC, VI.

JOHNSON & WALES INN & CONFERENCE CENTER   **Phone:** (508)336-8700   **15**
All Year [CP]   1P: $89- 139   2P/1B: $89- 139 2P/2B: $89- 139 XP: $10   F17
Motor Inn
Location: On US 44; 0.3 mi e of jct SR 114A. 213 Taunton Ave 02771-5320. Fax: 508/336-3414. **Terms:** Reserv deposit; weekly/monthly rates; package plans. **Facility:** 86 rooms. Friendly, attentive guest services in an educational facility of Johnson & Wales University. 4 stories; interior corridors. **Dining:** Audrey's Restaurant, see separate listing. **Services:** area transportation, to Amtrak & bus. **Some Rooms:** whirlpools. **Cards:** AE, CB, DI, DS, MC, VI.

RAMADA INN/PROVIDENCE-SEEKONK   Rates Subject to Change   **Phone:** 508/336-7300   **17**
All Year [BP]   1P: $60- 80   2P/1B: $65- 85 2P/2B: $70- 90 XP: $10   F18
Motor Inn
Location: On SR 114A at jct I-195 MA exit 1. 940 Fall River Ave 02771. Fax: 508/336-2107. **Facility:** 128 rooms. Inviting lobby with sweeping staircase & crystal chandelier. 2 stories; interior corridors; putting green; heated indoor pool; 2 tennis courts. **Cards:** AE, CB, DI, DS, MC, VI. (See color ad p 459)

SUSSE CHALET INN   Rates Subject to Change   **Phone:** (508)336-7900   **16**
All Year [CP]   1P: $50- 75   2P/1B: $60- 79 2P/2B: $60- 79 XP: $3   F17
Motel
Location: On US 6 at jct SR 114A; 0.5 mi s of I-195 MA exit 1. 341 Highland Ave 02771. Fax: 508/336-8518. **Facility:** 90 rooms. Set back from highway on sloping grounds with a center landscaped pool courtyard. 2 stories; interior corridors. **Cards:** AE, CB, DI, DS, MC, VI. (See ad p 460)

RESTAURANTS

AUDREY'S RESTAURANT   **Lunch:** $5-$9   **Dinner:** $11-$18   **Phone:** 508/336-4636   **25**
American
Location: On US 44; 0.3 mi e of jct SR 114A; in Johnson & Wales Inn & Conference Center. 213 Taunton Ave 02771. **Hours:** 6:30-10 am, 11:30-3 & 5-10 pm; Fri & Sat-11 pm, Sun 6:30 am-1 & 5-10 pm. Closed: 12/25. **Reservations:** suggested. **Features:** dressy casual; Sunday brunch; children's menu; carryout; cocktails; a la carte. Creative new American cuisine served in comfortable atmosphere. This is a Practicum of Johnson & Wales University. Smoke free premises. **Cards:** AE, CB, DI, DS, MC, VI.

BUGABOO CREEK STEAK HOUSE   **Lunch:** $5-$11   **Dinner:** $10-$20   **Phone:** 508/336-2200   **28**
Steakhouse
Location: Just s of jct SR 114A, 0.5 mi s of I-195 exit 1 in MA. 1125 Fall River Ave, Rt 6 02771. **Hours:** 11:30 am-10 pm, Fri-11:30, Sun noon-9 pm. Closed: 11/25 & 12/25. **Features:** casual dress; children's menu; cocktails & lounge. Friendly service in a mythical Canadian Rockies ski lodge with a North Country Gothic decor & "talking" mooseheads. Very popular, well worth the wait. Featuring dry-aged beef specialties, burgers & few chicken entrees. **Cards:** AE, DI, DS, MC, VI.

DARLING'S RESTAURANT & LOUNGE   **Lunch:** $6-$12   **Dinner:** $8-$15   **Phone:** 508/336-9222   **29**
American
Location: On SR 114A at jct I-195 MA exit 1; in Ramada Inn/Providence-Seekonk. 940 Fall River Ave. 02771. **Hours:** 7 am-10 pm, Fri & Sat-11 pm. Closed: 12/25. **Reservations:** suggested; weekends. **Features:** casual dress; children's menu; carryout; cocktails & lounge. Family-operated dining spot for over 60 years. Homestyle meals. Varied menu; seafood specialties. **Cards:** AE, CB, DI, DS, MC, VI.

FRANKIE'S RESTAURANT   **Lunch:** $4-$9   **Dinner:** $8-$14   **Phone:** 508/336-5648   **27**
Italian
Location: On US 6; 1.5 mi s of I-195, MA exit 1 via SR 114A. 1379 Fall River Ave 02771. **Hours:** 11:30 am-9:30 pm, Fri & Sat-10:30 pm, Sun & Mon noon-8 pm. Closed: 11/25, 12/24 & 12/25. **Features:** casual dress; children's menu; carryout; beer & wine only; a la carte. Cozy, lively family dining. All entrees cooked to order. **Cards:** MC, VI.

(See map p. 457)

THE OLD GRIST MILL TAVERN **Lunch:** $6-$11 **Dinner:** $12-$19 **Phone:** 508/336-8460 ㉖
🔺🔺
🔷🔷
Steak and
Seafood
Location: On SR 114A; 1.3 mi n of I-195, MA exit 1. 390 Fall River Ave 02771. **Hours:** 11:30 am-10 pm, Sun noon-9 pm. Closed: 11/25 & 12/25. **Features:** casual dress; children's menu; carryout; salad bar; cocktails & lounge. Charming dining room in a restored Colonial tavern overlooking a duck pond. Specializing in prime rib & fresh local seafood. Very popular weekends. **Cards:** AE, CB, DI, DS, MC, VI. ⊠

SHARON—See Boston p. 315.

SHEFFIELD

RESTAURANT

LIMEY'S **Lunch:** $6-$9 **Dinner:** $12-$20 **Phone:** 413/229-9000
🔷🔷
American
Location: 1 mi n on US 7. 650 N Main St 01257. **Hours:** 11:30 am-9:30 pm, Fri & Sat-10 pm, Sun-8 pm. Closed: 12/25 & Mon. **Reservations:** accepted. **Features:** casual dress; children's menu; carryout; cocktails & lounge. **Cards:** AE, DI, DS, MC, VI. 🎏 ⊠

SHIRLEY—See Boston p. 315.

SHREWSBURY—24,100

LODGING

DAYS INN WORCESTER/SHREWSBURY Rates Subject to Change **Phone:** (508)842-8500
🔷
Motel
All Year [CP] 1P: $59- 99 2P/1B: $65- 125 2P/2B: $65- 125 XP: $6-12 F13
Location: I-495 exit 23B, Rt 9 W 6 mi; I-90 exit 11A 495 n, 1 mi to exit 23B Rt 9 W. 889 Boston Tpk (SR 9) 01545. Fax: 508/842-3042. **Terms:** Reserv deposit. **Facility:** 101 rooms. 2 stories; interior corridors. **All Rooms:** combo or shower baths. **Cards:** AE, CB, DI, DS, JC, MC, VI.
[SAVE] [S/D] [icons...] [VCR] ⊟ ⊠

SOMERSET—17,700

LODGING

QUALITY INN-FALL RIVER/SOMERSET Rates Subject to Change **Phone:** (508)678-4545
🔷🔷
Motel
5/28-10/10 1P: $84- 104 2P/1B: $84- 104 2P/2B: $89- 104 XP: $10 F18
5/1-5/27 & 10/11-4/30 1P: $65- 85 2P/1B: $65- 95 2P/2B: $69- 95 XP: $10 F18
Location: At jct SR 103 & I-195, eastbound exit 4, westbound exit 4A. 1878 Wilbur Ave 02725. Fax: 508/678-9352. **Facility:** 105 rooms. Some units with balcony overlooking Lee's River. Variety of room sizes & decors. Suites, $115-$160; 2 stories; interior corridors; heated indoor pool. **Cards:** AE, CB, DI, DS, JC, MC, VI.
[SAVE] [S/D] [icons...] [VCR] ⊟ ⊠

SOMERVILLE—See Boston p. 315.

SOUTH ATTLEBORO (See map p. 457; index p. 456)

LODGING

DAYS INN **Phone:** (508)761-4825 ㊱
🔺🔺🔺 [SAVE]
🔷🔷
Motel
Fri & Sat 5/1-8/27 & 8/28-11/9 1P: $60- 89 2P/1B: $60- 89 2P/2B: $65- 95 XP: $5
Sun-Thurs 5/1-8/27 1P: $55- 85 2P/1B: $55- 85 2P/2B: $59- 95 XP: $5
11/10-4/30 1P: $45- 70 2P/1B: $45- 70 2P/2B: $50- 85 XP: $5
Location: On US 1; I-95 southbound exit 1; northbound exit 29 RI, 1 mi n on US 1 at the MA/RI border. 1116 Washington St 02703. Fax: 508/761-4825. **Terms:** Weekly rates. **Facility:** 40 rooms. Modern decor with oakwood furnishings. 2 stories; exterior corridors. **Cards:** AE, CB, DI, DS, MC, VI. **Special Amenities:** Free breakfast and free room upgrade (subject to availability with advanced reservations).
[icons...] ⊠

SOUTHBOROUGH—6,600

LODGING

RED ROOF INN Rates Subject to Change **Phone:** (508)481-3904
🔷🔷
Motel
5/1-10/31 1P: $51- 71 2P/1B: $61- 81 2P/2B: $61- 81 XP: $6-10 F18
4/1-4/30 1P: $51- 71 2P/1B: $61- 81 2P/2B: $61- 81 XP: $6-10 F18
11/1-3/31 1P: $46- 66 2P/1B: $51- 71 2P/2B: $51- 71 XP: $6-10 F18
Location: On SR 9 at jct I-495, exit 23A. 367 Turnpike Rd 01772. Fax: 508/481-3909. **Facility:** 108 rooms. 2 stories; exterior corridors. **Cards:** AE, CB, DI, DS, MC, VI.
[SAVE] [icons...] ⊟ ⊠

SOUTH CARVER—1,000   (See map p. 330; index p. 329)

RESTAURANT

CRANE BROOK RESTAURANT & TEA ROOM Historical   **Dinner:** $18-$28   **Phone:** 508/866-3235   (165)
◆◆◆   **Location:** From I-495 exit 2, 2.5 mi n on SR 58, 0.5 mi n on Tremont St, following signs to Myles Standish
Northern   State Park. 229 Tremont St 02366. **Hours:** 5:30 pm-8:30 pm, Sat 6 pm-9 pm, Sun 5:30 pm-8:30 pm; closing
American   hrs vary with reservations. Closed: 12/25, Mon, Tues, 1/1-1/7 & 7/3-7/9. **Reservations:** required; for dinner.
    Features: semi-formal attire; cocktails; a la carte. Restored foundry, featuring Early American antiques.
Overlooking scenic pond. Sun brunch 9/12-6/30, 11:30 am-2:30 pm. Changing creative gourmet entrees. Smoke free
premises. **Cards:** AE, MC, VI.   ⊠

SOUTH DEERFIELD—1,900—*See also DEERFIELD.*

RESTAURANT

CHANDLER'S TAVERN RESTAURANT   **Lunch:** $6-$9   **Dinner:** $16-$22   **Phone:** 413/665-1277
🅰🅰   **Location:** I-91 exit 24, 0.6 mi n. Rts 5 & 10 01373. **Hours:** 10:30 am-8 pm, Fri & Sat-9:30 pm. Closed:
    12/25. **Reservations:** suggested. **Features:** casual dress; children's menu; cocktails & lounge. Casual dining
◆◆◆   in an open rustic setting of a traditional yankee tavern. Smoke free premises. **Cards:** AE, DI, DS, MC, VI.
American   🅱 ⊠

SOUTH DENNIS—*See Cape Cod p. 377.*

SOUTH EGREMONT—500

LODGING

WEATHERVANE INN   Rates Subject to Change   **Phone:** 413/528-9580
◆◆◆   All Year [BP]   1P: $115- 130   2P/1B: $125- 165   2P/2B: $125- 165   XP: $20-30
Historic   **Location:** On Rt 23, 3.4 mi w of jct US 7. 17 Main St 01258 (PO Box 388). Fax: 413/528-1713. **Terms:** Age
Country Inn   restrictions may apply; reserv deposit, 15 day notice; handling fee imposed; $9 service charge; 3 night min
    stay, weekends 7/1-9/6. **Facility:** 11 rooms. Some small rooms. 1785 farmhouse listed in the National Register
of Historical Places. Suite avail; 2 stories; interior corridors; smoke free premises. **All Rooms:** combo or shower baths.
Cards: AE, MC, VI.   🅢 🅐 ⊠ 🅟🅥 🆃 🅕 ⊠

SOUTH HARWICH—*See Cape Cod p. 377.*

SOUTH LEE—500—*See also LEE.*

LODGING

HISTORIC MERRELL INN   Rates Subject to Change   **Phone:** 413/243-1794
◆◆◆   Fri-Sun 7/1-10/31 [BP]   2P/1B: $135- 165   2P/2B: $135- 165   XP: $15
Historic Bed   Fri & Sat 5/1-6/30 &
& Breakfast   11/1-4/30 [BP]   2P/1B: $85- 125   2P/2B: $85- 125   XP: $15
    Mon-Thurs 7/1-10/31 [BP]   2P/1B: $85- 115   2P/2B: $85- 115   XP: $15
    Sun-Thurs 5/1-6/30 &
    11/1-4/30 [BP]   2P/1B: $75- 105   2P/2B: $75- 105   XP: $15
Location: On SR 102, 3 mi w of I-90, exit 2. 1565 Pleasant St 01260. Fax: 413/243-2669. **Terms:** Age restrictions may
apply; reserv deposit, 14 day notice; 3 night min stay, 7/1-8/31 weekends. **Facility:** 10 rooms. 1794 brick building on the Housatonic River with 2 acres of park-like grounds. Antique furnishings. 4 rooms with fireplace. River view suite with fireplace,
$125-$215; 3 stories, no elevator; interior corridors; smoke free premises. **All Rooms:** combo or shower baths.
Some Rooms: color TV. **Cards:** MC, VI.   🆃 🅥 🆅🅲🆁 🅕 ⊠

SOUTH WELLFLEET—*See Cape Cod p. 377.*

SOUTH YARMOUTH—*See Cape Cod p. 378.*

ROOM RESERVATIONS:
Mail in your advance deposit
early to make certain that space is held for you.

SPRINGFIELD—157,000—*See also WEST SPRINGFIELD.*

LODGINGS

HOLIDAY INN   Phone: (413)781-0900

(AAA) [SAVE]
5/1-10/23	1P: $129- 149	2P/1B: $139- 159	2P/2B: $139- 159	XP: $10	F18
4/1-4/30	1P: $119	2P/1B: $129	2P/2B: $129	XP: $10	F18
3/1-3/31	1P: $99	2P/1B: $109	2P/2B: $109	XP: $10	F18
10/24-2/29	1P: $89	2P/1B: $99	2P/2B: $99	XP: $10	F18

◆◆◆
Hotel

Location: I-291 exit 2B westbound; exit 2A (Chestnut St) eastbound. 711 Dwight St 01104. Fax: 413/785-1410. **Terms:** Package plans; pets, $10 extra charge. **Facility:** 245 rooms. 1 two-bedroom unit. 12 stories; interior corridors; heated indoor pool. **Dining:** Restaurant; rooftop restaurant; 6:30-11 am, 11:30-2 & 5-10 pm; $6-$18; cocktails. **All Rooms:** extended cable TV. **Some Rooms:** whirlpools. **Cards:** AE, CB, DI, DS, JC, MC, VI. *(See color ad below)*

[icons]

SPRINGFIELD-MARRIOTT HOTEL   Rates Subject to Change   Phone: 413/781-7111

◆◆◆
Hotel
Sun-Thurs	1P: $99- 145	2P/1B: $109- 155	2P/2B: $109- 155	
Fri & Sat	1P: $64- 99	2P/1B: $64- 99	2P/2B: $64- 99	

Location: I-91 northbound exit 6, 0.3 mi s; just n. Boland Way & Columbus Ave 01115. Fax: 413/731-8932. **Terms:** Check-in 4 pm. **Facility:** 265 rooms. In downtown shopping mall. 15 stories; interior corridors; heated indoor pool. **Fee:** parking. **Cards:** AE, DI, DS, MC, VI.

[icons]

RESTAURANT

STUDENT PRINCE & FORT RESTAURANT   **Lunch:** $5-$10   **Dinner:** $8-$17   **Phone:** 413/734-7475

(AAA)

◆◆
German

Location: Between Main St & Columbus Ave. 8 Fort St 01103. **Hours:** 11 am-11 pm, Sun noon-10 pm. Closed: 12/25. **Reservations:** suggested. **Features:** casual dress; children's menu; carryout; cocktails; a la carte. Popular. Fine collection of steins. Friendly atmosphere. **Cards:** AE, DI, DS, MC, VI.   [X]

STERLING—6,500

LODGING

CHOCKSETT INN   Rates Subject to Change   Phone: 978/422-3355

◆◆◆
Bed & Breakfast

All Year [CP]   1P: $79- 125   2P/1B: $79- 125   2P/2B: $79- 125   XP: $20   F12
Location: 0.3 mi w of SR 12, 0.3 mi s of I-190, exit 6. 59 Laurelwood Rd 01564. Fax: 978/422-3187. **Facility:** 25 rooms. 1-bedroom suite & studios. Large redwood outdoor covered deck. Grocery services; 3 stories; interior corridors. **All Rooms:** kitchens. **Cards:** AE, CB, DI, JC, MC, VI.

[icons]

RESTAURANT

STERLING INN   Country Inn   **Lunch:** $4-$7   **Dinner:** $12-$18   **Phone:** 978/422-6592

◆◆
Regional American

Location: On SR 12; 2 mi s of I-190 exit 6. 240 Worcester Rd (SR 12) 01564. **Hours:** 11:30 am-3 & 5-9 pm, Sun 8 am-11 & noon-8 pm. Closed: 12/25, Mon & Sat for lunch. **Reservations:** suggested; for dinner. **Features:** casual dress; children's menu; cocktails & lounge; a la carte. 1908 New England inn. Informal dining. **Cards:** AE, DS, MC, VI.   [X]

CLASSIFICATION explanations are found in About Lodgings & Restaurants.

STOCKBRIDGE—2,400—See also WEST STOCKBRIDGE.

LODGING

THE INN AT STOCKBRIDGE
Rates Subject to Change
Phone: (413)298-3337

(AAA)

5/1-6/30 & 11/1-4/30 [BP]   1P: $110- 115   2P/1B: $170- 205   XP: $25
7/1-10/31 [BP]   1P: $115- 125   2P/1B: $200- 275   XP: $25

Location: 1.7 mi n on US 7. 30 East St 01262 (PO Box 618). Fax: 413/298-3406. **Terms:** Age restrictions

◆◆◆
Historic Bed
& Breakfast

may apply; reserv deposit, 14 day notice; handling fee imposed; 5% service charge; weekly rates; package plans, in winter; 2 night min stay, weekends; pet on premises. **Facility:** 12 rooms. 1906 Georgian Colonial Inn. 3 night min stay summer weekends; 2 stories; interior corridors; smoke free premises. **Recreation:** badminton, croquet. **All Rooms:** combo or shower baths, extended cable TV. **Some Rooms:** color TV, whirlpools. **Cards:** AE, DS, MC, VI.

🐕 🍴 🎦 VCR 🖨 🔒 ✕

RESTAURANT

THE RED LION INN DINING ROOM Country Inn   **Lunch:** $7-$12   **Dinner:** $15-$25   **Phone:** 413/298-5545
◆◆◆   **Location:** Center. 30 Main St 01262. **Hours:** 7:30-10:30 am, 11:30-2:30 & 5:30-9:30 pm, Sun 8-10:30 am,
American   noon-4 & 4-9 pm; 9/1-6/30 5:30 pm-8:30 pm. **Reservations:** suggested. **Features:** children's menu; health
conscious menu; cocktails & lounge; entertainment; a la carte. Pleasant country inn dining room. Also tavern
dining. Semi-formal evening attire. Smoke free premises. **Cards:** AE, CB, DI, DS, MC, VI.
✕

STOUGHTON—See Boston p. 315.

STURBRIDGE—7,800

LODGINGS

AMERICAN MOTOR LODGE-BEST WESTERN
Phone: (508)347-9121

(AAA) (SAVE)

5/1-11/30   1P: $75- 115   2P/1B: $95- 115 2P/2B: $95- 115 XP: $5-10   F12
12/1-4/30   1P: $65- 71   2P/1B: $79- 89 2P/2B: $79- 89 XP: $5-10   F12

Location: On US 20 at jct SR 131. 350 Main St 01566. Fax: 508/347-9121. **Terms:** Reserv deposit; small

◆◆
Motor Inn

pets only. **Facility:** 55 rooms. Traditional decor. 2 stories; interior corridors; heated indoor pool, saunas. **Dining:** Restaurant; 7 am-10:30 & 5:30-9 pm; $8-$14; cocktails. **All Rooms:** extended cable TV. **Cards:** AE, CB, DI, DS, MC. **Special Amenities:** Preferred room (subject to availability with advanced reservations).
(See ad below)

⌾ 🐕 🐾 🖨 🍴 🎦 🏊 🎦 🖨 ✕

BETHANY BED & BREAKFAST
◆◆
Bed & Breakfast

Rates Subject to Change
5/1-11/1 [BP] 1P: $85- 95 2P/1B: $95- 115 2P/2B: $95 XP: $25 F5
11/1-4/30 [BP] 1P: $75- 85 2P/1B: $95- 105 2P/2B: $75- 85 XP: $25 F5
Phone: (508)347-5993
Location: I-84 exit 3B; 1.5 mi w on US 20, then 2.3 mi s on Rt 131, then 4 mi e on Fiske Hill Rd, left on McGregory Rd, 2nd house on left. 5 McGregory Rd 01566. **Terms:** Reserv deposit, 7 day notice; handling fee imposed. **Facility:** 4 rooms. In quiet residential neighborhood. Antique ceiling fan in all rooms. 2 stories; interior corridors; smoke free premises. **Cards:** AE, MC, VI.

COMFORT SUITES AT CRYSTAL POND STURBRIDGE
[FYI]
Phone: (508)347-3306
Under construction. **Location:** 0.5 mi e of jct MA Tpk, I-90 exit 9 & I-84 exit 3A. US 20 01566 (PO Box 399). Fax: 508/347-3514. **Facility:** 78 rooms. Schedule to open, July 1999;

DAYS INN
[AAA] [SAVE]
◆◆
Motel

Phone: (508)347-3391
5/1-10/31 [CP] 1P: $55- 70 2P/1B: $60- 75 2P/2B: $65- 75 XP: $5 F12
11/1-4/30 [CP] 1P: $38- 49 2P/1B: $49- 59 2P/2B: $50- 60 XP: $5 F12
Location: At I-84 exit 2, following signs to SR 131, on I-84 service road. 66-68 Old Route 15, Haynes St 01566 (PO Box 185). **Terms:** Pets, $5 extra charge. **Facility:** 32 rooms. Wooded setting. 2 two-bedroom units. 2 stories; interior/exterior corridors. **All Rooms:** combo or shower baths, extended cable TV. **Cards:** AE, DI, DS, MC, VI. **Special Amenities:** Free breakfast and free local telephone calls. *(See ad below)*

ECONO LODGE
[AAA] [SAVE]
◆◆◆
Motel

Phone: (508)347-2324
5/1-10/31 1P: $55- 90 2P/1B: $55- 85 2P/2B: $55- 90 XP: $5 F16
11/1-4/30 1P: $50- 60 2P/1B: $50- 55 2P/2B: $50- 60 XP: $5 F16
Location: 2.6 mi w on US 20; I-84, exit 3B. 682 Main St (US 20) 01518. Fax: 508/347-7320. **Facility:** 52 rooms. Beautifully landscaped grounds. 1-2 stories; exterior corridors; playground. **Cards:** AE, CB, DI, JC, MC, VI. **Special Amenities:** Early check-in/late check-out and free local telephone calls.

GREEN ACRES MOTEL
[AAA] [SAVE]
◆◆
Motel

Phone: (508)347-3496
5/1-10/31 [CP] 1P: $55- 70 2P/1B: $65- 80 2P/2B: $70- 85 XP: $8 F12
11/1-4/30 [EP] 1P: $45- 50 2P/1B: $48- 55 2P/2B: $50- 58 XP: $5-8 F12
Location: Just off SR 131, 1.4 mi s of jct US 20. 2 Shepard Rd, Rt 131 01566 (PO Box 153). Fax: 508/347-2021. **Terms:** Small pets only. **Facility:** 16 rooms. Quiet area back from the road. 2 whirlpool rms, $98-$125; $85-$115 off season; exterior corridors. **Dining:** Restaurant nearby. **All Rooms:** extended cable TV. **Some Rooms:** 5 efficiencies. **Cards:** AE, DS, MC, VI. **Special Amenities:** Early check-in/late check-out and free local telephone calls.

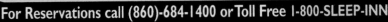

HOLIDAY INN EXPRESS-STURBRIDGE

Phone: (508)347-5141

(AAA) (SAVE)
◆◆◆
Motel

5/1-10/31 [CP]	1P:	$85- 130	2P/1B:	$85- 130	2P/2B:	$85- 130	XP: $8-10	F19
11/1-4/30 [CP]	1P:	$75- 130	2P/1B:	$75- 130	2P/2B:	$75- 130	XP: $8-10	F19

Location: On US 20; 1 mi w of jct SR 20 & 131. 478 Main St 01566 (P O Box 180). Fax: 508/347-2034. **Terms:** Reserv deposit. **Facility:** 64 rooms. 5 whirlpool rms, $99-$125; 3 stories; interior corridors. **All Rooms:** extended cable TV. **Cards:** AE, CB, DI, DS, JC, MC, VI. **Special Amenities: Free breakfast and free local telephone calls.** (See color ad below)

OLD STURBRIDGE VILLAGE LODGES

Guaranteed Rates   **Phone:** (508)347-3327

(AAA)
◆◆◆
Motel

11/1-4/30	1P:	$75- 110	2P/1B:	$75- 110	2P/2B:	$75- 110	XP: $5	F16
10/1-10/31	1P:	$85- 110	2P/1B:	$85- 110	2P/2B:	$85- 95	XP: $5	F16
7/1-9/30	1P:	$85- 105	2P/1B:	$85- 105	2P/2B:	$80- 90	XP: $5	F16
5/1-6/30	1P:	$80- 95	2P/1B:	$80- 95	2P/2B:	$80- 90	XP: $5	F16

Location: On US 20, 0.5 mi w of I-90 tpk, exit 9 & I-84, exit 3B. 391 Main St (Rt 20) 01566 (PO Box 481). Fax: 508/347-3018. **Terms:** Reserv deposit; package plans. **Facility:** 59 rooms. Back from hwy on extensive landscaped grounds. Attractive Colonial style rooms. 1 historic building dates to 1789. 2 stories; interior/exterior corridors; playground. **Dining:** Restaurant nearby. **All Rooms:** combo or shower baths. **Cards:** AE, DS, MC, VI.

PUBLICK HOUSE HISTORIC INN & COUNTY MOTOR LODGE

Phone: (508)347-3313

(AAA) (SAVE)
◆◆
Complex

7/1-10/31	1P:	$90- 155	2P/1B:	$90- 155	2P/2B:	$90- 155	XP: $90-155	F17
5/1-6/30 & 11/1-4/30	1P:	$70- 135	2P/1B:	$70- 135	2P/2B:	$70- 135	XP: $5-10	F17

Location: On the Common, SR 131; 0.5 mi s of jct US 20 on Rt 131; I-90 exit 9 & I-84 exit 3B. SR 131 01566 (PO Box 187). Fax: 508/347-1246. **Terms:** Handling fee imposed; CP, MAP avail; package plans; pets, $5 extra charge. **Facility:** 126 rooms. Motel units & country inn rooms in historic inn & farmhouse. Spacious landscaped grounds. 2 two-bedroom units. 2 stories; interior/exterior corridors; 1 tennis court; playground. **Dining:** 2 restaurants; 7:30 am-10:30 pm; $6-$28; cocktails; dining room, see separate listing. **Services:** giftshop. **All Rooms:** combo or shower baths, extended cable TV. **Some Rooms:** color TV. **Cards:** AE, CB, DI, MC, VI. **Special Amenities: Free local telephone calls and free room upgrade (subject to availability with advanced reservations).** (See ad below)

RODEWAY INN

Phone: (508)347-9673

(AAA) (SAVE)
◆◆
Motel

5/1-10/31 [CP]	1P:	$55- 110	2P/1B:	$55- 110	2P/2B:	$65- 120	XP: $5-10	F13
11/1-4/30 [CP]	1P:	$45- 65	2P/1B:	$45- 65	2P/2B:	$48- 68	XP: $5-7	F13

Location: On SR 131, 2 mi s of jct US 20 & SR 131. 172 Main St 01566 (PO Box 849 Rt 131). Fax: 508/347-3261. **Terms:** Reserv deposit; small pets only, $5 extra charge, $10 dep req. **Facility:** 17 rooms. 1 story; exterior corridors. **All Rooms:** combo or shower baths, extended cable TV. **Cards:** AE, DI, DS, MC, VI. **Special Amenities: Free breakfast and free local telephone calls.** (See ad p 424)

STURBRIDGE COACH MOTOR LODGE

CAAA (SAVE)

| | 5/1-10/31 | 1P: | $55- | 90 | 2P/1B: | $65- | 100 | 2P/2B: | $70- | 105 | XP: | $5 | F16 |
| | 11/1-4/30 | 1P: | $45- | 54 | 2P/1B: | $55- | 65 | 2P/2B: | $60- | 69 | XP: | $5 | F16 |

Phone: 508/347-7327

◆◆
Motel

Location: On US 20; 0.8 mi w of tpk exit 9 & I-84. 408 Main St (US 20) 01566. Fax: 508/347-2954.
Terms: Reserv deposit. **Facility:** 54 rooms. Traditional room decor. Attractively landscaped grounds. 2 stories; exterior corridors. **Some Rooms:** efficiency. **Cards:** AE, MC, VI. *(See color ad below)*   ⊠

STURBRIDGE HOST HOTEL AND CONFERENCE CENTER ON CEDAR LAKE

CAAA (SAVE)

| | All Year | 1P: | $119- | 159 | 2P/1B: | $119- | 159 | 2P/2B: | $119- | 159 | XP: | $15 | F18 |

Phone: (508)347-7393

◆◆◆
Motor Inn

Location: On US 20, w of I-90 tpk exit 9 & I-84, exit 3B. 366 Main St 01566. Fax: 508/347-3944.
Terms: Check-in 4 pm; reserv deposit, 10 day notice; weekly/monthly rates; package plans; small pets only.
Facility: 241 rooms. Some rooms with fireplace. 6 suites, $195-$280; 2-3 stories; interior corridors; beach, heated indoor pool, saunas, whirlpools; 1 tennis court. Fee: miniature golf; racquetball courts. **Dining:** Dining room, restaurant; 6:30 am-10 pm, Fri & Sat-11 pm; $9-$17; cocktails. **Services:** giftshop. **Recreation:** swimming. Fee: fishing. Rental: boats, paddleboats. **Cards:** AE, CB, DI, DS, MC.

🐾 🍸 📷 🛥 🍴 🍽 🎿 ⊠ 🏋 🏃 📺 🖨 🎱 ⊠ 🎣

RESTAURANTS

PUBLICK HOUSE HISTORIC RESORT   Historical   **Lunch:** $8-$23   **Dinner:** $16-$28   Phone: 508/347-3313

CAAA
◆◆
American

Location: On the Common, on SR 131, 0.5 mi s of jct US 20; I-90 exit 9 & I-84 exit 3B; in Publick House Historic Inn & Country Motor Lodge. On The Common, SR 131 01566. **Hours:** 7 am-11 & 11:30-8:30 pm, Fri & Sat-9 pm, Sun from 8 am. **Reservations:** suggested. **Features:** casual dress; children's menu; cocktails & lounge; a la carte. New England fare, lobster pie, clam chowder, homemade dessert, generous portions. American wine list. Entertainment Fri & Sat. **Cards:** AE, DI, MC, VI.   ⊠

ROM'S RESTAURANT   **Lunch:** $4-$8   **Dinner:** $8-$14   Phone: 508/347-3349

CAAA
◆
American

Location: 0.8 mi s of jct US 20 on SR 131. SR 131 01566. **Hours:** 11:30 am-9 pm, Fri & Sat-10 pm. Closed: 11/25 & 12/25. **Reservations:** suggested. **Features:** casual dress; children's menu; health conscious menu items; carryout; cocktails. Family atmosphere. Complete meals avail. Also Italian dishes. Buffet Wed 5-9 pm & Thurs 11:30 am-2 pm, dessert included. Picnic area avail. **Cards:** AE, DI, DS, MC, VI.   ⊠

THE WHISTLING SWAN   **Lunch:** $6-$13   **Dinner:** $17-$24   Phone: 508/347-2321

CAAA
◆◆◆
American

Location: On US 20; 2 mi w of jct SR 131. 502 Main St (US 20) 01566. **Hours:** 11:30 am-2:30 & 5:30-9:30 pm, Sun noon-8 pm. Closed: 11/25, 12/25 & Mon. **Reservations:** suggested. **Features:** children's menu; carryout; cocktails & lounge; entertainment; a la carte. Prepared with an international flair. Ugly Duckling Loft 11:30 am-midnight. Intimate dining in Greek Revival house. Smoking permitted in Ugly Duckling Loft. **Cards:** AE, CB, DI, DS, MC, VI.   ⊠

SUDBURY—*See Boston p. 316.*

SWANSEA—15,400

RESTAURANT

VENUS DE MILO RESTAURANT   **Lunch:** $5-$16   **Dinner:** $10-$19   Phone: 508/678-3901

◆◆
American

Location: On US 6, 1.8 mi e of I-95, exit 3 in MA. 75 GAR Hwy, Rt 6 02777. **Hours:** 11 am-3 & 4:30-9 pm, Fri & Sat-10 pm, Sun noon-9 pm. Closed: 12/25. **Reservations:** suggested; dinner. **Features:** casual dress; children's menu; health conscious menu items; carryout; cocktails & lounge; minimum charge-$3.50; a la carte. Pleasant family dining for over 30 years. Specializing in prime rib of beef & fresh lobsters. Newport Chowder Fest award-winning signature minestrone soup. Spacious, elegant lobby & ample banquet facilities. **Cards:** CB, DI, DS, MC, VI.   ♿ ⊠

TAUNTON—49,800

LODGING

HOLIDAY INN-TAUNTON/FOXBORO Phone: (508)823-0430

Ⓐ SAVE All Year 1P: $89- 119 2P/1B: $89- 119 2P/2B: $99- 129
◆◆◆ **Location:** 3 mi n, just off I-495, exit 9; in Myles Standish Industrial Park. 700 Myles Standish Blvd 02780.
Hotel Fax: 508/880-6483. **Terms:** BP avail; package plans. **Facility:** 155 rooms. Inviting public areas with mahogany, brass & marble accents. Traditional furnishing or country-style pine woods in variety of guest rooms. 7 stories; interior corridors; heated indoor pool, saunas, steamrooms, whirlpool. Fee: racquetball courts. **Dining:** Restaurant; 6:30 am-11 pm, Fri & Sat from 7 am; $10-$18; cocktails. **Services:** giftshop. **Cards:** AE, DI, DS, MC, VI. **Special Amenities: Free local telephone calls and free newspaper.**

RESTAURANT

BENJAMIN'S RESTAURANT Lunch: $7-$10 Dinner: $12-$20 Phone: 508/824-7532
◆◆ **Location:** 3 mi se of I-495, exit 9. 698 Bay St 02780. **Hours:** 11:30 am-3 & 3:30-10 pm, Sat from 5 pm, Sun
American & holidays noon-10 pm. Closed: 12/24 & 12/25. **Reservations:** accepted; except Sat. **Features:** semi-formal attire; children's menu; early bird specials; cocktails & lounge. A well-established, popular, family dining tradition for over 25 years. Warm country decor or relaxed garden rooms & elegant library lounge with sweeping staircases. **Cards:** AE, CB, DI, MC, VI.

TEWKSBURY—See Boston p. 316.

TYNGSBORO—See Boston p. 316.

UXBRIDGE—3,500

LODGING

QUAKER MOTOR LODGE Rates Subject to Change Phone: (508)278-2445

Ⓐ All Year [CP] 1P: $52- 60 2P/1B: $60 2P/2B: $60 XP: $4 F12
◆◆ **Location:** 1 mi e of SR 146 on SR 146A. 442 Quaker Hwy 01569. Fax: 508/278-2446. **Terms:** Weekly rates,
Motel in winter; small pets only, $10 extra charge. **Facility:** 22 rooms. 1 story; exterior corridors; heated pool. **All Rooms:** combo or shower baths. **Cards:** AE, MC, VI.

RESTAURANTS

COCK 'N KETTLE Dinner: $10-$22 Phone: 508/278-5517
◆◆ **Location:** On SR 122, 1 mi s of jct SR 16 at terminus of SR 146A. 240 South Main St 01569. **Hours:** 4
American pm-9 pm, Sat 5 pm-10 pm, Sun 1 pm-9 pm. Closed: 12/25 & Mon. **Reservations:** suggested. **Features:** casual dress; children's menu; early bird specials; cocktails & lounge. Colonial era mansion built by Revolutionary war officer Bazeel Taft. Four working fireplaces make for cozy dining. **Cards:** AE, DS, MC, VI.

THE OYSTER CABIN Dinner: $14-$24 Phone: 508/278-4440
◆◆◆ **Location:** On SR 146A; just e of jct SR 146 (1st MA exit). 785 Quaker Hwy 01569. **Hours:** 4:30 pm-9 pm,
American Sat-9:30, Sun 3 pm-8 pm. Closed: 12/24, 12/25 & Mon. **Reservations:** suggested. **Features:** dressy casual; children's menu; cocktails & lounge; a la carte. Seafood, beef, duck & veal. Upscale artistic presentations in rustic surroundings. Current chef is 3rd generation operator of this restaurant. Smoke free premises. **Cards:** AE, MC, VI.

WAKEFIELD—See Boston p. 317.

WALTHAM—See Boston p. 317.

WARE—9,800

LODGING

WILDWOOD INN BED & BREAKFAST Rates Subject to Change Phone: (413)967-7798
◆◆ 5/1-10/18 1P: $55- 90 2P/1B: $55- 90 2P/2B: $80- 90 XP: $15
Bed & 10/19-4/30 1P: $50- 80 2P/1B: $50- 80 2P/2B: $70- 80 XP: $15
Breakfast **Location:** 0.8 mi n of Hwy 9. 121 Church St 01082. Fax: 413/967-5167. **Terms:** Age restrictions may apply; check-in 4 pm; reserv deposit, 14 day notice. **Facility:** 9 rooms. Quiet, residential location; rooms have handmade quilts, hardwood floors. 3 stories, no elevator; interior corridors; smoke free premises. **Cards:** AE, DI, DS, MC, VI.

WELLESLEY—See Boston p. 318.

WELLFLEET—See Cape Cod & South Wellfleet p. 381.

WENHAM—See Boston p. 319.

WEST BARNSTABLE—See Cape Cod p. 382.

WESTBOROUGH—14,100

LODGINGS

COURTYARD BY MARRIOTT Rates Subject to Change **Phone:** 508/836-4800
◆◆◆   Sun-Thurs   1P: $119   2P/1B: $119   2P/2B: $119
Motel   Fri & Sat   1P: $89   2P/1B: $89   2P/2B: $89
    Location: Computer/Research Dr exit from SR 9, just w of I-495, exit 23B; 0.5 mi beyond the Marriott Hotel.
3 Technology Dr 01581. Fax: 508/870-5577. **Terms:** Reserv deposit, Sun-Thurs. **Facility:** 98 rooms. 3 stories; interior corridors; heated indoor pool. **All Rooms:** combo or shower baths. **Cards:** AE, CB, DI, DS, MC, VI.

RESIDENCE INN BY MARRIOTT BOSTON/WESTBOROUGH   Rates Subject to Change   **Phone:** 508/366-7700
◆◆◆   Sun-Thurs [CP]   2P/1B: $139- 169 2P/2B: $149- 189
Apartment   Fri & Sat [CP]   2P/1B: $99- 159 2P/2B: $109- 189
    Location: 0.3 mi s of SR 9, Computer Dr/Research Dr exit, just w of jct I-495, exit 23B. 25 Connector Rd
01581. Fax: 508/366-4334. **Terms:** Check-in 4 pm; reserv deposit. **Facility:** 109 rooms. Well equipped 1 & 2-bedroom suites.
25 two-bedroom units. Rates for up to 4 persons; 3 stories; interior/exterior corridors. **Recreation:** sports court.
All Rooms: efficiencies. **Cards:** AE, CB, DI, DS, JC, MC, VI.

SIERRA SUITES   Guaranteed Rates   **Phone:** (508)366-6100
◆◆◆   Sun-Thurs 5/1-10/31 [CP]   1P: $149   2P/1B: $149   2P/2B: $149
Extended Stay   Sun-Thurs 11/1-4/30 [CP] 1P: $129   2P/1B: $129   2P/2B: $129
Motel   Fri & Sat 5/1-5/31,
    10/2-10/31 & 1/1-4/30 [CP]   1P: $119   2P/1B: $119   2P/2B: $119
    Fri & Sat 6/1-10/1 &
    11/1-12/31 [CP]   1P: $99   2P/1B: $99   2P/2B: $99
Location: Just s of I-495, exit 23B on n side of SR 9. 1800 Computer Dr 01581. Fax: 508/366-9699. **Facility:** 113 rooms.
Rates for up to 4 persons; 3 stories; interior corridors; heated pool. **All Rooms:** efficiencies, combo or shower baths.
Cards: AE, DI, DS, JC, MC, VI.

WYNDHAM WESTBOROUGH HOTEL   Rates Subject to Change   **Phone:** 508/366-5511
◆◆◆   Sun-Thurs   1P: $134- 149 2P/1B: $144- 159 2P/2B: $144- 159 XP: $10   F
Motor Inn   Fri & Sat   1P: $79   2P/1B: $79   2P/2B: $79
    Location: Computer/Research Dr exit from SR 9, just w of I-495, exit 23B. 5400 Computer Dr 01581.
Fax: 508/870-5965. **Terms:** Check-in 4 pm. **Facility:** 223 rooms. Spacious guestrooms. 4 stories; interior corridors; heated indoor pool. **Services:** giftshop. **All Rooms:** combo or shower baths. **Cards:** AE, CB, DI, DS, MC, VI. *(See color ad below)*

WEST BROOKFIELD—3,500

RESTAURANT

SALEM CROSS INN   Historical   **Lunch:** $6-$9   **Dinner:** $10-$18   **Phone:** 508/867-2345
ⒶⒶⒶ   **Location:** 1.8 mi w on SR 9. SR 9 01585. **Hours:** 11:30 am-9 pm, Sat from 5 pm, Sun noon-8 pm. Closed:
◆◆◆   Mon & 1/2-1/14 & Mon-Wed 1/19-3/31. **Reservations:** suggested. **Features:** casual dress; children's menu;
American   early bird specials; cocktails & lounge; a la carte. Beautifully restored country homestead from 1705 with
            large number of exceptional antique implements & furnishings of Colonial America. Special events in summer
            & winter. Tours & museum. Smoke free premises. **Cards:** AE, MC, VI.

WEST DENNIS—See Cape Cod p. 382.

WESTMINSTER—6,200

LODGING

WACHUSETT VILLAGE INN & CONFERENCE CENTER   Phone: (978)874-2000

		1P:		2P/1B:		2P/2B:		XP:	
	12/4-4/30	1P: $149		2P/1B: $89- 149		2P/2B: $89- 149		XP: $10	F16
	6/1-10/25	1P: $139		2P/1B: $139		2P/2B: $139		XP: $10	F16
	10/26-12/3	1P: $129		2P/1B: $129		2P/2B: $129		XP: $10	F16
Motor Inn	5/1-5/31	1P: $119		2P/1B: $119		2P/2B: $119		XP: $10	F16

Location: 0.7 mi w on Village Inn Rd; SR 2, exit 27 westbound, 0.3 mi e on Village Inn Rd; SR 2, exit 26 eastbound. 9 Village Inn Rd 01473. Fax: 978/874-1753. **Terms:** Reserv deposit; weekly/monthly rates; package plans. **Facility:** 74 rooms. Motel rooms, Colonial style cottages, some with fireplace. 6 efficiency units, $149-$179; 1-2 stories; interior/exterior corridors; heated indoor pool, sauna, steamroom, whirlpool; 2 tennis courts; playground. **Dining:** Dining room, restaurant; 7 am-10 pm; $10-$20; cocktails. **Recreation:** game room. Fee: sleigh rides; hay rides. **All Rooms:** combo or shower baths. **Cards:** AE, DI, DS, MC, VI. **Special Amenities:** Early check-in/late check-out and preferred room (subject to availability with advanced reservations).

RESTAURANT

THE OLD MILL   **Lunch:** $6-$15   **Dinner:** $9-$17   **Phone:** 978/874-5941

Location: 0.8 mi e on SR 2A; SR 2, exit 25. SR 2A 01473. **Hours:** 11:30 am-9:15 pm, Fri & Sat-9:45 pm, Sun 9 am-8:15 pm. **Closed:** 12/25. **Reservations:** suggested. **Features:** casual dress; children's menu; early bird specials; senior's menu; health conscious menu items; cocktails & lounge; a la carte. Picturesque dining rooms in old mill overlooking pond, falls & covered bridge. Lunch buffet $8. Sun brunch 10 am-2 pm, $14. **Cards:** AE, DI, DS, MC, VI.

American

WESTPORT—13,900

LODGING

HAMPTON INN-FALL RIVER-WESTPORT   Rates Subject to Change   **Phone:** (508)675-8500

		1P:		2P/1B:		2P/2B:	
♦♦♦	6/20-9/11	1P: $89- 99		2P/1B: $99- 109		2P/2B: $99- 109	
Motel	9/12-10/23	1P: $76		2P/1B: $86		2P/2B: $86	
	5/16-6/19	1P: $74		2P/1B: $79		2P/2B: $79	
	5/1-5/15 & 10/24-4/30	1P: $67		2P/1B: $72		2P/2B: $72	

Location: I-195, eastbound exit 9, westbound exit 10; then 1.3 mi w on US 6. 53 Old Bedford Rd 02790. Fax: 508/675-0075. **Facility:** 133 rooms. Tastefully appointed, meticulously clean guest rooms. Quiet location. Many units overlook scenic Lake Watuppa. Brightly illuminated grounds. Excellent guest service. Rates for up to 5 persons; 4 stories; interior corridors; 1 tennis court. **Cards:** AE, CB, DI, DS, MC, VI.

RESTAURANT

THE PRISCILLA DINING ROOM AT WHITE'S   **Lunch:** $5-$9   **Dinner:** $9-$14   **Phone:** 508/675-7185

Location: Off I-195, eastbound exit 9; westbound exit 10, 1 mi w on Rt 6. 66 State Rd, Rt 6 02790. **Hours:** 11:30 am-10 pm. **Closed:** 12/25. **Reservations:** suggested. **Features:** casual dress; children's menu; early bird specials; carryout; cocktails & lounge; a la carte. Relaxing, family style dining overlooking Lake Watuppa. Elegant ambiance of the historic steamship "Priscilla" the inspiration here. Complete dinners offered. Fine hospitality for over 35 years. **Cards:** AE, DI, DS, MC, VI.

American

WESTPORT POINT—600

RESTAURANT

MOBY DICK WHARF RESTAURANT   **Lunch:** $7-$10   **Dinner:** $15-$20   **Phone:** 508/636-6500

Location: 11.5 mi s of I-195 exit 10; just w of SR 88 s of the drawbridge. 1 Bridge Rd 02791. **Hours:** Open 5/1-1/1 & 4/1-4/30; 11:30 am-10 pm, Fri & Sat-11 pm; Fri 4 pm-9 pm, Sat 11:30 am-9 pm, Sun noon-8 pm 10/1-12/31. **Closed:** 11/25 & 12/25. **Features:** casual dress; Sunday brunch; children's menu; early bird specials; cocktails & lounge; street parking. Upscale casual dining overlooking Westport harbor. Outdoor dining on the deck in season. **Cards:** AE, MC, VI.

Seafood

WEST SPRINGFIELD—27,500—*See also SPRINGFIELD.*

LODGINGS

BEST WESTERN SOVEREIGN HOTEL & CONFERENCE CENTER   Rates Subject to Change   **Phone:** (413)781-8750

		1P:		2P/1B:		2P/2B:		XP:	
♦♦	All Year [BP]	1P: $79- 110		2P/1B: $79- 110		2P/2B: $79- 110		XP: $10-15	F17

Motor Inn   **Location:** I-91 exit 13B, just s, on US 5. 1080 Riverdale St 01089. Fax: 413/733-8652. **Terms:** Weekend rates avail. **Facility:** 260 rooms. Featuring excellent courtyard tropical setting. 2-4 stories; interior corridors; heated indoor pool. **Cards:** AE, CB, DI, DS, MC, VI. *(See color ad inside front cover)*

HAMPTON INN   Rates Subject to Change   **Phone:** 413/732-1300

		1P:		2P/1B:		2P/2B:	
♦♦♦	All Year [CP]	1P: $80		2P/1B: $82		2P/2B: $82	

Motel   **Location:** On US 5, 0.3 mi s of jct I-91 exit 13B. 1011 Riverdale St (US 5) 01089. Fax: 413/732-9883. **Terms:** Reserv deposit. **Facility:** 126 rooms. Located in retail business area, contemporary lobby with breakfast area & comfortable compact rooms. Rates for up to 4 persons; 4 stories; interior corridors. **Cards:** AE, DI, DS, MC, VI. *(See color ad p 430)*

QUALITY INN   Rates Subject to Change   **Phone:** 413/739-7261

		1P:		2P/1B:		2P/2B:		XP:	
♦♦	All Year [CP]	1P: $50- 115		2P/1B: $55- 120		2P/2B: $65- 110		XP: $5-25	F18

Motor Inn   **Location:** At I-91 exit 13B; jct US 5. 1150 Riverdale St 01089. Fax: 413/737-8410. **Facility:** 114 rooms. Rooms range in size from small to spacious. 2 night min stay weekends 5/1-9/30; 5 stories; interior corridors. **Cards:** AE, CB, DI, DS, MC, VI.

RED CARPET INN   Phone: 413/733-6678

(AAA) SAVE
◆
Motel

5/1-9/30 [CP]	1P:	$55-	75	2P/1B:	$65-	75	2P/2B:	$65-	85	XP: $5-20	D10
10/1-12/31 [CP]	1P:	$45-	55	2P/1B:	$50-	60	2P/2B:	$55-	70	XP: $5-20	D10
1/1-4/30 [CP]	1P:	$40-	50	2P/1B:	$40-	55	2P/2B:	$48-	65	XP: $5-20	D10

Location: On US 5; 1.3 mi s of I-91 exit 13B. 560 Riverdale St 01089. Fax: 413/733-6678. **Terms:** Reserv deposit; small pets only, $10 extra charge. **Facility:** 28 rooms. 5 whirlpool rms, extra charge; 1 story; exterior corridors. **All Rooms:** combo or shower baths. **Some Rooms:** 4 efficiencies. **Cards:** AE, DI, MC, VI.

🐕 🏊 🎦 ▢ 🖪 ✕

RED ROOF INN   Rates Subject to Change   Phone: (413)731-1010

◆◆
Motel

5/1-11/30	1P:	$51-	71	2P/1B:	$56-	76	2P/2B:	$61-	81	XP:	$7	F18
4/1-4/30	1P:	$51-	71	2P/1B:	$56-	76	2P/2B:	$61-	81	XP:	$7	F18
12/1-3/31	1P:	$41-	61	2P/1B:	$46-	66	2P/2B:	$51-	71	XP:	$7	F18

Location: I-91, at exit 13A (US 5N). 1254 Riverdale (US 5) St 01089. Fax: 413/731-1009. **Facility:** 111 rooms. Well-kept property with modest rooms. 2 stories; exterior corridors. **Cards:** AE, CB, DI, DS, MC, VI.

SAVE 🐕 🎦 🍴 ⛽ 🎦 🖨 🛗 ✕ 🗎

RESTAURANTS

HOFBRAUHAUS RESTAURANT   Lunch: $6-$12   Dinner: $10-$23   Phone: 413/737-4905

◆◆◆
German

Location: Just w on SR 147, then just nw, from jct of US 5 & SR 147. 1105 Main St 01089. **Hours:** 11:30 am-2:30 & 5:30-9 pm; Fri 11:30 am-2:30 & 5-10 pm; Sat 5 pm-10 pm. Closed: 12/24 & 12/25. **Reservations:** suggested. **Features:** children's menu; cocktails. Bavarian decor dining room with servers in traditional dress. Lighter fare menu avail in tavern. **Cards:** AE, DI, DS, MC, VI.   ✕

STORROWTON TAVERN   Historical   Lunch: $7-$12   Dinner: $10-$20   Phone: 413/732-4188

(AAA)
◆◆
Continental

Location: On SR 147; 1.8 mi w of jct US 5. 1305 Memorial Ave 01089. **Hours:** 11:30 am-2 & 5-8 pm, Sat 11:30 am-2 & 5-9 pm. Closed major holidays & Sun. **Reservations:** suggested. **Features:** casual dress; children's menu; cocktails & lounge. Authentic 1795 New England tavern. Smoke free premises. **Cards:** AE, DS, MC, VI.   ✕

WEST STOCKBRIDGE—1,500—See also STOCKBRIDGE.

LODGING

PLEASANT VALLEY MOTEL   Rates Subject to Change   Phone: 413/232-8511

(AAA)
◆◆
Motel

Fri & Sat 6/15-10/31 [CP]	1P:	$100-	145	2P/1B:	$100-	145	2P/2B:	$100-	145	XP: $10	F12
Sun-Thurs 6/15-10/31 [CP]	1P:	$55-	75	2P/1B:	$55-	75	2P/2B:	$55-	75	XP: $10	F12
5/1-6/14 & 11/1-4/30 [CP]	1P:	$39-	65	2P/1B:	$39-	65	2P/2B:	$39-	65	XP: $10	F12

Location: Eastbound I-90 exit B3, 0.5 mi s on SR 22 & 3.5 mi e Rt 102; westbound I-90, exit 1, 0.4 mi e. Rt 102 01266. Fax: 413/232-8512. **Terms:** Reserv deposit, 10 day notice, 15 day 7/1-9/4; weekly/monthly rates; package plans; 2 night min stay, weekends 7/1-9/4; pets. **Facility:** 16 rooms. 1 story; exterior corridors. **Dining:** Continental breakfast Sat & Sun, 7/1-9/4. **All Rooms:** extended cable TV. **Some Rooms:** 2 efficiencies, no utensils. **Cards:** AE, DS, MC, VI. (See ad p 423)   🐕 🏊 ▢ 🖪 ✕

WEST YARMOUTH—See Cape Cod p. 382.

WILLIAMSBURG—2,500

RESTAURANT

WILLIAMS HOUSE   Lunch: $5-$10   Dinner: $13-$20   Phone: 413/268-7300

(AAA)
◆◆
American

Location: Center on SR 9. Four Main St 01096-0766. **Hours:** 11:30 am-8 pm, Fri & Sat-9 pm, Sun brunch 10:30 am-1 pm. Closed: 12/25 & Mon. **Reservations:** suggested. **Features:** casual dress; children's menu; cocktails. Casual contemporary dining with beef, fish, fowl & vegetarian entrees; lighter fare & patio dining also avail. Smoke free premises. **Cards:** AE, CB, DI, DS, MC, VI.   ✕

WILLIAMSTOWN—8,200

LODGINGS

BERKSHIRE HILLS MOTEL   Phone: (413)458-3950

(AAA) SAVE

◆◆◆ Motel

Fri & Sat 6/25-9/6 & 9/24-10/24 [EP]	1P: $109- 129	2P/1B: $119- 129	2P/2B: $119- 129	XP: $10	F3
Sun-Thurs 6/25-9/6 & 9/24-10/24 [CP]	1P: $99- 119	2P/1B: $99- 119	2P/2B: $109- 119	XP: $10	F3
5/1-6/24, 9/7-9/23 & 10/25-4/30 [CP]	1P: $59- 89	2P/1B: $59- 99	2P/2B: $59- 99	XP: $10	F3

Location: 2.3 mi s on US 7 & SR 2. 01267 (Rt 7). **Terms:** Reserv deposit, 10 day notice. **Facility:** 20 rooms. Lovely breakfast room & deck; attractive, well maintained rooms; beautiful grounds bordering brook. 2 night min stay weekends, 6/28-8/31 & 9/27-10/19; 2 stories; exterior corridors; heated pool. **Dining:** Restaurant nearby. **All Rooms:** combo or shower baths. **Cards:** AE, DI, DS, MC, VI. **Special Amenities:** Free breakfast. *(See color ad below)*

THE CHIMNEY MIRROR MOTEL   Rates Subject to Change   Phone: 413/458-5202

(AAA)

◆◆ Motel

Fri & Sat 6/21-9/5 & 9/25-10/24	2P/1B: $75	2P/2B: $90-	XP: $10	D10
Fri & Sat 5/1-6/20, Sun-Thurs 6/21-Thurs 5/1-6/8&8/6-9/24			XP: $10	D10
9/6-10/24	2P/1B: $65	2P/2B: $70-	XP: $10	D10
10/25-4/30	2P/1B: $55	2P/2B: $65-	XP: $10	D10
	2P/1B: $42- 45	2P/2B: $49-	XP: $10	D10

Location: 1 mi e on SR 2. 295 Main St 01267. **Terms:** Reserv deposit, 10 day notice; handling fee imposed; 2 night min stay, weekends in summer. **Facility:** 18 rooms. Small to medium country decor rooms. 1 story; exterior corridors. **Dining:** Restaurant nearby. **All Rooms:** combo or shower baths, extended cable TV. **Cards:** AE, DS, MC, VI.

COZY CORNER MOTEL   Rates Subject to Change   Phone: 413/458-8006

◆◆ Motel

Fri & Sat 7/1-10/25	1P: $83	2P/1B: $83	2P/2B: $93	XP: $10	F12
Sun-Thurs 7/1-10/25	1P: $67	2P/1B: $67	2P/2B: $75	XP: $10	F12
Fri & Sat 5/1-6/30 & 10/26-4/30	1P: $49	2P/1B: $49	2P/2B: $60	XP: $10	F12
Sun-Thurs 5/1-6/30 & 10/26-4/30	1P: $45	2P/1B: $45	2P/2B: $53	XP: $10	F12

Location: On US 7, 1.5 mi n of jct SR 2. 284 Sand Springs Rd & US 7 01267. Fax: 413/458-0237. **Terms:** Reserv deposit, 10 day notice; handling fee imposed. **Facility:** 12 rooms. Well-maintained motel with traditional room decor; exceptional housekeeping. 2 stories; exterior corridors. **All Rooms:** shower baths. **Cards:** AE, DI, DS, MC, VI.

THE 1896 HOUSE "BROOKSIDE" & "PONDSIDE"   Rates Subject to Change   Phone: (413)458-8125

(AAA)

◆◆◆ Motel

Fri & Sat 5/23-9/5 & 9/24-10/23 [CP]	1P: $100- 108	2P/1B: $100- 108	2P/2B: $100- 108	XP: $10	F8
Sun-Thurs 5/23-9/5 [CP]	1P: $81- 98	2P/1B: $90- 98	2P/2B: $90- 98	XP: $10	F8
Fri & Sat 5/1-5/22, 9/6-9/23 & Fri & Sat 4/2-4/30 [CP]	1P: $72- 90	2P/1B: $72- 90	2P/2B: $72- 90	XP: $10	F8
Sun-Thurs 5/1-5/22, 10/24-4/1 & Sun-Thurs 4/2-4/30 [CP]	1P: $45- 76	2P/1B: $50- 76	2P/2B: $50- 76	XP: $10	F8

Location: 1.8 mi s on US 7 & SR 2. 910 Cold Spring Rd 01267 (US 7). **Terms:** Reserv deposit, 3 day notice; package plans; 2 night min stay, weekends 6/23-9/4. **Facility:** 29 rooms. Attractive rooms in enchanting setting along brook or bucolic duck pond. 1-2 stories; exterior corridors; heated pool. **Recreation:** shuffleboard. **All Rooms:** combo or shower baths. **Some Rooms:** kitchen. **Cards:** AE, DI, DS, MC, VI. *(See ad p 432)*

FOUR ACRES MOTEL Rates Subject to Change Phone: 413/458-8158

Fri & Sat 6/25-9/4 &					
9/24-10/23 [CP]	1P: $79- 115	2P/1B: $79- 115	2P/2B: $99	XP: $10	
5/1-6/24 & 9/5-9/23 [CP]	1P: $58- 95	2P/1B: $58- 95	2P/2B: $69- 89	XP: $10	
Sun-Thurs 6/25-9/4 [CP]	1P: $60- 80	2P/1B: $60- 80	2P/2B: $74	XP: $10	
10/24-4/30 [CP]	1P: $55- 75	2P/1B: $55- 75	2P/2B: $65	XP: $10	

Location: 1 mi e on SR 2. 213 Main St 01267. Fax: 413/458-8158. **Terms:** Reserv deposit, 14 day notice; handling fee imposed. **Facility:** 31 rooms. Large attractive rooms, very well maintained. 1-2 stories; exterior corridors. **Dining:** Restaurant nearby. **Recreation:** barbecue grill, picnic table, shuffleboard. **All Rooms:** combo or shower baths, extended cable TV. **Some Rooms:** efficiency. **Cards:** AE, DI, DS, MC, VI.

MAPLE TERRACE MOTEL Guaranteed Rates Phone: (413)458-9677

[CP]	1P: $58- 83	2P/1B: $63- 83	2P/2B: $68- 88	XP: $5-10	F12
9/7-9/16 [CP]	1P: $49- 63	2P/1B: $54- 63	2P/2B: $59- 68	XP: $5-10	F12
5/1-5/27 & 10/25-4/30 [CP]	1P: $44- 54	2P/1B: $49- 54	2P/2B: $54- 59	XP: $5-10	F12

Location: On SR 2, 1 mi e of jct SR 7. 555 Main St 01267. Fax: 413/458-9677. **Terms:** Weekly/monthly rates. **Facility:** 17 rooms. Attractive setting, well-maintained units. 1 two-bedroom unit. 1 king deluxe with fireplace, 2 efficiencies $10 extra charge. 2 night min stay weekends 6/25-9/6 & 9/17-10/23; 1-2 stories; exterior corridors; heated pool. **All Rooms:** combo or shower baths, extended cable TV. **Cards:** AE, CB, DI, DS, MC, VI.

NORTHSIDE MOTEL Rates Subject to Change Phone: 413/458-8107

		1P:	2P/1B:	2P/2B:	XP:	
⚫⚫⚫	Fri & Sat 5/1-11/15 [CP]	1P: $68- 84	2P/1B: $71- 84	2P/2B: $71- 84	XP: $5	F5
	Sun-Thurs 5/1-11/15 [CP]	1P: $60- 72	2P/1B: $65- 72	2P/2B: $65- 72	XP: $5	F5
◆◆	11/16-4/30 [EP]	1P: $43- 60	2P/1B: $49- 60	2P/2B: $49- 60	XP: $5	F5

Motel **Location:** Williams College campus; jct US 7 & SR 2. 45 North St 01267. **Terms:** Reserv deposit, 7 day notice; handling fee imposed; weekly/monthly rates; 2 night min stay, weekends in season. **Facility:** 29 rooms. 1-2 stories; interior/exterior corridors; small pool. **Dining:** 7:30-10 am 6/1-11/15, closed Mon & Tues; coffee shop nearby. **All Rooms:** extended cable TV. **Cards:** AE, DS, MC, VI. ⚉ 🅙 ▢ 🄳

THE ORCHARDS Rates Subject to Change Phone: 413/458-9611

		1P:	2P/1B:	2P/2B:
◆◆◆◆	5/27-11/15	1P: $165- 230	2P/1B: $165- 230	2P/2B: $165- 230
Country Inn	5/1-5/26 & 11/16-4/30	1P: $125- 175	2P/1B: $125- 175	2P/2B: $125- 175

Location: 1 mi e on US 2. 222 Adams Rd 01267. Fax: 413/458-3273. **Terms:** Check-in 4 pm; reserv deposit, 7 day notice; 2 night min stay, weekends 5/15-11/15. **Facility:** 49 rooms. Spacious rooms furnished with English antiques; some with fireplace. 3 stories; interior corridors; small pool. **Cards:** AE, CB, DI, MC, VI.

🄴 🄿 ⚉ 🅙 🆈 🄰 🆆 🆆 🄰 🆅🄲🆁 🄻 🄳 🆇 🄰

THE VILLAGER MOTEL Rates Subject to Change Phone: 413/458-4046

		1P:	2P/1B:	2P/2B:	XP:	
⚫⚫⚫	Fri & Sat 5/20-10/31 [CP]	1P: $70- 75	2P/1B: $75- 80	2P/2B: $75- 80	XP: $5-10	F14
	Sun-Thurs 5/20-10/31 [CP]	1P: $55- 60	2P/1B: $55- 65	2P/2B: $55- 65	XP: $5-10	F14
◆◆	Fri & Sat 5/1-5/19 & 11/1-4/30 [CP]	1P: $50- 55	2P/1B: $55- 60	2P/2B: $55- 60	XP: $5	F14
Motel	Sun-Thurs 5/1-5/19 & 11/1-4/30 [CP]	1P: $45- 50	2P/1B: $50- 55	2P/2B: $50- 55	XP: $5	F14

Location: On US 7, 1.7 n of jct SR 2. 953 Simonds Rd 01267. **Terms:** Small pets only, by prior arrangement. **Facility:** 13 rooms. Charming motel, many rooms with knotty pine walls; quiet, semi-rural location. 1 story; exterior corridors. **Cards:** AE, DS, MC, VI. 🆂🄳 🛏 🆇🅿 🄳 🆇

THE WILLOWS MOTEL Rates Subject to Change Phone: 413/458-5768

		1P:	2P/1B:	2P/2B:	XP:	
⚫⚫⚫	Fri & Sat 5/20-11/14 [CP]	1P: $79- 84	2P/1B: $79- 84	2P/2B: $95- 99	XP: $10	F10
	Sun-Thurs 5/20-11/14 [CP]	1P: $55- 58	2P/1B: $63- 66	2P/2B: $70- 77	XP: $10	F10
◆◆	5/1-5/19 & 11/15-4/30 [CP]	1P: $49- 57	2P/1B: $55- 67	2P/2B: $58- 75		

Motel **Location:** 0.8 mi e on SR 2. 480 Main St 01267. Fax: 413/458-9317. **Terms:** Reserv deposit, 7 day notice, in season; handling fee imposed; weekly rates. **Facility:** 17 rooms. Bright & cheery rooms. 1 two-bedroom unit. 1-2 stories; exterior corridors; heated pool. **All Rooms:** combo or shower baths, extended cable TV. **Some Rooms:** kitchen. **Cards:** AE, MC, VI. ⚉ 💻 ▢ 🄳 🆇

RESTAURANTS

COZY CORNER RESTAURANT **Lunch:** $4-$8 **Dinner:** $5-$13 Phone: 413/458-3854

◆ **Location:** 1.5 mi n on US 7. 850 Simonds Rd 01267. **Hours:** 11 am-11 pm, Sat-1 am, Sun noon-9 pm; Fri & American Sat in summer-10 pm. Closed major holidays. **Reservations:** accepted; except Fri. **Features:** casual dress; children's menu; early bird specials; carryout; cocktails & lounge. Family atmosphere. Famous for fish & chips. **Cards:** AE, MC, VI.

THE 1896 HOUSE RESTAURANT **Dinner:** $10-$20 **Phone:** 413/458-1896
◆ ◆ **Location:** 1.7 mi s on US 7 & SR 2. 866 Cold Spring Rd 01267. **Hours:** 4:30 pm-9:30 pm; Sun Brunch
American 11:30 am-2 pm. Closed: 12/24 & 12/25. **Reservations:** suggested; Sat. **Features:** casual dress; children's
menu; early bird specials; cocktails & lounge. New England country cuisine in a vintage 19th century barn &
friendly open dining atmosphere. **Cards:** AE, DI, DS, MC, VI. *(See ad p 432)* ☒

HOBSON'S CHOICE **Lunch:** $5-$9 **Dinner:** $10-$20 **Phone:** 413/458-9101
AAA **Location:** On SR 43, 0.3 mi s of jct SR 2. 159 Water St 01267. **Hours:** 11:30 am-2 & 5-9:30 pm, Sat-Mon
from 5 pm. Closed: 1/1, 11/25 & 12/25. **Reservations:** suggested. **Features:** dressy casual; children's menu;
◆ ◆ carryout; salad bar; cocktails. Casual dining, very popular featuring blackened steak & seafood. Smoke free
Steak and premises. **Cards:** AE, MC, VI. ☒
Seafood

LE JARDIN RESTAURANT **Dinner:** $15-$22 **Phone:** 413/458-8032
◆ ◆ **Location:** 1.3 mi s on US 7 & SR 2. 777 Cold Spring Rd 01267. **Hours:** 5 pm-9 pm, Sat-10 pm. Closed:
Continental Tues. **Reservations:** accepted. **Features:** casual dress; Sunday brunch; health conscious menu; cocktails &
lounge; a la carte. Country Inn atmosphere with a very good selection of beef, chichen, fish, veal, lamb &
pasta. **Cards:** AE, DS, MC, VI. ☒

THE ORCHARDS DINING ROOM Country Inn **Lunch:** $8-$15 **Dinner:** $18-$30 **Phone:** 413/458-9611
◆ ◆ ◆ ◆ **Location:** In the Orchards. 222 Adams Rd 01267. **Hours:** 7 am-10, noon-2 & 5:30-9 pm, Sun 8 am-2 &
Continental 5:30-9 pm; off season to 8:30 pm. **Reservations:** suggested; Sunday brunch. **Features:** dressy casual; Sunday brunch;
children's menu; health conscious menu items; cocktails & lounge; a la carte. Finely appointed English dining
room overlooking courtyard garden. Terrace dining weather permitting. Continental cuisine with New England influences.
Smoking permitted in lounge. Smoke free premises. **Cards:** AE, CB, DI, MC, VI. ☒

THE TACONIC RESTAURANT **Lunch:** $7-$11 **Dinner:** $10-$19 **Phone:** 413/458-9499
◆ ◆ ◆ **Location:** 2.2 mi s on US 7,from jct SR 2. 1161 Cold Spring Rd 01267. **Hours:** 5 pm-9:30 pm, Sun noon-9
American pm. Closed: 12/24. **Reservations:** suggested; weekends. **Features:** casual dress; children's menu; health
conscious menu; cocktails & lounge. Steak, veal, chicken & fish dishes. Fine fireside dining on lower level
overlooking garden. Chef owned & operated. Smoke free premises. **Cards:** AE, DI, DS, MC, VI. ☒

WILD AMBER GRILL **Dinner:** $12-$19 **Phone:** 413/458-4000
◆ ◆ ◆ **Location:** 0.5 mi n on US 7, adjacent to Williams College campus. 101 North St 01267. **Hours:** noon-2 pm
American & 5:30-10 pm, Sun-9 pm. Closed: 1/1, 12/24, 12/25 & Tues. **Reservations:** suggested. **Features:** casual
dress; cocktails; a la carte. Contemporary American cuisine. **Cards:** AE, MC, VI. ☒

WINCHENDON—4,300

RESTAURANT

THE BRASS PINEAPPLE RESTAURANT **Lunch:** $3-$8 **Dinner:** $6-$20 **Phone:** 978/297-0312
AAA **Location:** 0.8 mi s on SR 12. 302 Spring St (SR 12) 01475. **Hours:** 11:30 am-2 & 4:30-9 pm, Sun noon-8
pm. Closed: 11/25, 12/25, Mon, Tues & for lunch Wed. **Reservations:** suggested. **Features:** casual dress;
◆ ◆ children's menu; carryout; cocktails & lounge; a la carte. Casual dining in cozy knotty pine dining room.
American Chef/owner. Also featuring veal, seafood, steak, chicken, pasta & creative specials Smaller portions of all
entrees avail. Smoke free premises. **Cards:** AE, DS, MC, VI. ☒

WOBURN—*See Boston p. 319.*

WOODS HOLE—*See Cape Cod p. 386.*

LODGINGS

BEECHWOOD HOTEL

Hotel

Phone: (508)754-5789

5/1-5/31 & 10/1-10/31 Mon-Thurs 6/1-9/30 & 11/1-4/30	1P: $149- 169	2P/1B: $149- 169	2P/2B: $149- 169	XP: $15	F16
Fri-Sun 6/1-6/30, 8/1-9/30 & 11/1-11/30	1P: $125- 149	2P/1B: $125- 149	2P/2B: $125- 149	XP: $15	F16
	1P: $99- 199	2P/1B: $99- 119	2P/2B: $99- 119	XP: $15	F16
Fri-Sun 7/1-7/31 & 12/1-4/30	1P: $79- 109	2P/1B: $79- 109	2P/2B: $79- 109	XP: $15	F16

Location: I-290, westbound exit 22N, 0.5 mi w on Lincoln St, 1.5 mi s; eastbound exit 21, 1.3 mi s. 363 Plantation St 01605. Fax: 508/752-2060. **Terms:** Package plans. **Facility:** 73 rooms. Circular guest room building with large rooms. 4 units with gas fireplace $20 extra charge; executive rooms & suites $209; 5 stories; interior corridors. **Dining:** Restaurant; 6:30-10:30 am, 11:30-2:30 & 6-10 pm; Sat from 7:30 am; Sun 7:30 am-2 & 5-9 pm; cocktails. **Services:** giftshop. **All Rooms:** combo or shower baths, extended cable TV. **Cards:** AE, DI, DS, MC, VI. **Special Amenities:** Free newspaper and free room upgrade (subject to availability with advanced reservations).

CROWNE PLAZA WORCESTER
Phone: 508/791-1600
◆◆◆ All Year
Hotel
Rates Subject to Change
1P: $119- 159   2P/1B: $119- 159   2P/2B: $119- 159   XP: $20   F14
Location: 0.3 n of I-290; exit 17 eastbound, exit 18 westbound. 10 Lincoln Sq 01608. Fax: 508/791-1796. **Facility:** 243 rooms. Medium size lobby with central fireplace. 7 one-bedroom suites $249-$299; 9 stories; interior corridors; heated indoor/outdoor pool. Fee: parking. **Services:** giftshop. **All Rooms:** combo or shower baths. **Cards:** AE, CB, DI, DS, MC, VI.

HAMPTON INN
Phone: (508)757-0400
AAA SAVE
5/1-12/31   1P: $100- 115   2P/1B: $100- 115   2P/2B: $100- 115
1/1-4/30   1P: $87- 100   2P/1B: $87- 100   2P/2B: $87- 100
◆◆◆
Motel
Location: Just n of I-290; exit 16. 110 Summer St 01608. Fax: 508/831-9839. **Terms:** Pets. **Facility:** 97 rooms. 2-story lobby with breakfast area. Large rooms. Rates for up to 4 persons; 5 stories; interior corridors. **Cards:** AE, CB, DI, DS, MC, VI. **Special Amenities:** Free breakfast and free local telephone calls.

HOLIDAY INN
Phone: (508)852-4000
◆◆◆
Motor Inn
5/1-5/31 & All Year
Rates Subject to Change
1P: $107   2P/1B: $107   2P/2B: $107   XP: $10   F19
Location: From I-290, exit 20; 0.5 mi n on Lincoln St; westbound following signs to SR 70. 500 Lincoln St 01605. Fax: 508/852-8521. **Facility:** 142 rooms. Central atrium with gazebo. 2 stories; interior corridors; heated indoor pool. **Services:** area transportation. **Cards:** AE, CB, DI, DS, MC, VI. (See color ad p 275)

THE REGENCY SUITES
Phone: (508)753-3512
AAA SAVE
All Year
1P: $75- 115   2P/1B: $85- 135   2P/2B: $105- 155   XP: $15
◆◆
Hotel
Location: I-290 exit 13, 0.5 mi n on SR 122. 70 Southbridge St 01608. Fax: 508/755-7104. **Terms:** Reserv deposit, 3 day notice; monthly rates; package plans. **Facility:** 108 rooms. Busy downtown location. 10 two-bedroom units. 10 stories; interior corridors; heated pool. **Dining:** 2 restaurants; 7 am-10 pm; $9-$13; cocktails. **All Rooms:** kitchens, extended cable TV. **Cards:** AE, CB, DI, MC, VI. **Special Amenities:** Free breakfast and free local telephone calls. (See color ad p 435)

RESTAURANTS

ARTURO'S RISTORANTE & PIZZERIA
Lunch: $6-$9   Dinner: $10-$15   Phone: 508/755-5640
◆◆◆
Northern
Italian
Location: 2 mi n on SR 122 (Chandler Sq Shopping Center); I-290, exit 13. 411 Chandler St 01602. **Hours:** 11:30 am-3 & 5-10 pm, Sat from 5 pm. Closed major holidays & Sun. **Reservations:** suggested; weekends. **Features:** casual dress; children's menu; carryout; cocktails & lounge; a la carte. Contemporary informal dining room. Pizzeria open 11:30 am-11 pm, Sun 1 pm-10 pm. **Cards:** AE, MC, VI.

MAXWELL SILVERMAN'S TOOLHOUSE
Lunch: $5-$8   Dinner: $10-$22   Phone: 508/755-1200
◆◆
American
Location: At Lincoln Square. 25 Union St 01608. **Hours:** 11:30 am-10 pm, Fri & Sat-11 pm, Sun 11 am-2:30 & 4-10 pm. Closed: 12/25. **Reservations:** suggested. **Features:** casual dress; Sunday brunch; children's menu; early bird specials; carryout; cocktails & lounge. Trendy dining rooms in restored factory building. **Cards:** AE, DI, MC, VI.

THE SOLE PROPRIETOR
Lunch: $7-$9   Dinner: $13-$20   Phone: 508/798-3474
◆◆
Seafood
Location: Downtown, 0.7 mi w of I-290 exit 17. 118 Highland St 01609. **Hours:** 11:30 am-10 pm, Fri & Sat-11 pm, Sun 4-9:30 pm. Closed: 11/25 & 12/25. **Reservations:** accepted. **Features:** casual dress; children's menu; senior's menu; carryout; cocktails & lounge; a la carte. Traditional & creative seafood served in upscale casual ambiance. Popular with locals. **Cards:** AE, DS, MC, VI.

YARMOUTH PORT—See Cape Cod p. 387.

Rhode Island

BLOCK ISLAND—800

RESTAURANT

FINN'S SEAFOOD RESTAURANT   **Lunch:** $7-$20   **Dinner:** $7-$20   **Phone:** 401/466-2473
◆
Seafood
Location: At Old Harbor opposite the ferry docks. 212 Water St 02807. **Hours:** Open 5/26-10/11; 11:30 am-10 pm, to 9 pm, 9/6-10/11, Fri & Sat-10:30 pm. **Features:** No A/C; casual dress; carryout; cocktails; street parking; a la carte. Relaxed, informal dining overlooking the harbor. Outdoor patio. **Cards:** AE, MC, VI.
   ✕

BRISTOL—21,600   (See map p. 446; index p. 444)

LODGINGS

BRADFORD-DIMOND-NORRIS HOUSE BED & BREAKFAST Rates Subject to Change **Phone:** (401)253-6338   **3**
◆ ◆ ◆   All Year [BP]   1P: $85- 100   2P/1B: $85- 100 2P/2B: $85- 100 XP: $20
Historic Bed   **Location:** Center on SR 114. 474 Hope St 02809. Fax: 401/253-4023. **Terms:** Age restrictions may apply;
& Breakfast   reserv deposit, 10 day notice. **Facility:** 4 rooms. Federal style with victorian updates, dating from 1792. Most rooms are large with canopy or 4-poster bed. 2 two-bedroom units. 3 stories; interior corridors; smoke free premises. **All Rooms:** shower baths. **Cards:** AE, MC, VI.
   ⌖ ⓩ 🖨 ✕

ROCKWELL HOUSE INN   Rates Subject to Change   **Phone:** (401)253-0040   **1**
◆ ◆ ◆   All Year [BP]   1P: $80- 130   2P/1B: $80- 130 2P/2B: $80- 130 XP: $30
Historic Bed   **Location:** Center on SR 114. 610 Hope St 02809-1945. Fax: 401/253-1811. **Terms:** Age restrictions may
& Breakfast   apply; reserv deposit, 14 day notice; 2 night min stay, weekends in season. **Facility:** 4 rooms. Restored 1809 inn with high ceilings & several fireplaces. 2 stories; interior corridors; smoke free premises.
All Rooms: combo or shower baths. **Cards:** AE, DS, MC, VI.
   ⌖ ⓩ Ⓚ 🖨 ✕

WILLIAM'S GRANT INN   Rates Subject to Change   **Phone:** 401/253-4222   **2**
◆ ◆ ◆   5/1-10/31 & 4/1-4/30 [BP]   1P: $95- 105   2P/1B: $95- 105   XP: $15
   11/1-3/31 [BP]   1P: $85- 95   2P/1B: $85- 95   XP: $10
Historic Bed   **Location:** From SR 114, just e on Constitution St, just s. 154 High St 02809. **Terms:** Age restrictions may
& Breakfast   apply; reserv deposit, 14 day notice; handling fee imposed; 2 night min stay, weekends in season. **Facility:** 5 rooms. Federal Colonial home circa 1808 with charming, individual & sometimes whimsical room decors. Quiet tree-lined setting. Gracious hospitality. 3 stories, no elevator; interior corridors; smoke free premises. **Cards:** AE, DS, MC, VI.
   ⌂ⓈK Ⓢ ⌖ ⓩ Ⓚ 🖨 ✕

CHARLESTOWN—6,500

LODGING

WILLOWS RESORT MOTEL   **Phone:** 401/364-7727
🅐🅐🅐 SAVE   6/18-9/6   2P/1B: $93- 122 2P/2B: $122- 135 XP: $16   F18
   5/14-6/17 & 9/7-10/12   2P/1B: $54- 69 2P/2B: $59- 75 XP: $16   F18
◆ ◆   **Location:** On US 1; 8 mi n of jct SR 78 Westerly bypass. 5310 Post Rd, Rt 1 02813 (PO Box 1260).
Motor Inn   Fax: 401/364-0576. **Terms:** Open 5/14-10/12; reserv deposit, 3 day notice, 42 days for efficiencies; handling fee imposed; weekly/monthly rates; BP, MAP avail; package plans; 2 night min stay, weekends in season.
Facility: 50 rooms. Peaceful setting with rolling, spacious grounds overlooking inlet. Variety of rooms. 3 two-bedroom units. 1 two-bedroom housekeeping apartment & efficiencies, $550-$1300 in season; 2 stories; exterior corridors; 1 tennis court; boat dock, boat ramp. **Dining:** Dining room; 5 pm-9 pm; also 7:30-10 am, 6/22-9/2; $12-$20; cocktails. **Recreation:** fishing, golf practice range; horseshoes, shuffleboard. Rental: boats, canoes, paddleboats. **All Rooms:** combo or shower baths. **Some Rooms:** 13 efficiencies. **Cards:** MC, VI.
   ➤ 🍴 ⌂ ✕ 🖥 ⛁ 🖨 🛄 ✕

RESTAURANT

NORDIC LODGE RESTAURANT   **Lunch:** $43   **Dinner:** $43   **Phone:** 401/783-4515
◆ ◆   **Location:** I-95 exit 3A, 6.5 mi e on SR 138, 4.8 mi s on SR 2, then 3 mi se following signs; or US 1, Kenyon
American   exit, 4.8 mi n on SR 2, then 3 mi se following signs. 178 E Pasquisett Tr 02813. **Hours:** Open 5/1-12/12 & 4/17-4/30; Fri 5 pm-9 pm, Sat from 3 pm, Sun 1 pm-7 pm; Thurs 5 pm-9 pm 7/9-8/23. **Features:** casual dress; children's menu; cocktails & lounge; buffet. A giant Viking smorgasbord featuring steamed lobster, shrimp, beef & Italian entrees. All you can eat in a jovial, rustic ambiance. Rural area. Call for detailed directions & complete menu. Dates are approx. Smoke free premises. **Cards:** AE, DI, DS, MC, VI.
   ✕

CHEPACHET—1,000

RESTAURANTS

PURPLE CAT RESTAURANT   **Lunch:** $4-$7   **Dinner:** $7-$17   **Phone:** 401/568-7161
◆◆   **Location:** Center on SR 100 at jct US 44 & SR 102. Money Hill Rd 02814. **Hours:** 11:30 am-2 & 4:30-9 pm,
American   Sat noon-9 pm, Sun noon-8 pm. Closed: 11/25, 12/25 & Mon. **Reservations:** accepted. **Features:** casual
dress; children's menu; carryout; cocktails. Featuring steak, chops, seafood & Italian specialties served in
casual country atmosphere. **Cards:** AE, DI, MC, VI.   ⊠

STAGECOACH TAVERN RESTAURANT   **Lunch:** $4-$10   **Dinner:** $8-$17   **Phone:** 401/568-2275
◆◆   **Location:** On US 44, just e of jct SR 102/100, in village center. Putnam Pike, Rt 44 02814. **Hours:** 11:30
American   am-9 pm, Fri & Sat-10 pm, Sun noon-9 pm. Closed: 12/25, also Mon & Tues except major holidays falling on
Mon. **Reservations:** suggested; for dinner. **Features:** casual dress; children's menu; carryout; salad bar;
cocktails & lounge. Friendly, relaxed, candlelit dining in a Colonial ambiance. A restored 1700's tavern, once a main stop
along the Providence to Massachusetts stagecoach lines. Family operated. **Cards:** AE, MC, VI.   ⊠

EAST GREENWICH—11,900   (See map p. 457; index p. 456)

RESTAURANT

TWENTY WATER STREET &
WAREHOUSE TAVERN   **Lunch:** $6-$10   **Dinner:** $14-$23   **Phone:** 401/885-3700   54
◆◆   **Location:** On the waterfront, 0.3 mi e of US 1, Main St, at foot of King St. 20 Water St 02818.
American   **Hours:** noon-2:30 & 6-9 pm, Fri-10 pm, Sat 6 pm-10 pm, Sun 4 pm-9 pm. Closed: 12/25.
Reservations: suggested; weekends. **Features:** casual dress; cocktails & lounge; a la carte. Overlooking
harbor. Seafood specialties. Valet parking 5/1-9/21. Casual tavern & outdoor deck serving light fare menu in season.
Cards: AE, DI, DS, MC, VI.   ⊠

EAST PROVIDENCE—50,400   (See map p. 457; index p. 456)

RESTAURANT

GREGG'S RESTAURANT & PUB   **Lunch:** $4-$7   **Dinner:** $6-$11   **Phone:** 401/438-5700   56
◆◆   **Location:** At jct SR 114, Pawtucket Ave & US 44, Taunton Ave. 1940 Pawtucket Ave, Rt 114 02914.
American   **Hours:** 11:30 am-midnight, Fri & Sat-1 am. Closed: 11/25 & 12/25. **Features:** casual dress; children's menu;
health conscious menu; carryout; cocktails & lounge. Very popular, bustling cheerful ambiance. Well worth
the short wait in line. Daily specials, sandwiches & salad. Famous for wide variety of homemade pastry & dessert. Friendly,
fast-paced service. **Cards:** AE, DS, MC, VI.   ♿ ⊠

GALILEE

LODGING

THE LIGHTHOUSE INN   Rates Subject to Change   **Phone:** 401/789-9341

◆◆	Fri & Sat 6/15-9/7	2P/1B: $130	2P/2B: $130	XP: $10	F12
Motor Inn	Sun-Thurs 6/15-9/7	2P/1B: $95	2P/2B: $95	XP: $10	F12
	Fri & Sat 5/1-6/14 & 9/8-4/30	2P/1B: $65- 95	2P/2B: $65- 95	XP: $10	F12
	Sun-Thurs 5/1-6/14 & 9/8-4/30	2P/1B: $55- 75	2P/2B: $55- 75	XP: $10	F12

Location: Opposite Block Island Ferry dock. 307 Great Island Rd 02882. Fax: 401/789-1590. **Terms:** Check-in 4 pm; reserv
deposit, 3 day notice. **Facility:** 100 rooms. 2 stories; interior/exterior corridors; heated indoor pool. **Cards:** AE, DS, MC, VI.

JAMESTOWN—5,000   (See map p. 446; index p. 445)

LODGING

THE BAY VOYAGE   Rates Subject to Change   **Phone:** (401)423-2100   48

AAA	5/1-10/31	2P/1B: $115- 260	2P/2B: $115- 260
	4/1-4/30	2P/1B: $75- 165	2P/2B: $75- 165
◆◆◆	11/1-3/31	2P/1B: $70- 135	2P/2B: $70- 135
Cottage			

Location: 0.5 mi s of SR 138 from Jamestown exit, just w of bridge toll. 150 Conanicus Ave 02835 (PO Box
2000, NEWPORT, 02840). Fax: 401/423-3209. **Terms:** Check-in 4 pm. **Facility:** 32 rooms. Overlooking the
harbor. A few rooms have deck. Nicely furnished units, some of which tend toward small. 3 stories; interior corridors; sauna,
whirlpool. **Dining:** Dining room; 5:30 pm-10:30 pm, Sun 10 am-2 pm; $18-$32. **All Rooms:** efficiencies. **Cards:** AE, CB, DI,
DS, MC, VI.

JOHNSTON—26,500   (See map p. 457; index p. 455)

LODGING

HI-WAY MOTOR INN   Rates Subject to Change   **Phone:** 401/351-7810   1
AAA   All Year   1P: $42- 46   2P/1B: $42- 46   2P/2B: $50- 54   XP: $5
◆   **Location:** On US 6; 0.3 mi e of I-295, exit 6. 1880 Hartford Ave 02919. **Terms:** Weekly rates, 9/1-4/30.
Motel   **Facility:** 35 rooms. At-door parking. Very good housekeeping. 2 two-bedroom units. 1 story; exterior corridors.
All Rooms: combo or shower baths. **Cards:** AE, MC, VI.

KINGSTON—6,500

LODGING

WELCOME INN Rates Subject to Change **Phone:** 401/884-9300
◆
| | 5/1-11/30 | 1P: | $59 | 2P/1B: | $75 | | 2P/2B: | $85 | XP: $10 | F5 |
| Motel | 12/1-4/30 | 1P: | $39 | 2P/1B: | $45 | | 2P/2B: | $55 | XP: $10 | F5 |

Location: On US 1, 1 mi s of jct SR 402 (Frenchtown Rd); or, 3.5 mi n of jct SR 102. 6481 Post Rd (US 1) 02852. Fax: 401/885-8260. **Facility:** 20 rooms. 2 whirlpool rms, $125; exterior corridors. **All Rooms:** combo or shower baths. **Cards:** AE, DS, MC, VI. ⬛⬛⬛⬛

MATUNUCK—500

RESTAURANT

SEA HORSE GRILL & CABARET **Dinner:** $13-$18 **Phone:** 401/789-3030
◆◆ **Location:** 1.5 mi se of US 1N, Matunuck Beach Rd exit, follow signs to Theatre-By-The-Sea. 364 Card's
American Pond Rd 02879. **Hours:** Open 6/1-9/22; 5:30 pm-10 pm, Sun-9 pm. Closed: Mon. **Reservations:** required; weekends. **Features:** casual dress; carryout; cocktails & lounge; entertainment; a la carte. Relaxed dining on grounds of Theatre-by-the Sea surrounded by lovely gardens & an harbor walk. Light fare avail until midnight during the Late Night Cabaret. **Cards:** AE, MC, VI. ⬛

MIDDLETOWN—19,500 (See map p. 446; index p. 445)

LODGINGS

THE BAY WILLOWS INN Rates Subject to Change **Phone:** (401)847-8400 **13**
AAA
| | Fri & Sat 5/14-10/30 | 1P: | $79- 119 | 2P/1B: | $79- 119 | 2P/2B: | $79- 119 | XP: $10 | F18 |
| | Sun-Thurs 5/14-10/30 | 1P: | $39- 79 | 2P/1B: | $39- 79 | 2P/2B: | $39- 79 | XP: $10 | F18 |
◆ | 5/1-5/13 & 10/31-4/30 | 1P: | $29- 59 | 2P/1B: | $29- 59 | 2P/2B: | $29- 59 | XP: $10 | F18 |
Motel **Location:** On SR 138A; at jct of SR 138, E Main Rd. 1225 Aquidneck Ave 02842. Fax: 401/841-9823.
Terms: Reserv deposit, 3 day notice; 2 night min stay, weekends in season; pets, $10 extra charge.
Facility: 21 rooms. Only minutes from Newport's ocean beaches. 1 story; exterior corridors. **All Rooms:** combo or shower baths. **Cards:** AE, DS, MC, VI. (See color ad p 447) ⬛⬛⬛⬛

BUDGET HOST INNS Rates Subject to Change **Phone:** 401/849-4700 **8**
AAA
| | 5/1-9/12 | 1P: | $68- 98 | 2P/1B: | $68- 98 | 2P/2B: | $68- 115 | XP: $10 | F18 |
| | 9/13-11/1 | 1P: | $48- 98 | 2P/1B: | $48- 98 | 2P/2B: | $48- 115 | XP: $5 | F18 |
◆◆ | 4/1-4/30 | 1P: | $38- 68 | 2P/1B: | $38- 68 | 2P/2B: | $38- 68 | XP: $5 | F18 |
Motel **Location:** On SR 114, 1.1 mi n of jct SR 138. 1185 W Main Rd 02842. Fax: 401/848-7704. **Terms:** Open
5/1-11/1 & 4/1-4/30; small pets only. **Facility:** 77 rooms. 2 stories; interior/exterior corridors. **Cards:** AE, DI,
DS, MC, VI. (See color ad p 438) ⬛⬛⬛

COURTYARD BY MARRIOTT-NEWPORT/MIDDLETOWN Rates Subject to Change **Phone:** 401/849-8000 **9**
◆◆◆
	6/26-9/18	1P: $209	2P/1B: $209	2P/2B: $209
Motel	5/14-6/25 & 9/19-10/15	1P: $159	2P/1B: $159	2P/2B: $159
	5/1-5/13	1P: $109	2P/1B: $109	2P/2B: $109
	10/16-4/30	1P: $69	2P/1B: $69	2P/2B: $69

Location: On SR 114 in Newport Corporate Park; 0.5 mi n of jct SR 138. 9 Commerce Dr 02842. Fax: 401/849-8313.
Terms: Check-in 4 pm; reserv deposit; handling fee imposed; 2 night min stay, weekends. **Facility:** 148 rooms. Many units with balcony or patio overlook an attractively landscaped center courtyard with gazebo. Maximum rate is for up to 5 persons; 3 stories; interior corridors; heated indoor/outdoor pool. **Cards:** AE, DI, DS, MC, VI. (See color ad p 448) ⬛⬛⬛⬛⬛⬛⬛⬛⬛⬛⬛

HOWARD JOHNSON INN-NEWPORT **Phone:** (401)849-2000 **14**
AAA SAVE
| | Fri & Sat 5/1-10/23 | 1P: | $74- 159 | 2P/1B: | $79- 159 | 2P/2B: | $84- 164 | XP: $5 | F18 |
| | Sun-Thurs 5/1-10/23 | 1P: | $49- 104 | 2P/1B: | $54- 104 | 2P/2B: | $59- 109 | XP: $5 | F18 |
◆◆ | Fri & Sat 10/24-4/30 | 1P: | $34- 79 | 2P/1B: | $39- 79 | 2P/2B: | $39- 84 | XP: $5 | F18 |
Motel | Sun-Thurs 10/24-4/30 | 1P: | $34- 54 | 2P/1B: | $39- 54 | 2P/2B: | $39- 59 | XP: $5 | F18 |
Location: On SR 114, 0.3 mi s of jct SR 138. 351 W Main Rd 02842. Fax: 401/849-6047. **Terms:** Weekly
rates; pets, selected rooms. **Facility:** 155 rooms. 2 stories; interior corridors; heated indoor pool, sauna, whirlpool; 2 tennis courts. **Dining:** Restaurant nearby. **Cards:** AE, CB, DI, DS, MC, VI. **Special Amenities:** Free local telephone calls and free newspaper. ⬛⬛⬛⬛⬛⬛⬛⬛⬛⬛⬛

POLLY'S PLACE Rates Subject to Change **Phone:** (401)847-2160 **15**
◆◆
	10/1-10/20 [BP]	1P:	$95- 135	2P/1B:	$95- 135
Bed &	5/1-5/31 & 10/21-4/30 [BP]	1P:	$85- 95	2P/1B:	$85- 95
Breakfast	6/1-9/30 [EP]	1P:	$80- 100	2P/1B:	$80- 100
Location: On SR 214, 0.5 mi se of jct SR 138. 349 Valley Rd 02842. **Terms:** Age restrictions may apply;
reserv deposit, 7 day notice; 2 night min stay, weekends in season. **Facility:** 4 rooms. A comfortable cape style home in a quiet residental area. Private bath $130, shared bath $90; 2 stories; interior corridors; smoke free premises. ⬛⬛⬛⬛⬛

ROYAL PLAZA HOTEL Rates Subject to Change **Phone:** (401)846-3555 **10**
AAA
| | 9/7-10/11 [CP] | 1P: | $79- 129 | 2P/1B: | $79- 179 | 2P/2B: | $99- 199 | XP: $20 | F13 |
| | 5/29-9/6 [EP] | 1P: | $79- 125 | 2P/1B: | $79- 125 | 2P/2B: | $99- 145 | XP: $20 | F13 |
◆◆◆ | 5/1-5/28 & 10/12-12/15 [EP] | 1P: | $39- 99 | 2P/1B: | $39- 99 | 2P/2B: | $49- 99 | XP: $20 | F13 |
Motel **Location:** At jct SR 138A. 425 E Main Rd, Rt 138 02842. Fax: 401/846-3666. **Terms:** Open 5/1-12/15; reserv deposit, 3 day notice; handling fee imposed; 2 night min stay, weekends 5/11-10/12. **Facility:** 75 rooms. A spacious, elegant lobby with Italian marble floors & sweeping staircase. Large, tastefully decorated guest rooms. Some 2-room suites & a few smaller 3rd floor rooms. 2 deluxe suites, $250 in season; 10 regular suites, $189 in season. Max of 4 persons per room; 2 stories; interior corridors. **Dining:** Cocktail lounge open weekends in season. **All Rooms:** combo or shower baths. **Some Rooms:** whirlpools. **Cards:** AE, DI, DS, MC, VI. ⬛⬛⬛⬛⬛⬛⬛⬛

(See map p. 446)

SEA BREEZE INN Phone: 401/849-1211 ⑱

(AAA) (SAVE) 5/7-10/11 1P: $125- 165 2P/1B: $125- 165
◆◆◆ 5/1-5/6 & 3/27-4/30 1P: $65- 95 2P/1B: $65- 95
Motel 10/12-3/26 1P: $55- 85 2P/1B: $55- 85

Location: 1.8 mi ne on SR 138A. 147 Aquidneck Ave 02842. Fax: 401/846-8335. **Terms:** Reserv deposit, 7 day notice; weekly/monthly rates; 2 night min stay, weekends in season. **Facility:** 8 rooms. All rooms open onto deck with view of either ocean or salt water pond. All rooms with hair dryer. 1 room with 2 queen beds, $165-$225; $85-$125 off season; 2 stories; interior corridors; smoke free premises. **Dining:** Coffee shop; breakfast & lunch served, light dinner in season; 8 am-10 pm, to 4 pm off season; $2-$7. **All Rooms:** combo or shower baths, extended cable TV. **Cards:** AE, MC, VI.

🆂🅳 🍽 🎬 💻 ▭ 🖨 🄴 ✕

SEAVIEW INN Rates Subject to Change Phone: (401)846-5000 ⑯

(AAA) Fri & Sat 5/14-10/30 [CP] 1P: $99- 159 2P/1B: $99- 159 2P/2B: $99- 159 XP: $20 F12
◆ Sun-Thurs 5/14-10/30 [CP] 1P: $59- 109 2P/1B: $59- 109 2P/2B: $59- 109 XP: $20 F12
Motel 5/1-5/13 & 10/31-4/30 [CP] 1P: $49- 89 2P/1B: $49- 89 2P/2B: $49- 89 XP: $20 F12

Location: On SR 138A at jct SR 214. 240 Aquidneck Ave 02842. Fax: 401/848-0873. **Terms:** Reserv deposit; weekly/monthly rates; 2 night min stay, weekends in season; $10 extra charge, $25 dep req. **Facility:** 41 rooms. On a small hill with large lawn & a panoramic view of the ocean. 1 two-bedroom unit. Suites, $100-$250 for up to 2 persons; 2 stories; exterior corridors. **Recreation:** bicycles. **All Rooms:** extended cable TV. **Some Rooms:** kitchen. **Cards:** AE, DS, MC, VI. (See color ad p 451)

🛏 ✕ 🚼 💻 🖨 🄴 ✕

SEA WHALE MOTEL Phone: (401)846-7071 ⑰

(AAA) (SAVE) 5/22-9/19 2P/1B: $78- 119 2P/2B: $78- 119 XP: $10 F12
◆◆ 9/20-10/12 2P/1B: $60- 90 2P/2B: $60- 90 XP: $10 F12
Motel 5/1-5/21 2P/1B: $60- 80 2P/2B: $60- 80 XP: $10 F12
10/13-4/30 2P/1B: $37- 47 2P/2B: $37- 47 XP: $10 F12

Location: 1.8 mi ne on SR 138A. 150 Aquidneck Ave 02842 (PO Box 3702, NEWPORT, 02840). **Terms:** Reserv deposit, 7 day notice; weekly rates. **Facility:** 16 rooms. Peaceful setting overlooking Easton's Pond. All rooms with garden patio or sun deck. Picnic grounds. 2 stories; exterior corridors. **All Rooms:** extended cable TV. **Cards:** AE, MC, VI. **Special Amenities:** Free local telephone calls and preferred room (subject to availability with advanced reservations).

🖨 🄴 ✕

WEST MAIN LODGE-NEWPORT/MIDDLETOWN Phone: (401)849-2718 ⑦

(AAA) (SAVE) Fri & Sat 7/1-9/6 2P/2B: $129 XP: $15 F12
◆◆ 5/1-6/30 & 9/7-10/31 2P/2B: $59- 105 XP: $10-15 F12
Motel Sun-Thurs 7/1-9/6 2P/2B: $69 XP: $10 F12
11/1-11/30 & 3/1-4/30 2P/2B: $39- 49 XP: $10 F12

Location: On SR 114; 1.4 mi n of jct SR 138. 1359 W Main Rd 02842. Fax: 401/849-2798. **Terms:** Open 5/1-11/30 & 3/1-4/30; reserv deposit, 3 day notice. **Facility:** 55 rooms. Second floor rooms have balcony. 2 stories; interior corridors. **All Rooms:** extended cable TV. **Cards:** AE, CB, DI, DS, JC, MC, VI. **Special Amenities:** Free local telephone calls and preferred room (subject to availability with advanced reservations). (See color ad p 450)

🆂🅳 🖨 🄴 ✕

RESTAURANTS

ANDREW'S GRILL & PASTA Lunch: $6-$11 Dinner: $12-$19 Phone: 401/848-5153 ④
◆◆◆ **Location:** On SR 138, 1 mi n of jct SR 138/138A; in Eastgate Center. 909 E Main Rd 02842. **Hours:** 11:30 am-2:30 & 4:30-9:30 pm, Fri & Sat-10 pm, Sun 10 am-9:30 pm. Closed: 11/25 & 12/25.
American **Reservations:** suggested. **Features:** casual dress; Sunday brunch; children's menu; early bird specials; carryout; cocktails & lounge. Wide variety of creative gourmet entrees featuring fresh local seafood, steak & unique pasta creations. Skilled chef/owner. **Cards:** AE, MC, VI. ✕

BATIK GARDEN RESTAURANT Lunch: $5-$12 Dinner: $5-$12 Phone: 401/848-0663 ⑤
◆ **Location:** On SR 138, just e of jct SR 114, in Aquidneck Shopping Center. 99 E Main Rd, Rt 138 02842.
Chinese **Hours:** 11 am-10 pm, Fri & Sat-11 pm, Sun noon-10 pm. **Reservations:** accepted. **Features:** casual dress; children's menu; carryout; cocktails; a la carte. Pleasant family dining featuring Szechuan, Hunan, Cantonese & Asian-Chinese cuisine. Also, curries & satay entrees. **Cards:** AE, DI, DS, MC, VI. ✕

JOHNNY'S ATLANTIC BEACH CLUB Lunch: $6-$11 Dinner: $6-$20 Phone: 401/847-2750 ⑥
◆◆ **Location:** On SR 138A at Easton's Beach. 55 Purgatory Rd 02842. **Hours:** 11:30 am-10 pm, Fri & Sat-11 pm. Closed: 12/25. **Reservations:** suggested. **Features:** casual dress; children's menu; early bird specials;
American carryout; cocktails & lounge. Popular, upscale dining with lovely ocean view. Featuring local fresh seafood. Lighter fare at beachfront grill in season. **Cards:** AE, CB, DI, DS, MC, VI. ✕

MISQUAMICUT—100

LODGING

BREEZEWAY RESORT MOTEL   Rates Subject to Change   **Phone:** 401/348-8953

(AAA)

♦♦♦   6/20-9/2 [CP]   1P: $124- 139   2P/1B: $124- 139   2P/2B: $124- 139   XP: $10-25
Motel   Fri & Sat 5/1-6/19 &
        9/3-10/23 & 4/9-4/30 [CP]   1P: $109   2P/1B: $109   2P/2B: $109   XP: $10-25
        Sun-Thurs 5/1-6/19 &
        9/3-10/23 & 4/9-4/30 [CP]   1P: $79   2P/1B: $79   2P/2B: $79   XP: $10-25

Location: 0.3 mi s of SR 1A, 0.3 mi n of beach. 70 Winnapaug Rd 02891 (PO Box 1368, WESTERLY). Fax: 401/596-3207.
Terms: Open 5/1-10/23 & 4/9-4/30; reserv deposit, 15 day notice; weekly rates; package plans; 3 night min stay, weekends in season. **Facility:** 45 rooms. Beautifully landscaped grounds with hand-crafted fountains. Wide variety of room styles & furnishings. 2 units are 0.3 mi from main property overlooking the ocean across the street & above restaurant. 3 efficiencies, $144 for up to 2 persons & 2 two-bedroom units, $980-$1540 weekly. 3 one-bedroom units, $149-$179; 1-2 stories; exterior corridors; heated pool; playground. **Recreation:** shuffleboard. **All Rooms:** combo or shower baths, extended cable TV. **Some Rooms:** whirlpools. **Cards:** AE, CB, DI, DS, MC, VI. *(See color ad below)*

NARRAGANSETT—3,700

LODGING

THE VILLAGE INN AT NARRAGANSETT PIER   Rates Subject to Change   **Phone:** 401/783-6767

(AAA)

♦♦   6/14-9/6   1P: $156- 201   2P/1B: $156- 201   2P/2B: $156- 201   XP: $1-10   F12
Motor Inn 5/22-6/13 & 9/7-11/1   1P: $114- 145   2P/1B: $114- 145   2P/2B: $114- 145   XP: $1-100   F12
        5/1-5/21   1P: $81- 111   2P/1B: $81- 111   2P/2B: $81- 111   XP: $1-10   F12
        11/2-4/30   1P: $70- 90   2P/1B: $70- 90   2P/2B: $70- 90   XP: $1-10   F12

Location: On SR 1A opposite the town beach & the post office. 1 Beach St 02882. Fax: 401/782-2220.
Terms: Reserv deposit, 7 day notice; package plans; 2 night min stay, weekends in season. **Facility:** 60 rooms. Near scenic Narragansett Bay & sandy beach. Some units with ocean view & some with private balcony. 3 stories; interior corridors; heated indoor pool, whirlpool. **Dining:** Restaurant, coffee shop; Coffeeshop 6 am-2 pm & restaurant noon-10 pm. **All Rooms:** extended cable TV. **Cards:** AE, CB, DI, DS, MC, VI. *(See color ad p 443)*

Choose an establishment with the next to its listing!

RESTAURANTS

BASIL'S
♦♦♦
Continental

Dinner: $15-$27

Location: Center, opposite shopping plaza. 22 Kingstown Rd 02882. **Hours:** 5:30 pm-10 pm. Closed: 11/25, 12/25, Mon & Tues 9/3-6/25. **Reservations:** suggested. **Features:** dressy casual; cocktails. Intimate dining in a cozy Victorian setting. Creative entrees with emphasis on French preparations. **Cards:** AE, DI, MC, VI.

Phone: 401/789-3743

SPAIN RESTAURANT
♦♦♦
Continental

Dinner: $10-$17

Location: 2 mi se of SR 108, Scarborough State Beach exit. 1144 Ocean Rd 02882. **Hours:** 4 pm-10 pm, Sun 1 pm-9 pm. Closed: 11/25, 12/24, 12/25 & Mon. **Features:** dressy casual; cocktails. Specializing in Mediterranean influenced European cuisine, served in informal elegance reminiscent of a Spanish Court. **Cards:** AE, CB, DI, DS, MC, VI.

Phone: 401/783-9770

SPANISH TAVERN RESTAURANT
♦♦
Continental

Lunch: $9-$12   **Dinner:** $15-$18

Location: On SR 1A opposite the town beach & the post office; in The Village Inn at Narragansett Pier. 1 Beach St 02882. **Hours:** noon-10 pm, Sat-11 pm, Sun-9 pm. Closed: 11/25, 12/24 & 12/25. **Features:** casual dress; carryout; cocktails & lounge; a la carte. Formal dining with gourmet Spanish cuisine, featuring fresh seafood & paella entrees. Overlooking Narragansett Bay. Smoke free premises. **Cards:** AE, CB, DI, DS, MC, VI.

Phone: 401/783-3550

NEWPORT
pop. 28,200

This index helps you "spot" where approved accommodations are located on the detailed maps that follow. Rate ranges are for comparison only and show the property's high season. Turn to the listing page for more detailed rate information and consult display ads for special promotions. Restaurant rate range is for dinner, unless only lunch (L) is served.

Spotter/Map Pg.Number	OA	NEWPORT - Lodgings	Rating	Rate	Listing Page
20 / p. 446	AAA	Motel 6 - 1219	◆◆	$79	450
21 / p. 446	AAA	Best Western Mainstay Inn - see ad p 447	◆◆	$99-189 SAVE	447
22 / p. 446	AAA	Stella Maris Inn	◆◆◆	$125-195	452
23 / p. 446	AAA	Vanderbilt Hall	◆◆◆◆	$195-745 SAVE	452
24 / p. 446	AAA	The Beechtree Inn	◆◆◆	$125-215	447
25 / p. 446		The Clarkeston	◆◆◆	$105-245	448
26 / p. 446	AAA	The Burbank Rose	◆◆	$109-169 SAVE	448
27 / p. 446		The Melville House	◆◆◆	$125-165	449
28 / p. 446	AAA	Pilgrim House Inn - see color ad p 451	◆◆	$100-205	451
29 / p. 446	AAA	Inn at Newport Beach	◆◆	$159-289 SAVE	449
30 / p. 446		Cleveland House Inn	◆◆	$125-225	448
31 / p. 446		Brinley Victorian Inn	◆◆	$135-225	447
32 / p. 446		James B Finch House B & B	◆◆	$135-195	449
33 / p. 446	AAA	Mill Street Inn	◆◆	$135-215	449
34 / p. 446	AAA	The Hotel Viking	◆◆◆	$139-309 SAVE	449
35 / p. 446	AAA	Hydrangea House Inn	◆◆◆	$145-225	449
36 / p. 446	AAA	Spring Street Inn	◆◆	$115-269	452
37 / p. 446		The Old Beach Inn	◆◆◆	$135-185	451
38 / p. 446	AAA	Long Wharf Resort	◆◆◆	$270-515	449
39 / p. 446		The Francis Malbone House Inn	◆◆◆	$175-255	449
41 / p. 446		Sarah Kendall House B&B	◆◆◆	$145-225	452
43 / p. 446	AAA	Doubletree Islander Hotel - see ad p 448	◆◆◆	$199-269 SAVE	448
45 / p. 446	AAA	Newport Harbor Hotel & Marina - see color ad p 450	◆◆◆	$129-309 SAVE	450
46 / p. 446		Newport Marriott Hotel	◆◆◆	$265-295	451
		NEWPORT - Restaurants			
11 / p. 446		White Horse Tavern	◆◆◆	$22-35	453
13 / p. 446	AAA	The Sea Fare's American Cafe	◆◆	$7-15	453
15 / p. 446		Brick Alley Pub & Restaurant	◆◆	$12-18	452
16 / p. 446		The Windward Grille	◆◆◆	$11-25	453
17 / p. 446		The Commodore's Room at the Black Pearl	◆◆◆	$20-30	452
18 / p. 446		The Mooring	◆◆	$16-24	452
20 / p. 446	AAA	Salas' Upstairs Dining Room	◆	$5-20	453
21 / p. 446		Christie's of Newport	◆◆	$18-28	452
23 / p. 446	AAA	The Pier	◆◆	$15-20	453
26 / p. 446		Puerini's	◆◆	$11-20	453
27 / p. 446		Castle Hill Inn & Resort Dining Room	◆◆◆	$22-36	452

Nearby Accommodations

Spotter/Map Pg.Number	OA	BRISTOL - Lodgings	Rating	Rate	Listing Page
1 / p. 446		Rockwell House Inn	◆◆◆	$80-130	438
2 / p. 446		William's Grant Inn	◆◆◆	$95-105	438
3 / p. 446		Bradford-Dimond-Norris House Bed & Breakfast	◆◆◆	$85-100	438
		PORTSMOUTH - Lodgings			
5 / p. 446	AAA	Best Western Bay Point Inn & Conference Center	◆◆	$95-125 SAVE	454
6 / p. 446	AAA	Founder's Brook Motel & Suites - see ad p 450	◆◆	$89-139 SAVE	455

Spotter/Map Pg.Number	OA	PORTSMOUTH - Restaurant	Rating	Rate	Listing Page
① / p. 446		15 Point Road Restaurant	◆◆	$11-18	455
		MIDDLETOWN - Lodgings			
⑦ / p. 446	⊕	West Main Lodge-Newport/Middletown - see color ad p 450	◆◆	$59-129 [SAVE]	441
⑧ / p. 446	⊕	Budget Host Inns - see color ad p 438	◆◆	$68-115	440
⑨ / p. 446		Courtyard by Marriott-Newport/Middletown - see color ad p 448	◆◆◆	$209	440
⑩ / p. 446	⊕	Royal Plaza Hotel	◆◆◆	$99-199	440
⑬ / p. 446	⊕	The Bay Willows Inn - see color ad p 447	◆	$79-119	440
⑭ / p. 446	⊕	Howard Johnson Inn-Newport	◆◆	$84-164 [SAVE]	440
⑮ / p. 446		Polly's Place	◆◆	$95-135	440
⑯ / p. 446	⊕	SeaView Inn - see color ad p 451	◆	$99-159	441
⑰ / p. 446	⊕	Sea Whale Motel	◆◆	$78-119 [SAVE]	441
⑱ / p. 446	⊕	Sea Breeze Inn	◆◆◆	$125-165 [SAVE]	441
		MIDDLETOWN - Restaurants			
④ / p. 446		Andrew's Grill & Pasta	◆◆◆	$12-19	441
⑤ / p. 446		Batik Garden Restaurant	◆	$5-12	441
⑥ / p. 446		Johnny's Atlantic Beach Club	◆◆	$6-20	441
		JAMESTOWN - Lodgings			
㊽ / p. 446	⊕	The Bay Voyage	◆◆◆	$115-260	439

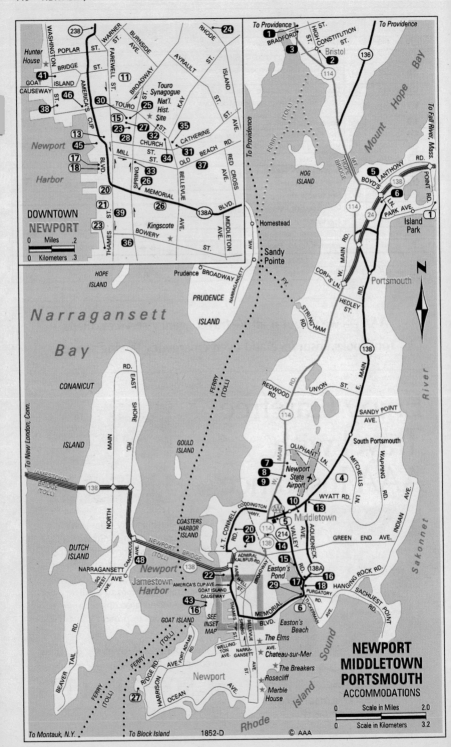

DOWNTOWN
NEWPORT

0   Miles   .2
0   Kilometers   .3

To Providence

To Providence

Hope Bay

Mount

Portsmouth

Narragansett

Bay

CONANICUT

ISLAND

Newport

Jamestown

Harbor

DUTCH

ISLAND

Sakonnet

River

NEWPORT
MIDDLETOWN
PORTSMOUTH
ACCOMMODATIONS

0   Scale in Miles   2.0
0   Scale in Kilometers   3.2

1852-D   © AAA

NEWPORT—28,200   (See map p. 446; index p. 444)

LODGINGS

THE BEECHTREE INN   Rates Subject to Change   **Phone:** (401)847-9794   **24**

Ⓐ Fri & Sat 5/1-10/31 [BP]   2P/1B: $125- 215 2P/2B: $125- 215 XP: $25   F12
Sun-Thurs 5/1-10/31 & Fri &
◆◆◆ Sat 11/1-4/30 [BP]   2P/1B: $79- 155 2P/2B: $79- 155 XP: $25   F12
Bed & Sun-Thurs 11/1-4/30 [BP]   2P/1B: $69- 125 2P/2B: $69- 125 XP: $25   F12
Breakfast **Location:** Just e of SR 114, 0.8 mi s of jct SR 138. 34 Rhode Island Ave 02840. Fax: 401/847-6824.
Terms: Reserv deposit, 14 day notice; handling fee imposed; weekly/monthly rates; 2 night min stay,
weekends. **Facility:** 7 rooms. Dating from 1887. 6 rooms with working fireplace; some with a deck. Water view from the 3rd
floor. 1 two-bedroom unit, 1 three-bedroom unit. 3 stories, no elevator; designated smoking area.
Services: Fee: massage. **All Rooms:** combo or shower baths, extended cable TV. **Some Rooms:** 2 kitchens, whirlpools.
Cards: AE, DS, MC, VI.

BEST WESTERN MAINSTAY INN   **Phone:** (401)849-9880   **21**

Ⓐ SAVE 7/2-9/5   1P: $99- 189 2P/1B: $99- 189 2P/2B: $99- 189 XP: $8   F12
5/14-7/1 & 9/6-10/30   1P: $68- 159 2P/1B: $68- 159 2P/2B: $68- 159 XP: $8   F12
◆◆ 5/1-5/13 & 1/1-4/30   1P: $40- 88 2P/1B: $40- 88 2P/2B: $40- 88 XP: $8   F12
Motor Inn 10/31-12/31   1P: $40- 68 2P/1B: $40- 68 2P/2B: $40- 68 XP: $8   F12
Location: On SR 138, opposite Jai Alai Fronton; from Newport Bridge, 2nd exit. 151 Admiral Kalbfus Rd
02840. Fax: 401/849-4391. **Terms:** 2 night min stay, 5/1-10/12. **Facility:** 165 rooms. Spacious guest rooms; many units with
2 double beds. Live entertainment Fri & Sat night. 3 stories, no elevator; interior corridors. **Dining:** Dining room; 6:30 am-10
pm; $10-$17; cocktails. **Cards:** AE, CB, DI, DS, MC, VI. **Special Amenities:** Early check-in/late check-out and free room
upgrade (subject to availability with advanced reservations). *(See ad below)*

BRINLEY VICTORIAN INN   Rates Subject to Change   **Phone:** (401)849-7645   **31**

◆◆ 5/1-11/1 [CP]   1P: $125- 199 2P/1B: $125- 199 2P/2B: $135- 225 XP: $15
Historic Bed 11/2-4/30 [CP]   1P: $95- 149 2P/1B: $95- 149 2P/2B: $125- 179 XP: $15
& Breakfast **Location:** Just e of Bellvue Ave between Kay & Catherine sts. 23 Brinley St 02840. Fax: 401/845-9634.
Terms: Age restrictions may apply; reserv deposit, 14 day notice; handling fee imposed; 2 night min stay,
weekends in season. **Facility:** 16 rooms. In quiet residential area. Circa 1850-1870, many Victorian furnishings. 1 suite with
working fireplace. 2 stories; interior corridors; smoke free premises. **All Rooms:** combo or shower baths. **Cards:** AE, MC,
VI.

(See map p. 446)

THE BURBANK ROSE Phone: (401)849-9457 26

AAA SAVE

◆◆

Historic Bed & Breakfast

5/1-10/1 [BP] 1P: $99- 149 2P/1B: $99- 169 2P/2B: $109- 169
10/2-4/30 [BP] 1P: $69- 129 2P/1B: $69- 129 2P/2B: $89- 129

Location: Just e on SR 138A. 111 Memorial Blvd W 02840. Fax: 401/848-9827. **Terms:** Age restrictions may apply; reserv deposit, 7 day notice; 2 night min stay, weekends in season. **Facility:** 4 rooms. Convenient to the waterfront. House dates to 1850. 3 stories, no elevator; interior corridors; smoke free premises. **All Rooms:** shower baths. **Some Rooms:** color TV. **Cards:** AE, DS. **Special Amenities:** Early check-in/late check-out and free local telephone calls.

THE CLARKESTON Rates Subject to Change Phone: 401/848-5300 25

◆◆◆

Historic Bed & Breakfast

5/24-10/13 [BP] 1P: $105- 245 2P/1B: $105- 245 2P/2B: $105- 195 XP: $15
5/1-5/23 & 10/14-4/30 [BP] 1P: $95- 225 2P/1B: $95- 225 2P/2B: $105- 175 XP: $15

Location: Downtown, just e of Thames St via Touro, follow right opposite Washington Sq onto narrow one-way Clarke St. 28 Clarke St 02840. Fax: 401/847-6071. **Terms:** Age restrictions may apply; reserv deposit, 15 day notice; handling fee imposed; 2 night min stay, weekends. **Facility:** 9 rooms. A 1705 Colonial. 5 rooms with working fireplace. Furnished with some antiques & reproductions. Featherbeds which may be removed upon request. 3 stories; interior corridors; smoke free premises. **All Rooms:** combo or shower baths. **Cards:** AE, MC, VI.

CLEVELAND HOUSE INN Rates Subject to Change Phone: 401/849-7397 30

◆◆

Bed & Breakfast

Fri & Sat 5/1-10/31 [CP] 2P/1B: $125- 225 2P/2B: $125- 225 XP: $15
Fri & Sat 11/1-4/30 [CP] 2P/1B: $65- 155 2P/2B: $65- 155 XP: $15
Sun-Thurs 5/1-10/31 [CP] 2P/1B: $75- 135 2P/2B: $75- 135 XP: $15
Sun-Thurs 11/1-4/30 [CP] 2P/1B: $65- 125 2P/2B: $65- 125 XP: $15

Location: Just e of Thames St via Touro, follow right opposite Washington Sq onto narrow one-way Clarke St. 27 Clarke St 02840. Fax: 401/847-6071. **Terms:** Age restrictions may apply; reserv deposit, 15 day notice; handling fee imposed; 2 night min stay, weekends. **Facility:** 12 rooms. A renovated Victorian home. Nicely decorated rooms. 3 stories; interior corridors; smoke free premises. **All Rooms:** combo or shower baths. **Cards:** AE, MC, VI.

DOUBLETREE ISLANDER HOTEL Phone: (401)849-2600 43

AAA SAVE

◆◆◆

Hotel

6/11-9/23 1P: $199- 269 2P/1B: $199- 269 2P/2B: $199- 269 XP: $15 F16
9/24-11/4 1P: $169- 229 2P/1B: $169- 229 2P/2B: $169- 229 XP: $15 F16
5/1-6/10 1P: $159- 219 2P/1B: $159- 219 2P/2B: $159- 219 XP: $15 F16
11/5-4/30 1P: $99- 144 2P/1B: $99- 144 2P/2B: $99- 144 XP: $15 F16

Location: 0.8 mi w of America's Cup Ave, following signs to Goat Island. Goat Island 02840. Fax: 401/846-7210. **Terms:** Check-in 4 pm; reserv deposit, 3 day notice; handling fee imposed; package plans; 2 night min stay, weekends in season. **Facility:** 264 rooms. Inviting public areas & vibrant modern room decors. Many units with harbor view. 1 two-bedroom unit. 2-9 stories; interior corridors; heated indoor pool, saunas, saltwater pool in season; 1 tennis court. **Dining:** Cocktails; also, The Windward Grille, see separate listing. **Services:** giftshop; area transportation, downtown. Fee: massage. **All Rooms:** combo or shower baths. **Some Rooms:** whirlpools. **Cards:** AE, CB, DI, DS, MC, VI. **Special Amenities:** Free local telephone calls and free newspaper. *(See ad below)*

(See map p. 446)

THE FRANCIS MALBONE HOUSE INN
◆◆◆
Historic Bed & Breakfast

Rates Subject to Change   Phone: 401/846-0392   39

5/1-10/31 [BP]	2P/1B: $175- 255	2P/2B: $225	XP: $30
11/1-4/30 [BP]	2P/1B: $145- 195	2P/2B: $175	XP: $30

Location: Downtown, just s of Memorial Blvd. 392 Thames St 02840. Fax: 401/848-5956. **Terms:** Age restrictions may apply; reserv deposit, 14 day notice; handling fee imposed; 3 night min stay, weekends 6/1-10/31. **Facility:** 18 rooms. A wonderful, extremely well-done Colonial mansion circa 1760. 15 rooms with working fireplace. Furnished with many reproductions & some antiques. 2 suites, $295-$355; 2-3 stories, no elevator; interior corridors; smoke free premises. **All Rooms:** combo or shower baths. **Some Rooms:** color TV. **Cards:** AE, MC, VI.

THE HOTEL VIKING
(AAA) [SAVE]
◆◆◆
Historic Hotel

Phone: (401)847-3300   34

Fri & Sat 5/1-10/31 & 4/1-4/30	1P: $139- 309	2P/1B: $139- 309	2P/2B: $139- 309	XP: $15	F17
Sun-Thurs 5/1-10/31 & 4/1-4/30	1P: $89- 189	2P/1B: $89- 189	2P/2B: $89- 189	XP: $15	F17
11/1-12/31	1P: $49- 129	2P/1B: $49- 129	2P/2B: $49- 129	XP: $15	F17
1/1-3/31	1P: $39- 109	2P/1B: $39- 109	2P/2B: $39- 109	XP: $39-109	F17

Location: Corner Kay, Bellevue & Church. One Bellevue Ave 02840. Fax: 401/848-4864. **Terms:** 3 night min stay, weekends. **Facility:** 185 rooms. Original portion on National Historic Register. Some small rooms. 1 two-bedroom unit. 5 stories; interior corridors; heated indoor pool, sauna, whirlpool. **Dining:** Dining room; 7 am-9 pm, Fri & Sat-10 pm 5/1-11/30; weekday hrs vary off season; $12-$20; cocktails. **Some Rooms:** color TV, whirlpools. **Cards:** AE, DI, DS, MC, VI.

HYDRANGEA HOUSE INN
(AAA)
◆◆◆
Historic Bed & Breakfast

Rates Subject to Change   Phone: 401/846-4435   35

Fri & Sat 5/1-6/30, 7/1-9/5 & Fri & Sat 9/6-10/31 [BP]	1P: $145- 225	2P/1B: $145- 225
Sun-Thurs 5/1-6/30 & 9/6-10/31 [BP]	1P: $125- 195	2P/1B: $125- 195
11/1-4/30 [BP]	1P: $100- 155	2P/1B: $100- 155

Location: Corner Kay, Bellevue & Church. 16 Bellevue Ave 02840. Fax: 401/846-6602. **Terms:** Age restrictions may apply; reserv deposit, 14 day notice; handling fee imposed; 3 night min stay, weekends; 2 weekdays; pets on premises. **Facility:** 6 rooms. Built in 1876. Many antiques & works of art. Elegant common room with fireplace. Suite with king bed, whirlpool, fireplace & color cable TV $280; $195 off season; 3 stories, no elevator; interior corridors; smoke free premises. **Dining:** Afternoon tea; restaurant nearby. **All Rooms:** combo or shower baths. **Cards:** AE, MC, VI.

INN AT NEWPORT BEACH
(AAA) [SAVE]
◆◆
Country Inn

Phone: (401)846-0310   29

Fri & Sat 5/1-10/31 & 4/1-4/30 [CP]	1P: $159- 289	2P/1B: $159- 289	2P/2B: $159- 289	XP: $15	F17
Sun-Thurs 5/1-10/31 & 4/1-4/30 [CP]	1P: $99- 159	2P/1B: $99- 159	2P/2B: $99- 159	XP: $15	F17
11/1-12/31 [CP]	1P: $39- 129	2P/1B: $39- 129	2P/2B: $39- 129	XP: $15	F17
1/1-3/31 [CP]	1P: $29- 99	2P/1B: $29- 99	2P/2B: $29- 99	XP: $15	F17

Location: 1.5 mi ne on SR 138A; across from Easton's Beach. Memorial Blvd 02840. Fax: 401/847-2621. **Terms:** Reserv deposit, 3 day notice; package plans; 2 night min stay, weekends in season. **Facility:** 50 rooms. Charming homey inn with a variety of room sizes & inviting individually-decorated, comfortably furnished units. Deluxe oceanview 4th level rooms. Relaxed setting opposite sandy ocean beach. 7 two-bedroom units. 3 deluxe suites, $250 for up to 2 persons; 4 stories; interior corridors. **All Rooms:** combo or shower baths. **Cards:** AE, DI, DS, MC, VI.

JAMES B FINCH HOUSE B & B
◆◆
Bed & Breakfast

Rates Subject to Change   Phone: 401/848-9700   32

5/1-11/1 [BP]	2P/1B: $135- 195	XP: $30
12/1-4/30 [BP]	2P/1B: $110- 165	XP: $30

Location: On Touro Street at Mt Vernon Street. 102 Touro St 02840. Fax: 401/848-9311. **Terms:** Open 5/1-11/1 & 12/1-4/30; check-in 4 pm; reserv deposit, 14 day notice; handling fee imposed. **Facility:** 6 rooms. Built in 1866 in the Renaissance Style by Champlin Mason a famous architect of the 'Newport Cottages'. 3 stories, no elevator; interior corridors; smoke free premises. **All Rooms:** combo or shower baths. **Cards:** MC, VI.

LONG WHARF RESORT
(AAA)
◆◆◆
Cottage

Rates Subject to Change   Phone: (401)847-7800   38

5/1-10/31	2P/2B: $270- 515
4/2-4/30	2P/2B: $165- 300
11/1-4/1	2P/2B: $135- 250

Location: Just w of America's Cup Blvd, behind the transportation center. 5 Washington St 02840 (PO Box 2000). Fax: 401/845-0127. **Terms:** Check-in 4 pm; 2 night min stay, weekends in season. **Facility:** 82 rooms. 73 two-bedroom units, 8 three-bedroom units. 4 stories; interior corridors; indoor pool, whirlpools. **Dining:** Restaurant nearby. **All Rooms:** kitchens. **Cards:** AE, CB, DI, DS, MC, VI.

THE MELVILLE HOUSE
◆◆◆
Historic Bed & Breakfast

Guaranteed Rates   Phone: (401)847-0640   27

5/1-10/31 [CP]	1P: $125- 165	2P/1B: $125- 165
11/1-12/3 [CP]	1P: $95- 125	2P/1B: $95- 125
12/4-4/30 [BP]	1P: $85- 125	2P/1B: $85- 125

Location: Downtown, just e of Thames St via Touro St, follow right opposite Washington Square onto narrow one-way Clarke St. 39 Clarke St 02840. Fax: 401/847-0956. **Terms:** Age restrictions may apply; reserv deposit, 14 day notice; handling fee imposed; 2 night min stay, weekends. **Facility:** 7 rooms. Colonial inn circa 1750 with antique furnishings. In the historic district. 1 fireplace suite avail 11/1-4/26. Suite with fireplace, $165; 2 stories; interior corridors; smoke free premises. **Recreation:** bicycles. **Cards:** AE, DS, MC, VI.

MILL STREET INN
(AAA)
◆◆
Suite Motel

Rates Subject to Change   Phone: (401)849-9500   33

7/1-9/30 [CP]	1P: $135- 215	2P/1B: $135- 215	2P/2B: $135- 215
5/1-6/30 & 10/1-10/31 [CP]	1P: $95- 155	2P/1B: $95- 155	2P/2B: $95- 155
11/1-11/30 [CP]	1P: $85- 115	2P/1B: $85- 115	2P/2B: $85- 115
12/1-4/30 [CP]	1P: $65- 105	2P/1B: $65- 105	2P/2B: $65- 105

Location: Off Thames St. 75 Mill St 02840. Fax: 401/848-5131. **Terms:** Reserv deposit, 5 day notice; handling fee imposed; package plans; 2 night min stay, weekends 3/1-10/31. **Facility:** 23 rooms. Contemporary 1-bedroom suites with living room in a restored 1815 saw mill. On the National Register of Historic Places. A few units with private harborview deck. Rooftop deck for continental breakfast in season. 2 stories; interior corridors. **Dining:** Afternoon tea. **All Rooms:** combo or shower baths, extended cable TV. **Cards:** AE, CB, DI, MC, VI.

(See map p. 446)

MOTEL 6 - 1219   Rates Subject to Change   **Phone:** 401/848-0600
All Year   1P: $69   2P/1B: $79   2P/2B: $79   XP: $6   F17
Location: 0.3 mi nw of Newport Bridge; near Newport Mall. 249 J T Connell Hwy 02840. Fax: 401/848-9966.
Terms: Pets, one pet per room. **Facility:** 77 rooms. Minutes from downtown Newport. Rates for up to 4 persons; 2 stories; interior corridors. **All Rooms:** combo or shower baths. **Cards:** AE, CB, DI, DS, MC, VI.

NEWPORT HARBOR HOTEL & MARINA   **Phone:** (401)847-9000
5/27-9/6   1P: $129- 309   2P/1B: $129- 309   2P/2B: $129- 309   XP: $15   F18
9/7-10/31   1P: $129- 269   2P/1B: $129- 269   2P/2B: $129- 269   XP: $15   F18
5/1-5/26   1P: $109- 199   2P/1B: $109- 199   2P/2B: $109- 199   XP: $15   F18
11/1-4/30   1P: $69- 189   2P/1B: $69- 189   2P/2B: $69- 189   XP: $15   F18
Location: On Newport Harbor. 49 America's Cup Ave 02840. Fax: 401/849-6380. **Terms:** Check-in 4 pm; reserv deposit, 3 day notice, 30 day 7/4-9/1; package plans; 2 night min stay, weekends in season. **Facility:** 133 rooms. Many rooms with harbor view. 4 stories; interior corridors; heated indoor pool, saunas; marina. Fee: parking. **Dining:** Dining room; 7 am-10 pm, Fri & Sat-11 pm; $15-$22; cocktails. **All Rooms:** combo or shower baths. **Cards:** AE, DI, DS, MC, VI.
Special Amenities: Free newspaper. (See color ad below)

(See map p. 446)

NEWPORT MARRIOTT HOTEL — Rates Subject to Change — Phone: (401)849-1000 **46**

◆◆◆ Hotel

	Rates Subject to Change			Phone: (401)849-1000
6/18-11/13	1P: $265- 295	2P/1B: $265- 295	2P/2B: $265- 295	
5/1-6/17 & 4/9-4/30	1P: $235- 265	2P/1B: $235- 265	2P/2B: $235- 265	
1/1-4/8	1P: $129- 149	2P/1B: $129- 149	2P/2B: $129- 149	
11/14-12/31	1P: $119- 139	2P/1B: $119- 139	2P/2B: $119- 139	

Location: Downtown on the Harbor; adjacent to Newport Visitor's Center. 25 America's Cup Ave 02840. Fax: 401/849-3422. **Terms:** Check-in 4 pm; reserv deposit, 3 day notice. **Facility:** 317 rooms. Historical town & harbor side location. Very large 7-story atrium; elegant public areas. Rates for up to 5 persons. 7 suites avail; 7 stories; interior corridors; heated indoor pool. Fee: parking; racquetball courts. **Services:** giftshop. Fee: massage. **Cards:** AE, DI, DS, MC, VI.

THE OLD BEACH INN

◆◆◆ Historic Bed & Breakfast

	Rates Subject to Change		Phone: 401/849-3479 **37**
5/1-10/31	1P: $135- 185	2P/1B: $135- 185	XP: $20
11/1-11/30 & 4/1-4/30	1P: $115- 165	2P/1B: $115- 165	XP: $20
12/1-3/31	1P: $85- 135	2P/1B: $85- 135	XP: $20

Location: Just e of Bellevue Ave. 19 Old Beach Rd 02840. Fax: 401/847-1236. **Terms:** Age restrictions may apply; reserv deposit, 15 day notice; handling fee imposed; 3 night min stay, weekends in season. **Facility:** 9 rooms. An 1879 Victorian home. Many period furnishings. 5 rooms with working fireplace. Relaxing landscaped courtyard. 3 stories; interior/exterior corridors; designated smoking area. **All Rooms:** combo or shower baths. **Some Rooms:** color TV. **Cards:** AE, DS, MC, VI.

PILGRIM HOUSE INN

ⓐⓐⓐ ◆◆ Bed & Breakfast

	Rates Subject to Change	Phone: (401)846-0040 **28**
8/1-8/31 [CP]	2P/1B: $100- 205	XP: $25
9/1-10/31 [CP]	2P/1B: $100- 175	XP: $25
11/1-4/30 [CP]	2P/1B: $55- 95	XP: $25
5/1-7/31 [CP]	2P/1B: $70- 165	XP: $25

Location: Just e of Thames St. 123 Spring St 02840. Fax: 401/848-0357. **Terms:** Age restrictions may apply; reserv deposit, 10 day notice; weekly rates; package plans; 2 night min stay, weekends. **Facility:** 11 rooms. A charming Victorian inn. Fee for parking 5/15-10/31. 3 stories, no elevator; interior corridors; designated smoking area; off site parking only. **Cards:** MC, VI. *(See color ad below)*

TAXES—state, city and local—are extra.
Allow for them; our listed rates do not.

(See map p. 446)

SARAH KENDALL HOUSE B&B — Rates Subject to Change — Phone: (401)846-7976 — **41**

Historic Bed & Breakfast

Fri & Sat 5/15-10/15 [BP]	1P: $145- 225	2P/1B: $145- 225	2P/2B: $145- 225	XP: $25	F12
Sun-Thurs 5/15-10/15 [BP]	1P: $125- 195	2P/1B: $125- 195	2P/2B: $125- 195	XP: $25	F12
Fri & Sat 5/1-5/14 & 3/16-4/30 [BP]	1P: $100- 195	2P/1B: $100- 195	2P/2B: $100- 195	XP: $25	F12
Sun-Thurs 5/1-5/14, 10/16-3/15 & Sun-Thurs 3/16-4/30 [BP]	1P: $75- 150	2P/1B: $75- 150	2P/2B: $75- 150	XP: $25	F12

Location: In historic district, just n from Newport Harbor, just nw of Gateway Visitor's Center between Elm & Bridge sts. 47 Washington St 02840. Fax: 401/849-2811. **Terms:** Age restrictions may apply; reserv deposit, 14 day notice; handling fee imposed; 2 night min stay, weekends. **Facility:** 4 rooms. Victorian home, circa 1871, facing the harbor. On the National Register of Historic Places. 3 stories, no elevator; interior corridors; designated smoking area. **All Rooms:** combo or shower baths. **Cards:** AE, MC, VI.

SPRING STREET INN — Rates Subject to Change — Phone: (401)847-4767 — **36**

Historic Bed & Breakfast

5/1-10/31 [BP]	1P: $115- 269	2P/1B: $115- 269	2P/2B: $115- 269	XP: $25
11/1-4/30 [BP]	1P: $75- 195	2P/1B: $75- 195	2P/2B: $75- 195	XP: $25

Location: Just e of Thames St. 353 Spring St 02840. **Terms:** Age restrictions may apply; reserv deposit, 10 day notice; handling fee imposed; weekly rates; package plans; 2 night min stay, weekends; pets on premises. **Facility:** 7 rooms. Afternoon refreshments. 1 two-bedroom unit. 1 one-bedroom with deck & harbor view, $165-$220 for up to 2 persons. 2-bedroom suite, $200-$269 for up to 4 persons in season; 3 stories, no elevator; interior corridors; smoke free premises. **All Rooms:** combo or shower baths. **Some Rooms:** kitchen. **Cards:** MC, VI.

STELLA MARIS INN — Rates Subject to Change — Phone: (401)849-2862 — **22**

Historic Bed & Breakfast

5/1-10/31 [CP]	1P: $115- 185	2P/1B: $125- 195	2P/2B: $125- 195	XP: $20	F10
11/1-4/30 [CP]	1P: $75- 140	2P/1B: $85- 150	2P/2B: $85- 150	XP: $20	F10

Location: In Historic District, 1 blk from Newport Harbor, 0.3 mi nw of Gateway Visitor's Center at jct Pine & Cherry sts. 91 Washington St 02840. **Terms:** Age restrictions may apply; reserv deposit, 6 day notice; handling fee imposed; weekly rates; 2 night min stay, weekends in season. **Facility:** 8 rooms. Stately red stone Victorian mansion with exterior porch circa 1861. Elegant public areas with 14-ft ceiling. Charming guest rooms, some units with oceanview & working fireplace. Antique furnishings. 3 stories; interior corridors; smoke free premises. **Dining:** Afternoon tea. **All Rooms:** combo or shower baths.

VANDERBILT HALL — Phone: (401)846-6200 — **23**

Historic Country Inn

5/29-10/12	1P: $195- 745	2P/1B: $195- 745	2P/2B: $195- 745	
5/1-5/28, 10/13-12/31 & 3/28-4/30	1P: $155- 565	2P/1B: $155- 565	2P/2B: $155- 565	
1/1-3/27	1P: $95- 460	2P/1B: $95- 460	2P/2B: $95- 460	

Location: Downtown, just n of Thames on one-way Mary St. 41 Mary St 02840. Fax: 401/846-0701. **Terms:** Reserv deposit, 14 day notice; handling fee imposed; 2 night min stay, weekends in season. **Facility:** 51 rooms. Restored 1909 hall, creating a grand house with elegant rooms, all individually appointed. In the Historic Hill District. 3 two-bedroom units. Junior & master suites $445-$720, in season; 4-5 stories; interior corridors; designated smoking area; heated indoor pool, sauna, steamroom, whirlpool. **Dining:** Dining room, restaurant; 4 & 5-course prix fixe $40-$50; 7:30 am-11 pm, also seasonal outdoor dining; $15-$22; cocktails; afternoon tea. **Services:** Fee: massage. **Recreation:** billiards room. **All Rooms:** extended cable TV. **Some Rooms:** whirlpools. **Cards:** AE, DI, DS, MC, VI.

RESTAURANTS

BRICK ALLEY PUB & RESTAURANT — Lunch: $6-$12 — Dinner: $12-$18 — Phone: 401/849-6334 — **15**
American
Location: Opposite the Brickmarket Place. 140 Thames St 02840. **Hours:** 11:30 am-9:30 pm, Fri & Sat-10:30 pm. Closed: 11/25, 12/24 for dinner & 12/25. **Reservations:** accepted. **Features:** casual dress; Sunday brunch; children's menu; early bird specials; carryout; cocktails; street parking; a la carte. Bustling casual dining in eclectic atmosphere. Limited menu, patio dining in season. Tex-Mex specialties Tuesdays. **Cards:** AE, CB, DI, DS, MC, VI.

CASTLE HILL INN & RESORT DINING ROOM — Country Inn — Lunch: $7-$12 — Dinner: $22-$36 — Phone: 401/849-3800 — **27**
Regional American
Location: 4.5 mi se on Ocean Ave via Ocean Dr. 590 Ocean Ave 02840. **Hours:** noon-3 & 6-9 pm, Fri & Sat-9:30 pm, Sun 11:30 am-3 & 6-9 pm. Closed: Sun for dinner. **Reservations:** required. **Features:** No A/C; dressy casual; Sunday brunch; cocktails & lounge; a la carte. Former summer home of Alexander Agassiz, geologist. Built in 1874. Overlooks Narragansett Bay. Smoke free premises. **Cards:** AE, DS, MC, VI.

CHRISTIE'S OF NEWPORT — Lunch: $6-$11 — Dinner: $18-$28 — Phone: 401/847-5400 — **21**
Steak and Seafood
Location: Off Thames St. Christie's Landing 02840. **Hours:** 11:30 am-9 pm, Fri-9:30 pm, Sat-10 pm, 5/1-10/31 11:30 am-10 pm, Fri-10:30 pm, Sat-11 pm. Closed: 11/25 & 12/25. **Reservations:** suggested. **Features:** casual dress; children's menu; carryout; cocktails & lounge; a la carte. Popular, lively harborside restaurant overlooking Newport Harbor. Outdoor upper deck dining in season. A local favorite since 1945. **Cards:** AE, DI, DS, MC, VI.

THE COMMODORE'S ROOM AT THE BLACK PEARL — Lunch: $7-$22 — Dinner: $20-$30 — Phone: 401/846-5264 — **17**
American
Location: At Bannister's Wharf. Bannister's Wharf 02840. **Hours:** Open 5/1-1/3 & 2/10-4/30; 11:30 am-3 & 6-10 pm. Closed: 11/25 & 12/25. **Reservations:** suggested; for diner. **Features:** semi-formal attire; cocktails; street parking. Intimate formal dining in warm candlelight, nautical setting. Lighter fare offered in the tavern. Lunch avail. Smoke free premises. **Cards:** AE, MC, VI.

THE MOORING — Lunch: $7-$14 — Dinner: $16-$24 — Phone: 401/846-2260 — **18**
Regional American
Location: Downtown on the waterfront. Sayer's Wharf 02840. **Hours:** 11:30 am-10 pm, Sat & Sun from noon, Fri & Sat in season-11 pm. Closed: 11/25 & 12/25. **Reservations:** suggested. **Features:** No A/C; casual dress; children's menu; carryout; cocktails; fee for parking; a la carte. Very popular. Outdoor patio dining in season. Contemporary New England cuisine. Fine yachting memorabilia in this original New York Yacht Club station house. **Cards:** AE, DI, DS, MC, VI.

(See map p. 446)

THE PIER
Ⓐ
◆◆
Steak and
Seafood

Lunch: $6-$12   Dinner: $15-$20   Phone: 401/849-3100   ㉓
Location: Off Thames St on W Howard St at W Howard Wharf. W Howard Wharf 02840. **Hours:** 11:30 am-10 pm, Fri & Sat-10:30 pm, Sun noon-10 pm. Closed: 1/1-2/28 & 12/25. **Features:** casual dress; children's menu; early bird specials; carryout; cocktails & lounge; a la carte. Popular harbor front dining rooms overlooking pier. Outdoor deck dining in season. Reservations suggested weekends & in season. **Cards:** AE, DI, DS, MC, VI.   ☒

PUERINI'S
◆◆
Italian

Dinner: $11-$20   Phone: 401/847-5506   ㉖
Location: Just w of Bellevue Ave. 24 Memorial Blvd W 02840. **Hours:** Open 5/1-2/1 & 3/1-4/30; 5 pm-9 pm, Fri & Sat-10 pm; 5/25-9/7 5 pm-10 pm, Fri & Sat-11 pm. Closed major holidays & Mon, except 5/25-9/8. **Features:** No A/C; casual dress; beer & wine only; street parking; a la carte. Intimate dining in casual atmosphere. Northern & Southern Italian cuisine with innovative touches. Smoke free premises. **Cards:** MC, VI.   ☒

SALAS' UPSTAIRS DINING ROOM
Ⓐ
◆
Italian

Dinner: $5-$20   Phone: 401/846-8772   ㉒
Location: Just off Memorial Blvd. 345 Thames St 02840. **Hours:** 5 pm-10 pm, Sat & Sun 4-10 pm. Closed: 11/25, 12/24 & 12/25. **Features:** No A/C; casual dress; carryout; cocktails & lounge; street parking; a la carte. Bustling, casual, family restaurant on 2nd floor. Oriental spaghetti a specialty. **Cards:** AE, DI, DS, MC, VI.   ☒

THE SEA FARE'S AMERICAN CAFE
Ⓐ
◆◆
American

Lunch: $7-$15   Dinner: $7-$15   Phone: 401/849-9188   ⑬
Location: America's Cup Ave & Thames St; at the Brick Marketplace. 151 Swinburne Row 02840. **Hours:** 11:30 am-9 pm, Fri & Sat-10 pm. Closed: 11/25, 12/24 & 12/25. **Reservations:** accepted. **Features:** casual dress; children's menu; carryout; cocktails & lounge; fee for parking. Relaxing, contemporary dining opposite harbor. Variety of gourmet entrees. Featuring pizza from a wood burning brick oven. Fresh seafood. Extensive wine list. **Cards:** AE, DI, DS, MC, VI.   ☒

WHITE HORSE TAVERN   Historical
◆◆◆
Continental

Lunch: $7-$16   Dinner: $22-$35   Phone: 401/849-3600   ⑪
Location: Corner of Marlborough & Farewell sts. **Hours:** noon-3 & 6-9:30 pm, Fri & Sat-10 pm. Closed: 12/24, 12/25 & Mon-Weds for lunch. **Reservations:** suggested; for dinner. **Features:** semi-formal attire; Sunday brunch; cocktails & lounge; a la carte. Gracious, formal dining in a historical setting. Extensive wine list. Smoke free premises. **Cards:** AE, DI, DS, MC, VI.   ☒

THE WINDWARD GRILLE
◆◆◆
Regional
American
VI.

Lunch: $6-$11   Dinner: $11-$25   Phone: 401/849-2600   ⑯
Location: 0.8 mi w of America's Cup Ave, following signs to Goat Island; in Doubletree Islander Hotel. Goat Island 02840. **Hours:** 6:30 am-10 pm 5/15-12/31; hours vary off season. **Reservations:** suggested; for dinner. **Features:** casual dress; Sunday brunch; children's menu; cocktails; a la carte. Casual dining overlooking Newport harbor. Specializing in fresh local seafood, steak & pasta. **Cards:** AE, CB, DI, DS, MC, VI.   ☒

NORTH KINGSTOWN—23,800

LODGINGS

BEST WESTERN-MONTE VISTA INN
◆◆
Motel

Rates Subject to Change

		1P:		2P/1B:		2P/2B:		XP:		
5/17-10/17		1P: $79		2P/1B: $89		2P/2B: $99		XP: $5		F18
5/1-5/16		1P: $69		2P/1B: $79		2P/2B: $79				
10/18-4/30		1P: $69		2P/1B: $69		2P/2B: $69				

Phone: (401)884-8000

Location: On US 1 at SR 403; opposite Quonset Point. 7075 Post Rd 02852. Fax: 401/884-5080. **Terms:** Reserv deposit, 3 day notice. **Facility:** 45 rooms. Meticulously clean units. At-door parking. Very atttractive landscaped pool area. 1 story; exterior corridors; heated pool. **Cards:** AE, CB, DI, DS, MC, VI.   ⊇ ⑪ ⚒ ▢ ⊟ ☒

HAMILTON VILLAGE INN
◆◆
Motel

Rates Subject to Change   Phone: (401)295-0700
5/1-12/1 & 4/1-4/30   1P: $70   2P/1B: $70   2P/2B: $70- 100   XP: $10
Location: On SR 1A, 1 mi s of jct SR 102. 642 Boston Neck Rd 02852. Fax: 401/294-9044. **Terms:** Open 5/1-12/1 & 4/1-4/30. **Facility:** 29 rooms. Grass picnic area. At-door parking. 4 one-bedroom housekeeping apts, $90 for up to 4 persons; 1 efficiency $80 for up to 4 persons; 1 story; exterior corridors. **All Rooms:** combo or shower baths. **Some Rooms:** 4 kitchens. **Cards:** AE, DS, MC, VI.   ⚒ ⑪ ⊿ ▢ ⊟

WICKFORD MOTOR INN
Ⓐ [SAVE]
◆
Motel

		1P:		2P/1B:		2P/2B:		XP:		
6/15-9/15		1P: $58		2P/1B: $68		2P/2B: $76		XP: $10		F8
5/1-6/14 & 9/16-10/15		1P: $54		2P/1B: $64		2P/2B: $66		XP: $7		F8
10/16-4/30		1P: $44		2P/1B: $48		2P/2B: $50		XP: $5		F8

Phone: (401)294-4852

Location: On US 1, 1 mi n of Wickford Village; 1 mi s of jct SR 403. 7650 Post Rd, Rt 1 02852. Fax: 401/294-3197. **Terms:** Reserv deposit; weekly rates; 2 night min stay, weekends in season. **Facility:** 18 rooms. 1st floor units are on basement level. 6 units with private sauna, $5 extra charge; 2 stories; interior corridors. **Dining:** Restaurant nearby. **All Rooms:** extended cable TV. **Some Rooms:** 4 efficiencies. **Cards:** AE, CB, DI, DS, MC, VI. **Special Amenities:** Free local telephone calls and preferred room (subject to availability with advanced reservations).   [SD] ⑪ ▢ ▢ ⊟ ⊟ ☒

RESTAURANT

GREGG'S RESTAURANT & PUB
◆
American

Lunch: $5-$8   Dinner: $7-$13   Phone: 401/294-5700
Location: On SR 2, 2 mi s of SR 4, southbound exit 4; or 0.5 mi ne of SR 4, northbound exit 5B. 4120 Quaker Ln, Rt 2 02852. **Hours:** 11:30 am-11 pm, Fri & Sat-midnight. Closed: 11/25 & 12/25. **Features:** casual dress; children's menu; health conscious menu; carryout; cocktails & lounge. Very popular, relaxed cheerful ambiance. Well worth a short wait in line. Famous for wide variety of homemade pastry. Friendly, fast-paced service. **Cards:** AE, DI, DS, MC, VI.   ☒

NORTH PROVIDENCE—32,100   (See map p. 457; index p. 456)

RESTAURANT

FLORENTINE GRILLE   **Dinner:** $10-$20   **Phone:** 401/354-8411 58
◆ ◆   **Location:** On SR 7; 0.6 mi s of SR 15. 1195 Douglas Ave 02904. **Hours:** 5 pm-10 pm, Fri & Sat-11 pm, Sun
Italian   4 pm-9 pm. **Closed:** 11/25, 12/24, 12/25 & Mon. **Reservations:** accepted. **Features:** dressy casual; health
conscious menu; cocktails & lounge. Open wood grill is the dining room focus. Grilled vegetables, artichokes,
prosciutto, pappa con pomidoro appetizers. Features wood-grilled T-bone steak & mashed red Bliss potatoes,
herb-marinated turkey breast. Ample desserts. **Cards:** AE, MC, VI.   ✕

NORTH SMITHFIELD—10,500—See also SMITHFIELD.

RESTAURANT

BEEF BARN INC   **Lunch:** $2-$5   **Dinner:** $2-$5   **Phone:** 401/762-9880
◆   **Location:** At jct of SR 146A & SR 104; 0.3 mi n of Park Square. 1 Greenville Rd (Rt 104) 02896. **Hours:** 11
American   am-10 pm, Sun from noon. Closed major holidays & 5/9. **Features:** casual dress; carryout. Friendly family
dining in a cozy, rustic, restored barn & silo, decorated with farmland collectibles. Menu limited to
sandwiches, homemade soup & pastry. Very popular for over 25 yrs. Disposable plates & utensils.   ✕

PAWTUCKET—72,600   (See map p. 457; index p. 455)

LODGING

COMFORT INN-PROVIDENCE/PAWTUCKET   Rates Subject to Change   **Phone:** 401/723-6700 3
◆ ◆   All Year [CP]   1P: $75- 150   2P/1B: $75- 150 2P/2B: $75- 150 XP: $10   F16
Motor Inn   **Location:** At I-95, exit 27. 2 George St 02860. **Fax:** 401/726-6380. **Facility:** 135 rooms. Family-owned & op-
erated. Many units with small private balcony or patio. 4 suites, $149; 5 stories; interior corridors. **Cards:** AE,
CB, DI, DS, JC, MC, VI. *(See color ad below)*   🖭 🖭 📶 📶 ⏸ 📶 📶 📶 📶 📶 📶 📶 ✕

PEACE DALE—3,200

RESTAURANT

PUMP HOUSE RESTAURANT   Historical   **Lunch:** $5-$11   **Dinner:** $13-$18   **Phone:** 401/789-4944
◆ ◆   **Location:** 0.5 mi n on SR 108. 1464 Kingstown Rd 02883. **Hours:** 11:30 am-10 pm, Fri & Sat-11 pm, Sun
American   noon-9 pm, Mon 4 pm-10 pm. **Closed:** 12/25. **Reservations:** suggested; weekends. **Features:** casual dress;
children's menu; carryout; salad bar; cocktails & lounge. Relaxed dining in a beautifully restored water
pumping stone building circa 1889. A comfortable, rustic ambiance. Smoking in lounge only. Smoke free premises.
Cards: AE, MC, VI.   ✕

PORTSMOUTH—16,900   (See map p. 446; index p. 444)

LODGINGS

BEST WESTERN BAY POINT INN & CONFERENCE CENTER   **Phone:** (401)683-3600 5
AAA SAVE   5/17-10/31   1P: $85- 119   2P/1B: $95- 125 2P/2B: $95- 125 XP: $10   F18
             5/1-5/16 & 3/1-4/30   1P: $65- 85   2P/1B: $75- 85   2P/2B: $75- 85   XP: $10   F18
◆ ◆   11/1-2/29   1P: $49- 53   2P/1B: $58- 63   2P/2B: $58- 63   XP: $10   F18
Motor Inn   **Location:** Just w of SR 138 & 24, exit 2. 144 Anthony Rd 02871. **Fax:** 401/683-6690. **Terms:** Reserv
deposit, 3 day notice; package plans; 2 night min stay, weekends in season. **Facility:** 85 rooms. Lovely lobby
with a sweeping double staircase, mirrored walls & brass accents. 2 stories; interior corridors; heated indoor pool, sauna.
Dining: Restaurant; 6:30 am-11 & 5-9 pm, Fri-10 pm, Sat & Sun 6:30 am-9:30 & 10-2 pm, also Sun dinner 5-9 pm; $8-$15;
cocktails. **Cards:** AE, DI, DS, MC, VI. **Special Amenities:** Free newspaper and preferred room (subject to availability
with advanced reservations).   🖭 🖭 📶 📶 📶 📶 📶 📶 📶 📶 📶 📶 ✕

(See map p. 446)

FOUNDER'S BROOK MOTEL & SUITES   Phone: (401)683-1244   **6**

(AAA) (SAVE)

5/1-9/5	2P/1B:	$69-	129	2P/2B:	$89- 139	XP: $10	F16
9/6-10/10	2P/1B:	$59-	99	2P/2B:	$69- 109	XP: $10	F16
10/11-4/30	2P/1B:	$39-	69	2P/2B:	$49- 79	XP: $10	F16

◆◆

Complex   **Location:** On SR 138 at jct SR 24, Mt Hope Bridge exit. 314 Boyd's Ln 02871. Fax: 401/683-9129. **Terms:** Reserv deposit, 3 day notice; weekly/monthly rates; CP avail, weekends; pets, $25 fee. **Facility:** 32 rooms. 2 whirlpool rms, $109-$149; $89-$139 off season. 8 motel units $69-$115; $39-$69 off season; 1 story; exterior corridors. **All Rooms:** combo or shower baths. **Some Rooms:** 24 efficiencies. **Cards:** AE, CB, DI, DS, MC, VI. **Special Amenities:** Free local telephone calls. *(See ad p 450)*

RESTAURANT

15 POINT ROAD RESTAURANT   **Dinner:** $11-$18   **Phone:** 401/683-3138   **1**
◆◆   **Location:** Island Park exit off SR 24, 0.5 mi e on Boyd's Ln, 1 mi n on Park Ave. 15 Point Rd 02871.
American   **Hours:** Open 5/1-12/31 & 2/5-4/30; 5 pm-9 pm, Fri & Sat-10 pm, Sun 2 pm-9 pm, 6/1-10/15 from 4 pm. Closed: 11/25, 12/24, 12/25, Mon & Tues. **Features:** casual dress; cocktails & lounge; a la carte. Intimate candlelit dining room overlooking Sakonnet River at Old Stone Bridge. Prix fixe meals avail off season. Featuring grilled meat, fresh local seafood & creative pasta entrees. Smoking permitted in lounge only. **Cards:** AE, DS, MC, VI.

PROVIDENCE
pop. 160,700

This index helps you "spot" where approved accommodations are located on the detailed maps that follow. Rate ranges are for comparison only and show the property's high season. Turn to the listing page for more detailed rate information and consult display ads for special promotions. Restaurant rate range is for dinner, unless only lunch (L) is served.

Spotter/Map Pg.Number	OA	PROVIDENCE - Lodgings	Rating	Rate	Listing Page
5 / p. 457		State House Inn - see color ad p 459	◆◆	$119-139	460
7 / p. 457	(AAA)	**Days Hotel on the Harbor - see color ad p 458**	◆◆	$79-149 (SAVE)	458
8 / p. 457		**Holiday Inn Downtown - see color ad p 458**	◆◆◆	$99-200 (SAVE)	460
9 / p. 457		Providence Marriott Hotel	◆◆◆	$139-350	460
10 / p. 457	(AAA)	**The Westin Providence**	◆◆◆◆	$149-265 (SAVE)	460
		PROVIDENCE - Restaurants			
8 / p. 457		Al Forno Restaurant	◆◆◆	$14-27	460
9 / p. 457		Angelos Civita Farnese Restaurant	◆	$2-10	460
10 / p. 457		Gatehouse Restaurant	◆◆◆	$20-26	461
11 / p. 457		DownCity Food & Cocktails	◆◆	$10-16	461
12 / p. 457		India Point Cafe	◆◆	$9-19	461
13 / p. 457		Barnsider's Mile And A Quarter	◆◆	$10-26	460
14 / p. 457		Gregg's Restaurant & Pub	◆◆	$6-16	461
15 / p. 457		Capriccio	◆◆◆	$17-30	460
16 / p. 457		Pot Au Feu Restaurant & Bistro	◆◆◆	$16-26	461
17 / p. 457	(AAA)	**The Capital Grille**	◆◆◆	$20-26	460
18 / p. 457		New Rivers	◆◆◆	$12-21	461
19 / p. 457	(AAA)	**Hemenway's Seafood Grill & Oyster Bar**	◆◆	$15-24	461
20 / p. 457		Walter's La Locanda del Coccio	◆◆◆	$14-30	461
21 / p. 457		Providence Bookstore Cafe	◆◆	$6-18	461
22 / p. 457		Union Station Brewery	◆◆	$10-15	461
23 / p. 457		Agora	◆◆◆	$24-28	460

Nearby Accommodations

Spotter/Map Pg.Number	OA	JOHNSTON - Lodgings	Rating	Rate	Listing Page
1 / p. 457	(AAA)	Hi-Way Motor Inn	◆	$50-54	439
		PAWTUCKET - Lodgings			
3 / p. 457		Comfort Inn-Providence/Pawtucket - see color ad p 454	◆◆	$75-150	454
		SEEKONK - Lodgings			
14 / p. 457	(AAA)	**Historic Jacob Hill Farm Bed & Breakfast/Inn**	◆◆◆	$120-180	419
15 / p. 457	(AAA)	**Johnson & Wales Inn & Conference Center**	◆◆◆	$89-139 (SAVE)	419

Spotter/Map Pg.Number	OA	SEEKONK - Lodgings (contd.)	Rating	Rate	Listing Page
16 / p. 457		Susse Chalet Inn - see ad p 459	◆◆	$60-79	419
17 / p. 457		Ramada Inn/Providence-Seekonk - see color ad p 459	◆◆◆	$70-90	419
		SEEKONK - Restaurants			
25 / p. 457		Audrey's Restaurant	◆◆◆	$11-18	419
26 / p. 457	AAA	**The Old Grist Mill Tavern**	◆ ◆	$12-19	420
27 / p. 457		Frankie's Restaurant	◆◆	$8-14	419
28 / p. 457	AAA	**Bugaboo Creek Steak House**	◆ ◆	$10-20	419
29 / p. 457		Darling's Restaurant & Lounge	◆	$8-15	419
		WARWICK - Lodgings			
23 / p. 457		Radisson Airport Hotel Providence	◆◆◆	$109	464
24 / p. 457		Susse Chalet Inn - see ad p 459	◆◆	$61-79	464
25 / p. 457		Sheraton Inn Providence Airport	◆◆◆	$135-185	464
26 / p. 457		Residence Inn by Marriott	◆◆◆	$149-179	464
27 / p. 457	AAA	**Open Gate Motel**	◆	$40-45	463
28 / p. 457	AAA	**MainStay Suites, Warwick - see color ad p 458**	◆◆◆	$70-100 SAVE	463
29 / p. 457	AAA	**Crowne Plaza Hotel**	◆◆◆	$145 SAVE	463
30 / p. 457		Master Hosts Inn	◆	$69-150	463
31 / p. 457		Comfort Inn-Airport - see color ad p 463	◆◆	$79-109	463
		WARWICK - Restaurants			
35 / p. 457		Gregg's Restaurant	◆	$6-13	465
38 / p. 457		Jefferson Grille	◆◆	$10-20	465
40 / p. 457		Bugaboo Creek Steak House	◆◆	$6-18	464
41 / p. 457		Legal Sea Foods	◆◆	$10-18	465
		SMITHFIELD - Lodgings			
34 / p. 457	AAA	**Susse Chalet Inn - see ad p 459**	◆◆	$80-85 SAVE	461
		SMITHFIELD - Restaurants			
45 / p. 457		Club 44 Restaurant	◆◆	$11-19	462
47 / p. 457		Cricket's of Smithfield	◆◆	$9-15	462
		SOUTH ATTLEBORO - Lodgings			
36 / p. 457	AAA	**Days Inn**	◆◆	$65-95 SAVE	420
		WEST WARWICK - Lodgings			
40 / p. 457		Fairfield Suites by Marriott	◆◆◆	$95	466
		EAST GREENWICH - Restaurant			
54 / p. 457		Twenty Water Street & Warehouse Tavern	◆◆	$14-23	439
		EAST PROVIDENCE - Restaurant			
56 / p. 457		Gregg's Restaurant & Pub	◆◆	$6-11	439
		NORTH PROVIDENCE - Restaurant			
58 / p. 457		Florentine Grille	◆◆	$10-20	454

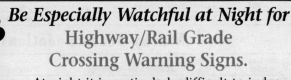

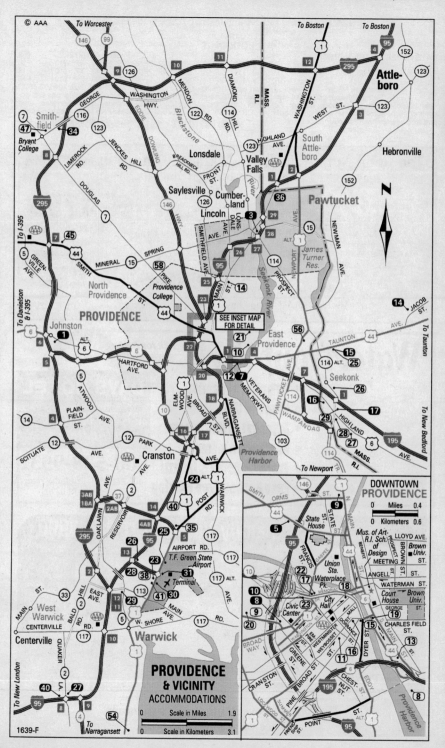

PROVIDENCE & VICINITY
ACCOMMODATIONS

DOWNTOWN PROVIDENCE

1639-F

PROVIDENCE—160,700   (See map p. 457; index p. 455)

LODGINGS

DAYS HOTEL ON THE HARBOR   Phone: (401)272-5577   ⑦

5/1-10/31	1P: $79- 149	2P/1B: $79- 149	2P/2B: $79- 149	XP: $10	F16
1/1-4/30	1P: $69- 149	2P/1B: $69- 149	2P/2B: $69- 149	XP: $10	F16
11/1-12/31	1P: $59- 129	2P/1B: $59- 129	2P/2B: $59- 129	XP: $10	F16

Location: From I-195 exit 3, then s, following signs. 220 India St 02903. Fax: 401/272-5577. **Terms:** Package plans. **Facility:** 136 rooms. Deluxe units overlook the harbor. Nicely appointed rooms. 6 stories; interior corridors; whirlpool. **Dining:** Restaurant; also, India Point Cafe, see separate listing. **Services:** area transportation. **Some Rooms:** whirlpools. **Cards:** AE, CB, DI, DS, MC, VI. **Special Amenities:** Free local telephone calls and free newspaper. (See color ad below)

The AAA Approved Auto Repair sign means service you can depend on.

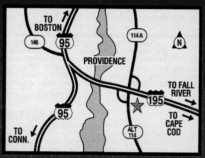

(See map p. 457)

HOLIDAY INN DOWNTOWN   Phone: (401)831-3900 [8]
(AAA) (SAVE)
     All Year   1P: $89- 200   2P/1B: $99- 200   2P/2B: $99- 200   XP: $10-15
◆◆◆   **Location:** I-95, exit 21 (Atwells Ave); adjacent to civic center. 21 Atwells Ave 02903. Fax: 401/751-0007.
Hotel   **Terms:** Package plans. **Facility:** 274 rooms. 14 stories; interior corridors; heated indoor pool, whirlpool. Fee: parking. **Dining:** Dining room; 6:30 am-10 pm; $13-$20; cocktails. **Services:** giftshop; area transportation, within 2 mi. **Cards:** AE, CB, DI, DS, JC, MC, VI. *(See color ad p 458)*

PROVIDENCE MARRIOTT HOTEL   Rates Subject to Change   Phone: (401)272-2400   [9]
◆◆◆
Hotel

11/21-3/4	1P: $89- 350	2P/1B: $89- 350	2P/2B: $89- 350	XP: $20	F16
5/1-9/4	1P: $129- 199	2P/1B: $129- 199	2P/2B: $129- 199	XP: $20	F16
9/5-11/20	1P: $139- 199	2P/1B: $139- 199	2P/2B: $139- 199	XP: $20	F16
3/5-4/30	1P: $109- 179	2P/1B: $109- 179	2P/2B: $109- 179	XP: $20	F16

Location: At I-95, exit 23 to state offices. One Orms Street 02904. Fax: 401/273-2686. **Facility:** 345 rooms. Vibrant contemporary room decor & mahogany traditional furnishings. Inviting lobby accented with marble & brass. Excellent guest services. 5-6 stories; interior corridors; heated indoor/outdoor pool. **Services:** giftshop. **Cards:** AE, CB, DI, DS, JC, MC, VI.

STATE HOUSE INN   Rates Subject to Change   Phone: (401)351-6111   [5]
◆◆
Bed &   Fri & Sat 5/1-10/31 &
Breakfast   3/1-4/30 [BP]

Fri & Sat 5/1-10/31 & 3/1-4/30 [BP]	1P: $119- 129	2P/1B: $119- 139	2P/2B: $119- 139	XP: $15	F10
Sun-Thurs 5/1-10/31 & 11/1-2/29 [BP]	1P: $89- 109	2P/1B: $99- 129	2P/2B: $99- 129	XP: $15	F10

Location: From I-95 exit 22, follow sign to downtown, 0.5 mi n on Francis St, 0.3 mi w on Smith St, left on Schaffer St. 43 Jewett St 02908. Fax: 401/351-4261. **Facility:** 10 rooms. In a quiet residential area. Cozy, cheerful rooms in Shaker & Colonial styles. Some canopy beds; 2 rooms with fireplace. 3 stories, no elevator; interior corridors; smoke free premises. **All Rooms:** combo or shower baths. **Cards:** AE, DS, MC, VI. *(See color ad p 459)*

THE WESTIN PROVIDENCE   Phone: (401)598-8000   [10]
(AAA) (SAVE)

5/1-6/30 & 8/30-11/19	1P: $149- 265	2P/1B: $149- 265	2P/2B: $149- 265	XP: $25	F18
7/1-8/29 & 11/20-4/30	1P: $129- 245	2P/1B: $129- 245	2P/2B: $129- 245	XP: $25	F18

◆◆◆◆   **Location:** From I-95 exit 22, downtown. One W Exchange St 02903. Fax: 401/598-8200. **Terms:** Check-in 4
Hotel   pm; reserv deposit, 14 day notice; package plans; small pets only, must be contained. **Facility:** 363 rooms. Neo-classical decor. Adjacent to the convention center, downtown. 25 stories; interior corridors; heated indoor pool, saunas, steamrooms, whirlpool. Fee: parking. **Dining:** Dining room; 6:30 am-11 pm; $15-$29; cocktails; also, Agora, see separate listing. **Services:** giftshop. Fee: massage. **Some Rooms:** whirlpools. **Cards:** AE, CB, DI, DS, MC, VI. **Special Amenities:** Free newspaper and free room upgrade (subject to availability with advanced reservations).

RESTAURANTS

AGORA   Dinner: $24-$28   Phone: 401-598-8011   [23]
◆◆◆
American   **Location:** From I-95 exit 22, downtown; in The Westin Providence. One West Exchange St 02903. **Hours:** 5:30 pm-9:30 pm, Fri & Sat-10 pm. Closed: 12/25 & Sun. **Reservations:** suggested. **Features:** semi-formal attire; cocktails & lounge; fee for parking & valet parking. Elegant dining overlooking downtown Providence. Creative American cuisine emphasizing local seafood. **Cards:** AE, CB, DI, DS, MC, VI.

AL FORNO RESTAURANT   Dinner: $14-$27   Phone: 401-273-9767   [8]
◆◆◆
Northern   **Location:** Downtown, I-195 exit 2, just s. 577 S Main St 02903. **Hours:** 5 pm-10 pm. Closed major holidays,
Italian   Sun & Mon. **Reservations:** not accepted. **Features:** casual dress; health conscious menu; cocktails & lounge; a la carte. Tuscany-style cuisine emphasizing fresh, seasonal ingredients. Made-to-order dessert. Carefully selected wines. Casual rustic elegance. Smoke free premises. **Cards:** AE, DI, MC, VI.

ANGELOS CIVITA FARNESE RESTAURANT   Lunch: $2-$10   Dinner: $2-$10   Phone: 401/621-8171   [9]
◆
Italian   **Location:** On Federal Hill, just n of I-95 exit 21 southbound, Broadway exit northbound. 141 Atwells Ave 02903. **Hours:** 11 am-8:30 pm, Fri & Sat-9 pm, Sun noon-6:30 pm. Closed major holidays & Sun 9/6-5/25. **Features:** casual dress; children's menu; carryout; cocktails & lounge; valet parking. A folksy, no-frills casual family restaurant offering standard Italo-American cooking; tripe, braciola, meatballs with French fries. Established in 1925. You may sit with strangers if you choose.

BARNSIDER'S MILE AND A QUARTER   Dinner: $10-$26   Phone: 401/351-7300   [13]
◆◆
Steak and   **Location:** I-195 exit 2 westbound, exit 1 eastbound, downtown exit. 375 S Main St 02903. **Hours:** 5 pm-10
Seafood   pm, Fri & Sat-11 pm, Sun 4 pm-9 pm. Closed: 7/4, 12/24 & 12/25. **Reservations:** suggested. **Features:** casual dress; children's menu; salad bar; cocktails & lounge. Upscale, popular dining in an authentically restored historic brick carriage depot. In financial district. Valet parking Fri & Sat. Dinner theatre pkgs Fri & Sat. **Cards:** AE, DI, DS, MC, VI.

THE CAPITAL GRILLE   Lunch: $8-$17   Dinner: $20-$26   Phone: 401/521-5600   [17]
(AAA)
    Location: From I-95 exit 22, on lower level of former Union Train Station; opposite Lafayette Park. 1 Cookson Pl 02903. **Hours:** 11:30 am-3 & 5-10 pm, Fri-11 pm, Sat 5 pm-11 pm, Sun 4 pm-9 pm. Closed:
◆◆◆   11/25 & 12/25. **Reservations:** suggested. **Features:** semi-formal attire; cocktails & lounge; fee for parking; a
Steak and   la carte. Fine dining in restored train station overlooking the State Capitol Building. Popular, bustling
Seafood   atmosphere. Dry-aged beef & fresh seafood. Extensive wine list. Impressive mahogany, brass & brick decor. Validated parking. **Cards:** AE, DI, DS, MC, VI.

CAPRICCIO   Lunch: $8-$12   Dinner: $17-$30   Phone: 401/421-1320   [15]
◆◆◆
Continental   **Location:** Downtown on corner Dyer & Pine sts; from I-195 exit 1. 2 Pine St 02903. **Hours:** 11:30 am-10 pm, Fri-10:30 pm, Sat 5 pm-10:30 pm, Sun 4 pm-9 pm. Closed: 1/1, 11/25 & 12/25. **Reservations:** suggested. **Features:** semi-formal attire; cocktails & lounge; valet parking. Creative continental cuisine with a Northern Italina accent served in formal romantic atmosphere. **Cards:** AE, CB, DI, DS, MC, VI.

(See map p. 457)

DOWNCITY FOOD & COCKTAILS   **Lunch:** $5-$7   **Dinner:** $10-$16   **Phone:** 401/331-9217   ⑪
◆◆
Regional
American
Location: Corner of Weybosset & Eddy. 151 Weybosset St 02903. **Hours:** 11:30 am-2 pm, 5:30 pm-9 pm; Sat 9 am-2 pm & 5:30-10 pm; Sun 9 am-2 pm. Closed: 11/25 & 12/25. **Reservations:** suggested. **Features:** casual dress; Sunday brunch; carryout; cocktails & lounge. Casual & fun atmosphere with stylish art deco elements. Specialities include Mom's meatloaf on Portuguese cornbread, Maine crab cakes with tomatillo salsa, grilled pork chops, & penne pasta with spinich, fresh mozzarella & tomatoes. **Cards:** AE, DI, MC, VI.   ⊠

GATEHOUSE RESTAURANT   **Lunch:** $9-$15   **Dinner:** $20-$26   **Phone:** 401/521-9229   ⑩
◆◆◆
Regional
American
Location: 1 mi ne of I-195 exit 3 via Gano & Pitman sts on the Seekonk River. 4 Richmond Sq 02906. **Hours:** noon-2:30 & 5:30-10 pm, Sun 11 am-2 & 5:30-10 pm. **Reservations:** suggested. **Features:** dressy casual; Sunday brunch; cocktails & lounge. New England cuisine with a New Orleans flair. Informal romantic setting in old brick gatehouse overlooking the Seekonk River. Live entertainment in lounge Wed-Sat. Smoke free premises. **Cards:** AE, DI, MC, VI.   ⊠

GREGG'S RESTAURANT & PUB   **Lunch:** $5-$8   **Dinner:** $6-$16   **Phone:** 401/831-5700   ⑭
◆◆
American
Location: I-95 exit 25, N Main St exit, 0.8 mi ne. 1303 N Main St 02904. **Hours:** 11:30 am-midnight, Fri & Sat to 1 am. Closed: 11/25 & 12/25. **Features:** casual dress; children's menu; health conscious menu; carryout; cocktails & lounge. Lively, cheerful family dining with friendly, fast-paced service. Well worth the short wait. Daily specials, sandwiches & salads. Very popular. Famous for wide variety of homemade pastry & dessert. **Cards:** AE, CB, DI, DS, MC, VI.   ⊠

HEMENWAY'S SEAFOOD GRILL & OYSTER BAR   **Lunch:** $7-$13   **Dinner:** $15-$24   **Phone:** 401/351-8570   ⑲
AAA
◆◆
Seafood
Location: Downtown on e side of the river at Crawford St bridge at s end of Providence River Park opposite the Old Stone Bank, Providence Washington Plaza. 1 Old Stone Sq 02903. **Hours:** 11:30 am-3 & 5-10 pm, Fri & Sat 11:30 am-3 & 4:30-11:30 pm, Sun noon-9 pm. Closed: 11/25 & 12/25. **Reservations:** suggested. **Features:** casual dress; children's menu; cocktails & lounge; valet parking. Popular, upscale dining. Impressive mahogany & brass decor. Excellent variety of fresh local seafood. Metered street parking. **Cards:** AE, CB, DI, DS, MC, VI.   ⊠

INDIA POINT CAFE   **Lunch:** $6-$9   **Dinner:** $9-$19   **Phone:** 401/272-5577   ⑫
◆◆
American
Location: From I-195 exit 3, then s, following signs; in Days Hotel on the Harbor. 220 India St 02903. **Hours:** 6:30 am-2 & 5-10 pm. **Reservations:** suggested. **Features:** casual dress; children's menu; cocktails & lounge. Charming intimate ambiance. Varied menu. Daily specials. **Cards:** AE, CB, DI, DS, MC, VI.   ⊠

NEW RIVERS   **Dinner:** $12-$21   **Phone:** 401/751-0350   ⑱
◆◆◆
American
Location: On an eastbound one-way st; corner of N Main & Steeple sts, opposite end of Waterman St. 7 Steeple St 02903. **Hours:** 5 pm-10 pm. Closed major holidays, Sun, Mon & Easter. **Reservations:** suggested. **Features:** casual dress; health conscious menu items; cocktails & lounge. Ethnic cuisine featured are Portuguese, Thai, Caribbean & Tuscan. Specialties include Jamaican jerk beef, grilled pork tenderloin & salmon filet. Dessert made-to-order, such as lemon tartlet with fresh blueberries. **Cards:** AE, MC, VI.   ⊠

POT AU FEU RESTAURANT & BISTRO   **Lunch:** $6-$10   **Dinner:** $16-$26   **Phone:** 401/273-8953   ⑯
◆◆◆
French
Location: Downtown; from I-95 exit 22, 0.3 mi s on Dorrance St, 3 blks e on Weybosset St to Custom House St. 44 Custom House St 02903. **Hours:** noon-1:30 & 6-9 pm, Sat 6 pm-9:30 pm. Closed: 11/25, 12/25, Mon, Sun 7/1-8/31 & 8/1-8/7. **Reservations:** suggested. **Features:** semi-formal attire; cocktails & lounge; a la carte. Formal, elegant dining in salon with fine French classic cuisine. Regional French entrees & lighter fare in casual lower level bistro open daily 11:30 am-2 & 5:30-10 pm. Smoke free premises. **Cards:** AE, CB, DI, MC, VI.   ⊠

PROVIDENCE BOOKSTORE CAFE   **Lunch:** $6-$18   **Dinner:** $6-$18   **Phone:** 401/521-5536   ㉑
◆◆
American
Location: At jct Angell St & Wayland Ave; in Wayland Square. 500 Angell St 02906. **Hours:** 11:30 am-midnight, Fri & Sat-1 am. Closed: 7/4, 11/25 & 12/25. **Reservations:** accepted. **Features:** casual dress; Sunday brunch; carryout; cocktails; street parking. Delightful dining amidst the classics in a comfortable library setting. A very popular east side cafe. **Cards:** AE, DI, DS, MC, VI.   ⊠

UNION STATION BREWERY   **Lunch:** $6-$8   **Dinner:** $10-$15   **Phone:** 401/274-2739   ㉒
◆◆
Regional
American
Location: From I-95 exit 22, on lower level of former Union Train Station; opposite Lafayette Park. 36 Exchange Terrace 02903. **Hours:** 11:30 am-4:30 & 4:45-10 pm, Fri & Sat-11 pm. Closed: 11/25 & 12/25. **Features:** casual dress; Sunday brunch; cocktails; fee for parking. Regional & creative American cuisine, served in casual, rustic atmosphere. Featuring a variety of micro brews to compliment the cuisine. **Cards:** AE, DI, DS, MC, VI.   ⊠

WALTER'S LA LOCANDA DEL COCCIO   **Lunch:** $5-$10   **Dinner:** $14-$30   **Phone:** 401/273-2652   ⑳
◆◆◆
Regional
Italian
Location: On Federal Hill; 0.4 mi nw of I-95 exit 21 southbound, Broadway exit northbound. 265 Atwells Ave 02903. **Hours:** noon-2:30 & 5 pm-10 pm, Sat 5 pm-10 pm. Closed major holidays & Sun. **Reservations:** suggested. **Features:** casual dress; health conscious menu items; cocktails & lounge; a la carte. Inviting atmosphere & warm Italian decor. Features spinach-filled tortellini, Tuscan farfalle pasta, fresh snapper, shrimp with shiitake mushrooms & pasta & risotto with spinach & shrimp. Outdoor dining in good weather. Smoke free premises. **Cards:** AE, DI, MC, VI.   ⊠

SMITHFIELD—19,200   (See map p. 457; index p. 456)—*See also NORTH SMITHFIELD.*

LODGING

SUSSE CHALET INN   **Phone:** (401)232-2400   ㉞
AAA SAVE
◆◆
Motel

	1P:	2P/1B:	2P/2B:	XP:	
All Year [CP]	$68- 79	$75- 82	$80- 85	$3	F17

Location: On SR 116; 0.6 mi e of jct SR 7, from I-295, exit 8B. 355 George Washington Hwy 02917 (PO Box 17309, ESMOND). Fax: 401/232-0235. **Facility:** 117 rooms. A quiet, rural setting with attractively landscaped sloping grounds & tree-lined incline driveway. Inviting rooms with soft pastel decors accented by mahogany & brass furnishings. 2 stories; interior corridors; heated pool, whirlpool. **Cards:** AE, CB, DI, DS, MC, VI. **Special Amenities:** Free breakfast and free local telephone calls. *(See ad p 460)*

⟨🅱 🏊 🛏 🅿 🍴 🖨 ⊠⟩

(See map p. 457)

RESTAURANTS

CLUB 44 RESTAURANT
♦♦
Steak and
Seafood
Location: On US 44, 0.3 mi s of jct I-295, exit 7A. 355 Putnam Ave 02917. **Hours:** 4 pm-9:30 pm, Sun from noon. Closed: 11/25, 12/24 & 12/25. **Reservations:** suggested; weekends. **Features:** casual dress; children's menu; carryout; cocktails & lounge. Family-operated business for over 40 years. Cozy, rustic ambiance, candlelit dinners, garden atrium. Generous portions. Lunch Fri & Sat 11:30 am-4 pm. **Cards:** AE, CB, DI, DS, MC, VI.
Dinner: $11-$19   **Phone:** 401/231-2240   ㊺   ☒

CRICKET'S OF SMITHFIELD
♦♦
American
Lunch: $5-$11   **Dinner:** $9-$15   **Phone:** 401/232-0300   ㊼
Location: On SR 116; 0.3 mi e of jct SR 7 from I-295, exit 8B. 280 George Washington Hwy 02917. **Hours:** 11:30 am-10 pm, Fri & Sat-11 pm, Sun noon-9 pm. Closed: 1/1 & 12/25. **Reservations:** suggested. **Features:** casual dress; children's menu; carryout; cocktails & lounge. A charming, country style ambiance. Features fresh seafood & Italian entrees. **Cards:** AE, DI, DS, MC, VI.   ☒

SOUTH KINGSTOWN—24,600

LODGINGS

HOLIDAY INN
♦♦
Motor Inn

		Rates Subject to Change					
5/1-10/31	1P: $80- 200	2P/1B: $80- 200	2P/2B: $80- 200	XP: $10	F15
11/1-4/30	1P: $65- 90	2P/1B: $65- 90	2P/2B: $65- 90	XP: $10	F15

Location: Just n of jct SR 138W on US 1. 3009 Tower Hill Rd 02874 (RFD 1, SAUNDERSTOWN). Fax: 401/789-0080. **Facility:** 105 rooms. 4 stories; interior corridors. **All Rooms:** combo or shower baths. **Cards:** AE, CB, DI, DS, MC, VI. *(See color ad below)*
Phone: 401/789-1051

☒☒☒☒☒☒☒☒☒

THE KINGS' ROSE BED & BREAKFAST INN
♦♦♦
Bed &
Breakfast

	Rates Subject to Change				
All Year	1P: $80- 115	2P/1B: $100- 135	2P/2B: $100- 135	XP: $25	F12

Location: On SR 138 10.5 mi e of I-95 exit 3A; 3.3 mi w of US 1. 1747 Mooresfield Rd 02879. **Terms:** Reserv deposit, 5 day notice; handling fee imposed. **Facility:** 5 rooms. A 1930's neo-colonial on 2 1/2 acres with spacious lawns & English gardens. 1 unit with working fireplace. Furnished with many antiques. 3 stories; interior corridors; designated smoking area; 1 tennis court. **Some Rooms:** color TV.
Phone: (401)783-5222

☒☒☒☒☒☒

WAKEFIELD—7,100

RESTAURANT

LARCHWOOD INN DINING ROOM   Country Inn
♦♦
American
Lunch: $4-$10   **Dinner:** $9-$14   **Phone:** 401/783-5454
Location: 0.3 mi w on scenic SR 1A; in Larchwood Inn & Holly House. 521 Main St 02879. **Hours:** 7:30 am-2:30 & 5:30-9 pm, Fri & Sat-10 pm, Sun 7:30 am-9 pm. Closed: 12/25. **Reservations:** suggested. **Features:** casual dress; children's menu; early bird specials; cocktails & lounge. Warm hospitality at 161 year-old manor house on mature grounds. Some dining areas with A/C. Featuring fresh seafood & prime rib of beef. **Cards:** AE, CB, DI, DS, MC, VI.   ☒

WARREN—11,400

RESTAURANT

NATHANIEL PORTER INN   Historical
♦♦♦
Regional
American
Lunch: $7-$10   **Dinner:** $14-$23   **Phone:** 401/245-6622
Location: On Water St, 0.3 mi sw of SR 114. 125 Water St 02885. **Hours:** 5 pm-9 pm, Sat 11 am-4 & 5-9 pm, Sun 10:30 am-8 pm. Closed major holidays except 11/25. **Reservations:** suggested. **Features:** casual dress; Sunday brunch; cocktails. Charming candlelit, cozy dining rooms in a restored 1795 sea captain's home. Creative traditional New England cuisine. Gracious hospitality. **Cards:** AE, DI, DS, MC, VI.   ☒

WARWICK—85,400 (See map p. 457; index p. 456)

✈ Airport Accommodations

Spotter/Map Pg. Number	OA	WARWICK	Rating	Rate	Listing Page
31 / p. 457		Comfort Inn-Airport, 0.8 mi n of airport terminal	◆◆	$79-109	463
28 / p. 457	⚫	**MainStay Suites, Warwick, 2 mi w of airport via Coronado Rd, Kilvert St & Metro Center**	◆◆◆	$70-100 🅢🅐🅥🅔	463
30 / p. 457		Master Hosts Inn, 0.5 mi s of airport	◆	$69-150	463
23 / p. 457		Radisson Airport Hotel Providence, 0.3 mi s of airport	◆◆◆	$109	464
26 / p. 457		Residence Inn by Marriott, 1.5 mi w of airport via Coronado Blvd & Kilvert St	◆◆◆	$149-179	464
25 / p. 457		Sheraton Inn Providence Airport, 0.5 mi n of airport terminal	◆◆◆	$135-185	464

LODGINGS

COMFORT INN-AIRPORT   Rates Subject to Change   **Phone: 401/732-0470**   **31**
◆◆   All Year [CP]   1P: $79- 109   2P/1B: $79- 109   2P/2B: $79- 109   XP: $10   F18
Motel   **Location:** from US 1; from I-95 airport exit 13 & Post Rd N. 1940 Post Rd 02886. Fax: 401/732-4247.
   Facility: 196 rooms. Some larger, well-appointed rooms in south wing. 4 stories; interior corridors.
Services: area transportation. **All Rooms:** combo or shower baths. **Cards:** AE, CB, DI, DS, MC, VI. *(See color ad below)*

CROWNE PLAZA HOTEL   **Phone: (401)732-6000**   **29**
⚫ 🅢🅐🅥🅔   All Year   1P: $135   2P/1B: $145   2P/2B: $145   XP: $10   F18
  Location: On SR 5, 0.3 mi e of I-95 exit 12A; northbound I-95 exit 12. 801 Greenwich Ave 02886.
◆◆◆   Fax: 401/732-4839. **Terms:** Small pets only. **Facility:** 266 rooms. Deluxe suites, $375-$525. 18 oversized
Hotel   whirlpool rms, $175 rates for 2 persons; 6 stories; interior corridors; heated indoor pool, sauna, whirlpool.
  Dining: Restaurant; 6 am-11 pm, Sat & Sun from 6:30 am; $10-$23; cocktails. **Services:** giftshop.
Cards: AE, CB, DI, DS, JC, MC, VI. **Special Amenities:** Free newspaper.

MAINSTAY SUITES, WARWICK   **Phone: (401)732-6667**   **28**
⚫ 🅢🅐🅥🅔   All Year [CP]   1P: $70- 100   2P/1B: $70- 100   2P/2B: $70- 100
  Location: I-95 exit 13 to Jefferson Blvd exit, 0.3 mi n to Kilvert St, 0.5 mi w to Metro Center Blvd, then 0.5
◆◆◆   mi s. 268 Metro Center Blvd 02886. Fax: 401/732-6668. **Terms:** Weekly/monthly rates; pets, $10 extra
Extended Stay   charge. **Facility:** 94 rooms. 3 stories; interior corridors; whirlpool. **Services:** complimentary evening
Motel   beverages, Mon, Wed. **Recreation:** sports court. **All Rooms:** efficiencies, combo or shower baths.
  Cards: AE, CB, DI, DS, MC, VI. **Special Amenities:** Early check-in/late check-out and free room
upgrade (subject to availability with advanced reservations). *(See color ad p 458)*

MASTER HOSTS INN   Rates Subject to Change   **Phone: (401)737-7400**   **30**
◆   All Year   1P: $59- 144   2P/1B: $65- 150   2P/2B: $69- 150   XP: $6   F18
Motel   **Location:** On US 1, from I-95 airport exit 13 & Post Rd N. 2138 Post Rd 02886. Fax: 401/739-6483.
  Facility: 103 rooms. Some spacious units. Located opposite airport runway with strong soundproofing. 3 stories; interior corridors. **Cards:** AE, CB, DI, DS, MC, VI.

OPEN GATE MOTEL   Rates Subject to Change   **Phone: 401/884-4490**   **27**
⚫   All Year   1P: $40- 45   2P/1B: $40- 45   2P/2B: $52   XP: $4   F14
  Location: On SR 2; from I-95 northbound, 0.5 mi n of exit 8B; from I-95 southbound, 0.5 mi n of exit 8. 840
◆   Quaker Ln 02818. **Terms:** Reserv deposit; weekly rates, 10/1-4/1. **Facility:** 23 rooms. Family-owned & oper-
Motel   ated. Minutes from Warwick Musical Theater & large shopping malls. Some cozy rooms. 1 story; exterior corridors. **Cards:** AE, CB, DI, DS, JC, MC, VI.

(See map p. 457)

RADISSON AIRPORT HOTEL PROVIDENCE   Rates Subject to Change   **Phone:** (401)739-3000   23
◆◆◆   All Year [CP]   1P: $109   2P/1B: $109   2P/2B: $109   XP: $15   F18
Motor Inn   **Location:** On US 1, from I-95, airport exit 13 & Post Rd N. 2081 Post Rd 02886. Fax: 401/732-9309.
    Facility: 111 rooms. Some deluxe suites with French doors. 2 sections surround lovely seasonal landscaped
courtyard. Attentive guest services in an educational facility of Johnson & Wales University. 2 stories; interior corridors.
All Rooms: combo or shower baths. **Cards:** AE, CB, DI, DS, MC, VI.

(ASK) [SÅVE] 🛏 🕭 🎦 🍴 🍸 🔫 🖑 📶 🖈 📶 🖥 🅱 🔌 ✕ 🖉

RESIDENCE INN BY MARRIOTT   Rates Subject to Change   **Phone:** (401)737-7100   26
◆◆◆   5/1-11/7 [CP]   1P: $149- 179   2P/1B: $149- 179   2P/2B: $149- 179   XP: $10   F19
Apartment   2/28-4/30 [CP]   1P: $135- 155   2P/1B: $135- 155   2P/2B: $135- 155   XP: $10   F19
    11/8-2/27 [CP]   1P: $119- 139   2P/1B: $119- 139   2P/2B: $119- 139   XP: $10   F19
Location: I-95 exit 13 to Jefferson Blvd exit; 0.3 mi to Jefferson Blvd, then 0.5 mi w. 500 Kilvert St 02886.
Fax: 401/739-2909. **Facility:** 96 rooms. Tudor-style brick & stucco buildings with attractively landscaped walkways. Inviting,
spacious studio & 2-level penthouse units, many with fireplace. **Recreation:** sports court. **All Rooms:** kitchens. **Cards:** AE, CB, DI, DS, MC, VI. 2 stories; exterior corridors; heated indoor pool. **Recreation:** sports court. **All Rooms:** kitchens. **Cards:** AE, CB, DI, DS, MC, VI.

(ASK) [SÅVE] 🛏 🕭 🎦 🍴 🍸 🔫 🖑 🐾 🚏 🔫 🍽 ▭ 🖥 ✕ 🖉

SHERATON INN PROVIDENCE AIRPORT   Rates Subject to Change   **Phone:** (401)738-4000   25
◆◆◆   5/1-11/30   1P: $135- 185   2P/1B: $135- 185   2P/2B: $135- 185
Hotel   12/1-4/30   1P: $115- 150   2P/1B: $115- 150   2P/2B: $115- 150
    Location: On US 1; from I-95 airport exit 13 & Post Rd N. 1850 Post Rd 02886. Fax: 401/738-8206.
Facility: 207 rooms. Some deluxe units. Efficient, friendly guest services. 5 stories; interior corridors; heated indoor pool.
Services: area transportation. **Cards:** AE, CB, DI, DS, JC, MC, VI.

(ASK) [SÅVE] 🛏 🕭 🎦 🍴 🍸 🔫 🖑 🐾 🚏 🔫 🍽 🖥 🅱 ✕ 🖉

SUSSE CHALET INN   Rates Subject to Change   **Phone:** (401)941-6600   24
◆◆   All Year [CP]   1P: $56- 76   2P/1B: $61- 79   2P/2B: $61- 79   XP: $3   F17
Motel   **Location:** At I-95, exit 15. 36 Jefferson Blvd 02888. Fax: 401/785-1260. **Facility:** 115 rooms. Cozy, inviting
    lobby with a greenhouse ambiance. 5 stories; interior corridors. **Cards:** AE, CB, DI, DS, MC, VI.
(See ad p 460)

🕭 🎦 🚏 🍴 🔫 🖑 🍽 🖥 ✕

RESTAURANTS

BUGABOO CREEK STEAK HOUSE   **Lunch:** $6-$11   **Dinner:** $6-$18   **Phone:** 401/781-1400   40
◆◆   **Location:** At I-95, exit 15. 30 Jefferson Blvd 02888. **Hours:** 11:30 am-10 pm, Fri & Sat-10:30 pm, Sun
Steakhouse   noon-9 pm. Closed: 11/25 & 12/25. **Features:** casual dress; children's menu; carryout; cocktails & lounge.
    Friendly sevice in a mythical Canadian Rockies ski lodge with a North Country Gothic decor & "talking"
mooseheads. A family favorite featuring dry-aged beef specialties & a few chicken entrees. **Cards:** AE, CB, DI, DS, MC, VI.

✕

(See map p. 457)

GREGG'S RESTAURANT Lunch: $5-$10 Dinner: $6-$13 Phone: 401/467-5700 35
◆
American **Location:** On US 1; 1.5 mi n of State Airport; 0.3 mi n of jct SR 37. 1359 Post Rd, Rt 1 02886.
Hours: 11:30 am-midnight, Fri & Sat-1 am. Closed: 11/25 & 12/25. **Features:** casual dress; children's menu; health conscious menu; carryout; cocktails. Very popular, bustling, cheerful ambiance. Also daily specials, sandwiches & salad. Famous for wide variety of homemade pastry & dessert. Friendly, fast-paced service. **Cards:** AE, DI, DS, MC, VI.
⊠

JEFFERSON GRILLE Lunch: $5-$7 Dinner: $10-$20 Phone: 401/737-1110 38
◆◆
American **Location:** 0.3 mi n of airport exit via Coronado Rd; at corner of Jefferson Blvd & Kilvert St. 137 Kilvert St 02886. **Hours:** 11 am-10 pm, Fri & Sat-11 pm. Closed major holidays & Sun; except Mother's Day. **Features:** casual dress; cocktails & lounge. Wood-grilled steak, chops, chicken & seafood. Some fresh game. Outdoor deck, weather permitting. **Cards:** AE, DI, DS, MC, VI.

LEGAL SEA FOODS Lunch: $7-$13 Dinner: $10-$18 Phone: 401/732-3663 41
◆◆
Seafood **Location:** On US 1, from I-95, airport exit 13 & Post Rd N. 2099 Post Road 02886. **Hours:** 11:30 am-10 pm, Fri-10:30 pm, Sat noon-10:30 pm, Sun noon-9 pm. Closed: 11/25 & 12/25. **Reservations:** suggested; weekends. **Features:** casual dress; children's menu; carryout; cocktails. Casual atmosphere serving grilled, broiled, fried cajun style seafood. **Cards:** AE, DI, DS, JC, MC, VI.
♿ ⊠

WESTERLY—16,500

LODGINGS

PINE LODGE Rates Subject to Change Phone: (401)322-0333

	6/15-9/15	1P:	$81- 92	2P/1B:	$81- 92		XP: $10	D16
	5/1-6/14 & 9/16-4/30	1P:	$45- 56	2P/1B:	$45- 56		XP: $10	D16

◆◆
Complex **Location:** On US 1; 1.8 mi ne of jct SR 78. 92 Old Post Rd 02891. Fax: 401/322-2010. **Terms:** Reserv deposit, 21 for cottages; weekly rates. **Facility:** 30 rooms. 1- & 2-bedroom cottages $483-$575 weekly; $284-$341 off season for up to 2 persons; 1 story; exterior corridors; playground. **Recreation:** horseshoes, shuffleboard & volleyball. **All Rooms:** kitchens, combo or shower baths. **Cards:** AE, MC, VI.
[ASK] 🆂 ⊠ 🎦 ▣ 🖥 ⊠

SAND DOLLAR INN Rates Subject to Change Phone: (401)322-2000

	Fri-Sun 6/11-9/6 [CP]	1P:	$90- 110	2P/1B:	$90- 110	2P/2B:	$100- 115	XP: $16	F12
	9/7-11/30 [CP]	1P:	$45- 100	2P/1B:	$45- 100	2P/2B:	$45- 100	XP: $16	F12
	Fri-Sun 5/1-6/10, Mon-Thurs 6/11-9/6 & Fri-Sun 3/1-4/30 [CP]	1P:	$65- 80	2P/1B:	$65- 80	2P/2B:	$75- 85	XP: $16	F12
	Mon-Thurs 5/1-6/10 3/1-4/30 [CP]	1P:	$45- 60	2P/1B:	$45- 60	2P/2B:	$50- 60	XP: $16	F12

◆◆
Motel **Location:** On US 1; 1.5 mi n of jct SR 78 Westerly Bypass. 171 Post Rd (US 1) 02891. Fax: 401/322-1590. **Terms:** Open 5/1-11/30 & 3/1; reserv deposit, 7 day notice; handling fee imposed; 2 night min stay, weekends in summer. **Facility:** 34 rooms. Set back from hwy. 1-bedroom efficiency $500 in season for up to 5 persons, 1-bedroom cottage $500 in season for up to 4 persons; 1 story; exterior corridors. **Recreation:** picnic area, badminton. **All Rooms:** combo or shower baths, extended cable TV. **Some Rooms:** 2 kitchens. **Cards:** AE, DS, MC, VI.
📺 🖨 🖥 ⊠

SHELTER HARBOR INN Rates Subject to Change Phone: 401/322-8883
◆◆
Country Inn

Fri & Sat 5/1-6/18, 6/19-9/7 & Fri & Sat 9/8-10/31 [BP]	2P/1B:	$102- 136	2P/2B:	$102- 136	XP: $15-25
Sun-Thurs 5/1-6/18, 9/8-10/31 & 11/1-4/30 [BP]	2P/1B:	$92- 126	2P/2B:	$92- 126	XP: $15-25

Location: 4 mi ne of jct SR 78 on US 1. 10 Wagner Rd 02891. Fax: 401/322-7907. **Terms:** Reserv deposit; 2 night min stay, weekends. **Facility:** 23 rooms. Warm, relaxing ambiance with inviting room decor in converted farmhouse, barn & coach buildings. Some units with fireplace. 1-3 stories, no elevator; interior/exterior corridors. **Services:** area transportation. **All Rooms:** combo or shower baths. **Cards:** AE, CB, DI, DS, MC, VI.
♿ 🍽 🎦 🖨

THE VILLA BED & BREAKFAST Rates Subject to Change Phone: 401/596-1054
◆◆◆
Bed & Breakfast

Fri & Sat 5/28-10/11 [BP]	1P: $155- 235	2P/1B:	$165- 245		XP: $25
Sun-Thurs 5/28-10/11 [BP]	1P: $125- 185	2P/1B:	$135- 195		XP: $25
Fri & Sat 5/1-5/27 & 10/12-4/30 [BP]	1P: $140- 175	2P/1B:	$150- 185		XP: $25
Sun-Thurs 5/1-5/27 & 10/12-4/30 [BP]	1P: $75- 130	2P/1B:	$85- 140		XP: $25

Location: On SR 1A, 2.5 mi e of US 1 via Airport & Winnapaug Rds. 190 Shore Rd 02891. Fax: 401/596-6268. **Terms:** Age restrictions may apply; reserv deposit, 14 day notice; handling fee imposed; 2 night min stay, weekends. **Facility:** 6 rooms. Lavishly landscaped grounds. The feel of a seaside villa retreat. 3 stories, no elevator; interior/exterior corridors. **All Rooms:** combo or shower baths. **Cards:** AE, DS, MC, VI.
🛥 [VCR] ▢ 🖥 🖨

WINNAPAUG INN-MISQUAMICUT/WESTERLY Rates Subject to Change Phone: (401)348-8350

	6/25-8/31 [CP]	2P/1B:	$99- 169	2P/2B:	$99- 169	XP: $10-25
	5/1-6/24 & 9/1-4/30 [CP]	2P/1B:	$59- 139	2P/2B:	$59- 139	XP: $10-20

◆◆◆
Motel **Location:** On SR 1A; 2 mi e of US 1 via Airport & Winnapaug rds. 169 Shore Rd 02891. Fax: 401/596-8654. **Terms:** Reserv deposit, 14 day notice; weekly/monthly rates; 3 night min stay, weekends in season. **Facility:** 54 rooms. Family oriented. Many units with balcony. 1.2 mi from private ocean beach. Quiet, scenic location. Adjacent to public 18-hole golf course. 1 two-bedroom unit. 7 suites, $129-$229; 3 housekeeping units, $169-$229 in season; 3 stories; interior/exterior corridors; heated pool. **Recreation:** shuffleboard, video game room. **All Rooms:** combo or shower baths. **Some Rooms:** whirlpools. **Cards:** AE, CB, DI, DS, MC, VI. *(See color ad p 442)*
♿ 🏊 🛥 ▣ ▢ 🖨 🖥 ♿ ⊠

RESTAURANT

SHELTER HARBOR INN Country Inn Lunch: $7-$12 Dinner: $14-$22 Phone: 401/322-8883
◆◆◆
Regional American **Location:** 4 mi ne of jct SR 78 on US 1; in Shelter Harbor Inn. 10 Wagner Rd 02891. **Hours:** 7:30-10:30 am, 11:30-3 & 5-10 pm, Sun 7:30 am-10 pm. **Reservations:** suggested. **Features:** semi-formal attire; Sunday brunch; cocktails & lounge. Gracious dining in a candlelit garden setting. Variety of homemade bread & pastry. **Cards:** AE, CB, DI, DS, MC, VI.
⊠

WEST GREENWICH—3,500

LODGING

BEST WESTERN WEST GREENWICH INN   Rates Subject to Change   **Phone:** 401/397-5494
◆◆◆   7/1-9/7 [CP]   1P: $69- 79 2P/1B: $75- 95 2P/2B: $75- 95 XP: $10   F12
Motel   5/1-6/30 & 9/8-4/30 [CP]   1P: $69- 79 2P/1B: $79- 89 2P/2B: $69- 89 XP: $10   F12
Location: From I-95 exit 6, 0.3 mi n on SR 3N. 101 Nooseneck Hill Rd 02817. Fax: 401/397-7185.
Facility: 56 rooms. An attractive modern brick building surrounded by pine trees in a quiet rural hillside setting. Large guest rooms with traditional furnishings. 2 stories; interior corridors; heated indoor pool. **Cards:** AE, CB, DI, DS, MC, VI.

WEST WARWICK—29,300   (See map p. 457; index p. 456)

LODGING

FAIRFIELD SUITES BY MARRIOTT   Rates Subject to Change   **Phone:** 401/822-1244 ㊵
◆◆◆   Fri-Sun 7/1-8/31 [CP]   1P: $95   2P/1B: $95   2P/2B: $95   XP: $6   F12
Suite Motel   Fri-Sun 9/1-10/31 [CP]   1P: $90   2P/1B: $90   2P/2B: $90   XP: $6   F12
    Mon-Thurs [CP]   1P: $85   2P/1B: $85   2P/2B: $85   XP: $6   F12
    Fri-Sun 5/1-6/30 & 11/1-4/30
    [CP]   1P: $80   2P/1B: $80   2P/2B: $80   XP: $6   F12
Location: Just nw I-95 exit 8 southbound; exit 8B northbound. 14 JP Murphy Hwy 02893. Fax: 401/828-3873.
Terms: Reserv deposit. **Facility:** 109 rooms. 4 stories; interior corridors; heated indoor pool. **Services:** area transportation.
All Rooms: combo or shower baths. **Cards:** AE, CB, DI, DS, MC, VI.

WOONSOCKET—43,900

LODGING

WOONSOCKET MOTOR INN   Rates Subject to Change   **Phone:** 401/762-1224
AAA   All Year   1P: $41- 45 2P/1B: $41- 45 2P/2B: $44- 48 XP: $5   D5
    Location: 0.5 mi n on SR 104; just n of police station. 333 Clinton St 02895. Fax: 401/765-5521.
◆◆   **Terms:** Reserv deposit. **Facility:** 38 rooms. Variety of furnishings in large, inviting guest rooms. A quiet setting
Motel   back from hwy. Family owned & operated. 2 stories; interior corridors. **Dining:** Restaurant nearby.
    Cards: AE, CB, DI, DS, MC, VI.

RESTAURANT

CHAN'S FINE ORIENTAL DINING   **Lunch:** $4-$5   **Dinner:** $7-$12   **Phone:** 401/765-1900
◆◆   **Location:** Downtown at Depot Square & jct of Main & Railroad sts; 0.3 mi w of Monument Square. 267 Main
Chinese   St 02895. **Hours:** 11:30 am-10 pm, Fri & Sat-12:30 am. **Reservations:** suggested; weekends.
    Features: casual dress; children's menu; carryout; cocktails & lounge. Traditional Oriental cuisine featuring
Cantonese, Szechwan-Hunan, Mandarin & Shanghai cooking styles. Popular since 1905. Acclaimed jazz/blues
entertainment Fri & Sat; call for details. Lunch buffet Mon-Fri. **Cards:** AE, DS, MC, VI.

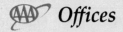 *Offices*

Cities with main offices are listed in **BOLD TYPE** and toll-free member service numbers in *ITALIC TYPE*.
All are closed Saturdays, Sundays and holidays unless otherwise indicated.

The type of service provided is designated below the name of the city where the office is located:
Auto travel services, including books/maps, marked maps and on-demand Triptik maps ✦
Auto travel services, including books/maps, marked maps, but no on-demand Triptik maps ●
Provides books/maps only. No marked maps or on-demand Triptik maps available ■
Travel agency services ▲

CONNECTICUT

AVON—AUTOMOBILE CLUB OF HARTFORD, 70 E MAIN ST, 06001. MON-FRI 8-5:30, SAT 10-2. (860) 236-3261.✦▲

BRANFORD—CONNECTICUT MOTOR CLUB, 143 CEDAR ST, 06405. MON-FRI 8:30-5:30, SAT 8:30-12. (203) 765-4222.✦▲

CROMWELL—AUTOMOBILE CLUB OF HARTFORD, 34 SHUNPIKE RD #20, 06416. MON-FRI 8:30-5:30, SAT 10-2. (860) 236-3261.●▲

DANBURY—CONNECTICUT MOTOR CLUB, 10 MAIN ST, 06810. MON-FRI 8:30-5:30, SAT 8:30-12. (203) 765-4222.✦▲

ENFIELD—AUTOMOBILE CLUB OF HARTFORD, 109 ELM ST, 06082. MON-FRI 8:30-5:30, SAT 10-2. (860) 236-3261.✦▲

HAMDEN—CONNECTICUT MOTOR CLUB, 2276 WHITNEY AVE, 06518. MON-FRI 8:30-5:30, SAT 8:30-12. (203) 765-4222.✦▲

MANCHESTER—AUTOMOBILE CLUB OF HARTFORD, 391 BROAD ST, 06040. MON-FRI 8:30-5:30, SAT 10-2. (860) 236-3261.✦▲

ORANGE—CONNECTICUT MOTOR CLUB, 527 BOSTON POST RD, 06477. MON-FRI 8:30-5:30, SAT 8:30-12. (203) 765-4222.✦▲

PLAINVILLE—AUTOMOBILE CLUB OF HARTFORD, 17 FARMINGTON AVE, 06062. MON-FRI 8:30-5:30, SAT 10-2. (860) 236-3261.✦▲

STAMFORD—CONNECTICUT MOTOR CLUB, 623 NEWFIELD AVE, 06905. MON-FRI 8:30-5:30, SAT 8:30-12. (203) 765-4222.✦▲

STRATFORD—CONNECTICUT MOTOR CLUB, 555 LORDSHIP BLVD, 06497. MON-FRI 8:30-5:30, SAT 8:30-12. (203) 765-4222.✦▲

WATERBURY—CONNECTICUT MOTOR CLUB, 720 WOLCOTT ST, 06705. MON-FRI 8:30-5:30, SAT 8:30-12. (203) 765-4222.✦▲

WATERFORD—AUTOMOBILE CLUB OF HARTFORD, 117 BOSTON POST RD, 06385. MON-FRI 8:30-5:30, SAT 10-2. (860) 236-3261.✦▲

WEST HARTFORD—AUTOMOBILE CLUB OF HARTFORD, 815 FARMINGTON AVE, 06119. MON-FRI 8:30-5:30, SAT 10-2. (860) 236-3261, *(800) 842-4320.*✦▲

WESTPORT—CONNECTICUT MOTOR CLUB, 20 SAUGATUCK AVE, 06880. MON-FRI 8:30-5:30, SAT 8:30-12. (203) 765-4222.✦▲

MASSACHUSETTS

AUBURN—AAA SOUTHERN NEW ENGLAND, 711 SOUTHBRIDGE ST, 01501-1833. MON-FRI 9-5, SAT 9-1. (508) 832-0200.✦▲

BOSTON—AAA SOUTHERN NEW ENGLAND, 125 HIGH ST, 02110. MON-FRI 9-5. (617) 443-9300.✦▲

BURLINGTON—AAA SOUTHERN NEW ENGLAND, 101 CAMBRIDGE ST #260, 01803. MON-FRI 9-5, SAT 9-1. (781) 272-3272.✦▲

FAIRHAVEN—AAA SOUTHERN NEW ENGLAND, 32 FAIRHAVEN COMMONS WAY, 02719. MON-FRI 9-5, SAT 9-1. (508) 997-7811.✦▲

FRAMINGHAM—AAA SOUTHERN NEW ENGLAND, 653 WORCESTER RD, 01701. MON-FRI 9-5, SAT 9-1. (508) 875-2000.✦▲

HAVERHILL—AAA MERRIMACK VALLEY, 90 KENOZA AVE, 01830-4140. MON-FRI 8:30-5:30, SAT 9-1. (978) 373-3611.✦▲

LAWRENCE—AAA MERRIMACK VALLEY, 155 PARKER ST, 01843. MON-FRI 8:30-5:30, SAT 9-1. (978) 681-9200.✦▲

LEOMINSTER—AAA SOUTHERN NEW ENGLAND, 20 COMMERCIAL RD, 01453-3306. MON-FRI 9-5, SAT 9-1. (978) 537-4000.✦▲

LOWELL—AAA MERRIMACK VALLEY, 585 PAWTUCKET BLVD, 01854-2098. MON-FRI 8:30-5:30, SAT 9-1. (978) 937-3061.✦▲

NEEDHAM—AAA SOUTHERN NEW ENGLAND, 175 HIGHLAND AVE, 02194. MON-FRI 9-5, SAT 9-1. (781) 449-7000.✦▲

NEWBURYPORT—AAA MERRIMACK VALLEY, 45 STOREY AVE, RT 113, 01950-1851. MON-FRI 8:30-5:30, SAT 9-1. (978) 499-4222.✦▲

NORWOOD—AAA SOUTHERN NEW ENGLAND, 111 LENOX ST, 02062. MON-FRI 9-5, SAT 9-1. (781) 551-0025.✦▲

PITTSFIELD—AAA BERKSHIRE COUNTY, 196 SOUTH ST, 01201. MON-FRI 8:30-5. (413) 445-5635, *(888) 222-2404.*✦▲

RAYNHAM—AAA SOUTHERN NEW ENGLAND, 350 NEW STATE HWY, 02767-1434. MON-FRI 9-5, SAT 9-1. (508) 823-6000.✦▲

ROCKLAND—AAA SOUTHERN NEW ENGLAND, 1050 HINGHAM ST, 02370. MON-FRI 9-5, SAT 9-1. (781) 871-5880.✦▲

SAUGUS—AAA SOUTHERN NEW ENGLAND, 190 BROADWAY, RT 1, 01906. MON-FRI 9-5, SAT 9-1. (781) 231-3000.✦▲

SOMERSET—AAA SOUTHERN NEW ENGLAND, 869 G.A.R. HWY, 02726-1204. MON-FRI 9-5, SAT 9-1. (508) 672-2600.✦▲

SOUTH ATTLEBORO—AAA SOUTHERN NEW ENGLAND, 405 WASHINGTON ST, 02703-5916. MON-FRI 9-5, SAT 9-1. (508) 399-9000.✦▲

SOUTH DENNIS—AAA SOUTHERN NEW ENGLAND, 6 ENTERPRISE RD, RT 134, 02660-3436. MON-FRI 9-5, SAT 9-1. (508) 760-4778.✦▲

SPRINGFIELD—AUTOMOBILE CLUB OF PIONEER VALLEY, 1826 ALLEN ST, 01118-1822. MON-FRI 8:30-5, THU 8:30-7, SAT 9-1. (413) 796-7252, *(800) 622-9211.*✦▲

WEST SPRINGFIELD—AUTOMOBILE CLUB OF PIONEER VALLEY, 150 CAPITAL DR, 01089-1351. MON-FRI 8:30-5, THU 8:30-7, SAT 9-12. (413) 785-1381, *(800) 622-9211.*✦▲

WORCESTER—AAA SOUTHERN NEW ENGLAND, 25 MOUNTAIN ST E, 01606-1498. MON-FRI 9-5, SAT 9-1. (508) 853-7000.✦▲

RHODE ISLAND

BARRINGTON—AAA SOUTHERN NEW ENGLAND, 18 MAPLE AVE, 02806-3518. MON-FRI 9-5, SAT 9-1. (401) 245-1050.✦▲

CRANSTON—AAA SOUTHERN NEW ENGLAND, 1035 RESERVOIR AVE, 02910-0758. MON-FRI 9-5, SAT 9-1. (401) 944-7300.✦▲

GREENVILLE—AAA SOUTHERN NEW ENGLAND, 445 PUTNAM PIKE, 02828-3022. MON-FRI 9-5, SAT 9-1. (401) 232-5100.✦▲

MIDDLETOWN—AAA SOUTHERN NEW ENGLAND, 99 E MAIN RD, 02842-4969. MON-FRI 9-5, SAT 9-1. (401) 841-5000.✦▲

NARRAGANSETT—AAA SOUTHERN NEW ENGLAND, 14 WOODRUFF AVE, 02882-3457. MON-FRI 9-5, SAT 9-1. (401) 789-3000.✦▲

PROVIDENCE—AAA SOUTHERN NEW ENGLAND, 55 DORRANCE ST, 02903-2200. MON-FRI 9-5. (401) 272-7100.✦▲

WARWICK—AAA SOUTHERN NEW ENGLAND, 501 CENTERVILLE RD, 02886-4390. MON-FRI 9-5, SAT 9-1. (401) 732-5000.▲

WOONSOCKET—AAA SOUTHERN NEW ENGLAND, 1500 DIAMOND HILL RD, 02895-1507. MON-FRI 9-5, SAT 9-1. (401) 765-5000.✦▲

Temperature Averages - Maximum/Minimum
From the records of the National Weather Service

	JAN	FEB	MAR	APR	MAY	JUN	JUL	AUG	SEP	OCT	NOV	DEC
CONNECTICUT												
Bridgeport	37 / 23	38 / 23	45 / 30	57 / 39	68 / 50	77 / 59	83 / 65	81 / 63	75 / 56	65 / 46	53 / 36	41 / 26
Hartford	36 / 18	37 / 19	45 / 26	59 / 37	71 / 47	79 / 56	83 / 61	81 / 59	73 / 51	64 / 41	51 / 32	38 / 21
New Haven	37 / 22	38 / 21	45 / 29	56 / 38	67 / 48	75 / 57	81 / 63	79 / 62	73 / 55	64 / 44	52 / 35	40 / 24
MASSACHUSETTS												
Boston	37 / 23	37 / 23	45 / 31	56 / 40	68 / 50	76 / 59	82 / 65	80 / 63	73 / 57	63 / 47	52 / 38	40 / 27
Nantucket	39 / 26	38 / 25	43 / 30	51 / 37	60 / 45	68 / 54	74 / 61	74 / 61	69 / 55	61 / 47	52 / 39	43 / 29
Pittsfield	31 / 13	32 / 13	40 / 22	53 / 33	66 / 43	75 / 52	79 / 56	78 / 55	69 / 47	59 / 37	46 / 29	34 / 17
Worcester	31 / 17	33 / 17	41 / 25	54 / 36	66 / 44	75 / 55	79 / 61	77 / 59	70 / 52	60 / 41	47 / 31	34 / 20
RHODE ISLAND												
Block Island	39 / 26	38 / 25	43 / 31	52 / 38	61 / 48	70 / 56	76 / 63	76 / 64	70 / 58	61 / 49	52 / 40	42 / 30
Providence	37 / 21	38 / 21	45 / 29	57 / 38	68 / 47	76 / 56	81 / 63	80 / 61	73 / 53	63 / 43	52 / 34	40 / 24

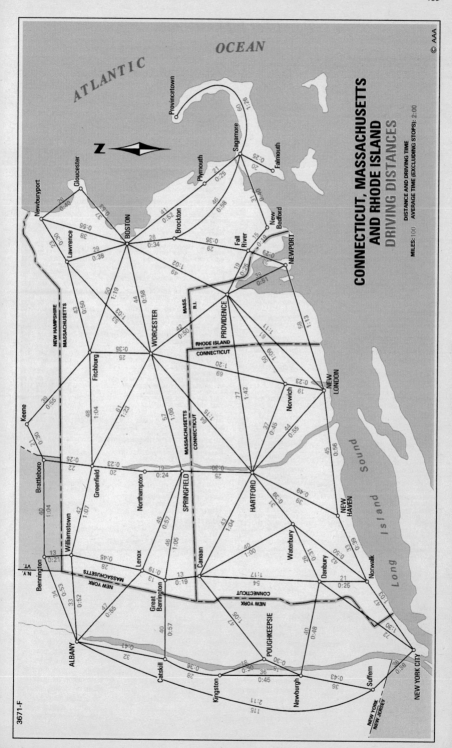

CONNECTICUT, MASSACHUSETTS AND RHODE ISLAND
DRIVING DISTANCES

MILES: 100 DISTANCE AND DRIVING TIME
AVERAGE TIME (EXCLUDING STOPS): 2:00

© AAA

3671-F

Points of Interest Index

INDEX ABBREVIATIONS

HISTORIC DOCUMENTS, MANUSCRIPTS & RARE BOOKS

HISTORIC SITES

HORSE FARMS

INDIAN BURIAL GROUNDS

INDIAN MOUNDS, REMAINS, RUINS

INDUSTRIAL TOURS

ISLANDS

JAILS

LAKES, PONDS & RESERVOIRS

LIBRARIES

MUSIC EVENTS

MUSIC HALLS & OPERA HOUSES

NATURAL BRIDGES

NATURAL PHENOMENA

NATURE CENTERS

NATURE TRAILS

🆂🅰🆅🅴 *Attraction Admission Discount Index*

Bed & Breakfast Lodgings Index

Some bed and breakfasts listed below might have historical significance. Those properties are also referenced in the Historical index. The indication that continental [CP] or full breakfast [BP] is included in the room rate reflects whether a property is a Bed-and-Breakfast facility.

Country Inns Index

Some of the following country inns can also be considered as bed-and-breakfast operations. The indication that continental [CP] or full breakfast [BP] is included in the room rate reflects whether a property is a Bed-and-Breakfast facility.

COUNTRY INNS (CONT'D)

Historical Lodgings & Restaurants Index

Some of the following historical lodgings can also be considered as bed-and-breakfast operations. The indication that con nental [CP] or full breakfast [BP] is included in the room rate reflects whether a property is a Bed-and-Breakfast facility.

RED ALERT!

When you pick up a AAA TourBook®, be alert for the establishments that display a bright red AAA logo beside their listing. These establishments place a high value on the patronage they receive from AAA members. They are telling you they're willing to go the extra mile to get your business. Some even offer special amenities designed just for you.

And don't forget to look for the establishments that display the familiar **icon to receive discounts.**

So, when you turn to the AAA TourBook to make your travel plans, be on the look out for the establishments that will give you the special treatment you deserve.

HISTORICAL LODGINGS & RESTAURANTS (CONT'D)

MASSACHUSETTS

ACCOMMODATIONS

RESTAURANTS

RHODE ISLAND

ACCOMMODATIONS

RESTAURANTS

Resorts Index

Many establishments are located in resort areas; however, the following places have extensive on-premises recreational facilities:

MASSACHUSETTS

ACCOMMODATIONS

Comprehensive City Index

Here is an alphabetical list of all cities appearing in this TourBook. Cities are presented by state/province. Page numbers under the POI column indicate where points of interest text begins. Page numbers under the L&R column indicate where lodging and restaurant listings begin.

COMPREHENSIVE CITY INDEX (CONT'D)

COMPREHENSIVE CITY INDEX (CONT'D)

Photo Credit Index

Kent Falls State Park, CT
© Marc Muench .... Cover, Title, Table of Contents

The Charles W. Morgan, Mystic, CT
© Mark E. Gibson .... Cover

CONNECTICUT

Housatonic River Valley
© David Muench .... 25, 205, Table of Contents
Cornwall covered bridge .... 26, Table of Contents

Hartford / Center Church
Andre Jenny / International Stock 46

Hartford / Sculpture "Stegosaurus" at Burr Mall
Andre Jenny / International Stock 47, 61, 233

MASSACHUSETTS

Mount Greylock State Reservation
© David Muench .... 81, 263, Table of Contents

Jenny Grist Mill, Plymouth
© David Muench .... 82, Table of Contents
Boston / Clear view of the city 98
Boston / Swan boat, Public Garden
R. Kord / H. Armstrong Roberts 99, 140, 320
Cape Cod / Town center, Chatham
W. Bertsch / H. Armstrong Roberts 142
Cape Cod / Provincetown Harbor
J. Nettis / H. Armstrong Roberts 143, 153, 387

RHODE ISLAND

Newport
© David Muench .... 177, 437, Table of Contents
Burlingame State Park
© David Muench 178

Now You Can Count on AAA for Financial Services Too!

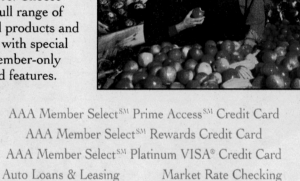

*N*ow, your AAA membership offers even more. Choose from a full range of financial products and services with special AAA member-only rates and features.

AAA Member Select[SM] Prime Access[SM] Credit Card

AAA Member Select[SM] Rewards Credit Card

AAA Member Select[SM] Platinum VISA® Credit Card

Auto Loans & Leasing   Market Rate Checking

Home Equity Loans[1]   Money Market Accounts

Personal Loans   Certificates of Deposit[2]

Financial Services

MAKE THE MOST OF YOUR MEMBERSHIP.[SM]

1-800-680-AAA4

24 HOURS A DAY. 7 DAYS A WEEK.

Available only through participating AAA clubs.

Equal Housing Lender

RED ALERT!

When you pick up a AAA TourBook®, be alert for the establishments that display a bright red AAA logo beside their listing. These establishments place a high value on the patronage they receive from AAA members. They are telling you they're willing to go the extra mile to get your business. Some even offer special amenities designed just for you.

And don't forget to look for the establishments that display the familiar **icon to receive discounts.**

So, when you turn to the AAA TourBook to make your travel plans, be on the look out for the establishments that will give you the special treatment you deserve.

492

Affordable Adventure

Make your next vacation an adventure - at a price that won't make paying the bill adventuresome. Travel consultants will help you plan a vacation that will meet all your needs. From a quiet getaway to a family gathering, AAA can arrange for the most economical or the most extravagant use of your vacation dollar. Come to your local AAA Travel Agency for the vacation adventure you can afford to enjoy.

Travel With Someone You Trust®

SPECIAL PEOPLE GET SPECIAL TREATMENT

WANT TO BE SURE YOU'LL BE TREATED RIGHT ON YOUR NEXT TRAVEL ADVENTURE?

Look for establishments that advertise in the AAA TourBook®. These are the businesses that cater to AAA members. They value the business they receive from AAA members, and are willing to go the extra mile to get it. And in turn, they pass value on to you.

So, when you're using the TourBook to make your travel plans, be sure to look for the establishments who advertise in the AAA TourBook.

494

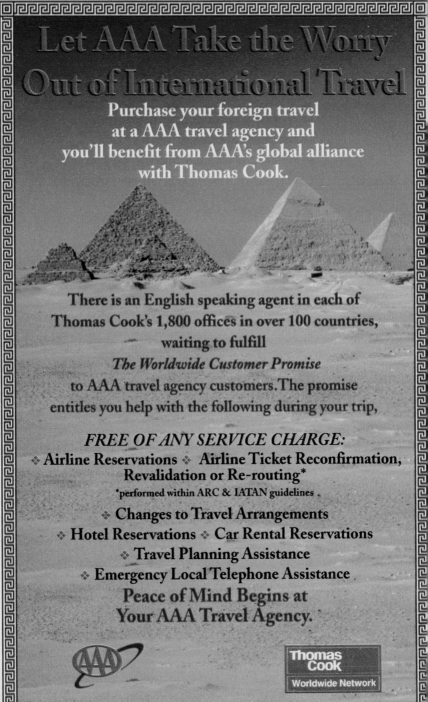